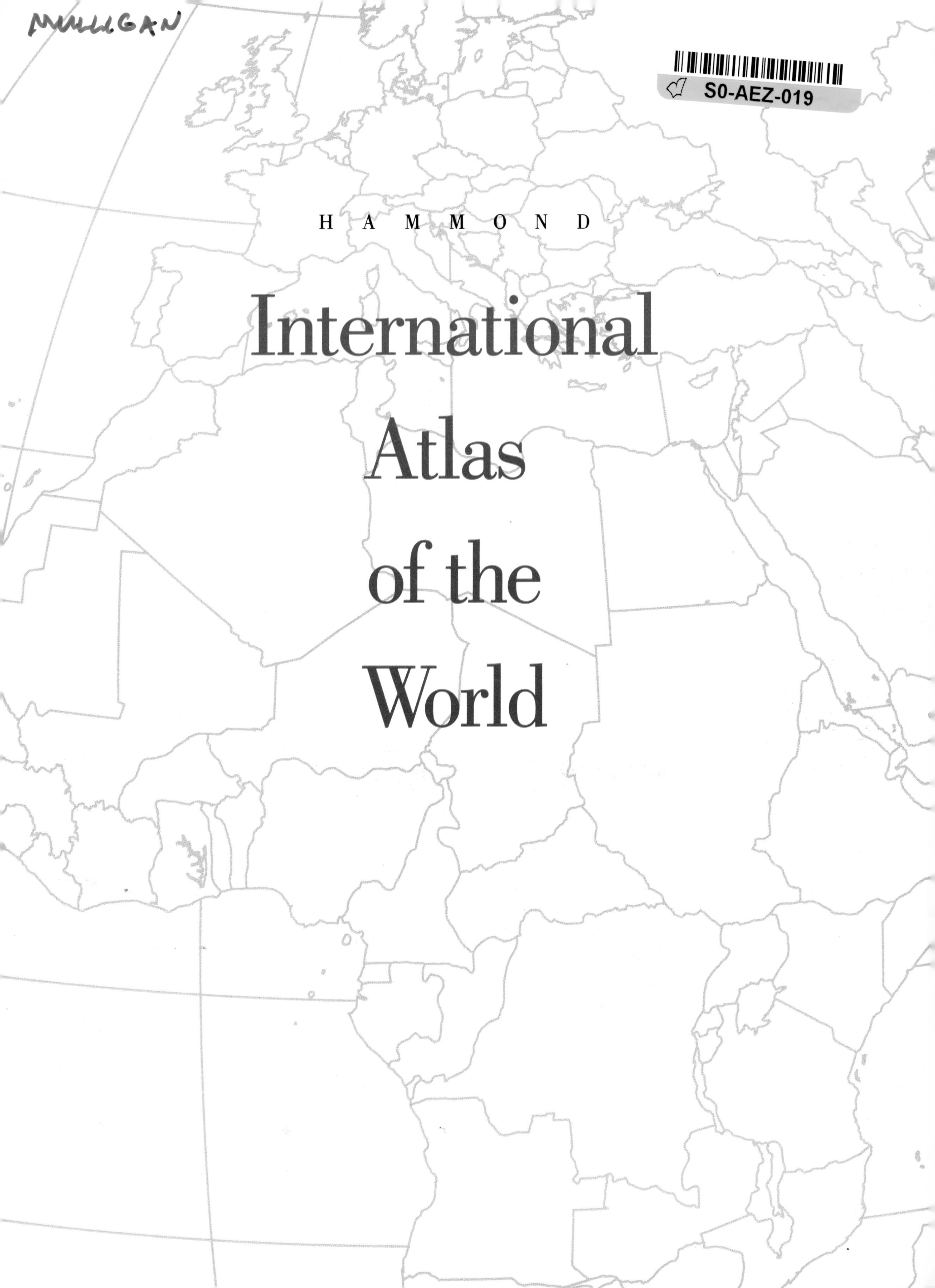

H A M M O N D

International Atlas of the World

Contents

Interpreting Maps

Designed to enhance your knowledge and enjoyment of maps, these pages explain map scales and projections, describe how to locate information quickly and show you how to weave together the sections of this atlas to gain a more dynamic world view.

4-5 Map Projections
6-7 Using This Atlas
Symbols, Abbreviations

World Reference Guide

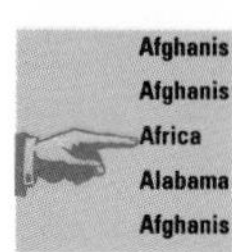

Afghanis
Afghanis
Africa
Alabama
Afghanis

These six pages contain flags and important facts about each independent country including area, population, capital, largest city, highest point and monetary unit.

8-13 World Flags & Reference Guide

Global Relationships

Maps, charts and graphs unveil the complex relationships between people and their environments. Coverage includes: demographic trends, population distribution and growth; assessing the consequences of pollution: acid rain, deforestation, ozone depletion and global warming; also revealing comparisons of GNP per capita and literacy and life expectancy around the globe.

14-15 Environmental Concerns
16-17 Population
18-19 Standards of Living

The Physical World

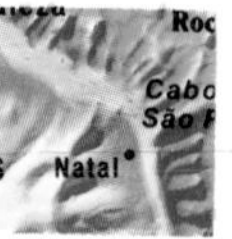

Natal

Seven pages of new physical maps present a comprehensive and accurate rendering of the earth's surface and the ocean floors. Created from Hammond's Digital Cartographic Database and with continents shown on a new map projection.

20-21 World
22 Europe
23 Asia
24 Africa
25 South America
26 North America

Maps of the World

Luxembourg
Thionville
Yutz

This entirely new collection of world maps is the first ever generated from a computer database structured by latitude and longitude. New maps artfully balance political detail while proprietary map projections present the most distortion-free views of the continents yet seen. Over 40 inset maps highlight metropolitan and special areas. Numbers following each entry indicate map scale (M= million, K= thousand).

28-29 World - Political Map 1:82M

Europe and Northern Asia

30 Europe 1:17.5M
31 Metropolitan London, Metropolitan Paris 1:587K
32-33 Northeastern Ireland, Northern England and Wales 1:1.17M
34-35 Southern England and Wales 1:1.17M
36 United Kingdom, Ireland 1:3.5M
37 Scandinavia and Finland 1:7M
Iceland 1:7M
38-39 North Central Europe 1:3.5M
40-41 Netherlands, Northwestern Germany 1:1.17M
42-43 Belgium, Northern France, Western Germany 1:1.17M
44-45 West Central Europe 1:3.5M
46-47 Spain, Portugal 1:3.5M
Barcelona, Madrid, Lisbon 1:1.17M
Azores, Canary Islands, Madeira 1:7M
48-49 Southern Italy, Albania, Greece 1:3.5M
Athens 1:1.17M
50-51 Hungary, Northern Balkan States 1:3.5M
52-53 Northeastern Europe 1:7M
St. Petersburg, Moscow 1:1.17M
54-55 Southeastern Europe 1:7M
56-57 Russia and Neighboring Countries 1:21M

Asia

58 Asia 1:49M
59 Turkey 1:8.8M
Eastern Mediterranean Region 1:3.5M
Central Israel and West Bank 1:1.17M
60-61 Southwestern Asia 1:10.5M
62-63 Eastern Asia 1:10.5M
64-65 Central and Southern Japan 1:3.5M
Tokyo, Osaka-Nagoya 1:1.17M
66 Northeastern China 1:7M
Beijing-Tianjin, Shanghai 1:3.5M
67 Southeastern China, Taiwan, Philippines 1:10.5M
68 Central Asia 1:10.5M
69 Eastern Burma, Thailand, Indochina 1:7M
70-71 Southern Asia 1:10.5M
72-73 Southeastern Asia 1:10.5M

Australia and Pacific

74-75 Australia 1:14M
New Zealand 1:10.5M
76 Northeastern Australia 1:7M
Brisbane, Sydney 1:1.17M
77 Southeastern Australia 1:7M
Melbourne 1:1.17M
78-79 Central Pacific Ocean 1:31.5M

Africa

80 Africa 1:31.5M
Cape Verde 1:7M
81 Northern Morocco, Algeria, Tunisia 1:3.5M
82-83 Northern Africa 1:17.5M
84-85 West Africa 1:7M
86 Northeastern Africa 1:7M
87 Southern Africa 1:17.5M
88 South Africa 1:7M
Cape Region, Witwatersrand, Mauritius and Réunion 1:3.5M
89 Madagascar 1:7M

South America, Antarctica

90 South America 1:28M
91 Southern South America 1:15M
92-93 Northern South America 1:15M
94 Northeastern Brazil 1:7M
95 Southeastern Brazil 1:7M
São Paulo-Rio de Janeiro 1:3.5M
96-97 Southern Chile and Argentina 1:7M
Santiago-Valparaíso, Río de la Plata 1:3.5M
98 Antarctica 1:28M

North America

99 North America 1:35M
100-101 Middle America and Caribbean 1:10.5M
102-103 Canada 1:14M
104-105 United States 1:14M
Hawaii 1:3.5M
Oahu 1:1.17M
106-107 Southwestern Canada, Northwestern United States 1:7M
108-109 Southwestern United States 1:7M
110-111 Southeastern Canada, Northeastern United States 1:7M
Montreal, Toronto-Buffalo 1:1.17M
112-113 Southeastern United States 1:7M
114 Alaska 1:10.5M
115 Los Angeles; New York-Philadelphia; Washington 1:1.17M
116 Seattle-Tacoma, Sacramento-San Francisco-San Jose, Detroit, Chicago-Milwaukee 1:1.17M

Statistical Tables and Index

68/B3 Flixecourt
69/D4 Flize, Fran
69/D4 Floing, Fra
69/H4 Flonheim,
68/F5 Florange, I
69/D3 Floreffe, B

Time Zones are shown for all countries. World Statistics gives the dimensions of the earth's major mountain peaks, longest rivers and largest lakes and islands. A 45,000-entry Master Index lists places and features appearing in this atlas, complete with page numbers and easy-to-use alpha-numeric references.

118-119 Time Zones of the World
120-121 World Statistics
122-168 Index of the World

Library of Congress
Cataloging-in-Publication Data

Hammond Incorporated.
Hammond international atlas of the world
p. cm.
Includes index.
ISBN 0–8437–1183–3
ISBN 0–8437–1184–1 (pbk.)
1. Atlases. I. Title.
II. Title: International atlas of the world
G1021.H2710 1994 <G&M>
912—dc20 94–7294
CIP
MAP

Map Projections

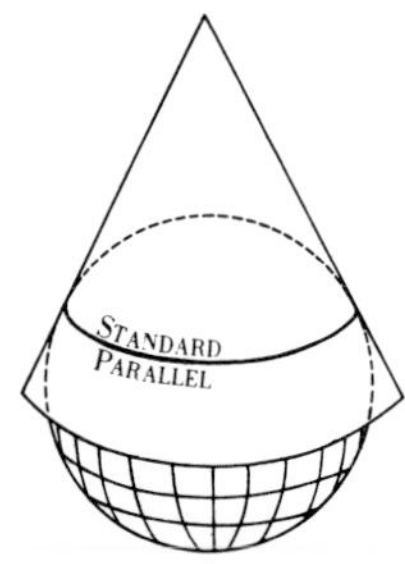
STANDARD
PARALLEL

FIGURE 3
Conic Projection
The original idea of a conic projection is to cap the globe with a cone, and then project onto the cone from the planet's center the lines of latitude and longitude (the parallels and meridians). To produce a working map, the cone is simply cut open and laid flat. The conic projection used here is a modification of this idea. A cone can be made tangent to any standard parallel you choose. One popular version of a conic projection, the Lambert Conformal Conic, uses two standard parallels near the top and bottom of the map to further reduce errors of scale.

FIGURE 4
Lambert Azimuthal Equal-Area Projection
Because this projection shows correct areas with relatively little distortion of shapes, it is commonly used to plot maps of the continents. However, because of improved accuracy, the Optimal Conformal projection was used for all of the continent maps in this atlas.

Simply stated, the mapmaker's challenge is to project the earth's curved surface onto a flat plane. To achieve this elusive goal, cartographers have developed map projections — equations which govern this conversion of geographic data.

This section explores some of the most widely used projections. It also introduces a new projection, Hammond's Optimal Conformal.

General Principles and Terms

The earth rotates around its axis once a day. Its end points are the North and South poles; the line circling the earth midway between the poles is the equator. The arc from the equator to either pole is divided into 90 degrees of latitude. The equator represents 0° latitude. Circles of equal latitude, called parallels, are traditionally shown at every fifth or tenth degree.

The equator is divided into 360 degrees. Lines circling the globe from pole to pole through the degree points on the equator are called meridians, or great circles. All meridians are equal in length, but by international agreement the meridian passing through the Greenwich Observatory near London has been chosen as the prime meridian or 0° longitude. The distance in degrees from the prime meridian to any point east or west is its longitude.

While meridians are all equal in length, parallels become shorter as they approach the poles. Whereas one degree of latitude represents approximately 69 miles (112 km.) anywhere on the globe, a degree of longitude varies from 69 miles (112 km.) at the equator to zero at the poles. Each degree of latitude and longitude is divided into 60 minutes. One minute of latitude equals one nautical mile (1.15 land miles or 1.85 km.).

How to Flatten a Sphere: The Art of Controlling Distortion

There is only one way to represent a sphere with absolute precision: on a globe. All attempts to project our planet's surface onto a plane unevenly stretch or tear the sphere as it flattens, inevitably distorting shapes, distances, area (sizes appear larger or smaller than actual size), angles or direction.

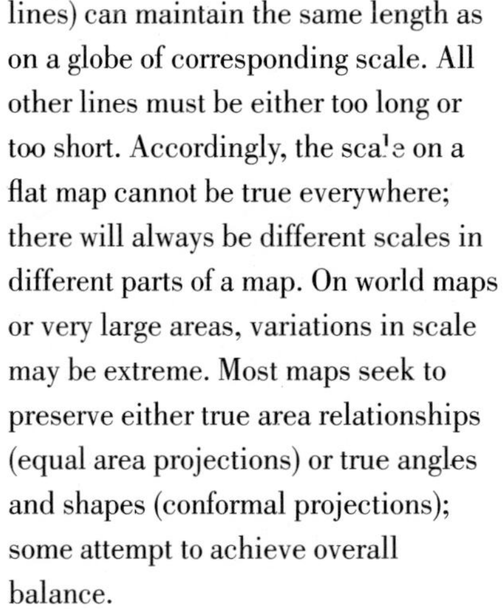

FIGURE 1 **Mercator Projection**

FIGURE 2 **Robinson Projection**

Since representing a sphere on a flat plane always creates distortion, only the parallels or the meridians (or some other set of lines) can maintain the same length as on a globe of corresponding scale. All other lines must be either too long or too short. Accordingly, the scale on a flat map cannot be true everywhere; there will always be different scales in different parts of a map. On world maps or very large areas, variations in scale may be extreme. Most maps seek to preserve either true area relationships (equal area projections) or true angles and shapes (conformal projections); some attempt to achieve overall balance.

Projections: Selected Examples

Mercator (Fig. 1): This projection is especially useful because all compass directions appear as straight lines, making it a valuable navigational tool. Moreover, every small region conforms to its shape on a globe — hence the name conformal. But because its meridians are evenly-spaced vertical lines which never converge (unlike the globe), the horizontal parallels must be drawn farther and farther apart at higher latitudes to maintain a correct relationship. Only the equator is true to scale, and the size of areas in the higher latitudes is dramatically distorted.

Robinson (Fig. 2): To create the thematic maps in Global Relationships and the two-page world map in the Maps of the World section, the Robinson projection was used. It combines elements of both conformal and equal area projections to show the whole earth with relatively true shapes and reasonably equal areas.

Conic (Fig. 3): This projection has been used frequently for air navigation charts and to create most of the national and regional maps in this atlas. (See text in margin at left).

Hammond's Optimal Conformal

As its name implies, this new conformal projection presents the optimal view of an area by reducing shifts in scale over an entire region to the minimum degree possible. While conformal maps generally preserve all small shapes, large shapes can become very distorted because of varying scales, causing considerable inaccuracy in distance measurements. The concept underlying the Optimal Conformal is that for any region on the globe, there is an ideal projection for which scale variation can be made as small as possible. Consequently, unlike other projections, the Optimal Conformal does not use one standard formula to construct a map. Each map is a unique projection — the optimal projection for that particular area.

In practice, the cartographer first defines the map subject, then, working on a computer, draws a band around the region to be mapped. Next, a sophisticated software program evaluates the size and shape of the region to determine the most accurate way to project it. The result is the most distortion-free conformal map possible, and the most

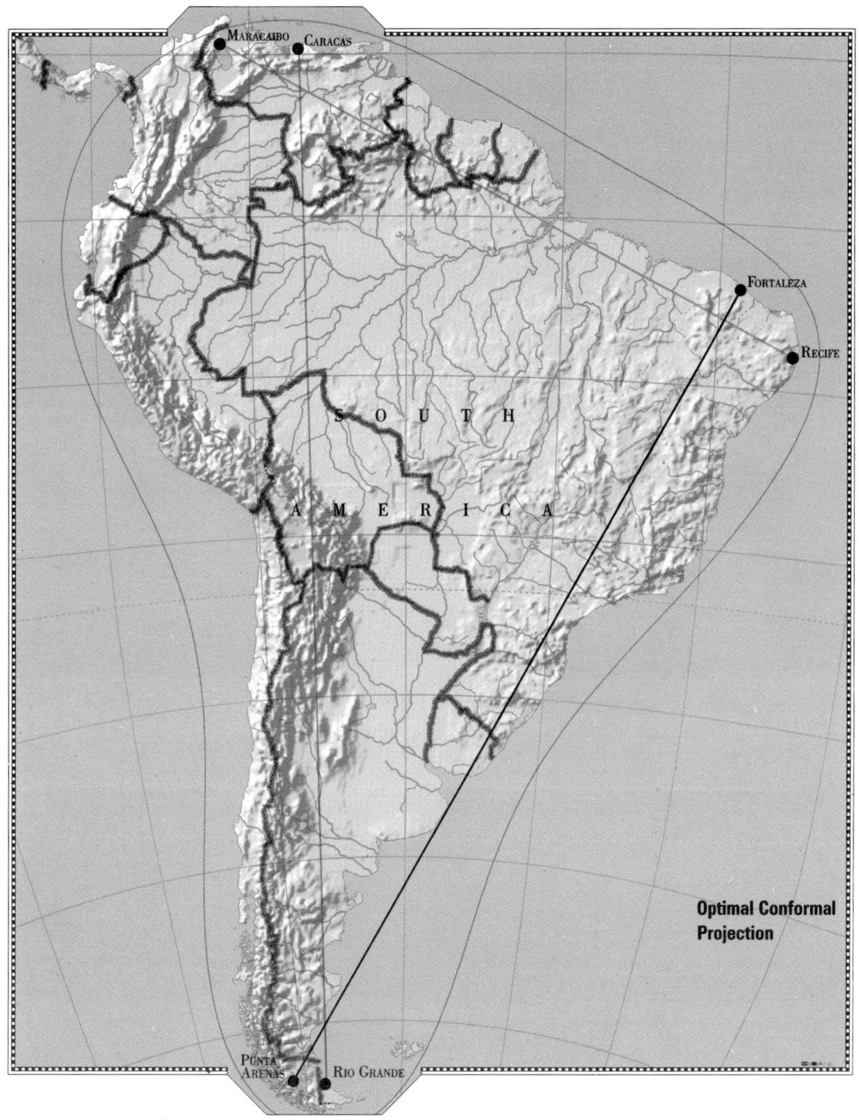
Maracaibo
Caracas
Fortaleza
Recife
South America
Optimal Conformal Projection
Punta Arenas
Rio Grande

Accuracy Compared

Cities	Spherical (True) Distance	Optimal Conformal Distance	Lambert Azimuthal Distance
Caracas to Rio Grande	4,443 mi. (7,149 km.)	4,429 mi. (7,126 km.)	4,316 mi. (6,944 km.)
Maracaibo to Recife	2,834 mi. (4,560 km.)	2,845 mi. (4,578 km.)	2,817 mi. (4,533 km.)
Fortaleza to Punta Arenas	3,882 mi. (6,246 km.)	3,907 mi. (6,266 km.)	3,843 mi. (6,163 km.)

Continent maps drawn using the Lambert Azimuthal Equal Area projection (Fig. 4) contain distortions ranging from 2.3 percent for Europe up to 15 percent for Asia. The Optimal Conformal cuts that distortion in half, improving distance measurements on these continent maps. Less distortion means greater visual fidelity, so the shape of a continent on an Optimal projection more closely represents its True shape. The table above compares measurements on the Optimal projection to those of the Lambert Azimuthal Equal Area projection for selected cities.

accurate projections that have ever been made. All of the continents maps in this atlas (with the exception of Antarctica) have been drawn using this projection.

Projections Compared

Because the true shapes of earth's landforms are unfamiliar to most people, distinguishing between various projections can be difficult. The following diagrams reveal the distortions introduced by several commonly used projections. By using a simple face with familiar shapes as the starting point (The Plan), it is easy to see the benefits — and drawbacks — of each. Think of the facial features as continents. Note that distortion appears not only in the features themselves, but in the changing shapes, angles and areas of the background grid, or graticule.

Figure 5: The Plan

The Plan indicates that the continents are either perfect concentric circles or are true straight lines *on the earth.* They should appear that way on a "perfect" map.

Figure 6: Orthographic Projection

This view shows the continents on the earth as seen from space. The facial features occupy half of the earth, which is all that you can see from this perspective. As you move outward towards the edge, note how the eyes become elliptical, the nose appears larger and less straight, and the mouth is curved into a smile.

Figure 7: Mercator

This cylindrical projection preserves angles exactly, but the mouth is now smiling broadly, and shows extreme distortion at the map's outer edge. This rapid expansion as you move away from the map's center is typified by the extreme enlargement of Greenland found on Mercator world maps (also see Fig. 1).

Figure 8: Peters

The Peters projection is a square equal area projection elongated, or stretched vertically, by a factor of two. While representing areas in their correct proportions, it does not closely resemble the Plan, and angles, local shapes and global relations are significantly distorted.

Figure 9: Hammond's Optimal Conformal

As you can see, this projection minimizes inaccuracies between the angles and shapes of the Plan, yielding a near-perfect map of the given area, up to a complete hemisphere. Like all conformal maps, the Optimal projection preserves every angle exactly, but it is more successful than previous projections at spreading the inevitable curvature across the entire map. Note that the sides of the triangle appear almost straight while correctly containing more than 180°. And though the eyes are slightly too large, it is the only map with eyes which appear concentric. Both mathematically and visually, it offers the best conformal map that can be made of the ideal Plan. All continent maps in this atlas are drawn on this projection.

Figure 5
The Plan

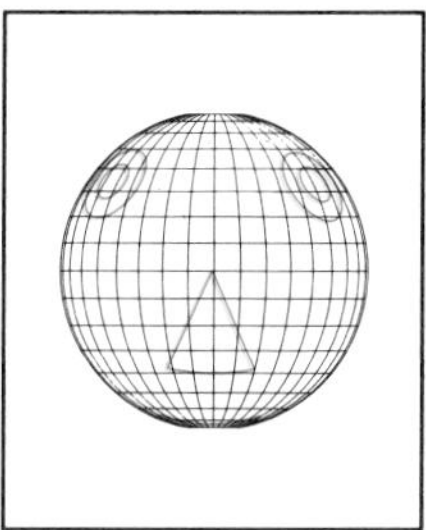

Figure 6
Orthographic Projection

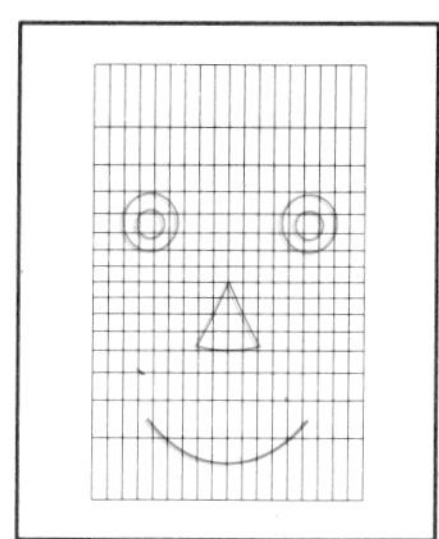

Figure 7
Mercator Projection

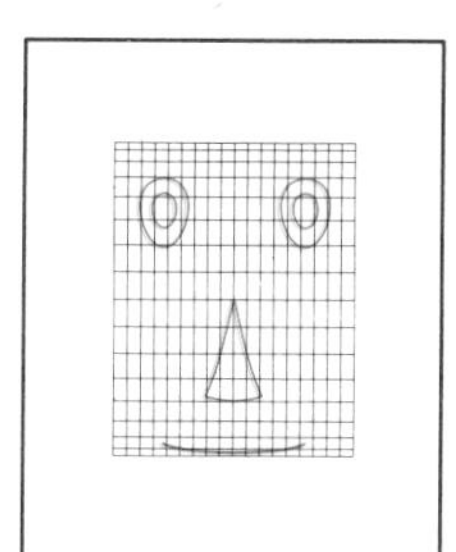

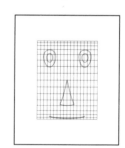

Figure 8
Peters Projection

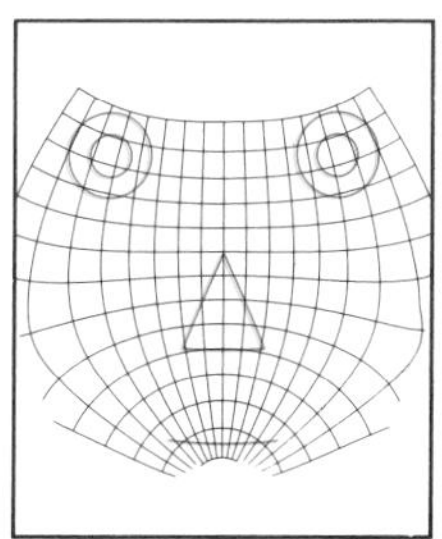

Figure 9
Optimal Conformal Projection

Using This Atlas

How to Locate Information Quickly
Our Maps of the World section is organized by continent. If you're looking for a major region of the world, consult the Contents on page two.

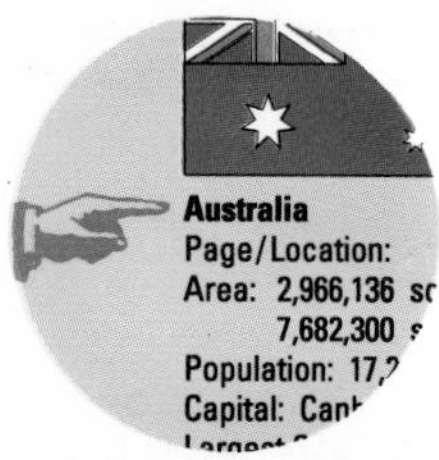

Australia
Page/Location:
Area: 2,966,136
7,682,300
Population:
Capital:

World Reference Guide
This concise guide lists the countries of the world alphabetically. If you're looking for the largest scale map of any country, you'll find a page and alpha-numeric reference at a glance, as well as information about each country, including its flag.

Merlimont, France
Mersch, Luxembourg
68/A3 Mers-les-Bains, France
69/F4 Mertert, Luxembourg
69/F4 Mertesdorf, Germany
69/G6 Mertzwiller, France
69/B5 Méru, France
68/B2 Merville, France
69/F2 Merzenich, Germany
69/F5 Merzig, Germany
Messancy, Belgium

Master Index
When you're looking for a specific place or physical feature, your quickest route is the Master Index. This 45,000-entry alphabetical index lists both the page number and alpha-numeric reference for major places and features in Maps of the World.

This new atlas is created from a unique digital database, and its computer-generated maps represent a new phase in map-making technology.

How Computer-Generated Maps Are Made

To build a digital database capable of generating this world atlas, the latitude and longitude of every significant town, river, coastline, boundary, transportation network and peak elevation was researched and digitized. Hundreds of millions of data points describing every important geographic feature are organized into thousands of different map feature codes.

There are no maps in this unique system. Rather, it consists entirely of coded points, lines and polygons. To create a map, cartographers simply determine what specific information they wish to show, based upon considerations of scale, size, density and importance of different features.

New technology developed by Hammond describes and re-configures coastlines, borders and other linework to fit a variety of map scales and projections. A computerized type placement program allows thousands of map labels to be placed accurately in minutes.

Each section of this atlas has been designed to be both easy and enjoyable to use. Familiarizing yourself with its organization will help you to benefit fully from its use.

World Flags and Reference Guide

This colorful section portrays each nation of the world, its flag, important geographical data, such as size, population and capital, and its location in the Maps of the World section.

Global Relationships

Three thematic chapters highlight social and cultural factors providing a fresh perspective on the world today.

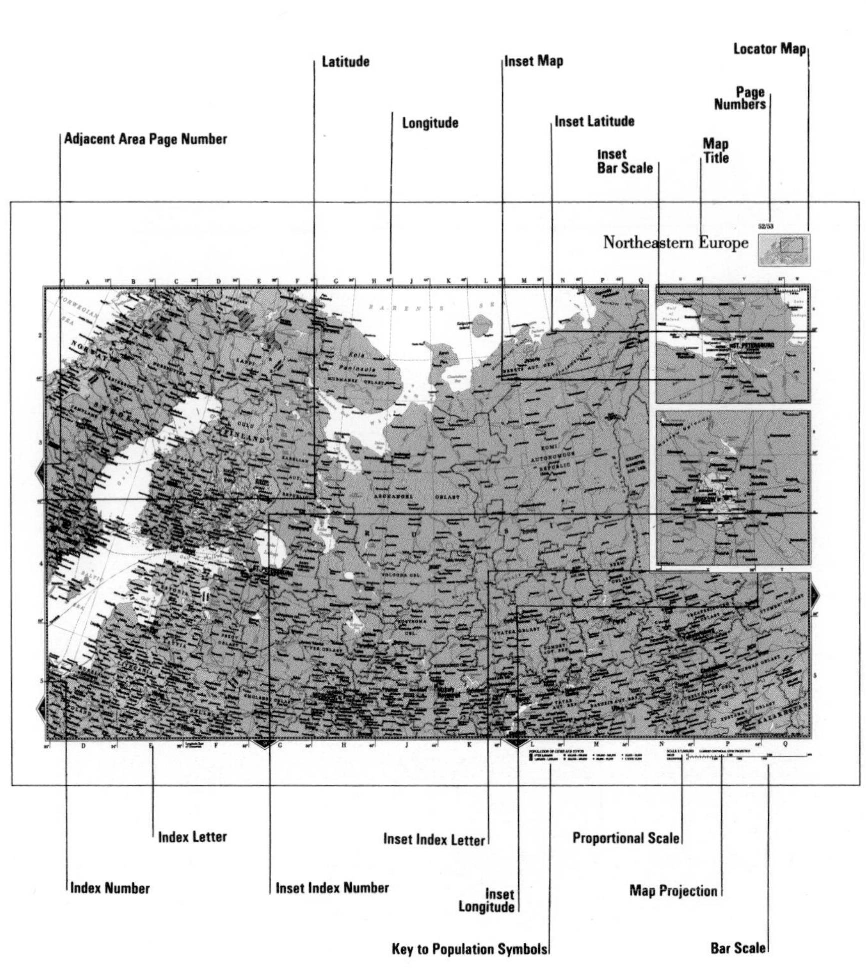

Latitude
Inset Map
Locator Map
Page Numbers
Longitude
Inset Latitude
Adjacent Area Page Number
Inset Bar Scale
Map Title
Northeastern Europe
Index Letter
Inset Index Letter
Proportional Scale
Index Number
Inset Index Number
Inset Longitude
Map Projection
Key to Population Symbols
Bar Scale

Symbols Used on Maps of the World

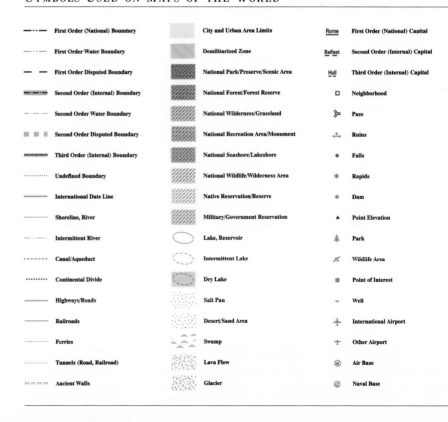

First Order (National) Boundary	City and Urban Area Limits	Rome — First Order (National) Capital
First Order Water Boundary	Demilitarized Zone	Belfast — Second Order (Internal) Capital
First Order Disputed Boundary	National Park/Preserve/Scenic Area	Hull — Third Order (Internal) Capital
Second Order (Internal) Boundary	National Forest/Forest Reserve	Neighborhood
Second Order Water Boundary	National Wilderness/Grassland	Pass
Second Order Disputed Boundary	National Recreation Area/Monument	Ruins
Third Order (Internal) Boundary	National Seashore/Lakeshore	Falls
Undefined Boundary	National Wildlife/Wilderness Area	Rapids
International Date Line	Native Reservation/Reserve	Dam
Shoreline, River	Military/Government Reservation	Point Elevation
Intermittent River	Lake, Reservoir	Park
Canal/Aqueduct	Intermittent Lake	Wildlife Area
Continental Divide	Dry Lake	Point of Interest
Highways/Roads	Salt Pan	Well
Railroads	Desert/Sand Area	International Airport
Ferries	Swamp	Other Airport
Tunnels (Road, Railroad)	Lava Flow	Air Base
Ancient Walls	Glacier	Naval Base

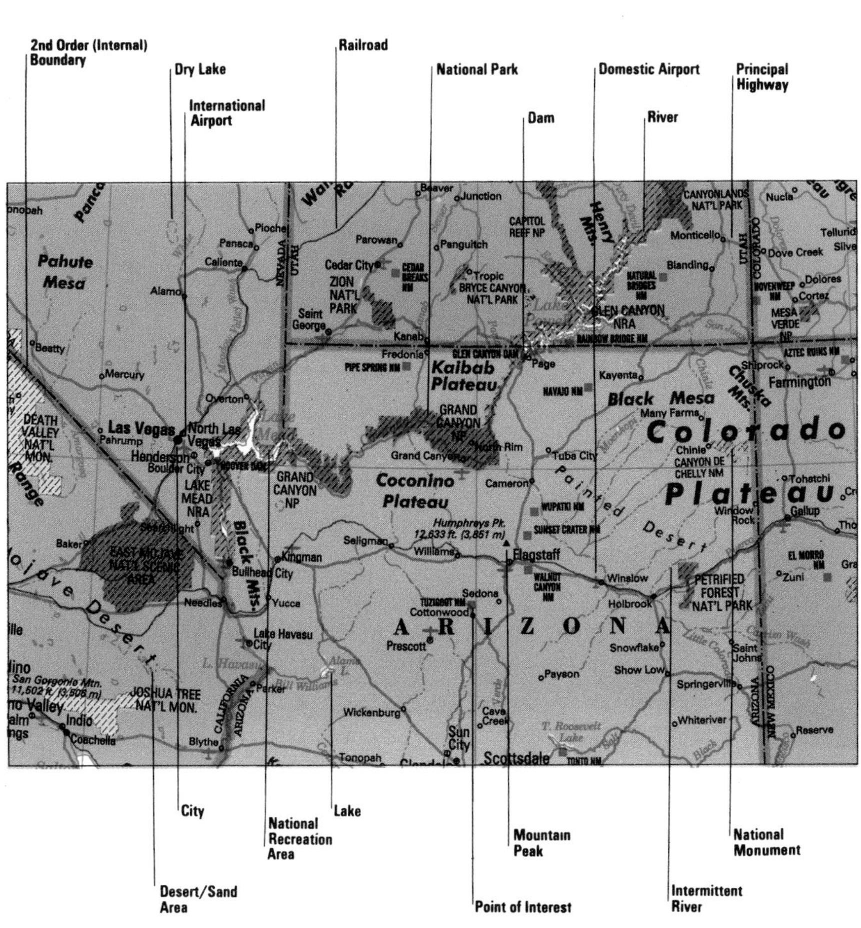

2nd Order (Internal) Boundary
Railroad
Dry Lake
International Airport
National Park
Dam
Domestic Airport
River
Principal Highway
Pahute Mesa
Kaibab Plateau
Black Mesa
Colorado Plateau
Coconino Plateau
ARIZONA
Las Vegas
Flagstaff
City
Lake
National Recreation Area
Mountain Peak
National Monument
Desert/Sand Area
Point of Interest
Intermittent River

Principal Map Abbreviations

Abor. Rsv.	Aboriginal Reserve	Ind. Res.	Indian Reservation	NWR	National Wildlife
Admin.	Administration	Int'l	International		Reserve
AFB	Air Force Base	IR	Indian Reservation	Obl.	Oblast
Amm. Dep.	Ammunition Depot	Isth.	Isthmus	Occ.	Occupied
Arch.	Archipelago	Jct.	Junction	Okr.	Okrug
Arpt.	Airport	L.	Lake	Par.	Parish
Aut.	Autonomous	Lag.	Lagoon	Passg.	Passage
B.	Bay	Lakesh.	Lakeshore	Pen.	Peninsula
Bfld.	Battlefield	Mem.	Memorial	Pk.	Peak
Bk.	Brook	Mil.	Military	Plat.	Plateau
Bor.	Borough	Miss.	Missile	PN	Park National
Br.	Branch	Mon.	Monument	Pref.	Prefecture
C.	Cape	Mt.	Mount	Prom.	Promontory
Can.	Canal	Mtn.	Mountain	Prov.	Province
Cap.	Capital	Mts.	Mountains	Prsv.	Preserve
C.G.	Coast Guard	Nat.	Natural	Pt.	Point
Chan.	Channel	Nat'l	National	R.	River
Co.	County	Nav.	Naval	RA	Recreation Area
Cr.	Creek	NB	National	Ra.	Range
Ctr.	Center		Battlefield	Rec.	Recreation(al)
Dep.	Depot	NBP	National	Ref.	Refuge
Depr.	Depression		Battlefield Park	Reg.	Region
Dept.	Department	NBS	National	Rep.	Republic
Des.	Desert		Battlefield Site	Res.	Reservoir,
Dist.	District	NHP	National Historical		Reservation
DMZ	Demilitarized Zone		Park	Rvwy.	Riverway
Dpcy.	Dependency	NHPP	National Historical	Sa.	Sierra
Eng.	Engineering		Park and Preserve	Sd.	Sound
Est.	Estuary	NHS	National Historic	Seash.	Seashore
Fd.	Fiord, Fjord		Site	So.	Southern
Fed.	Federal	NL	National Lakeshore	SP	State Park
Fk.	Fork	NM	National Monument	Spr., Sprs.	Spring, Springs
Fld.	Field	NMEMP	National Memorial	St.	State
For.	Forest		Park	Sta.	Station
Ft.	Fort	NMILP	National Military	Stm.	Stream
G.	Gulf		Park	Str.	Strait
Gov.	Governor	No.	Northern	Terr.	Territory
Govt.	Government	NP	National Park	Tun.	Tunnel
Gd.	Grand	NPP	National Park and	Twp.	Township
Gt.	Great		Preserve	Val.	Valley
Har.	Harbor	NPRSV	National Preserve	Vill.	Village
Hd.	Head	NRA	National	Vol.	Volcano
Hist.	Historic(al)		Recreation Area	Wild.	Wildlife,
Hts.	Heights	NRSV	National Reserve		Wilderness
I., Is.	Island(s)	NS	National Seashore	Wtr.	Water

The Physical World

These relief maps of the continents are derived from a digital cartographic database and drawn on a new Optimal Conformal Projection. They present the relationships of land and sea forms with startling realism.

Maps of the World

These detailed regional maps are arranged by continent, and introduced by a physical map of that continent which utilizes Hammond's new Optimal Conformal projection.

On the regional maps, individual colors for each country highlight political divisions. A country's color remains the same on all regional maps. These maps also provide considerable information by locating numerous political and physical geographic features.

World Statistics

World Statistics lists the dimensions of the earth's principal mountains, islands, rivers and lakes, along with other useful geographic information.

Master Index

This is an A-Z listing of names found on the political maps. It also has its own abbreviation list which, along with other Index keys, appears on page 122.

Map Scales

A map's scale is the relationship of any length on the map to an identical length on the earth's surface. A scale of 1:3,000,000 means that one inch on the map represents 3,000,000 inches (47 miles, 76 km.) on the earth's surface. A 1:1,000,000 scale is larger than a 1:3,000,000 scale, just as 1/1 is larger than 1/3.

The most densely populated areas are shown at a scale of 1:1,170,000, while selected metropolitan areas are covered at either 1:587,000 or 1:1,170,000. Other populous areas are presented at 1:3,500,000 and 1:7,000,000. Large regions and continent maps, as well as the United States, Canada, Russia, Pacific and World have smaller scales.

Boundary Policies

This atlas observes the boundary policies of the U.S. Department of State. Boundary disputes are customarily handled with a special symbol treatment, but de facto boundaries are favored if they seem to have any degree of permanence, in the belief that boundaries should reflect current geographic and political realities. The portrayal of independent nations in the atlas follows their recognition by the United Nations and/or the United States government.

The atlas uses

accepted conventional names for certain major foreign places. Usually, space permits the inclusion of the local form in parentheses. To make the maps more readily understandable to English-speaking readers, many foreign physical features are translated into more recognizable English forms.

A Word About Names

Our source for all foreign names and physical names in the United States is the decision lists of the U.S. Board of Geographic Names, which contain hundreds of thousands of place names. If a place is not listed, the Atlas follows the name form appearing on official foreign maps or in official gazetteers of the country concerned. For rendering domestic city, town and village names, this atlas follows the forms and spelling of the U.S. Postal Service.

World Flags and Reference Guide

Afghanistan
Page/Location: 61/H2
Area: 250,775 sq. mi.
649,507 sq. km.
Population: 16,450,000
Capital: Kabul
Largest City: Kabul
Highest Point: Noshaq
Monetary Unit: afghani

Albania
Page/Location: 49/F2
Area: 11,100 sq. mi.
28,749 sq. km.
Population: 3,335,000
Capital: Tiranë
Largest City: Tiranë
Highest Point: Korab
Monetary Unit: lek

Algeria
Page/Location: 82/F2
Area: 919,591 sq. mi.
2,381,740 sq. km.
Population: 26,022,000
Capital: Algiers
Largest City: Algiers
Highest Point: Tahat
Monetary Unit: Algerian dinar

Andorra
Page/Location: 47/F1
Area: 188 sq. mi.
487 sq. km.
Population: 53,000
Capital: Andorra la Vella
Largest City: Andorra la Vella
Highest Point: Coma Pedrosa
Monetary Unit: Fr. franc, Sp. peseta

Angola
Page/Location: 87/C3
Area: 481,351 sq. mi.
1,246,700 sq. km.
Population: 8,668,000
Capital: Luanda
Largest City: Luanda
Highest Point: Morro de Môco
Monetary Unit: kwanza

Antigua and Barbuda
Page/Location: 101/J4
Area: 171 sq. mi.
443 sq. km.
Population: 64,000
Capital: St. John's
Largest City: St. John's
Highest Point: Boggy Peak
Monetary Unit: East Caribbean dollar

Argentina
Page/Location: 91/C4
Area: 1,072,070 sq. mi.
2,776,661 sq. km.
Population: 32,664,000
Capital: Buenos Aires
Largest City: Buenos Aires
Highest Point: Cerro Aconcagua
Monetary Unit: Argentine peso

Armenia
Page/Location: 55/H5
Area: 11,506 sq. mi.
29,800 sq. km.
Population: 3,283,000
Capital: Yerevan
Largest City: Yerevan
Highest Point: Alagez
Monetary Unit: Armenian ruble

Australia
Page/Location: 74
Area: 2,966,136 sq. mi.
7,682,300 sq. km.
Population: 17,288,000
Capital: Canberra
Largest City: Sydney
Highest Point: Mt. Kosciusko
Monetary Unit: Australian dollar

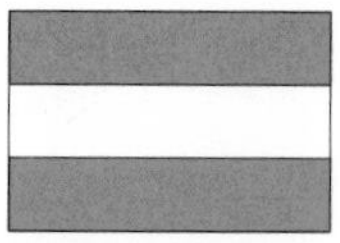

Austria
Page/Location: 45/L3
Area: 32,375 sq. mi.
83,851 sq. km.
Population: 7,666,000
Capital: Vienna
Largest City: Vienna
Highest Point: Grossglockner
Monetary Unit: schilling

Azerbaijan
Page/Location: 55/H4
Area: 33,436 sq. mi.
86,600 sq. km.
Population: 7,029,000
Capital: Baku
Largest City: Baku
Highest Point: Bazardyuzyu
Monetary Unit: Azerbaijani ruble

Bahamas
Page/Location: 101/F2
Area: 5,382 sq. mi.
13,939 sq. km.
Population: 252,000
Capital: Nassau
Largest City: Nassau
Highest Point: 207 ft. (63 m)
Monetary Unit: Bahamian dollar

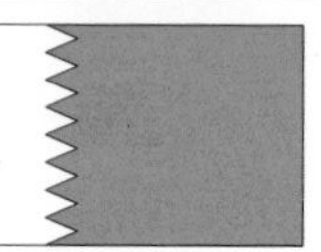

Bahrain
Page/Location: 60/F3
Area: 240 sq. mi.
622 sq. km.
Population: 537,000
Capital: Manama
Largest City: Manama
Highest Point: Jabal Dukhān
Monetary Unit: Bahraini dinar

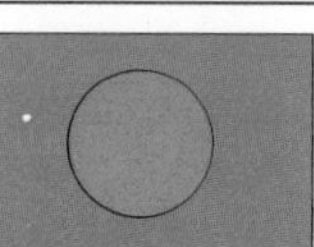

Bangladesh
Page/Location: 70/E3
Area: 55,126 sq. mi.
142,776 sq. km.
Population: 116,601,000
Capital: Dhaka
Largest City: Dhaka
Highest Point: Keokradong
Monetary Unit: taka

Barbados
Page/Location: 101/K5
Area: 166 sq. mi.
430 sq. km.
Population: 255,000
Capital: Bridgetown
Largest City: Bridgetown
Highest Point: Mt. Hillaby
Monetary Unit: Barbadian dollar

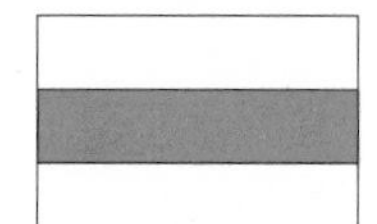

Belarus
Page/Location: 30/F3
Area: 80,154 sq. mi.
207,600 sq. km.
Population: 10,200,000
Capital: Minsk
Largest City: Minsk
Highest Point: Dzerzhinskaya
Monetary Unit: Belarusian ruble

Belgium
Page/Location: 42/C2
Area: 11,781 sq. mi.
30,513 sq. km.
Population: 9,922,000
Capital: Brussels
Largest City: Brussels
Highest Point: Botrange
Monetary Unit: Belgian franc

Belize
Page/Location: 100/D4
Area: 8,867 sq. mi.
22,966 sq. km.
Population: 228,000
Capital: Belmopan
Largest City: Belize City
Highest Point: Victoria Peak
Monetary Unit: Belize dollar

Benin
Page/Location: 85/F4
Area: 43,483 sq. mi.
112,620 sq. km.
Population: 4,832,000
Capital: Porto-Novo
Largest City: Cotonou
Highest Point: Nassoukou
Monetary Unit: CFA franc

Bhutan
Page/Location: 70/E2
Area: 18,147 sq. mi.
47,000 sq. km.
Population: 1,598,000
Capital: Thimphu
Largest City: Thimphu
Highest Point: Kula Kangri
Monetary Unit: ngultrum

Bolivia
Page/Location: 92/F7
Area: 424,163 sq. mi.
1,098,582 sq. km.
Population: 7,157,000
Capital: La Paz; Sucre
Largest City: La Paz
Highest Point: Nevado Ancohuma
Monetary Unit: Bolivian peso

Bosnia and Herzegovina
Page/Location: 50/C3
Area: 19,940 sq. mi.
51,129 sq. km.
Population: 4,124,256
Capital: Sarajevo
Largest City: Sarajevo
Highest Point: Maglič
Monetary Unit: —

Botswana
Page/Location: 87/D5
Area: 224,764 sq. mi.
582,139 sq. km.
Population: 1,258,000
Capital: Gaborone
Largest City: Gaborone
Highest Point: Tsodilo Hills
Monetary Unit: pula

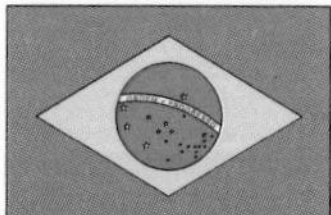

Brazil
Page/Location: 90/D3
Area: 3,284,426 sq. mi.
8,506,663 sq. km.
Population: 155,356,000
Capital: Brasília
Largest City: São Paulo
Highest Point: Pico da Neblina
Monetary Unit: cruzeiro real

Brunei
Page/Location: 72/D2
Area: 2,226 sq. mi.
5,765 sq. km.
Population: 398,000
Capital: Bandar Seri Begawan
Largest City: Bandar Seri Begawan
Highest Point: Bukit Pagon
Monetary Unit: Brunei dollar

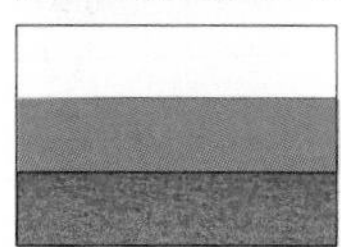

Bulgaria
Page/Location: 51/G4
Area: 42,823 sq. mi.
110,912 sq. km.
Population: 8,911,000
Capital: Sofia
Largest City: Sofia
Highest Point: Musala
Monetary Unit: lev

Burkina Faso
Page/Location: 85/E3
Area: 105,869 sq. mi.
274,200 sq. km.
Population: 9,360,000
Capital: Ouagadougou
Largest City: Ouagadougou
Highest Point: 2,405 ft. (733 m)
Monetary Unit: CFA franc

Burma
Page/Location: 71/G3
Area: 261,789 sq. mi.
678,034 sq. km.
Population: 42,112,000
Capital: Rangoon
Largest City: Rangoon
Highest Point: Hkakabo Razi
Monetary Unit: kyat

Burundi
Page/Location: 87/E1
Area: 10,747 sq. mi.
27,835 sq. km.
Population: 5,831,000
Capital: Bujumbura
Largest City: Bujumbura
Highest Point: 8,760 ft. (2,670 m)
Monetary Unit: Burundi franc

Cambodia
Page/Location: 69/D3
Area: 69,898 sq. mi.
181,036 sq. km.
Population: 7,146,000
Capital: Phnom Penh
Largest City: Phnom Penh
Highest Point: Phnum Aoral
Monetary Unit: riel

Cameroon
Page/Location: 82/H7
Area: 183,568 sq. mi.
475,441 sq. km.
Population: 11,390,000
Capital: Yaoundé
Largest City: Douala
Highest Point: Mt. Cameroon
Monetary Unit: CFA franc

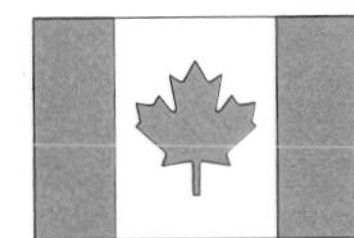

Canada
Page/Location: 102
Area: 3,851,787 sq. mi.
9,976,139 sq. km.
Population: 26,835,331
Capital: Ottawa
Largest City: Toronto
Highest Point: Mt. Logan
Monetary Unit: Canadian dollar

Cape Verde
Page/Location: 80/K9
Area: 1,557 sq. mi.
4,033 sq. km.
Population: 387,000
Capital: Praia
Largest City: Praia
Highest Point: 9,282 ft. (2,829 m)
Monetary Unit: Cape Verde escudo

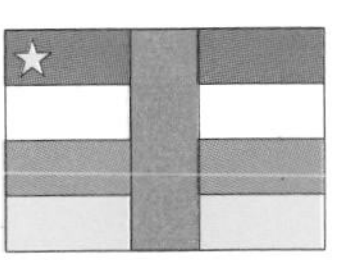

Central African Republic
Page/Location: 83/J6
Area: 242,000 sq. mi.
626,780 sq. km.
Population: 2,952,000
Capital: Bangui
Largest City: Bangui
Highest Point: Mt. Kayagangiri
Monetary Unit: CFA franc

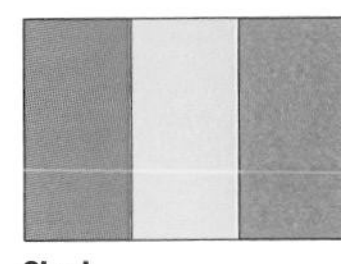

Chad
Page/Location: 83/J6
Area: 495,752 sq. mi.
1,283,998 sq. km.
Population: 5,122,000
Capital: N'Djamena
Largest City: N'Djamena
Highest Point: Emi Koussi
Monetary Unit: CFA franc

Chile
Page/Location: 91/B3
Area: 292,257 sq. mi.
756,946 sq. km.
Population: 13,287,000
Capital: Santiago
Largest City: Santiago
Highest Point: Nevado Ojos del Salado
Monetary Unit: Chilean peso

China
Page/Location: 58/J6
Area: 3,691,000 sq. mi.
9,559,690 sq. km.
Population: 1,151,487,000
Capital: Beijing
Largest City: Shanghai
Highest Point: Mt. Everest
Monetary Unit: yuan

Colombia
Page/Location: 92/D3
Area: 439,513 sq. mi.
1,138,339 sq. km.
Population: 33,778,000
Capital: Bogotá
Largest City: Bogotá
Highest Point: Pico Cristóbal Colón
Monetary Unit: Colombian peso

Comoros
Page/Location: 80/G6
Area: 719 sq. mi.
1,862 sq. km.
Population: 477,000
Capital: Moroni
Largest City: Moroni
Highest Point: Karthala
Monetary Unit: Comorian franc

Congo
Page/Location: 80/D5
Area: 132,046 sq. mi.
342,000 sq. km.
Population: 2,309,000
Capital: Brazzaville
Largest City: Brazzaville
Highest Point: Lékéti Mts.
Monetary Unit: CFA franc

Costa Rica
Page/Location: 100/E5
Area: 19,575 sq. mi.
50,700 sq. km.
Population: 3,111,000
Capital: San José
Largest City: San José
Highest Point: Cerro Chirripó Grande
Monetary Unit: Costa Rican colón

Croatia
Page/Location: 50/C3
Area: 22,050 sq. mi.
56,538 sq. km.
Population: 4,601,469
Capital: Zagreb
Largest City: Zagreb
Highest Point: Veliki Troglav
Monetary Unit: Croatian dinar

Cuba
Page/Location: 101/F3
Area: 44,206 sq. mi.
114,494 sq. km.
Population: 10,732,000
Capital: Havana
Largest City: Havana
Highest Point: Pico Turquino
Monetary Unit: Cuban peso

Cyprus
Page/Location: 59/J4
Area: 3,473 sq. mi.
8,995 sq. km.
Population: 709,000
Capital: Nicosia
Largest City: Nicosia
Highest Point: Olympus
Monetary Unit: Cypriot pound

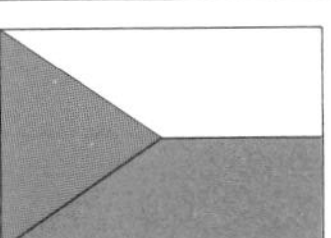

Czech Republic
Page/Location: 39/H4
Area: 30,449 sq. mi.
78,863 sq. km.
Population: 10,291,927
Capital: Prague
Largest City: Prague
Highest Point: Sněžka
Monetary Unit: Czech koruna

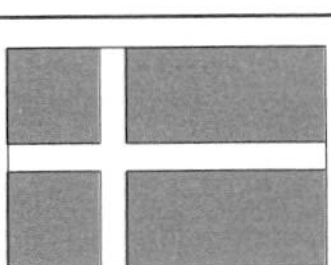

Denmark
Page/Location: 37/C5
Area: 16,629 sq. mi.
43,069 sq. km.
Population: 5,133,000
Capital: Copenhagen
Largest City: Copenhagen
Highest Point: Yding Skovhøj
Monetary Unit: Danish krone

Djibouti
Page/Location: 83/P5
Area: 8,880 sq. mi.
23,000 sq. km.
Population: 346,000
Capital: Djibouti
Largest City: Djibouti
Highest Point: Moussa Ali
Monetary Unit: Djibouti franc

Dominica
Page/Location: 101/J4
Area: 290 sq. mi.
751 sq. km.
Population: 86,000
Capital: Roseau
Largest City: Roseau
Highest Point: Morne Diablotin
Monetary Unit: Dominican dollar

Dominican Republic
Page/Location: 101/H4
Area: 18,704 sq. mi.
48,443 sq. km.
Population: 7,385,000
Capital: Santo Domingo
Largest City: Santo Domingo
Highest Point: Pico Duarte
Monetary Unit: Dominican peso

Ecuador
Page/Location: 92/C4
Area: 109,483 sq. mi.
283,591 sq. km.
Population: 10,752,000
Capital: Quito
Largest City: Guayaquil
Highest Point: Chimborazo
Monetary Unit: sucre

Egypt
Page/Location: 86/B3
Area: 386,659 sq. mi.
1,001,447 sq. km.
Population: 54,452,000
Capital: Cairo
Largest City: Cairo
Highest Point: Mt. Catherine
Monetary Unit: Egyptian pound

El Salvador
Page/Location: 100/D5
Area: 8,260 sq. mi.
21,393 sq. km.
Population: 5,419,000
Capital: San Salvador
Largest City: San Salvador
Highest Point: Santa Ana
Monetary Unit: Salvadoran colón

Equatorial Guinea
Page/Location: 82/G7
Area: 10,831 sq. mi.
28,052 sq. km.
Population: 379,000
Capital: Malabo
Largest City: Malabo
Highest Point: Pico de Santa Isabel
Monetary Unit: CFA franc

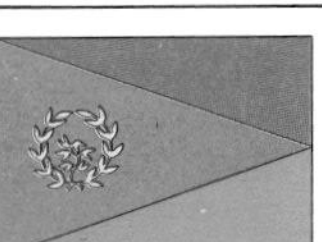

Eritrea
Page/Location: 83/N4
Area: 45,410 sq. mi.
117,600 sq. km.
Population: 2,614,700
Capital: Åsmera
Largest City: Åsmera
Highest Point: Soira
Monetary Unit: birr

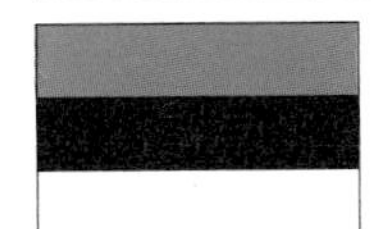

Estonia
Page/Location: 52/E4
Area: 17,413 sq. mi.
45,100 sq. km.
Population: 1,573,000
Capital: Tallinn
Largest City: Tallinn
Highest Point: Munamägi
Monetary Unit: kroon

Ethiopia
Page/Location: 83/N6
Area: 426,366 sq. mi.
1,104,300 sq. km.
Population: 50,576,300
Capital: Addis Ababa
Largest City: Addis Ababa
Highest Point: Ras Dashen Terara
Monetary Unit: birr

Fiji
Page/Location: 78/G6
Area: 7,055 sq. mi.
18,272 sq. km.
Population: 744,000
Capital: Suva
Largest City: Suva
Highest Point: Tomaniivi
Monetary Unit: Fijian dollar

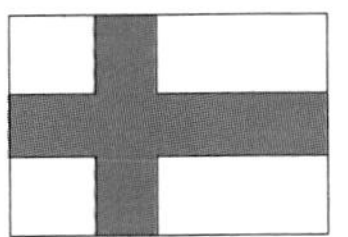

Finland
Page/Location: 37/H2
Area: 130,128 sq. mi.
337,032 sq. km.
Population: 4,991,000
Capital: Helsinki
Largest City: Helsinki
Highest Point: Kahperusvaara
Monetary Unit: markka

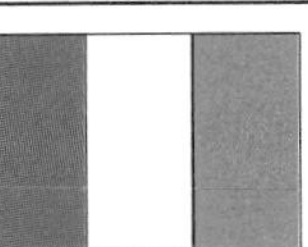

France
Page/Location: 44/D3
Area: 210,038 sq. mi.
543,998 sq. km.
Population: 56,596,000
Capital: Paris
Largest City: Paris
Highest Point: Mont Blanc
Monetary Unit: French franc

Gabon
Page/Location: 82/H7
Area: 103,346 sq. mi.
267,666 sq. km.
Population: 1,080,000
Capital: Libreville
Largest City: Libreville
Highest Point: Mt. Iboundji
Monetary Unit: CFA franc

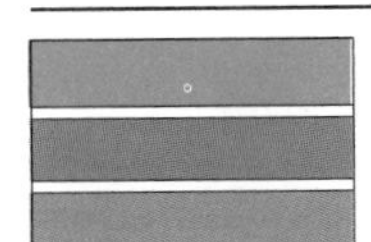

Gambia
Page/Location: 84/B3
Area: 4,127 sq. mi.
10,689 sq. km.
Population: 875,000
Capital: Banjul
Largest City: Banjul
Highest Point: 98 ft. (30 m)
Monetary Unit: dalasi

Georgia
Page/Location: 55/G4
Area: 26,911 sq. mi.
69,700 sq. km.
Population: 5,449,000
Capital: Tbilisi
Largest City: Tbilisi
Highest Point: Kazbek
Monetary Unit: Georgian ruble

Germany
Page/Location: 38/E3
Area: 137,753 sq. mi.
356,780 sq. km.
Population: 79,548,000
Capital: Berlin
Largest City: Berlin
Highest Point: Zugspitze
Monetary Unit: Deutsche mark

Ghana
Page/Location: 85/E4
Area: 92,099 sq. mi.
238,536 sq. km.
Population: 15,617,000
Capital: Accra
Largest City: Accra
Highest Point: Afadjoto
Monetary Unit: cedi

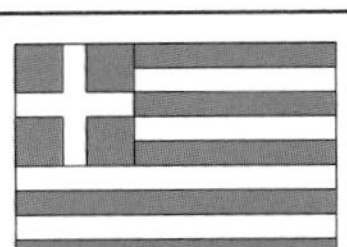

Greece
Page/Location: 49/G3
Area: 50,944 sq. mi.
131,945 sq. km.
Population: 10,043,000
Capital: Athens
Largest City: Athens
Highest Point: Mt. Olympus
Monetary Unit: drachma

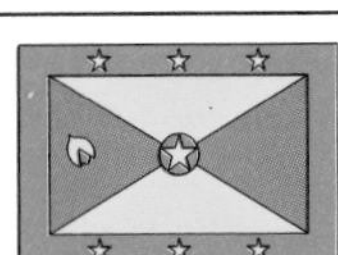

Grenada
Page/Location: 101/J5
Area: 133 sq. mi.
344 sq. km.
Population: 84,000
Capital: St. George's
Largest City: St. George's
Highest Point: Mt. St. Catherine
Monetary Unit: East Caribbean dollar

World Flags and Reference Guide

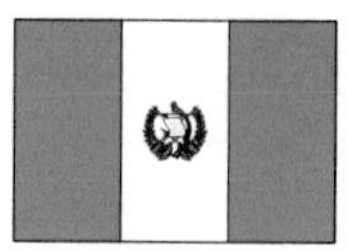

Guatemala
Page/Location: 100/C4
Area: 42,042 sq. mi.
108,889 sq. km.
Population: 9,266,000
Capital: Guatemala
Largest City: Guatemala
Highest Point: Tajumulco
Monetary Unit: quetzal

Guinea
Page/Location: 84/C4
Area: 94,925 sq. mi.
245,856 sq. km.
Population: 7,456,000
Capital: Conakry
Largest City: Conakry
Highest Point: Mt. Nimba
Monetary Unit: Guinea franc

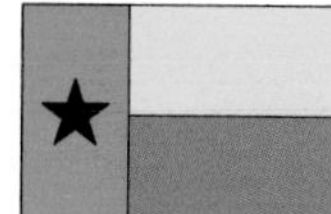

Guinea-Bissau
Page/Location: 84/B3
Area: 13,948 sq. mi.
36,125 sq. km.
Population: 943,000
Capital: Bissau
Largest City: Bissau
Highest Point: 689 ft. (210 m)
Monetary Unit: Guinea-Bissau peso

Guyana
Page/Location: 92/G2
Area: 83,000 sq. mi.
214,970 sq. km.
Population: 1,024,000
Capital: Georgetown
Largest City: Georgetown
Highest Point: Mt. Roraima
Monetary Unit: Guyana dollar

Haiti
Page/Location: 101/G4
Area: 10,694 sq. mi.
27,697 sq. km.
Population: 6,287,000
Capital: Port-au-Prince
Largest City: Port-au-Prince
Highest Point: Pic la Selle
Monetary Unit: gourde

Honduras
Page/Location: 100/D4
Area: 43,277 sq. mi.
112,087 sq. km.
Population: 4,949,000
Capital: Tegucigalpa
Largest City: Tegucigalpa
Highest Point: Cerro de las Minas
Monetary Unit: lempira

Hungary
Page/Location: 50/D2
Area: 35,919 sq. mi.
93,030 sq. km.
Population: 10,558,000
Capital: Budapest
Largest City: Budapest
Highest Point: Kékes
Monetary Unit: forint

Iceland
Page/Location: 37/N7
Area: 39,768 sq. mi.
103,000 sq. km.
Population: 260,000
Capital: Reykjavík
Largest City: Reykjavík
Highest Point: Hvannadalshnúkur
Monetary Unit: króna

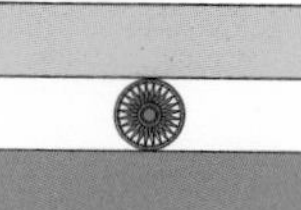

India
Page/Location: 70/C3
Area: 1,269,339 sq. mi.
3,287,558 sq. km.
Population: 869,515,000
Capital: New Delhi
Largest City: Calcutta
Highest Point: Nanda Devi
Monetary Unit: Indian rupee

Indonesia
Page/Location: 73/E4
Area: 788,430 sq. mi.
2, 042,034 sq. km.
Population: 19,560,000
Capital: Jakarta
Largest City: Jakarta
Highest Point: Puncak Jaya
Monetary Unit: rupiah

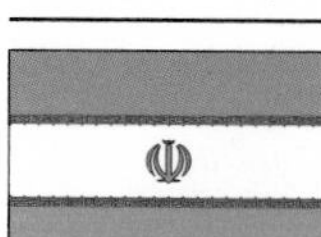

Iran
Page/Location: 60/F2
Area: 636,293 sq. mi.
1,648,000 sq. km.
Population: 59,051,000
Capital: Tehran
Largest City: Tehran
Highest Point: Qolleh-ye Damāvand
Monetary Unit: Iranian rial

Iraq
Page/Location: 60/D2
Area: 172,476 sq. mi.
446,713 sq. km.
Population: 19,525,000
Capital: Baghdad
Largest City: Baghdad
Highest Point: Haji Ibrahim
Monetary Unit: Iraqi dinar

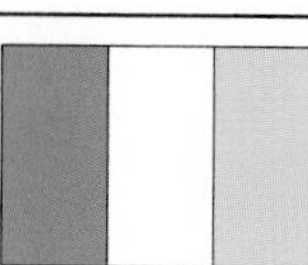

Ireland
Page/Location: 36/A4
Area: 27,136 sq. mi.
70,282 sq. km.
Population: 3,489,000
Capital: Dublin
Largest City: Dublin
Highest Point: Carrantuohill
Monetary Unit: Irish pound

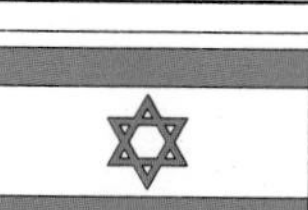

Israel
Page/Location: 59/K5
Area: 7,847 sq. mi.
20,324 sq. km.
Population: 4,558,000
Capital: Jerusalem
Largest City: Tel Aviv-Yafo
Highest Point: Har Meron
Monetary Unit: shekel

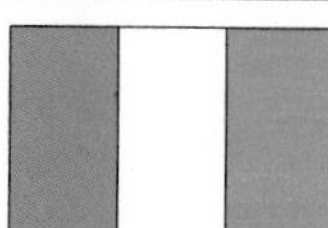

Italy
Page/Location: 30/E4
Area: 116,303 sq. mi.
301,225 sq. km.
Population: 57,772,000
Capital: Rome
Largest City: Rome
Highest Point: Monte Rosa
Monetary Unit: Italian lira

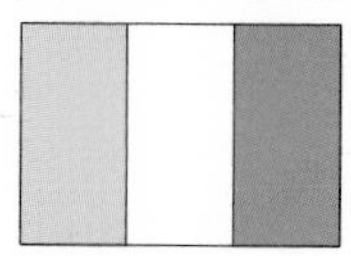

Ivory Coast
Page/Location: 84/D5
Area: 124,504 sq. mi.
322,465 sq. km.
Population: 12,978,000
Capital: Yamoussoukro
Largest City: Abidjan
Highest Point: Mt. Nimba
Monetary Unit: CFA franc

Jamaica
Page/Location: 101/F4
Area: 4,411 sq. mi.
11,424 sq. km.
Population: 2,489,000
Capital: Kingston
Largest City: Kingston
Highest Point: Blue Mountain Pk.
Monetary Unit: Jamaican dollar

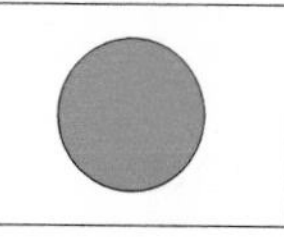

Japan
Page/Location: 63/M4
Area: 145,730 sq. mi.
377,441 sq. km.
Population: 124,017,000
Capital: Tokyo
Largest City: Tokyo
Highest Point: Fujiyama
Monetary Unit: yen

Jordan
Page/Location: 60/C2
Area: 35,000 sq. mi.
90,650 sq. km.
Population: 3,413,000
Capital: Amman
Largest City: Amman
Highest Point: Jabal Ramm
Monetary Unit: Jordanian dinar

Kazakhstan
Page/Location: 56/G5
Area: 1,048,300 sq. mi.
2,715,100 sq. km.
Population: 16,538,000
Capital: Alma-Ata
Largest City: Alma-Ata
Highest Point: Khan-Tengri
Monetary Unit: Kazakhstani ruble

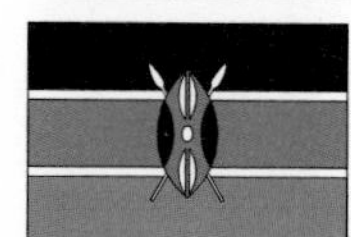

Kenya
Page/Location: 83/M7
Area: 224,960 sq. mi.
582,646 sq. km.
Population: 25,242,000
Capital: Nairobi
Largest City: Nairobi
Highest Point: Mt. Kenya
Monetary Unit: Kenya shilling

Kiribati
Page/Location: 79/H5
Area: 291 sq. mi.
754 sq. km.
Population: 71,000
Capital: Bairiki
Largest City: —
Highest Point: Banaba Island
Monetary Unit: Australian dollar

Korea, North
Page/Location: 63/K3
Area: 46,540 sq. mi.
120,539 sq. km.
Population: 21,815,000
Capital: P'yŏngyang
Largest City: P'yŏngyang
Highest Point: Paektu-san
Monetary Unit: North Korean won

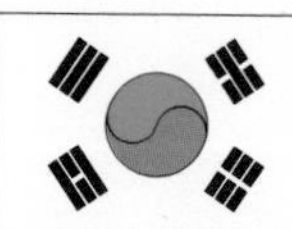

Korea, South
Page/Location: 63/K4
Area: 38,175 sq. mi.
98,873 sq. km.
Population: 43,134,000
Capital: Seoul
Largest City: Seoul
Highest Point: Halla-san
Monetary Unit: South Korean won

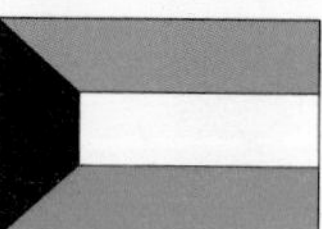

Kuwait
Page/Location: 60/E3
Area: 6,532 sq. mi.
16,918 sq. km.
Population: 2,204,000
Capital: Al Kuwait
Largest City: Al Kuwait
Highest Point: 951 ft. (290 m)
Monetary Unit: Kuwaiti dinar

Kyrgyzstan
Page/Location: 68/B3
Area: 76,641 sq. mi.
198,500 sq. km.
Population: 4,291,000
Capital: Bishkek
Largest City: Bishkek
Highest Point: Pik Pobedy
Monetary Unit: Kyrgyz ruble

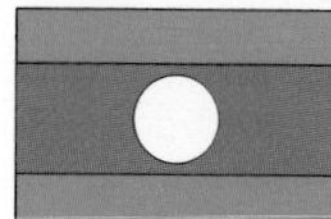

Laos
Page/Location: 69/C2
Area: 91,428 sq. mi.
236,800 sq. km.
Population: 4,113,000
Capital: Vientiane
Largest City: Vientiane
Highest Point: Phou Bia
Monetary Unit: kip

Latvia
Page/Location: 52/E4
Area: 24,595 sq. mi.
63,700 sq. km.
Population: 1,681,000
Capital: Riga
Largest City: Riga
Highest Point: Gaizina Kalns
Monetary Unit: Latvian ruble, lat

Lebanon
Page/Location: 59/K5
Area: 4,015 sq. mi.
10,399 sq. km.
Population: 3,385,000
Capital: Beirut
Largest City: Beirut
Highest Point: Qurnat as Sawdā'
Monetary Unit: Lebanese pound

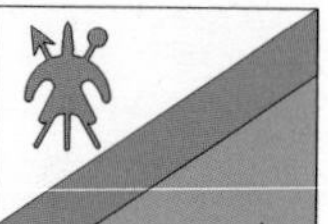

Lesotho
Page/Location: 88/E3
Area: 11,720 sq. mi.
30,355 sq. km.
Population: 1,801,000
Capital: Maseru
Largest City: Maseru
Highest Point: Thabana-Ntlenyana
Monetary Unit: loti

Liberia
Page/Location: 84/C4
Area: 43,000 sq. mi.
111,370 sq. km.
Population: 2,730,000
Capital: Monrovia
Largest City: Monrovia
Highest Point: Mt. Wuteve
Monetary Unit: Liberian dollar

Libya
Page/Location: 83/J2
Area: 679,358 sq. mi.
1,759,537 sq. km.
Population: 4,353,000
Capital: Tripoli
Largest City: Tripoli
Highest Point: Picco Bette
Monetary Unit: Libyan dinar

Liechtenstein
Page/Location: 45/H3
Area: 61 sq. mi.
158 sq. km.
Population: 28,000
Capital: Vaduz
Largest City: Vaduz
Highest Point: Grauspitz
Monetary Unit: Swiss franc

Lithuania
Page/Location: 52/D5
Area: 25,174 sq. mi.
65,200 sq. km.
Population: 3,690,000
Capital: Vilnius
Largest City: Vilnius
Highest Point: Nevaišių
Monetary Unit: talonas

Luxembourg
Page/Location: 43/F4
Area: 999 sq. mi.
2,587 sq. km.
Population: 388,000
Capital: Luxembourg
Largest City: Luxembourg
Highest Point: Ardennes Plateau
Monetary Unit: Luxembourg franc

Macedonia
Page/Location: 49/G2
Area: 9,889 sq. mi.
25,713 sq. km.
Population: 1,909,136
Capital: Skopje
Largest City: Skopje
Highest Point: Korab
Monetary Unit: denar

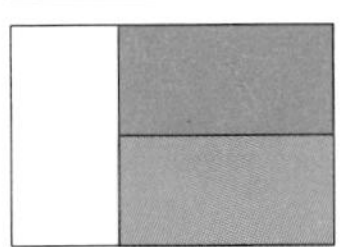

Madagascar
Page/Location: 89/H8
Area: 226,657 sq. mi.
587,041 sq. km.
Population: 12,185,000
Capital: Antananarivo
Largest City: Antananarivo
Highest Point: Maromokotro
Monetary Unit: Malagasy franc

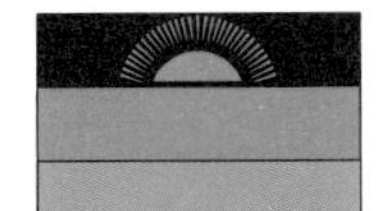

Malawi
Page/Location: 87/F3
Area: 45,747 sq. mi.
118, 485 sq. km.
Population: 9,438,000
Capital: Lilongwe
Largest City: Blantyre
Highest Point: Mulanje Mts.
Monetary Unit: Malawi kwacha

Malaysia
Page/Location: 73/C2
Area: 128,308 sq. mi.
332,318 sq. km.
Population: 17,982,000
Capital: Kuala Lumpur
Largest City: Kuala Lumpur
Highest Point: Gunung Kinabalu
Monetary Unit: ringgit

Maldives
Page/Location: 58/G9
Area: 115 sq. mi.
298 sq. km.
Population: 226,000
Capital: Male
Largest City: Male
Highest Point: 20 ft. (6 m)
Monetary Unit: rufiyaa

Mali
Page/Location: 82/E4
Area: 464,873 sq. mi.
1,204,021 sq. km.
Population: 8,339,000
Capital: Bamako
Largest City: Bamako
Highest Point: Hombori Tondo
Monetary Unit: CFA franc

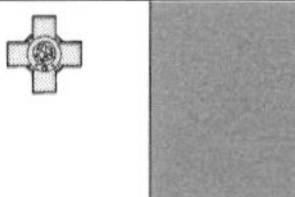

Malta
Page/Location: 48/D5
Area: 122 sq. mi.
316 sq. km.
Population: 356,000
Capital: Valletta
Largest City: Sliema
Highest Point: 830 ft. (253 m)
Monetary Unit: Maltese lira

Marshall Islands
Page/Location: 78/G3
Area: 70 sq. mi.
181 sq. km.
Population: 48,000
Capital: Majuro
Largest City: —
Highest Point: 20 ft. (6 m)
Monetary Unit: U.S. dollar

Mauritania
Page/Location: 82/C4
Area: 419,229 sq. mi.
1,085, 803 sq. km.
Population: 1,996,000
Capital: Nouakchott
Largest City: Nouakchott
Highest Point: Kediet Ijill
Monetary Unit: ouguiya

Mauritius
Page/Location: 89/S15
Area: 790 sq. mi.
2,046 sq. km.
Population: 1,081,000
Capital: Port Louis
Largest City: Port Louis
Highest Point: 2,713 ft. (827 m)
Monetary Unit: Mauritian rupee

Mexico
Page/Location: 100/A3
Area: 761,601 sq. mi.
1,972,546 sq. km.
Population: 90,007,000
Capital: Mexico City
Largest City: Mexico City
Highest Point: Citlaltépetl
Monetary Unit: Mexican peso

Micronesia
Page/Location: 78/D4
Area: 271 sq. mi.
702 sq. km.
Population: 108,000
Capital: Kolonia
Largest City: —
Highest Point: —
Monetary Unit: U.S. dollar

Moldova
Page/Location: 51/J2
Area: 13,012 sq. mi.
33,700 sq. km.
Population: 4,341,000
Capital: Kishinev
Largest City: Kishinev
Highest Point: 1,408 ft. (429 m)
Monetary Unit: Moldovan ruble

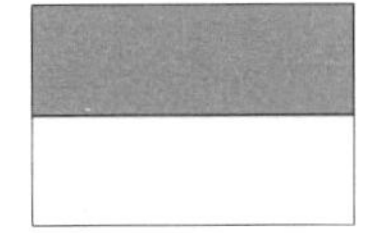

Monaco
Page/Location: 45/G5
Area: 368 acres
149 hectares
Population: 30,000
Capital: Monaco
Largest City: —
Highest Point: —
Monetary Unit: French franc

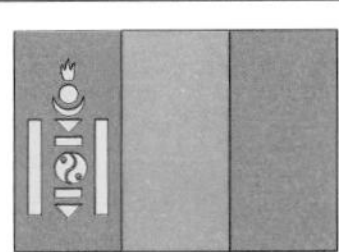

Mongolia
Page/Location: 62/D2
Area: 606,163 sq. mi.
1,569, 962 sq. km.
Population: 2,247,000
Capital: Ulaanbaatar
Largest City: Ulaanbaatar
Highest Point: Tavan Bogd Uul
Monetary Unit: tughrik

Morocco
Page/Location: 82/C1
Area: 172,414 sq. mi.
446,550 sq. km.
Population: 26,182,000
Capital: Rabat
Largest City: Casablanca
Highest Point: Jebel Toubkal
Monetary Unit: Moroccan dirham

Mozambique
Page/Location: 87/G4
Area: 303,769 sq. mi.
786,762 sq. km.
Population: 15,113,000
Capital: Maputo
Largest City: Maputo
Highest Point: Monte Binga
Monetary Unit: metical

Namibia
Page/Location: 87/C5
Area: 317,827 sq. mi.
823,172 sq. km.
Population: 1,521,000
Capital: Windhoek
Largest City: Windhoek
Highest Point: Brandberg
Monetary Unit: rand

Nauru
Page/Location: 78/F5
Area: 7.7 sq. mi.
20 sq. km.
Population: 9,000
Capital: Yaren (district)
Largest City: —
Highest Point: 230 ft. (70 m)
Monetary Unit: Australian dollar

Nepal
Page/Location: 70/D2
Area: 54,663 sq. mi.
141,557 sq. km.
Population: 19,612,000
Capital: Kathmandu
Largest City: Kathmandu
Highest Point: Mt. Everest
Monetary Unit: Nepalese rupee

Netherlands
Page/Location: 40/B5
Area: 15,892 sq. mi.
41,160 sq. km.
Population: 15,022,000
Capital: The Hague; Amsterdam
Largest City: Amsterdam
Highest Point: Vaalserberg
Monetary Unit: Netherlands guilder

New Zealand
Page/Location: 75/Q10
Area: 103,736 sq. mi.
268,676 sq. km.
Population: 3,309,000
Capital: Wellington
Largest City: Auckland
Highest Point: Mt. Cook
Monetary Unit: New Zealand dollar

Nicaragua
Page/Location: 100/D5
Area: 45,698 sq. mi.
118,358 sq. km.
Population: 3,752,000
Capital: Managua
Largest City: Managua
Highest Point: Pico Mogotón
Monetary Unit: córdoba

Niger
Page/Location: 82/G4
Area: 489,189 sq. mi.
1,267,000 sq. km.
Population: 8,154,000
Capital: Niamey
Largest City: Niamey
Highest Point: Bagzane
Monetary Unit: CFA franc

Nigeria
Page/Location: 82/G6
Area: 357,000 sq. mi.
924,630 sq. km.
Population: 122,471,000
Capital: Abuja
Largest City: Lagos
Highest Point: Dimlang
Monetary Unit: naira

Norway
Page/Location: 37/C3
Area: 125,053 sq. mi.
323,887 sq. km.
Population: 4,273,000
Capital: Oslo
Largest City: Oslo
Highest Point: Glittertjnden
Monetary Unit: Norwegian krone

Oman
Page/Location: 61/G4
Area: 120,000 sq. mi.
310,800 sq. km.
Population: 1,534,000
Capital: Muscat
Largest City: Muscat
Highest Point: Jabal ash Shām
Monetary Unit: Omani rial

Pakistan
Page/Location: 61/H3
Area: 310,403 sq. mi.
803,944 sq. km.
Population: 117,490,000
Capital: Islamabad
Largest City: Karachi
Highest Point: K2 (Godwin Austen)
Monetary Unit: Pakistani rupee

Panama
Page/Location: 101/E6
Area: 29,761 sq. mi.
77,082 sq. km.
Population: 2,476,000
Capital: Panamá
Largest City: Panamá
Highest Point: Barú
Monetary Unit: balboa

Papua New Guinea
Page/Location: 78/D5
Area: 183,540 sq. mi.
475,369 sq. km.
Population: 3,913,000
Capital: Port Moresby
Largest City: Port Moresby
Highest Point: Mt. Wilhelm
Monetary Unit: kina

Paraguay
Page/Location: 90/D5
Area: 157,047 sq. mi.
406,752 sq. km.
Population: 4,799,000
Capital: Asunción
Largest City: Asunción
Highest Point: Sierra de Amambay
Monetary Unit: guaraní

World Flags and Reference Guide

Peru
Page/Location: 92/C5
Area: 496,222 sq. mi.
1,285,215 sq. km.
Population: 22,362,000
Capital: Lima
Largest City: Lima
Highest Point: Nevado Huascarán
Monetary Unit: nuevo sol

Philippines
Page/Location: 67/D5
Area: 115,707 sq. mi.
299,681 sq. km.
Population: 65,759,000
Capital: Manila
Largest City: Manila
Highest Point: Mt. Apo
Monetary Unit: Philippine peso

Poland
Page/Location: 39/K2
Area: 120,725 sq. mi.
312,678 sq. km.
Population: 37,800,000
Capital: Warsaw
Largest City: Warsaw
Highest Point: Rysy
Monetary Unit: zloty

Portugal
Page/Location: 46/A3
Area: 35,549 sq. mi.
92,072 sq. km.
Population: 10,388,000
Capital: Lisbon
Largest City: Lisbon
Highest Point: Serra da Estrela
Monetary Unit: Portuguese escudo

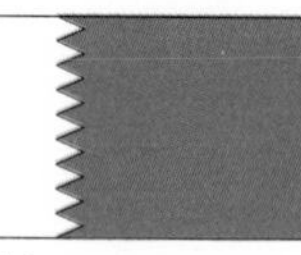

Qatar
Page/Location: 60/F3
Area: 4,247 sq. mi.
11,000 sq. km.
Population: 518,000
Capital: Doha
Largest City: Doha
Highest Point: Dukhān Heights
Monetary Unit: Qatari riyal

Romania
Page/Location: 51/F3
Area: 91,699 sq. mi.
237,500 sq. km.
Population: 23,397,000
Capital: Bucharest
Largest City: Bucharest
Highest Point: Moldoveanul
Monetary Unit: leu

Russia
Page/Location: 56/H3
Area: 6,592,812 sq. mi.
17,075,400 sq. km.
Population: 147,386,000
Capital: Moscow
Largest City: Moscow
Highest Point: El'brus
Monetary Unit: Russian ruble

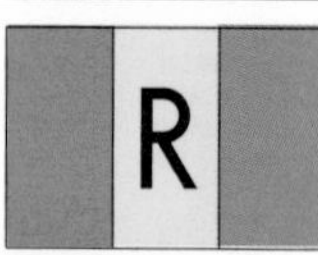

Rwanda
Page/Location: 87/E1
Area: 10,169 sq. mi.
26,337 sq. km.
Population: 7,903,000
Capital: Kigali
Largest City: Kigali
Highest Point: Karisimbi
Monetary Unit: Rwanda franc

Saint Kitts and Nevis
Page/Location: 101/J4
Area: 104 sq. mi.
269 sq. km.
Population: 40,000
Capital: Basseterre
Largest City: Basseterre
Highest Point: Mt. Misery
Monetary Unit: East Caribbean dollar

Saint Lucia
Page/Location: 101/J5
Area: 238 sq. mi.
616 sq. km.
Population: 153,000
Capital: Castries
Largest City: Castries
Highest Point: Mt. Gimie
Monetary Unit: East Caribbean dollar

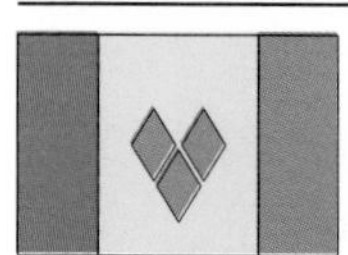

Saint Vincent and the Grenadines
Page/Location: 101/J5
Area: 150 sq. mi.
388 sq. km.
Population: 114,000
Capital: Kingstown
Largest City: Kingstown
Highest Point: Soufrière
Monetary Unit: East Caribbean dollar

San Marino
Page/Location: 45/K5
Area: 23.4 sq. mi.
60.6 sq. km.
Population: 23,000
Capital: San Marino
Largest City: San Marino
Highest Point: Monte Titano
Monetary Unit: Italian lira

São Tomé and Príncipe
Page/Location: 82/G7
Area: 372 sq. mi.
963 sq. km.
Population: 128,000
Capital: São Tomé
Largest City: São Tomé
Highest Point: Pico de São Tomé
Monetary Unit: dobra

Saudi Arabia
Page/Location: 60/D4
Area: 829,995 sq. mi.
2,149,687 sq. km.
Population: 17,870,000
Capital: Riyadh
Largest City: Riyadh
Highest Point: Jabal Sawdā'
Monetary Unit: Saudi riyal

Senegal
Page/Location: 84/B3
Area: 75,954 sq. mi.
196,720 sq. km.
Population: 7,953,000
Capital: Dakar
Largest City: Dakar
Highest Point: Fouta Djallon
Monetary Unit: CFA franc

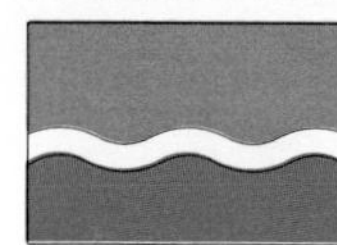

Seychelles
Page/Location: 80/H5
Area: 145 sq. mi.
375 sq. km.
Population: 69,000
Capital: Victoria
Largest City: Victoria
Highest Point: Morne Seychellois
Monetary Unit: Seychellois rupee

Sierra Leone
Page/Location: 84/B4
Area: 27,925 sq. mi.
72,325 sq. km.
Population: 4,275,000
Capital: Freetown
Largest City: Freetown
Highest Point: Loma Mansa
Monetary Unit: leone

Singapore
Page/Location: 72/B3
Area: 226 sq. mi.
585 sq. km.
Population: 2,756,000
Capital: Singapore
Largest City: Singapore
Highest Point: Bukit Timah
Monetary Unit: Singapore dollar

Slovakia
Page/Location: 39/K4
Area: 18,924 sq. mi.
49,014 sq. km.
Population: 4,991,168
Capital: Bratislava
Largest City: Bratislava
Highest Point: Gerlachovský Štít
Monetary Unit: Slovak koruna

Slovenia
Page/Location: 50/B3
Area: 7,898 sq. mi.
20,251 sq. km.
Population: 1,891,864
Capital: Ljubljana
Largest City: Ljubljana
Highest Point: Triglav
Monetary Unit: tolar

Solomon Islands
Page/Location: 78/E6
Area: 11,500 sq. mi.
29,785 sq. km.
Population: 347,000
Capital: Honiara
Largest City: Honiara
Highest Point: Mt. Makarakomburu
Monetary Unit: Solomon Islands dollar

Somalia
Page/Location: 83/Q6
Area: 246,200 sq. mi.
637,658 sq. km.
Population: 6,709,000
Capital: Mogadishu
Largest City: Mogadishu
Highest Point: Shimber Berris
Monetary Unit: Somali shilling

South Africa
Page/Location: 88/C3
Area: 455,318 sq. mi.
1,179,274 sq. km.
Population: 40,601,000
Capital: Cape Town; Pretoria
Largest City: Johannesburg
Highest Point: Injasuti
Monetary Unit: rand

Spain
Page/Location: 46/C2
Area: 194,881 sq. mi.
504,742 sq. km.
Population: 39,385,000
Capital: Madrid
Largest City: Madrid
Highest Point: Pico de Teide
Monetary Unit: peseta

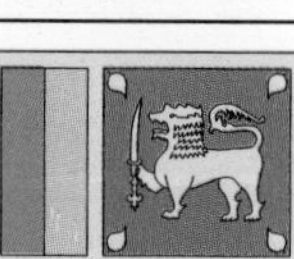

Sri Lanka
Page/Location: 70/D6
Area: 25,332 sq. mi.
65,610 sq. km.
Population: 17,424,000
Capital: Colombo
Largest City: Colombo
Highest Point: Pidurutalagala
Monetary Unit: Sri Lanka rupee

Sudan
Page/Location: 83/L5
Area: 967,494 sq. mi.
2,505,809 sq. km.
Population: 27,220,000
Capital: Khartoum
Largest City: Omdurman
Highest Point: Jabal Marrah
Monetary Unit: Sudanese pound

Suriname
Page/Location: 93/G3
Area: 55,144 sq. mi.
142,823 sq. km.
Population: 402,000
Capital: Paramaribo
Largest City: Paramaribo
Highest Point: Juliana Top
Monetary Unit: Suriname guilder

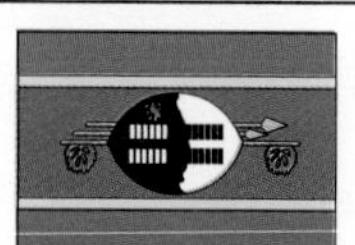

Swaziland
Page/Location: 89/E2
Area: 6,705 sq. mi.
17,366 sq. km.
Population: 859,000
Capital: Mbabane
Largest City: Mbabane
Highest Point: Emlembe
Monetary Unit: lilangeni

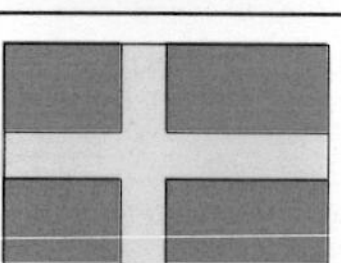

Sweden
Page/Location: 37/E3
Area: 173,665 sq. mi.
449,792 sq. km.
Population: 8,564,000
Capital: Stockholm
Largest City: Stockholm
Highest Point: Kebnekaise
Monetary Unit: krona

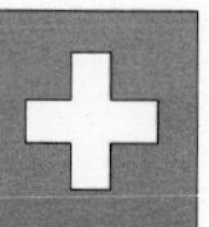

Switzerland
Page/Location: 45/H3
Area: 15,943 sq. mi.
41,292 sq. km.
Population: 6,784,000
Capital: Bern
Largest City: Zürich
Highest Point: Dufourspitze
Monetary Unit: Swiss franc

Syria
Page/Location: 60/C1
Area: 71,498 sq. mi.
185,180 sq. km.
Population: 12,966,000
Capital: Damascus
Largest City: Damascus
Highest Point: Jabal ash Shaykh
Monetary Unit: Syrian pound

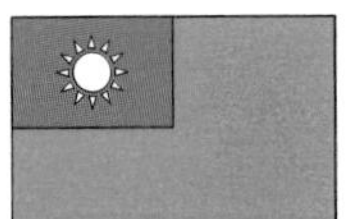

Taiwan
Page/Location: 67/D3
Area: 13,971 sq. mi.
36,185 sq. km.
Population: 16,609,961
Capital: Taipei
Largest City: Taipei
Highest Point: Yü Shan
Monetary Unit: new Taiwan dollar

Tajikistan
Page/Location: 56/H6
Area: 55,251 sq. mi.
143,100 sq. km.
Population: 5,112,000
Capital: Dushanbe
Largest City: Dushanbe
Highest Point: Communism Peak
Monetary Unit: Tajik ruble

Tanzania
Page/Location: 87/F2
Area: 363,708 sq. mi.
942,003 sq. km.
Population: 26,869,000
Capital: Dar es Salaam
Largest City: Dar es Salaam
Highest Point: Kilimanjaro
Monetary Unit: Tanzanian shilling

Thailand
Page/Location: 69/C3
Area: 198,455 sq. mi.
513,998 sq. km.
Population: 56,814,000
Capital: Bangkok
Largest City: Bangkok
Highest Point: Doi Inthanon
Monetary Unit: baht

Togo
Page/Location: 85/F4
Area: 21,622 sq. mi.
56,000 sq. km.
Population: 3,811,000
Capital: Lomé
Largest City: Lomé
Highest Point: Mt. Agou
Monetary Unit: CFA franc

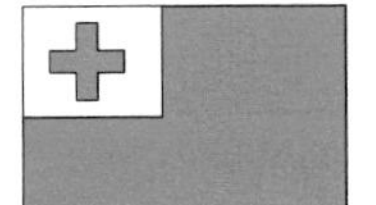

Tonga
Page/Location: 79/H7
Area: 270 sq. mi.
699 sq. km.
Population: 102,000
Capital: Nuku'alofa
Largest City: Nuku'alofa
Highest Point: Kao Island
Monetary Unit: pa'anga

Trinidad and Tobago
Page/Location: 101/J5
Area: 1,980 sq. mi.
5,128 sq. km.
Population: 1,285,000
Capital: Port-of-Spain
Largest City: Port-of-Spain
Highest Point: El Cerro del Aripo
Monetary Unit: Trin. & Tobago dollar

Tunisia
Page/Location: 82/G1
Area: 63,378 sq. mi.
164,149 sq. km.
Population: 8,276,000
Capital: Tunis
Largest City: Tunis
Highest Point: Jabal ash Sha'nabī
Monetary Unit: Tunisian dinar

Turkey
Page/Location: 59/C2
Area: 300,946 sq. mi.
779,450 sq. km.
Population: 58,581,000
Capital: Ankara
Largest City: Istanbul
Highest Point: Mt. Ararat
Monetary Unit: Turkish lira

Turkmenistan
Page/Location: 56/F6
Area: 188,455 sq. mi.
488,100 sq. km.
Population: 3,534,000
Capital: Ashkhabad
Largest City: Ashkhabad
Highest Point: Rize
Monetary Unit: Turkmen ruble

Tuvalu
Page/Location: 78/G5
Area: 9.8 sq. mi.
25.3 sq. km.
Population: 9,000
Capital: Fongafale
Largest City: —
Highest Point: 16 ft. (5 m)
Monetary Unit: Australian dollar

Uganda
Page/Location: 83/M7
Area: 91,076 sq. mi.
235,887 sq. km.
Population: 18,690,000
Capital: Kampala
Largest City: Kampala
Highest Point: Margherita Peak
Monetary Unit: Ugandan shilling

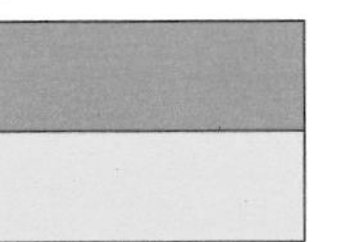

Ukraine
Page/Location: 54/D2
Area: 233,089 sq. mi.
603,700 sq. km.
Population: 51,704,000
Capital: Kiev
Largest City: Kiev
Highest Point: Goverla
Monetary Unit: Ukrainian ruble

United Arab Emirates
Page/Location: 60/F4
Area: 32,278 sq. mi.
83,600 sq. km.
Population: 2,390,000
Capital: Abu Dhabi
Largest City: Dubayy
Highest Point: Hajar Mts.
Monetary Unit: Emirian dirham

United Kingdom
Page/Location: 36
Area: 94,399 sq. mi.
244,493 sq. km.
Population: 57,515,000
Capital: London
Largest City: London
Highest Point: Ben Nevis
Monetary Unit: pound sterling

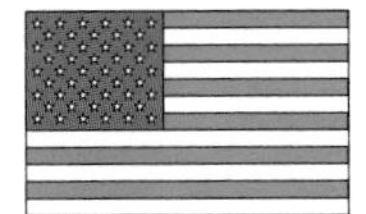

United States
Page/Location: 104
Area: 3,623,420 sq. mi.
9,384,658 sq. km.
Population: 252,502,000
Capital: Washington
Largest City: New York
Highest Point: Mt. McKinley
Monetary Unit: U.S. dollar

Uruguay
Page/Location: 91/E3
Area: 72,172 sq. mi.
186,925 sq. km.
Population: 3,121,000
Capital: Montevideo
Largest City: Montevideo
Highest Point: Cerro Catedral
Monetary Unit: Uruguayan peso

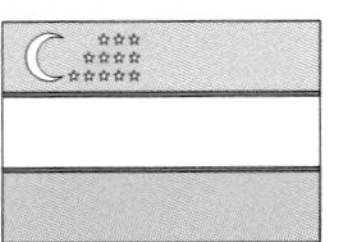

Uzbekistan
Page/Location: 56/G5
Area: 173,591 sq. mi.
449,600 sq. km.
Population: 19,906,000
Capital: Tashkent
Largest City: Tashkent
Highest Point: Khodzha-Pir'yakh
Monetary Unit: Uzbek ruble

Vanuatu
Page/Location: 78/F6
Area: 5,700 sq. mi.
14,763 sq. km.
Population: 170,000
Capital: Vila
Largest City: Vila
Highest Point: Tabwemasana
Monetary Unit: vatu

Vatican City
Page/Location: 48/C2
Area: 108.7 acres
44 hectares
Population: 1,000
Capital: —
Largest City: —
Highest Point: —
Monetary Unit: Italian lira

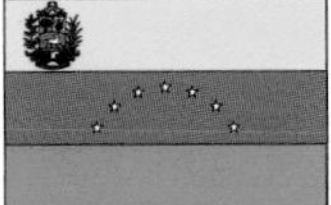

Venezuela
Page/Location: 92/E2
Area: 352,143 sq. mi.
912,050 sq. km.
Population: 20,189,000
Capital: Caracas
Largest City: Caracas
Highest Point: Pico Bolívar
Monetary Unit: bolívar

Vietnam
Page/Location: 69/D2
Area: 128,405 sq. mi.
332,569 sq. km.
Population: 67,568,000
Capital: Hanoi
Largest City: Ho Chi Minh City
Highest Point: Fan Si Pan
Monetary Unit: dong

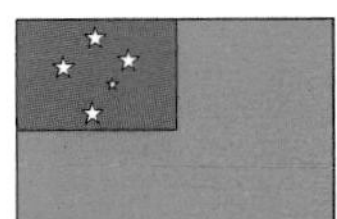

Western Samoa
Page/Location: 79/H6
Area: 1,133 sq. mi.
2,934 sq. km.
Population: 190,000
Capital: Apia
Largest City: Apia
Highest Point: Mt. Silisili
Monetary Unit: tala

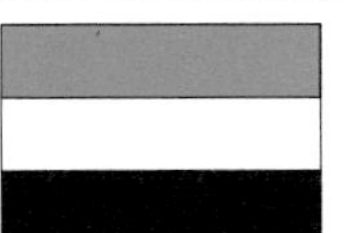

Yemen
Page/Location: 60/E5
Area: 188,321 sq. mi.
487,752 sq. km.
Population: 10,063,000
Capital: Sanaa
Largest City: Aden
Highest Point: Nabī Shu'ayb
Monetary Unit: Yemeni rial

Yugoslavia
Page/Location: 50/E3
Area: 38,989 sq. mi.
102,173 sq. km.
Population: 11,371,275
Capital: Belgrade
Largest City: Belgrade
Highest Point: Đaravica
Monetary Unit: Yugoslav new dinar

Zaire
Page/Location: 80/E5
Area: 905,063 sq. mi.
2,344,113 sq. km.
Population: 37,832,000
Capital: Kinshasa
Largest City: Kinshasa
Highest Point: Margherita Peak
Monetary Unit: zaire

Zambia
Page/Location: 87/E3
Area: 290,586 sq. mi.
752,618 sq. km.
Population: 8,446,000
Capital: Lusaka
Largest City: Lusaka
Highest Point: Sunzu
Monetary Unit: Zambian kwacha

Zimbabwe
Page/Location: 87/E4
Area: 150,803 sq. mi.
390,580 sq. km.
Population: 10,720,000
Capital: Harare
Largest City: Harare
Highest Point: Inyangani
Monetary Unit: Zimbabwe dollar

Environmental Concerns

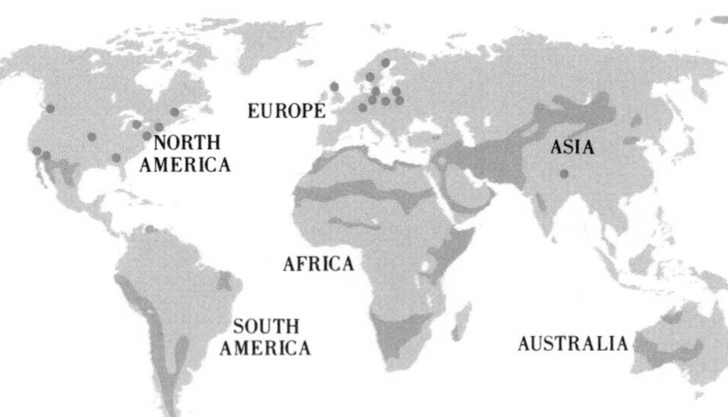

EUROPE
NORTH AMERICA
ASIA
AFRICA
SOUTH AMERICA
AUSTRALIA

DESERTIFICATION AND ACID RAIN DAMAGE

AREAS OF PRODUCTIVE DRYLANDS DESERTIFIED BY EARLY 1980's

AREAS OF DAMAGE FROM ACID RAIN AND OTHER AIRBORNE POLLUTANTS

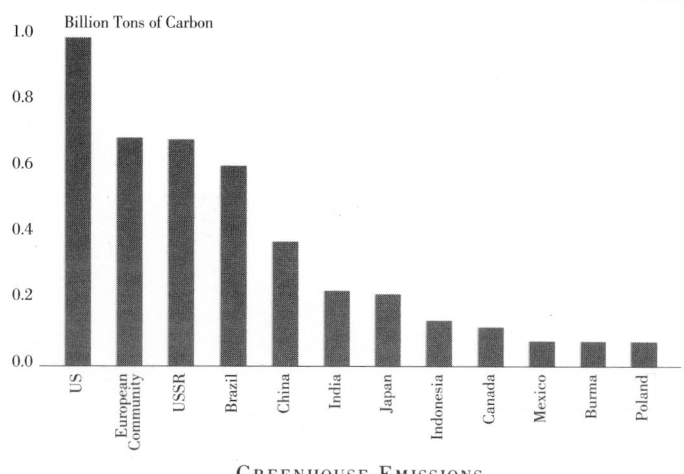

Billion Tons of Carbon
1.0
0.8
0.6
0.4
0.2
0.0
US
European Community
USSR
Brazil
China
India
Japan
Indonesia
Canada
Mexico
Burma
Poland

GREENHOUSE EMISSIONS

CARBON DIOXIDE EQUIVALENTS, 1987 NET EMISSIONS

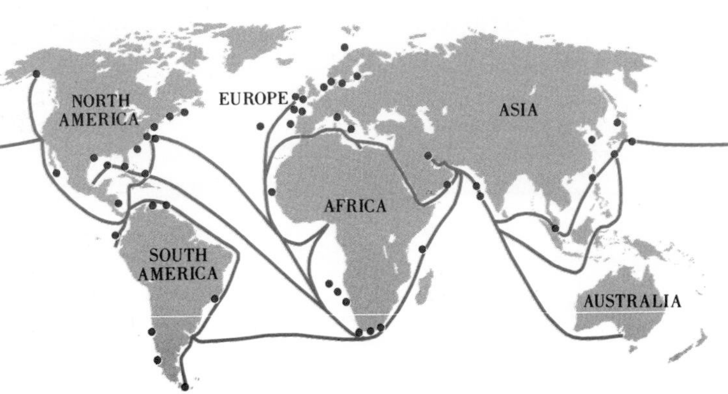

NORTH AMERICA
EUROPE
ASIA
AFRICA
SOUTH AMERICA
AUSTRALIA

MAIN TANKER ROUTES AND MAJOR OIL SPILLS

ROUTES OF VERY LARGE CRUDE OIL CARRIERS ● MAJOR OIL SPILLS

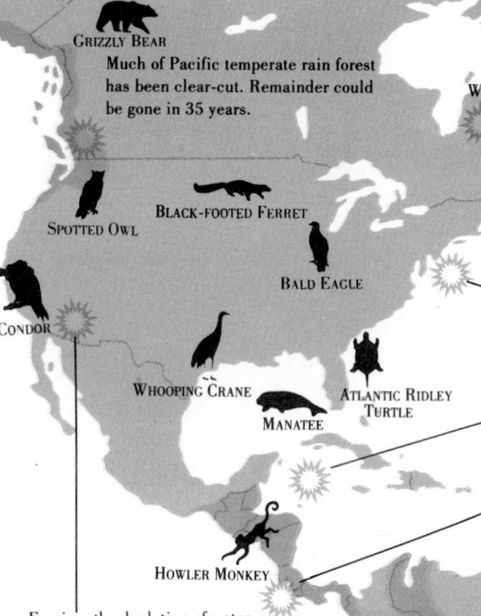

GRIZZLY BEAR
Much of Pacific temperate rain forest has been clear-cut. Remainder could be gone in 35 years.
SPOTTED OWL
BLACK-FOOTED FERRET
BALD EAGLE
CONDOR
WHOOPING CRANE
MANATEE
ATLANTIC RIDLEY TURTLE
WOODLAND CARIBOU

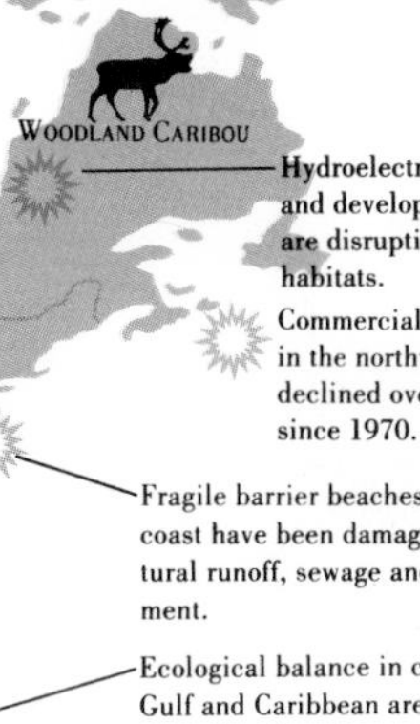

HUMPBACK W
Hydroelectric power proje and development in Queb are disrupting wildlife habitats.
Commercial fishing harves in the northwest Atlantic h declined over 30 percent since 1970.

Fragile barrier beaches of the Atlanti coast have been damaged by agricultural runoff, sewage and overdevelop ment.

Ecological balance in coral reefs of th Gulf and Caribbean area is being upset by a booming tourist industry.

At the present rate of clearing, half Central America's rain forest will di appear by the year 2000.

One-third of Guinea's tropical fores expected to disappear in the next decade.

HOWLER MONKEY

Erosion, the depletion of water resources for irrigation, and overgrazing have turned range and cropland into desert.

GALÁPAGOS TORTOISE

BLACK CAIMAN

JAGUAR

VICUNA

Every year over 5000 square miles (13,000 sq km) of rain forest is destroyed in Brazil's Amazon Basin.

GOLDEN LION TAMARIN

CHINCHILLA

GIANT ARMADILLO

The Atlantic waters off Patagonia have suffered fr over-fishing and oil spills

Southern Chile's rain forest is threatened by development.

BLUE WHALE

Acid Rain

Acid rain of nitric and sulfuric acids has killed all life in thousands of lakes, and over 15 million acres (6 million hectares) of virgin forest in Europe and North America are dead or dying.

Deforestation

Each year, 50 million acres (20 million hectares) of tropical rainforests are being felled by loggers. Trees remove carbon dioxide from the atmosphere and are vital to the prevention of soil erosion.

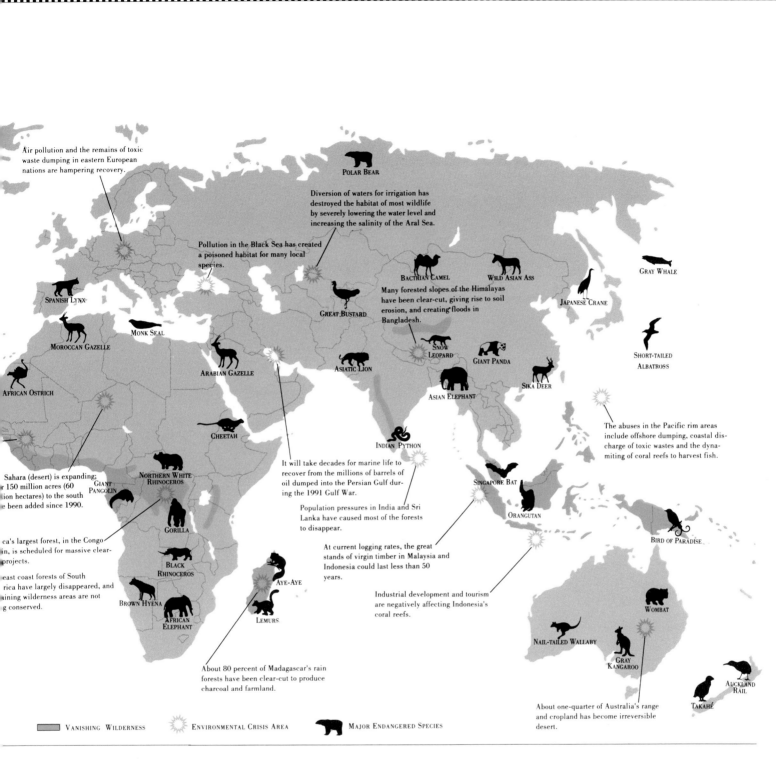

Air pollution and the remains of toxic waste dumping in eastern European nations are hampering recovery.

POLAR BEAR

Diversion of waters for irrigation has destroyed the habitat of most wildlife by severely lowering the water level and increasing the salinity of the Aral Sea.

Pollution in the Black Sea has created a poisoned habitat for many local species.

BACTRIAN CAMEL

WILD ASIAN ASS

GRAY WHALE

SPANISH LYNX

GREAT BUSTARD

Many forested slopes of the Himalayas have been clear-cut, giving rise to soil erosion, and creating floods in Bangladesh.

JAPANESE CRANE

MONK SEAL

MOROCCAN GAZELLE

SHORT-TAILED ALBATROSS

SNOW LEOPARD

GIANT PANDA

ARABIAN GAZELLE

ASIATIC LION

AFRICAN OSTRICH

SIKA DEER

ASIAN ELEPHANT

The abuses in the Pacific rim areas include offshore dumping, coastal discharge of toxic wastes and the dynamiting of coral reefs to harvest fish.

CHEETAH

INDIAN PYTHON

It will take decades for marine life to recover from the millions of barrels of oil dumped into the Persian Gulf during the 1991 Gulf War.

Sahara (desert) is expanding; 150 million acres (60 ion hectares) to the south e been added since 1990.

NORTHERN WHITE RHINOCEROS

GIANT PANGOLIN

SINGAPORE BAT

Population pressures in India and Sri Lanka have caused most of the forests to disappear.

ORANGUTAN

GORILLA

ca's largest forest, in the Congo in, is scheduled for massive clear- projects.

BIRD OF PARADISE

At current logging rates, the great stands of virgin timber in Malaysia and Indonesia could last less than 50 years.

BLACK RHINOCEROS

east coast forests of South rica have largely disappeared, and aining wilderness areas are not g conserved.

AYE-AYE

BROWN HYENA

Industrial development and tourism are negatively affecting Indonesia's coral reefs.

WOMBAT

AFRICAN ELEPHANT

LEMURS

NAIL-TAILED WALLABY

GRAY KANGAROO

About 80 percent of Madagascar's rain forests have been clear-cut to produce charcoal and farmland.

AUCKLAND RAIL

TAKAHÉ

About one-quarter of Australia's range and cropland has become irreversible desert.

VANISHING WILDERNESS

ENVIRONMENTAL CRISIS AREA

MAJOR ENDANGERED SPECIES

Extinction

Biologists estimate that over 50,000 plant and animal species inhabiting the world's rain forests are disappearing each year due to pollution, unchecked hunting and the destruction of natural habitats.

Air Pollution

Billions of tons of industrial emissions and toxic pollutants are released into the air each year, depleting our ozone layer, killing our forests and lakes with acid rain and threatening our health.

Water Pollution

Only 3 percent of the earth's water is fresh. Pollution from cities, farms and factories has made much of it unfit to drink. In the developing world, most sewage flows untreated into lakes and rivers.

Ozone Depletion

The layer of ozone in the stratosphere shields earth from harmful ultraviolet radiation. But man-made gases are destroying this vital barrier, increasing the risk of skin cancer and eye disease.

Population

Current Population Comparisons

Each Area's Size is Proportionate to Its Population

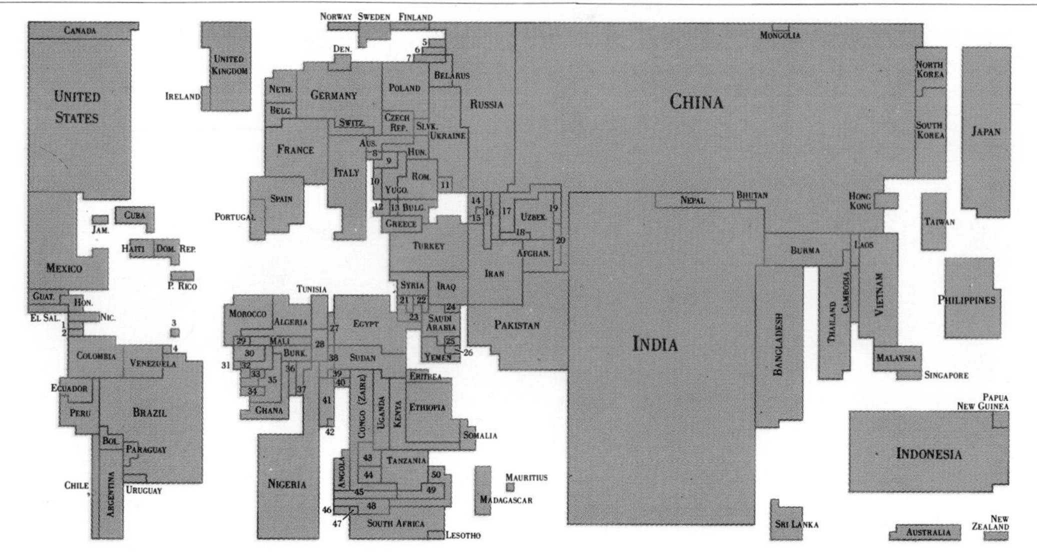

Canada
United States
Ireland
United Kingdom
Norway
Sweden
Finland
Den.
Neth.
Belg.
Germany
Poland
Belarus
Russia
China
Mongolia
North Korea
South Korea
Japan
Czech Rep.
Slvk.
Ukraine
Switz.
Aus.
Hun.
France
Italy
Rom.
Yugo.
Bulg.
Greece
Spain
Portugal
Turkey
Uzbek.
Afghan.
Iran
Iraq
Syria
Nepal
Bhutan
Hong Kong
Taiwan
Burma
Laos
Philippines
Thailand
Cambodia
Vietnam
Bangladesh
India
Pakistan
Malaysia
Singapore
Papua New Guinea
Indonesia
Sri Lanka
Australia
New Zealand
Cuba
Jam.
Haiti
Dom. Rep.
P. Rico
Mexico
Guat.
Hon.
El Sal.
Nic.
Colombia
Venezuela
Ecuador
Peru
Brazil
Bol.
Paraguay
Chile
Argentina
Uruguay
Tunisia
Morocco
Algeria
Egypt
Saudi Arabia
Yemen
Mali
Burk.
Sudan
Ghana
Eritrea
Ethiopia
Somalia
Nigeria
Congo (Zaire)
Uganda
Kenya
Tanzania
Angola
Mauritius
Madagascar
South Africa
Lesotho

Countries Indicated by Number

1 Costa Rica
2 Panama
3 Trinidad and Tobago
4 Guyana
5 Estonia
6 Latvia
7 Lithuania
8 Slovenia
9 Croatia
10 Bosnia and Hercegovina
11 Moldova
12 Albania
13 Macedonia
14 Georgia
15 Armenia
16 Azerbaijan
17 Kazakhstan
18 Turkmenistan
19 Kyrgyzstan
20 Tajikistan
21 Lebanon
22 Jordan
23 Israel
24 Kuwait
25 United Arab Emirates
26 Oman
27 Libya
28 Niger
29 Mauritania
30 Senegal
31 Guinea-Bissau
32 Guinea
33 Sierra Leone
34 Liberia
35 Ivory Coast
36 Togo
37 Benin
38 Chad
39 Central African Republic
40 Congo
41 Cameroon
42 Gabon
43 Rwanda
44 Burundi
45 Zambia
46 Namibia
47 Botswana
48 Zimbabwe
49 Mozambique
50 Malawi
51 Cyprus
52 Cape Verde
53 Gambia
54 Equatorial Guinea
55 Bahrain
56 Qatar
57 Brunei
58 Solomon Islands

Projected Population Comparisons - 2020

Each Area's Size is Proportionate to Its Population

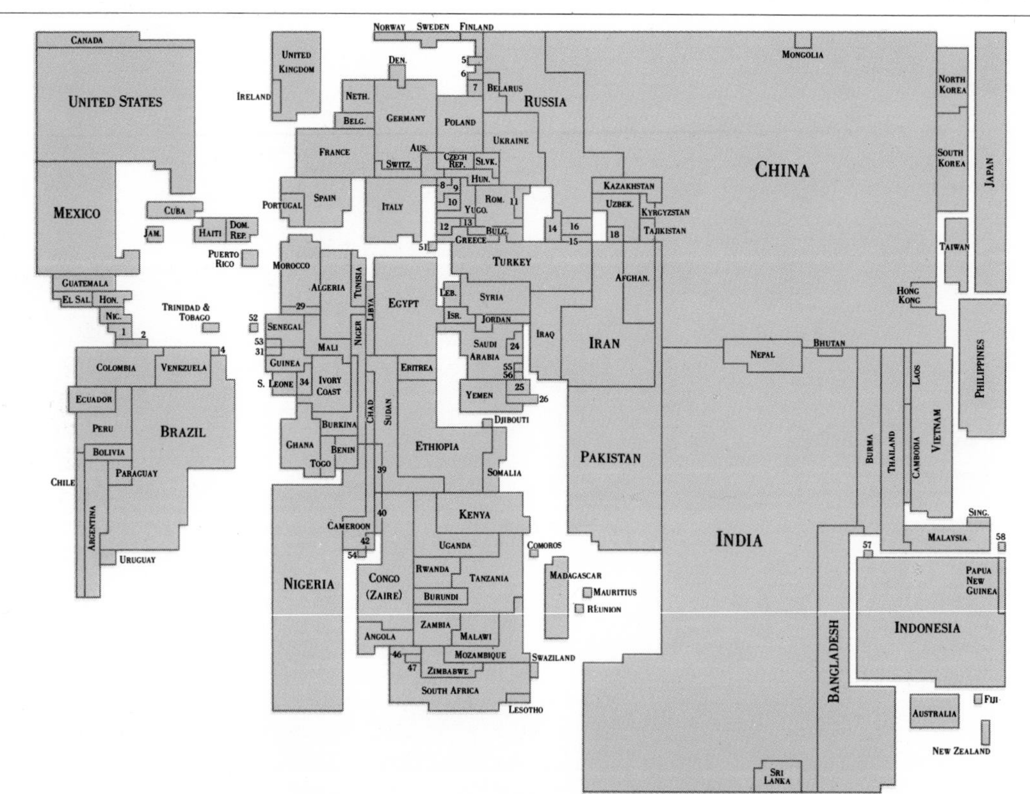

Canada
United States
Mexico
Ireland
United Kingdom
Norway
Sweden
Finland
Den.
Neth.
Belg.
Germany
Poland
Belarus
Russia
France
Aus.
Switz.
Czech Rep.
Slvk.
Ukraine
Hun.
Spain
Portugal
Italy
Rom.
Yugo.
Bulg.
Greece
Turkey
Kazakhstan
Uzbek.
Kyrgyzstan
Tajikistan
Afghan.
China
Mongolia
North Korea
South Korea
Japan
Taiwan
Hong Kong
Philippines
Cuba
Jam.
Haiti
Dom. Rep.
Puerto Rico
Guatemala
El Sal.
Hon.
Nic.
Trinidad & Tobago
Colombia
Venezuela
Ecuador
Peru
Brazil
Bolivia
Paraguay
Chile
Argentina
Uruguay
Morocco
Algeria
Tunisia
Libya
Egypt
Leb.
Syria
Isr.
Jordan
Iraq
Iran
Saudi Arabia
Yemen
Senegal
Guinea
Mali
Niger
S. Leone
Ivory Coast
Eritrea
Burkina
Benin
Ghana
Togo
Chad
Sudan
Djibouti
Ethiopia
Somalia
Pakistan
Nepal
Bhutan
Burma
Thailand
Laos
Cambodia
Vietnam
India
Bangladesh
Sri Lanka
Sing.
Malaysia
Papua New Guinea
Indonesia
Australia
Fiji
New Zealand
Nigeria
Cameroon
Kenya
Uganda
Congo (Zaire)
Rwanda
Burundi
Tanzania
Comoros
Madagascar
Mauritius
Réunion
Angola
Zambia
Malawi
Mozambique
Swaziland
Zimbabwe
South Africa
Lesotho

Alaska

3.5 PERCENT OR M

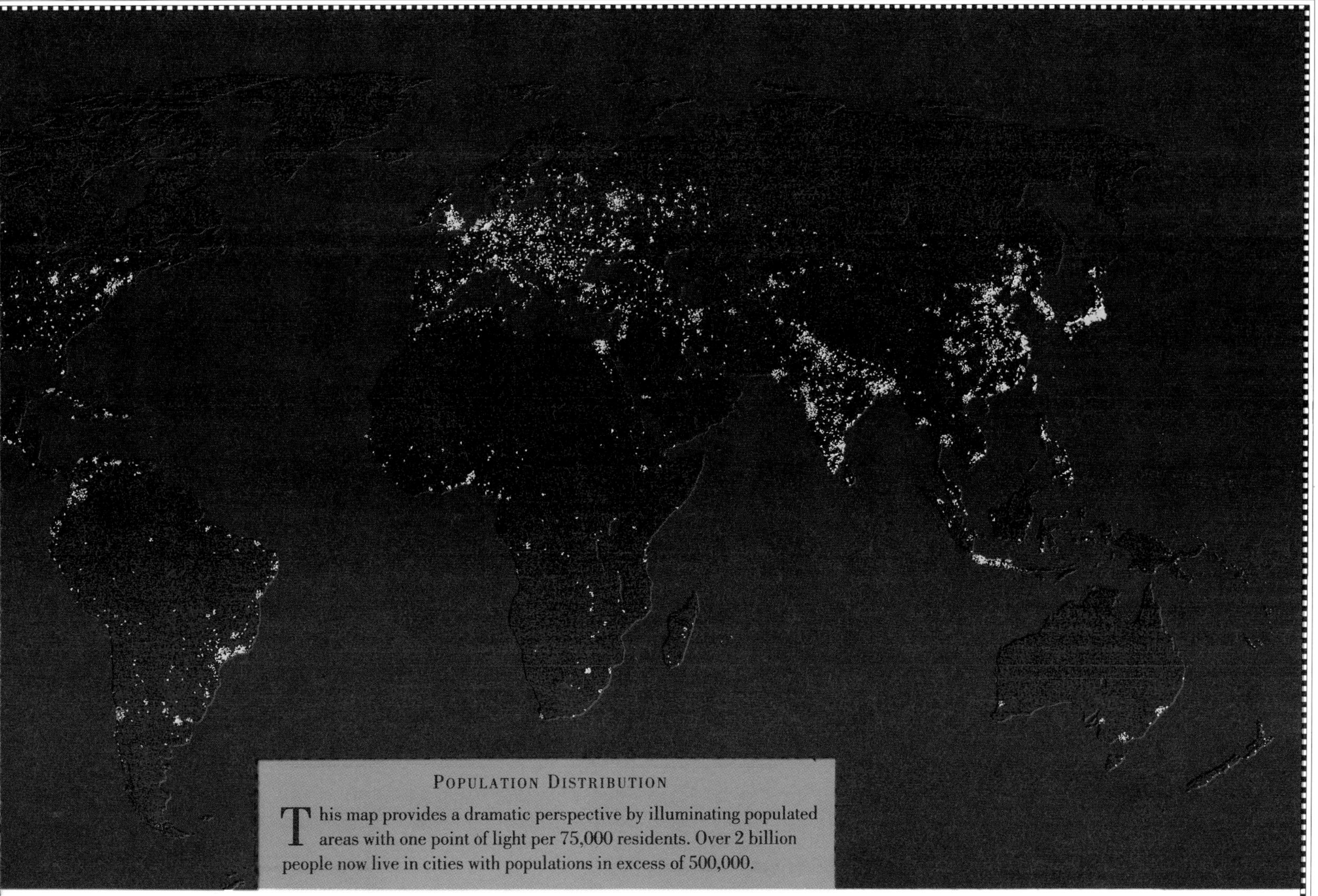

Population Distribution

This map provides a dramatic perspective by illuminating populated areas with one point of light per 75,000 residents. Over 2 billion people now live in cities with populations in excess of 500,000.

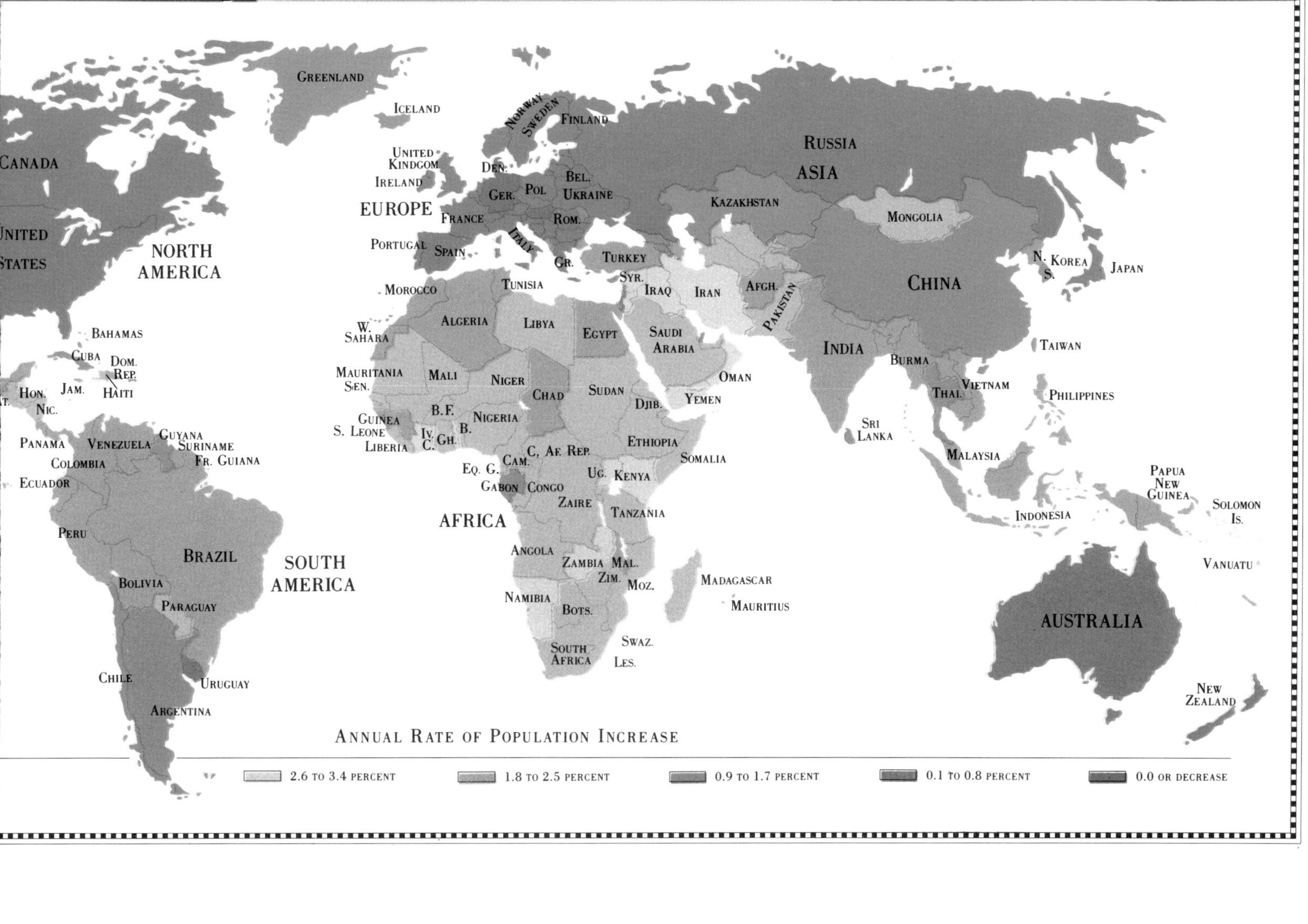

Greenland
Iceland
Norway
Sweden
Finland
Canada
United Kingdom
Ireland
Den.
Bel.
Russia
Asia
Ger.
Pol.
Ukraine
Europe
France
Rom.
Kazakhstan
Mongolia
United States
North America
Portugal
Spain
Italy
Gr.
Turkey
Syr.
Iraq
Iran
Afgh.
Pakistan
China
N. Korea
S.
Japan
Morocco
Tunisia
W. Sahara
Algeria
Libya
Egypt
Saudi Arabia
India
Burma
Taiwan
Bahamas
Cuba
Dom. Rep.
Haiti
Jam.
Hon.
Nic.
Mauritania
Sen.
Mali
Niger
Chad
Sudan
Oman
Djib.
Yemen
Thai.
Vietnam
Philippines
B.F.
Guinea
S. Leone
Liberia
Iv. C.
Gh.
B.
Nigeria
Ethiopia
Sri Lanka
Panama
Venezuela
Guyana
Suriname
Fr. Guiana
Colombia
Ecuador
C. Af. Rep.
Cam.
Eq. G.
Gabon
Congo
Ug.
Kenya
Somalia
Malaysia
Papua New Guinea
Solomon Is.
Zaire
Tanzania
Indonesia
Africa
Peru
Brazil
South America
Angola
Zambia
Mal.
Zim.
Moz.
Madagascar
Mauritius
Vanuatu
Bolivia
Paraguay
Namibia
Bots.
Australia
South Africa
Swaz.
Les.
Chile
Uruguay
Argentina
New Zealand
Annual Rate of Population Increase
2.6 to 3.4 percent
1.8 to 2.5 percent
0.9 to 1.7 percent
0.1 to 0.8 percent
0.0 or decrease

Standards of Living

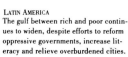

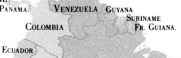

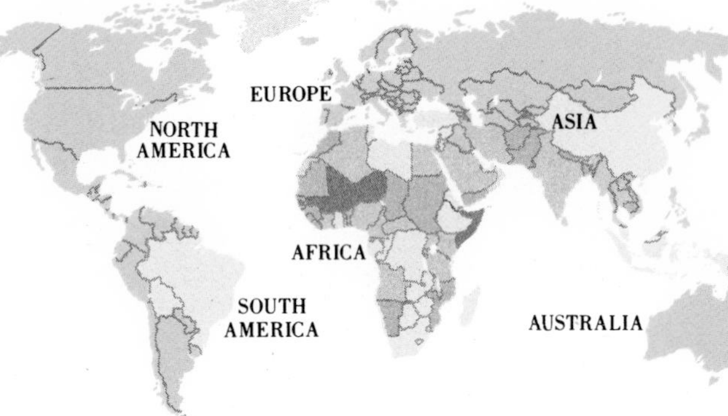

NORTH AMERICA
EUROPE
ASIA
AFRICA
SOUTH AMERICA
AUSTRALIA

Literate Percent of Population

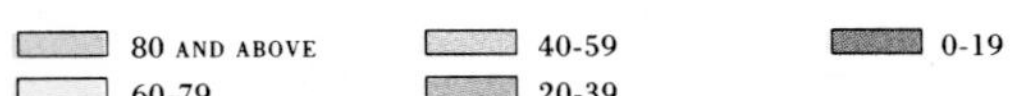

80 and above
60-79
40-59
20-39
0-19

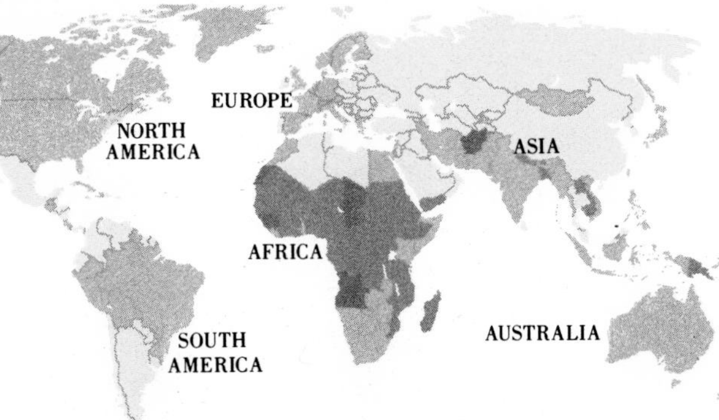

NORTH AMERICA
EUROPE
ASIA
AFRICA
SOUTH AMERICA
AUSTRALIA

Years of Life Expectancy (Men and Women)

70 and above
60-69
50-59
40-49
0-39

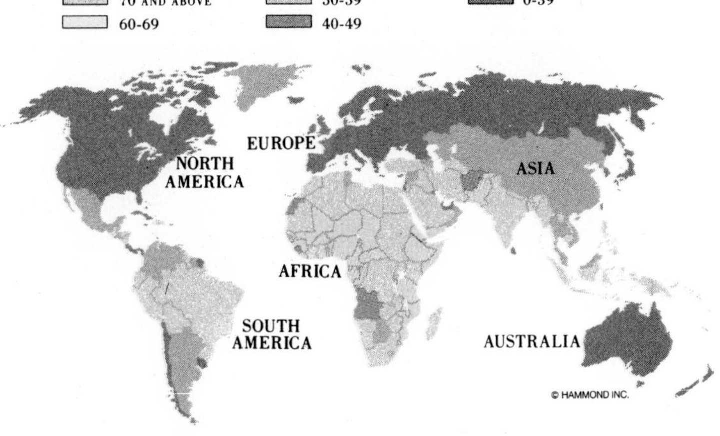

NORTH AMERICA
EUROPE
ASIA
AFRICA
SOUTH AMERICA
AUSTRALIA
© HAMMOND INC.

Infant Deaths per 1,000 Live Births

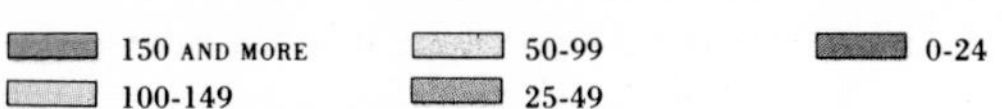

150 and more
100-149
50-99
25-49
0-24

United States
The economic and political influence of women has risen substantially. In a number of fields, women's salaries are now nearly equal to men's.

South America
Political unrest, rising inflation and slow economic growth continue to thwart efforts to bring unity and prosperity to the nations of South America.

Latin America
The gulf between rich and poor continues to widen, despite efforts to reform oppressive governments, increase literacy and relieve overburdened cities.

Comparison of European, U.S. and Japanese Workers

Country	Scheduled Weekly Hours	Annual Leave Days/Holidays	Annual Hours Worked
Germany	39	42	1708
Netherlands	40	43.5	1740
Belgium	38	31	1748
Austria	39.3	38	1751
France	39	34	1771
Italy	40	39	1776
United Kingdom	39	33	1778
Luxembourg	40	37	1792
Finland	40	37	1792
Sweden	40	37	1792
Spain	40	36	1800
Denmark	40	34	1816
Norway	40	30	1848
Greece	40	28	1864
Ireland	40	28	1864
United States	40	22	1912
Switzerland	41.5	30.5	1913
Portugal	45	36	2025
Japan	44	23.5	2116

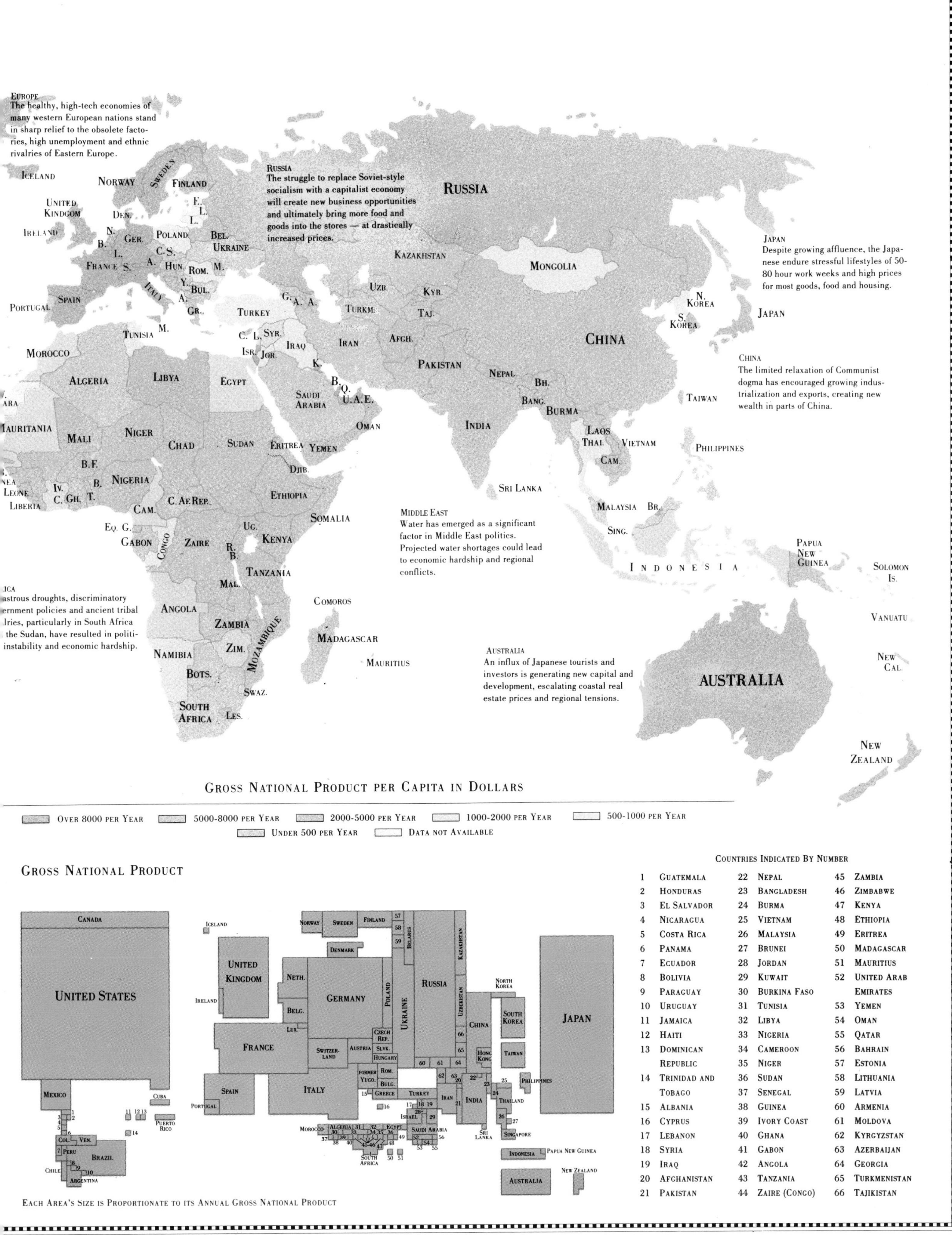
Europe
The healthy, high-tech economies of many western European nations stand in sharp relief to the obsolete factories, high unemployment and ethnic rivalries of Eastern Europe.
Russia
The struggle to replace Soviet-style socialism with a capitalist economy will create new business opportunities and ultimately bring more food and goods into the stores — at drastically increased prices.
Japan
Despite growing affluence, the Japanese endure stressful lifestyles of 50-80 hour work weeks and high prices for most goods, food and housing.
China
The limited relaxation of Communist dogma has encouraged growing industrialization and exports, creating new wealth in parts of China.
Middle East
Water has emerged as a significant factor in Middle East politics. Projected water shortages could lead to economic hardship and regional conflicts.
Australia
An influx of Japanese tourists and investors is generating new capital and development, escalating coastal real estate prices and regional tensions.
Iceland
Norway
Sweden
Finland
United Kingdom
Ireland
Den.
Ger.
Poland
Bel.
Ukraine
France
Spain
Portugal
Italy
Hun.
Rom.
Bul.
Gr.
Russia
Kazakhstan
Mongolia
Uzb.
Kyr.
Turkm.
Taj.
Turkey
Syr.
Iraq
Iran
Afgh.
Pakistan
Jor.
Isr.
Saudi Arabia
U.A.E.
Oman
Yemen
China
N. Korea
S. Korea
Japan
Nepal
Bh.
Bang.
Burma
India
Taiwan
Laos
Thai.
Vietnam
Cam.
Philippines
Sri Lanka
Malaysia
Br.
Sing.
Indonesia
Papua New Guinea
Solomon Is.
Vanuatu
New Cal.
Australia
New Zealand
Morocco
Algeria
Tunisia
Libya
Egypt
Mauritania
Mali
Niger
Chad
Sudan
Eritrea
Djib.
Ethiopia
Somalia
B.F.
Nigeria
C. Af. Rep.
Cam.
Liberia
Eq. G.
Gabon
Congo
Zaire
Ug.
Kenya
R.
B.
Tanzania
Mal.
Comoros
Angola
Zambia
Mozambique
Madagascar
Mauritius
Namibia
Zim.
Bots.
Swaz.
South Africa
Les.
...ica
...astrous droughts, discriminatory ...ernment policies and ancient tribal ...lries, particularly in South Africa ... the Sudan, have resulted in politi... instability and economic hardship.
Gross National Product per Capita in Dollars
Over 8000 per Year
5000-8000 per Year
2000-5000 per Year
1000-2000 per Year
500-1000 per Year
Under 500 per Year
Data not Available
Gross National Product
Canada
United States
Mexico
Cuba
Puerto Rico
Brazil
Argentina
Chile
Col.
Ven.
Peru
Iceland
United Kingdom
Ireland
Norway
Sweden
Finland
Denmark
Neth.
Germany
Belg.
Lux.
France
Spain
Portugal
Italy
Switzerland
Austria
Poland
Czech Rep.
Slvk.
Hungary
Former Yugo.
Rom.
Bulg.
Greece
Turkey
Belarus
Ukraine
Russia
Kazakhstan
Uzbekistan
Israel
Iran
Saudi Arabia
Morocco
Algeria
Egypt
South Africa
China
North Korea
South Korea
Hong Kong
Taiwan
India
Sri Lanka
Thailand
Philippines
Singapore
Indonesia
Papua New Guinea
Japan
Australia
New Zealand
Each Area's Size is Proportionate to its Annual Gross National Product
Countries Indicated By Number
1 Guatemala
2 Honduras
3 El Salvador
4 Nicaragua
5 Costa Rica
6 Panama
7 Ecuador
8 Bolivia
9 Paraguay
10 Uruguay
11 Jamaica
12 Haiti
13 Dominican Republic
14 Trinidad and Tobago
15 Albania
16 Cyprus
17 Lebanon
18 Syria
19 Iraq
20 Afghanistan
21 Pakistan
22 Nepal
23 Bangladesh
24 Burma
25 Vietnam
26 Malaysia
27 Brunei
28 Jordan
29 Kuwait
30 Burkina Faso
31 Tunisia
32 Libya
33 Nigeria
34 Cameroon
35 Niger
36 Sudan
37 Senegal
38 Guinea
39 Ivory Coast
40 Ghana
41 Gabon
42 Angola
43 Tanzania
44 Zaire (Congo)
45 Zambia
46 Zimbabwe
47 Kenya
48 Ethiopia
49 Eritrea
50 Madagascar
51 Mauritius
52 United Arab Emirates
53 Yemen
54 Oman
55 Qatar
56 Bahrain
57 Estonia
58 Lithuania
59 Latvia
60 Armenia
61 Moldova
62 Kyrgyzstan
63 Azerbaijan
64 Georgia
65 Turkmenistan
66 Tajikistan

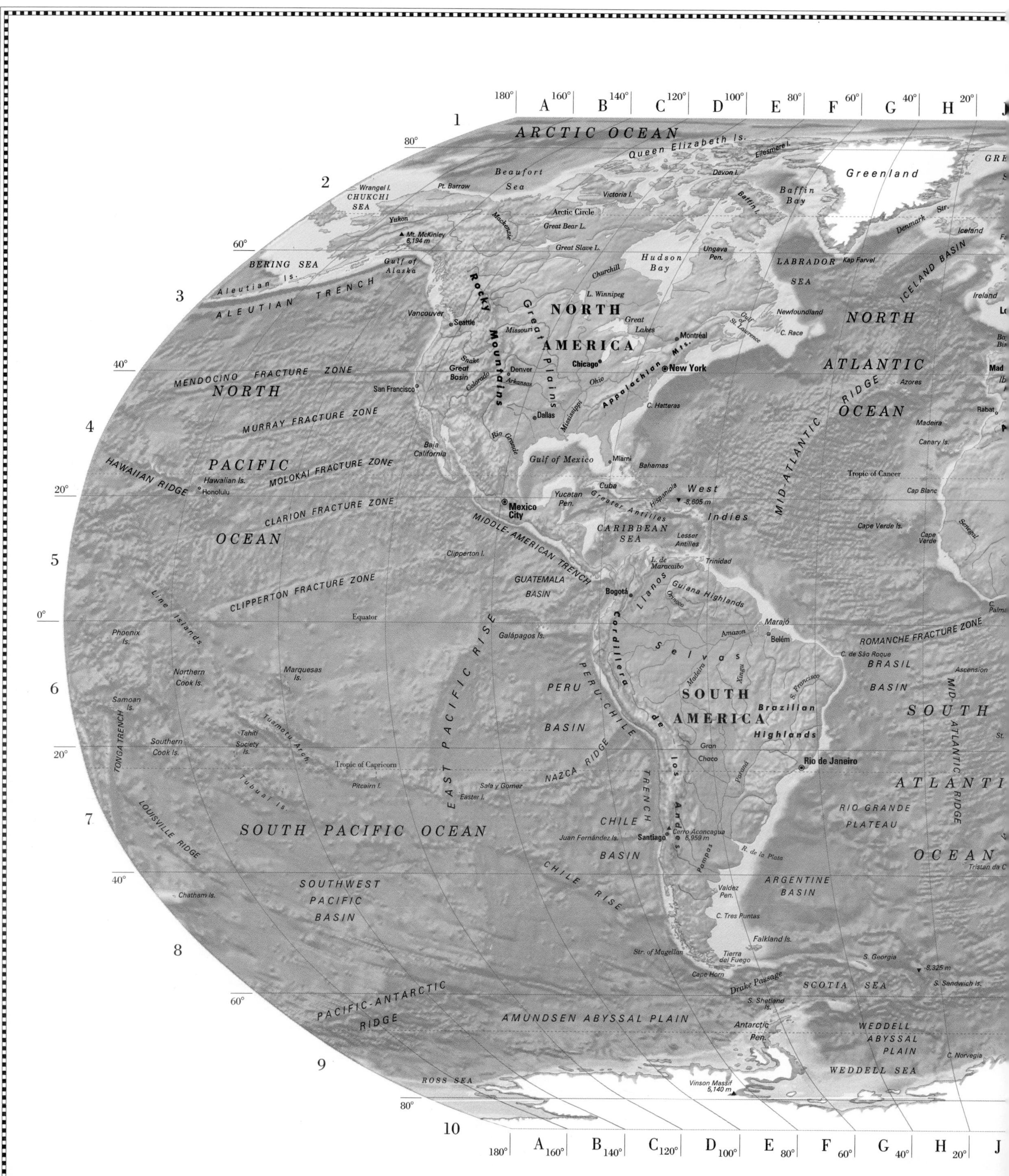
ARCTIC OCEAN
Queen Elizabeth Is.
Ellesmere I.
Greenland
Beaufort Sea
Devon I.
Victoria I.
Baffin Bay
Baffin I.
Wrangel I.
CHUKCHI SEA
Pt. Barrow
Yukon
Mt. McKinley 6,194 m
Mackenzie
Arctic Circle
Great Bear L.
Great Slave L.
Denmark Str.
Iceland
BERING SEA
Gulf of Alaska
Hudson Bay
Ungava Pen.
LABRADOR SEA
Kap Farvel
ICELAND BASIN
Aleutian Is.
ALEUTIAN TRENCH
Churchill
L. Winnipeg
Rocky Mountains
Great Plains
NORTH AMERICA
Great Lakes
Gulf of St. Lawrence
Newfoundland
C. Race
NORTH ATLANTIC OCEAN
Ireland
Vancouver
Seattle
Missouri
Montréal
Snake
Great Bosin
Denver
Colorado
Arkansas
Chicago
Ohio
Appalachian Mts.
New York
MENDOCINO FRACTURE ZONE
NORTH
San Francisco
Mississippi
C. Hatteras
MID-ATLANTIC RIDGE
Azores
Madeira
Rabat
MURRAY FRACTURE ZONE
Dallas
Rio Grande
Canary Is.
Baja California
Gulf of Mexico
Miami
Bahamas
HAWAIIAN RIDGE
PACIFIC
Hawaiian Is.
Honolulu
MOLOKAI FRACTURE ZONE
Tropic of Cancer
Cuba
Hispaniola
West Indies
8,605 m
Greater Antilles
Yucatan Pen.
Mexico City
Cap Blanc
CLARION FRACTURE ZONE
MIDDLE-AMERICAN TRENCH
CARIBBEAN SEA
Lesser Antilles
Cape Verde Is.
Cape Verde
Senegal
OCEAN
Clipperton I.
Trinidad
L. de Maracaibo
GUATEMALA BASIN
Bogotá
Llanos
Guiana Highlands
Orinoco
CLIPPERTON FRACTURE ZONE
Line Islands
Equator
Marajó
Belém
Amazon
Phoenix Is.
Galápagos Is.
Cordillera
Selvas
ROMANCHE FRACTURE ZONE
C. de São Roque
BRASIL BASIN
Ascension
Northern Cook Is.
Marquesas Is.
EAST PACIFIC RISE
PERU BASIN
PERU-CHILE TRENCH
Madeira
Xingu
S. Francisco
SOUTH AMERICA
Brazilian Highlands
SOUTH
MID-ATLANTIC RIDGE
Samoan Is.
TONGA TRENCH
Tuamotu Arch.
Tahiti
Society Is.
Southern Cook Is.
de los Andes
Gran Chaco
Paraná
Rio de Janeiro
Tropic of Capricorn
NAZCA RIDGE
Tubuai Is.
Pitcairn I.
Sala y Gomez
Easter I.
ATLANTI
RIO GRANDE PLATEAU
LOUISVILLE RIDGE
SOUTH PACIFIC OCEAN
CHILE BASIN
Juan Fernández Is.
Santiago
Cerro Aconcagua 6,959 m
Pampas
R. de la Plata
OCEAN
Tristan da C
CHILE RISE
SOUTHWEST PACIFIC BASIN
Chatham Is.
Valdez Pen.
ARGENTINE BASIN
C. Tres Puntas
Falkland Is.
Str. of Magellan
Tierra del Fuego
S. Georgia
8,325 m
Cape Horn
Drake Passage
SCOTIA SEA
S. Sandwich Is.
PACIFIC-ANTARCTIC RIDGE
AMUNDSEN ABYSSAL PLAIN
S. Shetland Is.
Antarctic Pen.
WEDDELL ABYSSAL PLAIN
C. Norvegia
WEDDELL SEA
ROSS SEA
Vinson Massif 5,140 m
180° A 160° B 140° C 120° D 100° E 80° F 60° G 40° H 20° J
80° 60° 40° 20° 0° 20° 40° 60° 80°
1 2 3 4 5 6 7 8 9 10

World

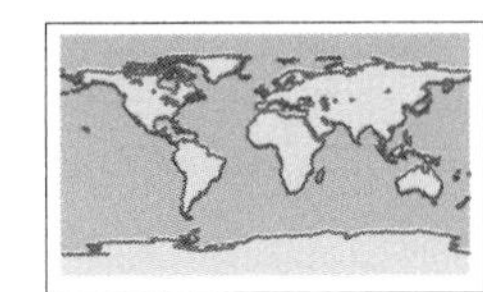

K 20° L 40° M 60° N 80° P 100° Q 120° R 140° S 160° T 180°

1 80°

ARCTIC OCEAN

-5,470 m Svalbard Franz Josef Land Severnaya Zemlya New Siberian Is.

Spitsbergen

2

BARENTS SEA Novaya Zemlya Kara Sea Yamal Pen. Nordkapp Kola Pen. White Sea

NORWEGIAN SEA Kjølen

Yenisey Central Lower Tunguska Siberian Plateau Lena Arctic Circle Kolyma Ra.

West Siberian Plain Ob Ural Mountains

60° BERING SEA

Stockholm L. Ladoga Moscow Baltic Sea

Angara Lena Aldan L. Baykal Kamchatka Pen. SEA OF OKHOTSK Sakhalin

3

EUROPE Paris Danube Carpathians Dnepr Alps Adriatic Rome

Kirgiz Steppe Aral Sea Volga Irtysh L. Balkhash ASIA Altai Mts. Gobi Amur Kuril Is.

Black Sea İstanbul Caucasus El'brus 5,642 m Caspian Sea Tian Shan

Hokkaido NORTHWEST PACIFIC BASIN 40°

Sea of Japan Beijing Honshu Tōkyō JAPAN TRENCH NORTH

MEDITERRANEAN SEA Sicily Aegean Sea Taurus Mts. Tigris Tehrān Amu Darya Hindu Kush Takla Makan Kunlun Shan Cyprus Euphrates Zagros Mts. Indus Himalaya Salween Huang Yellow Sea

Cairo Nile Hijāz Persian Gulf Karāchi Mt. Everest 8,848 m Ganges Chang East China Sea Ryukyu Is. RYUKYU TRENCH -7,507 m

4

Sahara Ahaggar Red Sea Arabian Pen. Narmada Irrawaddy Red Taiwan PHILIPPINE PACIFIC Tropic of Cancer 20°

AFRICA Red Sea Hills Rub' al Khali ARABIAN SEA Bombay BAY OF BENGAL Mekong Hainan SOUTH CHINA SEA Luzon Manila PHILIPPINE SEA BASIN Mariana Is. MARIANA TRENCH OCEAN

L. Chad Sudan Blue Nile Gulf of Aden Socotra Andaman Is. Isthmus of Kra Palawan Challenger Deep -11,033 m CENTRAL

Niger Lagos White Nile Ethiopian Plateau CARLSBERG RIDGE C. Comorin Sri Lanka Malay Pen. Sulu Sea Mindanao Marshall Is. PACIFIC BASIN

5

Bioko Congo Maldive Is. Celebes Sea Caroline Is. MELANESIAN BASIN

São Tomé Congo Basin SOMALI BASIN Equator INDIAN Borneo Halmahera 0°

Kilimanjaro 5,895 m L. Victoria Kinshasa L. Tanganyika Seychelles Chagos Arch. CENTRAL INDIAN RIDGE NINETYEAST RIDGE Sumatra Celebes Jakarta Java Sea Banda Sea New Guinea Bismarck Arch. New Britain Solomon Is. BASIN

6

ANGOLA BASIN L. Nyasa Comoros Is. OCEAN Java JAVA TRENCH -7,450 m Cocos Is. Timor Sea Arafura Sea Torres Str. Gulf of Carpentaria Cape York Pen. CORAL SEA New Hebrides Fiji Is.

Lusaka Zambezi Madagascar Mozambique Chan. Réunion Mauritius Great Barrier Reef

Namib Desert Kalahari Johannesburg Orange Drakensberg New Caledonia 20°

AUSTRALIA Great Dividing Ra.

BROKEN PLATEAU Great Victoria Desert

7

Cape of Good Hope SOUTHWEST INDIAN RIDGE C. Leeuwin Great Australian Bight Darling Murray Sydney Mt. Kosciusko 2,228 m Melbourne TASMAN SEA North C. North

SOUTHEAST INDIAN RIDGE Tasmania 40° South

Kerguélen McDonald Is. KERGUELEN PLATEAU

8

AUSTRALIAN-ANTARCTIC BASIN

ENDERBY ABYSSAL PLAIN 60°

C. Batterbee Antarctic Circle

C. Adare 9

ROSS SEA

ANTARCTICA

80°

10

K 20° L 40° M 60° N 80° P 100° Q 120° R 140° S 160° T 180°

POPULATION OF CITIES AND TOWNS
- ◉ OVER 5,000,000
- ● 2,000,000 - 4,999,999
- ⊙ 500,000 - 1,999,999
- ○ UNDER 500,000

SCALE 1:81,700,000 ROBINSON PROJECTION STANDARD PARALLELS 38°N AND 38°S

MILES 0 1000 2000 3000 4000

KILOMETERS 0 1000 2000 3000 4000

Europe

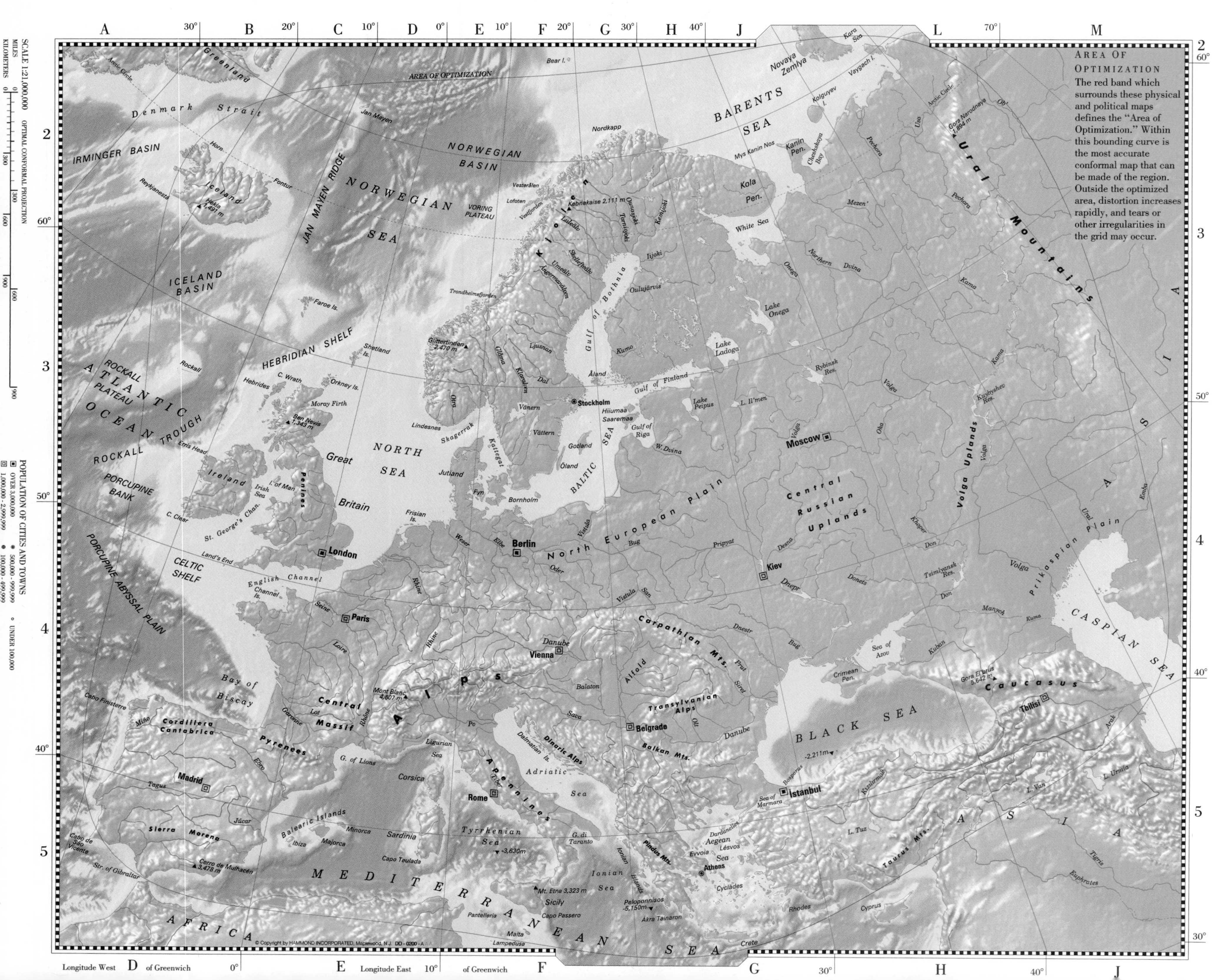
AREA OF OPTIMIZATION
The red band which surrounds these physical and political maps defines the "Area of Optimization." Within this bounding curve is the most accurate conformal map that can be made of the region. Outside the optimized area, distortion increases rapidly, and tears or other irregularities in the grid may occur.
Ural Mountains
Volga Uplands
Central Russian Uplands
North European Plain
Prikaspian Plain
CASPIAN SEA
BLACK SEA
BARENTS SEA
NORWEGIAN SEA
NORTH SEA
BALTIC SEA
MEDITERRANEAN SEA
ATLANTIC OCEAN
Carpathian Mts.
Transylvanian Alps
Balkan Mts.
Dinaric Alps
Apennines
Alps
Pyrenees
Caucasus
Moscow
Kiev
Istanbul
Athens
Belgrade
Vienna
Berlin
Stockholm
Paris
London
Rome
Madrid
Tbilisi
Iceland
Ireland
Great Britain
AFRICA
ASIA
© Copyright by HAMMOND INCORPORATED, Maplewood, N.J.
Longitude West of Greenwich
Longitude East of Greenwich
SCALE 1:21,000,000 OPTIMAL CONFORMAL PROJECTION
MILES 0 300 600 900
KILOMETERS 0 300 600 900
POPULATION OF CITIES AND TOWNS
OVER 3,000,000
1,000,000 - 2,999,999
500,000 - 999,999
100,000 - 499,999
UNDER 100,000

ARCTIC OCEAN
North Pole
NORWEGIAN SEA
NORTH SEA
English Chan.
BARENTS SEA
KARA SEA
LAPTEV SEA
EAST SIBERIAN SEA
CHUKCHI SEA
BERING SEA
NORTH AMERICA
Bering Str.
SVALBARD
Spitsbergen
Northeast Land
Edge I.
Bear I.
FRANZ JOSEF LAND
Novaya Zemlya
Kolguyev I.
Nordkapp
Komsomolets I.
October Revolution I.
Bol'shevik I.
SEVERNAYA ZEMLYA
NEW SIBERIAN IS.
Bol'shoy Lyakhov I.
Vrangelya I.
Chukchi Pen.
Gulf of Anadyr'
St. Lawrence I.
Taymyr Pen.
Yamal Pen.
Gyda Pen.
Gulf of Ob'
Gulf of Bothnia
Baltic Sea
White Sea
Arctic Circle
L. Ladoga
L. Onega
EUROPE
Rhine
Rhône
Loire
Danube
Oder
Vistula
W. Dvina
N. Dvina
Mezen'
Pechora
Dnepr
Prut
Don
Volga
Kama
Rybinsk Res.
Kuybyshev Res.
Adriatic Sea
Po
MEDITERRANEAN SEA
BLACK SEA
Crimea
Sea of Azov
Aegean Sea
Crete
Cyprus
Taurus Mts.
Caucasus
Mt. Ararat 5,165 m
CASPIAN SEA
Ural Mountains
Yekaterinburg
Ural
Tobol
Ishim
Irtysh
Ob'
West Siberian Plain
Taz
Yenisey
Central Siberian Plateau
Lower Tunguska
Stony Tunguska
Angara
Kotuy
Olenëk
Lena
Vilyuy
Aldan
Verkhoyansk Range
Cherskiy Range
Indigirka
Kolyma
Omolon
Anadyr'
Kolyma Range
Koryak Ra.
Karaginskiy I.
Komandorskiye Is.
Shelekhov Gulf
Kamchatka Pen.
Maya
Dzhugdzhur Range
Stanovoy Ra.
Shantar I.
SEA OF OKHOTSK
Mys Yelizavety
Mys Lopatka
Sakhalin
Paramushir
KURIL IS.
KURIL-KAMCHATKA TRENCH
Urup
Etorofu
Kunashiri
Hokkaido
La Perouse Str.
Tatar Str.
Amur
Zeya Res.
Sikhote-Alin
Khanka
L. Baykal
Vitim
Shilka
Yablonovyy Range
Argun
Da Hinggang Mts.
Nen
Songhua
Kerulen
Liao
Yalu
SEA OF JAPAN
Honshū
JAPAN TRENCH
Tokyo
Shikoku
Kyūshū
Kirgiz Steppe
Ustyurt Plateau
Aral Sea
Syrdar'ya
Amudar'ya
Kazakh Uplands
L. Balkhash
L. Zaysan
Ili
Alma-Ata
Tian Shan
Altai Mts.
Gobi
Beijing
Huang
Yellow Sea
EAST CHINA SEA
Communism Pk. 7,495 m
Takla Makan
Hindu Kush
Harirud
Indus
K2 (Godwin-Austen) 8,611 m
Altun Mts.
Qilian Mts.
Kunlun Shan
Tibet Plateau
Himalaya
Mt. Everest 8,848 m
Ganges Plain
Ganges
Brahmaputra
Mekong
Salween
Jinsha
Yalong
Han
Huai
Chang
Yuan
Xi
Red
Irrawaddy
Elburz Mts.
Tehrān
Zagros Mts.
Tigris
Euphrates
Damascus
Suez Canal
Sinai
G. of Aqaba
Nile
Nefud
Jabal al Hijaz
Dahana
Persian Gulf
Helmand
Tropic of Cancer
Arabian Peninsula
Rub' al Khali
RED SEA
Farasan Is.
Gulf of Oman
Ra's al Hadd
J. Masirah
Kuria Muria Is.
INDUS CONE
AFRICA
Gulf of Aden
Ras Asêr
Socotra
ARABIAN SEA
ARABIAN BASIN
Bombay
Narmada
Godavari
Krishna
Calcutta
Lakshadweep Is.
BAY OF BENGAL
Andaman Is.
Nicobar Is.
ANDAMAN SEA
C. Comorin
Gulf of Mannar
Sri Lanka
Dondra Head
CEYLON PLAIN
AREA OF OPTIMIZATION
Maldives
Seychelles
CARLSBERG RIDGE
SOMALI BASIN
Equator
CENTRAL INDIAN RIDGE
Chagos Arch.
Diego Garcia
CHAGOS TRENCH
MID-INDIAN OCEAN BASIN
NINETYEAST RIDGE
INDIAN OCEAN
COCOS BASIN
Cocos Is.
Christmas I.
INVESTIGATOR RIDGE
Hainan
Gulf of Tonkin
Korat Plateau
Bangkok
Gulf of Thailand
Isthmus of Kra
Mui Ca Mau
Malay Pen.
Str. of Malacca
Simeulue
Nias
Siberut
Mentawai Is.
Sumatra
Bangka
Billiton
Natuna Is.
SUNDA SHELF
Borneo
Kayan
SUNDA ISLANDS
Jakarta
Sunda Str.
Java
JAVA SEA
JAVA TRENCH
7,450 m
Bali
Lombok
Madura
Sumbawa
Sumba
Flores
FLORES SEA
Savu Sea
Timor
TIMOR SEA
Melville I.
AUSTRALIA
Great Sandy Desert
SOUTH CHINA SEA
SOUTH CHINA BASIN
Paracel Is.
Taiwan
Taiwan Str.
RYUKYU IS.
RYUKYU TRENCH
Amami Is.
Okinawa Is.
Sakishima Is.
Daito Is.
Okino-Tori-Shima (Parece Vela)
Batan Is.
Babuyan Is.
C. Engaño
Luzon
Manila
Mindoro
Panay
Palawan
Negros
Samar
Leyte
Philippines
PHILIPPINE BASIN
PHILIPPINE SEA
10,497 m
Mindanao
Sulu Sea
Sulu Arch.
Tinaca Pt.
Sangihe Is.
Talaud Is.
CELEBES SEA
Morotai
Halmahera
Palau
Celebes
Makassar Str.
G. of Tomini
Molucca Sea
Sula Is.
MOLUCCA ISLANDS
G. of Bone
Buru
Ceram
Buton
BANDA SEA
Wetar
Tanimbar Is.
New Guinea
PACIFIC OCEAN
© Copyright by HAMMOND INCORPORATED, Maplewood, N.J.
Longitude East of Greenwich
POPULATION OF CITIES AND TOWNS
OVER 3,000,000
1,000,000 - 2,999,999
500,000 - 999,999
100,000 - 499,999
UNDER 100,000
SCALE 1:49,000,000 OPTIMAL CONFORMAL PROJECTION
MILES 0 700 1400 2100
KILOMETERS 0 700 1400 2100

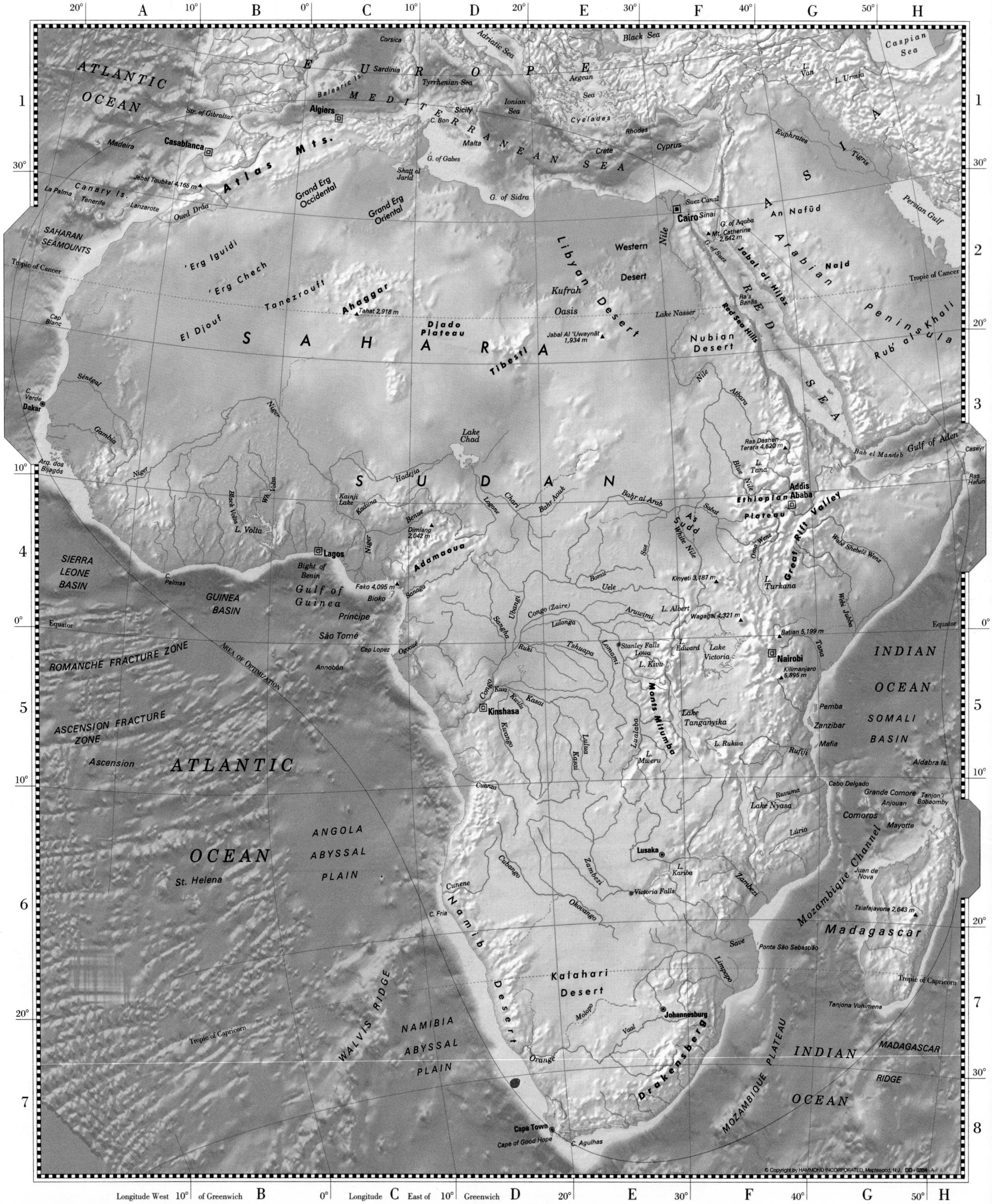

20° A 10° B 0° C 10° D 20° E 30° F 40° G 50° H

1

30°

ATLANTIC OCEAN
EUROPE
Corsica
Sardinia
Adriatic Sea
Black Sea
Caspian Sea
Balearic Is.
Tyrrhenian Sea
Aegean Sea
L. Van
L. Urmia
MEDITERRANEAN SEA
Str. of Gibraltar
Algiers
Sicily
Ionian Sea
Cyclades
C. Bon
Malta
Rhodes
Crete
Cyprus
Casablanca
Madeira
Atlas Mts.
Jebel Toubkal 4,165 m
G. of Gabes
Shatt al Jarid
Euphrates
Tigris
ASIA
La Palma
Canary Is.
Tenerife
Lanzarote
Oued Drâa
Grand Erg Occidental
Grand Erg Oriental
G. of Sidra
Suez Canal
Cairo
Sinai
G. of Aqaba
Mt. Catherine 2,642 m
G. of Suez
An Nafūd
Persian Gulf
SAHARAN SEAMOUNTS
'Erg Iguidi
'Erg Chech
Tanezrouft
Ahaggar
Tahat 2,918 m
Libyan Desert
Western Desert
Kufrah Oasis
Nile
Jabal al Hijāz
Arabian Peninsula
Najd
Tropic of Cancer
Cap Blanc
El Djouf
SAHARA
Djado Plateau
Tibesti
Jabal Al 'Uwaynāt 1,934 m
Lake Nasser
Nubian Desert
Ra's Banās
Red Sea Hills
RED SEA
Rub' al Khali
Sénégal
C. Verde
Dakar
Niger
Atbara
Gambia
Lake Chad
Ras Dashen Terara 4,620 m
Bab el Mandeb
Gulf of Aden
Caseyr
Arq. dos Bijagós
Hadejia
L. Tana
Blue Nile
SUDAN
Addis Ababa
Ras Hafun
Black Volta
Wh. Volta
Kainji Lake
Kaduna
Chari
Logone
Bahr Aouk
Bahr al Arab
Sobat
As Sudd
White Nile
Ethiopian Plateau
Great Rift Valley
Benue
Dimlang 2,042 m
Omo Wenz
Wabē Shebelē Wenz
L. Volta
Lagos
Adamaoua
Sue
SIERRA LEONE BASIN
Bight of Benin
C. Palmas
Fako 4,095 m
Bioko
Sanaga
Bomu
Uele
Kinyeti 3,187 m
L. Turkana
GUINEA BASIN
Gulf of Guinea
Príncipe
Ubangi
Sangha
Congo (Zaire)
Aruwimi
L. Albert
Wagagai 4,321 m
Lulonga
Weri Jubba
Equator
São Tomé
Cap Lopez
Ogooué
Ruki
Tshuapa
Lomami
Stanley Falls
Lowa
L. Edward
Lake Victoria
Batian 5,199 m
Nairobi
Tana
ROMANCHE FRACTURE ZONE
AREA OF OPTIMIZATION
Annobón
L. Kivu
Kilimanjaro 5,895 m
INDIAN OCEAN
Congo
Kwa
Kasai
Kwilu
Kinshasa
Kwango
Monts Mitumba
Lualaba
Lulua
Kasai
Lake Tanganyika
Pemba
Zanzibar
Mafia
SOMALI BASIN
ASCENSION FRACTURE ZONE
Ascension
ATLANTIC
L. Mweru
L. Rukwa
Rufiji
Aldabra Is.
Cuanza
Ruvuma
Cabo Delgado
Grande Comore
Tanjon' i Bobaomby
Anjouan
Lake Nyasa
Comoros
Mayotte
ANGOLA ABYSSAL PLAIN
OCEAN
St. Helena
Lúrio
Lusaka
L. Kariba
Cubango
Zambezi
Zambezi
Mozambique Channel
Juan de Nova
Cunene
Victoria Falls
C. Fria
Namib Desert
Okovango
Tsiafajavona 2,643 m
Madagascar
Save
Ponta São Sebastião
Limpopo
Kalahari Desert
Tropic of Capricorn
WALVIS RIDGE
NAMIBIA ABYSSAL PLAIN
Molopo
Johannesburg
Tanjona Vohimena
Vaal
Orange
Drakensberg
MOZAMBIQUE PLATEAU
INDIAN OCEAN
MADAGASCAR RIDGE
Cape Town
Cape of Good Hope
C. Agulhas

2 3 4 5 6 7 8
20° 10° 0° 10° 20° 30°

Longitude West 10° of Greenwich B 0° Longitude C East of 10° Greenwich D 20° E 30° F 40° G 50° H

SCALE 1:35,000,000 OPTIMAL CONFORMAL PROJECTION

MILES 0 500 1000 1500

KILOMETERS 0 500 1000 1500

POPULATION OF CITIES AND TOWNS

- OVER 3,000,000
- 1,000,000 - 2,999,999
- 500,000 - 999,999
- 100,000 - 499,999
- UNDER 100,000

South America

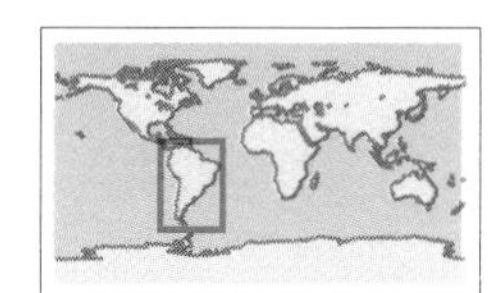

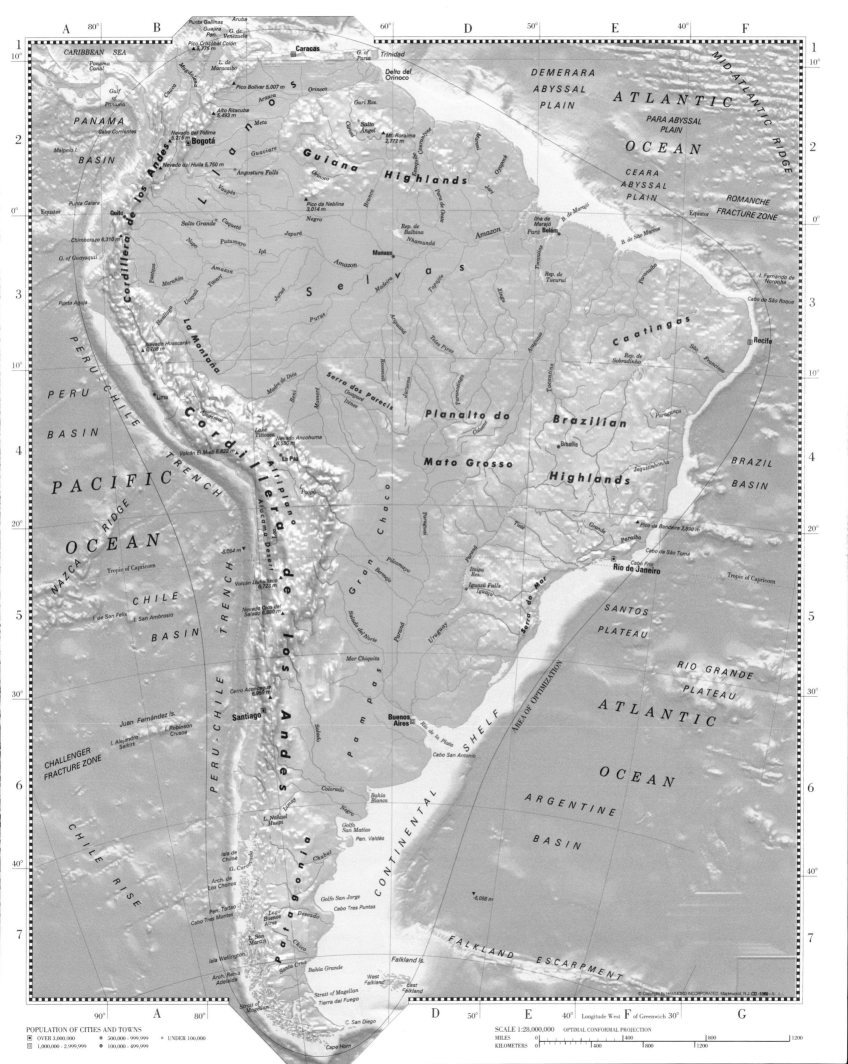

CARIBBEAN SEA
Punta Gallinas
Guajira Pen.
Aruba
G. de Venezuela
Pico Cristóbal Colón 5,775 m
Caracas
G. of Paria
Trinidad
Panama Canal
L. de Maracaibo
Delta del Orinoco
Magdalena
Cauca
Pico Bolívar 5,007 m
Orinoco
Gulf of Panama
Arauca
Guri Res.
Alto Ritacuba 5,493 m
Meta
Salto Angel
Caroni
Mt. Roraima 2,772 m
PANAMA BASIN
Cabo Corrientes
Nevado del Tolima 5,215 m
Bogotá
Malpelo I.
Guaviare
Nevado del Huila 5,750 m
Angostura Falls
Guiana Highlands
Llanos
Cordillera de los Andes
Vaupés
Pico da Neblina 3,014 m
Branco
Essequibo
Courantyne
Maroni
Oyapock
Jari
Paru de Oeste
Punta Galera
Quito
Equator
Negro
Caquetá
Salto Grande
Japurá
Rep. de Balbina
Nhamundá
Amazon
Ilha de Marajó
Pará
Belém
B. de Marajó
B. de São Marcos
Chimborazo 6,310 m
Napo
Putumayo
Içá
Manaus
G. of Guayaquil
Amazon
Pastaza
Marañón
Yavari
Ucayali
Juruá
Selvas
Madeira
Tapajós
Xingu
Tocantins
Rep. de Tucuruí
Parnaíba
I. Fernando de Noronha
Cabo de São Roque
Punta Aguja
Huallaga
La Montaña
Purus
Aripuanã
Teles Pires
Araguaia
Caatingas
Recife
Nevado Huascarán 6,768 m
Rep. de Sobradinho
São Francisco
Madre de Dios
Roosevelt
Juruena
Paranatinga
Tocantins
Serra dos Parecis
Beni
Mamoré
Guaporé
Iténez
Lima
PERU BASIN
Apurimac
Planalto do Brazilian
Culuene
Paraguaçu
Cordillera de los Andes
Lake Titicaca
Nevado Ancohuma 6,550 m
Brasília
La Paz
Volcán El Misti 5,822 m
Mato Grosso
Highlands
Jequitinhonha
Altiplano
L. Poopó
PACIFIC OCEAN
Chaco
Paraguai
Tietê
Grande
Pico de Bandeira 2,890 m
Paraíba
Atacama Desert
Cabo de São Tomé
Cabo Frio
Rio de Janeiro
Tropic of Capricorn
Pilcomayo
Bermejo
Paraná
Itaipu Res.
Iguazú Falls
Iguaçu
Serra do Mar
Volcán Llullaillaco 6,723 m
Gran Chaco
NAZCA RIDGE
CHILE BASIN
I. de San Felix
I. San Ambrosio
Nevado Ojos del Salado 6,880 m
Salado del Norte
Paraná
Uruguay
PERU-CHILE TRENCH
Mar Chiquita
Cerro Aconcagua 6,959 m
Santiago
Pampas
Buenos Aires
Río de la Plata
Cabo San Antonio
Juan Fernández Is.
I. Alejandro Selkirk
I. Robinson Crusoe
CHALLENGER FRACTURE ZONE
Salado
Colorado
Bahía Blanca
Limay
L. Nahuel Huapí
Negro
Golfo San Matías
Pen. Valdés
CHILE RISE
Isla de Chiloé
G. Corcovado
Chubut
Arch. de Los Chonos
Golfo San Jorge
Cabo Tres Puntas
Pen. Taitao
Cabo Tres Montes
Lago Buenos Aires
Deseado
L. San Martín
Chico
Isla Wellington
Patagonia
Santa Cruz
Bahía Grande
Falkland Is.
West Falkland
East Falkland
Arch. Reina Adelaida
Strait of Magellan
Tierra del Fuego
C. San Diego
Cape Horn
DEMERARA ABYSSAL PLAIN
ATLANTIC OCEAN
MID-ATLANTIC RIDGE
PARA ABYSSAL PLAIN
CEARA ABYSSAL PLAIN
ROMANCHE FRACTURE ZONE
BRAZIL BASIN
SANTOS PLATEAU
RIO GRANDE PLATEAU
ATLANTIC OCEAN
AREA OF OPTIMIZATION
CONTINENTAL SHELF
ARGENTINE BASIN
FALKLAND ESCARPMENT

A B C D E F G
80° 60° 50° 40° 90° 80° 50° 40° 30°
10° 0° 10° 20° 30° 40°
1 2 3 4 5 6 7

Longitude West of Greenwich

POPULATION OF CITIES AND TOWNS

- ▣ OVER 3,000,000
- ◎ 1,000,000 - 2,999,999
- ⊛ 500,000 - 999,999
- ⊕ 100,000 - 499,999
- ○ UNDER 100,000

SCALE 1:28,000,000 OPTIMAL CONFORMAL PROJECTION

MILES 0 400 800 1200

KILOMETERS 0 400 800 1200

North America

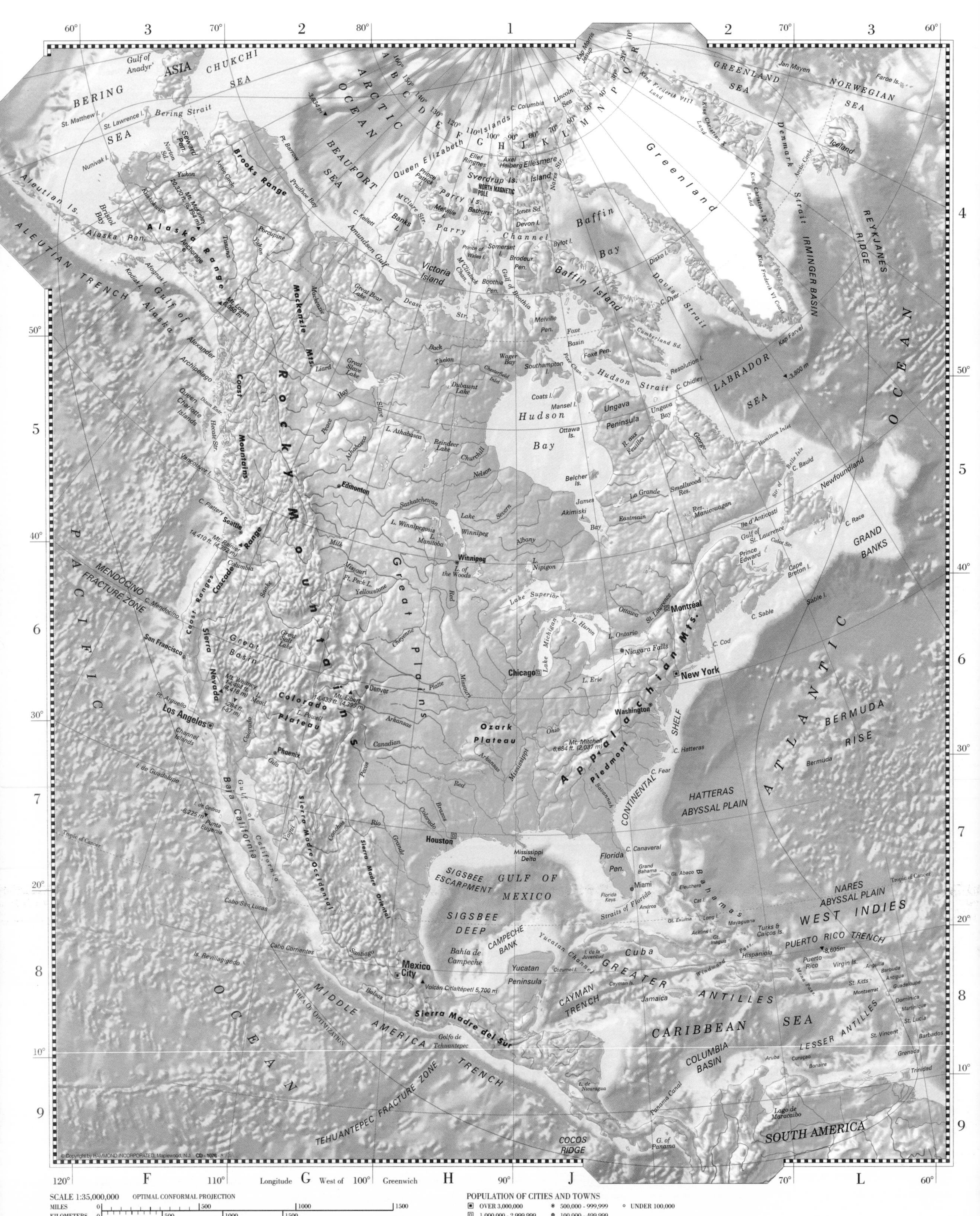

ASIA
Gulf of Anadyr'
CHUKCHI SEA
BERING SEA
Bering Strait
St. Matthew I.
St. Lawrence I.
Seward Pen.
Norton Sd.
Nunivak I.
Aleutian Is.
ALEUTIAN TRENCH
Bristol Bay
Alaska Pen.
Alaska Range
Brooks Range
Yukon
Mt. McKinley
Anchorage
Kodiak I.
Gulf of Alaska
Mt. Logan
Alexander Archipelago
Queen Charlotte Islands
Coast Mountains
Vancouver I.
C. Flattery
Seattle
Mt. Rainier
Cascade Range
Columbia
Coast Ranges
Sierra Nevada
San Francisco
Great Basin
Mt. Whitney
Los Angeles
Channel Islands
MENDOCINO FRACTURE ZONE
C. Mendocino
PACIFIC OCEAN
ARCTIC OCEAN
BEAUFORT SEA
Pt. Barrow
Prudhoe Bay
Mackenzie Mts.
Mackenzie
Great Bear Lake
Great Slave Lake
Rocky Mountains
Edmonton
Queen Elizabeth Islands
Sverdrup Is.
Ellesmere Island
Axel Heiberg I.
Ellef Ringnes I.
Prince Patrick I.
Melville I.
Bathurst I.
NORTH MAGNETIC POLE
Parry Is.
Banks I.
Victoria Island
Amundsen Gulf
Prince of Wales I.
Somerset I.
Devon I.
Jones Sd.
Lincoln Sea
C. Columbia
Kap Morris Jesup
Greenland
GREENLAND SEA
Jan Mayen
NORWEGIAN SEA
Faroe Is.
Iceland
Denmark Strait
IRMINGER BASIN
REYKJANES RIDGE
Kap Farvel
Baffin Bay
Baffin Island
Bylot I.
Disko I.
Davis Strait
Cumberland Sd.
Boothia Pen.
Gulf of Boothia
Melville Pen.
Foxe Basin
Foxe Pen.
Southampton I.
Hudson Strait
Resolution I.
C. Chidley
LABRADOR SEA
Hudson Bay
Coats I.
Mansel I.
Ungava Peninsula
Ungava Bay
Belcher Is.
James Bay
Akimiski I.
Churchill
Nelson
Reindeer Lake
L. Athabasca
Dubawnt Lake
Chesterfield Inlet
Wager Bay
Back
Thelon
Peace
Athabasca
Saskatchewan
L. Winnipegosis
L. Manitoba
Lake Winnipeg
Winnipeg
L. of the Woods
Severn
Albany
L. Nipigon
Lake Superior
La Grande
Eastmain
Smallwood Res.
Res. Manicouagan
Hamilton Inlet
C. Bauld
Newfoundland
Ile d'Anticosti
Gulf of St. Lawrence
Prince Edward I.
Cape Breton I.
C. Race
GRAND BANKS
Sable I.
C. Sable
Montréal
Ottawa
L. Huron
Lake Michigan
L. Ontario
L. Erie
Niagara Falls
Chicago
New York
Washington
Appalachian Mts.
Mt. Mitchell
Piedmont
C. Hatteras
C. Fear
C. Cod
CONTINENTAL SHELF
ATLANTIC OCEAN
BERMUDA RISE
Bermuda
HATTERAS ABYSSAL PLAIN
Great Plains
Missouri
Platte
Ft. Peck L.
Yellowstone
Great Salt Lake
Denver
Mt. Elbert
Colorado Plateau
L. Powell
L. Mead
Colorado
Phoenix
Gila
Arkansas
Canadian
Red
Ozark Plateau
Ohio
Mississippi
Pecos
Rio Grande
Brazos
Houston
Mississippi Delta
Florida Pen.
C. Canaveral
Miami
Florida Keys
Straits of Florida
Grand Bahama
Bahamas
Andros I.
SIGSBEE ESCARPMENT
GULF OF MEXICO
SIGSBEE DEEP
CAMPECHE BANK
Bahía de Campeche
Yucatan Peninsula
Yucatan Channel
Cuba
GREATER ANTILLES
Hispaniola
Jamaica
Cayman Is.
CAYMAN TRENCH
Puerto Rico
PUERTO RICO TRENCH
Turks & Caicos Is.
NARES ABYSSAL PLAIN
WEST INDIES
Virgin Is.
LESSER ANTILLES
Barbados
Trinidad
CARIBBEAN SEA
COLUMBIA BASIN
Aruba
Curaçao
Bonaire
Lago de Maracaibo
SOUTH AMERICA
G. of Panama
Panama Canal
L. de Nicaragua
COCOS RIDGE
TEHUANTEPEC FRACTURE ZONE
MIDDLE AMERICA TRENCH
Golfo de Tehuantepec
Sierra Madre del Sur
Mexico City
Volcán Citlaltépetl 5,700 m
Sierra Madre Oriental
Sierra Madre Occidental
Baja California
Gulf of California
Punta Eugenia
I. de Guadalupe
Cabo San Lucas
Cabo Corrientes
Is. Revillagigedo
Tropic of Cancer
AREA OF OPTIMIZATION
© Copyright by HAMMOND INCORPORATED, Maplewood, N.J.

Longitude West of Greenwich

SCALE 1:35,000,000 OPTIMAL CONFORMAL PROJECTION

MILES 0 500 1000 1500

KILOMETERS 0 500 1000 1500

POPULATION OF CITIES AND TOWNS

- OVER 3,000,000
- 1,000,000 - 2,999,999
- 500,000 - 999,999
- 100,000 - 499,999
- UNDER 100,000

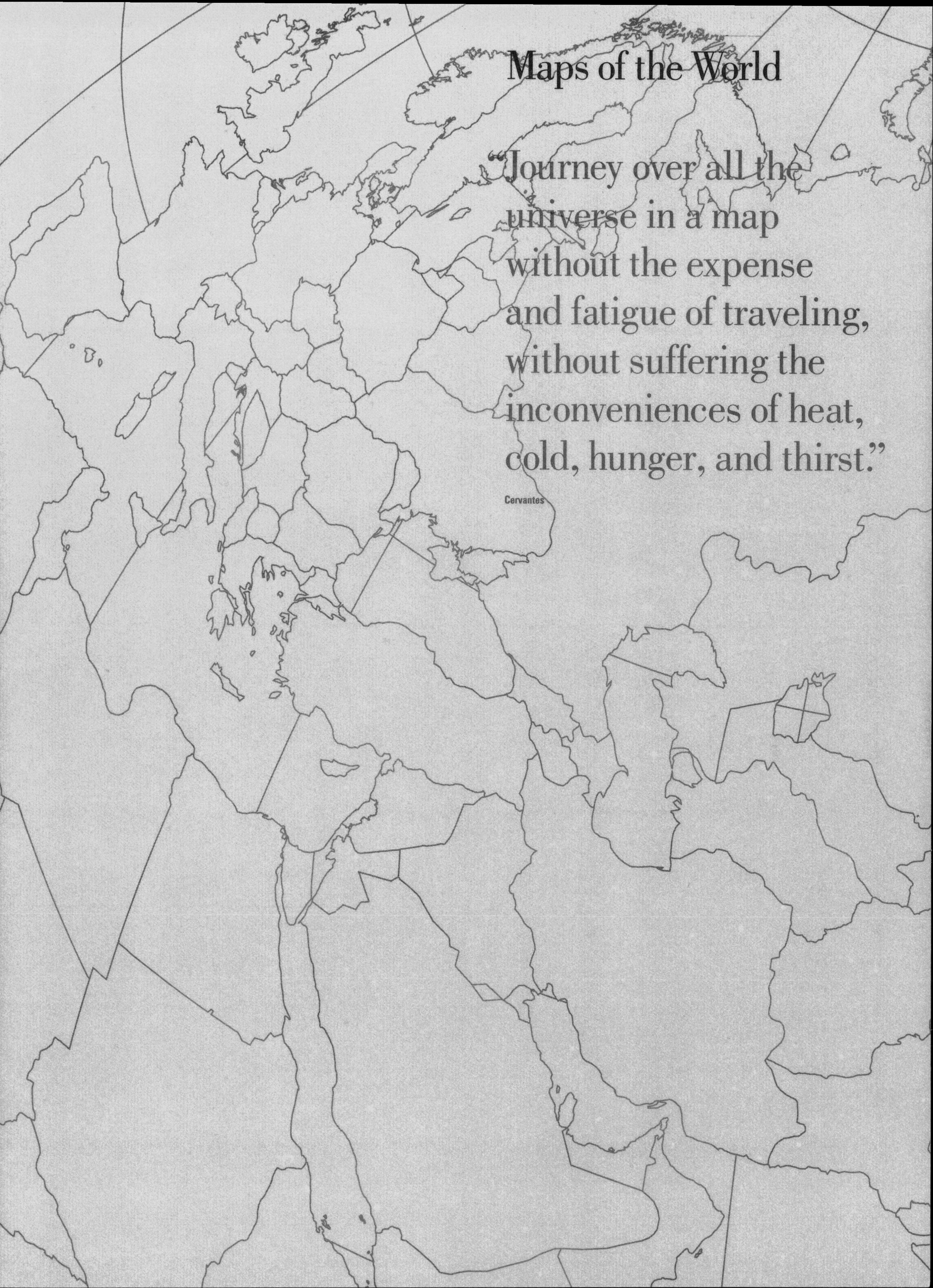

Maps of the World

> "Journey over all the universe in a map without the expense and fatigue of traveling, without suffering the inconveniences of heat, cold, hunger, and thirst."
>
> Cervantes

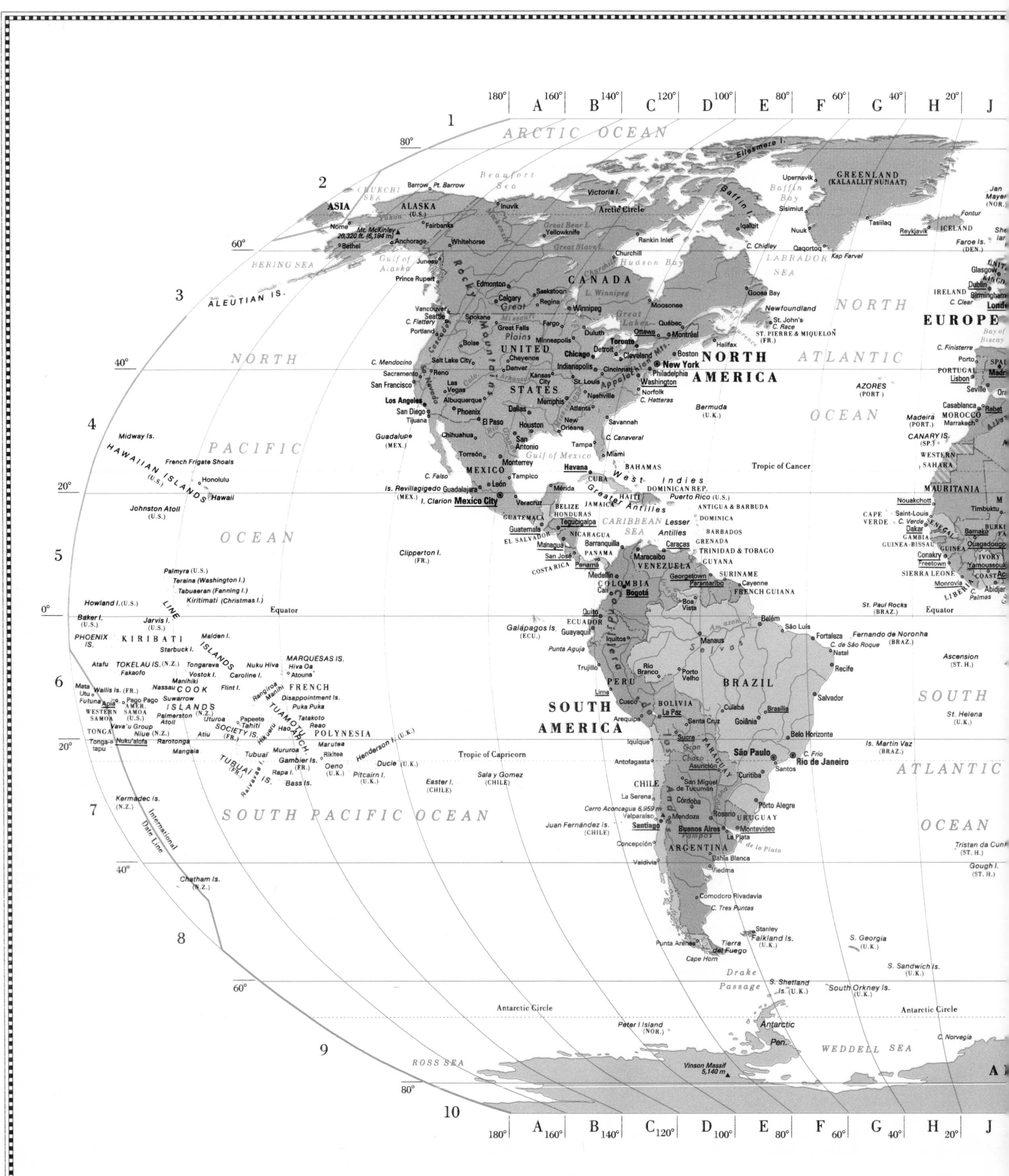
180°
A 160°
B 140°
C 120°
D 100°
E 80°
F 60°
G 40°
H 20°
J
1
2
3
4
5
6
7
8
9
10
80°
60°
40°
20°
0°
ARCTIC OCEAN
Ellesmere I.
GREENLAND (KALAALLIT NUNAAT)
Upernavik
Baffin Bay
Baffin I.
Sisimiut
Iqaluit
Nuuk
Tasiilaq
Qaqortoq
Kap Farvel
C. Chidley
Jan Mayen (NOR.)
Fontur
ICELAND
Reykjavik
Faroe Is. (DEN.)
Beaufort Sea
CHUKCHI SEA
Barrow
Pt. Barrow
Victoria I.
Arctic Circle
Inuvik
ASIA
ALASKA (U.S.)
Yukon
Fairbanks
Nome
Mt. McKinley 20,320 ft. (6,194 m)
Anchorage
Bethel
Whitehorse
Great Bear L.
Yellowknife
Great Slave L.
Rankin Inlet
Churchill
Hudson Bay
LABRADOR SEA
BERING SEA
Gulf of Alaska
Juneau
Prince Rupert
Rocky Mountains
Edmonton
CANADA
Saskatoon
Calgary
Regina
L. Winnipeg
Winnipeg
Goose Bay
Newfoundland
St. John's
C. Race
ST. PIERRE & MIQUELON (FR.)
Halifax
Moosonee
Québec
Montréal
Ottawa
Great Lakes
NORTH
ATLANTIC
OCEAN
IRELAND
Dublin
Glasgow
C. Clear
EUROPE
Bay of Biscay
C. Finisterre
Porto
PORTUGAL
Lisbon
Seville
ALEUTIAN IS.
Vancouver
Seattle
C. Flattery
Portland
Spokane
Missouri
Great Falls
Great Plains
Fargo
Minneapolis
Duluth
Toronto
Detroit
Cleveland
Chicago
Boston
New York
Philadelphia
Washington
Norfolk
C. Hatteras
NORTH AMERICA
Boise
Salt Lake City
Cheyenne
Denver
UNITED STATES
Indianapolis
Cincinnati
Kansas City
St. Louis
Nashville
Memphis
Atlanta
Appalachian Mts.
C. Mendocino
Sacramento
Reno
San Francisco
Las Vegas
Los Angeles
San Diego
Tijuana
Albuquerque
Phoenix
Dallas
El Paso
Houston
New Orleans
San Antonio
Savannah
Tampa
C. Canaveral
Miami
Bermuda (U.K.)
AZORES (PORT.)
Madeira (PORT.)
MOROCCO
Casablanca
Marrakech
CANARY IS. (SP.)
WESTERN SAHARA
MAURITANIA
Nouakchott
Guadalupe (MEX.)
Chihuahua
Torreón
Monterrey
MEXICO
Gulf of Mexico
Tampico
C. Falso
Is. Revillagigedo (MEX.)
Guadalajara
León
I. Clarion
Mexico City
Veracruz
Mérida
Havana
CUBA
BAHAMAS
West Indies
Greater Antilles
HAITI
DOMINICAN REP.
Puerto Rico (U.S.)
JAMAICA
BELIZE
HONDURAS
Tegucigalpa
GUATEMALA
Guatemala
EL SALVADOR
NICARAGUA
Managua
San José
COSTA RICA
PANAMA
Panamá
CARIBBEAN SEA
Lesser Antilles
ANTIGUA & BARBUDA
DOMINICA
BARBADOS
GRENADA
TRINIDAD & TOBAGO
GUYANA
SURINAME
FRENCH GUIANA
Barranquilla
Maracaibo
Caracas
VENEZUELA
Georgetown
Paramaribo
Cayenne
Medellín
COLOMBIA
Cali
Bogotá
Tropic of Cancer
CAPE VERDE
Saint-Louis
C. Verde
Dakar
GAMBIA
GUINEA-BISSAU
GUINEA
Conakry
Freetown
SIERRA LEONE
Monrovia
LIBERIA
Bamako
Timbuktu
Ouagadougou
IVORY COAST
Yamoussoukro
Abidjan
C. Palmas
St. Paul Rocks (BRAZ.)
Equator
Midway Is.
HAWAIIAN ISLANDS (U.S.)
French Frigate Shoals
Honolulu
Hawaii
PACIFIC
OCEAN
Johnston Atoll (U.S.)
Clipperton I. (FR.)
Palmyra (U.S.)
Teraina (Washington I.)
Tabuaeran (Fanning I.)
Kiritimati (Christmas I.)
LINE ISLANDS
Howland I. (U.S.)
Baker I. (U.S.)
Jarvis I. (U.S.)
PHOENIX IS.
KIRIBATI
Malden I.
Starbuck I.
Galápagos Is. (ECU.)
Quito
ECUADOR
Guayaquil
Iquitos
Belém
São Luís
Fortaleza
Fernando de Noronha (BRAZ.)
C. de São Roque
Natal
Recife
Amazon
Selvas
Manaus
Boa Vista
Punta Aguja
Trujillo
PERU
Lima
Cusco
Rio Branco
Porto Velho
BRAZIL
Salvador
SOUTH AMERICA
BOLIVIA
La Paz
Cuiabá
Brasília
Goiânia
Santa Cruz
Sucre
Arequipa
Iquique
Belo Horizonte
Ascension (ST. H.)
SOUTH
St. Helena (U.K.)
Atafu
TOKELAU IS. (N.Z.)
Fakaofo
Tongareva
Vostok I.
Manihiki
Nuku Hiva
MARQUESAS IS.
Hiva Oa
Atuona
Caroline I.
Flint I.
FRENCH
COOK ISLANDS
Wallis Is. (FR.)
Futuna
Apia
Pago Pago
WESTERN SAMOA
AMER. SAMOA (U.S.)
Nassau
Suwarrow
Palmerston Atoll
Disappointment Is.
Puka Puka
Rangiroa
Manihi
TUAMOTU ARCHIPELAGO
Tatakoto
Reao
Papeete
Tahiti
SOCIETY IS. (FR.)
Hao
POLYNESIA
TONGA
Vava'u Group
Niue (N.Z.)
Uturoa
Atiu
Tonga-tapu
Nuku'alofa
Rarotonga
Mangaia
Tubuai
TUBUAI IS.
Raivavae I.
Rapa I.
Mururoa
Marutea
Rikitea
Gambier Is. (FR.)
Oeno (U.K.)
Henderson I. (U.K.)
Ducie (U.K.)
Pitcairn I. (U.K.)
Bass Is.
Easter I. (CHILE)
Sala y Gomez (CHILE)
Tropic of Capricorn
Antofagasta
Gran Chaco
PARAGUAY
Asunción
São Paulo
C. Frio
Rio de Janeiro
Santos
Curitiba
Is. Martin Vaz (BRAZ.)
ATLANTIC
CHILE
San Miguel de Tucumán
La Serena
Córdoba
Porto Alegre
Cerro Aconcagua 6,959 m
Valparaíso
Mendoza
Rosario
URUGUAY
Juan Fernández Is. (CHILE)
Santiago
Buenos Aires
Montevideo
La Plata
Pampas
Río de la Plata
Concepción
ARGENTINA
Bahía Blanca
Valdivia
Viedma
Comodoro Rivadavia
C. Tres Puntas
Tristan da Cunha (ST. H.)
Gough I. (ST. H.)
Kermadec Is. (N.Z.)
SOUTH PACIFIC OCEAN
International Date Line
Chatham Is. (N.Z.)
Stanley
Falkland Is. (U.K.)
Punta Arenas
Tierra del Fuego
Cape Horn
S. Georgia (U.K.)
S. Sandwich Is. (U.K.)
Drake Passage
S. Shetland Is. (U.K.)
South Orkney Is. (U.K.)
Antarctic Circle
Peter I Island (NOR.)
Antarctic Pen.
WEDDELL SEA
C. Norvegia
ROSS SEA
Vinson Massif 5,140 m

World

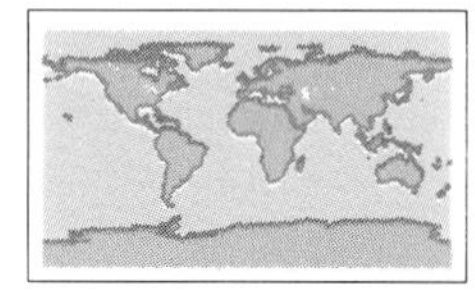

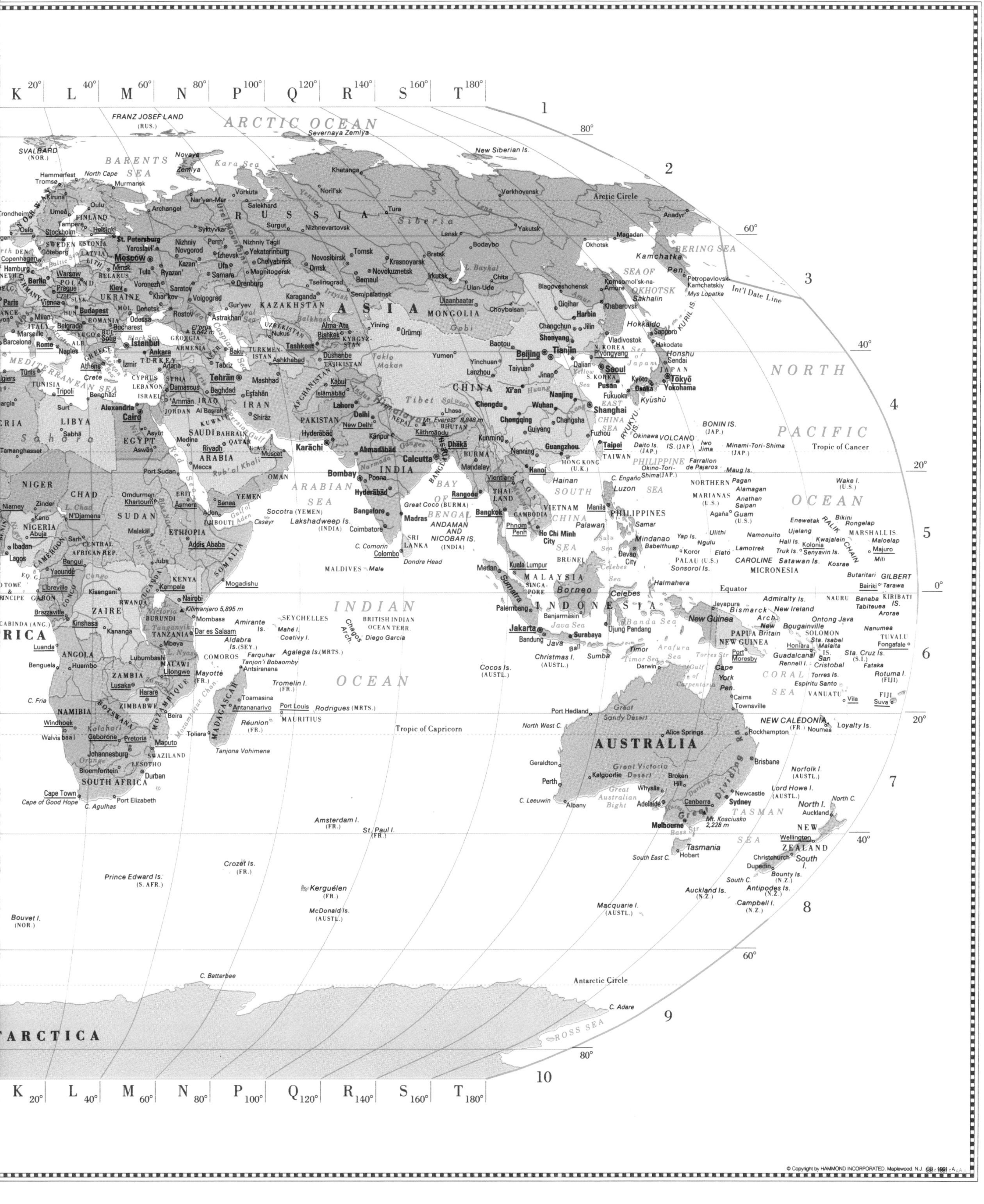

POPULATION OF CITIES AND TOWNS

- OVER 5,000,000
- 2,000,000 - 4,999,999
- 500,000 - 1,999,999
- UNDER 500,000

SCALE 1:81,700,000 ROBINSON PROJECTION STANDARD PARALLELS 38°N AND 38°S

MILES 0 1000 2000 3000 4000

KILOMETERS 0 1000 2000 3000 4000

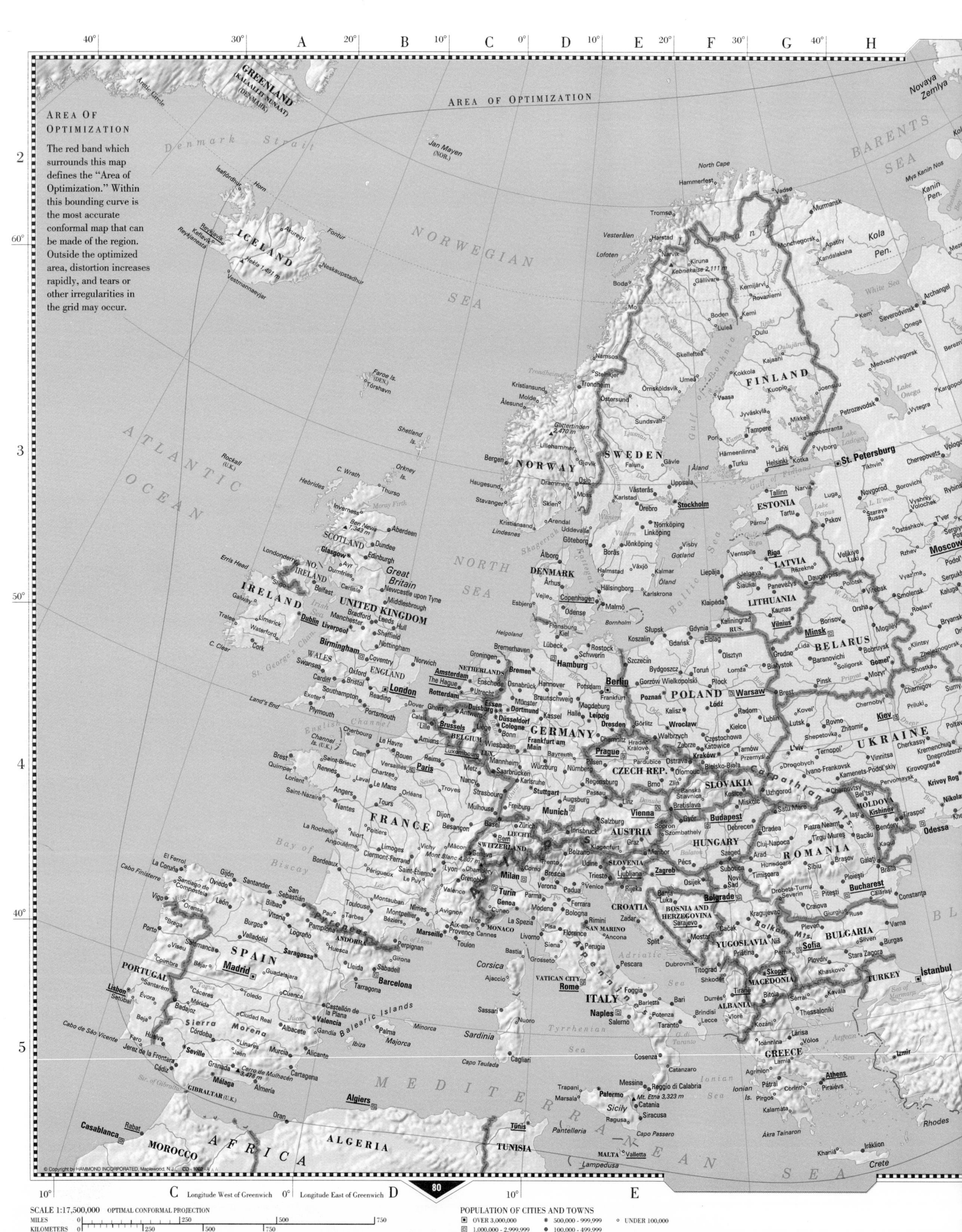
AREA OF OPTIMIZATION
The red band which surrounds this map defines the "Area of Optimization." Within this bounding curve is the most accurate conformal map that can be made of the region. Outside the optimized area, distortion increases rapidly, and tears or other irregularities in the grid may occur.
AREA OF OPTIMIZATION
GREENLAND (KALAALLIT NUNAAT) (DENMARK)
Denmark Strait
Jan Mayen (NOR.)
ICELAND
NORWEGIAN SEA
BARENTS SEA
Novaya Zemlya
Kola Pen.
Kanin Pen.
White Sea
Faroe Is. (DEN.)
Shetland Is.
Orkney Is.
ATLANTIC OCEAN
Rockall (U.K.)
NORTH SEA
NORWAY
SWEDEN
FINLAND
ESTONIA
LATVIA
LITHUANIA
RUS.
BELARUS
DENMARK
Baltic Sea
Gulf of Bothnia
Gulf of Finland
SCOTLAND
Great Britain
UNITED KINGDOM
NO. IRELAND
IRELAND
WALES
ENGLAND
English Channel
Channel Is. (U.K.)
NETHERLANDS
BELGIUM
LUX.
GERMANY
POLAND
CZECH REP.
SLOVAKIA
UKRAINE
MOLDOVA
AUSTRIA
HUNGARY
ROMANIA
SWITZERLAND
LIECHT.
FRANCE
Bay of Biscay
SPAIN
PORTUGAL
ANDORRA
Pyrenees
Balearic Islands
Sierra Morena
GIBRALTAR (U.K.)
ITALY
MONACO
SAN MARINO
VATICAN CITY
Corsica
Sardinia
Sicily
Adriatic Sea
Tyrrhenian Sea
Ionian Sea
SLOVENIA
CROATIA
BOSNIA AND HERZEGOVINA
YUGOSLAVIA
MACEDONIA
ALBANIA
BULGARIA
GREECE
TURKEY
Crete
Rhodes
MEDITERRANEAN SEA
MOROCCO
ALGERIA
TUNISIA
AFRICA
MALTA
Moscow
St. Petersburg
Kiev
Minsk
Warsaw
Berlin
Paris
London
Madrid
Lisbon
Rome
Vienna
Prague
Budapest
Bucharest
Sofia
Athens
Belgrade
Istanbul
Algiers
Tunis
Rabat
Casablanca
© Copyright by HAMMOND INCORPORATED, Maplewood, N.J.
C Longitude West of Greenwich 0° Longitude East of Greenwich D
E
SCALE 1:17,500,000 OPTIMAL CONFORMAL PROJECTION
MILES 0 250 500 750
KILOMETERS 0 250 500 750
POPULATION OF CITIES AND TOWNS
OVER 3,000,000
1,000,000 - 2,999,999
500,000 - 999,999
100,000 - 499,999
UNDER 100,000

Europe

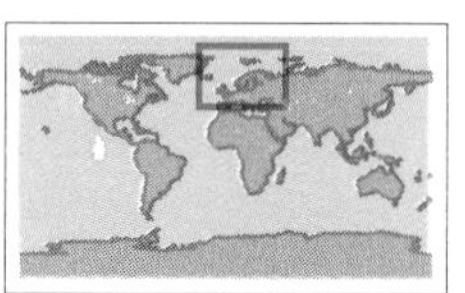

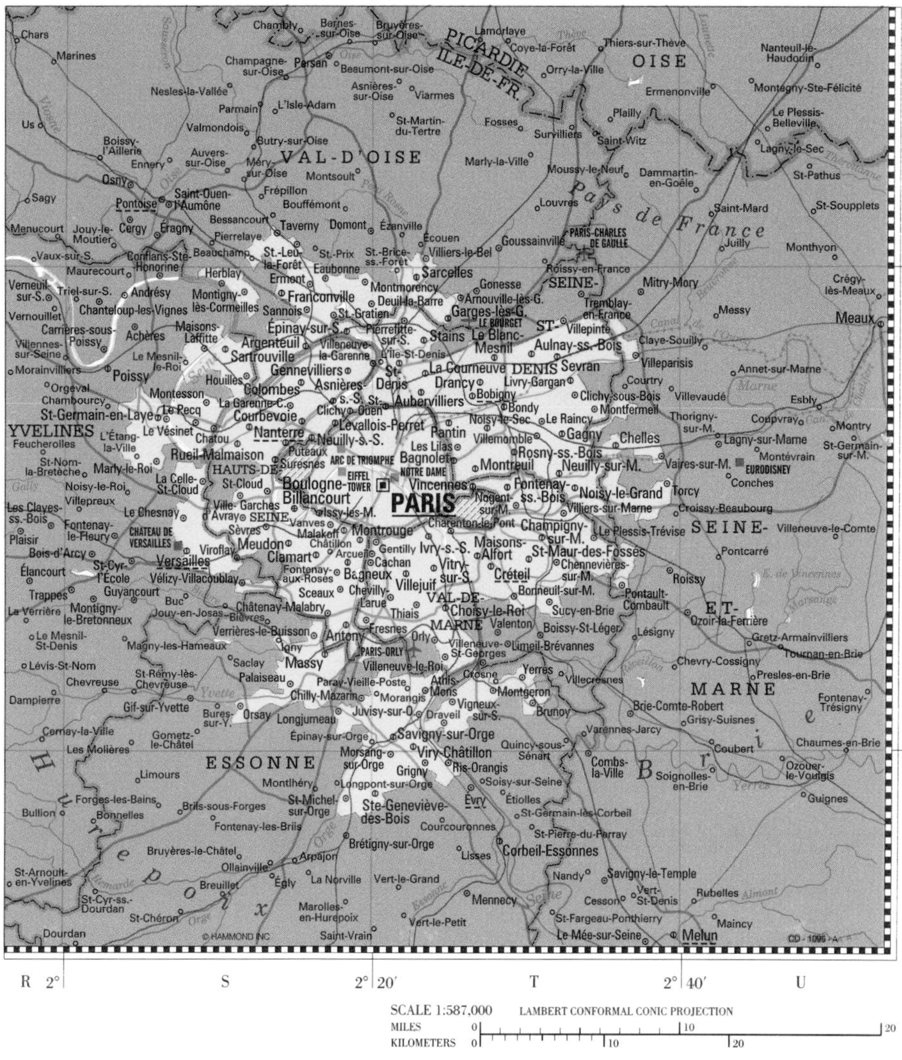

Boroughs indicated by number:
1 HAMMERSMITH & FULHAM
2 ISLINGTON
3 KENSINGTON & CHELSEA
4 CITY OF LONDON
5 SOUTHWARK
6 TOWER HAMLETS
7 WALTHAM FOREST
8 CITY OF WESTMINSTER

SCALE 1:587,000 LAMBERT CONFORMAL CONIC PROJECTION
MILES 0 10 20
KILOMETERS 0 10 20

7°
B
6°
C
5°
D
4°
E
36
A
2
3
4
5
6
55°
54° 30′
54°
53° 30′
53°
Kintyre
Rathlin I.
Mull of Kintyre
Southend
Sanda I.
Firth of Clyde
North Channel
Ailsa Craig
Inishowen
DONEGAL
Lough Foyle
IRELAND
U.K.
Londonderry
LONDONDERRY
LIMAVADY
COLERAINE
BALLYMONEY
MOYLE
Giant's Causeway
LARNE
BALLYMENA
ANTRIM
MAGHERAFELT
NORTHERN IRELAND
Lough Neagh
STRABANE
OMAGH
COOKSTOWN
CARRICKFERGUS
NORTH DOWN
Belfast
BELFAST
Bangor
ARDS
Ards Pen.
LISBURN
CRAIGAVON
DUNGANNON
BANBRIDGE
ARMAGH
DOWN
FERMANAGH
Ulster
MONAGHAN
MOURNE
Newry
Dundrum Bay
Isle of Man (U.K.)
Douglas
Calf of Man
Point of Ayre
Snaefell 621 m
STRATHCLYDE
DUMFRIES
SCOTLAND
Southern Uplands
The Rhinns
The Machars
Luce Bay
Wigtown Bay
Solway Firth
Mull of Galloway
Stranraer
Dumfries
Workington
Whitehaven
IRISH SEA
CAVAN
LOUTH
Dundalk
Dundalk Bay
MEATH
Drogheda
WESTMEATH
IRELAND
DUBLIN
Dublin
Dún Laoghaire
OFFALY
KILDARE
Leinster
LAOIS (LEIX)
CARLOW
WICKLOW
Wicklow Mts.
Lugnaquillia 926 m
WEXFORD
KILKENNY
Arklow
Wicklow
UNITED KINGDOM
IRELAND
St. George's Channel
Anglesey
Holyhead
Caernarfon Bay
GWYNEDD
SNOWDONIA NAT'L PARK
WALES
Lleyn Pen.
Tremadoc Bay
Cardigan Bay
Bardsey I.

Northeastern Ireland, Northern England and Wales

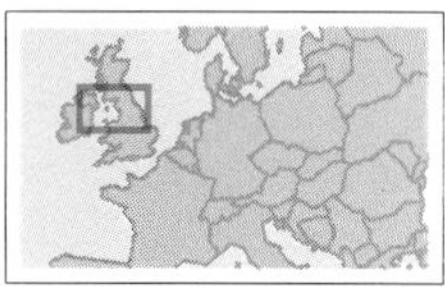

NORTH SEA

BORDERS · NORTHUMBERLAND · NORTHUMBERLAND NATIONAL PARK · CUMBRIA · LAKE DISTRICT NAT'L PARK · DURHAM · CLEVELAND · TYNE & WEAR · NORTH YORKSHIRE · NORTH YORK MOORS NAT'L PARK · YORKSHIRE DALES NAT'L PARK · LANCASHIRE · WEST YORKSHIRE · HUMBERSIDE · GREATER MANCHESTER · MERSEYSIDE · SOUTH YORKSHIRE · PEAK DISTRICT NAT'L PARK · CHESHIRE · STAFFORDSHIRE · DERBYSHIRE · NOTTINGHAMSHIRE · LINCOLNSHIRE · LEICESTERSHIRE · SHROPSHIRE · POWYS · NORFOLK · ENGLAND · SCOTLAND · WALES

35

Longitude West of Greenwich

POPULATION OF CITIES AND TOWNS

- OVER 2,000,000
- 1,000,000 - 1,999,999
- 500,000 - 999,999
- 250,000 - 499,999
- 100,000 - 249,999
- 30,000 - 99,999
- 10,000 - 29,999
- UNDER 10,000

SCALE 1:1,170,000 LAMBERT CONFORMAL CONIC PROJECTION

MILES 0 10 20 30 40 50

KILOMETERS 0 10 20 30 40 50

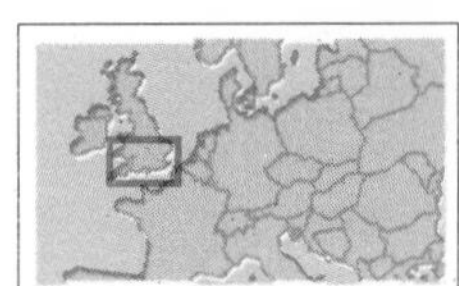

Southern England and Wales

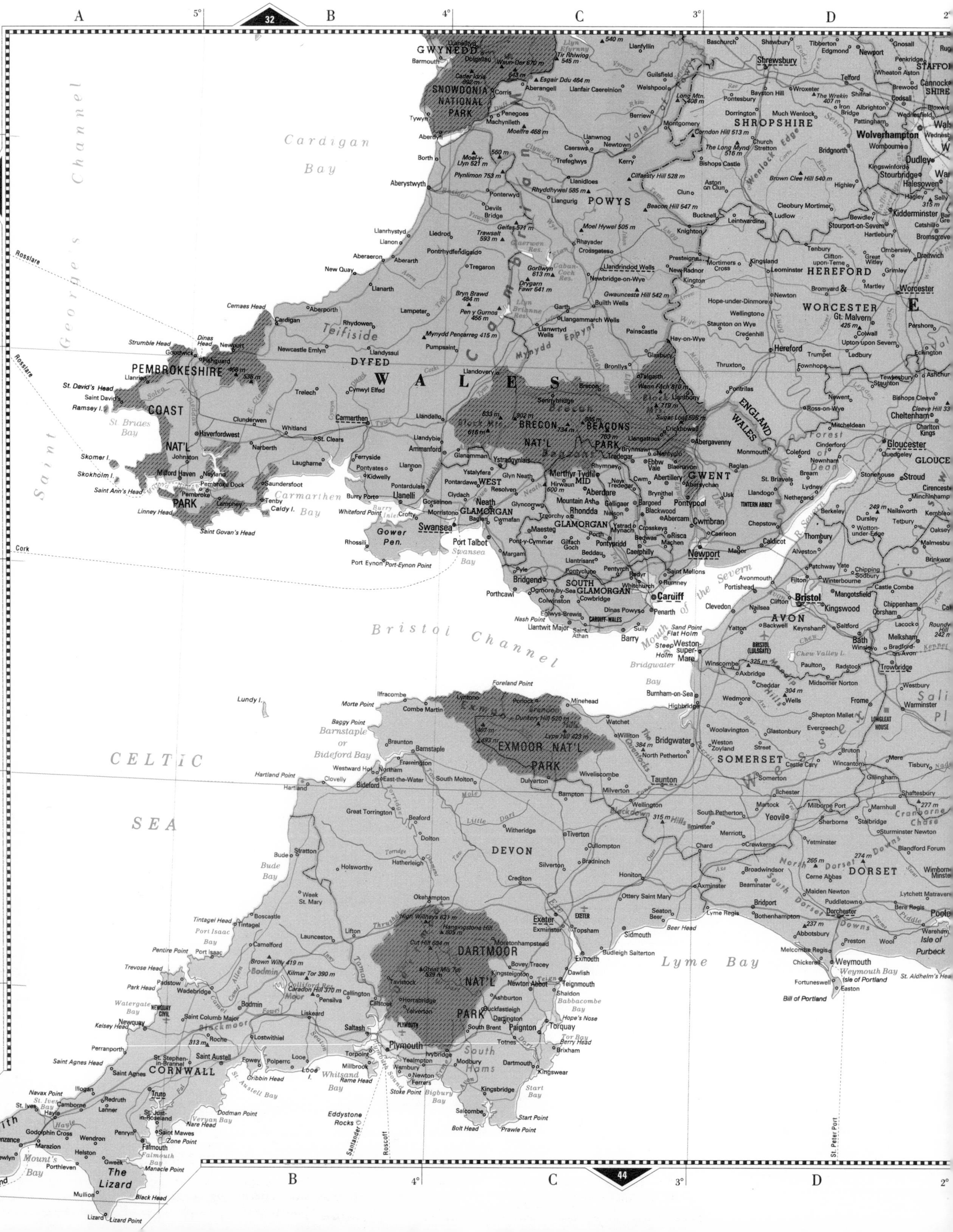

WALES
ENGLAND
Cardigan Bay
Saint George's Channel
Bristol Channel
CELTIC SEA
Lyme Bay
GWYNEDD
SNOWDONIA NATIONAL PARK
POWYS
DYFED
PEMBROKESHIRE COAST NAT'L PARK
BRECON BEACONS NAT'L PARK
WEST GLAMORGAN
MID GLAMORGAN
SOUTH GLAMORGAN
GWENT
SHROPSHIRE
HEREFORD & WORCESTER
AVON
SOMERSET
EXMOOR NAT'L PARK
DEVON
DARTMOOR NAT'L PARK
CORNWALL
DORSET
Shrewsbury
Wolverhampton
Hereford
Worcester
Gloucester
Cheltenham
Swansea
Cardiff
Newport
Bristol
Bath
Taunton
Exeter
Plymouth
Torquay
Weymouth
Dorchester
Carmarthen
Aberystwyth
Lundy I.
Land's End
The Lizard
Gower Pen.

Northeastern Ireland, Northern England and Wales

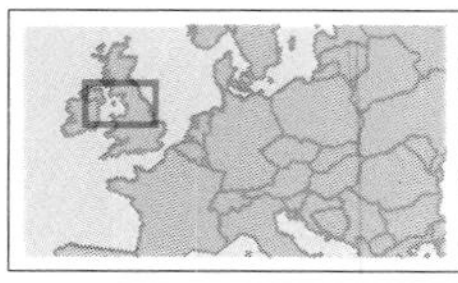

Longitude West of Greenwich

POPULATION OF CITIES AND TOWNS

- OVER 2,000,000
- 1,000,000 - 1,999,999
- 500,000 - 999,999
- 250,000 - 499,999
- 100,000 - 249,999
- 30,000 - 99,999
- 10,000 - 29,999
- UNDER 10,000

SCALE 1:1,170,000 LAMBERT CONFORMAL CONIC PROJECTION

MILES 0 10 20 30 40 50

KILOMETERS 0 10 20 30 40 50

35

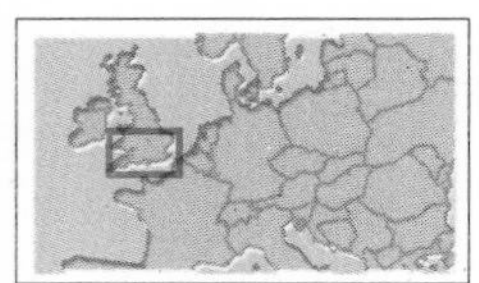

Southern England and Wales

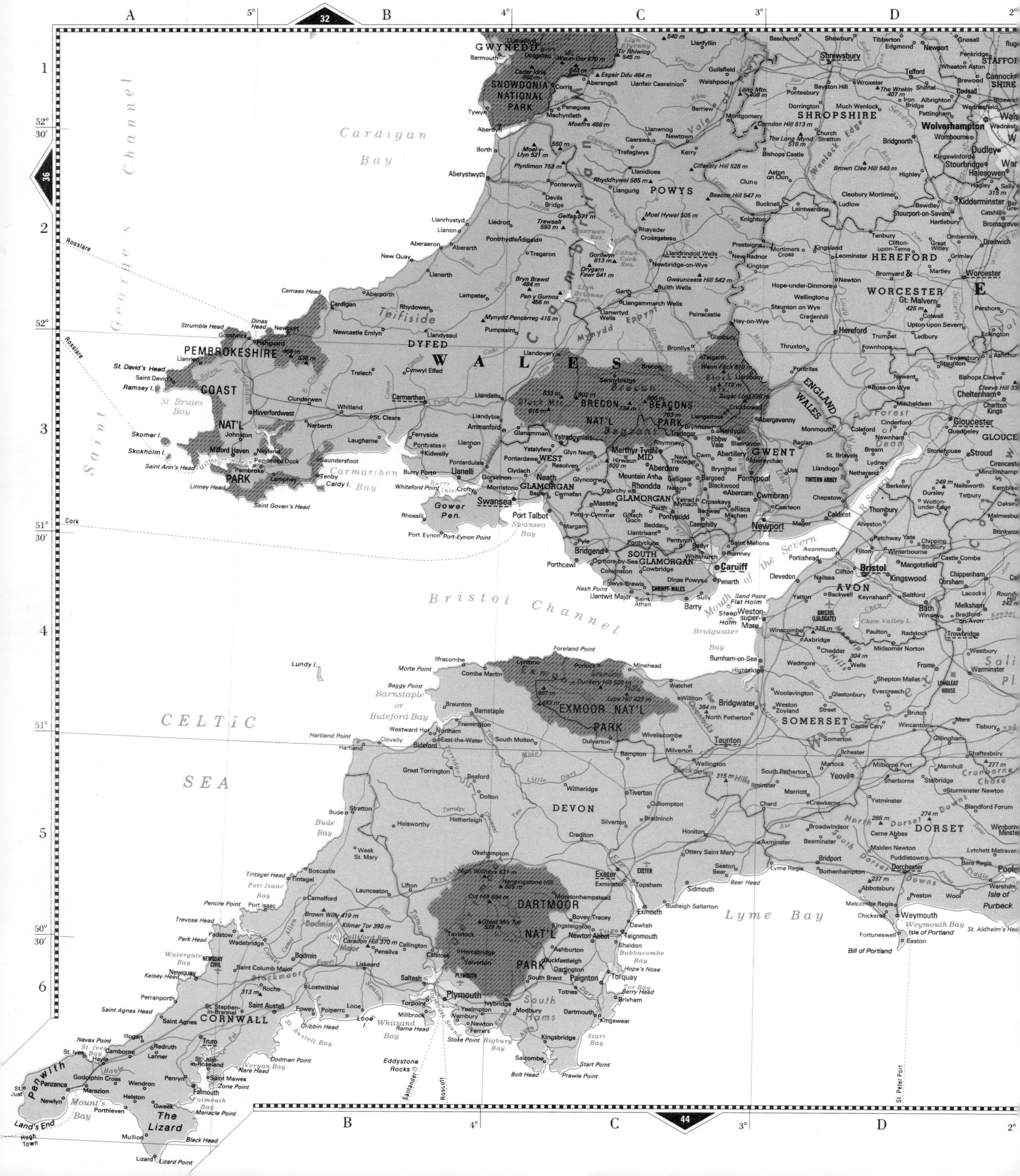

A 5° B 4° C 3° D 2°

1 2 3 4 5 6

52° 30′ 52° 51° 30′ 51° 50° 30′

32 36 44

Cardigan Bay
Saint George's Channel
Carmarthen Bay
Swansea Bay
Bristol Channel
Bridgwater Bay
Barnstaple or Bideford Bay
CELTIC SEA
Lyme Bay
Mount's Bay
St. Ives Bay
Bude Bay
Watergate Bay
Port Isaac Bay
St. Austell Bay
Whitsand Bay
Bigbury Bay
Start Bay
Tor Bay
Babbacombe Bay
Weymouth Bay
St. Brides Bay
Falmouth Bay
Veryan Bay

WALES
GWYNEDD
SNOWDONIA NATIONAL PARK
POWYS
DYFED
Teifiside
PEMBROKESHIRE COAST NAT'L PARK
BRECON BEACONS NAT'L PARK
WEST GLAMORGAN
MID GLAMORGAN
SOUTH GLAMORGAN
GWENT
ENGLAND
SHROPSHIRE
HEREFORD & WORCESTER
AVON
SOMERSET
EXMOOR NAT'L PARK
DEVON
DARTMOOR NAT'L PARK
CORNWALL
DORSET
South Hams
The Lizard
Penwith
Gower Pen.

Cader Idris 892 m
Plynlimon 753 m
Pen y Gurnos 456 m
Mynydd Pencarreg 415 m
Gorllwyn 613 m
Drygarn Fawr 641 m
Bryn Brawd 484 m
Gwaunceste Hill 542 m
Moel Hywel 505 m
Beacon Hill 547 m
Cilfaesty Hill 528 m
Corndon Hill 513 m
The Long Mynd 516 m
Long Mtn. 408 m
The Wrekin 407 m
Brown Clee Hill 540 m
Waun Fach 810 m
Sugar Loaf 596 m
Dunkery Hill 520 m
Lype Hill 423 m
High Willhays 621 m
Hangingstone Hill 603 m
Cut Hill 604 m
Great Mis Tor 539 m
Brown Willy 419 m
Kilmar Tor 390 m
Caradon Hill 370 m
Cleeve Hill 330 m

Barmouth, Dolgellau, Tywyn, Machynlleth, Aberdyfi, Borth, Aberystwyth, Devils Bridge, Llanrhystyd, Lledrod, Tregaron, Aberaeron, New Quay, Llanarth, Lampeter, Aberporth, Cardigan, Newport, Fishguard, Newcastle Emlyn, Llandysul, Pumpsaint, Llandovery, Llanwrtyd Wells, Builth Wells, Llandrindod Wells, Newbridge-on-Wye, Rhayader, Llanidloes, Llangurig, Newtown, Llanfyllin, Welshpool, Montgomery, Kerry, Knighton, Presteigne, New Radnor, Kington, Hay-on-Wye, Talgarth, Brecon, Crickhowell, Abergavenny, Monmouth, Raglan, Pontypool, Cwmbran, Newport, Caerleon, Chepstow, Caldicot, Ebbw Vale, Tredegar, Rhymney, Merthyr Tydfil, Aberdare, Hirwaun, Mountain Ash, Pontypridd, Caerphilly, Rhondda, Maesteg, Neath, Port Talbot, Swansea, Gorseinon, Llanelli, Burry Port, Kidwelly, Ammanford, Llandeilo, Carmarthen, St. Clears, Whitland, Narberth, Haverfordwest, Milford Haven, Pembroke, Pembroke Dock, Tenby, Saundersfoot, Laugharne, St. David's, Bridgend, Porthcawl, Cowbridge, Llantwit Major, Barry, Penarth, Cardiff, Rhossili, Port Eynon

Shrewsbury, Telford, Wolverhampton, Dudley, Stourbridge, Kidderminster, Stourport-on-Severn, Bridgnorth, Much Wenlock, Church Stretton, Bishops Castle, Ludlow, Cleobury Mortimer, Tenbury, Leominster, Bromyard, Hereford, Ledbury, Great Malvern, Worcester, Droitwich, Pershore, Tewkesbury, Cheltenham, Gloucester, Ross-on-Wye, Stroud, Cirencester, Tetbury, Dursley, Thornbury, Lydney, Coleford, Bristol, Avonmouth, Portishead, Clevedon, Weston-super-Mare, Nailsea, Keynsham, Bath, Kingswood, Chippenham, Melksham, Trowbridge, Frome, Warminster, Midsomer Norton, Wells, Cheddar, Axbridge, Burnham-on-Sea, Highbridge, Bridgwater, Glastonbury, Street, Shepton Mallet, Bruton, Wincanton, Castle Cary, Yeovil, Sherborne, Ilchester, Somerton, Langport, Taunton, Wellington, Ilminster, Chard, Crewkerne, Minehead, Watchet, Porlock, Lynton, Ilfracombe, Combe Martin, Barnstaple, Braunton, Bideford, Northam, South Molton, Dulverton, Tiverton, Great Torrington, Holsworthy, Bude, Okehampton, Crediton, Exeter, Exmouth, Sidmouth, Honiton, Axminster, Lyme Regis, Bridport, Dorchester, Weymouth, Poole, Wareham, Swanage, Teignmouth, Newton Abbot, Torquay, Paignton, Brixham, Dartmouth, Totnes, Kingsbridge, Salcombe, Ivybridge, Plymouth, Tavistock, Saltash, Launceston, Liskeard, Looe, Fowey, Lostwithiel, Bodmin, Wadebridge, Padstow, Camelford, Tintagel, Boscastle, Newquay, St. Austell, Truro, Perranporth, St. Agnes, Redruth, Camborne, Hayle, St. Ives, Penzance, Newlyn, St. Just, Helston, Falmouth, Penryn, Mullion

Lundy I., Caldy I., Skomer I., Skokholm I., Ramsey I., Flat Holm, Steep Holm, Isle of Portland, Isle of Purbeck, Land's End, Lizard Point, Start Point, Bolt Head, Hartland Point, Morte Point, Foreland Point, Trevose Head, St. Govan's Head, Strumble Head, St. David's Head, Worms Head, Bill of Portland, Eddystone Rocks

Rosslare, Cork, Santander, Roscoff, St. Peter Port

33
E
F
1°
0°
LINCOLNSHIRE
LEICESTERSHIRE
NORFOLK
NORTHAMPTON-SHIRE
CAMBRIDGESHIRE
WARWICKSHIRE
BEDFORDSHIRE
SUFFOLK
BUCKINGHAM-SHIRE
HERTFORD-SHIRE
ESSEX
OXFORDSHIRE
BERKSHIRE
WILTSHIRE
HAMPSHIRE
SURREY
KENT
WEST SUSSEX
EAST SUSSEX
ISLE OF WIGHT
GREATER LONDON
LONDON
East Anglia
The Fens
The Wash
NORTH SEA
ENGLISH CHANNEL
Strait of Dover
FRANCE
UNITED KINGDOM
FRANCE
Birmingham
Coventry
Leicester
Peterborough
Norwich
Cambridge
Ipswich
Northampton
Bedford
Luton
Oxford
Reading
Southampton
Portsmouth
Brighton
Hastings
Dover
Canterbury
Maidstone
Chelmsford
Colchester
Southend-on-Sea
Great Yarmouth
Lowestoft
King's Lynn
Boulogne-sur-Mer
Calais
40
44
1
2
3
4
52°
52° 30′
51° 30′
51°
© Copyright by HAMMOND INCORPORATED, Maplewood, N.J.
Longitude West of Greenwich
Longitude East of Greenwich
G
POPULATION OF CITIES AND TOWNS
OVER 2,000,000
1,000,000 - 1,999,999
500,000 - 999,999
250,000 - 499,999
100,000 - 249,999
30,000 - 99,999
10,000 - 29,999
UNDER 10,000
SCALE 1:1,170,000
LAMBERT CONFORMAL CONIC PROJECTION
MILES 0 10 20 30 40 50
KILOMETERS 0 10 20 30 40 50

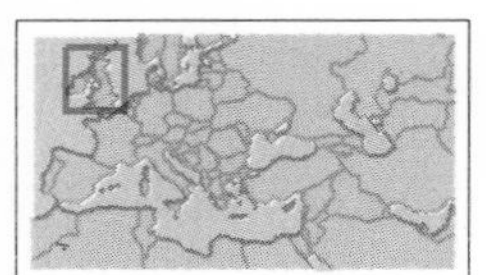

United Kingdom, Ireland

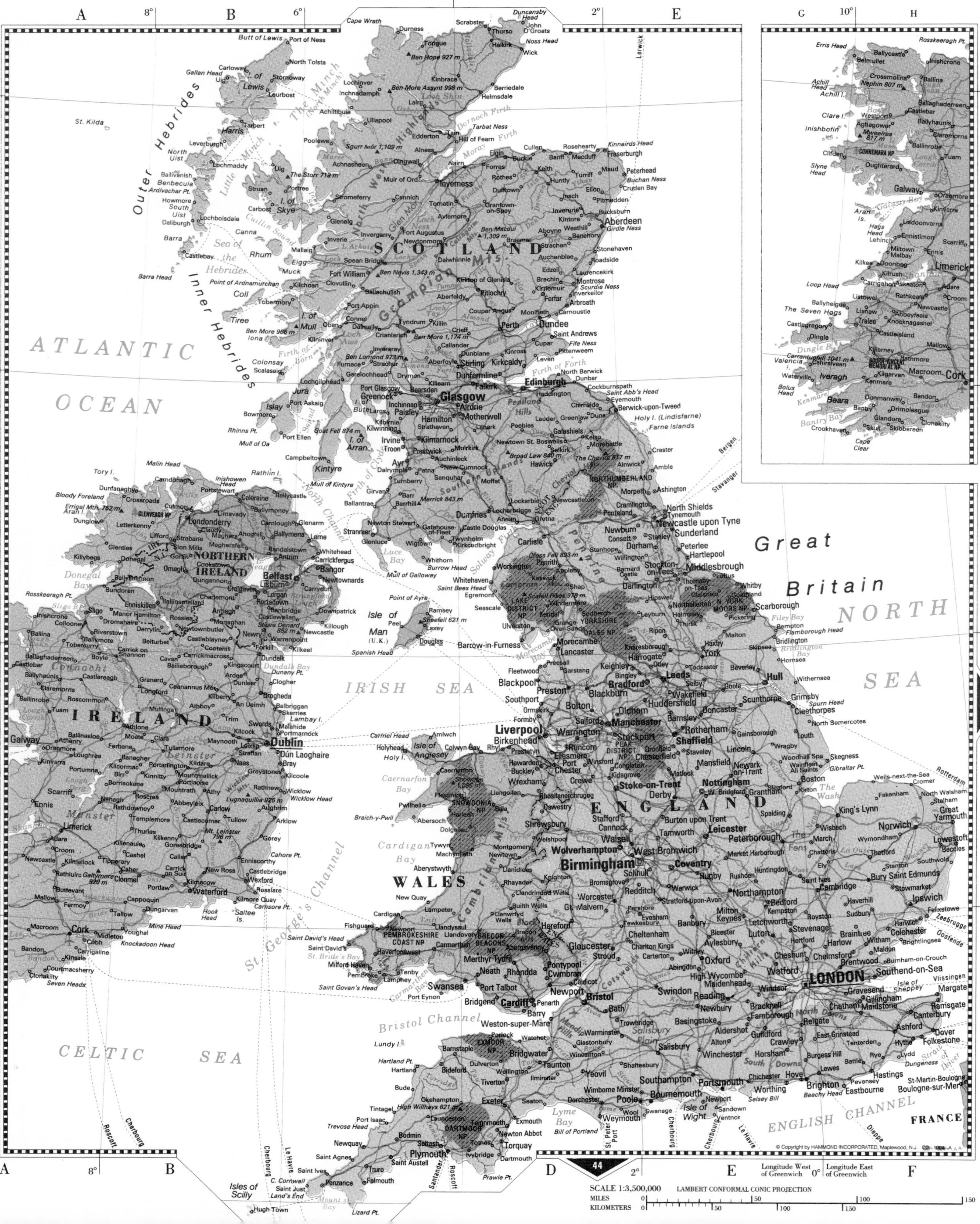

SCOTLAND

NORTHERN IRELAND

IRELAND

ENGLAND

WALES

Great Britain

ATLANTIC OCEAN

NORTH SEA

IRISH SEA

CELTIC SEA

ENGLISH CHANNEL

FRANCE

SCALE 1:3,500,000 LAMBERT CONFORMAL CONIC PROJECTION

MILES 0 50 100 150

KILOMETERS 0 50 100 150

Longitude West of Greenwich 0° Longitude East of Greenwich

Scandinavia and Finland, Iceland

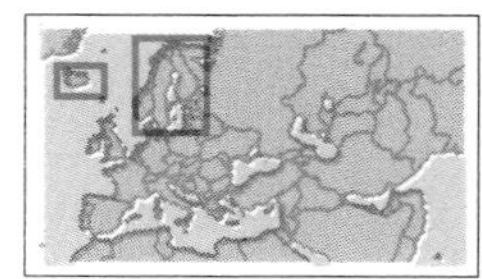

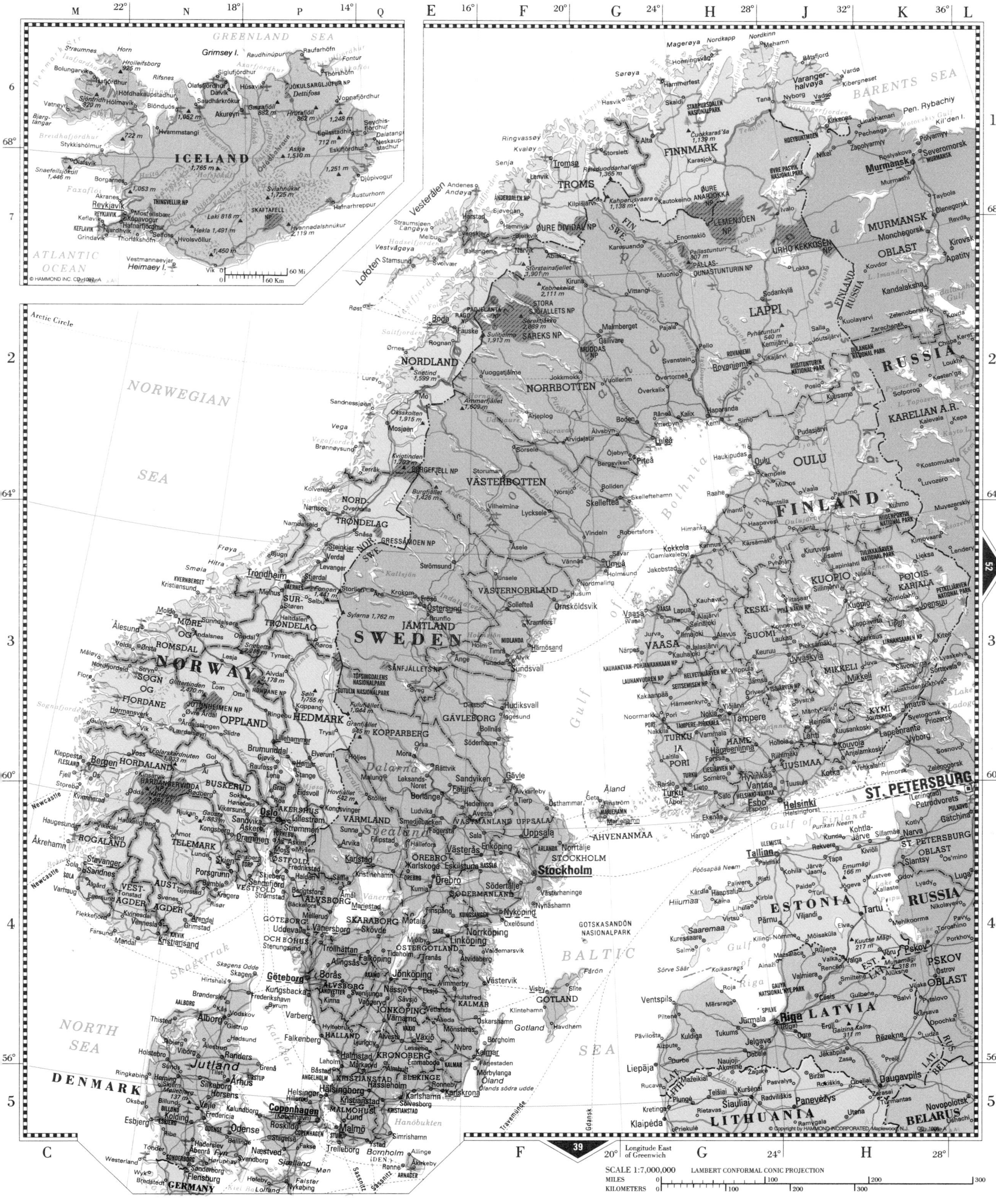

ICELAND

GREENLAND SEA

ATLANTIC OCEAN

NORWEGIAN SEA

NORTH SEA

BARENTS SEA

BALTIC SEA

Gulf of Bothnia

Gulf of Finland

NORWAY

SWEDEN

FINLAND

DENMARK

RUSSIA

ESTONIA

LATVIA

LITHUANIA

BELARUS

GERMANY

52

39

Longitude East of Greenwich

SCALE 1:7,000,000

LAMBERT CONFORMAL CONIC PROJECTION

MILES 0 100 200 300

KILOMETERS 0 100 200 300

A
2°
B
4°
C
6°
D
8°
E
10°
37
F
12°
1
2
3
4
5
54°
52°
50°
48°
36
44
45
Longitude East of Greenwich
NORTH SEA
DENMARK
Copenhagen
FYN
SØNDERJYLLAND
North Frisian Islands
Helgoländer Bucht
East Frisian Islands
West Frisian Islands
Great Britain
U.K.
Hamburg
Bremen
Hannover
LOWER SAXONY
SCHLESWIG-HOLSTEIN
MECKLENBURG-WEST
Amsterdam
The Hague
Rotterdam
NETHERLANDS
Brussels
BELGIUM
LUXEMBOURG
Dortmund
Essen
Düsseldorf
Cologne
Bonn
NORTH RHINE-WESTPHALIA
GERMANY
HESSE
Frankfurt am Main
RHINELAND-PALATINATE
SAARLAND
BADEN-WÜRTTEMBERG
Stuttgart
BAVARIA
Munich
Nürnberg
THURINGIA
SAXONY-ANHALT
Magdeburg
Leipzig
PARIS
ILE-DE-FRANCE
CHAMPAGNE-ARDENNE
LORRAINE
ALSACE
FRANCE
PICARDIE
NORD-PAS-DE-CALAIS
CENTRE
BOURGOGNE
FRANCHE-COMTÉ
SWITZERLAND
AUSTRIA
Strasbourg
Basel
Dijon

North Central Europe

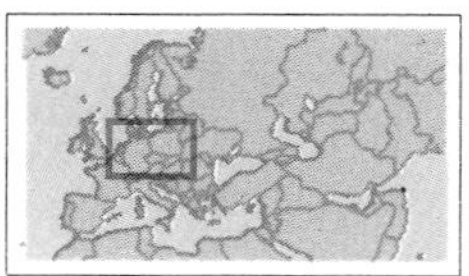

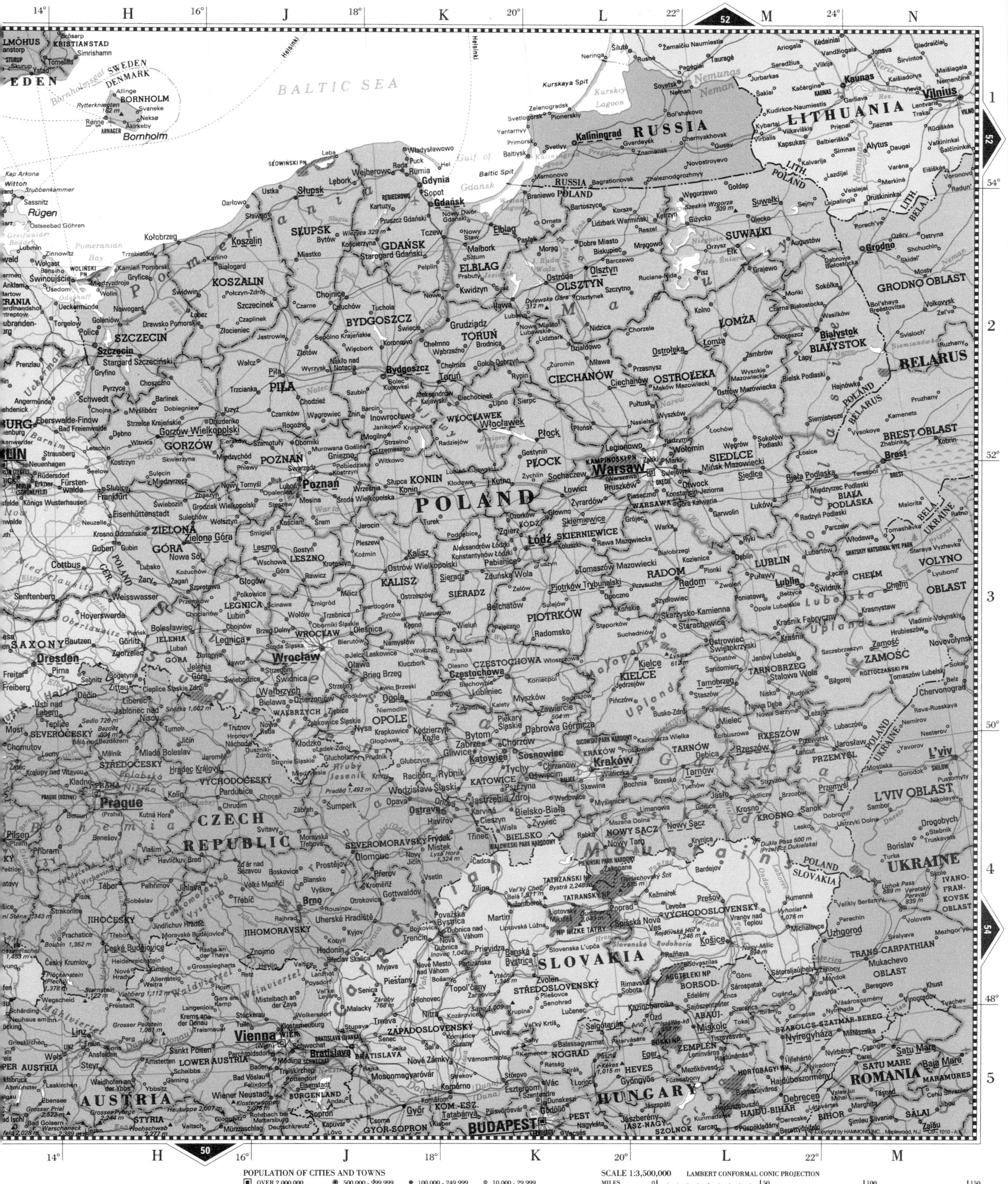

POPULATION OF CITIES AND TOWNS

- OVER 2,000,000
- 1,000,000 - 1,999,999
- 500,000 - 999,999
- 250,000 - 499,999
- 100,000 - 249,999
- 30,000 - 99,999
- 10,000 - 29,999
- UNDER 10,000

SCALE 1:3,500,000 LAMBERT CONFORMAL CONIC PROJECTION

MILES 0 50 100 150

KILOMETERS 0 50 100 150

Netherlands, Northwestern Germany

A
B
C
D
4°
5°
6°
7°
53° 30′
53°
52° 30′
52°
51° 30′
51°
1
2
3
4
5
6
7
Longitude East of Greenwich
42
43
NORTH SEA
West Frisian Islands
Waddenzee
IJsselmeer
Markerwaard
Texel
Vlieland
Terschelling
Ameland
Schiermonnikoog
Borkum
Juist
Rottumerplaat
Rottumeroog
Griend
Richel
Noorderhaaks
Den Helder
De Cocksdorp
Den Burg
De Koog
Oudeschild
West-Terschelling
Oosterend
Oost-Vlieland
Hollum
Nes
Buren
Harlingen
Franeker
Leeuwarden
Dokkum
Sneek
Bolsward
Drachten
Heerenveen
Joure
Wolvega
Lemmer
Sloten
Balk
Stavoren
Hindeloopen
Workum
Makkum
Gaast
Cornwerd
LORENTZSLUIZEN
AFSLUITDIJK
STEVINSLUIZEN
HOUTRIBDIJK
FRIESLAND
GRONINGEN
Groningen
Delfzijl
Appingedam
Uithuizen
Warffum
Winsum
Zuidhorn
Leek
Hoogezand
Sappemeer
Slochteren
Veendam
Assen
DRENTHE
Beilen
Westerbork
Hoogeveen
Meppel
Steenwijk
Emmeloord
Urk
Noordoostpolder
Kampen
Zwolle
Dedemsvaart
Hardenberg
Ommen
Coevorden
Emmen
OVERIJSSEL
Almelo
Hengelo
Enschede
Oldenzaal
Twente
Salland
Deventer
Apeldoorn
Zutphen
Doetinchem
Winterswijk
Graafschap
Lelystad
Dronten
FLEVOLAND
Oostelijk Flevoland
Zuidelijk Flevoland
Almere
Harderwijk
Elburg
Nunspeet
Ermelo
Epe
Veluwe
NATIONAAL PARK DE HOGE VELUWE
RIJKSMUSEUM KRÖLLER-MÜLLER
GELDERLAND
Arnhem
Nijmegen
Ede
Wageningen
Tiel
Betuwe
Culemborg
Zaltbommel
Schiermonnikoog
Wieringermeerpolder
Wieringerwerf
Medemblik
Enkhuizen
Hoorn
Schagen
Alkmaar
Heerhugowaard
Purmerend
Edam
Volendam
Monnickendam
Marken
NORTH HOLLAND
Callantsoog
Bergen aan Zee
Egmond aan Zee
Castricum
Heemskerk
Beverwijk
IJmuiden
NATIONAAL PARK DE KENNEMERDUINEN
Zaandam
Haarlem
Zandvoort
Amsterdam
AMSTERDAM (SCHIPHOL)
Amstelveen
Hoofddorp
Aalsmeer
Hilversum
Bussum
Naarden
Huizen
Soest
Amersfoort
Barneveld
Nijkerk
UTRECHT
Utrecht
Zeist
De Bilt
Woerden
Alphen aan de Rijn
Leiden
Katwijk aan Zee
Noordwijk aan Zee
Lisse
Hillegom
Wassenaar
Scheveningen
The Hague
('s-Gravenhage)
Zoetermeer
Rijswijk
Delft
Gouda
Hoek van Holland
EUROPOORT
Maassluis
Schiedam
Vlaardingen
Rotterdam
Dordrecht
Gorinchem
Brielle
Hellevoetsluis
SOUTH HOLLAND
Voorne
Goeree
Overflakkee
Hoekse Waard
Schouwen
Zierikzee
Tholen
Walcheren
Middelburg
Vlissingen
Zuidbeveland
Goes
Westerschelde
Oosterschelde
ZEELAND
Bergen op Zoom
Roosendaal
Breda
Tilburg
's-Hertogenbosch
Oss
Eindhoven
Helmond
NORTH BRABANT
Venlo
Roermond
LIMBURG
Sittard
Maastricht
De Peel
Weert
NETHERLANDS
BELGIUM
GERMANY
NETH.
BELG.
Terneuzen
Antwerp
(Antwerpen)
ANTWERP
Turnhout
Mechelen
Gent
EAST FLANDERS
BRABANT
Harwich
Sheerness
Hull
Emmerich
Kleve
Wesel
Bocholt
Borken
Rees
Xanten
Moers
Duisburg
Oberhausen
Gelsenkirchen
Bottrop
Krefeld
Mönchengladbach
Düsseldorf
Neuss
Viersen
Grevenbroich
Dormagen
Leverkusen
Cologne
Ruhr
Rhine
Maas
Waal
Lek
IJssel

38

LOWER SAXONY

GERMANY

NORTH RHINE-WESTPHALIA

HESSE

THURINGIA

SAXONY-ANHALT

SCHLESWIG-HOLSTEIN

MECKLENBURG-WESTERN POMERANIA

HAMBURG

BREMEN

E 8° F 9° G 10° H

45

POPULATION OF CITIES AND TOWNS

OVER 2,000,000	500,000 - 999,999	100,000 - 249,999
1,000,000 - 1,999,999	250,000 - 499,999	30,000 - 99,999
10,000 - 29,999	UNDER 10,000	

SCALE 1:1,170,000 LAMBERT CONFORMAL CONIC PROJECTION

MILES 0 10 20 30 40 50

KILOMETERS 0 10 20 30 40 50

1°
A
2°
B
3°
C
4°
D
51°
50° 30′
50°
49° 30′
49°
1
2
3
4
5
6
35
44
UNITED KINGDOM
Aylesham
Eastry
Deal
Saint Margaret's at Cliffe
South Foreland
Capel le Ferne
Dover
Hythe
Folkestone
Ramsgate
Channel Tunnel
STRAIT OF DOVER
UNITED KINGDOM
FRANCE
Calais
Cap Blanc Nez
Cap Gris Nez
Wissant
Ambleteuse
Wimereux
Boulogne-sur-Mer
Le Portel
Équihen -Plage
Hardelot-Plage
Le Touquet-Paris-Plage
Étaples
Montreuil
Berck
Fort-Mahon-Plage
Pointe du Hourdel
Cayeux-sur-Mer
St-Valéry-sur-Somme
Ault
Mers-les-Bains
Le Tréport
Criel-sur-Mer
Dieppe
Felixstowe
Hull
Cadzand-Bad
Breskens
Knokke-Heist
Blankenberge
Zeebrugge
Sluis
Oostburg
Terneuzen
NETHERLANDS
BELG.
Hoek
Axel
De Haan
Oostende
Bredene
Middelkerke
Brugge
Damme
Maldegem
Eeklo
Sas Van Gent
Zelzate
Antwerp
Merksem
Borgerhout
Berchem
Hoboken
Sint-Niklaas
Beveren
Nieuwpoort
Koksijde
De Panne
Veurne
Bray-Dunes
Dunkerque
Fort-Mardyck
Grand-Fort-Philippe
Gravelines
Grande-Synthe
Coudekerque-Branche
Bergues
Hondschoote
Diksmuide
Roeselare
Tielt
Gent
Lokeren
Dendermonde
Mechelen
Aalst
Wetteren
Vilvoorde
Zaventem
Schaerbeek
Brussels
Etterbeek
Auderghem
Halle
Ninove
Flanders
WEST FLANDERS
EAST FLANDERS
BELGIUM
FRANCE
Poperinge
Ieper
Zonnebeke
Kortrijk
Menen
Wevelgem
Comines
Mouscron
Tourcoing
Roubaix
Wattrelos
Marcq-en-Barœul
Lille
Villeneuve-d'Ascq
Armentières
Hazebrouck
Cassel
Saint-Omer
Arques
Aire-s.-la-Lys
Lillers
Béthune
Bruay-en-Artois
Lens
Liévin
Douai
Arras
Saint-Pol-s.-Ternoise
Hesdin
HAINAUT
Tournai
Ath
Geraardsbergen
Ronse
Enghien
Braine-l'Alleud
Waterloo
Soignies
Mons
La Louvière
Charleroi
Binche
Valenciennes
Maubeuge
Jeumont
BELGIQUE
Collines de l'Artois
Artois
PAS-DE-CALAIS
NORD-PAS-DE-CALAIS
PICARDIE
NORD
Cambrai
Le Cateau
Caudry
Bapaume
Doullens
Abbeville
Crécy-en-Ponthieu
Rue
Le Crotoy
Somme
SOMME
Amiens
Albert
Péronne
Corbie
Poix-de-Picardie
Boves
Moreuil
Roye
Montdidier
Nesle
Ham
Saint-Quentin
Guise
Hirson
Fourmies
La Capelle
AISNE
La Fère
Tergnier
Chauny
Laon
Noyon
Soissons
Compiègne
Reims
REIMS (CHAMPAGNE)
CATHÉDRALE DE REIMS
Rethel
Rocroi
Chimay
Couvin
Philippeville
BELGIUM
CHAMPAGNE-ARDENNE
ARD
HAUTE-NORMANDIE
SEINE-MARITIME
Neufchâtel-en-Bray
Aumale
Forges-les-Eaux
Gournay-en-Bray
Rouen
Elbeuf
Louviers
Évreux
EURE
Les Andelys
Gisors
Vernon
NORMANDIE
Picardy
OISE
Beauvais
Clermont
Creil
Chantilly
Senlis
Crépy-en-Valois
Villers-Cotterêts
Château-Thierry
Épernay
Châlons-sur-Marne
ILE-DE-FRANCE
VAL-D'OISE
Pontoise
Cergy
Mantes-la-Jolie
YVELINES
Versailles
Saint-Germain-en-Laye
Nanterre
PARIS
PARIS (CHARLES DE GAULLE)
SEINE-SAINT-DENIS
Boulogne-Billancourt
Vincennes
Créteil
Meaux
EURODISNEY
SEINE-ET-MARNE
Coulommiers
ESSONNE
Évry
Massy
Rambouillet
Dreux
EURE-ET-LOIR
CENTRE
FRANCE
Champagne
MARNE
Brie
AUBE
Sézanne
Fère-Champenoise
Vitry-le-François
Longitude East of Greenwich

Belgium, Northern France, Western Germany

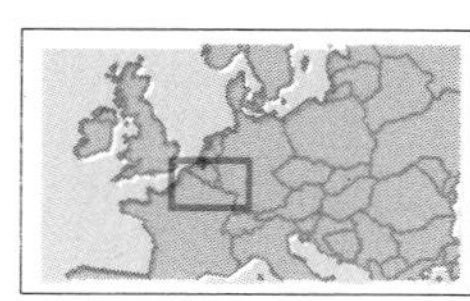

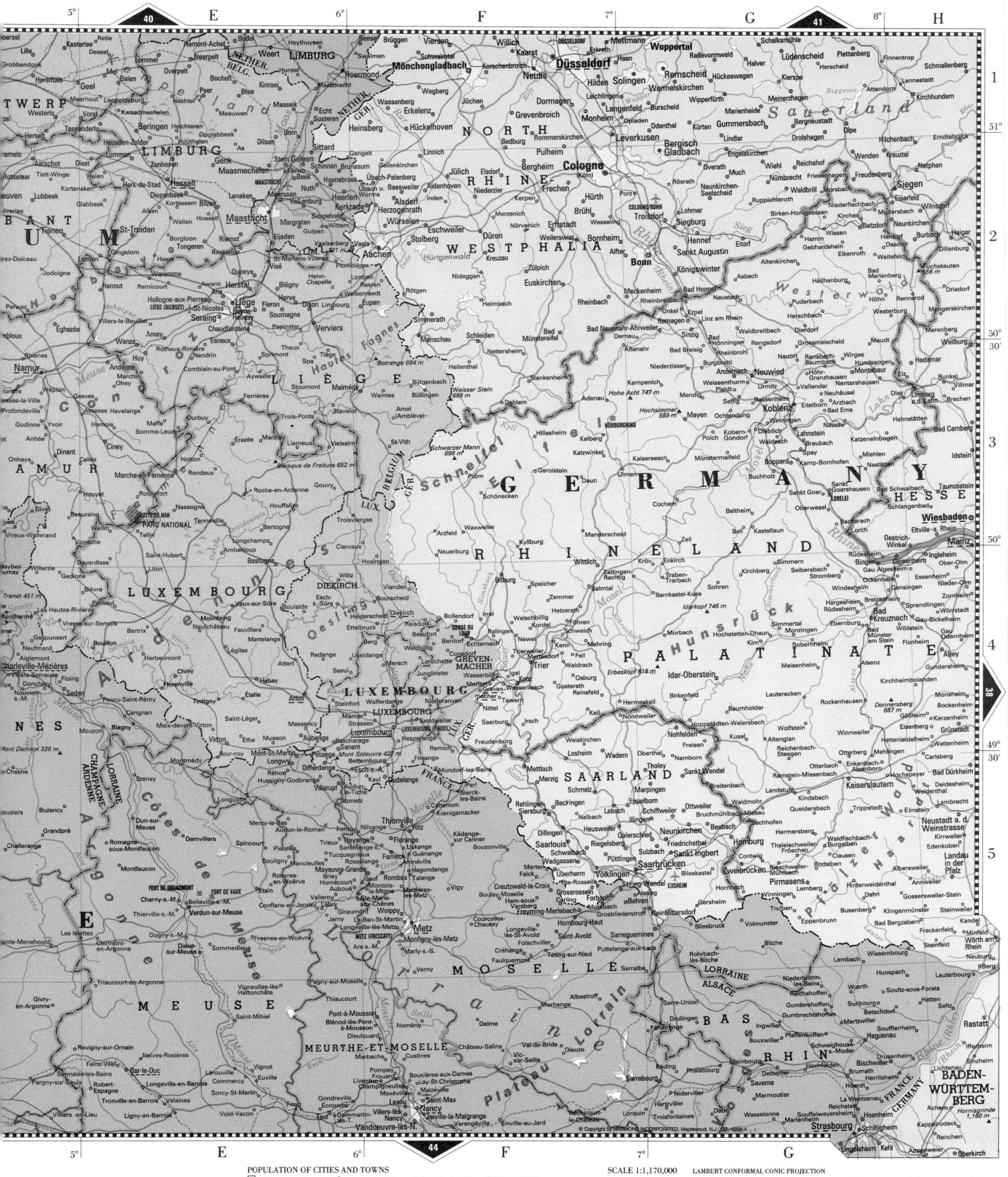

POPULATION OF CITIES AND TOWNS

▣ OVER 2,000,000	◉ 500,000 - 999,999	◉ 100,000 - 249,999	◎ 10,000 - 29,999
◻ 1,000,000 - 1,999,999	◉ 250,000 - 499,999	◉ 30,000 - 99,999	○ UNDER 10,000

SCALE 1:1,170,000 LAMBERT CONFORMAL CONIC PROJECTION

MILES 0 10 20 30 40 50

KILOMETERS 0 10 20 30 40 50

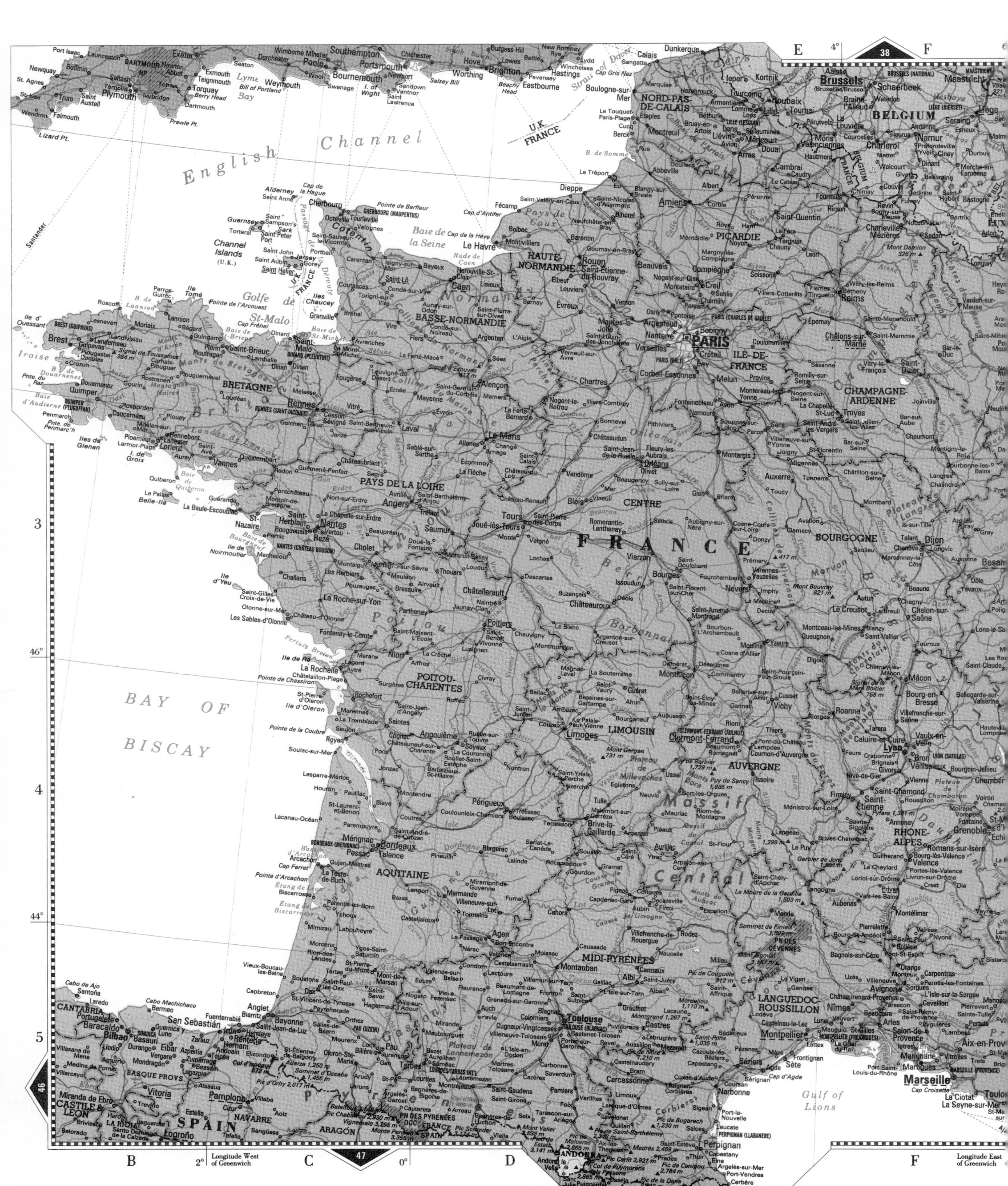

English Channel
BAY OF BISCAY
Gulf of Lions
FRANCE
BELGIUM
SPAIN
ANDORRA
U.K.
Channel Islands (U.K.)
NORD-PAS-DE-CALAIS
PICARDIE
HAUTE-NORMANDIE
BASSE-NORMANDIE
BRETAGNE
PAYS DE LA LOIRE
CENTRE
ILE-DE-FRANCE
CHAMPAGNE-ARDENNE
BOURGOGNE
POITOU-CHARENTES
LIMOUSIN
AUVERGNE
RHONE-ALPES
AQUITAINE
MIDI-PYRÉNÉES
LANGUEDOC-ROUSSILLON
CANTABRIA
BASQUE PROVS.
NAVARRE
ARAGÓN
CATALONIA
CASTILE & LEON
LA RIOJA
Massif Central
PARIS
Brussels
Bordeaux
Toulouse
Marseille
Lyon
Nantes
Rennes
Le Havre
Plymouth
Southampton
Bay of Biscay
E
F
B
C
D
4°
2°
0°
46°
44°
3
4
5
38
46
47
Longitude West of Greenwich
Longitude East of Greenwich

West Central Europe

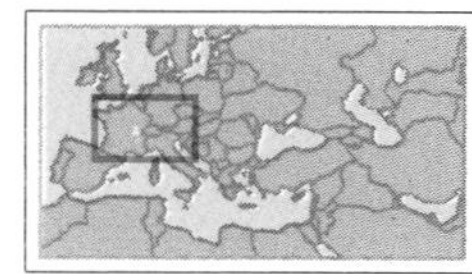

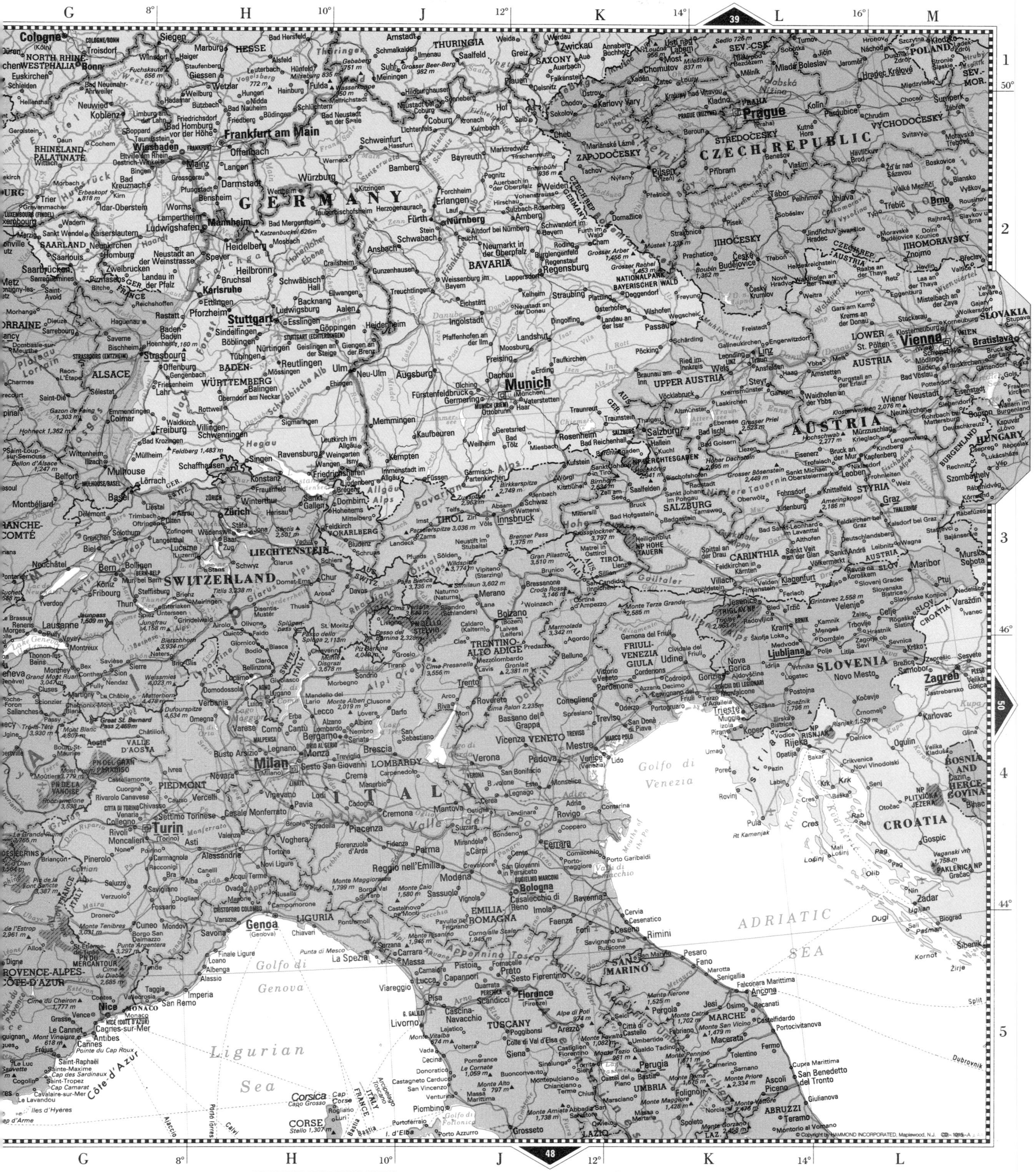

POPULATION OF CITIES AND TOWNS

- OVER 2,000,000
- 1,000,000 - 1,999,999
- 500,000 - 999,999
- 250,000 - 499,999
- 100,000 - 249,999
- 30,000 - 99,999
- 10,000 - 29,999
- UNDER 10,000

SCALE 1:3,500,000 LAMBERT CONFORMAL CONIC PROJECTION

MILES 0 50 100 150

KILOMETERS 0 50 100 150

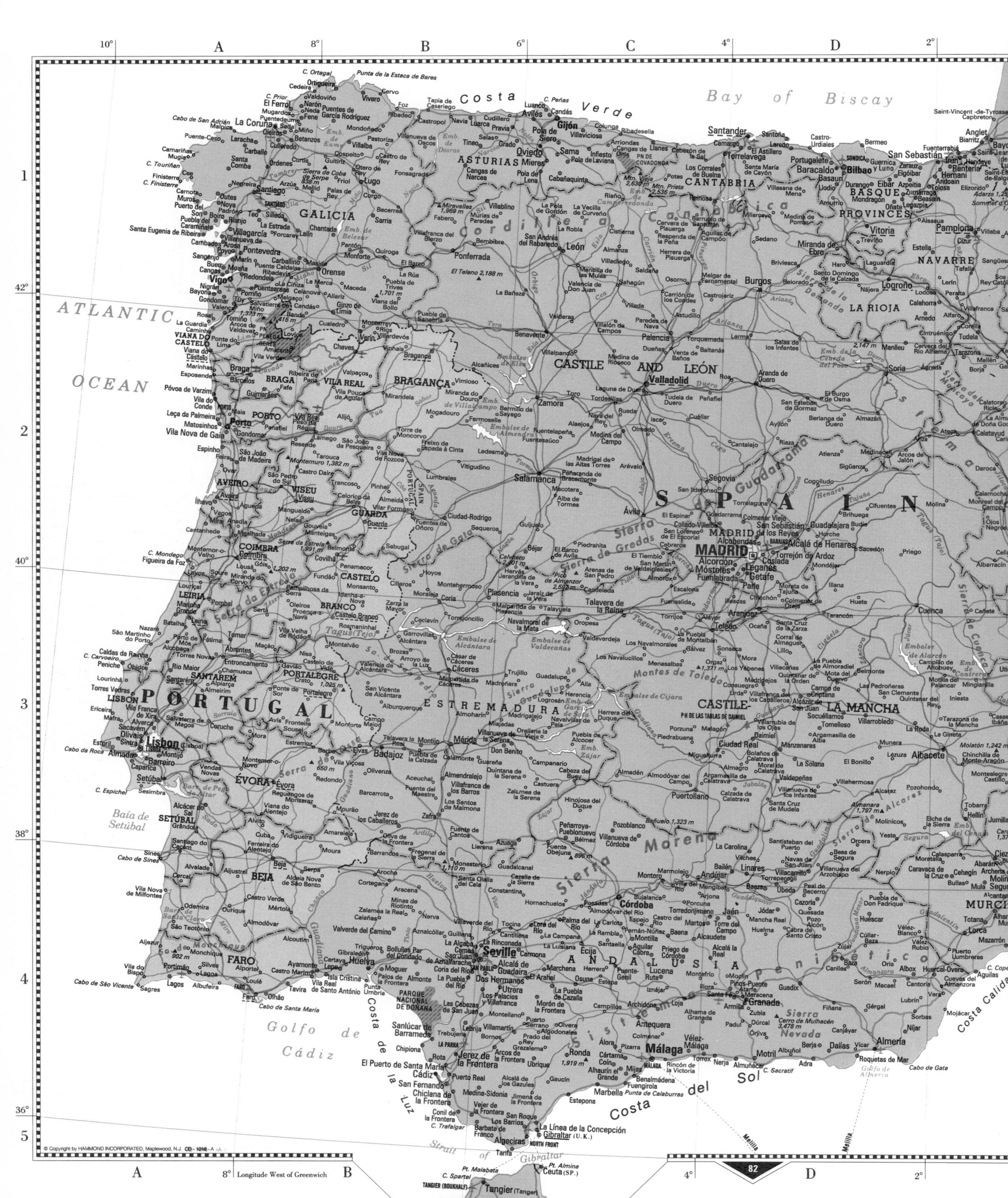

10°
A
8°
B
6°
C
4°
D
2°
Bay of Biscay
Costa Verde
ATLANTIC
OCEAN
SPAIN
PORTUGAL
GALICIA
ASTURIAS
CANTABRIA
BASQUE PROVINCES
NAVARRE
LA RIOJA
CASTILE AND LEÓN
CASTILE-LA MANCHA
ESTREMADURA
ANDALUSIA
MURCIA
MADRID
Lisbon
Porto
Seville
Córdoba
Granada
Málaga
Valladolid
Salamanca
Bilbao
Santander
Gijón
Oviedo
León
Burgos
Vigo
La Coruña
Toledo
Badajoz
Cádiz
Gibraltar (U.K.)
Ceuta (SP.)
Tangier
Tétouan
MOROCCO
Cordillera Cantábrica
Sierra de Guadarrama
Sierra de Gredos
Sierra Morena
Sierra Nevada
Sistema Penibético
Montes de Toledo
Golfo de Cádiz
Costa de la Luz
Costa del Sol
Costa Calida
Strait of Gibraltar
Baía de Setúbal
Cabo de São Vicente
Cabo da Roca
C. Finisterre
C. Ortegal
Cabo de Gata
Melilla
42°
40°
38°
36°
1
2
3
4
5
Longitude West of Greenwich

Spain, Portugal

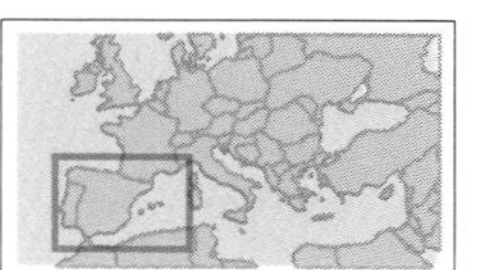

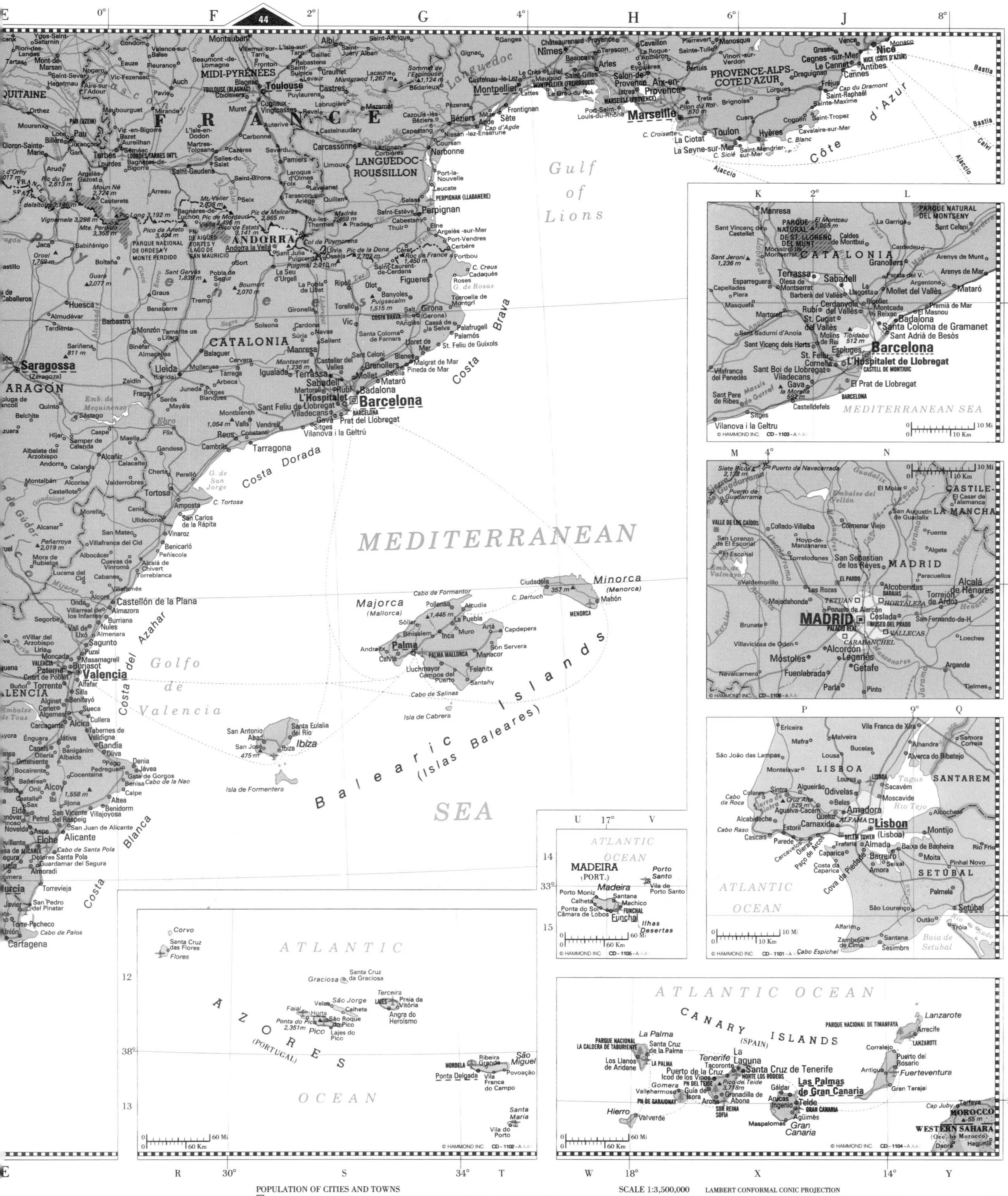

POPULATION OF CITIES AND TOWNS

- OVER 2,000,000
- 1,000,000 - 1,999,999
- 500,000 - 999,999
- 250,000 - 499,999
- 100,000 - 249,999
- 30,000 - 99,999
- 10,000 - 29,999
- UNDER 10,000

SCALE 1:3,500,000 LAMBERT CONFORMAL CONIC PROJECTION

MILES 0 50 100 150

KILOMETERS 0 50 100 150

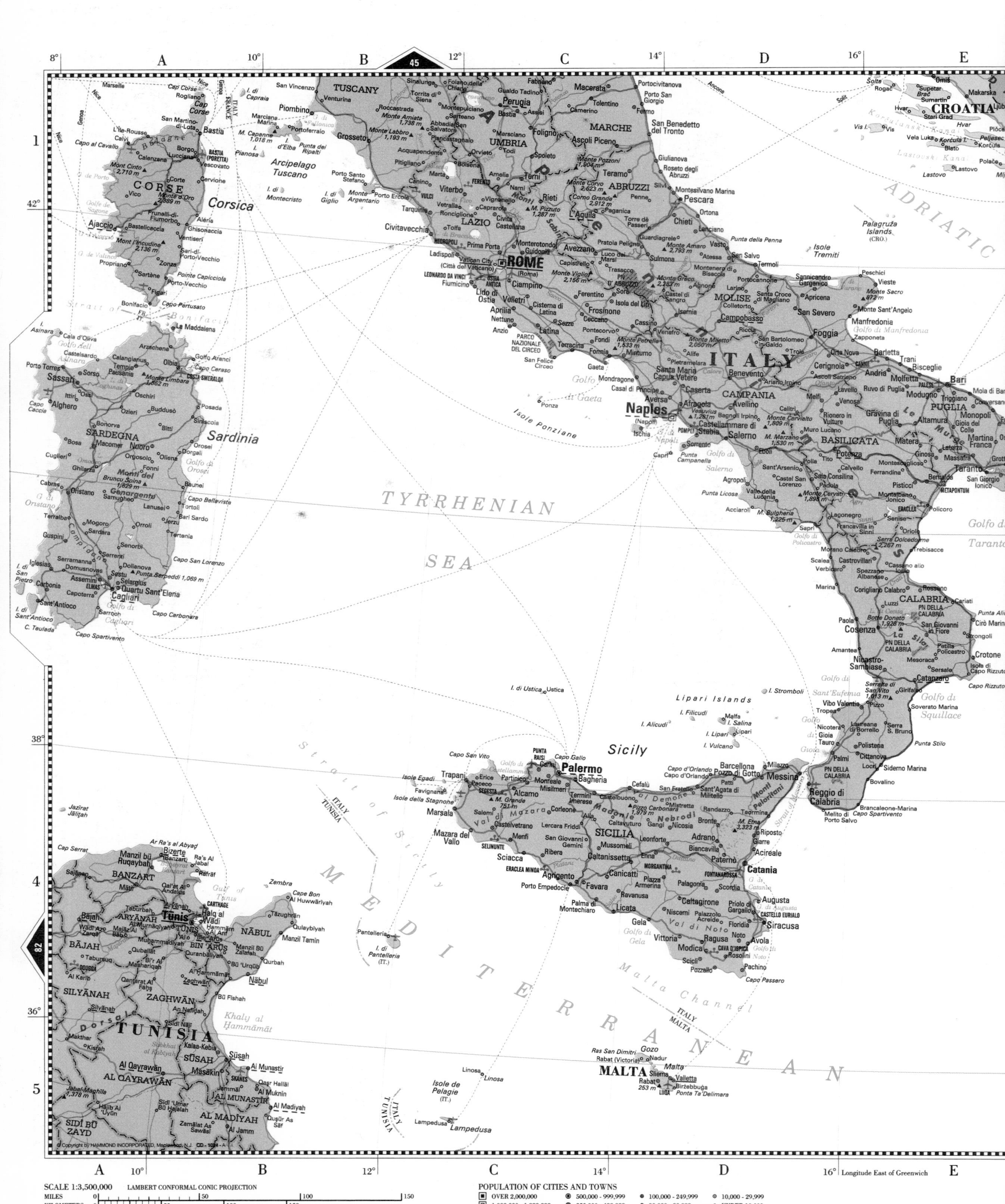

45
82
8°
10°
12°
14°
16°
A
B
C
D
E
1
4
5
42°
38°
36°
ITALY
TUSCANY
UMBRIA
LAZIO
MARCHE
ABRUZZI
MOLISE
CAMPANIA
PUGLIA
BASILICATA
CALABRIA
SICILIA
SARDEGNA
CORSE
Corsica
Sardinia
Sicily
CROATIA
TUNISIA
MALTA
ROME
(Roma)
Naples
(Napoli)
Palermo
Bari
Catania
Messina
Cagliari
Tunis
Florence
Perugia
Pescara
L'Aquila
Foggia
Taranto
Cosenza
Catanzaro
Reggio di Calabria
Siracusa
Agrigento
Trapani
Marsala
Sassari
Olbia
Nuoro
Oristano
Ajaccio
Bastia
Bonifacio
Civitavecchia
Grosseto
Piombino
Salerno
Potenza
Benevento
Avellino
Caserta
Latina
Frosinone
Viterbo
Rieti
Terni
Ancona
Split
Valletta
Sūsah
Al Munastīr
Nābul
Bizerte
TYRRHENIAN
SEA
MEDITERRANEAN
ADRIATIC
Strait of Bonifacio
Strait of Sicily
Strait of Messina
Malta Channel
Golfo di Gaeta
Golfo di Salerno
Golfo di Policastro
Golfo di Taranto
Golfo di Squillace
Golfo di Cagliari
Gulf of Tunis
Khalij al Ḩammāmāt
Lipari Islands
Isole Ponziane
Arcipelago Toscano
Isole Egadi
Isole Tremiti
Isole de Pelagie (IT.)
Lampedusa
Linosa
Pantelleria
I. di Ustica
Capri
Ischia
Monte Cinto 2,710 m
M. Etna 3,323 m
Gran Sasso
M. Pollino
Longitude East of Greenwich
© Copyright by HAMMOND INCORPORATED, Maplewood, N.J.

SCALE 1:3,500,000 LAMBERT CONFORMAL CONIC PROJECTION

MILES 0 50 100 150

KILOMETERS 0 50 100 150

POPULATION OF CITIES AND TOWNS

- ■ OVER 2,000,000
- ◉ 500,000 - 999,999
- ● 100,000 - 249,999
- ● 10,000 - 29,999
- □ 1,000,000 - 1,999,999
- ◎ 250,000 - 499,999
- ● 30,000 - 99,999
- ○ UNDER 10,000

Southern Italy, Albania, Greece

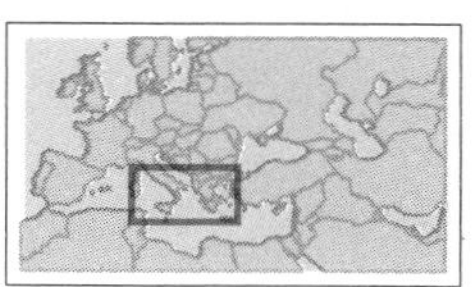

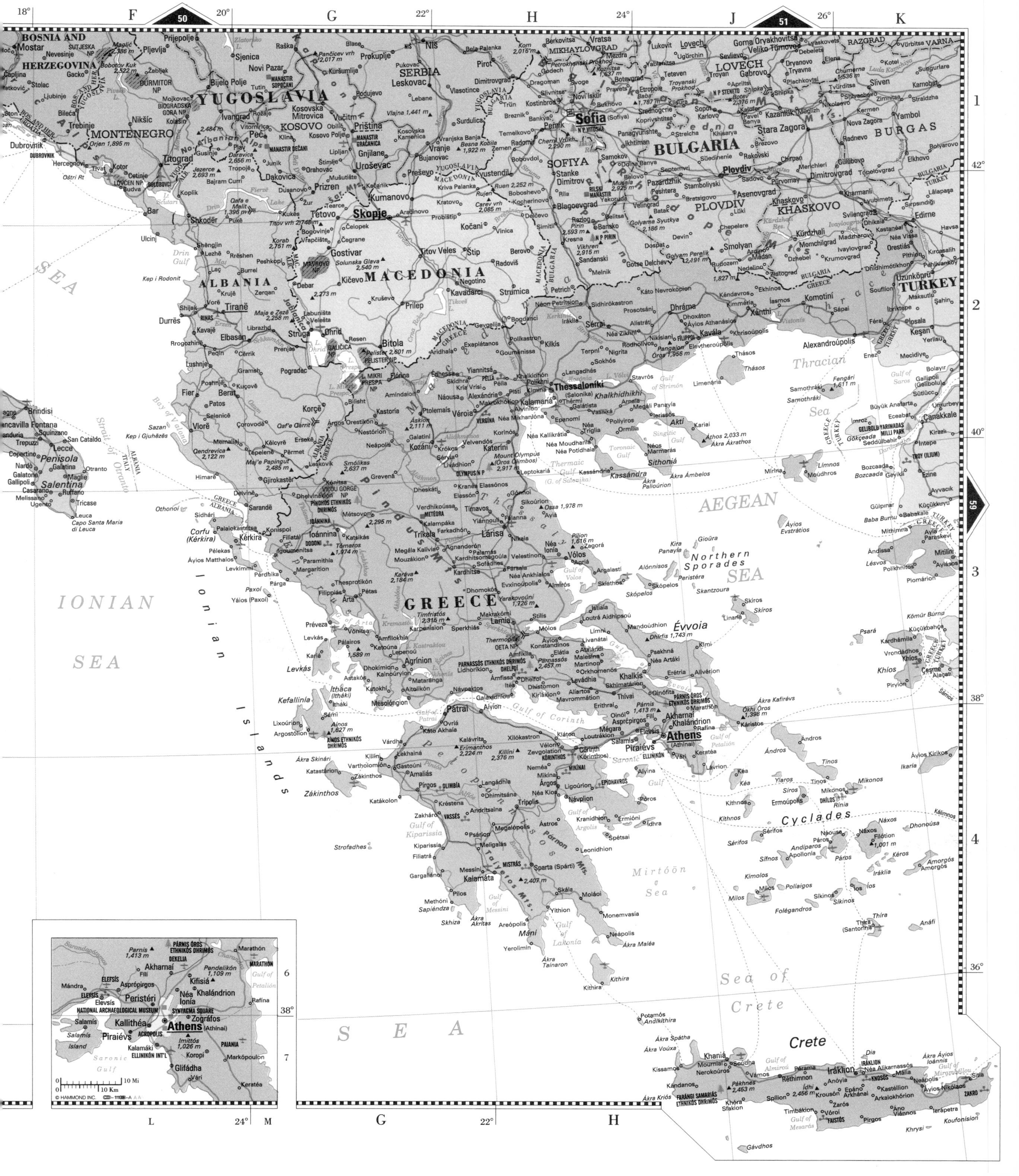

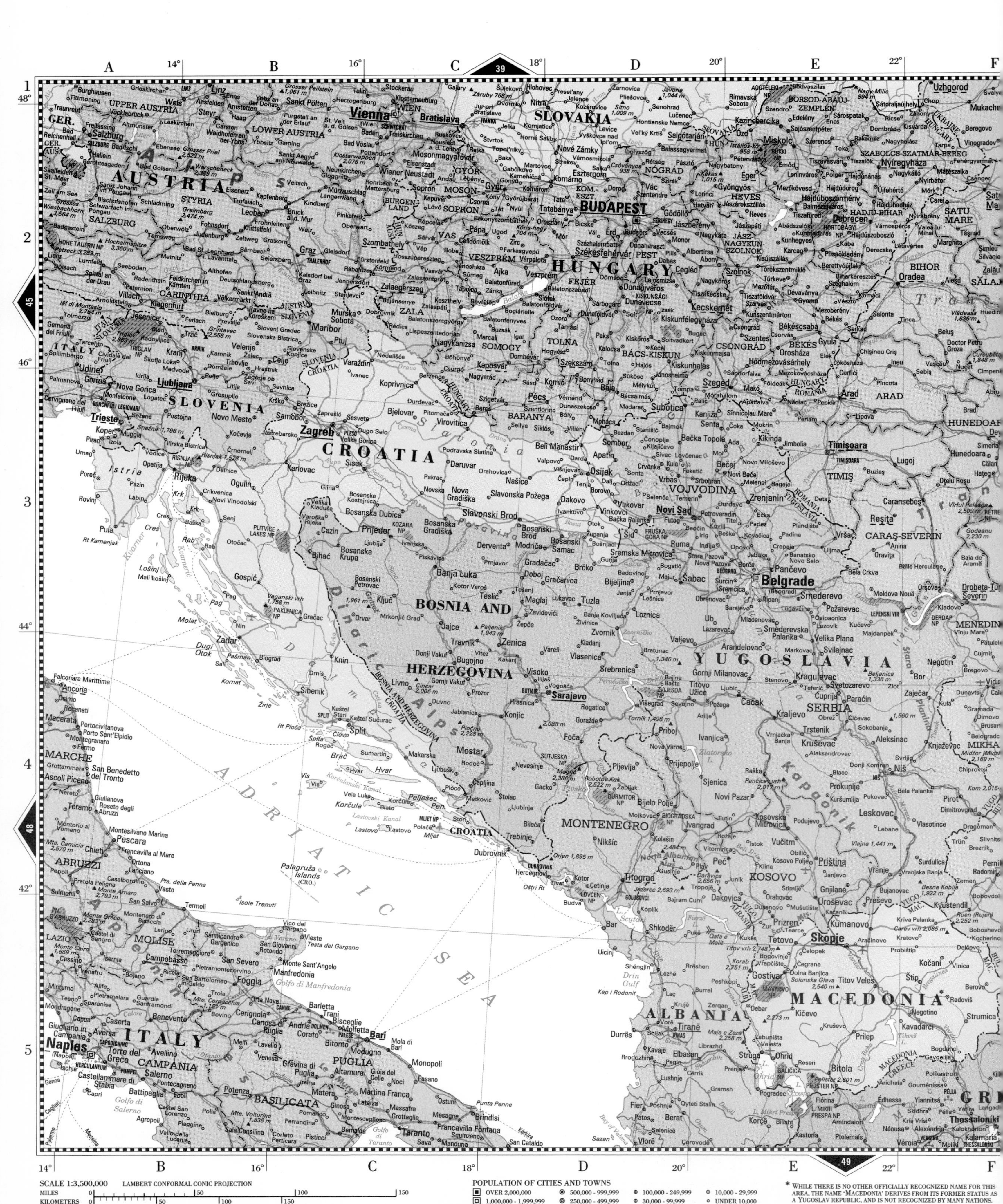

39
45
48
49
A
B
C
D
E
F
14°
16°
18°
20°
22°
48°
46°
44°
42°
1
2
3
4
5
AUSTRIA
UPPER AUSTRIA
LOWER AUSTRIA
STYRIA
SALZBURG
CARINTHIA
Alps
SLOVAKIA
HUNGARY
SLOVENIA
CROATIA
BOSNIA AND HERZEGOVINA
Dinaric Alps
Dalmatia
YUGOSLAVIA
SERBIA
VOJVODINA
MONTENEGRO
KOSOVO
ALBANIA
MACEDONIA*
ITALY
ABRUZZI
MOLISE
MARCHE
LAZIO
CAMPANIA
PUGLIA
BASILICATA
Apennines
ADRIATIC SEA
Vienna
(Wien)
Bratislava
BUDAPEST
Ljubljana
Zagreb
Sarajevo
Belgrade
(Beograd)
Skopje
Tiranë
Naples
(Napoli)
Bari
Trieste
Graz
Linz
Salzburg
Maribor
Rijeka
Split
Dubrovnik
Zadar
Osijek
Novi Sad
Pécs
Szeged
Debrecen
Miskolc
Timişoara
Arad
Niš
Titograd
Mostar
Banja Luka
Tuzla
Pescara
Foggia
Taranto
Brindisi
Thessaloníki
Lake Balaton
Drin Gulf
Golfo di Manfredonia
Golfo di Taranto
Golfo di Salerno
Palagruža Islands (CRO.)

SCALE 1:3,500,000 LAMBERT CONFORMAL CONIC PROJECTION

MILES 0 50 100 150

KILOMETERS 0 50 100 150

POPULATION OF CITIES AND TOWNS

OVER 2,000,000	1,000,000 - 1,999,999
500,000 - 999,999	250,000 - 499,999
100,000 - 249,999	30,000 - 99,999
10,000 - 29,999	UNDER 10,000

* WHILE THERE IS NO OTHER OFFICIALLY RECOGNIZED NAME FOR THIS AREA, THE NAME 'MACEDONIA' DERIVES FROM ITS FORMER STATUS AS A YUGOSLAV REPUBLIC, AND IS NOT RECOGNIZED BY MANY NATIONS.

Hungary, Northern Balkan States

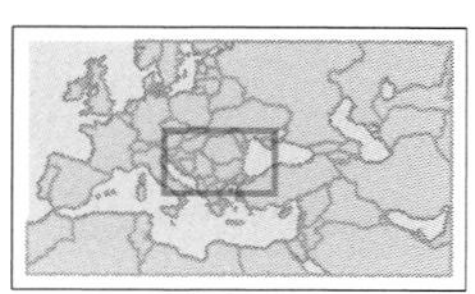

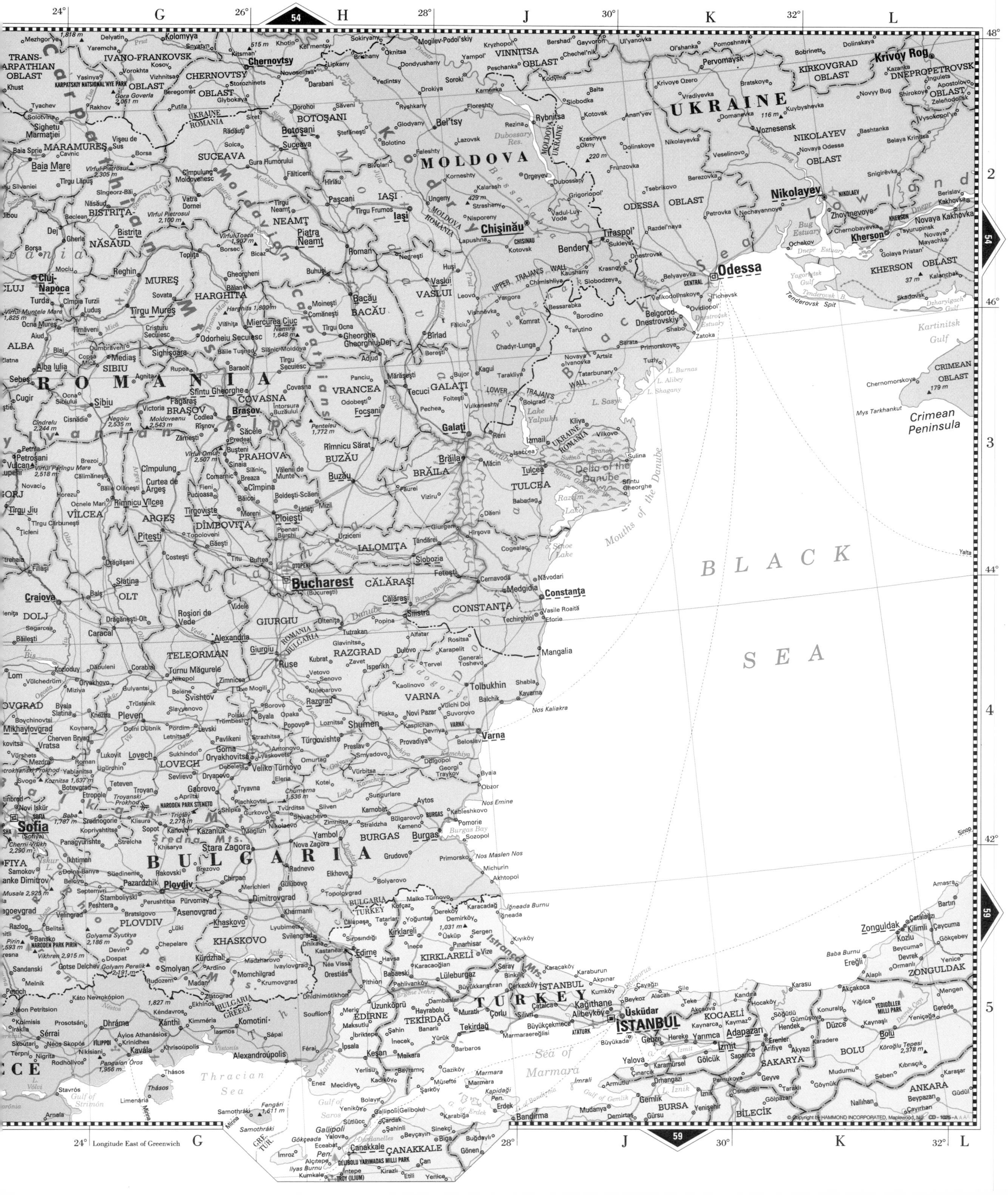

24° G 26° 54 H 28° J 30° K 32° L

48° 2 46° 3 44° 4 42° 5

UKRAINE

MOLDOVA

ROMANIA

BULGARIA

TURKEY

BLACK SEA

Crimean Peninsula

Sea of Marmara

Thracian Sea

Carpathian Mts.

Transylvanian Alps

Walachia

Dobruja

Rhodope Mts.

Delta of the Danube

Mouths of the Danube

Odessa

Bucharest (București)

Sofia

Istanbul

Chișinău

Constanța

Varna

Burgas

Kherson

Nikolayev

Krivoy Rog

Sevastopol

Crimean Oblast

ODESSA OBLAST

NIKOLAYEV OBLAST

KHERSON OBLAST

24° Longitude East of Greenwich G 28° J 59 30° K 32° L

8°
A
12°
B
16°
C
20°
D
24°
E
28°
F
32°
G
36°
H
40°
J
2
3
4
5
64°
60°
56°
37
39
NORWEGIAN SEA
Arctic Circle
BARENTS
NORWAY
SWEDEN
FINLAND
ESTONIA
LATVIA
LITHUANIA
RUSSIA
POLAND
BELARUS
Kola Peninsula
MURMANSK OBLAST
KARELIAN AUT. REPUBLIC
ARCHANGEL
White Sea
Gulf of Bothnia
Gulf of Finland
Gulf of Riga
BALTIC SEA
Lake Ladoga
Lake Onega
Rybinsk Res.
Lake Peipus
Dvina Bay
Onega Bay
Kandalaksha Gulf
Onega Pen.
Solovetskiy Is.
Pen. Rybachiy
LAPPI
OULU
VAASA
KUOPIO
MIKKELI
TURKU JA PORI
HÄME
KYMI
USIMAA
AHVENANMAA
Åland
NORRBOTTEN
VÄSTERBOTTEN
JAMTLAND
VÄSTERNORRLAND
GÄVLEBORG
KOPPARBERG
NORDLAND
FINNMARK
TROMS
PSKOV OBLAST
NOVGOROD OBL.
T'VER OBLAST
SMOLENSK OBLAST
VOLOGDA OBL.
YAROSLAVL' OBL.
KOSTROMA OBL.
SAINT PETERSBURG OBLAST
KALININGRAD OBL.
MOSCOW OBL.
KALUGA OBL.
RYAZAN' OBL.
VLADIMIR OBL.
IVANOVO OBL.
Murmansk
Archangel
Petrozavodsk
Oulu
Helsinki (Helsingfors)
Tallinn
Riga
Vilnius
Minsk
Stockholm
ST. PETERSBURG (Leningrad)
MOSCOW (Moskva)
Novgorod
Pskov
Vologda
Yaroslavl'
Kostroma
Rybinsk
Cherepovets
T'ver
Smolensk
Vitebsk
Kaunas
Kaliningrad
Gdańsk
Gdynia
Białystok
Grodno
Mogilev
Kaluga
Ryazan'
Tampere
Turku (Åbo)
Jyväskylä
Kuopio
Joensuu
Rovaniemi
Luleå
Umeå
Sundsvall
Uppsala
Vaasa (Vasa)
Kokkola (Gamlakarleby)
Tartu
Pärnu
Narva
Daugavpils
Liepāja
Klaipėda
Šiauliai
Panevėžys
Longitude East of Greenwich
20°
24°
28°
32°
36°
40°
D
E
F
G
H
J
54

Northeastern Europe

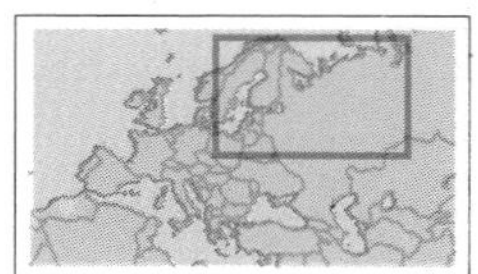

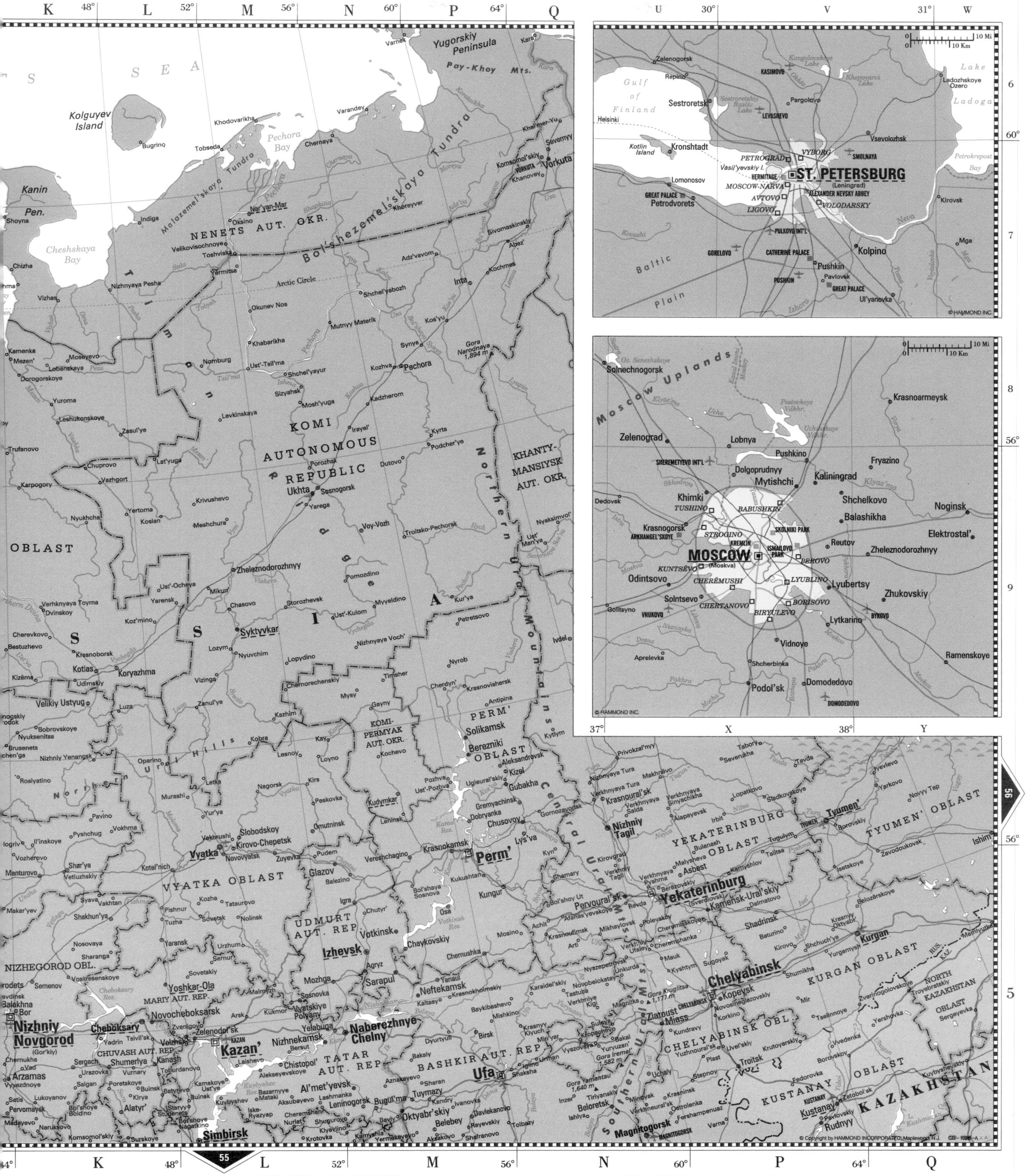

NENETS AUT. OKR.

KOMI AUTONOMOUS REPUBLIC

KHANTY-MANSIYSK AUT. OKR.

KOMI-PERMYAK AUT. OKR.

PERM' OBLAST

VYATKA OBLAST

UDMURT AUT. REP.

MARIY AUT. REP.

CHUVASH AUT. REP.

TATAR AUT. REP.

BASHKIR AUT. REP.

YEKATERINBURG OBLAST

TYUMEN' OBLAST

CHELYABINSK OBL.

KURGAN OBLAST

KUSTANAY OBLAST

NORTH KAZAKHSTAN OBLAST

KAZAKHSTAN

NIZHEGOROD OBL.

ST. PETERSBURG (Leningrad)

MOSCOW (Moskva)

56

55

POPULATION OF CITIES AND TOWNS

OVER 2,000,000	500,000 - 999,999	100,000 - 249,999	10,000 - 29,999
1,000,000 - 1,999,999	250,000 - 499,999	30,000 - 99,999	UNDER 10,000

SCALE 1:7,000,000 LAMBERT CONFORMAL CONIC PROJECTION

MILES 0 100 200 300

KILOMETERS 0 100 200 300

A
B
C
D
E
20°
24°
28°
32°
52
1
2
3
4
5
52°
48°
44°
40°
39
49
59
MOSCOW
POLAND
Warsaw
BELARUS
Minsk
UKRAINE
KIEV
HUNGARY
ROMANIA
Bucharest
MOLDOVA
Chişinău
YUGOSLAVIA
Belgrade
BULGARIA
Sofia
MACEDONIA
GREECE
Athens
TURKEY
ANKARA
İSTANBUL
İzmir
BLACK SEA
AEGEAN SEA
Sea of Azov
Sea of Marmara
Odessa
Khar'kov
Dnepropetrovsk
Donetsk
Crimean Pen.
Longitude East of Greenwich

SCALE 1:7,000,000 LAMBERT CONFORMAL CONIC PROJECTION

MILES 0 100 200 300

KILOMETERS 0 100 200 300

POPULATION OF CITIES AND TOWNS

- OVER 2,000,000
- 1,000,000 - 1,999,999
- 500,000 - 999,999
- 250,000 - 499,999
- 100,000 - 249,999
- 30,000 - 99,999
- 10,000 - 29,999
- UNDER 10,000

Southeastern Europe

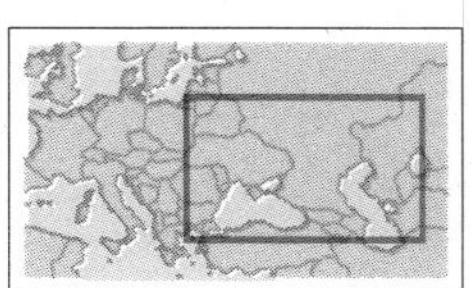

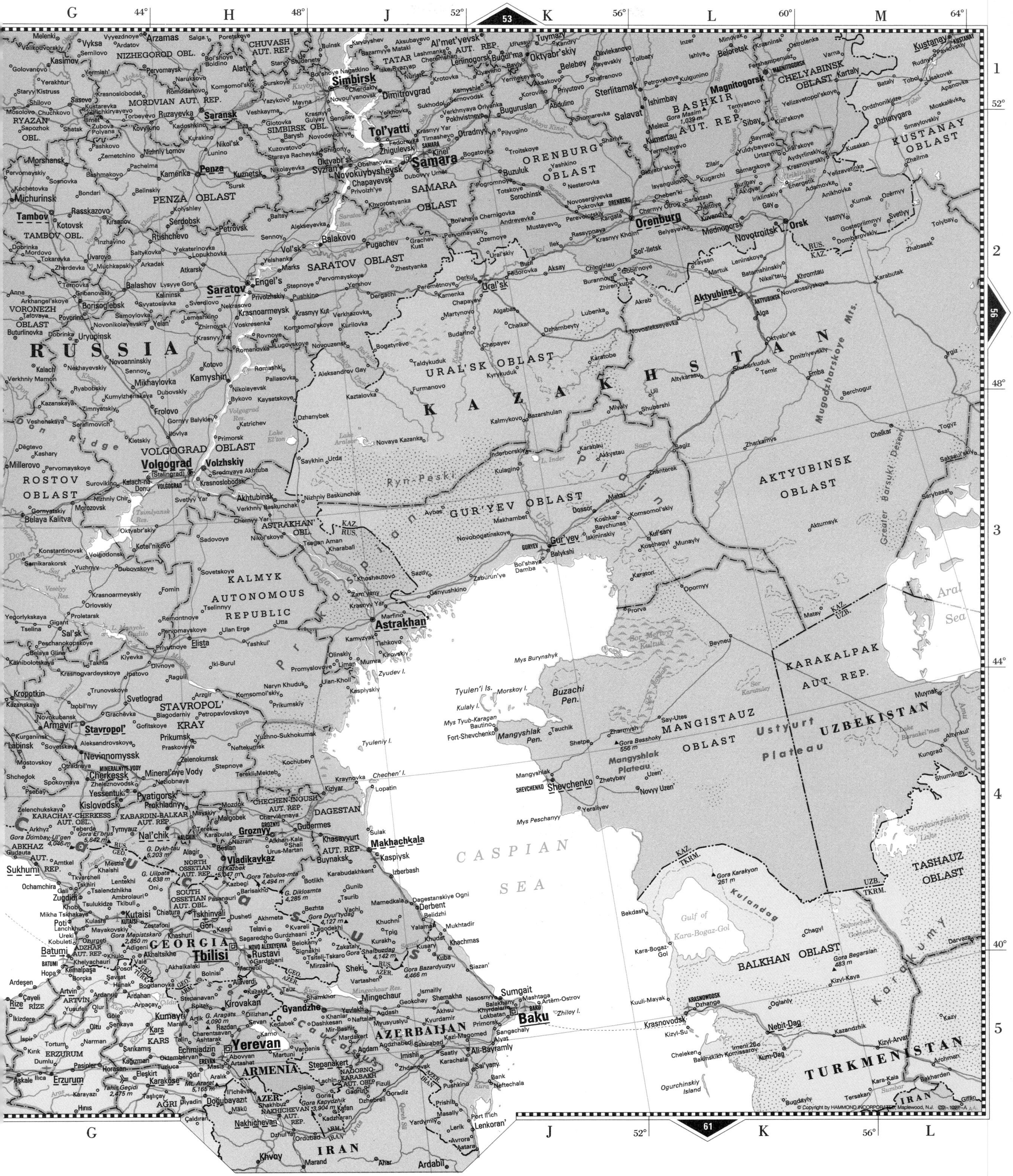

G 44° H 48° J 52° 53 K 56° L 60° M 64°

RUSSIA

KAZAKHSTAN

NIZHEGOROD OBL.

CHUVASH AUT. REP.

TATAR AUT. REP.

BASHKIR AUT. REP.

CHELYABINSK OBLAST

KUSTANAY OBLAST

MORDVIAN AUT. REP.

SIMBIRSK OBL.

SAMARA OBLAST

ORENBURG OBLAST

RYAZAN' OBL.

PENZA OBLAST

TAMBOV OBL.

SARATOV OBLAST

VORONEZH OBLAST

URAL'SK OBLAST

VOLGOGRAD OBLAST

ROSTOV OBLAST

AKTYUBINSK OBLAST

GUR'YEV OBLAST

ASTRAKHAN' OBL.

KALMYK AUTONOMOUS REPUBLIC

KARAKALPAK AUT. REP.

STAVROPOL' KRAY

MANGISTAUZ OBLAST

UZBEKISTAN

DAGESTAN AUT. REP.

CHECHEN-INGUSH AUT. REP.

KARACHAY-CHERKESS AUT. OBL.

KABARDIN-BALKAR AUT. REP.

NORTH OSSETIAN AUT. REP.

SOUTH OSSETIAN AUT. OBL.

ABKHAZ AUT. REP.

ADZHAR AUT. REP.

GEORGIA

ARMENIA

AZERBAIJAN

NAGORNO-KARABAKH AUT. OBL.

NAKHICHEVAN AUT. REP.

TASHAUZ OBLAST

BALKHAN OBLAST

TURKMENISTAN

IRAN

CASPIAN SEA

Aral Sea

Ryn-Peski

Ustyurt Plateau

Mangyshlak Plateau

Mugodzharskoye Mts.

Greater Barsuki Desert

Karakumy

Gulf of Kara-Bogaz-Gol

Caucasus

Don Ridge

1 2 3 4 5

52° 48° 44° 40°

56

G J 52° 61 K 56° L

© Copyright by HAMMOND INCORPORATED, Maplewood, N.J.

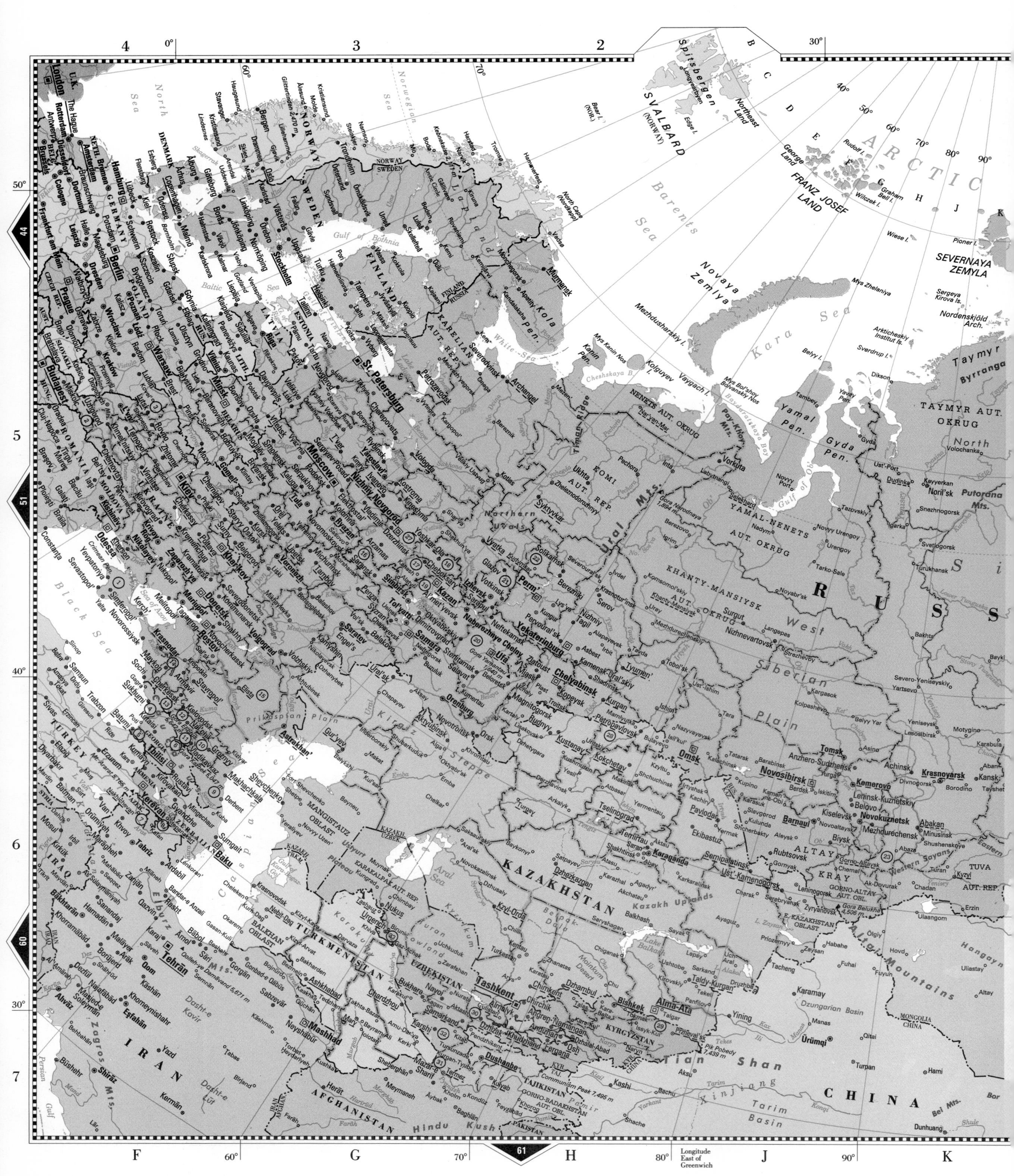

4
3
2
B C D E F G H J K
ARCTIC
SVALBARD
(NORWAY)
Spitsbergen
Northeast Land
FRANZ JOSEF LAND
SEVERNAYA ZEMLYA
Barents Sea
Novaya Zemlya
Kara Sea
Norwegian Sea
North Sea
NORWAY
SWEDEN
FINLAND
DENMARK
GERMANY
POLAND
ESTONIA
LATVIA
LITH.
Gulf of Bothnia
Baltic Sea
Kola Pen.
White Sea
KARELIAN AUT. REP.
Murmansk
Archangel
St. Petersburg
Moscow
Stockholm
Helsinki
Oslo
Copenhagen
Berlin
Warsaw
Prague
Budapest
Minsk
Kiev
Riga
Tallinn
Vilnius
Amsterdam
London
Brussels
Hamburg
Nizhniy Novgorod
Kazan'
Samara
Saratov
Volgograd
Rostov
Kharkov
Odessa
Black Sea
Sea of Azov
ROMANIA
TURKEY
IRAQ
IRAN
Tehrān
Baku
Tbilisi
Yerevan
Caspian Sea
Aral Sea
Ural Mts.
Timan Ridge
Northern Uvals
KOMI AUT. REP.
NENETS AUT. OKRUG
YAMAL-NENETS AUT. OKRUG
KHANTY-MANSIYSK AUT. OKRUG
TAYMYR AUT. OKRUG
Yamal Pen.
Gyda Pen.
Gulf of Ob'
Taymyr
Putorana Mts.
West Siberian Plain
RUSSIA
Perm'
Yekaterinburg
Chelyabinsk
Ufa
Orenburg
Omsk
Novosibirsk
Tomsk
Krasnoyarsk
Barnaul
Novokuznetsk
KAZAKHSTAN
Kazakh Uplands
Caspian Plain
Kirgiz Steppe
Turan Lowland
Kyzyl Kum
Karakum
TURKMENISTAN
UZBEKISTAN
KYRGYZSTAN
TAJIKISTAN
AFGHANISTAN
PAKISTAN
Tashkent
Alma-Ata
Bishkek
Dushanbe
Ashkhabad
Mashhad
Hindu Kush
Pamir
Tian Shan
Tarim Basin
Xinjiang
Dzungarian Basin
Altai Mountains
ALTAY KRAY
GORNO-ALTAY AUT. OBL.
TUVA AUT. REP.
Western Sayans
Lake Balkhash
CHINA
MONGOLIA
Ürümqi
Kashi
Elburz Mts.
Zagros Mts.
Dasht-e Kavīr
Dasht-e Lūt
Persian Gulf
Communism Peak 7,495 m
Pik Pobedy 7,439 m
44
51
60
61
Longitude East of Greenwich

Russia and Neighboring Countries

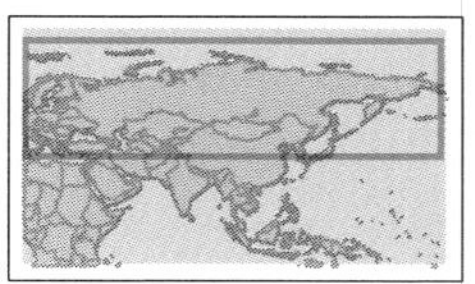

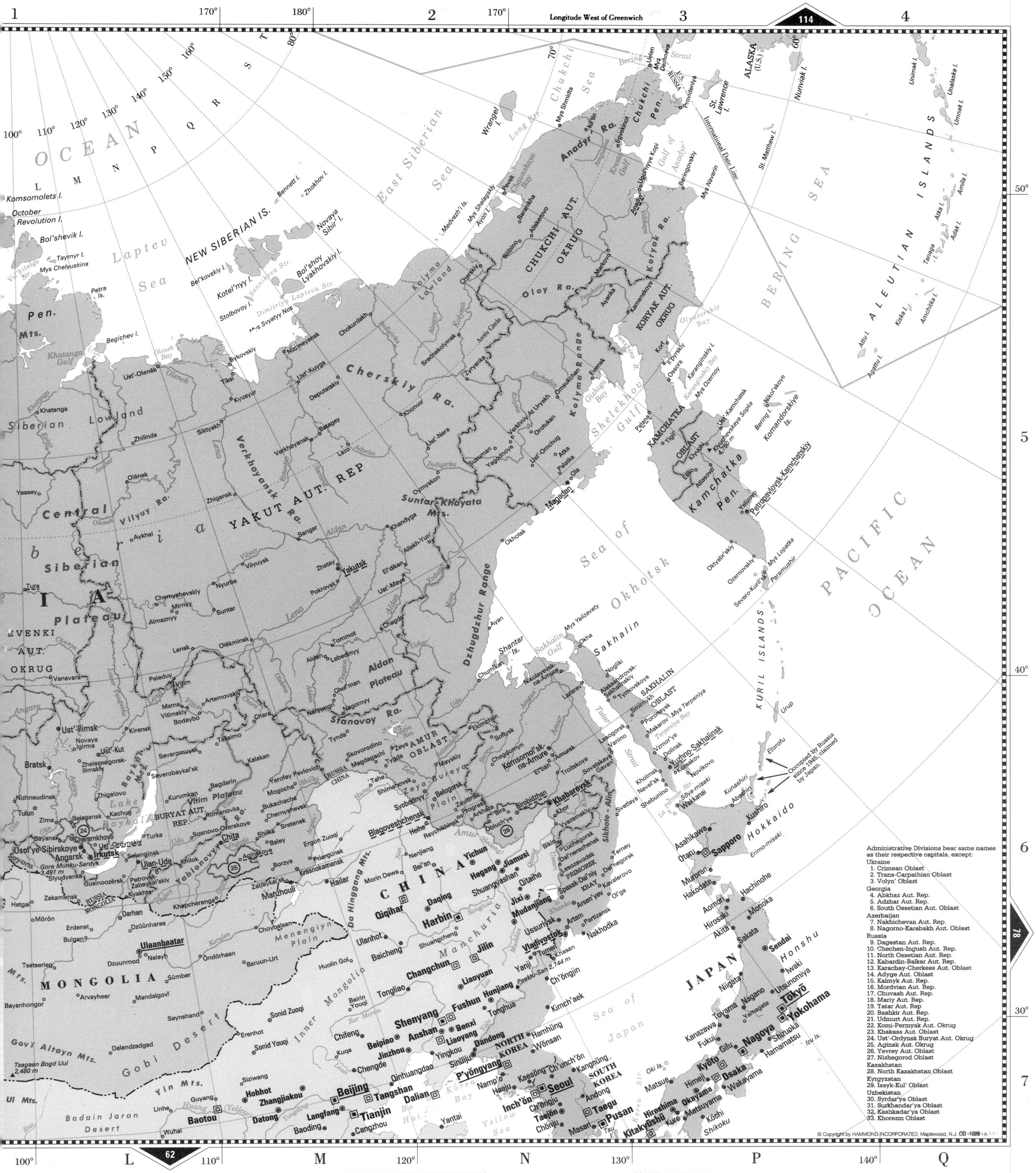

Administrative Divisions bear same names as their respective capitals, except:

Ukraine
1. Crimean Oblast
2. Trans-Carpathian Oblast
3. Volyn' Oblast

Georgia
4. Abkhaz Aut. Rep.
5. Adzhar Aut. Rep.
6. South Ossetian Aut. Oblast

Azerbaijan
7. Nakhichevan Aut. Rep.
8. Nagorno-Karabakh Aut. Oblast

Russia
9. Dagestan Aut. Rep.
10. Chechen-Ingush Aut. Rep.
11. North Ossetian Aut. Rep.
12. Kabardin-Balkar Aut. Rep.
13. Karachay-Cherkess Aut. Oblast
14. Adyge Aut. Oblast
15. Kalmyk Aut. Rep.
16. Mordvian Aut. Rep.
17. Chuvash Aut. Rep.
18. Mariy Aut. Rep.
19. Tatar Aut. Rep
20. Bashkir Aut. Rep.
21. Udmurt Aut. Rep.
22. Komi-Permyak Aut. Okrug
23. Khakass Aut. Oblast
24. Ust'-Ordynsk Buryat Aut. Okrug
25. Aginsk Aut. Okrug
26. Yevrey Aut. Oblast
27. Nizhegorod Oblast

Kazakhstan
28. North Kazakhstan Oblast

Kyrgyzstan
29. Issyk-Kul' Oblast

Uzbekistan
30. Syrdar'ya Oblast
31. Surkhandar'ya Oblast
32. Kashkadar'ya Oblast
33. Khorezm Oblast

POPULATION OF CITIES AND TOWNS

- OVER 2,000,000
- 1,000,000 - 1,999,999
- 500,000 - 999,999
- 100,000 - 499,999
- 50,000 - 99,999
- UNDER 50,000

SCALE 1:21,000,000 LAMBERT CONFORMAL CONIC PROJECTION

MILES 0 300 600 900

KILOMETERS 0 300 600 900

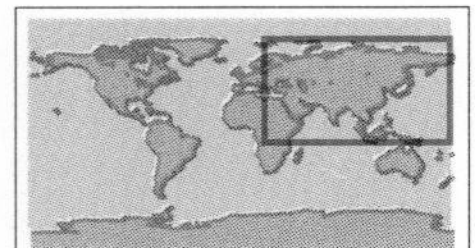

Asia

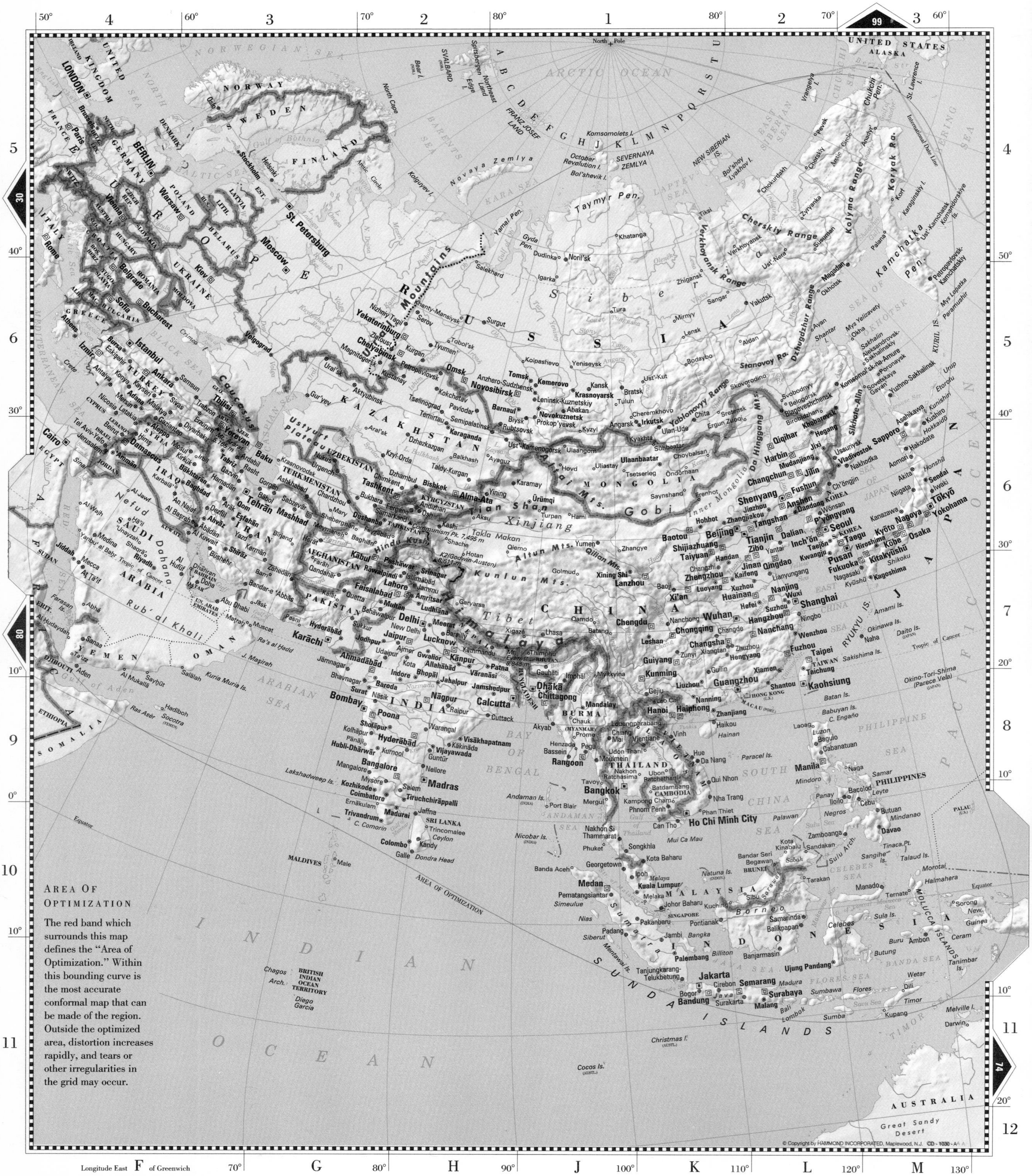

Area Of Optimization

The red band which surrounds this map defines the "Area of Optimization." Within this bounding curve is the most accurate conformal map that can be made of the region. Outside the optimized area, distortion increases rapidly, and tears or other irregularities in the grid may occur.

Longitude East of Greenwich

SCALE 1:49,000,000 OPTIMAL CONFORMAL PROJECTION

MILES 0 700 1400 2100

KILOMETERS 0 700 1400 2100

POPULATION OF CITIES AND TOWNS

- OVER 3,000,000
- 1,000,000 - 2,999,999
- 500,000 - 999,999
- 100,000 - 499,999
- UNDER 100,000

Eastern Mediterranean Region

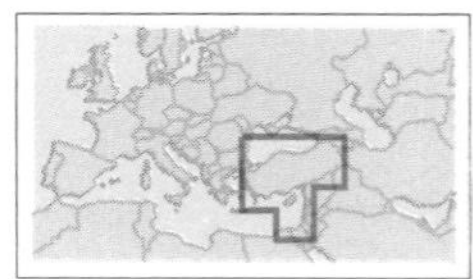

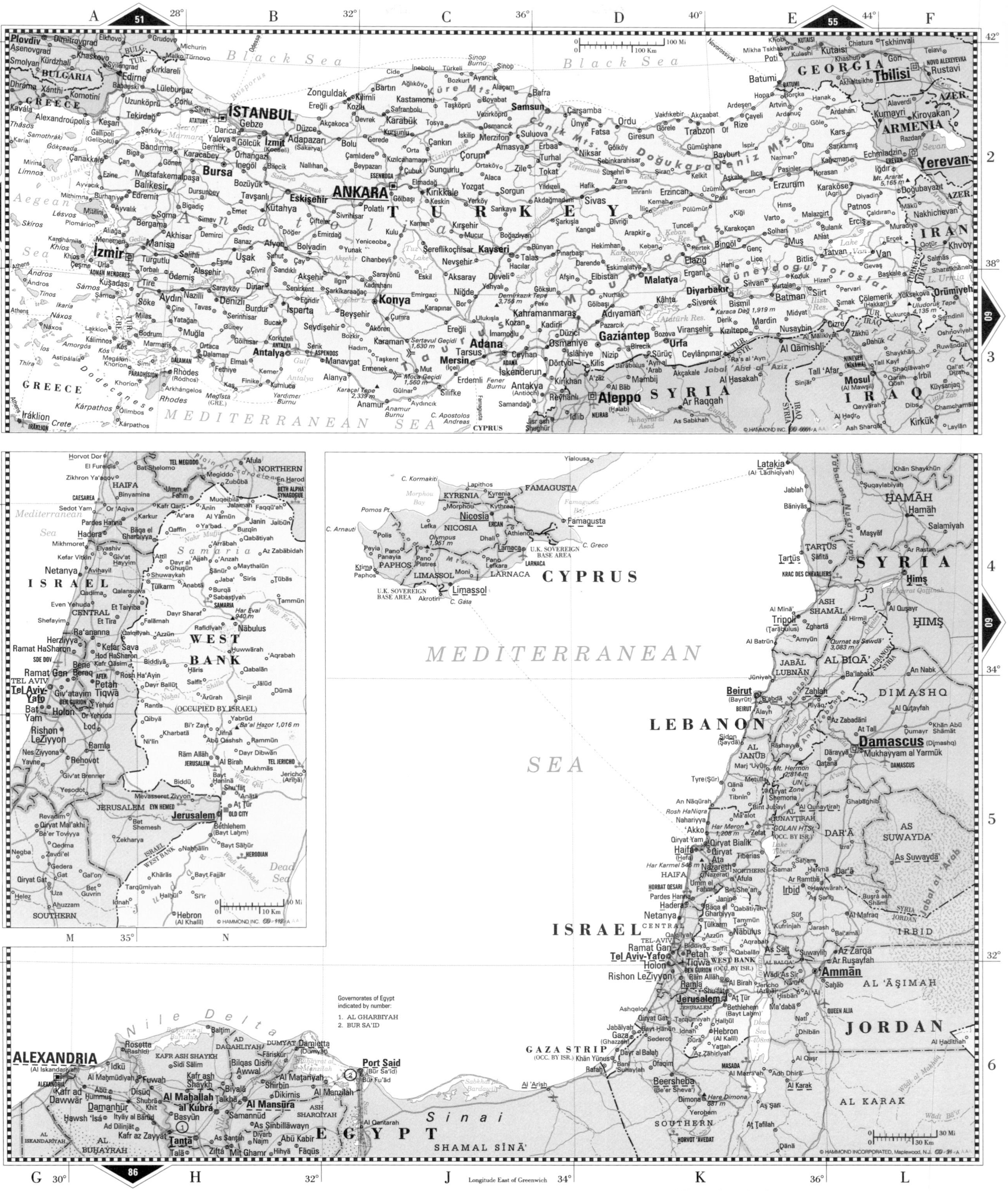

Governorates of Egypt indicated by number:

1. AL GHARBIYAH
2. BUR SA'ID

0 100 Mi
0 100 Km

Longitude East of Greenwich

POPULATION OF CITIES AND TOWNS

- OVER 2,000,000
- 1,000,000 - 1,999,999
- 500,000 - 999,999
- 250,000 - 499,999
- 100,000 - 249,999
- 50,000 - 99,999
- 10,000 - 29,999
- UNDER 10,000

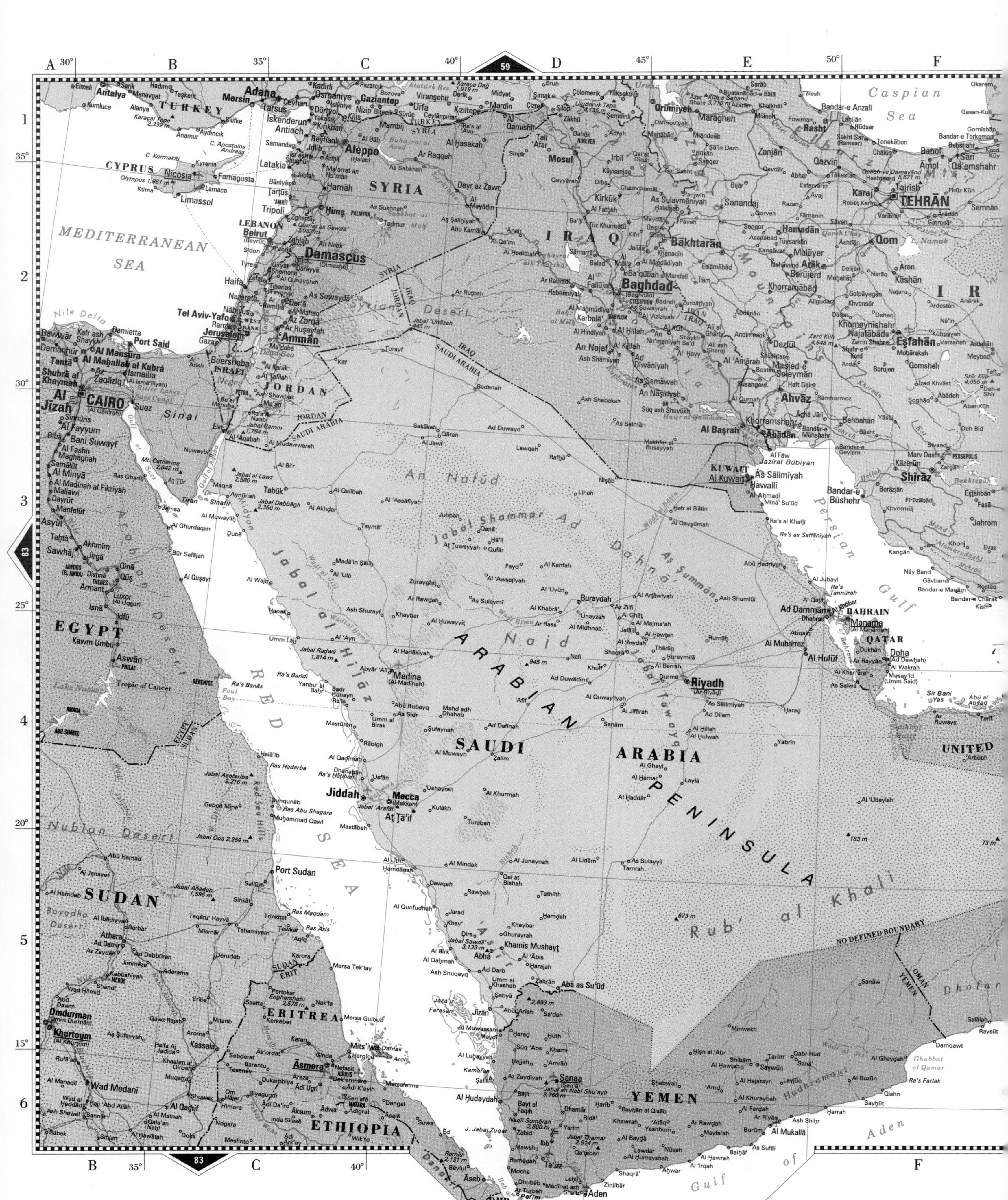

A
B
C
D
E
F
30°
35°
40°
45°
50°
59
83
1
2
3
4
5
6
TURKEY
CYPRUS
SYRIA
IRAQ
LEBANON
ISRAEL
JORDAN
KUWAIT
BAHRAIN
QATAR
UNITED
EGYPT
SUDAN
ERITREA
ETHIOPIA
DJIB.
YEMEN
SAUDI
ARABIA
ARABIAN PENINSULA
MEDITERRANEAN SEA
Caspian Sea
RED SEA
Persian Gulf
Gulf of Aden
Sinai
An Nafūd
Ad Dahnā'
Aş Şummān
Najd
Jabal al Ḩijāz
Rub' al Khali
Syrian Desert
Arabian Desert
Nubian Desert
Nile Delta
Tropic of Cancer
NO DEFINED BOUNDARY
Adana
Mersin
Antalya
Gaziantep
Urfa
Mardin
Aleppo
Latakia
Nicosia
Famagusta
Limassol
Ḩamāh
Ḩimş
Tripoli
Beirut
Damascus
Haifa
Tel Aviv-Yafo
Jerusalem
'Ammān
Port Said
Al Manşūra
Ismailia
Suez
CAIRO
Al Jīzah
Luxor
Aswān
Al Mawşil
Mosul
Kirkūk
Baghdad
Karbalā'
An Najaf
Al Başrah
Ābādān
Khorramshahr
Al Kuwayt
Tabūk
Medina
Jiddah
Mecca
Aţ Ţā'if
Riyadh
Buraydah
Al Hufūf
Ad Dammām
Manama
Doha
Khamis Mushayţ
Abhā
Jīzān
Sanaa
Al Ḩudaydah
Ta'izz
Aden
Al Mukallā
Port Sudan
Khartoum
Omdurman
Wad Medani
Kassala
Āsmera
Mits'iwa
Tehrān
Qom
Eşfahān
Shīrāz
Hamadān
Bākhtarān
Tabrīz
Rasht
Ahvāz
Dezfūl
Būshehr

Southwestern Asia

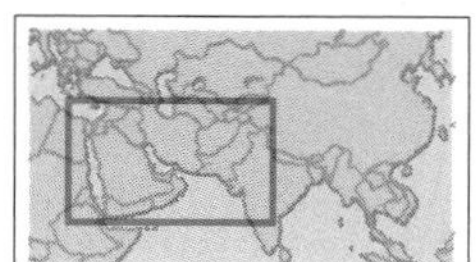

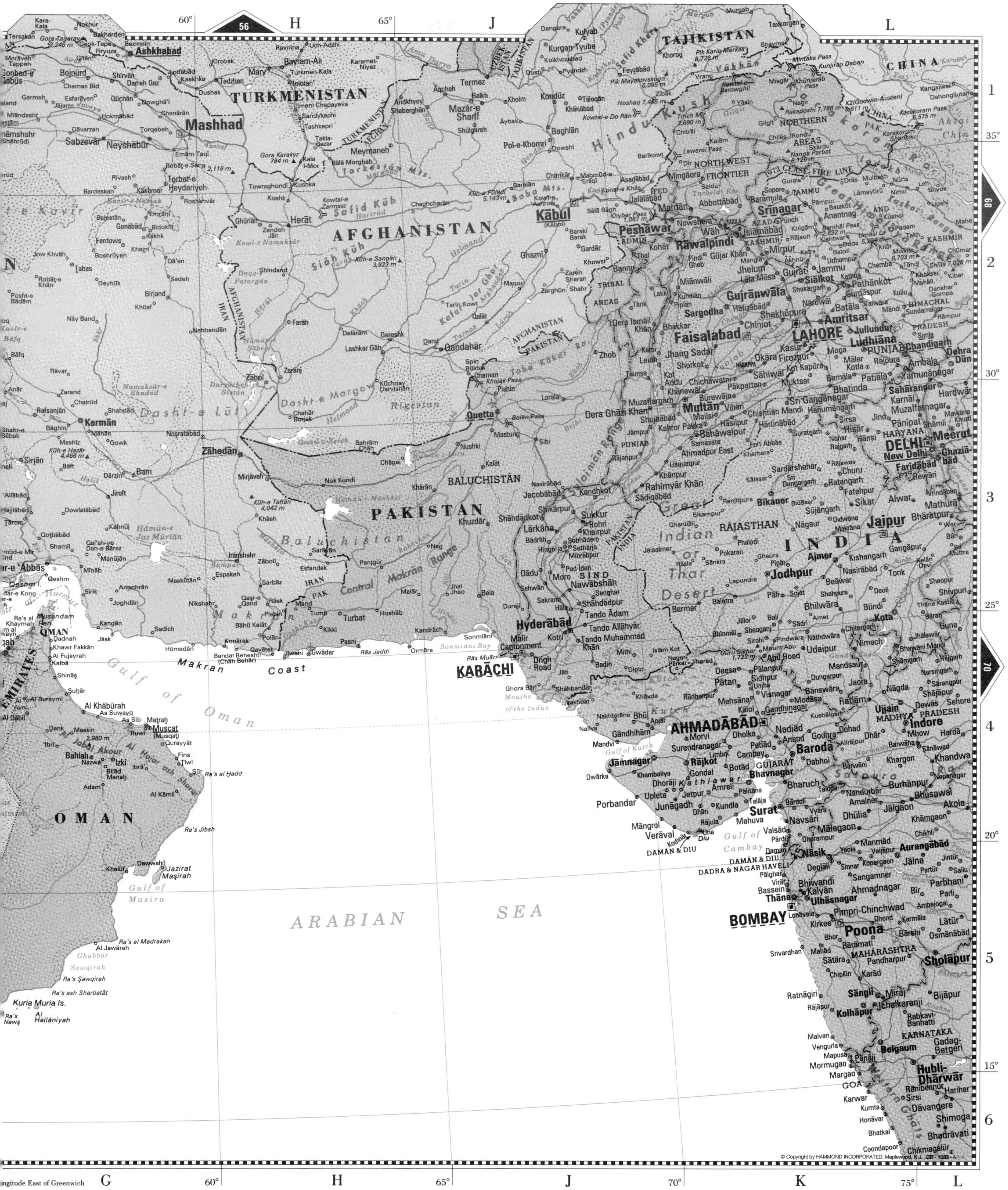

Longitude East of Greenwich

POPULATION OF CITIES AND TOWNS

▣ OVER 2,000,000	◉ 500,000 - 999,999	● 100,000 - 249,999	◦ 10,000 - 29,999
▢ 1,000,000 - 1,999,999	◎ 250,000 - 499,999	⊙ 30,000 - 99,999	○ UNDER 10,000

SCALE 1:10,500,000 LAMBERT CONFORMAL CONIC PROJECTION

MILES 0 150 300 450

KILOMETERS 0 150 300 450

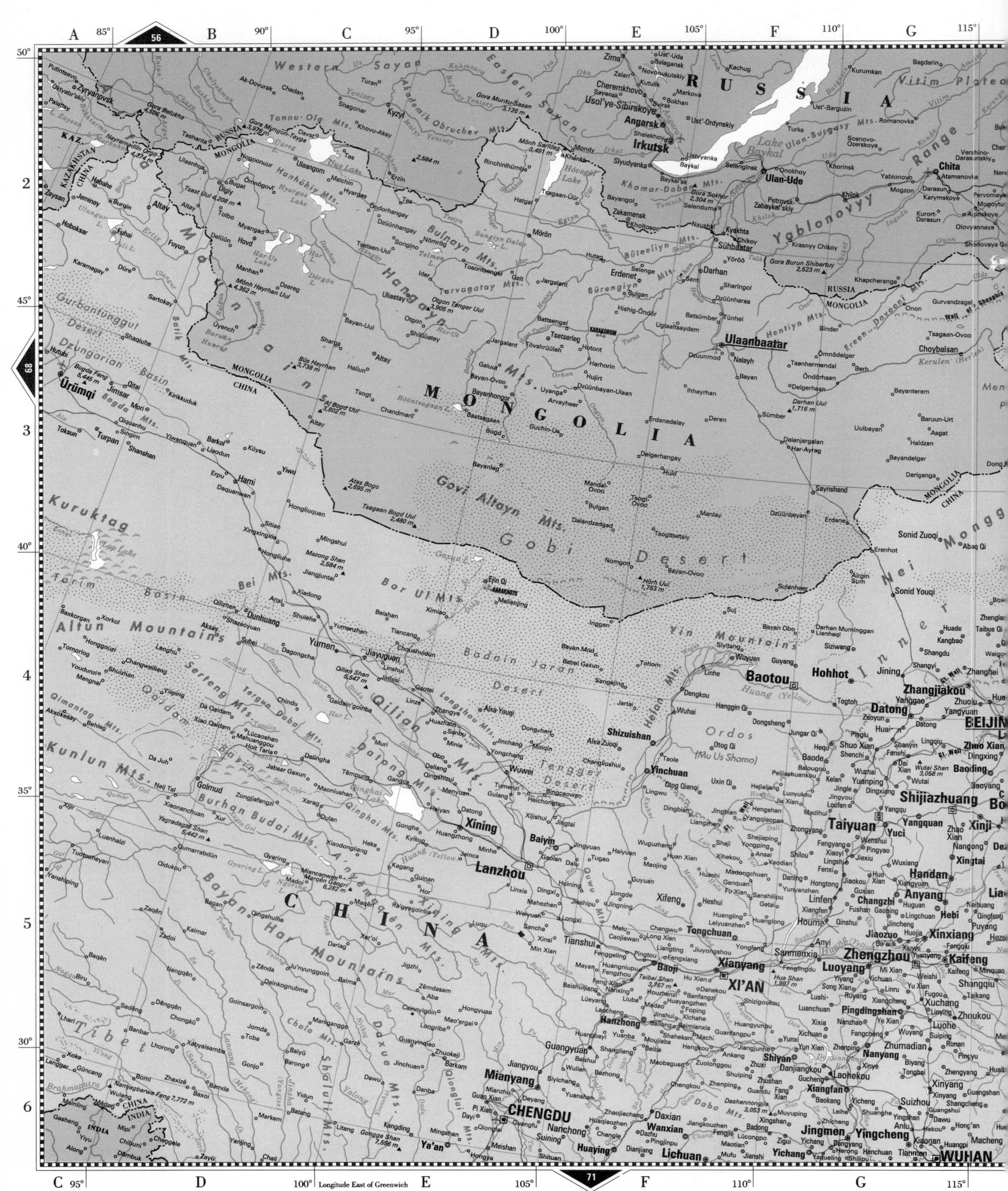

A
85°
56
B
90°
C
95°
D
100°
E
105°
F
110°
G
115°
50°
45°
40°
35°
30°
2
3
4
5
6
68
R U S S I A
M O N G O L I A
C H I N A
KAZAKHSTAN
KAZ.
INDIA
Western Sayan
Eastern Sayan
Tannu-Ola Mts.
Akademik Obruchev Mts.
Lake Baykal
Irkutsk
Angarsk
Usol'ye-Sibirskoye
Cheremkhovo
Ulan-Ude
Chita
Khamar-Daban Mts.
Ulan-Burgasy Mts.
Yablonovyy Range
Vitim Plateau
Gora Munku-Sasan 3,126 m
Mönh Saridag 3,491 m
Hövsgöl Lake
Uvs Lake
Har Us Lake
Hyargas Lake
Hanhöhiy Mts.
Bulnayn Mts.
Tarvagatay Mts.
Hangayn Mts.
Büreengiyn Mts.
Hentiyn Mts.
Ulaanbaatar
Karakorum
Darhan
Erdenet
Sühbaatar
Kyakhta
Mongol Altai Mts.
Gora Belukha 4,506 m
Nayramadlin Orgil 4,374 m
Mönh Hayrhan Uul 4,362 m
Otgon Tenger Uul 3,905 m
Büs Hayrhan 3,736 m
Ih Bogd Uul 3,957 m
Govi Altayn Mts.
Gobi Desert
Atas Bogd 2,695 m
Tsagaan Bogd Uul 2,480 m
Hörh Uul 1,763 m
Darhan Uul 1,716 m
Choybalsan
Sayn Shand
Erenhot
Gurbantünggüt Desert
Dzungarian Basin
Bogda Feng 5,445 m
Ürümqi
Turpan
Hami
Kuruktag
Lop Lake
Tarim Basin
Bei Mts.
Altun Mountains
Dunhuang
Bor Ul Mts.
Badain Jaran Desert
Yin Mountains
Baotou
Hohhot
Zhangjiakou
Datong
BEIJING
Qilian Mts.
Qilian Shan 5,547 m
Jiayuguan
Yumen
Mazong Shan 2,584 m
Qaidam Basin
Serteng Mts.
Kunlun Mts.
Golmud
Qinghai Lake
Xining
Lanzhou
Tengger Desert
Helan Mts.
Ordos (Mu Us Shamo)
Yinchuan
Shizuishan
Taiyuan
Shijiazhuang
Handan
Anyang
Xinxiang
Zhengzhou
Kaifeng
Luoyang
XI'AN
Xianyang
Baoji
Taibai Shan 3,767 m
Hua Shan 1,997 m
Tianshui
Hanzhong
Burhan Budai Mts.
A'nyêmaqên Mts.
Bayan Har Mountains
Amnê Machin 6,282 m
Tibet
Chola Mts.
Daxue Mts.
Shaluli Mts.
Qionglai Mts.
Gongga Shan 7,556 m
Namjagbarwa Feng 7,772 m
Mianyang
CHENGDU
Ya'an
Nanchong
Daxian
Wanxian
Daba Mts.
Dashennongjia 3,053 m
Shiyan
Xiangfan
Jingmen
Yingcheng
WUHAN
Nanyang
Pingdingshan
Zhumadian
Wutai Shan 3,058 m
Great Wall
Huang (Yellow)
Longitude East of Greenwich
71

Eastern Asia

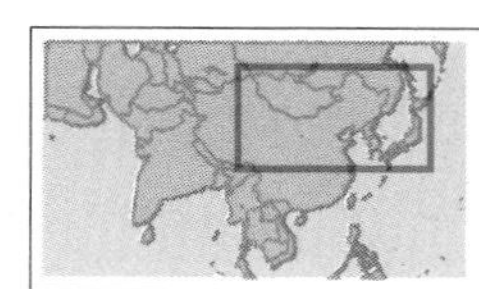

Longitude East of Greenwich

POPULATION OF CITIES AND TOWNS

- OVER 2,000,000
- 1,000,000 - 1,999,999
- 500,000 - 999,999
- 250,000 - 499,999
- 100,000 - 249,999
- 30,000 - 99,999
- 10,000 - 29,999
- UNDER 10,000

SCALE 1:10,500,000 LAMBERT CONFORMAL CONIC PROJECTION

MILES 0 150 300 450

KILOMETERS 0 150 300 450

128°
A
130°
B
132°
C
134°
D
136°
38°
36°
34°
32°
2
3
4
5
63
SORAKSAN NAT'L PARK
Inje
Yangyang
Soyang Lake
Hongch'ŏn
ODAESAN NAT'L PARK
Kangnŭng
Nogwak-san 1,321 m
Paektŏk-san 1,350 m
Samch'ŏk
P'yŏngch'ang
Wŏnju
KANGWŎN-DO
CH'UNGCH'ŎNG-BUKTO
Yŏngwŏl
Chech'ŏn
KYŎNGSANG-BUKTO
Ponghwa
Ulchin
Yŏngju
SOUTH
Ch'ŏmch'ŏn
Yŏng-yang
Andong Lake
Sangju
Andong
CHUWANG-SAN NAT'L PARK
Ch'ŏngsong
Sŏnsan
Ŭisŏng
Yŏngdŏk
KOREA
Kumi
Kimch'ŏn
P'algong-san 1,192 m
P'ohang
Sŏngju
TAEGU-JIKHALSI
Yŏngch'ŏn
Changgi-ap
Taegu
SILLA TOMBS
Kyŏngsan
Kyŏngju
KYŎNGJU NAT'L PARK
KYONGSANG-BUKTO
PULGUK-SA
Hwayang
KYONGSANG-NAMDO
Kaji-san 1,240 m
Miryang
Ulsan
Naktong
Ŭiryŏng
Samnangjin
Ch'angwŏn
Kimhae
Masan
Chinhae
PUSAN-JIKHALSI
UNITED NATIONS MEMORIAL CEM.
PUSAN
Kosŏng
Ch'ungmu
Koje Island
Samch'ŏnp'o
HALLYO HAESANG NAT'L PARK
Western Channel
KOREA STRAIT
SOUTH KOREA
JAPAN
Kara-saki
Tsu Island
Cheju
TSUSHIMA
Izuhara
Ko-saki
Eastern Channel
Ullŭng I.
(South Korea)
Liancourt Rocks
(Disputed between Japan and South Korea)
SEA OF JAPAN
OKI ISLANDS
Dōgo
Saigō
OKI
Dōzen
DAISEN-OKI NAT'L PARK
SAN'IN KAIGIN NATIONAL PARK
Kyōga-misaki
Wakasa Bay
Sakaiminato
Jizō-zaki
Hino-misaki
Hirata
Matsue
YONAGO
Yonago
TOTTORI
Kurayoshi
Tottori
Iwami
Toyo'oka
Miyazu
Maizuru
Obama
Tsuruga
Mikuni
Sakai
Fukui
Takefu
Taisha
Izumo
Yasugi
Dai-sen 1,711 m
Hyō-no-sen 1,510 m
Oda
DAISEN-OKI NAT'L PARK
SHIMANE
Wakasa
Fukuchiyama
Ayabe
KYŌTO
Kyōto
Ōtsu
Hikone
Gōtsu
Hamada
Niimi
Tsuyama
OKAYAMA
CHŪGOKU
KINKI
HYŌGO
Ikuno
Nishiwaki
Kameoka
Sonobe
Kasai
Shōbara
Tojō
Takahashi
HIMEJI CASTLE
Himeji
Yokawa
Sanda
Ono
Takatsuki
Masuda
HIROSHIMA
Miyoshi
Sōja
Kurashiki
KORAKUEN GARDEN
Akō
Kōbe
Hirakata
Nara
Yao
Hagi
Kanmuri-yama 1,339 m
Fuchū
Ibara
Kasaoka
Okayama
Harima Sea
Akashi
Awaji
ŌSAKA
Nagato
PEACE MEMORIAL PARK
Hiroshima
Fukuyama
Mihara
Onomichi
Shōdo I.
Kishiwada
Izumi
Yamatotakada
NARA
Kashihara
YAMAGUCHI
Yamaguchi
Takehara
Kure
Ōtake
Iwakuni
SETO-NAIKAI NAT'L PARK
Marugame
Takamatsu
Sakaide
Zentsūji
KAGAWA
Izumi-Sano
Sumoto
Misaki
Hashimoto
Gose
Gojō
Katsuragi
YOSHINO-KUMANO
Shimonoseki
Onoda
Hōfu
Tokuyama
Kudamatsu
Yanai
Kan'onji
Imabari
Niihama
Naruto
Tokushima
Wakayama
Arida
Kainan
Hakken-san 1,915 m
Kitakyūshū
Ube
Sea of Suo
CHŪGOKU
KYŪSHŪ
SETO-NAIKAI NAT'L PARK
Hōjō
Matsuyama
Saijō
Iyo
TOKUSHIMA
Komatsushima
Anan
Kii Channel
Gobō
Iki
Fukuoka
Nogata
Yukuhashi
Iizuka
Tagawa
Nakatsu
FUKUOKA
Usa
Amagi
Sea of Iyo
Nagahama
EHIME
Ishizuchi-san 1,982 m
KŌCHI
Tsurugi-san 1,955 m
Tanabe
Shingū
WAKAYAMA
Hirado
Karatsu
Tosu
ŌITA
Ōzu
Kōchi
Nankoku
SAIKAI NAT'L PARK
Imari
Saga
SAGA
Kurume
Beppu
Ōita
Yawatahama
Aki
Tosa
Muroto
Kushimoto
Shio-no-misaki
Nachi-Katsuura
GOTŌ ISLANDS
Sasebo
Kashima
Okawa
Yanagawa
Beppu Bay
SHIKOKU
KYŪSHŪ
Yoshida
Uwajima
Susaki
Tosa Bay
Muroto-zaki
NAGASAKI
Ōmuta
ASO NAT'L PARK
Kuju-san 1,787 m
Usuki
Ōmura
Unzen-dake 1,359 m
KUMAMOTO
Yamaga
Taketa
Tsukumi
Kubokawa
Shikoku
Nagasaki
Isahaya
Kumamoto
Aso-san 1,592 m
Mie
Saiki
SAIKAI NAT'L PARK
Fukue
Fukue I.
NAGASAKI PEACE PARK
Shimabara
JAPAN
Nakamura
Sukumo
Tosashimizu
Ashizuri-misaki
Nomo-zaki
Tachibana Bay
Shimabara Bay
Nobeoka
Hondo
Yatsushiro
Kunimi-dake 1,739 m
Amakusa Sea
UNZEN-AMAKUSA NATIONAL PARK
Hyūga
Ushibuka
Minamata
Hitoyoshi
MIYAZAKI
PACIFIC
Akune
Saito
Takanabe
Izumi
Ōkuchi
Sadowara
Miyanojō
Kobayashi
EAST
Kirishima-yama 1,700 m
Sendai
Miyazaki
Shimo-koshiki I.
Kushikino
Kokubu
Ijūin
Miyakonojō
Kyūshū
Kagoshima
Nichinan
CHINA
Tarumizu
Nomo-misaki
KAGOSHIMA
Kaseda
Kanoya
Kushima
OCEAN
Makurazaki
Kōyama
Shibushi Bay
Kagoshima Bay
Ōsumi Pen.
SEA
Sata-misaki
Ōsumi Strait
Nishino'omote
ŌSUMI ISLANDS
Tanega I.
Yaku I.
Nakatane
KIRISHIMA-YAKU NAT'L PARK
© Copyright by HAMMOND INCORPORATED, Maplewood, N.J.
Longitude East of Greenwich

Central and Southern Japan

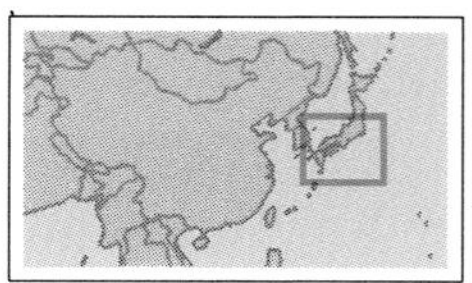

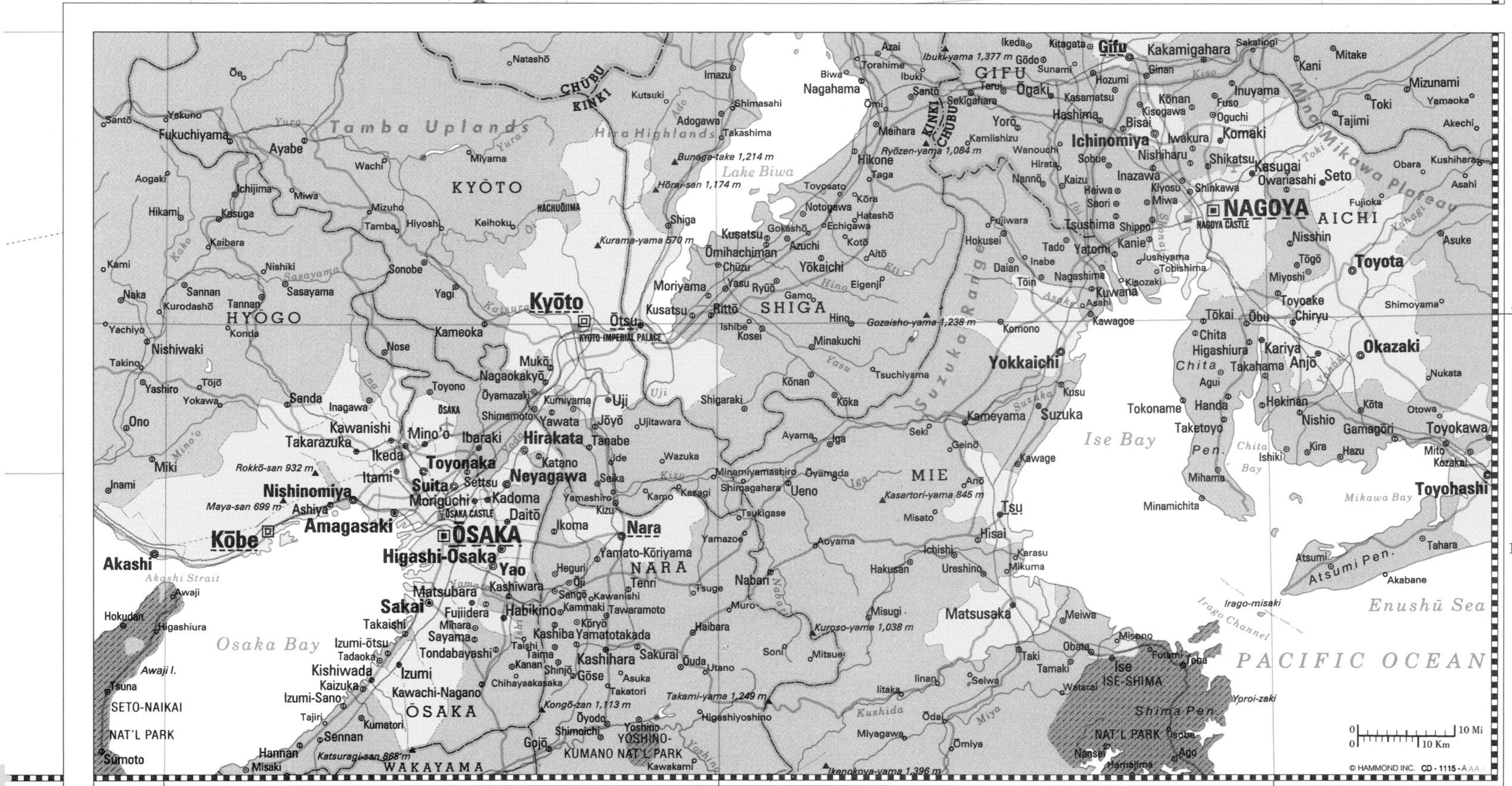

POPULATION OF CITIES AND TOWNS

■ OVER 2,000,000	◉ 500,000 - 999,999	● 100,000 - 249,999	◎ 10,000 - 29,999
▣ 1,000,000 - 1,999,999	◉ 250,000 - 499,999	● 30,000 - 99,999	○ UNDER 10,000

SCALE 1:3,500,000 LAMBERT CONFORMAL CONIC PROJECTION

MILES 0 10 20 30 40 50

KILOMETERS 0 10 20 30 40 50

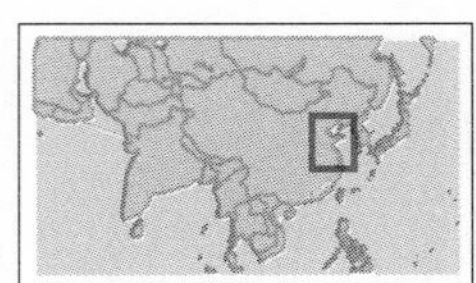

Northeastern China

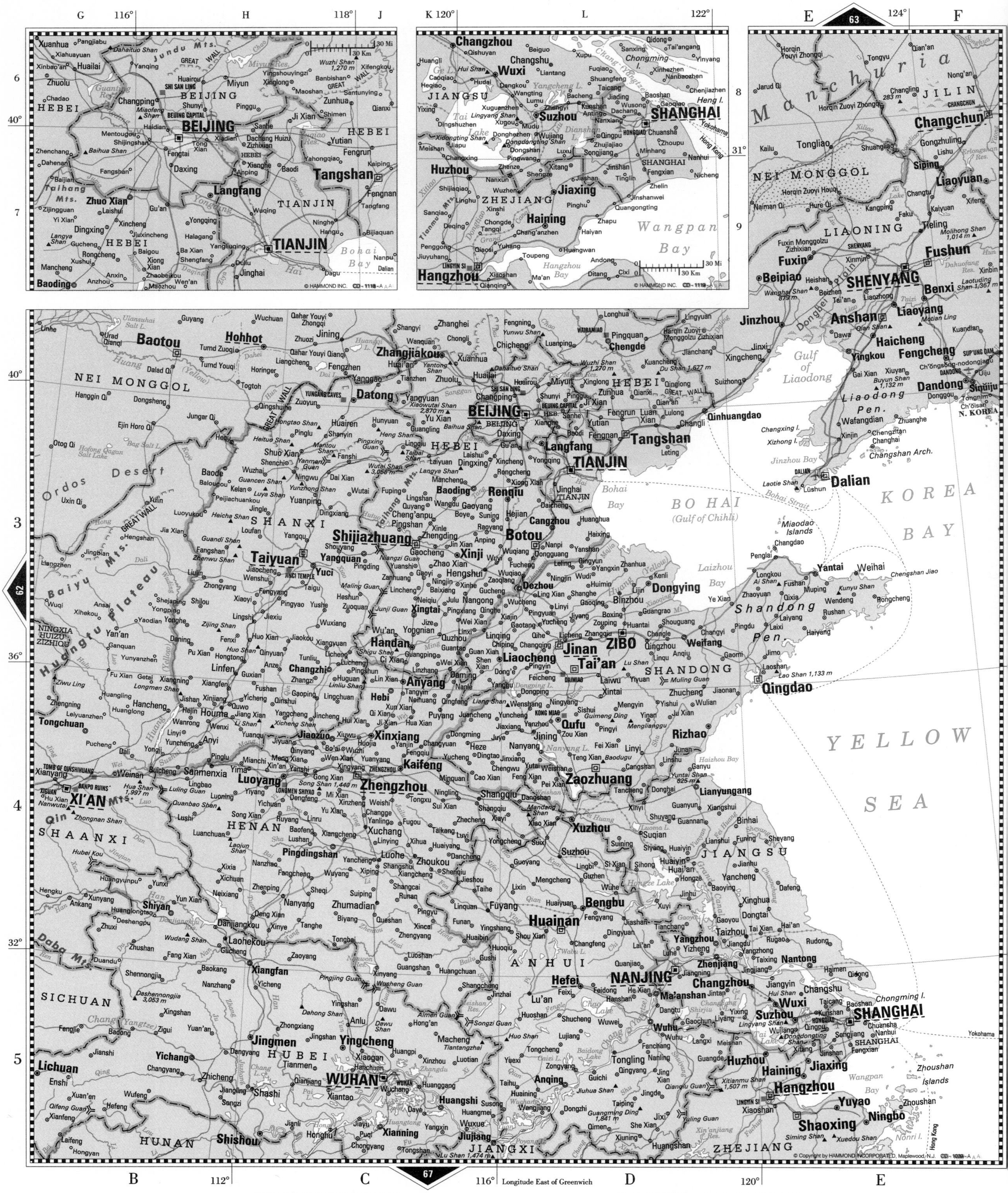

POPULATION OF CITIES AND TOWNS

- OVER 2,000,000
- 1,000,000 - 1,999,999
- 500,000 - 999,999
- 250,000 - 499,999
- 100,000 - 249,999
- 30,000 - 99,999
- 10,000 - 29,999
- UNDER 10,000

SCALE 1:7,000,000 LAMBERT CONFORMAL CONIC PROJECTION

MILES 0 100 200 300

KILOMETERS 0 100 200 300

Longitude East of Greenwich

Southeastern China, Taiwan, Philippines

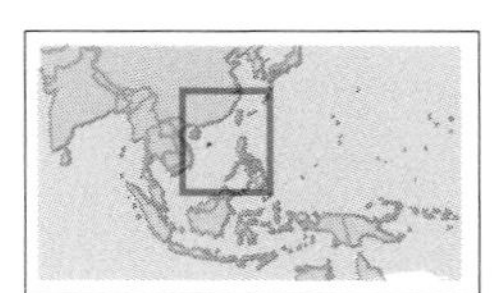

CHINA

TAIWAN

PHILIPPINES

VIETNAM

MALAYSIA

EAST CHINA SEA

PACIFIC OCEAN

PHILIPPINE SEA

SOUTH CHINA SEA

Sulu Sea

CELEBES SEA

Gulf of Tonkin

Taiwan Strait

Bashi Channel

Ryukyu Islands

Paracel Islands (Sovereignty disputed)

Spratly Islands (Sovereignty disputed)

Tropic of Cancer

WUHAN · Hangzhou · CHONGQING · Changsha · Nanchang · Fuzhou · TAIPEI · Kaohsiung · GUANGZHOU (Canton) · Dongguan · KOWLOON · Victoria · HONG KONG (U.K.) · MACAU (PORT.) · Haikou · Hainan · Manila · Quezon City · Cebu · Davao · Zamboanga · Luzon · Mindanao · Palawan

SCALE 1:10,500,000 LAMBERT CONFORMAL CONIC PROJECTION

MILES 0 150 300 450

KILOMETERS 0 150 300 450

Longitude East of Greenwich

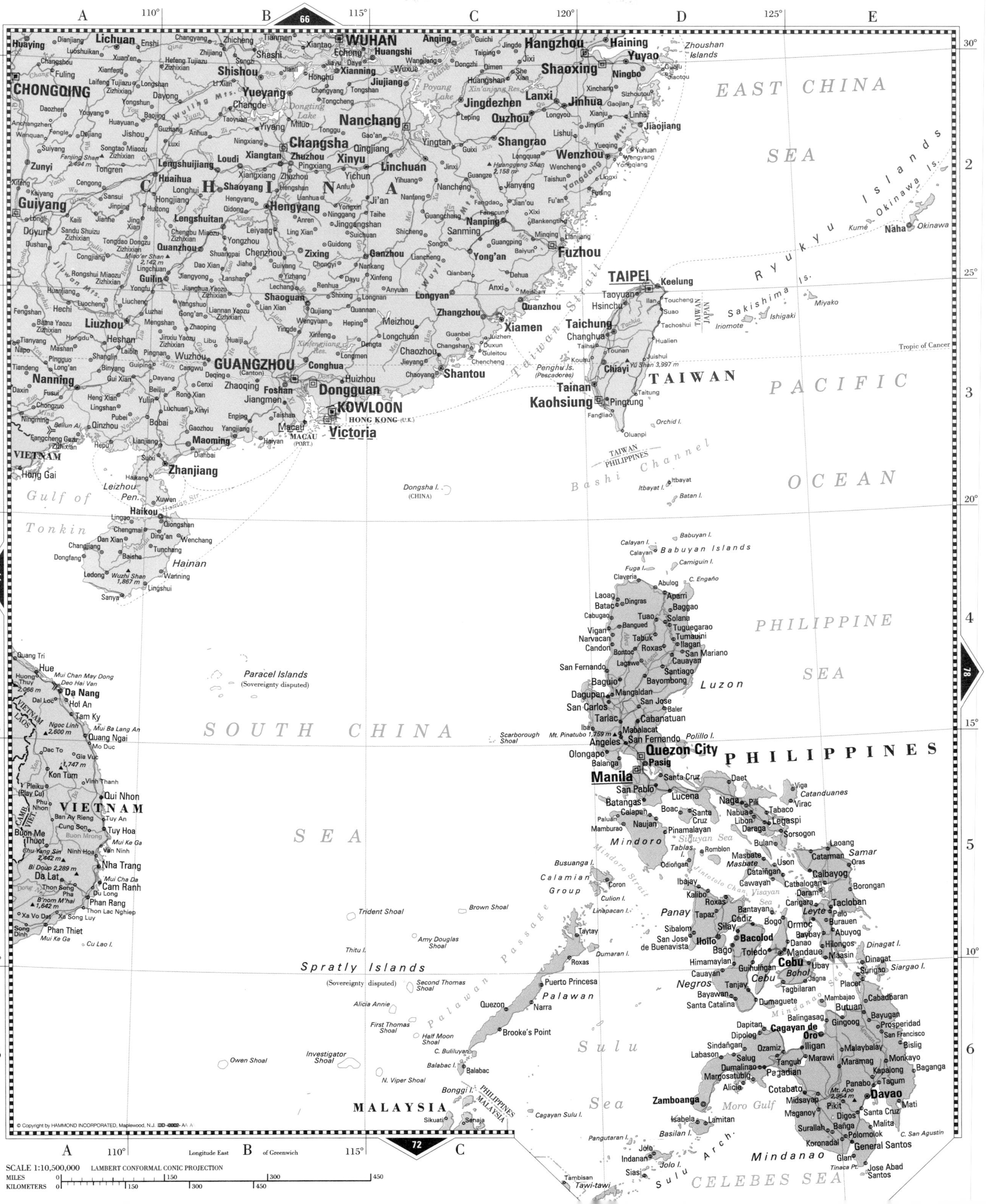

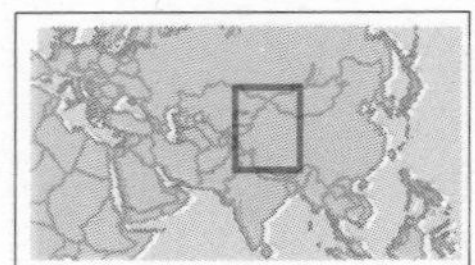

Central Asia

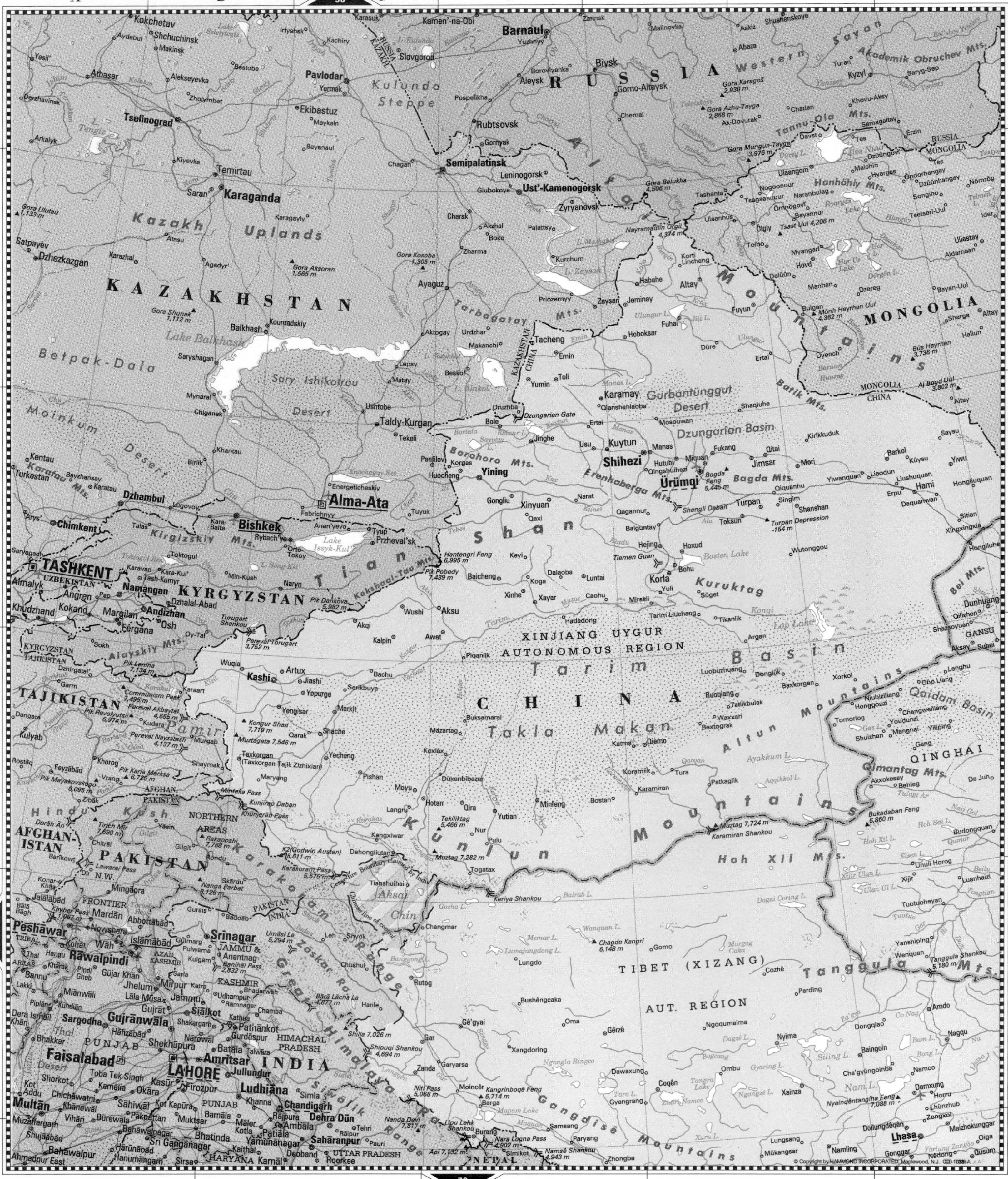

SCALE 1:10,500,000 LAMBERT CONFORMAL CONIC PROJECTION

MILES 0 150 300 450

KILOMETERS 0 150 300 450

Longitude East of Greenwich

POPULATION OF CITIES AND TOWNS

- OVER 2,000,000
- 1,000,000 - 1,999,999
- 500,000 - 999,999
- 250,000 - 499,999
- 100,000 - 249,999
- 30,000 - 99,999
- 10,000 - 29,999
- UNDER 10,000

Eastern Burma, Thailand, Indochina

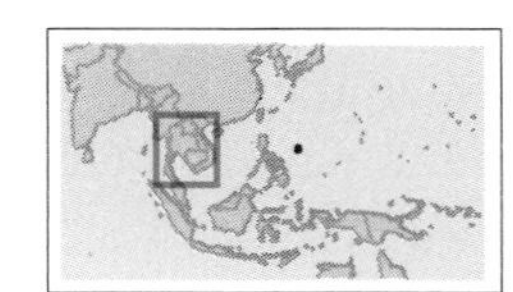

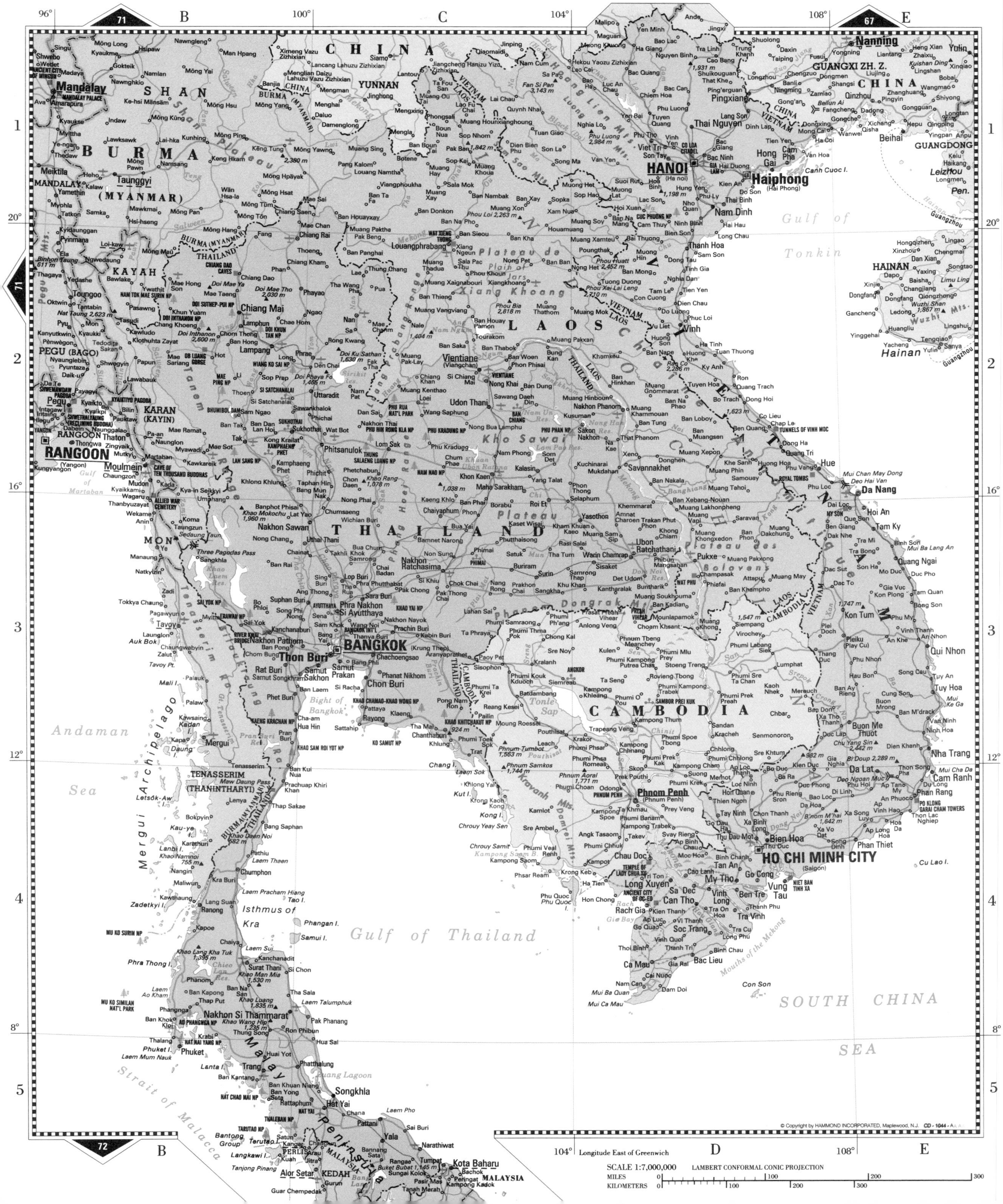

SCALE 1:7,000,000 LAMBERT CONFORMAL CONIC PROJECTION

MILES 0 100 200 300

KILOMETERS 0 100 200 300

Longitude East of Greenwich

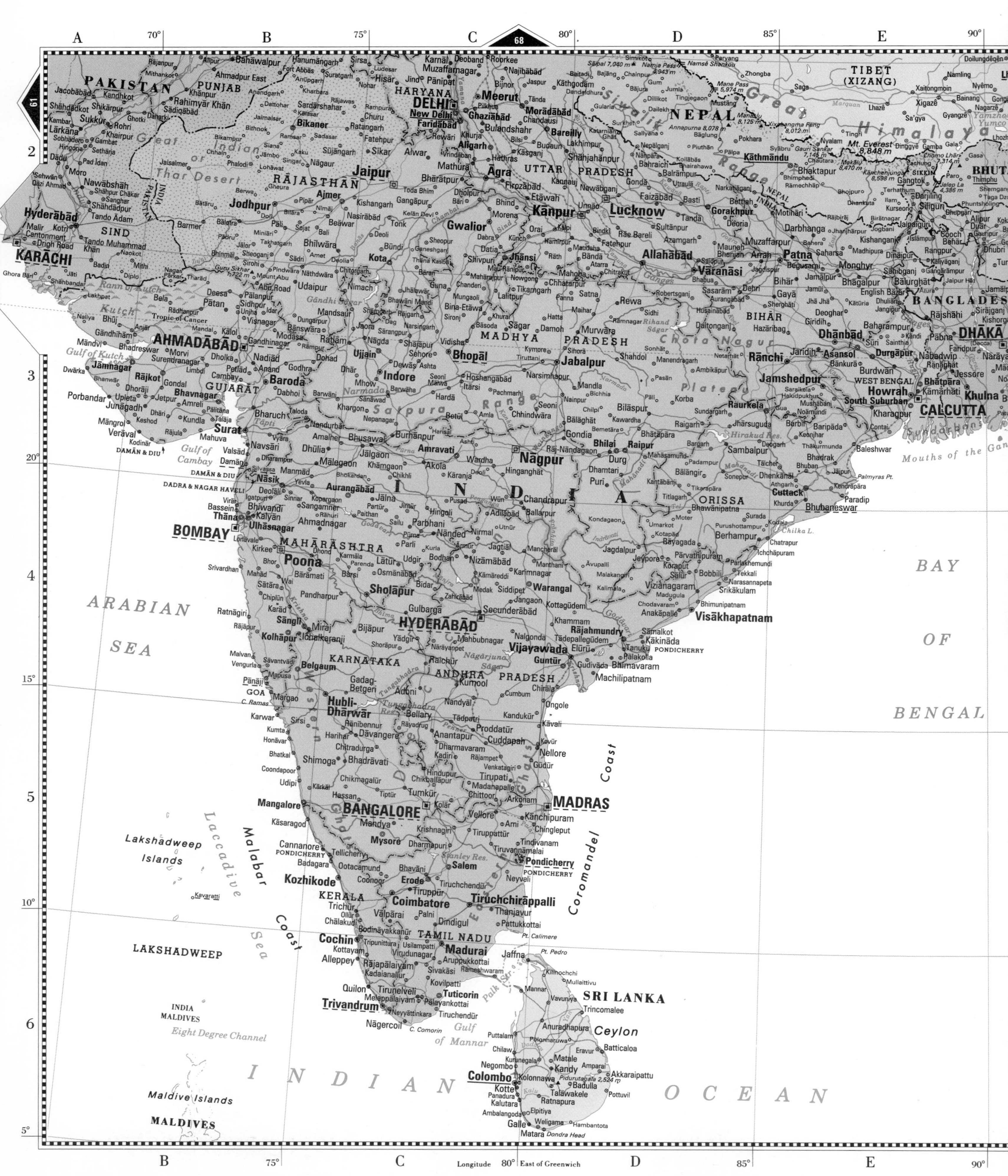

A
70°
B
75°
C
68
80°
D
85°
E
90°
61
2
3
4
5
6
20°
15°
10°
5°
PAKISTAN
PUNJAB
SIND
KARĀCHI
Hyderābād
Bahāwalpur
Sukkur
Great Indian or Thar Desert
RĀJASTHĀN
Jaipur
Jodhpur
Bikaner
Ajmer
Udaipur
Kota
HARYANA
DELHI
New Delhi
Meerut
Ghaziābād
Farīdābād
Āgra
Alīgarh
Morādābād
Bareilly
UTTAR PRADESH
Kānpur
Lucknow
Allahābād
Vārānasi
Gwalior
Jhānsi
NEPAL
Kāthmāndu
Mt. Everest 8,848 m
Annapurna 8,078 m
Great Himalaya
TIBET (XIZANG)
SIKKIM
Patna
BIHĀR
Gayā
Rānchi
Jamshedpur
Dhanbād
Asansol
WEST BENGAL
Howrah
CALCUTTA
South Suburban
BANGLADESH
DHĀKA
Khulna
Rājshāhi
Mouths of the Ganges
Rann of Kutch
Kutch
Gulf of Kutch
Tropic of Cancer
AHMADĀBĀD
GUJARĀT
Rājkot
Jāmnagar
Bhavnagar
Junāgadh
Porbandar
Baroda
Surat
Gulf of Cambay
DAMĀN & DIU
DADRA & NAGAR HAVELI
MADHYA PRADESH
Bhopāl
Indore
Ujjain
Jabalpur
Sāgar
Narmada
Satpura Range
Chota Nagpur Plateau
Nāgpur
Raipur
Bhilai
Durg
INDIA
MAHĀRĀSHTRA
BOMBAY
Thāna
Ulhāsnagar
Kalyān
Nāsik
Aurangābād
Poona
Sholāpur
Amravati
Akola
ORISSA
Cuttack
Bhubaneswar
Sambalpur
Raurkela
Berhampur
Chilka L.
ANDHRA PRADESH
HYDERĀBĀD
Secunderābād
Warangal
Vijayawada
Guntūr
Rājahmundry
Visākhapatnam
Kākināda
Machilipatnam
Nellore
Kurnool
Godāvari
Krishna
PONDICHERRY
KARNATAKA
Belgaum
Hubli-Dhārwār
GOA
Panaji
Mangalore
Mysore
BANGALORE
Deccan
Western Ghats
Eastern Ghats
MADRAS
Kānchipuram
Vellore
Salem
Pondicherry
Coromandel Coast
Malabar Coast
Kozhikode
KERALA
Coimbatore
Tiruchchirāppalli
Thanjavur
TAMIL NADU
Madurai
Cochin
Alleppey
Quilon
Trivandrum
Tirunelveli
Tuticorin
Nāgercoil
C. Comorin
Gulf of Mannar
Palk Strait
Pt. Calimere
Pt. Pedro
Jaffna
SRI LANKA
Ceylon
Trincomalee
Anurādhapura
Batticaloa
Kandy
Colombo
Kotte
Galle
Matara
Dondra Head
Pidurutalagala 2,524 m
ARABIAN SEA
BAY OF BENGAL
INDIAN OCEAN
Lakshadweep Islands
Laccadive Sea
Kavaratti
LAKSHADWEEP
INDIA
MALDIVES
Eight Degree Channel
Maldive Islands
MALDIVES
Longitude 80° East of Greenwich

Southern Asia

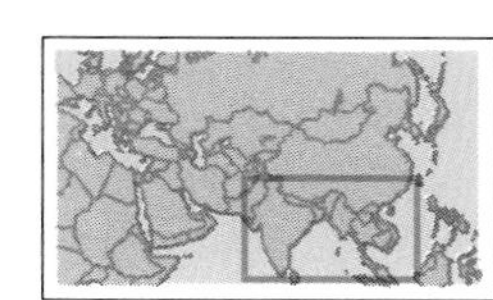

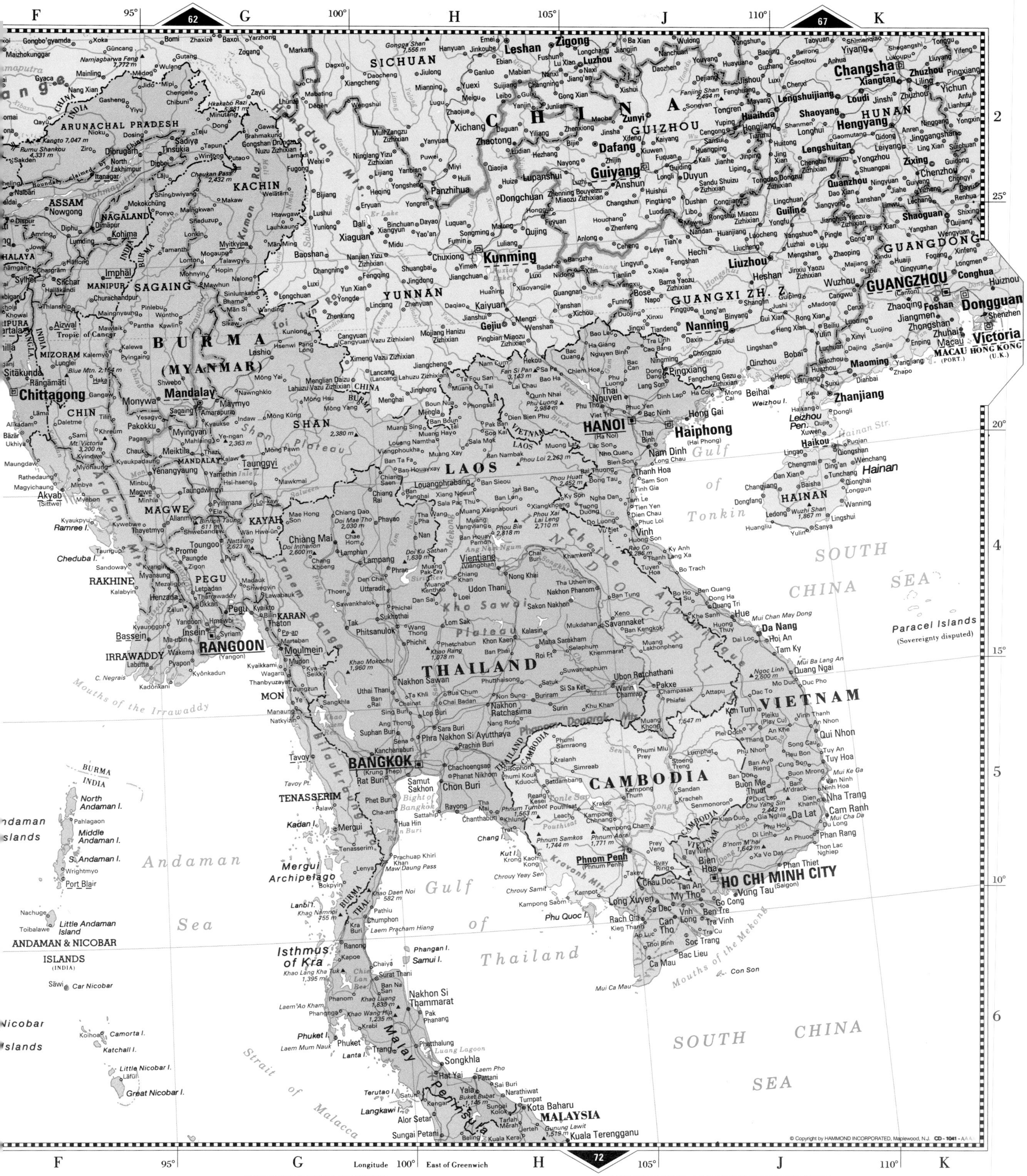

POPULATION OF CITIES AND TOWNS

- ■ OVER 2,000,000
- ▣ 1,000,000 - 1,999,999
- ◉ 500,000 - 999,999
- ◎ 250,000 - 499,999
- ● 100,000 - 249,999
- ◦ 30,000 - 99,999
- ◉ 10,000 - 29,999
- ○ UNDER 10,000

SCALE 1:10,500,000 LAMBERT CONFORMAL CONIC PROJECTION

MILES 0 150 300 450

KILOMETERS 0 150 300 450

Longitude 100° East of Greenwich

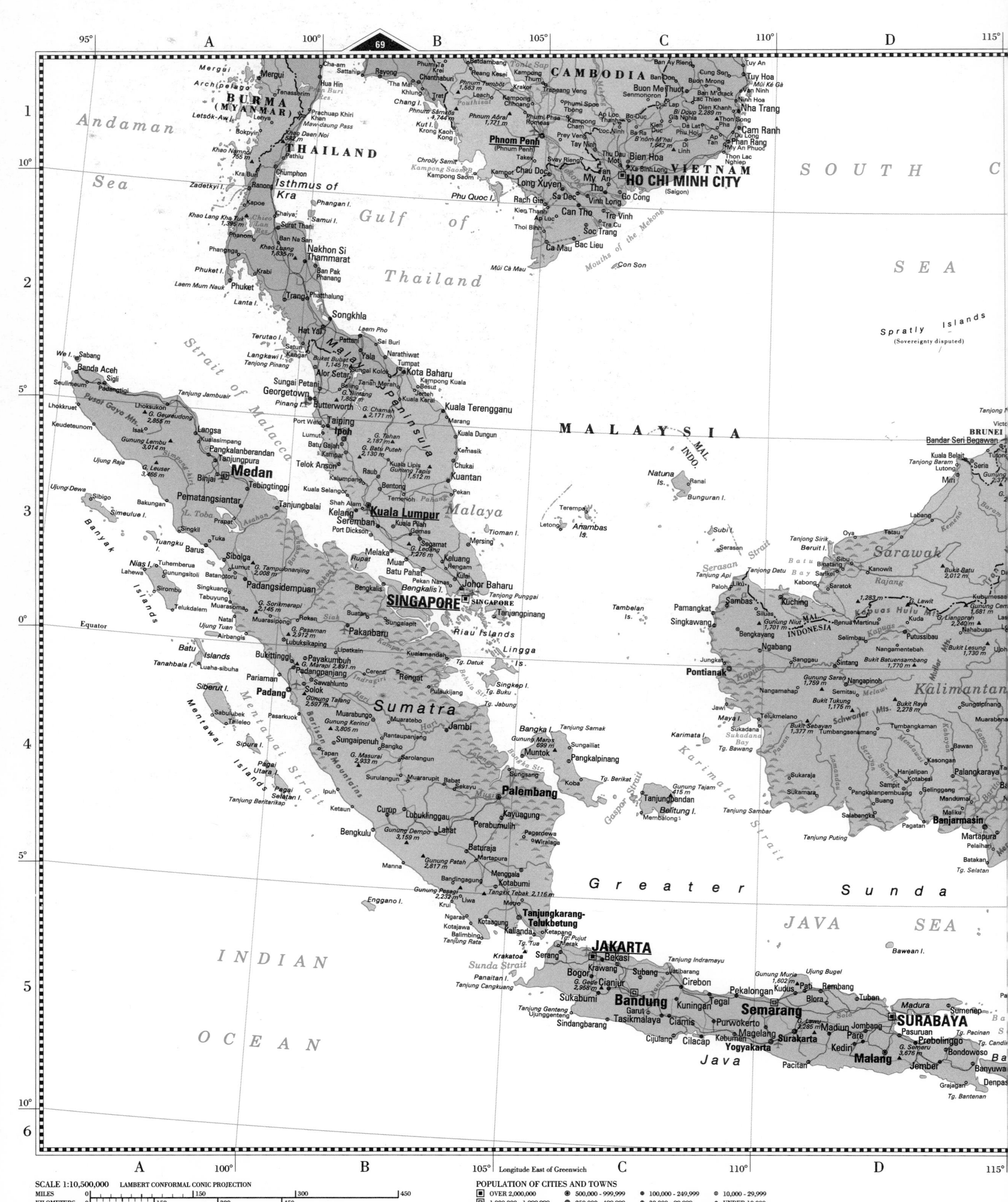

69
95°
100°
105°
110°
115°
A
B
C
D
1
2
3
4
5
6
10°
5°
0°
Equator
Andaman Sea
BURMA (MYANMAR)
Mergui Archipelago
Mergui
THAILAND
Isthmus of Kra
Gulf of Thailand
CAMBODIA
Phnom Penh
(Phnom Penh)
VIETNAM
HO CHI MINH CITY
(Saigon)
Mouths of the Mekong
SOUTH CHINA SEA
Spratly Islands
(Sovereignty disputed)
MALAYSIA
Malay Peninsula
Malaya
Kuala Lumpur
SINGAPORE
Strait of Malacca
BRUNEI
Bandar Seri Begawan
Sarawak
Kalimantan
Natuna Is.
Anambas Is.
Tambelan Is.
Riau Islands
Lingga Is.
Sumatra
Medan
Padang
Palembang
Jambi
Pakanbaru
Bengkulu
Banda Aceh
Barisan Mountains
Mentawai Islands
Mentawai Strait
Banyak Islands
Batu Islands
Bangka I.
Belitung I.
Karimata Strait
Gaspar Strait
Pontianak
Banjarmasin
Greater Sunda
JAVA SEA
JAKARTA
Bandung
Semarang
Yogyakarta
Surakarta
Malang
SURABAYA
Madura
Java
Sunda Strait
Krakatoa
Tanjungkarang-Telukbetung
INDIAN OCEAN
Enggano I.
Longitude East of Greenwich
SCALE 1:10,500,000
LAMBERT CONFORMAL CONIC PROJECTION
MILES 0 150 300 450
KILOMETERS 0 150 300 450
POPULATION OF CITIES AND TOWNS
OVER 2,000,000
1,000,000 - 1,999,999
500,000 - 999,999
250,000 - 499,999
100,000 - 249,999
30,000 - 99,999
10,000 - 29,999
UNDER 10,000

Southeastern Asia

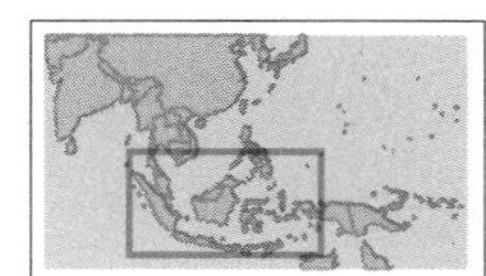

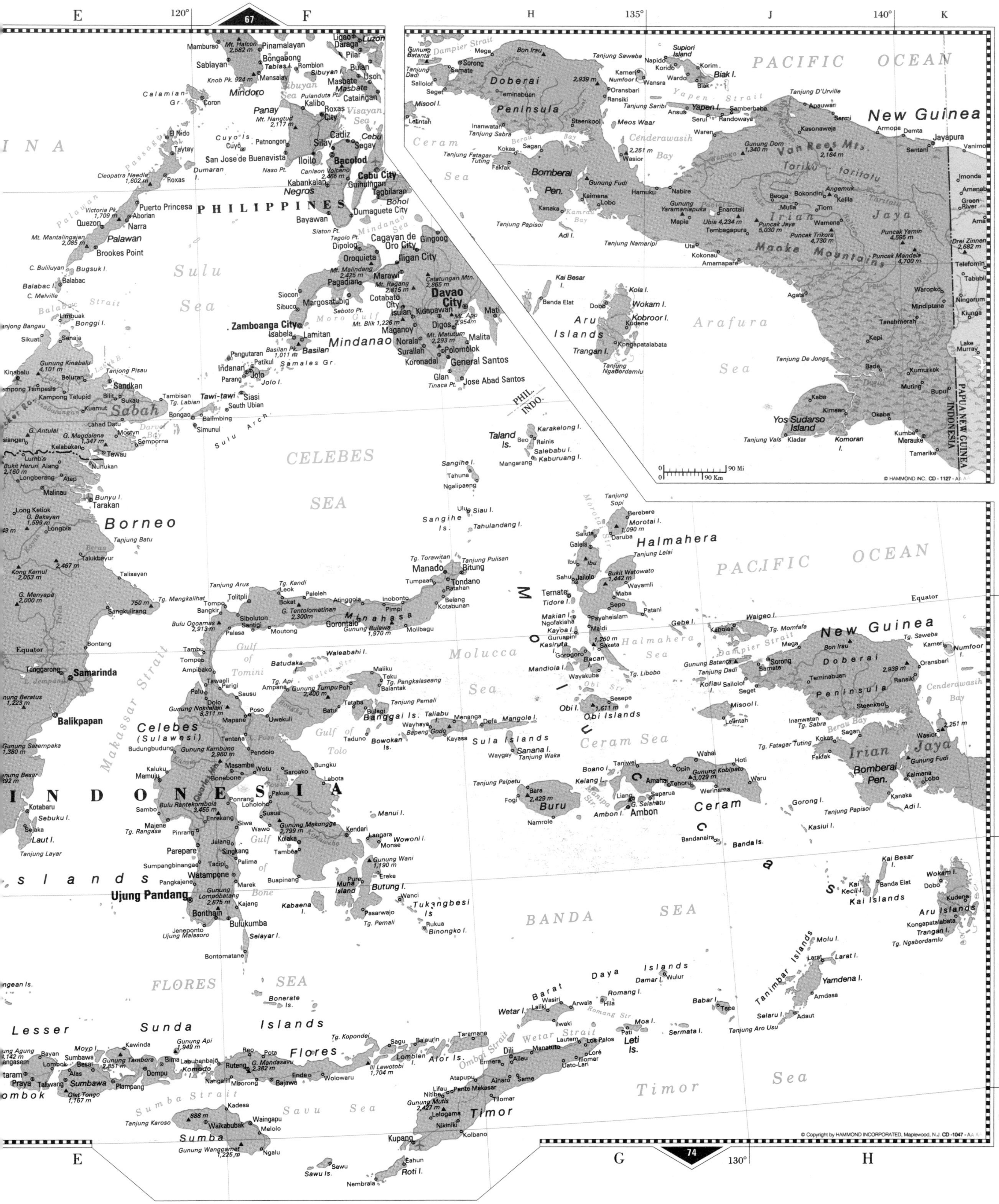

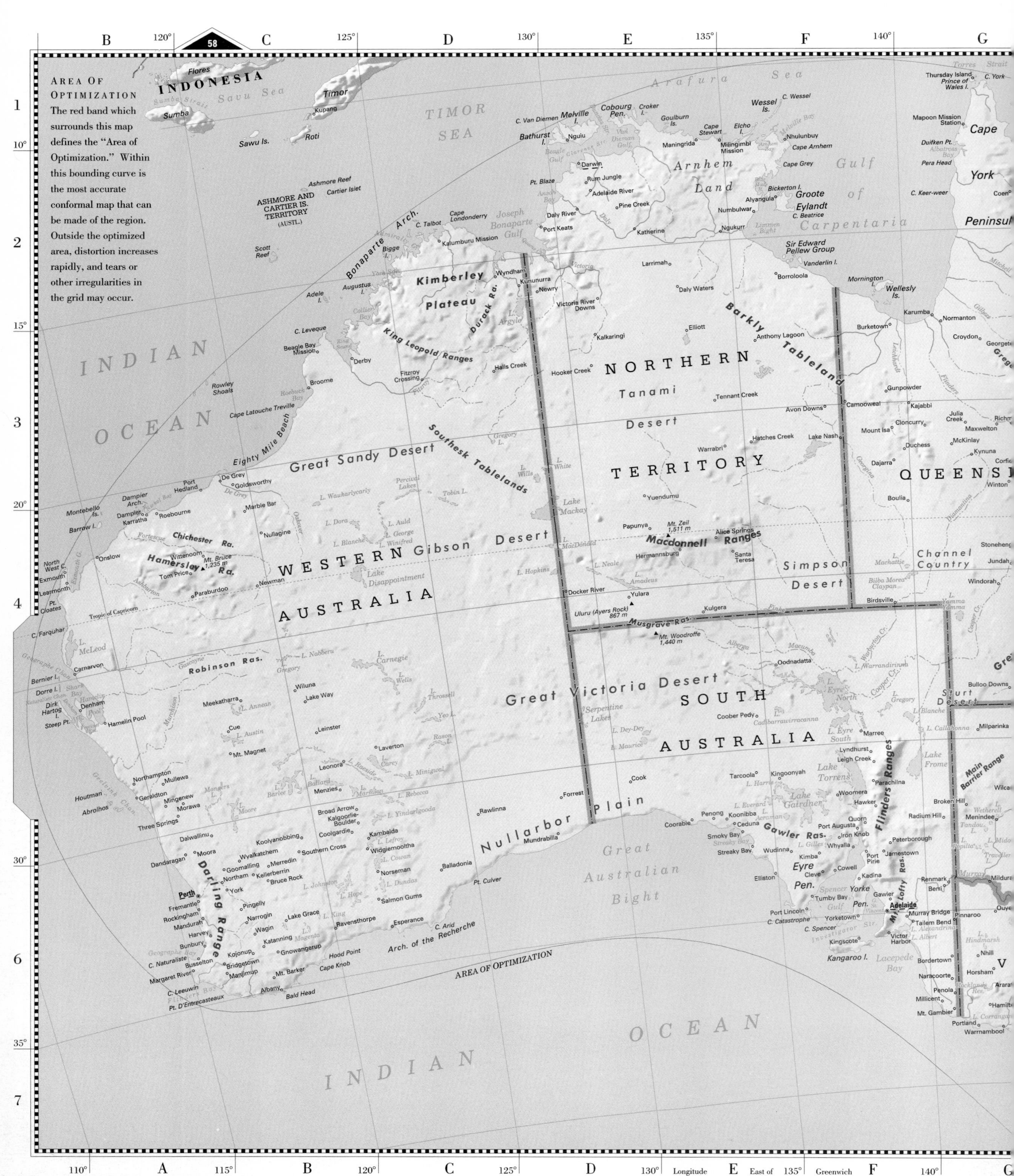

AREA OF OPTIMIZATION
The red band which surrounds this map defines the "Area of Optimization." Within this bounding curve is the most accurate conformal map that can be made of the region. Outside the optimized area, distortion increases rapidly, and tears or other irregularities in the grid may occur.
58
INDONESIA
Flores
Sumba
Sumba Strait
Savu Sea
Timor
Kupang
Roti
Sawu Is.
TIMOR SEA
Arafura Sea
ASHMORE AND CARTIER IS. TERRITORY (AUSTL.)
Ashmore Reef
Cartier Islet
Scott Reef
INDIAN OCEAN
Rowley Shoals
Cape Latouche Treville
Eighty Mile Beach
Bonaparte Arch.
Kimberley Plateau
King Leopold Ranges
Durack Ra.
Joseph Bonaparte Gulf
C. Talbot
Cape Londonderry
Kalumburu Mission
Wyndham
Kununurra
Newry
Derby
Broome
Fitzroy Crossing
Halls Creek
Beagle Bay Mission
C. Leveque
Adele I.
Augustus I.
Bigge I.
Great Sandy Desert
Southesk Tablelands
De Grey
Goldsworthy
Port Hedland
Dampier Arch.
Dampier
Karratha
Roebourne
Marble Bar
Nullagine
Montebello Is.
Barrow I.
Chichester Ra.
Hamersley Ra.
Mt. Bruce 1,235 m
Wittenoom
Tom Price
Paraburdoo
Newman
Onslow
North West C.
Exmouth
Learmonth
Pt. Cloates
Tropic of Capricorn
C. Farquhar
Carnarvon
Bernier I.
Dorre I.
Dirk Hartog I.
Steep Pt.
Denham
Hamelin Pool
WESTERN AUSTRALIA
Gibson Desert
Lake Disappointment
Robinson Ras.
Wiluna
Lake Way
Meekatharra
Cue
Mt. Magnet
Leinster
Laverton
Leonora
Menzies
Northampton
Mullewa
Geraldton
Mingenew
Morawa
Houtman Abrolhos
Three Springs
Dalwallinu
Moora
Dandaragan
Darling Range
Perth
Fremantle
Rockingham
Mandurah
Harvey
Bunbury
Busselton
C. Naturaliste
Margaret River
C. Leeuwin
Pt. D'Entrecasteaux
Albany
Bald Head
Mt. Barker
Manjimup
Bridgetown
Kojonup
Katanning
Gnowangerup
Wagin
Narrogin
Pingelly
York
Northam
Goomalling
Wyalkatchem
Merredin
Kellerberrin
Bruce Rock
Koolyanobbing
Southern Cross
Kalgoorlie-Boulder
Coolgardie
Kambalda
Widgiemooltha
Norseman
Salmon Gums
Esperance
Ravensthorpe
Lake Grace
Hood Point
Cape Knob
Arch. of the Recherche
C. Arid
Broad Arrow
Balladonia
Pt. Culver
Rawlinna
Nullarbor Plain
Forrest
Mundrabilla
Cook
Great Victoria Desert
Great Australian Bight
AREA OF OPTIMIZATION
INDIAN OCEAN
NORTHERN TERRITORY
Tanami Desert
Darwin
Rum Jungle
Adelaide River
Pine Creek
Daly River
Port Keats
Katherine
Bathurst I.
Melville I.
C. Van Diemen
Nguiu
Cobourg Pen.
Croker I.
Goulburn Is.
Maningrida
Cape Stewart
Milingimbi Mission
Elcho I.
Wessel Is.
C. Wessel
Nhulunbuy
Cape Arnhem
Cape Grey
Arnhem Land
Pt. Blaze
Bickerton I.
Groote Eylandt
C. Beatrice
Alyangula
Numbulwar
Ngukurr
Gulf of Carpentaria
Sir Edward Pellew Group
Vanderlin I.
Borroloola
Larrimah
Daly Waters
Victoria River Downs
Kalkaringi
Elliott
Barkly Tableland
Anthony Lagoon
Hooker Creek
Tennant Creek
Warrabri
Hatches Creek
Lake Nash
Avon Downs
Yuendumu
Papunya
Mt. Zeil 1,511 m
Macdonnell Ranges
Alice Springs
Hermannsburg
Santa Teresa
Simpson Desert
Docker River
Yulara
Uluru (Ayers Rock) 867 m
Kulgera
Musgrave Ras.
Mt. Woodroffe 1,440 m
TERRITORY
SOUTH AUSTRALIA
Oodnadatta
Coober Pedy
L. Eyre North
L. Eyre South
Marree
Lyndhurst
Leigh Creek
Lake Torrens
Tarcoola
Kingoonyah
Woomera
Lake Gairdner
Flinders Ranges
Parachilna
Hawker
Quorn
Port Augusta
Iron Knob
Whyalla
Port Pirie
Gawler Ras.
Penong
Koonibba
Ceduna
Coorabie
Smoky Bay
Streaky Bay
Wudinna
Kimba
Cleve
Cowell
Eyre Pen.
Elliston
Port Lincoln
C. Catastrophe
C. Spencer
Tumby Bay
Yorke Pen.
Yorketown
Kadina
Gawler
Adelaide
Kingscote
Kangaroo I.
Victor Harbor
Murray Bridge
Tailem Bend
Pinnaroo
Bordertown
Naracoorte
Penola
Millicent
Mt. Gambier
Portland
Warrnambool
Horsham
Renmark
Berri
Peterborough
Jamestown
Radium Hill
Broken Hill
Menindee
Wilcannia
Milparinka
Lake Frome
Main Barrier Range
Sturt Desert
Bulloo Downs
Birdsville
Bilba Morea Claypan
Channel Country
Windorah
Jundah
Stonehenge
Boulia
Dajarra
Mount Isa
Cloncurry
Duchess
Julia Creek
McKinlay
Kynuna
Maxwelton
Camooweal
Gunpowder
Kajabbi
Burketown
Karumba
Normanton
Croydon
Mornington I.
Wellesly Is.
QUEENSLAND
Thursday Island
Prince of Wales I.
C. York
Torres Strait
Mapoon Mission Station
Duifken Pt.
Pera Head
C. Keer-weer
Cape York Peninsula
Lacepede Bay
1
2
3
4
6
7
10°
15°
20°
30°
35°
120°
125°
130°
135°
140°
110°
115°
B C D E F G A
Longitude East of Greenwich

Australia, New Zealand

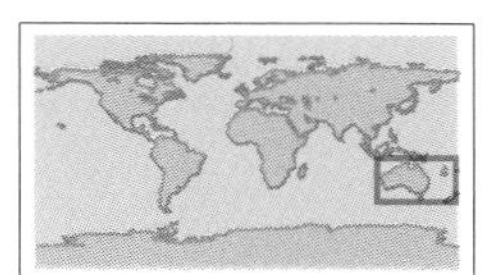

145° H 150° J 155° Q 170° R 175° S

PAPUA NEW GUINEA
Louisiade Arch.
Misima I.
Tagula I.
Rossel I.
Pocklington Reef
Grenville
Great Barrier Reef
Osprey Reef
Cape Melville
Cape Flattery
Cooktown
Bougainville Reef
CORAL SEA ISLANDS TERRITORY (AUSTL.)
CORAL SEA
Willis Islets
Magdelaine Cays
Coringa Islets
Holmes Reefs
Mossman
Cairns
Mareeba
Gordonvale
Atherton
Bartle Frere 1,622 m
Innisfail
Ravenshoe
Flinders Reefs
Lihou Reef and Kays
Mellish Reef
Hinchinbrook I.
Palm Is.
Ingham
Townsville
C. Bowling Green
Ayr
Home Hill
Marion Reef
Charters Towers
Bowen
Whitsunday I.
Hughenden
Proserpine
Repulse Bay
Walkerston
Mackay
Sarina
Frederick Reef
Kenn Reef
Swain Reefs
Percy Isles
Saumarez Reef
Stamford
Great Dividing Range
Drummond Ra.
Clermont
Capricorn Channel
West Islet
Bird Islet
Wreck Reef
Morella
Longreach
Ogmore
C. Manifold
Yeppoon
Rockhampton
Curtis I.
Cato I.
Barcaldine
Alpha
Emerald
Blackwater
Gladstone
Blackall
Bilpela
Moura
Monto
Bundaberg
Hervey Bay
Sandy Cape
Fraser I.
Warrego Ra.
Chesterton Ra.
Mundubbera
Maryborough
Augathella
Charleville
Mitchell
Roma
Miles
Gympie
Tewantin-Noosa
Caloundra
Quilpie
Cooladdi
Chinchilla
Surat
Dalby
Moreton I.
Toowoomba
Brisbane
Darling Downs
Saint George
Beenleigh
N. Stradbroke I.
Cunnamulla
Bollon
Warwick
Gold Coast
Tweed Heads
Goondiwindi
Stanthorpe
Dirranbandi
Boomi
Casino
Lismore
Tenterfield
Moree
Inverell
Glen Innes
Grafton
Brewarrina
Walgett
Bourke
Narrabri
Armidale
Coffs Harbour
Coonamble
Gunnedah
Tamworth
Kempsey
NEW SOUTH WALES
Cobar
Nyngan
Gilgandra
Port Macquarie
Warren
Narromine
Dubbo
Taree
Wellington
Mudgee
Singleton
Sugarloaf Pt.
Condobolin
Parkes
Maitland
Port Stephens
Newcastle
Hillston
Forbes
Orange
Bathurst
Lithgow
Katoomba
West Wyalong
Cowra
Sydney
Griffith
Young
Camden
Hay
Leeton
Temora
Cootamundra
Wollongong
Narrandera
Goulburn
Bomaderry
Jervis Bay
Wagga Wagga
Tumut
Canberra
Queanbeyan
AUSTL. CAP. TERR.
Riverina
AUSTRALIAN CAPITAL TERR.
Deniliquin
Finley
Echuca
Albury
Wodonga
Cooma
Shepparton
Mt. Kosciusko 2,228 m
Wangaratta
Australian Alps
VICTORIA
Bendigo
Seymour
Bega
Melton
Orbost
C. Howe
Melbourne
Moe
Sale
Bairnsdale
Morwell
Traralgon
Wonthaggi
Corner Inlet
C. Otway
Wilsons Promontory
South East Pt.
Bass Strait
King I.
Furneaux Group
Flinders I.
Hunter I.
Cape Barren I.
Smithton
Wynyard
George Town
Eddystone Pt.
West Pt.
Ulverstone
Devonport
Launceston
Mt. Ossa 1,617 m
Queenstown
TASMANIA
Macquarie Hbr.
New Norfolk
Hobart
Tasman Pen.
South West C.

Three Kings Is.
North C.
C. Maria van Diemen
Te Kao
C. Kerikeri
C. Brett
Kaitaia
Kaikohe
Whangarei
TASMAN SEA
Dargaville
Great Barrier I.
Kaipara Har.
Warkworth
Waitemata
Takapuna
Coromandel
Coromandel Peninsula
Auckland
Manukau
Thames
North Island
Huntly
Te Aroha
Bay of Plenty
Mount Maunganui
Te Araroa
Hamilton
Tauranga
Whakatane
East C.
Te Awamutu
Cambridge
Hikurangi 1,754 m
Tokoroa
Rotorua
Kawerau
Te Kuiti
Murupara
North Taranaki Bight
Taupo
Gisborne
NEW ZEALAND
New Plymouth
Turangi
Wairoa
C. Egmont
Waitara
Stratford
Mt Ngauruhoe 2,291 m
Mt Egmont 2,518 m
Hawera
Mt Ruapehu 2,797 m
Mahia Pen.
Hawke Bay
Hastings
Napier
South Taranaki Bight
Havelock North
Wanganui
Dannevirke
Ashhurst
Waipukurau
C. Farewell
Tasman Bay
Palmerston North
Collingwood
Levin
Karamea Bight
Paraparaumu
Masterton
Motueka
Porirua
Karamea
Wellington
Upper Hutt
Mt Owen 1,875 m
Nelson
Blenheim
Lower Hutt
C. Palliser
Westport
Cook Strait
C. Foulwind
Ward
Murchison
Reefton
Mt Una 2,301 m
Clarence
Greymouth
Lewis Pass
Kaikoura
Hokitika
Otira
Waikari
Arthur's Pass
Pegasus Bay
Rangiora
Fox Glacier
Darfield
Kaiapoi
Mt Cook 3,764 m
Christchurch
Haast
Banks Pen.
Southern Alps
Ashburton
Geraldine
Mt Aspiring 3,027 m
Temuka
South Island
Twizel
Canterbury Bight
Timaru
Wanaka
Waimate
Queenstown
Cromwell
Oamaru
PACIFIC OCEAN
Te Anau
Alexandra
Palmerston
Lumsden
West C.
Mosgiel
Dunedin
Milton
Gore
Balclutha
Riverton
Invercargill
Bluff
Foveaux Strait
Mt Anglem 980 m
Oban
South C.
Stewart I.
Snares Is.

SCALE 1:10,500,000 LAMBERT CONFORMAL CONIC PROJECTION
MILES 0 150 300
KILOMETERS 0 150 300

Norfolk I. (AUSTL.)
Kingston
Lord Howe I. (N.S. WALES)
PACIFIC OCEAN
TASMAN SEA
Three Kings Is.
North C.
NEW ZEALAND
North Island
Great Barrier I.
Auckland

9 10 11 12 5 6 7
35° 40° 45° 30° 35°

J 155° K 160° L 165° M 170° N 175° P

POPULATION OF CITIES AND TOWNS
OVER 2,000,000
1,000,000 - 1,999,999
500,000 - 999,999
100,000 - 499,999
50,000 - 99,999
UNDER 50,000

SCALE 1:14,000,000 OPTIMAL CONFORMAL PROJECTION
MILES 0 200 400 600
KILOMETERS 0 200 400 600

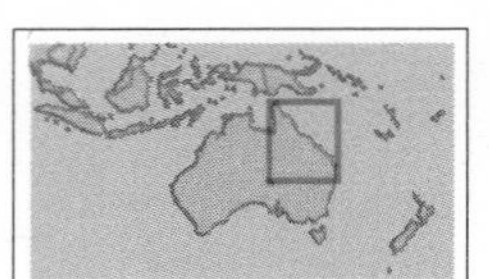

Northeastern Australia

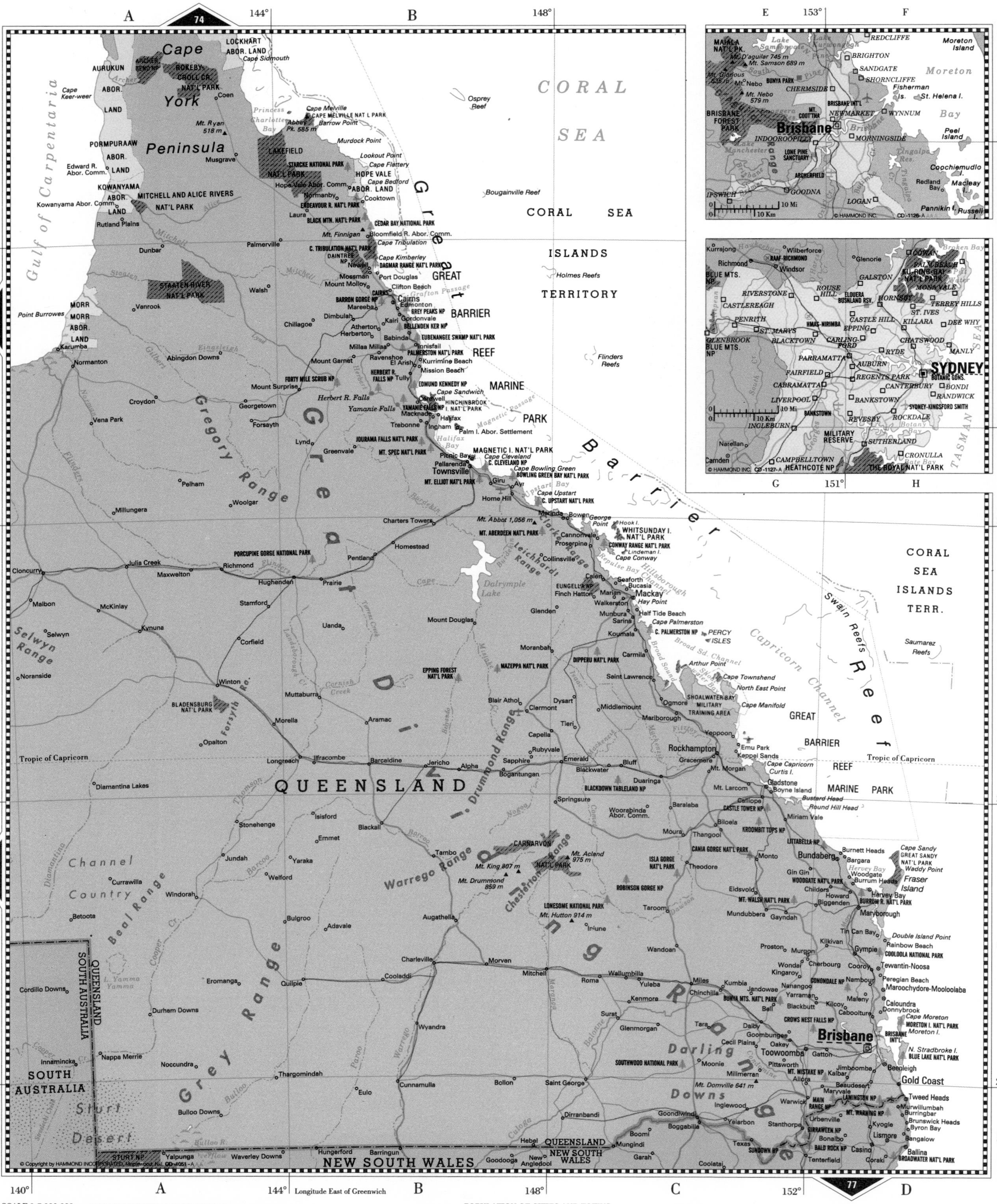

SCALE 1:7,000,000 LAMBERT CONFORMAL CONIC PROJECTION

MILES 0 100 200 300

KILOMETERS 0 100 200 300

Longitude East of Greenwich

POPULATION OF CITIES AND TOWNS

- OVER 2,000,000
- 1,000,000 - 1,999,999
- 500,000 - 999,999
- 250,000 - 499,999
- 100,000 - 249,999
- 30,000 - 99,999
- 10,000 - 29,999
- UNDER 10,000

Southeastern Australia

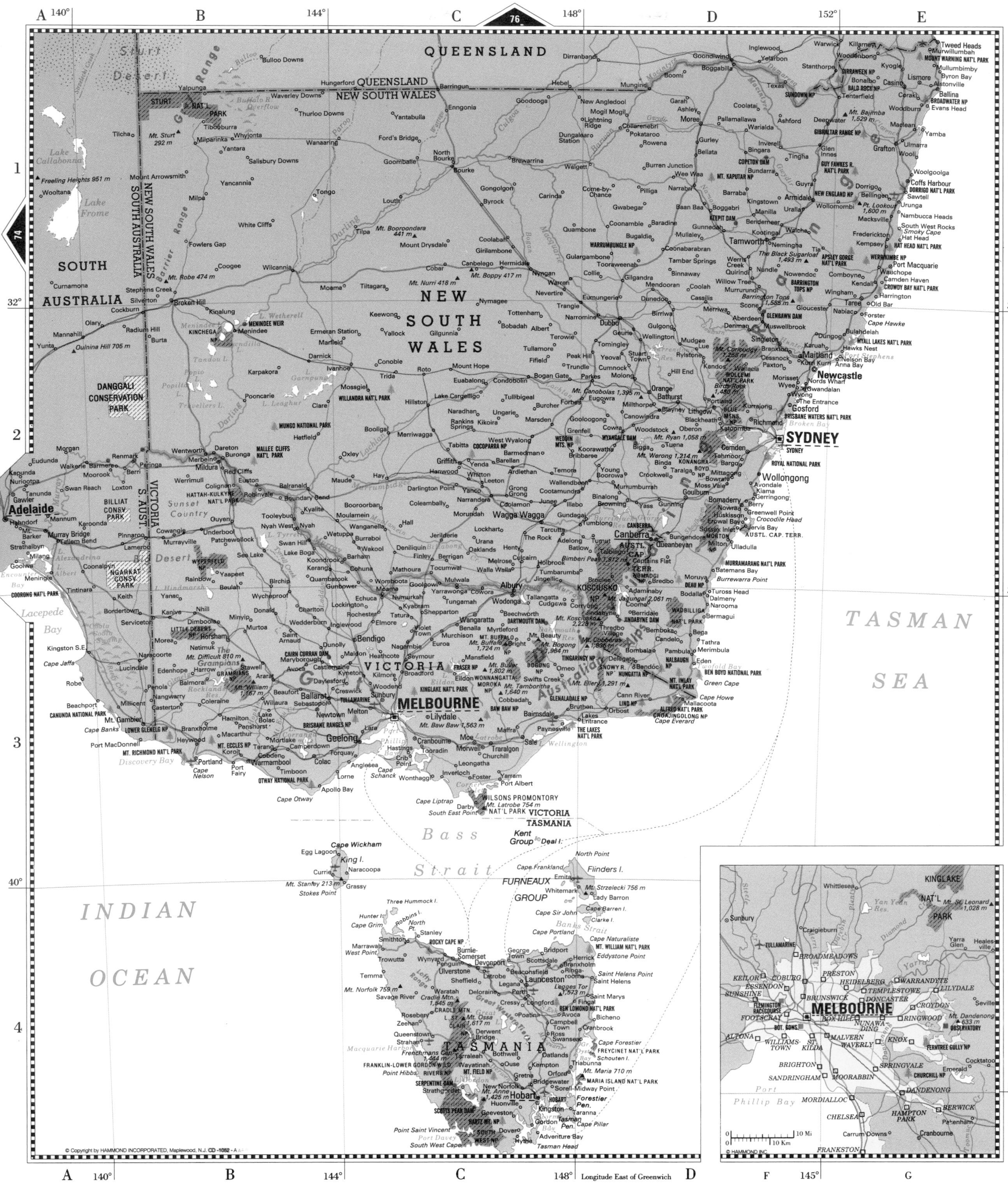

QUEENSLAND

NEW SOUTH WALES

SOUTH AUSTRALIA

VICTORIA

TASMANIA

AUSTL. CAP. TERR.

INDIAN OCEAN

TASMAN SEA

Bass Strait

SYDNEY

MELBOURNE

Adelaide

Canberra

Hobart

Newcastle

Wollongong

Geelong

Launceston

Longitude East of Greenwich

SCALE 1:7,000,000 LAMBERT CONFORMAL CONIC PROJECTION

MILES 0 100 200 300

KILOMETERS 0 100 200 300

POPULATION OF CITIES AND TOWNS

- OVER 2,000,000
- 1,000,000 - 1,999,999
- 500,000 - 999,999
- 250,000 - 499,999
- 100,000 - 249,999
- 30,000 - 99,999
- 10,000 - 29,999
- UNDER 10,000

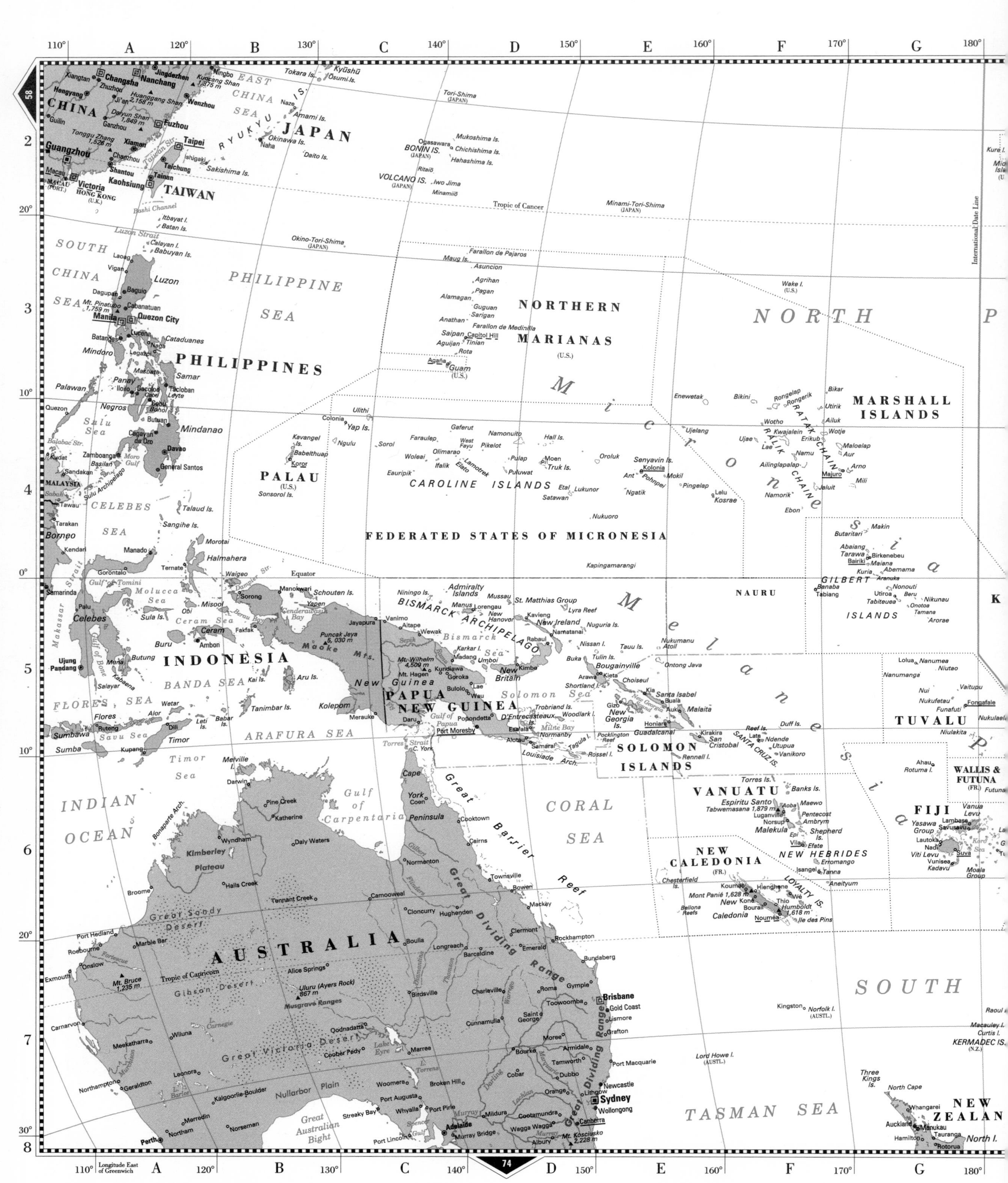

58
74
110°
120°
130°
140°
150°
160°
170°
180°
A
B
C
D
E
F
G
2
3
4
5
6
7
8
20°
10°
0°
30°
Longitude East of Greenwich
CHINA
Xiangtan
Changsha
Jingdezhen
Nanchang
Ningbo
Kuocang Shan 1,375 m
Hengyang
Zhuzhou
Ji'an
Huanggang Shan 2,158 m
Wenzhou
Guilin
Daiyun Shan 1,849 m
Ganzhou
Fuzhou
Tonggu Zhang 1,526 m
Xiamen
Guangzhou
Chaozhou
Shantou
Macau
MACAU (PORT.)
Victoria
HONG KONG (U.K.)
Taipei
Taichung
Tainan
Kaohsiung
TAIWAN
Bashi Channel
Taiwan Str.
EAST CHINA SEA
RYUKYU IS.
Tokara Is.
Kyūshū
Ōsumi Is.
Naze
Amami Is.
JAPAN
Okinawa Is.
Naha
Daito Is.
Ishigaki
Sakishima Is.
Tori-Shima (JAPAN)
Mukoshima Is.
Ogasawara
BONIN IS. (JAPAN)
Chichishima Is.
Hahashima Is.
Ritaiō
VOLCANO IS. (JAPAN)
Iwo Jima
Minamiiō
Tropic of Cancer
Minami-Tori-Shima (JAPAN)
International Date Line
Kure I.
Itbayat I.
Batan Is.
Luzon Strait
Calayan I.
Babuyan Is.
SOUTH CHINA SEA
Okino-Tori-Shima (JAPAN)
Laoag
Vigan
Luzon
PHILIPPINE SEA
Dagupan
Baguio
Mt. Pinatubo 1,759 m
Cabanatuan
Manila
Quezon City
Batangas
Lucena
Naga
Catanduanes
Mindoro
Legazpi
PHILIPPINES
Masbate
Samar
Palawan
Panay
Iloilo
Bacolod
Cebu
Tacloban
Leyte
Negros
Bohol
Quezon
Sulu Sea
Butuan
Cagayan de Oro
Mindanao
Balabac Str.
Zamboanga
Davao
Kudat
Basilan
Moro Gulf
General Santos
Sandakan
MALAYSIA
Sabah
Sulu Archipelago
Tawau
CELEBES SEA
Talaud Is.
Sangihe Is.
Tarakan
Borneo
Kendari
Manado
Morotai
Halmahera
Ternate
Gorontalo
Gulf of Tomini
Waigeo
Dampier Str.
Equator
Samarinda
Makassar Strait
Molucca Sea
Sorong
Manokwari
Schouten Is.
Yapen
Palu
Misool
Obi
Celebes
Sula Is.
Ceram Sea
Berau Bay
Cenderawasih Bay
Jayapura
Ceram
Fakfak
Buru
Ambon
Puncak Jaya 5,030 m
Maoke Mts.
Gulf of Bone
Ujung Pandang
Butung
Muna
Kabaena
INDONESIA
Salayar
BANDA SEA
Kai Is.
Aru Is.
New Guinea
FLORES SEA
Wetar
Alor
Tanimbar Is.
Kolepom
Merauke
Flores
Ruteng
Sumbawa
Savu Sea
Leti Is.
Babar Is.
Dili
Timor
ARAFURA SEA
Sumba
Kupang
Timor Sea
Melville I.
Darwin
INDIAN OCEAN
Bonaparte Arch.
Pine Creek
Katherine
Gulf of Carpentaria
Wyndham
Daly Waters
Kimberley Plateau
Halls Creek
Broome
Tennant Creek
Camooweal
Great Sandy Desert
Port Hedland
Marble Bar
Roebourne
Onslow
Exmouth
Mt. Bruce 1,235 m
Tropic of Capricorn
Gibson Desert
AUSTRALIA
Alice Springs
Uluru (Ayers Rock) 867 m
Musgrave Ranges
Carnarvon
Wiluna
Meekatharra
Oodnadatta
Great Victoria Desert
Coober Pedy
Lake Eyre
Marree
Leonora
Northampton
Geraldton
Kalgoorlie-Boulder
Nullarbor Plain
Woomera
Port Augusta
Whyalla
Port Pirie
Broken Hill
Merredin
Northam
Perth
Norseman
Great Australian Bight
Streaky Bay
Port Lincoln
Spencer Gulf
Adelaide
Murray Bridge
Murray
Mildura
Ninigo Is.
Admiralty Islands
Manus
Lorengau
Mussau
St. Matthias Group
BISMARCK ARCHIPELAGO
New Hanover
Kavieng
New Ireland
Lyra Reef
Vanimo
Aitape
Wewak
Sepik
Bismarck Sea
Rabaul
Namatanai
Karkar I.
Madang
Umboi
Mt. Wilhelm 4,509 m
Mt. Hagen
Kundiawa
Goroka
New Britain
Kimbe
Bulolo
Lae
Wau
PAPUA NEW GUINEA
Solomon Sea
Fly
Daru
Gulf of Papua
Popondetta
Port Moresby
D'Entrecasteaux Is.
Trobriand Is.
Woodlark I.
Milne Bay
Esa'ala
Alotau
Samarai
Normanby
Louisiade Arch.
Tagula I.
Rossel I.
Torres Strait
C. York
Cape York Peninsula
Coen
Cooktown
Cairns
Great Barrier Reef
Normanton
Gilbert
Flinders
Townsville
Bowen
Cloncurry
Hughenden
Mackay
Great Dividing Range
Boulia
Clermont
Emerald
Rockhampton
Longreach
Barcaldine
Bundaberg
Diamantina
Thomson
Birdsville
Charleville
Roma
Gympie
Brisbane
Gold Coast
Toowoomba
Lismore
Grafton
Cunnamulla
Saint George
Moree
Armidale
Bourke
Tamworth
Port Macquarie
Darling
Dubbo
Cobar
Newcastle
Lachlan
Orange
Lithgow
Sydney
Wollongong
Cootamundra
Wagga Wagga
Canberra
Albury
Mt. Kosciusko 2,228 m
CORAL SEA
Farallon de Pajaros
Maug Is.
Asuncion
Agrihan
Pagan
Alamagan
Guguan
Sarigan
Anathan
Farallon de Medinilla
Saipan
Capitol Hill
Tinian
Aguijan
Rota
Agaña
Guam (U.S.)
NORTHERN MARIANAS (U.S.)
Micronesia
Wake I. (U.S.)
NORTH P
Ulithi
Colonia
Yap Is.
Ngulu
Sorol
Faraulep
Gaferut
West Fayu
Namonuito
Hall Is.
Kayangel Is.
Babelthuap
Koror
Woleai
Olimarao
Ifalik
Elato
Lamotrek
Pikelot
Pulap
Puluwat
Moen
Truk Is.
Oroluk
Senyavin Is.
Kolonia
Pohnpei
Mokil
Pingelap
PALAU (U.S.)
Sonsorol Is.
Eauripik
CAROLINE ISLANDS
Etal
Satawan
Lukunor
Ant
Ngatik
Lelu
Kosrae
Nukuoro
FEDERATED STATES OF MICRONESIA
Kapingamarangi
Enewetak
Bikini
Rongelap
Rongerik
Bikar
Utirik
Ailuk
Ujelang
Wotho
Kwajalein
Erikub
Wotje
Ujae
Lae
RATAK CHAIN
RALIK CHAIN
Namu
Maloelap
Aur
Ailinglapalap
Arno
Majuro
Mili
Namorik
Jaluit
Ebon
MARSHALL ISLANDS
Makin
Butaritari
Abaiang
Tarawa
Birkenebeu
Bairiki
Maiana
Abemama
Kuria
Aranuka
GILBERT ISLANDS
Banaba
Tabiang
Nonouti
Utiroa
Tabiteuea
Beru
Nikunau
Onotoa
Tamana
Arorae
NAURU
K
Melanesia
Nukumanu Atoll
Tauu Is.
Nissan I.
Buka
Tulin Is.
Bougainville
Arawa
Kieta
Ontong Java
Shortland I.
Choiseul
New Georgia
Gizo
New Georgia Is.
Kia
Santa Isabel
Buala
Auki
Malaita
Honiara
Guadalcanal
Pocklington Reef
SOLOMON ISLANDS
Kirakira
San Cristobal
Rennell I.
Reef Is.
Lata
Ndende
Utupua
Vanikoro
SANTA CRUZ IS.
Duff Is.
Lolua
Nanumea
Niutao
Nanumanga
Nui
Vaitupu
Nukufetau
Funafuti
Fongafale
TUVALU
Nukulaela
Niulakita
Polynesia
Ahau
Rotuma I.
WALLIS & FUTUNA (FR.)
Futuna
Torres Is.
Banks Is.
VANUATU
Espiritu Santo
Tabwemasana 1,879 m
Aoba
Maewo
Luganville
Pentecost
Norsup
Ambrym
Malekula
Epi
Shepherd Is.
Vila
Efate
NEW HEBRIDES
Erromango
Isangel
Tanna
Aneityum
FIJI
Vanua Levu
Lambasa
Yasawa Group
Savusavu
Lautoka
Nadi
Viti Levu
Vunisea
Kadavu
Suva
Koro Sea
Moala Group
NEW CALEDONIA (FR.)
Chesterfield Is.
Mont Panié 1,628 m
Koumac
Hienghène
Wé
LOYALTY IS.
New Caledonia
Koné
Bourail
Thio
Humboldt 1,618 m
Bellona Reefs
Nouméa
Île des Pins
SOUTH
Kingston
Norfolk I. (AUSTL.)
Raoul I.
Macauley I.
Curtis I.
KERMADEC IS. (N.Z.)
Lord Howe I. (AUSTL.)
TASMAN SEA
Three Kings Is.
North Cape
Whangarei
NEW ZEALAN
Auckland
Manukau
Tauranga
Hamilton
Rotorua
North I.

Central Pacific Ocean

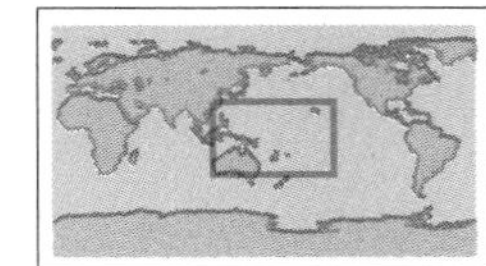

H 170° J 160° K 150° L 140° M

Pearl and Hermes Reef
Lisianski I.
Laysan I.
Maro Reef
HAWAIIAN
HAWAII
(U.S.)
French Frigate Shoals
Necker I.
Nihoa
Tropic of Cancer
Kauai
Niihau
Oahu
Honolulu
Molokai
Maui
Lanai
ISLANDS
Hilo
Hawaii
PACIFIC
Johnston Atoll
(U.S.)
OCEAN
Polynesia
Kingman Reef (U.S.)
Palmyra
(U.S.)
Teraina (Washington I.)
Tabuaeran (Fanning I.)
LINE
Kiritimati (Christmas I.)
Howland I. (U.S.)
Baker I. (U.S.)
Equator
Jarvis I.
(U.S.)
KIRIBATI
PHOENIX IS.
Abariringa (Canton)
Enderbury
McKean
Birnie
Rawaki (Phoenix)
Nikumaroro (Gardner)
Orona (Hull)
Manra (Sydney)
Malden I.
ISLANDS
Starbuck I.
Atafu
TOKELAU
(N.Z.)
Nukunonu
Fakaofo
Tongareva (Penrhyn)
Rakahanga
Caroline I.
Vostok I.
Swains I.
Manihiki
Pukapuka
NORTHERN
Nassau
COOK IS.
Flint I.
WESTERN SAMOA
AMERICAN SAMOA
Mt. Silisili 1,858 m
Asau
Apia
Pago Pago
Savai'i
Upolu
Tutuila
Manua Is.
Suwarrow
COOK ISLANDS
(N.Z.)
Niuafo'ou
Rose I.
Niuatoputapu Group
Palmerston Atoll
Aitutaki Atoll
Amuri
Manuae Atoll
Mitiaro
Atiu
Mauke
SOUTHERN
COOK IS.
Neiafu
Vava'u Group
Alofi
Niue
Tofua
Pangai
Ha'apai Group
NIUE
(N.Z.)
Nuku'alofa
Eua
TONGA
Avarua
Rarotonga
Mangaia
Eiao
MARQUESAS ISLANDS
Nuku Hiva
Taiohae
Hakahau
Ua Pou
Ua Huka
Hiva Oa
Atuona
Tahuata
Fatu Hiva
King George Is.
Disappointment Is.
Iles sous le Vent
Bellingshausen
Maupiti
Tupai
Bora Bora
Tikehau
Rangiroa
Manihi
Takaroa
Takapoto
Tepoto
Napuka
Pukapuka
Tiputa
Makatea
Arutua
Apataki
Kaukura
Toau
Fakarava
Huahine
Raiatea
Uturoa
Tetiaroa
Moorea
Papeete
Faaa
Tahiti
Iles du Vent
SOCIETY IS.
Anaa
Takanea
Makemo
Raroia
Fangatau
Fakahina
TUAMOTU ARCHIPELAGO
Hikueru
Marokau
Amanu
Otepa
Hao
Tatakoto
Pukarua
Reao
Vahitahi
Nukutavake
FRENCH POLYNESIA
Hereheretue
Duke of Gloucester Is.
Vanavaro
Tureia
Actaeon Group
Maria I.
Moerai
Rurutu
Rimatara
Mataura
Tubuai
AUSTRAL ISLANDS (Tubuai Islands)
Raivavae
Fangataufa
Mururoa
Marutea
Maria
Morane
Rikitea
Taravai
Mangareva
Temoe
GAMBIER IS.
PITCAIRN ISLANDS
(U.K.)
Oeno I.
Henderson I.
Adamstown
Pitcairn I.
Ducie I.
Tropic of Capricorn
PACIFIC
OCEAN
Rapa
Marotiri (Bass Is.)
Easter Island (Isla de Pascua)
(CHILE)
International Date Line

H 170° J 160° K 150° L 140° M 130° N 120° P 110° Longitude West of Greenwich Q 100°

R 172° S 171° T

Cape Mulinu'u
Savai'i
Asau
Mt. Silisili 1,858 m
WESTERN SAMOA
Sala'ilua
Satupaitea
Apolima Str.
Faleolo
Apia
Upolu
APIA (FALEOLO)
APIA (FAGALI)
Mt. Fito 1,113 m
Tiavea
WESTERN SAMOA
AMERICAN SAMOA
AMERICAN SAMOA
PACIFIC OCEAN
Pago Pago
Tutuila
PAGO PAGO INT'L
0 30 Mi
0 30 Km
© HAMMOND INC. CD - 1132

164° U 166° V 168°

Ile Art
Iles Bélep
Ile Baaba
NEW CALEDONIA
(FRANCE)
Ile Yandé
Ile Balabio
PACIFIC OCEAN
Loyalty Islands
Mont Panié 1,628 m
Koumac
Hienghene
Lagon d'Ouvéa
Ouvéa
Chépénéhé
Wé
New Caledonia
Voh
Lifou
Koné
Ile Tiga
CORAL SEA
Bourail
Canala
Thio
Tadine
Maré
Humboldt 1,618 m
NOUMEA (TONTOUTA)
Nouméa
Canal de la Havannah
I. Ouen
Ile des Pins
0 60 Mi
0 60 Km
© HAMMOND INC. CD - 131

W 150° X 149°

Tetiaroa
FRENCH POLYNESIA
Moorea
Papetoai
Mt. Tohivea 1,207 m
Afareaitu
Pte Nuupere
Faaa
Pte Vénus
Papenoo
Papeete
PAPEETE (FAAA)
Mahaena
Maiao
Punaauia
Mt. Orohena 2,241 m
Tahiti
Tautira
Papara
PACIFIC OCEAN
Iles du Vent
Taiarapu Pen.
Mt Roniu 1,323 m
0 30 Mi
0 30 Km
© HAMMOND INC. CD - 1133

177° Y 179° Z

Undu Pt.
PACIFIC OCEAN
Vanua Levu
Labasa
Natewa Bay
Rambi
FIJI
Nasorolevu 1,032 m
Yasawa Group
Waiyevo
Taveuni
Bligh Water
Nanuku Passage
Koro
Koro Sea
Lautoka
Vatukoula
Ba
Ovalau
NADI (INTERNATIONAL)
Tomanivi 1,323 m
Levuka
Nadi
Thithia
SUVA (NASORI)
Ngau
Viti Levu
Suva
Mbengga
Kandavu Passage
0 60 Mi
0 60 Km
© HAMMOND INC. CD - 1131

9 14° 10 11 20° 12 22° 13 14 17° 15 18° 16 17 17° 18 20° 7 30° 8

POPULATION OF CITIES AND TOWNS
- OVER 3,000,000
- 1,000,000 - 2,999,999
- 500,000 - 999,999
- 100,000 - 499,999
- UNDER 100,000

SCALE 1:31,500,000 LAMBERT AZIMUTHAL EQUAL-AREA PROJECTION
MILES 0 400 800 1200
KILOMETERS 0 400 800 1200

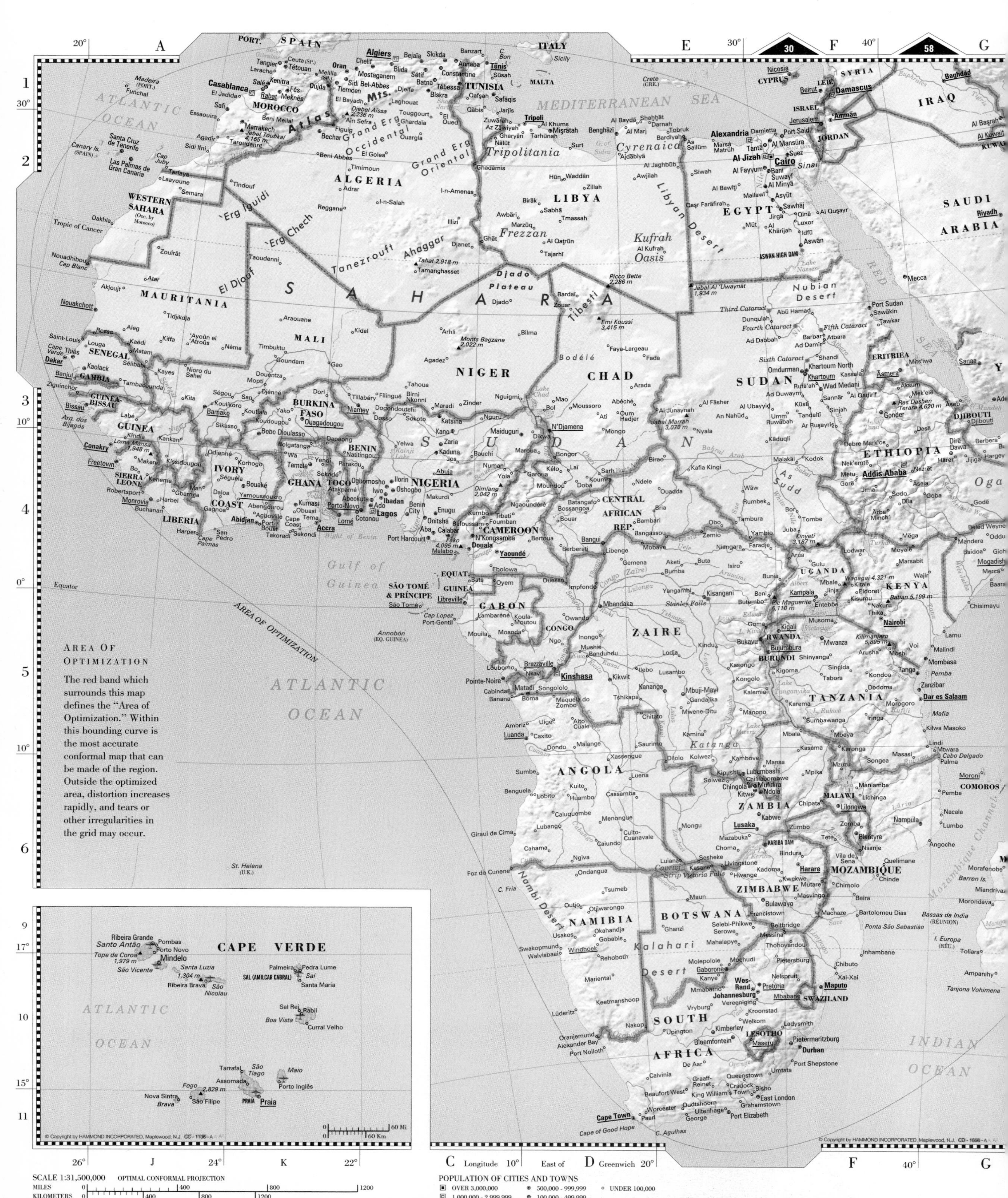

ATLANTIC OCEAN
MEDITERRANEAN SEA
PORT.
SPAIN
ITALY
Sicily
MALTA
Crete (GRE.)
CYPRUS
Nicosia
SYRIA
LEB.
Beirut
Damascus
IRAQ
Baghdad
ISRAEL
Jerusalem
'Ammān
JORDAN
Al Başrah
Al Kuwait
SAUDI ARABIA
Riyadh
Mecca
RED SEA
MOROCCO
Rabat
Casablanca
Marrakech
Jebel Toubkal 4,165 m
Atlas Mts.
Madeira (PORT.)
Funchal
Canary Is. (SPAIN)
Santa Cruz de Tenerife
Las Palmas de Gran Canaria
ALGERIA
Algiers
Oran
Grand Erg Occidental
Grand Erg Oriental
TUNISIA
Tūnis
LIBYA
Tripoli
Tripolitania
Cyrenaica
Benghāzī
Frezzan
Kufrah Oasis
Libyan Desert
EGYPT
Cairo
Alexandria
Al Jīzah
Aswān
ASWAN HIGH DAM
Lake Nasser
Sinai
WESTERN SAHARA (Occ. by Morocco)
Tropic of Cancer
MAURITANIA
Nouakchott
SAHARA
El Djouf
Erg Iguidi
Erg Chech
Tanezrouft
Ahaggar
Tahat 2,918 m
Djado Plateau
Tibesti
Emi Koussi 3,415 m
MALI
NIGER
CHAD
SUDAN
Nubian Desert
Khartoum
Third Cataract
Fourth Cataract
Fifth Cataract
Sixth Cataract
SENEGAL
Dakar
GAMBIA
Banjul
GUINEA-BISSAU
Bissau
GUINEA
Conakry
SIERRA LEONE
Freetown
LIBERIA
Monrovia
IVORY COAST
Abidjan
BURKINA FASO
Ouagadougou
GHANA
Accra
TOGO
Lomé
BENIN
Porto-Novo
NIGERIA
Lagos
Niamey
Bamako
N'Djamena
Lake Chad
Bodélé
Monts Bagzane 2,022 m
Jabal Marrah 3,070 m
SUDAN
Gulf of Guinea
Bight of Benin
CAMEROON
Yaoundé
Douala
Fako 4,095 m
EQUAT. GUINEA
Malabo
SÃO TOMÉ & PRÍNCIPE
São Tomé
GABON
Libreville
Cap Lopez
Annobón (EQ. GUINEA)
CONGO
Brazzaville
CENTRAL AFRICAN REP.
Bangui
ZAIRE
Kinshasa
Congo (Zaire)
As Sudd
ERITREA
Asmera
ETHIOPIA
Addis Ababa
Ras Dashen Terara 4,620 m
DJIBOUTI
Djibouti
UGANDA
Kampala
KENYA
Nairobi
Batian 5,199 m
Margherita 5,110 m
Lake Victoria
RWANDA
Kigali
BURUNDI
Bujumbura
TANZANIA
Dar es Salaam
Kilimanjaro 5,895 m
Lake Tanganyika
ANGOLA
Luanda
Katanga
ZAMBIA
Lusaka
MALAWI
Lilongwe
MOZAMBIQUE
Maputo
Mozambique Channel
COMOROS
Moroni
ZIMBABWE
Harare
Victoria Falls
KARIBA DAM
Caprivi Strip
NAMIBIA
Windhoek
Namib Desert
BOTSWANA
Gaborone
Kalahari Desert
SOUTH AFRICA
Pretoria
Johannesburg
SWAZILAND
Mbabane
LESOTHO
Maseru
Cape Town
Cape of Good Hope
C. Agulhas
Durban
Port Elizabeth
INDIAN OCEAN
St. Helena (U.K.)
Bassas da India (RÉUNION)
I. Europa (RÉU.)
Equator
AREA OF OPTIMIZATION
Area Of Optimization
The red band which surrounds this map defines the "Area of Optimization." Within this bounding curve is the most accurate conformal map that can be made of the region. Outside the optimized area, distortion increases rapidly, and tears or other irregularities in the grid may occur.
CAPE VERDE
Santo Antão
Mindelo
São Vicente
Santa Luzia
São Nicolau
Sal
Boa Vista
Maio
São Tiago
Fogo 2,829 m
Brava
PRAIA
Praia
30
58
© Copyright by HAMMOND INCORPORATED, Maplewood, N.J.
C Longitude 10° East of D Greenwich 20°
SCALE 1:31,500,000 OPTIMAL CONFORMAL PROJECTION
MILES 0 400 800 1200
KILOMETERS 0 400 800 1200
POPULATION OF CITIES AND TOWNS
OVER 3,000,000
1,000,000 - 2,999,999
500,000 - 999,999
100,000 - 499,999
UNDER 100,000

Africa

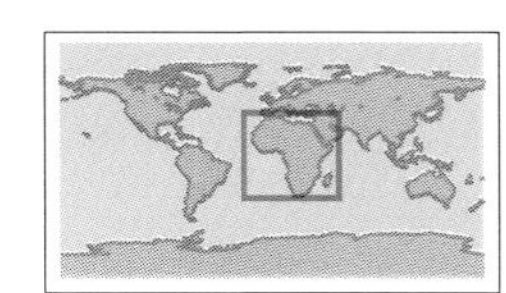

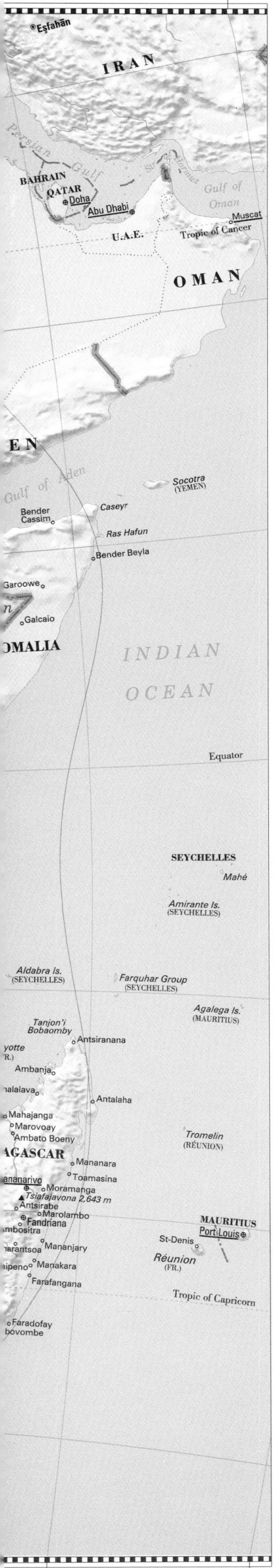

IRAN
BAHRAIN
QATAR
Doha
Abu Dhabi
U.A.E.
Muscat
Tropic of Cancer
OMAN
Gulf of Aden
Socotra (YEMEN)
SOMALIA
INDIAN OCEAN
Equator
SEYCHELLES
Mahé
Amirante Is. (SEYCHELLES)
Aldabra Is. (SEYCHELLES)
Farquhar Group (SEYCHELLES)
Agalega Is. (MAURITIUS)
Tromelin (RÉUNION)
MAURITIUS
Port Louis
St-Denis
Réunion (FR.)
Tropic of Capricorn
ATLANTIC OCEAN
MEDITERRANEAN SEA
SPAIN
Strait of Gibraltar
Gibraltar (U.K.)
Ceuta (SP.)
Tangier
Tétouan
Larache
Kenitra
Salé
Rabat
Casablanca
Meknès
Fès
Taza
Nador
Melilla (SP.)
Oujda
MOROCCO
Er Rif
Atlas Mts.
ALG.
Algiers
Blida
Médéa
Chlef
Mostaganem
Oran
Sidi Bel-Abbes
Tlemcen
Tiaret
Saïda
Djelfa
M'Sila
Bejaïa
ALGERIA
Tell Atlas
Atlas Mts.
Skikda
Annaba
Constantine
Sétif
Batna
Tébessa
Khenchela
Souk Ahras
Bizerte
Tunis
Sūsah
Al Qayrawān
Al Qaşrayn
TUNISIA
Dorsale
Mts. de Tebessa
Gulf of Tunis
© HAMMOND INC.

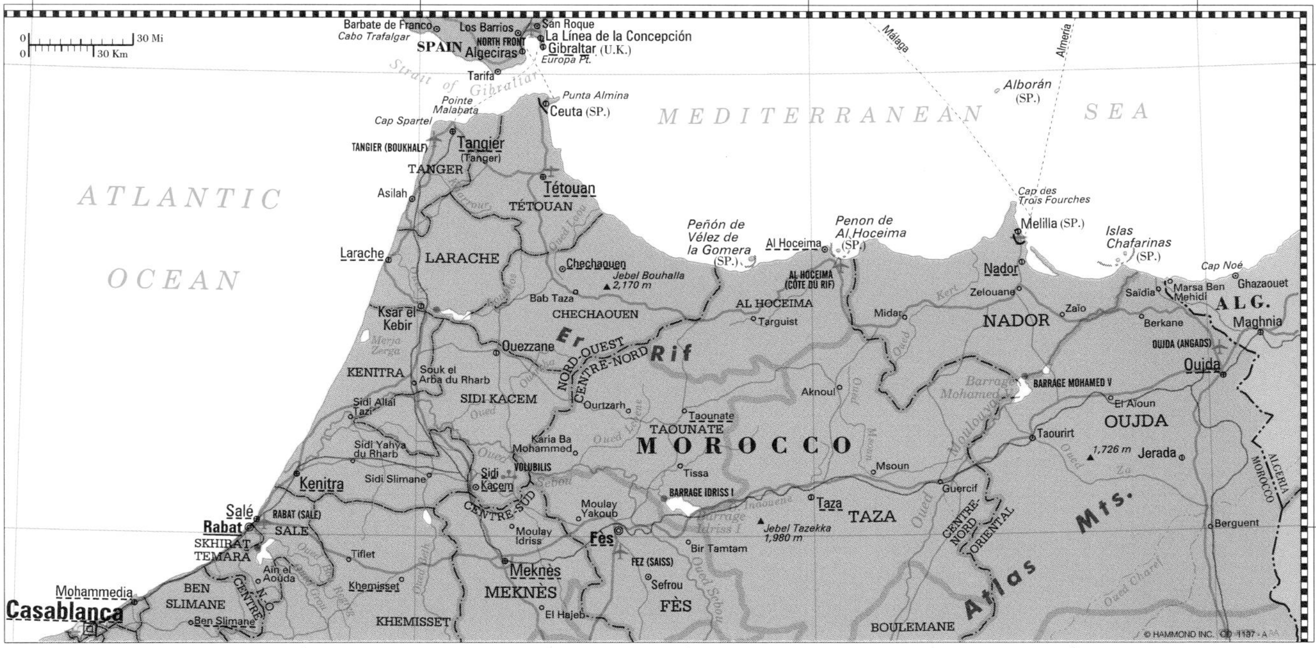

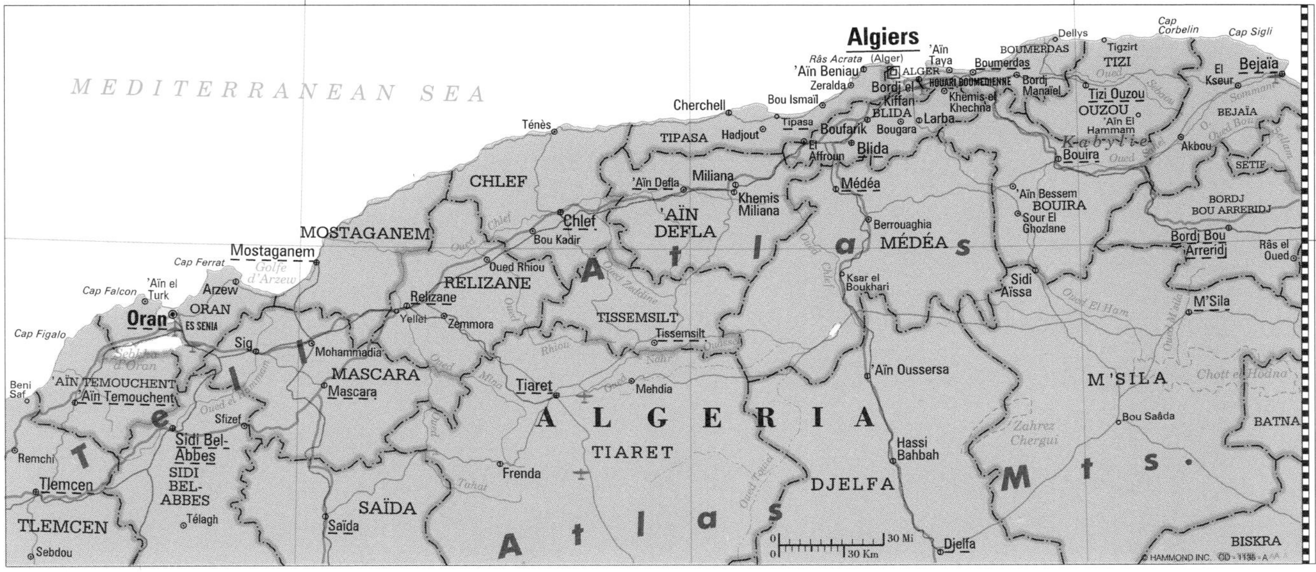

A
B
C
D
E
F
G
H
J
1
2
3
4
5
6
7
8
30°
25°
20°
15°
10°
5°
0°
Longitude West of Greenwich
Longitude East of Greenwich
ATLANTIC OCEAN
Mediterranean Sea
Canary Is. (SP.)
Madeira (PORT.)
Funchal
Santa Cruz de Tenerife
Las Palmas de Gran Canaria
Tenerife
La Palma
Gomera
Hierro
Gran Canaria
Lanzarote
Fuerteventura
Arrecife
Pico de Teide 3,718 m
SPAIN
Marbella
Almería
Gibraltar (U.K.)
Str. of Gibraltar
Tangier (Tanger)
Ceuta (SP.)
Tétouan
Melilla (SP.)
Larache
Kenitra
Salé
Rabat
Casablanca
El Jadida
Safi
Essaouira
Marrakech
Agadir
Inezgane
Sidi Ifni
Tiznit
Tata
Tan-Tan
Tarfaya
Cap Juby
Meknès
Fès
Taza
Oujda
Er Rif
Moyen Atlas
Haut Atlas
Anti-Atlas
Jebel Toubkal 4,165 m
Adrar bou Nasser 3,340 m
Jebel Mesrouh 2,714 m
Adrar Mkorn 3,222 m
Ouarzazate
Er Rachidia
Tinrhir
Erfoud
Taroudannt
Khouribga
Beni Mellal
Oued Zem
Khenifra
MOROCCO
Al Maghrib
Hamada du Drâa
WESTERN SAHARA (occ. by Morocco)
Laayoune
Cabo Bojador
Semara
Dakhla
Guelta Zemmur
Tifariti
Zug
Tichla
Agûenit
Tropic of Cancer
ALGERIA
Algiers (El Djezaïr)
Oran
Tlemcen
Sidi Bel-Abbes
Mostaganem
Relizane
Tiaret
Saïda
Mascara
Cherchell
Blida
Bouira
Béjaïa
Jijel
Skikda
Annaba
Constantine
Sétif
Batna
Biskra
Tébessa
Souk Ahras
Djelfa
Laghouat
El Bayadh
Aïn Sefra
Figuig
Beni Ounif
Bechar
Taghit
Beni Abbes
Tabelbala
Kerzaz
Timimoun
El Golea
Ghardaïa
Ouargla
Touggourt
El Oued
Hassi Messaoud
Atlas Saharien
Djebel Aïssa 2,236 m
Djebel Mahmel 2,321 m
Grand Erg Occidental
Grand Erg Oriental
Hamada du Tinrhert
Plateau du Tademaït
Adrar
Reggane
Aoulef
In-Salah
Tidikelt
Erg Iguidi
Erg Chech
El Eglab
Tindouf
Illizi
Djanet
Tassili
Ahaggar
Tahat 2,918 m
Tamanghasset
Silet
In Ebeggi
Garet el Djenoun 2,327 m
Azao 2,158 m
Djebel Telertheba 2,455 m
Tanezrouft
Poste Weygand
Poste Maurice Cortier
Tessalit
Aguelhok
Adrar des Iforas
TUNISIA
Tunis
Bizerte (Banzart)
Cape Bon
Nabul
Susah
Safaqis
Qafsah
Al Qayrawan
Gulf of Gabes
Qabis
Jaz. Jarbah
Tatawin
Pantelleria (IT.)
Pelagie (IT.)
Valletta
MALTA
Tripoli (Tarabulus)
Al Khums
Misratah
Tarhunah
Gharyan
Az Zawiyah
Nalut
Tripolitania
Al Hamadah al Hamra
Ghadamis
Hamadat Tinghert
Sahra Awbari
Fezzan
Sabha
Awbari
Murzuq
Sahra Marzuq
Al Qatrun
Tajarhi
Ghat
Plateau du Djado
Passe de Korizo
Madama
Ténéré du Tafassasset
Djado
Chirfa
Séguédine
Pic Toussidé 3,315 m
Bardai
Zouar
SAHARA
NIGER
Agadez
Aïr
Mont Tamgak 1,988 m
Monts Bagzane 2,022 m
Arlit
Timia
Talak
Erg du Ténéré
Grand Erg de Bilma
Bilma
Dirkou
Fachi
Achegour
Tchin Tabaradene
Tahoua
Dakoro
Maradi
Zinder
Tessaoua
Madaoua
Birni Nkonni
Dogondoutchi
Niamey
Tillabéry
Ouallam
Filingué
Dosso
Gouré
Nguigmi
Diffa
Mainé-Soroa
Lake Chad
Kanem
N'Djamena
MAURITANIA
Nouakchott
Nouadhibou
Cap Blanc
Parc National du Banc d'Arguin
Akjoujt
Atar
Zouîrât
Fdérik
Kediet Ijill 915 m
Adrar
Ouadane
Ouarane
El Khatt
El Djouf
Tidjikdja
Tichit
Trarza
Boutilimit
Aleg
Boûmdeïd
Kiffa
Aoukâr
'Ayoûn el 'Atroûs
Néma
Oualâta
Rosso
Bogué
Kaédi
Matam
Sélibabi
MALI
Araouane
Taoudenni
Azaouâd
Tombouctou (Timbuktu)
Gourma-Rharous
Goundam
Bourem
Gao
Ansongo
Ménaka
Kidal
Anefis I-n-Darane
Hombori Tondo 1,155 m
Douentza
Mopti
Djenné
Bandiagara
Ségou
Bamako
Kati
Kita
Kayes
Nioro du Sahel
Nara
Diéma
Koulikoro
Sikasso
Koutiala
San
Niono
Niger
Bani
PN de la Boucle du Baoulé
SENEGAL
Dakar
Thiès
Saint-Louis
Louga
Linguère
Diourbel
Kaolack
Kaffrine
Tambacounda
Bakel
Kolda
Ziguinchor
Kédougou
C. Verde
Cap Roxo
PN du Niokolo-Koba
GAMBIA
Banjul
GUINEA-BISSAU
Bissau
Arquipélago dos Bijagós
Bafatá
Bubaque
Catió
GUINEA
Conakry
Kindia
Labé
Mamou
Dabola
Kouroussa
Kankan
Faranah
Siguiri
Boké
Fouta Djallon
Kissidougou
Macenta
Nzérékoré
Guéckédou
Beyla
Mont Nimba 1,752 m
SIERRA LEONE
Freetown
Makeni
Bo
Kenema
Loma Mansa 1,948 m
Port Loko
Kambia
C. Sierra Leone
LIBERIA
Monrovia
Robertsport
Harbel
Buchanan
Gbarnga
Greenville
Harper
C. Palmas
C. Saint Ann
Grain Coast
PN de Taï
IVORY COAST (CÔTE D'IVOIRE)
Abidjan
Yamoussoukro
Bouaké
Korhogo
Odienné
Séguéla
Man
Daloa
Gagnoa
Divo
Dimbokro
San Pédro
Tabou
Grand-Bassam
Port-Bouët
Bondoukou
Katiola
Mankono
Ferkessédougou
Barrage de Kossou
PN de la Comoé
Ivory Coast
BURKINA FASO
Ouagadougou
Bobo Dioulasso
Koudougou
Ouahigouya
Kaya
Dori
Fada-N'Gourma
Tenkodogo
Banfora
Gaoua
Dédougou
Djibo
Gorom Gorom
Léo
Po
Black Volta
GHANA
Accra
Kumasi
Tamale
Bole
Wa
Yendi
Sunyani
Wenchi
Obuasi
Koforidua
Cape Coast
Takoradi
Sekondi
Tema
Ashanti Uplands
Lake Volta
Akosombo Dam
C. Three Points
Gold Coast
TOGO
Lomé
Sokodé
Lama-Kara
Bassari
Dapaong
Atakpamé
Kpalimé
BENIN
Porto-Novo
Cotonou
Abomey
Parakou
Djougou
Natitingou
Kandi
Malanville
Savé
Ouidah
PN de la Pendjari
PN du W du Niger
Bight of Benin
NIGERIA
Lagos
Ibadan
Abeokuta
Ogbomosho
Oshogbo
Ilorin
Iseyin
Oyo
Iwo
Ife
Ilesha
Owo
Ado
Benin City
Onitsha
Enugu
Aba
Owerri
Port Harcourt
Calabar
Warri
Ogoja
Lokoja
Bida
Minna
Abuja
Kaduna
Zaria
Kano
Katsina
Sokoto
Gusau
Kontagora
Yelwa
Wawa
Kainji Dam
Bauchi
Jos
Jos Plateau
Kafanchan
Makurdi
Wukari
Potiskum
Maiduguri
Dikwa
Nguru
Gashua
Damaturu
Biu
Yola
Numan
Mubi
Jalingo
Sokoto Plains
Plateau of Yorubaland
Kano
Hadejia
Benue
Gongola
Mouths of the Niger
Bight of Biafra
CAMEROON
Yaoundé
Douala
Garoua
Maroua
Mora
Kousseri
Ngaoundéré
Bertoua
Batouri
Bafoussam
Bamenda
Kumba
Buea
Edéa
Kribi
Ebolowa
Foumban
Sangmélima
Mbalmayo
Tibati
Meiganga
Adamaoua
Tchabal Mbabo 2,460 m
Mont Kayagangiri 1,420 m
Dimlang 2,042 m
Barrage de Lagdo
PN de la Bénoué
PN du Faro
Fako 4,095 m
Chari
Logone
Parc National de Kalamaloué
Baguirmi
EQUATORIAL GUINEA
Malabo
Bioko
Luba
Pico de Santa Isabel 3,008 m
Bata
Ebebiyin
Mbini
Monte Mitra 1,200 m
Gulf of Guinea
SÃO TOMÉ AND PRÍNCIPE
São Tomé
Príncipe
Santo António
Annobón (EQ. G.)
Palé
Equator
GABON
Libreville
Cap Esterias
Cap Lopez
Port-Gentil
Lambaréné
Oyem
Bitam
Mitzic
Makokou
Booué
N'Djolé
Koula-Moutou
Lastoursville
Franceville
Moanda
Mouila
Tchibanga
Mayumba
Omboué
Mont Iboundji 980 m
Monts de Cristal
Mongoungou
CONGO
Ouesso
Owando
Mbinda
Makabana
Mossendjo
Djambala
Plateau Batéké
PN d'Odzala
Bolobo
Ngo
C.A.R.
Moloundou
Yokadouma
ZAIRE

Northern Africa

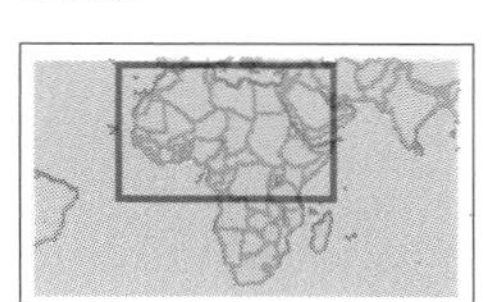

POPULATION OF CITIES AND TOWNS

- ■ OVER 2,000,000
- □ 1,000,000 - 1,999,999
- ● 500,000 - 999,999
- • 100,000 - 499,999
- ◦ 50,000 - 99,999
- ○ UNDER 50,000

SCALE 1:17,500,000 POLYCONIC PROJECTION

MILES 0 250 500 750

KILOMETERS 0 250 500 750

82
A
B
C
D
16°
12°
8°
4°
20°
16°
8°
1
2
4
5
MAURITANIA
SENEGAL
GAMBIA
GUINEA-BISSAU
GUINEA
SIERRA LEONE
LIBERIA
IVORY COAST
(CÔTE D'IVOIRE)
ATLANTIC
OCEAN
Grain Coast
Ivory Coast
B. d'Arguin
DAKHLET NOUADHIBOU
Cap Ioulk
Ile Tidra
Cap Timiris
Nouâmghâr
PN DU BANC D'ARGUIN
Akjoujt
Bennichchab
INCHIRI
Atar
Chinguetti
Ouâdâne
Oujeft
ADRAR
Ntergoent
Dhar de Chinguetti
El Djouf
TOMBOUCTOU
HODH ECH CHARGUI
Tâmassoumît
Tidjikdja
Lekhcheb
Tichît
Arhrîjît
TAGANT
Nouakchott
NOUAKCHOTT
Jreïda
Aguîlâl Faï
Ouâd Nâga
TRARZA
Boutilimit
Moudjéria
Aoukar
Oualâta
Boûmdeïd
Tamchaket
Tîguent
Mederdra
Rkîz
Aleg
BRAKNA
Keur Massène
Rosso
Podor
Bogué
Ndiago
Richard Toll
Dagana
Saint-Louis
Kiffa
Guérou
EL ACÂBA
Ayoûn el Atroûs
HODH EL GHARBI
Aïoun el Atroûs
Néma
Timbédra
Dendâra
Kobenni
Djiguéni
Amourj
Bassikounou
Adel Bagrou
Fassala-Néré
SAINT-LOUIS
GORGOL
Kaédi
M'Bout
Sélibabi
GUIDIMAKA
Ould Yenjé
Matam
Louga
LOUGA
Linguère
Dahra
Kébémer
Mboro
DAKAR
Dakar
Thiès
THIES
DIOURBEL
Diourbel
M'Bour
Joal
Kaolack
KAOLACK
FATICK
Fatick
Kaffrine
Koungheul
Tambacounda
TAMBACOUNDA
Banjul
Georgetown
Brikama
Basse Santa Su
KOLDA
Kolda
ZIGUINCHOR
Ziguinchor
Bignona
Sédhiou
PN DU NIOKOLO-KOBA
Kédougou
Bakel
Kidira
Kayes
KAYES
Bafoulabé
PN DE LA BOUCLE DU BAOULÉ
RÉSERVE DE KENIÉ-BAOULÉ
Bamako
BAMAKO
Kati
Kita
Nioro du Sahel
Diéma
Mourdiah
Ségou
SÉGOU
Mopti
MOPTI
Djenné
San
Koutiala
Sikasso
SIKASSO
Bougouni
Nara
Bissau
Bafatá
Gabú
Bolama
Arq. dos Bijagós
Cacheu
Boké
BOKÉ
Labé
LABÉ
Mamou
Kindia
KINDIA
Conakry
CONAKRY
Faranah
FARANAH
Kankan
KANKAN
Siguiri
Kouroussa
Dabola
Kissidougou
Guéckédou
Macenta
Nzérékoré
NZÉRÉKORÉ
Fouta Djallon
Freetown
WESTERN AREA
NORTHERN
SOUTHERN
EASTERN
Makeni
Bo
Kenema
Kailahun
Sherbro Island
Turtle Is.
Robertsport
GRAND CAPE MOUNT
MONTSERRADO
Monrovia
LOFA
BONG
NIMBA
GRAND BASSA
Buchanan
SINO
GRAND JIDE
MARYLAND
Harper
C. Palmas
Greenville
River Cess
Odienné
Korhogo
Ferkéssédougou
Boundiali
Séguéla
Man
Daloa
Bouaké
Yamoussoukro
Dimbokro
Gagnoa
Divo
Abidjan
Grand-Bassam
San Pédro
Sassandra
Tabou
PARC NATIONAL DE LA COMOÉ
PN DE TAÏ
Bobo Dioulasso
Banfora
Ouagadougou
ATLANTIC OCEAN
SCALE 1:7,000,000 POLYCONIC PROJECTION
MILES 0 100 200 300
KILOMETERS 0 100 200 300
Longitude West of Greenwich
© Copyright by HAMMOND INCORPORATED, Maplewood, N.J.

West Africa

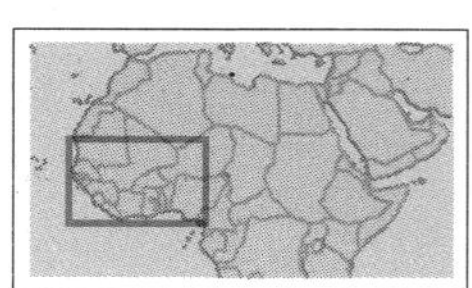

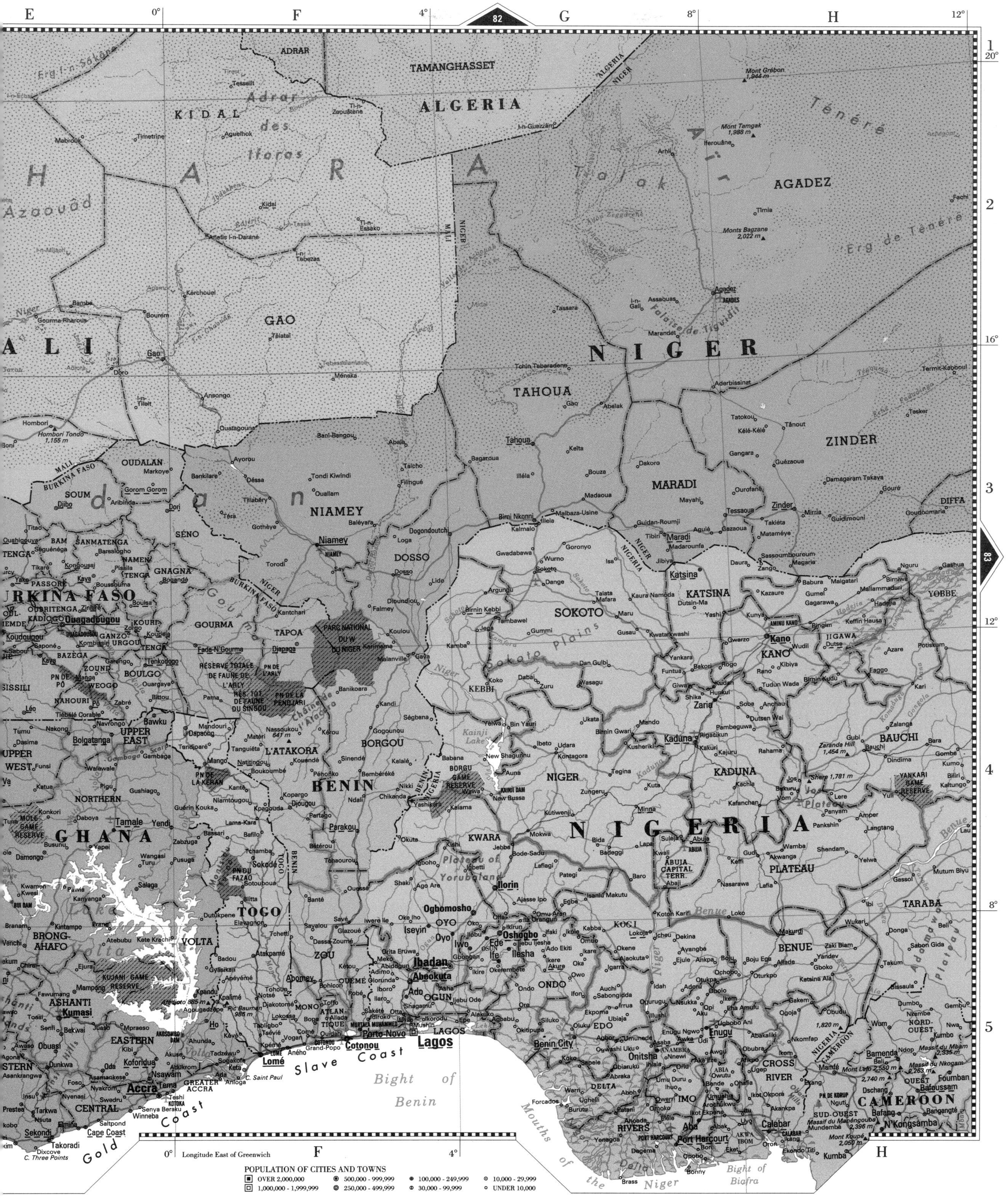

82

83

NIGER

NIGERIA

ALGERIA

BENIN

TOGO

GHANA

BURKINA FASO

CAMEROON

Bight of Benin

Slave Coast

Gold Coast

Longitude East of Greenwich

POPULATION OF CITIES AND TOWNS

OVER 2,000,000	500,000 - 999,999	100,000 - 249,999	10,000 - 29,999
1,000,000 - 1,999,999	250,000 - 499,999	30,000 - 99,999	UNDER 10,000

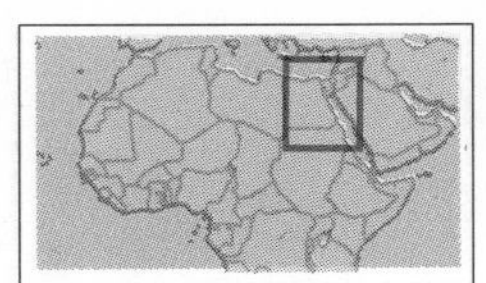

Northeastern Africa

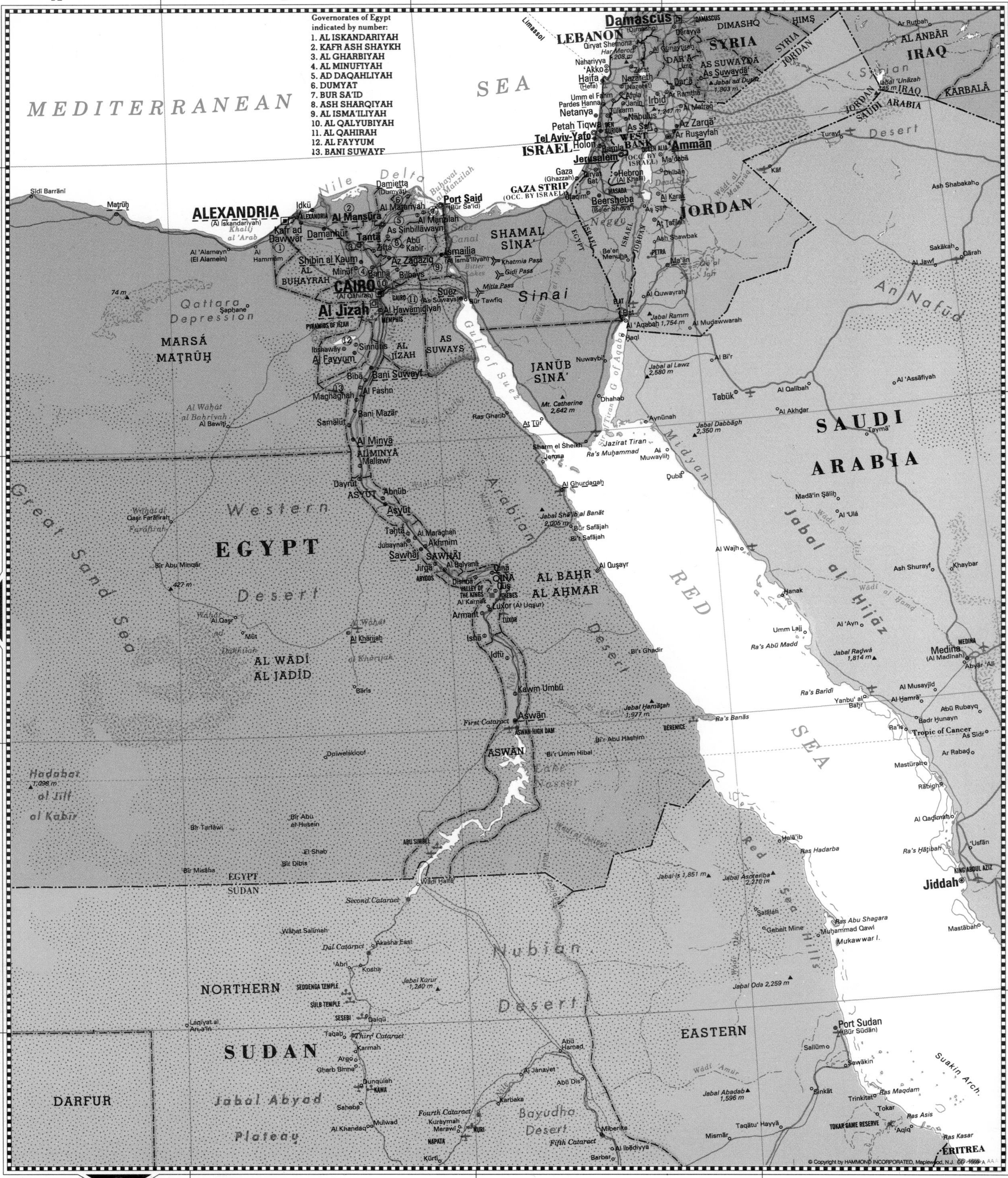

Governorates of Egypt indicated by number:

1. AL ISKANDARIYAH
2. KAFR ASH SHAYKH
3. AL GHARBIYAH
4. AL MINUFIYAH
5. AD DAQAHLIYAH
6. DUMYAT
7. BUR SA'ID
8. ASH SHARQIYAH
9. AL ISMA'ILIYAH
10. AL QALYUBIYAH
11. AL QAHIRAH
12. AL FAYYUM
13. BANI SUWAYF

Longitude East of Greenwich

POPULATION OF CITIES AND TOWNS

- OVER 2,000,000
- 1,000,000 - 1,999,999
- 500,000 - 999,999
- 250,000 - 499,999
- 100,000 - 249,999
- 30,000 - 99,999
- 10,000 - 29,999
- UNDER 10,000

SCALE 1:7,000,000 POLYCONIC PROJECTION

MILES 0 100 200 300

KILOMETERS 0 100 200 300

Southern Africa

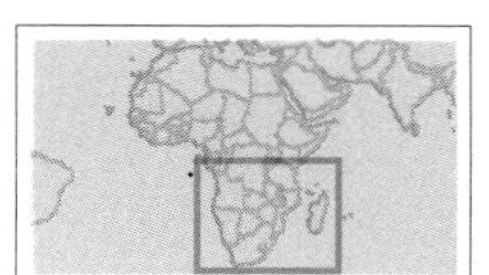

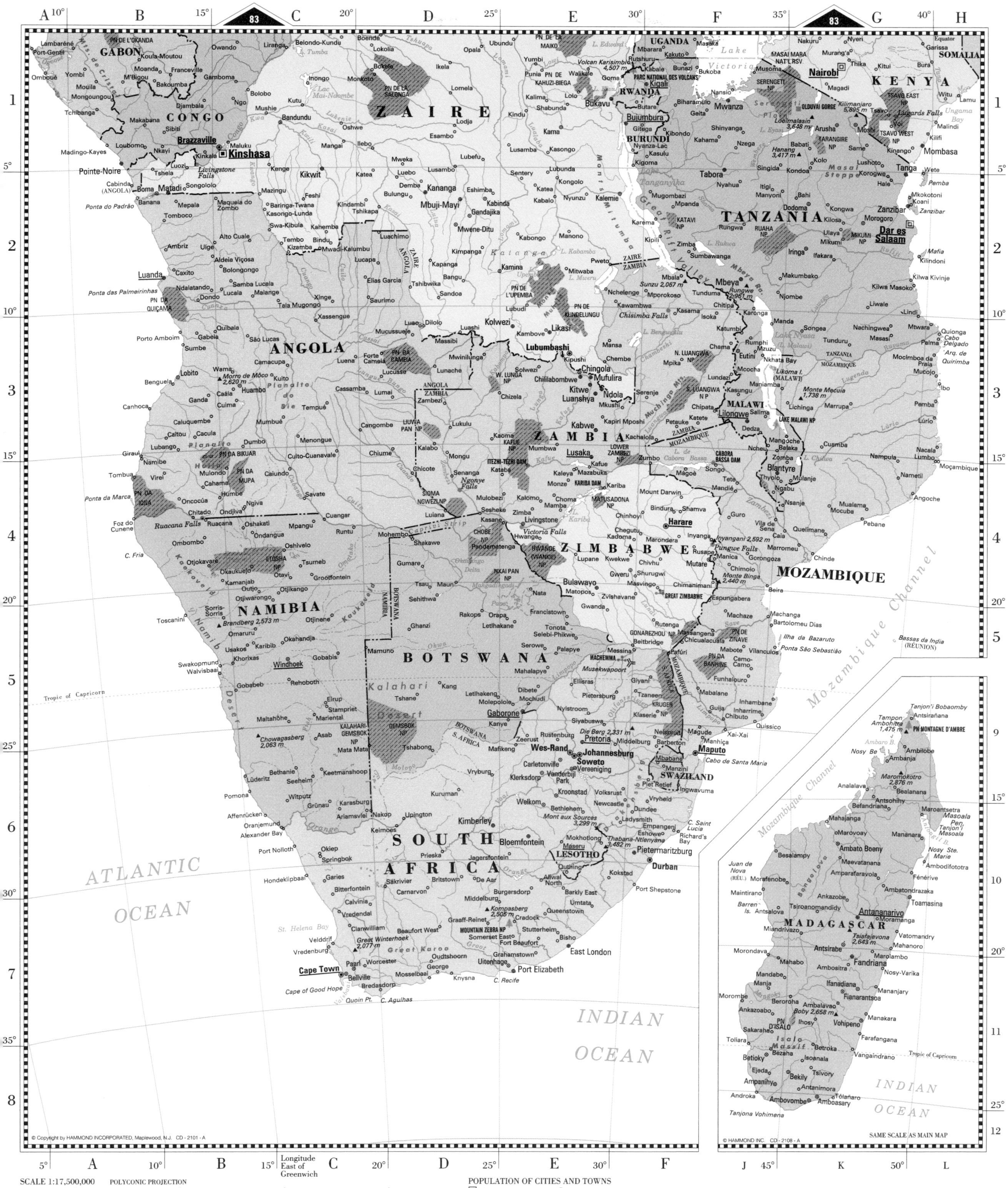

SCALE 1:17,500,000 POLYCONIC PROJECTION

MILES 0 250 500 750

KILOMETERS 0 250 500 750

Longitude East of Greenwich

POPULATION OF CITIES AND TOWNS

■ OVER 2,000,000	● 500,000 - 999,999	● 50,000 - 99,999
▣ 1,000,000 - 1,999,999	● 100,000 - 499,999	○ UNDER 50,000

SAME SCALE AS MAIN MAP

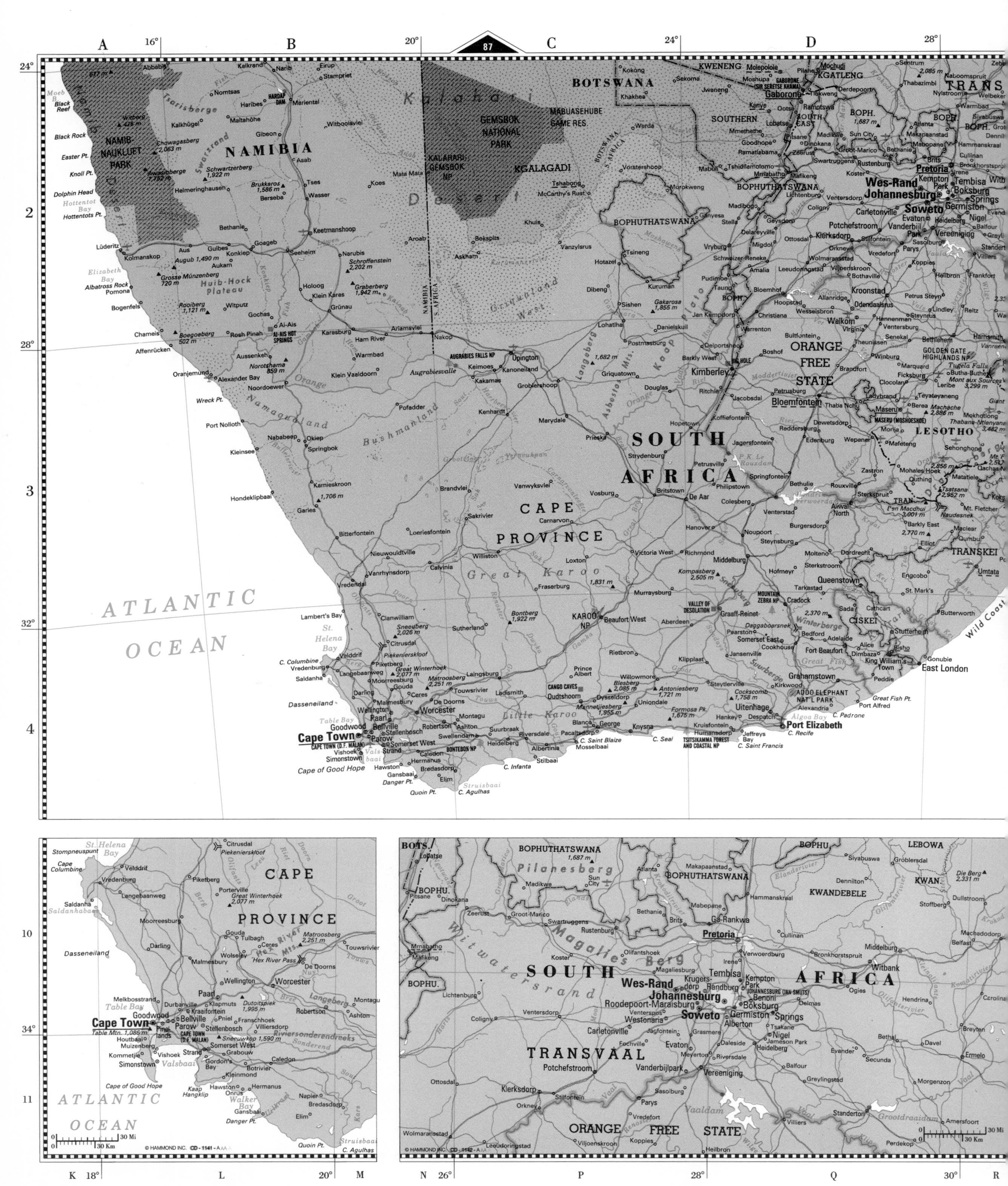

87
A
B
C
D
16°
20°
24°
28°
2
3
4
32°
NAMIBIA
BOTSWANA
SOUTH AFRICA
CAPE PROVINCE
ORANGE FREE STATE
LESOTHO
TRANSKEI
CISKEI
BOPHUTHATSWANA
KGALAGADI
SOUTHERN
KWENENG
KGATLENG
ATLANTIC OCEAN
Kalahari Desert
GEMSBOK NATIONAL PARK
MABUASEHUBE GAME RES.
KALAHARI-GEMSBOK NP
NAMIB-NAUKLUFT PARK
AUGRABIES FALLS NP
KAROO NP
VALLEY OF DESOLATION
MOUNTAIN ZEBRA NP
ADDO ELEPHANT NAT'L PARK
TSITSIKAMMA FOREST AND COASTAL NP
BONTEBOK NP
CANGO CAVES
AI-AIS HOT SPRINGS
HARDAP DAM
Great Karoo
Little Karoo
Bushmanland
Namaqualand
Griqualand West
Huib-Hock Plateau
Windhoek
Lüderitz
Keetmanshoop
Mariental
Gibeon
Bethanie
Karasburg
Oranjemund
Alexander Bay
Port Nolloth
Springbok
Upington
Kimberley
Bloemfontein
Maseru
Gaborone
Mafikeng
Pretoria
Wes-Rand
Johannesburg
Soweto
Vereeniging
Welkom
Kroonstad
De Aar
Colesberg
Beaufort West
Graaff-Reinet
Cradock
Queenstown
Grahamstown
East London
Port Elizabeth
Uitenhage
Knysna
George
Oudtshoorn
Mosselbaai
Worcester
Paarl
Stellenbosch
Cape Town
CAPE TOWN (D.F. MALAN)
Simonstown
Cape of Good Hope
C. Agulhas
Saldanha
Vredenburg
Calvinia
Vredendal
Clanwilliam
Table Bay
Algoa Bay
St. Helena Bay
Wild Coast
Mafeteng
Umtata
K
L
M
N
P
Q
R
10
11
18°
26°
30°
34°
CAPE PROVINCE
ATLANTIC OCEAN
Hex River Pass
Hex River Mts.
Table Mtn. 1,086 m
Dutoitspiek 1,995 m
Valsbaai
Walker Bay
Kaap Hangklip
SOUTH AFRICA
TRANSVAAL
ORANGE FREE STATE
BOPHUTHATSWANA
LEBOWA
KWANDEBELE
Witwatersrand
Magaliesberg
Pilanesberg
Roodepoort-Maraisburg
Krugersdorp
Randburg
Tembisa
Kempton Park
Benoni
Boksburg
Germiston
Springs
Alberton
Nigel
Heidelberg
Vanderbijlpark
Sasolburg
Potchefstroom
Klerksdorp
Rustenburg
Brits
Witbank
Middelburg
Standerton
Vaaldam
© HAMMOND INC. CD-1141-A
© HAMMOND INC. CD-1142-A
30 Mi
30 Km

South Africa

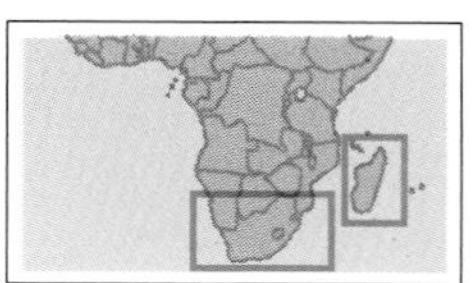

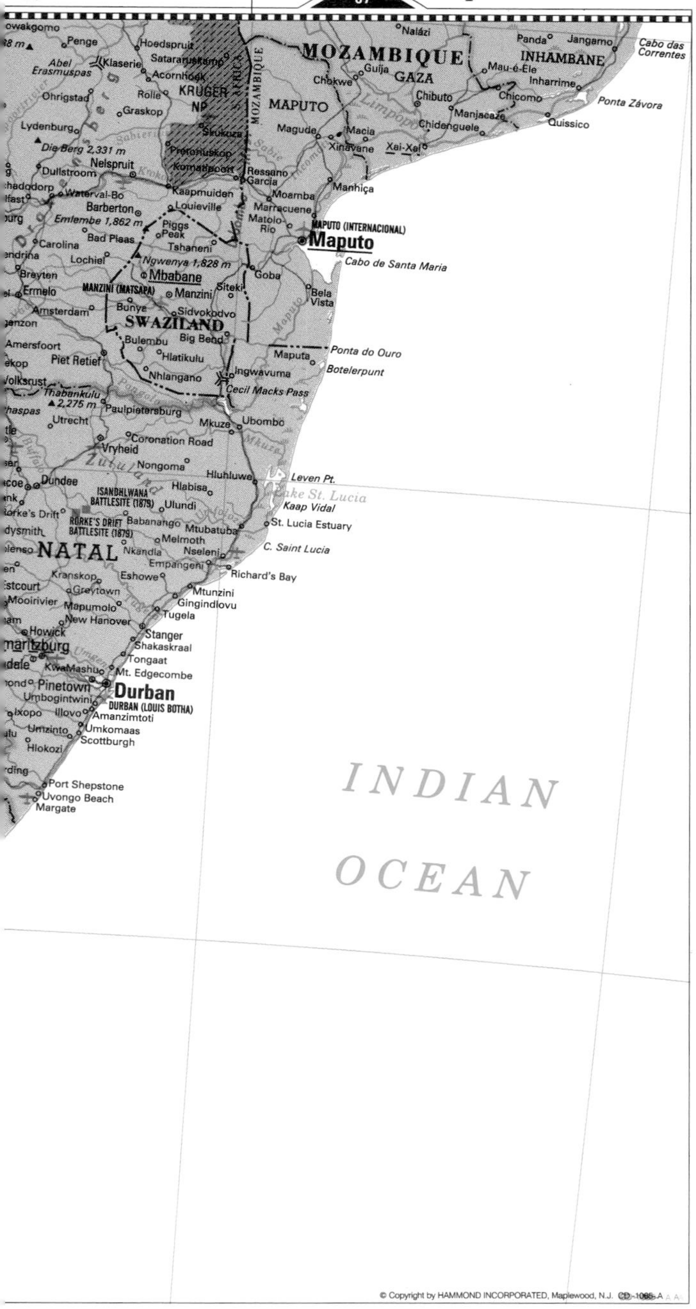

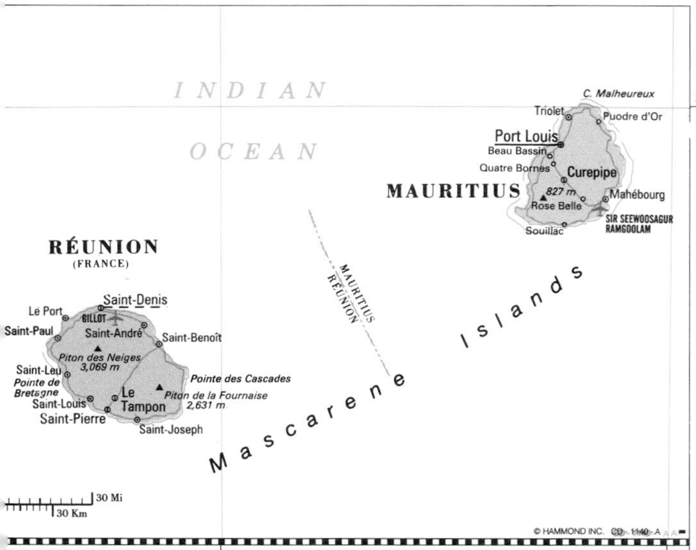

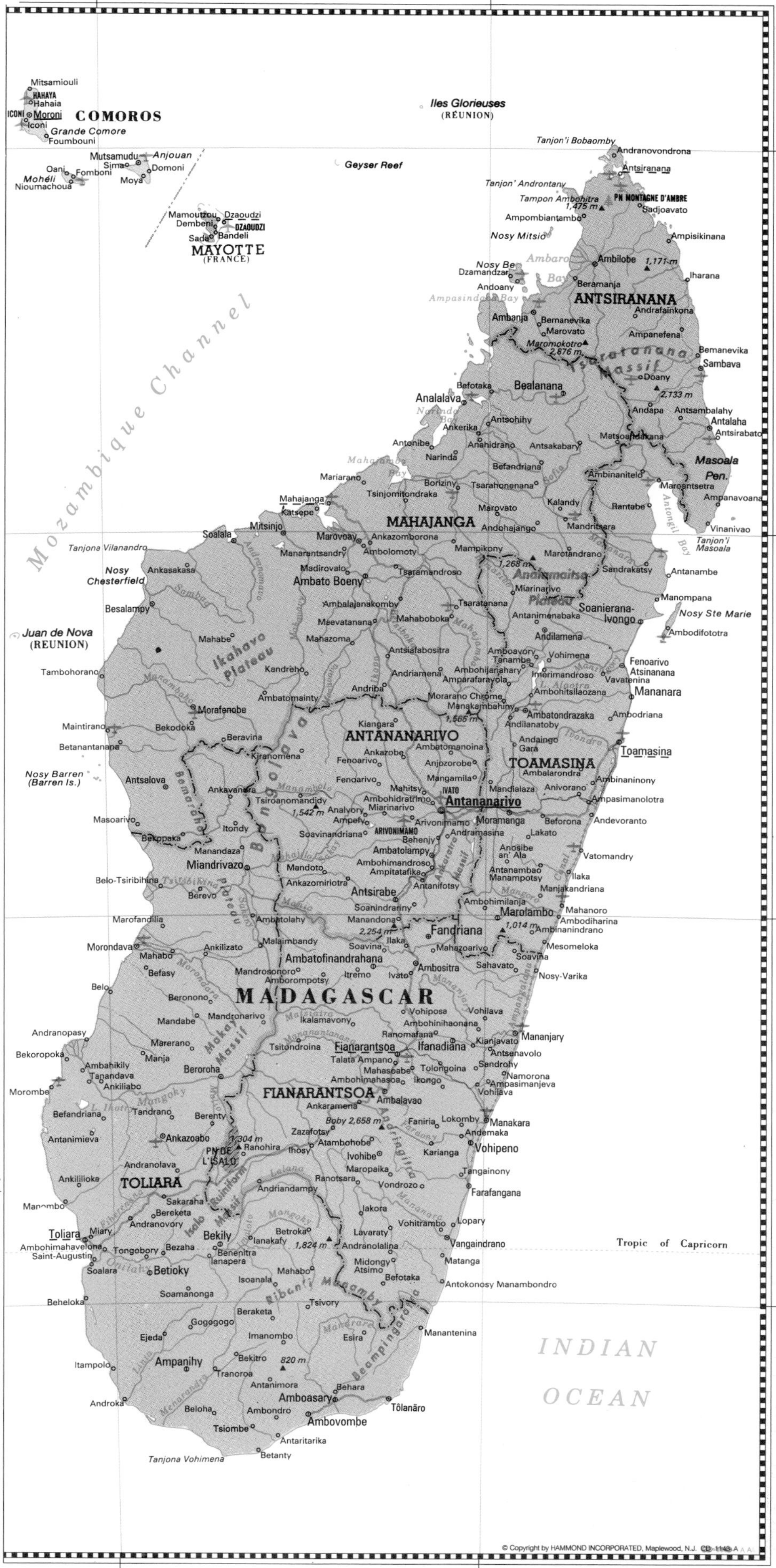

87

MOZAMBIQUE

SWAZILAND

NATAL

Maputo

Durban

INDIAN OCEAN

COMOROS

MAYOTTE (FRANCE)

Mozambique Channel

MADAGASCAR

ANTSIRANANA

MAHAJANGA

ANTANANARIVO

TOAMASINA

FIANARANTSOA

TOLIARA

Antananarivo

Tropic of Capricorn

INDIAN OCEAN

INDIAN OCEAN

MAURITIUS

Port Louis

RÉUNION (FRANCE)

Saint-Denis

Mascarene Islands

30 Mi

30 Km

POPULATION OF CITIES AND TOWNS

- OVER 2,000,000
- 1,000,000 - 1,999,999
- 500,000 - 999,999
- 250,000 - 499,999
- 100,000 - 249,999
- 30,000 - 99,999
- 10,000 - 29,999
- UNDER 10,000

SCALE 1:7,000,000 LAMBERT CONFORMAL CONIC PROJECTION

MILES 0 100 200 300

KILOMETERS 0 100 200 300

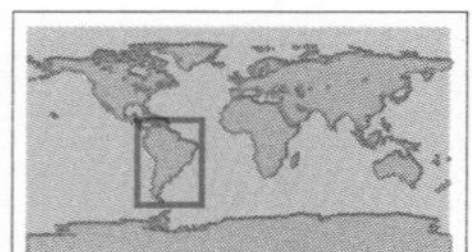

South America

AREA OF OPTIMIZATION

The red band which surrounds this map defines the "Area of Optimization." Within this bounding curve is the most accurate conformal map that can be made of the region. Outside the optimized area, distortion increases rapidly, and tears or other irregularities in the grid may occur.

POPULATION OF CITIES AND TOWNS

- OVER 3,000,000
- 1,000,000 - 2,999,999
- 500,000 - 999,999
- 100,000 - 499,999
- UNDER 100,000

SCALE 1:28,000,000 OPTIMAL CONFORMAL PROJECTION

MILES 0 400 800 1200

KILOMETERS 0 400 800 1200

Longitude West of Greenwich

Southern South America

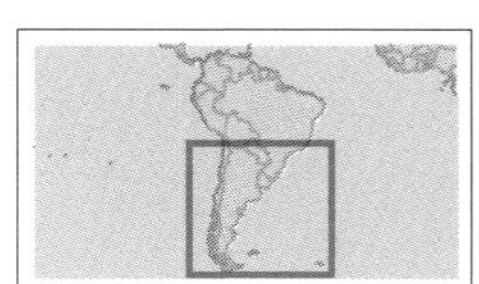

POPULATION OF CITIES AND TOWNS

- ■ OVER 2,000,000
- ▣ 1,000,000 - 1,999,999
- ◉ 500,000 - 999,999
- ● 100,000 - 499,999
- ⊙ 50,000 - 99,999
- ○ UNDER 50,000

SCALE 1:15,000,000 LAMBERT CONFORMAL CONIC PROJECTION

MILES 0 200 400 600

KILOMETERS 0 200 400 600

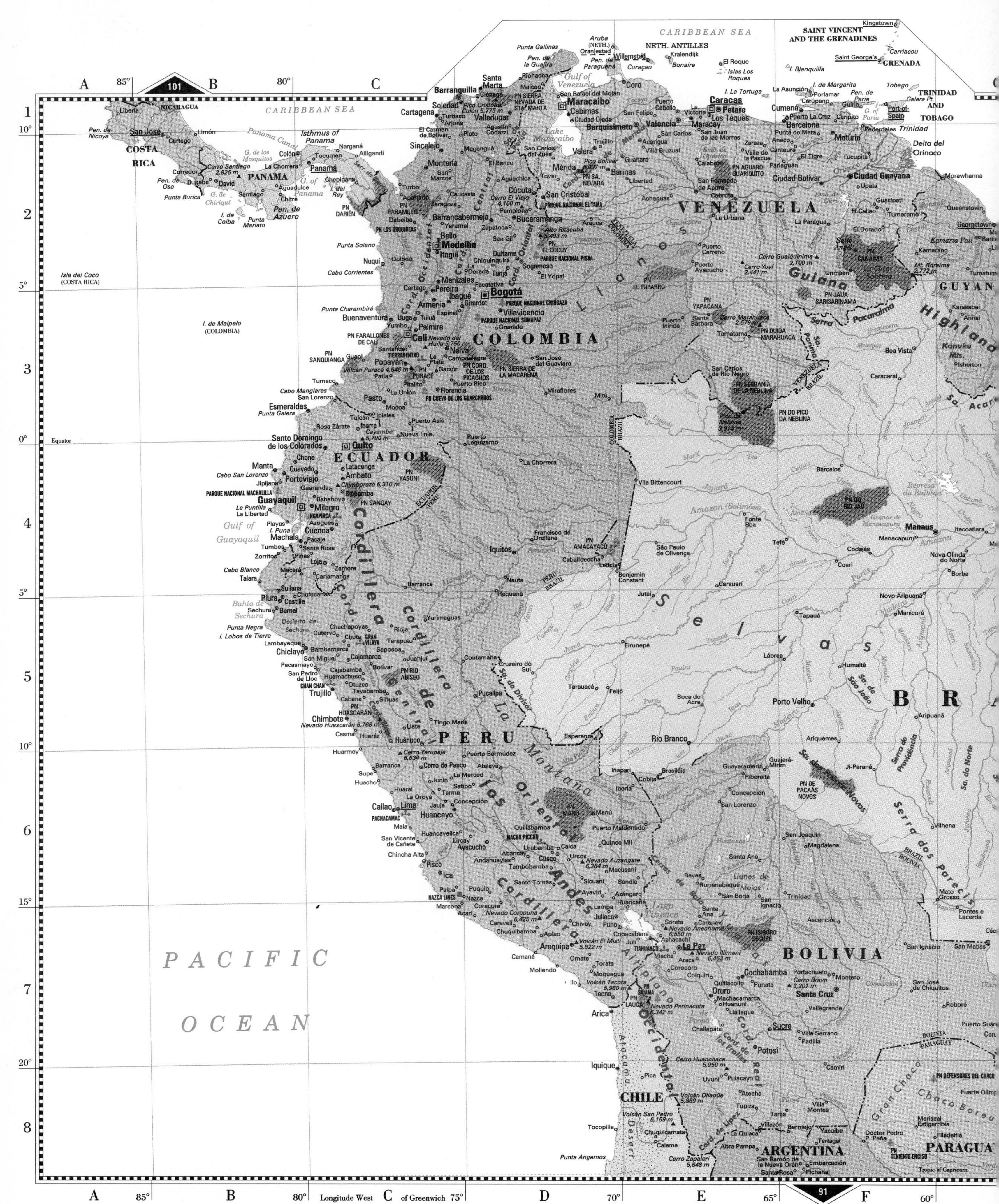

CARIBBEAN SEA
SAINT VINCENT AND THE GRENADINES
Kingstown
NETH. ANTILLES
Aruba (NETH.)
Oranjestad
Willemstad
Curaçao
Kralendijk
Bonaire
Saint George's
GRENADA
TRINIDAD AND TOBAGO
Port-of-Spain
Trinidad
Tobago
NICARAGUA
COSTA RICA
San José
PANAMA
Panamá
Isthmus of Panama
Panama Canal
Colón
G. of Panama
Pen. de Azuero
Pen. de Nicoya
Pen. de Osa
David
Punta Burica
I. de Coiba
Punta Mariato
Gulf of Venezuela
Pen. de la Guajira
Punta Gallinas
Pen. de Paraguaná
Lake Maracaibo
Maracaibo
Barranquilla
Cartagena
Santa Marta
Valledupar
Riohacha
Coro
Barquisimeto
Valencia
Caracas
Petare
Los Teques
Maracay
Cumaná
Barcelona
Maturín
Ciudad Bolívar
Ciudad Guayana
Delta del Orinoco
Orinoco
VENEZUELA
Mérida
Barinas
San Cristóbal
Cúcuta
Bucaramanga
Medellín
Manizales
Pereira
Ibagué
Bogotá
Villavicencio
Cali
Popayán
Pasto
Neiva
Buenaventura
Tumaco
COLOMBIA
Llanos
Guiana Highlands
Sierra Pacaraima
Salto Angel
Mt. Roraima 2,772 m
GUYANA
Georgetown
Isla del Coco (COSTA RICA)
I. de Malpelo (COLOMBIA)
Equator
Esmeraldas
Quito
ECUADOR
Santo Domingo de los Colorados
Manta
Portoviejo
Guayaquil
Gulf of Guayaquil
Chimborazo 6,310 m
Ambato
Cuenca
Machala
Loja
Tumbes
Talara
Piura
Chiclayo
Trujillo
Chimbote
Nevado Huascarán 6,768 m
Iquitos
Leticia
Amazon
Amazon (Solimões)
Manaus
Selvas
PERU
Cordillera Occidental
Cordillera Central
Cordillera Oriental
La Montaña
Lima
Callao
Huancayo
Ayacucho
Cusco
Arequipa
Tacna
Ica
Lago Titicaca
La Paz
BOLIVIA
Cochabamba
Santa Cruz
Oruro
Sucre
Potosí
Altiplano
Llanos de Mojos
Cordillera Real
Arica
Iquique
Antofagasta
CHILE
Atacama Desert
Calama
Tocopilla
ARGENTINA
PARAGUAY
Gran Chaco
Chaco Boreal
Tropic of Capricorn
Porto Velho
Rio Branco
Humaitá
Serra dos Parecis
BRAZIL
PACIFIC OCEAN
Longitude West of Greenwich

Northern South America

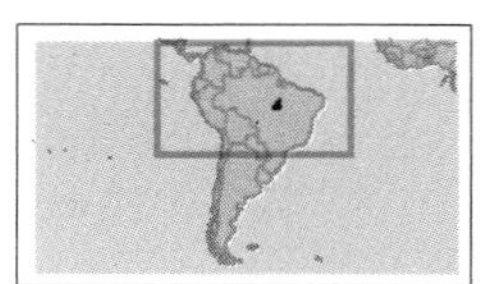

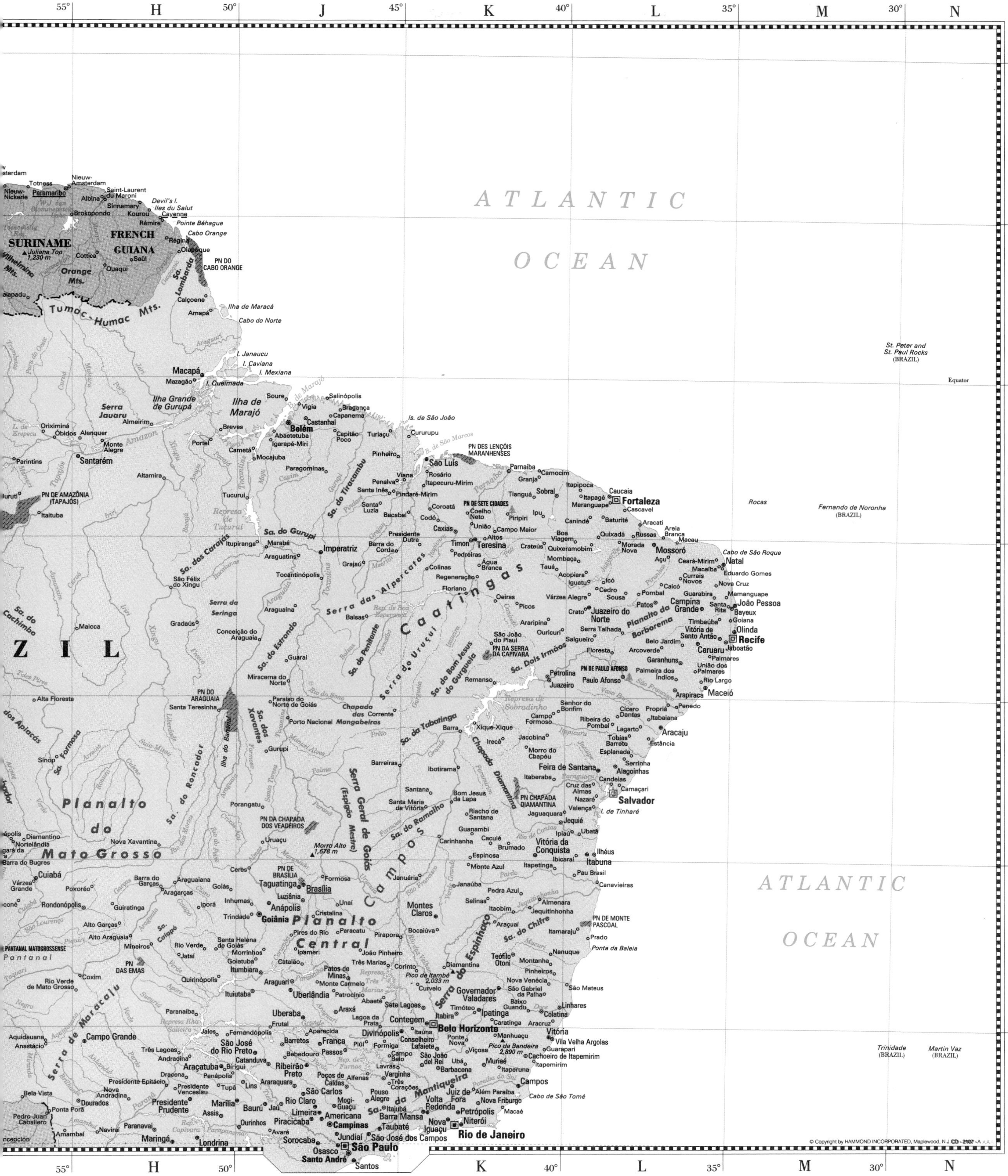

POPULATION OF CITIES AND TOWNS

- ■ OVER 2,000,000
- ▣ 1,000,000 - 1,999,999
- ◉ 500,000 - 999,999
- ● 100,000 - 499,999
- ◎ 50,000 - 99,999
- ○ UNDER 50,000

SCALE 1:15,000,000 LAMBERT CONFORMAL CONIC PROJECTION

MILES 0 200 400 600

KILOMETERS 0 200 400 600

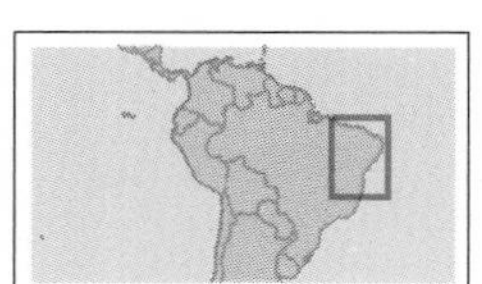

Northeastern Brazil

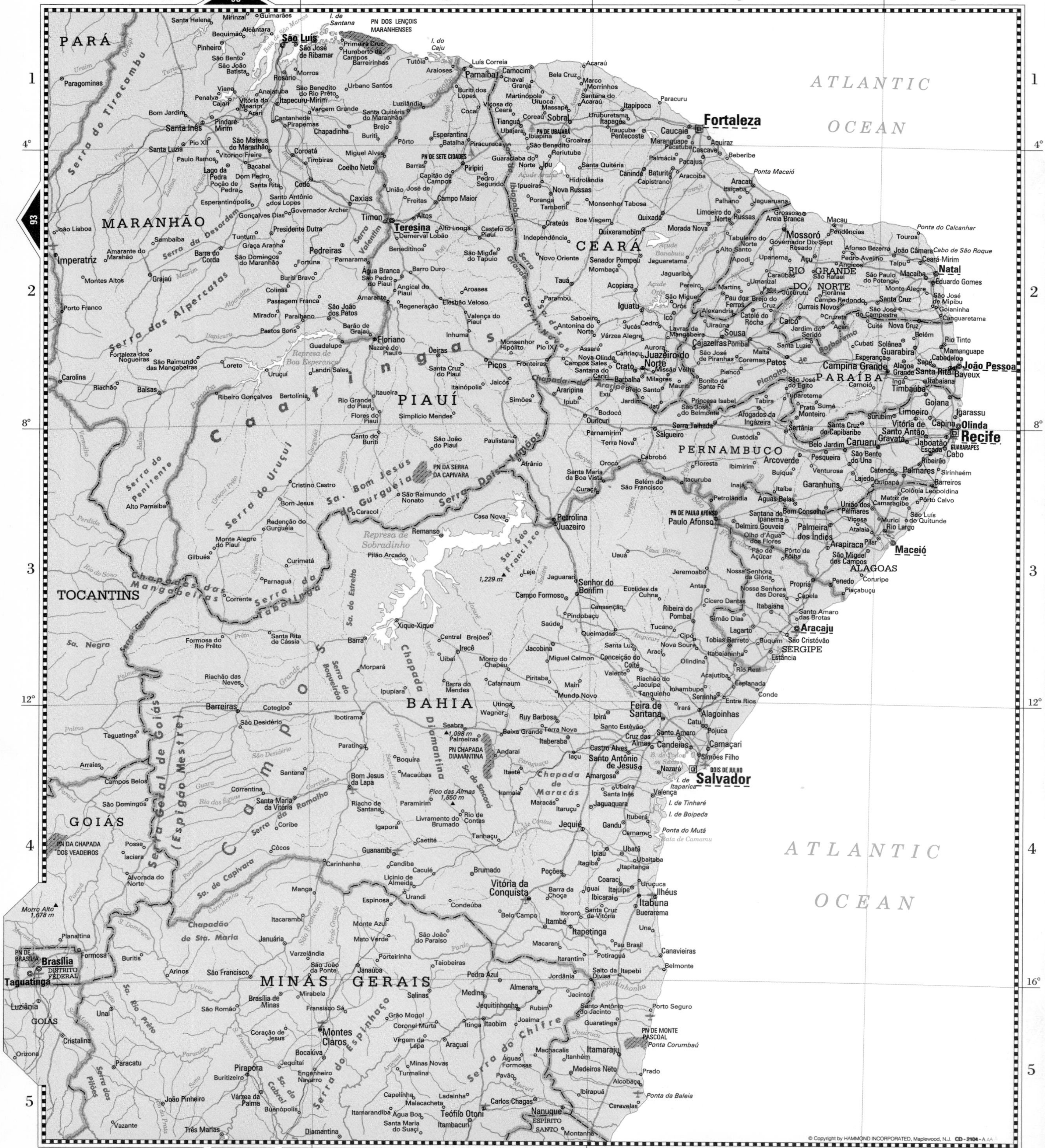

A B C D

SCALE 1:7,000,000 LAMBERT CONFORMAL CONIC PROJECTION

MILES 0 100 200 300

KILOMETERS 0 100 200 300

44° Longitude West of Greenwich

POPULATION OF CITIES AND TOWNS

- OVER 2,000,000
- 1,000,000 - 1,999,999
- 500,000 - 999,999
- 250,000 - 499,999
- 100,000 - 249,999
- 30,000 - 99,999
- 10,000 - 29,999
- UNDER 10,000

Southeastern Brazil

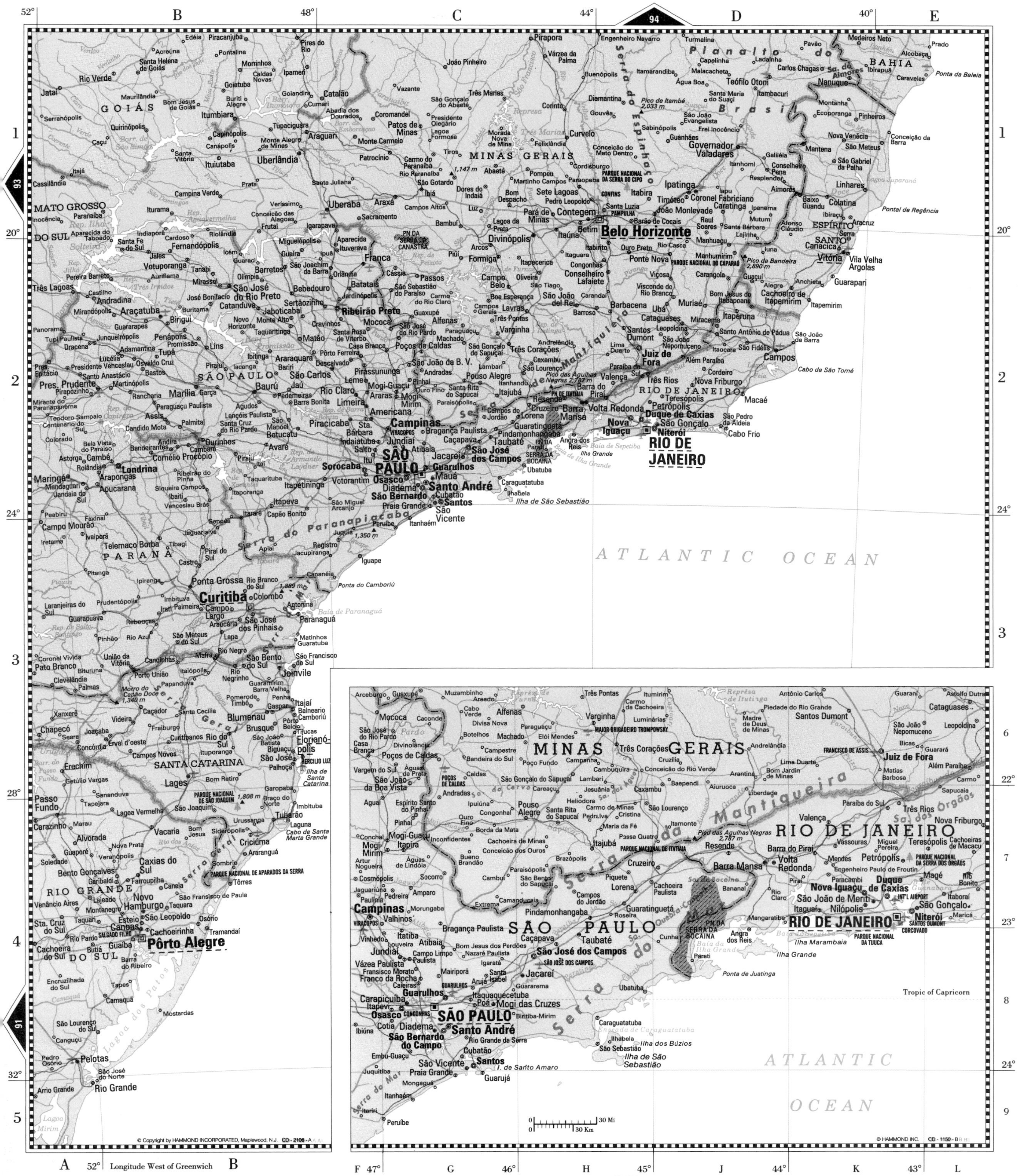

ATLANTIC OCEAN

Longitude West of Greenwich

POPULATION OF CITIES AND TOWNS

- OVER 2,000,000
- 1,000,000 - 1,999,999
- 500,000 - 999,999
- 250,000 - 499,999
- 100,000 - 249,999
- 30,000 - 99,999
- 10,000 - 29,999
- UNDER 10,000

SCALE 1:7,000,000 LAMBERT CONFORMAL CONIC PROJECTION

MILES 0 100 200 300

KILOMETERS 0 100 200 300

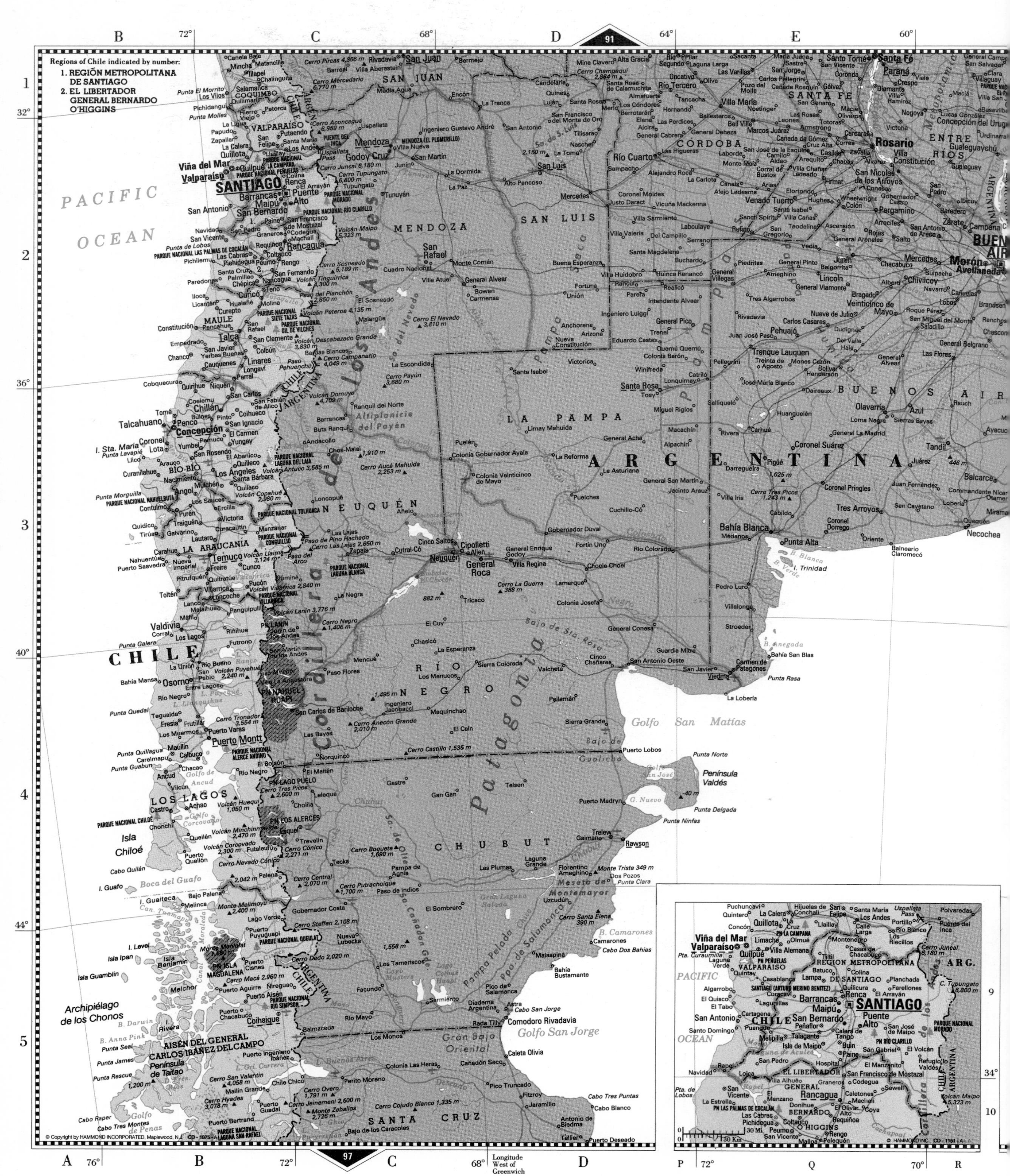

91
97
Regions of Chile indicated by number:
1. REGIÓN METROPOLITANA DE SANTIAGO
2. EL LIBERTADOR GENERAL BERNARDO O'HIGGINS
PACIFIC OCEAN
CHILE
ARGENTINA
SAN JUAN
MENDOZA
SAN LUIS
CÓRDOBA
SANTA FE
ENTRE RÍOS
BUENOS AIRES
LA PAMPA
NEUQUÉN
RÍO NEGRO
CHUBUT
SANTA CRUZ
COQUIMBO
VALPARAÍSO
MAULE
BÍO-BÍO
LA ARAUCANIA
LOS LAGOS
AISÉN DEL GENERAL CARLOS IBÁÑEZ DEL CAMPO
Cordillera de los Andes
Patagonia
Pampa Seca
Altiplanicie del Payén
SANTIAGO
Valparaíso
Viña del Mar
Mendoza
San Juan
San Luis
Río Cuarto
Rosario
Santa Fe
Paraná
Santa Rosa
Bahía Blanca
Neuquén
Concepción
Talcahuano
Temuco
Valdivia
Osorno
Puerto Montt
Coihaique
Rawson
Trelew
Puerto Madryn
Viedma
Comodoro Rivadavia
Isla Chiloé
Península Valdés
Golfo San Matías
Golfo San Jorge
Archipiélago de los Chonos
Península de Taitao
Golfo de Penas
Meseta de Montemayor
Gran Bajo Oriental
Bajo de Gualicho
Bajo de Sta. Rosa
Longitude West of Greenwich
© Copyright by HAMMOND INCORPORATED, Maplewood, N.J.
REGION METROPOLITANA
EL LIBERTADOR GENERAL BERNARDO O'HIGGINS
Rancagua
Puente Alto
San Bernardo
Maipú
San Antonio
© HAMMOND INC.

Southern Chile and Argentina

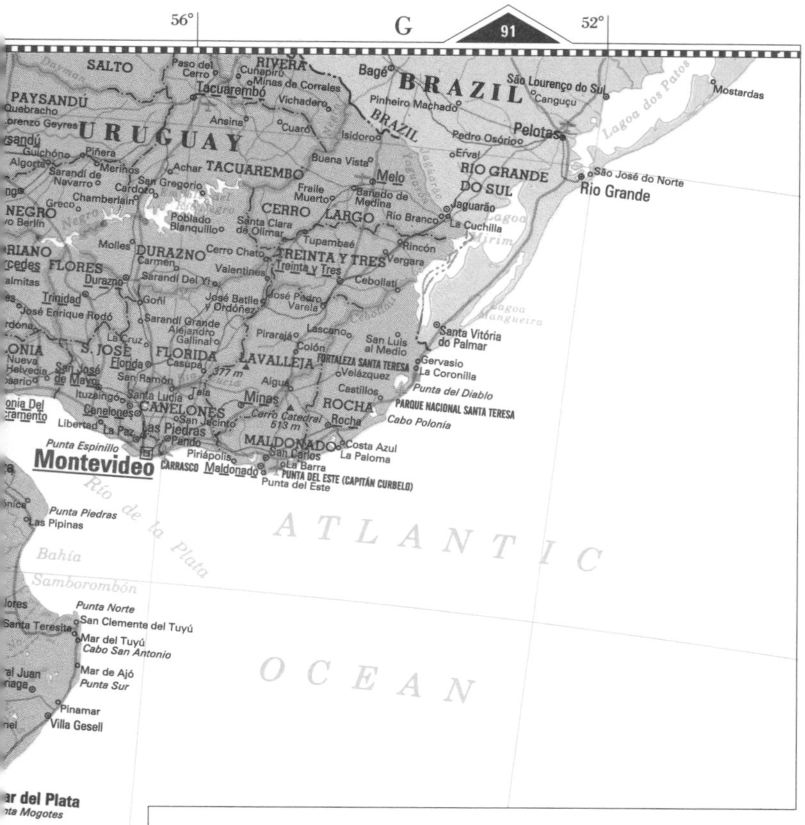

91

POPULATION OF CITIES AND TOWNS

OVER 2,000,000	500,000 - 999,999	100,000 - 249,999	10,000 - 29,999
1,000,000 - 1,999,999	250,000 - 499,999	30,000 - 99,999	UNDER 10,000

SCALE 1:7,000,000 LAMBERT CONFORMAL CONIC PROJECTION

MILES 0 100 200 300

KILOMETERS 0 100 200 300

Antarctica

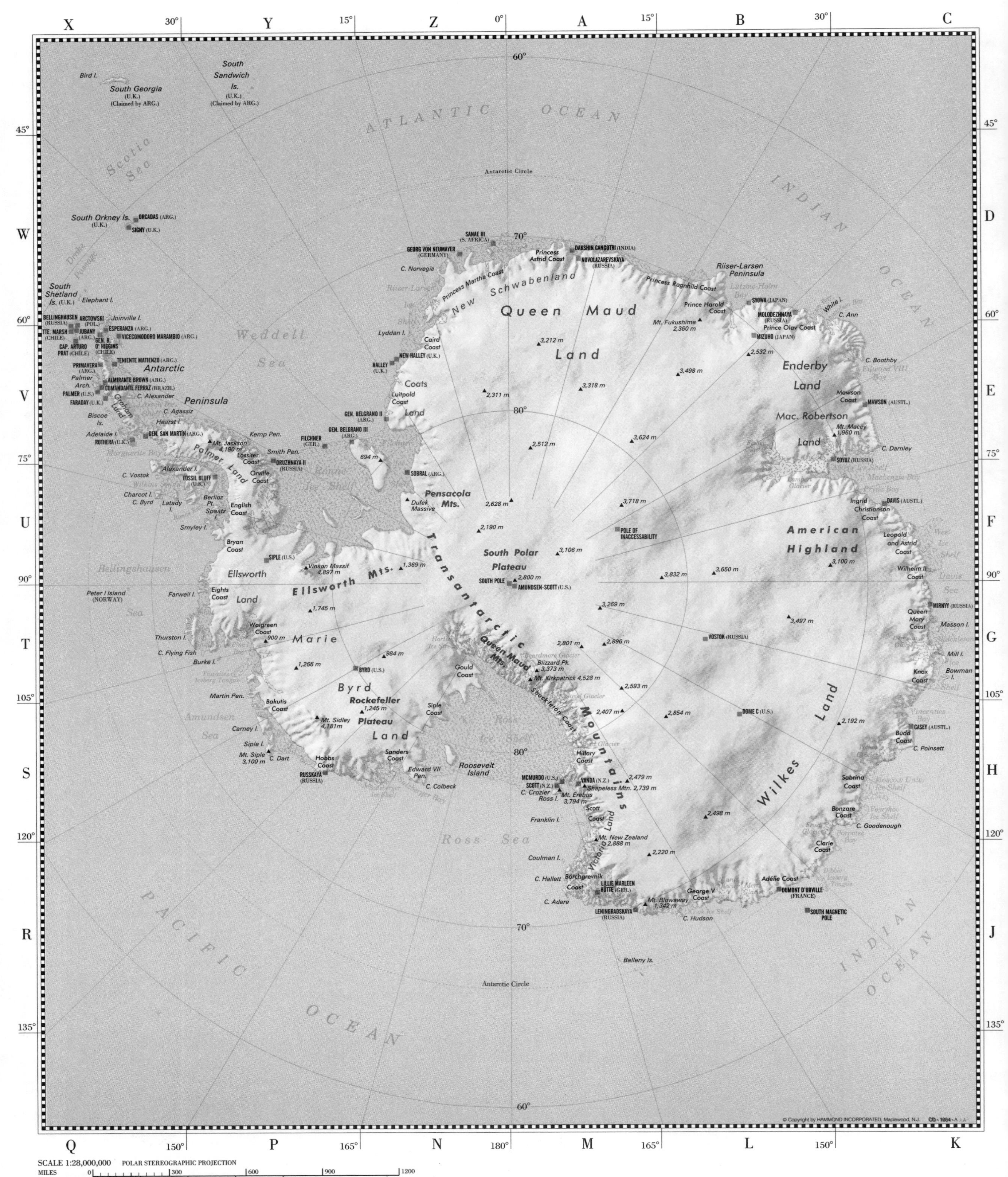
ATLANTIC OCEAN
INDIAN OCEAN
PACIFIC OCEAN
Antarctic Circle
South Georgia (U.K.) (Claimed by ARG.)
South Sandwich Is. (U.K.) (Claimed by ARG.)
Scotia Sea
South Orkney Is. (U.K.)
Drake Passage
South Shetland Is. (U.K.)
Weddell Sea
Antarctic Peninsula
Queen Maud Land
New Schwabenland
Princess Martha Coast
Princess Astrid Coast
Princess Ragnhild Coast
Riiser-Larsen Peninsula
Prince Harold Coast
Prince Olav Coast
Enderby Land
Mac. Robertson Land
Coats Land
Luitpold Coast
Ronne Ice Shelf
Pensacola Mts.
Dufek Massive
Transantarctic Mts.
Queen Maud Mts.
South Polar Plateau
SOUTH POLE
AMUNDSEN-SCOTT (U.S.)
POLE OF INACCESSABILITY
American Highland
Ellsworth Land
Ellsworth Mts.
Vinson Massif 4,897 m
Marie Byrd Land
Rockefeller Plateau
Bellingshausen Sea
Amundsen Sea
Ross Ice Shelf
Ross Sea
Roosevelt Island
Shackleton Coast
Victoria Land
Wilkes Land
VOSTOK (RUSSIA)
DOME C (U.S.)
MIRNYY (RUSSIA)
CASEY (AUSTL.)
DAVIS (AUSTL.)
MAWSON (AUSTL.)
MCMURDO (U.S.)
SCOTT (N.Z.)
Mt. Erebus 3,794 m
Mt. Kirkpatrick 4,528 m
DUMONT D'URVILLE (FRANCE)
SOUTH MAGNETIC POLE
Adélie Coast
George V Coast
Balleny Is.
Peter I Island (NORWAY)
© Copyright by HAMMOND INCORPORATED, Maplewood, N.J.
SCALE 1:28,000,000
POLAR STEREOGRAPHIC PROJECTION
MILES
KILOMETERS

North America

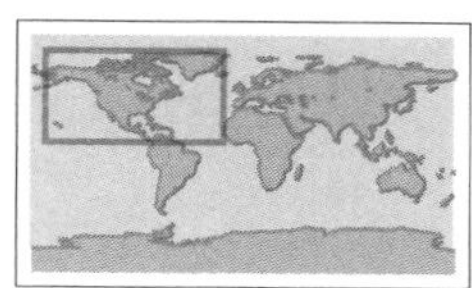

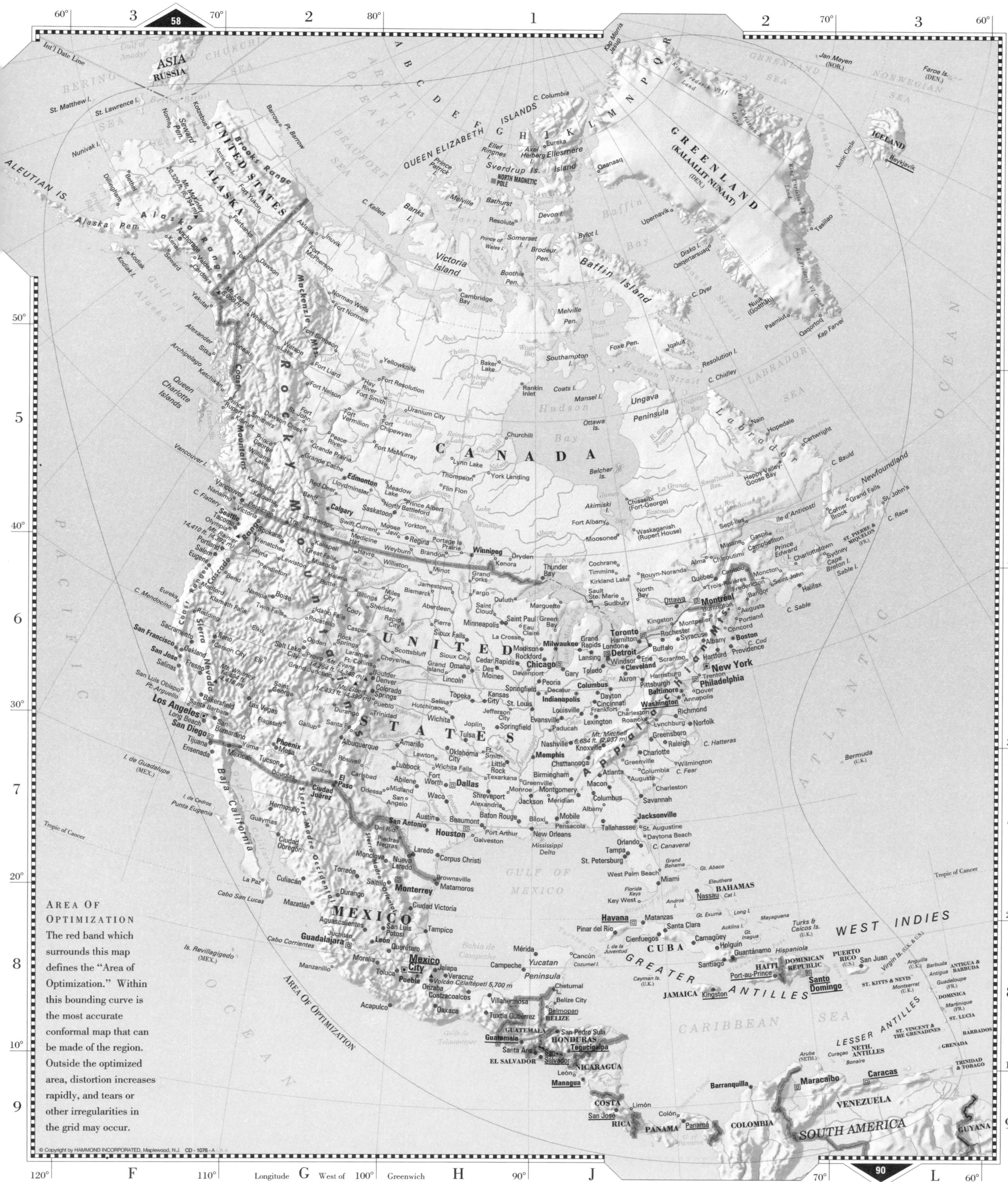

Area Of Optimization

The red band which surrounds this map defines the "Area of Optimization." Within this bounding curve is the most accurate conformal map that can be made of the region. Outside the optimized area, distortion increases rapidly, and tears or other irregularities in the grid may occur.

Longitude West of Greenwich

SCALE 1:35,000,000 OPTIMAL CONFORMAL PROJECTION

MILES 0 500 1000 1500

KILOMETERS 0 500 1000 1500

POPULATION OF CITIES AND TOWNS

- ▣ OVER 3,000,000
- ◻ 1,000,000 - 2,999,999
- ◉ 500,000 - 999,999
- ● 100,000 - 499,999
- ○ UNDER 100,000

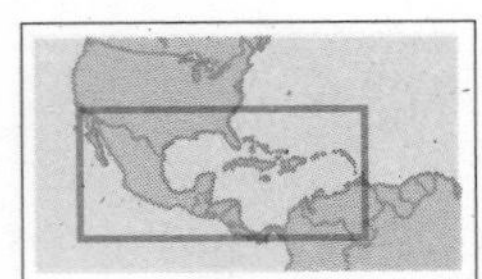

Middle America and Caribbean

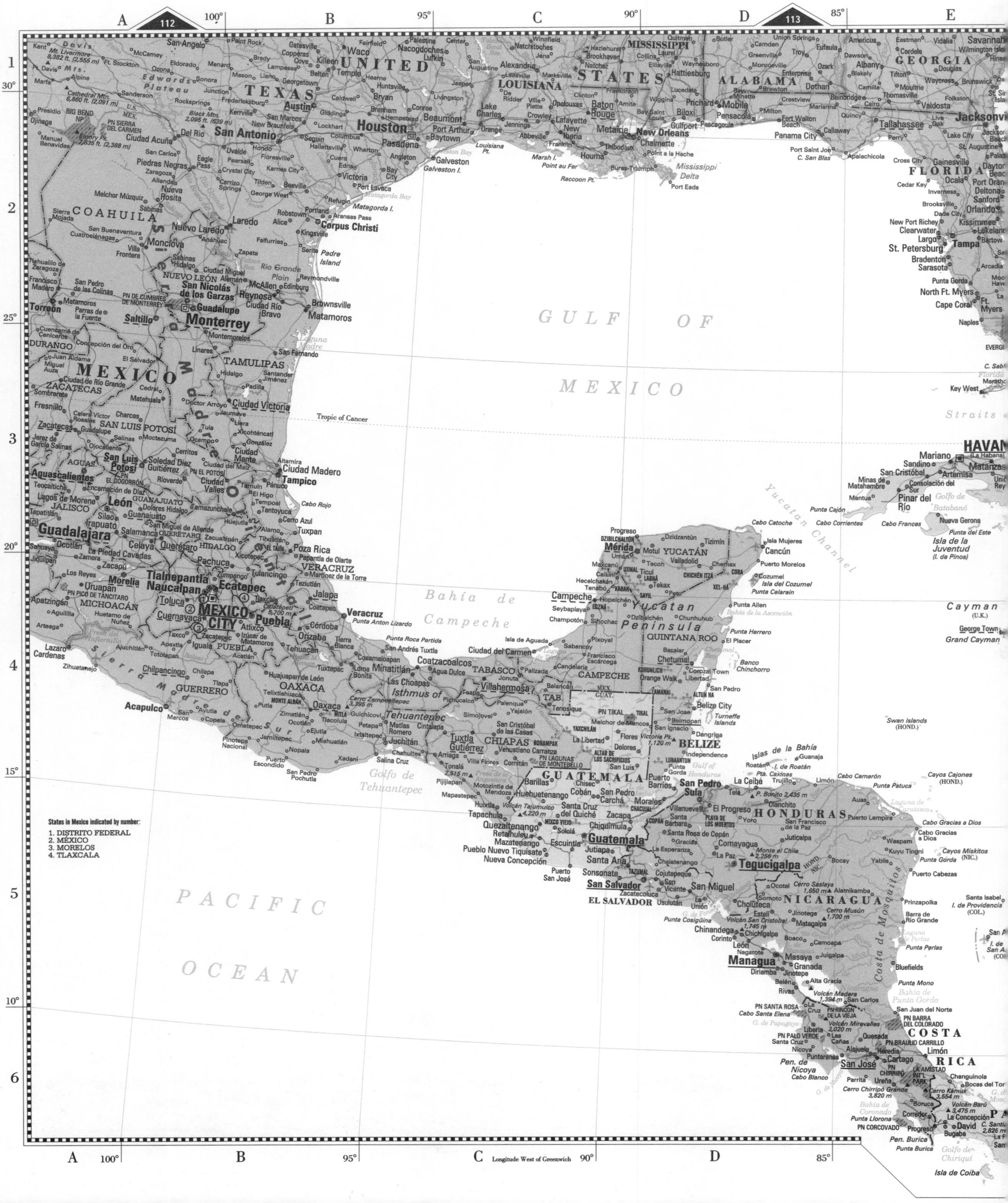

States in Mexico indicated by number:

1. DISTRITO FEDERAL
2. MÉXICO
3. MORELOS
4. TLAXCALA

Longitude West of Greenwich

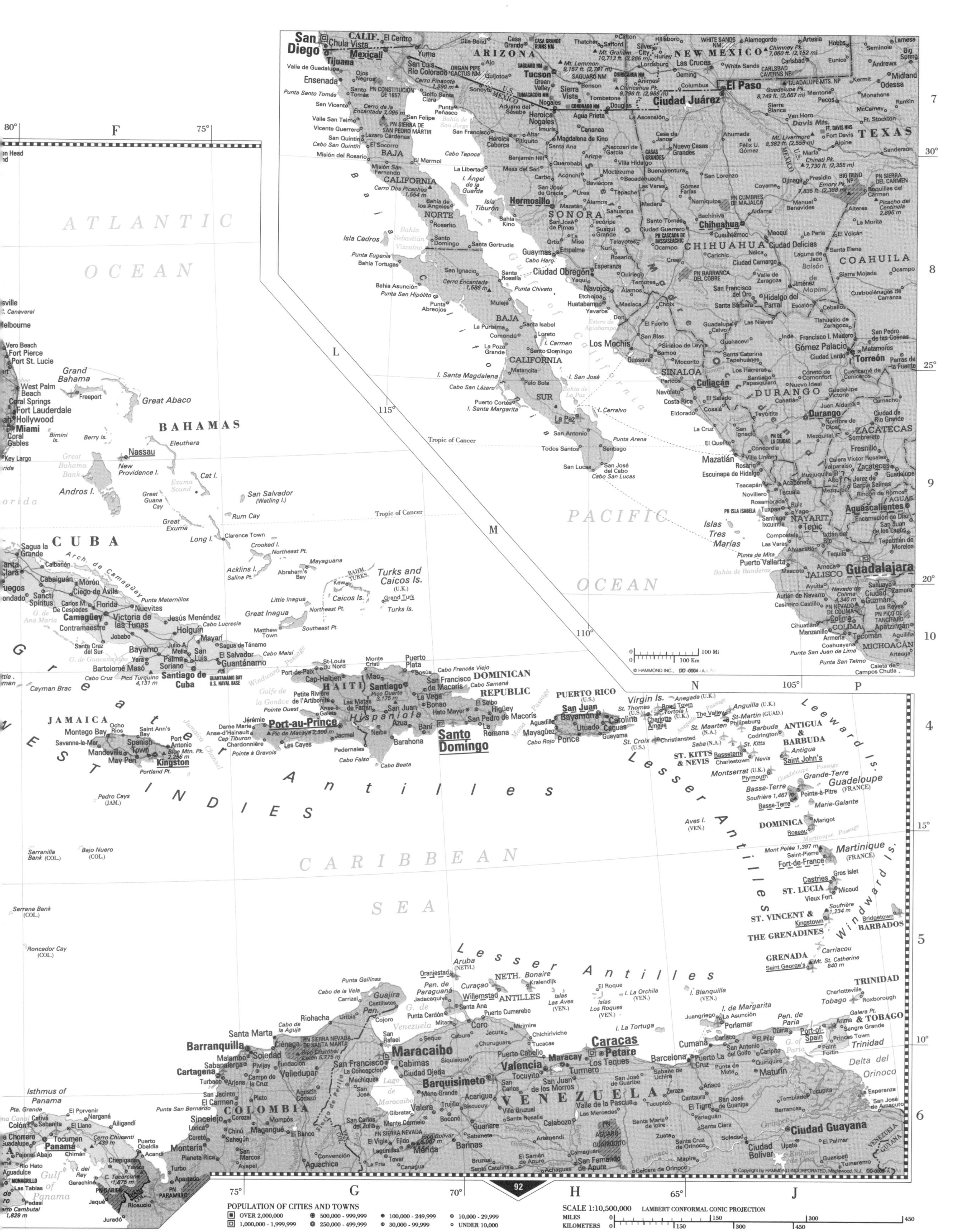

ATLANTIC OCEAN
PACIFIC OCEAN
CARIBBEAN SEA
Gulf of California
Greater Antilles
Lesser Antilles
WEST INDIES
Leeward Is.
Windward Is.
BAHAMAS
CUBA
JAMAICA
HAITI
DOMINICAN REPUBLIC
Hispaniola
PUERTO RICO (U.S.)
Virgin Is.
Turks and Caicos Is. (U.K.)
ANTIGUA & BARBUDA
ST. KITTS & NEVIS
Guadeloupe (FRANCE)
DOMINICA
Martinique (FRANCE)
ST. LUCIA
ST. VINCENT & THE GRENADINES
BARBADOS
GRENADA
TRINIDAD & TOBAGO
NETH. ANTILLES
Aruba (NETH.)
VENEZUELA
COLOMBIA
PANAMA
ARIZONA
NEW MEXICO
TEXAS
CALIF.
BAJA CALIFORNIA NORTE
BAJA CALIFORNIA SUR
SONORA
CHIHUAHUA
COAHUILA
SINALOA
DURANGO
ZACATECAS
NAYARIT
JALISCO
COLIMA
MICHOACÁN
AGUAS
Tropic of Cancer
San Diego
Tijuana
Mexicali
Tucson
El Paso
Ciudad Juárez
Hermosillo
Chihuahua
Ciudad Obregón
Los Mochis
Culiacán
Mazatlán
Torreón
Durango
Tepic
Guadalajara
Aguascalientes
La Paz
Havana
Nassau
Miami
Santiago de Cuba
Guantánamo
Kingston
Port-au-Prince
Santo Domingo
San Juan
Caracas
Maracaibo
Barranquilla
Cartagena
Valencia
Barquisimeto
Ciudad Guayana
Port-of-Spain
Saint John's
Basse-Terre
Roseau
Fort-de-France
Castries
Kingstown
Saint George's
Bridgetown
Plymouth
Oranjestad
Willemstad
92
POPULATION OF CITIES AND TOWNS
OVER 2,000,000
1,000,000 - 1,999,999
500,000 - 999,999
250,000 - 499,999
100,000 - 249,999
30,000 - 99,999
10,000 - 29,999
UNDER 10,000
SCALE 1:10,500,000
LAMBERT CONFORMAL CONIC PROJECTION
MILES 0 150 300 450
KILOMETERS 0 150 300 450
© HAMMOND INC.
© Copyright by HAMMOND INCORPORATED, Maplewood, N.J.

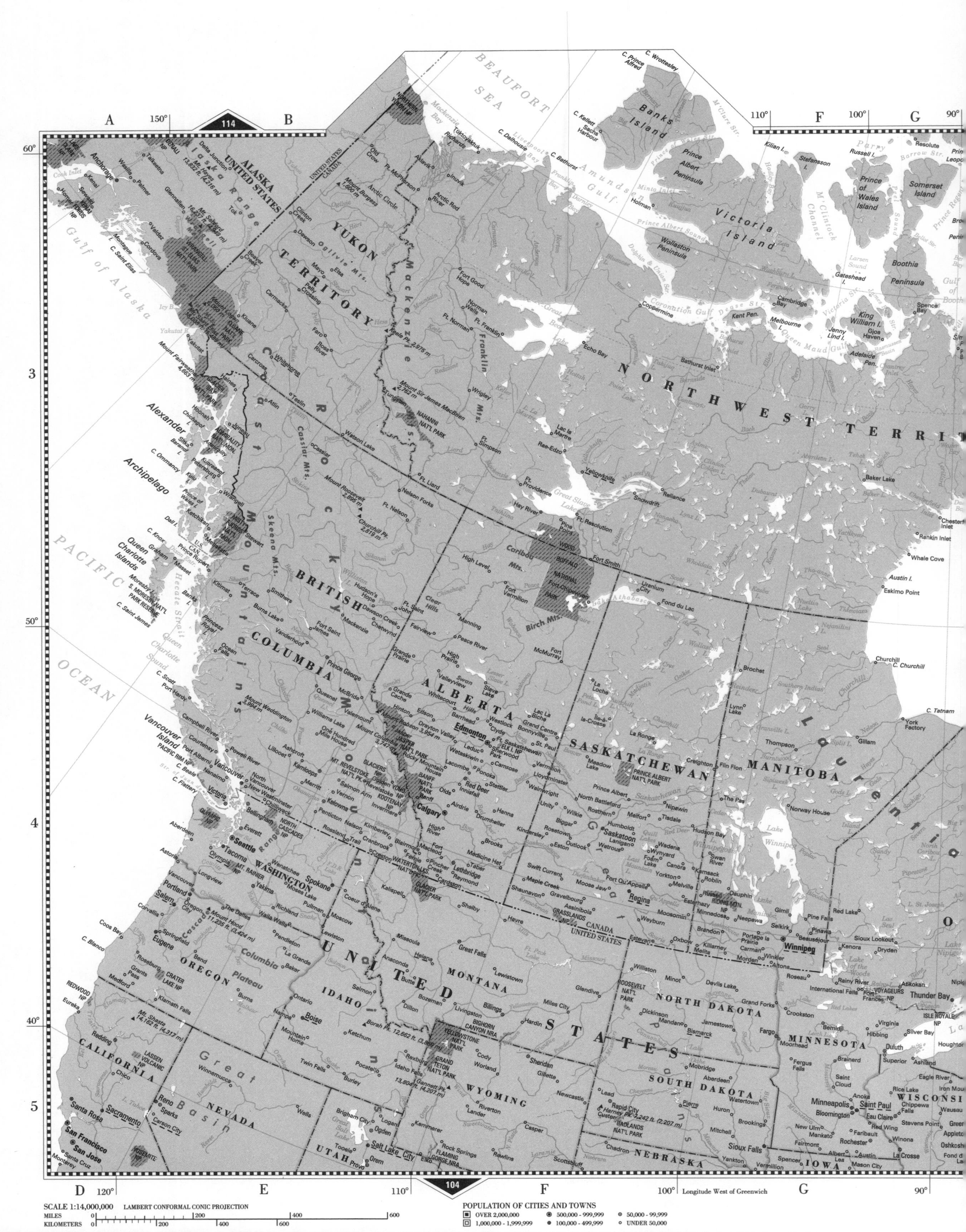

114
104
A
B
D
E
F
G
150°
110°
100°
90°
120°
60°
50°
40°
3
4
5
BEAUFORT SEA
Banks Island
Victoria Island
Prince of Wales Island
Somerset Island
Boothia Peninsula
Prince Albert Peninsula
Wollaston Peninsula
Amundsen Gulf
M'Clintock Channel
Queen Maud Gulf
Coronation Gulf
King William I.
ALASKA
UNITED STATES
CANADA
Anchorage
Alaska Range
Gulf of Alaska
Mt. McKinley 20,320 ft. (6,194 m)
Mount Logan 5,951 m
Mount Fairweather 4,663 m
YUKON TERRITORY
Dawson
Whitehorse
Mackenzie
Mount Sir James MacBrien 2,762 m
NAHANNI NAT'L PARK
NORTHWEST TERRITORIES
Great Bear Lake
Great Slave Lake
Yellowknife
WOOD BUFFALO NATIONAL PARK
Fort Smith
Baker Lake
Rankin Inlet
Whale Cove
Eskimo Point
Churchill
Alexander Archipelago
Queen Charlotte Islands
Juneau
Ketchikan
Prince Rupert
Coast Mountains
Rocky Mountains
BRITISH COLUMBIA
Prince George
Mount Robson 3,954 m
PACIFIC OCEAN
Vancouver Island
Vancouver
Victoria
ALBERTA
Edmonton
Calgary
Lake Athabasca
SASKATCHEWAN
Saskatoon
Regina
PRINCE ALBERT NAT'L PARK
MANITOBA
Lake Winnipeg
Winnipeg
Laurentian Plateau
Ontario
Thunder Bay
UNITED STATES
WASHINGTON
Seattle
Tacoma
Spokane
Olympia
Mount Rainier
OREGON
Portland
Salem
Eugene
Mount Hood 11,235 ft. (3,424 m)
Columbia Plateau
CRATER LAKE NP
IDAHO
Boise
Borah Pk. 12,662 ft. (3,859 m)
MONTANA
Helena
Billings
Great Falls
Missoula
YELLOWSTONE NAT'L PARK
GRAND TETON NAT'L PARK
Gannett Pk. 13,804 ft. (4,207 m)
WYOMING
Casper
NORTH DAKOTA
Bismarck
Fargo
SOUTH DAKOTA
Pierre
Rapid City
Sioux Falls
Harney Pk. 7,242 ft. (2,207 m)
BADLANDS NAT'L PARK
Great Plains
NEBRASKA
MINNESOTA
Minneapolis
Saint Paul
Duluth
WISCONSIN
IOWA
CALIFORNIA
Mt. Shasta 14,162 ft. (4,317 m)
LASSEN VOLCANIC NP
Redding
Sacramento
San Francisco
San Jose
YOSEMITE NP
NEVADA
Great Basin
Reno
Carson City
UTAH
Great Salt Lake
Salt Lake City
Ogden
Provo
Longitude West of Greenwich
SCALE 1:14,000,000 LAMBERT CONFORMAL CONIC PROJECTION
MILES 0 200 400 600
KILOMETERS 0 200 400 600
POPULATION OF CITIES AND TOWNS
OVER 2,000,000
1,000,000 - 1,999,999
500,000 - 999,999
100,000 - 499,999
50,000 - 99,999
UNDER 50,000

Canada

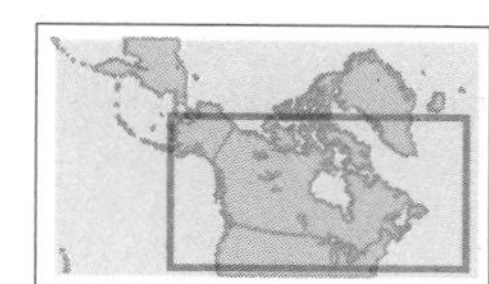

H 80° J 70° K 60° L 50°

Map continued at right

GREENLAND (KALAALLIT NUNAAT) (DEN.)

Upernavik

C. Sherard

Lancaster Sound

C. Liverpool

Bylot Island

Arctic Bay

Borden Pen.

Pond Inlet

Baffin Bay

Disko I.

Qeqertarsuaq

C. Adair

Baffin Island

Davis Strait

Koch I.

Jens Muck I.

Bray I.

Igloolik

Rowley I.

Foley I.

Broughton Island

AUYUITTUQ NATIONAL PARK

Hall Beach

Spicer Is.

Prince Charles Island

Air Force I.

Arctic Circle

C. Dyer

Cumberland Peninsula

Pangnirtung

C. Walsingham

Melville Peninsula

Rae Isthmus

C. Wilson

Foxe Basin

Repulse Bay

C. Mercy

Cumberland Sound

Vansittart I.

C. Dorchester

Foxe Pen.

Brevoort I.

Southampton Island

Coral Harbour

Mill I.

Seahorse Pt.

Bell Pen.

Cape Dorset

Salisbury I.

Iqaluit

Hall Pen.

Lake Harbour

Meta Incognita Pen.

Loks I.

Edgell I.

Resolution I.

Big I.

Nottingham I.

C. Low

Coats I.

Charles I.

Hudson Strait

C. Southampton

Mansel I.

Ivujivik

Kangiqsujuaq

Cap Hopes Advance

Quaqtaq

Port Burwell

Killinek I.

C. Chidley

N. Aulatsivik I.

Akpatok I.

Kangirsuk

LABRADOR SEA

Smith I.

Cape Smith

Ungava Peninsula

Ungava Bay

Hudson Bay

Povungnituk

Ottawa Is.

Kangiqsualujjuaq

Cod I.

Okak I.

S. Aulatsivik I.

Nain

Tunungayualuk I.

Kuujjuaq (Fort-Chimo)

Hopedale

Makkovik

C. Harrison

Inukjuak

King George Is.

Sleeper Is.

Nastapoka Is.

Mount Benedict 739 m

Rigolet

Cartwright

NEWFOUNDLAND

Belcher Islands

Schefferville

Smallwood Res.

Labrador

Churchill Falls

Happy Valley-Goose Bay

C. Bauld

Saint Anthony

Kuujjuarapik

Winisk

C. Henrietta Maria

Pointe Louis XIV

Labrador City

Chisasibi (Fort-George)

La Tabatière

James Bay

Akimiski I.

Attawapiskat

Wemindji

Gagnon

GROS MORNE NP

Gros Morne 806 m

Baie Verte

Gander

Bonavista

TERRA NOVA NP

Harbour Grace

St. John's

Grand Falls

Corner Brook

Stephenville

NEWFOUNDLAND

Avalon Pen.

C. Race

Marystown

Havre-Saint-Pierre

Ile de Anticosti

Pointe Heath

Fort Albany

Waskaganish (Rupert House)

Charlton I.

QUÉBEC

Sept-Îles

Port-Cartier

Port-Menier

Gulf of St. Lawrence

C. St. George

C. Ray

Channel-Port aux Basques

Grand Bank

Burin Pen.

ST. PIERRE & MIQUELON (FR.)

Moosonee

Baie-du-Poste

Mont Jacques Cartier 1,268 m

Gaspé

PN DE FORILLON

Percé

Chandler

Cabot Strait

Îles de la Madeleine

Plateau

ONTARIO

Chibougamau

Baie-Comeau

Hauterive

Cap-Chat

Matane

Gaspé Pen.

Mont-Joli

Rimouski

North C.

PRINCE EDWARD ISLAND

CAPE BRETON HIGHLANDS NP

532 m

Glace Bay

Sydney

Cape Breton I.

Geraldton

Hearst

Kapuskasing

Cochrane

Dolbeau

Mistassini

Alma

Chicoutimi

Roberval

Jonquière

Campbellton

Mount Carleton 820 m

NEW BRUNSWICK

Bathurst

Chatham

Souris

Inverness

Iroquois Falls

La Sarre

Amos

Rouyn-Noranda

Val-d'Or

Rivière-du-Loup

Baie-Saint-Paul

Edmundston

Grand Falls

CAN. U.S.

KOUCHIBOUGUAC NP

Charlottetown

Antigonish

C. Canso

White River

PUKASKWA NP

Wawa

Timmins

Kirkland Lake

Caribou

Presque Isle

Woodstock

Moncton

Amherst

New Glasgow

Truro

NOVA SCOTIA

Sable I.

ATLANTIC OCEAN

Chapleau

New Liskeard

Haileybury

La Tuque

PN DE LA MAURICIE

Québec

Lévis

Shawinigan

Trois-Rivières

Houlton

Fredericton

Oromocto

FUNDY NP

Saint John

Dartmouth

Halifax

Ogidaki Mountain 665 m

Lake Superior

Mont-Laurier

Victoriaville

Mt. Katahdin 5,268 ft. (1,606 m)

Thetford Mines

Millinocket

Saint Stephen

Calais

Kentville

Bridgewater

Liverpool

Sault Sainte Marie

Sudbury

North Bay

Joliette

Drummondville

Sherbrooke

MAINE

Bangor

Bay of Fundy

Digby

KEJIMKUJIK NP

Sault Ste. Marie

Elliot Lake

Sturgeon Falls

Deep River

Pembroke

Renfrew

Hull

Hawkesbury

Laval

Montréal

Rumford

ACADIA NP

Yarmouth

C. Sable

MICHIGAN

Manitoulin I.

Parry Sound

Huntsville

Ottawa

Cornwall

Massena

Plattsburgh

Burlington

Berlin

Augusta

Lewiston

Escanaba

Georgian Bay

Lake Huron

Alpena

Owen Sound

Orillia

Peterborough

Brockville

Kingston

Ogdensburg

Montpelier

VT.

N.H.

Portland

Gulf of Maine

Traverse City

Barrie

Belleville

NEW YORK

Watertown

Rutland

Laconia

Portsmouth

C. Ann

Toronto

Oshawa

Mississauga

Lake Ontario

Rochester

Oswego

Glens Falls

Concord

Manchester

Ludington

Bay City

Kitchener

Hamilton

Buffalo

Rome

Utica

Syracuse

Schenectady

Albany

Nashua

Lowell

Boston

Saginaw

Flint

Port Huron

London

Auburn

Springfield

MASS.

Worcester

Providence

C. Cod

Pontiac

Sarnia

Lansing

Detroit

Windsor

Ann Arbor

Lake Erie

Pt. Pelee

Jamestown

Erie

PA.

Cleveland

Toledo

OHIO

40°

50°

4

5

H J 70° K 60° L

140° Q 120° R 100° S 80° T 60°

0 120 Mi

0 120 Km

ARCTIC OCEAN

C. Columbia

Alert

Alert Pt.

Barbour Pt. 2616 m

ELLESMERE ISLAND NP

Queen Elizabeth Islands

C. Colgate

C. Stallworthy

Ellesmere Island

Meighen I.

C. Isachsen

Sverdrup Islands

Axel Heiberg Island

Eureka

Fosheim Pen.

Borden I.

Isachsen

Ellef Ringnes I.

Amund Ringnes I.

Stor I.

Raanes Pen.

GREENLAND (KALAALLIT NUNAAT)

CANADA GREENLAND

Hayes Pen.

Qaanaaq

Brock I.

Mackenzie King I.

Prince Patrick I.

Mould Bay

C. Manning

Lougheed I.

King Christian I.

NORTH MAGNETIC POLE

Cornwall I.

Graham I.

Bjorne Pen.

Svendsen Pen.

Clarence Head

Thule Air Base

Parry Islands

C. Prince Alfred

Eglinton I.

C. Scott

Cameron I.

I. Vanier

412 m

Grinnel Pen.

C. Wrottesley

778 m

Melville Island

Bathurst I.

Grise Fiord

Coburg I.

Banks Island

472 m

Dundas Pen.

Byam Martin I.

Cornwallis I.

Devon Island

Baffin Bay

Victoria Island

Kilian I.

Stefansson I.

Viscount Melville Sound

Russel I.

Resolute

C. Sherard

6

80°

7

Map continued at left

140° 135° 130° A 125° B 120° C 115° 102 110° E 105° F 100°
45° 40° 35° 30°
3
4
5
PACIFIC OCEAN
BRITISH COLUMBIA
ALBERTA
SASKATCHEWAN
CANADA
UNITED STATES
WASHINGTON
MONTANA
NORTH DAKOTA
OREGON
IDAHO
SOUTH DAKOTA
WYOMING
NEBRASKA
NEVADA
UTAH
COLORADO
CALIFORNIA
ARIZONA
NEW MEXICO
SONORA
CHIHUAHUA
COAHUILA
NUEVO LEON
MEXICO
ZACATECAS
SAN LUIS POTOSÍ
JALISCO
GUANAJUATO
Vancouver Island
Vancouver
Victoria
Seattle
Tacoma
Olympia
Spokane
Portland
Salem
Eugene
Calgary
Regina
Saskatoon
Great Falls
Helena
Billings
Boise
Great Salt Lake
Salt Lake City
Reno
Sacramento
San Francisco
Oakland
San Jose
Fresno
Los Angeles
San Diego
Tijuana
Mexicali
Las Vegas
Phoenix
Tucson
Albuquerque
Santa Fe
El Paso
Ciudad Juárez
Denver
Colorado Springs
Cheyenne
Lubbock
Amarillo
Monterrey
Saltillo
Guadalajara
León
Great Basin
Coast Ranges
Sierra Nevada
Mojave Desert
Painted Desert
YELLOWSTONE NAT'L PARK
GRAND CANYON NAT'L PARK
UNITED STATES
MEXICO
See p. 114 for map of Alaska.
R 160° S 158°
9
10
22°
HAWAII
Kauai
Niihau
Kauai Channel
Oahu
Honolulu
Kaiwi Channel
Molokai
Lanai
Maui
Kahoolawe
Alenuihaha Channel
Hawaii
Hilo
PACIFIC OCEAN
T 156° U
20°
11
12
13
21° 30′
Kauai Channel
PACIFIC OCEAN
HONOLULU
Oahu
Pearl City
Kaneohe
Kailua
Waipahu
Diamond Head
© HAMMOND INC.
V 158° W 158° T 156° U F 100 100°

United States

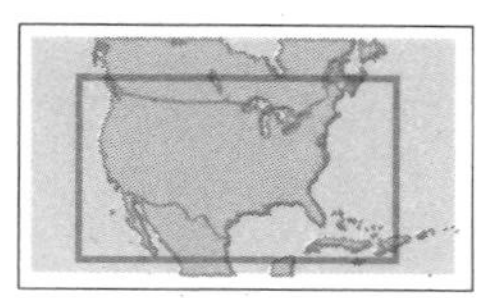

103

100

Longitude West of Greenwich

POPULATION OF CITIES AND TOWNS

- OVER 2,000,000
- 1,000,000 - 1,999,999
- 500,000 - 999,999
- 100,000 - 499,999
- 50,000 - 99,999
- UNDER 50,000

SCALE 1:14,000,000 LAMBERT CONFORMAL CONIC PROJECTION

MILES 0 200 400 600

KILOMETERS 0 200 400 600

CD - 1079 - A

A
128°
102
B
124°
C
120°
D
116°
E
112°
F
108°
114
2
3
4
5
6
52°
48°
44°
40°
PACIFIC
OCEAN
ALBERTA
BRITISH COLUMBIA
SASK
WASHINGTON
OREGON
IDAHO
MONTANA
WYOMING
CALIFORNIA
NEVADA
UTAH
CANADA
UNITED STATES
Coast Mountains
Interior
BRITISH
COLUMBIA
Plateau
Columbia Mts.
Cariboo Mts.
Monashee Mts.
Selkirk Mts.
Purcell Mts.
Livingstone Ra.
Continental Ranges
Pacific Ras
Vancouver Island
Cascade Range
Columbia Plateau
Blue Mts.
Wallowa Mts.
Clearwater Mts.
Salmon River Mts.
Bitterroot Range
Lewis Ra.
Coast Ranges
Klamath Mts.
Great Basin
Sierra Nevada
Wasatch Ra.
Wind River Ra.
Bighorn Mts.
Absaroka Ra.
Beartooth Mts.
Centennial Mts.
Snake River Plain
Great Salt Lake Desert
Great Divide Basin
Swan Hills
Pelican Mts.
Saddle Hills
Cypress Hills
Bearpaw Mts.
High Desert
Harney Valley
JASPER NATIONAL PARK
BANFF NAT'L PARK
GLACIER NP
WATERTON LAKES NP
YELLOWSTONE NAT'L PARK
OLYMPIC NAT'L PARK
NORTH CASCADES NP
MT. RAINIER NP
CRATER LAKE NP
LASSEN VOLCANIC NP
REDWOOD NAT'L PARK
HELLS CANYON NRA
SAWTOOTH NRA
Edmonton
Calgary
Vancouver
Victoria
Seattle
Tacoma
Olympia
Spokane
Portland
Salem
Eugene
Boise
Missoula
Helena
Great Falls
Billings
Butte
Idaho Falls
Pocatello
Ogden
Salt Lake City
Lethbridge
Medicine Hat
Red Deer
Kamloops
Kelowna
Prince George
Redding
Medford
Longitude West of Greenwich
108

Southwestern Canada, Northwestern United States

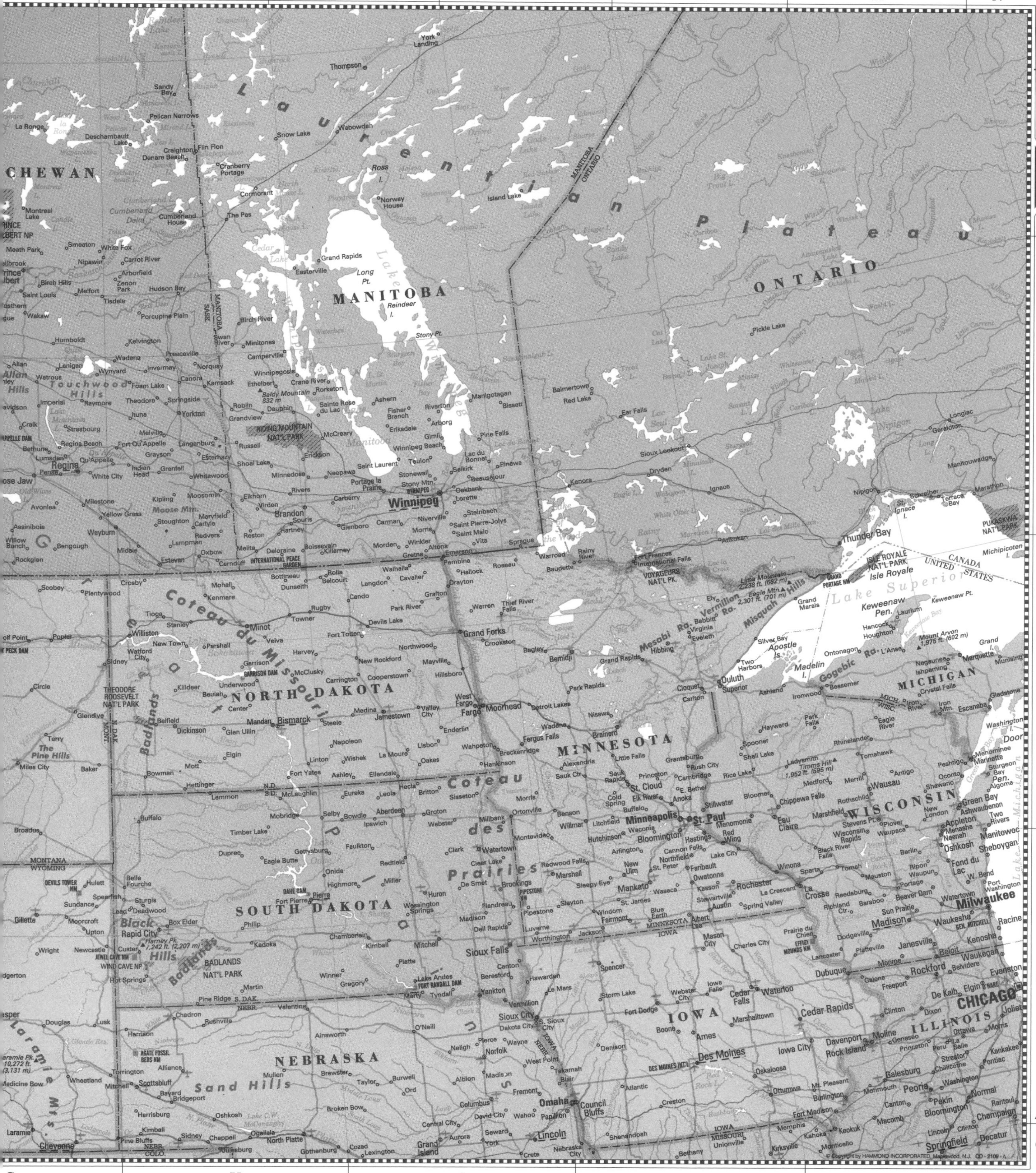

POPULATION OF CITIES AND TOWNS

- OVER 2,000,000
- 1,000,000 - 1,999,999
- 500,000 - 999,999
- 250,000 - 499,999
- 100,000 - 249,999
- 30,000 - 99,999
- 10,000 - 29,999
- UNDER 10,000

SCALE 1:7,000,000 LAMBERT CONFORMAL CONIC PROJECTION

MILES 0 100 200 300

KILOMETERS 0 100 200 300

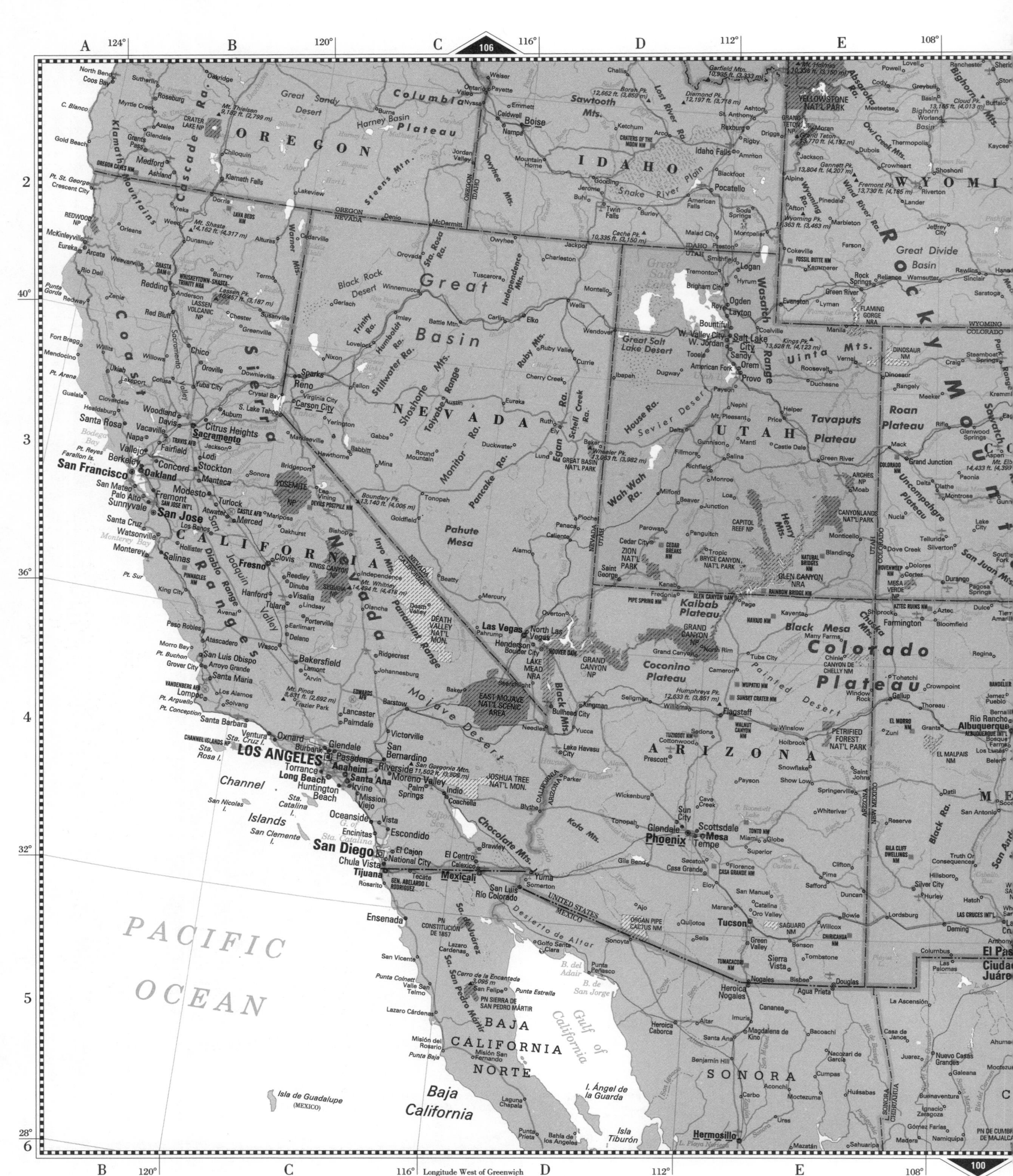
A
124°
B
120°
C
106
116°
D
112°
E
108°
40°
36°
32°
28°
2
3
4
5
6
Longitude West of Greenwich
100
PACIFIC OCEAN
OREGON
IDAHO
WYOMING
NEVADA
UTAH
CALIFORNIA
ARIZONA
BAJA CALIFORNIA NORTE
SONORA
Baja California
Gulf of California
Great Sandy Desert
Columbia Plateau
Harney Basin
Steens Mtn.
Cascade Ra.
Klamath Mountains
Coast Ranges
Sierra Nevada
Great Basin
Black Rock Desert
Sawtooth Mts.
Lost River Ra.
Snake River Plain
Great Salt Lake Desert
Wasatch Range
Uinta Mts.
Rocky Mountains
Great Divide Basin
Wind River Ra.
Wyoming Ra.
Owl Creek Mts.
Bighorn Mts.
Absaroka Ra.
Tavaputs Plateau
Roan Plateau
Sevier Desert
House Ra.
Wah Wah Ra.
Henry Mts.
Uncompahgre Plateau
Kaibab Plateau
Coconino Plateau
Black Mesa
Colorado Plateau
Painted Desert
Mojave Desert
Chocolate Mts.
Panamint Range
Pahute Mesa
Toiyabe Range
Shoshone Mts.
Monitor Ra.
Ruby Mts.
Independence Mts.
Trinity Ra.
Humboldt Ra.
Stillwater Ra.
Diablo Range
San Joaquin Valley
Sacramento Valley
Black Mts.
Kofa Mts.
Desierto de Altar
Channel Islands
Sierra de Juárez
Sierra San Pedro Mártir
Isla de Guadalupe (MEXICO)
I. Ángel de la Guarda
Isla Tiburón
YELLOWSTONE NAT'L PARK
GRAND TETON NP
CRATER LAKE NP
LASSEN VOLCANIC NP
YOSEMITE NP
KINGS CANYON NP
SEQUOIA NP
DEATH VALLEY NAT'L MON.
EAST MOJAVE NAT'L SCENIC AREA
JOSHUA TREE NAT'L MON.
LAKE MEAD NRA
GRAND CANYON NP
ZION NAT'L PARK
BRYCE CANYON NAT'L PARK
CAPITOL REEF NP
CANYONLANDS NAT'L PARK
ARCHES NP
GLEN CANYON NRA
GREAT BASIN NAT'L PARK
PETRIFIED FOREST NAT'L PARK
ORGAN PIPE CACTUS NM
SAGUARO NM
Mt. Whitney 14,494 ft. (4,418 m)
Mt. Shasta 14,162 ft. (4,317 m)
Lassen Pk. 10,457 ft. (3,187 m)
Humphreys Pk. 12,633 ft. (3,851 m)
Kings Pk. 13,528 ft. (4,123 m)
Wheeler Pk. 13,063 ft. (3,982 m)
Boundary Pk. 13,140 ft. (4,005 m)
San Gorgonio Mtn. 11,502 ft. (3,506 m)
Gannett Pk. 13,804 ft. (4,207 m)
Grand Teton 13,770 ft. (4,197 m)
Borah Pk. 12,662 ft. (3,859 m)
Boise
Sacramento
Carson City
Salt Lake City
Phoenix
San Francisco
Oakland
San Jose
Fresno
Bakersfield
LOS ANGELES
Long Beach
Anaheim
Santa Ana
San Diego
Tijuana
Mexicali
Las Vegas
Reno
Tucson
Mesa
Scottsdale
Flagstaff
Yuma
Albuquerque
Hermosillo
Ensenada
Ogden
Provo
Pocatello
Idaho Falls
Medford
Klamath Falls
Eureka
Redding
Stockton
Modesto
Santa Barbara
Oxnard
Riverside
San Bernardino
El Paso
Ciudad Juárez
Farmington
Grand Junction
Nogales
Heroica Nogales
Douglas
Agua Prieta
UNITED STATES
MEXICO

Southwestern United States

POPULATION OF CITIES AND TOWNS

OVER 2,000,000	500,000 - 999,999	100,000 - 249,999	10,000 - 29,999	
1,000,000 - 1,999,999	250,000 - 499,999	30,000 - 99,999	UNDER 10,000	

SCALE 1:7,000,000 LAMBERT CONFORMAL CONIC PROJECTION

MILES 0 100 200 300

KILOMETERS 0 100 200 300

Southeastern Canada, Northeastern United States

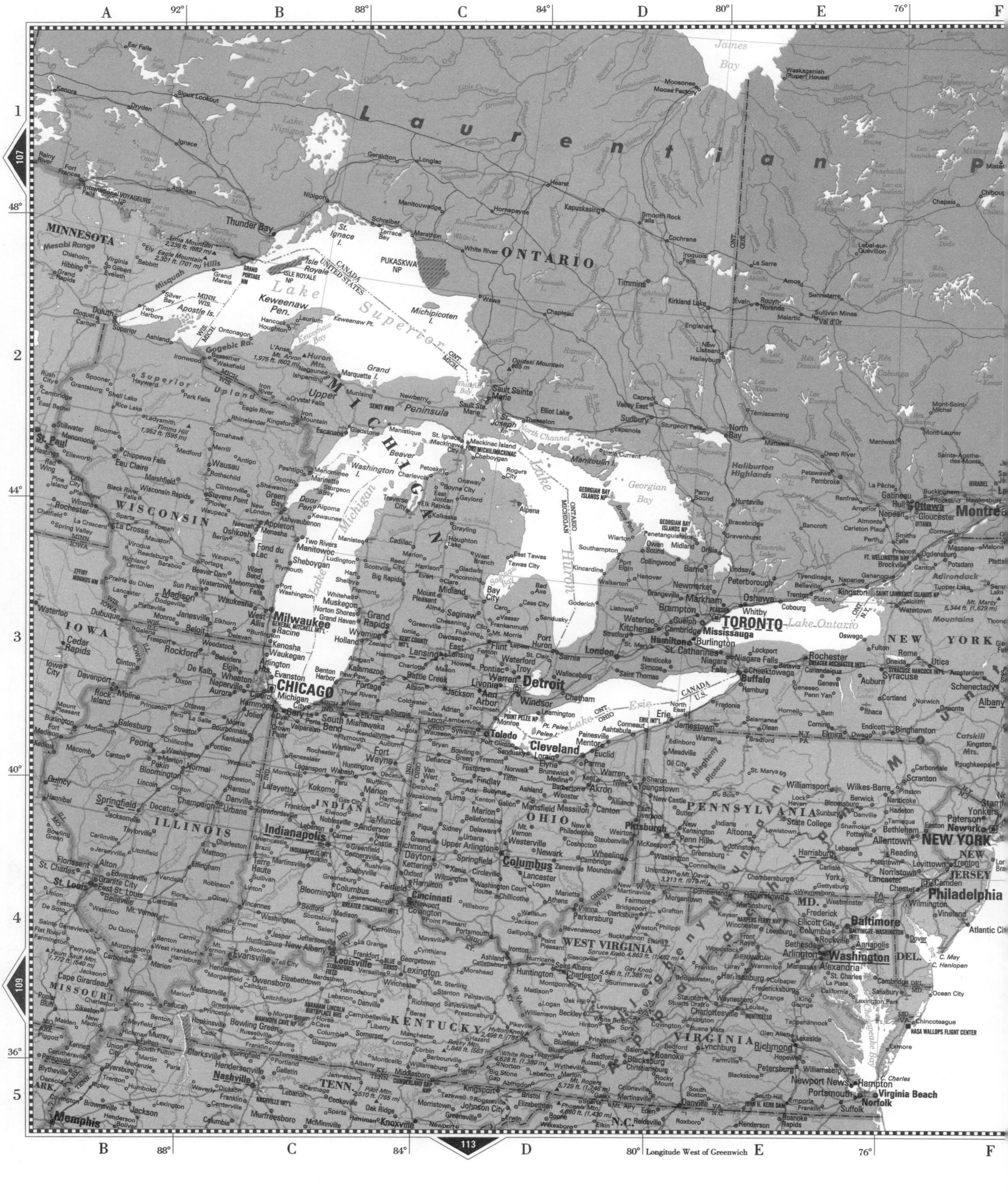

A 92° B 88° C 84° D 80° E 76° F

1

2

3

4

5

48°

44°

40°

36°

107

109

113

B 88° C 84° D 80° Longitude West of Greenwich E 76° F

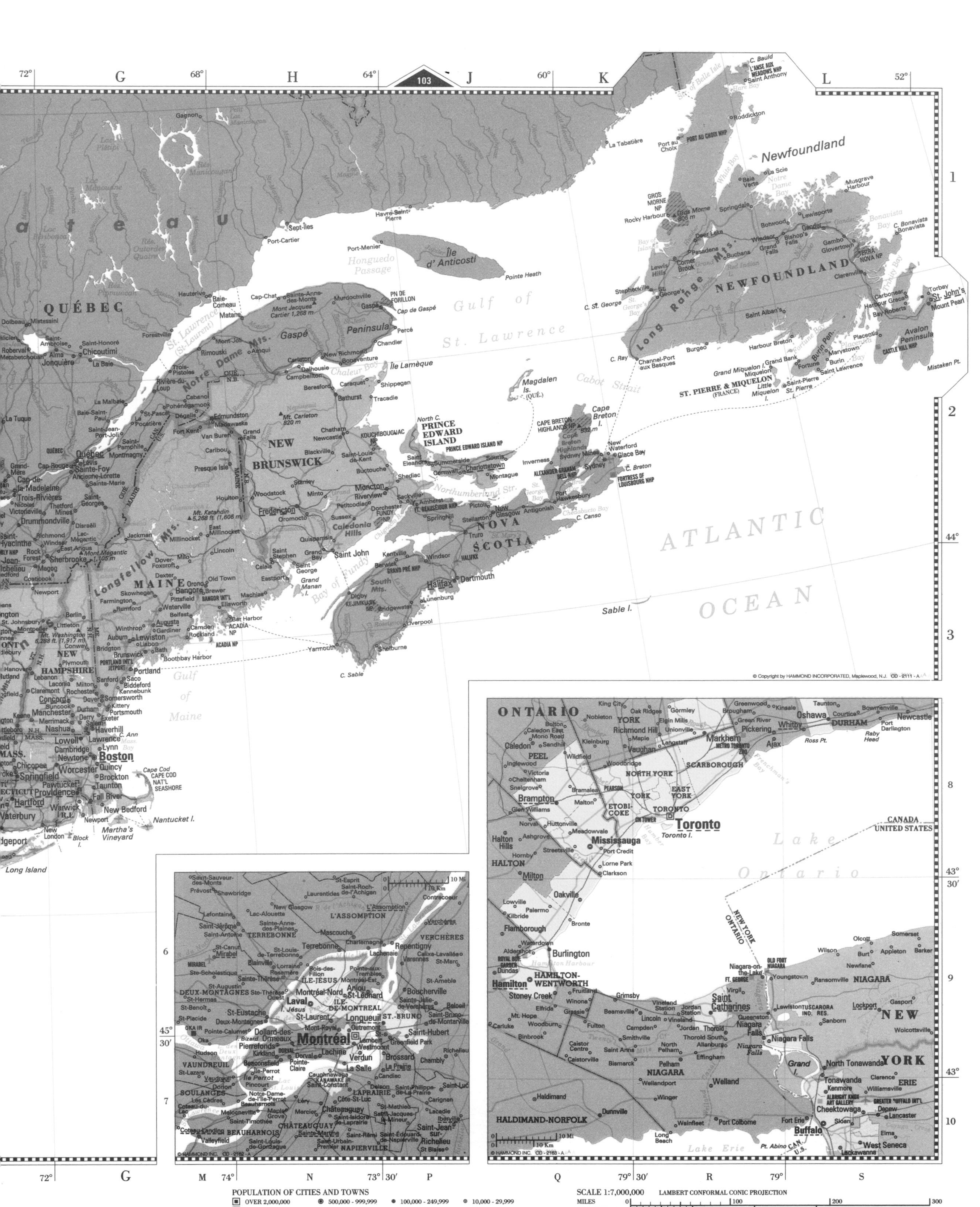
72°
G
68°
H
64°
J
60°
K
L
52°
1
2
3
44°
Newfoundland
NEWFOUNDLAND
Long Range Mts.
C. Bauld
L'ANSE AUX MEADOWS NHP
Saint Anthony
Roddickton
Port au Choix
PORT AU CHOIX NHP
La Tabatière
La Scie
Baie Verte
Notre Dame Bay
Musgrave Harbour
GROS MORNE NP
Gros Morne 806 m
Rocky Harbour
Springdale
Lewisporte
Gander
Bonavista Bay
C. Bonavista
Bonavista
Botwood
Bishop's Falls
Deer Lake
Windsor
Grand Falls
Gambo
Glovertown
TERRA NOVA NP
Pasadena
Corner Brook
Buchans
Lewis Hills
Clarenville
Trinity Bay
Stephenville
St. George's
St. George's Bay
C. St. George
Torbay
St. John's
Mount Pearl
Carbonear
Harbour Grace
Bay Roberts
Saint Alban's
Avalon Peninsula
Placentia
Placentia Bay
CASTLE HILL NHP
Burgeo
Harbour Breton
Fortune Bay
Burin Pen.
Marystown
Burin
Grand Bank
Fortune
Saint Lawrence
Mistaken Pt.
C. Ray
Channel-Port aux Basques
Grand Miquelon I.
Miquelon
Little Miquelon I.
Saint-Pierre
St. Pierre I.
ST. PIERRE & MIQUELON (FRANCE)
Cabot Strait
Gulf of St. Lawrence
Gagnon
Rés. Manicouagan
Sept-Îles
Port-Cartier
Havre-Saint-Pierre
Port-Menier
Île d' Anticosti
Honguedo Passage
Pointe Heath
QUÉBEC
Baie-Comeau
Hauterive
Matane
Cap-Chat
Sainte-Anne-des-Monts
Murdochville
Mont Jacques Cartier 1,268 m
Gaspé
PN DE FORILLON
Cap de Gaspé
Gaspé Peninsula
Percé
Chandler
Notre Dame Mts.
Mont-Joli
Rimouski
Amqui
New Richmond
Bonaventure
Carleton
Dalhousie
Campbellton
Chaleur Bay
Île Lamèque
Shippegan
Caraquet
Bathurst
Tracadie
Beresford
St. Lawrence (St-Laurent)
Forestville
Dolbeau
Mistassini
Saint-Honoré
Chicoutimi
Alma
Jonquière
La Baie
Roberval
Trois-Pistoles
Rivière-du-Loup
La Malbaie
Baie-Saint-Paul
La Pocatière
Saint-Jean-Port-Joli
Edmundston
Madawaska
Dégelis
Pohénégamook
Fort Kent
Van Buren
Grand Falls
Caribou
Presque Isle
Mt. Carleton 820 m
NEW BRUNSWICK
Chatham
Newcastle
KOUCHIBOUGUAC NP
Blackville
Saint-Louis-de-Kent
Buctouche
Shediac
Moncton
Riverview
Sackville
Amherst
Petitcodiac
Dorchester
FUNDY NP
FT. BEAUSÉJOUR NHP
Woodstock
Fredericton
Oromocto
Sussex
Caledonia Hills
Quispamsis
Saint John
Grand Bay
Saint George
St. Stephen
Calais
Eastport
Grand Manan I.
Bay of Fundy
North C.
PRINCE EDWARD ISLAND
PRINCE EDWARD ISLAND NP
Summerside
Charlottetown
Montague
Souris
Northumberland Str.
Magdalen Is. (QUÉ.)
CAPE BRETON HIGHLANDS NP
532 m
Cape Breton I.
Inverness
ALEXANDER GRAHAM BELL NHP
Sydney Mines
New Waterford
Glace Bay
Sydney
C. Breton
FORTRESS OF LOUISBOURG NHP
Port Hawkesbury
C. Canso
Antigonish
New Glasgow
Pictou
Stellarton
Truro
NOVA SCOTIA
Springhill
Kentville
Windsor
Berwick
GRAND PRÉ NHP
Halifax
Dartmouth
Digby
South Mts.
KEJIMKUJIK NP
Bridgewater
Lunenburg
Liverpool
Yarmouth
Shelburne
C. Sable
Sable I.
ATLANTIC OCEAN
Québec
Lévis
Sainte-Foy
Ancienne-Lorette
Cap-Rouge
Montmagny
Cap-de-la-Madeleine
Trois-Rivières
Thetford Mines
Victoriaville
Drummondville
Saint-Georges
Disraeli
Lac-Mégantic
Richmond
Windsor
East Angus
Mont Mégantic 1,105 m
Sherbrooke
Rock Forest
Magog
Coaticook
Jackman
Millinocket
East Millinocket
Mt. Katahdin 5,268 ft. (1,606 m)
Houlton
MAINE
Longfellow Mts.
Lincoln
Dover-Foxcroft
Milo
Old Town
Orono
Bangor
Brewer
BANGOR INT'L
Ellsworth
Machias
Skowhegan
Farmington
Pittsfield
Rumford
Waterville
Belfast
Bar Harbor
ACADIA NP
Camden
Rockland
Augusta
Gardiner
Winthrop
Auburn
Lewiston
Lisbon
Bath
Brunswick
Boothbay Harbor
Portland
PORTLAND INT'L JETPORT
Saco
Biddeford
Sanford
Kennebunk
Gulf of Maine
Newport
Berlin
St. Johnsbury
Montpelier
Littleton
Mt. Washington 6,288 ft. (1,917 m)
Conway
NEW HAMPSHIRE
Plymouth
Hanover
Lebanon
Laconia
Milton
Rochester
Claremont
Concord
Dover
Somersworth
Kittery
Portsmouth
Exeter
Durham
Derry
Keene
Manchester
Merrimack
Nashua
Haverhill
Lowell
Lawrence
C. Ann
Cambridge
Lynn
Mass. Bay
Boston
Newton
Quincy
Worcester
Chicopee
Springfield
Brockton
Cape Cod
CAPE COD NAT'L SEASHORE
Taunton
Pawtucket
Providence
Fall River
Hartford
Warwick
New Bedford
Waterbury
R.I.
Newport
Nantucket I.
Martha's Vineyard
New London
Block I.
Long Island
MASS.
N.H.
© Copyright by HAMMOND INCORPORATED, Maplewood, N.J. CD - 2111 - A
6
7
45°
30'
Saint-Sauveur-des-Monts
Prévost
Shawbridge
Saint-Esprit
Saint-Roch-de-l'Achigan
Laurentides
L'Assomption
L'ASSOMPTION
Contrecoeur
Lafontaine
Lac-Aloutte
New Glasgow
Sainte-Anne-des-Plaines
Saint-Jérôme
Saint-Antoine
TERREBONNE
Mascouche
Verchères
VERCHÈRES
Saint-Canut
Mirabel
MIRABEL
Terrebonne
Charlemagne
Repentigny
Lachenaie
Saint-Louis-de-Terrebonne
Blainville
Lorraine
Rosemère
Bois-des-Fillion
Pointe-aux-Trembles
Varennes
Calixa-Lavallée
St-Marc
Ste-Scholastique
Sainte-Thérèse
ÎLE-JÉSUS
Montréal-Est
Anjou
St-Léonard
Boucherville
St-Augustin
DEUX-MONTAGNES
St-Hermas
St-Benoît
St-Placide
St-Eustache
Deux-Montagnes
Laval
Î. Jésus
Montréal-Nord
ÎLE-DE-MONTRÉAL
St-Laurent
Longueuil
ST.-BRUNO
Sainte-Julie
Beloeil
Saint-Bruno-de-Montarville
Oka
Pointe-Calumet
Dollard-des-Ormeaux
Pierrefonds
Mont-Royal
Outremont
Montréal
Westmount
Saint-Hubert
Greenfield Park
Hudson
Kirkland
DORVAL
Dorval
Lachine
Verdun
Brossard
Chambly
Richelieu
VAUDREUIL
St-Lazare
Vaudreuil
Île-Perrot
Pointe-Claire
Beaconsfield
La Salle
La Prairie
Dorion
Pincourt
Caughnawaga
KAHNAWAKE I.R.
Saint-Constant
Candiac
Delson
SOULANGES
Les Cèdres
Coteau-du-Lac
Notre-Dame-de-l'Île-Perrot
Beauharnois
LAPRAIRIE
Côte-St-Luc
Saint-Philippe-de-La-Prairie
Saint-Luc
Carignan
Léry
Châteauguay
St-Mathieu
Saint-Jacques-le-Mineur
Melocheville
Maple Grove
Mercier
Saint-Timothée
Saint-Isidore-de-Laprairie
Iberville
Lacadie
Coteau-Landing
Valleyfield
BEAUHARNOIS
CHÂTEAUGUAY
Sainte-Martine
Saint-Rémi
Saint-Édouard-de-Napierville
Saint-Jean-sur-Richelieu
Saint-Louis-de-Gonzague
Saint-Urbain-Premier
NAPIERVILLE
St Blaise
© HAMMOND INC. CD - 2162 - A
0 10 Mi
0 10 Km
M
74°
N
73°
30'
P
ONTARIO
King City
Oak Ridges
Gormley
Greenwood
Kinsale
Taunton
Bowmanville
Newcastle
Nobleton
YORK
Elgin Mills
Brougham
Green River
Oshawa
Courtice
DURHAM
Port Darlington
Bolton
Caledon East
Mono Road
Richmond Hill
Unionville
Markham
Pickering
Whitby
Raby Head
Caledon
Sandhill
Kleinburg
Maple
Langstaff
METRO TORONTO ZOO
Ajax
Ross Pt.
PEEL
Wildfield
Vaughan
Woodbridge
SCARBOROUGH
Inglewood
Victoria
Cheltenham
Snelgrove
NORTH YORK
Bramalea
PEARSON
EAST YORK
Brampton
Malton
YORK
Glen Williams
ETOBICOKE
TORONTO
CN TOWER
Toronto
Toronto I.
Norval
Huttonville
Halton Hills
Ashgrove
Meadowvale
Mississauga
Hornby
Streetsville
Port Credit
HALTON
Lorne Park
Clarkson
Milton
Lake Ontario
CANADA
UNITED STATES
NEW YORK
ONTARIO
Oakville
Lowville
Palermo
Kilbride
Bronte
Flamborough
Waterdown
Aldershot
Burlington
ROYAL BOT. GARDEN
Dundas
Hamilton Harbour
Hamilton
HAMILTON-WENTWORTH
Stoney Creek
Grimsby
Winona
Fruitland
Vineland Station
Jordan Station
Saint Catharines
Niagara-on-the-Lake
OLD FORT NIAGARA
FT. GEORGE
Youngstown
Virgil
Olcott
Somerset
Wilson
Burt
Appleton
Barker
Newfane
Ransomville
NIAGARA
Lockport
Gasport
Lewiston
TUSCARORA IND. RES.
Sanborn
NEW
Elfrida
Grassie
Beamsville
Lincoln
Vineland
Queenston
Niagara Falls
Mt. Hope
Carluke
Woodburn
Fulton
Campden
Jordan
Thorold
Thorold South
Allanburg
Binbrook
Smithville
Caistor Centre
Saint Anns
North Pelham
Pelham
Effingham
Caistorville
Bismarck
NIAGARA
Welland
Wellandport
Grand I.
North Tonawanda
YORK
Tonawanda
Kenmore
Clarence
Williamsville
ERIE
ALBRIGHT KNOX ART GALLERY
GREATER BUFFALO INT'L
Cheektowaga
Depew
Lancaster
Haldimand
Winger
Dunnville
HALDIMAND-NORFOLK
Wainfleet
Port Colborne
Fort Erie
Buffalo
Sloan
Elma
Long Beach
Lake Erie
Pt. Abino
CAN. U.S.
West Seneca
Lackawanna
Woolcottsville
© HAMMOND INC. CD - 2163 - A
8
9
10
43°
30'
Q
79°
R
S
POPULATION OF CITIES AND TOWNS
OVER 2,000,000
1,000,000 - 1,999,999
500,000 - 999,999
250,000 - 499,999
100,000 - 249,999
30,000 - 99,999
10,000 - 29,999
UNDER 10,000
SCALE 1:7,000,000
LAMBERT CONFORMAL CONIC PROJECTION
MILES 0 100 200 300
KILOMETERS 0 100 200 300

A
108°
B
104°
C
109
100°
D
96°
E
2
36°
108
3
32°
4
28°
5
24°
6
100
Longitude West of Greenwich
92°
COLORADO
Rocky Mts.
Grand Junction
Colorado Springs
Pikes Pk. 14,110 ft. (4,301 m)
Mount Elbert 14,433 ft. (4,399 m)
Pueblo
Trinidad
Durango
Burlington
La Junta
Lamar
KANSAS
Great Plains
Wichita
Hutchinson
Salina
Topeka
Manhattan
Lawrence
Dodge City
Garden City
Liberal
Kansas City
Overland Park
Independence
Saint Joseph
Springfield
Joplin
MISSOURI
Ozark Plateau
Ozark Mts.
Boston Mts.
ARKANSAS
Fort Smith
Fayetteville
Hot Springs National Park
Texarkana
NEW MEXICO
Albuquerque
Santa Fe
Los Alamos
Rio Rancho
Roswell
Clovis
Las Cruces
Alamogordo
Carlsbad
Hobbs
Sierra Blanca 12,003 ft. (3,659 m)
Sangre de Cristo Mts.
Wheeler Pk. 13,161 ft. (4,011 m)
OKLAHOMA
Oklahoma City
Tulsa
Norman
Lawton
Enid
Stillwater
Muskogee
Bartlesville
Ouachita Mts.
Wichita Mts.
TEXAS
Amarillo
Lubbock
Llano Estacado
Cap Rock Escarpment
Wichita Falls
Abilene
Midland
Odessa
El Paso
Guadalupe Pk. 8,749 ft. (2,667 m)
Fort Worth
Dallas
Arlington
Irving
Plano
Garland
Mesquite
Denton
Tyler
Waco
Killeen
Temple
Austin
San Antonio
San Angelo
Edwards Plateau
Stockton Plateau
Balcones Escarpment
Houston
Pasadena
Baytown
Beaumont
Port Arthur
Galveston
Corpus Christi
Laredo
Brownsville
Harlingen
McAllen
Victoria
Bryan
College Station
Del Rio
Gulf Coastal Plain
Shreveport
LOUISIANA
Lake Charles
Lafayette
Matagorda I.
Padre I.
PADRE ISLAND NAT'L SEASHORE
Laguna Madre
MEXICO
CHIHUAHUA
Chihuahua
Ciudad Juárez
Ciudad Delicias
Hidalgo del Parral
COAHUILA
Monclova
Saltillo
Torreón
Gómez Palacio
Piedras Negras
Ciudad Acuña
Nuevo Laredo
NUEVO LEÓN
Monterrey
Guadalupe
Reynosa
Matamoros
DURANGO
Durango
ZACATECAS
TAMULIPAS
Sierra Madre Oriental
Bolsón de Mapimí

Southeastern United States

POPULATION OF CITIES AND TOWNS

- OVER 2,000,000
- 1,000,000 - 1,999,999
- 500,000 - 999,999
- 250,000 - 499,999
- 100,000 - 249,999
- 30,000 - 99,999
- 10,000 - 29,999
- UNDER 10,000

SCALE 1:7,000,000 LAMBERT CONFORMAL CONIC PROJECTION

MILES 0 100 200 300

KILOMETERS 0 100 200 300

Alaska

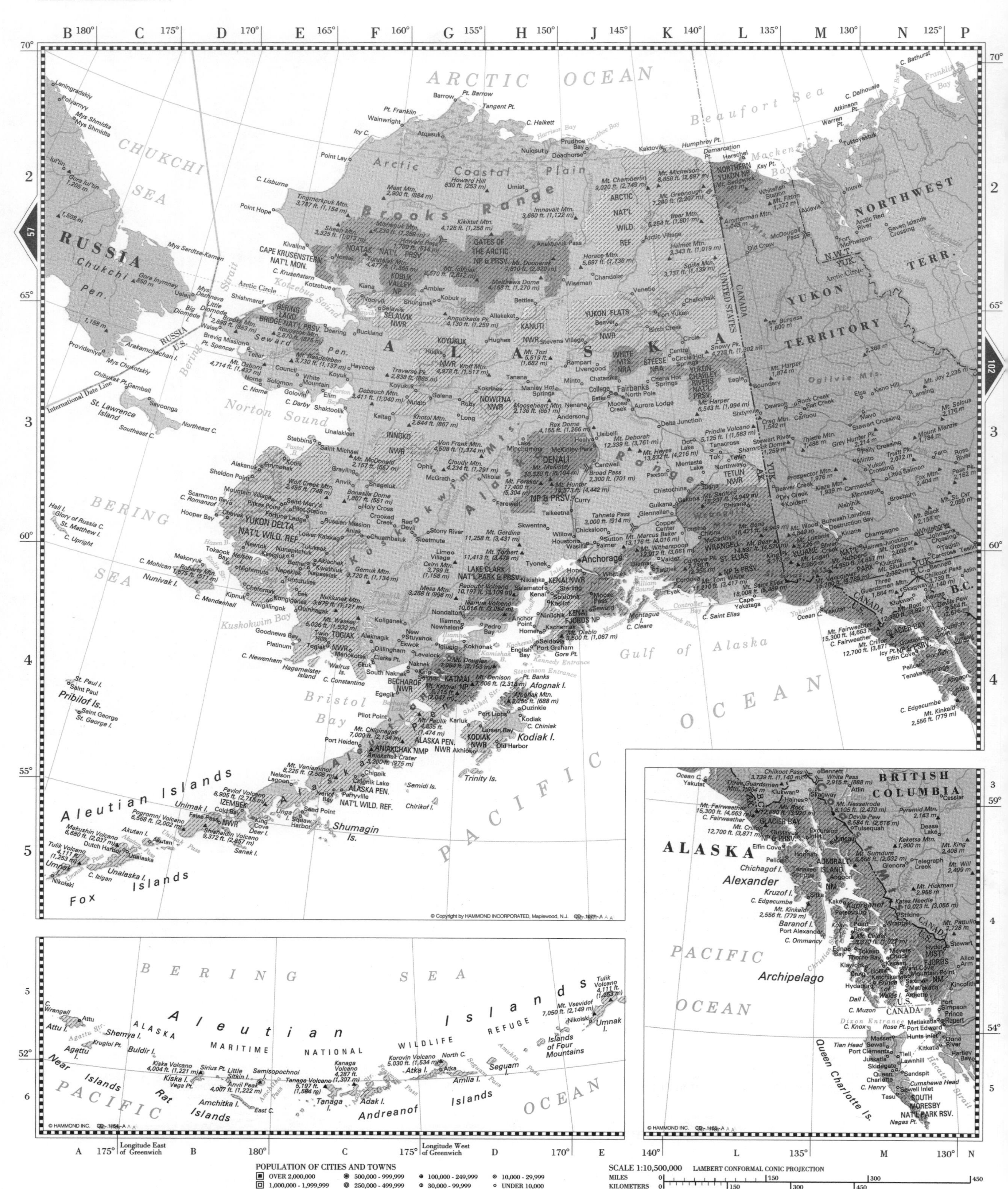
ARCTIC OCEAN
Beaufort Sea
CHUKCHI SEA
RUSSIA
Chukchi Pen.
Arctic Coastal Plain
Brooks Range
ALASKA
Seward Pen.
Norton Sound
Kotzebue Sound
Bering Strait
BERING SEA
YUKON DELTA NAT'L WILD. REF.
Kuskokwim Mts.
Alaska Range
Kuskokwim Bay
Bristol Bay
Gulf of Alaska
PACIFIC OCEAN
Aleutian Islands
Fox Islands
Kodiak I.
Pribilof Is.
St. Lawrence Island
Nunivak I.
Unimak I.
Shumagin Is.
Anchorage
Fairbanks
Barrow
Nome
Kotzebue
Juneau
Sitka
Ketchikan
DENALI NAT'L PARK & PRSV.
Mt. McKinley 20,320 ft. (6,194 m)
GATES OF THE ARCTIC NP & PRSV.
ARCTIC NAT'L WILD. REF.
YUKON TERRITORY
NORTHWEST TERR.
BRITISH COLUMBIA
CANADA
UNITED STATES
Ogilvie Mts.
Alexander Archipelago
Queen Charlotte Is.
Aleutian Islands ALASKA MARITIME NATIONAL WILDLIFE REFUGE
Near Islands
Rat Islands
Andreanof Islands
Islands of Four Mountains
Longitude East of Greenwich
Longitude West of Greenwich
© Copyright by HAMMOND INCORPORATED, Maplewood, N.J.
© HAMMOND INC.
POPULATION OF CITIES AND TOWNS
OVER 2,000,000
1,000,000 - 1,999,999
500,000 - 999,999
250,000 - 499,999
100,000 - 249,999
30,000 - 99,999
10,000 - 29,999
UNDER 10,000
SCALE 1:10,500,000
LAMBERT CONFORMAL CONIC PROJECTION
MILES 0 150 300 450
KILOMETERS 0 150 300 450

Los Angeles, New York-Philadelphia-Washington

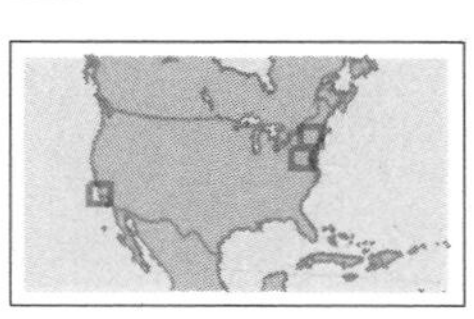

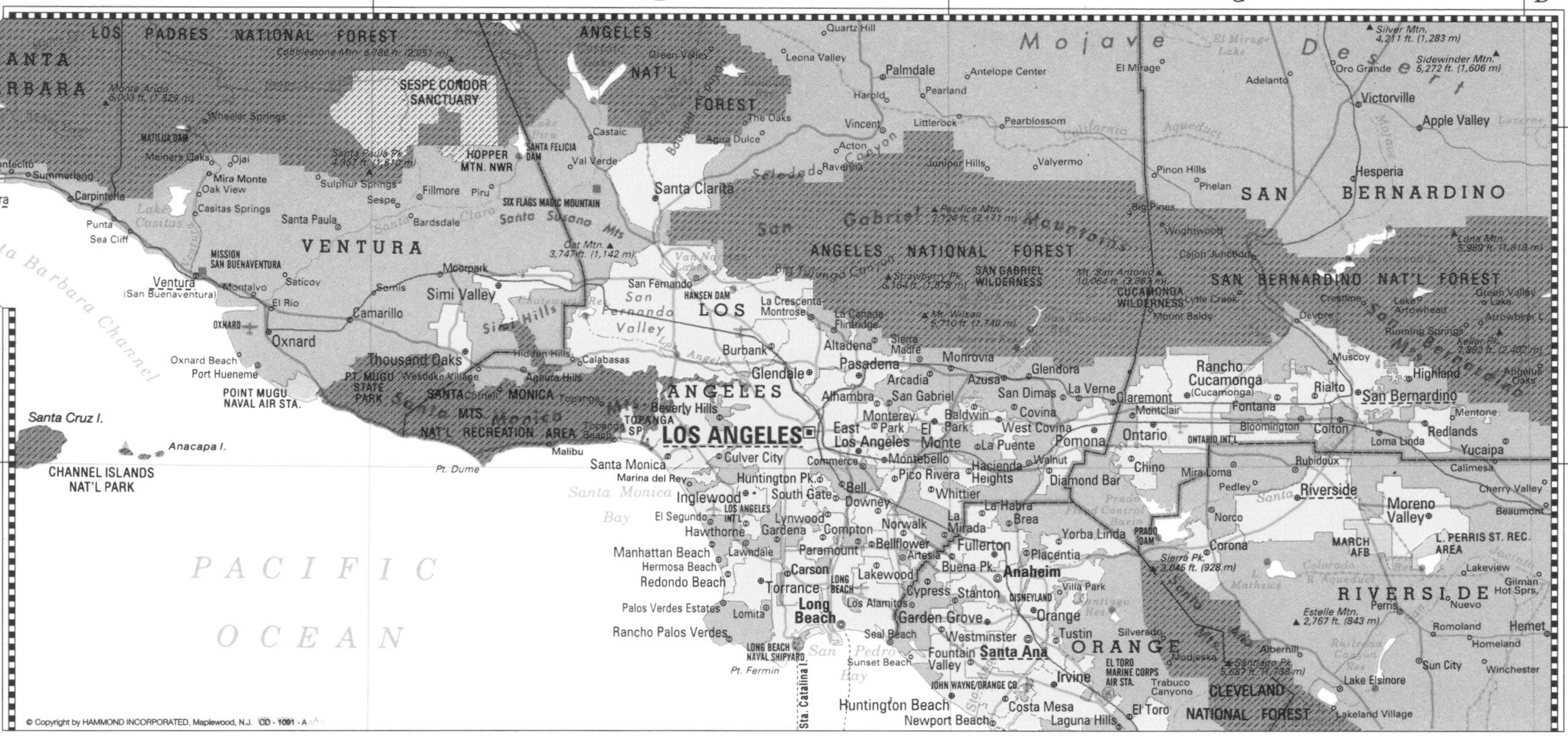

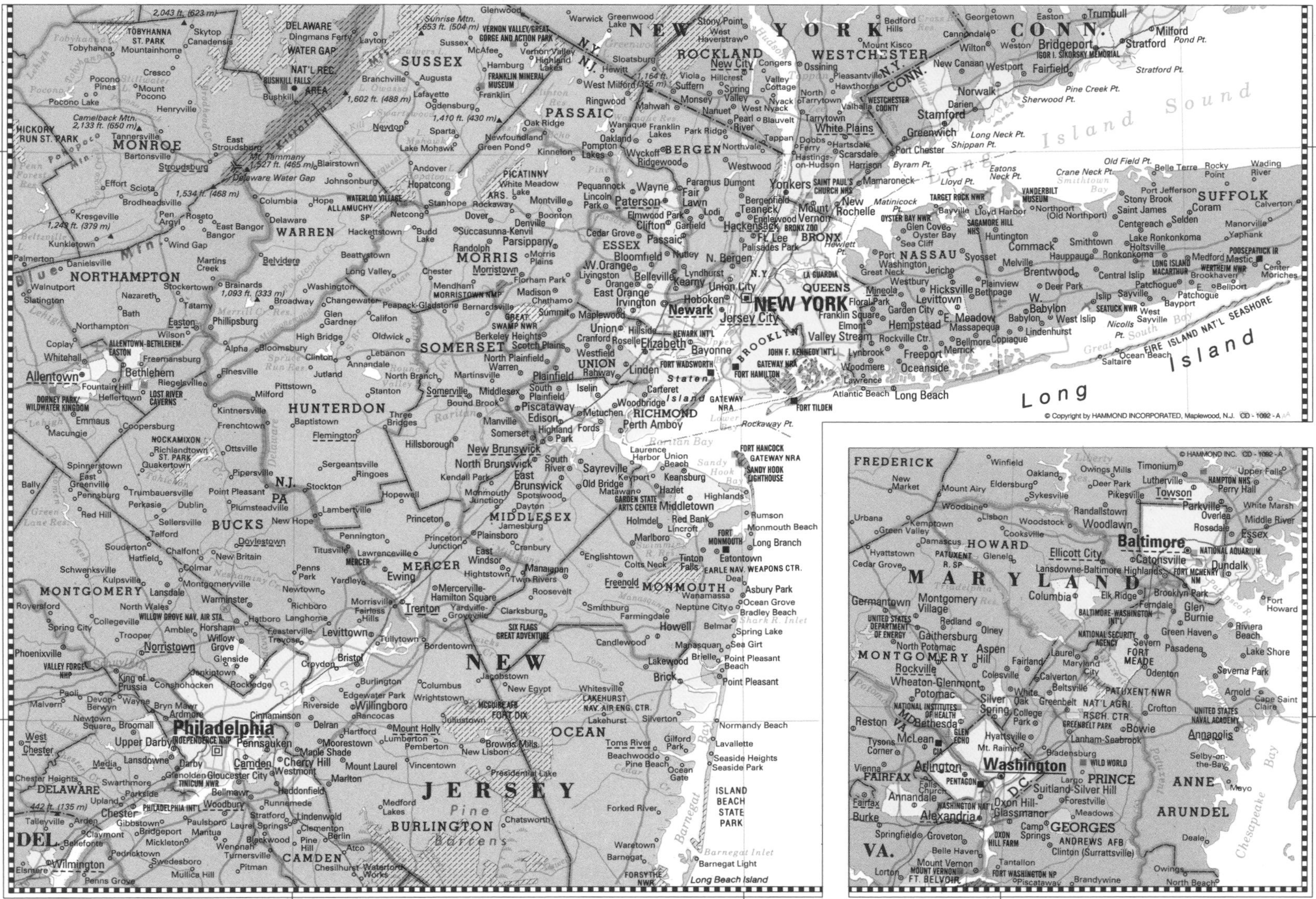

Longitude West of Greenwich

POPULATION OF CITIES AND TOWNS

- OVER 2,000,000
- 1,000,000 - 1,999,999
- 500,000 - 999,999
- 250,000 - 499,999
- 100,000 - 249,999
- 30,000 - 99,999
- 10,000 - 29,999
- UNDER 10,000

SCALE 1:1,170,000 LAMBERT CONFORMAL CONIC PROJECTION

MILES 0 10 20 30 40 50

KILOMETERS 0 10 20 30 40 50

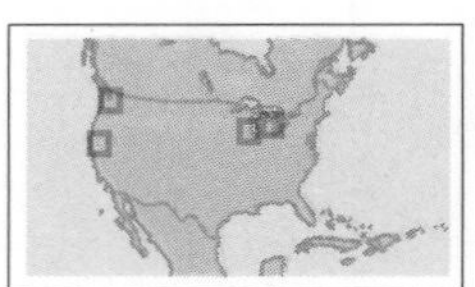

Seattle, San Francisco, Detroit, Chicago

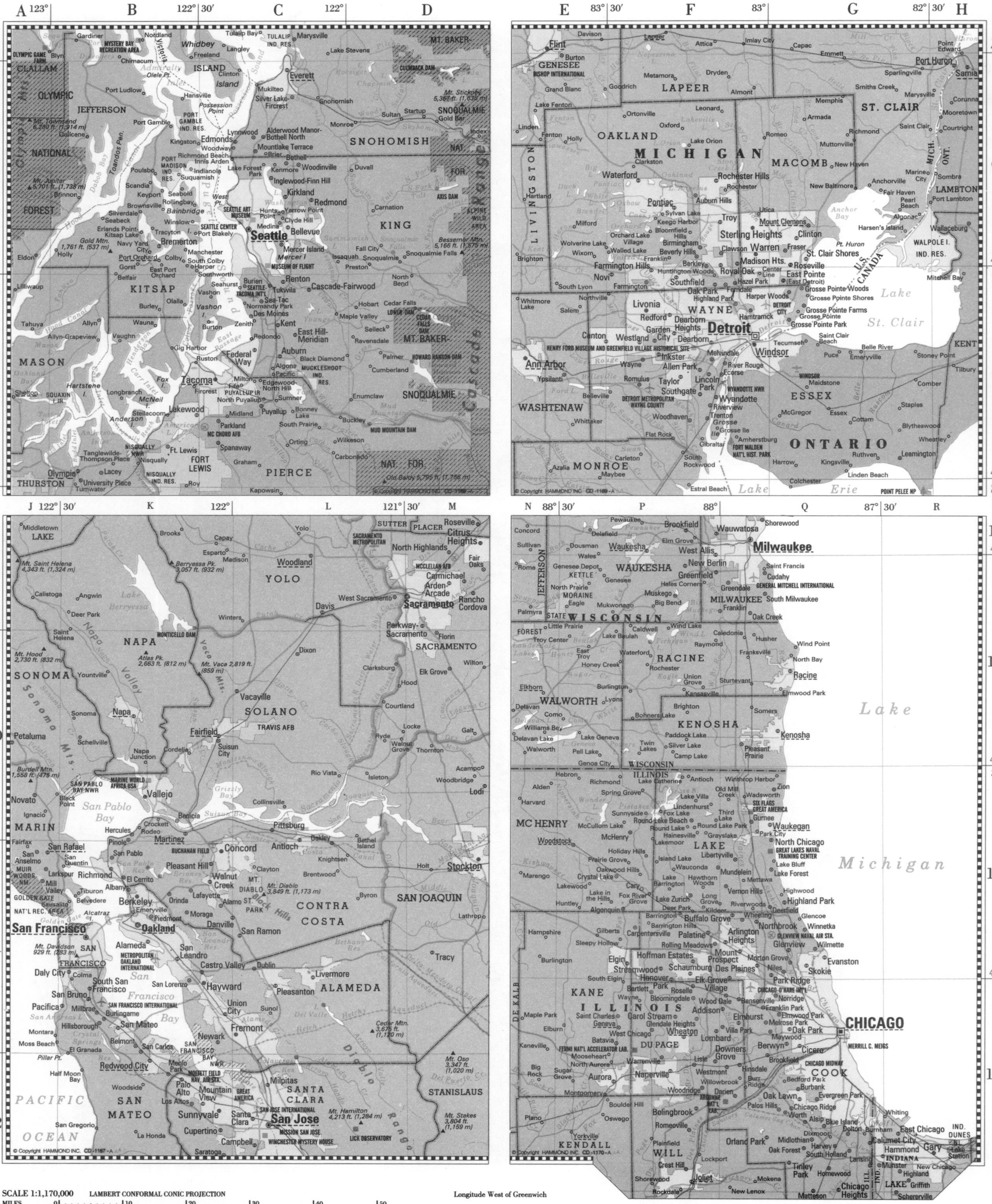

SCALE 1:1,170,000 LAMBERT CONFORMAL CONIC PROJECTION

MILES 0 10 20 30 40 50

KILOMETERS 0 10 20 30 40 50

Longitude West of Greenwich

Statistical Tables and Index

"I am not born for one corner; the whole world is my native land."

Seneca (The Younger)

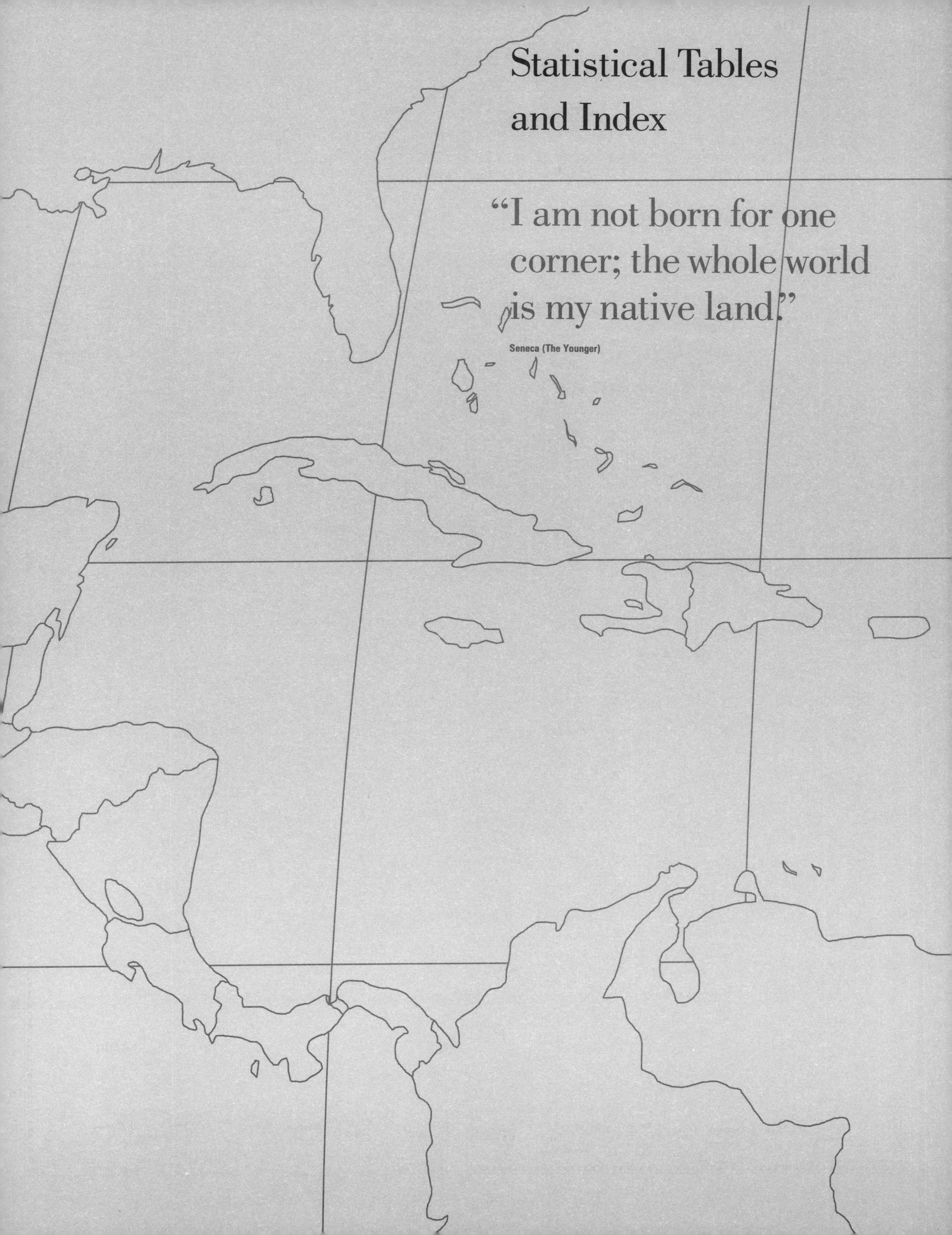

Time Zones of the World

165° W
150° W
135° W
120° W
105° W
90° W
75° W
60° W
45° W
30° W
15° W
0°
1 A.M.
2 A.M.
3 A.M.
4 A.M.
5 A.M.
6 A.M.
7 A.M.
8 A.M.
9 A.M.
10 A.M.
11 A.M.
NOON
ARCTIC OCEAN
GREENLAND
9 A.M.
11 A.M.
3 A.M.
ALASKA
Anchorage
Whitehorse
Nuuk
ICELAND
Reykjavik
CANADA
Edmonton
Winnipeg
NEWFOUNDLAND
8:30 A.M.
IRELAND
UNITED KINGDOM
London
Paris
Seattle
Boise
Montreal
Halifax
Detroit
Chicago
Denver
UNITED STATES
New York
Washington
San Francisco
Los Angeles
Phoenix
Atlanta
AZORES
PORTUGAL
Madrid
SPAIN
ANDORRA
Algiers
BERMUDA
Houston
MOROCCO
ATLANTIC
CANARY Is.
W. SAHARA
MEXICO
Miami
BAHAMAS
Honolulu
HAWAII
Mexico City
CUBA
HAITI
DOM. REP.
PUERTO RICO
ANT. & BARB.
BELIZE
JAMAICA
ST. KITTS & NEVIS
MAURITANIA
MALI
HONDURAS
DOMINICA
ST. LUCIA
BARBADOS
GRENADA
CAPE VERDE
Dakar
SENEGAL
GAMBIA
GUATEMALA
EL SALVADOR
NICARAGUA
ST. VINC. & GRENS.
PACIFIC
COSTA RICA
PANAMA
TRINIDAD AND TOBAGO
GUINEA-BISSAU
GUINEA
BURKINA FASO
SIERRA LEONE
IVORY COAST
LIBERIA
GHANA
VENEZUELA
GUYANA
Bogota
COLOMBIA
SUR.
FR. GUIANA
ECUADOR
Manaus
OCEAN
KIRIBATI
2:30 A.M.
MARQUESAS Is.
PERU
BRAZIL
Recife
ASCENSION
OCEAN
Lima
La Paz
BOLIVIA
TAHITI
FRENCH POLYNESIA
3:30 A.M.
PITCAIRN I.
PARAGUAY
Rio de Janeiro
EASTER I.
CHILE
Santiago
URUGUAY
Buenos Aires
ARGENTINA
TRISTAN DA CUNHA
TIME ZONES OF THE WORLD
STANDARD TIME ZONES
3 A.M.
4 A.M.
5 A.M.
6 A.M.
FALKLAND Is.
AREAS USING HALF HOUR DEVIATIONS
5:30 P.M.
SOUTH GEORGIA
© Copyright HAMMOND INCORPORATED, Maplewood, N.J.
1 A.M.
2 A.M.
3 A.M.
4 A.M.
5 A.M.
6 A.M.
7 A.M.
8 A.M.
9 A.M.
10 A.M.
11 A.M.
NOON

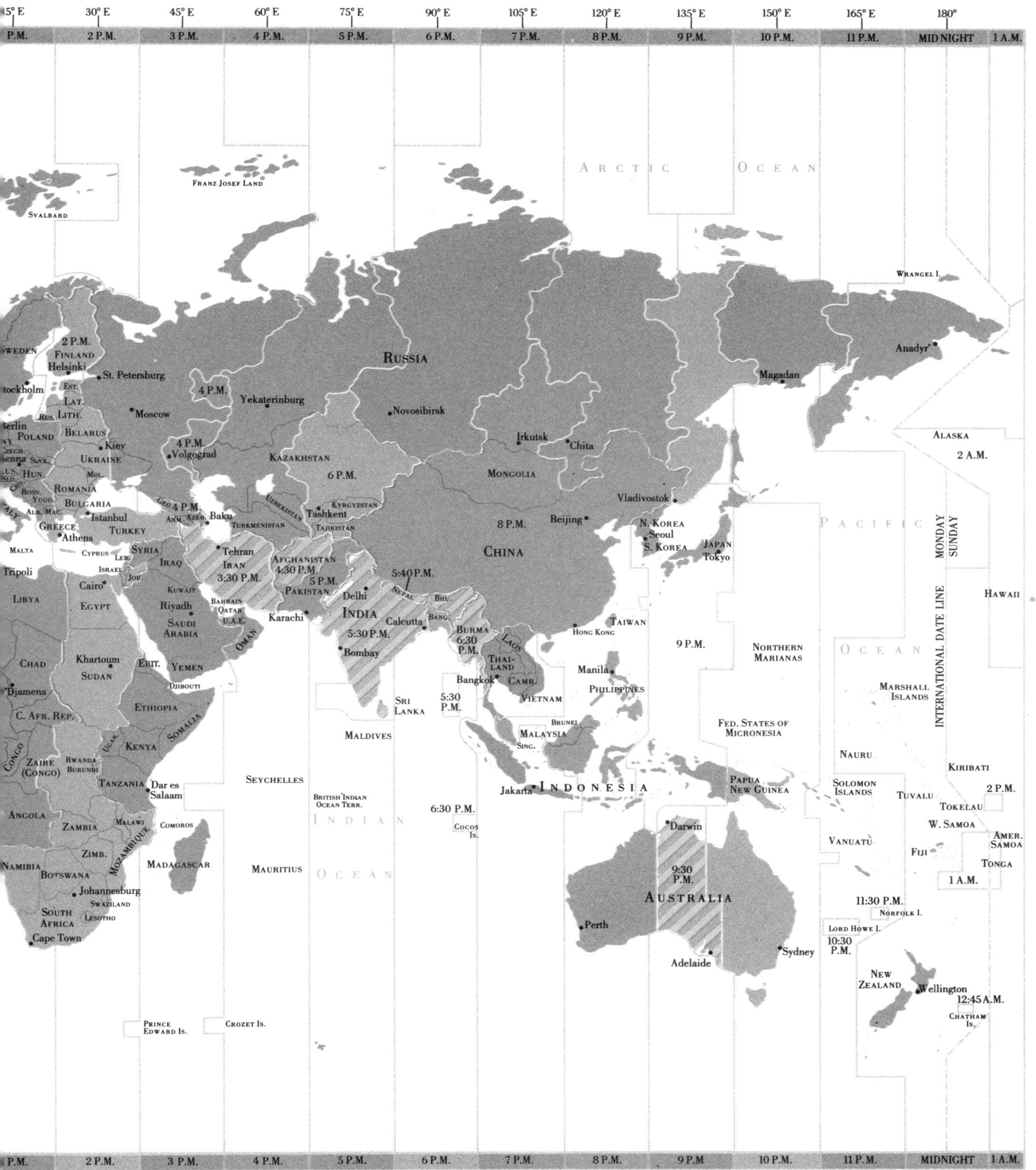

30° E
45° E
60° E
75° E
90° E
105° E
120° E
135° E
150° E
165° E
180°
2 P.M.
3 P.M.
4 P.M.
5 P.M.
6 P.M.
7 P.M.
8 P.M.
9 P.M.
10 P.M.
11 P.M.
MIDNIGHT
1 A.M.
ARCTIC OCEAN
FRANZ JOSEF LAND
SVALBARD
WRANGEL I.
RUSSIA
FINLAND
Helsinki
St. Petersburg
Moscow
Yekaterinburg
Novosibirsk
Irkutsk
Chita
Magadan
Anadyr'
ALASKA
2 A.M.
EST.
LAT.
LITH.
RUS.
POLAND
BELARUS
Kiev
UKRAINE
MOL.
HUN.
ROMANIA
BULGARIA
GREECE
Athens
Istanbul
TURKEY
Volgograd
KAZAKHSTAN
6 P.M.
MONGOLIA
Vladivostok
Beijing
N. KOREA
Seoul
S. KOREA
JAPAN
Tokyo
8 P.M.
CHINA
Baku
TURKMENISTAN
UZBEKISTAN
KYRGYZSTAN
Tashkent
TAJIKISTAN
Tehran
IRAN
3:30 P.M.
AFGHANISTAN
4:30 P.M.
PAKISTAN
5 P.M.
Delhi
INDIA
NEPAL
5:40 P.M.
BHU.
BANG.
Calcutta
5:30 P.M.
Bombay
Karachi
MALTA
CYPRUS
SYRIA
LEB.
ISRAEL
JOR.
IRAQ
KUWAIT
Riyadh
SAUDI ARABIA
BAHRAIN
QATAR
U.A.E.
OMAN
YEMEN
Tripoli
LIBYA
Cairo
EGYPT
CHAD
Khartoum
SUDAN
ERIT.
DJIBOUTI
ETHIOPIA
SOMALIA
C. AFR. REP.
KENYA
UGAN.
CONGO
ZAIRE (CONGO)
RWANDA
BURUNDI
TANZANIA
Dar es Salaam
ANGOLA
ZAMBIA
MALAWI
COMOROS
MOZAMBIQUE
ZIMB.
NAMIBIA
BOTSWANA
Johannesburg
SWAZILAND
LESOTHO
SOUTH AFRICA
Cape Town
MADAGASCAR
MAURITIUS
SEYCHELLES
MALDIVES
BRITISH INDIAN OCEAN TERR.
INDIAN OCEAN
PRINCE EDWARD IS.
CROZET IS.
SRI LANKA
5:30 P.M.
BURMA
6:30 P.M.
LAOS
THAILAND
Bangkok
CAMB.
VIETNAM
TAIWAN
HONG KONG
Manila
PHILIPPINES
BRUNEI
MALAYSIA
SING.
Jakarta
INDONESIA
6:30 P.M.
COCOS IS.
9 P.M.
NORTHERN MARIANAS
FED. STATES OF MICRONESIA
PAPUA NEW GUINEA
Darwin
9:30 P.M.
AUSTRALIA
Perth
Adelaide
Sydney
PACIFIC OCEAN
MONDAY
SUNDAY
INTERNATIONAL DATE LINE
HAWAII
MARSHALL ISLANDS
NAURU
KIRIBATI
SOLOMON ISLANDS
TUVALU
2 P.M.
TOKELAU
W. SAMOA
AMER. SAMOA
VANUATU
FIJI
TONGA
1 A.M.
11:30 P.M.
NORFOLK I.
LORD HOWE I.
10:30 P.M.
NEW ZEALAND
Wellington
12:45 A.M.
CHATHAM IS.

World Statistics

Elements of the Solar System

	Mean Distance from Sun: in Miles	in Kilometers	Period of Revolution around Sun	Period of Rotation on Axis	Equatorial Diameter in Miles	in Kilometers	Surface Gravity (Earth = 1)	Mass (Earth = 1)	Mean Density (Water = 1)	Number of Satellites
Mercury	35,990,000	57,900,000	87.97 days	59 days	3,032	4,880	0.38	0.055	5.5	0
Venus	67,240,000	108,200,000	224.70 days	243 days†	7,523	12,106	0.90	0.815	5.25	0
Earth	93,000,000	149,700,000	365.26 days	23h 56m	7,926	12,755	1.00	1.00	5.5	1
Mars	141,730,000	228,100,000	687.00 days	24h 37m	4,220	6,790	0.38	0.107	4.0	2
Jupiter	483,880,000	778,700,000	11.86 years	9h 50m	88,750	142,800	2.87	317.9	1.3	16
Saturn	887,130,000	1,427,700,000	29.46 years	10h 39m	74,580	120,020	1.32	95.2	0.7	23
Uranus	1,783,700,000	2,870,500,000	84.01 years	17h 24m†	31,600	50,900	0.93	14.6	1.3	15
Neptune	2,795,500,000	4,498,800,000	164.79 years	17h 50m	30,200	48,600	1.23	17.2	1.8	8
Pluto	3,667,900,000	5,902,800,000	247.70 years	6.39 days(?)	1,500	2,400	0.03(?)	0.01(?)	0.7(?)	1

† Retrograde motion

Dimensions of the Earth

	Area in: Sq. Miles	Sq. Kilometers
Superficial area	196,939,000	510,073,000
Land surface	57,506,000	148,941,000
Water surface	139,433,000	361,132,000
	Distance in: Miles	**Kilometers**
Equatorial circumference	24,902	40,075
Polar circumference	24,860	40,007
Equatorial diameter	7,926.4	12,756.4
Polar diameter	7,899.8	12,713.6
Equatorial radius	3,963.2	6,378.2
Polar radius	3,949.9	6,356.8
Volume of the Earth	2.6×10^{11} cubic miles	10.84×10^{11} cubic kilometers
Mass or weight	6.6×10^{21} short tons	6.0×10^{21} metric tons
Maximum distance from Sun	94,600,000 miles	152,000,000 kilometers
Minimum distance from Sun	91,300,000 miles	147,000,000 kilometers

Oceans and Major Seas

	Area in: Sq. Miles	Sq. Kms.	Greatest Depth in: Feet	Meters
Pacific Ocean	64,186,000	166,241,700	36,198	11,033
Atlantic Ocean	31,862,000	82,522,600	28,374	8,648
Indian Ocean	28,350,000	73,426,500	25,344	7,725
Arctic Ocean	5,427,000	14,056,000	17,880	5,450
Caribbean Sea	970,000	2,512,300	24,720	7,535
Mediterranean Sea	969,000	2,509,700	16,896	5,150
South China Sea	895,000	2,318,000	15,000	4,600
Bering Sea	875,000	2,266,250	15,800	4,800
Gulf of Mexico	600,000	1,554,000	12,300	3,750
Sea of Okhotsk	590,000	1,528,100	11,070	3,370
East China Sea	482,000	1,248,400	9,500	2,900
Yellow Sea	480,000	1,243,200	350	107
Sea of Japan	389,000	1,007,500	12,280	3,740
Hudson Bay	317,500	822,300	846	258
North Sea	222,000	575,000	2,200	670
Black Sea	185,000	479,150	7,365	2,245
Red Sea	169,000	437,700	7,200	2,195
Baltic Sea	163,000	422,170	1,506	459

The Continents

	Area in: Sq. Miles	Sq. Kms.	Percent of World's Land
Asia	17,128,500	44,362,815	29.5
Africa	11,707,000	30,321,130	20.2
North America	9,363,000	24,250,170	16.2
South America	6,875,000	17,806,250	11.8
Antarctica	5,500,000	14,245,000	9.5
Europe	4,057,000	10,507,630	7.0
Australia	2,966,136	7,682,300	5.1

Major Ship Canals

	Length in: Miles	Kms.	Minimum Depth in: Feet	Meters
Volga-Baltic, Russia	225	362	–	–
Baltic-White Sea, Russia	140	225	16	5
Suez, Egypt	100.76	162	42	13
Albert, Belgium	80	129	16.5	5
Moscow-Volga, Russia	80	129	18	6
Volga-Don, Russia	62	100	–	–
Göta, Sweden	54	87	10	3
Kiel (Nord-Ostsee), Germany	53.2	86	38	12
Panama Canal, Panama	50.72	82	41.6	13
Houston Ship, U.S.A.	50	81	36	11

Largest Islands

	Area in: Sq. Miles	Sq. Kms.
Greenland	840,000	2,175,600
New Guinea	305,000	789,950
Borneo	290,000	751,100
Madagascar	226,400	586,376
Baffin, Canada	195,928	507,454
Sumatra, Indonesia	164,000	424,760
Honshu, Japan	88,000	227,920
Great Britain	84,400	218,896
Victoria, Canada	83,896	217,290
Ellesmere, Canada	75,767	196,236
Celebes, Indonesia	72,986	189,034
South I., New Zealand	58,393	151,238
Java, Indonesia	48,842	126,501
North I., New Zealand	44,187	114,444
Newfoundland, Canada	42,031	108,860
Cuba	40,533	104,981
Luzon, Philippines	40,420	104,688
Iceland	39,768	103,000
Mindanao, Philippines	36,537	94,631
Ireland	31,743	82,214
Sakhalin, Russia	29,500	76,405
Hispaniola, Haiti & Dom. Rep.	29,399	76,143

	Area in: Sq. Miles	Sq. Kms.
Hokkaido, Japan	28,983	75,066
Banks, Canada	27,038	70,028
Ceylon,Sri Lanka	25,332	65,610
Tasmania, Australia	24,600	63,710
Svalbard, Norway	23,957	62,049
Devon, Canada	21,331	55,247
Novaya Zemlya (north isl.), Russia	18,600	48,200
Marajó, Brazil	17,991	46,597
Tierra del Fuego, Chile & Argentina	17,900	46,360
Alexander, Antarctica	16,700	43,250
Axel Heiberg, Canada	16,671	43,178
Melville, Canada	16,274	42,150
Southhampton, Canada	15,913	41,215
New Britain, Papua New Guinea	14,100	36,519
Taiwan, China	13,836	35,835
Kyushu, Japan	13,770	35,664
Hainan, China	13,127	33,999
Prince of Wales, Canada	12,872	33,338
Spitsbergen, Norway	12,355	31,999
Vancouver, Canada	12,079	31,285
Timor, Indonesia	11,527	29,855
Sicily, Italy	9,926	25,708

	Area in: Sq. Miles	Sq. Kms.
Somerset, Canada	9,570	24,786
Sardinia, Italy	9,301	24,090
Shikoku, Japan	6,860	17,767
New Caledonia, France	6,530	16,913
Nordaustlandet, Norway	6,409	16,599
Samar, Philippines	5,050	13,080
Negros, Philippines	4,906	12,707
Palawan, Philippines	4,550	11,785
Panay, Philippines	4,446	11,515
Jamaica	4,232	10,961
Hawaii, United States	4,038	10,458
Viti Levu, Fiji	4,010	10,386
Cape Breton, Canada	3,981	10,311
Mindoro, Philippines	3,759	9,736
Kodiak, Alaska, U.S.A.	3,670	9,505
Cyprus	3,572	9,251
Puerto Rico, U.S.A.	3,435	8,897
Corsica, France	3,352	8,682
New Ireland, Papua New Guinea	3,340	8,651
Crete, Greece	3,218	8,335
Anticosti, Canada	3,066	7,941
Wrangel, Russia	2,819	7,301

Principal Mountains

	Height in : Feet	Meters
Everest, Nepal-China	29,028	8,848
K2 (Godwin Austen), Pakistan-China	28,250	8,611
Makalu, Nepal-China	27,789	8,470
Dhaulagiri, Nepal	26,810	8,172
Nanga Parbat, Pakistan	26,660	8,126
Annapurna, Nepal	26,504	8,078
Rakaposhi, Pakistan	25,550	7,788
Kongur Shan, China	25,325	7,719
Tirich Mir, Pakistan	25,230	7,690
Gongga Shan, China	24,790	7,556
Communism Peak, Tajikistan	24,590	7,495
Pobedy Peak, Kyrgyzstan	24,406	7,439
Chomo Lhari, Bhutan-China	23,997	7,314
Muztag, China	23,891	7,282
Cerro Aconcagua, Argentina	22,831	6,959
Ojos del Salado, Chile-Argentina	22,572	6,880
Bonete, Chile-Argentina	22,546	6,872
Tupungato, Chile-Argentina	22,310	6,800
Pissis, Argentina	22,241	6,779
Mercedario, Argentina	22,211	6,770
Huascarán, Peru	22,205	6,768

	Height in : Feet	Meters
Llullaillaco, Chile-Argentina	22,057	6,723
Nevada Ancohuma, Bolivia	21,489	6,550
Chimborazo, Ecuador	20,561	6,267
McKinley, Alaska	20,320	6,194
Logan, Yukon, Canada	19,524	5,951
Cotopaxi, Ecuador	19,347	5,897
Kilimanjaro, Tanzania	19,340	5,895
El Misti, Peru	19,101	5,822
Pico Cristóbal Colón, Colombia	18,947	5,775
Huila, Colombia	18,865	5,750
Citlaltépetl (Orizaba), Mexico	18,701	5,700
Damavand, Iran	18,606	5,671
El'brus, Russia	18,510	5,642
St. Elias, Alaska, U.S.A.-Yukon, Canada	18,008	5,489
Dykh-tau, Russia	17,070	5,203
Batian (Kenya), Kenya	17,058	5,199
Ararat, Turkey	16,946	5,165
Vinson Massif, Antarctica	16,864	5,140
Margherita (Ruwenzori), Africa	16,795	5,119
Kazbek, Georgia-Russia	16,558	5,047
Puncak Jaya, Indonesia	16,503	5,030

	Height in : Feet	Meters
Blanc, France	15,771	4,807
Klyuchevskaya Sopka, Russia	15,584	4,750
Fairweather, Br. Col., Canada	15,300	4,663
Dufourspitze (Mte. Rosa), Italy-Switzerland	15,203	4,634
Ras Dashen, Ethiopia	15,157	4620
Matterhorn, Switzerland	14,691	4,478
Whitney, California, U.S.A.	14,494	4,418
Elbert, Colorado, U.S.A.	14,433	4,399
Rainier, Washington, U.S.A.	14,410	4,392
Shasta, California, U.S.A.	14,162	4,317
Pikes Peak, Colorado, U.S.A.	14,110	4,301
Finsteraarhorn, Switzerland	14,022	4, 274
Mauna Kea, Hawaii, U.S.A.	13,796	4,205
Mauna Loa, Hawaii, U.S.A.	13,677	4,169
Jungfrau, Switzerland	13,642	4,158
Grossglockner, Austria	12,457	3,797
Fujiyama, Japan	12,389	3,776
Cook, New Zealand	12,349	3,764
Etna, Italy	10,902	3,323
Kosciusko, Australia	7,310	2,228
Mitchell, North Carolina, U.S.A.	6,684	2,037

Longest Rivers

	Length in: Miles	Kms.
Nile, Africa	4,145	6,671
Amazon, S. America	3,915	6,300
Chang Jiang (Yangtze), China	3,900	6,276
Mississippi-Missouri-Red Rock, U.S.A.	3,741	6,019
Ob'-Irtysh-Black Irtysh, Russia-Kazakhstan	3,362	5,411
Yenisey-Angara, Russia	3,100	4,989
Huang He (Yellow), China	2,877	4,630
Amur-Shilka-Onon, Asia	2,744	4,416
Lena, Russia	2,734	4,400
Congo (Zaire), Africa	2,718	4,374
Mackenzie-Peace-Finlay,Canada	2,635	4,241
Mekong, Asia	2,610	4,200
Missouri-Red Rock, U.S.A.	2,564	4,125
Niger, Africa	2,548	4,101
Paraná-La Plata, S. America	2,450	3,943
Mississippi, U.S.A.	2,348	3,778
Murray-Darling, Australia	2,310	3,718
Volga, Russia	2,194	3,531
Madeira, S. America	2,013	3,240
Purus, S. America	1,995	3,211
Yukon, Alaska-Canada	1,979	3,185
St. Lawrence, Canada-U.S.A.	1,900	3,058
Rio Grande, Mexico-U.S.A.	1,885	3,034
Syrdar'ya-Naryn, Asia	1,859	2,992
São Francisco, Brazil	1,811	2,914

	Length in: Miles	Kms.
Indus, Asia	1,800	2,897
Danube, Europe	1,775	2,857
Salween, Asia	1,770	2,849
Brahmaputra, Asia	1,700	2,736
Euphrates, Asia	1,700	2,736
Tocantins, Brazil	1,677	2,699
Xi (Si), China	1,650	2,601
Amudar'ya, Asia	1,616	2,601
Nelson-Saskatchewan, Canada	1,600	2,575
Orinoco, S. America	1,600	2,575
Zambezi, Africa	1,600	2,575
Paraguay, S. America	1,584	2,549
Kolyma, Russia	1,562	2,514
Ganges, Asia	1,550	2,494
Ural, Russia-Kazakhstan	1,509	2,428
Japurá, S. America	1,500	2,414
Arkansas, U.S.A.	1,450	2,334
Colorado, U.S.A.-Mexico	1.450	2,334
Negro, S. America	1,400	2,253
Dnieper, Russia-Belarus-Ukraine	1,368	2,202
Orange, Africa	1,350	2,173
Irrawaddy, Burma	1,325	2,132
Brazos, U.S.A.	1,309	2,107
Ohio-Allegheny, U.S.A.	1,306	2,102
Kama, Russia	1,252	2,031

	Length in: Miles	Kms.
Don, Russia	1,222	1,967
Red, U.S.A.	1,222	1,966
Columbia, U.S.A.-Canada	1,214	1,953
Saskatchewan, Canada	1,205	1,939
Peace-Finlay, Canada	1,195	1,923
Tigris, Asia .	1,181	1,901
Darling, Australia	1,160	1,867
Angara, Russia	1,135	1,827
Sungari, Asia	1,130	1,819
Pechora, Russia	1,124	1,809
Snake, U.S.A.	1,038	1,670
Churchill, Canada	1,000	1,609
Pilcomayo, S. America	1,000	1,609
Uruguay, S. America	994	1.600
Platte-N. Platte, U.S.A.	990	1,593
Ohio, U.S.A.	981	1,578
Magdalena, Colombia	956	1,538
Pecos, U.S.A.	926	1,490
Oka, Russia	918	1,477
Canadian, U.S.A.	906	1,458
Colorado, Texas, U.S.A.	894	1,439
Dniester, Ukraine-Moldova	876	1,410
Fraser, Canada	850	1,369
Rhine, Europe	820	1,319
Northern Dvina, Russia	809	1,302

Principal Natural Lakes

	Area in:		Max. Depth in:	
	Sq. Miles	Sq. Kms.	Feet	Meters
Caspian Sea, Asia	143,243	370,999	3,264	995
Lake Superior, U.S.A.-Canada	31,820	82,414	1,329	405
Lake Victoria, Africa	26,724	69,215	270	82
Lake Huron, U.S.A.-Canada	23,010	59,596	748	228
Lake Michigan, U.S.A.	22,400	58,016	923	281
Aral Sea, Kazakhstan-Uzbekistan	15,830	41,000	213	65
Lake Tanganyika, Africa	12,650	32,764	4,700	1,433
Lake Baykal, Russia	12,162	31,500	5,316	1,620
Great Bear Lake, Canada	12,096	31,328	1,356	413
Lake Nyasa (Malawi), Africa	11,555	29,928	2,320	707
Great Slave Lake, Canada	11,031	28,570	2,015	614
Lake Erie, U.S.A.-Canada	9,940	25,745	210	64
Lake Winnipeg, Canada	9,417	24,390	60	18
Lake Ontario, U.S.A.-Canada	7,540	19,529	775	244
Lake Ladoga, Russia	7,104	18,399	738	225
Lake Balkhash, Kazakhstan	7,027	18,200	87	27
Lake Maracaibo, Venezuela	5,120	13,261	100	31
Lake Chad, Africa	4,000 – 10,000	10,360 – 25,900	25	8
Lake Onega, Russia	3,710	9,609	377	115

	Area in:		Max. Depth in:	
	Sq. Miles	Sq. Kms.	Feet	Meters
Lake Eyre, Australia	3,500-0	9,000-0	–	–
Lake Titicaca, Peru-Bolivia	3,200	8,288	1, 000	305
Lake Nicaragua, Nicaragua	3,100	8,029	230	70
Lake Athabasca, Canada	3,064	7,936	400	122
Reindeer Lake, Canada	2,568	6,651	–	–
Lake Turkana (Rudolf), Africa	2,463	6,379	240	73
Issyk-Kul', Kyrgyzstan	2,425	6,281	2,303	702
Lake Torrens, Australia	2,230	5,776	–	–
Vänern, Sweden	2,156	5,584	328	100
Nettilling Lake, Canada	2,140	5,543	–	–
Lake Winnipegosis, Canada	2,075	5,374	38	12
Lake Mobutu Sese Seko (Albert), Africa	2,075	5,374	160	49
Kariba Lake, Zambia-Zimbabwe	2,050	5,310	295	90
Lake Nipigon, Canada	1,872	4,848	540	165
Lake Mweru, Zaire-Zambia	1,800	4,662	60	18
Lake Manitoba, Canada	1,799	4,659	12	4
Lake Taymyr, Russia	1,737	4,499	85	26
Lake Khanka, China-Russia	1,700	4,403	33	10
Lake Kioga, Uganda	1,700	4,403	25	8
Lake of the Woods, U.S.A.-Canada	1,679	4,349	70	21

Index of the World

This index is a comprehensive listing of the places and geographic features found in the atlas. Names are arranged in strict alphabetical order, without regard to hyphens or spaces. Every name is followed by the country or area to which it belongs. Except for cities, towns, countries and cultural areas, all entries include a reference to feature type, such as province, river, island, peak, and so on. The page number and alpha-numeric code appear in green to the left of each listing. The page number directs you to the largest scale map on which the name can be found. The code refers to the grid squares formed by the horizontal and vertical lines of latitude and longitude on each map. Following the letters from left to right and the numbers from top to bottom helps you to locate quickly the square containing the place or feature. Inset maps have their own alpha-numeric codes. Names that are accompanied by a point symbol are indexed to the symbol's location on the map. Other names are indexed to the initial letter of the name. When a map name contains a subordinate or alternate name, both names are listed in the index. To conserve space and provide room for more entries, many abbreviations are used in this index. The primary abbreviations are listed below.

Index Abbreviations

A	**Ab,Can**	Alberta
	Acad.	Academy
	ACT	Australian Capital Territory
	A.F.B.	Air Force Base
	Afld.	Airfield
	Afg.	Afghanistan
	Afr.	Africa
	Ak,US	Alaska
	Al,US	Alabama
	Alb.	Albania
	Alg.	Algeria
	Amm. Dep.	Ammunition Depot
	And.	Andorra
	Ang.	Angola
	Angu.	Anguilla
	Ant.	Antarctica
	Anti.	Antigua and Barbuda
	Ar,US	Arkansas
	Arch.	Archipelago
	Arg.	Argentina
	Arm.	Armenia
	Arpt.	Airport
	Aru.	Aruba
	ASam.	American Samoa
	Ash.	Ashmore and Cartier Islands
	Aus.	Austria
	Austl.	Australia
	Aut.	Autonomous
	Az,US	Arizona
	Azer.	Azerbaijan
	Azor.	Azores
B	**Bahm.**	Bahamas
	Bahr.	Bahrain
	Bang.	Bangladesh
	Bar.	Barbados
	BC,Can	British Columbia
	Bela.	Belarus
	Belg.	Belgium
	Belz.	Belize
	Ben.	Benin
	Berm.	Bermuda
	Bfld.	Battlefield
	Bhu.	Bhutan
	Bol.	Bolivia
	Bor.	Borough
	Bosn.	Bosnia and Hercegovina
	Bots.	Botswana
	Braz.	Brazil
	Brln.	British Indian Ocean Territory
	Bru.	Brunei
	Bul.	Bulgaria
	Burk.	Burkina
	Buru.	Burundi
	BVI	British Virgin Islands
C	**Ca,US**	California
	CAfr.	Central African Republic
	Camb.	Cambodia
	Camr.	Cameroon
	Can.	Canada
	Can.	Canal
	Canl.	Canary Islands
	Cap.	Capital
	Cap. Dist.	Capital District
	Cap. Terr.	CapitalTerritory
	Cay.	Cayman Islands
	C.G.	Coast Guard
	Chan.	Channel
	Chl.	Channel Islands
	Co.	County
	Co,US	Colorado
	Col.	Colombia
	Com.	Comoros
	Cont.	Continent
	CpV.	Cape Verde Islands
	CR	Costa Rica
	Cr.	Creek
	Cro.	Croatia
	CSea.	Coral Sea Islands Territory
	Ct,US	Connecticut
	Ctr.	Center
	Ctry.	Country
	Cyp.	Cyprus
	Czh.	Czech Republic
D	**DC,US**	District of Columbia
	De,US	Delaware
	Den.	Denmark
	Depr.	Depression
	Dept.	Department
	Des.	Desert
	DF	Distrito Federal
	Dist.	District
	Djib.	Djibouti
	Dom.	Dominica
	Dpcy.	Dependency
	DRep.	Dominican Republic
E	**Ecu.**	Ecuador
	Emb.	Embankment
	Eng.	Engineering
	Eng,UK	England
	EqG.	Equatorial Guinea
	Erit..	Eritrea
	ESal.	El Salvador
	Est.	Estonia
	Eth.	Ethiopia
	Eur.	Europe
F	**Falk.**	Falkland Islands
	Far.	Faroe Islands
	Fed. Dist.	Federal District
	Fin.	Finland
	Fl,US	Florida
	For.	Forest
	Fr.	France
	FrAnt.	French Southern and Antarctic Lands
	FrG.	French Guiana
	FrPol.	French Polynesia
G	**Ga,US**	Georgia
	Galp.	Galapagos Islands
	Gam.	Gambia
	Gaza	Gaza Strip
	GBis.	Guinea-Bissau
	Geo.	Georgia
	Ger.	Germany
	Gha.	Ghana
	Gib.	Gibraltar
	Glac.	Glacier
	Gov.	Governorate
	Govt.	Government
	Gre.	Greece
	Grld.	Greenland
	Gren.	Grenada
	Grsld.	Grassland
	Guad.	Guadeloupe
	Guat.	Guatemala
	Gui.	Guinea
	Guy.	Guyana
H	**Har.**	Harbor
	Hi,US	Hawaii
	Hist.	Historic(al)
	HK	Hong Kong
	Hon.	Honduras
	Hts.	Heights
	Hun.	Hungary
I	**Ia,US**	Iowa
	Ice.	Iceland
	Id,US	Idaho
	Il,US	Illinois
	IM	Isle of Man
	In,US	Indiana
	Ind. Res.	Indian Reservation
	Indo.	Indonesia
	Int'l	International
	Ire.	Ireland
	Isl., Isls.	Island, Islands
	Isr.	Israel
	Isth.	Isthmus
	It.	Italy
	IvC.	Ivory Coast
J	**Jam.**	Jamaica
	Jor.	Jordan
K	**Kaz.**	Kazakhstan
	Kiri.	Kiribati
	Ks,US	Kansas
	Kuw.	Kuwait
	Ky,US	Kentucky
	Kyr.	Kyrgyzstan
L	**La,US**	Louisiana
	Lab.	Laboratory
	Lag.	Lagoon
	Lakesh.	Lakeshore
	Lat.	Latvia
	Lcht.	Liechtenstein
	Ldg.	Landing
	Leb.	Lebanon
	Les.	Lesotho
	Libr.	Liberia
	Lith.	Lithuania
	Lux.	Luxembourg
M	**Ma,US**	Massachusetts
	Macd.	Macedonia
	Madg.	Madagascar
	Madr.	Madeira
	Malay.	Malaysia
	Mald.	Maldives
	Malw.	Malawi
	Mart.	Martinique
	May.	Mayotte
	Mb,Can	Manitoba
	Md,US	Maryland
	Me,US	Maine
	Mem.	Memorial
	Mex.	Mexico
	Mi,US	Michigan
	Micr.	Micronesia, Federated States of
	Mil.	Military
	Mn,US	Minnesota
	Mo,US	Missouri
	Mol.	Moldova
	Mon.	Monument
	Mona.	Monaco
	Mong.	Mongolia
	Monts.	Montserrat
	Mor.	Morocco
	Moz.	Mozambique
	Mrsh.	Marshall Islands
	Mrta.	Mauritania
	Mrts.	Mauritius
	Ms,US	Mississippi
	Mt.	Mount
	Mt,US	Montana
	Mtn., Mts.	Mountain, Mountains
	Mun. Arpt.	Municipal Airport
N	**NAm.**	North America
	Namb.	Namibia
	NAnt.	Netherlands Antilles
	Nat'l	National
	Nav.	Naval
	NB,Can	New Brunswick
	Nbrhd.	Neighborhood
	NC,US	North Carolina
	NCal.	New Caledonia
	ND,US	North Dakota
	Ne,US	Nebraska
	Neth.	Netherlands
	Nf,Can	Newfoundland
	Nga.	Nigeria
	NH,US	New Hampshire
	NI,UK	Northern Ireland
	Nic.	Nicaragua
	NJ,US	New Jersey
	NKor.	North Korea
	NM,US	New Mexico
	NMar.	Northern Mariana Islands
	Nor.	Norway
	NS,Can	Nova Scotia
	Nv,US	Nevada
	NW,Can	Northwest Territories
	NY,US	New York
	NZ	New Zealand
O	**Obl.**	Oblast
	Oh,US	Ohio
	Ok,US	Oklahoma
	On,Can	Ontario
	Or,US	Oregon
P	**Pa,US**	Pennsylvania
	PacUS	Pacific Islands, U.S.
	Pak.	Pakistan
	Pan.	Panama
	Par.	Paraguay
	Par.	Parish
	PE,Can	Prince Edward Island
	Pen.	Peninsula
	Phil.	Philippines
	Phys. Reg.	Physical Region
	Pitc.	Pitcairn Islands
	Plat.	Plateau
	PNG	Papua New Guinea
	Pol.	Poland
	Port.	Portugal
	Poss.	Possession
	Pkwy.	Parkway
	PR	Puerto Rico
	Pref.	Prefecture
	Prov.	Province
	Prsv.	Preserve
	Pt.	Point
Q	**Qu,Can**	Quebec
R	**Rec.**	Recreation(al)
	Ref.	Refuge
	Reg.	Region
	Rep.	Republic
	Res.	Reservoir, Reservation
	Reun.	Réunion
	RI,US	Rhode Island
	Riv.	River
	Rom.	Romania
	Rsv.	Reserve
	Rus.	Russia
	Rvwy.	Riverway
	Rwa.	Rwanda
S	**SAfr.**	South Africa
	SAm.	South America
	SaoT.	São Tomé and Príncipe
	SAr.	Saudi Arabia
	Sc,UK	Scotland
	SC,US	South Carolina
	SD,US	South Dakota
	Seash.	Seashore
	Sen.	Senegal
	Sey.	Seychelles
	SGeo.	South Georgia and Sandwich Islands
	Sing.	Singapore
	Sk,Can	Saskatchewan
	SKor.	South Korea
	SLeo.	Sierra Leone
	Slov.	Slovenia
	Slvk.	Slovakia
	SMar.	San Marino
	Sol.	Solomon Islands
	Som.	Somalia
	Sp.	Spain
	Spr., Sprs.	Spring, Springs
	SrL.	Sri Lanka
	Sta.	Station
	StH.	Saint Helena
	Str.	Strait
	StK.	Saint Kitts and Nevis
	StL.	Saint Lucia
	StP.	Saint Pierre and Miquelon
	StV.	Saint Vincent and the Grenadines
	Sur.	Suriname
	Sval.	Svalbard
	Swaz.	Swaziland
	Swe.	Sweden
	Swi.	Switzerland
T	**Tah.**	Tahiti
	Tai.	Taiwan
	Taj.	Tajikistan
	Tanz.	Tanzania
	Ter.	Terrace
	Terr.	Territory
	Thai.	Thailand
	Tn,US	Tennessee
	Tok.	Tokelau
	Trg.	Training
	Trin.	Trinidad and Tobago
	Trkm.	Turkmenistan
	Trks.	Turks and Caicos Islands
	Tun.	Tunisia
	Tun.	Tunnel
	Turk.	Turkey
	Tuv.	Tuvalu
	Twp.	Township
	Tx,US	Texas
U	**UAE**	United Arab Emirates
	Ugan.	Uganda
	UK	United Kingdom
	Ukr.	Ukraine
	Uru.	Uruguay
	US	United States
	USVI	U.S. Virgin Islands
	Ut,US	Utah
	Uzb.	Uzbekistan
V	**Va,US**	Virginia
	Val.	Valley
	Van.	Vanuatu
	VatC.	Vatican City
	Ven.	Venezuela
	Viet.	Vietnam
	Vill.	Village
	Vol.	Volcano
	Vt,US	Vermont
W	**Wa,US**	Washington
	Wal,UK	Wales
	Wall.	Wallis and Futuna
	WBnk.	West Bank
	Wi,US	Wisconsin
	Wild.	Wildlife, Wilderness
	WSah.	Western Sahara
	WSam.	Western Samoa
	WV,US	West Virginia
	Wy,US	Wyoming
Y	**Yem.**	Yemen
	Yk,Can	Yukon Territory
	Yugo.	Yugoslavia
Z	**Zam.**	Zambia
	Zim.	Zimbabwe

A

42/B2 Aa (riv.), Fr.
40/D5 Aa (riv.), Ger.
41/G5 Aa (riv.), Ger.
43/F2 Aachen, Ger.
40/C5 Aalburg, Neth.
45/J2 Aalen, Ger.
40/B4 Aalsmeer, Neth.
42/D2 Aalst, Belg.
40/D5 Aalten, Neth.
42/C1 Aalter, Belg.
45/H3 Aarau, Swi.
45/H3 Aare (riv.), Swi.
43/D2 Aarschot, Belg.
42/D1 Aartselaar, Belg.
62/E5 Aba, China
85/G5 Aba, Nga.
83/M7 Aba, Zaire
60/D5 Abā as Su'ūd, SAr.
92/G5 Abacaxis (riv.), Braz.
86/C5 Abadab, Jabal (peak), Sudan
60/E2 Ābādān, Iran
60/F2 Ābādeh, Iran
95/C1 Abaeté, Braz.
93/J4 Abaetetuba, Braz.
78/G4 Abaiang (atoll), Kiri.
104/D4 Abajo (mts.), Ut,US
56/K4 Abakan, Rus.
92/D6 Abancay, Peru
62/G3 Abaq Qi, China
46/E3 Abarán, Sp.
79/H5 Abariringa (Canton) (atoll), Kiri.
60/F2 Abar Kūh, Iran
63/N3 Abashiri, Japan
56/H5 Abay, Kaz.
83/N6 Ābaya Hayk' (lake), Eth.
68/F1 Abaza, Rus.
48/B1 Abbadia San Salvatore, It.
42/A3 Abbeville, Fr.
112/E4 Abbeville, La,US
113/H3 Abbeville, SC,US
32/E2 Abbey Head (pt.), Sc,UK
76/B3 Abbot (mt.), Austl.
98/T Abbot Ice Shelf, Ant.
33/G6 Abbots Bromley, Eng,UK
34/D5 Abbotsbury, Eng,UK
31/M6 Abbots Langley, Eng,UK
61/K2 Abbottābād, Pak.
40/B4 Abcoude, Neth.
59/E3 'Abd al 'Azīz, Jabal (mts.), Syria
55/K1 Abdulino, Rus.
83/K5 Abéché, Chad
89/E2 Abel Erasmuspas (pass), SAfr.
78/G4 Abemama (atoll), Kiri.
84/E5 Abengourou, IvC.
38/E1 Åbenrå, Den.
45/J2 Abens (riv.), Ger.
85/F5 Abeokuta, Nga.
32/D5 Aber, Wal,UK
34/B2 Aberaeron, Wal,UK
34/C1 Aberangell, Wal,UK
34/B2 Aberath, Wal,UK
34/C3 Abercarn, Wal,UK
34/C3 Aberdare, Wal,UK
32/D6 Aberdaron, Wal,UK
102/G2 Aberdeen (lake), NW,Can
36/D2 Aberdeen, Sc,UK
113/F3 Aberdeen, Ms,US
107/J4 Aberdeen, SD,US
106/C4 Aberdeen, Wa,US
34/B1 Aberdyfi, Wal,UK
36/D2 Aberfeldy, Sc,UK
36/C2 Aberfoyle, Sc,UK
34/C3 Abergavenny, Wal,UK
32/E5 Abergele, Wal,UK
34/B2 Aberporth, Wal,UK
32/D6 Abersoch, Wal,UK
34/C3 Abersychan, Wal,UK
108/B2 Abert (lake), Or,US
34/C3 Abertillery, Wal,UK
34/B2 Aberystwyth, Wal,UK
60/D5 Abhá, SAr.
60/E1 Abhar, Iran
83/P5 Abhe Bad (lake), Djib., Eth.
84/D5 Abidjan, IvC.
65/J7 Abiko, Japan
109/H3 Abilene, Ks,US
112/D3 Abilene, Tx,US
35/E3 Abingdon, Eng,UK
110/D4 Abingdon, Va,US
111/R10 Abino (pt.), On,Can
109/F3 Abiquiu, NM,US
110/E1 Abitibi (lake), On,Can
110/D1 Abitibi (riv.), On,Can
55/G4 Abkhaz Aut. Rep., Geo.
86/B3 Abnūb, Egypt
84/E5 Aboisso, IvC.
85/F5 Abomey, Ben.
50/E2 Abony, Hun.
73/E2 Aborlan, Phil.
37/G3 Åbo (Turku), Fin.
36/D2 Aboyne, Sc,UK
67/D4 Abra (riv.), Phil.
101/G3 Abraham's Bay, Bahm.
46/A3 Abrantes, Port.
91/C1 Abra Pampa, Arg.
86/B4 'Abrī, Sudan
31/P7 Abridge, Eng,UK
50/F2 Abrud, Rom.
48/C1 Abruzzi (reg.), It.
48/C2 Abruzzo Nat'l Park, It.
106/F4 Absaroka (range), Mt, Wy,US
60/F4 Abū al Abyaḑ (isl.), UAE
61/F4 Abu Dhabi (Abū Ẓaby) (cap.), UAE
86/C5 Abū Dīs, Sudan
86/B4 Abu el-Husein, Bîr (well), Egypt
86/C5 Abū Hamad, Sudan
86/C4 Abu Hashim, Bi'r (well), Egypt
59/H6 Abū Ḩummuş, Egypt
85/G4 Abuja (cap.), Nga.
85/G4 Abuja Cap. Terr., Nga.
59/H6 Abū Kabīr, Egypt
60/D2 Abū Kamāl, Syria
65/G2 Abukuma (hills), Japan
65/G2 Abukuma (riv.), Japan
67/D4 Abulog, Phil.
86/A3 Abu Minqâr, Bîr (well), Egypt
92/E6 Abuná (riv.), Bol.
92/E5 Abunã, Braz.
70/B3 Abu Road, India
86/D4 Abu Shagara, Ras (cape), Sudan
86/B4 Abu Simbel (ruins), Egypt
83/N5 Ābuyē Mēda (peak), Eth.
67/E5 Abuyog, Phil.
61/F4 Abū Ẓaby (Abu Dhabi) (cap.), UAE
48/A4 Abyaḑ, Ar Ra's al (cape), Tun.
86/B3 Abydos (ruins), Egypt
111/G2 Acadia Nat'l Park, Me,US
94/C3 Acajutiba, Braz.
101/N9 Acaponeta, Mex.
100/B4 Acapulco, Mex.
94/B1 Acaraú, Braz.
94/B1 Acaraú (riv.), Braz.
94/C2 Acari, Braz.
92/G5 Acari (riv.), Braz.
101/H6 Acarigua, Ven.
100/B4 Acatlán, Mex.
85/E5 Accra (cap.), Gha.
33/F4 Accrington, Eng,UK
96/B4 Achao, Chile
85/H2 Achegour (well), Niger
63/K2 Acheng, China
31/S10 Achères, Fr.
42/B3 Achicourt, Fr.
42/B3 Achiet-le-Grand, Fr.
111/N6 Achigan (riv.), Qu,Can
56/K4 Achinsk, Rus.
84/D2 Achmîm (well), Mrta.
36/C2 Achnasheen, Sc,UK
43/G3 Acht, Hohe (peak), Ger.
48/D4 Acireale, It.
101/G3 Acklins (isl.), Bahm.
33/G4 Ackworth Moor Top, Eng,UK
76/C4 Acland (peak), Austl.
35/H1 Acle, Eng,UK
96/C2 Aconcagua, Cerro (peak), Arg.
94/C2 Acopiara, Braz.
45/H4 Acqui Terme, It.
74/F6 Acraman (lake), Austl.
92/E6 Acre (riv.), Braz., Peru
95/B1 Acreúna, Braz.
49/L7 Acropolis, Gre.
79/M7 Actaeon Group (isls.), FrPol.
31/N7 Acton, Eng,UK
115/B2 Acton, Ca,US
94/C2 Açu, Braz.
96/Q9 Aculeo (lake), Chile
110/D3 Ada, Oh,US
109/H4 Ada, Ok,US
50/E3 Ada, Yugo.
103/J1 Adair (cape), NW,Can
46/C2 Adaja (riv.), Sp.
114/C6 Adak (isl.), Ak,US
114/C6 Adak (str.), Ak,US
97/M7 Adam (peak), Falk.
95/B2 Adamantina, Braz.
85/H5 Adamawa (plat.), Camr., Nga.
106/D3 Adams (lake), BC,Can
106/C4 Adams (peak), Wa,US
59/C3 Adana, Turk.
51/K5 Adapazarı, Turk.
98/M Adare (cape), Ant.
44/C5 Adarza (mtn.), Fr.
45/H4 Adda (riv.), It.
83/M4 Ad Dabbah, Sudan
60/D3 Ad Dahnā' (des.), SAr.
83/M5 Ad Damazin, Sudan
83/M4 Ad Dāmir, Sudan
60/F3 Ad Dammām, SAr.
59/H6 Ad Daqahlīyah (gov.), Egypt
60/F3 Ad Dawḩah (Doha) (cap.), Qatar
59/H6 Ad Dilinjāt, Egypt
83/N6 Addis Ababa (cap.), Eth.
116/Q16 Addison, Il,US
60/D2 Ad Dīwānīyah, Iraq
31/M7 Addlestone, Eng,UK
88/D4 Addo Elephant Nat'l Park, SAfr.
83/M5 Ad Duwaym, Sudan
98/V Adelaide (isl.), Ant.
77/A2 Adelaide, Austl.
102/G2 Adelaide (pen.), NW,Can
88/D4 Adelaide, SAfr.
115/C1 Adelanto, Ca,US
74/C3 Adèle (isl.), Austl.
41/G5 Adelebsen, Ger.
98/K Adélie (coast), Ant.
83/Q5 Aden (gulf), Afr., Asia
60/D6 Aden, Yem.
41/H2 Adendorf, Ger.
73/H4 Adi (isl.), Indo.
45/J4 Adige (Etsch) (riv.), It.
83/N5 Ādīgrat, Eth.
70/C4 Adilābād, India
85/E2 Adiora (well), Mali
110/F2 Adirondack (mts.), NY,US
83/N6 Ādīs Ābeba (Addis Ababa) (cap.), Eth.
83/N5 Ādīs Zemen, Eth.
60/C6 Ādī Ugri, Erit.
59/D3 Adıyaman, Turk.
51/H2 Adjud, Rom.
100/B3 Adjuntas (res.), Mex.
33/F4 Adlington, Eng,UK
74/D2 Admiralty (gulf), Austl.
103/H1 Admiralty (inlet), NW,Can
78/D5 Admiralty (isls.), PNG
116/B2 Admiralty (inlet), Wa,US
114/M4 Admiralty I. Nat'l Mon., Ak,US
65/L9 Ado (riv.), Japan
85/F5 Ado, Nga.
65/M9 Adogawa, Japan
70/C4 Ādoni, India
44/C5 Adour (riv.), Fr.
46/D4 Adra, Sp.
48/D4 Adrano, It.
82/E2 Adrar, Alg.
84/B1 Adrar (reg.), Mrta.
82/E1 Adrar bou Nasser (peak), Mor.
85/F1 Adrar des Iforas (mts.), Mali
83/K5 Adré, Chad
45/K4 Adria, It.
110/C3 Adrian, Mi,US
35/F5 Adur (riv.), Eng,UK
83/N5 Ādwa, Eth.
33/G4 Adwick le Street, Eng,UK
57/P3 Adycha (riv.), Rus.
55/G4 Adzhar Aut. Rep., Geo.
53/N2 Adz'va (riv.), Rus.
49/J3 Aegean (sea), Gre., Turk.
38/F1 Aerø (isl.), Den.
34/B2 Aeron (riv.), Wal,UK
32/E1 Ae, Water of (riv.), Sc,UK
85/F5 Afadjoto (peak), Gha.
79/X15 Afareaitu, FrPol.
59/M8 Afek Nat'l Park, Isr.
44/B3 Aff (riv.), Fr.
61/H2 Afghanistan
83/Q7 Afgooye, Som.
94/C2 Afogados da Ingazeira, Braz.
114/H4 Afognak (isl.), Ak,US
114/H4 Afognak (mtn.), Ak,US
84/C2 Afollé (reg.), Mrta.
95/D2 Afonso Cláudio, Braz.
48/D2 Afragola, It.
80/* Africa
59/D2 Afşin, Turk.
40/C2 Afsluitdijk (IJsselmeer) (dam), Neth.
41/F5 Afte (riv.), Ger.
106/F5 Afton, Wy,US
59/K5 'Afula, Isr.
59/B2 Afyon, Turk.
82/H4 Agadem, Niger
85/G2 Agadez, Niger
85/H2 Agadez (dept.), Niger
82/D1 Agadir, Mor.
81/H6 Agalega (isls.), Mrts.
85/F2 Agamor (well), Mali
78/D3 Agaña (cap.), Guam
85/F2 Agano (riv.), Japan
83/N6 Āgaro, Eth.
71/F3 Agartala, India
98/V Agassiz (cape), Ant.
103/T6 Agassiz (ice field), NW,Can
109/G2 Agate Fossil Beds Nat'l Mon., Ne,US
114/A5 Agattu (isl.), Ak,US
114/A5 Agattu (str.), Ak,US
85/G5 Agbor, Nga.
84/D5 Agboville, IvC.
55/H5 Agdam, Azer.
44/E5 Agde, Fr.
44/E5 Agde, Cap d' (cape), Fr.
44/D4 Agen, Fr.
65/H7 Ageo, Japan
38/E1 Agerbæk, Den.
41/E6 Agger (riv.), Ger.
50/E1 Aggteleki Nat'l Park, Hun.
32/B3 Aghagallon, NI,UK
60/E2 Āghā Jārī, Iran
101/N8 Agiabampo, Estero de (bay), Mex.
62/G1 Aginskoye, Rus.
32/B1 Agivey, NI,UK
44/E5 Agly (riv.), Fr.
51/G3 Agnita, Rom.
65/M10 Ago, Japan
45/H4 Agogna (riv.), It.
115/B2 Agoura Hills, Ca,US
44/D5 Agout (riv.), Fr.
70/C2 Āgra, India
48/E2 Agri (riv.), It.
55/H5 Ağri (Ararat) (peak), Turk.
48/C4 Agrigento, It.
78/D3 Agrihan (isl.), NMar.
49/G3 Agrínion, Gre.
96/C3 Agrio (riv.), Arg.
48/D2 Agropoli, It.
53/M4 Agryz, Rus.
101/G6 Aguachica, Col.
101/H4 Aguadilla, PR
100/C4 Agua Dulce, Mex.
101/E6 Aguadulce, Pan.
95/F7 Aguaí, Braz.
47/P10 Agualva-Cacém, Port.
100/D4 Aguan (riv.), Hon.
95/B2 Aguapeí (riv.), Braz.
101/N7 Agua Prieta, Mex.
101/H6 Aguaro-Guariquito Nat'l Park, Ven.
95/H6 Águas (hills), Braz.
94/C3 Águas Belas, Braz.
100/A3 Aguascalientes, Mex.
100/A3 Aguascalientes (state), Mex.
95/G6 Águas da Prata, Braz.
95/G7 Águas de Lindóia, Braz.
94/B5 Águas Formosas, Braz.
95/B1 Aguavermelha (res.), Braz.
95/B2 Agudos, Braz.
46/A2 Águeda, Port.
46/B2 Agueda (riv.), Sp.
82/C3 Agüenit, WSah.
65/M10 Agui, Japan
78/D3 Aguijan (isl.), NMar.
46/C4 Aguilar, Sp.
46/C1 Aguilar de Campóo, Sp.
91/C2 Aguilares, Arg.
46/E4 Aguilas, Sp.
101/P10 Aguililla de Iturbide, Mex.
47/X17 Agüimes, Canl.,Sp.
101/G5 Aguja (cape), Col.
88/M11 Agulhas (cape), SAfr.
95/C2 Agulhas Negras (peak), Braz.
73/E5 Agung (vol.), Indo.
67/E6 Agusan (riv.), Phil.
101/G5 Agustín Codazzi, Col.
82/G3 Ahaggar (plat.), Alg.
40/E4 Ahaus, Ger.
43/F3 Ahbach (riv.), Ger.
59/E2 Ahlat, Turk.
41/E5 Ahlen, Ger.
70/B3 Ahmadābād, India
70/B4 Ahmadnagar, India
61/K3 Ahmadpur East, Pak.
83/P6 Ahmar (mts.), Eth.
32/B2 Ahoghill, NI,UK
43/F3 Ahr (riv.), Ger.
41/H1 Ahrensburg, Ger.
41/F5 Ahse (riv.), Ger.
101/P9 Ahuacatlán, Mex.
104/W13 Ahuimanu, Hi,US
101/N7 Ahumada, Mex.
60/E2 Ahvāz, Iran
37/F4 Ahvenanmaa (prov.), Fin.
88/B2 Ai-Ais Hot Springs, Namb.
66/B2 Aibag Gol (riv.), China
65/E3 Aichi (pref.), Japan
104/W13 Aiea, Hi,US
44/E4 Aigoual (mtn.), Fr.
44/F4 Aigues (riv.), Fr.
47/F1 Aigues Tortes y Lago de San Mauricio Nat'l Park, Sp.
81/Q16 Aiguille, Cap de l' (cape), Alg.
65/F1 Aikawa, Japan
113/H3 Aiken, SC,US
101/F6 Ailigandí, Pan.
78/F4 Ailinglapalap (atoll), Mrsh.
32/C1 Ailsa Craig (isl.), Sc,UK
78/G3 Ailuk (atoll), Mrsh.
66/C5 Aimen Guan (pass), China
95/D1 Aimorés, Braz.
44/F4 Ain (riv.), Fr.
81/V18 'Aïn Beïda, Alg.
81/S15 'Aïn Beniau, Alg.
82/D2 Aïn Ben Tili, Mrta.
81/S15 'Aïn Bessem, Alg.
81/R15 'Aïn Defla, Alg.
81/Q16 'Aïn el Turk, Alg.
81/V17 'Aïn Fakroun, Alg.
81/V17 'Aïn M'Lila, Alg.
49/G3 Aínos (peak), Gre.
49/G3 Aínos Nat'l Park, Gre.
81/U18 'Aïn Oulmene, Alg.
81/S16 'Aïn Oussersa, Alg.
33/E4 Ainsdale, Eng,UK
82/E1 'Aïn Sefra, Alg.
109/H2 Ainsworth, Ne,US
81/S15 'Aïn Taya, Alg.
81/Q16 'Aïn Temouchent, Alg.
81/U18 'Aïn Touta, Alg.
85/G2 Aïr (plat.), Niger
106/E3 Airdrie, Ab,Can
36/D3 Airdrie, Sc,UK
42/D5 Aire (riv.), Fr.
33/G4 Aire (riv.), Eng,UK
42/B2 Aire, Canal de (can.), Fr.
33/E5 Aire, Point of (pt.), Wal,UK
42/B2 Aire-sur-la-Lys, Fr.
103/J2 Air Force (isl.), NW,Can
33/F3 Airton, Eng,UK
45/J2 Aisch (riv.), Ger.
42/D3 Aiseau-Presles, Belg.
96/B5 Aisén del General Carlos Ibáñez del Campo (reg.), Chile
66/E3 Ai Shan (mtn.), China
114/L3 Aishihik, Yk,Can
43/E3 Aisne (riv.), Belg.
42/C4 Aisne (dept.), Fr.
42/C5 Aisne (riv.), Fr.
82/E1 Aïssa (peak), Alg.
65/M9 Aitō, Japan
79/J6 Aitutaki (atoll), CookIs.
51/F2 Aiud, Rom.
95/J7 Aiuruoca (riv.), Braz.
44/F5 Aix-en-Provence, Fr.
44/F4 Aix-les-Bains, Fr.
49/H4 Aíyina, Gre.
49/H3 Aíyion, Gre.
65/F2 Aizu-Wakamatsu, Japan
71/F3 Aīzwal, India
48/A2 Ajaccio, Fr.
48/A2 Ajaccio (gulf), Fr.
111/R8 Ajax, On,Can
62/D3 Aj Bogd (peak), Mong.
82/K1 Ajdābiyā, Libya
86/C5 Aj Janayet, Sudan
50/C2 Ajka, Hun.
70/B2 Ajmer, India
108/D4 Ajo, Az,US
46/D1 Ajo, Cabo de (cape), Sp.
100/A4 Ajuchitlán, Mex.
65/F1 Aka (riv.), Japan
65/N10 Akabane, Japan
68/F1 Akademik Obruchev (mts.), Rus.
65/F3 Akaishi-dake (mtn.), Japan
86/B4 Akasha East, Sudan
64/D3 Akashi, Japan
65/K10 Akashi (str.), Japan
68/B4 Akbaytal (pass), Taj.
81/T15 Akbou, Alg.
59/D2 Akçaabat, Turk.
59/D3 Akçakale, Turk.
51/K5 Akçakoca, Turk.
84/B2 Akchâr (reg.), Mrta.
59/C2 Akdağmadeni, Turk.
60/G4 Akdar, Al Jabal (mts.), Oman
65/N9 Akechi, Japan
37/D3 Akershus (co.), Nor.
83/K7 Aketi, Zaire
55/G4 Akhaltsikhe, Geo.
49/H3 Akharnaí, Gre.
49/G3 Akhelóos (riv.), Gre.
59/A2 Akhisar, Turk.
86/B3 Akhmīm, Egypt
55/H3 Akhtuba (riv.), Rus.
55/H2 Akhtubinsk, Rus.
54/E2 Akhtyrka, Ukr.
64/C4 Aki, Japan
65/H7 Aki (riv.), Japan
65/H7 Akigawa, Japan
103/H3 Akimiski (isl.), NW,Can
65/H7 Akishima, Japan
63/N4 Akita, Japan
84/B2 Akjoujt, Mrta.
70/D6 Akkaraipattu, SrL.
59/K5 'Akko, Isr.
84/D2 'Aklé 'Aouâna (dune), Mali, Mrta.
64/D3 Akō, Japan
82/H7 Akoga, Gabon
70/C3 Akola, India
83/N4 Āk'ordat, Erit.
85/F5 Akosombo (dam), Gha.
103/K2 Akpatok (isl.), NW,Can
68/C3 Akqi, China
49/J2 Akrathos, Akra (cape), Gre.
37/C4 Åkrehamn, Nor.
49/G4 Akrítas, Akra (cape), Gre.
109/G2 Akron, Co,US
110/D3 Akron, Oh,US
68/C4 Aksai Chin (reg.), China, India
59/C2 Aksaray, Turk.
62/C4 Aksay, China
55/K2 Aksay, Kaz.
59/B2 Akşehir, Turk.
59/B2 Akşehir (lake), Turk.
68/C2 Aksoran (peak), Kaz.
68/D3 Aksu, China
68/C3 Aksu (riv.), China
68/C2 Aksu (riv.), Kaz.
83/N5 Āksum, Eth.
49/J2 Aktí (pen.), Gre.
55/L2 Aktyubinsk, Kaz.
55/L3 Aktyubinsk Obl., Kaz.
64/B4 Akune, Japan
37/N6 Akureyri, Ice.
114/E5 Akutan (isl.), Ak,US
114/E5 Akutan (passg.), Ak,US
85/G5 Akwa Ibom (state), Nga.
71/F3 Akyab (Sittwe), Burma
55/L2 Ak"yar, Rus.
51/K5 Akyazı, Turk.
62/B3 Ala (riv.), China
113/G3 Alabama (state), US
113/G3 Alabama (riv.), Al,US
113/G3 Alabaster, Al,US
59/C2 Alaca, Turk.
59/C2 Alaçam, Turk.
113/H4 Alachua, Fl,US
55/H4 Alagir, Rus.
44/E4 Alagnon (riv.), Fr.
94/D2 Alagoa Grande, Braz.
94/C3 Alagoas (state), Braz.
94/C4 Alagoinhas, Braz.
46/B2 Alagón (riv.), Sp.
37/G3 Alajärvi, Fin.
100/E5 Alajuela, CR
68/D2 Alakol' (lake), Kaz.
86/B2 Al 'Alamayn (El Alamein), Egypt
78/D3 Alamagan (isl.), NMar.
60/E2 Al 'Amārah, Iraq
60/F3 'Alāmarvdasht (riv.), Iran
116/K11 Alameda, Ca,US
100/E5 Alamikamba, Nic.
100/B3 Alamo, Mex.
108/D4 Alamo (lake), Az,US
116/K11 Alamo, Ca,US
108/D3 Alamo, Nv,US
109/F4 Alamogordo, NM,US
101/N8 Alamos, Mex.
109/F3 Alamosa, Co,US
37/G3 Åland (isls.), Fin.
38/F2 Aland (riv.), Ger.
59/C3 Alanya, Turk.
89/J7 Alaotra (lake), Madg.
113/H4 Alapaha (riv.), Ga,US
51/K5 Alaplı, Turk.
46/D3 Alarcón (res.), Sp.
59/B2 Alaşehir, Turk.
59/L6 Al 'Āsimah (gov.), Jor.
114/* Alaska (state), US
114/J4 Alaska (gulf), Ak,US
114/F4 Alaska (pen.), Ak,US
114/H3 Alaska (range), Ak,US
114/B5 Alaska Maritime Nat'l Wild. Ref., Ak,US
114/G4 Alaska Pen. Nat'l Wild. Ref., Ak,US
45/H5 Alassio, It.
53/K5 Alatyr', Rus.
55/H4 Alaverdi, Arm.
37/G3 Alavus, Fin.
32/D5 Alaw (riv.), Wal,UK
32/D5 Alaw, Llyn (lake), Wal,UK
68/B4 Alayskiy (mts.), Kyr.
57/R3 Alazeya (riv.), Rus.
60/E2 Al 'Azīzīyah, Iraq
82/H1 Al 'Azīzīyah, Libya
45/H4 Alba, It.
51/F2 Alba (co.), Rom.
59/D3 Al Bāb, Syria
46/E3 Albacete, Sp.
86/C3 Al Baḩr al Aḩmar (gov.), Egypt
51/F2 Alba Iulia, Rom.
59/K5 Al Balqā' (gov.), Jor.
86/C3 Al Balyanā, Egypt
111/F1 Albanel (lake), Qu,Can
49/F2 Albania
74/B5 Albany, Austl.
103/H3 Albany (riv.), On,Can
116/K11 Albany, Ca,US
113/G4 Albany, Ga,US
110/C4 Albany, Ky,US
110/F3 Albany (cap.), NY,US
106/C4 Albany, Or,US
60/E2 Al Başrah, Iraq
74/G2 Albatross (bay), Austl.
88/A2 Albatross (pt.), Namb.
86/B2 Al Bawīţī, Egypt
83/K1 Al Bayḑā, Libya
113/H3 Albemarle, NC,US
113/J2 Albemarle (sound), NC,US
45/H4 Albenga, It.
46/C2 Alberche (riv.), Sp.
74/E5 Alberga (riv.), Austl.
77/A2 Albert (inlet), Austl.
74/F7 Albert (lake), Austl.
43/E2 Albert (can.), Belg.
42/B4 Albert, Fr.
83/M7 Albert (lake), Ugan., Zaire
102/E3 Alberta (prov.), Can.
96/E2 Alberti, Arg.
50/D2 Albertirsa, Hun.
107/K5 Albert Lea, Mn,US
83/M7 Albert Nile (riv.), Ugan.
97/J8 Alberto de Agostini Nat'l Park, Chile
88/Q13 Alberton, SAfr.
45/G4 Albertville, Fr.
113/G3 Albertville, Al,US
44/E5 Albi, Fr.
45/H4 Albino, It.
110/C3 Albion, Mi,US
109/H2 Albion, Ne,US
59/L4 Al Biqā' (gov.), Leb.
59/K5 Al Biqā' (Bekaa) (val.), Leb.
59/K6 Al Bīrah, WBnk.
40/B5 Alblasserdam, Neth.
37/D4 Ålborg, Den.
46/D4 Albox, Sp.
34/D1 Albrighton, Eng,UK
46/A4 Albufeira, Port.
59/H6 Al Buḩayrah (gov.), Egypt
45/H3 Albula (riv.), Swi.
108/F4 Albuquerque, NM,US
46/B3 Alburquerque, Sp.
77/C3 Albury, Austl.
47/P10 Alcabideche, Port.
46/A3 Alcácer do Sal, Port.
46/C4 Alcalá de Guadaira, Sp.
46/D2 Alcalá de Henares, Sp.
46/D4 Alcalá la Real, Sp.
48/C4 Alcamo, It.
47/E2 Alcanadre (riv.), Sp.
47/E2 Alcanar, Sp.
47/E2 Alcañiz, Sp.
46/B3 Alcantara (res.), Sp.
46/E4 Alcantarilla, Sp.
46/D3 Alcarez (range), Sp.
116/K11 Alcatraz (isl.), Ca,US
46/C4 Alcaudete, Sp.
46/D3 Alcázar de San Juan, Sp.
35/E2 Alcester, Eng,UK
47/E3 Alcira, Sp.
113/H3 Alcoa, Tn,US
46/D2 Alcobendas, Sp.
47/Q10 Alcochete, Port.
47/E2 Alcora, Sp.
46/D2 Alcorcón, Sp.
113/H3 Alcovy (riv.), Ga,US
47/E3 Alcoy, Sp.
81/G5 Aldabra (isls.), Sey.
112/B4 Aldama, Mex.
57/N4 Aldan, Rus.
57/N4 Aldan (plat.), Rus.
57/P3 Aldan (riv.), Rus.
68/G2 Aldarhaan, Mong.
35/E4 Aldbourne, Eng,UK
33/H4 Aldbrough, Eng,UK
35/H2 Alde (riv.), Eng,UK
35/H2 Aldeburgh, Eng,UK
87/B2 Aldeia Viçosa, Ang.
43/F2 Aldenhoven, Ger.
32/B2 Aldergrove, NI,UK
33/F5 Alderley Edge, Eng,UK
35/E4 Aldermaston, Eng,UK
111/Q9 Aldershot, On,Can
35/F4 Aldershot, Eng,UK
116/C2 Alderwood Manor-Bothell North, Wa,US
112/E4 Aldine, Tx,US
35/E1 Aldridge, Eng,UK
84/B2 Aleg, Mrta.
95/D2 Alegre, Braz.
91/E2 Alegrete, Braz.
90/A6 Alejandro Selkirk (isl.), Chile
54/E2 Aleksandriya, Ukr.
52/H4 Aleksandrov, Rus.
53/N4 Aleksandrovsk, Rus.
63/N1 Aleksandrovsk-Sakhalinskiy, Rus.
39/K2 Aleksandrów Kujawski, Pol.
39/K3 Aleksandrów Łódzki, Pol.
68/B1 Alekseyevka, Kaz.
54/F2 Alekseyevka, Rus.
52/H5 Aleksin, Rus.
50/E4 Aleksinac, Yugo.
95/L6 Além Paraíba, Braz.
44/D2 Alençon, Fr.
93/H4 Alenquer, Braz.
104/T10 Alenuihaha (chan.), Hi,US
59/D3 Aleppo (Ḩalab), Syria
96/B4 Alerce Andino Nat'l Park, Chile
103/S6 Alert (pt.), NW,Can
50/F2 Aleşd, Rom.
45/H4 Alessandria, It.
37/C3 Ålesund, Nor.
114/E5 Aleutian (isls.), Ak,US
114/G4 Aleutian (range), Ak,US
98/V Alexander (cape), Ant.
98/V Alexander (isl.), Ant.
114/L4 Alexander (arch.), Ak,US
113/G3 Alexander City, Al,US
75/Q12 Alexandra, NZ
94/C2 Alexandria, Braz.
49/H2 Alexándria, Gre.
51/G4 Alexandria, Rom.
112/E4 Alexandria, La,US
107/K4 Alexandria, Mn,US
115/J8 Alexandria, Va,US
59/G6 Alexandria (Al Iskandarīyah), Egypt
77/A2 Alexandrina (lake), Austl.
49/J2 Alexandroúpolis, Gre.
106/C2 Alexis Creek, BC,Can
68/D1 Aley (riv.), Rus.
68/D1 Aleysk, Rus.
47/E3 Alfafar, Sp.
60/D2 Al Fallūjah, Iraq
47/P10 Alfama, Port.
47/P11 Alfarim, Port.
46/E1 Alfaro, Sp.
83/L5 Al Fāsher, Sudan
86/B2 Al Fashn, Egypt
60/D1 Al Fatḩah, Iraq
60/E3 Al Fāw, Iraq
86/B2 Al Fayyum, Egypt
43/F3 Alfbach (riv.), Ger.
41/G5 Alfeld, Ger.
95/H6 Alfenas, Braz.
49/G4 Alfiós (riv.), Gre.
33/J5 Alford, Eng,UK
77/D3 Alfred Nat'l Park, Austl.
33/G5 Alfreton, Eng,UK
35/G5 Alfriston, Eng,UK
43/G2 Alfter, Ger.
55/L2 Alga, Kaz.
37/C4 Ålgård, Nor.
46/C4 Algeciras, Sp.
47/E3 Algemesí, Sp.
81/S15 Alger (Algiers) (cap.), Alg.
82/F2 Algeria
41/G4 Algermissen, Ger.
47/N8 Algete, Sp.
86/B2 Al Gharbīyah (gov.), Egypt
48/A2 Alghero, It.
86/C3 Al Ghurdaqah, Egypt
81/S15 Algiers (Alger) (cap.), Alg.
47/E3 Alginet, Sp.
88/D4 Algoa (bay), SAfr.
94/D2 Algodón (riv.), Peru
116/P15 Algonquin, Il,US
47/P10 Algueirão, Port.
60/D2 Al Ḩadīthah, Iraq
59/E3 Al Ḩadr, Iraq
61/G4 Al Ḩajar ash Sharqī (mts.), Oman
61/G5 Al Ḩallānīyah (isl.), Oman
46/D4 Alhama de Granada, Sp.
46/E4 Alhama de Murcia, Sp.
115/B2 Alhambra, Ca,US
86/B2 Al Ḩammām, Egypt
47/Q10 Alhandra, Port.
59/E3 Al Ḩasakah, Syria
46/C4 Alhaurín el Grande, Sp.
86/B2 Al Ḩawāmidīyah, Egypt
60/E2 Al Ḩayy, Iraq
60/D2 Al Ḩillah, Iraq
60/D2 Al Hindīyah, Iraq
81/N13 Al Hoceima, Mor.
81/N13 Al Hoceima (isl.), Sp.
60/E3 Al Hufūf, SAr.
59/A2 Aliağa, Turk.
49/G2 Aliákmon (riv.), Gre.
49/G2 Aliákmonos (lake), Gre.
60/E2 'Alī al Gharbī, Iraq
60/E2 'Alī ash Sharqī, Iraq
112/C3 Alibates Flint Quarries Nat'l Mon., Tx,US
55/J5 Ali-Bayramly, Azer.
86/C5 Al Ibēdiyya, Sudan
51/J5 Alibeyköy, Turk.
47/E3 Alicante, Sp.
76/A1 Alice (riv.), Austl.
48/E3 Alice (pt.), It.
112/D5 Alice, Tx,US
74/E4 Alice Springs, Austl.
113/F3 Aliceville, Al,US
67/D6 Alicia, Phil.
67/C6 Alicia Annie (shoal)
48/D3 Alicudi (isl.), It.
70/C2 Alīgarh, India
60/E2 Alīgudarz, Iran
82/J8 Alima (riv.), Congo
37/E4 Alingsås, Swe.
70/B2 Alīpur, Pak.
70/E2 Alīpur Duār, India
59/G6 Al Iskandarīyah (gov.), Egypt
59/G6 Al Iskandarīyah (Alexandria), Egypt
86/C2 Al Ismā'īlīyah (gov.), Egypt
86/C2 Al Ismā'īlīyah (Ismalia), Egypt
88/D3 Aliwal North, SAfr.
83/K2 Al Jaghbūb, Libya
81/X18 Al Jamm, Tun.
59/K5 Al Janūb (gov.), Leb.
86/B2 Al Jīzah, Egypt
86/B2 Al Jīzah (gov.), Egypt
83/K5 Al Junaynah, Sudan
46/A4 Aljustrel, Port.
81/W17 Al Kāf, Tun.
81/W17 Al Kāf (gov.), Tun.
59/K6 Al Karak, Jor.
59/L6 Al Karak (gov.), Jor.
86/C3 Al Karnak, Egypt
43/E2 Alken, Belg.
61/G4 Al Khābūrah, Oman
59/K6 Al Khalīl (Hebron), WBnk.
60/D2 Al Khāliş, Iraq
86/B5 Al Khandaq, Sudan
86/B3 Al Khārijah, Egypt
83/M4 Al Kharţūm Baḩrī (Khartoum North), Sudan
60/F3 Al Khobar, SAr.
82/H1 Al Khums, Libya
40/B3 Alkmaar, Neth.
82/H3 Alkoum (well), Alg.
60/D2 Al Kūfah, Iraq
83/K3 Al Kufrah, Libya
60/E2 Al Kūt, Iraq
60/E3 Al Kuwait (Kuwait) (cap.), Kuw.
59/K4 Al Lādhiqīyah (Latakia), Syria
70/D2 Allahābād, India
107/G3 Allan, Sk,Can
107/G3 Allan (hills), Sk,Can
111/R9 Allanburg, On,Can
71/G4 Allanmyo, Burma
107/L3 Allan Water (riv.), On,Can
82/H1 'Allāq (well), Libya
86/C4 'Allāqi, Wādī al (dry riv.), Egypt
110/C3 Allegan, Mi,US
105/K4 Allegheny (mts.), US
110/E3 Allegheny (plat.), Pa,US
110/E3 Allegheny (riv.), Pa,US
96/D3 Allen, Arg.
34/B5 Allen (riv.), Eng,UK
32/B5 Allen, Bog of (swamp), Ire.
33/F2 Allendale, Eng,UK
113/H3 Allendale, SC,US
100/A2 Allende, Mex.
116/F7 Allen Park, Mi,US
115/E5 Allentown, Pa,US
70/C6 Alleppey, India
41/G3 Aller (riv.), Ger.
41/H4 Allerkanal (can.), Ger.
45/J3 Allgäu (mts.), Aus., Ger.
109/G2 Alliance, Ne,US
110/D3 Alliance, Oh,US
44/E3 Allier (riv.), Fr.
44/D3 Allones, Fr.
111/G1 Alma, Qu,Can
110/C3 Alma, Mi,US
109/H2 Alma, Ne,US
68/C3 Alma-Ata (cap.), Kaz.
46/A3 Almada, Port.
46/C3 Almadén, Sp.
60/B3 Al Madīnah al Fikrīyah, Egypt
81/X18 Al Madīyah, Tun.
81/X18 Al Madīyah (gov.), Tun.
59/L5 Al Mafraq, Jor.
96/D2 Almafuerte, Arg.
82/E1 Al Maghrib (reg.), Alg., Mor.
46/D3 Almagro, Sp.
59/H6 Al Maḩallah al Kubrá, Egypt
59/H6 Al Maḩmūdīyah, Egypt
60/D2 Al Maḩmūdīyah, Iraq
59/E3 Al Mālikīyah, Syria
68/A3 Almalyk, Uzb.
60/F3 Al Manāmah (Manama) (cap.), Bahr.
108/B2 Almanor (lake), Ca,US
47/E3 Almansa, Sp.
59/H6 Al Mansūra, Egypt

59/H6 **Al Manzilah**, Egypt
46/D4 **Almanzora** (riv.), Sp.
46/C2 **Almanzor, Pico de** (peak), Sp.
86/B3 **Al Marāghah**, Egypt
82/K1 **Al Marj**, Libya
94/B4 **Almas** (peak), Braz.
93/J6 **Almas** (riv.), Braz.
59/J6 **Al Maṭarīyah**, Egypt
59/E3 **Al Mawṣil** (Mosul), Iraq
60/D1 **Al Mayādin**, Syria
47/E3 **Almazora**, Sp.
41/F5 **Alme** (riv.), Ger.
46/A3 **Almeirim**, Port.
40/D4 **Almelo**, Neth.
94/B5 **Almenara**, Braz.
46/D3 **Almenara** (mtn.), Sp.
46/B2 **Almendra** (res.), Sp.
46/B3 **Almendralejo**, Sp.
40/C4 **Almere**, Neth.
46/D4 **Almería**, Sp.
47/D4 **Almería** (gulf), Sp.
53/M5 **Al'met'yevsk**, Rus.
37/E4 **Älmhult**, Swe.
46/C5 **Almina** (pt.), Sp.
86/B2 **Al Minūfīyah** (gov.), Egypt
86/B2 **Al Minyā**, Egypt
86/B3 **Al Minyā** (gov.), Egypt
60/D2 **Al Miqdādiyah**, Iraq
97/J7 **Almirante Montt** (gulf), Chile
49/H3 **Almirós**, Gre.
49/J5 **Almiroú** (gulf), Gre.
46/C3 **Almodóvar del Campo**, Sp.
46/C4 **Almodóvar del Río**, Sp.
36/D2 **Almond** (riv.), Sc,UK
31/U11 **Almont** (riv.), Fr.
110/E2 **Almonte**, On,Can
46/B4 **Almonte**, Sp.
47/E3 **Almoradí**, Sp.
95/D1 **Almores** (range), Braz.
60/E3 **Al Mubarraz**, SAr.
83/L5 **Al Muglad**, Sudan
81/X18 **Al Muknīn**, Tun.
81/X18 **Al Munastīr**, Tun.
81/X18 **Al Munastīr** (gov.), Tun.
46/D4 **Almuñécar**, Sp.
36/C2 **Alness**, Sc,UK
79/J6 **Alofi** (cap.), Niue
78/H6 **Alofi** (isl.), Wall.
71/G2 **Along**, India
49/H3 **Alónnisos** (isl.), Gre.
73/F5 **Alor** (isls.), Indo.
46/C4 **Álora**, Sp.
72/B2 **Alor Setar**, Malay.
78/E6 **Alotau**, PNG
40/D5 **Alpen**, Ger.
110/D2 **Alpena**, Mi,US
94/A2 **Alpercatas** (mts.), Braz.
94/A2 **Alpercatas** (riv.), Braz.
40/B4 **Alphen aan de Rijn**, Neth.
46/A3 **Alpiarça**, Port.
112/C4 **Alpine**, Tx,US
106/F5 **Alpine**, Wy,US
46/B4 **Alportel**, Port.
45/G4 **Alps** (mts.), Eur.
65/F3 **Alps-Minami Nat'l Park**, Japan
61/G4 **Al Qābil**, Oman
83/N5 **Al Qaḍārif**, Sudan
86/B2 **Al Qāhirah** (Cairo) (cap.), Egypt
59/E3 **Al Qāmishlī**, Syria
86/B3 **Al Qaṣr**, Egypt
81/W18 **Al Qaṣrayn**, Tun.
81/W18 **Al Qaṣrayn** (gov.), Tun.
83/M5 **Al Qaṭaynah**, Sudan
82/H3 **Al Qaṭrūn**, Libya
81/X18 **Al Qayrawān**, Tun.
81/W18 **Al Qayrawān** (gov.), Tun.
59/K5 **Al Qunayṭirah** (prov.), Syria
86/C3 **Al Quṣayr**, Egypt
59/L4 **Al Quṣayr**, Syria
59/L5 **Al Quṭayfah**, Syria
35/E1 **Alrewas**, Eng,UK
38/F1 **Als** (isl.), Den.
45/G2 **Alsace** (reg.), Fr.
38/D5 **Alsace, Ballon d'** (mtn.), Fr.
33/F5 **Alsager**, Eng,UK
106/F3 **Alsask**, Sk,Can
46/D1 **Alsasua**, Sp.
43/F2 **Alsdorf**, Ger.
38/E3 **Alsfeld**, Ger.
116/Q16 **Alsip**, Il,US
41/H1 **Alster** (riv.), Ger.
33/F2 **Alston**, Eng,UK
33/F4 **Alt** (riv.), Eng,UK
37/G1 **Alta**, Nor.
115/B2 **Altadena**, Ca,US
93/G6 **Alta Floresta**, Braz.
96/D1 **Alta Gracia**, Arg.
100/D5 **Alta Gracia**, Nic.
68/D1 **Altai** (mts.), Asia
113/H4 **Altamaha** (riv.), Ga,US
93/H4 **Altamira**, Braz.
100/B3 **Altamira**, Mex.
113/H4 **Altamonte Springs**, Fl,US
48/E2 **Altamura**, It.
100/C4 **Altar de los Sacrificios** (ruins), Guat.
62/B2 **Altay**, China
56/J4 **Altay** (kray), Rus.
45/H3 **Altdorf**, Swi.
45/J2 **Altdorf bei Nürnberg**, Ger.
47/E3 **Altea**, Sp.
41/E6 **Altena**, Ger.
41/F5 **Altenau** (riv.), Ger.
41/F5 **Altenbeken**, Ger.
38/G3 **Altenburg**, Ger.
39/G2 **Altentreptow**, Ger.
101/P8 **Alteres**, Mex.
40/D5 **Alter Rhein** (riv.), Ger.
41/G1 **Altes Land** (reg.), Ger.
33/H4 **Althorpe**, Eng,UK
92/E7 **Altiplano** (plat.), Bol., Peru
38/F2 **Altmark** (reg.), Ger.
45/J2 **Altmühl** (riv.), Ger.
45/K3 **Altmünster**, Aus.
94/A4 **Alto** (peak), Braz.
93/H7 **Alto Araguaia**, Braz.
87/C2 **Alto Cuale**, Ang.
35/F4 **Alton**, Eng,UK
110/B4 **Alton**, Il,US
77/F5 **Altona**, Austl.
107/J3 **Altona**, Mb,Can
110/E3 **Altoona**, Pa,US
94/A3 **Alto Parnaíba**, Braz.
92/D6 **Alto Purús** (riv.), Peru
94/B2 **Altos**, Braz.
94/C2 **Alto Santo**, Braz.
33/F5 **Altrincham**, Eng,UK
62/C4 **Altun** (mts.), China
100/D4 **Altun Ha** (ruins), Belz.
108/B2 **Alturas**, Ca,US
109/H4 **Altus**, Ok,US
109/H4 **Altus** (res.), Ok,US
109/H4 **Altus A.F.B.**, Ok,US
83/M5 **Al Ubayyiḍ**, Sudan
83/L5 **Al Uḍayyah**, Sudan
32/E5 **Alun** (riv.), Wal,UK
86/C3 **Al Uqṣur** (Luxor), Egypt
54/E3 **Alushta**, Ukr.
83/L3 **Al 'Uwaynāt** (peak), Sudan
109/H3 **Alva**, Ok,US
35/E2 **Alvechurch**, Eng,UK
46/A3 **Alverca**, Port.
47/P10 **Alverca do Ribatejo**, Port.
37/E4 **Alvesta**, Swe.
34/D4 **Alveston**, Eng,UK
112/E4 **Alvin**, Tx,US
37/F3 **Älvkarleby**, Swe.
37/E4 **Älvsborg** (co.), Swe.
37/G2 **Älvsbyn**, Swe.
86/B3 **Al Wādī al Jadīd** (gov.), Egypt
70/C2 **Alwar**, India
62/E4 **Alxa Youqi**, China
62/F4 **Alxa Zuoqi**, China
39/N1 **Alytus**, Lith.
45/K2 **Alz** (riv.), Ger.
45/H4 **Alzano Lombardo**, It.
43/F4 **Alzette** (riv.), Lux.
86/C2 **Al `Aqabah**, Jor.
92/D4 **Amacayacú Nat'l Park**, Col.
60/B4 **Amada** (ruins), Egypt
74/E4 **Amadeus** (lake), Austl.
83/M6 **Amadi**, Sudan
103/J2 **Amadjuak** (lake), NW,Can
46/A3 **Amadora**, Port.
65/L10 **Amagasaki**, Japan
64/B4 **Amagi**, Japan
65/F3 **Amagi-san** (mtn.), Japan
73/G4 **Amahai**, Indo.
64/A4 **Amakusa** (sea), Japan
37/E4 **Åmål**, Swe.
62/G1 **Amalat** (riv.), Rus.
49/G4 **Amaliás**, Gre.
70/C3 **Amalner**, India
91/E1 **Amambaí**, Braz.
93/H8 **Amambaí** (riv.), Braz.
78/B2 **Amami** (isls.), Japan
48/E3 **Amantea**, It.
79/L6 **Amanu** (atoll), FrPol.
94/B2 **Amarante**, Braz.
46/A2 **Amarante**, Port.
69/B1 **Amarapura**, Burma
94/C4 **Amargosa**, Braz.
108/C3 **Amargosa** (dry riv.), Ca, Nv,US
112/C3 **Amarillo**, Tx,US
48/D1 **Amaro** (peak), It.
59/C2 **Amasya**, Turk.
65/J7 **Amatsukominato**, Japan
43/E2 **Amay**, Belg.
93/H4 **Amazon** (riv.), SAm.
93/G4 **Amazônia** (Tapajós) Nat'l Park, Braz.
70/C4 **Ambajogai**, India
61/L2 **Ambāla**, India
70/D6 **Ambalangoda**, SrL.
89/H8 **Ambalavao**, Madg.
89/J6 **Ambanja**, Madg.
89/H6 **Ambaro** (bay), Madg.
92/C4 **Ambato**, Ecu.
89/H7 **Ambato Boeny**, Madg.
89/H8 **Ambatofinandrahana**, Madg.
89/H7 **Ambatolampy**, Madg.
89/J7 **Ambatondrazaka**, Madg.
49/H4 **Ambelos, Ákra** (cape), Gre.
45/J2 **Amberg**, Ger.
33/G5 **Ambergate**, Eng,UK
70/D3 **Ambikāpur**, India
89/J6 **Ambilobe**, Madg.
89/J7 **Ambinaninony**, Madg.
33/G1 **Amble**, Eng,UK
115/E5 **Ambler**, Pa,US
33/F3 **Ambleside**, Eng,UK
42/A2 **Ambleteuse**, Fr.
43/F3 **Amblève** (riv.), Belg.
89/H9 **Amboasary**, Madg.
89/J6 **Ambohitra, Tampon** (peak), Madg.
73/G4 **Ambon**, Indo.
73/G4 **Ambon** (isl.), Indo.
89/H8 **Ambositra**, Madg.
89/H9 **Ambovombe**, Madg.
87/B2 **Ambriz**, Ang.
78/F6 **Ambrym** (isl.), Van.
114/B6 **Amchitka** (isl.), Ak,US
114/B6 **Amchitka** (passg.), Ak,US
101/P9 **Ameca**, Mex.
43/F3 **Amel**, Belg.
40/C2 **Ameland** (isl.), Neth.
40/B5 **Amer** (chan.), Neth.
98/F **American** (highland), Ant.
116/M9 **American** (riv.), Ca,US
116/B3 **American** (lake), Wa,US
95/C2 **Americana**, Braz.
106/E5 **American Falls**, Id,US
108/D2 **American Falls** (res.), Id,US
108/E2 **American Fork**, Ut,US
79/J6 **American Samoa** (terr.), US
113/G3 **Americus**, Ga,US
45/L3 **Ameringkogel** (peak), Aus.
40/C4 **Amersfoort**, Neth.
35/F3 **Amersham**, Eng,UK
98/E **Amery Ice Shelf**, Ant.
107/K5 **Ames**, Ia,US
35/E4 **Amesbury**, Eng,UK
49/H3 **Ámfissa**, Gre.
57/N3 **Amga** (riv.), Rus.
57/T3 **Amguema** (riv.), Rus.
63/M1 **Amgun'** (riv.), Rus.
111/H2 **Amherst**, NS,Can
116/F7 **Amherstburg**, On,Can
48/B1 **Amiata** (peak), It.
42/B4 **Amiens**, Fr.
57/U4 **Amila** (isl.), Ak,US
81/H5 **Amirante** (isls.), Sey.
107/H2 **Amisk** (lake), Sk,Can
112/C4 **Amistad** (res.), Mex., US
109/G5 **Amistad Nat'l Rec. Area**, Tx,US
109/K5 **Amite** (riv.), La,US
70/C3 **Amla**, India
114/D6 **Amlia** (isl.), Ak,US
32/D5 **Amlwch**, Wal,UK
59/K6 **'Ammān** (cap.), Jor.
34/C3 **Amman** (riv.), Wal,UK
34/C3 **Ammanford**, Wal,UK
37/E2 **Ammarfjället** (peak), Swe.
114/K2 **Ammerman** (mtn.), Yk,Can
45/J2 **Ammersee** (lake), Ger.
106/F5 **Ammon**, Id,US
69/D3 **Amnat Charoen**, Thai.
43/F5 **Amnéville**, Fr.
60/F1 **Āmol**, Iran
47/P10 **Amora**, Port.
49/J4 **Amorgós** (isl.), Gre.
113/F3 **Amory**, Ms,US
110/E1 **Amos**, Qu,Can
89/J8 **Ampangalana** (can.), Madg.
89/H9 **Ampanihy**, Madg.
70/D6 **Amparai**, SrL.
95/G7 **Amparo**, Braz.
89/J6 **Ampasindava** (bay), Madg.
47/F2 **Amposta**, Sp.
35/F2 **Ampthill**, Eng,UK
111/H1 **Amqui**, Qu,Can
70/C3 **Amravati**, India
70/B3 **Amreli**, India
60/C2 **'Amrīt** (ruins), Syria
61/K2 **Amritsar**, India
38/E1 **Amrun** (isl.), Ger.
40/B4 **Amstel** (riv.), Neth.
40/B4 **Amstelveen**, Neth.
29/N7 **Amsterdam** (isl.), FrAnt.
40/B4 **Amsterdam** (cap.), Neth.
110/F3 **Amsterdam**, NY,US
40/C5 **Amsterdam-Rijnkanaal** (can.), Neth.
45/L2 **Amstetten**, Aus.
83/K5 **Am Timan**, Chad
58/F5 **Amudar'ya** (riv.), Asia
114/D5 **Amukta** (passg.), Ak,US
103/S7 **Amund Rignes** (isl.), NW,Can
98/D **Amundsen** (bay), Ant.
98/S **Amundsen** (sea), Ant.
102/D1 **Amundsen** (gulf), NW,Can
98/A **Amundsen-Scott**, Ant.
63/M1 **Amur** (riv.), China, Rus.
79/K6 **Amuri**, Cookls.
57/N4 **Amur Obl.**, Rus.
46/D1 **Amurrio**, Sp.
63/M1 **Amursk**, Rus.
86/C5 **'Amur, Wādī** (dry riv.), Sudan
67/C5 **Amy Douglas** (shoal)
59/K4 **Amyūn**, Leb.
79/L6 **Anaa** (atoll), FrPol.
57/L3 **Anabar** (riv.), Rus.
115/A2 **Anacapa** (isl.), Ca,US
101/J6 **Anaco**, Ven.
106/E4 **Anaconda**, Mt,US
109/H4 **Anadarko**, Ok,US
57/T3 **Anadyr'**, Rus.
57/U3 **Anadyr'** (gulf), Rus.
57/T3 **Anadyr'** (range), Rus.
58/S3 **Anadyr'** (riv.), Rus.
49/J4 **Anáfi** (isl.), Gre.
60/D2 **'Ānah**, Iraq
115/C3 **Anaheim**, Ca,US
106/B2 **Anahim Lake**, BC,Can
100/A2 **Anáhuac**, Mex.
112/E4 **Anahuac**, Tx,US
70/D4 **Anakāpalle**, India
89/H6 **Analalava**, Madg.
89/J7 **Analamaitso** (plat.), Madg.
101/F3 **Ana María** (gulf), Cuba
72/C3 **Anambas** (isls.), Indo.
85/G5 **Anambra** (state), Nga.
59/C3 **Anamur**, Turk.
59/C3 **Anamur** (pt.), Turk.
64/D4 **Anan**, Japan
70/B3 **Anand**, India
70/C5 **Anantapur**, India
61/L2 **Anantnag**, India
68/C3 **Anan'yevo**, Kyr.
54/F3 **Anapa**, Rus.
97/K7 **Añapi** (peak), Arg.
93/J7 **Anápolis**, Braz.
93/H4 **Anapu** (riv.), Braz.
93/G8 **Anastácio**, Braz.
78/D3 **Anathan** (isl.), NMar.
59/B2 **Anatolia** (reg.), Turk.
91/D2 **Añatuya**, Arg.
92/F3 **Anauá** (riv.), Braz.
111/Q9 **Ancaster**, On,Can
67/A2 **Anchangzhen**, China
116/G6 **Anchor** (bay), Mi,US
114/J3 **Anchorage**, Ak,US
111/G2 **Ancienne-Lorette**, Qu,Can
92/E7 **Ancohuma** (peak), Bol.
45/K5 **Ancona**, It.
96/B4 **Ancud**, Chile
96/B4 **Ancud** (gulf), Chile
62/C3 **Anda**, China
92/D6 **Andahuaylas**, Peru
89/J7 **Andaingo Gara**, Madg.
37/C3 **Åndalsnes**, Nor.
46/C4 **Andalusia** (aut. comm.), Sp.
113/G4 **Andalusia**, Al,US
71/F5 **Andaman** (sea), Asia
71/F5 **Andaman** (isls.), India
71/F5 **Andaman & Nicobar Is.** (terr.), India
89/J6 **Andapa**, Madg.
42/A4 **Andelle** (riv.), Fr.
37/F1 **Andenes**, Nor.
43/E3 **Andenne**, Belg.
37/F1 **Ånderdalen Nat'l Park**, Nor.
42/D3 **Anderlues**, Belg.
43/G3 **Andernach**, Ger.
114/N2 **Anderson** (riv.), NW,Can
108/B2 **Anderson**, Ca,US
110/C3 **Anderson**, In,US
113/H3 **Anderson**, SC,US
112/E4 **Anderson**, Tx,US
116/B3 **Anderson** (isl.), Wa,US
90/C4 **Andes** (mts.), SAm.
37/F1 **Andfjorden** (fjord), Nor.
70/C4 **Andhra Pradesh** (state), India
49/H5 **Andikíthira** (isl.), Gre.
89/J7 **Andilamena**, Madg.
60/E2 **Andīmeshk**, Iran
49/J4 **Andíparos** (isl.), Gre.
95/B2 **Andira**, Braz.
68/B3 **Andizhan**, Uzb.
46/D1 **Andoain**, Sp.
64/A2 **Andong**, SKor.
64/A2 **Andong** (lake), SKor.
47/F1 **Andorra**
47/E2 **Andorra**, Sp.
47/F1 **Andorra la Vella** (cap.), And.
35/E4 **Andover**, Eng,UK
115/F5 **Andover**, NJ,US
37/E1 **Andøya** (isl.), Nor.
95/G7 **Andradas**, Braz.
95/B2 **Andradina**, Braz.
47/G3 **Andraitx**, Sp.
89/H7 **Andranomavo** (riv.), Madg.
114/C6 **Andreanof** (isls.), Ak,US
95/J6 **Andrelândia**, Braz.
31/S10 **Andrésy**, Fr.
112/C3 **Andrews**, Tx,US
48/E2 **Andria**, It.
89/H8 **Andringitra** (mts.), Madg.
89/J6 **Androntany** (cape), Madg.
101/F3 **Andros** (isl.), Bahm.
49/J4 **Ándros** (isl.), Gre.
110/G2 **Androscoggin** (riv.), Me, NH,US
46/C3 **Andújar**, Sp.
96/C4 **Anecón Grande** (peak), Arg.
96/E4 **Anegada** (bay), Arg.
101/J4 **Anegada** (isl.), BVi.
101/J4 **Anegada** (passage), NAm.
85/F5 **Anécho**, Togo
78/G7 **Aneityum** (isl.), Van.
47/F1 **Aneto, Pico de** (peak), Sp.
67/B2 **Anfu**, China
91/B1 **Angamos** (pt.), Chile
62/E1 **Angara** (riv.), Rus.
62/E1 **Angarsk**, Rus.
37/E3 **Ånge**, Swe.
41/E5 **Angel** (riv.), Ger.
101/M8 **Ángel de la Guarda** (isl.), Mex.
67/D4 **Angeles**, Phil.
115/B2 **Angeles Nat'l Forest**, Ca,US
112/E4 **Angelina** (riv.), Tx,US
38/E1 **Angeln** (reg.), Ger.
92/F2 **Angel, Salto** (falls), Ven.
116/F6 **Angelus** (lake), Mi,US
73/J4 **Angemuk** (mtn.), Indo.
37/E2 **Ångermanälven** (riv.), Swe.
39/H2 **Angermünde**, Ger.
44/C3 **Angers**, Fr.
94/C2 **Angicos**, Braz.
69/C3 **Angkor** (ruins), Camb.
69/D4 **Angk Tasaom**, Camb.
75/Q12 **Anglem** (peak), NZ
32/D5 **Anglesey** (isl.), Wal,UK
44/C5 **Anglet**, Fr.
112/E4 **Angleton**, Tx,US
44/D3 **Anglin** (riv.), Fr.
69/C2 **Ang Nam Ngum** (lake), Laos
83/L7 **Ango**, Zaire
96/B3 **Angol**, Chile
87/C3 **Angola**
116/L10 **Angola**, In,US
110/C3 **Angola**, NY,US
100/C4 **Angostura** (res.), Mex.
44/D4 **Angoulême**, Fr.
47/S12 **Angra do Heroísmo**, Azor.,Port.
95/J8 **Angra dos Reis**, Braz.
68/B3 **Angren**, Uzb.
69/C3 **Ang Thong**, Thai.
83/K7 **Angu**, Zaire
101/J4 **Anguilla** (isl.), UK
114/G2 **Angutikada** (peak), Ak,US
93/H8 **Anhanduí** (riv.), Braz.
43/D3 **Anhée**, Belg.
71/K2 **Anhua**, China
66/D4 **Anhui** (prov.), China
114/G4 **Aniakchak** (crater), Ak,US
114/G4 **Aniakchak Nat'l Mon. & Prsv.**, Ak,US
42/C3 **Aniche**, Fr.
108/F3 **Animas** (riv.), Co, NM,US
50/E3 **Anina**, Rom.
63/N2 **Aniva** (bay), Rus.
37/H3 **Anjalankoski**, Fin.
70/B3 **Anjār**, India
65/N10 **Anjō**, Japan
111/N6 **Anjou**, Qu,Can
44/C3 **Anjou** (hist. reg.), Fr.
89/H6 **Anjouan** (isl.), Com.
59/C2 **Ankara** (cap.), Turk.
89/H7 **Ankaratra, Massif** (plat.), Madg.
112/C2 **Ankaree** (riv.), Co,US
89/H8 **Ankazoabo**, Madg.
69/E3 **An Khe**, Viet.
39/G2 **Anklam**, Ger.
69/D3 **Anlong Veng**, Camb.
40/D2 **Anloo**, Neth.
66/C5 **Anlu**, China
98/D **Ann** (cape), Ant.
111/G3 **Ann** (cape), Ma,US
110/E4 **Anna** (lake), Va,US
81/V17 **Annaba**, Alg.
45/K1 **Annaberg-Buchholz**, Ger.
59/L4 **An Nabk**, Syria
32/B3 **Annaclone**, NI,UK
60/C3 **An Nafūd** (des.), SAr.
83/L5 **An Nahūd**, Sudan
60/D2 **An Najaf**, Iraq
36/B3 **Annalee** (riv.), Ire.
32/C3 **Annalong**, NI,UK
69/D2 **Annamitique, Chaîne** (mts.), Laos, Viet.
33/E2 **Annan**, Sc,UK
36/D3 **Annan** (riv.), Sc,UK
115/J8 **Annandale**, Va,US
40/B3 **Anna Pavlowna**, Neth.
96/B5 **Anna Pink** (bay), Chile
115/K8 **Annapolis** (cap.), Md,US
70/D2 **Annapurna** (mtn.), Nepal
60/C3 **An Naqb, Ra's**, Jor.
116/E7 **Ann Arbor**, Mi,US
60/E2 **An Nāṣirīyah**, Iraq
77/C4 **Anne** (peak), Austl.
74/B5 **Annean** (lake), Austl.
45/G4 **Annecy**, Fr.
31/U10 **Annet-sur-Marne**, Fr.
69/E3 **An Nhon**, Viet.
113/G3 **Anniston**, Al,US
82/F8 **Annobón** (isl.), EqG.
44/F4 **Annonay**, Fr.
60/E2 **An Nu'manīyah**, Iraq
65/M10 **Anō**, Japan
47/K7 **Anoia** (riv.), Sp.
107/K4 **Anoka**, Mn,US
89/J7 **Anosibe an' Ala**, Madg.
85/G2 **Ânou-Zeggarene** (wadi), Niger
69/E4 **An Phuoc**, Viet.
66/D5 **Anqing**, China
41/F5 **Anröchte**, Ger.
43/E2 **Ans**, Belg.
45/J2 **Ansbach**, Ger.
101/G4 **Anse-d'Hainault**, Haiti
45/L2 **Ansfelden**, Aus.
71/J2 **Anshun**, China
74/D2 **Anson** (bay), Austl.
112/D3 **Anson**, Tx,US
63/K4 **Ansŏng**, SKor.
78/E4 **Ant** (atoll), Micr.
35/H1 **Ant** (riv.), Eng,UK
59/D3 **Antakya** (Antioch), Turk.
89/J6 **Antalaha**, Madg.
59/B3 **Antalya**, Turk.
59/B3 **Antalya** (gulf), Turk.
89/H7 **Antananarivo** (cap.), Madg.
89/H7 **Antananarivo** (prov.), Madg.
98/W **Antarctic** (pen.), Ant.
98/* **Antarctica**
95/B4 **Antas** (riv.), Braz.
42/D5 **Ante** (riv.), Fr.
46/C4 **Antequera**, Sp.
109/H3 **Anthony**, Ks,US
108/F4 **Anthony**, NM,US
82/D2 **Anti-Atlas** (mts.), Mor.
45/G5 **Antibes**, Fr.
111/J1 **Anticosti** (isl.), Qu,Can
44/D2 **Antifer, Cap d'** (cape), Fr.
110/B2 **Antigo**, Wi,US
111/J2 **Antigonish**, NS,Can
101/J4 **Antigua** (isl.), Ant. & Barb.
101/J4 **Antigua and Barbuda**
59/K5 **Anti-Lebanon** (mts.), Leb.
116/L10 **Antioch**, Ca,US
116/P15 **Antioch**, Il,US
59/D3 **Antioch** (Antakya), Turk.
29/T8 **Antipodes** (isls.), NZ
109/J4 **Antlers**, Ok,US
91/B1 **Antofagasta**, Chile
42/C2 **Antoing**, Belg.
89/J6 **Antongil** (bay), Madg.
88/C4 **Antoniesberg** (peak), SAfr.
95/B3 **Antonina**, Braz.
109/F3 **Antonito**, Co,US
100/B4 **Anton Lizardo** (pt.), Mex.
31/S10 **Antony**, Fr.
32/B2 **Antrim**, NI,UK
32/B2 **Antrim** (dist.), NI,UK
32/B1 **Antrim** (mts.), NI,UK
89/H7 **Antsalova**, Madg.
89/H7 **Antsirabe**, Madg.
89/J6 **Antsiranana**, Madg.
89/J6 **Antsiranana** (prov.), Madg.
89/H6 **Antsohihy**, Madg.
96/C3 **Antuco** (vol.), Chile
43/E1 **Antwerp** (prov.), Belg.
42/D1 **Antwerp** (Antwerpen), Belg.
70/D6 **Anuradhapura**, SrL.
114/B6 **Anvil** (vol.), Ak,US
67/C2 **Anxi**, China
66/C3 **Anyang**, China
62/D4 **A'nyêmaqên** (mts.), China
66/B4 **Anyi**, China
63/M2 **Anyuy** (riv.), Rus.
42/C2 **Anzegem**, Belg.
56/J4 **Anzhero-Sudzhensk**, Rus.
42/C3 **Anzin**, Fr.
48/C2 **Anzio**, It.
65/L9 **Aogaki**, Japan
69/B4 **Ao Kham** (pt.), Thai.
63/N3 **Aomori**, Japan
49/G2 **Aóos** (riv.), Gre.
69/B4 **Ao Phangnga Nat'l Park**, Thai.
69/D3 **Aoral** (peak), Camb.
45/G4 **Aosta**, It.
84/C2 **Aoudaghost** (ruins), Mrta.
83/K5 **Aouk** (riv.), CAfr., Chad
84/C2 **Aoukar** (reg.), Mrta.
82/F2 **Aoulef**, Alg.
65/M10 **Aoyama**, Japan
82/J3 **Aozou**, Chad
112/B4 **Apache** (mts.), Tx,US
113/G4 **Apalachicola**, Fl,US
95/B4 **Aparados da Serra Nat'l Park**, Braz.
95/C2 **Aparecida**, Braz.
95/B2 **Aparecida do Taboado**, Braz.
67/D4 **Aparri**, Phil.
101/F6 **Apartado**, Col.
79/L6 **Apataki**, FrPol.
50/D3 **Apatin**, Yugo.
52/G2 **Apatity**, Rus.
101/P10 **Apatzingán**, Mex.
100/B4 **Apaxtla**, Mex.
69/D4 **Ap Binh Chau**, Viet.
40/C4 **Apeldoorn**, Neth.
40/D4 **Apeldoornsch** (can.), Neth.
41/E2 **Apen**, Ger.
30/E4 **Apennines** (mts.), It.
72/C3 **Api** (cape), Indo.
73/E5 **Api** (peak), Indo.
68/D5 **Api** (mtn.), Nepal
79/H6 **Apia** (cap.), WSam.
93/G6 **Apiacás** (mts.), Braz.
95/B3 **Apiaí**, Braz.
69/D4 **Ap Loc Thanh**, Viet.
69/E4 **Ap Long Hoa**, Viet.
69/D4 **Ap Luc**, Viet.
67/E6 **Apo** (mt.), Phil.
94/C2 **Apodi**, Braz.
94/C2 **Apodi** (riv.), Braz.
79/R9 **Apolima** (str.), WSam.
95/B1 **Aporé** (riv.), Braz.
110/B2 **Apostle** (isls.), Wi,US
91/E2 **Apóstoles**, Arg.
59/C3 **Apostolos Andreas** (cape), Cyp.
105/K4 **Appalachian** (mts.), US
40/D2 **Appingedam**, Neth.
33/F2 **Appleby**, Eng,UK
35/E1 **Appleby Magna**, Eng,UK
111/S9 **Appleton**, NY,US
110/B2 **Appleton**, Wi,US
115/C1 **Apple Valley**, Ca,US
48/D2 **Apricena**, It.
48/C2 **Aprilia**, It.
54/F3 **Apsheronsk**, Rus.
77/E1 **Apsley Gorge Nat'l Park**, Austl.
69/E4 **Ap Tan My**, Viet.
104/U11 **Apua** (pt.), Hi,US
45/J4 **Apuane** (mts.), It.
95/B2 **Apucarana**, Braz.
101/H6 **Apure** (riv.), Ven.
92/D6 **Apurímac** (riv.), Peru
69/E4 **Ap Vinh Hao**, Viet.
86/C2 **Aqaba** (gulf), Asia
60/B3 **Aqaba** (gulf), Egypt, SAr.
86/D5 **'Aqīq**, Sudan
68/E4 **Aqqikkol** (lake), China
60/D1 **'Aqrah**, Iraq
93/G8 **Aquidauana**, Braz.
93/G8 **Aquidauana** (riv.), Braz.
94/C1 **Aquiraz**, Braz.
44/C4 **Aquitaine** (reg.), Fr.
62/D4 **Ar** (riv.), China
65/F2 **Ara** (riv.), Japan
83/L5 **'Arab** (riv.), Sudan
113/G3 **Arab**, Al,US
86/C2 **'Arabah, Wādī** (dry riv.), Egypt
60/D3 **Arabian** (pen.), Asia
61/H5 **Arabian** (sea), Asia
86/C3 **Arabian** (des.), Egypt
59/L5 **'Arab, Jabal al** (mts.), Syria
86/B2 **'Arab, Kalīj al** (gulf), Egypt
54/E4 **Araç** (riv.), Turk.
94/C3 **Aracaju**, Braz.
94/C2 **Aracati**, Braz.
95/B2 **Araçatuba**, Braz.
46/B4 **Aracena**, Sp.
94/C3 **Araci**, Braz.
95/D1 **Aracruz**, Braz.
94/B5 **Araçuaí**, Braz.
94/B5 **Araçuaí** (riv.), Braz.
50/E2 **Arad**, Rom.
50/E2 **Arad** (co.), Rom.
83/K4 **Arada**, Chad
60/F1 **Arādān**, Iran
60/D4 **'Arafāt, Jabal** (mtn.), SAr.
78/C5 **Arafura** (sea), Austl., Indo.
93/H7 **Aragarças**, Braz.
55/H4 **Aragats, Gora** (peak), Arm.
47/E2 **Aragon** (aut. comm.), Sp.
46/E1 **Aragón** (riv.), Sp.
93/J5 **Araguaia** (riv.), Braz.
93/H5 **Araguaia Nat'l Park**, Braz.
93/J5 **Araguaína**, Braz.
95/B1 **Araguari**, Braz.
93/H3 **Araguari** (riv.), Braz.
93/J7 **Araguari** (riv.), Braz.
95/C1 **Araguari** (Valhas) (riv.), Braz.
93/J5 **Araguatins**, Braz.
65/F2 **Arai**, Japan
94/B1 **Araioses**, Braz.
60/E2 **Arāk**, Iran
114/D3 **Arakamchechan** (isl.), Rus.
71/F3 **Arakan** (mts.), Burma
49/G3 **Arákhthos** (riv.), Gre.
31/H5 **Araks** (riv.), Eur., Asia
56/G5 **Aral** (sea), Uzb., Kaz.
56/G5 **Aral'sk**, Kaz.
55/H2 **Aralsor** (lake), Kaz.
60/F2 **Ārān**, Iran
36/H7 **Aran** (isl.), Ire.
36/A4 **Aran** (isls.), Ire.
46/D2 **Aranda de Duero**, Sp.
50/E3 **Arandelovac**, Yugo.
46/D2 **Aranjuez**, Sp.
32/E6 **Aran Mawddwy** (mtn.), Wal,UK
112/D5 **Aransas Pass**, Tx,US
78/G4 **Aranuka** (atoll), Kiri.
94/C3 **Arapiraca**, Braz.
59/D2 **Arapkir**, Turk.
95/B2 **Arapongas**, Braz.
95/B4 **Araranguá**, Braz.
95/B2 **Araraquara**, Braz.
95/C2 **Araras**, Braz.
77/B3 **Ararat**, Austl.
94/A1 **Arari**, Braz.
94/B2 **Araripe** (hills), Braz.
94/B2 **Araripina**, Braz.
55/H5 **Aras** (riv.), Asia
84/C2 **Aratane** (well), Mrta.
94/B2 **Aratas** (res.), Braz.
92/F4 **Arauá** (riv.), Braz.
92/D2 **Arauca**, Col.
95/B3 **Araucária**, Braz.
78/E5 **Arawa**, PNG
95/C1 **Araxá**, Braz.
83/N6 **Ārba Minch'**, Eth.
107/H2 **Arborfield**, Sk,Can
107/J3 **Arborg**, Mb,Can
36/D2 **Arbroath**, Sc,UK
44/F5 **Arc** (riv.), Fr.
45/G4 **Arc** (riv.), Fr.
44/C4 **Arcachon**, Fr.
44/C4 **Arcachon** (lag.), Fr.
44/C4 **Arcachon, Pointe d'** (pt.), Fr.
115/B2 **Arcadia**, Ca,US
113/H5 **Arcadia**, Fl,US
108/A2 **Arcata**, Ca,US
31/S10 **Arc de Triomphe**, Fr.
52/J2 **Archangel** (Arkhangel'sk), Rus.
52/H3 **Archangel Obl.**, Rus.
46/E3 **Archena**, Sp.
76/A1 **Archer** (riv.), Austl.
76/A1 **Archer Bend Nat'l Park**, Austl.
112/D3 **Archer City**, Tx,US
108/E3 **Arches Nat'l Park**, Ut,US
46/C4 **Archidona**, Sp.
96/C3 **Arco** (pass), Arg.
45/J4 **Arco**, It.
106/E5 **Arco**, Id,US
95/C2 **Arcos**, Braz.
46/C4 **Arcos de la Frontera**, Sp.
94/C3 **Arcoverde**, Braz.
28/A1 **Arctic** (ocean)
114/F2 **Arctic** (coast. pl.), Ak,US
114/J2 **Arctic Nat'l Wild. Ref.**, Ak,US
114/M2 **Arctic Red River**, NW,Can
51/G5 **Arda** (riv.), Bul.
59/E2 **Ardahan**, Turk.
60/F2 **Ardakān**, Iran
37/C3 **Årdalstangen**, Nor.
59/E2 **Ardanuç**, Turk.
33/E6 **Arddleen**, Wal,UK
44/F4 **Ardèche** (riv.), Fr.
116/M9 **Arden-Arcade**, Ca,US
43/E4 **Ardennes** (for.), Eur.
42/D4 **Ardennes** (dept.), Fr.
43/D4 **Ardennes, Canal des** (can.), Fr.
59/E2 **Ardeşen**, Turk.
32/C3 **Ardglass**, NI,UK
46/B3 **Ardila** (riv.), Sp.
109/H4 **Ardmore**, Ok,US
115/E5 **Ardmore**, Pa,US
42/C2 **Ardooie**, Belg.
32/C2 **Ards** (dist.), NI,UK
32/C3 **Ards** (pen.), NI,UK
37/E3 **Åre**, Swe.
95/G6 **Areado**, Braz.
94/C2 **Areia Branca**, Braz.
101/N9 **Arena** (pt.), Mex.
108/B3 **Arena** (pt.), Ca,US
93/G6 **Arenápolis**, Braz.
46/C2 **Arenas de San Pedro**, Sp.
97/K8 **Arenas, Punta de** (pt.), Arg.
37/D4 **Arendal**, Nor.
40/C6 **Arendonk**, Belg.
32/E6 **Arenig Fawr** (mtn.), Wal,UK
47/L6 **Arenys de Mar**, Sp.
47/L6 **Arenys de Munt**, Sp.
92/D7 **Arequipa**, Peru
46/C2 **Arévalo**, Sp.
45/J5 **Arezzo**, It.
44/C5 **Arga** (riv.), Sp.
46/D3 **Argamasilla de Alba**, Sp.
46/C3 **Argamasilla de Calatrava**, Sp.
47/N9 **Arganda**, Sp.
45/G5 **Argens** (riv.), Fr.
44/C2 **Argentan**, Fr.
45/G4 **Argentera** (peak), It.
31/S10 **Argenteuil**, Fr.
91/C4 **Argentina**
97/J7 **Argentino** (lake), Arg.
47/L6 **Argentona**, Sp.
51/G3 **Argeş** (co.), Rom.
51/G3 **Argeş** (riv.), Rom.
61/J2 **Arghandab** (riv.), Afg.
86/B5 **Argo**, Sudan
49/H4 **Argolis** (gulf), Gre.
43/E5 **Argonne** (for.), Fr.
49/H4 **Árgos**, Gre.
49/G3 **Argostólion**, Gre.
42/A4 **Argueil**, Fr.
108/B4 **Arguello** (pt.), Ca,US
84/A1 **Arguin** (bay), Mrta.
63/H1 **Argun** (riv.), China, Rus.
68/E2 **Argut** (riv.), Rus.
74/D3 **Argyle** (lake), Austl.
82/C3 **Arhreijît** (well), Mrta.
37/D4 **Århus**, Den.
48/D2 **Ariano Irpino**, It.
46/C1 **Arianza** (riv.), Sp.
92/D7 **Arica**, Chile
74/C6 **Arid** (cape), Austl.
64/D3 **Arida**, Japan
115/A1 **Arido** (mt.), Ca,US
44/D5 **Ariège** (riv.), Fr.
51/K5 **Arifiye**, Turk.
59/K6 **Arīḥā** (Jericho), WBnk.
109/G3 **Arikaree** (riv.), Co,US
101/J5 **Arima**, Trin.
93/G6 **Arinos** (riv.), Braz.
92/F5 **Aripuanā** (riv.), Braz.
92/F5 **Ariquemes**, Braz.
86/C2 **'Arīsh, Wādī al** (dry riv.), Egypt
89/H7 **Arivonimamo**, Madg.
47/F1 **Arize** (riv.), Fr.
108/D4 **Arizona** (state), US
101/F5 **Arjona**, Col.
46/C4 **Arjona**, Sp.
112/E3 **Arkadelphia**, Ar,US
36/C2 **Arkaig, Loch** (lake), Sc,UK
68/A1 **Arkalyk**, Kaz.
109/K4 **Arkansas** (riv.), US
112/E3 **Arkansas** (state), US
109/H3 **Arkansas City**, Ks,US
83/K3 **Arkanū** (peak), Libya
52/J2 **Arkhangel'sk** (Archangel), Rus.
32/B6 **Arklow**, Ire.
39/G1 **Arkona, Kap** (cape), Ger.
70/C5 **Arkonam**, India
33/G4 **Arksey**, Eng,UK
56/H2 **Arkticheskiy Institut** (isls.), Rus.
46/C1 **Arlanza** (riv.), Sp.
46/C1 **Arlazón** (riv.), Sp.
44/F5 **Arles**, Fr.
42/C3 **Arleux**, Fr.
113/G4 **Arlington**, Ga,US
107/K4 **Arlington**, Mn,US
112/D3 **Arlington**, Tx,US
115/J8 **Arlington**, Va,US

116/Q15 **Arlington Heights,** Il,US
43/E4 **Arlon,** Belg.
85/F4 **Arly Nat'l Park,** Burk.
116/G6 **Armada,** Mi,US
32/B3 **Armagh,** NI,UK
32/B3 **Armagh** (dist.), NI,UK
44/F3 **Armançon** (riv.), Fr.
95/B2 **Armando Laydner** (res.), Braz.
86/C3 **Armant,** Egypt
55/G3 **Armavir,** Rus.
45/G5 **Arme, Cap d'** (cape), Fr.
55/H4 **Armenia**
92/C3 **Armenia,** Col.
42/B2 **Armentières,** Fr.
101/P10 **Armería,** Mex.
77/D1 **Armidale,** Austl.
46/D4 **Armilla,** Sp.
32/B1 **Armoy,** NI,UK
96/E2 **Armstrong,** Arg.
106/D3 **Armstrong,** BC,Can
33/G4 **Armthorpe,** Eng,UK
70/C4 **Ārmūr,** India
103/J3 **Arnaud** (riv.), Qu,Can
59/J4 **Arnauti** (cape), Cyp.
35/E3 **Arncott,** Eng,UK
46/D1 **Arnedo,** Sp.
42/B2 **Arnèke,** Fr.
109/H3 **Arnett,** Ok,US
74/F2 **Arnhem** (bay), Austl.
74/F2 **Arnhem** (cape), Austl.
40/C5 **Arnhem,** Neth.
74/E2 **Arnhem Land** (reg.), Austl.
70/C5 **Arni,** India
45/J5 **Arno** (riv.), It.
78/G4 **Arno** (atoll), Mrsh.
33/G5 **Arnold,** Eng,UK
45/K3 **Arnoldstein,** Aus.
44/E3 **Arnon** (riv.), Fr.
31/T10 **Arnouville-lès-Gonesse,** Fr.
110/E2 **Arnprior,** On,Can
41/F6 **Arnsberg,** Ger.
33/F3 **Arnside,** Eng,UK
38/F3 **Arnstadt,** Ger.
41/G6 **Arolsen,** Ger.
44/E3 **Aron** (riv.), Fr.
47/X16 **Arona,** Canl.
42/B4 **Aronde** (riv.), Fr.
78/G5 **Arorae** (atoll), Kiri.
73/H5 **Aro Usu** (cape), Indo.
31/S11 **Arpajon,** Fr.
42/B2 **Arques,** Fr.
70/D2 **Arrah,** India
83/M5 **Ar Rahad,** Sudan
93/H6 **Arraias** (riv.), Braz.
33/H4 **Arram,** Eng,UK
60/D2 **Ar Ramādī,** Iraq
59/L5 **Ar Ramthā,** Jor.
36/C3 **Arran** (isl.), Sc,UK
59/D3 **Ar Raqqah,** Syria
42/B3 **Arras,** Fr.
59/L4 **Ar Rastan,** Syria
47/F1 **Arrats** (riv.), Fr.
47/Y16 **Arrecife,** Canl.
96/E2 **Arrecifes,** Arg.
44/B2 **Arrée** (mts.), Fr.
100/C4 **Arriaga,** Mex.
95/A5 **Arrio Grande,** Braz.
60/E4 **Ar Riyāḑ** (Riyadh) (cap.), SAr.
44/F3 **Arroux** (riv.), Fr.
46/B3 **Arroyo de la Luz,** Sp.
108/B4 **Arroyo Grande,** Ca,US
59/L5 **Ar Ruşayfah,** Jor.
83/M5 **Ar Ruşayriş,** Sudan
60/F4 **Ar Ruways,** SAr.
63/L3 **Arsen'yev,** Rus.
79/T11 **Art** (isl.), NCal.
49/G3 **Árta,** Gre.
49/G3 **Arta** (gulf), Gre.
46/A1 **Arteijo,** Sp.
63/L3 **Artem,** Rus.
100/E3 **Artemisa,** Cuba
115/B3 **Artesia,** Ca,US
109/F4 **Artesia,** NM,US
76/C3 **Arthur** (pt.), Austl.
75/R11 **Arthur's** (pass), NZ
91/E3 **Artigas,** Uru.
42/A2 **Artois** (reg.), Fr.
42/B2 **Artois, Collines de l'** (hills), Fr.
95/F7 **Artur Nogueira,** Braz.
68/C4 **Artux,** China
59/E2 **Artvin,** Turk.
73/H5 **Aru** (isls.), Indo.
83/M7 **Arua,** Ugan.
101/H5 **Aruba** (isl.), Neth.
95/G8 **Arujá,** Braz.
35/F5 **Arun** (riv.), Eng,UK
71/F2 **Arunachal Pradesh** (state), India
35/F5 **Arundel,** Eng,UK
70/C6 **Aruppukkottai,** India
73/F3 **Arus** (cape), Indo.
87/G1 **Arusha,** Tanz.
79/L6 **Arutua** (atoll), FrPol.
83/L7 **Aruwimi** (riv.), Zaire
62/E2 **Arvayheer,** Mong.
37/F2 **Arvidsjaur,** Swe.
37/E4 **Arvika,** Swe.
108/C4 **Arvin,** Ca,US
110/B2 **Arvon** (peak), Mi,US
81/X17 **Aryānah** (gov.), Tun.
68/A3 **Arys',** Kaz.
44/B3 **Arz** (riv.), Fr.
53/J5 **Arzamas,** Rus.
41/G4 **Arzen,** Ger.
81/Q16 **Arzew,** Alg.
43/F3 **Arzfeld,** Ger.
46/A1 **Arzúa,** Sp.
43/E1 **As,** Belg.
45/K1 **Aš,** Czh.
37/D4 **Ås,** Nor.
60/E2 **Asadābād,** Iran
84/D5 **Asagny Nat'l Park,** IvC.
72/A3 **Asahan** (riv.), Indo.
64/C3 **Asahi** (riv.), Japan
65/G2 **Asahi-Bandai Nat'l Park,** Japan
63/N3 **Asahi-dake** (mtn.), Japan
63/N3 **Asahikawa,** Japan
65/H7 **Asaka,** Japan
65/M9 **Asake** (riv.), Japan
83/P5 **Āsalē,** Erit.
65/F2 **Asama-yama** (mtn.), Japan
70/E3 **Asansol,** India
82/J3 **Asawanwah** (well), Libya
53/P4 **Asbest,** Rus.
88/C3 **Asbestos** (mts.), SAfr.
115/F5 **Asbury Park,** NJ,US
100/D4 **Ascención** (bay), Mex.
28/J6 **Ascension** (isl.), StH.
41/E5 **Ascheberg,** Ger.
38/F3 **Aschersleben,** Ger.
48/A1 **Asco** (riv.), Fr.
48/C1 **Ascoli Piceno,** It.
48/D2 **Ascoli Satriano,** It.
35/F4 **Ascot,** Eng,UK
83/P5 **Āseb,** Erit.
83/N6 **Āsela,** Eth.
51/G4 **Asenovgrad,** Bul.
62/G2 **Asgat,** Mong.
35/G4 **Ash,** Eng,UK
35/E4 **Ashampstead,** Eng,UK
85/E5 **Ashanti** (reg.), Gha.
85/E5 **Ashanti** (uplands), Gha.
33/G5 **Ashbourne,** Eng,UK
74/B4 **Ashburton** (riv.), Austl.
75/R11 **Ashburton,** NZ
34/C5 **Ashburton,** Eng,UK
35/E1 **Ashby** (can.), Eng,UK
33/G6 **Ashby-de-la-Zouch,** Eng,UK
34/D3 **Ashchurch,** Eng,UK
106/C3 **Ashcroft,** BC,Can
113/J3 **Asheboro,** NC,US
107/J3 **Ashern,** Mb,Can
113/H3 **Asheville,** NC,US
107/M2 **Asheweig** (riv.), On,Can
31/M7 **Ashford,** Eng,UK
35/F1 **Ashfordby,** Eng,UK
111/Q8 **Ashgrove,** On,Can
75/S11 **Ashhurst,** NZ
33/G1 **Ashington,** Eng,UK
65/L10 **Ashiya,** Japan
64/C4 **Ashizuri-misaki** (cape), Japan
81/W17 **Ashkal** (lake), Tun.
61/G1 **Ashkhabad** (cap.), Trkm.
109/H3 **Ashland,** Ks,US
110/D4 **Ashland,** Ky,US
110/D3 **Ashland,** Oh,US
106/C5 **Ashland,** Or,US
110/B2 **Ashland,** Wi,US
107/J4 **Ashley,** ND,US
31/M6 **Ashley Green,** Eng,UK
74/C2 **Ashmore** (reef), Austl.
74/C2 **Ashmore and Cartier Is.** (terr.), Austl.
59/L4 **Ash Shamāl** (gov.), Leb.
60/D2 **Ash Shāmīyah,** Iraq
61/G3 **Ash Shāriqah,** UAE
59/E3 **Ash Sharqāt,** Iraq
59/H6 **Ash Sharqīyah** (gov.), Egypt
70/C3 **Ashta,** India
110/D3 **Ashtabula,** Oh,US
31/N8 **Ashtead,** Eng,UK
106/F4 **Ashton,** Id,US
33/F5 **Ashton-in-Makerfield,** Eng,UK
33/F5 **Ashton-under-Lyne,** Eng,UK
110/B2 **Ashwaubenon,** Wi,US
35/F2 **Ashwell,** Eng,UK
58/* **Asia**
81/L13 **Asilah,** Mor.
48/A2 **Asinara** (gulf), It.
48/A2 **Asinara** (isl.), It.
56/J4 **Asino,** Rus.
60/D5 **'Asīr** (mts.), SAr., Yemen
86/D5 **Asis, Ras** (cape), Sudan
59/E2 **Aşkale,** Turk.
33/E3 **Askam in Furness,** Eng,UK
37/D4 **Asker,** Nor.
33/G4 **Askern,** Eng,UK
37/D4 **Askim,** Nor.
49/G2 **Áskion** (peak), Gre.
37/P6 **Askja** (crater), Ice.
83/N4 **Āsmera** (cap.), Erit.
31/T9 **Asnières-sur-Oise,** Fr.
31/S10 **Asnières-sur-Seine,** Fr.
64/B4 **Aso Nat'l Park,** Japan
83/M5 **Āsosa,** Eth.
64/B4 **Aso-san** (mtn.), Japan
86/D4 **Asoteriba, Jabal** (peak), Sudan
33/E2 **Aspatria,** Eng,UK
47/E3 **Aspe,** Sp.
108/F3 **Aspen,** Co,US
115/J7 **Aspen Hill,** Md,US
112/C3 **Aspermont,** Tx,US
47/F1 **Aspin, Col d'** (pass), Fr.
75/Q11 **Aspiring** (peak), NZ
49/H3 **Asprópirgos,** Gre.
106/G2 **Asquith,** Sk,Can
84/C2 **'Assâba, Massif de l'** (reg.), Mrta.
59/D3 **As Sabkhah,** Syria
59/K6 **Aş Şāfī,** Jor.
60/E3 **As Sālimīyah,** Kuw.
60/E4 **As Sālimīyah,** SAr.
83/L1 **As Sallūm,** Egypt
59/K5 **As Salţ,** Jor.
71/F2 **Assam** (state), India
60/E2 **As Samāwah,** Iraq
59/H6 **As Santah,** Egypt
59/K5 **Aş Şarīḩ,** Jor.
42/D2 **Asse,** Belg.
48/A3 **Assemini,** It.
40/D2 **Assen,** Neth.
42/C1 **Assenede,** Belg.
82/J1 **As Sidr,** Libya
59/H6 **As Sinbillāwayn,** Egypt
107/G3 **Assiniboia,** Sk,Can
106/E3 **Assiniboine** (peak), BC,Can
107/J3 **Assiniboine** (riv.), Mb,Can
110/F1 **Assinika** (lake), Qu,Can
95/B2 **Assis,** Braz.
47/G1 **Assou** (riv.), Fr.
83/M6 **As Sudd** (reg.), Sudan
60/E1 **As Sulaymānīyah,** Iraq
60/E3 **Aş Şummān** (mts.), SAr.
59/L5 **As Suwaydā',** Syria
59/L5 **As Suwaydā'** (dist.), Syria
60/D2 **Aş Şuwayrah,** Iraq
86/C2 **As Suways** (gov.), Egypt
86/C2 **As Suways** (Suez), Egypt
40/C6 **Asten,** Neth.
45/H4 **Asti,** It.
95/L6 **Astolfo Dutra,** Braz.
35/E2 **Aston,** Eng,UK
34/D2 **Aston on Clun,** Eng,UK
95/B2 **Astorga,** Braz.
106/C4 **Astoria,** Or,US
55/J3 **Astrakhan',** Rus.
55/H3 **Astrakhan Obl.,** Rus.
46/B1 **Asturias** (aut. comm.), Sp.
35/E2 **Astwood Bank,** Eng,UK
65/L10 **Asuka,** Japan
65/N9 **Asuke,** Japan
78/D3 **Asuncion** (isl.), NMar.
91/E2 **Asunción** (cap.), Par.
100/B4 **Asunción Ixtaltepec,** Mex.
83/M7 **Aswa** (riv.), Ugan.
86/C3 **Aswān,** Egypt
86/C4 **Aswān** (gov.), Egypt
86/C4 **Aswan High** (dam), Egypt
86/B3 **Asyūt,** Egypt
86/B3 **Asyūt** (gov.), Egypt
86/C2 **Asyūţī, Wādī al** (dry riv.), Egypt
91/C2 **Atacama** (des.), Chile
91/C1 **Atacama, Puna de** (plat.), Arg.
85/F4 **Atacora** (range), Ben.
79/H5 **Atafu** (atoll), Tok.
85/F5 **Atakpamé,** Togo
94/C3 **Atalaia,** Braz.
65/F3 **Atami,** Japan
84/B1 **Atar,** Mrta.
46/D4 **Atarfe,** Sp.
70/D2 **Atarra,** India
62/D3 **Atas Bogd** (peak), Mong.
108/B4 **Atascadero,** Ca,US
59/D3 **Atatürk** (res.), Turk.
83/M4 **Atbara,** Sudan
83/M4 **Atbara** (Atbarah) (riv.), Eth., Sudan
68/A1 **Atbasar,** Kaz.
109/K5 **Atchafalaya** (bay), La,US
113/F4 **Atchafalaya** (riv.), La,US
109/J3 **Atchison,** Ks,US
85/E5 **Atebubu,** Gha.
37/G1 **Ateelva** (riv.), Nor.
101/P9 **Atengo** (riv.), Mex.
48/C1 **Aterno** (riv.), It.
42/C2 **Ath,** Belg.
106/E2 **Athabasca,** Ab,Can
102/E3 **Athabasca** (riv.), Ab,Can
102/F3 **Athabasca** (lake), Ab, Sk,Can
107/H2 **Athapapuskow** (lake), Mb,Can
82/K1 **Āthār Ţulmaythah** (Ptolemaïs) (ruins), Libya
113/G3 **Athens,** Al,US
113/H3 **Athens,** Ga,US
110/D4 **Athens,** Oh,US
113/G3 **Athens,** Tn,US
112/E3 **Athens,** Tx,US
49/H4 **Athens** (Athínai) (cap.), Gre.
49/L7 **Athens** (Athínai) (inset) (cap.), Gre.
35/E1 **Atherstone,** Eng,UK
33/F4 **Atherton,** Eng,UK
31/T10 **Athis-Mons,** Fr.
36/B4 **Athlone,** Ire.
49/J2 **Áthos** (peak), Gre.
82/J5 **Ati,** Chad
95/G8 **Atibaia,** Braz.
95/G7 **Atíbaia** (riv.), Braz.
110/B1 **Atikokan,** On,Can
79/K7 **Atiu** (isl.), CookIs.
114/C5 **Atka** (isl.), Ak,US
55/H2 **Atkarsk,** Rus.
114/M2 **Atkinson** (pt.), NW,Can
113/G3 **Atlanta** (cap.), Ga,US
112/E3 **Atlanta,** Tx,US
28/G3 **Atlantic** (ocean)
107/K5 **Atlantic,** Ia,US
115/G5 **Atlantic Beach,** NY,US
85/F5 **Atlantique** (prov.), Ben.
82/E2 **Atlas** (mts.), Afr.
116/K10 **Atlas** (peak), Ca,US
82/E1 **Atlas Saharien** (mts.), Alg., Mor.
114/M4 **Atlin** (lake), BC,Can
100/B4 **Atlixco,** Mex.
113/G4 **Atmore,** Al,US
82/B3 **Atoui** (dry riv.), Mrta.
61/G1 **Atrak** (riv.), Iran
92/C2 **Atrato** (riv.), Col.
65/H7 **Atsugi,** Japan
65/N10 **Atsumi,** Japan
65/N10 **Atsumi** (pen.), Japan
59/K6 **Aţ Ţafīlah,** Jor.
60/D4 **Aţ Ţā'if,** SAr.
59/L5 **At Tall,** Syria
113/G3 **Attalla,** Al,US
103/H3 **Attawapiskat** (riv.), On,Can
41/E6 **Attendorn,** Ger.
45/K3 **Attersee** (lake), Aus.
42/C5 **Attichy,** Fr.
35/E2 **Attleborough,** Eng,UK
35/H2 **Attleborough,** Eng,UK
114/A5 **Attu** (isl.), Ak,US
86/C2 **Aţ Ţūr,** Egypt
59/K6 **Aţ Ţūr,** WBnk.
60/D6 **At Turbah,** Yem.
96/D2 **Atuel** (riv.), Arg.
37/F4 **Åtvidaberg,** Swe.
108/B3 **Atwater,** Ca,US
109/G3 **Atwood,** Ks,US
100/E4 **Auas,** Hon.
43/E4 **Aubange,** Belg.
42/D6 **Aube** (dept.), Fr.
44/F2 **Aube** (riv.), Fr.
44/F4 **Aubenas,** Fr.
31/T10 **Aubervilliers,** Fr.
42/C6 **Aubetin** (riv.), Fr.
42/A5 **Aubette** (riv.), Fr.
44/E4 **Aubin,** Fr.
44/E4 **Aubrac** (mts.), Fr.
113/G3 **Auburn,** Al,US
108/B3 **Auburn,** Ca,US
110/C3 **Auburn,** In,US
111/G2 **Auburn,** Me,US
109/J2 **Auburn,** Ne,US
110/E3 **Auburn,** NY,US
116/C3 **Auburn,** Wa,US
116/F6 **Auburn Hills,** Mi,US
96/C3 **Aucá Mahuida** (peak), Arg.
44/D5 **Auch,** Fr.
42/B3 **Auchel,** Fr.
36/D2 **Auchenblae,** Sc,UK
32/E2 **Auchencairn,** Sc,UK
36/C3 **Auchinleck,** Sc,UK
75/R10 **Auckland,** NZ
29/S8 **Auckland** (isls.), NZ
44/E5 **Aude** (riv.), Fr.
42/D2 **Auderghem,** Belg.
44/A3 **Audierne** (bay), Fr.
33/F6 **Audlem,** Eng,UK
33/F5 **Audley,** Eng,UK
83/P6 **Audo** (range), Eth.
43/E5 **Audun-le-Tiche,** Fr.
45/K1 **Aue,** Ger.
41/E2 **Aue** (riv.), Ger.
41/F3 **Aue** (riv.), Ger.
45/K1 **Auerbach,** Ger.
45/J2 **Auerbach in der Oberpfalz,** Ger.
32/A3 **Augher,** NI,UK
32/B3 **Aughnacloy,** NI,UK
88/C3 **Augrabies Falls Nat'l Park,** SAfr.
88/C3 **Augrabiesvalle** (falls), SAfr.
45/J2 **Augsburg,** Ger.
88/A2 **Augub** (peak), Namb.
48/D4 **Augusta,** It.
48/D4 **Augusta** (gulf), It.
113/H3 **Augusta,** Ga,US
111/G2 **Augusta** (cap.), Me,US
41/F5 **Augustdorf,** Ger.
39/M2 **Augustów,** Pol.
74/C3 **Augustus** (isl.), Austl.
69/B3 **Auk Bok** (isl.), Burma
74/C4 **Auld** (lake), Austl.
47/M9 **Aulencia** (riv.), Sp.
31/T10 **Aulnay-sous-Bois,** Fr.
44/B2 **Aulne** (riv.), Fr.
42/C3 **Aulnoye-Aymeries,** Fr.
42/B5 **Aunette** (riv.), Fr.
88/B2 **Auob** (dry riv.), Namb.
88/C2 **Auobrivier** (dry riv.), SAfr.
78/G4 **Aur** (atoll), Mrsh.
70/C4 **Aurangābād,** India
70/D3 **Aurangābād,** India
44/B3 **Auray,** Fr.
44/D5 **Aureilhan,** Fr.
41/E2 **Aurich,** Ger.
95/B2 **Auriflama,** Braz.
44/E4 **Aurillac,** Fr.
94/C2 **Aurora,** Braz.
109/F3 **Aurora,** Co,US
116/P16 **Aurora,** Il,US
109/J3 **Aurora,** Mo,US
109/H2 **Aurora,** Ne,US
76/A1 **Aurukun Abor. Land,** Austl.
110/C2 **Au Sable** (riv.), Mi,US
39/K3 **Auschwitz** (Oświęcim), Pol.
44/E5 **Aussillon,** Fr.
37/C4 **Aust-Agder** (co.), Nor.
74/B5 **Austin** (lake), Austl.
102/G2 **Austin** (isl.), NW,Can
107/K5 **Austin,** Mn,US
108/C3 **Austin,** Nv,US
112/D4 **Austin** (cap.), Tx,US
74/* **Australia**
77/C3 **Australian Alps** (mts.), Austl.
77/D3 **Australian Cap. Terr.,** Austl.
45/L3 **Austria**
37/P7 **Austurhorn** (pt.), Ice.
42/B3 **Authie** (riv.), Fr.
101/P10 **Autlán de Navarro,** Mex.
42/B5 **Automne** (riv.), Fr.
44/F3 **Autun,** Fr.
44/E4 **Auvergne** (reg.), Fr.
31/S9 **Auvers-sur-Oise,** Fr.
44/D4 **Auvézère** (riv.), Fr.
44/E3 **Auxerre,** Fr.
44/F3 **Auxonne,** Fr.
110/D2 **Aux Sables** (riv.), On,Can
103/K2 **Auyuittuq Nat'l Park,** NW,Can
92/D6 **Auzangate** (peak), Peru
44/E3 **Avallon,** Fr.
111/K2 **Avalon** (pen.), Nf,Can
95/B2 **Avaré,** Braz.
35/E4 **Avebury,** Eng,UK
46/A2 **Aveiro,** Port.
46/A2 **Aveiro** (dist.), Port.
31/P7 **Aveley,** Eng,UK
42/C2 **Avelgem,** Belg.
96/F2 **Avellaneda,** Arg.
48/D2 **Avellino,** It.
42/A4 **Avelon** (riv.), Fr.
108/B3 **Avenal,** Ca,US
42/A46 **Aver** (riv.), Fr.
48/D2 **Aversa,** It.
101/J4 **Aves** (isl.), Ven.
37/F3 **Avesta,** Swe.
44/D4 **Aveyron** (riv.), Fr.
48/C1 **Avezzano,** It.
36/D2 **Aviemore,** Sc,UK
44/F5 **Avignon,** Fr.
46/C2 **Ávila de los Caballeros,** Sp.
46/C1 **Avilés,** Sp.
42/B3 **Avion,** Fr.
46/B3 **Avis,** Port.
32/B6 **Avoca,** Ire.
32/B6 **Avoca** (riv.), Ire.
48/D4 **Avola,** It.
44/E2 **Avon,** Fr.
34/D4 **Avon** (co.), Eng,UK
34/C6 **Avon** (riv.), Eng,UK
34/D4 **Avon** (riv.), Eng,UK
35/E2 **Avon** (riv.), Eng,UK
35/E5 **Avon** (riv.), Eng,UK
32/B6 **Avonbeg** (riv.), Ire.
107/G3 **Avonlea,** Sk,Can
32/B6 **Avonmore** (riv.), Ire.
34/D4 **Avonmouth,** Eng,UK
44/C2 **Avranches,** Fr.
42/B4 **Avre** (riv.), Fr.
44/C3 **Avrillé,** Fr.
65/L10 **Awaji,** Japan
64/D3 **Awaji** (isl.), Japan
59/L5 **A'waj, Nahr al** (riv.), Syria
43/E2 **Awans,** Belg.
83/N6 **Āwasa,** Eth.
83/P5 **Āwash Wenz** (riv.), Eth.
88/A2 **Awasibberge** (peak), Namb.
82/H2 **Awbārī,** Libya
36/C2 **Awe, Loch** (lake), Sc,UK
83/K2 **Awjilah,** Libya
37/P6 **Axarfjördhur** (bay), Ice.
34/D4 **Axbridge,** Eng,UK
34/D4 **Axe** (riv.), Eng,UK
34/D5 **Axe** (riv.), Eng,UK
40/A6 **Axel,** Neth.
103/S7 **Axel Heiberg** (isl.), NW,Can
85/E5 **Axim,** Gha.
49/H2 **Axios** (riv.), Gre.
34/D5 **Axminster,** Eng,UK
53/N5 **Ay** (riv.), Rus.
64/D3 **Ayabe,** Japan
96/F3 **Ayacucho,** Arg.
92/D6 **Ayacucho,** Peru
68/D2 **Ayaguz,** Kaz.
68/D2 **Ayaguz** (riv.), Kaz.
68/E4 **Ayakkum** (lake), China
65/M10 **Ayama,** Japan
84/E5 **Ayamé, Barrage d'** (dam), IvC.
46/B4 **Ayamonte,** Sp.
59/C2 **Ayancık,** Turk.
101/F6 **Ayapel,** Col.
65/H7 **Ayase,** Japan
92/D6 **Ayaviri,** Peru
61/J1 **Āybak,** Afg.
59/N8 **'Aybāl, Jabal** (Har Eval) (mtn.), WBnk.
59/A3 **Aydın,** Turk.
59/C3 **Aydıncık,** Turk.
74/E5 **Ayers Rock** (Uluru) (peak), Austl.
49/J3 **Áyios Evstrátios** (isl.), Gre.
49/J5 **Áyios Ioánnis, Ákra** (cape), Gre.
49/J5 **Áyios Nikólaos,** Gre.
35/F3 **Aylesbury,** Eng,UK
35/G4 **Aylesford,** Eng,UK
35/H4 **Aylesham,** Eng,UK
102/F2 **Aylmer** (lake), NW,Can
35/H1 **Aylsham,** Eng,UK
59/D3 **'Ayn al 'Arab,** Syria
83/K2 **'Ayn Ath Tha'lab,** Libya
60/D1 **'Ayn, Ra's al,** Syria
83/K3 **'Ayn Zuwayyah** (well), Libya
57/S3 **Ayon** (isl.), Rus.
47/E3 **Ayora,** Sp.
82/D3 **'Ayoûn 'Abd el Mâlek** (well), Mrta.
76/B2 **Ayr,** Austl.
36/C3 **Ayr,** Sc,UK
36/C3 **Ayr** (riv.), Sc,UK
32/D3 **Ayre, Point of** (pt.), Eng,UK
33/H3 **Ayton,** Eng,UK
51/H4 **Aytos,** Bul.
44/C3 **Aytré,** Fr.
100/B4 **Ayutla,** Mex.
69/C3 **Ayutthaya** (ruins), Thai.
59/A2 **Ayvacık,** Turk.
59/A2 **Ayvalık,** Turk.
43/E3 **Aywaille,** Belg.
47/F3 **Azahar** (coast), Sp.
65/M9 **Azaj,** Japan
106/C5 **Azalea,** Or,US
70/D2 **Azamgarh,** India
92/D6 **Azángaro,** Peru
82/G2 **Azao** (peak), Alg.
85/E2 **Azaouād** (reg.), Mali
85/G2 **Azaouak, Vallée de l'** (wadi), Mali, Niger
59/D3 **A'zāz,** Syria
55/H4 **Azerbaijan**
83/N5 **Āzezo,** Eth.
68/E1 **Azhu-Tayga, Gora** (peak), Rus.
92/C4 **Azogues,** Ecu.
47/R12 **Azores** (aut. reg.), Port.
47/R12 **Azores** (isls.), Port.
54/F3 **Azov,** Rus.
54/E3 **Azov** (sea), Rus., Ukr.
46/D1 **Azpeitia,** Sp.
108/F3 **Aztec,** NM,US
108/E3 **Aztec Ruins Nat'l Mon.,** NM,US
101/G4 **Azua,** DRep.
46/C3 **Azuaga,** Sp.
65/M9 **Azuchi,** Japan
101/F6 **Azuero** (pen.), Pan.
96/F3 **Azul,** Arg.
65/G2 **Azuma-san** (mtn.), Japan
65/F2 **Azumaya-san** (mtn.), Japan
45/G5 **Azur, Côte d'** (coast), Fr.
115/C2 **Azuza,** Ca,US
81/V17 **Azzaba,** Alg.
59/L5 **Az Zabadānī,** Syria
86/B2 **Az Zagāzīg,** Egypt
45/K4 **Azzano Decimo,** It.
59/L5 **Az Zarqā',** Jor.
82/H1 **Az Zāwiyah,** Libya

B

79/Y18 **Ba,** Fiji
69/E3 **Ba** (riv.), Viet.
79/U11 **Baaba** (isl.), NCal.
59/N9 **Ba'al Ḫazor** (Tall 'Āsūr) (mtn.), WBnk.
45/H3 **Baar,** Swi.
80/G4 **Baarawe,** Som.
40/C4 **Baarn,** Neth.
62/D2 **Baatsagaan,** Mong.
61/J2 **Baba** (mts.), Afg.
51/F4 **Baba** (peak), Bul.
54/D4 **Baba Burnu** (pt.), Turk.
51/J3 **Babadag,** Rom.
51/H5 **Babaeski,** Turk.
92/C4 **Babahoyo,** Ecu.
73/G5 **Babar** (isl.), Indo.
87/G1 **Babati,** Tanz.
34/C5 **Babbacombe** (bay), Eng,UK
107/L4 **Babbitt,** Mn,US
108/C3 **Babbitt,** Nv,US
81/G3 **Bab el Mandeb** (str.), Afr., Asia
78/C4 **Babelthuap** (isl.), Palau
54/A2 **Babia Gora** (peak), Pol.
71/H3 **Babian** (riv.), China
106/B2 **Babine** (lake), BC,Can
102/D3 **Babine** (riv.), BC,Can
60/F1 **Bābol,** Iran
67/D4 **Babuyan** (isls.), Phil.
60/D2 **Babylon** (ruins), Iraq
115/G5 **Babylon,** NY,US
94/A2 **Bacabal,** Braz.
93/H4 **Bacajá** (riv.), Braz.
73/G4 **Bacan** (isl.), Indo.
51/H2 **Bacău,** Rom.
51/H2 **Bacău** (co.), Rom.
69/D1 **Bac Can,** Viet.
69/D1 **Bac Giang,** Viet.
102/G2 **Back** (riv.), NW,Can
110/E2 **Back** (lake), On,Can
115/K7 **Back** (riv.), Md,US
50/D3 **Bačka** (reg.), Yugo.
50/D3 **Bačka Palanka,** Yugo.
50/D3 **Bačka Topola,** Yugo.
45/H2 **Backnang,** Ger.
34/D4 **Backwell,** Eng,UK
69/D4 **Bac Lieu,** Viet.
69/D1 **Bac Ninh,** Viet.
67/D5 **Bacolod,** Phil.
69/D1 **Bac Quang,** Viet.
50/D2 **Bácsalmás,** Hun.
50/D2 **Bács-Kiskun** (co.), Hun.
35/H1 **Bacton,** Eng,UK
33/F4 **Bacup,** Eng,UK
107/H4 **Bad** (riv.), SD,US
70/C5 **Badagara,** India
62/E3 **Badain Jaran** (des.), China
46/B3 **Badajoz,** Sp.
47/L7 **Badalona,** Sp.
110/D3 **Bad Axe,** Mi,US
41/F6 **Bad Berleberg,** Ger.
43/G2 **Bad Breisig,** Ger.
38/F1 **Bad Doberan,** Ger.
41/G5 **Bad Driburg,** Ger.
45/M2 **Baden,** Aus.
45/H2 **Baden-Baden,** Ger.
45/H2 **Baden-Württemberg** (state), Ger.
41/F4 **Bad Essen,** Ger.
39/H2 **Bad Freienwalde,** Ger.
41/H5 **Bad Gandersheim,** Ger.
45/K3 **Bad Goisern,** Aus.
41/H5 **Bad Harzburg,** Ger.
38/E3 **Bad Hersfeld,** Ger.
45/H1 **Bad Homburg vor der Höhe,** Ger.
43/G2 **Bad Honnef,** Ger.
61/J4 **Badīn,** Pak.
45/K3 **Bad Ischl,** Aus.
45/G2 **Bad Kreuznach,** Ger.
45/G3 **Bad Krozingen,** Ger.
107/H4 **Badlands** (uplands), ND,US
107/H5 **Badlands** (hills), SD,US
107/H5 **Badlands Nat'l Park,** SD,US
41/H6 **Bad Langensalza,** Ger.
41/H5 **Bad Lauterberg,** Ger.
41/F3 **Bad Lippspringe,** Ger.
45/H2 **Bad Mergentheim,** Ger.
41/G4 **Bad Munder am Deister,** Ger.
43/F2 **Bad Münstereifel,** Ger.
45/H1 **Bad Nauheim,** Ger.
41/G4 **Bad Nenndorf,** Ger.
43/G2 **Bad Neuenahr-Ahrweiler,** Ger.
45/J1 **Bad Neustadt an der Saale,** Ger.
41/F4 **Bad Oeynhausen,** Ger.
38/F2 **Bad Oldesloe,** Ger.
41/G5 **Bad Pyrmont,** Ger.
61/J3 **Bādrāh,** Pak.
38/G5 **Bad Reichenhall,** Ger.
41/H5 **Bad Sachsa,** Ger.
41/H4 **Bad Salzdetfurth,** Ger.
41/F4 **Bad Salzuflen,** Ger.
38/F3 **Bad Salzungen,** Ger.
41/F5 **Bad Sassendorf,** Ger.
38/F2 **Bad Schwartau,** Ger.
38/F2 **Bad Segeberg,** Ger.
41/G6 **Bad Sooden-Allendorf,** Ger.
45/J3 **Bad Tölz,** Ger.
70/D6 **Badulla,** SrL.
45/M3 **Bad Vöslau,** Aus.
41/G6 **Bad Wildungen,** Ger.
41/E2 **Bad Zwischenahn,** Ger.
46/C4 **Baena,** Sp.
95/J6 **Baependi,** Braz.
43/F2 **Baesweiler,** Ger.
46/D4 **Baeza,** Sp.
85/H5 **Bafang,** Camr.
103/H1 **Baffin** (isl.), NW,Can
103/K1 **Baffin** (bay), Can.,Grld.
112/D5 **Baffin** (bay), Tx,US
82/H7 **Bafia,** Camr.
84/D4 **Bafing** (riv.), Gui., IvC.
84/C3 **Bafing** (riv.), Gui., Mali
85/H5 **Bafoussam,** Camr.
59/C2 **Bafra,** Turk.
84/B2 **Bafrechié** (well), Mrta.
83/L7 **Bafwasende,** Zaire
66/B3 **Bag** (salt lake), China
82/H5 **Baga,** Nga.
67/E6 **Baganga,** Phil.
85/G3 **Bagaroua,** Niger
68/E3 **Bagda** (mts.), China
97/G1 **Bagé,** Braz.
67/D4 **Baggao,** Phil.
34/B4 **Baggy** (pt.), Eng,UK
60/D2 **Baghdad** (Baghdād) (cap.), Iraq
48/C3 **Bagheria,** It.
61/J1 **Baghlān,** Afg.
34/C3 **Baglan,** Wal,UK
107/K4 **Bagley,** Mn,US
44/D5 **Bagnères-de-Bigorre,** Fr.
31/S10 **Bagneux,** Fr.
31/T10 **Bagnolet,** Fr.
44/F4 **Bagnols-sur-Cèze,** Fr.
67/D5 **Bago,** Phil.
84/D3 **Bagoe** (riv.), IvC., Mali
69/B2 **Bago** (Pegu) (div.), Burma
67/D4 **Baguio,** Phil.
82/J5 **Baguirmi** (reg.), Chad
85/H2 **Bagzane** (peak), Niger
101/F2 **Bahamas**
70/E3 **Baharampur,** India
68/B6 **Bahāwalnagar,** Pak.
61/K3 **Bahāwalpur,** Pak.
87/G2 **Bahi,** Tanz.
94/B4 **Bahia** (state), Braz.
100/D4 **Bahía** (isls.), Hon.
101/M8 **Bahia Asunción,** Mex.
96/E3 **Bahía Blanca,** Arg.
101/M8 **Bahía de los Angeles,** Mex.
70/D3 **Bahía Honda,** Cuba
101/M8 **Bahía Kino,** Mex.
101/M8 **Bahía Tortugas,** Mex.
83/N5 **Bahir Dar,** Eth.
61/G4 **Bahlah,** Oman
70/D2 **Bahraich,** India
60/F3 **Bahrain**
60/F3 **Bahrain** (gulf), Bahr., SAr.
80/E3 **Baḩr al Arab** (riv.), Sudan
60/D2 **Baḩr al Milḩ** (lake), Iraq
80/D4 **Bahr Aouk** (riv.), CAfr., Chad
86/B2 **Baḩrīyah, Al Wāḩāt al** (oasis), Egypt
66/C2 **Bai** (riv.), China
66/C4 **Bai** (riv.), China
51/F2 **Baia Mare,** Rom.
51/F2 **Baia Sprie,** Rom.
82/J6 **Baïbokoum,** Chad
63/J2 **Baicheng,** China
68/D3 **Baicheng,** China
51/G3 **Băicoi,** Rom.
83/P7 **Baidoa,** Som.
66/D5 **Baidong** (lake), China
111/G1 **Baie-Comeau,** Qu,Can
103/J3 **Baie-du-Poste,** Qu,Can
111/G2 **Baie-Saint-Paul,** Qu,Can
111/K1 **Baie Verte,** Nf,Can
66/G7 **Baigou** (riv.), China
66/C3 **Baihua Shan** (mtn.), China
60/D2 **Ba'ījī,** Iraq
57/L4 **Baikal** (Baykal) (lake), Rus.
33/G4 **Baildon,** Eng,UK
46/D3 **Bailén,** Sp.
51/F3 **Băileşti,** Rom.
42/B2 **Bailleul,** Fr.
62/E5 **Bailong** (riv.), China
66/C4 **Bailu** (riv.), China
33/H5 **Bain** (riv.), Eng,UK
113/G4 **Bainbridge,** Ga,US
116/B2 **Bainbridge** (isl.), Wa,US
68/D4 **Bairab** (lake), China
114/F3 **Baird** (inlet), Ak,US
112/D3 **Baird,** Tx,US
78/G4 **Bairiki** (cap.), Kiri.
77/C3 **Bairnsdale,** Austl.
59/L6 **Bā'ir, Wādī** (riv.), Jor.
44/D5 **Baïse** (riv.), Fr.
70/D2 **Baitadi,** Nepal
69/D2 **Bai Thuong,** Viet.
47/P10 **Baixa de Banheira,** Port.
94/B4 **Baixa Grande,** Braz.
95/D1 **Baixo Guandu,** Braz.
62/E4 **Baiyin,** China
66/B3 **Baiyu** (mts.), China
67/C2 **Baiyun,** China
97/J7 **Baja** (pt.), Chile
50/D2 **Baja,** Hun.
101/L8 **Baja California** (pen.), Mex.
101/L7 **Baja California Norte** (state), Mex.
101/M8 **Baja California Sur** (state), Mex.
81/W17 **Bājah,** Tun.
81/W17 **Bājah** (gov.), Tun.
73/F5 **Bajawa,** Indo.
50/D4 **Bajina Bašta,** Yugo.
77/E1 **Bajmba** (peak), Austl.
50/D3 **Bajmok,** Yugo.
101/F4 **Bajo Nuero** (isl.), Col.
68/C2 **Bakanas** (riv.), Kaz.
73/E3 **Bakayan** (peak), Indo.
84/B3 **Bakel,** Sen.
102/G2 **Baker** (lake), NW,Can
97/J6 **Baker** (riv.), Chile
79/H4 **Baker** (isl.), PacUS
108/C4 **Baker,** Ca,US
107/G4 **Baker,** Mt,US
108/D3 **Baker,** Nv,US
106/D4 **Baker,** Or,US
106/C3 **Baker** (peak), Wa,US
108/C4 **Bakersfield,** Ca,US
33/G5 **Bakewell,** Eng,UK
54/E3 **Bakhchisaray,** Ukr.
54/E2 **Bakhmach,** Ukr.
60/E2 **Bākhtarān,** Iran
60/F3 **Bakhtegān** (lake), Iran
37/P6 **Bakkaflói** (bay), Ice.
87/B1 **Bakoumba,** Gabon
84/C4 **Bakoye** (riv.), Gui., Mali
55/J4 **Baku** (cap.), Azer.
98/S **Bakutis** (coast), Ant.
92/E6 **Bala** (mts.), Bol.
32/E6 **Bala,** Wal,UK
73/E2 **Balabac** (str.), Malay., Phil.
67/C6 **Balabac,** Phil.
67/C6 **Balabac** (isl.), Phil.
59/L5 **Ba'labakk,** Leb.
79/U12 **Balabio** (isl.), NCal.
60/D2 **Balad,** Iraq
70/D3 **Bālāghāt,** India
48/A1 **Balagne** (range), Fr.
47/F2 **Balaguer,** Sp.
44/C5 **Balaïtous** (mtn.), Fr.
87/F3 **Balaka,** Malw.
53/J4 **Balakhna,** Rus.
55/H1 **Balakovo,** Rus.
61/H1 **Bālā Morghab,** Afg.
51/G2 **Bălan,** Rom.
100/C4 **Balancán,** Mex.
67/D5 **Balanga,** Phil.
69/E3 **Ba Lang An** (cape), Viet.
70/D3 **Bālāngir,** India
53/X9 **Balashikha,** Rus.
55/G2 **Balashov,** Rus.
50/D1 **Balassagyarmat,** Hun.
50/C2 **Balaton** (lake), Hun.
50/C2 **Balatonfüred,** Hun.
92/F4 **Balbina** (res.), Braz.
96/F3 **Balcarce,** Arg.
32/E2 **Balcary** (pt.), Sc,UK
51/J4 **Balchik,** Bul.
75/Q12 **Balclutha,** NZ
35/F4 **Balcombe,** Eng,UK
112/D4 **Balcones Escarpment** (plat.), Tx,US
74/B7 **Bald** (pt.), Austl.
113/H2 **Bald** (peak), Va,US
35/F3 **Baldock,** Eng,UK
77/E1 **Bald Rock Nat'l Park,** Austl.
115/C2 **Baldwin Park,** Ca,US
107/H3 **Baldy** (peak), Mb,Can

Balea – Bellv

47/F3 **Balearic** (Baleares) (isls.), Sp.
95/E1 **Baleia, Ponta da** (pt.), Braz.
103/K3 **Baleine** (riv.), Qu,Can
103/J3 **Baleine, Grande Rivière de la** (riv.), Qu,Can
103/J3 **Baleine, Petite Rivière de la** (riv.), Qu,Can
83/N6 **Bale Mountains Nat'l Park**, Eth.
43/E1 **Balen**, Belg.
67/D4 **Baler**, Phil.
70/E3 **Baleshwar**, India
62/H1 **Baley**, Rus.
70/B2 **Bali**, India
72/D5 **Bali** (isl.), Indo.
72/D5 **Bali** (sea), Indo.
59/A2 **Balıkesir**, Turk.
73/E4 **Balikpapan**, Indo.
67/D6 **Balingasag**, Phil.
45/H2 **Balingen**, Ger.
30/F4 **Balkan** (mts.), Eur.
55/K4 **Balkhan Obl.**, Trkm.
68/C2 **Balkhash**, Kaz.
68/B2 **Balkhash** (lake), Kaz.
32/B4 **Ballagan** (pt.), Ire.
32/C1 **Ballantrae**, Sc,UK
77/B3 **Ballarat**, Austl.
74/C5 **Ballard** (lake), Austl.
70/C4 **Ballarpur**, India
32/D3 **Ballaugh**, IM,UK
98/L **Balleny** (isls.), Ant.
77/E1 **Ballina**, Austl.
36/A3 **Ballina**, Ire.
36/A4 **Ballinasloe**, Ire.
32/B2 **Ballinderry** (riv.), NI,UK
112/D4 **Ballinger**, Tx,US
32/B1 **Ballintoy**, NI,UK
45/G3 **Ballon d'Alsace** (mtn.), Fr.
32/C2 **Ballycarry**, NI,UK
32/B1 **Ballycastle**, NI,UK
32/B2 **Ballyclare**, NI,UK
32/C2 **Ballyeaston**, NI,UK
32/C2 **Ballygawley**, NI,UK
32/C3 **Ballygowan**, NI,UK
32/C3 **Ballyhalbert**, NI,UK
32/A1 **Ballykelly**, NI,UK
32/B2 **Ballymena**, NI,UK
32/B2 **Ballymena** (dist.), NI,UK
32/B1 **Ballymoney**, NI,UK
32/B1 **Ballymoney** (dist.), NI,UK
32/C3 **Ballynahinch**, NI,UK
32/C2 **Ballynure**, NI,UK
32/C3 **Ballyquintin** (pt.), NI,UK
32/C2 **Ballywalter**, NI,UK
97/J7 **Balmaceda** (peak), Chile
50/E2 **Balmazújváros**, Hun.
107/K3 **Balmertown**, On,Can
95/B3 **Balneario Camboriú**, Braz.
97/T12 **Balneario Carras**, Uru.
76/C4 **Balonne** (riv.), Austl.
70/B2 **Bālotra**, India
66/B3 **Balougou**, China
70/D2 **Balrāmpur**, India
51/G3 **Balş**, Rom.
35/E2 **Balsall Common**, Eng,UK
94/A2 **Balsas**, Braz.
94/A3 **Balsas** (riv.), Braz.
100/A4 **Balsas** (riv.), Mex.
37/F4 **Baltic** (sea), Eur.
39/K1 **Baltic** (spit), Pol., Rus.
59/H6 **Balṭīm**, Egypt
115/K7 **Baltimore**, Md,US
115/K7 **Baltimore Highlands-Lansdown**, Md,US
39/K1 **Baltiysk**, Rus.
41/E1 **Baltrum** (isl.), Ger.
61/H3 **Baluchistan** (reg.), Iran, Pak.
70/E2 **Bālurghāt**, India
41/E6 **Balve**, Ger.
55/J3 **Balykshi**, Kaz.
85/E3 **Bam** (prov.), Burk.
68/F5 **Bam** (lake), China
61/G3 **Bam**, Iran
82/H5 **Bama**, Nga.
110/A1 **Bamaji** (lake), On,Can
84/D3 **Bamako** (cap.), Mali
84/D3 **Bamako** (reg.), Mali
92/C5 **Bambamarca**, Peru
83/K6 **Bambari**, CAfr.
45/J2 **Bamberg**, Ger.
113/H3 **Bamberg**, SC,US
33/F4 **Bamber Ridge**, Eng,UK
37/D4 **Bamble**, Nor.
95/C2 **Bambuí**, Braz.
85/H5 **Bamenda**, Camr.
61/J2 **Bāmiān**, Afg.
83/K6 **Bamingui-Bangoran Nat'l Park**, CAfr.
101/N8 **Bamoa**, Mex.
34/C5 **Bampton**, Eng,UK
61/H3 **Bampūr** (riv.), Iran
78/F5 **Banaba** (isl.), Kiri.
94/C2 **Banabuiu** (res.), Braz.
84/D3 **Banamba**, Mali
84/B4 **Banana** (isls.), SLeo.
87/B2 **Banana**, Zaire
70/B2 **Banās** (riv.), India
86/C4 **Banās, Ra's** (pt.), Egypt
50/E3 **Banatsko Novo Selo**, Yugo.
59/B2 **Banaz**, Turk.
32/B3 **Banbridge**, NI,UK
32/B3 **Banbridge** (dist.), NI,UK
35/E2 **Banbury**, Eng,UK
82/B3 **Banc d'Arguin Nat'l Park**, Mrta.
69/C2 **Ban Chiang** (ruins), Thai.
36/D2 **Banchory**, Sc,UK
100/D4 **Banco Chinchorro** (isls.), Mex.
110/E2 **Bancroft**, On,Can
73/H4 **Banda** (isls.), Indo.
73/G5 **Banda** (sea), Indo.
72/A2 **Banda Aceh**, Indo.
65/G2 **Bandai-Asahi Nat'l Park**, Japan
65/G2 **Bandai-san** (mtn.), Japan
84/D5 **Bandama** (riv.), IvC.
84/D4 **Bandama Blanc** (riv.), IvC.
84/D4 **Bandama Rouge** (riv.), IvC.
61/H3 **Bandar Beheshtī** (Chāh Behār), Iran
61/G3 **Bandar-e 'Abbās**, Iran
60/E1 **Bandar-e Anzalī**, Iran
60/F3 **Bandar-e Būshehr**, Iran
60/E2 **Bandar-e Māhshahr**, Iran
60/F1 **Bandar-e Torkeman**, Iran
72/D3 **Bandar Seri Begawan** (cap.), Bru.
95/D2 **Bandeira** (peak), Braz.
108/F4 **Bandelier Nat'l Mon.**, NM,US
112/D4 **Bandera**, Tx,US
101/N9 **Banderas** (bay), Mex.
84/E3 **Bandiagara**, Mali
68/B5 **Bandipura**, India
51/H5 **Bandırma**, Turk.
51/J5 **Bandırma** (gulf), Turk.
71/J5 **Ban Don**, Viet.
87/C1 **Bandundu**, Zaire
72/C5 **Bandung**, Indo.
47/E3 **Bañeres**, Sp.
36/D2 **Banff**, Sc,UK
106/E3 **Banff Nat'l Park**, Ab, BC,Can
84/D4 **Banfora**, Burk.
67/D6 **Bañga**, Phil.
70/C5 **Bangalore**, India
85/H5 **Bangangté**, Camr.
83/K7 **Bangassou**, CAfr.
73/E2 **Bangau, Tanjong** (cape), Malay.
73/F4 **Banggai** (isls.), Indo.
68/C5 **Banggong** (lake), China
69/D2 **Banghiang** (riv.), Laos
72/C4 **Bangka** (isl.), Indo.
72/B4 **Bangka** (str.), Indo.
69/C3 **Bangkok** (bight), Thai.
69/C3 **Bangkok** (Krung Thep) (cap.), Thai.
70/E3 **Bangladesh**
69/C5 **Bang Lang** (res.), Thai.
32/C2 **Bangor**, NI,UK
32/D5 **Bangor**, Wal,UK
111/G2 **Bangor**, Me,US
33/F6 **Bangor-is-y-Coed**, Wal,UK
87/D2 **Bangu**, Zaire
67/D4 **Bangued**, Phil.
83/J7 **Bangui** (cap.), CAfr.
86/B2 **Banhā**, Egypt
87/F5 **Banhine Nat'l Park**, Moz.
101/G4 **Baní**, DRep.
84/D3 **Bani** (riv.), Mali
84/D3 **Banifing** (riv.), Burk., Mali
61/L2 **Banihāl** (pass), India
86/B2 **Banī Mazār**, Egypt
113/J2 **Banister** (riv.), Va,US
59/K6 **Banī Suhaylah**, Gaza
86/B2 **Banī Suwayf**, Egypt
86/B2 **Banī Suwayf** (gov.), Egypt
59/K4 **Bāniyās**, Syria
50/C3 **Banja Luka**, Bosn.
72/D4 **Banjarmasin**, Indo.
84/A3 **Banjul** (cap.), Gam.
69/B5 **Ban Kantang**, Thai.
71/J4 **Ban Kengkok**, Laos
67/C2 **Bankengting**, China
69/D3 **Ban Khampho**, Laos
69/C5 **Ban Khuan Niang**, Thai.
77/B3 **Banks** (cape), Austl.
77/C4 **Banks** (str.), Austl.
102/C3 **Banks** (isl.), BC,Can
102/D1 **Banks** (isl.), NW,Can
75/R11 **Banks** (pen.), NZ
114/H4 **Banks** (pt.), Ak,US
106/D4 **Banks** (lake), Wa,US
78/F6 **Banks** (isls.), Van.
76/H8 **Bankstown**, Austl.
70/E3 **Bānkura**, India
49/H1 **Bankya**, Bul.
69/D2 **Ban Loboy**, Laos
69/E3 **Ban Mdrack**, Viet.
69/D2 **Ban Mong**, Viet.
69/D2 **Ban Muangsen**, Laos
36/B4 **Bann** (riv.), Ire.
32/B2 **Bann** (riv.), NI,UK
69/D2 **Ban Nape**, Laos
61/K2 **Bannu**, Pak.
50/D3 **Banovići**, Bosn.
69/C4 **Ban Pak Phanang**, Thai.
69/D3 **Ban Phon**, Laos
66/B4 **Banpo** (ruins), China
69/C2 **Ban Sieou**, Laos
39/K4 **Banská Bystrica**, Slvk.
51/F5 **Bansko**, Bul.
31/N8 **Banstead**, Eng,UK
70/B3 **Bānswāra**, India
67/D5 **Bantayan**, Phil.
72/D5 **Bantenan** (cape), Indo.
69/C2 **Ban Thabok**, Laos
69/B5 **Bantong Group** (isls.), Thai.
46/C3 **Bañuelo** (mtn.), Sp.
69/D3 **Ban Xebang-Nouan**, Laos
72/A3 **Banyak** (isls.), Indo.
47/G1 **Banyoles**, Sp.
72/D5 **Banyuwangi**, Indo.
98/J **Banzare** (coast), Ant.
81/W17 **Banzart** (gov.), Tun.
81/W17 **Banzart** (lake), Tun.
81/W17 **Banzart** (Bizerte), Tun.
66/B3 **Baode**, China
66/D3 **Baodi**, China
66/C3 **Baoding**, China
66/D4 **Baodugu** (mtn.), China
69/D1 **Bao Ha**, Viet.
62/F5 **Baoji**, China
71/J2 **Baojing**, China
69/D1 **Bao Lac**, Viet.
69/D4 **Bao Loc**, Viet.
66/E5 **Baoshan**, China
71/G2 **Baoshan**, China
66/B2 **Baotou**, China
84/D4 **Baoulé** (riv.), IvC., Mali
84/C3 **Baoulé** (riv.), Mali
70/D4 **Bāpatla**, India
59/K5 **Bāqa el Gharbiyya**, Isr.
69/D4 **Ba Quan** (cape), Viet.
60/D2 **Ba'qūbah**, Iraq
42/D5 **Bar** (riv.), Fr.
50/D4 **Bar**, Yugo.
69/D4 **Ba Ra**, Viet.
83/P7 **Baraawe**, Som.
72/E4 **Barabai**, Indo.
56/H4 **Barabinsk**, Rus.
110/B3 **Baraboo**, Wi,US
46/D1 **Baracaldo**, Sp.
59/L5 **Baradá** (riv.), Syria
96/F2 **Baradero**, Arg.
83/M5 **Bārah**, Sudan
101/G4 **Barahona**, DRep.
68/C5 **Bāra Lācha La** (pass), India
72/D3 **Baram** (cape), Malay.
72/D3 **Baram** (riv.), Malay.
92/G2 **Barama** (riv.), Guy.
70/B4 **Bārāmati**, India
61/K2 **Baramula**, India
70/C2 **Bāran**, India
114/L4 **Baranof** (isl.), Ak,US
54/C1 **Baranovichi**, Bela.
50/C3 **Baranya** (co.), Hun.
95/D1 **Barão de Cocais**, Braz.
51/G2 **Baraolt**, Rom.
43/E3 **Baraque de Fraiture** (hill), Belg.
73/G5 **Barat Daya** (isls.), Indo.
95/D2 **Barbacena**, Braz.
101/J5 **Barbados**
94/C2 **Barbalha**, Braz.
86/C5 **Barbar**, Sudan
47/F1 **Barbastro**, Sp.
46/C4 **Barbate de Franco**, Sp.
103/T6 **Barbeau** (peak), NW,Can
47/L6 **Barbera del Valles**, Sp.
104/V13 **Barbers** (pt.), Hi,US
89/E2 **Barberton**, SAfr.
110/D3 **Barberton**, Oh,US
44/C4 **Barbezieux-Saint-Hilaire**, Fr.
70/E3 **Barbil**, India
33/F3 **Barbon**, Eng,UK
110/D4 **Barbourville**, Ky,US
101/J4 **Barbuda** (isl.), Ant. & Barb.
50/F2 **Barcău** (riv.), Rom.
48/D3 **Barcellona Pozzo di Gotto**, It.
47/G2 **Barcelona**, Sp.
101/J5 **Barcelona**, Ven.
47/L7 **Barcelona** (inset), Sp.
46/A2 **Barcelos**, Port.
39/J2 **Barcin**, Pol.
76/A4 **Barcoo** (riv.), Austl.
50/C3 **Barcs**, Hun.
39/L2 **Barczewo**, Pol.
82/J3 **Bardaï**, Chad
59/J6 **Bardawīl, Sabkhat al** (lag.), Egypt
39/L4 **Bardejov**, Slvk.
83/P7 **Bardheere**, Som.
33/H5 **Bardney**, Eng,UK
70/B3 **Bārdoli**, India
32/D6 **Bardsey** (isl.), Wal,UK
110/C4 **Bardstown**, Ky,US
83/R5 **Bareeda**, Som.
70/C2 **Bareilly**, India
40/B5 **Barendrecht**, Neth.
44/D2 **Barentin**, Fr.
29/L2 **Barents** (sea)
83/N4 **Barentu**, Erit.
44/C2 **Barfleur, Pointe de** (pt.), Fr.
70/D3 **Bargarh**, India
34/C3 **Bargoed**, Wal,UK
41/H1 **Bargteheide**, Ger.
62/F1 **Barguzin** (riv.), Rus.
70/D2 **Barhaj**, India
111/G2 **Bar Harbor**, Me,US
35/G2 **Bar Hill**, Eng,UK
70/C2 **Bāri**, India
48/E2 **Bari**, It.
81/U18 **Barika**, Alg.
100/C4 **Barillas**, Guat.
101/G6 **Barinas**, Ven.
87/C2 **Baringa-Twana**, Zaire
70/E3 **Baripāda**, India
95/B2 **Bariri**, Braz.
86/B3 **Bārīs**, Egypt
70/F3 **Barisāl**, Bang.
72/B4 **Barisan** (mts.), Indo.
72/D4 **Barito** (riv.), Indo.
91/C1 **Baritu Nat'l Park**, Arg.
111/S9 **Barker**, NY,US
31/P7 **Barking & Dagenham** (bor.), Eng,UK
106/B3 **Barkley** (sound), BC,Can
110/C4 **Barkley** (lake), Ky,US
74/E3 **Barkly** (tablelands), Austl.
33/F6 **Barlaston**, Eng,UK
33/G4 **Barlby**, Eng,UK
43/E6 **Bar-le-Duc**, Fr.
74/B5 **Barlee** (lake), Austl.
48/E2 **Barletta**, It.
42/B3 **Barlin**, Fr.
39/H2 **Barlinek**, Pol.
91/E2 **Barmejo** (riv.), Arg.
70/B2 **Barmer**, India
34/B1 **Barmouth**, Wal,UK
41/G1 **Barmstedt**, Ger.
61/L2 **Barnāla**, India
33/G2 **Barnard Castle**, Eng,UK
68/D1 **Barnaul**, Rus.
115/F6 **Barnegat** (bay), NJ,US
31/N7 **Barnet**, Eng,UK
31/N7 **Barnet** (bor.), Eng,UK
40/C4 **Barneveld**, Neth.
39/G2 **Barnim** (reg.), Ger.
33/F4 **Barnoldswick**, Eng,UK
33/G4 **Barnsley**, Eng,UK
34/B4 **Barnstaple**, Eng,UK
34/B4 **Barnstaple** (Bideford) (bay), Eng,UK
34/E2 **Barnt Green**, Eng,UK
41/G5 **Barntrup**, Ger.
113/H3 **Barnwell**, SC,US
70/B3 **Baroda**, India
61/K1 **Barowghīl** (Khyber) (pass), Afg.
70/F2 **Barpeta**, India
101/H5 **Barquisimeto**, Ven.
32/D1 **Barr**, Sc,UK
94/B3 **Barra**, Braz.
95/B2 **Barra Bonita**, Braz.
95/B2 **Barra Bonita** (res.), Braz.
94/B4 **Barra da Choça**, Braz.
100/E5 **Barra del Colorado Nat'l Park**, CR
100/E5 **Barra de Rio Grande**, Nic.
93/G7 **Barra do Bugres**, Braz.
94/A2 **Barra do Corda**, Braz.
93/H7 **Barra do Garças**, Braz.
95/K7 **Barra do Piraí**, Braz.
95/B4 **Barra do Ribeiro**, Braz.
95/J7 **Barra Mansa**, Braz.
92/C4 **Barranca**, Peru
92/C6 **Barranca**, Peru
92/D2 **Barrancabermeja**, Col.
101/N8 **Barranca del Cobre Nat'l Park**, Mex.
96/C2 **Barrancas**, Chile
101/G5 **Barranquilla**, Col.
94/B2 **Barras**, Braz.
95/B3 **Barra Velha**, Braz.
94/A4 **Barreiras**, Braz.
94/B1 **Barreirinhas**, Braz.
46/A3 **Barreiro**, Port.
94/D3 **Barreiros**, Braz.
89/G7 **Barren, Nosy** (isls.), Madg.
95/B2 **Barretos**, Braz.
106/E2 **Barrhead**, Ab,Can
32/D1 **Barrhill**, Sc,UK
110/E2 **Barrie**, On,Can
77/B1 **Barrier** (range), Austl.
106/C3 **Barrière**, BC,Can
116/P15 **Barrington**, Il,US
116/P15 **Barrington Hills**, Il,US
77/D1 **Barrington Tops** (peak), Austl.
77/D1 **Barrington Tops Nat'l Park**, Austl.
76/B2 **Barron Gorge Nat'l Park**, Austl.
95/D2 **Barroso**, Braz.
74/A4 **Barrow** (isl.), Austl.
76/B1 **Barrow** (pt.), Austl.
102/G1 **Barrow** (str.), NW,Can
36/B4 **Barrow** (riv.), Ire.
114/G1 **Barrow** (pt.), Ak,US
33/H6 **Barrowby**, Eng,UK
33/F4 **Barrowford**, Eng,UK
33/E3 **Barrow-in-Furness**, Eng,UK
34/C4 **Barry**, Wal,UK
55/L4 **Barsakel'mes** (salt pan), Uzb.
61/L5 **Bārshi**, India
41/G4 **Barsinghausen**, Ger.
41/E2 **Barssel**, Ger.
108/C4 **Barstow**, Ca,US
44/F2 **Bar-sur-Aube**, Fr.
68/B4 **Bartang** (riv.), Taj.
38/G1 **Barth**, Ger.
51/L5 **Bartın**, Turk.
75/H3 **Bartle Frere** (peak), Austl.
109/J3 **Bartlesville**, Ok,US
116/P16 **Bartlett**, Il,US
101/F3 **Bartolomé Masó**, Cuba
87/G5 **Bartolomeu Dias**, Moz.
35/F3 **Barton in the Clay**, Eng,UK
35/E5 **Barton on Sea**, Eng,UK
35/E1 **Barton under Needwood**, Eng,UK
33/H4 **Barton-upon-Humber**, Eng,UK
39/L1 **Bartoszyce**, Pol.
113/H5 **Bartow**, Fl,US
100/E6 **Barú** (vol.), Pan.
72/B3 **Barumun** (riv.), Indo.
72/A3 **Barus**, Indo.
62/C2 **Baruun Huuray** (reg.), Mong.
62/G2 **Baruun-Urt**, Mong.
70/C3 **Barwāha**, India
70/B3 **Barwāni**, India
77/D1 **Barwon** (riv.), Austl.
39/J3 **Barycz** (riv.), Pol.
55/H1 **Barysh**, Rus.
83/J7 **Basankusu**, Zaire
46/D1 **Basauri**, Sp.
96/F2 **Basavilbaso**, Arg.
34/D1 **Baschurch**, Eng,UK
45/G3 **Basel**, Swi.
48/E2 **Basento** (riv.), It.
88/E3 **Bashee** (riv.), SAfr.
67/D3 **Bashi** (chan.), Phil., Tai.
68/E1 **Bashkaus** (riv.), Rus.
53/M5 **Bashkir Aut. Rep.**, Rus.
67/D6 **Basilan** (isl.), Phil.
73/F2 **Basilan** (peak), Phil.
35/G3 **Basildon**, Eng,UK
48/D2 **Basilicata** (reg.), It.
70/C3 **Bāsim**, India
106/F4 **Basin**, Wy,US
35/E4 **Basingstoke**, Eng,UK
31/M8 **Basingstoke** (can.), Eng,UK
59/F2 **Başkale**, Turk.
110/F2 **Baskatong** (res.), Qu,Can
70/C3 **Bāsoda**, India
83/K7 **Basoko**, Zaire
46/D1 **Basque Provinces** (aut. comm.), Sp.
77/C3 **Bass** (str.), Austl.
79/L7 **Bass** (isls.), FrPol.
49/G4 **Bassae** (ruins), Gre.
106/E3 **Bassano**, Ab,Can
45/J4 **Bassano del Grappa**, It.
87/G5 **Bassas da India** (isl.), Reun.
71/F4 **Bassein**, Burma
71/F4 **Bassein** (riv.), Burma
70/B4 **Bassein**, India
43/E2 **Bassenge**, Belg.
44/C2 **Basse-Normandie** (reg.), Fr.
32/E2 **Bassenthwaite** (lake), Eng,UK
101/J4 **Basse-Terre** (cap.), Guad.
101/J4 **Basse-Terre** (isl.), Guad.
101/J4 **Basseterre** (cap.), StK.
41/F3 **Bassum**, Ger.
110/B1 **Basswood** (lake), On,Can, Mn,US
37/E4 **Båstad**, Swe.
70/D2 **Bastī**, India
48/A1 **Bastia**, Fr.
48/C1 **Bastia**, It.
43/E3 **Bastogne**, Belg.
95/B2 **Bastos**, Braz.
112/F3 **Bastrop**, La,US
112/D4 **Bastrop**, Tx,US
59/H6 **Basyūn**, Egypt
82/G7 **Bata**, EqG.
100/E3 **Batabanó** (gulf), Cuba
67/D4 **Batac**, Phil.
57/P3 **Batagay**, Rus.
61/L2 **Batāla**, India
46/A3 **Batalha**, Port.
67/D3 **Batan** (isl.), Phil.
83/J6 **Batangafo**, CAfr.
67/D5 **Batangas**, Phil.
73/H4 **Batanta** (mtn.), Indo.
95/C2 **Batatais**, Braz.
116/P16 **Batavia**, Il,US
110/E3 **Batavia**, NY,US
54/F3 **Bataysk**, Rus.
71/H5 **Batdambang**, Camb.
76/H9 **Bate** (bay), Austl.
82/H8 **Batéké** (plat.), Congo
77/D2 **Batemans Bay**, Austl.
113/H3 **Batesburg**, SC,US
113/F3 **Batesville**, Ar,US
113/F3 **Batesville**, Ms,US
34/D4 **Bath**, Eng,UK
111/G3 **Bath**, Me,US
110/E3 **Bath**, NY,US
77/D2 **Bathurst**, Austl.
111/H2 **Bathurst**, NB,Can
74/D2 **Bathurst** (isl.), Austl.
114/N1 **Bathurst** (cape), NW,Can
102/F2 **Bathurst** (inlet), NW,Can
103/R7 **Bathurst** (isl.), NW,Can
83/P5 **Batī**, Eth.
83/N8 **Batian** (peak), Kenya
68/F2 **Batik** (mts.), China
60/E3 **Bāṭin, Wādī al** (dry riv.), SAr.
33/G4 **Batley**, Eng,UK
59/E3 **Batman**, Turk.
81/V18 **Batna**, Alg.
82/H7 **Batouri**, Camr.
111/F2 **Batsican** (riv.), Qu,Can
115/F6 **Batsto** (riv.), NJ,US
62/F2 **Batsümber**, Mong.
29/M9 **Batterbee** (cape), Ant.
33/G3 **Battersby**, Eng,UK
31/N7 **Battersea**, Eng,UK
70/D6 **Batticaloa**, SrL.
106/F2 **Battle** (riv.), Ab, Sk,Can
35/G5 **Battle**, Eng,UK
106/F3 **Battle** (cr.), Mt,US
110/C3 **Battle Creek**, Mi,US
106/F2 **Battleford**, Sk,Can
108/C2 **Battle Mountain**, Nv,US
50/E2 **Battonya**, Hun.
62/E2 **Battsengel**, Mong.
83/N6 **Batu** (peak), Eth.
73/E3 **Batu** (cape), Indo.
72/A4 **Batu** (isls.), Indo.
72/D3 **Batu** (bay), Malay.
72/D3 **Batu** (peak), Malay.
73/F4 **Batudaka** (isl.), Indo.
72/D3 **Batuensambang** (peak), Indo.
72/B3 **Batu Gajah**, Malay.
55/G4 **Batumi**, Geo.
72/B3 **Batu Pahat**, Malay.
72/B3 **Batu Puteh** (peak), Malay.
72/B4 **Baturaja**, Indo.
94/C2 **Baturité**, Braz.
59/M8 **Bat Yam**, Isr.
85/H4 **Bauchi** (state), Nga.
107/K3 **Baudette**, Mn,US
103/L1 **Bauld** (cape), Nf,Can
85/F5 **Bauman** (peak), Togo
41/G6 **Baunatal**, Ger.
95/B2 **Baurú**, Braz.
39/H3 **Bautzen**, Ger.
45/J2 **Bavaria** (state), Ger.
45/J3 **Bavarian Alps** (mts.), Aus., Ger.
72/C4 **Bawang** (cape), Indo.
77/C3 **Baw Baw** (peak), Austl.
77/C3 **Baw Baw Nat'l Park**, Austl.
72/D5 **Bawean** (isl.), Indo.
85/E4 **Bawku**, Gha.
101/F3 **Bayamo**, Cuba
101/H4 **Bayamón**, PR
62/D5 **Bayan Har** (mts.), China
62/E2 **Bayanhongor**, Mong.
62/E3 **Bayanleg**, Mong.
68/F2 **Bayannur**, Mong.
62/E2 **Bayan-Ovoo**, Mong.
62/D2 **Bayan-Uul**, Mong.
109/G2 **Bayard**, Ne,US
67/D6 **Bayawan**, Phil.
43/G3 **Baybach** (riv.), Ger.
67/D5 **Baybay**, Phil.
59/E2 **Bayburt**, Turk.
110/D3 **Bay City**, Mi,US
112/E4 **Bay City**, Tx,US
56/G2 **Baydaratskaya** (bay), Rus.
83/P7 **Baydhabo** (Baidoa), Som.
62/D2 **Baydrag** (riv.), Mong.
45/K2 **Bayerischer Wald Nat'l Park**, Ger.
94/D2 **Bayeux**, Braz.
44/C2 **Bayeux**, Fr.
97/T11 **Baygorria, Artificial de** (res.), Uru.
60/E6 **Bayḥān al Qiṣāb**, Yem.
57/L4 **Baykal** (mts.), Rus.
62/F1 **Baykal** (Baikal) (lake), Rus.
113/G4 **Bay Minette**, Al,US
67/D4 **Bayombong**, Phil.
46/A1 **Bayona**, Sp.
113/H4 **Bayonet Point**, Fl,US
44/C5 **Bayonne**, Fr.
115/F5 **Bayonne**, NJ,US
115/G5 **Bayport**, NY,US
61/H1 **Bayram-Ali**, Trkm.
51/H5 **Bayramiç**, Turk.
45/J2 **Bayreuth**, Ger.
59/K5 **Bayrūt** (Beirut) (cap.), Leb.
110/E2 **Bays** (lake), On,Can
113/F4 **Bay Saint Louis**, Ms,US
47/E1 **Bayse** (riv.), Fr.
34/D1 **Bayston Hill**, Eng,UK
59/K6 **Bayt Laḥm** (Bethlehem), WBnk.
112/E4 **Baytown**, Tx,US
86/C5 **Bayudha** (des.), Sudan
67/E6 **Bayugan**, Phil.
115/G5 **Bayville**, NY,US
46/D4 **Baza**, Sp.
55/H4 **Bazardyuzyu, Gora** (peak), Rus.
87/G5 **Bazaruto** (isl.), Moz.
85/E4 **Bazèga** (prov.), Burk.
110/F2 **Bazin** (riv.), Qu,Can
115/F6 **Beachwood**, NJ,US
35/G5 **Beachy Head** (pt.), Eng,UK
34/C2 **Beacon** (hill), Wal,UK
111/N7 **Beaconsfield**, Qu,Can
35/F3 **Beaconsfield**, Eng,UK
34/B5 **Beaford**, Eng,UK
74/E2 **Beagle** (gulf), Austl.
76/A4 **Beal** (mts.), Austl.
89/J6 **Bealanana**, Madg.
106/B3 **Beale** (cape), BC,Can
109/G4 **Beals** (cr.), Tx,US
34/D5 **Beaminster**, Eng,UK
89/H9 **Beampingaratra** (ridge), Madg.
111/R9 **Beamsville**, On,Can
107/J3 **Bear** (lake), Mb,Can
56/C2 **Bear** (isl.), Nor.
114/K2 **Bear** (mtn.), Ak,US
114/K3 **Bear** (mtn.), Ak,US
106/F5 **Bear** (lake), Id, Ut,US
106/F5 **Bear** (riv.), Id, Ut,US
98/M **Beardmore** (glac.), Ant.
106/F3 **Bearpaw** (mts.), Mt,US
36/C3 **Bearsden**, Sc,UK
106/F4 **Beartooth** (mts.), Mt, Wy,US
113/F4 **Bear Town**, Ms,US
46/D1 **Beasain**, Sp.
46/D3 **Beas de Segura**, Sp.
101/G4 **Beata** (cape), DRep.
74/F2 **Beatrice** (cape), Austl.
109/H2 **Beatrice**, Ne,US
32/E1 **Beattock**, Sc,UK
108/C3 **Beatty**, Nv,US
44/F5 **Beaucaire**, Fr.
31/S9 **Beauchamp**, Fr.
99/C2 **Beaufort** (sea), Can., US
113/H3 **Beaufort**, SC,US
88/C4 **Beaufort West**, SAfr.
44/D3 **Beaugency**, Fr.
111/N7 **Beauharnois**, Qu,Can
44/F4 **Beaujolais** (mts.), Fr.
35/E5 **Beaulieu**, Eng,UK
32/D5 **Beaumaris**, Wal,UK
42/B3 **Beaumetz-les-Loges**, Fr.
115/C3 **Beaumont**, Ca,US
112/E4 **Beaumont**, Tx,US
31/S9 **Beaumont-sur-Oise**, Fr.
44/F3 **Beaune**, Fr.
44/C3 **Beaupréau**, Fr.
43/D3 **Beauraing**, Belg.
107/J3 **Beauséjour**, Mb,Can
42/B5 **Beauvais**, Fr.
106/G2 **Beauval**, Sk,Can
106/F2 **Beaver** (riv.), Ab, Sk,Can
102/D2 **Beaver** (riv.), Yk,Can
109/G3 **Beaver** (riv.), Co,US
109/G3 **Beaver** (riv.), Ks, Ne,US
110/C2 **Beaver** (isl.), Mi,US
109/G3 **Beaver** (riv.), NM, Ok,US
109/G3 **Beaver**, Ok,US
108/D3 **Beaver**, Ut,US
114/K3 **Beaver Creek**, Yk,Can
110/B3 **Beaver Dam**, Wi,US
106/E4 **Beaverhead** (riv.), Mt,US
106/D2 **Beaverlodge**, Ab,Can
107/L2 **Beaver Stone** (riv.), On,Can
70/B2 **Beāwar**, India
95/B2 **Bebedouro**, Braz.
33/E5 **Bebington**, Eng,UK
41/G7 **Bebra**, Ger.
35/H2 **Beccles**, Eng,UK
50/E3 **Bečej**, Yugo.
82/E1 **Bechar**, Alg.
114/G4 **Becharof** (lake), Ak,US
114/G4 **Becharof Nat'l Wild. Ref.**, Ak,US
31/N7 **Beckenham**, Eng,UK
43/F5 **Beckingen**, Ger.
33/H5 **Beckingham**, Eng,UK
110/D4 **Beckley**, WV,US
41/F5 **Beckum**, Ger.
51/G2 **Beclean**, Rom.
33/G3 **Bedale**, Eng,UK
40/D7 **Bedburg**, Ger.
40/D5 **Bedburg-Hau**, Ger.
34/C3 **Beddau**, Wal,UK
32/D5 **Beddgelert**, Wal,UK
76/B1 **Bedford** (cape), Austl.
111/F2 **Bedford**, Qu,Can
35/F2 **Bedford**, Eng,UK
110/C4 **Bedford**, In,US
110/E4 **Bedford**, Va,US
35/G2 **Bedford Level** (reg.), Eng,UK
35/F2 **Bedfordshire** (co.), Eng,UK
33/G1 **Bedlington**, Eng,UK
31/M6 **Bedmond**, Eng,UK
82/H4 **Bedouaram** (well), Niger
40/D2 **Bedum**, Neth.
34/C3 **Bedwas**, Wal,UK
35/E2 **Bedworth**, Eng,UK
76/D4 **Beenleigh**, Austl.
34/C5 **Beer**, Eng,UK
34/C5 **Beer Head** (pt.), Eng,UK
42/C1 **Beernem**, Belg.
59/K6 **Beersheba** (Be'er Sheva'), Isr.
43/D1 **Beerzel**, Belg.
40/D6 **Beesel**, Neth.
33/G6 **Beeston**, Eng,UK
112/D4 **Beeville**, Tx,US
83/K7 **Befale**, Zaire
41/F5 **Bega** (riv.), Ger.
70/C3 **Begamganj**, India
55/K4 **Begarslan** (peak), Trkm.
50/E3 **Bega Veche** (riv.), Rom.
57/M2 **Begichev** (isl.), Rus.
32/B2 **Beg, Lough** (lake), NI,UK
37/D3 **Begna** (riv.), Nor.
70/E2 **Begusarai**, India
93/H3 **Béhague** (pt.), FrG.
72/B4 **Behala** (str.), Indo.
60/F2 **Behbahān**, Iran
43/F5 **Behren-lès-Forbach**, Fr.
60/F1 **Behshahr**, Iran
68/F3 **Bei** (mts.), China
67/A2 **Bei** (riv.), China
63/K2 **Bei'an**, China
62/D4 **Beida** (riv.), China
69/E1 **Beihai**, China
66/D3 **Beijing** (cap.), China
66/H6 **Beijing** (prov.), China
66/H7 **Beijing** (inset) (cap.), China
40/D3 **Beilen**, Neth.
62/C5 **Beilu** (riv.), China
69/D1 **Beilun** (pass), China
66/E2 **Beipiao**, China
87/F4 **Beira**, Moz.
66/C4 **Beiru** (riv.), China
59/K5 **Beirut** (Bayrūt) (cap.), Leb.
87/E5 **Beitbridge**, Zim.
50/F2 **Beiuş**, Rom.
46/B3 **Beja**, Port.
46/A4 **Beja** (dist.), Port.
81/T15 **Bejaïa**, Alg.
46/C2 **Béjar**, Sp.
61/J3 **Bejhi** (riv.), Pak.
59/K5 **Bekaa** (Al Biqā') (val.), Leb.
72/C5 **Bekasi**, Indo.
50/E2 **Békés**, Hun.
50/E2 **Békés** (co.), Hun.
50/E2 **Békéscsaba**, Hun.
89/H8 **Bekily**, Madg.
85/E5 **Bekwai**, Gha.
70/B3 **Bela**, India
61/J3 **Bela**, Pak.
50/E3 **Bela Crkva**, Yugo.
94/B1 **Bela Cruz**, Braz.
50/F4 **Bela Palanka**, Yugo.
30/F3 **Belarus**
47/P10 **Belas**, Port.
93/G8 **Bela Vista**, Braz.
95/B2 **Bela Vista do Paraíso**, Braz.
53/M5 **Belaya** (riv.), Rus.
55/G2 **Belaya Kalitva**, Rus.
54/D2 **Belaya Tserkov'**, Ukr.
39/K3 **Bełchatów**, Pol.
103/S7 **Belcher** (chan.), NW,Can
103/H3 **Belcher** (isls.), NW,Can
107/J3 **Belcourt**, ND,US
53/M5 **Belebey**, Rus.
83/Q7 **Beled Weyne**, Som.
94/D2 **Belém**, Braz.
94/C3 **Belém de São Francisco**, Braz.
91/C2 **Belén**, Arg.
108/F4 **Belen**, NM,US
97/S12 **Belén de Escobar**, Arg.
51/G4 **Belene**, Bul.
46/B1 **Belesar** (res.), Sp.
83/N5 **Beles Wenz** (riv.), Eth.
54/F1 **Belev**, Rus.
32/C2 **Belfast** (cap.), NI,UK
32/C2 **Belfast** (dist.), NI,UK
111/G2 **Belfast**, Me,US
32/C2 **Belfast Lough** (inlet), NI,UK
107/H4 **Belfield**, ND,US
45/G3 **Belfort**, Fr.
70/B4 **Belgaum**, India
38/C3 **Belgium**
54/F2 **Belgorod**, Rus.
54/D3 **Belgorod-Dnestrovskiy**, Ukr.
54/F2 **Belgorod Obl.**, Rus.
106/F4 **Belgrade**, Mt,US
50/E3 **Belgrade** (Beograd) (cap.), Yugo.
50/E4 **Beli Drim** (riv.), Yugo.
50/D3 **Beli Manastir**, Cro.
50/F4 **Beli Timok** (riv.), Yugo.
72/C4 **Belitung** (isl.), Indo.
100/D4 **Belize**
100/D4 **Belize City**, Belz.
50/E3 **Beljanica** (peak), Yugo.
57/P2 **Bel'kovskiy** (isl.), Rus.
103/H2 **Bell** (pen.), NW,Can
110/E1 **Bell** (riv.), Qu,Can
115/B3 **Bell**, Ca,US
106/B2 **Bella Coola**, BC,Can
32/B2 **Bellaghy**, NI,UK
70/C4 **Bellary**, India
91/E2 **Bella Vista**, Arg.
48/A3 **Bellavista** (cape), It.
116/G7 **Belle** (riv.), On,Can
116/G6 **Belle** (riv.), Mi,US
42/C5 **Belleau**, Fr.
32/B3 **Belleek**, NI,UK
110/D3 **Bellefontaine**, Oh,US
107/G4 **Belle Fourche** (riv.), SD, Wy,US
44/F3 **Bellegarde-sur-Valserine**, Fr.
113/H5 **Belle Glade**, Fl,US
115/J8 **Belle Haven**, Va,US
44/B3 **Belle-Ile** (isl.), Fr.
111/K1 **Belle Isle** (str.), Nf, Qu,Can
76/B2 **Bellenden Ker Nat'l Park**, Austl.
44/E3 **Bellerive-sur-Allier**, Fr.
110/E2 **Belleville**, On,Can
110/B4 **Belleville**, Il,US
109/H3 **Belleville**, Ks,US
115/F5 **Belleville**, NJ,US
116/C2 **Bellevue**, Wa,US
115/B3 **Bellflower**, Ca,US
33/F1 **Bellingham**, Eng,UK
106/C3 **Bellingham**, Wa,US
98/U **Bellingshausen** (sea), Ant.
79/K6 **Bellingshausen** (isl.), FrPol.
41/E2 **Bellingwolde**, Neth.
45/H4 **Bellinzona**, Swi.
115/E6 **Bellmawr**, NJ,US
115/G5 **Bellmore**, NY,US
92/C2 **Bello**, Col.
78/F7 **Bellona** (reefs), NCal.
102/G1 **Bellot** (str.), NW,Can
104/W13 **Bellows A.F.B.**, Hi,US
115/H5 **Bellport**, NY,US
36/C3 **Bellshill**, Sc,UK
45/K3 **Belluno**, It.
96/E2 **Bell Ville**, Arg.
88/B4 **Bellville**, SAfr.
112/D4 **Bellville**, Tx,US

41/F4 **Belm**, Ger.
115/F5 **Belmar**, NJ,US
116/K11 **Belmont**, Ca,US
94/C4 **Belmonte**, Braz.
100/D4 **Belmopan** (cap.), Belz.
42/C2 **Beloeil**, Belg.
111/P6 **Beloeil**, Qu,Can
63/K1 **Belogorsk**, Rus.
50/F4 **Belogradchik**, Bul.
95/D1 **Belo Horizonte**, Braz.
109/H3 **Beloit**, Ks,US
110/B3 **Beloit**, Wi,US
94/C3 **Belo Jardim**, Braz.
52/G2 **Belomorsk**, Rus.
87/C1 **Belondo-Kundu**, Zaire
54/F3 **Belorechensk**, Rus.
53/N5 **Beloretsk**, Rus.
50/E4 **Beloševac**, Yugo.
51/H4 **Beloslav**, Bul.
56/J4 **Belovo**, Rus.
52/H3 **Beloye** (lake), Rus.
33/G5 **Belper**, Eng,UK
33/G1 **Belsay**, Eng,UK
106/F4 **Belt**, Mt,US
40/D3 **Belterwijde** (lake), Neth.
35/H1 **Belton**, Eng,UK
112/D4 **Belton**, Tx,US
115/K7 **Beltsville**, Md,US
51/H2 **Bel'tsy**, Mol.
115/E5 **Beltzville** (lake), Pa,US
68/E2 **Belukha, Gora** (peak), Rus.
110/B3 **Belvidere**, Il,US
76/B3 **Belyando** (riv.), Austl.
56/G2 **Belyy** (isl.), Rus.
38/G2 **Belzig**, Ger.
39/M3 **Bełżyce**, Pol.
89/H7 **Bemaraha** (plat.), Madg.
89/H7 **Bemarivo** (riv.), Madg.
46/B1 **Bembibre**, Sp.
35/E5 **Bembridge**, Eng,UK
107/K4 **Bemidji**, Mn,US
40/C5 **Bemmel**, Neth.
33/H3 **Bempton**, Eng,UK
77/C3 **Benalla**, Austl.
46/C4 **Benalmádena**, Sp.
46/C2 **Benavente**, Sp.
112/D5 **Benavides**, Tx,US
32/B1 **Benbane Head** (pt.), NI,UK
77/D3 **Ben Boyd Nat'l Park**, Austl.
32/B3 **Benburb**, NI,UK
106/C4 **Bend**, Or,US
85/G5 **Bendel** (state), Nga.
114/F2 **Bendeleben** (mtn.), Ak,US
51/J2 **Bendery**, Mol.
77/C3 **Bendigo**, Austl.
59/M8 **Bene Beraq**, Isr.
103/L3 **Benedict** (mtn.), Nf,Can
32/D1 **Beneraid** (hill), Sc,UK
45/L2 **Benešov**, Czh.
48/D2 **Benevento**, It.
35/G3 **Benfleet**, Eng,UK
70/E4 **Bengal** (bay), Asia
66/D4 **Bengbu**, China
83/K1 **Benghāzī**, Libya
69/D3 **Ben Giang**, Viet.
72/B3 **Bengkalis**, Indo.
72/B3 **Bengkalis** (isl.), Indo.
72/C3 **Bengkayang**, Indo.
72/B4 **Bengkulu**, Indo.
107/G3 **Bengough**, Sk,Can
37/E4 **Bengtsfors**, Swe.
87/B3 **Benguela**, Ang.
87/F3 **Bengweulu** (lake), Zam.
92/E6 **Beni** (riv.), Bol.
83/L7 **Beni**, Zaire
82/E1 **Beni Abbes**, Alg.
47/F2 **Benicarló**, Sp.
116/K10 **Benicia**, Ca,US
47/E3 **Benidorm**, Sp.
47/E3 **Benifayó**, Sp.
82/D1 **Beni Mellal**, Mor.
85/F4 **Benin**
85/F5 **Benin** (bight), Ben., Nga.
85/G5 **Benin City**, Nga.
82/E1 **Beni Ounif**, Alg.
47/F3 **Benisa**, Sp.
96/B5 **Benjamin** (isl.), Chile
112/D3 **Benjamin**, Tx,US
92/D4 **Benjamin Constant**, Braz.
101/M7 **Benjamín Hill**, Mex.
109/G2 **Benkelman**, Ne,US
32/D5 **Benllech**, Wal,UK
36/C2 **Ben Lomond** (mtn.), Sc,UK
77/C4 **Ben Lomond Nat'l Park**, Austl.
36/D2 **Ben Macdui** (mtn.), Sc,UK
36/C2 **Ben More** (mtn.), Sc,UK
32/C1 **Bennane Head** (pt.), Sc,UK
57/R2 **Bennett** (isl.), Rus.
113/J3 **Bennettsville**, SC,US
36/C2 **Ben Nevis** (mtn.), Sc,UK
111/F3 **Bennington**, Vt,US
88/Q13 **Benoni**, SAfr.
89/J6 **Be, Nosy** (isl.), Madg.
82/H6 **Bénoué Nat'l Park**, Camr.
69/D2 **Ben Quang**, Viet.
116/Q16 **Bensenville**, Il,US
45/H2 **Bensheim**, Ger.
108/E5 **Benson**, Az,US
107/K4 **Benson**, Mn,US
33/F3 **Bentham**, Eng,UK
41/E4 **Bentheim**, Ger.
83/L6 **Bentiu**, Sudan
33/G4 **Bentley**, Eng,UK
95/B4 **Bento Gonçalves**, Braz.
112/E3 **Benton**, Ar,US
110/B4 **Benton**, Il,US
110/B4 **Benton**, Ky,US
72/B3 **Bentong**, Malay.
110/C3 **Benton Harbor**, Mi,US
112/E2 **Bentonville**, Ar,US
69/D4 **Ben Tre**, Viet.
85/G4 **Benue** (riv.), Nga.
85/G5 **Benue** (state), Nga.
50/D3 **Beočin**, Yugo.
50/E3 **Beograd** (Belgrade) (cap.), Yugo.
64/B4 **Beppu**, Japan
64/B4 **Beppu** (bay), Japan
82/E1 **Beraber** (well), Alg.
32/A2 **Beragh**, NI,UK
49/F2 **Berat**, Alb.
73/E4 **Beratus** (peak), Indo.
73/H4 **Berau** (bay), Indo.
73/E3 **Berau** (riv.), Indo.
83/Q5 **Berbera**, Som.
82/J7 **Berberati**, CAfr.
92/G2 **Berbice** (riv.), Guy.
42/D1 **Berchem**, Belg.
45/K3 **Berchtesgaden**, Ger.
45/K3 **Berchtesgaden Nat'l Park**, Ger.
42/A3 **Berck**, Fr.
54/D2 **Berdichev**, Ukr.
56/J4 **Berdsk**, Rus.
54/F3 **Berdyansk**, Ukr.
110/C4 **Berea**, Ky,US
54/B2 **Beregovo**, Ukr.
85/E5 **Berekum**, Gha.
86/C4 **Berenice** (ruins), Egypt
34/D5 **Bere Regis**, Eng,UK
111/H2 **Beresford**, NB,Can
107/J5 **Beresford**, SD,US
50/E2 **Berettyo** (riv.), Hun.
50/E2 **Berettyóújfalu**, Hun.
54/D1 **Berezina** (riv.), Bela.
53/N4 **Berezniki**, Rus.
88/B4 **Berg** (riv.), SAfr.
59/A2 **Bergama**, Turk.
45/H4 **Bergamo**, It.
40/B3 **Bergen**, Neth.
37/C3 **Bergen**, Nor.
41/G3 **Bergen-Belsen**, Ger.
115/F5 **Bergenfield**, NJ,US
40/B6 **Bergen op Zoom**, Neth.
44/D4 **Bergerac**, Fr.
40/C6 **Bergeyk**, Neth.
43/F2 **Bergheim**, Ger.
41/E6 **Bergisch Gladbach**, Ger.
41/E5 **Bergkamen**, Ger.
41/E6 **Bergneustadt**, Ger.
40/C2 **Bergum**, Neth.
40/D2 **Bergumermeer** (lake), Neth.
70/D4 **Berhampur**, India
72/C4 **Berikat** (cape), Indo.
57/S4 **Bering** (isl.), Rus.
114/E3 **Bering** (str.), Rus., Ak,US
43/E1 **Beringen**, Belg.
114/E2 **Bering Land Bridge Nat'l Prsv.**, Ak,US
72/B4 **Beritarikap** (cape), Indo.
46/D4 **Berja**, Sp.
40/D4 **Berkel** (riv.), Ger.
40/B5 **Berkel**, Neth.
34/D3 **Berkeley**, Eng,UK
116/K11 **Berkeley**, Ca,US
115/F5 **Berkeley Heights**, NJ,US
31/M6 **Berkhamsted**, Eng,UK
116/F6 **Berkley**, Mi,US
98/W **Berkner** (isl.), Ant.
51/F4 **Berkovitsa**, Bul.
35/E4 **Berkshire** (co.), Eng,UK
35/E4 **Berkshire Downs** (uplands), Eng,UK
42/C1 **Berlare**, Belg.
40/C5 **Berlicum**, Neth.
39/G2 **Berlin** (cap.), Ger.
111/G2 **Berlin**, NH,US
98/V **Berlioz** (pt.), Ant.
90/C5 **Bermejo** (riv.), Arg.
91/D1 **Bermejo**, Bol.
46/D1 **Bermeo**, Sp.
99/L6 **Bermuda** (isl.), UK
45/G3 **Bern** (cap.), Swi.
92/B5 **Bernal**, Peru
48/E2 **Bernalda**, It.
108/F4 **Bernalillo**, NM,US
102/D1 **Bernard** (riv.), NW,Can
97/J7 **Bernardo O'Higgins Nat'l Park**, Chile
115/G5 **Bernardsville**, NJ,US
44/D2 **Bernay**, Fr.
38/F3 **Bernburg**, Ger.
41/F2 **Berne** (riv.), Ger.
45/G3 **Bernese Alps** (range), Swi.
31/S9 **Bernes-sur-Oise**, Fr.
74/A4 **Bernier** (isl.), Austl.
102/G1 **Bernier** (bay), NW,Can
45/J3 **Bernina, Passo del** (pass), Swi.
42/C3 **Bernissart**, Belg.
43/G4 **Bernkastel-Kues**, Ger.
89/H8 **Beroroha**, Madg.
45/L2 **Beroun**, Czh.
45/K2 **Berounka** (riv.), Czh.
50/F5 **Berovo**, Macd.
44/F5 **Berre** (lag.), Fr.
34/C1 **Berriew**, Wal,UK
81/S15 **Berrouaghia**, Alg.
101/F2 **Berry** (isls.), Bahm.
44/D3 **Berry** (hist. reg.), Fr.
116/K9 **Berryessa** (lake), Ca,US
116/K9 **Berryessa** (peak), Ca,US
34/C6 **Berry Head** (pt.), Wal,UK
112/E2 **Berryville**, Ar,US
82/H7 **Bertoua**, Camr.
97/J7 **Bertrand** (peak), Arg.
43/E4 **Bertrix**, Belg.
78/G5 **Beru** (atoll), Kiri.
72/D3 **Beruit** (isl.), Malay.
77/G5 **Berwick**, Austl.
111/H2 **Berwick**, NB,Can
36/D3 **Berwick-upon-Tweed**, Eng,UK
32/E6 **Berwyn** (mts.), Wal,UK
116/Q16 **Berwyn**, Il,US
115/E5 **Berwyn-Devon**, Pa,US
44/E4 **Bès** (riv.), Fr.
89/H7 **Besalampy**, Madg.
44/G3 **Besançon**, Fr.
73/E4 **Besar** (peak), Indo.
44/E3 **Besbre** (riv.), Fr.
56/F6 **Beshahr**, Iran
50/E3 **Beška**, Yugo.
39/K4 **Beskids** (mts.), Pol.
55/H4 **Beslan**, Rus.
50/F4 **Besna Kobila** (peak), Yugo.
107/G2 **Besnard** (lake), Sk,Can
33/G4 **Bessacarr**, Eng,UK
31/S9 **Bessancourt**, Fr.
51/J2 **Bessarabia** (reg.), Mol.
32/B3 **Bessbrook**, NI,UK
113/G3 **Bessemer**, Al,US
110/B2 **Bessemer**, Mi,US
116/D2 **Bessemer** (mtn.), Wa,US
55/K3 **Besshoky, Gora** (peak), Kaz.
40/C6 **Best**, Neth.
41/F6 **Bestwig**, Ger.
46/A1 **Betanzos**, Sp.
81/M14 **Beth** (riv.), Mor.
59/N7 **Beth Alpha Synagogue Nat'l Park**, Isr.
109/J2 **Bethany**, Mo,US
32/D5 **Bethesda**, Wal,UK
115/J8 **Bethesda**, Md,US
88/E3 **Bethlehem**, SAfr.
115/E5 **Bethlehem**, Pa,US
59/K6 **Bethlehem** (Bayt Laḩm), WBnk.
115/G5 **Bethpage**, NY,US
107/G3 **Bethune**, Sk,Can
42/B2 **Béthune**, Fr.
42/A4 **Béthune** (riv.), Fr.
95/C1 **Betim**, Braz.
89/H8 **Betioky**, Madg.
68/A2 **Betpak-Dala** (des.), Kaz.
43/G6 **Betschdorf**, Fr.
59/K5 **Bet She'an**, Isr.
59/M9 **Bet Shemesh**, Isr.
111/G1 **Betsiamites** (riv.), Qu,Can
89/H7 **Betsiboka** (riv.), Madg.
83/J3 **Bette** (peak), Libya
43/F4 **Bettembourg**, Lux.
70/D2 **Bettiah**, India
70/C3 **Betūl**, India
40/C5 **Betuwe** (reg.), Neth.
32/E5 **Betws-y-Coed**, Wal,UK
43/G2 **Betzdorf**, Ger.
107/H4 **Beulah**, ND,US
40/D3 **Beulakerwijde** (lake), Neth.
35/G4 **Beult** (riv.), Eng,UK
40/C5 **Beuningen**, Neth.
44/D3 **Beuvron** (riv.), Fr.
31/U10 **Beuvronne** (riv.), Fr.
42/B2 **Beuvry**, Fr.
41/H2 **Bevensen**, Ger.
41/E4 **Bever** (riv.), Ger.
42/D1 **Beveren**, Belg.
33/H4 **Beverley**, Eng,UK
115/B2 **Beverly Hills**, Ca,US
116/F6 **Beverly Hills**, Mi,US
41/G5 **Beverungen**, Ger.
40/B4 **Beverwijk**, Neth.
33/F1 **Bewcastle**, Eng,UK
34/D2 **Bewdley**, Eng,UK
35/G4 **Bewl Bridge** (res.), Eng,UK
43/G5 **Bexbach**, Ger.
35/G5 **Bexhill**, Eng,UK
31/P7 **Bexley** (bor.), Eng,UK
51/J5 **Beykoz**, Turk.
43/E2 **Beyne-Heusay**, Belg.
51/K5 **Beypazarı**, Turk.
59/B3 **Beyşehir**, Turk.
59/B3 **Beyşehir** (lake), Turk.
50/D3 **Bezdan**, Yugo.
45/L1 **Bezděz** (peak), Czh.
52/H4 **Bezhetsk**, Rus.
44/E5 **Béziers**, Fr.
70/D2 **Bhabua**, India
70/E3 **Bhadrak**, India
70/C5 **Bhadrāvati**, India
70/A3 **Bhadreswar**, India
70/E2 **Bhāgalpur**, India
61/K2 **Bhakkar**, Pak.
70/E2 **Bhaktapur**, Nepal
71/G3 **Bhamo**, Burma
70/C2 **Bhārātpur**, India
70/B3 **Bharuch**, India
70/D3 **Bhātāpāra**, India
61/K2 **Bhatinda**, India
70/B5 **Bhatkal**, India
70/E3 **Bhātpāra**, India
70/C5 **Bhavāni**, India
70/B3 **Bhavnagar**, India
70/C3 **Bhawāni Mandi**, India
70/D4 **Bhawānipatna**, India
70/D3 **Bhilai**, India
70/B2 **Bhīlwāra**, India
70/C4 **Bhīma** (riv.), India
70/D4 **Bhīmavaram**, India
70/D4 **Bhimunipatnam**, India
70/C2 **Bhind**, India
70/B3 **Bhīnmāl**, India
70/B4 **Bhiwandi**, India
70/E2 **Bhojpur**, Nepal
70/C3 **Bhopāl**, India
70/B4 **Bhor**, India
70/E3 **Bhuban**, India
70/E3 **Bhubaneswar**, India
70/A3 **Bhūj**, India
69/B2 **Bhumibol** (dam), Thai.
70/C3 **Bhusawal**, India
70/E2 **Bhutan**
68/F5 **Bi** (riv.), China
92/E4 **Biá** (riv.), Braz.
84/E5 **Bia** (riv.), Gui., IvC.
42/B3 **Biache-Saint-Vaast**, Fr.
82/G7 **Biafra** (bight), Afr.
73/J4 **Biak** (isl.), Indo.
39/M2 **Biała Podlaska**, Pol.
39/M3 **Biała Podlaska** (prov.), Pol.
39/L3 **Białobrzegi**, Pol.
39/J2 **Białogard**, Pol.
39/K4 **Białowieski Nat'l Park**, Pol.
39/M2 **Białystok**, Pol.
39/M2 **Białystok** (prov.), Pol.
45/J3 **Bianca** (peak), It.
48/D4 **Biancavilla**, It.
83/L7 **Biaro**, Zaire
44/C5 **Biarritz**, Fr.
86/B2 **Bibā**, Egypt
95/K6 **Bicas**, Braz.
51/H2 **Bicaz**, Rom.
35/E3 **Bicester**, Eng,UK
74/F2 **Bickerton** (isl.), Austl.
50/D2 **Bicske**, Hun.
84/D5 **Bidaga** (rapids), IvC.
70/C4 **Bīdar**, India
111/G3 **Biddeford**, Me,US
33/F5 **Biddulph**, Eng,UK
34/B4 **Bideford**, Eng,UK
34/B4 **Bideford** (Barnstaple) (bay), Eng,UK
35/E2 **Bidford on Avon**, Eng,UK
69/E3 **Bi Doup** (peak), Viet.
47/E1 **Bidouze** (riv.), Fr.
87/B4 **Bíe** (plat.), Ang.
39/M2 **Biebzra** (riv.), Pol.
45/G3 **Biel**, Swi.
39/J3 **Bielawa**, Pol.
41/F4 **Bielefeld**, Ger.
103/J1 **Bieler** (lake), NW,Can
39/K4 **Bielsko** (prov.), Pol.
39/K4 **Bielsko-Biała**, Pol.
39/M2 **Bielsk Podlaski**, Pol.
69/D4 **Bien Hoa**, Viet.
69/D1 **Bien Son**, Viet.
103/J3 **Bienville** (lake), Qu,Can
40/B5 **Biesbosch** (reg.), Neth.
40/D5 **Biesme** (riv.), Fr.
45/G3 **Bietschhorn** (peak), Swi.
31/S10 **Bièvre** (riv.), Fr.
31/S10 **Bièvres**, Fr.
48/D2 **Biferno** (riv.), It.
77/B2 **Big** (des.), Austl.
103/J2 **Big** (isl.), NW,Can
102/D1 **Big** (riv.), NW,Can
51/H5 **Biga**, Turk.
59/B2 **Bigadiç**, Turk.
106/F4 **Big Belt** (mts.), Mt,US
112/C4 **Big Bend Nat'l Park**, Tx,US
109/K4 **Big Black** (riv.), Ms,US
109/H2 **Big Blue** (riv.), Ks, Ne,US
34/C6 **Bigbury** (bay), Eng,UK
114/D2 **Big Diomede** (isl.), Rus.
107/K4 **Big Fork** (riv.), Mn,US
106/G2 **Biggar**, Sk,Can
43/G1 **Biggasee** (lake), Ger.
74/D2 **Bigge** (isl.), Austl.
41/E6 **Bigge** (riv.), Ger.
41/E6 **Biggesee** (res.), Ger.
31/P8 **Biggin Hill**, Eng,UK
35/F2 **Biggleswade**, Eng,UK
88/D3 **Big Hole**, SAfr.
106/E4 **Big Hole** (riv.), Mt,US
106/F4 **Bighorn** (lake), Mt, Wy,US
106/G4 **Bighorn** (mts.), Mt, Wy,US
106/G4 **Bighorn** (riv.), Mt, Wy,US
108/E1 **Bighorn** (basin), Wy,US
102/F4 **Bighorn Canyon Nat'l Rec. Area**, Mt,US
112/C4 **Big Lake**, Tx,US
108/D2 **Big Lost** (riv.), Id,US
116/P14 **Big Muskego** (lake), Wi,US
84/A3 **Bignona**, Sen.
110/C3 **Big Rapids**, Mi,US
106/G2 **Big River**, Sk,Can
116/N16 **Big Rock** (cr.), Il,US
113/H4 **Big Saltilla** (cr.), Ga,US
109/G3 **Big Sandy** (cr.), Co,US
113/F2 **Big Sandy** (riv.), Tn,US
108/E2 **Big Sandy** (riv.), Wy,US
107/J5 **Big Sioux** (riv.), Ia, SD,US
112/C3 **Big Spring**, Tx,US
107/J4 **Big Stone** (lake), Mn, SD,US
110/D4 **Big Stone Gap**, Va,US
106/F4 **Big Timber**, Mt,US
102/H3 **Big Trout** (lake), On,Can
115/B2 **Big Tujunga** (canyon), Ca,US
95/B3 **Biguaçu**, Braz.
108/D2 **Big Wood** (riv.), Id,US
50/B3 **Bihać**, Yugo.
70/E2 **Bihār**, India
70/D3 **Bihār** (state), India
50/F2 **Bihor** (co.), Rom.
42/A4 **Bihorel**, Fr.
84/A4 **Bijagós** (isls.), GBis.
70/C4 **Bījāpur**, India
60/E1 **Bījār**, Iran
50/D3 **Bijeljina**, Bosn.
50/D4 **Bijelo Polje**, Yugo.
70/C2 **Bijnor**, India
70/B2 **Bīkaner**, India
78/G3 **Bikar** (atoll), Mrsh.
63/L2 **Bikin**, Rus.
63/M2 **Bikin** (riv.), Rus.
78/F3 **Bikini** (atoll), Mrsh.
87/C4 **Bikuar Nat'l Park**, Moz.
69/B3 **Bilauktaung** (range), Burma, Thai.
74/G5 **Bilba Morea Claypan** (lake), Austl.
46/D1 **Bilbao**, Sp.
86/B2 **Bilbays**, Egypt
50/D4 **Bileća**, Bosn.
59/B2 **Bilecik**, Turk.
51/K5 **Bilecik** (prov.), Turk.
39/M3 **Biłgoraj**, Pol.
57/S3 **Bilibino**, Rus.
69/B2 **Bilin** (riv.), Burma
77/C2 **Billabong** (cr.), Austl.
41/H1 **Bille** (riv.), Ger.
41/E5 **Billerbeck**, Ger.
44/C5 **Billère**, Fr.
35/G3 **Billericay**, Eng,UK
77/B2 **Billiat Consv. Park**, Austl.
33/F5 **Billinge**, Eng,UK
33/G2 **Billingham**, Eng,UK
106/F4 **Billings**, Mt,US
35/F4 **Billingshurst**, Eng,UK
58/K10 **Billiton** (isl.), Indo.
108/D4 **Bill Williams** (riv.), Az,US
76/C4 **Biloela**, Austl.
113/F4 **Biloxi**, Ms,US
70/C2 **Bilsi**, India
43/E2 **Bilzen**, Belg.
73/E5 **Bima**, Indo.
77/D2 **Bimberi** (peak), Austl.
101/F2 **Bimini** (isls.), Bahm.
70/C3 **Bina-Etāwa**, India
81/X17 **Bin 'Arūs** (gov.), Tun.
111/Q9 **Binbrook**, On,Can
33/H5 **Binbrook**, Eng,UK
42/D3 **Binche**, Belg.
62/G2 **Binder**, Mong.
70/D2 **Bindki**, India
87/C2 **Bindu**, Zaire
87/F4 **Bindura**, Zim.
47/F2 **Binéfar**, Sp.
35/F4 **Binfield**, Eng,UK
87/F4 **Binga** (mtn.), Moz.
45/G2 **Bingen**, Ger.
84/E5 **Bingerville**, IvC.
33/H6 **Bingham**, Eng,UK
110/F3 **Binghamton**, NY,US
33/G4 **Bingley**, Eng,UK
59/E2 **Bingöl**, Turk.
66/D4 **Binhai**, China
69/D4 **Binh Chanh**, Viet.
69/D4 **Binh Chau**, Viet.
71/G4 **Binhon** (peak), Burma
69/E3 **Binh Son**, Viet.
72/A3 **Binjai**, Indo.
73/F5 **Binongko** (isl.), Indo.
72/B2 **Bintang** (peak), Malay.
71/J3 **Binyang**, China
66/D3 **Binzhou**, China
96/B3 **Bío-Bío** (reg.), Chile
96/B3 **Bío-Bío** (riv.), Chile
50/B4 **Biograd**, Cro.
50/D4 **Biogradska Nat'l Park**, Yugo.
82/G7 **Bioko** (isl.), EqG.
70/C4 **Bīr**, India
82/H2 **Birāk**, Libya
82/H2 **Bi'r al Ghuzayyil** (well), Libya
83/K2 **Bi'r al Ḩarash** (well), Libya
70/E2 **Birātnagar**, Nepal
102/E3 **Birch** (mts.), Ab,Can
107/G2 **Birch Hills**, Sk,Can
107/H2 **Birch River**, Mb,Can
98/X **Bird** (isl.), Ant.
75/K4 **Bird Islet** (isl.), Austl.
77/D2 **Birds Rock** (peak), Austl.
59/D3 **Birecik**, Turk.
95/B2 **Birigui**, Braz.
95/G8 **Biritiba-Mirim**, Braz.
61/G2 **Bīrjand**, Iran
78/G4 **Birkenebeu**, Kiri.
33/E5 **Birkenhead**, Eng,UK
45/J3 **Birkkarspitze** (peak), Aus.
51/H2 **Bîrlad**, Rom.
51/H2 **Bîrlad** (riv.), Rom.
68/B3 **Birlik**, Kaz.
35/E2 **Birmingham**, Eng,UK
113/G3 **Birmingham**, Al,US
116/F6 **Birmingham**, Mi,US
45/K3 **Birnhorn** (peak), Aus.
79/H5 **Birnie** (isl.), Kiri.
85/G3 **Birni Nkonni**, Niger
63/L2 **Birobidzhan**, Rus.
82/E3 **Bîr Ounâne** (well), Mali
45/G3 **Birse** (riv.), Swi.
53/M5 **Birsk**, Rus.
52/E4 **Biržai**, Lith.
51/F4 **Bis** (lake), Rom.
65/M9 **Bisai**, Japan
108/E5 **Bisbee**, Az,US
44/C4 **Biscarrosse**, Fr.
44/C4 **Biscarrosse** (lag.), Fr.
44/B4 **Biscay** (bay), Eur.
113/H5 **Biscayne Nat'l Park**, Fl,US
48/E2 **Bisceglie**, It.
45/G2 **Bischheim**, Fr.
45/K3 **Bischofshofen**, Aus.
43/G6 **Bischwiller**, Fr.
98/V **Biscoe** (isls.), Ant.
101/H6 **Biscucuy**, Ven.
60/D4 **Bīshah** (dry riv.), SAr.
68/B3 **Bishkek** (cap.), Kyr.
108/C3 **Bishop**, Ca,US
33/G2 **Bishop Auckland**, Eng,UK
34/D2 **Bishops Castle**, Eng,UK
34/D3 **Bishops Cleeve**, Eng,UK
111/L1 **Bishop's Falls**, Nf,Can
35/G3 **Bishop's Stortford**, Eng,UK
35/E5 **Bishops Waltham**, Eng,UK
33/H4 **Bishop Wilton**, Eng,UK
82/G1 **Biskra**, Alg.
39/L2 **Biskupiec**, Pol.
67/E6 **Bislig**, Phil.
111/Q9 **Bismarck**, On,Can
78/D5 **Bismarck** (arch.), PNG
78/D5 **Bismarck** (sea), PNG
107/H4 **Bismarck** (cap.), ND,US
59/E3 **Bismil**, Turk.
84/B4 **Bissau** (cap.), GBis.
41/F4 **Bissendorf**, Ger.
107/K3 **Bissett**, Mb,Can
51/G2 **Bistriţa**, Rom.
51/G2 **Bistriţa-Năsăud** (co.), Rom.
92/E2 **Bita** (riv.), Col.
82/H7 **Bitam**, Gabon
43/F4 **Bitburg**, Ger.
43/G5 **Bitche**, Fr.
82/J5 **Bitkin**, Chad
59/E2 **Bitlis**, Turk.
50/E5 **Bitola**, Macd.
50/C5 **Bitonto**, It.
51/G2 **Bitriţa** (riv.), Rom.
86/C2 **Bitter** (lakes), Egypt
106/E4 **Bitterroot** (range), Id, Mt,US
73/G3 **Bitung**, Indo.
82/H5 **Biu**, Nga.
65/M9 **Biwa**, Japan
64/E3 **Biwa** (lake), Japan
109/J4 **Bixby**, Ok,US
59/H6 **Biyalā**, Egypt
68/E1 **Biysk**, Rus.
111/N7 **Bizard** (isl.), Qu,Can
81/W17 **Bizerte** (Banzart), Tun.
37/M6 **Bjargtangar** (pt.), Ice.
38/G1 **Bjärred**, Swe.
50/C3 **Bjelovar**, Cro.
103/S7 **Bjorne** (pen.), NW,Can
35/E1 **Blaby**, Eng,UK
39/K3 **Blachownia**, Pol.
54/D4 **Black** (sea), Asia, Eur.
110/B1 **Black** (bay), On,Can
107/L2 **Black** (riv.), On,Can
114/M3 **Black** (mtn.), Yk,Can
69/C1 **Black** (riv.), China
54/D4 **Black** (sea), Eur.
45/H2 **Black** (for.), Ger.
88/A2 **Black** (pt.), Namb.
34/A6 **Black** (pt.), Eng,UK
34/C3 **Black** (mtn.), Wal,UK
34/C3 **Black** (mts.), Wal,UK
109/K3 **Black** (riv.), Ar, Mo,US
108/D4 **Black** (mts.), Az,US
108/E4 **Black** (riv.), Az,US
116/L11 **Black** (hills), Ca,US
116/G5 **Black** (riv.), Mi,US
108/F4 **Black** (range), NM,US
110/F3 **Black** (riv.), NY,US
107/H5 **Black** (hills), SD, Wy,US
107/L4 **Black** (riv.), Wi,US
35/E3 **Black Bourton**, Eng,UK
33/F4 **Blackburn**, Eng,UK
32/D1 **Blackcraig** (hill), Sc,UK
69/C1 **Black** (Da) (riv.), Viet.
106/E3 **Black Diamond**, Ab,Can
35/F4 **Blackdown** (hill), Eng,UK
34/C5 **Blackdown** (hills), Eng,UK
76/C3 **Blackdown Tableland Nat'l Park**, Austl.
106/F4 **Black Eagle**, Mt,US
106/E5 **Blackfoot**, Id,US
106/F5 **Blackfoot** (res.), Id,US
33/G2 **Blackhall Rocks**, Eng,UK
32/C2 **Black Head** (pt.), NI,UK
108/E3 **Black Mesa** (upland), Az,US
34/B6 **Blackmoor** (upland), Eng,UK
31/P6 **Blackmore**, Eng,UK
76/B1 **Black Mountain Nat'l Park**, Austl.
33/E4 **Blackpool**, Eng,UK
88/A2 **Black Reef** (pt.), Namb.
110/B2 **Black River Falls**, Wi,US
108/C2 **Black Rock** (des.), Nv,US
33/F4 **Blackrod**, Eng,UK
110/D4 **Blacksburg**, Va,US
113/H3 **Blackshear** (lake), Ga,US
110/E4 **Blackstone**, Va,US
77/D1 **Black Sugarloaf** (peak), Austl.
76/G8 **Blacktown**, Austl.
111/H2 **Blackville**, NB,Can
84/E4 **Black Volta** (riv.), Afr.
113/G3 **Black Warrior** (riv.), Al,US
76/C3 **Blackwater**, Austl.
32/B4 **Blackwater** (riv.), Ire.
36/A4 **Blackwater** (riv.), Ire.
35/G3 **Blackwater** (riv.), Eng,UK
32/B3 **Blackwater** (riv.), NI,UK
109/J3 **Blackwater** (riv.), Mo,US
109/H3 **Blackwell**, Ok,US
34/C3 **Blackwood**, Wal,UK
115/K8 **Bladensburg**, Md,US
76/A3 **Bladensburg Nat'l Park**, Austl.
32/D2 **Bladnoch** (riv.), Sc,UK
32/E6 **Blaenau-Ffestiniog**, Wal,UK
34/C3 **Blaenavon**, Wal,UK
44/D5 **Blagnac**, Fr.
51/F4 **Blagoevgrad**, Bul.
63/K1 **Blagoveshchensk**, Rus.
106/G2 **Blaine Lake**, Sk,Can
111/N6 **Blainville**, Qu,Can
109/H2 **Blair**, Ne,US
106/E3 **Blairmore**, Ab,Can
115/F5 **Blairstown**, NJ,US
44/F2 **Blaise** (riv.), Fr.
51/F2 **Blaj**, Rom.
113/G4 **Blakely**, Ga,US
82/B3 **Blanc** (cape), Mrta.
96/E3 **Blanca** (bay), Arg.
92/C5 **Blanca** (range), Peru
46/E3 **Blanca**, Sp.
47/E4 **Blanca** (coast), Sp.
109/F4 **Blanca** (peak), NM,US
74/C4 **Blanche** (lake), Austl.
74/G5 **Blanche** (lake), Austl.
45/G4 **Blanc, Mont** (mtn.), Fr., It.
42/A2 **Blanc Nez** (cape), Fr.
97/K6 **Blanco** (riv.), Arg.
97/K8 **Blanco** (lake), Chile
96/C1 **Blanco** (riv.), Chile
100/D6 **Blanco** (cape), CR
92/B4 **Blanco** (cape), Peru
106/B5 **Blanco** (cape), Or,US
109/H5 **Blanco** (riv.), Tx,US
34/D5 **Blandford Forum**, Eng,UK
108/E3 **Blanding**, Ut,US
47/G2 **Blanes**, Sp.
47/G1 **Blanes, Serre de** (mtn.), Fr.
39/G4 **Blanice** (riv.), Czh.
42/C1 **Blankenberge**, Belg.
43/F3 **Blankenheim**, Ger.
101/J5 **Blanquilla** (isl.), Ven.
39/J4 **Blansko**, Czh.
87/G4 **Blantyre**, Malw.
44/F3 **Blanzy**, Fr.
40/C4 **Blaricum**, Neth.
38/E1 **Blåvands Huk** (pt.), Den.
44/B2 **Blavet** (riv.), Fr.
74/D2 **Blaze** (pt.), Austl.
41/H2 **Bleckede**, Ger.
43/E2 **Blégny**, Belg.
42/C2 **Bléharies**, Belg.
50/B2 **Bleiburg**, Aus.
41/H6 **Bleicherode**, Ger.
40/B4 **Bleiswijk**, Neth.
37/E4 **Blekinge** (co.), Swe.
75/R11 **Blenheim**, NZ
35/E3 **Blenheim Palace**, Eng,UK
45/G4 **Bléone** (riv.), Fr.
42/C4 **Blérancourt**, Fr.
88/C4 **Blesberg** (peak), SAfr.
31/N8 **Bletchingley**, Eng,UK
35/F2 **Bletchley**, Eng,UK
35/E3 **Blewbury**, Eng,UK
81/S15 **Blida**, Alg.
33/G5 **Blidworth**, Eng,UK
43/G5 **Blies** (riv.), Fr., Ger.
43/G5 **Bliesbruck**, Fr.
43/G5 **Blieskastel**, Ger.
79/Y18 **Bligh Water** (sound), Fiji
73/F2 **Blik** (mt.), Phil.
33/G6 **Blithfield** (res.), Eng,UK
98/L **Blizzard** (peak), Ant.
40/B4 **Bloemendaal**, Neth.
88/D3 **Bloemfontein**, SAfr.
88/D2 **Bloemhofdam** (res.), SAfr.
44/D3 **Blois**, Fr.
40/C3 **Blokker**, Neth.
107/J3 **Bloodvein** (riv.), Mb, On,Can
36/A3 **Bloody Foreland** (pt.), Ire.
110/B2 **Bloomer**, Wi,US
115/F5 **Bloomfield**, NJ,US
108/F3 **Bloomfield**, NM,US
116/F6 **Bloomfield Hills**, Mi,US
116/P16 **Bloomingdale**, Il,US
115/C2 **Bloomington**, Ca,US
110/B3 **Bloomington**, Il,US
110/C4 **Bloomington**, In,US
107/K4 **Bloomington**, Mn,US
72/D5 **Blora**, Indo.
113/G4 **Blountstown**, Fl,US
98/L **Blowaway** (peak), Ant.
35/E3 **Bloxham**, Eng,UK
34/E1 **Bloxwich**, Eng,UK
45/K1 **Blšanka** (riv.), Czh.
45/H3 **Bludenz**, Aus.
71/F3 **Blue** (mtn.), India
112/D3 **Blue** (riv.), Ok,US
106/D4 **Blue** (mts.), Or, Wa,US
107/K5 **Blue Earth**, Mn,US
110/D4 **Bluefield**, Va,US
110/D4 **Bluefield**, WV,US
100/E5 **Bluefields**, Nic.
116/Q16 **Blue Island**, Il,US
108/C2 **Bluejoint** (lake), Or,US
76/D4 **Blue Lake Nat'l Park**, Austl.
108/F3 **Blue Mesa** (res.), Co,US
101/F4 **Blue Mountain** (pk.), Jam.
77/D2 **Blue Mountains Nat'l Park**, Austl.
74/F2 **Blue Mud** (bay), Austl.
83/M5 **Blue Nile** (riv.), Eth., Sudan
102/E2 **Bluenose** (lake), NW,Can
113/G3 **Blue Ridge**, Ga,US
113/H2 **Blue Ridge** (mts.), NC, Va,US
75/Q12 **Bluff**, NZ
110/C3 **Bluffton**, In,US
95/B3 **Blumenau**, Braz.
33/G1 **Blyth**, Eng,UK
33/G5 **Blyth**, Eng,UK
35/H2 **Blyth** (riv.), Eng,UK
33/F6 **Blythe** (riv.), Eng,UK
108/D4 **Blythe**, Ca,US
33/F6 **Blythe Bridge**, Eng,UK
113/F3 **Blytheville**, Ar,US
69/D4 **B'nom M'hai** (peak), Viet.
84/C5 **Bo**, SLeo.
67/D5 **Boac**, Phil.
100/D5 **Boaco**, Nic.
95/C2 **Boa Esperança**, Braz.
94/A2 **Boa Esperança** (res.), Braz.
73/G4 **Boano** (isl.), Indo.
103/H2 **Boas** (riv.), NW,Can
94/C2 **Boa Viagem**, Braz.
92/F3 **Boa Vista**, Braz.
80/K10 **Boa Vista** (isl.), CpV.
113/G3 **Boaz**, Al,US
71/J3 **Bobai**, China
81/G6 **Bobaomby** (cape), Madg.
70/D4 **Bobbili**, India
42/B6 **Bobigny**, Fr.
45/H2 **Böblingen**, Ger.
84/D4 **Bobo Dioulasso**, Burk.
50/D4 **Bobotov Kuk** (peak), Yugo.
50/F4 **Bobovdol**, Bul.
39/H3 **Bóbr** (riv.), Pol.
54/G2 **Bobrov**, Rus.
54/D1 **Bobruysk**, Bela.
89/H8 **Boby** (peak), Madg.
92/E5 **Boca do Acre**, Braz.
95/J7 **Bocaina** (mts.), Braz.
94/B5 **Bocaiúva**, Braz.
113/H5 **Boca Raton**, Fl,US
100/D5 **Bocay**, Nic.
39/L4 **Bochnia**, Pol.
43/E1 **Bocholt**, Belg.
40/D5 **Bocholt**, Ger.
41/E6 **Bochum**, Ger.
41/H4 **Bockenem**, Ger.
35/G3 **Bocking**, Eng,UK
101/G6 **Boconó**, Ven.
43/D3 **Bocq** (riv.), Belg.
82/J7 **Boda**, CAfr.
57/M4 **Bodaybo**, Rus.
38/F3 **Bode** (riv.), Ger.
108/B3 **Bodega** (bay), Ca,US
40/B4 **Bodegraven**, Neth.
82/J4 **Bodélé** (depr.), Chad
37/G2 **Boden**, Swe.
45/H3 **Bodensee** (Constance) (lake), Ger., Swi.
70/C4 **Bodhan**, India
70/C5 **Bodināyakkanūr**, India
34/B6 **Bodmin**, Eng,UK
34/B5 **Bodmin Moor** (upland), Eng,UK
37/E2 **Bodø**, Nor.
62/C2 **Bodonchiyn** (riv.), Mong.
50/E1 **Bodrog** (riv.), Hun.
59/A3 **Bodrum**, Turk.
69/D4 **Bo Duc**, Viet.
88/A2 **Boegoeberg** (peak), Namb.
40/C5 **Boekel**, Neth.
87/D1 **Boende**, Zaire
109/K4 **Boeuf** (riv.), Ar, La,US
113/F4 **Bogalusa**, La,US
77/C1 **Bogan** (riv.), Austl.
85/E3 **Bogandé**, Burk.
50/D3 **Bogatić**, Yugo.
39/H3 **Bogatynia**, Pol.
59/C2 **Boğazlıyan**, Turk.
68/E5 **Bogcang** (riv.), China
62/E2 **Bogd**, Mong.
62/B3 **Bogda** (mts.), China
68/E3 **Bogda Feng** (peak), China
35/F5 **Bognor Regis**, Eng,UK
43/D4 **Bogny-sur-Meuse**, Fr.
67/D5 **Bogo**, Phil.
77/C3 **Bogong** (peak), Austl.
77/C3 **Bogong Nat'l Park**, Austl.

Bogor - Bucur

72/C5 **Bogor**, Indo.
92/D3 **Bogotá** (cap.), Col.
50/E5 **Bogovinje**, Macd.
70/E3 **Bogra**, Bang.
32/E1 **Bogrie** (hill), Sc,UK
84/B2 **Bogué**, Mrta.
66/D3 **Bohai** (bay), China
66/E3 **Bohai** (str.), China
66/D3 **Bo Hai (Chihli)** (gulf), China
42/C4 **Bohain-en-Vermandois**, Fr.
45/K1 **Bohemia** (reg.), Czh.
41/G3 **Böhme** (riv.), Ger.
41/F4 **Bohmte**, Ger.
67/D6 **Bohol** (isl.), Phil.
71/J4 **Bo Ho Su**, Viet.
48/D2 **Boiano**, It.
94/C4 **Boipeda** (isl.), Braz.
46/A1 **Boiro**, Sp.
95/B1 **Bois** (riv.), Braz.
31/S10 **Bois-d'Arcy**, Fr.
106/D5 **Boise** (cap.), Id,US
106/E5 **Boise** (riv.), Id,US
109/G3 **Boise City**, Ok,US
42/A5 **Bois-Guillaume**, Fr.
107/H3 **Boissevain**, Mb,Can
31/S9 **Boissy-l'Aillerie**, Fr.
31/T10 **Boissy-Saint-Léger**, Fr.
41/H2 **Boizenburg**, Ger.
82/C2 **Bojador** (cape), WSah.
39/J4 **Bojkovice**, Czh.
61/G1 **Bojnūrd**, Iran
84/B4 **Boké** (comm.), Gui.
87/D1 **Bokele**, Zaire
37/C4 **Boknafjorden** (fjord), Nor.
83/N7 **Bokol** (peak), Kenya
82/J5 **Bokoro**, Chad
88/E2 **Boksburg**, SAfr.
84/B4 **Bolama**, GBis.
61/J3 **Bolān** (pass), Pak.
46/D3 **Bolaños de Calatrava**, Sp.
44/D2 **Bolbec**, Fr.
51/H3 **Boldeşti-Scăeni**, Rom.
33/G2 **Boldon**, Eng,UK
85/E4 **Bole**, Gha.
39/H3 **Bolesławiec**, Pol.
85/E4 **Bolgatanga**, Gha.
116/P16 **Bolingbrook**, Il,US
96/E3 **Bolívar**, Arg.
109/J3 **Bolivar**, Mo,US
110/B5 **Bolivar**, Tn,US
101/G6 **Bolívar** (pk.), Ven.
92/F7 **Bolivia**
43/F4 **Bollendorf**, Ger.
44/F4 **Bollène**, Fr.
45/G3 **Bolligen**, Swi.
33/F5 **Bollin** (riv.), Eng,UK
33/F5 **Bollington**, Eng,UK
37/F3 **Bollnäs**, Swe.
46/B4 **Bollullos Par del Condado**, Sp.
35/F5 **Bolney**, Eng,UK
87/C1 **Bolobo**, Zaire
45/J4 **Bologna**, It.
52/G4 **Bologoye**, Rus.
83/J7 **Bolomba**, Zaire
63/M2 **Bolon'** (lake), Rus.
87/C2 **Bolongongo**, Ang.
69/D3 **Bolovens** (plat.), Laos
48/B1 **Bolsena** (lake), It.
55/K2 **Bol'shaya Khobda** (riv.), Kaz.
55/K1 **Bol'shaya Kinel'** (riv.), Rus.
53/P2 **Bol'shaya Rogovaya** (riv.), Rus.
53/N2 **Bol'shaya Synya** (riv.), Rus.
63/L2 **Bol'shaya Ussurka** (riv.), Rus.
57/L2 **Bol'shevik** (isl.), Rus.
53/M2 **Bol'shezemel'skaya** (tundra), Rus.
56/F2 **Bol'shoy Bolvanskiy Nos** (pt.), Rus.
55/H2 **Bol'shoy Irgiz** (riv.), Rus.
57/Q2 **Bol'shoy Lyakhovskiy** (isl.), Rus.
55/J2 **Bol'shoy Uzen'** (riv.), Kaz., Rus.
62/D1 **Bol'shoy Yenisey** (riv.), Rus.
33/G5 **Bolsover**, Eng,UK
40/C2 **Bolsward**, Neth.
34/C6 **Bolt Head** (pt.), Wal,UK
111/Q8 **Bolton**, On,Can
33/F4 **Bolton**, Eng,UK
33/G4 **Bolton Abbey**, Eng,UK
51/K5 **Bolu**, Turk.
51/K5 **Bolu** (prov.), Turk.
59/B2 **Bolvadin**, Turk.
87/B2 **Boma**, Zaire
77/D2 **Bomaderry**, Austl.
70/B4 **Bombay**, India
73/H4 **Bomberai** (pen.), Indo.
94/C3 **Bom Conselho**, Braz.
95/C1 **Bom Despacho**, Braz.
71/G2 **Bomi**, China
94/A1 **Bom Jardim**, Braz.
95/J6 **Bom Jardim de Minas**, Braz.
94/A3 **Bom Jesus**, Braz.
95/B4 **Bom Jesus**, Braz.
94/B3 **Bom Jesus da Gurguéia** (mts.), Braz.
94/B4 **Bom Jesus da Lapa**, Braz.
95/B1 **Bom Jesus de Goiás**, Braz.
95/D2 **Bom Jesus do Itabapoana**, Braz.
95/G8 **Bom Jesus dos Perdões**, Braz.
41/G3 **Bomlitz**, Ger.
95/B3 **Bom Retiro**, Braz.
83/L6 **Bomu** (riv.), Zaire
81/X17 **Bon** (cape), Tun.
114/K3 **Bona** (mtn.), Ak,US
101/H5 **Bonaire** (isl.), NAnt.
100/C4 **Bonampak** (ruins), Mex.
101/G4 **Bonao**, DRep.
74/C2 **Bonaparte** (arch.), Austl.
114/F3 **Bonasila** (mtn.), Ak,US
111/H1 **Bonaventure**, Qu,Can
111/H1 **Bonaventure** (riv.), Qu,Can
111/L1 **Bonavista** (bay), Nf,Can
111/L1 **Bonavista** (cape), Nf,Can
45/J4 **Bondeno**, It.
76/H8 **Bondi**, Austl.
83/K7 **Bondo**, Zaire
84/E4 **Bondoukou**, IvC.
72/D5 **Bondowoso**, Indo.
73/F4 **Bone** (gulf), Indo.
41/E5 **Bönen**, Ger.
73/F5 **Bonerate** (isls.), Indo.
68/F5 **Bong** (lake), China
84/C5 **Bong** (co.), Libr.
84/C5 **Bong** (range), Libr.
73/F1 **Bongabong**, Phil.
83/K7 **Bongandanga**, Zaire
73/E2 **Bongao**, Phil.
73/E2 **Bonggi** (isl.), Malay.
73/F4 **Bongka** (riv.), Indo.
89/H7 **Bongolava** (uplands), Madg.
82/J5 **Bongor**, Chad
83/K6 **Bongos** (mts.), CAfr.
69/E3 **Bong Son**, Viet.
112/D3 **Bonham**, Tx,US
42/D1 **Bonheiden**, Belg.
48/A2 **Bonifacio** (str.), Fr., It.
113/G4 **Bonifay**, Fl,US
78/D2 **Bonin** (isls.), Japan
113/H5 **Bonita Springs**, Fl,US
100/D4 **Bonito** (pk.), Hon.
43/G2 **Bonn**, Ger.
31/S11 **Bonnelles**, Fr.
106/D3 **Bonners Ferry**, Id,US
106/E4 **Bonner-West Riverside**, Mt,US
107/K3 **Bonnet** (lake), Mb,Can
31/T10 **Bonneuil-sur-Marne**, Fr.
45/G3 **Bonneville**, Fr.
106/C4 **Bonneville** (dam), Or, Wa,US
116/C3 **Bonney Lake**, Wa,US
106/F2 **Bonnyville**, Ab,Can
88/C4 **Bontberg** (peak), SAfr.
88/C4 **Bontebok Nat'l Park**, SAfr.
73/E5 **Bonthain**, Indo.
84/B5 **Bonthe**, SLeo.
67/D4 **Bontoc**, Phil.
50/D2 **Bonyhád**, Hun.
98/J **Bonzare** (coast), Ant.
42/D1 **Boom**, Belg.
107/K5 **Boone**, Ia,US
113/H2 **Boone**, NC,US
113/F3 **Booneville**, Ms,US
115/F5 **Boonton**, NJ,US
62/D2 **Bööntsagaan** (lake), Mong.
110/C4 **Boonville**, In,US
77/C1 **Booroondara** (peak), Austl.
42/A5 **Boos**, Fr.
111/G3 **Boothbay Harbor**, Me,US
98/D **Boothby** (cape), Ant.
102/G1 **Boothia** (gulf), NW,Can
102/G1 **Boothia** (pen.), NW,Can
33/E5 **Bootle**, Eng,UK
82/H8 **Booué**, Gabon
88/D2 **Bophuthatswana** (ind. homeland), SAfr.
43/G3 **Boppard**, Ger.
77/C1 **Boppy** (peak), Austl.
94/B3 **Boqueirão** (mts.), Braz.
96/C4 **Boquete** (peak), Arg.
83/N7 **Bor** (dry riv.), Kenya
53/K4 **Bor**, Rus.
83/M6 **Bor**, Sudan
59/C3 **Bor**, Turk.
50/F3 **Bor**, Yugo.
79/K6 **Bora Bora** (isl.), FrPol.
106/E4 **Borah** (peak), Id,US
37/E4 **Borås**, Swe.
60/F3 **Borāzjān**, Iran
92/G4 **Borba**, Braz.
44/D3 **Borbonnais** (hist. reg.), Fr.
94/C2 **Borborema** (plat.), Braz.
50/E3 **Borča**, Yugo.
41/F5 **Borchen**, Ger.
98/M **Borchgrevink** (coast), Ant.
59/E2 **Borçka**, Turk.
40/D4 **Borculo**, Neth.
95/G7 **Borda da Mata**, Braz.
44/C4 **Bordeaux**, Fr.
103/R7 **Borden** (isl.), NW,Can
103/H2 **Borden** (pen.), NW,Can
115/F5 **Bordentown**, NJ,US
33/F1 **Borders** (reg.), Sc,UK
81/T15 **Bordj Bou Arreridj**, Alg.
47/G4 **Bordj el Bahri** (cape), Alg.
81/S15 **Bordj el Kiffan**, Alg.
81/S15 **Bordj Manaïel**, Alg.
82/G2 **Bordj Omar Driss**, Alg.
35/F4 **Bordon**, Eng,UK
31/N7 **Borehamwood**, Eng,UK
37/E2 **Børgefjell Nat'l Park**, Nor.
41/G5 **Borgentreich**, Ger.
40/D3 **Borger**, Neth.
112/C3 **Borger**, Tx,US
42/D1 **Borgerhout**, Belg.
37/F4 **Borgholm**, Swe.
41/F4 **Borgholzhausen**, Ger.
41/E4 **Borghorst**, Ger.
45/G4 **Borgo San Dalmazzo**, It.
85/F4 **Borgou** (prov.), Ben.
85/F4 **Borgu Game Rsv.**, Nga.
54/B2 **Borislav**, Ukr.
55/G2 **Borisoglebsk**, Rus.
52/F5 **Borisov**, Bela.
89/H6 **Boriziny**, Madg.
40/D5 **Borken**, Ger.
40/D1 **Borkum** (isl.), Ger.
37/E3 **Borlänge**, Swe.
45/H4 **Bormida** (riv.), It.
40/C6 **Born**, Neth.
38/G3 **Borna**, Ger.
40/C2 **Borndiep** (chan.), Neth.
40/D4 **Borne**, Neth.
42/D1 **Bornem**, Belg.
72/E3 **Borneo** (isl.), Asia
43/F2 **Bornheim**, Ger.
39/H1 **Bornholm** (co.), Den.
39/H1 **Bornholm** (isl.), Den.
39/H1 **Bornholmsgat** (chan.), Swe.
85/H3 **Borno** (state), Nga.
46/C4 **Bornos**, Sp.
82/H5 **Bornu** (plains), Nga.
83/L6 **Boro** (riv.), Sudan
68/D3 **Borohoro** (mts.), China, Kaz.
67/E5 **Borongan**, Phil.
33/G3 **Boroughbridge**, Eng,UK
52/G4 **Borovichi**, Rus.
50/D3 **Borovo**, Cro.
54/B3 **Borşa**, Rom.
63/H1 **Borshchovochnyy** (mts.), Rus.
50/E1 **Borsod-Abaúj-Zemplén** (co.), Hun.
40/A6 **Borssele**, Neth.
68/D3 **Bortala** (riv.), China
34/B2 **Borth**, Wal,UK
60/F2 **Borūjen**, Iran
60/E2 **Borūjerd**, Iran
62/D3 **Bor Ul** (mts.), China
62/H1 **Borzya**, Rus.
48/A2 **Bosa**, It.
50/C3 **Bosanska Dubica**, Bosn.
50/C3 **Bosanska Gradiška**, Bosn.
50/C3 **Bosanska Kostajnica**, Bosn.
50/C3 **Bosanska Krupa**, Bosn.
50/D3 **Bosanski Brod**, Bosn.
50/C3 **Bosanski Petrovac**, Bosn.
50/D3 **Bosanski Šamac**, Bosn.
83/Q5 **Bosaso** (Bender Cassim), Som.
34/B5 **Boscastle**, Eng,UK
71/J3 **Bose**, China
35/F5 **Bosham**, Eng,UK
40/B4 **Boskoop**, Neth.
39/J4 **Boskovice**, Czh.
50/D3 **Bosna** (riv.), Bosn.
50/C3 **Bosnia and Hercegovina**
65/G3 **Bōsō** (pen.), Japan
83/J7 **Bosobolo**, Zaire
51/J5 **Bosporus** (str.), Turk.
108/F4 **Bosque Farms**, NM,US
97/K6 **Bosques Petrificados Natural Mon.**, Arg.
82/J6 **Bossangoa**, CAfr.
112/E3 **Bossier City**, La,US
68/E3 **Bosten** (lake), China
33/H6 **Boston**, Eng,UK
112/E3 **Boston** (mts.), Ar,US
111/G3 **Boston** (cap.), Ma,US
112/E3 **Boston**, Tx,US
50/D3 **Bosut** (riv.), Cro.
70/B3 **Botād**, India
76/H8 **Botany** (bay), Austl.
113/H3 **Boteler** (peak), NC,US
89/F2 **Botelerpunt** (pt.), SAfr.
95/G6 **Botelhos**, Braz.
49/J1 **Botev** (peak), Bul.
51/F4 **Botevgrad**, Bul.
89/E2 **Bothaspas** (pass), SAfr.
33/E2 **Bothel**, Eng,UK
116/C2 **Bothell**, Wa,US
34/D5 **Bothenhampton**, Eng,UK
37/G2 **Bothnia** (gulf), Fin., Swe.
54/C3 **Botoşani**, Rom.
51/H2 **Botoşani** (co.), Rom.
66/D3 **Botou**, China
69/D2 **Bo Trach**, Viet.
43/F3 **Botrange** (mtn.), Belg.
87/D5 **Botswana**
48/E3 **Botte Donato** (peak), It.
33/H4 **Bottesford**, Eng,UK
33/H6 **Bottesford**, Eng,UK
107/H3 **Bottineau**, ND,US
40/D5 **Bottrop**, Ger.
95/B2 **Botucatu**, Braz.
111/L1 **Botwood**, Nf,Can
84/D4 **Bou** (riv.), IvC.
84/D5 **Bouaflé**, IvC.
84/D5 **Bouaké**, IvC.
82/J6 **Bouar**, CAfr.
45/K2 **Boubín** (peak), Czh.
83/J6 **Bouca**, CAfr.
111/P6 **Boucherville**, Qu,Can
84/C3 **Boucle du Baoulé Nat'l Park**, Mali
82/E1 **Boudenib**, Mor.
85/E2 **Boû Djébéha** (well), Mali
81/S15 **Boufarik**, Alg.
31/S9 **Bouffémont**, Fr.
76/B1 **Bougainville** (reef), Austl.
97/N7 **Bougainville** (cape), Falk.
78/E5 **Bougainville** (isl.), PNG
81/S15 **Bougara**, Alg.
81/V17 **Bougar'oûn** (cape), Alg.
84/D4 **Bougouni**, Mali
84/E4 **Bougouriba** (prov.), Burk.
44/C3 **Bouguenais**, Fr.
81/M13 **Bouhalla** (peak), Mor.
81/V17 **Bou Hamdane** (riv.), Alg.
81/S15 **Bouira**, Alg.
81/S15 **Bou Ismaïl**, Alg.
81/R15 **Bou Kadir**, Alg.
78/B8 **Boulder**, Austl.
109/F2 **Boulder**, Co,US
106/E4 **Boulder**, Mt,US
108/D4 **Boulder City**, Nv,US
116/P16 **Boulder Hill**, Il,US
85/E4 **Boulgo** (prov.), Burk.
85/E3 **Boulkiemde** (prov.), Burk.
44/C3 **Boulogne** (riv.), Fr.
31/S10 **Boulogne-Billancourt**, Fr.
42/A2 **Boulogne-sur-Mer**, Fr.
33/F4 **Boulsworth** (hill), Eng,UK
81/S15 **Boumerdas**, Alg.
47/F1 **Boumort** (mtn.), Sp.
114/K3 **Boundary**, Yk,Can
108/C3 **Boundary** (peak), Nv,US
115/F5 **Bound Brook**, NJ,US
84/D4 **Boundiali**, IvC.
108/E2 **Bountiful**, Ut,US
29/T8 **Bounty** (isls.), NZ
115/B2 **Bouquet** (canyon), Ca,US
110/C3 **Bourbonnais**, Il,US
42/B2 **Bourbourg**, Fr.
81/L14 **Bou Regreg** (riv.), Mor.
85/F2 **Bouressa** (wadi), Mali
44/F3 **Bourg-en-Bresse**, Fr.
44/E3 **Bourges**, Fr.
44/F4 **Bourg-lès-Valence**, Fr.
44/B3 **Bourgneuf** (bay), Fr.
42/D5 **Bourgogne**, Fr.
44/E3 **Bourgogne** (reg.), Fr.
44/F4 **Bourgoin-Jallieu**, Fr.
35/F1 **Bourne**, Eng,UK
31/M8 **Bourne** (riv.), Eng,UK
35/F3 **Bourne End**, Eng,UK
35/E5 **Bournemouth**, Eng,UK
35/E2 **Bournville**, Eng,UK
36/A4 **Bourn-Vincent Mem. Nat'l Park**, Ire.
41/E3 **Bourtanger Moor** (reg.), Ger.
35/E3 **Bourton on the Water**, Eng,UK
81/T15 **Bou Sellam** (riv.), Alg.
84/B2 **Boutilimit**, Mrta.
29/K8 **Bouvet** (isl.), Nor.
42/C5 **Bouzy**, Fr.
41/G5 **Bovenden**, Ger.
40/D3 **Bovenwijde** (lake), Neth.
34/C5 **Bovey Tracey**, Eng,UK
31/M6 **Bovingdon**, Eng,UK
45/J4 **Bovolone**, It.
106/E3 **Bow** (riv.), Ab,Can
107/J4 **Bowdle**, SD,US
33/F5 **Bowdon**, Eng,UK
76/C3 **Bowen**, Austl.
40/C5 **Bowen Merwede** (can.), Neth.
33/G3 **Bowes**, Eng,UK
108/E4 **Bowie**, Az,US
115/K8 **Bowie**, Md,US
106/F3 **Bow Island**, Ab,Can
76/B2 **Bowling Green** (cape), Austl.
110/C4 **Bowling Green**, Ky,US
109/K3 **Bowling Green**, Mo,US
110/D3 **Bowling Green**, Oh,US
76/B2 **Bowling Green Bay Nat'l Park**, Austl.
98/G **Bowman** (isl.), Ant.
103/J2 **Bowman** (bay), NW,Can
107/H4 **Bowman**, ND,US
111/S8 **Bowmanville**, On,Can
33/E2 **Bowness-on-Solway**, Eng,UK
73/F4 **Bowokan** (isls.), Indo.
77/D2 **Bowral**, Austl.
106/C2 **Bowron** (riv.), BC,Can
107/H4 **Box Elder**, SD,US
77/C3 **Box Hill**, Austl.
77/G5 **Box Hill**, Austl.
40/C5 **Boxmeer**, Neth.
40/C5 **Boxtel**, Neth.
59/C2 **Boyabat**, Turk.
77/D2 **Boyd-Konangra Nat'l Park**, Austl.
107/K5 **Boyer** (riv.), Ia,US
106/E2 **Boyle**, Ab,Can
32/B4 **Boyne** (riv.), Ire.
110/C2 **Boyne City**, Mi,US
113/H5 **Boynton Beach**, Fl,US
106/F5 **Boysen** (res.), Wy,US
49/J3 **Bozcaada** (isl.), Turk.
106/F4 **Bozeman**, Mt,US
59/C3 **Bozkır**, Turk.
82/J6 **Bozoum**, CAfr.
59/B2 **Bozüyük**, Turk.
45/G4 **Bra**, It.
42/D2 **Brabant** (prov.), Belg.
35/G4 **Brabourne Lees**, Eng,UK
50/C4 **Brač** (isl.), Cro.
48/B1 **Bracciano** (lake), It.
110/E2 **Bracebridge**, On,Can
52/B3 **Bräcke**, Swe.
112/C4 **Brackettville**, Tx,US
35/E2 **Brackley**, Eng,UK
35/F4 **Bracknell**, Eng,UK
95/B4 **Braço do Norte**, Braz.
50/F2 **Brad**, Rom.
48/D2 **Bradano** (riv.), It.
32/D3 **Bradda Head** (pt.), IM,UK
113/H5 **Bradenton**, Fl,US
33/G4 **Bradford**, Eng,UK
110/E3 **Bradford**, Pa,US
34/D4 **Bradford on Avon**, Eng,UK
35/E5 **Brading**, Eng,UK
115/F5 **Bradley Beach**, NJ,US
34/C5 **Bradninch**, Eng,UK
112/D4 **Brady**, Tx,US
114/L3 **Braeburn**, Yk,Can
36/D2 **Braemar**, Sc,UK
46/A2 **Braga**, Port.
46/A2 **Braga** (dist.), Port.
96/E2 **Bragado**, Arg.
93/J4 **Bragança**, Braz.
46/B2 **Bragança**, Port.
46/B2 **Bragança** (dist.), Port.
95/G7 **Bragança Paulista**, Braz.
58/J7 **Brahmaputra** (riv.), Asia
32/D6 **Braich-y-Pwll** (pt.), Wal,UK
32/B2 **Braid** (riv.), NI,UK
51/H3 **Brăila**, Rom.
51/H3 **Brăila** (co.), Rom.
42/D2 **Braine-l'Alleud**, Belg.
42/D2 **Braine-le-Comte**, Belg.
107/K4 **Brainerd**, Mn,US
35/G3 **Braintree**, Eng,UK
88/C3 **Brak** (riv.), SAfr.
41/F2 **Brake**, Ger.
42/C2 **Brakel**, Belg.
41/G5 **Brakel**, Ger.
84/B2 **Brakna** (reg.), Mrta.
111/Q8 **Bramalea**, On,Can
33/G4 **Bramhope**, Eng,UK
111/Q8 **Brampton**, On,Can
33/F2 **Brampton**, Eng,UK
41/E4 **Bramsche**, Ger.
92/F4 **Branco** (riv.), Braz.
87/B5 **Brandberg** (peak), Namb.
38/G2 **Brandenburg**, Ger.
38/G2 **Brandenburg** (state), Ger.
33/H4 **Brandesburton**, Eng,UK
107/J3 **Brandon**, Mb,Can
35/G2 **Brandon**, Eng,UK
113/H5 **Brandon**, Fl,US
113/F3 **Brandon**, Ms,US
96/F2 **Brandsen**, Arg.
39/K1 **Braniewo**, Pol.
35/E5 **Bransgore**, Eng,UK
111/J2 **Bras d'Or** (lake), NS,Can
94/A4 **Brasília** (cap.), Braz.
94/A5 **Brasília de Minas**, Braz.
94/A4 **Brasília Nat'l Park**, Braz.
95/D1 **Brasil, Planalto do** (plat.), Braz.
51/G3 **Braşov**, Rom.
51/G3 **Braşov** (co.), Rom.
40/B6 **Brasschaat**, Belg.
113/H3 **Brasstown Bald** (peak), Ga,US
39/J4 **Bratislava** (cap.), Slvk.
39/J4 **Bratislava** (reg.), Slvk.
57/L4 **Bratsk**, Rus.
111/F3 **Brattleboro**, Vt,US
100/E5 **Braulio Carrillo**, CR
45/K2 **Braunau am Inn**, Aus.
41/H5 **Braunlage**, Ger.
41/H4 **Braunschweig** (Brunswick), Ger.
34/B4 **Braunton**, Eng,UK
80/J11 **Brava** (isl.), CpV.
47/G2 **Brava** (coast), Sp.
97/T12 **Brava** (pt.), Uru.
92/F7 **Bravo** (peak), Bol.
108/D4 **Brawley**, Ca,US
103/J2 **Bray** (isl.), NW,Can
32/B5 **Bray**, Ire.
44/D3 **Braye** (riv.), Fr.
32/B5 **Bray Head** (pt.), Ire.
42/B4 **Bray-sur-Somme**, Fr.
90/D3 **Brazil**
110/C4 **Brazil**, In,US
90/E4 **Brazilian** (plat.), Braz.
95/H7 **Brazópolis**, Braz.
112/D4 **Brazos** (riv.), Tx,US
97/K7 **Brazo Sur** (riv.), Arg.
87/C1 **Brazzaville** (cap.), Congo
50/D3 **Brčko**, Bosn.
38/J2 **Brda** (riv.), Pol.
45/K2 **Brdy** (mts.), Czh.
115/C3 **Brea**, Ca,US
34/D3 **Bream**, Eng,UK
51/G3 **Breaza**, Rom.
36/D2 **Brechin**, Sc,UK
40/B6 **Brecht**, Belg.
107/J4 **Breckenridge**, Mn,US
41/E6 **Breckerfeld**, Ger.
35/G2 **Breckland** (reg.), Eng,UK
97/K8 **Brecknock** (pen.), Chile
39/J4 **Břeclav**, Czh.
34/C3 **Brecon**, Wal,UK
34/C3 **Brecon Beacons** (mts.), Wal,UK
34/C3 **Brecon Beacons Nat'l Park**, Wal,UK
40/B5 **Breda**, Neth.
42/B1 **Bredene**, Belg.
43/E1 **Bree**, Belg.
88/L10 **Breë** (riv.), SAfr.
50/F5 **Bregalnica** (riv.), Macd.
45/H3 **Bregenz**, Aus.
37/M6 **Breidhafjördhur** (bay), Ice.
94/B1 **Brejo**, Braz.
94/C2 **Brejo Santo**, Braz.
41/F2 **Bremen**, Ger.
41/F2 **Bremen** (state), Ger.
76/E7 **Bremer** (riv.), Austl.
41/F1 **Bremerhaven**, Ger.
116/B2 **Bremerton**, Wa,US
41/G2 **Bremervörde**, Ger.
34/C4 **Brendon** (hills), Eng,UK
112/D4 **Brenham**, Tx,US
32/E5 **Brenig, Llyn** (lake), Wal,UK
44/F3 **Brenne** (riv.), Fr.
45/J3 **Brenner** (Brennerpass) (pass), Aus.
31/N7 **Brent** (bor.), Eng,UK
31/N7 **Brent** (res.), Eng,UK
31/N7 **Brent** (riv.), Eng,UK
45/J4 **Brenta** (riv.), It.
31/P7 **Brentwood**, Eng,UK
116/L11 **Brentwood**, Ca,US
115/G5 **Brentwood**, NY,US
45/J4 **Brescia**, It.
42/A4 **Bresle** (riv.), Fr.
45/J3 **Bressanone**, It.
44/C3 **Bressuire**, Fr.
39/M2 **Brest**, Bela.
44/A2 **Brest**, Fr.
39/M2 **Brest Obl.**, Bela.
44/B2 **Bretagne** (mts.), Fr.
44/B2 **Bretagne** (reg.), Fr.
89/R15 **Bretagne** (pt.), Reun.
31/S11 **Brétigny-sur-Orge**, Fr.
106/E2 **Breton**, Ab,Can
111/K2 **Breton** (cape), NS,Can
75/R10 **Brett** (cape), NZ
31/S11 **Breuillet**, Fr.
40/B4 **Breukelen**, Neth.
93/H4 **Breves**, Braz.
103/K2 **Brevoort** (isl.), NW,Can
111/G2 **Brewer**, Me,US
34/D1 **Brewood**, Eng,UK
109/H2 **Brewster**, Ne,US
106/D3 **Brewster**, Wa,US
113/G4 **Brewton**, Al,US
50/B3 **Brežice**, Slov.
51/G3 **Brezoi**, Rom.
83/K6 **Bria**, CAfr.
45/G4 **Briançon**, Fr.
34/C2 **Brianne, Lyn** (res.), Wal,UK
115/F5 **Brick**, NJ,US
31/M6 **Bricket Wood**, Eng,UK
36/A4 **Bride** (riv.), Ire.
32/D3 **Bride**, IM,UK
112/E4 **Bridge City**, Tx,US
34/C4 **Bridgend**, Wal,UK
108/C3 **Bridgeport**, Ca,US
111/F3 **Bridgeport**, Ct,US
109/G2 **Bridgeport**, Ne,US
110/D4 **Bridgeport**, WV,US
106/F4 **Bridger**, Mt,US
101/K5 **Bridgetown** (cap.), Bar.
77/C4 **Bridgewater**, Austl.
111/H2 **Bridgewater**, NS,Can
110/E4 **Bridgewater**, Va,US
34/D1 **Bridgnorth**, Eng,UK
111/G2 **Bridgton**, Me,US
34/D4 **Bridgwater**, Eng,UK
34/C4 **Bridgwater** (bay), Eng,UK
33/H3 **Bridlington**, Eng,UK
33/H3 **Bridlington** (bay), Eng,UK
34/D5 **Bridport**, Eng,UK
31/U10 **Brie** (reg.), Fr.
31/T10 **Brie-Comte-Robert**, Fr.
39/J3 **Brieg Brzeg**, Pol.
40/B5 **Brielle**, Neth.
115/F5 **Brielle**, NJ,US
33/F4 **Brierfield**, Eng,UK
45/G3 **Brig**, Swi.
33/H4 **Brigg**, Eng,UK
45/H3 **Brig-Glis**, Swi.
108/D2 **Brigham City**, Ut,US
33/G4 **Brighouse**, Eng,UK
35/E5 **Brighstone**, Eng,UK
35/H3 **Brightlingsea**, Eng,UK
76/F6 **Brighton**, Austl.
77/F5 **Brighton**, Austl.
35/F5 **Brighton**, Eng,UK
109/F3 **Brighton**, Co,US
44/F4 **Brignais**, Fr.
44/G5 **Brignoles**, Fr.
31/S11 **Briis-sous-Forges**, Fr.
84/A3 **Brikama**, Gam.
35/E3 **Brill**, Eng,UK
93/H8 **Brillante** (riv.), Braz.
41/F6 **Brilon**, Ger.
33/G5 **Brimington**, Eng,UK
49/E2 **Brindisi**, It.
34/E3 **Brinkworth**, Eng,UK
46/A1 **Brion**, Sp.
116/K11 **Briones** (res.), Ca,US
76/D4 **Brisbane** , Austl.
76/F6 **Brisbane** (riv.), Austl.
76/E6 **Brisbane For. Park**, Austl.
76/E6 **Brisbane** (inset), Austl.
77/C3 **Brisbane Ranges Nat'l Park**, Austl.
77/D2 **Brisbane Waters Nat'l Park**, Austl.
34/B4 **Bristol** (chan.), UK
34/D4 **Bristol**, Eng,UK
114/F4 **Bristol** (bay), Ak,US
115/F5 **Bristol**, Pa,US
113/H2 **Bristol**, Tn,US
109/H4 **Bristow**, Ok,US
114/K2 **British** (mts.), Yk,Can, Ak,US
102/D3 **British Columbia** (prov.), Can.
103/S6 **British Empire** (range), NW,Can
58/G10 **British Indian Ocean Terr.**
88/P12 **Brits**, SAfr.
44/B2 **Brittany** (reg.), Fr.
107/J4 **Britton**, SD,US
44/D4 **Brive-la-Gaillarde**, Fr.
34/C6 **Brixham**, Eng,UK
35/F2 **Brixworth**, Eng,UK
39/J4 **Brno**, Czh.
76/C3 **Broad** (sound), Austl.
114/J3 **Broad** (pass), Ak,US
113/H3 **Broad** (riv.), NC, SC,US
110/E1 **Broadback** (riv.), Qu,Can
36/D3 **Broad Law** (mtn.), Sc,UK
77/F5 **Broadmeadows**, Austl.
76/C3 **Broad Sound** (chan.), Austl.
35/H4 **Broadstairs**, Eng,UK
35/E5 **Broadstone**, Eng,UK
107/G4 **Broadus**, Mt,US
77/E1 **Broadwater Nat'l Park**, Austl.
35/E2 **Broadway**, Eng,UK
35/E2 **Broadway** (hill), Eng,UK
34/D5 **Broadwindsor**, Eng,UK
103/R7 **Brock** (isl.), NW,Can
41/H5 **Brocken** (peak), Ger.
35/E5 **Brockenhurst**, Eng,UK
111/G3 **Brockton**, Ma,US
110/F2 **Brockville**, On,Can
102/G1 **Brodeur** (pen.), NW,Can
115/E4 **Brodhead** (cr.), Pa,US
39/K2 **Brodnica**, Pol.
40/B3 **Broek Op Langedijk**, Neth.
77/D2 **Broken** (bay), Austl.
109/J3 **Broken Arrow**, Ok,US
109/H2 **Broken Bow**, Ne,US
109/J4 **Broken Bow**, Ok,US
109/J4 **Broken Bow** (lake), Ok,US
77/B1 **Broken Hill**, Austl.
112/B3 **Brokeoff** (mts.), NM,US
31/P7 **Bromley**, Eng,UK
31/P7 **Bromley** (bor.), Eng,UK
31/P7 **Bromley Common**, Eng,UK
34/D2 **Bromsgrove**, Eng,UK
34/D2 **Bromyard**, Eng,UK
44/F4 **Bron**, Fr.
37/D4 **Brønderslev**, Den.
85/E5 **Brong-Ahafo** (reg.), Gha.
45/H4 **Broni**, It.
34/C3 **Bronllys**, Wal,UK
37/E2 **Brønnøysund**, Nor.
111/Q9 **Bronte**, On,Can
48/D4 **Bronte**, It.
115/G5 **Bronx** (co.), NY,US
67/C6 **Brooke's Point**, Phil.
116/Q16 **Brookfield**, Il,US
109/J3 **Brookfield**, Mo,US
116/P13 **Brookfield**, Wi,US
113/F4 **Brookhaven**, Ms,US
115/H5 **Brookhaven**, NY,US
107/J4 **Brookings**, SD,US
115/G5 **Brooklyn (Kings)** (co.), NY,US
115/K7 **Brooklyn Park**, Md,US
31/N6 **Brookmans Park**, Eng,UK
106/F3 **Brooks**, Ab,Can
114/H2 **Brooks** (mtn.), Ak,US
114/F2 **Brooks** (range), Ak,US
113/H4 **Brooksville**, Fl,US
115/E6 **Broomall**, Pa,US
111/P7 **Brossard**, Qu,Can
33/H2 **Brotton**, Eng,UK
33/F2 **Brough**, Eng,UK
111/R8 **Brougham**, On,Can
32/B2 **Broughshane**, NI,UK
35/F2 **Broughton**, Eng,UK
33/E3 **Broughton in Furness**, Eng,UK
35/G4 **Broughton Street**, Eng,UK
40/A5 **Brouwersdam** (dam), Neth.
67/C5 **Brown** (shoal)
34/D2 **Brown Clee** (hill), Eng,UK
112/C3 **Brownfield**, Tx,US
35/E1 **Brownhills**, Eng,UK
106/E3 **Browning**, Mt,US
35/E5 **Brownsea** (isl.), Eng,UK
115/F6 **Browns Mills**, NJ,US
113/F3 **Brownsville**, Tn,US
112/D5 **Brownsville**, Tx,US
34/B5 **Brown Willy** (hill), Eng,UK
112/D4 **Brownwood**, Tx,US
31/N6 **Broxbourne**, Eng,UK
42/B3 **Bruay-en-Artois**, Fr.
42/C3 **Bruay-sur-l'Escaut**, Fr.
74/B4 **Bruce** (peak), Austl.
110/D2 **Bruce** (pen.), On,Can
45/G2 **Bruche** (riv.), Fr.
43/G5 **Bruchmühlbach-Miesau**, Ger.
45/H2 **Bruchsal**, Ger.
41/G5 **Brucht** (riv.), Ger.
45/K3 **Bruck an der Grossglockner-strasse**, Aus.
50/C1 **Bruck an der Leitha**, Aus.
45/L3 **Bruck an der Mur**, Aus.
38/F5 **Bruckmühl**, Ger.
34/D4 **Brue** (riv.), Eng,UK
42/C1 **Bruges** (Brugge), Belg.
40/D6 **Brüggen**, Ger.
43/F2 **Brühl**, Ger.
88/B2 **Brukkaros** (peak), Namb.
94/B4 **Brumado**, Braz.
43/G6 **Brumath**, Fr.
40/D4 **Brummen**, Neth.
37/D3 **Brumunddal**, Nor.
48/A2 **Bruncu Spina** (peak), It.
35/H1 **Brundall**, Eng,UK
42/D4 **Brune** (riv.), Fr.
108/D2 **Bruneau** (riv.), Id, Nv,US
72/D2 **Brunei**
45/J3 **Brunico**, It.
31/T10 **Brunoy**, Fr.
41/G1 **Brunsbüttel**, Ger.
43/E2 **Brunssum**, Neth.
77/F5 **Brunswick**, Austl.
97/J8 **Brunswick** (pen.), Chile
113/H4 **Brunswick**, Ga,US
111/G3 **Brunswick**, Me,US
110/D3 **Brunswick**, Oh,US
41/H4 **Brunswick** (Braunschweig), Ger.
95/B3 **Brusque**, Braz.
42/D2 **Brussels** (Bruxelles) (cap.), Belg.
34/D4 **Bruton**, Eng,UK
31/S11 **Bruyères-le-Châtel**, Fr.
31/S9 **Bruyères-sur-Oise**, Fr.
44/C2 **Bruz**, Fr.
98/U **Bryan** (coast), Ant.
110/C3 **Bryan**, Oh,US
112/D4 **Bryan**, Tx,US
54/E1 **Bryansk**, Rus.
54/E1 **Bryansk Obl.**, Rus.
108/D3 **Bryce Canyon Nat'l Park**, Ut,US
33/E5 **Brymbo**, Wal,UK
34/C2 **Bryn Brawd** (mtn.), Wal,UK
34/C3 **Brynithel**, Wal,UK
34/C3 **Brynmawr**, Wal,UK
39/J3 **Brzeg Dolny**, Pol.
39/L4 **Brzesko**, Pol.
39/M4 **Brzozów**, Pol.
69/C3 **Bua Yai**, Thai.
84/B4 **Buba**, GBis.
84/B4 **Bubaque**, GBis.
60/E3 **Būbiyan** (isl.), Kuw.
31/S10 **Buc**, Fr.
59/B3 **Bucak**, Turk.
92/D2 **Bucaramanga**, Col.
47/P10 **Bucelas**, Port.
103/J1 **Buchan** (gulf), NW,Can
84/C5 **Buchanan**, Libr.
109/H5 **Buchanan** (lake), Tx,US
111/K1 **Buchans**, Nf,Can
51/H3 **Bucharest** (Bucureşti) (cap.), Rom.
41/G2 **Buchholz in der Nordheide**, Ger.
108/B4 **Buchon** (pt.), Ca,US
33/F3 **Buckden Pike** (mtn.), Eng,UK
41/G4 **Bückeburg**, Ger.
34/C6 **Buckfastleigh**, Eng,UK
110/D4 **Buckhannon**, WV,US
31/P7 **Buckhurst Hill**, Eng,UK
36/D2 **Buckie**, Sc,UK
110/F2 **Buckingham**, Qu,Can
35/F3 **Buckingham**, Eng,UK
31/N7 **Buckingham Palace**, Eng,UK
35/F3 **Buckinghamshire** (co.), Eng,UK
33/E5 **Buckley**, Wal,UK
34/D2 **Bucknell**, Eng,UK
36/D2 **Bucksburn**, Sc,UK
111/H2 **Buctouche**, NB,Can
51/H3 **Bucureşti** (Bucharest) (cap.), Rom.

110/D3 **Bucyrus**, Oh,US
50/D2 **Budaörs**, Hun.
50/D2 **Budapest** (cap.), Hun.
70/C2 **Budaun**, India
98/H **Budd** (coast), Ant.
116/B3 **Budd** (inlet), Wa,US
115/F5 **Budd Lake**, NJ,US
34/B5 **Bude**, Eng,UK
34/B5 **Bude** (bay), Eng,UK
40/C6 **Budel**, Neth.
38/E1 **Büdelsdorf**, Ger.
45/H1 **Büdingen**, Ger.
83/J7 **Budjala**, Zaire
34/C5 **Budleigh Salterton**, Eng,UK
50/D4 **Budva**, Yugo.
51/J2 **Budzhak** (reg.), Mol., Ukr.
82/G7 **Buea**, Camr.
115/C3 **Buena Park**, Ca,US
92/C3 **Buenaventura**, Col.
109/F3 **Buena Vista**, Co,US
110/E4 **Buena Vista**, Va,US
96/B4 **Bueno** (riv.), Chile
96/F2 **Buenos Aires** (cap.), Arg.
96/C5 **Buenos Aires** (lake), Arg.
96/E3 **Buenos Aires** (prov.), Arg.
97/S12 **Buenos Aires** (inset) (cap.), Arg.
94/C4 **Buerarema**, Braz.
46/A1 **Bueu**, Sp.
77/C3 **Buffalo** (peak), Austl.
106/E2 **Buffalo** (lake), Ab,Can
89/E2 **Buffalo** (riv.), SAfr.
112/E2 **Buffalo** (riv.), Ar,US
107/K4 **Buffalo**, Mn,US
109/J3 **Buffalo**, Mo,US
111/S10 **Buffalo**, NY,US
109/H3 **Buffalo**, Ok,US
107/H4 **Buffalo**, SD,US
113/G3 **Buffalo** (riv.), Tn,US
106/G4 **Buffalo**, Wy,US
116/Q15 **Buffalo Grove**, Il,US
106/F2 **Buffalo Narrows**, Sk,Can
77/B1 **Buffalo Riv. Overflow** (swamp), Austl.
88/B3 **Buffelsrivier** (dry riv.), SAfr.
113/G3 **Buford**, Ga,US
51/G3 **Buftea**, Rom.
54/B1 **Bug** (riv.), Eur.
51/K2 **Bug** (estuary), Ukr.
92/C3 **Buga**, Col.
100/E6 **Bugaba**, Pan.
44/E5 **Bugarach, Pic de** (peak), Fr.
35/E2 **Bugbrooke**, Eng,UK
72/D5 **Bugel** (pt.), Indo.
42/D1 **Buggenhout**, Belg.
50/C3 **Bugojno**, Bosn.
73/E2 **Bugsuk** (isl.), Phil.
53/M5 **Bugul'ma**, Rus.
55/K1 **Buguruslan**, Rus.
62/D4 **Buh** (riv.), China
59/D3 **Buhayrat al Asad** (lake), Turk.
60/D2 **Buḩayrat ath Tharthār** (lake), Iraq
106/E5 **Buhl**, Id,US
51/H2 **Buhuşi**, Rom.
85/E4 **Bui** (dam), Gha.
85/E4 **Bui Gorge** (res.), Gha.
34/C2 **Builth Wells**, Wal,UK
96/Q9 **Buin**, Chile
46/C4 **Bujalance**, Sp.
50/E4 **Bujanovac**, Yugo.
51/H3 **Bujor**, Rom.
87/E1 **Bujumbura** (cap.), Buru.
39/J2 **Buk**, Pol.
78/E5 **Buka** (isl.), PNG
62/H1 **Bukachacha**, Rus.
68/F4 **Bukadaban Feng** (peak), China
60/E1 **Būkān**, Iran
87/E1 **Bukavu**, Zaire
69/C5 **Buket Bubat** (peak), Malay.
56/G6 **Bukhara**, Uzb.
62/A2 **Bukhtarma** (riv.), Kaz.
72/B4 **Bukittinggi**, Indo.
50/E1 **Bükki Nat'l Park**, Hun.
87/F1 **Bukoba**, Tanz.
72/B4 **Buku** (cape), Indo.
67/D5 **Bulan**, Phil.
70/C2 **Bulandshahr**, India
59/E2 **Bulanık**, Turk.
73/F3 **Bulawa** (peak), Indo.
87/E5 **Bulawayo**, Zim.
114/B5 **Buldir** (isl.), Ak,US
62/C2 **Bulgan** (riv.), Mong.
51/G4 **Bulgaria**
48/D2 **Bulgheria** (peak), It.
67/C6 **Bulilyan** (cape), Phil.
76/F7 **Bulimba** (cr.), Austl.
35/E2 **Bulkington**, Eng,UK
106/B2 **Bulkley** (riv.), BC,Can
32/B1 **Bull** (pt.), NI,UK
46/E3 **Bullas**, Sp.
77/C3 **Buller** (peak), Austl.
108/D4 **Bullhead City**, Az,US
43/F3 **Büllingen**, Belg.
31/R11 **Bullion**, Fr.
76/A5 **Bulloo** (riv.), Austl.
109/J3 **Bull Shoals** (lake), Ar, Mo,US
42/B3 **Bully-les-Mines**, Fr.
62/D2 **Bulnayn** (mts.), Mong.
96/B3 **Bulnes**, Chile
78/D5 **Bulolo**, PNG
31/Q7 **Bulphan**, Eng,UK
73/F5 **Bulukumba**, Indo.
87/D2 **Bulungu**, Zaire
83/K7 **Bumba**, Zaire
83/N7 **Buna**, Kenya
65/L9 **Bunaga-take** (peak), Japan
87/F1 **Bunazi**, Tanz.
74/B6 **Bunbury**, Austl.
76/D4 **Bundaberg**, Austl.
41/F4 **Bünde**, Ger.
70/C2 **Būndi**, India
35/H2 **Bungay**, Eng,UK
72/C3 **Bunguran** (isl.), Indo.
83/M7 **Bunia**, Zaire
113/H4 **Bunnell**, Fl,US
40/C4 **Bunnik**, Neth.
47/E3 **Buñol**, Sp.
40/C4 **Bunschoten**, Neth.
35/F3 **Buntingford**, Eng,UK
76/C4 **Bunya Mountains Nat'l Park**, Austl.
59/C2 **Bünyan**, Turk.
76/E6 **Bunya Park**, Austl.
73/E3 **Bunyu** (isl.), Indo.
69/E3 **Buon Me Thuot**, Viet.
69/E3 **Buon Mrong**, Viet.
94/C3 **Buquim**, Braz.
83/N8 **Bura**, Kenya
83/L5 **Buram**, Sudan
83/M7 **Buranga** (pass), Ugan.
83/Q6 **Burao** (Burco), Som.
113/F4 **Buras-Triumph**, La,US
67/D5 **Burauen**, Phil.
60/D3 **Buraydah**, SAr.
43/H2 **Burbach**, Ger.
115/B2 **Burbank**, Ca,US
116/Q16 **Burbank**, Il,US
83/Q6 **Burco** (Burao), Som.
76/B3 **Burdekin** (riv.), Austl.
116/J10 **Burdell** (mtn.), Ca,US
59/B3 **Burdur**, Turk.
70/E3 **Burdwān**, India
35/H1 **Bure** (riv.), Eng,UK
41/F5 **Büren**, Ger.
40/C5 **Buren**, Neth.
62/E2 **Bürengiyn** (mts.), Mong.
31/S10 **Bures-sur-Yvette**, Fr.
61/K2 **Būrewāla**, Pak.
63/L1 **Bureya** (mts.), Rus.
63/L1 **Bureya** (riv.), Rus.
35/E3 **Burford**, Eng,UK
51/H4 **Burgas**, Bul.
51/H4 **Burgas** (bay), Bul.
51/H4 **Burgas** (reg.), Bul.
41/H4 **Burgdorf**, Ger.
45/M3 **Burgenland** (prov.), Aus.
111/K2 **Burgeo**, Nf,Can
88/D3 **Burgersdorp**, SAfr.
114/L2 **Burgess** (mtn.), Yk,Can
35/F5 **Burgess Hill**, Eng,UK
37/E2 **Burgfjället** (peak), Swe.
33/J5 **Burgh le Marsh**, Eng,UK
45/K2 **Burglengenfeld**, Ger.
46/D1 **Burgos**, Sp.
41/E4 **Burgsteinfurt**, Ger.
44/F3 **Burgundy** (hist. reg.), Fr.
41/G3 **Burgwedel**, Ger.
62/D4 **Burhan Budai** (mts.), China
59/A2 **Burhaniye**, Turk.
70/C3 **Burhānpur**, India
100/E6 **Burica** (pen.), CR, Pan.
100/E6 **Burica** (pt.), Pan.
116/C3 **Burien**, Wa,US
111/L2 **Burin**, Nf,Can
111/K2 **Burin** (pen.), Nf,Can
69/C3 **Buriram**, Thai.
95/B2 **Buritama**, Braz.
94/B1 **Buriti**, Braz.
95/B1 **Buriti Alegre**, Braz.
94/B2 **Buriti Bravo**, Braz.
94/A4 **Buritis**, Braz.
95/C1 **Buritizeiro**, Braz.
47/E3 **Burjasot**, Sp.
112/D3 **Burkburnett**, Tx,US
98/S **Burke** (isl.), Ant.
115/J8 **Burke**, Va,US
106/B2 **Burke Channel** (inlet), BC,Can
85/E3 **Burkina Faso**
106/E5 **Burley**, Id,US
116/K11 **Burlingame**, Ca,US
111/Q9 **Burlington**, On,Can
109/G3 **Burlington**, Co,US
107/L5 **Burlington**, Ia,US
109/J3 **Burlington**, Ks,US
113/J2 **Burlington**, NC,US
115/F5 **Burlington**, NJ,US
111/F2 **Burlington**, Vt,US
116/P14 **Burlington**, Wi,US
71/G2 **Burma** (Myanmar)
51/K3 **Burnas** (lake), Ukr.
112/D4 **Burnet**, Tx,US
97/J8 **Burney** (peak), Chile
108/B2 **Burney**, Ca,US
35/G3 **Burnham on Crouch**, Eng,UK
34/D4 **Burnham on Sea**, Eng,UK
77/C4 **Burnie-Somerset**, Austl.
33/F4 **Burnley**, Eng,UK
106/D5 **Burns**, Or,US
102/E2 **Burnside** (riv.), NW,Can
106/B2 **Burns Lake**, BC,Can
107/J2 **Burntwood** (riv.), Mb,Can
35/E1 **Burntwood**, Eng,UK
77/B2 **Buronga**, Austl.
62/B2 **Burqin** (riv.), China
75/H6 **Burragorang** (lake), Austl.
49/G2 **Burrel**, Alb.
77/D2 **Burrendong** (res.), Austl.
77/D2 **Burrewarra** (pt.), Austl.
47/E3 **Burriana**, Sp.
77/D2 **Burrinjuck** (res.), Austl.
76/A2 **Burrowes** (pt.), Austl.
32/D2 **Burrow Head** (pt.), Sc,UK
116/Q16 **Burr Ridge**, Il,US
76/D4 **Burrum River Nat'l Park**, Austl.
34/B3 **Burry** (inlet), Wal,UK
34/B3 **Burry Port**, Wal,UK
51/J5 **Bursa**, Turk.
51/J5 **Bursa** (prov.), Turk.
86/C3 **Būr Safājah**, Egypt
59/J6 **Būr Sa'īd** (gov.), Egypt
59/J6 **Būr Sa'īd** (Port Said), Egypt
41/E6 **Burscheid**, Ger.
33/F4 **Burscough Bridge**, Eng,UK
86/D5 **Būr Sūdān** (Port Sudan), Sudan
111/S9 **Burt**, NY,US
86/C2 **Būr Tawfīq**, Egypt
35/E5 **Burton**, Eng,UK
116/E6 **Burton**, Mi,US
35/F2 **Burton Latimer**, Eng,UK
35/E1 **Burton upon Trent**, Eng,UK
73/G4 **Buru** (isl.), Indo.
59/H6 **Burullus, Buḩayrat al** (lag.), Egypt
87/E1 **Burundi**
62/F2 **Burun Shibertuy** (peak), Rus.
94/A2 **Buruticupu** (riv.), Braz.
114/L3 **Burwash Landing**, Yk,Can
35/G2 **Burwell**, Eng,UK
109/H2 **Burwell**, Ne,US
35/F5 **Bury**, Eng,UK
57/M4 **Buryat Aut. Rep.**, Rus.
55/J3 **Burynshyk** (pt.), Kaz.
35/G2 **Bury Saint Edmunds**, Eng,UK
45/H4 **Busalla**, It.
32/B1 **Bush** (riv.), NI,UK
62/C2 **Büs Hayrhan** (peak), Mong.
31/M7 **Bushey**, Eng,UK
115/E4 **Bushkill** (falls), Pa,US
88/B3 **Bushmanland** (reg.), SAfr.
32/B1 **Bushmills**, NI,UK
83/K7 **Businga**, Zaire
37/D3 **Buskerud** (co.), Nor.
39/L3 **Busko-Zdrój**, Pol.
74/B6 **Busselton**, Austl.
83/L6 **Busseri** (riv.), Sudan
40/C4 **Bussum**, Neth.
97/K7 **Bustamente** (pt.), Arg.
76/C4 **Bustard** (pt.), Austl.
51/G3 **Buşteni**, Rom.
45/H4 **Busto Arsizio**, It.
67/C5 **Busuanga** (isl.), Phil.
83/K7 **Buta**, Zaire
87/E1 **Butare**, Rwa.
78/G4 **Butaritari** (atoll), Kiri.
106/B3 **Bute** (inlet), BC,Can
36/C3 **Bute** (isl.), Sc,UK
62/E2 **Büteeliyn** (mts.), Mong.
83/L7 **Butembo**, Zaire
95/B4 **Butiá**, Braz.
110/E3 **Butler**, Pa,US
73/F5 **Buton** (isl.), Indo.
31/S9 **Butry-sur-Oise**, Fr.
106/E4 **Butte**, Mt,US
72/B2 **Butterworth**, Malay.
73/F5 **Butung** (isl.), Indo.
55/G2 **Buturlinovka**, Rus.
45/H1 **Butzbach**, Ger.
38/F2 **Bützow**, Ger.
83/Q7 **Buulo Berde**, Som.
83/P7 **Buur Hakaba**, Som.
41/G2 **Buxtehude**, Ger.
33/G5 **Buxton**, Eng,UK
52/J4 **Buy**, Rus.
55/H4 **Buynaksk**, Rus.
84/D5 **Buyo, Barrage de** (dam), IvC.
63/H2 **Buyr** (lake), Mong.
51/J5 **Büyükçekmece**, Turk.
59/B3 **Büyük Menderes** (riv.), Turk.
66/E2 **Buyun Shan** (peak), China
55/J3 **Buzachi** (pen.), Kaz.
51/H3 **Buzău**, Rom.
51/H3 **Buzău** (co.), Rom.
51/H3 **Buzău** (riv.), Rom.
50/E3 **Buziaş**, Rom.
95/H8 **Búzios** (isl.), Braz.
55/K1 **Buzuluk**, Rus.
51/F4 **Byala Slatina**, Bul.
103/R7 **Byam Martin** (chan.), NW,Can
103/R7 **Byam Martin** (isl.), NW,Can
39/J2 **Bydgoszcz**, Pol.
39/J2 **Bydgoszcz** (prov.), Pol.
35/E2 **Byfield**, Eng,UK
31/M8 **Byfleet**, Eng,UK
54/D1 **Bykhov**, Bela.
32/E5 **Bylchau**, Wal,UK
103/J1 **Bylot** (isl.), NW,Can
115/G5 **Byram** (pt.), NY,US
98/U **Byrd** (cape), Ant.
98/U **Byrd** (glac.), Ant.
97/J6 **Byron** (isl.), Chile
56/K2 **Byrranga** (mts.), Rus.
39/K4 **Bystrá** (peak), Slvk.
57/N3 **Bytantay** (riv.), Rus.
39/K3 **Bytom**, Pol.
39/J1 **Bytów**, Pol.

C

69/D2 **Ca** (riv.), Viet.
87/C3 **Caála**, Ang.
94/B2 **Caatingas** (reg.), Braz.
67/E6 **Cabadbaran**, Phil.
101/F3 **Cabaiguán**, Cuba
108/F4 **Caballo** (res.), NM,US
46/C1 **Cabañaquinta**, Sp.
67/D4 **Cabanatuan**, Phil.
34/C2 **Caban Coch** (res.), Wal,UK
111/G2 **Cabano**, Qu,Can
94/D2 **Cabedelo**, Braz.
44/E5 **Cabestany**, Fr.
46/C3 **Cabeza del Buey**, Sp.
46/C1 **Cabezón de la Sal**, Sp.
101/G5 **Cabimas**, Ven.
87/B2 **Cabinda**, Ang.
94/D3 **Cabo**, Braz.
82/C2 **Cabo Bojador**, WSah.
95/D2 **Cabo Frio**, Braz.
110/E2 **Cabonga** (res.), Qu,Can
76/D4 **Caboolture**, Austl.
93/H3 **Cabo Orange Nat'l Park**, Braz.
87/F4 **Cabora Bassa** (lake), Moz.
111/J2 **Cabot** (str.), Nf, NS,Can
95/G6 **Cabo Verde**, Braz.
46/C4 **Cabra**, Sp.
94/A5 **Cabral** (mts.), Braz.
76/G8 **Cabramatta**, Austl.
48/A3 **Cabras**, It.
47/G3 **Cabrera** (isl.), Sp.
106/F3 **Cabri**, Sk,Can
46/E3 **Cabriel** (riv.), Sp.
94/C3 **Cabrobó**, Braz.
67/D4 **Cabugao**, Phil.
101/H5 **Cabure**, Ven.
95/B3 **Caçador**, Braz.
50/E4 **Čačak**, Yugo.
95/H8 **Caçapava**, Braz.
48/A2 **Caccia** (cape), It.
92/G7 **Cáceres**, Braz.
46/B3 **Cáceres**, Sp.
31/S10 **Cachan**, Fr.
96/Q10 **Cachapoal** (riv.), Chile
108/B3 **Cache** (cr.), Ca,US
106/E5 **Cache** (peak), Id,US
106/C3 **Cache Creek**, BC,Can
84/A3 **Cacheu**, GBis.
93/G5 **Cachimbo** (mts.), Braz.
95/A4 **Cachoeira do Sul**, Braz.
95/J7 **Cachoeira Paulista**, Braz.
95/L7 **Cachoeiras de Macacu**, Braz.
95/B4 **Cachoeirinha**, Braz.
95/D2 **Cachoeiro de Itapemirim**, Braz.
95/G6 **Caconde**, Braz.
95/B1 **Caçu**, Braz.
87/B3 **Cacula**, Ang.
94/B4 **Caculé**, Braz.
47/G1 **Cadaques**, Sp.
39/K4 **Čadca**, Slvk.
112/E3 **Caddo** (mts.), Ar,US
34/C1 **Cader Idris** (mtn.), Wal,UK
74/E5 **Cadibarrawirracanna** (lake), Austl.
110/C2 **Cadillac**, Mi,US
67/D5 **Cadiz**, Phil.
46/B4 **Cádiz**, Sp.
46/B4 **Cádiz** (gulf), Sp.
110/C4 **Cadiz**, Ky,US
35/E5 **Cadnam**, Eng,UK
44/C2 **Caen**, Fr.
34/D3 **Caerleon**, Wal,UK
32/D5 **Caernarfon**, Wal,UK
32/D5 **Caernarfon** (bay), Wal,UK
34/C3 **Caerphilly**, Wal,UK
34/C1 **Caersws**, Wal,UK
59/M7 **Caesarea Nat'l Park**, Isr.
42/B2 **Caëstre**, Fr.
94/B4 **Caetité**, Braz.
91/C2 **Cafayate**, Arg.
67/D6 **Cagayan de Oro**, Phil.
67/C6 **Cagayan Sulu** (isl.), Phil.
48/A3 **Cagliari**, It.
48/A3 **Cagliari** (gulf), It.
45/G5 **Cagnes-sur-Mer**, Fr.
92/D3 **Caguán** (riv.), Col.
101/H4 **Caguas**, PR
87/B4 **Cahama**, Ang.
36/B4 **Cahore** (pt.), Ire.
44/D4 **Cahors**, Fr.
95/B4 **Caí** (riv.), Braz.
93/H7 **Caiapó** (mts.), Braz.
93/H7 **Caiapó** (riv.), Braz.
101/F3 **Caibarién**, Cuba
94/C2 **Caicó**, Braz.
101/G3 **Caicos** (isls.), Trks.
95/G8 **Caieiras**, Braz.
42/A4 **Cailly** (riv.), Fr.
69/D4 **Cai Nuoc**, Viet.
98/Y **Caird** (coast), Ant.
114/G3 **Cairn** (mtn.), Ak,US
77/B3 **Cairn Curran** (dam), Austl.
36/D2 **Cairngorm** (mts.), Sc,UK
32/C2 **Cairn Pat** (hill), Sc,UK
32/C2 **Cairnryan**, Sc,UK
76/B2 **Cairns**, Austl.
32/D1 **Cairnsmore of Carsphairn** (mtn.), Sc,UK
113/G4 **Cairo**, Ga,US
110/B4 **Cairo**, Il,US
86/B2 **Cairo** (Al Qāhirah) (cap.), Egypt
35/H1 **Caister on Sea**, Eng,UK
33/H5 **Caistor**, Eng,UK
111/Q9 **Caistor Centre**, On,Can
111/Q9 **Caistorville**, On,Can
87/B3 **Caitou**, Ang.
87/C4 **Caiundo**, Ang.
66/C5 **Caizi** (lake), China
92/C5 **Cajabamba**, Peru
92/C5 **Cajamarca**, Peru
94/C2 **Cajazeiras**, Braz.
100/E3 **Cajón** (pt.), Cuba
94/B1 **Caju** (isl.), Braz.
85/G5 **Calabar**, Nga.
101/H6 **Calabozo**, Ven.
48/E3 **Calabria** (reg.), It.
48/E3 **Calabria Nat'l Park**, It.
46/C4 **Calaburras, Punta de** (pt.), Sp.
50/F4 **Calafat**, Rom.
46/E1 **Calahorra**, Sp.
42/A2 **Calais**, Fr.
111/H2 **Calais**, Me,US
42/A2 **Calais, Canal de** (can.), Fr.
91/C2 **Calalaste** (mts.), Arg.
91/C1 **Calama**, Chile
67/C5 **Calamian Group** (isls.), Phil.
50/F3 **Călan**, Rom.
67/D5 **Calapan**, Phil.
51/H3 **Călăraşi**, Rom.
51/H3 **Călăraşi** (co.), Rom.
46/E3 **Calasparra**, Sp.
46/E2 **Calatayud**, Sp.
116/L12 **Calaveras** (res.), Ca,US
67/D4 **Calayan**, Phil.
67/D4 **Calayan** (isl.), Phil.
67/D5 **Calbayog**, Phil.
96/B4 **Calbuco**, Chile
92/D6 **Calca**, Peru
94/D2 **Calcanhar, Ponta do** (pt.), Braz.
112/E4 **Calcasieu** (riv.), La,US
110/F2 **Calcium**, NY,US
70/E3 **Calcutta**, India
46/A3 **Caldas da Rainha**, Port.
95/B1 **Caldas Novas**, Braz.
33/E2 **Caldbeck**, Eng,UK
41/G6 **Calden**, Ger.
33/G4 **Calder** (riv.), Eng,UK
114/M4 **Calder** (mtn.), Ak,US
47/L6 **Caldes de Montbui**, Sp.
33/F2 **Caldew** (riv.), Eng,UK
34/D3 **Caldicot**, Wal,UK
106/D5 **Caldwell**, Id,US
112/D4 **Caldwell**, Tx,US
34/B3 **Caldy** (isl.), Wal,UK
88/D3 **Caledon** (riv.), Les., SAfr.
111/Q8 **Caledon East**, On,Can
111/H2 **Caledonia** (hills), NB,Can
47/G2 **Calella**, Sp.
96/Q9 **Calera de Tango**, Chile
101/P9 **Calera Víctor Rosales**, Mex.
101/P10 **Caleta de Campos Chutla**, Mex.
96/D5 **Caleta Olivia**, Arg.
108/D4 **Calexico**, Ca,US
33/F3 **Calf, The** (mtn.), Eng,UK
106/E3 **Calgary**, Ab,Can
47/S12 **Calheta**, Azor.,Port.
47/U15 **Calheta**, Madr.,Port.
113/G3 **Calhoun**, Ga,US
110/C4 **Calhoun**, Ky,US
92/C3 **Cali**, Col.
46/E4 **Calida, Costa** (coast), Sp.
108/D3 **Caliente**, Nv,US
101/M8 **California** (gulf), Mex.
108/B3 **California** (state), US
110/E4 **California**, Md,US
109/J3 **California**, Mo,US
91/D1 **Calilegua Nat'l Park**, Arg.
51/G3 **Călimăneşti**, Rom.
70/C5 **Calimere** (pt.), India
115/C2 **Calimesa**, Ca,US
100/C3 **Calkiní**, Mex.
77/A1 **Callabonna** (lake), Austl.
36/C2 **Callander**, Sc,UK
92/C6 **Callao**, Peru
113/G4 **Callaway**, Fl,US
96/Q9 **Calle Larga**, Chile
34/B6 **Callington**, Eng,UK
47/E3 **Callosa de Ensarriá**, Sp.
47/E3 **Callosa de Segura**, Sp.
34/D4 **Calne**, Eng,UK
42/B3 **Calonne-Ricouart**, Fr.
48/D2 **Calore** (riv.), It.
76/D4 **Caloundra**, Austl.
47/F3 **Calpe**, Sp.
34/B6 **Calstock**, Eng,UK
48/D4 **Caltagirone**, It.
48/D4 **Caltanissetta**, It.
44/F4 **Caluire-et-Cuire**, Fr.
116/Q16 **Calumet** (riv.), Il,US
116/Q16 **Calumet City**, Il,US
87/B3 **Caluquembe**, Ang.
106/A3 **Calvert** (isl.), BC,Can
33/G5 **Calverton**, Eng,UK
115/K7 **Calverton**, Md,US
115/H5 **Calverton**, NY,US
47/G3 **Calviá**, Sp.
88/B3 **Calvinia**, SAfr.
46/C2 **Calvitero** (mtn.), Sp.
35/G2 **Cam** (riv.), Eng,UK
94/C4 **Camaçari**, Braz.
87/C3 **Camacupa**, Ang.
101/F3 **Camagüey**, Cuba
101/F3 **Camagüey** (arch.), Cuba
45/J5 **Camaiore**, It.
94/C4 **Camamu**, Braz.
94/C4 **Camamu** (bay), Braz.
92/D7 **Camaná**, Peru
95/B4 **Camaquã**, Braz.
95/A4 **Camaquã** (riv.), Braz.
47/V15 **Câmara de Lobos**, Madr.,Port.
45/G5 **Camarat** (cape), Fr.
46/D1 **Camargo**, Sp.
115/A2 **Camarillo**, Ca,US
46/A1 **Camariñas**, Sp.
100/D4 **Camarón** (cape), Hon.
96/D5 **Camarones** (bay), Arg.
46/B4 **Camas**, Sp.
69/D4 **Ca Mau**, Viet.
69/D4 **Ca Mau** (cape), Viet.
46/A1 **Cambados**, Sp.
95/B2 **Cambará**, Braz.
70/B3 **Cambay**, India
70/B3 **Cambay** (gulf), India
95/B2 **Cambé**, Braz.
35/F4 **Camberley Frimley**, Eng,UK
31/N7 **Camberwell**, Eng,UK
69/D3 **Cambodia**
95/C3 **Camboriú, Ponta do** (pt.), Braz.
34/A6 **Camborne**, Eng,UK
42/C3 **Cambrai**, Fr.
34/C2 **Cambrian** (mts.), Wal,UK
110/D3 **Cambridge**, On,Can
75/S10 **Cambridge**, NZ
35/G2 **Cambridge**, Eng,UK
111/G3 **Cambridge**, Ma,US
110/E4 **Cambridge**, Md,US
107/K4 **Cambridge**, Mn,US
110/D3 **Cambridge**, Oh,US
35/G2 **Cambridgeshire** (co.), Eng,UK
47/F2 **Cambrils**, Sp.
95/G7 **Cambuí**, Braz.
95/H6 **Cambuquira**, Braz.
101/E6 **Cambutal** (mt.), Pan.
77/D2 **Camden**, Austl.
31/N7 **Camden** (bor.), Eng,UK
113/G4 **Camden**, Al,US
112/E3 **Camden**, Ar,US
111/G2 **Camden**, Me,US
115/F5 **Camden**, NJ,US
113/H3 **Camden**, SC,US
109/J3 **Camdenton**, Mo,US
87/D3 **Cameia Nat'l Park**, Ang.
34/B6 **Camel** (riv.), Eng,UK
115/E4 **Camelback** (mtn.), Pa,US
34/B5 **Camelford**, Eng,UK
103/R7 **Cameron** (isl.), NW,Can
108/E4 **Cameron**, Az,US
112/E4 **Cameron**, La,US
109/J3 **Cameron**, Mo,US
112/D4 **Cameron**, Tx,US
82/H7 **Cameroon**
93/J4 **Cametá**, Braz.
42/A2 **Camiers**, Fr.
67/D4 **Camiguin** (isl.), Phil.
113/G4 **Camilla**, Ga,US
92/F8 **Camiri**, Bol.
87/F5 **Camo-Camo**, Moz.
94/B1 **Camocim**, Braz.
71/F6 **Camorta** (isl.), India
42/A3 **Campagne**, Fr.
96/F2 **Campana**, Arg.
97/J7 **Campana** (isl.), Chile
96/C2 **Campanario** (peak), Arg.
48/D2 **Campanella** (cape), It.
95/H6 **Campanha**, Braz.
48/D2 **Campania** (reg.), It.
29/T8 **Campbell** (isl.), NZ
116/L12 **Campbell**, Ca,US
106/A2 **Campbell Island**, BC,Can
106/B3 **Campbell River**, BC,Can
110/C4 **Campbellsville**, Ky,US
111/H2 **Campbellton**, NB,Can
76/G9 **Campbelltown**, Austl.
111/Q9 **Campbellville**, On,Can
111/R9 **Campden**, On,Can
100/C4 **Campeche**, Mex.
100/C4 **Campeche** (bay), Mex.
100/C4 **Campeche** (state), Mex.
107/H3 **Camperville**, Mb,Can
95/G6 **Campestre**, Braz.
69/D1 **Cam Pha**, Viet.
48/A3 **Campidano** (range), It.
46/C4 **Campillos**, Sp.
94/D2 **Campina Grande**, Braz.
95/F7 **Campinas**, Braz.
95/B1 **Campina Verde**, Braz.
92/C3 **Campoalegre**, Col.
48/D2 **Campobasso**, It.
95/C2 **Campo Belo**, Braz.
46/D3 **Campo de Criptana**, Sp.
101/G5 **Campo de la Cruz**, Col.
94/B3 **Campo Formoso**, Braz.
93/H8 **Campo Grande**, Braz.
91/G2 **Campo Largo**, Braz.
95/G8 **Campo Limpo Paulista**, Braz.
94/B2 **Campo Maior**, Braz.
46/B3 **Campo Maior**, Port.
45/H4 **Campomorone**, It.
95/A3 **Campo Mourão**, Braz.
94/C2 **Campo Redondo**, Braz.
46/C1 **Camporredondo** (res.), Sp.
95/D2 **Campos**, Braz.
94/A4 **Campos** (reg.), Braz.
95/C1 **Campos Altos**, Braz.
94/A4 **Campos Belos**, Braz.
47/G3 **Campos del Puerto**, Sp.
95/H7 **Campos do Jordão**, Braz.
95/C2 **Campos Gerais**, Braz.
95/B3 **Campos Novos**, Braz.
94/B2 **Campos Sales**, Braz.
115/K8 **Camp Springs**, Md,US
112/E4 **Campti**, La,US
69/E4 **Cam Ranh**, Viet.
106/E2 **Camrose**, Ab,Can
69/D1 **Cam Thuy**, Viet.
102/* **Canada**
96/E2 **Cañada de Gómez**, Arg.
109/H4 **Canadian** (riv.), US
112/C3 **Canadian**, Tx,US
96/C5 **Cañadon Grande** (mts.), Arg.
101/G6 **Canagua**, Ven.
92/F2 **Canaima Nat'l Park**, Ven.
51/H5 **Çanakkale**, Turk.
51/H5 **Çanakkale** (prov.), Turk.
79/U12 **Canala**, NCal.
96/E2 **Canals**, Arg.
47/E3 **Canals**, Sp.
110/E3 **Canandaigua**, NY,US
101/M7 **Cananea**, Mex.
95/C3 **Cananéia**, Braz.
47/X16 **Canary Islands** (aut. comm.), Sp.
100/D5 **Cañas**, CR
101/P9 **Canatlán**, Mex.
113/H4 **Canaveral** (cape), Fl,US
94/C4 **Canavieiras**, Braz.
77/D2 **Canberra** (cap.), Austl.
42/A3 **Canche** (riv.), Fr.
100/D3 **Cancún**, Mex.
46/C1 **Candás**, Sp.
111/N7 **Candiac**, Qu,Can
95/B2 **Candido Mota**, Braz.
72/D5 **Canding** (cape), Indo.
107/G2 **Candle** (lake), Sk,Can
107/J3 **Cando**, ND,US
67/D4 **Candon**, Phil.
95/B4 **Canela**, Braz.
45/H4 **Canelli**, It.
97/F2 **Canelones**, Uru.
97/F2 **Canelones** (dept.), Uru.
46/A1 **Cangas**, Sp.
46/B1 **Cangas de Narcea**, Sp.
46/C1 **Cangas de Onís**, Sp.
72/C5 **Cangkuang** (cape), Indo.
88/C4 **Cango Caves**, SAfr.
87/D3 **Cangombe**, Ang.
97/J7 **Cangrejo** (peak), Arg.
94/D2 **Canguaretama**, Braz.
95/A4 **Canguçu**, Braz.
66/D3 **Cangzhou**, China
69/D1 **Canh Cuoc** (isl.), Viet.
87/B3 **Canhoca**, Ang.
76/C4 **Cania Gorge Nat'l Park**, Austl.
103/K3 **Caniapiscau** (lake), Qu,Can
103/K3 **Caniapiscau** (riv.), Qu,Can
48/C4 **Canicattì**, It.
44/E5 **Canigou, Pic de** (peak), Fr.
59/D2 **Canik** (mts.), Turk.
46/D4 **Caniles**, Sp.
94/C2 **Canindé**, Braz.
94/B2 **Canindé** (riv.), Braz.
59/C2 **Çankırı**, Turk.
73/F1 **Canlaon** (vol.), Phil.
106/E3 **Canmore**, Ab,Can
70/C5 **Cannanore**, India
48/E2 **Canne** (ruins), It.
43/F5 **Canner** (riv.), Fr.
45/G5 **Cannes**, Fr.
36/C2 **Cannich**, Sc,UK
34/D1 **Cannock**, Eng,UK
107/H4 **Cannonball** (riv.), ND,US
107/K4 **Cannon Falls**, Mn,US
95/B4 **Canoas**, Braz.
95/B3 **Canoas** (riv.), Braz.
77/D2 **Canobolas** (peak), Austl.
106/F2 **Canoe** (lake), Sk,Can
95/B3 **Canoinhas**, Braz.
33/F1 **Canonbie**, Sc,UK
109/F3 **Canon City**, Co,US
107/H3 **Canora**, Sk,Can
111/J2 **Canso** (cape), Can.
46/C1 **Cantabria** (aut. comm.), Sp.
44/E4 **Cantal** (plat.), Fr.
46/A2 **Cantanhede**, Port.
101/J6 **Cantaura**, Ven.
76/H8 **Canterbury**, Austl.
75/R11 **Canterbury** (bight), NZ
35/H4 **Canterbury**, Eng,UK
69/D4 **Can Tho**, Viet.
46/C4 **Cantillana**, Sp.
94/B3 **Canto do Buriti**, Braz.
110/B3 **Canton**, Il,US
116/E7 **Canton**, Mi,US
113/F3 **Canton**, Ms,US
110/F2 **Canton**, NY,US
110/D3 **Canton**, Oh,US
109/H3 **Canton**, Ok,US
107/J5 **Canton**, SD,US
112/E3 **Canton**, Tx,US
79/H5 **Canton** (Abariringa) (atoll), Kiri.
67/B3 **Canton** (Guangzhou), China
45/H4 **Cantù**, It.
96/F2 **Cañuelas**, Arg.
77/B3 **Canunda Nat'l Park**, Austl.
35/G3 **Canvey Island**, Eng,UK
106/G2 **Canwood**, Sk,Can
112/C3 **Canyon**, Tx,US
108/E3 **Canyon de Chelly Nat'l Mon.**, Az,US
108/E3 **Canyonlands Nat'l Park**, Ut,US
69/D1 **Cao Bang**, Viet.
67/A2 **Caodu** (riv.), China
69/D1 **Cao Lanh**, Viet.
92/E2 **Capanaparo** (riv.), Ven.
93/J4 **Capanema**, Braz.
48/B1 **Capanne** (peak), It.
45/J5 **Capannori**, It.
95/B3 **Capão Bonito**, Braz.
95/D2 **Caparaó Nat'l Park**, Braz.
46/A3 **Caparica**, Port.
111/H1 **Cap-Chat**, Qu,Can
111/F2 **Cap-de-la-Madeleine**, Qu,Can
76/B3 **Cape** (riv.), Austl.
88/C3 **Cape** (prov.), SAfr.
77/D4 **Cape Barren** (isl.), Austl.
111/J2 **Cape Breton** (highlands), NS,Can
111/J2 **Cape Breton** (isl.), NS,Can
111/J2 **Cape Breton Highlands Nat'l Park**, NS,Can
76/B2 **Cape Cleveland Nat'l Park**, Austl.
85/E5 **Cape Coast**, Gha.
111/G3 **Cape Cod Nat'l Seashore**, Ma,US
113/H5 **Cape Coral**, Fl,US
113/J3 **Cape Fear** (riv.), NC,US
109/K3 **Cape Girardeau**, Mo,US
113/K3 **Cape Hatteras Nat'l Seashore**, NC,US
114/E2 **Cape Krusenstern Nat'l Mon.**, Ak,US
31/Q8 **Capel**, Eng,UK
94/C3 **Capela**, Braz.
32/E5 **Capel-Curig**, Wal,UK
95/D1 **Capelinha**, Braz.
47/K6 **Capellades**, Sp.
35/H4 **Capel le Ferne**, Eng,UK
113/J3 **Cape Lookout Nat'l Seashore**, NC,US
35/H2 **Capel Saint Mary**, Eng,UK
76/B1 **Cape Melville Nat'l Park**, Austl.
76/C3 **Cape Palmerston Nat'l Park**, Austl.
115/K7 **Cape Saint Claire**, Md,US
88/B4 **Cape Town** (cap.), SAfr.
76/B2 **Cape Tribulation Nat'l Park**, Austl.
76/B2 **Cape Upstart Nat'l Park**, Austl.
80/K9 **Cape Verde**
76/A1 **Cape York** (pen.), Austl.
101/G4 **Cap-Haïtien**, Haiti
48/A2 **Capicciola** (pt.), Fr.
93/J4 **Capim** (riv.), Braz.
94/D2 **Capina**, Braz.
95/B1 **Capinópolis**, Braz.
95/B2 **Capirara** (res.), Braz.
112/B3 **Capitan** (mts.), NM,US
93/J4 **Capitão Poco**, Braz.
108/E3 **Capitol Reef Nat'l Park**, Ut,US
94/A4 **Capivara** (mts.), Braz.
93/H8 **Capivara** (res.), Braz.
95/J6 **Capivari** (riv.), Braz.
50/C4 **Čapljina**, Bosn.
48/D3 **Capo d'Orlando**, It.
48/A3 **Capoterra**, It.
48/A1 **Capraia** (isl.), It.
110/D2 **Capreol**, On,Can
48/D2 **Capri**, It.
76/C3 **Capricorn** (cape), Austl.
76/C3 **Capricorn** (chan.), Austl.
87/D4 **Caprivi Strip** (reg.), Namb.
112/C3 **Cap Rock Escarpment** (cliffs), Tx,US
112/C3 **Caprock, The** (cliffs), NM,US
111/G2 **Cap-Rouge**, Qu,Can
45/G5 **Cap Roux, Pointe du** (pt.), Fr.
109/G3 **Capulin Volcano Nat'l Mon.**, NM,US
92/D4 **Caquetá** (riv.), Col.
47/N9 **Carabanchel** (nrbhd.), Sp.
51/G3 **Caracal**, Rom.
101/H5 **Caracas** (cap.), Ven.
34/B5 **Caradon** (hill), Eng,UK
95/H8 **Caraguatatuba**, Braz.
95/H8 **Caraguatatuba** (bay), Braz.
96/D3 **Carahue**, Chile
93/H5 **Carajás** (mts.), Braz.

95/D2 Carandaí, Braz.
95/D2 Carangola, Braz.
50/F3 Caransebeş, Rom.
48/D2 Carapelle (riv.), It.
95/G8 Carapicuíba, Braz.
111/H2 Caraquet, NB,Can
50/E3 Caraş-Severin (co.), Rom.
100/E4 Caratasca (lag.), Hon.
95/D1 Caratinga, Braz.
92/E4 Carauari, Braz.
94/C2 Caraúbas, Braz.
46/E3 Caravaca de la Cruz, Sp.
84/A4 Caravela (isl.), GBis.
91/F2 Carazinho, Braz.
46/A1 Carballino, Sp.
46/A1 Carballo, Sp.
107/J3 Carberry, Mb,Can
81/U17 Carbon (cape), Alg.
116/C3 Carbon (riv.), Wa,US
48/A3 Carbonara (cape), It.
48/D4 Carbonara, Pizzo (peak), It.
110/B4 Carbondale, Il,US
110/F3 Carbondale, Pa,US
48/A3 Carbonia, It.
47/E3 Carcagente, Sp.
96/E2 Carcaraña, Arg.
44/E5 Carcassonne, Fr.
47/P10 Carcavelos, Port.
46/E3 Carche (mtn.), Sp.
102/C2 Carcross, Yt,Can
47/L6 Cardedeu, Sp.
97/K7 Cardiel (lake), Arg.
34/C4 Cardiff (cap.), Wal,UK
34/B2 Cardigan, Wal,UK
47/F2 Cardona, Sp.
95/B2 Cardoso, Braz.
106/E3 Cardston, Ab,Can
50/F2 Carei, Rom.
44/C2 Carentan, Fr.
50/F4 Carev vrh (peak), Macd.
74/C5 Carey (lake), Austl.
44/B2 Carhaix-Plouguer, Fr.
96/E3 Carhué, Arg.
95/D2 Cariacica, Braz.
101/J5 Cariaco, Ven.
92/C4 Cariamanga, Ecu.
48/E3 Cariati, It.
101/G5 Caribbean (sea)
106/C2 Cariboo (mts.), BC,Can
102/E3 Caribou (mts.), Ab,Can
110/B1 Caribou (lake), On,Can
114/L3 Caribou, Yk,Can
106/F5 Caribou (range), Id,US
111/G2 Caribou, Me,US
67/D5 Carigara, Phil.
94/B4 Carinhanha, Braz.
94/A4 Carinhanha (riv.), Braz.
48/C3 Carini, It.
45/K3 Carinthia (prov.), Aus.
101/J5 Caripito, Ven.
94/B2 Cariri Novos (mts.), Braz.
109/G3 Carizzo (cr.), NM, Tx,US
47/E3 Carlet, Sp.
111/H2 Carleton (peak), NB,Can
111/H2 Carleton (riv.), NS,Can
111/H1 Carleton, Qu,Can
88/D2 Carletonville, SAfr.
108/C2 Carlin, Nv,US
76/H8 Carlingford, Austl.
32/B3 Carlingford (mtn.), Ire.
32/B3 Carlingford Lough (inlet), Ire.
110/B4 Carlinville, Il,US
110/D3 Carlisle, On,Can
33/F2 Carlisle, Eng,UK
44/D5 Carlit (peak), Fr.
96/E2 Carlos Casares, Arg.
95/D1 Carlos Chagas, Braz.
101/F3 Carlos M. De Cespedes, Cuba
32/B6 Carlow, Ire.
32/B6 Carlow (co.), Ire.
109/F4 Carlsbad, NM,US
109/F4 Carlsbad Caverns Nat'l Park, NM,US
33/G6 Carlton, Eng,UK
107/K4 Carlton, Mn,US
111/Q9 Carluke, On,Can
107/H3 Carlyle, Sk,Can
109/K3 Carlyle (lake), Il,US
102/C2 Carmacks, Yk,Can
45/G4 Carmagnola, It.
107/J3 Carman, Mb,Can
34/B3 Carmarthen, Wal,UK
34/B3 Carmarthen (bay), Wal,UK
44/E4 Carmaux, Fr.
110/C4 Carmel, In,US
32/D5 Carmel Head (pt.), Wal,UK
59/K5 Carmel, Mount (Har Karmel) (mtn.), Isr.
96/F2 Carmelo, Uru.
101/M8 Carmen (isl.), Mex.
101/N7 Carmen (riv.), Mex.
110/B4 Carmi, Il,US
116/M9 Carmichael, Ca,US
95/L6 Carmo, Braz.
95/C1 Carmo do Paranaíba, Braz.
95/C2 Carmo do Rio Claro, Braz.
46/C4 Carmona, Sp.
32/B1 Carnanmore (mtn.), NI,UK
74/A4 Carnarvon, Austl.
88/C3 Carnarvonleegte (dry riv.), SAfr.
76/B4 Carnarvon Nat'l Park, Austl.
47/P10 Carnaxide, Port.
32/C2 Carncastle, NI,UK
107/H3 Carnduff, Sk,Can
32/D5 Carnedd Dafydd (mtn.), Wal,UK
32/E5 Carnedd Llewelyn (mtn.), Wal,UK
74/C5 Carnegie (lake), Austl.
98/S Carney (isl.), Ant.
33/F3 Carnforth, Eng,UK
42/C3 Carnières, Fr.
32/B2 Carnlough, NI,UK
94/C2 Carnoió, Braz.
82/J7 Carnot, CAfr.
46/A1 Carnota, Sp.
36/D2 Carnoustie, Sc,UK
36/B4 Carnsore (pt.), Ire.
102/D2 Carnwath (riv.), NW,Can
110/D3 Caro, Mi,US
94/A2 Carolina, Braz.
101/H4 Carolina, PR
79/K5 Caroline (isl.), Kiri.
78/D4 Caroline (isls.), Micr.
116/P16 Carol Stream, Il,US
54/B2 Carpathian (mts.), Eur.
45/J4 Carpenedolo, It.
74/F2 Carpentaria (gulf), Austl.
116/P15 Carpentersville, Il,US
44/F4 Carpentras, Fr.
45/J4 Carpi, It.
115/A2 Carpinteria, Ca,US
116/B3 Carr (inlet), Wa,US
113/G4 Carrabelle, Fl,US
45/J4 Carrara, It.
32/D6 Carreg Ddu (pt.), Wal,UK
101/J5 Carriacou (isl.), Gren.
32/C2 Carrickfergus, NI,UK
32/C2 Carrickfergus (dist.), NI,UK
32/A2 Carrickmore, NI,UK
31/S10 Carrières-sous-Poissy, Fr.
32/B3 Carrigatuke (mtn.), NI,UK
107/J4 Carrington, ND,US
46/C1 Carrión (riv.), Sp.
101/G5 Carrizal, Col.
104/E4 Carrizo (mts.), Az,US
112/C2 Carrizo (cr.), NM,US
112/D4 Carrizo Springs, Tx,US
109/F4 Carrizozo, NM,US
113/G3 Carrollton, Ga,US
110/C4 Carrollton, Ky,US
109/J3 Carrollton, Mo,US
107/H2 Carrot (riv.), Sk,Can
107/H2 Carrot River, Sk,Can
32/C2 Carrowdore, NI,UK
32/C2 Carryduff, NI,UK
59/D2 Çarşamba, Turk.
115/B3 Carson, Ca,US
108/C3 Carson (riv.), Nv,US
108/C3 Carson (sink), Nv,US
108/C3 Carson City (cap.), Nv,US
32/D1 Carsphairn, Sc,UK
106/E3 Carstairs, Ab,Can
96/Q9 Cartagena, Chile
101/F5 Cartagena, Col.
47/E4 Cartagena, Sp.
92/C3 Cartago, Col.
100/E6 Cartago, CR
46/C4 Cártama, Sp.
46/A3 Cartaxo, Port.
46/B4 Cartaya, Sp.
76/A1 Carter (peak), Austl.
115/F5 Carteret, NJ,US
113/G3 Cartersville, Ga,US
35/E3 Carterton, Eng,UK
48/B4 Carthage (ruins), Tun.
109/J3 Carthage, Mo,US
113/F3 Carthage, Ms,US
113/G2 Carthage, Tn,US
112/E3 Carthage, Tx,US
74/C2 Cartier Islet (isl.), Austl.
103/L3 Cartwright, Nf,Can
94/D3 Caruaru, Braz.
92/F1 Carúpano, Ven.
109/K3 Caruthersville, Mo,US
42/B2 Carvin, Fr.
46/A3 Carvoeiro (cape), Port.
116/P15 Cary, Il,US
113/J3 Cary, NC,US
81/L14 Casablanca, Mor.
95/F6 Casa Branca, Braz.
101/N7 Casa de Janos, Mex.
108/E4 Casa Grande, Az,US
108/E4 Casa Grande Nat'l Mon., Az,US
48/D2 Casal di Principe, It.
45/J4 Casalecchio di Reno, It.
45/H4 Casale Monferrato, It.
84/A3 Casamance (riv.), Sen.
94/B3 Casa Nova, Braz.
49/F3 Casarano, It.
101/N7 Casas Grandes (ruins), Mex.
101/N8 Cascada de Bassaseachic Nat'l Park, Mex.
106/C5 Cascade (range), Can., US
106/D4 Cascade (res.), Id,US
116/C3 Cascade-Fairwood, Wa,US
89/R15 Cascades (pt.), Reun.
47/P10 Cascais, Port.
111/H1 Cascapédia (riv.), Qu,Can
94/C2 Cascavel, Braz.
45/J5 Cascina-Navacchio, It.
116/B3 Case (inlet), Wa,US
48/D2 Caserta, It.
98/H Casey, Ant.
98/D Casey (bay), Ant.
81/H3 Caseyr (cape), Som.
106/C4 Cashmere, Wa,US
96/E2 Casilda, Arg.
101/P10 Casimiro Castillo, Mex.
77/E1 Casino, Austl.
115/A2 Casitas (lake), Ca,US
92/C5 Casma, Peru
47/E2 Caspe, Sp.
107/G5 Casper, Wy,US
56/F6 Caspian (sea), Eur., Asia
47/G2 Cassà de la Selva, Sp.
87/D3 Cassai (riv.), Ang.
87/D3 Cassamba, Ang.
48/E3 Cassano allo Ionio, It.
110/D3 Cass City, Mi,US
95/C2 Cássia, Braz.
102/C3 Cassiar (mts.), BC,Can
95/B1 Cassilândia, Braz.
48/C2 Cassino, It.
109/J3 Cassville, Mo,US
115/B2 Castaic, Ca,US
115/B1 Castaic (lake), Ca,US
47/E3 Castalla, Sp.
93/J4 Castanhal, Braz.
48/D4 Castelbuono, It.
45/K5 Castelfidardo, It.
48/C3 Castellammare (gulf), It.
48/D2 Castellammare di Stabia, It.
45/G4 Castellamonte, It.
47/G2 Castellar del Vallès, Sp.
47/K7 Castelldefels, Sp.
47/L7 Castell de Montjuic, Sp.
48/D4 Castello Eurialo (ruins), It.
47/E3 Castellón de la Plana, Sp.
59/N9 Castel Nat'l Park, Isr.
44/D5 Castelnaudary, Fr.
44/E5 Castelnau-le-Lez, Fr.
46/B3 Castelo Branco, Port.
46/B2 Castelo Branco (dist.), Port.
94/B2 Castelo do Piauí, Braz.
44/D4 Castelsarrasin, Fr.
48/C4 Castelvetrano, It.
95/B2 Castilho, Braz.
92/B5 Castilla, Peru
46/C2 Castille and León (aut. comm.), Sp.
46/D3 Castille-La Mancha (aut. comm.), Sp.
101/G5 Castilletes, Col.
96/C4 Castillo (peak), Arg.
113/H4 Castillo de San Marcos Nat'l Mon., Fl,US
97/G2 Castillos, Uru.
35/G1 Castle Acre, Eng,UK
36/A4 Castlebar, Ire.
34/D4 Castle Cary, Eng,UK
32/B3 Castlecaulfield, NI,UK
34/D4 Castle Combe, Eng,UK
108/E3 Castle Dale, Ut,US
32/B2 Castledawson, NI,UK
33/G6 Castle Donnington, Eng,UK
32/E2 Castle Douglas, Sc,UK
33/G4 Castleford, Eng,UK
106/D3 Castlegar, BC,Can
76/H8 Castle Hill, Austl.
32/D2 Castle Kennedy, Sc,UK
77/C3 Castlemaine, Austl.
76/G8 Castlereagh, Austl.
32/B1 Castlerock, NI,UK
109/F3 Castle Rock, Co,US
107/L5 Castle Rock (lake), Wi,US
76/C4 Castle Tower Nat'l Park, Austl.
32/D3 Castletown, IM,UK
32/C3 Castlewellan, NI,UK
106/F2 Castor, Ab,Can
82/D6 Castos (riv.), Libr.
44/E5 Castres, Fr.
40/B3 Castricum, Neth.
101/J5 Castries (cap.), StL.
95/B3 Castro, Braz.
96/B4 Castro, Chile
94/C4 Castro Alves, Braz.
46/C4 Castro del Río, Sp.
46/B1 Castro de Rey, Sp.
41/E5 Castrop-Rauxel, Ger.
46/D1 Castro-Urdiales, Sp.
116/K11 Castro Valley, Ca,US
48/E3 Castrovillari, It.
46/C3 Castuera, Sp.
101/F3 Cat (isl.), Bahm.
107/K3 Cat (lake), On,Can
78/B3 Catanduanes (isl.), Phil.
95/L6 Cataguases, Braz.
67/D5 Cataiñgan, Phil.
73/F1 Cataiñgan, Phil.
51/K5 Çatalağzı, Turk.
95/C1 Catalão, Braz.
51/J5 Çatalca, Turk.
108/E4 Catalina, Az,US
47/F2 Catalonia (aut. comm.), Sp.
91/C2 Catamarca, Arg.
67/D5 Catanduanes (isl.), Phil.
95/B2 Catanduva, Braz.
48/D4 Catania, It.
48/D4 Catania (gulf), It.
48/E3 Catanzaro, It.
73/F1 Catarman, Indo.
67/D5 Catarman, Phil.
47/E3 Catarroja, Sp.
74/E7 Catastrophe (cape), Austl.
101/G6 Catatumbo (riv.), Col., Ven.
73/F2 Catatungan (mtn.), Phil.
113/H3 Catawba (riv.), NC, SC,US
67/D5 Catbalogan, Phil.
97/G2 Catedral (peak), Uru.
94/D3 Catende, Braz.
31/N8 Caterham, Eng,UK
86/C2 Catherine, Mount (Jabal Katrīnah) (mtn.), Egypt
101/F6 Cativá, Pan.
110/D4 Catlettsburg, Ky,US
75/K4 Cato (isl.), Austl.
100/D3 Catoche (cape), Mex.
94/C2 Catolé do Rocha, Braz.
45/K5 Catria (peak), It.
92/F3 Catrimani (riv.), Braz.
34/D2 Catshill, Eng,UK
110/F3 Catskill (mts.), NY,US
43/F5 Cattenom, Fr.
33/G3 Catterick, Eng,UK
94/C4 Catu, Braz.
67/D4 Cauayan, Phil.
67/D6 Cauayan, Phil.
92/C2 Cauca (riv.), Col.
94/C1 Caucaia, Braz.
92/C2 Caucasia, Col.
54/G4 Caucasus (mts.), Eur.
47/E3 Caudete, Sp.
42/C3 Caudry, Fr.
33/F1 Cauldcleuch (mtn.), Sc,UK
96/B2 Cauquenes, Chile
44/D4 Caussade, Fr.
48/D4 Cava d'Ispica (ruins), It.
46/B2 Cávado (riv.), Port.
44/F5 Cavaillon, Fr.
107/J3 Cavalier, ND,US
82/D6 Cavalla (riv.), IvC., Libr.
84/D5 Cavalla (Cavally) (riv.), IvC., Libr.
48/A1 Cavallo, Capo al (cape), Fr.
32/A4 Cavan (co.), Ire.
108/E4 Cave Creek, Az,US
93/J3 Caviana, Braz.
51/F2 Cavnic, Rom.
67/D5 Cawayan, Phil.
77/B2 Cawndilla (lake), Austl.
33/G4 Cawood, Eng,UK
35/H1 Cawston, Eng,UK
95/J6 Caxambu, Braz.
94/B2 Caxias, Braz.
95/B4 Caxias do Sul, Braz.
100/D4 Caxinas (pt.), Hon.
87/B2 Caxito, Ang.
59/B2 Çay, Turk.
92/C3 Cayambe (vol.), Ecu.
113/H3 Cayce, SC,US
51/L5 Çaycuma, Turk.
59/E2 Çayeli, Turk.
93/H3 Cayenne (cap.), FrG.
101/F4 Cayman Brac (isl.), Cay.
100/E4 Cayman Islands, UK
100/E4 Cayos Cajones (isls.), Hon.
100/E5 Cayos Miskitos (isls.), Nic.
50/B3 Cazin, Bosn.
46/D4 Cazorla, Sp.
46/C1 Cea (riv.), Sp.
94/C3 Ceará (state), Braz.
94/D2 Ceará-Mirim, Braz.
97/G2 Cebollatí (riv.), Uru.
67/D5 Cebu, Phil.
67/D6 Cebu (isl.), Phil.
48/C2 Ceccano, It.
89/E2 Cecil Macks (pass), Swaz.
45/J5 Cecina, It.
48/E3 Cecita (lake), It.
107/H2 Cedar (lake), Mb,Can
110/E2 Cedar (lake), On,Can
116/L11 Cedar (mtn.), Ca,US
107/L5 Cedar (riv.), Ia,US
115/F6 Cedar (cr.), NJ,US
116/C3 Cedar (riv.), Wa,US
76/B1 Cedar Bay Nat'l Park, Austl.
109/G3 Cedar Bluff (res.), Ks,US
108/D3 Cedar Breaks Nat'l Mon., Ut,US
108/D3 Cedar City, Ut,US
112/D3 Cedar Creek (res.), Tx,US
107/K5 Cedar Falls, Ia,US
115/F5 Cedar Grove, NJ,US
113/H4 Cedar Key, Fl,US
107/L5 Cedar Rapids, Ia,US
113/G3 Cedartown, Ga,US
108/B2 Cedarville, Ca,US
46/A1 Cedeira, Sp.
94/C2 Cedro, Braz.
101/L8 Cedros (isl.), Mex.
46/A1 Cee, Sp.
83/Q7 Ceel Dheere, Som.
83/Q5 Ceerigaabo (Erigabo), Som.
48/D3 Cefalù, It.
32/D5 Cefni (riv.), Wal,UK
33/E6 Cefn-mawr, Wal,UK
46/C2 Cega (riv.), Sp.
50/D2 Cegléd, Hun.
46/E3 Cehegín, Sp.
51/F2 Cehu Silvaniei, Rom.
33/E6 Ceiriog (riv.), Wal,UK
54/F4 Çekerek (riv.), Turk.
46/B1 Celanova, Sp.
100/D3 Celarain (pt.), Mex.
100/A3 Celaya, Mex.
32/B5 Celbridge, Ire.
73/F3 Celebes (sea), Asia
73/E4 Celebes (Sulawesi) (isl.), Indo.
110/C3 Celina, Oh,US
50/B2 Celje, Slov.
50/C2 Celldömölk, Hun.
44/E2 Celle (riv.), Fr.
41/H3 Celle, Ger.
34/A4 Celtic (sea), Eur.
34/B2 Cemaes Head (pt.), Wal,UK
72/D3 Cemaru (peak), Indo.
46/E3 Cenajo (res.), Sp.
73/H4 Cenderawasih (bay), Indo.
91/C4 Centenario, Arg.
95/B2 Centenario do Sul, Braz.
108/D4 Centennial (wash), Az,US
106/E4 Centennial (mts.), Id,US
107/H4 Center, ND,US
112/E4 Center, Tx,US
115/G5 Centereach, NY,US
116/F7 Center Line, Mi,US
115/H5 Center Moriches, NY,US
113/G3 Center Point, Al,US
113/G3 Centerville, Tn,US
112/E4 Centerville, Tx,US
45/J4 Cento, It.
96/C4 Central (peak), Arg.
94/B3 Central, Braz.
85/E5 Central (reg.), Gha.
59/K5 Central (dist.), Isr.
83/J6 Central African Republic
106/G3 Central Butte, Sk,Can
109/H2 Central City, Ne,US
92/C5 Central, Cordillera (range), SAm.
110/B4 Centralia, Il,US
106/C4 Centralia, Wa,US
115/G5 Central Islip, NY,US
61/H3 Central Makrān (range), Pak.
44/E4 Central, Massif (plat.), Fr.
93/J7 Central, Planalto (plat.), Braz.
106/C5 Central Point, Or,US
57/L3 Central Siberian (plat.), Rus.
53/N4 Central Ural (mts.), Rus.
44/D3 Centre (reg.), Fr.
81/L14 Centre (reg.), Mor.
81/M13 Centre Nord (reg.), Mor.
81/M14 Centre Sud (reg.), Mor.
113/G3 Centreville, Al,US
44/D4 Céou (riv.), Fr.
50/D3 Čepin, Cro.
73/G4 Ceram (isl.), Indo.
73/G4 Ceram (sea), Indo.
48/A2 Ceraso (cape), It.
47/L7 Cerdanyola del Vallès, Sp.
44/D4 Cère (riv.), Fr.
45/J4 Cerea, It.
91/D2 Ceres, Arg.
93/J7 Ceres, Braz.
88/B4 Ceres, SAfr.
101/F6 Cereté, Col.
31/S9 Cergy, Fr.
48/D2 Cerignola, It.
51/J5 Çerkezköy, Turk.
51/J3 Černavodă, Rom.
31/R10 Cernay-la-Ville, Fr.
34/D5 Cerne Abbas, Eng,UK
101/N9 Cerralvo (isl.), Mex.
32/E5 Cerrig-y-Druidion, Wal,UK
49/F2 Cërrik, Alb.
100/A3 Cerritos, Mex.
100/B3 Cerro Azul, Mex.
96/C3 Cerro Colorados (res.), Arg.
101/L7 Cerro de la Encantada (peak), Mex.
101/M8 Cerro Dos Picachos (peak), Mex.
101/M8 Cerro Encantada (peak), Mex.
97/G2 Cerro Largo (dept.), Uru.
101/M7 Cerro Pinacote (peak), Mex.
48/D2 Cervaro (riv.), It.
48/D2 Cervati (peak), It.
47/F2 Cervera, Sp.
45/K4 Cervia, It.
48/D2 Cervialto (peak), It.
45/K4 Cervignano del Friuli, It.
95/H7 Cervo (hills), Braz.
46/B1 Cervo, Sp.
101/G5 César (riv.), Col.
45/K4 Cesena, It.
45/K4 Cesenatico, It.
52/E4 Cēsis, Lat.
45/L2 České Budějovice, Czh.
39/H4 Českomoravská Vysočina (upland), Czh.
45/L2 Český Krumlov, Czh.
50/C3 Česma (riv.), Cro.
49/K3 Çeşme, Turk.
59/A2 Çeşme, Turk.
31/T11 Cesson, Fr.
44/C2 Cesson-Sévigné, Fr.
84/C5 Cestos (riv.), Libr.
50/C4 Cetina (riv), Cro.
50/D4 Cetinje, Yugo.
46/D2 Ceurda del Pozo (res.), Sp.
46/C5 Ceuta, Sp.
44/E5 Cévennes (mts.), Fr.
44/E4 Cévennes Nat'l Park, Fr.
59/C3 Ceyhan, Turk.
59/E3 Ceylânpınar, Turk.
70/D6 Ceylon (isl.), SrL.
44/F4 Cèze (riv.), Fr.
44/C5 Chabarrou (peak), Fr.
96/E2 Chacabuco, Arg.
92/C5 Chachapoyas, Peru
69/C3 Chachoengsao, Thai.
108/F3 Chaco (dry riv.), NM,US
112/B3 Chaco (mesa), NM,US
91/D2 Chaco Austral (plain), Arg.
92/G8 Chaco Boreal (plain), Par.
91/D1 Chaco Central (plain), Arg.
91/E2 Chaco Nat'l Park, Arg.
100/D4 Chacujal (ruins), Guat.
83/J4 Chad
82/H5 Chad (lake), Afr.
69/E4 Cha Da (cape), Viet.
35/E3 Chadlington, Eng,UK
109/G2 Chadron, Ne,US
51/J2 Chadyr-Lunga, Mol.
81/N13 Chafarinas (isls.), Sp.
68/D5 Chagdo Kangri (peak), China
58/G10 Chagos (arch.), Brln.
61/H3 Chāh Behār (Bandar Beheshtī), Iran
100/C4 Chahuites, Mex.
69/C3 Chainat, Thai.
69/C3 Chaiyaphum, Thai.
70/C5 Chālakudi, India
100/D5 Chalatenango, ESal.
83/N7 Chalbi (des.), Kenya
63/H2 Chalchyn (riv.), Mong.
111/H2 Chaleur (bay), NB, Qu,Can
31/M7 Chalfont Saint Giles, Eng,UK
31/M7 Chalfont Saint Peter, Eng,UK
35/E3 Chalgrove, Eng,UK
31/U10 Chalifert (can.), Fr.
112/C4 Chalk (mts.), Tx,US
44/C3 Challans, Fr.
103/T6 Challenger (mtn.), NW,Can
43/D5 Challerange, Fr.
106/E4 Challis, Id,US
35/G4 Challock, Eng,UK
42/D6 Châlons-sur-Marne, Fr.
44/F3 Chalon-sur-Saône, Fr.
60/F1 Chālūs, Iran
45/K2 Cham, Ger.
108/F3 Chama (riv.), Co, NM,US
72/B2 Chamah (peak), Malay.
61/J2 Chaman, Pak.
61/L2 Chamba, India
70/C2 Chambal (riv.), India
44/F4 Chambaran (plat.), Fr.
111/G2 Chamberlain (lake), Me,US
107/J5 Chamberlain, SD,US
114/K2 Chamberlin (mtn.), Ak,US
110/E4 Chambersburg, Pa,US
44/F4 Chambéry, Fr.
87/F3 Chambeshi (riv.), Zam.
111/P7 Chambly, Qu,Can
31/S9 Chambly, Fr.
31/S10 Chambourcy, Fr.
59/F3 Chamchamāl, Iraq
44/F4 Chamechaude (mtn.), Fr.
91/C3 Chamical, Arg.
45/G4 Chamonix-Mont-Blanc, Fr.
114/L3 Champagne, Yk,Can
42/C6 Champagne (reg.), Fr.
44/F2 Champagne-Ardennes (reg.), Fr.
31/S9 Champagne-sur-Oise, Fr.
110/B3 Champaign, Il,US
96/D1 Champaqui (peak), Arg.
43/F6 Champigneulles, Fr.
31/T10 Champigny-sur-Marne, Fr.
110/F2 Champlain (lake), Can., US
100/C4 Champotón, Mex.
42/B6 Champs-sur-Marne, Fr.
91/B2 Chañaral, Chile
46/B4 Chança (riv.), Port.
92/C5 Chan Chan (ruins), Peru
96/B2 Chanco, Chile
114/J2 Chandalar (riv.), Ak,US
70/C2 Chandausi, India
70/C3 Chanderi, India
61/L2 Chandigarh, India
111/H1 Chandler, Qu,Can
114/H2 Chandler (riv.), Ak,US
112/D3 Chandler, Ok,US
70/C4 Chandrapur, India
66/C5 Chang (lake), China
66/L8 Chang (riv.), China
69/C3 Chang (isl.), Thai.
63/K3 Changbai (peak), China
63/K3 Changbai (mts.), China, NKor.
66/F2 Changchun, China
66/D5 Changdang (lake), China
67/B2 Changde, China
64/A2 Changgi-ap (cape), SKor.
67/D3 Changhua, Tai.
63/K5 Changhŭng, SKor.
66/D3 Changli, China
66/D2 Changping, China
63/J4 Changsan-got (cape), NKor.
67/B2 Changsha, China
66/E5 Changshu, China
71/J2 Changshun, China
63/K4 Changsŏng, SKor.
100/E6 Changuinola, Pan.
64/A3 Ch'angwŏn, SKor.
66/E3 Changxing (isl.), China
66/D5 Chang (Yangtze) (riv.), China
66/C3 Changzhi, China
66/D5 Changzhou, China
69/E2 Chan May Dong (cape), Viet.
35/H4 Channel (tunnel), UK, Fr.
108/C4 Channel (isls.), Ca,US
76/A4 Channel Country (plain), Austl.
44/B2 Channel Islands, UK
108/B4 Channel Islands Nat'l Park, Ca,US
111/K2 Channel-Port aux Basques, Nf,Can
46/B1 Chantada, Sp.
31/S10 Chanteloup-les-Vignes, Fr.
69/C3 Chanthaburi, Thai.
42/B5 Chantilly, Fr.
102/G2 Chantrey (inlet), NW,Can
109/J3 Chanute, Ks,US
66/D5 Chao (lake), China
63/H4 Chaobai (riv.), China
69/C3 Chao Phraya (riv.), Thai.
63/J2 Chaor (riv.), China
67/C3 Chaoyang, China
67/C3 Chaozhou, China
94/B4 Chapada Diamantina Nat'l Park, Braz.
94/A4 Chapada dos Veadeiros Nat'l Park, Braz.
94/B1 Chapadinha, Braz.
110/F1 Chapais, Qu,Can
101/P9 Chapala (lake), Mex.
55/J1 Chapayevsk, Rus.
95/A3 Chapecó, Braz.
33/G5 Chapel en le Frith, Eng,UK
33/F2 Chapelfell Top (mtn.), Eng,UK
113/J3 Chapel Hill, NC,US
42/D3 Chapelle-Lez-Herlaimont, Belg.
33/J5 Chapel Saint Leonards, Eng,UK
33/G5 Chapeltown, Eng,UK
116/D2 Chaplain (lake), Wa,US
69/D2 Chap Le, Viet.
110/D2 Chapleau, On,Can
106/G3 Chaplin, Sk,Can
109/G2 Chappell, Ne,US
57/M4 Chara (riv.), Rus.
92/C3 Charambirá (pt.), Col.
49/L6 Charandra (riv.), Gre.
91/D2 Charata, Arg.
100/A3 Charcas, Mex.
98/U Charcot (isl.), Ant.
34/D5 Chard, Eng,UK
56/G6 Chardzhou, Trkm.
81/N14 Charef, Oued (riv.), Mor.
44/C4 Charente (riv.), Fr.
31/T10 Charenton-le-Pont, Fr.
82/J5 Chari (riv.), Chad
61/J1 Chārīkār, Afg.
35/G4 Charing, Eng,UK
109/J2 Chariton (riv.), Ia, Mo,US
35/E3 Charlbury, Eng,UK
32/B3 Charlemont, NI,UK
42/D3 Charleroi, Belg.
42/D2 Charleroi à Bruxelles, Canal de (can.), Belg.
103/J2 Charles (isl.), NW,Can
110/F4 Charles (cape), Va,US
107/K5 Charles City, Ia,US
110/B4 Charleston, Il,US
109/K3 Charleston, Mo,US
113/F3 Charleston, Ms,US
108/D2 Charleston, Nv,US
113/J3 Charleston, SC,US
110/D4 Charleston (cap.), WV,US
43/D4 Charleville-Mézières, Fr.
110/C2 Charlevoix, Mi,US
106/B2 Charlotte (lake), BC,Can
110/C3 Charlotte, Mi,US
113/H3 Charlotte, NC,US
101/J4 Charlotte Amalie (cap.), USVI
110/E4 Charlottesville, Va,US
111/J2 Charlottetown (cap.), PE,Can
101/J5 Charlotteville, Trin.
103/H3 Charlton (isl.), NW,Can
34/D3 Charlton Kings, Eng,UK
31/N8 Charlwood, Eng,UK
44/F3 Charolais (mts.), Fr.
31/R9 Chars, Fr.
68/D2 Charsk, Kaz.
76/B3 Charters Towers, Austl.
44/D2 Chartres, Fr.
68/C3 Charyn (riv.), Kaz.
68/D1 Charysh (riv.), Rus.
96/F2 Chascomús, Arg.
106/D3 Chase, BC,Can
44/F4 Chassezac (riv.), Fr.
44/C3 Chassiron, Pointe de (pt.), Fr.
44/C3 Châteaubriant, Fr.
44/C3 Château-d'Olonne, Fr.
44/D2 Châteaudun, Fr.
111/N7 Châteauguay, Qu,Can
44/F5 Châteaurenard-Provence, Fr.
44/D3 Château-Renault, Fr.
44/D3 Châteauroux, Fr.
42/C5 Château-Thierry, Fr.
42/D3 Châtelet, Belg.
44/D3 Châtellerault, Fr.
31/S10 Châtenay-Malabry, Fr.
109/J2 Chatfield, Mn,US
111/H2 Chatham, NB,Can
110/D3 Chatham, On,Can
97/J7 Chatham (isl.), Chile
35/G4 Chatham, Eng,UK
115/F5 Chatham, NJ,US
31/S10 Châtillon, Fr.
44/F3 Châtillon-sur-Seine, Fr.
31/S10 Chatou, Fr.
70/D4 Chatrapur, India
76/H8 Chatswood, Austl.
115/B2 Chatsworth (res.), Ca,US
113/G3 Chatsworth, Ga,US
113/G4 Chattahoochee, Fl,US
113/G4 Chattahoochee (riv.), Fl, Ga,US
113/G3 Chattanooga, Tn,US
35/G2 Chatteris, Eng,UK
44/C2 Chaucey (isls.), Fr.
43/E2 Chaudfontaine, Belg.
111/G2 Chaudière (riv.), Qu,Can
69/D4 Chau Doc, Viet.
71/F3 Chauk, Burma
71/G2 Chaukan (pass), India
42/B4 Chaulnes, Fr.
31/U10 Chaumes-en-Brie, Fr.
44/F2 Chaumont, Fr.
42/A5 Chaumont-en-Vexin, Fr.
42/D4 Chaumont-Porcien, Fr.
57/T3 Chaunskaya (bay), Rus.
42/C4 Chauny, Fr.
110/E3 Chautauqua (lake), NY,US
44/D3 Chauvigny, Fr.
94/B1 Chaval, Braz.
46/B2 Chaves, Port.
69/D1 Chay (riv.), Viet.
92/E7 Chayana (riv.), Bol.
53/M4 Chaykovskiy, Rus.
33/G6 Cheadle, Eng,UK
113/G3 Cheaha (peak), Al,US
45/K1 Cheb, Czh.
53/K4 Cheboksary, Rus.
53/K4 Cheboksary (res.), Rus.
110/C2 Cheboygan, Mi,US
81/M13 Chechaouene, Mor.
55/H4 Chechen' (isl.), Rus.
55/H4 Chechen-Ingush Aut. Rep., Rus.
82/D3 Chech, 'Erg (des.), Afr.
64/A2 Chech'ŏn, SKor.
109/J4 Checotah, Ok,US
111/J2 Chedabucto (bay), NS,Can
34/D4 Cheddar, Eng,UK
71/F4 Cheduba (isl.), Burma
111/S10 Cheektowaga, NY,US
110/D1 Cheepash (riv.), On,Can
110/D1 Cheepay (riv.), On,Can
63/L1 Chegdomyn, Rus.
87/F4 Chegutu, Zim.
106/C4 Chehalis, Wa,US
45/G5 Cheiron, Cime du (peak), Fr.
63/K5 Cheju, SKor.
63/K5 Cheju (isl.), SKor.
63/K5 Cheju (str.), SKor.
106/C4 Chelan, Wa,US
106/C4 Chelan (lake), Wa,US
33/F5 Chelford, Eng,UK
81/V17 Chelghoum El Aïd, Alg.
55/L3 Chelkar, Kaz.
31/T10 Chelles, Fr.
39/M3 Chełm, Pol.
39/M3 Chełm (prov.), Pol.
35/G3 Chelmer (riv.), Eng,UK
39/K2 Chełmno, Pol.
35/G3 Chelmsford, Eng,UK
39/K2 Chełmża, Pol.
77/G6 Chelsea, Austl.
31/N7 Chelsea, Eng,UK
31/N7 Chelsea & Kensington (bor.), Eng,UK
111/Q8 Cheltenham, On,Can
34/D3 Cheltenham, Eng,UK
53/P5 Chelyabinsk, Rus.
53/P5 Chelyabinsk Obl., Rus.
57/L2 Chelyuskina (cape), Rus.
87/E3 Chembe, Zam.
38/G3 Chemnitz, Ger.
67/A2 Chen (riv.), China

61/K2 Chenāb (riv.), India, Pak.
82/E2 Chenachane (well), Alg.
106/D4 Cheney, Wa,US
66/C3 Cheng'anpu, China
66/D2 Chengde, China
66/E3 Chengshan Jiao (cape), China
31/T10 Chennevières-sur-Marne, Fr.
44/F3 Chenôve, Fr.
67/B2 Chenzhou, China
51/G5 Chepelare, Bul.
79/V12 Chépénéhé, NCal.
96/C2 Chépica, Chile
101/F6 Chepigana, Pan.
34/D3 Chepstow, Wal,UK
53/M4 Cheptsa (riv.), Rus.
44/D3 Cher (riv.), Fr.
113/J3 Cheraw, SC,US
44/C2 Cherbourg, Fr.
81/S15 Cherchell, Alg.
62/E1 Cheremkhovo, Rus.
52/H4 Cherepovets, Rus.
81/V17 Cherf (riv.), Alg.
81/S16 Chergui (lake), Alg.
81/V18 Cheria, Alg.
54/E2 Cherkassy, Ukr.
54/D2 Cherkassy Obl., Ukr.
55/G3 Cherkessk, Rus.
76/E6 Chermside, Austl.
53/M2 Chernaya (riv.), Rus.
54/D2 Chernigov, Ukr.
54/D2 Chernigov Obl., Ukr.
51/H4 Cherni Lom (riv.), Bul.
51/F4 Cherni Vrŭkh (peak), Bul.
54/C2 Chernovtsy, Ukr.
54/C2 Chernovtsy Obl., Ukr.
53/N4 Chernushka, Rus.
62/H1 Chernyshevsk, Rus.
109/H3 Cherokee, Ok,US
112/E2 Cherokees (lake), Ok,US
71/F2 Cherrapunjee, India
108/D3 Cherry Creek, Nv,US
115/E6 Cherry Hill, NJ,US
115/D3 Cherry Valley, Ca,US
57/Q3 Cherskiy (range), Rus.
31/M7 Chertsey, Eng,UK
51/G4 Cherven Bryag, Bul.
54/C2 Chervonograd, Ukr.
35/E3 Cherwell (riv.), Eng,UK
110/C3 Chesaning, Mi,US
110/E4 Chesapeake (bay), Md, Va,US
35/F3 Chesham, Eng,UK
33/F5 Cheshire (co.), Eng,UK
33/F5 Cheshire (plain), Eng,UK
53/K2 Cheshskaya (bay), Rus.
31/N6 Cheshunt, Eng,UK
33/F5 Chester, Eng,UK
108/B2 Chester, Ca,US
106/F3 Chester, Mt,US
115/F5 Chester, NJ,US
115/E6 Chester, Pa,US
113/H3 Chester, SC,US
102/G2 Chesterfield (inlet), NW,Can
78/E7 Chesterfield (isls.), NCal.
33/G5 Chesterfield, Eng,UK
89/H7 Chesterfield, Nosy (isl.), Madg.
33/G2 Chester-le-Street, Eng,UK
76/B3 Chesterton (range), Austl.
111/G2 Chesuncook (lake), Me,US
100/D4 Chetumal (bay), Belz., Mex.
100/D4 Chetumal, Mex.
106/C2 Chetwynd, BC,Can
31/T10 Chevilly-Larue, Fr.
31/S10 Chevreuse, Fr.
31/T10 Chevry-Cossigny, Fr.
34/D4 Chew (riv.), Eng,UK
106/D3 Chewelah, Wa,US
34/D4 Chew Valley (lake), Eng,UK
109/H4 Cheyenne, Ok,US
107/H4 Cheyenne (riv.), SD, Wy,US
107/G5 Cheyenne (cap.), Wy,US
109/G3 Cheyenne Wells, Co,US
70/C3 Chhatarpur, India
70/C3 Chhindwāra, India
69/D3 Chhlong, Camb.
66/D4 Chi (riv.), China
69/C2 Chi (riv.), Thai.
69/B2 Chiang Dao (caves), Thai.
69/B2 Chiang Mai, Thai.
69/B2 Chiang Rai, Thai.
48/C1 Chiani (riv.), It.
100/C4 Chiapas (state), Mex.
55/G4 Chiatura, Geo.
45/H4 Chiavari, It.
45/H3 Chiavenna, It.
67/D3 Chiayi, Tai.
65/G3 Chiba, Japan
65/G3 Chiba (pref.), Japan
110/F1 Chibougamau, Qu,Can
110/F1 Chibougamau (lake), Qu,Can
110/F1 Chibougamau (riv.), Qu,Can
114/D3 Chibukak (pt.), Ak,US
89/F2 Chibuto, Moz.
116/Q16 Chicago, Il,US
116/Q16 Chicago Heights, Il,US
116/Q16 Chicago Ridge, Il,US
114/L4 Chichagof (isl.), Ak,US
61/K2 Chīchāwatni, Pak.
66/C2 Chicheng, China
100/D3 Chichén Itzá (ruins), Mex.
74/B4 Chichester (range), Austl.
35/F5 Chichester, Eng,UK
65/F3 Chichibu, Japan
65/F3 Chichibu-Tama Nat'l Park, Japan
100/D5 Chichigalpa, Nic.
78/D2 Chichishima (isls.), Japan
113/G3 Chickamauga (lake), Tn,US
109/H4 Chickasha, Ok,US
34/D5 Chickerell, Eng,UK
46/B4 Chiclana de la Frontera, Sp.
92/C5 Chiclayo, Peru
96/C4 Chico (riv.), Arg.
96/D5 Chico (riv.), Arg.
108/B3 Chico, Ca,US
111/F3 Chicopee, Ma,US
87/D4 Chicote, Ang.
111/G1 Chicoutimi, Qu,Can
31/P8 Chiddingstone, Eng,UK
103/K2 Chidley (cape), Nf,Can
113/H4 Chiefland, Fl,US
69/D1 Chiem Hoa, Viet.
45/K3 Chiemsee (lake), Ger.
48/C1 Chienti (riv.), It.
69/B4 Chieo Lan (res.), Thai.
43/E5 Chiers (riv.), Fr.
45/J3 Chiese (riv.), It.
48/D1 Chieti, It.
35/E4 Chieveley, Eng,UK
63/H3 Chifeng, China
94/B5 Chifre (mts.), Braz.
65/F3 Chigasaki, Japan
114/G4 Chiginagak (mtn.), Ak,US
111/H2 Chignecto (bay), NB,Can
31/P7 Chigwell, Eng,UK
65/L10 Chihayaakasaka, Japan
66/D3 Chihli (Bo Hai) (gulf), China
101/N8 Chihuahua, Mex.
101/N8 Chihuahua (state), Mex.
109/H3 Chikaskia (riv.), Ks,US
70/C5 Chikballāpur, India
70/C3 Chikhli, India
70/C5 Chikmagalūr, India
62/G1 Chikoy (riv.), Rus.
64/B4 Chikugo (riv.), Japan
65/F2 Chikuma (riv.), Japan
65/H8 Chikura, Japan
70/D4 Chilakalūrupet, India
100/B4 Chilapa, Mex.
70/C6 Chilaw, SrL.
106/C3 Chilcotin (riv.), BC,Can
113/G3 Childersburg, Al,US
112/C3 Childress, Tx,US
90/B6 Chile
100/D5 Chile (mt.), Hon.
91/C2 Chilecito, Arg.
87/E3 Chililabombwe, Zam.
70/E4 Chilka (lake), India
106/C3 Chilko (lake), BC,Can
114/L4 Chilkoot (pass), BC,Can, Ak,US
96/B3 Chillán, Chile
110/B3 Chillicothe, Il,US
109/J3 Chillicothe, Mo,US
110/D4 Chillicothe, Oh,US
106/C3 Chilliwack, BC,Can
31/S10 Chilly-Mazarin, Fr.
96/B4 Chiloé (isl.), Chile
96/B4 Chiloé Nat'l Park, Chile
106/C5 Chiloquin, Or,US
100/B4 Chilpancingo, Mex.
35/F3 Chiltern (hills), Eng,UK
87/G4 Chilwa (lake), Malw.
101/F6 Chimán, Pan.
42/D3 Chimay, Belg.
56/F5 Chimbay, Uzb.
92/C4 Chimborazo (vol.), Ecu.
92/C5 Chimbote, Peru
68/A3 Chimkent, Kaz.
101/N7 Chimney (peak), NM.,US
71/F3 Chin (state), Burma
63/K5 Chin (isl.), SKor.
58/J6 China
100/D5 Chinandega, Nic.
112/B4 Chinati (mts.), Tx,US
101/P8 Chinati (peak), Tx.,US
92/C6 Chincha Alta, Peru
102/E3 Chinchaga (riv.), Ab,Can
110/F4 Chincoteague, Va,US
71/F3 Chindwin (riv.), Burma
92/D3 Chingaza Nat'l Park, Col.
31/P7 Chingford, Eng,UK
70/C5 Chingleput, India
87/E3 Chingola, Zam.
84/B1 Chinguetti, Dhar de (hills), Mrta.
64/A3 Chinhae, SKor.
87/F4 Chinhoyi, Zim.
114/H4 Chiniak (cape), Ak,US
61/K2 Chiniot, Pak.
69/D3 Chinit (riv.), Camb.
83/K6 Chinko (riv.), CAfr.
108/E3 Chinle (dry riv.), Az, Ut,US
35/F3 Chinnor, Eng,UK
65/F3 Chino, Japan
115/C2 Chino, Ca,US
106/F3 Chinook, Mt,US
101/F6 Chinú, Col.
87/F3 Chipata, Zam.
66/D3 Chiping, China
46/B4 Chipiona, Sp.
113/G4 Chipley, Fl,US
70/B4 Chiplūn, India
113/G4 Chipola (riv.), Fl,US
34/D4 Chippenham, Eng,UK
107/K4 Chippewa (riv.), Mn,US
110/B2 Chippewa (riv.), Wi,US
110/B2 Chippewa Falls, Wi,US
35/E2 Chipping Campden, Eng,UK
35/E3 Chipping Norton, Eng,UK
31/P6 Chipping Ongar, Eng,UK
34/D3 Chipping Sodbury, Eng,UK
31/N8 Chipstead, Eng,UK
111/H2 Chiputneticook (lakes), NB,Can, Me,US
100/D5 Chiquimula, Guat.
92/D2 Chiquinquirá, Col.
90/C6 Chiquita, Mar (lake), Arg.
90/A3 Chira (riv.), Peru
70/D4 Chīrāla, India
68/A3 Chirchik, Uzb.
82/H3 Chirfa, Niger
101/N7 Chiricahua (peak), Az.,US
108/E4 Chiricahua Nat'l Mon., Az,US
114/G4 Chirikof (isl.), Ak,US
100/E6 Chiriquí (gulf), Pan.
33/E6 Chirk, Eng,UK
36/D3 Chirnside, Sc,UK
51/G4 Chirpan, Bul.
100/E6 Chirripó Grande (mt.), CR
100/E6 Chirripó Nat'l Park, CR
65/N10 Chiryu, Japan
103/J3 Chisasibi (Fort-George), Qu,Can
100/C4 Chisec, Guat.
35/E3 Chiseldon, Eng,UK
110/A2 Chisholm, Mn,US
61/K3 Chishtiān Mandi, Pak.
83/P8 Chisimayu, Som.
50/E2 Chişineu Criş, Rom.
53/L5 Chistopol', Rus.
31/M6 Chiswell Green, Eng,UK
31/N7 Chiswick, Eng,UK
35/M10 Chita, Japan
65/M10 Chita (bay), Japan
65/M10 Chita (pen.), Japan
62/G1 Chita, Rus.
87/B4 Chitado, Ang.
87/F2 Chitipa, Malw.
70/B3 Chitorgarh, India
63/N3 Chitose, Japan
70/C5 Chitradurga, India
70/D2 Chitrakut, India
101/E6 Chitré, Pan.
71/F3 Chittagong, Bang.
70/C5 Chittoor, India
87/D4 Chiume, Ang.
45/G4 Chivasso, It.
101/M8 Chivato (pt.), Mex.
96/E2 Chivilcoy, Arg.
81/R15 Chlef, Alg.
81/R15 Chlef (riv.), Alg.
69/D3 Choam Khsant, Camb.
96/C1 Choapa (riv.), Chile
87/D4 Chobe Nat'l Park, Bots.
39/K4 Choč (peak), Slvk.
39/J4 Choceň, Czh.
39/H3 Chocianów, Pol.
108/D4 Chocolate (mts.), Ca,US
45/K1 Chodov, Czh.
39/J2 Chodzież, Pol.
65/F3 Chōfu, Japan
65/H7 Chōfu, Japan
78/E5 Choiseul (isl.), Sol.
31/T10 Choisy-le-Roi, Fr.
39/H2 Chojna, Pol.
39/J2 Chojnice, Pol.
39/H3 Chojnów, Pol.
63/N4 Chokai-san (mtn.), Japan
112/D4 Choke Canyon (res.), Tx,US
62/D5 Chola (mts.), China
44/C3 Cholet, Fr.
35/E3 Cholsey, Eng,UK
100/D5 Choluteca (riv.)
100/D5 Choluteca, Hon.
87/E4 Choma, Zam.
64/A2 Chŏmch'ŏn, SKor.
70/E2 Chomo Lhāri (mtn.), Bhu.
45/K1 Chomutov, Czh.
65/J7 Chōnan, Japan
63/K4 Ch'ŏnan, SKor.
69/C3 Chon Buri, Thai.
96/B4 Chonchi, Chile
92/B4 Chone, Ecu.
63/K3 Ch'ŏngjin, NKor.
63/K4 Ch'ŏngju, SKor.
69/C3 Chong Kal, Camb.
66/L8 Chongming (isl.), China
67/A2 Chongqing, China
64/A2 Ch'ŏngsong, SKor.
63/K4 Chŏnju, SKor.
96/A5 Chonos (arch.), Chile
69/D4 Chon Thanh, Viet.
33/F4 Chorley, Eng,UK
31/M7 Chorleywood, Eng,UK
54/C2 Chortkov, Ukr.
39/K3 Chorzów, Pol.
65/G3 Chōshi, Japan
39/H2 Choszczno, Pol.
92/C5 Chota, Peru
106/E4 Choteau, Mt,US
88/A2 Chowagasberg (peak), Namb.
113/J2 Chowan (riv.), NC,US
62/G2 Choybalsan, Mong.
75/R11 Christchurch, NZ
35/E5 Christchurch, Eng,UK
35/E5 Christchurch (bay), Eng,UK
114/L4 Christian (sound), Ak,US
88/D2 Christiana, SAfr.
110/D4 Christiansburg, Va,US
106/F2 Christine (riv.), Ab,Can
58/K11 Christmas (isl.), Austl.
79/K4 Christmas (Kiritimati) (atoll), Kiri.
39/H4 Chrudim, Czh.
39/K3 Chrzanów, Pol.
68/B3 Chu (riv.), Kaz.
69/D2 Chu (riv.), Viet.
66/E4 Chuanchang (riv.), China
106/E5 Chubbuck, Id,US
65/F2 Chūbu (prov.), Japan
96/C4 Chubut (prov.), Arg.
96/D4 Chubut (riv.), Arg.
101/F6 Chucanti (mt.), Pan.
64/C3 Chūgoku (mts.), Japan
64/C3 Chūgoku (prov.), Japan
72/B3 Chukai, Malay.
63/M1 Chukchagirskoye (lake), Rus.
57/U3 Chukchi (pen.), Rus.
57/S3 Chukchi Aut. Okr., Rus.
114/D3 Chukotskiy, Mys (pt.), Rus.
108/C4 Chula Vista, Ca,US
92/B5 Chulucanas, Peru
56/J4 Chulym (riv.), Rus.
68/E1 Chulyshman (riv.), Rus.
51/G4 Chumerna (peak), Bul.
69/B4 Chumphon, Thai.
56/K4 Chuna (riv.), Rus.
63/K4 Ch'unch'ŏn, SKor.
63/K4 Ch'ungju, SKor.
64/A3 Ch'ungmu, SKor.
57/L3 Chunya (riv.), Rus.
91/C1 Chuquicamata, Chile
45/H3 Chur, Swi.
71/F3 Churachandpur, India
33/F4 Church, Eng,UK
102/D3 Churchill (peak), BC,Can
102/G3 Churchill, Mb,Can
102/G3 Churchill (cape), Mb,Can
102/G3 Churchill (riv.), Mb, Sk,Can
103/K3 Churchill (riv.), Nf,Can
106/F1 Churchill (lake), Sk,Can
102/G3 Churchill (riv.), Mb, Sk,Can
77/G5 Churchill Nat'l Park, Austl.
34/D1 Church Stretton, Eng,UK
33/G6 Churnet (riv.), Eng,UK
70/B2 Churu, India
101/H5 Churuguara, Ven.
108/E3 Chuska (mts.), Az, NM,US
53/N4 Chusovaya (riv.), Rus.
53/N4 Chusovoy, Rus.
53/K5 Chuvash Aut. Rep., Rus.
64/A2 Chuwang-san Nat'l Park, SKor.
71/H2 Chuxiong, China
62/B1 Chuya (riv.), Rus.
69/E3 Chu Yang Sin (peak), Viet.
65/M9 Chūzu, Japan
72/C5 Ciamis, Indo.
48/C2 Ciampino, It.
72/C5 Cianjur, Indo.
116/Q16 Cicero, Il,US
94/C3 Cícero Dantas, Braz.
48/C2 Cicero Nat'l Park, It.
59/C2 Cide, Turk.
39/L2 Ciechanów, Pol.
39/K2 Ciechanów (prov.), Pol.
39/K2 Ciechocinek, Pol.
101/F3 Ciego de Avilla, Cuba
101/G5 Ciénaga, Col.
101/E3 Cienfuegos, Cuba
39/H3 Cieplice Śląskie Zdrój, Pol.
39/K4 Cieszyn, Pol.
46/E3 Cieza, Sp.
59/B2 Çifteler, Turk.
46/D3 Cigüela (riv.), Sp.
59/C2 Cihanbeyli, Turk.
101/P10 Cihuatlán, Mex.
46/C3 Cijara (res.), Sp.
72/C5 Cijulang, Indo.
72/C5 Cilacap, Indo.
34/C2 Cilfaesty (hill), Wal,UK
109/G3 Cimarron, Ks,US
109/H3 Cimarron (riv.), Ks, Ok,US
112/B2 Cimarron (range), NM,US
50/F2 Cîmpeni, Rom.
51/F2 Cîmpia Turzii, Rom.
51/G3 Cîmpina, Rom.
51/G3 Cîmpulung, Rom.
51/G2 Cîmpulung Moldovenesc, Rom.
47/F1 Cinca (riv.), Sp.
50/C4 Cincar (peak), Bosn.
110/C4 Cincinnati, Oh,US
96/C3 Cinco Saltos, Arg.
34/D3 Cinderford, Eng,UK
51/F3 Cîndrelu (peak), Rom.
59/B3 Çine, Turk.
43/E3 Ciney, Belg.
115/F6 Cinnaminson, NJ,US
100/C4 Cintalapa, Mex.
48/A1 Cinto (mtn.), Fr.
50/C4 Čiovo (isl.), Cro.
96/D3 Cipolletti, Arg.
107/G4 Circle, Mt,US
110/D4 Circleville, Oh,US
72/C5 Cirebon, Indo.
34/E3 Cirencester, Eng,UK
48/E3 Cirò Marina, It.
44/C4 Ciron (riv.), Fr.
88/D4 Ciskei (ind. homeland), SAfr.
51/G3 Cisnădie, Rom.
96/B5 Cisnes (riv.), Chile
44/D3 Cisse (riv.), Fr.
48/C2 Cisterna di Latina, It.
100/B4 Citlaltépetl (mt.), Mex.
116/M9 Citrus Heights, Ca,US
45/K5 Città di Castello, It.
48/E3 Cittanova, It.
100/A2 Ciudad Acuna, Mex.
101/J6 Ciudad Bolívar, Ven.
101/N8 Ciudad Camargo, Mex.
100/C4 Ciudad del Carmen, Mex.
101/N8 Ciudad Delicias, Mex.
101/P9 Ciudad de Río Grande, Mex.
47/G3 Ciudadela, Sp.
101/J6 Ciudad Guayana, Ven.
101/N8 Ciudad Guerrero, Mex.
101/P10 Ciudad Guzmán, Mex.
101/N7 Ciudad Juárez, Mex.
101/P8 Ciudad Lerdo, Mex.
100/B3 Ciudad Madero, Mex.
100/B3 Ciudad Mante, Mex.
100/B2 Ciudad Miguel Alemán, Mex.
101/N8 Ciudad Obregón, Mex.
101/G5 Ciudad Ojeda, Ven.
46/D3 Ciudad Real, Sp.
100/B2 Ciudad Río Bravo, Mex.
46/B2 Ciudad-Rodrigo, Sp.
100/B3 Ciudad Valles, Mex.
100/B3 Ciudad Victoria, Mex.
54/F4 Civa Burnu (pt.), Turk.
45/K3 Cividale del Friuli, It.
48/C1 Civita Castellana, It.
48/B1 Civitavecchia, It.
59/B2 Çivril, Turk.
66/C3 Ci Xian, China
59/E3 Cizre, Turk.
46/E1 Cizur, Sp.
35/H3 Clacton on Sea, Eng,UK
34/C2 Claerwen (res.), Wal,UK
44/D3 Clain (riv.), Fr.
102/E3 Claire (lake), Ab,Can
108/B2 Clair Engle (lake), Ca,US
44/D3 Claise (riv.), Fr.
31/S10 Clamart, Fr.
35/F5 Clanfield, Eng,UK
113/G3 Clanton, Al,US
111/Q9 Clappison's Corners, On,Can
96/D4 Clara (pt.), Arg.
36/A4 Clare (riv.), Ire.
110/C3 Clare, Mi,US
115/C2 Claremont, Ca,US
111/F3 Claremont, NH,US
109/J3 Claremore, Ok,US
77/E1 Clarence (riv.), Austl.
74/E2 Clarence (str.), Austl.
103/T7 Clarence (pt.), NW,Can
75/R11 Clarence, NZ
111/S9 Clarence, NY,US
101/G3 Clarence Town, Bahm.
112/C3 Clarendon, Tx,US
106/E3 Claresholm, BC,Can
98/J Clarie (coast), Ant.
107/J4 Clark, SD,US
77/D4 Clarke (isl.), Austl.
76/B3 Clarke (range), Austl.
106/E3 Clark Fork (riv.), Id, Mt,US
113/H3 Clark Hill (lake), Ga, SC,US
110/D4 Clarksburg, WV,US
113/F3 Clarksdale, Ms,US
111/Q8 Clarkson, On,Can
116/F6 Clarkston, Mi,US
106/D4 Clarkston, Wa,US
112/E3 Clarksville, Ar,US
113/G2 Clarksville, Tn,US
112/E3 Clarksville, Tx,US
95/B1 Claro (riv.), Braz.
42/C3 Clary, Fr.
32/D1 Clatteringshaws Loch (lake), Sc,UK
32/A2 Claudy, NI,UK
41/H5 Clausthal-Zellerfeld, Ger.
67/D4 Claveria, Phil.
116/F6 Clawson, Mi,US
109/H3 Clay Center, Ks,US
33/G5 Clay Cross, Eng,UK
35/H2 Claydon, Eng,UK
31/U10 Claye-Souilly, Fr.
31/M7 Claygate, Eng,UK
32/D3 Clay Head (pt.), IM,UK
115/E6 Claymont, De,US
116/L11 Clayton, Ca,US
113/H3 Clayton, Ga,US
109/G3 Clayton, NM,US
109/J4 Clayton, Ok,US
33/F4 Clayton-le-Moors, Eng,UK
97/S11 Clé (stream), Arg.
102/E3 Clear (hills), Ab,Can
36/H8 Clear (cape), Ire.
108/B3 Clear (lake), Ca,US
114/J4 Cleare (cape), Ak,US
107/J4 Clear Lake, SD,US
106/C3 Clearwater, BC,Can
113/H5 Clearwater, Fl,US
106/D4 Clearwater (mts.), Id,US
107/K4 Clearwater (riv.), Mn,US
32/E2 Cleator Moor, Eng,UK
112/D3 Cleburne, Tx,US
33/H4 Cleethorpes, Eng,UK
34/D3 Cleeve (hill), Eng,UK
113/H3 Clemson, SC,US
34/D2 Cleobury Mortimer, Eng,UK
73/E1 Cleopatra Needle (mtn.), Phil.
42/A4 Clères, Fr.
43/E3 Clerf (riv.), Belg., Lux.
42/B5 Clermont, Fr.
34/D4 Clevedon, Eng,UK
76/B2 Cleveland (cape), Austl.
33/G2 Cleveland (co.), Eng,UK
33/G3 Cleveland (hills), Eng,UK
113/F3 Cleveland, Ms,US
106/E3 Cleveland (peak), Mt,US
110/D3 Cleveland, Oh,US
113/G3 Cleveland, Tn,US
112/E4 Cleveland, Tx,US
95/A3 Clevelândia, Braz.
36/A4 Clew (bay), Ire.
113/H5 Clewiston, Fl,US
42/B6 Clichy, Fr.
31/T10 Clichy-sous-Bois, Fr.
34/D4 Clifton, Eng,UK
108/E4 Clifton, Az,US
115/F5 Clifton, NJ,US
112/D4 Clifton, Tx,US
113/J2 Clifton Forge, Va,US
34/D2 Clifton upon Teme, Eng,UK
42/C5 Clignon (riv.), Fr.
113/H3 Clingmans (mtn.), Tn,US
106/C3 Clinton, BC,Can
107/L5 Clinton, Ia,US
110/B3 Clinton, Il,US
113/F4 Clinton, La,US
116/G6 Clinton, Mi,US
116/F6 Clinton (riv.), Mi,US
109/J3 Clinton, Mo,US
113/F3 Clinton, Ms,US
113/J3 Clinton, NC,US
115/F5 Clinton, NJ,US
115/F4 Clinton (res.), NJ,US
109/H4 Clinton, Ok,US
113/H3 Clinton, SC,US
102/F2 Clinton-Colden (lake), NW,Can
102/B2 Clinton Creek, Yk,Can
115/K8 Clinton (Surratts-ville), Md,US
110/D3 Clio, Mi,US
28/D5 Clipperton (isl.), Fr.
35/F2 Clipston, Eng,UK
33/F4 Clitheroe, Eng,UK
74/A4 Cloates (pt.), Austl.
32/B4 Clogherhead, Ire.
32/B4 Clogher Head (pt.), Ire.
32/C3 Cloghy, NI,UK
36/B4 Clonmel, Ire.
41/F3 Cloppenburg, Ger.
107/K4 Cloquet, Mn,US
91/E2 Clorinda, Arg.
32/E1 Closeburn, Sc,UK
106/G4 Cloud (peak), Wy,US
112/B3 Cloudcroft, NM,US
114/G3 Cloudy (mtn.), Ak,US
32/B2 Cloughmills, NI,UK
33/H3 Cloughton, Eng,UK
34/B4 Clovelly, Eng,UK
108/B3 Cloverdale, Ca,US
108/C3 Clovis, Ca,US
109/G4 Clovis, NM,US
36/C2 Clovullin, Sc,UK
33/G5 Clowne, Eng,UK
51/F2 Cluj (co.), Rom.
51/F2 Cluj-Napoca, Rom.
34/C2 Clun, Eng,UK
34/B3 Clunderwen, Wal,UK
45/G3 Cluses, Fr.
45/H4 Clusone, It.
32/E5 Clwyd (co.), Wal,UK
33/E5 Clwyd (riv.), Wal,UK
33/E5 Clwydian (range), Wal,UK
34/C3 Clydach, Wal,UK
111/H2 Clyde (riv.), NS,Can
106/E2 Clyde, NW,Can
36/C3 Clyde (riv.), Sc,UK
36/C3 Clyde, Firth of (inlet), Sc,UK
34/C2 Clywedog (riv.), Wal,UK
111/R8 CN Tower, On,Can
46/B2 Côa (riv.), Port.
108/C4 Coachella, Ca,US
32/B2 Coagh, NI,UK
100/A2 Coahuila (state), Mex.
106/E3 Coaldale, Ab,Can
109/H4 Coalgate, Ok,US
106/E3 Coalhurst, Ab,Can
32/B2 Coalisland, NI,UK
35/E1 Coalville, Eng,UK
108/E2 Coalville, Ut,US
94/C4 Coaraci, Braz.
92/F4 Coari, Braz.
92/F5 Coari (riv.), Braz.
102/C2 Coast (mts.), BC, Yk,Can
104/B4 Coast (ranges), Ca,US
113/H4 Coastal (plain), US
100/B4 Coatepec, Mex.
111/G2 Coaticook, Qu,Can
103/H2 Coats (isl.), NW,Can
98/Y Coats Land (reg.), Ant.
100/C4 Coatzacoalcos, Mex.
100/D3 Coba (ruins), Mex.
46/B1 Coba de Serpe, Sierra de (mtn.), Sp.
100/C4 Cobán, Guat.
77/D3 Cobberas (peak), Austl.
115/B1 Cobblestone (mtn.), Ca,US
107/K2 Cobham (riv.), Mb, On,Can
31/M8 Cobham, Eng,UK
74/E2 Cobourg (pen.), Austl.
110/E3 Cobourg, On,Can
96/B3 Cobquecura, Chile
77/F5 Coburg, Austl.
103/T7 Coburg (isl.), NW,Can
45/J1 Coburg, Ger.
47/E3 Cocentaina, Sp.
92/E7 Cochabamba, Bol.
70/C6 Cochin, India
113/H3 Cochran, Ga,US
106/E3 Cochrane, Ab,Can
110/D1 Cochrane, On,Can
97/J8 Cockburn (chan.), Chile
36/D3 Cockburnspath, Sc,UK
33/E2 Cockermouth, Eng,UK
88/D4 Cockscomb (peak), SAfr.
92/A2 Coco (isl.), CR
100/E5 Coco (riv.), Hon.
113/H4 Cocoa, Fl,US
108/D4 Coconino (plat.), Az,US
77/C2 Cocoparra Nat'l Park, Austl.
58/J11 Cocos (Keeling) (isls.), Austl.
103/K3 Cod (isl.), Nf,Can
33/G3 Cod Beck (riv.), Eng,UK
96/C2 Codegua, Chile
51/G3 Codlea, Rom.
94/B2 Codó, Braz.
45/H4 Codogno, It.
101/J4 Codrington, Anti.
45/K4 Codroipo, It.
34/D1 Codsall, Eng,UK
106/F4 Cody, Wy,US
94/B2 Coelho Neto, Braz.
41/E5 Coesfeld, Ger.
29/M6 Coetivy (isl.), Sey.
106/D4 Coeur d'Alene, Id,US
106/D4 Coeur d'Alene (lake), Id,US
40/D3 Coevorden, Neth.
109/J3 Coffeyville, Ks,US
77/E1 Coffs Harbour, Austl.
35/G3 Coggeshall, Eng,UK
48/A2 Coghinas (lake), It.
44/C4 Cognac, Fr.
100/E6 Coiba (isl.), Pan.
97/K7 Coig (riv.), Arg.
96/B5 Coihaique, Chile
96/C3 Coihueco, Chile
70/C5 Coimbatore, India
46/A2 Coimbra, Port.
46/A2 Coimbra (dist.), Port.
46/C4 Coín, Sp.
47/P10 Coina (riv.), Port.
44/F4 Coise (riv.), Fr.
92/E2 Cojedes (riv.), Ven.
101/G5 Cojoro, Ven.
96/C5 Cojudo Blanco (peak), Arg.
100/D5 Cojutepeque, ESal.
106/F5 Cokeville, Wy,US
77/B3 Colac, Austl.
109/H2 Colamus (riv.), Ne,US
47/P10 Colares, Port.
95/D1 Colatina, Braz.
98/P Colbeck (cape), Ant.
96/C2 Colbún, Chile
109/G3 Colby, Ks,US
35/G3 Colchester, Eng,UK
106/F2 Cold (lake), Ab, Sk,Can
33/F2 Cold Fell (mtn.), Eng,UK
106/F2 Cold Lake, Ab,Can
107/K4 Cold Spring, Mn,US
112/E4 Coldspring, Tx,US
109/H3 Coldwater, Ks,US
110/C3 Coldwater, Mi,US
35/E3 Cole (riv.), Eng,UK
34/D3 Coleford, Eng,UK
112/D4 Coleman, Tx,US
59/E3 Çölemerik, Turk.
32/B1 Coleraine, NI,UK
32/B1 Coleraine (dist.), NI,UK
88/D3 Colesberg, SAfr.
35/E2 Coleshill, Eng,UK
115/J7 Colesville, Md,US
106/D4 Colfax, Wa,US
103/S6 Colgate (cape), NW,Can
96/C5 Colhué Huapí (lake), Arg.
69/D2 Co Lieu, Viet.
101/P10 Colima, Mex.
101/P10 Colima (state), Mex.
96/C2 Colina, Chile
94/A2 Colinas, Braz.
46/D2 Collado-Villalba, Sp.
114/J3 College, Ak,US
115/K8 College Park, Md,US
112/D4 College Station, Tx,US
45/G4 Collegno, It.
77/D1 Collie, Austl.
74/C3 Collier (bay), Austl.
33/G2 Collier Law (hill), Eng,UK
113/F3 Collierville, Tn,US
34/B6 Colliford (res.), Eng,UK
33/G4 Collingham, Eng,UK
110/D2 Collingwood, On,Can
75/R11 Collingwood, NZ
113/F4 Collins, Ms,US
109/J3 Collinsville, Ok,US
110/E4 Collinsville, Va,US
81/V17 Collo, Alg.
45/G2 Colmar, Fr.
46/D2 Colmenar Viejo, Sp.
97/J7 Colmillo (cape), Chile
32/D1 Colmonell, Sc,UK
35/E3 Coln (riv.), Eng,UK
33/F4 Colne, Eng,UK
35/G3 Colne (riv.), Eng,UK
31/N6 Colney Heath, Eng,UK
43/F2 Cologne (Köln), Ger.
31/S10 Colombes, Fr.
92/D3 Colombia
95/B3 Colombo, Braz.
70/C6 Colombo (cap.), SrL.
44/D5 Colomiers, Fr.
96/E2 Colón, Arg.
96/F2 Colón, Arg.
101/F6 Colón, Pan.
78/C4 Colonia, Micro.
97/F2 Colonia (dept.), Uru.
97/F2 Colonia Del Sacramento, Uru.
94/D3 Colônia Leopoldina, Braz.
97/K7 Colorado (peak), Arg.
96/D3 Colorado (riv.), Arg.
95/B2 Colorado, Braz.
108/D4 Colorado (riv.), Mex., US
108/E3 Colorado (plat.), US
108/F3 Colorado (state), US
112/D4 Colorado (riv.), Tx,US
109/F3 Colorado City, Co,US
112/C3 Colorado City, Tx,US
108/E3 Colorado Nat'l Mon., Co,US
91/C2 Colorados, Desagües de los (marsh), Arg.
109/F3 Colorado Springs, Co,US
92/E7 Colquiri, Bol.
106/G4 Colstrip, Mt,US
32/D1 Colt (hill), Sc,UK
96/C2 Coltauco, Chile
35/H1 Coltishall, Eng,UK
115/C2 Colton, Ca,US
115/F5 Colts Neck, NJ,US
90/D4 Coluene (riv.), Braz.
102/E3 Columbia (mtn.), Ab,Can
106/C2 Columbia (mts.), BC,Can
103/T6 Columbia (cape), NW,Can
106/C4 Columbia (riv.), Can., US
106/D4 Columbia (plat.), US
110/C4 Columbia, Ky,US
112/E3 Columbia, La,US
115/K7 Columbia, Md,US
109/J3 Columbia, Mo,US
113/F4 Columbia, Ms,US
113/H3 Columbia (cap.), SC,US
113/G3 Columbia, Tn,US
106/E3 Columbia Falls, Mt,US
88/B4 Columbine (cape), SAfr.
113/G3 Columbus, Ga,US
110/C4 Columbus, In,US
113/F3 Columbus, Ms,US
106/F4 Columbus, Mt,US
109/H2 Columbus, Ne,US
115/F5 Columbus, NJ,US
108/F5 Columbus, NM,US
110/D4 Columbus (cap.), Oh,US
112/D4 Columbus, Tx,US
108/B3 Colusa, Ca,US
102/D2 Colville (lake), NW,Can
114/H2 Colville (riv.), Ak,US
106/D3 Colville, Wa,US
116/B3 Colvos (passg.), Wa,US
34/D2 Colwall, Eng,UK
34/C4 Colwinston, Wal,UK
32/E5 Colwyn Bay, Wal,UK
45/K4 Comacchio, It.
45/K4 Comacchio, Valli di (lag.), It.
112/D4 Comanche, Tx,US
96/F3 Comandante Nicanor Otamendi, Arg.
51/H2 Comăneşti, Rom.
51/G3 Comarnic, Rom.
100/D5 Comayagua, Hon.
91/B3 Combarbalá, Chile
34/B4 Combe Martin, Eng,UK
32/C2 Comber, NI,UK
31/T11 Combs-la-Ville, Fr.
76/C4 Comet (riv.), Austl.
71/F3 Comilla, Bang.
42/B2 Comines, Belg.
42/C2 Comines, Fr.
115/G5 Commack, NY,US
44/E3 Commentry, Fr.
115/B2 Commerce, Ca,US
43/E6 Commercy, Fr.

103/H2 **Committee** (bay), NW,Can
68/B4 **Communism** (Kommunizma) (peak), Taj.
45/H4 **Como**, It.
45/H3 **Como** (lake), It.
116/P14 **Como** (lake), Wi,US
96/D5 **Comodoro Rivadavia**, Arg.
84/D4 **Comoé** (prov.), Burk.
84/E4 **Comoé Nat'l Park**, IvC.
70/C6 **Comorin** (cape), India
89/G5 **Comoros**
106/B3 **Comox**, BC,Can
42/B5 **Compiègne**, Fr.
101/P9 **Compostela**, Mex.
115/B3 **Compton**, Ca,US
112/C4 **Comstock**, Tx,US
84/B4 **Conakry** (cap.), Gui.
84/B4 **Conakry** (comm.), Gui.
44/B3 **Concarneau**, Fr.
95/E1 **Conceição da Barra**, Braz.
95/B1 **Conceição das Alagoas**, Braz.
93/J5 **Conceição do Araguaia**, Braz.
94/C3 **Conceição do Coité**, Braz.
95/D1 **Conceição do Mato Dentro**, Braz.
95/H6 **Conceição do Rio Verde**, Braz.
92/F7 **Concepción** (lake), Bol.
96/B3 **Concepción**, Chile
91/E1 **Concepción**, Par.
92/C6 **Concepción**, Peru
100/A3 **Concepción del Oro**, Mex.
96/F2 **Concepción del Uruguay**, Arg.
108/B4 **Conception** (pt.), Ca,US
95/F7 **Conchal**, Braz.
109/F4 **Conchas** (lake), NM,US
31/U10 **Conches**, Fr.
109/G5 **Concho** (riv.), Tx,US
101/N8 **Conchos** (riv.), Mex.
116/K11 **Concord**, Ca,US
113/H3 **Concord**, NC,US
111/G3 **Concord** (cap.), NH,US
91/E3 **Concordia**, Arg.
95/A3 **Concórdia**, Braz.
109/H3 **Concordia**, Ks,US
106/C3 **Concrete**, Wa,US
69/D2 **Con Cuong**, Viet.
101/F3 **Condado**, Cuba
75/J5 **Condamine** (riv.), Austl.
42/C3 **Condé-sur-L'Escaut**, Fr.
44/C2 **Condé-sur-Noireau**, Fr.
76/C4 **Condomine** (riv.), Austl.
106/C4 **Condon**, Or,US
43/D3 **Condroz** (plat.), Belg.
113/G4 **Conecuh** (riv.), Al,US
45/K4 **Conegliano**, It.
112/B2 **Conejos**, Co,US
31/S10 **Conflans-Sainte-Honorine**, Fr.
115/G4 **Congers**, NY,US
67/B3 **Conghua**, China
33/F5 **Congleton**, Eng,UK
80/D5 **Congo**
83/K7 **Congo** (basin), Afr.
87/C1 **Congo** (riv.), Afr.
95/D2 **Congonhas**, Braz.
96/C3 **Conguillio Nat'l Park**, Chile
96/C4 **Cónico, Cerro** (Nevado) (peak), Arg., Chile
46/B4 **Conil de la Frontera**, Sp.
33/H5 **Coningsby**, Eng,UK
33/G5 **Conisbrough**, Eng,UK
33/E3 **Coniston**, Eng,UK
33/E3 **Coniston Water** (lake), Eng,UK
32/C2 **Conlig**, NI,UK
103/J1 **Conn** (lake), NW,Can
36/A4 **Connacht** (prov.), Ire.
33/E5 **Connah's Quay**, Wal,UK
110/D3 **Conneaut**, Oh,US
111/G2 **Connecticut** (riv.), US
111/F3 **Connecticut** (state), US
36/C2 **Connel**, Sc,UK
110/E3 **Connellsville**, Pa,US
36/H7 **Connemara Nat'l Park**, Ire.
110/C4 **Connersville**, In,US
36/A3 **Conn, Lough** (lake), Ire.
97/K7 **Cono Grande** (peak), Arg.
76/D4 **Conondale Nat'l Park**, Austl.
44/E4 **Conques**, Fr.
106/F3 **Conrad**, Mt,US
100/B1 **Conroe**, Tx.,US
112/E4 **Conroe**, Tx,US
95/D2 **Conselheiro Lafaiete**, Braz.
95/D1 **Conselheiro Pena**, Braz.
33/G2 **Consett**, Eng,UK
115/E5 **Conshohocken**, Pa,US
100/E3 **Consolación del Sur**, Cuba
69/D4 **Con Son** (isl.), Viet.
45/H3 **Constance** (Bodensee) (lake), Ger., Swi.
51/J3 **Constanța**, Rom.
51/J3 **Constanța** (co.), Rom.
47/F2 **Constantí**, Sp.
46/C4 **Constantina**, Sp.
81/V17 **Constantine**, Alg.
81/V17 **Constantine** (gov.), Alg.
114/G4 **Constantine** (cape), Ak,US
96/B2 **Constitución**, Chile
97/T11 **Constitución** (res.), Uru.
101/L7 **Constitución de 1857 Nat'l Park**, Mex.
46/D3 **Consuegra**, Sp.
70/E3 **Contai**, India
45/K4 **Contarina**, It.
94/B4 **Contas** (riv.), Braz.
95/C1 **Contegem**, Braz.
42/B4 **Contigny**, Fr.
106/C2 **Continental** (ranges), Ab, BC,Can
116/L11 **Contra Costa** (can.), Ca,US
101/F3 **Contramaestre**, Cuba
46/E3 **Contreras** (res.), Sp.
114/J3 **Controller** (bay), Ak,US
96/B3 **Contulmo**, Chile
102/E2 **Contwoyto** (lake), NW,Can
42/B4 **Conty**, Fr.
101/G6 **Convención**, Col.
48/E2 **Conversano**, It.
76/C3 **Conway** (cape), Austl.
112/E3 **Conway**, Ar,US
111/G3 **Conway**, NH,US
113/J3 **Conway**, SC,US
76/C3 **Conway Range Nat'l Park**, Austl.
32/E5 **Conway, Vale of** (val.), Wal,UK
32/E5 **Conwy**, Wal,UK
32/D5 **Conwy** (bay), Wal,UK
32/E5 **Conwy** (riv.), Wal,UK
70/E2 **Cooch Behār**, India
76/F7 **Coochiemudlo** (isl.), Austl.
97/K8 **Cook** (bay), Chile
75/R11 **Cook** (str.), NZ
114/H3 **Cook** (inlet), Ak,US
113/G2 **Cookeville**, Tn,US
98/L **Cook Ice Shelf**, Ant.
79/J6 **Cook Islands** (terr.), NZ
75/R11 **Cook, Mount** (peak), NZ
32/B2 **Cookstown**, NI,UK
32/B2 **Cookstown** (dist.), NI,UK
77/B3 **Coola Coola** (swamp), Austl.
32/B4 **Cooley** (pt.), Ire.
76/D4 **Cooloola Nat'l Park**, Austl.
77/D3 **Cooma**, Austl.
70/B5 **Coondapoor**, India
70/C5 **Coonoor**, India
74/F5 **Cooper** (cr.), Austl.
112/E3 **Cooper**, Tx,US
107/J4 **Cooperstown**, ND,US
77/A3 **Coorong Nat'l Park**, Austl.
113/G3 **Coosa** (riv.), Al,US
106/B5 **Coos Bay**, Or,US
77/D2 **Cootamundra**, Austl.
115/G5 **Copague**, NY,US
96/C3 **Copahué** (vol.), Chile
100/D5 **Copán** (ruins), Hon.
46/E4 **Cope** (cape), Sp.
32/C2 **Copeland** (isl.), NI,UK
38/G1 **Copenhagen** (København) (cap.), Den.
49/F2 **Copertino**, It.
77/D1 **Copeton** (dam), Austl.
91/B2 **Copiapó**, Chile
45/J4 **Copparo**, It.
41/G4 **Coppenbrügge**, Ger.
112/D4 **Copperas Cove**, Tx,US
102/E2 **Coppermine** (riv.), NW,Can
33/F4 **Coppull**, Eng,UK
51/G2 **Copșa Mică**, Rom.
33/F1 **Coquet** (riv.), Eng,UK
33/G1 **Coquet Dale** (val.), Eng,UK
91/B2 **Coquimbo**, Chile
96/C1 **Coquimbo** (reg.), Chile
51/G4 **Corabia**, Rom.
94/A5 **Coração de Jesus**, Braz.
76/C1 **Coral** (sea)
113/H5 **Coral Gables**, Fl,US
75/J2 **Coral Sea Is.** (terr.), Austl.
113/H5 **Coral Springs**, Fl,US
115/H5 **Coram**, NY,US
44/E2 **Corbeil-Essonnes**, Fr.
81/T15 **Corbelin** (cape), Alg.
42/B4 **Corbie**, Fr.
44/E5 **Corbieres** (mts.), Fr.
110/C4 **Corbin**, Ky,US
33/F2 **Corbridge**, Eng,UK
35/F2 **Corby**, Eng,UK
95/K7 **Corcovado** (mon.), Braz.
96/B4 **Corcovado** (gulf), Chile
96/B4 **Corcovado** (vol.), Chile
100/E6 **Corcovado Nat'l Park**, CR
95/D2 **Cordeiro**, Braz.
113/H4 **Cordele**, Ga,US
109/H4 **Cordell** (New Cordell), Ok,US
45/K4 **Cordenons**, It.
92/D3 **Cordillera de los Picachos Nat'l Park**, Col.
91/D3 **Córdoba**, Arg.
91/D3 **Córdoba** (mts.), Arg.
96/E2 **Córdoba** (prov.), Arg.
100/B4 **Córdoba**, Mex.
46/C4 **Córdoba**, Sp.
114/J3 **Cordova** (peak), Ak,US
46/E1 **Corella**, Sp.
94/C2 **Coremas**, Braz.
92/G3 **Corentyne** (riv.), Guy.
49/F3 **Corfu** (Kérkira) (isl.), Gre.
46/B3 **Coria**, Sp.
46/B4 **Coria del Río**, Sp.
77/D2 **Coricudgy** (peak), Austl.
48/E3 **Corigliano Calabro**, It.
75/J3 **Coringa Islets** (isls.), Austl.
49/H4 **Corinth** (ruins), Gre.
113/F3 **Corinth**, Ms,US
49/H4 **Corinth** (Kórinthos), Gre.
95/C1 **Corinto**, Braz.
100/D5 **Corinto**, Nic.
46/A1 **Coristanco**, Sp.
48/C4 **Corleone**, It.
51/H5 **Çorlu**, Turk.
42/D5 **Cormontreuil**, Fr.
107/H2 **Cormorant**, Mb,Can
107/H2 **Cormorant** (lake), Mb,Can
34/C1 **Corndon** (hill), Wal,UK
95/B2 **Cornélio Procópio**, Braz.
103/K2 **Cornelius Grinnel** (bay), NW,Can
47/L7 **Cornella**, Sp.
77/C3 **Corner** (inlet), Austl.
111/K1 **Corner Brook**, Nf,Can
110/E3 **Corning**, NY,US
76/B3 **Cornish** (cr.), Austl.
45/J4 **Corno alle Scale** (peak), It.
97/L8 **Cornú** (peak), Arg.
103/S7 **Cornwall** (isl.), NW,Can
110/F2 **Cornwall**, On,Can
111/J2 **Cornwall**, PE,Can
34/B6 **Cornwall** (co.), Eng,UK
103/S7 **Cornwallis** (isl.), NW,Can
101/H5 **Coro**, Ven.
80/J9 **Coroa** (mtn.), CpV.
94/A2 **Coroatá**, Braz.
92/E7 **Corocoro**, Bol.
95/C1 **Coromandel**, Braz.
70/D5 **Coromandel** (coast), India
75/S10 **Coromandel**, NZ
75/S10 **Coromandel** (pen.), NZ
67/D5 **Coron**, Phil.
115/C3 **Corona**, Ca,US
109/F4 **Corona**, NM,US
100/E6 **Coronado** (bay), CR
106/F2 **Coronation**, Ab,Can
102/E2 **Coronation** (gulf), NW,Can
96/E1 **Coronda**, Arg.
96/B3 **Coronel**, Chile
96/E3 **Coronel Dorrego**, Arg.
95/D1 **Coronel Fabriciano**, Braz.
96/D2 **Coronel Moldes**, Arg.
91/E2 **Coronel Oviedo**, Par.
96/E3 **Coronel Pringles**, Arg.
96/E3 **Coronel Suárez**, Arg.
95/A3 **Coronel Vivida**, Braz.
92/D7 **Coropuna** (peak), Peru
101/F6 **Corozal**, Col.
100/D4 **Corozal Town**, Belz.
112/D5 **Corpus Christi**, Tx,US
46/D3 **Corral de Almaguer**, Sp.
96/E2 **Corral de Bustos**, Arg.
47/Y16 **Corralejo**, Canl.
77/B3 **Corrangamite** (lake), Austl.
100/E6 **Corredor**, CR
94/A3 **Corrente**, Braz.
94/A4 **Corrente** (riv.), Braz.
95/B1 **Corrente** (riv.), Braz.
36/A4 **Corrib, Lough** (lake), Ire.
91/E2 **Corrientes**, Arg.
100/E3 **Corrientes** (cape), Cuba
92/C4 **Corrientes** (riv.), Ecu., Peru
34/C1 **Corris**, Wal,UK
48/A1 **Corse** (cape), Fr.
48/A1 **Corse** (reg.), Fr.
32/D1 **Corserine** (mtn.), Sc,UK
32/C1 **Corsewall** (pt.), Sc,UK
34/D4 **Corsham**, Eng,UK
48/A1 **Corsica** (Corse) (isl.), Fr.
112/D3 **Corsicana**, Tx,US
48/A1 **Corte**, Fr.
108/E3 **Cortez**, Co,US
45/K3 **Cortina d'Ampezzo**, It.
110/E3 **Cortland**, NY,US
84/B4 **Corubal** (riv.), GBis.
46/A3 **Coruche**, Port.
59/E2 **Çoruh** (riv.), Turk.
92/G7 **Corumbá**, Braz.
95/B1 **Corumbá** (riv.), Braz.
94/C5 **Corumbaú** (pt.), Braz.
94/C3 **Coruripe**, Braz.
106/C4 **Corvallis**, Or,US
34/D2 **Corve** (riv.), Eng,UK
47/R12 **Corvo** (isl.), Azor.
48/C1 **Corvo** (peak), It.
33/E6 **Corwen**, Wal,UK
48/E3 **Cosenza**, It.
110/D3 **Coshocton**, Oh,US
100/D5 **Cosigüina** (pt.), Nic.
46/D2 **Coslada**, Sp.
95/F7 **Cosmópolis**, Braz.
44/E3 **Cosne-Cours-sur-Loire**, Fr.
46/B1 **Cospeito**, Sp.
91/D3 **Cosquín**, Arg.
44/D3 **Cosson** (riv.), Fr.
115/C3 **Costa Mesa**, Ca,US
100/E5 **Costa Rica**
101/N9 **Costa Rica**, Mex.
35/H1 **Costessey**, Eng,UK
51/G3 **Costești**, Rom.
116/M10 **Cosumnes** (riv.), Ca,US
67/D6 **Cotabato**, Phil.
84/D5 **Côte d'Ivoire** (Ivory Coast)
44/F3 **Côte d'Or** (uplands), Fr.
94/A4 **Cotegipe**, Braz.
44/C2 **Cotentin** (pen.), Fr.
111/N7 **Côte-Saint-Luc**, Qu,Can
34/B3 **Cothi** (riv.), Wal,UK
95/G8 **Cotia**, Braz.
85/F5 **Cotonou**, Ben.
34/D4 **Cotswolds** (hills), Eng,UK
106/C5 **Cottage Grove**, Or,US
39/H3 **Cottbus**, Ger.
35/G2 **Cottenham**, Eng,UK
108/D4 **Cottonwood**, Az,US
112/D2 **Cottonwood** (riv.), Ks,US
109/F5 **Cottonwood** (dry riv.), Tx,US
112/D4 **Cotulla**, Tx,US
31/U10 **Coubert**, Fr.
44/C4 **Coubre, Pointe de la** (pt.), Fr.
42/C5 **Coucy-le-Château-Auffrique**, Fr.
42/B1 **Coudekerque-Branche**, Fr.
44/E5 **Couguille, Pic de** (peak), Fr.
44/D2 **Coulaines**, Fr.
106/D4 **Coulee City**, Wa,US
98/M **Coulman** (isl.), Ant.
42/C6 **Coulommiers**, Fr.
110/E2 **Coulonge** (riv.), Qu,Can
44/D4 **Coulounieix-Chamiers**, Fr.
31/N8 **Coulsdon**, Eng,UK
106/D4 **Council**, Id,US
107/K5 **Council Bluffs**, Ia,US
109/H3 **Council Grove**, Ks,US
36/D2 **Coupar Angus**, Sc,UK
31/U10 **Coupvray**, Fr.
31/S10 **Courbevoie**, Fr.
42/D3 **Courcelles**, Belg.
43/F5 **Courcelles-Chaussy**, Fr.
31/T11 **Courcouronnes**, Fr.
44/E4 **Cournon-d'Auvergne**, Fr.
102/D4 **Courtenay**, BC,Can
111/S8 **Courtice**, On,Can
42/C2 **Courtrai** (Kortrijk), Belg.
31/T10 **Courtry**, Fr.
44/C2 **Coutances**, Fr.
106/F3 **Coutts**, Ab,Can
42/D3 **Couvin**, Belg.
47/P10 **Cova da Piedade**, Port.
46/C1 **Covadonga Nat'l Park**, Sp.
51/H3 **Covasna**, Rom.
50/G3 **Covasna** (co.), Rom.
35/E2 **Coventry**, Eng,UK
35/E1 **Coventry** (can.), Eng,UK
46/B2 **Covilhã**, Port.
115/C2 **Covina**, Ca,US
113/H3 **Covington**, Ga,US
110/C4 **Covington**, Ky,US
113/F3 **Covington**, Tn,US
110/E4 **Covington**, Va,US
76/H8 **Cowan**, Austl.
74/C6 **Cowan** (lake), Austl.
34/C4 **Cowbridge**, Wal,UK
35/E5 **Cowes**, Eng,UK
33/F2 **Cow Green** (res.), Eng,UK
106/C4 **Cowlitz** (riv.), Wa,US
113/H3 **Cowpens Nat'l Bfld.**, SC,US
77/D2 **Cowra**, Austl.
33/G2 **Coxhoe**, Eng,UK
93/H7 **Coxim**, Braz.
31/T9 **Coye-la-Forêt**, Fr.
109/H2 **Cozad**, Ne,US
100/D3 **Cozumel**, Mex.
100/D3 **Cozumel** (isl.), Mex.
77/C4 **Cradle** (peak), Austl.
77/C4 **Cradle Mountain-Lake Saint Clair Nat'l Park**, Austl.
88/D4 **Cradock**, SAfr.
114/K3 **Crag** (mtn.), Yk,Can
33/F3 **Crag** (hill), Eng,UK
108/F2 **Craig**, Co,US
32/C2 **Craigavad**, NI,UK
32/B3 **Craigavon**, NI,UK
32/B3 **Craigavon** (dist.), NI,UK
77/F5 **Craigieburn**, Austl.
107/G3 **Craik**, Sk,Can
45/J2 **Crailsheim**, Ger.
51/F3 **Craiova**, Rom.
33/G1 **Cramlington**, Eng,UK
32/A1 **Crana** (riv.), Ire.
107/H2 **Cranberry Portage**, Mb,Can
34/D5 **Cranborne Chase** (for.), Eng,UK
77/C3 **Cranbourne**, Austl.
106/E3 **Cranbrook**, BC,Can
35/G4 **Cranbrook**, Eng,UK
115/F5 **Cranbury**, NJ,US
112/C4 **Crane**, Tx,US
107/J3 **Crane River**, Mb,Can
115/F5 **Cranford**, NJ,US
35/F4 **Cranleigh**, Eng,UK
42/C5 **Craonne**, Fr.
51/F2 **Crasna** (riv.), Rom.
106/C5 **Crater** (lake), Or,US
106/C5 **Crater Lake Nat'l Park**, Or,US
106/E5 **Craters of the Moon Nat'l Mon.**, Id,US
94/B2 **Crateús**, Braz.
48/E3 **Crati** (riv.), It.
94/C2 **Crato**, Braz.
95/C2 **Cravinhos**, Braz.
110/C3 **Crawfordsville**, In,US
113/G4 **Crawfordville**, Fl,US
35/F4 **Crawley**, Eng,UK
31/P7 **Cray** (riv.), Eng,UK
31/P7 **Crayford**, Eng,UK
106/F4 **Crazy** (mts.), Mt,US
42/A3 **Crécy-en-Ponthieu**, Fr.
34/D2 **Credenhill**, Eng,UK
111/Q8 **Credit** (riv.), On,Can
34/C5 **Crediton**, Eng,UK
102/F3 **Cree** (lake), Sk,Can
102/F3 **Cree** (riv.), Sk,Can
32/D2 **Cree** (riv.), Sc,UK
32/D2 **Creetown**, Sc,UK
31/U10 **Crégy-lès-Meaux**, Fr.
107/H2 **Creighton**, Sk,Can
42/B5 **Creil**, Fr.
45/H4 **Crema**, It.
41/H4 **Cremlingen**, Ger.
45/J4 **Cremona**, It.
42/B5 **Crépy-en-Valois**, Fr.
50/B3 **Cres** (isl.), Cro.
108/A2 **Crescent City**, Ca,US
96/E2 **Crespo**, Arg.
44/F4 **Crest**, Fr.
116/P16 **Crest Hill**, Il,US
115/C2 **Crestline**, Ca,US
106/D3 **Creston**, BC,Can
107/K5 **Creston**, Ia,US
113/G4 **Crestview**, Fl,US
33/G5 **Creswell**, Eng,UK
49/J5 **Crete** (isl.), Gre.
49/J5 **Crete** (sea), Gre.
109/H2 **Crete**, Ne,US
31/T10 **Créteil**, Fr.
47/G1 **Creus** (cape), Sp.
44/D3 **Creuse** (riv.), Fr.
43/F5 **Creutzwald-la-Croix**, Fr.
45/J4 **Crevalcore**, It.
47/E3 **Crevillente**, Sp.
33/F5 **Crewe**, Eng,UK
34/D5 **Crewkerne**, Eng,UK
36/C2 **Crianlarich**, Sc,UK
32/D6 **Criccieth**, Wal,UK
95/B4 **Criciúma**, Braz.
34/C3 **Crickhowell**, Wal,UK
35/E3 **Cricklade**, Eng,UK
36/D2 **Crieff**, Sc,UK
42/A3 **Criel-sur-Mer**, Fr.
32/E2 **Criffell** (hill), Eng,UK
54/E3 **Crimean** (pen.), Ukr.
54/E3 **Crimean Obl.**, Ukr.
82/H7 **Cristal** (mts.), Gabon
94/A5 **Cristalina**, Braz.
101/G5 **Cristóbal** (pk.), Col.
50/F2 **Criștul Alb** (riv.), Rom.
51/G2 **Cristuru Secuiesc**, Rom.
50/E2 **Crișul Negru** (riv.), Rom.
93/H6 **Crixás-Açu** (riv.), Braz.
49/G2 **Crna Reka** (riv.), Macd.
77/D3 **Croajingolong Nat'l Park**, Austl.
50/B3 **Croatia**
111/F2 **Croche** (riv.), Qu,Can
72/E3 **Crocker** (range), Malay.
32/E1 **Crocketford**, Sc,UK
112/E4 **Crockett**, Tx,US
77/D2 **Crocodile** (pt.), Austl.
115/K7 **Crofton**, Md,US
34/B3 **Crofty**, Wal,UK
32/B6 **Croghan** (mtn.), Ire.
44/F5 **Croisette** (cape), Fr.
31/T10 **Croissy-Beaubourg**, Fr.
107/L3 **Croix** (lake), Can., US
74/E2 **Croker** (isl.), Austl.
35/H1 **Cromer**, Eng,UK
75/Q12 **Cromwell**, NZ
69/E3 **Crong A Na** (riv.), Viet.
76/H9 **Cronulla**, Austl.
33/G2 **Crook**, Eng,UK
101/G3 **Crooked** (isl.), Bahm.
107/J4 **Crookston**, Mn,US
33/E5 **Crosby**, Eng,UK
107/H3 **Crosby**, ND,US
112/C3 **Crosbyton**, Tx,US
31/T10 **Crosne**, Fr.
85/H5 **Cross** (riv.), Camr., Nga.
107/J2 **Cross** (lake), Mb,Can
113/H4 **Cross City**, Fl,US
112/F3 **Crossett**, Ar,US
33/F2 **Cross Fell** (mtn.), Eng,UK
106/E3 **Crossfield**, Ab,Can
32/C3 **Crossgar**, NI,UK
34/C2 **Crossgates**, Wal,UK
32/D1 **Crosshill**, Sc,UK
34/C3 **Crosskeys**, Wal,UK
32/B3 **Crossmaglen**, NI,UK
32/E2 **Crossmichael**, Sc,UK
85/H5 **Cross River** (state), Nga.
113/G3 **Crossville**, Tn,US
33/F4 **Croston**, Eng,UK
48/E3 **Crotone**, It.
35/G3 **Crouch** (riv.), Eng,UK
42/C5 **Crouy-sur-Ourq**, Fr.
106/G4 **Crow Agency**, Mt,US
35/G4 **Crowborough**, Eng,UK
77/E1 **Crowdy Bay Nat'l Park**, Austl.
110/E2 **Crowe** (riv.), On,Can
106/F5 **Crowheart**, Wy,US
35/F1 **Crowland**, Eng,UK
33/H4 **Crowle**, Eng,UK
112/E4 **Crowley**, La,US
113/F3 **Crowley's** (ridge), Ar,US
107/K4 **Crow, North Fork** (riv.), Mn,US
110/C3 **Crown Point**, In,US
108/E4 **Crownpoint**, NM,US
103/H1 **Crown Prince Frederik** (isl.), NW,Can
76/D4 **Crows Nest Falls Nat'l Park**, Austl.
35/F4 **Crowthorne**, Eng,UK
31/M7 **Croxley Green**, Eng,UK
77/G5 **Croydon**, Austl.
31/N7 **Croydon** (bor.), Eng,UK
29/M8 **Crozet** (isls.), FrAnt.
98/M **Crozier** (cape), Ant.
44/A2 **Crozon**, Fr.
36/E2 **Cruden Bay**, Sc,UK
32/B2 **Crumlin**, NI,UK
33/E2 **Crummock Water** (lake), Eng,UK
43/E5 **Crusnes** (riv.), Fr.
101/F4 **Cruz** (cape), Cuba
96/E2 **Cruz Alta**, Arg.
91/F2 **Cruz Alta**, Braz.
47/P10 **Cruz Alta** (mtn.), Port.
94/C4 **Cruz das Almas**, Braz.
91/D3 **Cruz del Eje**, Arg.
95/J7 **Cruzeiro**, Braz.
92/D5 **Cruzeiro do Sul**, Braz.
95/J6 **Cruzília**, Braz.
50/D3 **Crvenka**, Yugo.
33/E5 **Cryn-y-Brain** (mtn.), Wal,UK
108/C3 **Crystal Bay**, Nv,US
112/D4 **Crystal City**, Tx,US
110/B2 **Crystal Falls**, Mi,US
116/P15 **Crystal Lake**, Il,US
50/E2 **Csongrád**, Hun.
50/E2 **Csongrád** (co.), Hun.
50/C2 **Csorna**, Hun.
50/E2 **Csorvás**, Hun.
50/D2 **Csóványos** (peak), Hun.
60/D2 **Ctesiphon** (ruins), Iraq
87/D4 **Cuando** (riv.), Ang.
87/C4 **Cuangar**, Ang.
87/C2 **Cuango** (riv.), Ang.
87/B2 **Cuanza** (riv.), Ang.
47/E3 **Cuart de Poblet**, Sp.
96/D2 **Cuarto** (riv.), Arg.
100/A2 **Cuatrociénagas**, Mex.
101/F3 **Cuba**
109/K3 **Cuba**, Mo,US
87/C4 **Cubango** (riv.), Ang.
95/G8 **Cubatão**, Braz.
59/C2 **Çubuk**, Turk.
115/C2 **Cucamonga** (Rancho Cucamonga), Ca,US
92/E2 **Cuchivero** (riv.), Ven.
35/F4 **Cuckfield**, Eng,UK
35/G5 **Cuckmere** (riv.), Eng,UK
69/D1 **Cuc Phuong Nat'l Park**, Viet.
92/D2 **Cúcuta**, Col.
116/Q14 **Cudahy**, Wi,US
70/C5 **Cuddalore**, India
70/C5 **Cuddapah**, India
33/F5 **Cuddington**, Eng,UK
46/B1 **Cudillero**, Sp.
33/G4 **Cudworth**, Eng,UK
46/C2 **Cuéllar**, Sp.
92/C4 **Cuenca**, Ecu.
46/D2 **Cuenca**, Sp.
46/E2 **Cuenca** (range), Sp.
100/B4 **Cuernavaca**, Mex.
112/D4 **Cuero**, Tx,US
44/G5 **Cuers**, Fr.
92/C3 **Cueva de los Guarcharos Nat'l Park**, Col.
46/E4 **Cuevas del Almanzora**, Sp.
31/N6 **Cuffley**, Eng,UK
51/F3 **Cugir**, Rom.
44/D5 **Cugnaux-Vingtcasses**, Fr.
93/G7 **Cuiabá**, Braz.
93/G7 **Cuiabá** (riv.), Braz.
40/C5 **Cuijk**, Neth.
87/C2 **Cuilo** (riv.), Ang.
87/C3 **Cuima**, Ang.
94/C2 **Cuité**, Braz.
87/C4 **Cuito** (riv.), Ang.
87/C4 **Cuito-Cuanavale**, Ang.
92/F4 **Cuiuni** (riv.), Braz.
59/E3 **Çukurca**, Turk.
69/E4 **Cu Lao** (isl.), Viet.
32/A1 **Culdaff** (riv.), Ire.
40/C5 **Culemborg**, Neth.
93/H6 **Culene** (riv.), Braz.
77/C1 **Culgoa** (riv.), Austl.
101/N9 **Culiacán**, Mex.
67/D5 **Culion** (isl.), Phil.
46/D4 **Cúllar Baza**, Sp.
36/D2 **Cullen**, Sc,UK
47/E3 **Cullera**, Sp.
46/A1 **Culleredo**, Sp.
113/G3 **Cullman**, Al,US
34/C5 **Cullompton**, Eng,UK
32/B2 **Cullybackey**, NI,UK
32/A1 **Culmore**, NI,UK
76/B5 **Culoga** (riv.), Austl.
110/E4 **Culpeper**, Va,US
74/C6 **Culver** (pt.), Austl.
115/B2 **Culver City**, Ca,US
101/J5 **Cumaná**, Ven.
103/K2 **Cumberland** (pen.), NW,Can
103/K2 **Cumberland** (sound), NW,Can
107/H2 **Cumberland** (lake), Sk,Can
113/G3 **Cumberland** (plat.), US
113/H4 **Cumberland** (isl.), Ga,US
113/G2 **Cumberland** (falls), Ky,US
110/C4 **Cumberland** (lake), Ky,US
113/G2 **Cumberland** (riv.), Ky, Tn,US
110/E4 **Cumberland**, Md,US
110/D4 **Cumberland Gap Nat'l Hist. Park**, Tn,US
107/H2 **Cumberland House**, Sk,Can
101/N8 **Cumbres de Majalca Nat'l Park**, Mex.
100/A2 **Cumbres de Monterrey Nat'l Park**, Mex.
33/F2 **Cumbria** (co.), Eng,UK
33/E3 **Cumbrian** (mts.), Eng,UK
70/C4 **Cumbum**, India
59/C3 **Çumra**, Turk.
114/M5 **Cumshewa** (pt.), BC,Can
96/B3 **Cunco**, Chile
87/B4 **Cunene** (riv.), Ang.
45/G4 **Cuneo**, It.
69/E3 **Cung Son**, Viet.
95/J8 **Cunha**, Braz.
37/H1 **Čuokkaraš'ša** (peak), Nor.
45/G4 **Cuorgnè**, It.
36/D2 **Cupar**, Sc,UK
116/K12 **Cupertino**, Ca,US
50/E4 **Ćuprija**, Yugo.
101/H5 **Curaçao** (isl.), NAnt.
96/C3 **Curacautín**, Chile
96/B3 **Curanilahue**, Chile
92/C4 **Curaray** (riv.), Ecu., Peru
96/Q9 **Curaumilla** (pt.), Chile
50/F2 **Curcubăta** (peak), Rom.
44/E3 **Cure** (riv.), Fr.
89/S15 **Curepipe**, Mrts.
96/B2 **Curepto**, Chile
96/C2 **Curicó**, Chile
95/B3 **Curitiba**, Braz.
95/B3 **Curitibanos**, Braz.
32/B5 **Curragh, The**, Ire.
94/C2 **Currais Novos**, Braz.
109/K3 **Current** (riv.), Ar, Mo,US
108/D2 **Currie**, Nv,US
51/G3 **Curtea de Argeș**, Rom.
50/E2 **Curtici**, Rom.
76/C3 **Curtis** (isl.), Austl.
78/H8 **Curtis** (isl.), NZ
93/G4 **Curuá** (riv.), Braz.
93/H5 **Curuá** (riv.), Braz.
92/D5 **Curuçá** (riv.), Braz.
72/B4 **Curup**, Indo.
94/A2 **Cururupu**, Braz.
91/E2 **Curuzú Cuatiá**, Arg.
95/C1 **Curvelo**, Braz.
105/J2 **Curwood** (mtn.), Mi,US
92/D6 **Cusco**, Peru
32/B1 **Cushendall**, NI,UK
32/B3 **Cusher** (riv.), NI,UK
109/H4 **Cushing**, Ok,US
44/E3 **Cusset**, Fr.
113/G3 **Cusseta**, Ga,US
106/G4 **Custer**, Mt,US
107/H5 **Custer**, SD,US
94/C3 **Custódia**, Braz.
34/C5 **Cut** (hill), Eng,UK
106/E3 **Cut Bank**, Mt,US
92/C5 **Cutervo**, Peru
113/G4 **Cuthbert**, Ga,US
106/F2 **Cut Knife**, Sk,Can
96/C3 **Cutral-Có**, Arg.
70/E3 **Cuttack**, India
41/F1 **Cuxhaven**, Ger.
108/C4 **Cuyama** (riv.), Ca,US
73/F1 **Cuyo**, Phil.
73/F1 **Cuyo** (isls.), Phil.
92/F2 **Cuyuni** (riv.), Guy., Ven.
34/C3 **Cwm**, Wal,UK
34/C3 **Cwmafan**, Wal,UK
34/C3 **Cwmbran**, Wal,UK
107/H5 **C.W. McConaughy** (lake), Ne,US
49/J4 **Cyclades** (isls.), Gre.
110/C4 **Cynthiana**, Ky,US
34/B3 **Cynwyl Elfed**, Wal,UK
106/F3 **Cypress** (hills), Ab, Sk,Can
115/B3 **Cypress**, Ca,US
59/J4 **Cyprus**
83/K1 **Cyrenaica** (reg.), Libya
34/B3 **Cywyn** (riv.), Wal,UK
39/J2 **Czaplinek**, Pol.
39/M2 **Czarna Białostocka**, Pol.
39/J2 **Czarnków**, Pol.
39/H4 **Czech Republic**
39/K3 **Częstochowa**, Pol.
39/K3 **Częstochowa** (prov.), Pol.
39/J2 **Człuchów**, Pol.

D

67/D2 **Da** (riv.), China
66/B4 **Daba** (mts.), China
50/D2 **Dabas**, Hun.
60/C3 **Dabbāgh, Jabal** (mtn.), SAr.
92/C2 **Dabeiba**, Col.
70/B3 **Dabhoi**, India
69/D1 **Da** (Black) (riv.), Viet.
116/B2 **Dabob** (bay), Wa,US
83/Q6 **Daborow**, Som.
84/D5 **Dabou**, IvC.
70/C2 **Dabra**, India
39/M2 **Dąbrowa Białostocka**, Pol.
39/K3 **Dąbrowa Górnicza**, Pol.
45/J2 **Dachau**, Ger.
69/D3 **Dac Sut**, Viet.
69/D3 **Dac To**, Viet.
113/H4 **Dade City**, Fl,US
73/H4 **Dadi** (cape), Indo.
70/B4 **Dadra & Nagar Haveli** (terr.), India
61/J3 **Dādu**, Pak.
70/D6 **Daduru** (riv.), SrL.
69/B4 **Daen Noi** (peak), Thai.
67/D5 **Daet**, Phil.
71/J2 **Dafang**, China
84/B2 **Dagana**, Sen.
55/H3 **Dagestan Aut. Rep.**, Rus.
88/D4 **Daggaboersnek** (pass), SAfr.
76/B2 **Dagmar Range Nat'l Park**, Austl.
71/H2 **Daguan**, China
76/E6 **D'Aguilar** (mtn.), Austl.
76/E6 **D'Aguilar** (range), Austl.
63/K2 **Daguokui** (peak), China
67/D4 **Dagupan**, Phil.
68/E5 **Dagzê** (lake), China
66/C2 **Dahaituo Shan** (mtn.), China
58/D7 **Dahana** (des.), SAr.
70/B4 **Dāhānu**, India
70/A2 **Daharki**, Pak.
66/B2 **Dahei** (riv.), China
63/K2 **Daheiding** (peak), China
63/J2 **Da Hinggang** (mts.), China
83/N4 **Dahlak** (arch.), Erit.
113/H3 **Dahlonega**, Ga,US
39/G3 **Dahme** (riv.), Ger.
69/D4 **Da Hoa**, Viet.
66/C5 **Dahong** (mtn.), China
59/E3 **Dahūk**, Iraq
66/C2 **Dai** (lake), China
65/M9 **Daian**, Japan
65/G2 **Daigo**, Japan
70/D2 **Dailekh**, Nepal
32/D1 **Dailly**, Sc,UK
69/E3 **Dai Loc**, Viet.
46/D3 **Daimiel**, Sp.
112/E3 **Daingerfield**, Tx,US
76/B2 **Daintree Nat'l Park**, Austl.
65/E3 **Daiō-zaki** (pt.), Japan
96/E3 **Daireaux**, Arg.
64/C3 **Dai-sen** (mtn.), Japan
64/C3 **Daisen-Oki Nat'l Park**, Japan
65/L10 **Daitō**, Japan
78/C2 **Daito** (isls.), Japan
84/A3 **Dakar** (cap.), Sen.
84/A3 **Dakar** (reg.), Sen.
86/B3 **Dākhilah, Wāḥāt ad** (oasis), Egypt
82/B3 **Dakhla**, WSah.
84/A1 **Dakhlet Nouadhibou** (reg.), Mrta.
69/D3 **Dak Nhe**, Viet.
85/G3 **Dakoro**, Niger
109/H2 **Dakota City**, Ne,US
50/E4 **Đakovica**, Yugo.
50/D3 **Đakovo**, Yugo.
98/A **Dakshin Gangotri**, Ant.
30/E2 **Dal** (riv.), Swe.
62/H3 **Dalai** (salt lake), China
59/B3 **Dalaman**, Turk.
62/F2 **Dalanjargalan**, Mong.
37/E3 **Dalarna** (reg.), Swe.
69/E4 **Da Lat**, Viet.
37/Q6 **Dalatangi** (pt.), Ice.
32/E2 **Dalbeattie**, Sc,UK
76/C4 **Dalby**, Austl.
86/B4 **Dal Cataract** (falls), Sudan
40/D4 **Dalfsen**, Neth.
112/C2 **Dalhart**, Tx,US
111/H1 **Dalhousie**, NB,Can
114/N1 **Dalhousie** (cape), NW,Can
71/H2 **Dali**, China
66/B3 **Dali** (riv.), China
46/D4 **Dalías**, Sp.
63/H3 **Daling** (riv.), China
50/D3 **Dalj**, Cro.
114/M4 **Dall** (isl.), Ak,US
114/F3 **Dall** (lake), Ak,US
112/D3 **Dallas**, Tx,US
106/C4 **Dalles, The**, Or,US
85/F3 **Dallol Bosso** (wadi), Mali, Niger
36/C2 **Dalmally**, Sc,UK
50/C4 **Dalmatia** (reg.), Cro.
32/D1 **Dalmellington**, Sc,UK
63/M3 **Dal'negorsk**, Rus.
63/L2 **Dal'nerechensk**, Rus.
84/D5 **Daloa**, IvC.
86/B4 **Dalqū**, Sudan

76/B3 Dalrymple (lake), Austl.
36/C3 Dalrymple, Sc,UK
113/G3 Dalton, Ga,US
70/D3 Daltonganj, India
33/E3 Dalton-in-Furness, Eng,UK
36/C2 Dalwhinnie, Sc,UK
74/E2 Daly (riv.), Austl.
102/H2 Daly (bay), NW,Can
116/K11 Daly City, Ca,US
68/F5 Dam (riv.), China
70/B3 Damān, India
70/B3 Damān & Diu (terr.), India
59/H6 Damanhūr, Egypt
73/G5 Damar (isl.), Indo.
115/J7 Damascus, Md,US
59/L5 Damascus (Dimashq) (cap.), Syria
82/H5 Damaturu, Nga.
60/F1 Damavand (mtn.), Iran
69/D4 Dam Doi, Viet.
35/E5 Damerham, Eng,UK
61/F1 Dāmghān, Iran
59/H6 Damietta (Dumyāţ), Egypt
66/C3 Daming, China
43/D4 Damion (mtn.), Fr.
31/U9 Dammartin-en-Goële, Fr.
42/C1 Damme, Belg.
41/F3 Damme, Ger.
70/C3 Damoh, India
85/E4 Damongo, Gha.
74/B4 Dampier (arch.), Austl.
73/H4 Dampier (str.), Indo.
69/C4 Damrei (mts.), Camb.
40/D2 Damsterdiep (riv.), Neth.
43/E5 Damvillers, Fr.
66/B4 Dan (riv.), China
113/H2 Dan (riv.), NC,US
83/P5 Danakil (reg.), Djib.
84/C5 Danané, IvC.
69/E2 Da Nang, Viet.
67/D5 Danao, Phil.
35/G3 Danbury, Eng,UK
77/G5 Dandenong, Austl.
77/G5 Dandenong (cr.), Austl.
77/G5 Dandenong (mtn.), Austl.
33/F5 Dane (riv.), Eng,UK
62/D4 Dang (riv.), China
88/B4 Danger (pt.), SAfr.
77/B2 Danggali Consv. Park, Austl.
83/N5 Dangila, Eth.
100/D4 Dangriga, Belz.
52/J4 Danilov, Rus.
66/B4 Danjiangkou, China
66/B4 Danjiangkou (res.), China
54/F1 Dankov, Rus.
68/C3 Dankova, Pik (peak), Kyr.
113/G3 Dannelly (res.), Al,US
38/F2 Dannenberg, Ger.
75/S11 Dannevirke, NZ
30/F4 Danube (riv.), Eur.
51/J3 Danube (delta), Rom.
51/H3 Danube, Borcea Branch (riv.), Rom.
51/J3 Danube, Mouths of the, Rom.
51/J3 Danube, Sfîntu Gheorghe Branch (riv.), Rom.
51/J3 Danube, Sulina Branch (riv.), Rom.
116/L11 Danville, Ca,US
110/C3 Danville, Il,US
110/C4 Danville, Ky,US
110/E4 Danville, Va,US
85/F4 Dapaong, Togo
113/G4 Daphne, Al,US
67/D6 Dapitan, Phil.
63/K2 Daqing, China
66/H7 Daqing (riv.), China
61/H2 Daqq-e Patargān (lake), Afg., Iran
59/L5 Dar'ā, Syria
61/F3 Dārāb, Iran
51/H1 Darabani, Rom.
67/D5 Daraga, Phil.
67/D5 Daram, Phil.
50/E4 Đaravica (peak), Yugo.
59/L5 Dārayyā, Syria
70/E2 Darbhanga, India
114/F3 Darby (cape), Ak,US
115/E6 Darby, Pa,US
50/D3 Darda, Cro.
109/J4 Dardanelle (lake), Ar,US
51/H5 Dardanelles (str.), Turk.
77/G5 Darebin (cr.), Austl.
59/D2 Darende, Turk.
31/P8 Darent (riv.), Eng,UK
87/G2 Dar es Salaam (cap.), Tanz.
75/R11 Darfield, NZ
45/J4 Darfo, It.
75/R10 Dargaville, NZ
32/B5 Dargle (riv.), Ire.
62/F2 Darhan (peak), Mong.
83/Q6 Darie (hills), Som.
115/G4 Darien, Ct,US
113/H4 Darien, Ga,US
116/Q16 Darien, Il,US
101/F6 Darien Nat'l Park, Pan.
62/G2 Dariganga, Mong.
70/E2 Darjiling, India
74/B6 Darling (range), Austl.
77/B2 Darling (riv.), Austl.
76/C4 Darling Downs (upland), Austl.
33/G2 Darlington, Eng,UK
113/J3 Darlington, SC,US
39/J1 Darłowo, Pol.
45/H2 Darmstadt, Ger.
83/K1 Darnah, Libya
81/W18 Darnāya, Tun.
42/A5 Darnétal, Fr.
98/E Darnley (cape), Ant.
102/D2 Darnley (bay), NW,Can
33/G1 Darras Hall, Eng,UK
61/G1 Darreh Gaz, Iran
83/K6 Dar Rounga (reg.), CAfr.
98/R Dart (cape), Ant.
34/C6 Dart (riv.), Eng,UK
31/P7 Dartford, Eng,UK
34/C6 Dartington, Eng,UK
34/B5 Dartmoor (upland), Eng,UK
34/C5 Dartmoor Nat'l Park, Eng,UK
77/C3 Dartmouth (res.), Austl.
111/J2 Dartmouth, NS,Can
34/C6 Dartmouth, Eng,UK
33/G4 Darton, Eng,UK
47/G3 Dartuch (cape), Sp.
78/D5 Daru, PNG
50/C3 Daruvar, Cro.
73/E3 Darvel (bay), Malay.
33/F4 Darwen, Eng,UK
74/E2 Darwin, Austl.
96/B5 Darwin (bay), Chile
97/K8 Darwin (mts.), Chile
61/H2 Daryācheh-ye Sīstān (lake), Iran
63/H3 Dashengtang (peak), China
66/B5 Dashennongjia (peak), China
83/N5 Dashen, Ras (peak), Eth.
61/F2 Dasht-e Kavīr (des.), Iran
61/G2 Dasht-e Lūt (des.), Iran
61/H2 Dasht-e Mārgow (des.), Afg.
61/H3 Dasht Kaur (riv.), Pak.
41/G5 Dassel, Ger.
88/B4 Dasseneiland (isl.), SAfr.
31/M7 Datchet, Eng,UK
69/D4 Dat Do, Viet.
70/C2 Datia, India
108/F4 Datil, NM,US
66/C2 Datong, China
62/D4 Datong (mts.), China
62/D4 Datong (riv.), China
41/E5 Datteln, Ger.
72/C3 Datu (cape), Malay.
72/B3 Datuk (cape), Indo.
37/H4 Daugava (riv.), Lat.
52/E4 Daugava (riv.), Lat.
52/E5 Daugavpils, Lat.
43/F3 Daun, Ger.
69/B3 Daung (isl.), Burma
107/H3 Dauphin, Mb,Can
107/J3 Dauphin (lake), Mb,Can
70/C5 Dāvangere, India
67/E6 Davao, Phil.
107/L5 Davenport, Ia,US
106/D4 Davenport, Wa,US
35/E2 Daventry, Eng,UK
103/T6 Davgaard-Jensen (reg.), Grld.
100/E6 David, Pan.
109/H2 David City, Ne,US
107/G3 Davidson, Sk,Can
116/K11 Davidson (mtn.), Ca,US
98/F Davis (sea), Ant.
98/F Davis (sta.), Ant.
99/M3 Davis (str.), Can., Grld.
116/L9 Davis, Ca,US
110/E4 Davis (peak), Pa,US
112/B4 Davis (mts.), Tx,US
53/M5 Davlekanovo, Rus.
84/D5 Davo (riv.), IvC.
45/H3 Davos, Swi.
62/C1 Davst, Mong.
83/N7 Dawa Wenz (riv.), Afr.
66/D4 Dawen (riv.), China
34/C5 Dawlish, Eng,UK
76/C4 Dawson (riv.), Austl.
114/L3 Dawson, Yk,Can
97/K8 Dawson (isl.), Chile
113/G4 Dawson, Ga,US
106/C2 Dawson Creek, BC,Can
66/C5 Dawu Shan (mtn.), China
60/G4 Dawwah, Oman
44/C5 Dax, Fr.
66/D3 Daxing, China
71/G3 Daying (riv.), China
97/F1 Dayman (riv.), Uru.
67/B2 Dayong, China
59/K6 Dayr al Balaḩ, Gaza
60/D1 Dayr az Zawr, Syria
86/B3 Dayrūt, Egypt
106/E2 Daysland, Ab,Can
110/C4 Dayton, Oh,US
113/G3 Dayton, Tn,US
106/D4 Dayton, Wa,US
113/H4 Daytona Beach, Fl,US
88/D3 De Aar, SAfr.
59/K6 Dead (sea), Isr., Jor.
107/H4 Deadwood, SD,US
77/C3 Deal (isl.), Austl.
35/H4 Deal, Eng,UK
115/G5 Deal, NJ,US
106/B2 Dean (riv.), BC,Can
34/D3 Dean, Forest of (for.), Eng,UK
91/D3 Deán Funes, Arg.
116/F7 Dearborn, Mi,US
116/F7 Dearborn Heights, Mi,US
33/G4 Dearne, Eng,UK
33/G4 Dearne (riv.), Eng,UK
114/N4 Dease (riv.), BC,Can
102/F2 Dease (str.), NW,Can
108/C3 Death Valley Nat'l Mon., Ca, Nv,US
50/E5 Debar, Macd.
114/G3 Debauch (mtn.), Ak,US
35/H2 Deben (riv.), Eng,UK
35/H2 Debenham, Eng,UK
39/L3 Dębica, Pol.
40/C4 De Bilt, Neth.
39/L3 Dęblin, Pol.
39/H2 Dębno, Pol.
114/J3 Deborah (mtn.), Ak,US
83/N6 Debre Birhan, Eth.
50/E2 Debrecen, Hun.
83/N5 Debre Mark'os, Eth.
83/N5 Debre Tabor, Eth.
83/N6 Debre Zeyit, Eth.
113/G3 Decatur, Al,US
113/G3 Decatur, Ga,US
110/B4 Decatur, Il,US
110/C3 Decatur, In,US
112/D3 Decatur, Tx,US
44/E4 Decazeville, Fr.
70/C5 Deccan (plat.), India
39/H3 Děčín, Czh.
44/E3 Decize, Fr.
35/E3 Deddington, Eng,UK
40/D3 Dedemsvaart, Neth.
96/C5 Dedo (peak), Arg.
84/E3 Dédougou, Burk.
87/F3 Dedza, Malw.
32/B4 Dee (riv.), Ire.
32/D1 Dee (riv.), Sc,UK
36/D2 Dee (riv.), Sc,UK
33/E5 Dee (riv.), Wal,UK
32/A4 Deel (riv.), Ire.
35/F1 Deeping Saint James, Eng,UK
110/E2 Deep River, On,Can
114/F5 Deer (isl.), Ak,US
116/Q15 Deerfield, Il,US
111/K1 Deer Lake, Nf,Can
42/C2 Deerlijk, Belg.
106/E4 Deer Lodge, Mt,US
115/G5 Deer Park, NY,US
106/D4 Deer Park, Wa,US
70/B3 Deesa, India
76/H8 Dee Why, Austl.
83/Q6 Deex Nugaaleed (dry river), Som.
92/F8 Defensores del Chaco Nat'l Park, Par.
110/C3 Defiance, Oh,US
113/G4 De Funiak Springs, Fl,US
32/E5 Deganwy, Wal,UK
83/P6 Degeh Bur, Eth.
111/G2 Dégelis, Qu,Can
45/K2 Deggendorf, Ger.
74/B4 De Grey (riv.), Austl.
42/C1 De Haan, Belg.
83/P4 Dehalak (isl.), Erit.
83/P4 Dehalak Marine Nat'l Park, Erit.
61/L2 Dehra Dūn, India
70/D3 Dehri, India
42/C2 Deinze, Belg.
41/G4 Deister (mts.), Ger.
51/F2 Dej, Rom.
110/B3 De Kalb, Il,US
83/N4 Dek'emhāre, Eth.
113/H4 De Land, Fl,US
108/C4 Delano, Ca,US
61/H2 Delārām, Afg.
106/G2 Delaronde (lake), Sk,Can
116/N14 Delavan, Wi,US
110/F3 Delaware (riv.), US
110/F4 Delaware (state), US
110/D3 Delaware, Oh,US
115/F4 Delaware Water Gap Nat'l Rec. Area, NJ, Pa,US
41/F5 Delbrück, Ger.
96/D2 Del Campillo, Arg.
50/F5 Delčevo, Macd.
40/D4 Delden, Neth.
40/D2 De Leijen (lake), Neth.
45/G3 Delémont, Swi.
40/B5 Delft, Neth.
40/D2 Delfzijl, Neth.
96/E4 Delgada (pt.), Arg.
87/H3 Delgado (cape), Moz.
62/D2 Delger (riv.), Mong.
62/F2 Delgerhaan, Mong.
62/E2 Delgerhangay, Mong.
70/C2 Delhi, India
54/E5 Delice (riv.), Turk.
40/B5 De Lier, Neth.
48/D5 Delimara, Ponta Ta' (pt.), Malta
106/G3 Delisle, Sk,Can
41/G5 Delligsen, Ger.
107/J5 Dell Rapids, SD,US
88/Q13 Delmas, SAfr.
43/F6 Delme, Fr.
41/F3 Delme (riv.), Ger.
41/F2 Delmenhorst, Ger.
94/C3 Delmiro Gouveia, Braz.
109/F3 Del Norte, Co,US
107/H3 Deloraine, Mb,Can
49/J4 Delos (ruins), Gre.
49/H3 Delphi (ruins), Gre.
110/C3 Delphos, Oh,US
115/F5 Delran, NJ,US
113/H5 Delray Beach, Fl,US
112/C4 Del Rio, Tx,US
108/E3 Delta, Co,US
108/D3 Delta, Ut,US
97/T12 Delta del Tigre, Uru.
116/M11 Delta-Mendota (can.), Ca,US
113/H4 Deltona, Fl,US
62/C2 Delüün, Mong.
116/L11 Del Valle (lake), Ca,US
53/M5 Dëma (riv.), Rus.
46/D1 Demanda (range), Sp.
114/K2 Demarcation (pt.), Ak,US
87/D2 Demba, Zaire
83/M6 Dembī Dolo, Eth.
40/B7 Demer (riv.), Belg.
108/F4 Deming, NM,US
92/F3 Demini (riv.), Braz.
38/G2 Demmin, Ger.
113/G3 Demopolis, Al,US
72/B4 Dempo (peak), Indo.
42/C3 Denain, Fr.
83/P5 Denakil (reg.), Erit., Eth.
114/H3 Denali Nat'l Park & Prsv., Ak,US
107/H2 Denare Beach, Sk,Can
33/E5 Denbigh, Wal,UK
40/B2 Den Burg, Neth.
33/G4 Denby Dale, Eng,UK
42/D2 Dender (riv.), Belg.
42/D2 Denderleeuw, Belg.
42/D1 Dendermonde, Belg.
40/D4 Denekamp, Neth.
74/A5 Denham (sound), Austl.
40/D4 Den Ham, Neth.
31/M7 Denham, Eng,UK
40/B3 Den Helder, Neth.
33/G4 Denholme, Eng,UK
47/F3 Denia, Sp.
77/C2 Deniliquin, Austl.
108/C2 Denio, Nv,US
114/H4 Denison (mtn.), Ak,US
107/K5 Denison, Ia,US
112/D3 Denison, Tx,US
59/B3 Denizli, Turk.
98/G Denman (glac.), Ant.
37/C5 Denmark
99/Q3 Denmark (str.), NAm
72/E5 Denpasar, Indo.
42/C2 Dentergem, Belg.
35/G5 Denton, Eng,UK
112/D3 Denton, Tx,US
74/A6 D'Entrecasteaux (pt.), Austl.
78/D5 D'Entrecasteaux (isls.), PNG
109/F3 Denver (cap.), Co,US
115/F5 Denville, NJ,US
70/C2 Deoband, India
70/D3 Deogarh, India
70/E3 Deoghar, India
70/B4 Deolāli, India
70/C2 Deoli, India
44/D3 Déols, Fr.
70/D2 Deoria, India
42/B1 De Panne, Belg.
40/C6 De Peel (reg.), Neth.
111/S10 Depew, NY,US
42/C2 De Pinte, Belg.
31/N7 Deptford, Eng,UK
83/P7 Dera (dry riv.), Som.
60/E2 Dera Ghāzi Khān, Pak.
61/K2 Dera Ismāīl Khān, Pak.
55/J4 Derbent, Rus.
33/G6 Derby, Eng,UK
109/H3 Derby, Ks,US
33/G6 Derbyshire (co.), Eng,UK
51/F3 Đerdap Nat'l Park, Yugo.
50/E2 Derecske, Hun.
62/F2 Deren, Mong.
36/A4 Derg, Lough (lake), Ire.
112/E4 De Ridder, La,US
59/E3 Derik, Turk.
44/B2 Déroute (passg.), Fr., Chl,UK
32/A4 Derravaragh, Lough (lake), Ire.
32/B6 Derry (riv.), Ire.
111/G3 Derry, NH,US
32/C3 Derryboy, NI,UK
36/B3 Derrylin, NI,UK
35/G1 Dersingham, Eng,UK
50/C3 Derventa, Bosn.
32/B1 Dervock, NI,UK
77/C4 Derwent (riv.), Austl.
33/F2 Derwent (res.), Eng,UK
33/E2 Derwent (riv.), Eng,UK
33/G5 Derwent (riv.), Eng,UK
33/H4 Derwent (riv.), Eng,UK
32/E2 Derwent Water (lake), Eng,UK
96/D2 Desaguadero (riv.), Arg.
92/E7 Desaguadero (riv.), Bol.
35/F2 Desborough, Eng,UK
96/C2 Descabezado Grande (vol.), Chile
95/C2 Descalvado, Braz.
107/H2 Deschambault Lake, Sk,Can
108/B2 Deschutes (riv.), Or,US
83/N5 Desē, Eth.
91/C6 Deseado (riv.), Arg.
97/L8 Deseado (cape), Chile
97/L7 Desengaño (pt.), Arg.
47/V15 Desertas (isl.), Madr.,Port.
66/B4 Deshengpu, China
107/J4 De Smet, SD,US
107/K5 Des Moines (cap.), Ia,US
107/K5 Des Moines (riv.), Ia, Mo,US
116/C3 Des Moines, Wa,US
54/D2 Desna (riv.), Rus., Ukr.
97/J8 Desolación (isl.), Chile
88/D4 Desolation, Valley of (val.), SAfr.
94/A2 Desordem (mts.), Braz.
109/K3 De Soto, Mo,US
88/D4 Despatch, SAfr.
116/Q15 Des Plaines, Il,US
116/P16 Des Plaines (riv.), Il,US
38/G3 Dessau, Ger.
43/E1 Dessel, Belg.
42/C1 Destelbergen, Belg.
114/L3 Destruction Bay, Yk,Can
50/E3 Deta, Rom.
41/F5 Detmold, Ger.
116/F7 Detroit, Mi,US
116/F7 Detroit (riv.), On,Can, Mi,US
107/K4 Detroit Lakes, Mn,US
37/P6 Dettifoss (falls), Ice.
77/D2 Deua Nat'l Park, Austl.
31/S10 Deuil-la-Barre, Fr.
42/B2 Deûle (riv.), Fr.
40/B6 Deurne, Belg.
40/C6 Deurne, Neth.
45/L3 Deutschlandsberg, Aus.
111/N6 Deux-Montagnes, Qu,Can
111/M7 Deux-Montagnes (lake), Qu,Can
50/F3 Deva, Rom.
50/E2 Dévaványa, Hun.
59/C2 Develi, Turk.
40/D4 Deventer, Neth.
36/D2 Deveron (riv.), Sc,UK
93/H2 Devil's (isl.), FrG.
109/G5 Devils (riv.), Tx,US
107/J3 Devils Lake, ND,US
114/M4 Devils Paw (mtn.), BC,Can, Ak,US
108/C3 Devils Postpile Nat'l Mon., Ca,US
107/G4 Devils Tower Nat'l Mon., Wy,US
51/G5 Devin, Bul.
112/D4 Devine, Tx,US
35/E4 Devizes, Eng,UK
51/H4 Devnya, Bul.
49/G2 Devoll (riv.), Alb.
106/E2 Devon, Ab,Can
103/S7 Devon (isl.), NW,Can
34/C5 Devon (co.), Eng,UK
77/C4 Devonport, Austl.
51/K5 Devrek, Turk.
54/D4 Devrek (riv.), Turk.
54/E4 Devrez (riv.), Turk.
72/A3 Dewa (pt.), Indo.
70/C3 Dewās, India
112/E2 Dewey, Ok,US
109/H2 De Witt, Ne,US
33/G4 Dewsbury, Eng,UK
111/G2 Dexter, Me,US
74/D5 Dey-Dey (lake), Austl.
60/E2 Dez (riv.), Iran
60/E2 Dezfūl, Iran
114/E2 Dezhneva, Mys (pt.), Rus.
66/D3 Dezhou, China
86/C2 Dhahab, Egypt
70/F3 Dhākā (Dacca) (cap.), Bang.
70/D3 Dhamtari, India
70/E3 Dhānbād, India
70/E2 Dhankuta, Nepal
70/C3 Dhār, India
70/B3 Dharampur, India
70/B3 Dhāri, India
70/C5 Dharmapuri, India
70/C5 Dharmavaram, India
70/D2 Dhaulāgiri (peak), Nepal
49/H3 Dhelfoí (Delphi) (ruins), Gre.
70/E3 Dhenkānāl, India
49/K2 Dhidhimótikhon, Gre.
49/H3 Dhírfis (peak), Gre.
60/F5 Dhofar (reg.), Oman
70/B3 Dholka, India
70/C2 Dholpur, India
70/B4 Dhond, India
49/J4 Dhonoúsa (isl.), Gre.
70/B3 Dhorāji, India
49/J2 Dhráma, Gre.
43/F4 Dhronbach (riv.), Ger.
70/E2 Dhubri, India
70/B3 Dhūlia, India
70/E3 Dhuliān, India
70/E2 Dhupgāri, India
49/J5 Día (isl.), Gre.
45/G4 Diable, Cime du (peak), Fr.
114/H4 Diablo (mtn.), Ak,US
116/L11 Diablo (mt.), Ca,US
108/B3 Diablo (range), Ca,US
112/B4 Diablo (plat.), Tx,US
97/G2 Diablo, Punta del (pt.), Uru.
95/G8 Diadema, Braz.
96/E2 Diamante, Arg.
96/D2 Diamante (riv.), Arg.
74/G4 Diamantina (riv.), Austl.
95/D1 Diamantina, Braz.
94/B3 Diamantina (mts.), Braz.
93/G6 Diamantino, Braz.
77/G5 Diamond (cr.), Austl.
106/E4 Diamond (peak), Id,US
115/C3 Diamond Bar, Ca,US
104/W13 Diamond Head (crater), Hi,US
66/L8 Dianshan (lake), China
85/F3 Diapaga, Burk.
98/J Dibble Iceberg Tongue, Ant.
87/E5 Dibete, Bots.
86/B4 Dibis, Bīr (well), Egypt
112/E4 Diboll, Tx,US
71/F2 Dibrugarh, India
59/F3 Dibs, Iraq
112/C3 Dickens, Tx,US
107/H4 Dickinson, ND,US
113/G2 Dickson, Tn,US
59/E3 Dicle (riv.), Turk.
40/D5 Didam, Neth.
35/E3 Didcot, Eng,UK
106/E3 Didsbury, Ab,Can
61/K3 Didwāna, India
89/E2 Die Berg (peak), SAfr.
84/E4 Diébougou, Burk.
102/F3 Diefenbaker (lake), Sk,Can
97/J7 Diego de Almagro (isl.), Chile
58/G10 Diego Garcia (isl.), BrIn.
43/E4 Diekirch (dist.), Lux.
41/F5 Diemel (riv.), Ger.
40/B4 Diemen, Neth.
69/C1 Dien Bien Phu, Viet.
69/D2 Dien Chau, Viet.
69/E3 Dien Khanh, Viet.
43/E2 Diepenbeek, Belg.
40/D4 Diepenveen, Neth.
41/F3 Diepholz, Ger.
42/A4 Dieppe, Fr.
43/E2 Diest, Belg.
83/P7 Dif, Kenya
85/H3 Diffa (dept.), Niger
43/E4 Differdange, Lux.
77/B3 Difficult (peak), Austl.
71/G2 Digboi, India
111/H2 Digby, NS,Can
45/G4 Digne, Fr.
44/E3 Digoin, Fr.
67/E6 Digos, Phil.
70/C3 Digras, India
42/D2 Dijle (Dyle) (riv.), Belg.
44/F3 Dijon, Fr.
83/P5 Dikhil, Djib.
59/H6 Dikirnis, Egypt
55/H4 Diklosmta, Gora (peak), Geo.
42/B1 Diksmuide, Belg.
82/H5 Dikwa, Nga.
83/N6 Dīla, Eth.
42/D2 Dilbeek, Belg.
73/G5 Dili, Indo.
43/H2 Dillenburg, Ger.
83/L5 Dilling, Sudan
43/F5 Dillingen, Ger.
113/J3 Dillon, SC,US
87/D3 Dilolo, Zaire
43/E1 Dilsen, Belg.
71/F2 Dimāpur, India
59/L5 Dimashq (Damascus) (cap.), Syria
84/D5 Dimbokro, IvC.
51/G3 Dîmboviţa (co.), Rom.
57/P2 Dimitriya Lapteva (str.), Rus.
51/G4 Dimitrovgrad, Bul.
55/J1 Dimitrovgrad, Rus.
50/F4 Dimitrovgrad, Yugo.
82/H6 Dimlang (peak), Nga.
59/K6 Dimona, Isr.
59/K6 Dimona, Hare (mtn.), Isr.
67/E6 Dinagat, Phil.
67/E5 Dinagat (isl.), Phil.
70/E2 Dinājpur, Bang.
44/B2 Dinan, Fr.
43/D3 Dinant, Belg.
59/B2 Dinar, Turk.
44/B2 Dinard, Fr.
49/E1 Dinaric Alps (range), Bosn., Cro.
34/B2 Dinas (pt.), Wal,UK
34/C4 Dinas Powys, Wal,UK
83/N5 Dinder Nat'l Park, Eth.
70/C5 Dindigul, India
45/K2 Dingolfing, Ger.
67/D4 Dingras, Phil.
36/C2 Dingwall, Sc,UK
66/C3 Dingxing, China
66/D4 Dingyuan, China
69/D1 Dinh Lap, Viet.
41/E5 Dinkel (riv.), Ger.
41/F3 Dinklage, Ger.
33/G1 Dinnington, Eng,UK
108/E2 Dinosaur, Co,US
108/E2 Dinosaur Nat'l Mon., Co, Ut,US
40/D5 Dinslaken, Ger.
106/G3 Dinsmore, Sk,Can
40/B5 Dintel Mark (riv.), Neth.
108/C3 Dinuba, Ca,US
40/D5 Dinxperlo, Neth.
84/C4 Dion (riv.), Gui.
84/A3 Diourbel, Sen.
84/A3 Diourbel (reg.), Sen.
71/F2 Diphu, India
61/J4 Diplo, Pak.
67/D6 Dipolog, Phil.
76/C3 Dipperu Nat'l Park, Austl.
84/E2 Diré, Mali
75/G2 Direction (cape), Austl.
83/P6 Dirē Dawa, Eth.
100/D5 Diriamba, Nic.
74/A5 Dirk Hartog (isl.), Austl.
82/H4 Dirkou, Niger
40/B5 Dirksland, Neth.
108/E3 Dirty Devil (riv.), Ut,US
74/C4 Disappointment (lake), Austl.
79/L6 Disappointment (isls.), FrPol.
77/B3 Discovery (bay), Austl.
86/C3 Dishnā, Egypt
103/L2 Disko (isl.), Grld.
33/F5 Disley, Eng,UK
115/C3 Disneyland, Ca,US
43/E2 Dison, Belg.
70/F2 Dispur, India
111/G2 Disraëli, Qu,Can
35/H2 Diss, Eng,UK
41/F4 Dissen am Teutoburger Wald, Ger.
32/E2 Distington, Eng,UK
115/J8 District of Columbia (cap.), US
97/S12 Distrito Federal (fed. dist.), Arg.
94/A4 Distrito Federal (fed. dist.), Braz.
100/B4 Distrito Federal (state), Mex.
59/H6 Disūq, Egypt
35/F5 Ditchling Beacon (hill), Eng,UK
48/D4 Dittaino (riv.), It.
61/K4 Diu (isl.), India
70/B3 Diu, Damān and (terr.), India
50/D4 Diva (riv.), Yugo.
44/D3 Dive (riv.), Fr.
95/C2 Divinópolis, Braz.
32/B2 Divis (mtn.), NI,UK
92/D5 Divisor (mts.), Braz.
84/D5 Divo, IvC.
59/D2 Divriği, Turk.
114/M4 Dixon (chan.), Ak,US
116/L10 Dixon, Ca,US
110/B3 Dixon, Il,US
102/C3 Dixon Entrance (chan.), BC,Can
59/E2 Diyadin, Turk.
59/E3 Diyarbakır, Turk.
59/H6 Diyarb Najm, Egypt
82/H3 Djado, Niger
82/H3 Djado (plat.), Niger
82/G1 Djamaa, Alg.
87/B1 Djambala, Congo
82/G3 Djanet, Alg.
81/S16 Djelfa, Alg.
81/U17 Djemila (ruins), Alg.
84/D3 Djénné, Mali
85/E3 Djibo, Burk.
83/P5 Djibouti
83/P5 Djibouti (cap.), Djib.
32/B5 Djouce (mtn.), Ire.
85/F4 Djougou, Ben.
83/M7 Djugu, Zaire
30/G3 Dnepr (riv.), Eur.
54/E2 Dneprodzerzhinsk, Ukr.
54/E2 Dnepropetrovsk, Ukr.
54/E2 Dnepropetrovsk Obl., Ukr.
54/D3 Dnestr (riv.), Eur.
62/E5 Do (riv.), China
85/E3 Do (lake), Mali
82/J6 Doba, Chad
115/G4 Dobbs Ferry, NY,US
52/D4 Dobele, Lat.
38/G3 Döbeln, Ger.
73/H4 Doberai (pen.), Indo.
50/D3 Doboj, Bosn.
39/L2 Dobre Miasto, Pol.
51/H4 Dobruja (reg.), Bul., Rom.
54/D1 Dobrush, Bela.
53/N4 Dobryanka, Rus.
95/D1 Doce (riv.), Braz.
35/G1 Docking, Eng,UK
113/H4 Dock Junction, Ga,US
91/D1 Doctor Pedro P. Peña, Par.
50/F2 Doctor Petru Groza, Rom.
110/F1 Doda (lake), Qu,Can
32/B5 Dodder (riv.), Ire.
31/P7 Doddinghurst, Eng,UK
59/A3 Dodecanese (isls.), Turk.
109/G3 Dodge City, Ks,US
110/B3 Dodgeville, Wi,US
34/B6 Dodman (pt.), Wal,UK
87/G2 Dodoma, Tanz.
49/G3 Dodoni (ruins), Gre.
106/F3 Dodsland, Sk,Can
33/G4 Dodworth, Eng,UK
40/D4 Doesburg, Neth.
40/D5 Doetinchem, Neth.
68/E5 Dogai Coring (lake), China
59/D2 Doğankent (riv.), Turk.
64/C2 Dōgo (isl.), Japan
85/G3 Dogondoutchi, Niger
59/F2 Doğubayazıt, Turk.
59/E2 Doğukaradeniz (mts.), Turk.
60/F3 Doha (Ad Dawḩah) (cap.), Qatar
70/B3 Dohad, India
69/B2 Doi Inthanon Nat'l Park, Thai.
69/B2 Doi Khun Tan Nat'l Park, Thai.
46/B1 Doiras (res.)
94/B3 Dois Irmãos (mts.), Braz.
69/B2 Doi Suthep-Pui Nat'l Park, Thai.
40/D2 Dokkum, Neth.
40/C2 Dokkumer Ee (riv.), Neth.
111/F1 Dolbeau, Qu,Can
44/F3 Dôle, Fr.
34/C1 Dolgellau, Wal,UK
48/A3 Dolianova, It.
63/N2 Dolinsk, Rus.
51/F3 Dolj (co.), Rom.
111/N7 Dollard-des-Ormeaux, Qu,Can
41/E2 Dollard (Dollart) (bay), Ger., Neth.
38/D5 Doller (riv.), Fr.
50/C5 Dolmen (ruins), It.
45/J3 Dolomite Alps (Alpi Dolomitiche) (range), It.
97/F3 Dolores, Arg.
100/D4 Dolores, Guat.
47/E3 Dolores, Sp.
96/F2 Dolores, Uru.
108/E3 Dolores, Co,US
108/E3 Dolores (riv.), Co, Ut,US
100/A3 Dolores Hidalgo, Mex.
97/N7 Dolphin (cape), Falk.
88/A2 Dolphin (pt.), Namb.
102/E1 Dolphin and Union (str.), NW,Can
33/F4 Dolphinholme, Eng,UK
34/B5 Dolton, Eng,UK
116/Q16 Dolton, Il,US
69/D2 Do Luong, Viet.
73/J4 Dom (peak), Indo.
45/H3 Domat-Ems, Swi.
45/K2 Domažlice, Czh.
45/G2 Dombasle-sur-Meurthe, Fr.
55/G4 Dombay-Ul'gen, Gora (peak), Geo.
50/D2 Dombóvár, Hun.
44/E3 Domérat, Fr.
91/C1 Domeyko (mts.), Chile
101/J4 Dominica
101/H4 Dominican Republic
40/C6 Dommel (riv.), Belg., Neth.
69/D3 Dom Noi (res.), Thai.
53/X9 Domodedovo, Rus.
45/H3 Domodossola, It.
31/S9 Domont, Fr.
91/F3 Dom Pedrito, Braz.
94/A2 Dom Pedro, Braz.
73/E5 Dompu, Indo.
50/D2 Dömsöd, Hun.
48/A3 Domusnovas, It.
96/C3 Domuyo (vol.), Arg.
76/C5 Domvilk (peak), Austl.
50/B2 Domžale, Slov.
44/C3 Don (riv.), Fr.
101/N8 Don, Mex.
55/G2 Don (ridge), Rus.
55/G3 Don (riv.), Rus.
33/G5 Don (riv.), Eng,UK
36/D2 Don (riv.), Sc,UK
32/C2 Donaghadee, NI,UK
32/B2 Donaghmore, NI,UK
113/F4 Donaldsonville, La,US
46/B4 Doñana Nat'l Park, Sp.
44/E5 Dona, Pic de la (peak), Fr.
39/H4 Donau (Danube) (riv.), Aus., Ger.
46/C3 Don Benito, Sp.
77/G5 Doncaster, Austl.
33/G4 Doncaster, Eng,UK
87/B2 Dondo, Ang.
70/D6 Dondra Head (pt.), SrL.
36/A3 Donegal (bay), Ire.
32/A1 Donegal (co.), Ire.
54/F3 Donetsk, Ukr.
54/F3 Donetsk Obl., Ukr.
67/B3 Dong (riv.), China
71/J5 Dong (riv.), Viet.
85/H5 Donga (riv.), Camr., Nga.
71/H2 Dongchuan, China
71/J3 Dong Dang, Viet.
66/E5 Dongdongting Shan (mtn.), China
40/B5 Dongen, Neth.
67/B3 Dongguan, China
69/D2 Dong Ha, Viet.
69/D2 Donghen, Laos
69/D2 Dong Hoi, Viet.
66/E2 Dongliao (riv.), China
69/D4 Dong Noi (riv.), Viet.
66/D3 Dongping (lake), China
67/C3 Dongsha (isl.), China
66/E4 Dongtai, China
66/L9 Dongtaio (riv.), China
69/D2 Dong Tau, Viet.
67/B2 Dongting (lake), China
66/D3 Dongying, China
96/Q10 Donihue, Chile
33/H6 Donington, Eng,UK
102/C2 Donjek (riv.), Yk,Can
50/C3 Donji Vakuf, Bosn.
32/D1 Doon (riv.), Sc,UK
114/H2 Doonerak (mtn.), Ak,US
32/D1 Doon, Loch (lake), Sc,UK
110/C2 Door (pen.), Wi,US
40/C4 Doorn, Neth.
88/B3 Doorn (riv.), SAfr.
74/C4 Dora (lake), Austl.
47/F2 Dorada (coast), Sp.
61/K1 Do Rāh (pass), Afg.
68/B4 Dorāh Ān (pass), Pak.
45/G4 Dora Riparia (riv.), It.
111/H2 Dorchester, NB,Can
103/J2 Dorchester (cape), NW,Can
34/D5 Dorchester, Eng,UK
44/D4 Dordogne (riv.), Fr.
40/B5 Dordrecht, Neth.
106/G2 Dore (lake), Sk,Can
44/E4 Dore (mts.), Fr.
44/E4 Dore (riv.), Fr.
95/C1 Dores do Indaiá, Braz.
48/A2 Dorgali, It.
62/C2 Dörgön (lake), Mong.
85/E3 Dori, Burk.
111/M7 Dorion, Qu,Can
31/N8 Dorking, Eng,UK

40/D6 **Dormagen**, Ger.
31/P8 **Dormans Land**, Eng,UK
45/H3 **Dornbirn**, Aus.
50/D2 **Dorog**, Hun.
51/H2 **Dorohoi**, Rom.
74/A5 **Dorre** (isl.), Austl.
35/E2 **Dorridge**, Eng,UK
77/E1 **Dorrigo Nat'l Park**, Austl.
34/D1 **Dorrington**, Eng,UK
108/B2 **Dorris**, Ca,US
81/W17 **Dorsale** (mts.), Tun.
34/D5 **Dorset** (co.), Eng,UK
40/D5 **Dorsten**, Ger.
41/E5 **Dortmund**, Ger.
41/E4 **Dortmund-Ems** (can.), Ger.
59/D3 **Dörtyol**, Turk.
111/N7 **Dorval**, Qu,Can
41/G3 **Dörverden**, Ger.
96/D5 **Dos Bahias** (cape), Arg.
116/A2 **Dosewallips** (riv.), Wa,US
46/C4 **Dos Hermanas**, Sp.
65/H7 **Dōshi** (riv.), Japan
69/D1 **Do Son**, Viet.
101/M8 **Dos Picachos** (mt.), Mex.
38/G2 **Dosse** (riv.), Ger.
85/F3 **Dosso**, Niger
85/F3 **Dosso** (dept.), Niger
55/K3 **Dossor**, Kaz.
113/G4 **Dothan**, Al,US
42/C3 **Douai**, Fr.
82/G7 **Douala**, Camr.
44/A2 **Douarnenez**, Fr.
44/A2 **Douarnenez** (bay), Fr.
76/D4 **Double I.** (pt.), Austl.
44/F3 **Doubs** (riv.), Fr.
42/C3 **Douchy-les-Mines**, Fr.
44/C3 **Doué-la-Fontaine**, Fr.
84/E3 **Douentza**, Mali
81/W17 **Dougga** (ruins), Tun.
32/D3 **Douglas**, IM,UK
114/H4 **Douglas** (mtn.), Ak,US
108/E5 **Douglas**, Az,US
113/H4 **Douglas**, Ga,US
107/G5 **Douglas**, Wy,US
42/B3 **Doullens**, Fr.
45/K1 **Doupovské Hory** (mts.), Czh.
42/C3 **Dour**, Belg.
93/H8 **Dourados**, Braz.
31/S11 **Dourdan**, Fr.
44/E4 **Dourdou** (riv.), Fr.
46/B2 **Douro** (riv.), Port.
44/F4 **Doux** (riv.), Fr.
44/C4 **Douze** (riv.), Fr.
33/G6 **Dove** (riv.), Eng,UK
33/H3 **Dove** (riv.), Eng,UK
35/H2 **Dove** (riv.), Eng,UK
108/E3 **Dove Creek**, Co,US
42/A2 **Dover** (str.), Fr., UK
35/H4 **Dover**, Eng,UK
111/G3 **Dover**, NH,US
115/F5 **Dover**, NJ,US
111/G2 **Dover-Foxcroft**, Me,US
33/G6 **Doveridge**, Eng,UK
32/C3 **Down** (dist.), NI,UK
116/P16 **Downers Grove**, Il,US
115/B3 **Downey**, Ca,US
35/G1 **Downham Market**, Eng,UK
108/B3 **Downieville**, Ca,US
32/C3 **Downpatrick**, NI,UK
35/H4 **Downs, The** (har.), Eng,UK
35/E4 **Downton**, Eng,UK
115/E5 **Doylestown**, Pa,US
64/C3 **Dōzen** (isl.), Japan
110/E2 **Dozois** (res.), Qu,Can
82/D2 **Drâa** (plat.), Alg., Mor.
82/D2 **Drâa** (wadi), Alg., Mor.
44/F4 **Drac** (riv.), Fr.
95/B2 **Dracena**, Braz.
40/D2 **Drachten**, Neth.
51/G3 **Drăgănești-Olt**, Rom.
51/G3 **Drăgășani**, Rom.
45/G5 **Draguignan**, Fr.
97/L8 **Drake** (passage), Arg., Chile
87/E6 **Drakensberg** (range), Afr.
37/D4 **Drammen**, Nor.
31/T10 **Drancy**, Fr.
32/B2 **Draperstown**, NI,UK
45/L3 **Drau** (riv.), Aus.
50/C3 **Drava** (riv.), Eur.
42/B6 **Draveil**, Fr.
39/H2 **Drawa** (riv.), Pol.
39/H2 **Drawsko Pomorskie**, Pol.
107/J3 **Drayton**, ND,US
106/E2 **Drayton Valley**, Ab,Can
73/K4 **Drei Zinnen** (peak), PNG
41/E5 **Drensteinfurt**, Ger.
40/D3 **Drenthe** (prov.), Neth.
40/D3 **Drentse Hoofdvaart** (can.), Neth.
39/G3 **Dresden**, Ger.
42/A6 **Dreux**, Fr.
39/H2 **Drezdenko**, Pol.
40/C4 **Driebergen**, Neth.
106/F5 **Driggs**, Id,US
61/J4 **Drigh Road**, Pak.
49/F2 **Drin** (gulf), Alb.
49/F1 **Drin** (riv.), Alb.
50/D3 **Drina** (riv.), Bosn., Yugo.
50/E5 **Drinizi** (riv.), Alb.
50/F3 **Drobeta-Turnu Severin**, Rom.
41/G1 **Drochtersen**, Ger.
32/B4 **Drogheda**, Ire.
54/B2 **Drogobych**, Ukr.
34/D2 **Droitwich**, Eng,UK
43/G6 **Drolingen**, Fr.
41/E6 **Drolshagen**, Ger.
44/F4 **Drôme** (riv.), Fr.
32/A3 **Dromore** (riv.), Ire.
32/B3 **Dromore**, NI,UK
33/G5 **Dronfield**, Eng,UK
44/D4 **Dronne** (riv.), Fr.
40/C3 **Dronten**, Neth.
44/D4 **Dropt** (riv.), Fr.
42/A6 **Drouette** (riv.), Fr.
110/C1 **Drowning** (riv.), On,Can
32/C3 **Drumaness**, NI,UK
32/C2 **Drumbeg**, NI,UK
106/E3 **Drumheller**, Ab,Can
32/B5 **Drumleck** (pt.), Ire.
76/B4 **Drummond** (peak), Austl.
76/B4 **Drummond** (range), Austl.
111/F2 **Drummondville**, Qu,Can
32/D2 **Drummore**, Sc,UK
32/A2 **Drumnakilly**, NI,UK
40/C5 **Drunen**, Neth.
33/G1 **Druridge** (bay), Eng,UK
39/M1 **Druskininkai**, Lith.
40/C5 **Druten**, Neth.
50/C3 **Drvar**, Bosn.
39/K2 **Drwęca** (riv.), Pol.
51/G4 **Dryanovo**, Bul.
114/K3 **Dry Creek**, Yk,Can
110/A1 **Dryden**, On,Can
112/C4 **Dryden**, Tx,US
34/C2 **Drygarn Fawr** (mtn.), Wal,UK
36/C2 **Drymen**, Sc,UK
85/H5 **Dschang**, Camr.
66/B4 **Du** (riv.), China
34/B3 **Duad** (riv.), Wal,UK
101/H4 **Duarte** (pk.), DRep.
102/F2 **Dubawnt** (lake), NW,Can
102/F2 **Dubawnt** (riv.), NW,Can
61/G3 **Dubayy**, UAE
77/D2 **Dubbo**, Austl.
32/B5 **Dublin** (bay), Ire.
32/B5 **Dublin** (cap.), Ire.
32/B5 **Dublin** (co.), Ire.
116/L11 **Dublin**, Ca,US
113/H3 **Dublin**, Ga,US
52/H4 **Dubna**, Rus.
39/K4 **Dubnica nad Váhom**, Slvk.
54/C2 **Dubno**, Ukr.
110/E3 **Du Bois**, Pa,US
106/F5 **Dubois**, Wy,US
51/J2 **Dubossary** (res.), Mol.
50/D4 **Dubrovnik**, Cro.
107/L5 **Dubuque**, Ia,US
108/E2 **Duchesne**, Ut,US
108/E2 **Duchesne** (riv.), Ut,US
79/N7 **Ducie** (atoll), Pitc.
113/G3 **Duck** (riv.), Tn,US
116/A2 **Duckabush** (riv.), Wa,US
107/G2 **Duck Lake**, Sk,Can
108/D3 **Duckwater**, Nv,US
69/D3 **Duc Lap**, Viet.
69/E3 **Duc Pho**, Viet.
69/D4 **Duc Phong**, Viet.
33/E3 **Dudden** (riv.), Eng,UK
43/F5 **Dudelange**, Lux.
41/H5 **Duderstadt**, Ger.
56/J3 **Dudinka**, Rus.
34/D2 **Dudley**, Eng,UK
46/C2 **Duero (Douro)** (riv.), Sp.
98/W **Dufek Massive** (mtn.), Ant.
78/F5 **Duff** (isl.), Sol.
42/D1 **Duffel**, Belg.
33/G6 **Duffield**, Eng,UK
36/D2 **Dufftown**, Sc,UK
45/G4 **Dufourspitze** (Punta Dufour) (peak), It., Swi.
50/B3 **Dugi Otok** (isl.), Cro.
108/D2 **Dugway**, Ut,US
92/E3 **Duida Marahuaca Nat'l Park**, Ven.
75/G2 **Duifken** (pt.), Austl.
40/D6 **Duisburg**, Ger.
92/D2 **Duitama**, Col.
40/D5 **Duiven**, Neth.
79/L7 **Duke of Gloucester** (isls.), FrPol.
39/L4 **Dukla** (Przełęcz Dukielska) (pass), Pol.
62/D4 **Dulan**, China
91/D2 **Dulce** (riv.), Arg.
108/F3 **Dulce**, NM,US
71/J2 **Duliu** (riv.), China
41/E5 **Dülmen**, Ger.
51/H4 **Dulovo**, Bul.
107/K4 **Duluth**, Mn,US
34/C4 **Dulverton**, Eng,UK
59/L5 **Dūmā**, Syria
115/B2 **Duma** (pt.), Ca,US
67/D6 **Dumaguete**, Phil.
67/D6 **Dumalinao**, Phil.
67/C5 **Dumaran** (isl.), Phil.
77/D1 **Dumaresq** (riv.), Austl.
112/F3 **Dumas**, Ar,US
112/C3 **Dumas**, Tx,US
39/K4 **Ďumbier** (peak), Slvk.
87/C3 **Dumbo**, Ang.
51/G2 **Dumbrăveni**, Rom.
32/E1 **Dumfries**, Sc,UK
32/D1 **Dumfries & Galloway** (reg.), Sc,UK
41/F3 **Dümmer** (lake), Ger.
110/E2 **Dumoine** (lake), Qu,Can
110/E2 **Dumoine** (riv.), Qu,Can
115/F5 **Dumont**, NJ,US
98/K **Dumont d'Urville**, Ant.
59/H6 **Dumyāt** (gov.), Egypt
59/H6 **Dumyāt** (Damietta), Egypt
39/K5 **Duna** (Danube) (riv.), Hun.
50/D2 **Dunaföldvár**, Hun.
50/D2 **Dunaharaszti**, Hun.
39/K5 **Dunaj** (Danube) (riv.), Slvk.
39/L4 **Dunajec** (riv.), Pol.
39/K5 **Dunakeszi**, Hun.
32/B4 **Dunany** (pt.), Ire.
50/D2 **Dunaújváros**, Hun.
36/D3 **Dunbar**, Sc,UK
36/D2 **Dunblane**, Sc,UK
108/E4 **Duncan**, Az,US
109/H4 **Duncan**, Ok,US
112/D3 **Duncanville**, Tx,US
32/B3 **Dundalk**, Ire.
32/B4 **Dundalk** (bay), Ire.
115/K7 **Dundalk**, Md,US
74/C6 **Dundas** (lake), Austl.
74/E2 **Dundas** (str.), Austl.
103/R7 **Dundas** (pen.), NW,Can
111/Q9 **Dundas**, On,Can
89/E3 **Dundee**, SAfr.
36/D2 **Dundee**, Sc,UK
32/C3 **Dundrum**, NI,UK
32/C3 **Dundrum** (bay), NI,UK
106/G3 **Dundurn**, Sk,Can
75/R12 **Dunedin**, NZ
113/H4 **Dunedin**, Fl,US
36/D2 **Dunfermline**, Sc,UK
32/B2 **Dungannon**, NI,UK
32/B3 **Dungannon** (dist.), NI,UK
70/B3 **Dungarpur**, India
36/B4 **Dungarvan**, Ire.
97/K8 **Dungeness** (pt.), Arg.
35/G5 **Dungeness** (pt.), Eng,UK
32/B2 **Dungiven**, NI,UK
83/L7 **Dungu**, Zaire
63/K3 **Dunhua**, China
62/C3 **Dunhuang**, China
34/C4 **Dunkery** (hill), Eng,UK
42/B1 **Dunkirk** (Dunkerque), Fr.
85/E5 **Dunkwa**, Gha.
32/B5 **Dún Laoghaire**, Ire.
32/B2 **Dunloy**, NI,UK
32/B2 **Dunmurry**, NI,UK
113/J3 **Dunn**, NC,US
32/A2 **Dunnamanagh**, NI,UK
32/B2 **Dunnamore**, NI,UK
33/H4 **Dunnington**, Eng,UK
111/Q10 **Dunnville**, On,Can
86/B5 **Dunqulah**, Sudan
32/D2 **Dunragit**, Sc,UK
36/D3 **Duns**, Sc,UK
32/E1 **Dunscore**, Sc,UK
107/H3 **Dunseith**, ND,US
32/B1 **Dunseverick**, NI,UK
108/B2 **Dunsmuir**, Ca,US
35/F3 **Dunstable**, Eng,UK
43/E5 **Dun-sur-Meuse**, Fr.
63/J1 **Duobukur** (riv.), China
116/P16 **Du Page** (riv.), Il,US
107/H4 **Dupree**, SD,US
95/K7 **Duque de Caxias**, Braz.
97/J7 **Duque de York** (isl.), Chile
110/B4 **Du Quoin**, Il,US
74/D3 **Durack** (range), Austl.
44/F5 **Durance** (riv.), Fr.
101/N9 **Durango** (state), Mex.
46/D1 **Durango**, Sp.
108/F3 **Durango**, Co,US
101/P9 **Durango de Victoria**, Mex.
109/H4 **Durant**, Ok,US
97/F2 **Durazno**, Uru.
97/F2 **Durazno** (dept.), Uru.
89/E3 **Durban**, SAfr.
88/L10 **Durbanville**, SAfr.
43/E3 **Durbuy**, Belg.
50/C2 **Đurđevac**, Cro.
43/F2 **Düren**, Ger.
70/D3 **Durg**, India
70/E3 **Durgāpur**, India
33/G2 **Durham**, Eng,UK
33/F2 **Durham** (co.), Eng,UK
113/J3 **Durham**, NC,US
111/G3 **Durham**, NH,US
35/E5 **Durlston Head** (pt.), Eng,UK
42/D1 **Durme** (riv.), Belg.
50/D4 **Durmitor Nat'l Park**, Yugo.
49/F2 **Durrës**, Alb.
35/E4 **Durrington**, Eng,UK
34/D3 **Dursley**, Eng,UK
59/B2 **Dursunbey**, Turk.
73/J4 **D'Urville** (cape), Indo.
110/C1 **Dusey** (riv.), On,Can
66/D2 **Du Shan** (peak), China
56/G6 **Dushanbe** (cap.), Taj.
40/D6 **Düsseldorf**, Ger.
33/H4 **Dutch** (riv.), Eng,UK
41/F4 **Düte** (riv.), Ger.
88/L10 **Dutoitspiek** (peak), SAfr.
71/J2 **Duyun**, China
51/K5 **Düzce**, Turk.
59/D3 **Düzici**, Turk.
52/H2 **Dvina** (bay), Rus.
53/J3 **Dvina, Northern** (riv.), Rus.
52/F5 **Dvina, Western** (riv.), Bel., Rus.
70/A3 **Dwārka**, India
106/D4 **Dworshak** (res.), Id,US
32/D6 **Dwyfor** (riv.), Wal,UK
88/C4 **Dwyka** (riv.), SAfr.
54/E1 **Dyat'kovo**, Rus.
103/K2 **Dyer** (cape), NW,Can
97/J7 **Dyer** (cape), Chile
110/C3 **Dyer**, In,US
113/F2 **Dyersburg**, Tn,US
34/B3 **Dyfed** (co.), Wal,UK
32/D6 **Dyffryn**, Wal,UK
34/C1 **Dyfi** (riv.), Wal,UK
39/J4 **Dyje** (riv.), Czh.
55/G4 **Dykh-tau, Gora** (peak), Rus.
42/D2 **Dyle** (Dijle) (riv.), Belg.
39/K2 **Dylewska Gora** (peak), Pol.
35/G4 **Dymchurch**, Eng,UK
55/H4 **Dyul'tydag, Gora** (peak), Rus.
89/H6 **Dzaoudzi** (cap.), May.
62/C2 **Dzavhan** (riv.), Mong.
54/F3 **Dzenzik, Mys** (pt.), Ukr.
62/C2 **Dzereg**, Mong.
52/J4 **Dzerzhinsk**, Rus.
68/B3 **Dzhalal-Abad**, Kyr.
68/B3 **Dzhambul**, Kaz.
54/E3 **Dzhankoy**, Ukr.
55/M1 **Dzhetygara**, Kaz.
68/A2 **Dzhezkazgan**, Kaz.
56/G5 **Dzhizak**, Uzb.
57/P4 **Dzhugdzhur** (range), Rus.
39/L2 **Działdowo**, Pol.
100/D3 **Dzibilchaltún** (ruins), Mex.
100/D3 **Dzidzantún**, Mex.
39/J3 **Dzierżoniów**, Pol.
62/B3 **Dzungarian** (basin), China
68/D3 **Dzungarian Gate** (pass), China
62/E2 **Dzüünbayan-Ulaan**, Mong.
68/F2 **Dzüüngovĭ**, Mong.
62/D2 **Dzüünhangay**, Mong.
62/F2 **Dzüünharaa**, Mong.

E

109/G3 **Eads**, Co,US
103/L3 **Eagle** (riv.), Nf,Can
110/A1 **Eagle** (lake), On,Can
106/F3 **Eagle** (riv.), Sk,Can
108/B2 **Eagle** (lake), Ca,US
108/F3 **Eagle**, Co,US
107/L4 **Eagle** (peak), Mn,US
116/P14 **Eagle** (lake), Wi,US
107/H4 **Eagle Butte**, SD,US
112/C4 **Eagle Pass**, Tx,US
33/E1 **Eaglesfield**, Sc,UK
31/M7 **Ealing** (bor.), Eng,UK
33/F4 **Earby**, Eng,UK
110/A1 **Ear Falls**, On,Can
35/G2 **Earith**, Eng,UK
108/C4 **Earlimart**, Ca,US
35/F2 **Earls Barton**, Eng,UK
35/G3 **Earls Colne**, Eng,UK
35/H2 **Earl Stonham**, Eng,UK
112/D4 **Early**, Tx,US
36/D2 **Earn** (riv.), Sc,UK
33/G2 **Easington**, Eng,UK
33/G3 **Easingwold**, Eng,UK
113/H3 **Easley**, SC,US
75/S10 **East** (cape), NZ
114/B6 **East** (cape), Ak,US
35/G2 **East Anglia** (reg.), Eng,UK
111/G2 **East Angus**, Qu,Can
31/N7 **East Barnet**, Eng,UK
35/H3 **East Bergholt**, Eng,UK
107/K4 **East Bethel**, Mn,US
35/G5 **Eastbourne**, Eng,UK
115/F5 **East Brunswick**, NJ,US
33/G1 **East Chevington**, Eng,UK
116/R16 **East Chicago**, In,US
67/D2 **East China** (sea)
31/M8 **East Clandon**, Eng,UK
34/B3 **East Cleddau** (riv.), Wal,UK
34/C5 **East Dart** (riv.), Eng,UK
35/G1 **East Dereham**, Eng,UK
116/G7 **East Detroit** (East Pointe), Mi,US
79/Q7 **Easter** (isl.), Chile
88/A2 **Easter** (pt.), Namb.
85/E5 **Eastern** (reg.), Gha.
84/C4 **Eastern** (prov.), SLeo.
86/C5 **Eastern** (reg.), Sudan
33/H4 **Eastern** (plain), Eng,UK
64/A4 **Eastern Channel** (str.), Japan
70/C5 **Eastern Ghats** (uplands), India
56/K4 **Eastern Sayans** (mts.), Rus.
107/J2 **Easterville**, Mb,Can
97/N8 **East Falkland** (isl.), Falk.
42/C2 **East Flanders** (prov.), Belg.
41/E1 **East Frisian** (isls.), Ger.
35/F1 **East Glen** (riv.), Eng,UK
35/F4 **East Grinstead**, Eng,UK
106/F4 **East Helena**, Mt,US
116/C2 **East Hill-Meridian**, Wa,US
31/M8 **East Horsley**, Eng,UK
110/C2 **East Jordan**, Mi,US
56/J5 **East Kazakhstan Obl.**, Kaz.
112/D3 **Eastland**, Tx,US
110/C3 **East Lansing**, Mi,US
33/G6 **East Leake**, Eng,UK
35/E5 **Eastleigh**, Eng,UK
110/D3 **East Liverpool**, Oh,US
88/D4 **East London**, SAfr.
115/B2 **East Los Angeles**, Ca,US
110/F1 **Eastmain** (riv.), Qu,Can
113/H3 **Eastman**, Ga,US
115/G5 **East Meadow**, NY,US
111/G2 **East Millinocket**, Me,US
31/M7 **East Molesey**, Eng,UK
107/K5 **East Nishnabotna** (riv.), Ia,US
34/D5 **Easton**, Eng,UK
115/E5 **Easton**, Pa,US
115/F5 **East Orange**, NJ,US
115/H5 **East Patchogue**, NY,US
113/G3 **East Point**, Ga,US
116/G7 **East Pointe** (East Detroit), Mi,US
111/H2 **Eastport**, Me,US
33/H5 **East Retford**, Eng,UK
33/E2 **Eastriggs**, Sc,UK
35/H4 **Eastry**, Eng,UK
110/B4 **East Saint Louis**, Il,US
57/S2 **East Siberian** (sea), Rus.
115/E5 **East Stroudsburg**, Pa,US
35/G5 **East Sussex** (co.), Eng,UK
110/D2 **East Tawas**, Mi,US
34/B4 **East the Water**, Eng,UK
106/C4 **East Wenatchee**, Wa,US
115/F5 **East Windsor**, NJ,US
35/F5 **East Wittering**, Eng,UK
33/G6 **Eastwood**, Eng,UK
111/R8 **East York**, On,Can
35/E2 **Eatington**, Eng,UK
109/F2 **Eaton**, Co,US
106/F3 **Eatonia**, Sk,Can
35/F2 **Eaton Socon**, Eng,UK
115/F5 **Eatontown**, NJ,US
33/H5 **Eau** (riv.), Eng,UK
31/S10 **Eaubonne**, Fr.
103/J3 **Eau Claire** (lake), Qu,Can
110/B2 **Eau Claire**, Wi,US
42/A4 **Eaulne** (riv.), Fr.
78/D4 **Eauripik** (atoll), Micr.
35/E4 **Ebble** (riv.), Eng,UK
34/C3 **Ebbw Vale**, Wal,UK
82/G3 **Ebeggi** (well), Alg.
45/K3 **Ebensee**, Aus.
39/G2 **Eberswalde-Finow**, Ger.
63/N3 **Ebetsu**, Japan
65/H7 **Ebina**, Japan
68/D3 **Ebinur** (lake), China
84/D3 **Ebo** (lake), Mali
48/D2 **Eboli**, It.
82/H7 **Ebolowa**, Camr.
78/F4 **Ebon** (atoll), Mrsh.
47/F2 **Ebro** (riv.), Sp.
100/B4 **Ecatepec**, Mex.
33/E1 **Ecclefechan**, Sc,UK
33/F5 **Eccles**, Eng,UK
33/F6 **Eccleshall**, Eng,UK
85/H3 **Éché Fadadinga** (wadi), Niger
67/B1 **Echeng**, China
65/M9 **Echigawa**, Japan
44/F4 **Echirolles**, Fr.
55/H4 **Echmiadzin**, Arm.
102/E2 **Echo Bay**, NW,Can
107/L2 **Echoing** (riv.), Mb, On,Can
40/C6 **Echt**, Neth.
77/C3 **Echuca**, Austl.
46/C4 **Écija**, Sp.
38/E1 **Eckernförde**, Ger.
32/D2 **Eckington**, Eng,UK
103/H1 **Eclipse** (sound), NW,Can
95/D1 **Ecoporanga**, Braz.
116/F7 **Ecorse**, Mi,US
42/A5 **Écos**, Fr.
31/T9 **Écouen**, Fr.
44/D2 **Écouves, Signal d'** (peak), Fr.
92/C4 **Ecuador**
83/P5 **Ed**, Erit.
36/C2 **Edderton**, Sc,UK
77/D4 **Eddystone** (pt.), Austl.
34/B6 **Eddystone** (rocks), Eng,UK
40/C4 **Ede**, Neth.
85/G5 **Ede**, Nga.
82/H7 **Edéa**, Camr.
42/D1 **Edegem**, Belg.
95/B1 **Edéia**, Braz.
50/E1 **Edelény**, Hun.
41/H4 **Edemissen**, Ger.
33/F2 **Eden** (riv.), Eng,UK
113/J2 **Eden**, NC,US
31/P8 **Edenbridge**, Eng,UK
89/E3 **Edendale**, SAfr.
33/F2 **Edenside** (val.), Eng,UK
41/G6 **Eder** (riv.), Ger.
41/F6 **Eder-Stausee** (res.), Ger.
41/E2 **Edewecht**, Ger.
35/E2 **Edgbaston**, Eng,UK
56/C2 **Edge** (isl.), Sval.
114/L4 **Edgecumbe** (cape), Ak,US
103/K2 **Edgell** (isl.), NW,Can
107/G5 **Edgerton**, Wy,US
116/C3 **Edgewood-North Hill**, Wa,US
34/D1 **Edgmond**, Eng,UK
31/N7 **Edgware**, Eng,UK
49/H2 **Édhessa**, Gre.
110/D3 **Edinboro**, Pa,US
112/D5 **Edinburg**, Tx,US
36/D3 **Edinburgh** (cap.), Sc,UK
51/H5 **Edirne**, Turk.
51/H5 **Edirne** (prov.), Turk.
115/F5 **Edison**, NJ,US
113/H3 **Edisto** (riv.), SC,US
113/H3 **Edisto Island**, SC,US
85/F2 **Édjérir** (wadi), Mali
116/C2 **Edmonds**, Wa,US
106/E2 **Edmonton** (cap.), Ab,Can
31/N7 **Edmonton**, Eng,UK
107/K2 **Edmund** (lake), Mb,Can
76/B2 **Edmund Kennedy Nat'l Park**, Austl.
111/G2 **Edmundston**, NB,Can
112/D4 **Edna**, Tx,US
65/H7 **Edo** (riv.), Japan
59/A2 **Edremit**, Turk.
54/C5 **Edremit** (gulf), Turk.
106/D2 **Edson**, Ab,Can
94/D2 **Eduardo Gomes**, Braz.
83/L8 **Edward** (lake), Ugan., Zaire
109/K2 **Edwards** (riv.), Il,US
112/C4 **Edwards** (plat.), Tx,US
110/B4 **Edwardsville**, Il,US
98/P **Edward VII** (pen.), Ant.
98/D **Edward VIII** (bay), Ant.
36/D2 **Edzell**, Sc,UK
100/C4 **Edzná** (ruins), Mex.
42/C1 **Eeklo**, Belg.
108/B3 **Eel** (riv.), Ca,US
40/D2 **Eelde-Paterswolde**, Neth.
40/C4 **Eem** (riv.), Neth.
40/D2 **Eems (Ems)** (riv.), Neth.
40/D2 **Eemshaven** (har.), Neth.
40/D2 **Eemskanaal** (can.), Neth.
40/C6 **Eersel**, Neth.
78/F6 **Efate** (isl.), Van.
107/L5 **Effigy Mounds Nat'l Mon.**, Ia,US
111/R9 **Effingham**, On,Can
31/M8 **Effingham**, Eng,UK
110/B4 **Effingham**, Il,US
51/J3 **Eforie**, Rom.
32/E6 **Efyrnwy, Llyn** (lake), Wal,UK
48/C3 **Egadi** (isls.), It.
108/D3 **Egan** (range), Nv,US
45/K1 **Eger** (riv.), Ger.
50/E2 **Eger**, Hun.
37/C4 **Egersund**, Nor.
41/F5 **Eggegebirge** (ridge), Ger.
33/G3 **Egglescliffe**, Eng,UK
33/G2 **Eggleston**, Eng,UK
31/M7 **Egham**, Eng,UK
43/D2 **Éghezée**, Belg.
62/E1 **Egiyn** (riv.), Mong.
103/R7 **Eglinton** (isl.), NW,Can
32/A1 **Eglinton**, NI,UK
34/C4 **Eglwys Brewis**, Wal,UK
31/S11 **Égly**, Fr.
40/B3 **Egmond aan Zee**, Neth.
75/R10 **Egmont** (cape), NZ
75/R10 **Egmont** (peak), NZ
32/E3 **Egremont**, Eng,UK
59/B3 **Eğridir**, Turk.
94/A4 **Eguas** (riv.), Braz.
86/B3 **Egypt**
64/C4 **Ehime** (pref.), Japan
45/H1 **Ehringshausen**, Ger.
79/L5 **Eiao** (isl.), FrPol.
46/D1 **Eibar**, Sp.
40/D4 **Eibergen**, Neth.
43/G6 **Eichel** (riv.), Fr.
45/J2 **Eichstätt**, Ger.
37/D3 **Eidsvoll**, Nor.
43/F3 **Eifel** (plat.), Ger.
31/S10 **Eiffel Tower**, Fr.
65/M9 **Eigenji**, Japan
70/B6 **Eight Degree** (chan.), India, Mald.
98/T **Eights** (coast), Ant.
74/C3 **Eighty Mile** (beach), Austl.
40/B2 **Eijerlandsee Gat** (chan.), Neth.
43/E2 **Eijsden**, Neth.
77/C3 **Eildon** (lake), Austl.
76/A2 **Einasleigh** (riv.), Austl.
41/G5 **Einbeck**, Ger.
40/C6 **Eindhoven**, Neth.
92/E5 **Eirunepé**, Braz.
43/E4 **Eisch** (riv.), Lux.
41/H7 **Eisenach**, Ger.
45/L3 **Eisenerz**, Aus.
39/H2 **Eisenhüttenstadt**, Ger.
45/M3 **Eisenstadt**, Aus.
43/G2 **Eiserfeld**, Ger.
41/F3 **Eiter** (riv.), Ger.
43/G2 **Eitorf**, Ger.
47/E1 **Ejea de los Caballeros**, Sp.
101/G6 **Ejido**, Ven.
40/B6 **Ekeren**, Belg.
68/C1 **Ekibastuz**, Kaz.
37/E4 **Eksjö**, Swe.
103/H3 **Ekwan** (riv.), On,Can
84/C2 **El 'Acâba** (reg.), Mrta.
81/S15 **El Affroun**, Alg.
86/B2 **El Alamein** (Al 'Alamayn), Egypt
60/B3 **El Amra** (Abydos) (ruins), Egypt
34/C2 **Elan** (riv.), Wal,UK
31/R10 **Élancourt**, Fr.
88/P12 **Elands** (riv.), SAfr.
88/Q12 **Elandsrivier** (riv.), SAfr.
81/V18 **El Aouinet**, Alg.
46/C4 **El Arahal**, Sp.
76/B2 **El Arish**, Austl.
82/F1 **El Asnam**, Alg.
49/H3 **Elassón**, Gre.
46/D1 **El Astillero**, Sp.
86/C2 **Elat**, Isr.
78/D4 **Elato** (atoll), Micr.
59/D2 **Elazığ**, Turk.
48/B1 **Elba** (isl.), It.
113/G4 **Elba**, Al,US
101/G6 **El Banco**, Col.
46/B1 **El Barco**, Sp.
49/G2 **Elbasan**, Alb.
82/F1 **El Bayadh**, Alg.
38/E2 **Elbe** (riv.), Ger.
108/F3 **Elbert** (mtn.), Co,US
113/H3 **Elberton**, Ga,US
41/H2 **Elbe-Seitenkanal** (can.), Ger.
44/D2 **Elbeuf**, Fr.
59/D2 **Elbistan**, Turk.
39/K1 **Elbląg**, Pol.
39/K2 **Elbląg** (prov.), Pol.
106/G3 **Elbow**, Sk,Can
55/G4 **El'brus, Gora** (peak), Rus.
40/C4 **Elburg**, Neth.
60/E1 **Elburz** (mts.), Iran
108/C4 **El Cajon**, Ca,US
112/D4 **El Campo**, Tx,US
106/E4 **El Capitan** (peak), Mt,US
96/B3 **El Carmen**, Chile
101/F6 **El Carmen**, Col.
47/N8 **El Casar de Talamanca**, Sp.
108/D4 **El Centro**, Ca,US
116/K11 **El Cerrito**, Ca,US
47/E3 **Elche**, Sp.
74/F2 **Elcho** (isl.), Austl.
96/C3 **El Chocón** (res.), Arg.
92/D2 **El Cocuy Nat'l Park**, Col.
91/E2 **El Colorado**, Arg.
47/E3 **Elda**, Sp.
38/G2 **Elde** (riv.), Ger.
115/K7 **Eldersburg**, Md,US
84/C1 **El Djouf** (des.), Mali, Mrta.
91/F2 **Eldorado**, Arg.
101/N9 **Eldorado**, Mex.
112/E3 **El Dorado**, Ar,US
112/D2 **El Dorado**, Ks,US
112/C4 **Eldorado**, Tx,US
83/N7 **Eldoret**, Kenya
104/W13 **Eleao** (peak), Hi,US
82/D2 **El Eglab** (plat.), Alg.
50/E2 **Elek**, Hun.
52/H5 **Elektrostal'**, Rus.
51/G4 **Elena**, Bul.
98/W **Elephant** (isl.), Ant.
94/B2 **Elesbão Veloso**, Braz.
47/M8 **El Escorial**, Sp.
81/U17 **El Eulma**, Alg.
101/F2 **Eleuthera** (isl.), Bahm.
109/K3 **Eleven Point** (riv.), Ar, Mo,US
49/L6 **Elevsís**, Gre.
46/A1 **El Ferrol**, Sp.
111/Q9 **Elfrida**, On,Can
101/N8 **El Fuerte**, Mex.
36/D2 **Elgin**, Sc,UK
116/P15 **Elgin**, Il,US
107/H4 **Elgin**, ND,US
112/D4 **Elgin**, Tx,US
111/R8 **Elgin Mills**, On,Can
100/A3 **Elgogorrón Nat'l Park**, Mex.
46/D1 **Elgóibar**, Sp.
82/F1 **El Golea**, Alg.
83/N7 **Elgon** (mtn.), Kenya, Ugan.
81/T16 **El Ham** (riv.), Alg.
100/B3 **El Higo**, Mex.
87/D2 **Elias Garcia**, Ang.
109/G4 **Elida**, NM,US
112/C4 **El Indio**, Tx,US
35/E5 **Eling**, Eng,UK
55/H3 **Elista**, Rus.
88/A2 **Elizabeth** (bay), Namb.
115/F5 **Elizabeth**, NJ,US
113/J2 **Elizabeth City**, NC,US
113/H2 **Elizabethton**, Tn,US
110/C4 **Elizabethtown**, Ky,US
82/D1 **El Jadida**, Mor.
39/M2 **Ełk**, Pol.
112/B2 **Elk** (mts.), Co,US
113/H2 **Elk** (riv.), WV,US
109/H4 **Elk City**, Ok,US
116/M10 **Elk Grove**, Ca,US
116/Q15 **Elk Grove Village**, Il,US
110/C3 **Elkhart**, In,US
109/G3 **Elkhart**, Ks,US
82/D3 **El Khatt** (escarp.), Mrta.
107/H3 **Elkhorn**, Mb,Can
109/H2 **Elkhorn** (riv.), Ne,US
51/H4 **Elkhovo**, Bul.
113/H2 **Elkin**, NC,US
110/E4 **Elkins**, WV,US
106/E2 **Elk Island Nat'l Park**, Ab,Can
108/D2 **Elko**, Nv,US
106/F2 **Elk Point**, Ab,Can
110/C2 **Elk Rapids**, Mi,US
115/K7 **Elk Ridge**, Md,US
107/K4 **Elk River**, Mn,US
81/V17 **El Kroub**, Alg.
81/T15 **El Kseur**, Alg.
33/G4 **Elland**, Eng,UK
43/F2 **Elle** (riv.), Ger.
103/R7 **Ellef Ringnes** (isl.), NW,Can
33/E2 **Ellen** (riv.), Eng,UK
107/J4 **Ellendale**, ND,US
106/C4 **Ellensburg**, Wa,US
41/H5 **Eller** (riv.), Ger.
43/G4 **Ellerbach** (riv.), Ger.
77/D3 **Ellery** (peak), Austl.
103/T6 **Ellesmere** (isl.), NW,Can
103/T6 **Ellesmere Island Nat'l Park**, NW,Can
33/F5 **Ellesmere Port**, Eng,UK
96/C2 **El Libertador General Bernardo O'Higgins** (reg.), Chile
102/F2 **Ellice** (riv.), NW,Can
115/K7 **Ellicott City**, Md,US
110/D2 **Elliot Lake**, On,Can
113/J2 **Elliott** (peak), Va,US
87/E5 **Ellisras**, SAfr.
101/F6 **El Llano**, Pan.
36/D2 **Ellon**, Sc,UK
33/H4 **Elloughton**, Eng,UK
98/T **Ellsworth** (mts.), Ant.
109/H3 **Ellsworth**, Ks,US
111/G2 **Ellsworth**, Me,US
110/A2 **Ellsworth**, Wi,US
98/U **Ellsworth Land** (reg.), Ant.
45/J2 **Ellwangen**, Ger.
111/S10 **Elma**, NY,US
59/C2 **Elmadağ**, Turk.
59/B3 **Elmalı**, Turk.
108/F4 **El Malpais Nat'l Mon.**, NM,US
101/M8 **El Marmol**, Mex.
47/L7 **El Masnou**, Sp.
116/P13 **Elm Grove**, Wi,US
116/Q16 **Elmhurst**, Il,US
81/V17 **El Milia**, Alg.
85/E5 **Elmina**, Gha.
110/E3 **Elmira**, NY,US
92/D7 **El Misti** (vol.), Peru
47/N8 **El Molar**, Sp.
115/G5 **Elmont**, NY,US
47/L6 **El Montcau** (peak), Sp.
115/B2 **El Monte**, Ca,US
96/C1 **El Morrito** (pt.), Chile
108/E4 **El Morro Nat'l Mon.**, NM,US
84/C2 **El Mreyyé** (reg.), Mrta.
41/G1 **Elmshorn**, Ger.
35/G2 **Elmswell**, Eng,UK
116/Q16 **Elmwood Park**, Il,US
115/F5 **Elmwood Park**, NJ,US
82/D2 **El Mzereb** (well), Mali
96/C2 **El Nevado** (peak), Arg.
73/E1 **El Nido**, Phil.
95/H6 **Elói Mendes**, Braz.
44/A2 **Elorn** (riv.), Fr.
82/G1 **El Oued**, Alg.
108/E4 **Eloy**, Az,US
101/J6 **El Palmar**, Ven.
96/F1 **El Palmar Nat'l Park**, Arg.
47/N8 **El Pardo**, Sp.
112/B4 **El Paso**, Tx,US
101/J5 **El Pilar**, Ven.
70/D6 **Elpitiya**, SrL.
100/D4 **El Placer**, Mex.
101/F6 **El Porvenir**, Pan.
100/B3 **El Potosí Nat'l Park**, Mex.
47/G2 **El Prat de Llobregat**, Sp.
100/D4 **El Progreso**, Hon.
46/B4 **El Puerto de Santa María**, Sp.
101/N9 **El Quelite**, Mex.
109/H4 **El Reno**, Ok,US
115/A2 **El Rio**, Ca,US
101/H5 **El Roque**, Ven.
106/F3 **Elrose**, Sk,Can
114/L3 **Elsa**, Yk,Can
45/J5 **Elsa** (riv.), It.
46/B2 **Elsa** (res.), Sp.
46/C1 **Elsa** (riv.), Sp.
101/N9 **El Salado**, Mex.
100/D5 **El Salvador**
101/F3 **El Salvador**, Cuba
100/A3 **El Salvador**, Mex.
101/H6 **El Samán de Apure**, Ven.
41/F4 **Else** (riv.), Ger.
115/B3 **El Segundo**, Ca,US
101/H4 **El Seibo**, DRep.
68/F4 **Elsen** (lake), China
41/F2 **Elsfleth**, Ger.
86/B4 **El Shab** (well), Egypt
115/C3 **Elsinore** (lake), Ca,US
101/J7 **El Socorro**, Mex.
40/C5 **Elst**, Neth.
35/F4 **Elstead**, Eng,UK
100/B3 **El Tajín** (ruins), Mex.
92/D2 **El Tama Nat'l Park**, Ven.
81/V17 **El Tarf** (gov.), Alg.
46/B1 **El Teleno** (mtn.), Sp.
31/P7 **Eltham**, Eng,UK
101/J6 **El Tigre**, Ven.
55/H2 **El'ton** (lake), Rus.
115/C3 **El Toro**, Ca,US
92/E3 **El Tuparro Nat'l Park**, Col.
45/H1 **Eltville am Rhein**, Ger.
70/D4 **Elūru**, India
46/B3 **Elvas**, Port.
37/D3 **Elverum**, Nor.
92/D2 **El Viejo** (peak), Col.
101/G6 **El Vigía**, Ven.
101/P8 **El Volcán**, Mex.
83/P7 **El Wak**, Kenya
106/F3 **Elwell** (lake), Mt,US
110/C3 **Elwood**, In,US

32/E5 Elwy (riv.), Wal,UK
35/G2 Ely, Eng,UK
107/L4 Ely, Mn,US
108/D3 Ely, Nv,US
35/G2 Ely, Isle of (reg.), Eng,UK
110/D3 Elyria, Oh,US
43/G3 Elzbach (riv.), Ger.
41/G4 Elze, Ger.
61/F1 Emāmshahr, Iran
93/H7 Emas Nat'l Park, Braz.
55/L2 Emba, Kaz.
55/K3 Emba (riv.), Kaz.
91/D1 Embarcación, Arg.
113/E2 Embarras (riv.), Il,US
92/D5 Embira (riv.), Braz.
95/C1 Emborcaçao (res.), Braz.
95/G8 Embu-Guaçu, Braz.
41/E2 Emden, Ger.
71/H2 Emei, China
77/G5 Emerald, Austl.
107/J3 Emerson, Mb,Can
116/K11 Emeryville, Ca,US
59/B2 Emet, Turk.
45/J4 Emilia-Romagna (reg.), It.
68/D2 Emin (riv.), China
109/K3 Eminence, Mo,US
51/H4 Emine, Nos (cape), Bul.
59/B2 Emirdağ, Turk.
59/C3 Emirgazi, Turk.
89/E2 Emlembe (peak), Swaz.
40/D3 Emlichheim, Ger.
37/E4 Emmaboda, Swe.
115/E5 Emmaus, Pa,US
40/C3 Emmeloord, Neth.
40/D3 Emmen, Neth.
45/G2 Emmendingen, Ger.
41/G5 Emmer (riv.), Ger.
41/E5 Emmerbach (riv.), Ger.
40/D5 Emmerich, Ger.
106/D5 Emmett, Id,US
35/G1 Emneth, Eng,UK
112/E3 Emory, Tx,US
101/P8 Emory (peak), Tx.,US
101/M8 Empalme, Mex.
89/E3 Empangeni, SAfr.
91/E2 Empedrado, Arg.
96/B2 Empedrado, Chile
109/H3 Emporia, Ks,US
110/E4 Emporia, Va,US
41/E4 Emsbüren, Ger.
41/E4 Emsdetten, Ger.
40/D2 Ems (Eems) (riv.), Ger., Neth.
41/E2 Ems-Jade (can.), Ger.
41/E3 Emsland (reg.), Ger.
41/F3 Emstek, Ger.
37/H4 Emumägi (hill), Est.
63/J1 Emur (riv.), China
65/E3 Ena, Japan
106/G5 Encampment, Wy,US
101/L7 Encantada (mt.), Mex.
101/M8 Encantado (mt.), Mex.
91/E2 Encarnación, Par.
101/P9 Encarnación de Díaz, Mex.
84/E5 Enchi, Gha.
108/C4 Encinitas, Ca,US
77/A2 Encounter (bay), Austl.
95/A4 Encruzilhada do Sul, Braz.
73/F5 Ende, Indo.
76/B1 Endeavour River Nat'l Park, Austl.
79/H5 Enderbury (atoll), Kiri.
106/D3 Enderby, BC,Can
98/D Enderby Land (reg.), Ant.
107/J4 Enderlin, ND,US
110/E3 Endicott, NY,US
92/D6 Ene (riv.), Peru
78/F3 Enewetak (atoll), Mrsh.
31/N7 Enfield, Eng,UK
31/N7 Enfield (bor.), Eng,UK
67/D4 Engaño (cape), Phil.
55/H2 Engel's, Rus.
43/G2 Engelskirchen, Ger.
40/D2 Engelsmanplaat (isl.), Neth.
95/K7 Engenheiro Paulo de Frontin, Braz.
41/F4 Enger, Ger.
72/B5 Enggano (isl.), Indo.
83/N4 Enghershatu (peak), Erit.
42/D2 Enghien, Belg.
36/D4 England, UK
110/E2 Englehart, On,Can
115/F5 Englewood, NJ,US
115/G5 Englewood, NJ,US
98/V English (coast), Ant.
107/K3 English (riv.), On,Can
44/B2 English (chan.), Eur.
70/E3 English Bāzār, India
115/F5 Englishtown, NJ,US
109/H3 Enid, Ok,US
40/C3 Enkhuizen, Neth.
37/F4 Enköping, Swe.
48/D4 Enna, It.
83/K4 Ennedi (plat.), Chad
41/E6 Ennepe (riv.), Ger.
41/E6 Ennepetal, Ger.
31/S9 Ennery, Fr.
41/F5 Enningerloh, Ger.
106/F4 Ennis, Mt,US
112/D3 Ennis, Tx,US
45/L3 Enns (riv.), Aus.
76/E6 Enoggera (res.), Austl.
113/H3 Enoree (riv.), SC,US
40/D4 Enschede, Neth.
41/E6 Ense, Ger.
101/L7 Ensenada, Mex.
66/B5 Enshi, China
83/M7 Entebbe, Ugan.
45/K2 Entenbühl (peak), Ger.
113/G4 Enterprise, Al,US
96/F2 Entre Ríos (prov.), Arg.
94/C3 Entre Rios, Braz.
46/A3 Entroncamento, Port.
85/G5 Enugu, Nga.
116/D3 Enumclaw, Wa,US
65/N10 Enushū (sea), Japan
42/A4 Envermeu, Fr.
45/H2 Enz (riv.), Ger.
65/F3 Enzan, Japan
43/F4 Enzbach (riv.), Ger.
40/C4 Epe, Neth.
42/C5 Epernay, Fr.
78/F6 Epi (isl.), Van.
49/H4 Epidaurus (ruins), Gre.
45/G2 Epinal, Fr.
31/S10 Epinay-sur-Orge, Fr.
31/S10 Epinay-sur-Seine, Fr.
49/G3 Epirus (reg.), Gre.
43/F5 Eppelborn, Ger.
76/H8 Epping, Austl.
31/P6 Epping, Eng,UK
76/B3 Epping Forest Nat'l Park, Austl.
31/N8 Epsom, Eng,UK
33/H4 Epworth, Eng,UK
82/G7 Equatorial Guinea
71/H2 Er (lake), China
48/E2 Eraclea (ruins), It.
48/C4 Eraclea Minoa (ruins), It.
31/S9 Eragny, Fr.
70/D6 Eravur, SrL.
69/B3 Erawan Nat'l Park, Thai.
45/H4 Erba, It.
59/D2 Erbaa, Turk.
38/D4 Erbeskopf (peak), Ger.
96/B3 Ercilla, Chile
59/E2 Erciş, Turk.
42/C3 Erclin (riv.), Fr.
50/D2 Érd, Hun.
63/K3 Erdao (riv.), China
51/H5 Erdek, Turk.
51/H5 Erdek (gulf), Turk.
59/C3 Erdemli, Turk.
62/G3 Erdene, Mong.
62/E2 Erdenedalay, Mong.
83/K4 Erdi-Ma (plat.), Chad
45/J2 Erding, Ger.
44/C3 Erdre (riv.), Fr.
98/M Erebus (vol.), Ant.
95/A3 Erechim, Braz.
62/G2 Ereen Davaanī (mts.), Mong.
51/K5 Ereğli, Turk.
59/C3 Ereğli, Turk.
68/D3 Erenhaberga (mts.), China
62/G3 Erenhot, China
51/K5 Erenler, Turk.
93/G4 Erepecu (lake), Braz.
46/C2 Eresma (riv.), Sp.
82/E1 Erfoud, Mor.
43/F1 Erft (riv.), Ger.
43/F2 Erftstadt, Ger.
38/F3 Erfurt, Ger.
59/D2 Ergani, Turk.
82/D3 'Erg Chech (des.), Afr.
82/H4 'Erg du Ténéré (des.), Niger
51/H5 Ergene Nehri (riv.), Turk.
82/D2 'Erg Iguidi (des.), Afr.
82/J5 Erguig (riv.), Chad
63/H1 Ergun (riv.), China, Rus.
106/D3 Erickson, BC,Can
107/J3 Erickson, Mb,Can
110/D3 Erie (lake), Can., US
111/S9 Erie (can.), NY,US
110/D3 Erie, Pa,US
83/Q5 Erigabo, Som.
107/J3 Eriksdale, Mb,Can
78/F4 Erikub (atoll), Mrsh.
49/G4 Erímanthos (peak), Gre.
63/N3 Erimo-misaki (cape), Japan
83/N4 Eritrea
40/D6 Erkelenz, Ger.
39/G2 Erkner, Ger.
40/D6 Erkrath, Ger.
45/J2 Erlangen, Ger.
66/F2 Erlongshan (res.), China
34/C6 Erme (riv.), Eng,UK
40/C4 Ermelo, Neth.
89/E2 Ermelo, SAfr.
59/C3 Ermenek, Turk.
31/T9 Ermenonville, Fr.
31/S10 Ermont, Fr.
49/J4 Ermoúpolis, Gre.
43/H2 Erndtebrück, Ger.
44/C2 Ernée (riv.), Fr.
70/C5 Erode, India
42/D3 Erquelinnes, Belg.
82/E1 Er Rachidīa, Mor.
81/M13 Er Rif (mts.), Mor.
36/A3 Errigal (mtn.), Ire.
78/F6 Erromango (isl.), Van.
41/H4 Erse (riv.), Ger.
62/B2 Ertix (riv.), China
95/B3 Erval d'Oeste, Braz.
110/D4 Erwin, Tn,US
41/F5 Erwitte, Ger.
49/F2 Erzen (riv.), Alb.
45/K1 Erzgebirge (Krušné Hory) (mts.), Czh., Ger.
59/D2 Erzincan, Turk.
59/E2 Erzurum, Turk.
78/D5 Esa'ala, PNG
87/D1 Esambo, Zaire
63/N3 Esashi, Japan
37/D5 Esbjerg, Den.
31/U10 Esbly, Fr.
37/H3 Esbo (Espoo), Fin.
94/D3 Escada, Braz.
108/E3 Escalante (riv.), Ut,US
113/G4 Escambia (riv.), Fl,US
110/C2 Escanaba, Mi,US
42/C3 Escaudain, Fr.
42/C3 Escaut (riv.), Belg., Fr.
43/E6 Esch (riv.), Fr.
42/B5 Esches (riv.), Fr.
43/E5 Esch-sur-Alzette, Lux.
41/H6 Eschwege, Ger.
43/F2 Eschweiler, Ger.
108/C4 Escondido, Ca,US
101/N9 Escuinapa de Hidalgo, Mex.
100/C5 Escuintla, Guat.
59/N7 Esdraelon, Plain of (plain), Isr.
82/H7 Eséka, Camr.
41/E1 Esens, Ger.
47/F1 Esera (riv.), Sp.
60/F2 Eşfahān, Iran
34/C1 Esgair Ddu (mtn.), Wal,UK
33/G2 Esh, Eng,UK
31/M7 Esher, Eng,UK
87/D2 Eshimba, Zaire
33/G2 Esh Winning, Eng,UK
33/E2 Esk (riv.), Eng,UK
33/H3 Esk (riv.), Eng,UK
33/E1 Eskdale (val.), Sc,UK
59/C2 Eskil, Turk.
37/F4 Eskilstuna, Swe.
59/D2 Eskimalatya, Turk.
114/M2 Eskimo (lakes), NW,Can
59/B2 Eskişehir, Turk.
46/C1 Esla (riv.), Sp.
60/E2 Eslāmābād, Iran
41/F6 Eslohe, Ger.
59/B2 Eşme, Turk.
92/C3 Esmeraldas, Ecu.
43/E2 Esneux, Belg.
110/D2 Espanola, On,Can
109/F4 Española, NM,US
47/K6 Esparreguera, Sp.
41/F4 Espelkamp, Ger.
94/D2 Esperança, Braz.
74/C6 Esperance, Austl.
94/B1 Esperantina, Braz.
94/A2 Esperantinópolis, Braz.
106/B3 Esperanza (inlet), BC,Can
46/A3 Espichel (cape), Port.
92/D3 Espinal, Col.
94/B5 Espinhaço (mts.), Braz.
46/A2 Espinho, Port.
97/F2 Espinillo (pt.), Uru.
94/B4 Espinosa, Braz.
95/D1 Espírito Santo (state), Braz.
95/G7 Espírito Santo do Pinhal, Braz.
78/F6 Espiritu Santo (isl.), Van.
94/C3 Esplanada, Braz.
47/L7 Espluges, Sp.
37/H3 Espoo (Esbo), Fin.
96/C4 Esquel, Arg.
91/E3 Esquina, Arg.
82/D1 Essaouira, Mor.
41/G5 Esse (riv.), Ger.
40/B6 Essen, Belg.
40/E6 Essen, Ger.
77/F5 Essendon, Austl.
92/G2 Essequibo (riv.), Guy.
116/G7 Essex, On,Can
31/P6 Essex (co.), Eng,UK
115/K7 Essex, Md,US
45/H2 Esslingen, Ger.
31/S11 Essonne (dept.), Fr.
31/T11 Essonne (riv.), Fr.
97/L8 Estados (isl.), Arg.
60/F3 Eşţahbān, Iran
94/C3 Estância, Braz.
97/L8 Estancia La Carmen, Arg.
97/L8 Estancia La Sera, Arg.
47/F1 Estats, Pico de (peak), Sp.
89/E3 Estcourt, SAfr.
100/E3 Este (pt.), Cuba
41/G2 Este (riv.), Ger.
45/J4 Este, It.
95/B4 Esteio, Braz.
100/D5 Estelí, Nic.
46/D1 Estella, Sp.
115/C3 Estelle (mtn.), Ca,US
46/C4 Estepa, Sp.
46/C4 Estepona, Sp.
107/H3 Esterhazy, Sk,Can
82/G7 Esterias (cape), Gabon
45/G5 Estéron (riv.), Fr.
107/H3 Estevan, Sk,Can
42/D3 Estinnes-Au-Mont, Belg.
33/G2 Eston, Eng,UK
52/E4 Estonia
46/A3 Estoril, Port.
46/B2 Estrela, Serra da (mtn.), Port.
46/A3 Estrela, Serra da (range), Port.
94/B3 Estrelto (mts.), Braz.
46/B3 Estremadura (aut. comm.), Sp.
46/B3 Estremoz, Port.
93/J5 Estrondo (mts.), Braz.
50/D2 Esztergom, Hun.
78/E4 Etal (atoll), Micr.
42/A2 Étaples, Fr.
70/C2 Etāwah, India
107/H3 Ethelbert, Mb,Can
83/N5 Ethiopia
83/N6 Ethiopian (plat.), Eth.
65/M9 Eti (riv.), Japan
31/T11 Étiolles, Fr.
48/D4 Etna, Monte (Mount Etna) (vol.), It.
111/Q8 Etobicoke, On,Can
114/E3 Etolin (str.), Ak,US
63/P2 Etorofu (isl.), Rus.
87/C4 Etosha Nat'l Park, Namb.
87/C4 Etosha Pan (salt pan), Namb.
51/G4 Etropole, Bul.
65/F2 Etsu-Joshin Kogen Nat'l Park, Japan
59/M8 Et Taiyiba, Isr.
43/F4 Ettelbruck, Lux.
40/B5 Etten-Leur, Neth.
42/D2 Etterbeek, Belg.
59/M8 Et Tīra, Isr.
45/H2 Ettlingen, Ger.
33/E1 Ettrick Pen (mtn.), Sc,UK
42/A3 Eu, Fr.
79/H7 Eua (isl.), Tonga
76/B2 Eubenangee Swamp Nat'l Park, Austl.
110/D3 Euclid, Oh,US
94/C3 Euclides da Cunha, Braz.
75/H7 Eucumbene (lake), Austl.
113/F3 Eudora, Ar,US
113/G4 Eufaula, Al,US
109/J4 Eufaula, Ok,US
109/H4 Eufaula (lake), Ok,US
106/C4 Eugene, Or,US
101/L8 Eugenia (pt.), Mex.
46/B1 Eume (lake), Sp.
76/C3 Eungella Nat'l Park, Austl.
112/E4 Eunice, La,US
109/G4 Eunice, NM,US
43/F2 Eupen, Belg.
58/D6 Euphrates (riv.), Asia
44/D2 Eure (riv.), Fr.
103/S6 Eureka, NW,Can
103/S7 Eureka (sound), NW,Can
108/A2 Eureka, Ca,US
106/E3 Eureka, Mt,US
108/D3 Eureka, Nv,US
107/J4 Eureka, SD,US
42/B6 Eurodisney, Fr.
81/M12 Europa (pt.), Gib.
87/G5 Europa (isl.), Reun.
30/* Europe
40/B5 Europoort, Neth.
43/F2 Euskirchen, Ger.
113/H4 Eustis, Fl,US
38/F1 Eutin, Ger.
87/F3 Eutini, Malw.
106/B2 Eutsuk (lake), BC,Can
33/F4 Euxton, Eng,UK
110/E1 Evain, Qu,Can
103/H2 Evans (str.), NW,Can
110/E1 Evans (lake), Qu,Can
109/F2 Evans, Co,US
109/F3 Evans (mtn.), Co,US
116/Q15 Evanston, Il,US
106/F5 Evanston, Wy,US
110/C4 Evansville, In,US
109/F2 Evansville, Wy,US
110/C3 Evart, Mi,US
88/D2 Evaton, SAfr.
60/F3 Evaz, Iran
107/K4 Eveleth, Mn,US
57/L3 Evenki Aut. Okr., Rus.
35/E3 Evenlode (riv.), Eng,UK
77/D3 Everard (cape), Austl.
74/F6 Everard (lake), Austl.
34/D4 Evercreech, Eng,UK
116/C2 Everett, Wa,US
42/C1 Evergem, Belg.
113/H5 Everglades Nat'l Park, Fl,US
113/G4 Evergreen, Al,US
116/Q16 Evergreen Park, Il,US
35/F3 Eversholt, Eng,UK
41/E5 Everswinkel, Ger.
35/E2 Evesham, Eng,UK
49/G3 Evinos (riv.), Gre.
46/B3 Évora, Port.
46/A3 Évora (dist.), Port.
42/A5 Évreux, Fr.
44/C2 Évron, Fr.
49/H4 Evrótas (riv.), Gre.
31/T11 Évry, Fr.
49/H3 Évvoia (gulf), Gre.
49/H3 Évvoia (isl.), Gre.
104/V13 Ewa, Hi,US
104/V13 Ewa Beach, Hi,US
31/N7 Ewell, Eng,UK
115/F5 Ewing, NJ,US
109/J3 Excelsior Springs, Mo,US
34/C5 Exe (riv.), Eng,UK
34/C5 Exeter, Eng,UK
111/G3 Exeter, NH,US
34/C5 Exminster, Eng,UK
34/C4 Exmoor Nat'l Park, Eng,UK
110/F4 Exmore, Va,US
74/A4 Exmouth (gulf), Austl.
97/J7 Exmouth (pen.), Chile
34/C5 Exmouth, Eng,UK
103/L4 Exploits (riv.), Nf,Can
95/G7 Extrema, Braz.
94/C2 Exu, Braz.
101/F3 Exuma (sound), Bahm.
33/G5 Eyam, Eng,UK
87/F1 Eyasi (lake), Tanz.
35/H2 Eye, Eng,UK
35/F1 Eye (brook), Eng,UK
36/D3 Eyemouth, Sc,UK
59/N9 Eyn Hemed Nat'l Park, Isr.
31/P7 Eynsford, Eng,UK
74/F6 Eyre (pen.), Austl.
74/F5 Eyre North (lake), Austl.
74/F5 Eyre South (lake), Austl.
31/T9 Ézanville, Fr.
49/K3 Ezine, Turk.
82/H3 Ezzane (well), Alg.

F

79/L6 Faaa, FrPol.
112/B4 Fabens, Tx,US
46/B1 Fabero, Sp.
38/F1 Fåborg, Den.
45/K5 Fabriano, It.
92/D3 Facatativá, Col.
42/C2 Faches-Thumesnil, Fr.
83/K4 Fada, Chad
85/F3 Fada-N'Gourma, Burk.
45/J4 Faenza, It.
83/J6 Fafa (riv.), CAfr.
46/A2 Fafe, Port.
83/P6 Fafen Shet' (riv.), Eth.
51/G3 Făgăraş, Rom.
37/E4 Fagersta, Swe.
97/L8 Fagnano (lake), Arg.
84/D2 Faguibine (lake), Mali
47/S12 Faial (isl.), Azor.,Port.
33/F4 Failsworth, Eng,UK
114/J3 Fairbanks, Ak,US
116/J11 Fairfax, Ca,US
115/J8 Fairfax, Va,US
76/G8 Fairfield, Austl.
116/K10 Fairfield, Ca,US
115/G4 Fairfield, Ct,US
106/F4 Fairfield, Mt,US
110/C4 Fairfield, Oh,US
112/D4 Fairfield, Tx,US
35/E3 Fairford, Eng,UK
111/F3 Fair Haven, Vt,US
32/B1 Fair Head (pt.), NI,UK
115/K7 Fairland, Md,US
115/F5 Fair Lawn, NJ,US
115/F5 Fairless Hills, Pa,US
35/G5 Fairlight, Eng,UK
107/K5 Fairmont, Mn,US
110/D4 Fairmont, WV,US
116/M9 Fair Oaks, Ca,US
112/B2 Fairplay, Co,US
106/D1 Fairview, Ab,Can
109/H3 Fairview, Ok,US
114/L4 Fairweather (cape), Ak,US
114/L4 Fairweather (mtn.), BC,Can, Ak,US
116/C3 Fairwood-Cascade, Wa,US
61/K2 Faisalabad, Pak.
49/J5 Faistós (ruins), Gre.
70/D2 Faizābād, India
79/M6 Fakahina (isl.), FrPol.
79/H5 Fakaofo (atoll), Tok.
79/L6 Fakarava (atoll), FrPol.
35/G1 Fakenham, Eng,UK
82/G7 Fako (peak), Camr.
38/G1 Fakse Bugt (bay), Den.
34/B6 Fal (riv.), Eng,UK
81/Q16 Falcon (cape), Alg.
112/D5 Falcon (res.), Mex., US
45/K5 Falconara Marittima, It.
84/C3 Falémé (riv.), Mali, Sen.
79/S9 Faleolo, WSam.
112/D5 Falfurrias, Tx,US
106/D2 Falher, Ab,Can
37/E4 Falkenberg, Swe.
35/H2 Falkenham, Eng,UK
97/M8 Falkland Islands (Islas Malvinas) (dpcy.), UK
37/E4 Falköping, Swe.
41/G3 Fallingbostel, Ger.
108/C3 Fallon, Nv,US
111/G3 Fall River, Ma,US
115/J8 Falls Church, Va,US
109/J2 Falls City, Ne,US
34/A6 Falmouth, Eng,UK
34/A6 Falmouth (bay), Eng,UK
101/G4 Falso (cape), DRep.
97/K8 Falso Cabo de Hornos (cape), Chile
38/G1 Falster (isl.), Den.
51/H2 Fălticeni, Rom.
37/E3 Falun, Swe.
59/J4 Famagusta, Cyp.
43/F5 Fameck, Fr.
43/E3 Famenne (reg.), Belg.
66/D5 Fanchang, China
81/G7 Fandriana, Madg.
32/B4 Fane (riv.), Ire.
79/L6 Fangatau (isl.), FrPol.
79/L7 Fangataufa (isl.), FrPol.
67/C2 Fangcun, China
67/C2 Fangdao, China
67/D3 Fangliao, Tai.
67/A2 Fanjing (peak), China
79/K4 Fanning (Tabuaeran) (atoll), Kiri.
38/E1 Fanø (isl.), Den.
45/K5 Fano, It.
69/C1 Fan Si Pan (peak), Viet.
59/H6 Fāqūs, Egypt
83/L7 Faradje, Zaire
81/G7 Faradofay, Madg.
81/G7 Farafangana, Madg.
86/A3 Farāfirah, Wāḩāt al (oasis), Egypt
61/H2 Farāh, Afg.
61/H2 Farāh (riv.), Afg.
108/B3 Farallon (isls.), Ca,US
78/D3 Farallon de Medinilla (isl.), NMar.
78/D2 Farallon de Pajaros (isl.), NMar.
92/C3 Farallones de Cali Nat'l Park, Col.
84/C4 Faranah (comm.), Gui.
89/H8 Faraony (riv.), Madg.
78/D4 Faraulep (atoll), Micr.
42/D3 Farciennes, Belg.
35/E5 Fareham, Eng,UK
75/R11 Farewell (cape), NZ
107/J4 Fargo, ND,US
107/K4 Faribault, Mn,US
70/C2 Farīdābād, India
70/E3 Farīdpur, Bang.
35/E3 Faringdon, Eng,UK
59/H6 Fāriskūr, Egypt
111/G2 Farmington, Me,US
116/F7 Farmington, Mi,US
109/K3 Farmington, Mo,US
108/E3 Farmington, NM,US
116/F7 Farmington Hills, Mi,US
110/E4 Farmville, Va,US
35/F4 Farnborough, Eng,UK
35/F4 Farnham, Eng,UK
31/P7 Farningham, Eng,UK
33/F4 Farnworth, Eng,UK
102/C2 Faro, Yk,Can
46/B4 Faro, Port.
46/A4 Faro (dist.), Port.
30/D2 Faroe (isls.), Den.
37/F4 Fårön (isl.), Swe.
82/H6 Faro Nat'l Park, Camr.
74/A4 Farquhar (cape), Austl.
81/H5 Farquhar (isls.), Sey.
95/B4 Farroupilha, Braz.
70/C2 Farrukhābād, India
49/H3 Fársala, Gre.
106/F5 Farson, Wy,US
37/C4 Farsund, Nor.
60/F5 Fartak, Ra's (pt.), Yem.
99/N4 Farvel (cape), Grld.
98/T Farwell (isl.), Ant.
60/F3 Fasā, Iran
48/E2 Fasano, It.
41/H3 Fassberg, Ger.
54/D2 Fastov, Ukr.
73/H4 Fatagar Tuting (cape), Indo.
29/T6 Fataka (isl.), Sol.
70/B2 Fatehpur, India
70/D2 Fatehpur, India
84/A3 Fatick (reg.), Sen.
46/A3 Fátima, Port.
60/C4 Fāţimah (dry riv.), SAr.
59/D2 Fatsa, Turk.
79/M6 Fatu Hiva (isl.), FrPol.
44/F2 Faucilles (mts.), Fr.
32/A2 Faughan (riv.), NI,UK
107/J4 Faulkton, SD,US
37/E2 Fauske, Nor.
48/C4 Favara, It.
35/G4 Faversham, Eng,UK
35/E5 Fawley, Eng,UK
102/H3 Fawn (riv.), On,Can
37/M7 Faxaflói (bay), Ice.
95/B2 Faxinal, Braz.
83/J4 Faya-Largeau, Chad
113/G3 Fayette, Al,US
109/J3 Fayette, Mo,US
113/F4 Fayette, Ms,US
112/E2 Fayetteville, Ar,US
113/G3 Fayetteville, Ga,US
113/J3 Fayetteville, NC,US
113/G3 Fayetteville, Tn,US
85/F4 Fazao (mts.), Gha., Togo
85/F4 Fazao Nat'l Park, Togo
36/A4 Feale (riv.), Ire.
113/J3 Fear (cape), NC,US
108/B3 Feather (riv.), Ca,US
33/G4 Featherstone, Eng,UK
42/A2 Fécamp, Fr.
116/C3 Federal Way, Wa,US
32/A2 Feeny, NI,UK
50/F2 Fehérgyarmat, Hun.
38/F1 Fehmarn (isl.), Ger.
38/F1 Fehmarn Belt (str.), Ger., Den.
66/D4 Fei (riv.), China
95/D2 Feia (lake), Braz.
42/C3 Feignies, Fr.
66/D4 Fei Huang (riv.), China
94/C4 Feira de Santana, Braz.
45/L3 Feistritz (riv.), Aus.
50/D2 Fejér (co.), Hun.
47/G3 Felanitx, Sp.
45/H3 Feldberg (peak), Ger.
45/H3 Feldkirch, Aus.
45/L3 Feldkirchen in Kärnten, Aus.
35/H3 Felixstowe, Eng,UK
101/N7 Félix U. Gómez, Mex.
33/G2 Felling, Eng,UK
41/G6 Felsberg, Ger.
31/M7 Feltham, Eng,UK
35/G2 Feltwell, Eng,UK
66/C4 Fen (riv.), China
46/A1 Fene, Sp.
59/C3 Fener (pt.), Turk.
43/G6 Fénétrange, Fr.
49/J2 Fengári (peak), Gre.
63/J3 Fengcheng, China
66/D5 Fengle (riv.), China
66/D3 Fengnan, China
66/D3 Fengrun, China
66/D3 Fengshui (peak), China
66/C2 Fengzhen, China
114/C5 Fenimore (passg.), Ak,US
35/G2 Fens, The (reg.), Eng,UK
116/E6 Fenton, Mi,US
54/E3 Feodosiya, Ukr.
81/V17 Fer, Cap de (cape), Alg.
61/G2 Ferdows, Iran
48/C2 Ferentino, It.
48/C1 Ferento (ruins), It.
68/B3 Fergana, Uzb.
107/J4 Fergus Falls, Mn,US
102/F2 Ferguson (lake), NW,Can
84/D4 Ferkéssédougou, IvC.
45/L3 Ferlach, Aus.
82/C4 Ferlo (reg.), Sen.
84/B3 Ferlo, Vallée du (wadi), Sen.
32/A3 Fermanagh (dist.), NI,UK
115/B3 Fermin (pt.), Ca,US
48/C1 Fermo, It.
113/H4 Fernandina Beach, Fl,US
93/M4 Fernando de Noronha (isl.), Braz.
95/B2 Fernandópolis, Braz.
46/C4 Fernán-Núñez, Sp.
115/K7 Ferndale, Md,US
116/F7 Ferndale, Mi,US
35/E5 Ferndown, Eng,UK
106/E3 Fernie, BC,Can
77/G5 Ferntree Gully Nat'l Park, Austl.
48/E2 Ferrandina, It.
45/J4 Ferrara, It.
46/A3 Ferreira do Alentejo, Port.
44/C4 Ferret (cape), Fr.
112/F4 Ferriday, La,US
113/F4 Ferriday, La,US
33/G2 Ferryhill, Eng,UK
34/B3 Ferryside, Wal,UK
45/M3 Fertő (Neusiedler See) (lake), Aus., Hun.
40/C2 Ferwerd, Neth.
81/M13 Fès, Mor.
87/C2 Feshi, Zaire
113/F2 Festus, Mo,US
31/M8 Fetcham, Eng,UK
51/H3 Feteşti, Rom.
31/R10 Feucherolles, Fr.
45/J2 Feucht, Ger.
103/J3 Feuilles (lake), Qu,Can
103/J3 Feuilles (riv.), Qu,Can
44/F4 Feurs, Fr.
61/K1 Feyzābād, Afg.
82/H2 Fezzan (reg.), Libya
32/E6 Ffestiniog, Wal,UK
81/G7 Fianarantsoa, Madg.
89/H8 Fianarantsoa (prov.), Madg.
82/J6 Fianga, Chad
88/D3 Ficksburg, SAfr.
45/J4 Fidenza, It.
84/C4 Fié (riv.), Gui., Mali
51/G3 Fieni, Rom.
49/F2 Fier, Alb.
49/G1 Fierzë (lake), Alb.
36/D2 Fife Ness (pt.), Sc,UK
81/Q16 Figalo (cape), Alg.
44/E4 Figeac, Fr.
46/A2 Figueira da Foz, Port.
47/G1 Figueres, Sp.
82/E1 Figuig, Mor.
89/G8 Fiherenana (riv.), Madg.
78/G6 Fiji
98/X Filchner Ice Shelf, Ant.
33/H3 Filey, Eng,UK
33/H3 Filey (bay), Eng,UK
51/F3 Filiaşi, Rom.
48/D3 Filicudi (isl.), It.
85/F3 Filingué, Niger
49/J2 Filippoi (ruins), Gre.
37/E4 Filipstad, Swe.
115/B2 Fillmore, Ca,US
108/D3 Fillmore, Ut,US
79/S9 Filo (peak), WSam.
34/D3 Filton, Eng,UK
98/Z Fimbul Ice Shelf, Ant.
82/J8 Fimi (riv.), Zaire
45/H4 Finale Ligure, It.
84/C3 Fina Rsv., Mali
31/N7 Finchley, Eng,UK
36/D2 Findhorn (riv.), Sc,UK
110/D3 Findlay, Oh,US
77/D4 Fingal, Austl.
103/K2 Finger (lake), On,Can
110/E3 Finger (lakes), NY,US
44/E4 Finiels, Sommet de (peak), Fr.
59/B3 Finike, Turk.
46/A1 Finisterre (cape), Sp.
74/F5 Finke (riv.), Austl.
45/K3 Finkenstein, Aus.
37/H2 Finland
52/E4 Finland (gulf), Eur.
102/D3 Finlay (riv.), BC,Can
112/B4 Finlay (mts.), Tx,US
41/E6 Finnentrop, Ger.
116/C2 Finn Hill-Inglewood, Wa,US
76/B1 Finnigan (peak), Austl.
37/G1 Finnmark (co.), Nor.
37/E4 Finspång, Swe.
32/A3 Fintona, NI,UK
81/H8 Fiora (riv.), It.
45/H4 Fiorenzuola d'Arda, It.
116/C2 Fircrest-Silver Lake, Wa,US
45/J5 Firenze (Florence), It.
96/E2 Firmat, Arg.
44/F4 Firminy, Fr.
70/C2 Fīrozābād, India
61/K2 Fīrozpur, India
60/F3 Fīrūzābād, Iran
45/L3 Fischbacher (mts.), Aus.
88/B2 Fish (riv.), Namb.
88/C3 Fish (riv.), SAfr.
33/G2 Fishburn, Eng,UK
98/E Fisher (glac.), Ant.
107/J3 Fisher (bay), Mb,Can
103/H2 Fisher (str.), NW,Can
107/J3 Fisher Branch, Mb,Can
76/F6 Fisherman (isl.), Austl.
34/B3 Fishguard, Wal,UK
54/F4 Fisht, Gora (peak), Rus.
33/J6 Fishtoft, Eng,UK
79/S8 Fito (peak), WSam.
114/L2 Fitton (mtn.), Yk,Can
113/H4 Fitzgerald, Ga,US
106/B3 Fitz Hugo (sound), BC,Can
97/J7 Fitzroy (peak), Arg.
76/C3 Fitzroy (riv.), Austl.
103/R7 Fitzwilliam (str.), NW,Can
48/C2 Fiumicino, It.
32/A3 Fivemiletown, NI,UK
37/C3 Fjell, Nor.
35/F3 Flackwell Heath, Eng,UK
109/G3 Flagler, Co,US
113/H4 Flagler Beach, Fl,US
108/E4 Flagstaff, Az,US
110/B2 Flambeau (riv.), Wi,US
111/Q9 Flamborough, On,Can
33/H3 Flamborough, Eng,UK
33/H3 Flamborough Head (pt.), Eng,UK
38/G2 Fläming (hills), Ger.
106/F5 Flaming Gorge Nat'l Rec. Area, Ut, Wy,US
107/K2 Flanagan (riv.), On,Can
42/B2 Flanders (reg.), Belg., Fr.
107/J4 Flandreau, SD,US
114/L3 Flat Creek, Yk,Can
106/E4 Flathead (lake), Mt,US
106/E4 Flathead (riv.), Mt,US
34/C4 Flat Holm (isl.), Eng,UK
109/K3 Flat River, Mo,US
116/F7 Flat Rock, Mi,US
76/B1 Flattery (cape), Austl.
106/B3 Flattery (cape), Wa,US
35/F4 Fleet, Eng,UK
33/E4 Fleetwood, Eng,UK
37/C4 Flekkefjord, Nor.
115/F5 Flemington, NJ,US
38/E1 Flensburg, Ger.
43/E2 Fleron, Belg.
44/C2 Flers, Fr.
42/D3 Fleurus, Belg.
44/D3 Fleury-les-Aubrais, Fr.
40/C4 Flevoland (prov.), Neth.
32/E2 Flimby, Eng,UK
74/A6 Flinders (bay), Austl.
77/D3 Flinders (isl.), Austl.
74/F6 Flinders (ranges), Austl.
76/C2 Flinders (reefs), Austl.
76/A2 Flinders (riv.), Austl.
107/L3 Flindt (riv.), On,Can
107/H2 Flin Flon, Mb,Can
103/J2 Flint (lake), NW,Can
79/K6 Flint (isl.), Kiri.
33/E5 Flint, Wal,UK
113/G4 Flint (riv.), Ga,US
109/H3 Flint (hills), Ks,US
116/E5 Flint, Mi,US
35/F3 Flitwick, Eng,UK
41/F1 Flögelner See (lake), Ger.
39/G3 Flöha (riv.), Ger.
110/B4 Flora, Il,US
115/G5 Floral Park, NY,US
43/F5 Florange, Fr.
43/D3 Floreffe, Belg.
113/G3 Florence, Al,US
108/E4 Florence, Az,US
109/F3 Florence, Co,US
113/J3 Florence, SC,US
45/J5 Florence (Firenze), It.
92/C3 Florencia, Col.
42/D3 Florennes, Belg.
96/E3 Flores (riv.), Arg.
106/B3 Flores (isl.), BC,Can
100/D4 Flores, Guat.
73/F5 Flores (isl.), Indo.
73/E5 Flores (sea), Indo.
47/R12 Flores (isl.), Azor.,Port.
97/F2 Flores (dept.), Uru.
94/C3 Floresta, Braz.
112/D4 Floresville, Tx,US
115/F5 Florham Park, NJ,US
94/B2 Floriano, Braz.
95/B3 Florianópolis, Braz.
101/F3 Florida, Cuba
101/E3 Florida (str.), NAm.
97/F2 Florida, Uru.
97/F2 Florida (dept.), Uru.
113/H4 Florida (state), US
113/H5 Florida (bay), Fl,US
113/H5 Florida Keys (isls.), Fl,US
48/D4 Floridia, It.
116/M10 Florin, Ca,US
49/G2 Flórina, Gre.
109/K3 Florissant, Mo,US
37/C3 Florø, Nor.
112/C3 Floydada, Tx,US
40/D3 Fluessen (lake), Neth.
48/A3 Flumendosa (riv.), It.
110/D3 Flushing, Mi,US
40/A6 Flushing (Vlissingen), Neth.
78/D5 Fly (riv.), PNG
98/T Flying Fish (cape), Ant.
37/P6 Fnjóská (riv.), Ice.
107/H3 Foam Lake, Sk,Can
50/D4 Foča, Bosn.

Focşa – Geret

51/H3 Focşani, Rom.
48/D2 Foggia, It.
80/J10 Fogo (isl.), CpV.
45/L3 Fohnsdorf, Aus.
38/E1 Föhr (isl.), Ger.
44/D5 Foix, Fr.
37/C3 Folarskardnuten (peak), Nor.
37/D2 Folda (fjord), Nor.
49/J4 Folégandros (isl.), Gre.
103/J2 Foley (isl.), NW,Can
48/C1 Foligno, It.
35/H4 Folkestone, Eng,UK
113/H4 Folkston, Ga,US
48/B1 Follonica (gulf), It.
102/F3 Fond du Lac (riv.), Sk,Can
110/B3 Fond du Lac, Wi,US
48/C2 Fondi, It.
37/D3 Fongen (peak), Nor.
46/B1 Fonsagrada, Sp.
100/D5 Fonseca (gulf), NAm.
44/F4 Fontaine, Fr.
44/E2 Fontainebleau, Fr.
42/D3 Fontaine-L'Evêque, Belg.
115/C2 Fontana, Ca,US
44/C3 Fontenay-le-Comte, Fr.
31/S10 Fontenay-le-Fleury, Fr.
31/S11 Fontenay-les-Briis, Fr.
31/T10 Fontenay-sous-Bois, Fr.
31/U10 Fontenay-Trésigny, Fr.
106/F5 Fontenelle (res.), Wy,US
45/G4 Font Sancte, Pic de la (peak), Fr.
37/P6 Fontur (pt.), Ice.
77/F5 Footscray, Austl.
114/H3 Foraker (mtn.), Ak,US
43/F5 Forbach, Fr.
77/D2 Forbes, Austl.
46/A1 Forcarey, Sp.
45/J2 Forchheim, Ger.
116/E7 Ford (lake), Mi,US
35/E5 Fordingbridge, Eng,UK
112/E3 Fordyce, Ar,US
34/C4 Foreland (pt.), Eng,UK
35/E5 Foreland, The (pt.), Eng,UK
106/E3 Foremost, Ab,Can
35/H4 Foreness (pt.), Eng,UK
113/F3 Forest, Ms,US
77/D4 Forestier (cape), Austl.
111/G1 Forestville, Qu,Can
115/K8 Forestville, Md,US
44/E4 Forez (mts.), Fr.
36/D2 Forfar, Sc,UK
31/S11 Forges-les-Bains, Fr.
111/H1 Forillon Nat'l Park, Qu,Can
32/B3 Forkill, NI,UK
45/K4 Forlì, It.
33/E4 Formby, Eng,UK
33/E4 Formby (pt.), Eng,UK
47/F3 Formentera (isl.), Sp.
47/G3 Formentor, Cabo de (cape), Sp.
48/C2 Formia, It.
95/C2 Formiga, Braz.
91/E2 Formosa, Arg.
94/A4 Formosa, Braz.
93/G6 Formosa (mts.), Braz.
84/A4 Formosa (isl.), GBis.
88/C4 Formosa (peak), SAfr.
94/A4 Formoso (riv.), Braz.
45/J5 Fornacelle, It.
36/D2 Forres, Sc,UK
113/F3 Forrest City, Ar,US
37/G3 Forssa, Fin.
76/A3 Forsyth (range), Austl.
113/H3 Forsyth, Ga,US
106/G4 Forsyth, Mt,US
61/K3 Fort Abbās, Pak.
94/C1 Fortaleza, Braz.
97/G2 Fortaleza Santa Teresa, Uru.
88/D4 Fort Beaufort, SAfr.
106/F4 Fort Benton, Mt,US
108/B3 Fort Bragg, Ca,US
109/H4 Fort Cobb (res.), Ok,US
109/F2 Fort Collins, Co,US
112/C4 Fort Davis, Tx,US
43/E5 Fort de Douaumont, Fr.
101/J5 Fort-de-France (cap.), Mart.
43/E5 Fort de Vaux, Fr.
107/K5 Fort Dodge, Ia,US
87/D3 Forte Cameia, Ang.
111/S10 Fort Erie, On,Can
74/B4 Fortescue (riv.), Austl.
110/A1 Fort Frances, On,Can
113/F4 Fort Gaines, Al,US
111/R9 Fort George, On,Can
103/J3 Fort-George (Chisasibi), Qu,Can
109/J4 Fort Gibson, Ok,US
112/E2 Fort Gibson (lake), Ok,US
82/C3 Fort-Gouraud, Mrta.
36/C2 Forth (riv.), Sc,UK
36/D2 Forth, Firth of (inlet), Sc,UK
111/G2 Fort Kent, Me,US
113/H5 Fort Lauderdale, Fl,US
115/F5 Fort Lee, NJ,US
109/F2 Fort Lupton, Co,US
106/E3 Fort Macleod, Ab,Can
107/L5 Fort Madison, Ia,US
113/H4 Fort Matanzas Nat'l Mon., Fl,US
102/E3 Fort McMurray, Ab,Can
110/C2 Fort Michilimackinac, Mi,US
109/G2 Fort Morgan, Co,US
113/J3 Fort Moultrie, SC,US
113/H5 Fort Myers, Fl,US
102/D3 Fort Nelson (riv.), BC,Can
33/F4 Forton, Eng,UK
48/D2 Fortore (riv.), It.
113/G3 Fort Payne, Al,US
106/G4 Fort Peck (lake), Mt,US
113/H5 Fort Pierce, Fl,US
107/H4 Fort Pierre, SD,US
83/M7 Fort Portal, Ugan.
107/H3 Fort Qu'Appelle, Sk,Can
107/J5 Fort Randall (dam), SD,US
106/B2 Fort Saint James, BC,Can
102/D3 Fort Saint John, BC,Can
106/E2 Fort Saskatchewan, Ab,Can
109/J3 Fort Scott, Ks,US
55/J3 Fort-Shevchenko, Kaz.
112/E3 Fort Smith, Ar,US
112/C4 Fort Stockton, Tx,US
109/F4 Fort Sumner, NM,US
107/J4 Fort Totten, ND,US
94/A2 Fortuna, Braz.
111/L2 Fortune, Nf,Can
111/L2 Fortune (bay), Nf,Can
34/D5 Fortuneswell, Eng,UK
109/F4 Fort Union Nat'l Mon., NM,US
113/G4 Fort Walton Beach, Fl,US
115/J8 Fort Washington Park, Md,US
110/C3 Fort Wayne, In,US
36/C2 Fort William, Sc,UK
112/D3 Fort Worth, Tx,US
107/H4 Fort Yates, ND,US
76/B2 Forty Mile Scrub Nat'l Park, Austl.
67/B3 Foshan, China
103/S7 Fosheim (pen.), NW,Can
33/G3 Foss (riv.), Eng,UK
45/G4 Fossano, It.
31/T9 Fosses, Fr.
43/D3 Fosses-la-Ville, Belg.
106/C4 Fossil, Or,US
106/F5 Fossil Butte Nat'l Mon., Wy,US
110/D3 Fostoria, Oh,US
44/C2 Fougères, Fr.
83/N3 Foul (bay), Egypt, Sudan
35/G3 Foulness (isl.), Eng,UK
35/G3 Foulness (pt.), Eng,UK
33/H4 Foulness (riv.), Eng,UK
35/H1 Foulsham, Eng,UK
85/H5 Foumban, Camr.
109/F3 Fountain, Co,US
115/C3 Fountain Valley, Ca,US
112/E3 Fourche La Fave (riv.), Ar,US
35/E4 Four Marks, Eng,UK
42/D4 Fourmies, Fr.
114/D5 Four Mountains (isls.), Ak,US
89/R15 Fournaise, Piton de la (peak), Reun.
84/B4 Fouta Djallon (reg.), Gha.
75/Q12 Foveaux (str.), NZ
34/B6 Fowey, Eng,UK
34/B6 Fowey (riv.), Eng,UK
77/B1 Fowlers Gap, Austl.
60/E1 Fowman, Iran
114/M3 Fox (mtn.), Yk,Can
114/E5 Fox (isls.), Ak,US
110/B3 Fox (riv.), Il, Wi,US
106/D2 Fox Creek, Ab,Can
103/H2 Foxe (chan.), NW,Can
103/J2 Foxe (pen.), NW,Can
103/J2 Foxe Basin (sound), NW,Can
75/R11 Fox Glacier, NZ
116/P15 Fox Lake, Il,US
35/G2 Foxton, Eng,UK
106/F3 Fox Valley, Sk,Can
32/A2 Foyle (riv.), NI,UK
32/A1 Foyle, Lough (inlet), Ire., NI,UK
46/B1 Foz, Sp.
87/B4 Foz do Cunene, Ang.
91/F2 Foz do Iguaçu, Braz.
47/F2 Fraga, Sp.
95/B3 Fraiburgo, Braz.
92/E7 Frailes (range), Bol.
42/C3 Frameries, Belg.
35/H2 Framlingham, Eng,UK
95/C2 Franca, Braz.
49/E2 Francavilla Fontana, It.
44/D3 France
31/T9 France, Pays de (plain), Fr.
44/E5 France, Roc de (mtn.), Fr.
102/C2 Frances (lake), Yk,Can
100/E3 Frances (cape), Cuba
101/H4 Francés Viejo (cape), DRep.
87/B1 Franceville, Gabon
45/G3 Franche-Comté (reg.), Fr.
107/J5 Francis Case (lake), SD,US
100/C4 Francisco Escárcega, Mex.
101/P8 Francisco I. Madero, Mex.
87/E5 Francistown, Bots.
95/G8 Franco da Rocha, Braz.
106/B2 François (lake), BC,Can
31/S10 Franconville, Fr.
40/C2 Franeker, Neth.
41/F6 Frankenberg-Eder, Ger.
110/D3 Frankenmuth, Mi,US
110/C3 Frankfort, In,US
110/C4 Frankfort (cap.), Ky,US
39/H2 Frankfurt, Ger.
45/H1 Frankfurt am Main, Ger.
45/J2 Frankische Alb (mts.), Ger.
45/H1 Fränkische Saale (riv.), Ger.
45/J2 Fränkische Schweiz (reg.), Ger.
77/C3 Frankland (cape), Austl.
98/M Franklin (isl.), Ant.
114/N1 Franklin (bay), NW,Can
102/D2 Franklin (mts.), NW,Can
114/G1 Franklin (pt.), Ak,US
110/C4 Franklin, In,US
110/C4 Franklin, Ky,US
113/H3 Franklin, NC,US
113/G3 Franklin, Tn,US
112/D4 Franklin, Tx,US
110/E4 Franklin, Va,US
116/P14 Franklin, Wi,US
110/E4 Franklin, WV,US
106/D3 Franklin D. Roosevelt (lake), Wa,US
115/F4 Franklin Lakes, NJ,US
77/C4 Franklin-Lower Gordon Wild Rivers Nat'l Park, Austl.
116/Q16 Franklin Park, Il,US
115/G5 Franklin Square, NY,US
91/F2 Fransisco Beltrão, Braz.
95/G8 Fransisco Morato, Braz.
94/B5 Fransisco Sá, Braz.
56/F2 Franz Josef Land (arch.), Rus.
76/D4 Fraser (isl.), Austl.
106/B2 Fraser (lake), BC,Can
106/C3 Fraser (riv.), BC,Can
116/G6 Fraser, Mi,US
36/D2 Fraserburgh, Sc,UK
106/B2 Fraser Lake, BC,Can
77/F5 Fraser Nat'l Park, Austl.
45/H3 Frauenfeld, Swi.
96/F2 Fray Bentos, Uru.
108/C4 Frazier Park, Ca,US
43/F2 Frechen, Ger.
74/A5 Frecinet (estuary), Austl.
88/E3 Fred (mtn.), SAfr.
38/E1 Fredericia, Den.
75/J4 Frederick (reef), Austl.
110/E4 Frederick, Md,US
109/H4 Frederick, Ok,US
112/D4 Fredericksburg, Tx,US
110/E4 Fredericksburg, Va,US
111/H2 Fredericton (cap.), NB,Can
37/D4 Frederikshavn, Den.
108/D3 Fredonia, Az,US
109/J3 Fredonia, Ks,US
110/E3 Fredonia, NY,US
37/D4 Fredrikstad, Nor.
109/H3 Freedom, Ok,US
115/F5 Freehold, NJ,US
77/A1 Freeling Heights (peak), Austl.
101/F2 Freeport, Bahm.
110/B3 Freeport, Il,US
115/G5 Freeport, NY,US
112/E4 Freeport, Tx,US
112/D5 Freer, Tx,US
84/B4 Freetown (cap.), SLeo.
44/B2 Fréhel (cape), Fr.
38/G3 Freib (riv.), Ger.
39/G3 Freiberg, Ger.
38/G3 Freiberger Mulde (riv.), Ger.
95/D1 Frei Inocêncio, Braz.
96/B3 Freire, Chile
43/G4 Freisen, Ger.
45/J2 Freising, Ger.
45/L2 Freistadt, Aus.
39/G3 Freital, Ger.
45/G5 Fréjus, Fr.
34/B4 Fremington, Eng,UK
116/L11 Fremont, Ca,US
110/C3 Fremont, Mi,US
109/H2 Fremont, Ne,US
110/D3 Fremont, Oh,US
108/E3 Fremont (riv.), Ut,US
106/F5 Fremont (peak), Wy,US
110/D2 French (riv.), On,Can
79/J2 French Frigate (shoals), Hi,US
93/H3 French Guiana (dpcy.), Fr.
106/G3 Frenchman (riv.), Can., US
109/G2 Frenchman (cr.), Ne,US
111/R8 Frenchman's (bay), On,Can
77/C4 Frenchmans Cap (peak), Austl.
79/M6 French Polynesia (terr.), Fr.
81/R16 Frenda, Alg.
31/S9 Frépillon, Fr.
93/H5 Fresco (riv.), Braz.
35/E5 Freshwater, Eng,UK
96/B4 Fresia, Chile
31/S10 Fresnes, Fr.
101/P9 Fresnillo de González Echeverría, Mex.
108/C3 Fresno, Ca,US
77/D4 Freycinet Nat'l Park, Austl.
43/F5 Freyming-Merlebach, Fr.
45/K2 Freyung, Ger.
87/B4 Fria (cape), Namb.
91/C2 Frías, Arg.
45/G3 Fribourg, Swi.
45/H1 Friedberg, Ger.
41/E2 Friedeburg, Ger.
45/H1 Friedrichsdorf, Ger.
45/H3 Friedrichshafen, Ger.
43/G5 Friedrichsthal, Ger.
41/G7 Frielendorf, Ger.
45/G2 Friesenheim, Ger.
40/C2 Friesland (prov.), Neth.
41/E2 Friesoythe, Ger.
35/F4 Frimley, Eng,UK
35/H3 Frinton, Eng,UK
28/G7 Frio (cape), Braz.
109/H5 Frio (riv.), Tx,US
41/G6 Fritzlar, Ger.
45/K3 Friuli-Venezia Giulia (reg.), It.
32/E2 Frizington, Eng,UK
103/K2 Frobisher (bay), NW,Can
106/F1 Frobisher (lake), Sk,Can
33/F5 Frodsham, Eng,UK
37/D3 Frohavet (bay), Nor.
42/D3 Froidchapelle, Belg.
55/G2 Frolovo, Rus.
77/B1 Frome (lake), Austl.
74/F5 Frome (riv.), Austl.
34/D4 Frome, Eng,UK
34/D2 Frome (riv.), Eng,UK
34/D5 Frome (riv.), Eng,UK
109/F2 Front (range), Co,US
44/E5 Frontignan, Fr.
110/E4 Front Royal, Va,US
48/C2 Frosinone, It.
37/E3 Frösö, Swe.
98/J Frost (glac.), Ant.
43/F6 Frouard, Fr.
37/D3 Frøya (isl.), Nor.
103/H2 Frozen (str.), NW,Can
111/Q9 Fruitland, On,Can
50/D3 Fruška Gora Nat'l Park, Yugo.
95/B2 Frutal, Braz.
96/B4 Frutillar, Chile
39/K4 Frýdek-Místek, Czh.
66/C5 Fu (riv.), China
66/D3 Fucheng, China
38/E3 Fuchskaute (peak), Ger.
43/H2 Fuchskauten (peak), Ger.
64/C3 Fuchū, Japan
66/D5 Fuchun (riv.), China
73/H4 Fudi (mtn.), Indo.
67/D2 Fuding, China
47/Y16 Fuenaventura (isl.), Canl.
46/C4 Fuengirola, Sp.
46/D2 Fuenlabrada, Sp.
47/N8 Fuente, Sp.
47/E4 Fuente-Álamo, Sp.
46/B3 Fuente del Maestre, Sp.
46/C3 Fuente Obejuna, Sp.
46/E1 Fuenterrabía, Sp.
46/C4 Fuentes de Andalucía, Sp.
101/N8 Fuerte (riv.), Mex.
67/D4 Fuga (isl.), Phil.
38/F3 Fuhne (riv.), Ger.
41/H4 Fuhse (riv.), Ger.
65/F3 Fuji, Japan
65/F3 Fuji (riv.), Japan
65/F3 Fujieda, Japan
65/F3 Fuji-Hakone-Izu Nat'l Park, Japan
65/L10 Fujiidera, Japan
65/H7 Fujimi, Japan
65/H7 Fujino, Japan
65/F3 Fujinomiya, Japan
65/F2 Fujioka, Japan
65/F3 Fujisawa, Japan
65/J7 Fujishiro, Japan
65/M9 Fujiwara, Japan
65/F3 Fujiyama (mtn.), Japan
65/F3 Fujiyoshida, Japan
64/D3 Fukuchiyama, Japan
64/A4 Fukue, Japan
64/A4 Fukue (isl.), Japan
64/E2 Fukui, Japan
64/E3 Fukui (pref.), Japan
64/B4 Fukuoka, Japan
64/B4 Fukuoka (pref.), Japan
65/E3 Fukuroi, Japan
98/C Fukushima (peak), Ant.
65/G2 Fukushima, Japan
65/F2 Fukushima (pref.), Japan
64/C3 Fukuyama, Japan
61/J2 Fūlādī (mtn.), Afg.
35/G2 Fulbourn, Eng,UK
45/H1 Fulda, Ger.
33/G4 Fulford, Eng,UK
67/A2 Fuling, China
115/C3 Fullerton, Ca,US
115/E5 Fullerton (Whitehall), Pa,US
111/Q9 Fulton, On,Can
110/B4 Fulton, Ky,US
109/K3 Fulton, Mo,US
110/E3 Fulton, NY,US
37/E3 Fulufjället (peak), Swe.
33/F4 Fulwood, Eng,UK
44/D4 Fumel, Fr.
65/H7 Funabashi, Japan
78/G5 Funafuti (atoll), Tuv.
101/G5 Fundación, Col.
111/H2 Fundy (bay), NB, NS,Can
111/H2 Fundy Nat'l Park, NB,Can
87/F5 Funhalouro, Moz.
52/J4 Furmanov, Rus.
36/C2 Furnace, Sc,UK
95/H6 Furnas (res.), Braz.
77/C4 Furneaux Group (isls.), Austl.
41/E3 Fürstenau, Ger.
50/C2 Fürstenfeld, Aus.
45/J2 Fürstenfeldbruck, Ger.
39/H2 Fürstenwalde, Ger.
45/K2 Furth im Wald, Ger.
63/N4 Furukawa, Japan
103/H2 Fury and Hecla (str.), NW,Can
66/B4 Fushan, China
66/E3 Fushan, China
63/J3 Fushun, China
65/M9 Fuso, Japan
65/H7 Fussa, Japan
45/J3 Füssen, Ger.
65/M10 Futami, Japan
50/D3 Futog, Yugo.
96/B4 Futrono, Chile
65/F3 Futtsu, Japan
78/H6 Futuna (isl.), Wall.
59/H6 Fuwah, Egypt
71/H3 Fuxian (lake), China
63/J3 Fuxin, China
66/C4 Fuyang, China
67/B2 Fuyi (riv.), China
63/J2 Fuyu, China
39/L5 Füzesabony, Hun.
67/C2 Fuzhou, China
31/P6 Fyfield, Eng,UK
38/F1 Fyn (co.), Den.
37/D5 Fyn (isl.), Den.

G

83/Q6 Gaalkacyo (Galcaio), Som.
40/D5 Gaanderen, Neth.
40/C2 Gaast, Neth.
44/C5 Gabas (riv.), Fr.
108/C3 Gabbs, Nv,US
87/B3 Gabela, Ang.
82/H1 Gabes (gulf), Tun.
82/H7 Gabon
88/D2 Gaborone (cap.), Bots.
51/G4 Gabrovo, Bul.
50/D4 Gacko, Bosn.
70/C4 Gadag-Betgeri, India
113/G3 Gadsden, Al,US
51/G3 Găeşti, Rom.
48/C2 Gaeta, It.
48/C2 Gaeta (gulf), It.
113/H3 Gaffney, SC,US
52/G5 Gagarin, Rus.
84/D5 Gagnoa, IvC.
111/G1 Gagnon, Qu,Can
31/T10 Gagny, Fr.
54/G4 Gagra, Geo.
50/A2 Gail (riv.), Aus.
44/D5 Gaillac, Fr.
45/K3 Gailtaler Alps (mts.), Aus.
96/D4 Gaiman, Arg.
113/H4 Gainesville, Fl,US
113/H3 Gainesville, Ga,US
109/J3 Gainesville, Mo,US
112/D3 Gainesville, Tx,US
33/G2 Gainford, Eng,UK
33/H5 Gainsborough, Eng,UK
74/F6 Gairdner (lake), Austl.
115/J7 Gaithersburg, Md,US
52/E4 Gaizina Kalns (peak), Lat.
88/C2 Gakarosa (peak), SAfr.
46/D2 Galapagar, Sp.
36/D3 Galashiels, Sc,UK
51/J3 Galaţi, Rom.
51/H3 Galaţi (co.), Rom.
49/F2 Galatina, It.
49/F2 Galatone, It.
110/D4 Galax, Va,US
49/H3 Galaxidhiou, Gre.
73/G3 Galela, Indo.
110/B3 Galena, Il,US
96/B3 Galera (pt.), Chile
92/B3 Galera (pt.), Ecu.
101/J5 Galera (pt.), Trin.
110/B3 Galesburg, Il,US
36/A4 Galey (riv.), Ire.
32/B2 Galgorm, NI,UK
52/J4 Galich, Rus.
39/L3 Galicia (reg.), Pol., Ukr.
46/A1 Galicia (aut. comm.), Sp.
50/E5 Galičica Nat'l Park, Macd.
59/K5 Galilee, Sea of (Tiberias) (lake), Isr.
110/D3 Galion, Oh,US
113/G2 Gallatin, Tn,US
70/D6 Galle, SrL.
97/K7 Gallegos (riv.), Arg.
101/G5 Gallinas (pt.), Col.
112/B3 Gallinas (mts.), NM,US
49/E2 Gallipoli, It.
51/H5 Gallipoli (pen.), Turk.
51/H5 Gallipoli (Gelibolu), Turk.
110/D4 Gallipolis, Oh,US
37/G2 Gällivare, Swe.
48/C3 Gallo (cape), It.
32/D2 Galloway, Mull of (pt.), Sc,UK
108/E4 Gallup, NM,US
31/R10 Gally (riv.), Fr.
62/D2 Galt, Mong.
116/M10 Galt, Ca,US
36/A4 Galtymore (mtn.), Ire.
62/E2 Galuut, Mong.
96/B3 Galvarino, Chile
112/E4 Galveston, Tx,US
112/E4 Galveston (bay), Tx,US
112/E4 Galveston (isl.), Tx,US
96/E2 Gálvez, Arg.
36/A4 Galway, Ire.
36/A4 Galway (bay), Ire.
69/D1 Gam (riv.), Viet.
88/C2 Gamagara (dry riv.), SAfr.
65/E3 Gamagōri, Japan
70/E2 Gamba, China
85/E4 Gambaga Scarp (escarp.), Gha., Togo
70/A2 Gambat, Pak.
83/M6 Gambēla, Eth.
83/M6 Gambela Nat'l Park, Eth.
84/B3 Gambia
84/A3 Gambia (Gambie) (riv.), Afr.
79/M7 Gambier (isls.), FrPol.
111/L1 Gambo, Nf,Can
87/C1 Gamboma, Congo
88/C4 Gamka (riv.), SAfr.
88/B3 Gamkab (dry riv.), Namb.
35/F2 Gamlingay, Eng,UK
52/D2 Gammelstad, Swe.
65/M9 Gamo, Japan
39/G5 Gamsfeld (peak), Aus.
83/N7 Gamud (peak), Eth.
67/C2 Gan (riv.), China
110/E2 Gananoque, On,Can
87/D2 Gandajika, Zaire
111/L1 Gander, Nf,Can
111/L1 Gander (lake), Nf,Can
41/F2 Ganderkesee, Ger.
70/B3 Gāndhīhām, India
70/B3 Gandhinagar, India
70/B3 Gāndhi Sāgar (res.), India
47/E3 Gandía, Sp.
94/C4 Gandu, Braz.
82/C4 Ganeb (well), Mrta.
70/C2 Gangāpur, India
70/E2 Gangārāmpur, India
68/D5 Gangdisê (mts.), China
43/F2 Gangelt, Ger.
70/E3 Ganges (riv.), India
48/D4 Gangi, It.
70/E2 Gangtok, India
59/N8 Gan Hashlosha Nat'l Park, Isr.
106/F5 Gannett (peak), Wy,US
68/F4 Gansu (prov.), China
82/H6 Ganye, Nga.
67/B2 Ganzhou, China
85/E3 Ganzourgou (prov.), Burk.
85/E2 Gao, Mali
85/E2 Gao (reg.), Mali
66/C3 Gaocheng, China
67/D2 Gaojian, China
84/E4 Gaoua, Burk.
66/C3 Gaoyang, China
66/D4 Gaoyou (lake), China
45/G4 Gap, Fr.
62/D5 Gar (riv.), China
70/E3 Garai (riv.), Bang.
83/L7 Garamba Nat'l Park, Zaire
94/C3 Garanhuns, Braz.
83/N7 Garba Tula, Kenya
38/E2 Garbsen, Ger.
95/B2 Garça, Braz.
94/B3 Garças (riv.), Braz.
31/S10 Garches, Fr.
46/C3 Garcia de Sota (res.), Sp.
44/F5 Gard (riv.), Fr.
45/J4 Garda (lake), It.
81/V17 Garde, Cap de (cape), Alg.
38/F2 Gardelegen, Ger.
115/B3 Gardena, Ca,US
113/H3 Garden City, Ga,US
109/G3 Garden City, Ks,US
116/F7 Garden City, Mi,US
115/G5 Garden City, NY,US
106/A2 Gardener Canal (inlet), BC,Can
115/C3 Garden Grove, Ca,US
61/J2 Gardēz, Afg.
111/G2 Gardiner, Me,US
106/F4 Gardiner, Mt,US
79/H5 Gardner (Nikumaroro) (atoll), Kiri.
36/C2 Garelochhead, Sc,UK
82/G2 Garet el Djenoun (peak), Alg.
106/E4 Garfield (peak), Mt,US
115/F5 Garfield, NJ,US
33/G4 Garforth, Eng,UK
44/D4 Gargan (mtn.), Fr.
31/T10 Garges-lès-Gonesse, Fr.
33/F4 Gargrave, Eng,UK
70/C3 Garhākotā, India
95/B4 Garibaldi, Braz.
83/N8 Garissa, Kenya
112/D3 Garland, Tx,US
32/D2 Garlieston, Sc,UK
45/J3 Garmisch-Partenkirchen, Ger.
109/J3 Garnett, Ks,US
77/B2 Garnpung (lake), Austl.
44/D4 Garonne (riv.), Fr.
85/E2 Garou (lake), Mali
82/H6 Garoua, Camr.
82/H6 Garoua Boulaï, Camr.
47/K7 Garraf (range), Sp.
32/D6 Garreg, Wal,UK
41/F3 Garrel, Ger.
107/H4 Garrison, ND,US
107/H4 Garrison (dam), ND,US
32/C1 Garron (pt.), NI,UK
103/H2 Garry (bay), NW,Can
102/F2 Garry (lake), NW,Can
33/F4 Garstang, Eng,UK
45/L2 Garsten, Aus.
41/H6 Garte (riv.), Ger.
44/D3 Gartempe (riv.), Fr.
34/C2 Garth, Wal,UK
72/C5 Garut, Indo.
32/B2 Garvagh, NI,UK
39/L3 Garwolin, Pol.
116/R16 Gary, In,US
92/C3 Garzón, Col.
68/F4 Gas (lake), China
37/P6 Gæsafjöll (peak), Ice.
110/C3 Gas City, In,US
109/J3 Gasconade (riv.), Mo,US
44/C5 Gascony (reg.), Fr.
74/B5 Gascoyne (riv.), Austl.
95/B3 Gaspar, Braz.
72/C4 Gaspar (riv.), Indo.
111/H1 Gaspé, Qu,Can
111/H1 Gaspé (pen.), Qu,Can
111/H1 Gaspé, Cap de (cape), Qu,Can
111/S9 Gasport, NY,US
113/J2 Gaston (lake), NC, Va,US
113/H3 Gastonia, NC,US
59/J4 Gata (cape), Cyp.
46/B2 Gata (range), Sp.
46/D4 Gata, Cabo de (cape), Sp.
52/F4 Gatchina, Rus.
32/D2 Gatehouse-of-Fleet, Sc,UK
102/F1 Gateshead (isl.), NW,Can
33/G2 Gateshead, Eng,UK
114/H2 Gates of the Arctic Nat'l Pk. & Prsv., Ak,US
112/D4 Gatesville, Tx,US
115/G5 Gateway Nat'l Rec. Area, NJ, NY,US
44/C3 Gâtine (hills), Fr.
110/F2 Gatineau, Qu,Can
110/F2 Gatineau (riv.), Qu,Can
43/H4 Gau-Bickelheim, Ger.
71/F2 Gauhāti, India
33/G2 Gaunless (riv.), Eng,UK
70/E2 Gauripur, India
70/E2 Gauri Sankar (mtn.), Nepal
37/D4 Gausta (peak), Nor.
52/E4 Gauja Nat'l Park, Lat.
47/G2 Gavà, Sp.
49/J5 Gávdhos (isl.), Gre.
46/E1 Gave de Pau (riv.), Fr.
42/C2 Gavere, Belg.
37/F3 Gävle, Swe.
37/E3 Gävleborg (co.), Swe.
77/A2 Gawler, Austl.
74/F6 Gawler (ranges), Austl.
62/D3 Gaxun (lake), China
55/L2 Gay, Rus.
110/D4 Gay (peak), WV,US
63/K3 Gaya (riv.), China
70/E3 Gayā, India
85/F4 Gaya, Niger
110/C2 Gaylord, Mi,US
54/D2 Gaysin, Ukr.
59/K6 Gaza (Ghazzah), Gaza
59/J6 Gaza Strip
59/D3 Gaziantep, Turk.
63/H1 Gazimur (riv.), Rus.
45/G2 Gazon de Faing (peak), Fr.
83/K7 Gbadolite, Zaire
84/C5 Gbarnga, Libr.
39/K1 Gdańsk, Pol.
39/K1 Gdańsk (prov.), Pol.
39/K1 Gdańsk (gulf), Pol., Rus.
39/K1 Gdynia, Pol.
66/D5 Ge (lake), China
45/J1 Gebaberg (peak), Ger.
73/G3 Gebe (isl.), Indo.
86/D4 Gebeit Mine, Sudan
51/J5 Gebze, Turk.
72/C5 Gede (peak), Indo.
59/M9 Gedera, Isr.
59/B2 Gediz, Turk.
59/A2 Gediz (riv.), Turk.
43/E1 Geel, Belg.
77/C3 Geelong, Austl.
74/A5 Geelvink (chan.), Austl.
41/E3 Geeste, Ger.
41/F2 Geeste (riv.), Ger.
41/H2 Geesthacht, Ger.
68/D5 Gê'gyai, China
41/G4 Gehrden, Ger.
34/C2 Geifas (mtn.), Wal,UK
102/F3 Geikie (riv.), Sk,Can
43/F2 Geilenkirchen, Ger.
65/M10 Geinō, Japan
45/H2 Geislingen an der Steige, Ger.
71/H3 Gejiu, China
83/L6 Gel (riv.), Sudan
48/D4 Gela, It.
48/D4 Gela (gulf), It.
83/Q6 Geladī, Eth.
40/C4 Gelderland (prov.), Neth.
40/C5 Geldermalsen, Neth.
40/D5 Geldern, Ger.
40/C6 Geldrop, Neth.
43/E2 Geleen, Neth.
54/F3 Gelendzhik, Rus.
51/H5 Gelibolu (Gallipoli), Turk.
34/C3 Gelligaer, Wal,UK
40/E5 Gelsenkirchen, Ger.
43/D2 Gembloux, Belg.
83/J7 Gemena, Zaire
40/C5 Gemert, Neth.
51/J5 Gemlik, Turk.
51/J5 Gemlik (gulf), Turk.
45/K3 Gemona del Friuli, It.
88/C2 Gemsbok-Kalahari Nat'l Park, SAfr.
88/C2 Gemsbok Nat'l Park, Bots.
114/G3 Gemuk (mtn.), Ak,US
63/J1 Gen (riv.), China
83/N6 Genalē Wenz (riv.), Eth.
42/D2 Genappe, Belg.
48/A3 Genargentu (mts.), It.
59/E2 Genç, Turk.
40/D5 Gendringen, Neth.
40/C5 Gendt, Neth.
40/D3 Genemuiden, Neth.
96/D3 General Acha, Arg.
96/D2 General Alvear, Arg.
96/F2 General Belgrano, Arg.
96/E2 General Cabrera, Arg.
96/B5 General Carrera (lake), Chile
97/F3 General Juan Madariaga, Arg.
97/S12 General Las Heras, Arg.
91/C1 General Martín Miguel de Güemes, Arg.
96/E2 General Pico, Arg.
91/D2 General Pinedo, Arg.
67/E6 General Santos, Phil.
51/J4 General-Toshevo, Bul.
96/E2 General Viamonte, Arg.
96/E2 General Villegas, Arg.
110/E3 Genesee (riv.), NY,US
107/L5 Geneseo, Il,US
110/E3 Geneseo, NY,US
113/G4 Geneva, Al,US
116/P16 Geneva, Il,US
109/H2 Geneva, Ne,US
110/E3 Geneva, NY,US
116/P14 Geneva (lake), Wi,US
45/G3 Geneva (Genève), Swi.
45/G3 Geneva (Léman) (lake), Fr., Swi.
45/H2 Gengenbach, Ger.
54/E3 Genichesk, Ukr.
46/C4 Genil (riv.), Sp.
43/E2 Genk, Belg.
40/C5 Gennep, Neth.
31/S10 Gennevilliers, Fr.
45/H4 Genoa (Genova), It.
45/H4 Genoa (gulf), It.
42/C1 Gent-Brugge (can.), Belg.
72/C5 Genteng (cape), Indo.
42/C1 Gent (Ghent), Belg.
74/A6 Geographe (bay), Austl.
74/A4 Geographe (chan.), Austl.
74/C4 George (lake), Austl.
77/D2 George (lake), Austl.
76/C3 George (pt.), Austl.
103/K3 George (riv.), Qu,Can
88/C4 George, SAfr.
113/H4 George (lake), Fl,US
56/E1 George Land (isl.), Rus.
76/G9 Georges (riv.), Austl.
111/Q8 Georgetown, On,Can
100/E4 George Town (cap.), Cay.
92/G2 Georgetown (cap.), Guy.
113/H4 Georgetown, Ga,US
110/C4 Georgetown, Ky,US
113/J3 Georgetown, SC,US
112/D4 Georgetown, Tx,US
98/L George V (coast), Ant.
98/V George VI (sound), Ant.
112/D4 George West, Tx,US
55/G4 Georgia
106/B3 Georgia (str.), Can., US
113/G3 Georgia (state), US
110/D2 Georgian Bay Islands Nat'l Park, On,Can
74/F4 Georgina (riv.), Austl.
51/H4 Georgi Traykov, Bul.
41/F4 Georgsmarienhütte, Ger.
38/G3 Gera, Ger.
42/C2 Geraardsbergen, Belg.
94/A3 Geral (mts.), Braz.
94/A4 Geral de Goiás (Espigão Mestre) (range), Braz.
75/R11 Geraldine, NZ
74/A5 Geraldton, Austl.
110/C1 Geraldton, On,Can
44/F4 Gerbier de Jonc (mtn.), Fr.
41/H3 Gerdau (riv.), Ger.
114/H3 Gerdine (mtn.), Ak,US
51/L5 Gerede, Turk.
61/H2 Gereshk, Afg.
45/J3 Geretsried, Ger.

108/C2 **Gerlach**, Nv,US
39/L4 **Gerlachovský Štít** (peak), Slvk.
115/J7 **Germantown**, Md,US
113/F3 **Germantown**, Tn,US
38/E3 **Germany**
45/J2 **Germering**, Ger.
88/E2 **Germiston**, SAfr.
43/F3 **Gerolstein**, Ger.
47/G2 **Gerona** (Girona), Sp.
47/E1 **Ger, Pic du** (peak), Fr.
42/D3 **Gerpinnes**, Belg.
31/M7 **Gerrards Cross**, Eng,UK
44/D5 **Gers** (riv.), Fr.
43/G5 **Gersheim**, Ger.
40/E5 **Gescher**, Ger.
41/F5 **Geseke**, Ger.
83/P6 **Gestro Wenz** (riv.), Eth.
46/D2 **Getafe**, Sp.
43/E2 **Gete** (riv.), Belg.
107/J4 **Gettysburg**, SD,US
95/A3 **Getúlio Vargas**, Braz.
98/S **Getz Ice Shelf**, Ant.
43/E2 **Geul** (riv.), Belg., Neth.
72/A3 **Geureudong** (peak), Indo.
59/E2 **Gevaş**, Turk.
41/E6 **Gevelsberg**, Ger.
50/F5 **Gevgelija**, Macd.
83/P5 **Gewanē**, Eth.
89/H6 **Geyser** (reef), Madg.
51/K5 **Geyve**, Turk.
68/B4 **Gez** (riv.), China
82/G1 **Ghadāmis**, Libya
86/C3 **Ghadir, Bi'r** (well), Egypt
85/E4 **Ghana**
87/D5 **Ghanzi**, Bots.
86/B5 **Gharb Binna**, Sudan
82/F1 **Ghardaïa**, Alg.
82/H1 **Gharyān**, Libya
82/H3 **Ghāt**, Libya
82/J5 **Ghazal** (riv.), Chad
81/P13 **Ghazaouet**, Alg.
70/C2 **Ghaziābād**, India
61/J2 **Ghaznī**, Afg.
59/K6 **Ghazzah** (Gaza), Gaza
62/G2 **Ghengis Khan Wall** (ruins), Mong.
42/C1 **Ghent** (Gent), Belg.
51/H2 **Gheorghe Gheorghiu-Dej**, Rom.
51/G2 **Gheorgheni**, Rom.
51/F2 **Gherla**, Rom.
96/C5 **Ghio** (lake), Arg.
70/A2 **Ghotki**, Pak.
51/H2 **Ghūrīān**, Afg.
69/D4 **Gia Nghia**, Viet.
88/E3 **Giant's Castle** (peak), SAfr.
48/D4 **Giarre**, It.
69/E3 **Gia Vuc**, Viet.
106/E2 **Gibbons**, Ab,Can
46/B4 **Gibraleón**, Sp.
46/B4 **Gibraltar** (str.), Afr., Eur.
111/R8 **Gibraltar** (pt.), On,Can
46/C4 **Gibraltar** (dpcy.), UK
116/F7 **Gibraltar**, Mi,US
77/E1 **Gibraltar Range Nat'l Park**, Austl.
74/D4 **Gibson** (des.), Austl.
112/D4 **Giddings**, Tx,US
86/C2 **Gidi** (pass), Egypt
83/N6 **Gidolē**, Eth.
44/E3 **Gien**, Fr.
45/J2 **Giengen an der Brenz**, Ger.
44/F4 **Gier** (riv.), Fr.
45/H1 **Giessen**, Ger.
40/B5 **Giessendam**, Neth.
42/B6 **Gif**, Fr.
103/H1 **Gifford** (riv.), NW,Can
113/H5 **Gifford**, Fl,US
41/H4 **Gifhorn**, Ger.
31/S10 **Gif-sur-Yvette**, Fr.
65/E3 **Gifu**, Japan
65/E3 **Gifu** (pref.), Japan
33/F3 **Giggleswick**, Eng,UK
48/B1 **Giglio** (isl.), It.
46/C1 **Gijón**, Sp.
108/D4 **Gila** (riv.), Az, NM,US
108/D4 **Gila Bend**, Az,US
108/E4 **Gila Cliff Dwellings Nat'l Mon.**, NM,US
33/H4 **Gilberdyke Newport**, Eng,UK
76/A2 **Gilbert** (riv.), Austl.
78/G5 **Gilbert** (isls.), Kiri.
110/A2 **Gilbert**, Mn,US
96/C2 **Gil de Vilches Nat'l Park**, Chile
34/C3 **Gilfach Goch**, Wal,UK
32/B3 **Gilford**, NI,UK
115/F6 **Gilford Park**, NJ,US
61/K1 **Gilgit** (riv.), Pak.
74/F6 **Gilles** (lake), Austl.
107/G4 **Gillette**, Wy,US
106/B3 **Gillies Bay**, BC,Can
34/D4 **Gillingham**, Eng,UK
35/G4 **Gillingham**, Eng,UK
112/E3 **Gilmer**, Tx,US
61/K1 **Gilqit** (riv.), Pak.
63/K1 **Gilyuy** (riv.), Rus.
40/B5 **Gilze**, Neth.
83/N6 **Gīmbī**, Eth.
107/J3 **Gimli**, Mb,Can
47/F1 **Gimone** (riv.), Fr.
65/M9 **Ginan**, Japan
43/E2 **Gingelom**, Belg.
67/E6 **Gingoog**, Phil.
48/E2 **Ginosa**, It.
46/B1 **Ginzo de Limia**, Sp.
83/Q7 **Giohar**, Som.
48/D3 **Gioia** (gulf), It.
48/E2 **Gioia del Colle**, It.
48/D3 **Gioia Tauro**, It.
49/J3 **Gioūra** (isl.), Gre.
35/G2 **Gipping** (riv.), Eng,UK
92/D3 **Girardot**, Col.
87/B4 **Giraul**, Ang.
80/D6 **Giraul de Cima**, Ang.
59/D2 **Giresun**, Turk.
70/E3 **Girīdīh**, India
48/E3 **Girifalco**, It.
31/N7 **Girling** (res.), Eng,UK
47/G2 **Girona** (Gerona), Sp.
44/C4 **Gironde** (riv.), Fr.
77/D1 **Girraween Nat'l Park**, Austl.
35/G2 **Girton**, Eng,UK
32/D1 **Girvan**, Sc,UK
32/D1 **Girvan, Water of** (riv.), Sc,UK
75/S10 **Gisborne**, NZ
42/A5 **Gisors**, Fr.
42/B1 **Gistel**, Belg.
87/E1 **Gitega**, Buru.
52/B2 **Gittsfjället** (peak), Swe.
45/H3 **Giubiasco**, Swi.
48/C1 **Giulianova**, It.
51/G4 **Giurgiu**, Rom.
51/G3 **Giurgiu** (co.), Rom.
59/M8 **Giv'atayim**, Isr.
43/D3 **Givet**, Fr.
44/F4 **Givors**, Fr.
43/D6 **Givry-en-Argonne**, Fr.
87/F5 **Giyani**, SAfr.
83/N6 **Giyon**, Eth.
86/B2 **Giza, Pyramids of** (Jīzah) (ruins), Egypt
57/R3 **Gizhiga** (bay), Rus.
39/L1 **Giżycko**, Pol.
49/G2 **Gjirokastër**, Alb.
37/D3 **Gjøvik**, Nor.
49/F2 **Gjuhëzës, Kep i** (cape), Alb.
111/K2 **Glace Bay**, NS,Can
106/D3 **Glacier**, BC,Can
106/C3 **Glacier** (peak), Wa,US
114/L4 **Glacier Bay Nat'l Park & Prsv.**, Ak,US
106/D3 **Glacier Nat'l Park**, Can., US
40/D5 **Gladbeck**, Ger.
76/C3 **Gladstone**, Austl.
110/C3 **Gladwin**, Mi,US
33/H3 **Glaisdale**, Eng,UK
30/E2 **Glâma** (riv.), Nor.
43/G4 **Glan** (riv.), Ger.
67/E6 **Glan**, Phil.
34/C3 **Glanamman**, Wal,UK
42/D4 **Gland** (riv.), Fr.
45/H3 **Glarus Alps** (range), Swi.
34/C2 **Glasbury**, Wal,UK
36/C3 **Glasgow**, Sc,UK
110/C4 **Glasgow**, Ky,US
106/G3 **Glasgow**, Mt,US
32/D6 **Glaslyn** (riv.), Wal,UK
32/D3 **Glass** (riv.), IM,UK
112/D2 **Glass** (mts.), Ok,US
112/C4 **Glass** (mts.), Tx,US
115/K8 **Glassmanor-Oxon Hill**, Md,US
34/D4 **Glastonbury**, Eng,UK
53/M4 **Glazov**, Rus.
35/G2 **Glemsford**, Eng,UK
33/H6 **Glen** (riv.), Eng,UK
77/C3 **Glenaladale Nat'l Park**, Austl.
110/E4 **Glen Allen**, Va,US
32/C2 **Glenarm**, NI,UK
32/C2 **Glenarm** (riv.), NI,UK
32/B2 **Glenavy**, NI,UK
77/D2 **Glenbawn** (dam), Austl.
107/J3 **Glenboro**, Mb,Can
76/G8 **Glenbrook**, Austl.
115/K7 **Glen Burnie**, Md,US
108/E3 **Glen Canyon Nat'l Rec. Area**, Az, Ut,US
32/E1 **Glencaple**, Sc,UK
89/E3 **Glencoe**, SAfr.
116/Q15 **Glencoe**, Il,US
115/G5 **Glen Cove**, NY,US
108/D4 **Glendale**, Az,US
115/B2 **Glendale**, Ca,US
106/C5 **Glendale**, Or,US
116/P16 **Glendale Heights**, Il,US
107/G4 **Glendive**, Mt,US
109/F2 **Glendo** (res.), Wy,US
115/C2 **Glendora**, Ca,US
32/B1 **Glendun** (riv.), NI,UK
77/B3 **Glenelg** (riv.), Austl.
32/A2 **Glenelly** (riv.), NI,UK
32/D2 **Glenluce**, Sc,UK
36/C2 **Glen Mòr** (val.), Sc,UK
115/E6 **Glenolden**, Pa,US
114/M4 **Glenora**, BC,Can
76/H8 **Glenorie**, Austl.
109/H4 **Glenpool**, Ok,US
112/D3 **Glen Rose**, Tx,US
110/F3 **Glens Falls**, NY,US
32/B2 **Glenshane** (pass), NI,UK
115/E5 **Glenside**, Pa,US
32/D1 **Glentrool**, Sc,UK
107/H4 **Glen Ullin**, ND,US
116/Q15 **Glenview**, Il,US
111/Q8 **Glen Williams**, On,Can
108/F3 **Glenwood Springs**, Co,US
49/L7 **Glifáhda**, Gre.
41/H1 **Glinde**, Ger.
37/D3 **Glittertinden** (peak), Nor.
39/K3 **Gliwice**, Pol.
108/E4 **Globe**, Az,US
39/H5 **Gloggnitz**, Aus.
39/J3 **Głogów**, Pol.
39/J3 **Głogówek**, Pol.
89/H5 **Glorieuses, Iles** (isls.), Reun.
76/E6 **Glorious** (mtn.), Austl.
114/D3 **Glory of Russia** (cape), Ak,US
33/G5 **Glossop**, Eng,UK
110/F2 **Gloucester**, On,Can
34/D3 **Gloucester**, Eng,UK
115/E6 **Gloucester City**, NJ,US
34/D3 **Gloucestershire** (co.), Eng,UK
34/D3 **Gloucester, Vale of** (val.), Eng,UK
111/L1 **Glovertown**, Nf,Can
39/K3 **Głowno**, Pol.
39/J3 **Głubczyce**, Pol.
39/J3 **Głuchołazy**, Pol.
38/E1 **Glücksburg**, Ger.
41/G1 **Glückstadt**, Ger.
54/E2 **Glukhov**, Ukr.
32/B4 **Glyde** (riv.), Ire.
34/C3 **Glyncorrwg**, Wal,UK
32/C2 **Glynn**, NI,UK
34/C3 **Glyn Neath**, Wal,UK
39/H4 **Gmünd**, Aus.
85/E3 **Gnagna** (prov.), Burk.
41/G2 **Gnarrenburg**, Ger.
39/J2 **Gniezno**, Pol.
50/E4 **Gnjilane**, Yugo.
34/D1 **Gnosall**, Eng,UK
64/C3 **Gō** (riv.), Japan
70/B4 **Goa** (state), India
70/F2 **Goālpāra**, India
36/C3 **Goat Fell** (mtn.), Sc,UK
33/H3 **Goathland**, Eng,UK
83/N6 **Goba**, Eth.
87/C5 **Gobabeb**, Namb.
62/E3 **Gobi** (des.), China, Mong.
64/D4 **Gobō**, Japan
33/E6 **Gobowen**, Eng,UK
40/D5 **Goch**, Ger.
69/D4 **Go Cong**, Viet.
35/F4 **Godalming**, Eng,UK
69/D4 **Go Dau Ha**, Viet.
70/D4 **Godāvari** (riv.), India
83/P6 **Godē**, Eth.
50/F3 **Godeanu** (peak), Rom.
110/D3 **Goderich**, On,Can
70/B3 **Godhra**, India
35/F2 **Godmanchester**, Eng,UK
73/F4 **Godo** (mtn.), Indo.
65/M9 **Gōdo**, Japan
50/D2 **Gödöllő**, Hun.
34/A6 **Godolphin Cross**, Eng,UK
96/C2 **Godoy Cruz**, Arg.
107/K2 **Gods** (lake), Mb,Can
107/K2 **Gods** (riv.), Mb,Can
103/H2 **Gods Mercy** (bay), NW,Can
31/N8 **Godstone**, Eng,UK
99/M3 **Godthåb** (Nuuk), Grld.
68/C4 **Godwin Austen** (K2) (peak), China, Pak.
110/E1 **Goéland** (lake), Qu,Can
40/A5 **Goerce**, Neth.
40/A6 **Goes**, Neth.
110/B2 **Gogebic** (range), Mi,US
70/D2 **Gogra** (riv.), India
41/G3 **Gohbach** (riv.), Ger.
94/D2 **Goiana**, Braz.
93/J7 **Goiânia**, Braz.
94/D2 **Goianinha**, Braz.
93/H7 **Goiás**, Braz.
95/B1 **Goiás** (state), Braz.
95/B1 **Goiatuba**, Braz.
40/C5 **Goirle**, Neth.
64/D3 **Gojō**, Japan
54/E4 **Gök** (riv.), Turk.
64/B4 **Gokase** (riv.), Japan
65/M9 **Gokashō**, Japan
51/G5 **Gökçeada** (isl.), Turk.
59/D2 **Göksun**, Turk.
59/K5 **Golan Heights** (reg.), Syria
59/C2 **Gölbaşı**, Turk.
59/D3 **Gölbaşı**, Turk.
33/F5 **Golborne**, Eng,UK
39/M1 **Gołdap**, Pol.
106/B5 **Gold Beach**, Or,US
76/D4 **Gold Coast**, Austl.
85/E5 **Gold Coast** (reg.), Gha.
106/D3 **Golden**, BC,Can
109/F3 **Golden**, Co,US
106/C4 **Goldendale**, Wa,US
38/F3 **Goldene Aue** (reg.), Ger.
116/J11 **Golden Gate** (chan.), Ca,US
88/E3 **Golden Gate Highlands Nat'l Park**, SAfr.
106/B3 **Golden Hinde** (peak), BC,Can
41/F3 **Goldenstedt**, Ger.
108/C3 **Goldfield**, Nv,US
106/B3 **Gold River**, BC,Can
113/J3 **Goldsboro**, NC,US
112/D4 **Goldthwaite**, Tx,US
59/E2 **Göle**, Turk.
39/H2 **Goleniów**, Pol.
59/B3 **Gölhisar**, Turk.
112/D4 **Goliad**, Tx,US
59/D2 **Gölköy**, Turk.
62/C4 **Golmud**, China
60/F2 **Golpāyegān**, Iran
51/K5 **Gölpazarı**, Turk.
39/K2 **Golub-Dobrzyń**, Pol.
51/H4 **Golyama Kamchiya** (riv.), Bul.
51/G5 **Golyama Syutkya** (peak), Bul.
51/G5 **Golyam Perelik** (peak), Bul.
87/E1 **Goma**, Zaire
54/D1 **Gomel'**, Bela.
54/C2 **Gomel' Obl.**, Bela.
47/X16 **Gomera** (isl.), Canl.
31/S10 **Gometz-le-Châtel**, Fr.
101/P8 **Gómez Palacio**, Mex.
38/F2 **Gommern**, Ger.
35/F4 **Gomshall**, Eng,UK
61/G2 **Gonābād**, Iran
87/F5 **Gonarezhou Nat'l Park**, Zim.
101/G4 **Gonâve** (gulf), Haiti
61/G1 **Gonbad-e Qābūs**, Iran
94/A2 **Gonçalves Dias**, Braz.
70/D2 **Gondā**, India
70/B3 **Gondal**, India
83/N5 **Gonder**, Eth.
70/D3 **Gondia**, India
46/A2 **Gondomar**, Port.
46/A1 **Gondomar**, Sp.
51/H5 **Gönen**, Turk.
31/T10 **Gonesse**, Fr.
71/F2 **Gongbo'gyamda**, China
71/H2 **Gongga** (peak), China
62/E4 **Gonghe**, China
85/H4 **Gongola** (riv.), Nga.
85/H4 **Gongola** (state), Nga.
77/C1 **Gongolgon**, Austl.
66/F2 **Gongzhuling**, China
112/D4 **Gonzales**, Tx,US
100/B3 **González**, Mex.
98/J **Goodenough** (cape), Ant.
88/B4 **Good Hope, Cape of** (cape), SAfr.
106/E5 **Gooding**, Id,US
109/G3 **Goodland**, Ks,US
76/E7 **Goodna**, Austl.
34/B3 **Goodwick**, Wal,UK
88/B4 **Goodwood**, SAfr.
40/C4 **Gooimeer** (lake), Neth.
33/H4 **Goole**, Eng,UK
40/D4 **Goor**, Neth.
107/H2 **Goose** (lake), Mb,Can
104/B3 **Goose** (lake), Ca, Or,US
103/K3 **Goose Bay-Happy Valley**, Nf,Can
33/F5 **Goostrey**, Eng,UK
45/H2 **Göppingen**, Ger.
69/D4 **Go Quao**, Viet.
39/J3 **Góra**, Pol.
39/L3 **Góra Kalwaria**, Pol.
70/D2 **Gorakhpur**, India
50/D4 **Goražde**, Bosn.
100/E5 **Gorda** (pt.), Nic.
108/A2 **Gorda** (pt.), Ca,US
77/C4 **Gordon** (lake), Austl.
82/J6 **Goré**, Chad
83/N6 **Gorē**, Eth.
75/Q12 **Gore**, NZ
35/G1 **Gore** (pt.), Eng,UK
114/H4 **Gore** (pt.), Ak,US
59/D2 **Görele**, Turk.
44/B2 **Gorey**, Chl,UK
61/F1 **Gorgān**, Iran
43/F4 **Gorge du Loup**, Lux.
84/B3 **Gorgol** (reg.), Mrta.
84/B2 **Gorgol** (riv.), Mrta.
55/H4 **Gori**, Geo.
40/B5 **Gorinchem**, Neth.
35/E3 **Goring**, Eng,UK
35/F5 **Goring by Sea**, Eng,UK
45/K4 **Gorizia**, It.
51/F3 **Gorj** (co.), Rom.
54/D1 **Gorki**, Bela.
52/J4 **Gor'kiy** (res.), Rus.
53/K4 **Gor'kiy** (Nizhniy Novgorod), Rus.
39/L4 **Gorlice**, Pol.
39/H3 **Görlitz**, Ger.
34/C2 **Gorllwyn** (mtn.), Wal,UK
54/F2 **Gorlovka**, Ukr.
32/B4 **Gormanston**, Ire.
111/R8 **Gormley**, On,Can
51/G4 **Gorna Oryakhovitsa**, Bul.
50/E3 **Gornji Milanovac**, Yugo.
50/C4 **Gornji Vakuf**, Bosn.
56/J4 **Gorno-Altay Aut. Obl.**, Rus.
68/E1 **Gorno-Altaysk**, Rus.
56/H6 **Gorno-Badakhstan Aut. Obl.**, Taj.
53/J4 **Gorodets**, Rus.
78/D5 **Goroka**, PNG
73/H4 **Gorong** (isl.), Indo.
73/F3 **Gorontalo**, Indo.
34/B3 **Gorseinon**, Wal,UK
40/D4 **Gorssel**, Neth.
32/A2 **Gortin**, NI,UK
54/C2 **Goryn'** (riv.), Bela., Ukr.
39/H2 **Gorzów** (prov.), Pol.
39/H2 **Gorzów Wielkopolski**, Pol.
64/D3 **Gōse**, Japan
65/F2 **Gosen**, Japan
33/G2 **Gosforth**, Eng,UK
63/N3 **Goshogawara**, Japan
41/H5 **Goslar**, Ger.
50/B3 **Gospić**, Cro.
35/E5 **Gosport**, Eng,UK
50/E5 **Gostivar**, Macd.
39/J3 **Gostyń**, Pol.
39/K2 **Gostynin**, Pol.
37/D4 **Göteborg**, Swe.
37/D4 **Göteborg och Bohus** (co.), Swe.
82/H6 **Gotel** (mts.), Camr., Nga.
65/F3 **Gotemba**, Japan
41/H7 **Gotha**, Ger.
109/G2 **Gothenburg**, Ne,US
37/F4 **Gotland** (isl.), Swe.
64/A4 **Gotō** (isls.), Japan
51/F5 **Gotse Delchev**, Bul.
37/F4 **Gotska Sandön Nat'l Park**, Swe.
64/C3 **Gōtsu**, Japan
41/G5 **Göttingen**, Ger.
40/B4 **Gouda**, Neth.
28/J8 **Gough** (isl.), StH.
110/F1 **Gouin** (res.), Qu,Can
110/C2 **Goulais** (riv.), On,Can
77/D2 **Goulburn**, Austl.
74/E2 **Goulburn** (isls.), Austl.
77/D2 **Goulburn** (riv.), Austl.
98/P **Gould** (coast), Ant.
112/F3 **Gould**, Ar,US
84/E2 **Goundam**, Mali
85/H3 **Gouré**, Niger
88/C4 **Gourits** (riv.), SAfr.
85/F3 **Gourma** (prov.), Burk.
85/F3 **Gourma** (reg.), Burk.
85/E2 **Gourma-Rharous**, Mali
42/A5 **Gournay-en-Bray**, Fr.
83/J4 **Gouro**, Chad
31/T9 **Goussainville**, Fr.
59/D2 **Gouşu** (riv.), Turk.
95/D1 **Gouvêa**, Braz.
42/B5 **Gouvieux**, Fr.
54/C2 **Goverla** (peak), Ukr.
95/D1 **Governador Valadares**, Braz.
62/D3 **Govĭ Altayn** (mts.), Mong.
61/H3 **Gowd-e-Zereh** (lake), Afg.
34/B3 **Gower** (pen.), Wal,UK
33/H4 **Goxhill**, Eng,UK
91/E2 **Goya**, Arg.
33/F5 **Goyt** (riv.), Eng,UK
65/M9 **Gozaisho-yama** (peak), Japan
68/D4 **Gozha** (lake), China
48/D4 **Gozo** (isl.), Malta
88/D4 **Graaff-Reinet**, SAfr.
40/D4 **Graafschap** (reg.), Neth.
88/B2 **Graberberg** (peak), Namb.
38/F2 **Grabow**, Ger.
50/B3 **Gračac**, Cro.
50/D3 **Gračanica**, Bosn.
113/G4 **Graceville**, Fl,US
100/E5 **Gracias a Dios** (cape), Nic.
47/S12 **Graciosa** (isl.), Azor.,Port.
50/D3 **Gradačac**, Bosn.
93/H5 **Gradaús**, Braz.
46/B1 **Grado**, Sp.
35/F2 **Grafham Water** (lake), Eng,UK
77/E1 **Grafton**, Austl.
76/B2 **Grafton** (passg.), Austl.
107/J3 **Grafton**, ND,US
110/D4 **Grafton**, WV,US
102/C3 **Graham** (isl.), BC,Can
103/S7 **Graham** (isl.), NW,Can
101/N7 **Graham** (peak), Az,US
112/D3 **Graham**, Tx,US
116/C3 **Graham**, Wa,US
56/G1 **Graham Bell** (isl.), Rus.
98/V **Graham Land** (reg.), Ant.
88/D4 **Grahamstown**, SAfr.
35/G4 **Grain**, Eng,UK
84/C5 **Grain Coast** (reg.), Libr.
94/A2 **Grajaú**, Braz.
93/J4 **Grajaú** (riv.), Braz.
39/M2 **Grajewo**, Pol.
44/D4 **Gramat** (plat.), Fr.
36/C2 **Grampian** (mts.), Sc,UK
77/B3 **Grampians Nat'l Park**, Austl.
40/D3 **Gramsbergen**, Neth.
37/D3 **Gran**, Nor.
92/D3 **Granada**, Col.
100/D5 **Granada**, Nic.
46/D4 **Granada**, Sp.
97/K7 **Gran Altiplanicie Central** (plat.), Arg.
97/K7 **Gran Bajo de San Julián** (val.), Arg.
96/C5 **Gran Bajo Oriental** (val.), Arg.
112/D3 **Granbury**, Tx,US
109/F2 **Granby**, Co,US
47/X17 **Gran Canaria** (isl.), Canl.
90/C5 **Gran Chaco** (plain), SAm.
111/H2 **Grand** (lake), NB,Can
111/K1 **Grand** (lake), Nf,Can
103/J3 **Grand** (riv.), Qu,Can
66/D4 **Grand** (can.), China
32/B5 **Grand** (can.), Ire.
108/D3 **Grand** (canyon), Az,US
109/J3 **Grand** (riv.), Ia, Mo,US
109/J5 **Grand** (lake), La,US
110/C2 **Grand** (isl.), Mi,US
112/E2 **Grand** (riv.), Mo,US
111/S9 **Grand** (isl.), NY,US
107/H4 **Grand** (riv.), SD,US
101/F2 **Grand Bahama** (isl.), Bahm.
111/L2 **Grand Bank**, Nf,Can
84/C5 **Grand Bassa** (co.), Libr.
84/E5 **Grand-Bassam**, IvC.
111/H2 **Grand Bay**, NB,Can
116/E6 **Grand Blanc**, Mi,US
108/D3 **Grand Canyon Nat'l Park**, Az,US
84/C5 **Grand Cape Mount** (co.), Libr.
100/E4 **Grand Cayman** (isl.), Cay.
106/F2 **Grand Centre**, Ab,Can
106/D4 **Grand Coulee** (dam), Wa,US
97/K7 **Grande** (bay), Arg.
97/K8 **Grande** (riv.), Arg.
92/F7 **Grande** (riv.), Bol.
95/K8 **Grande** (isl.), Braz.
95/J7 **Grande** (riv.), Braz.
101/F6 **Grande** (pt.), Pan.
97/T11 **Grande** (stream), Uru.
106/D2 **Grande Cache**, Ab,Can
89/G5 **Grande Comore** (isl.), Com.
48/C1 **Grande, Corno** (peak), It.
93/H4 **Grande de Gurupá**, Braz.
48/C4 **Grande, Monte** (peak), It.
106/D2 **Grande Prairie**, Ab,Can
82/H4 **Grand 'Erg de Bilma** (des.), Niger
82/E1 **Grand Erg Occidental** (des.), Alg.
82/G1 **Grand Erg Oriental** (des.), Alg.
112/C4 **Grande, Rio** (riv.), Mex., US
42/B1 **Grande-Synthe**, Fr.
101/J4 **Grande-Terre** (isl.), Guad.
111/H2 **Grand Falls**, NB,Can
111/L1 **Grand Falls**, Nf,Can
106/D3 **Grand Forks**, BC,Can
107/J4 **Grand Forks**, ND,US
42/B2 **Grand-Fort-Philippe**, Fr.
110/C3 **Grand Haven**, Mi,US
109/H2 **Grand Island**, Ne,US
113/F4 **Grand Isle**, La,US
84/D5 **Grand Jide** (co.), Libr.
108/E3 **Grand Junction**, Co,US
109/J3 **Grand Lake O'The Cherokees** (lake), Ok,US
111/H2 **Grand Manan** (isl.), NB,Can
107/L4 **Grand Marais**, Mn,US
42/C6 **Grand Morin** (riv.), Fr.
111/F2 **Grand-Mère**, Qu,Can
111/K2 **Grand Miquelon** (isl.), StP.
45/G3 **Grand Mont Ruan** (mtn.), Fr.
46/A3 **Grândola**, Port.
107/L4 **Grand Portage Nat'l Mon.**, Mn,US
43/D5 **Grandpré**, Fr.
107/J2 **Grand Rapids**, Mb,Can
110/C3 **Grand Rapids**, Mi,US
107/K4 **Grand Rapids**, Mn,US
44/F5 **Grand Rhône** (riv.), Fr.
106/F5 **Grand Teton Nat'l Park**, Wy,US
101/G3 **Grand Turk**, Trks.
31/M6 **Grand Union** (can.), Eng,UK
107/H3 **Grandview**, Mb,Can
106/D4 **Grandview**, Wa,US
96/C2 **Graneros**, Chile
37/E3 **Granfjället** (peak), Swe.
33/F3 **Grange**, Eng,UK
114/L3 **Granger** (mtn.), Yk,Can
106/D4 **Grangeville**, Id,US
106/B2 **Granisle**, BC,Can
106/F4 **Granite** (peak), Mt,US
110/B4 **Granite City**, Il,US
94/B1 **Granja**, Braz.
96/D5 **Gran Laguna Salada** (lake), Arg.
47/G2 **Granollers**, Sp.
45/G4 **Gran Paradiso Nat'l Park**, It.
45/J3 **Gran Pilastro** (peak), It.
47/Y16 **Gran Tarajal**, Canl.,Sp.
33/H6 **Grantham**, Eng,UK
36/D2 **Grantown-on-Spey**, Sc,UK
108/F4 **Grants**, NM,US
110/A2 **Grantsburg**, Wi,US
106/C5 **Grants Pass**, Or,US
92/C5 **Gran Vilaya** (ruins), Peru
107/H1 **Granville** (lake), Mb,Can
44/C2 **Granville**, Fr.
116/B3 **Grapeview-Allyn**, Wa,US
41/F2 **Grasberg**, Ger.
33/E3 **Grasmere**, Eng,UK
45/G5 **Grasse**, Fr.
111/Q9 **Grassie**, On,Can
33/G3 **Grassington**, Eng,UK
106/G3 **Grasslands Nat'l Park**, Sk,Can
50/B2 **Gratkorn**, Aus.
44/E5 **Graulhet**, Fr.
94/D3 **Gravatá**, Braz.
40/C5 **Grave**, Neth.
106/G3 **Gravelbourg**, Sk,Can
42/B2 **Gravelines**, Fr.
110/E2 **Gravenhurst**, On,Can
31/Q7 **Gravesend**, Eng,UK
42/A5 **Gravigny**, Fr.
48/E2 **Gravina di Puglia**, It.
101/G4 **Gravois** (pt.), Haiti
44/F3 **Gray**, Fr.
110/C2 **Grayling**, Mi,US
31/P7 **Grays**, Eng,UK
106/F5 **Grays** (lake), Id,US
106/B4 **Grays** (har.), Wa,US
116/P15 **Grayslake**, Il,US
107/H3 **Grayson**, Sk,Can
45/L3 **Graz**, Aus.
77/C4 **Great** (lake), Austl.
107/G3 **Great** (plains), Can., US
28/E3 **Great** (lakes), NAm.
108/C2 **Great** (basin), US
101/F2 **Great Abaco** (isl.), Bahm.
39/L5 **Great Alföld** (plain), Hun.
74/D6 **Great Australian** (bight), Austl.
101/F3 **Great Bahama** (bank), Bahm.
35/F2 **Great Barford**, Eng,UK
75/S10 **Great Barrier** (isl.), NZ
76/B2 **Great Barrier Reef Marine Park**, Austl.
35/G2 **Great Barton**, Eng,UK
108/D3 **Great Basin Nat'l Park**, Nv,US
102/D2 **Great Bear** (lake), NW,Can
109/H3 **Great Bend**, Ks,US
31/M8 **Great Bookham**, Eng,UK
88/C3 **Great Brak** (riv.), SAfr.
36/E3 **Great Britain** (isl.), UK
29/P5 **Great Coco** (isl.), Burma
35/G2 **Great Cornard**, Eng,UK
106/F5 **Great Divide** (basin), Wyo,US
75/H7 **Great Dividing** (range), Austl.
33/H4 **Great Driffield**, Eng,UK
35/G3 **Great Dunmow**, Eng,UK
85/F5 **Greater Accra** (reg.), Gha.
101/G4 **Greater Antilles** (arch.), NAm.
55/L3 **Greater Barsuki** (des.), Kaz.
31/P7 **Greater London** (co.), Eng,UK
33/F5 **Greater Manchester** (co.), Eng,UK
72/C4 **Greater Sunda** (isls.), Indo.
101/F3 **Great Exuma** (isl.), Bahm.
106/F4 **Great Falls**, Mt,US
88/D4 **Great Fish** (pt.), SAfr.
88/D4 **Great Fish** (riv.), SAfr.
35/F2 **Great Gransden**, Eng,UK
101/F3 **Great Guana Cay** (isl.), Bahm.
33/G2 **Greatham**, Eng,UK
33/F4 **Great Harwood**, Eng,UK
70/D2 **Great Himalaya** (range), Asia
101/G3 **Great Inagua** (isl.), Bahm.
70/A2 **Great Indian** (des.), India, Pak.
88/C3 **Great Karoo** (reg.), SAfr.
88/D4 **Great Kei** (riv.), SAfr.
34/D2 **Great Malvern**, Eng,UK
35/E3 **Great Milton**, Eng,UK
34/B5 **Great Mis Tor** (hill), Eng,UK
115/G5 **Great Neck**, NY,US
71/F6 **Great Nicobar** (isl.), India
35/G1 **Great Ouse** (riv.), Eng,UK
77/C4 **Great Oyster** (bay), Austl.
113/J3 **Great Pee Dee** (riv.), SC,US
87/F2 **Great Rift** (val.), Afr.
87/F2 **Great Ruaha** (riv.), Tanz.
108/D2 **Great Salt** (lake), Ut,US
108/D2 **Great Salt Lake** (des.), Ut,US
109/F3 **Great Sand Dunes Nat'l Mon.**, Co,US
86/A3 **Great Sand Sea** (des.), Egypt, Libya
74/C4 **Great Sandy** (des.), Austl.
108/B2 **Great Sandy** (des.), Or,US
76/D4 **Great Sandy Nat'l Park**, Austl.
84/B4 **Great Scarcies** (riv.), Gui., SLeo.
35/G2 **Great Shelford**, Eng,UK
33/F3 **Great Shunner Fell** (mtn.), Eng,UK
102/E2 **Great Slave** (lake), NW,Can
113/H3 **Great Smoky Mts. Nat'l Park**, NC, Tn,US
115/G5 **Great South** (bay), NY,US
35/G4 **Great Stour** (riv.), Eng,UK
69/B3 **Great Tenasserim** (riv.), Burma
34/B5 **Great Torrington**, Eng,UK
74/D5 **Great Victoria** (des.), Austl.
66/B3 **Great Wall** (ruins), China
31/P7 **Great Warley**, Eng,UK
77/C4 **Great Western Tiers** (mts.), Austl.
88/B4 **Great Winterhoek** (peak), SAfr.
34/D2 **Great Witley**, Eng,UK
35/H1 **Great Yarmouth**, Eng,UK
59/F3 **Great Zab** (riv.), Iraq, Turk.
87/F5 **Great Zimbabwe** (ruins), Zim.
85/H2 **Grébon** (peak), Niger
59/K4 **Greco** (cape), Cyp.
48/D2 **Greco** (peak), It.
46/C2 **Gredos** (range), Sp.
30/F5 **Greece**
109/F2 **Greeley**, Co,US
103/S6 **Greely** (fjord), NW,Can
77/D3 **Green** (cape), Austl.
110/C4 **Green** (riv.), Ky,US
107/M4 **Green** (bay), Mi, Wi,US
108/E3 **Green** (riv.), Ut, Wy,US
111/G3 **Green** (mts.), Vt,US
110/B2 **Green Bay**, Wi,US
115/K7 **Greenbelt**, Md,US
110/C4 **Greencastle**, In,US
113/H4 **Green Cove Springs**, Fl,US
116/Q14 **Greendale**, Wi,US
113/H2 **Greeneville**, Tn,US
110/C4 **Greenfield**, In,US
111/F3 **Greenfield**, Ma,US
116/P14 **Greenfield**, Wi,US
111/P7 **Greenfield Park**, Qu,Can
115/K7 **Green Haven**, Md,US
32/C2 **Greenisland**, NI,UK
99/R2 **Greenland** (sea)
99/N2 **Greenland** (Kalaallit Nunaat) (dpcy.), Den.
36/D3 **Greenlaw**, Sc,UK
36/C3 **Greenock**, Sc,UK
114/K2 **Greenough** (mtn.), Ak,US
111/R8 **Green River**, On,Can
108/E3 **Green River**, Ut,US
106/F5 **Green River**, Wy,US
113/G3 **Greensboro**, Al,US
113/J2 **Greensboro**, NC,US
110/C4 **Greensburg**, In,US
110/E3 **Greensburg**, Pa,US
111/Q9 **Greensville**, On,Can
108/E5 **Green Valley**, Az,US
115/J7 **Green Valley**, Md,US
84/C5 **Greenville**, Libr.
113/G4 **Greenville**, Al,US
108/B2 **Greenville**, Ca,US
110/C4 **Greenville**, Ky,US
110/C3 **Greenville**, Mi,US
113/F3 **Greenville**, Ms,US
113/J3 **Greenville**, NC,US
110/C3 **Greenville**, Oh,US
113/H3 **Greenville**, SC,US
112/D3 **Greenville**, Tx,US
116/D3 **Greenwater** (riv.), Wa,US
31/P7 **Greenwich** (bor.), Eng,UK
115/G4 **Greenwich**, Ct,US
111/R8 **Greenwood**, On,Can
113/F3 **Greenwood**, Ms,US
115/F4 **Greenwood** (lake), NJ, NY,US
113/H3 **Greenwood**, SC,US
113/H3 **Greenwood** (lake), SC,US
109/J4 **Greers Ferry** (lake), Ar,US
32/B6 **Greese** (riv.), Ire.
40/D6 **Grefrath**, Ger.
92/D5 **Gregório** (riv.), Braz.
74/C5 **Gregory** (lake), Austl.
74/D4 **Gregory** (lake), Austl.
74/F5 **Gregory** (lake), Austl.
76/A2 **Gregory** (range), Austl.
107/J5 **Gregory**, SD,US
39/G1 **Greifswald**, Ger.
39/G1 **Greifswalder Bodden** (bay), Ger.
50/B2 **Greimberg** (peak), Aus.
38/G3 **Greiz**, Ger.
53/N4 **Gremyachinsk**, Rus.
37/D4 **Grenå**, Den.
101/J5 **Grenada**
113/F3 **Grenada**, Ms,US
45/G3 **Grenchen**, Swi.
107/H3 **Grenfell**, Sk,Can
44/F4 **Grenoble**, Fr.
74/G2 **Grenville** (cape), Austl.
37/E2 **Gressåmoen Nat'l Park**, Nor.
33/E2 **Greta** (riv.), Eng,UK
33/F3 **Greta** (riv.), Eng,UK
107/J3 **Gretna**, Mb,Can
33/E2 **Gretna**, Sc,UK
113/F4 **Gretna**, La,US
35/F1 **Gretton**, Eng,UK
31/U10 **Gretz-Armainvilliers**, Fr.
40/B5 **Grevelingendam** (dam), Neth.
41/E4 **Greven**, Ger.
49/G2 **Grevená**, Gre.
40/D6 **Grevenbroich**, Ger.
43/F4 **Grevenmacher** (dist.), Lux.
38/F2 **Grevesmühlen**, Ger.
40/A5 **Grevlingen** (chan.), Neth.
74/F2 **Grey** (cape), Austl.
76/A5 **Grey** (range), Austl.
111/K2 **Grey** (riv.), Nf,Can
32/C2 **Grey** (pt.), NI,UK
32/C2 **Grey Abbey**, NI,UK
106/F4 **Greybull**, Wy,US
114/L3 **Grey Hunter** (peak), Yk,Can
75/R11 **Greymouth**, NZ
76/B2 **Grey Peaks Nat'l Park**, Austl.

33/F2 Greystoke, Eng,UK
32/B5 Greystones, Ire.
89/E3 Greytown, SAfr.
43/D2 Grez-Doiceau, Belg.
34/B6 Gribbin (pt.), Eng,UK
40/C2 Griend (isl.), Neth.
113/G3 Griffin, Ga,US
77/C2 Griffith, Austl.
116/R16 Griffith, In,US
42/B6 Grigny, Fr.
77/C4 Grim (cape), Austl.
42/D2 Grimbergen, Belg.
34/D2 Grimley, Eng,UK
38/G1 Grimmen, Ger.
111/Q9 Grimsby, On,Can
33/H4 Grimsby, Eng,UK
37/N6 Grimsey (isl.), Ice.
37/D4 Grimstad, Nor.
103/S7 Grinnel (pen.), NW,Can
50/B2 Grintavec (peak), Slov.
88/E3 Griqualand East (reg.), SAfr.
88/C2 Griqualand West (reg.), SAfr.
42/A2 Gris Nez (cape), Fr.
31/U10 Grisy-Suisnes, Fr.
116/K10 Grizzly (bay), Ca,US
50/C3 Grmeč (mtn.), Bosn.
43/D1 Grobbendonk, Belg.
39/J3 Grodków, Pol.
39/M2 Grodno, Bela.
52/E5 Grodno Obl., Bela.
39/J2 Grodzisk Wielkopolski, Pol.
40/D4 Groenlo, Neth.
112/D4 Groesbeck, Tx,US
40/C5 Groesbeek, Neth.
44/B3 Groix (isl.), Fr.
39/L3 Grójec, Pol.
38/F1 Grömitz, Ger.
40/E4 Gronau, Ger.
40/D2 Groningen, Neth.
40/D2 Groningen (prov.), Neth.
45/J3 Gronlait (peak), It.
88/C4 Groot (riv.), SAfr.
74/F2 Groote Eylandt (isl.), Austl.
40/D2 Grootegast, Neth.
87/C4 Grootfontein, Namb.
88/D2 Groot-Marico (riv.), SAfr.
88/C3 Grootvloer (salt pan), SAfr.
101/J5 Gros Islet, StL.
111/K1 Gros Morne (peak), Nf,Can
111/K1 Gros Morne Nat'l Park, Nf,Can
44/F3 Grosne (riv.), Fr.
41/G6 Grossalmerode, Ger.
41/E3 Grosse Aa (riv.), Ger.
116/F7 Grosse Ile, Mi,US
88/A2 Grosse Münzenberg (peak), Namb.
43/G2 Grosse Nister (riv.), Ger.
41/F3 Grossenkneten, Ger.
116/G7 Grosse Pointe, Mi,US
116/G7 Grosse Pointe Farms, Mi,US
116/G7 Grosse Pointe Park, Mi,US
116/G7 Grosse Pointe Shores, Mi,US
116/G7 Grosse Pointe Woods, Mi,US
45/K2 Grosser Arber (peak), Ger.
41/G3 Grosser Aue (riv.), Ger.
38/F3 Grosser Beer-Berg (peak), Ger.
45/L3 Grosser Bösenstein (peak), Aus.
41/F1 Grosser Knechtsand (isl.), Ger.
39/H4 Grosser Peilstein (peak), Aus.
45/L3 Grosser Priel (peak), Aus.
39/H5 Grosser Pyhrgas (peak), Aus.
45/K2 Grosser Rachel (peak), Ger.
41/E2 Grosses Meer (lake), Ger.
50/A2 Grosses Wiesbachhorn (peak), Aus.
48/B1 Grosseto, It.
45/H2 Grossgerau, Ger.
45/K3 Grossglockner (peak), Aus.
41/H1 Grosshansdorf, Ger.
45/H5 Grosso (cape), Fr.
43/F5 Grossrosseln, Ger.
43/E2 Grote Gete (riv.), Belg.
43/D1 Grote Nete (riv.), Belg.
107/J4 Groton, SD,US
48/E2 Grottaglie, It.
43/E3 Grotte de Han, Belg.
47/E1 Grottes de Bétharram, Fr.
81/L14 Grou (riv.), Mor.
106/D2 Grouard Mission, Ab,Can
110/D1 Groundhog (riv.), On,Can
40/C2 Grouw, Neth.
35/E3 Grove, Eng,UK
109/J3 Grove, Ok,US
108/B4 Grover City, Ca,US
112/E4 Groves, Tx,US
115/J8 Groveton, Va,US
55/H4 Groznyy, Rus.
51/H4 Grudovo, Bul.
39/K2 Grudziądz, Pol.
33/E2 Grune (pt.), Eng,UK
54/F1 Gryazi, Rus.
39/H2 Gryfice, Pol.
39/H2 Gryfino, Pol.
96/B4 Guabun (pt.), Chile
101/F3 Guacanayabo (gulf), Cuba
95/D2 Guaçuí, Braz.
101/P9 Guadalajara, Mex.
46/D2 Guadalajara, Sp.
78/E6 Guadalcanal (isl.), Sol.
46/E4 Guadalentín (riv.), Sp.
46/D3 Guadalimlar (riv.), Sp.
47/N8 Guadalix (riv.), Sp.
47/E2 Guadalope (riv.), Sp.
46/D4 Guadalquivir (riv.), Sp.
94/B2 Guadalupe, Braz.
101/F6 Guadalupe, Pan.
46/C3 Guadalupe (range), Sp.
112/B4 Guadalupe (peak), Tx,US
112/D4 Guadalupe (riv.), Tx,US
112/B4 Guadalupe Mts. Nat'l Park, Tx,US
47/M8 Guadarrama (pass), Sp.
46/C2 Guadarrama (range), Sp.
46/C3 Guadarrama (riv.), Sp.
101/J4 Guadeloupe (dpcy.), Fr.
101/J4 Guadeloupe (passage), NAm.
46/B4 Guadiana (riv.), Sp., Port.
46/D4 Guadiana Menor (riv.), Sp.
46/D4 Guadix, Sp.
96/B4 Guafo (chan.), Chile
96/B4 Guafo (isl.), Chile
95/B4 Guaíba, Braz.
95/B4 Guaíba (riv.), Braz.
92/F2 Guaiquinima (peak), Ven.
95/B2 Guaíra, Braz.
96/B4 Guaiteca (isl.), Chile
92/E6 Guajará-Mirim, Braz.
101/G5 Guajira (pen.), Col., Ven.
108/B3 Gualala, Ca,US
48/C1 Gualdo Tadino, It.
96/F2 Gualeguay, Arg.
96/F2 Gualeguay (riv.), Arg.
96/F2 Gualeguaychú, Arg.
96/D4 Gualicho (val.), Arg.
78/D3 Guam (isl.), PacUS
96/B5 Guamblin (isl.), Chile
95/K7 Guanabara (bay), Braz.
100/A3 Guanajuato, Mex.
100/A3 Guanajuato (state), Mex.
94/B4 Guanambi, Braz.
101/H6 Guanare, Ven.
101/H6 Guanare (riv.), Ven.
66/C3 Guancen Shan (mtn.), China
66/B3 Guandi Shan (mtn.), China
71/K3 Guangdong (prov.), China
66/D5 Guangming Ding (peak), China
71/J3 Guangxi Zhuangzu Zizhiqu (aut. reg.), China
67/C2 Guangze, China
67/B3 Guangzhou (Canton), China
95/D1 Guanhães, Braz.
101/J6 Guanipa (riv.), Ven.
101/F3 Guantánamo, Cuba
66/G6 Guanting (res.), China
66/D4 Guanyun, China
95/B4 Guaporé, Braz.
92/F6 Guaporé (riv.), Braz.
94/A4 Guara (riv.), Braz.
47/E1 Guara (peak), Sp.
94/D2 Guarabira, Braz.
93/J5 Guaraí, Braz.
95/B3 Guaramirim, Braz.
92/C4 Guaranda, Ecu.
95/D2 Guarapari, Braz.
95/B3 Guarapuava, Braz.
95/B2 Guararapes, Braz.
95/B4 Guararema, Braz.
94/C5 Guaratinga, Braz.
95/H7 Guaratinguetá, Braz.
95/B3 Guaratuba, Braz.
46/B2 Guarda, Port.
46/B2 Guarda (dist.), Port.
46/B3 Guareña, Sp.
92/E2 Guárico (res.), Ven.
92/E2 Guárico (riv.), Ven.
95/G9 Guarujá, Braz.
95/G8 Guarulhos, Braz.
101/N8 Guasave, Mex.
100/C4 Guatemala
100/C5 Guatemala (cap.), Guat.
95/G6 Guaxupé, Braz.
101/H4 Guayama, PR
92/C4 Guayaquil, Ecu.
92/B4 Guayaquil (gulf), Ecu.
92/E6 Guayaramerín, Bol.
101/M8 Guaymas, Mex.
53/N4 Gubakha, Rus.
39/H3 Guben, Ger.
39/H3 Gubin, Pol.
54/F2 Gubkin, Rus.
62/E2 Guchin-Us, Mong.
47/E2 Gúdar (range), Sp.
41/G6 Gudensberg, Ger.
55/H4 Gudermes, Rus.
70/D4 Gudivāda, India
70/C5 Güdūr, India
46/D1 Guecho, Sp.
84/B1 Guelb Azefal (mts.), Mrta.
81/V17 Guelma, Alg.
110/D3 Guelph, On,Can
82/C2 Guelta Zemmur, WSah.
43/F5 Guénange, Fr.
44/B3 Guérande, Fr.
44/D3 Guéret, Fr.
46/D1 Guernica y Luno, Sp.
44/B2 Guernsey (isl.), ChI,UK
100/B4 Guerrero (state), Mex.
44/F3 Gueugnon, Fr.
85/H3 Guézaoua, Niger
83/N6 Gugē (peak), Eth.
78/D3 Guguan (isl.), NMar.
67/B3 Gui (riv.), China
47/X16 Guía de Isora, Sp.
92/F2 Guiana Highlands (mts.), SAm.
100/B4 Guichicovi, Mex.
82/H6 Guidder, Camr.
84/B3 Guidimaka (reg.), Mrta.
48/C2 Guidonia, It.
84/D5 Guiglo, IvC.
31/U11 Guignes, Fr.
42/C5 Guignicourt, Fr.
67/D5 Guihulngan, Phil.
31/M8 Guildford, Eng,UK
44/F4 Guilherand, Fr.
71/K2 Guilin, China
103/J3 Guillaume-Delisle (lake), Qu,Can
46/B4 Guillena, Sp.
34/C1 Guilsfield, Wal,UK
46/A2 Guimarães, Port.
66/D4 Guimeng Ding (mtn.), China
84/C4 Guinea
82/F7 Guinea (gulf), Afr.
84/B3 Guinea-Bissau
44/B2 Guingamp, Fr.
44/A2 Guipavas, Fr.
93/H7 Guiratinga, Braz.
101/J5 Güiria, Ven.
33/G2 Guisborough, Eng,UK
42/C4 Guise, Fr.
33/G4 Guiseley, Eng,UK
46/B1 Guitiriz, Sp.
67/B2 Guiyang, China
71/J2 Guiyang, China
71/J2 Guizhou (prov.), China
44/C4 Gujan-Mestras, Fr.
70/B3 Gujarāt (state), India
61/K2 Gūjar Khān, Pak.
61/K2 Gujrānwāla, Pak.
61/K2 Gujrāt, Pak.
54/F2 Gukovo, Rus.
62/E4 Gulang, China
70/C4 Gulbarga, India
43/G3 Guldenbach (riv.), Ger.
67/C3 Guleitou, China
113/F4 Gulfport, Ms,US
113/G4 Gulf Shores, Al,US
56/G5 Gulistan, Uzb.
63/J2 Guliya (peak), China
32/B2 Gulladuff, NI,UK
106/F3 Gull Lake, Sk,Can
59/C3 Gülnar, Turk.
43/E2 Gulpen, Neth.
83/M7 Gulu, Ugan.
51/G4 Gülübovo, Bul.
87/D4 Gumare, Bots.
65/F2 Gumma (pref.), Japan
41/E6 Gummersbach, Ger.
54/E4 Gümüşhacıköy, Turk.
59/D2 Gümüşhane, Turk.
83/N5 Guna (peak), Eth.
70/C3 Guna, India
59/E2 Güneydogu Toroslar (mts.), Turk.
107/J2 Gunisao (lake), Mb,Can
107/J2 Gunisao (riv.), Mb,Can
77/D1 Gunnedah, Austl.
108/F3 Gunnison, Co,US
108/F3 Gunnison (riv.), Co,US
108/E3 Gunnison, Ut,US
68/B4 Gunt (riv.), Taj.
113/G3 Guntersville, Al,US
113/G3 Guntersville (lake), Al,US
70/D4 Guntūr, India
45/J2 Günz (riv.), Ger.
45/J2 Gunzenhausen, Ger.
66/C4 Guo (riv.), China
83/N6 Gurage (peak), Eth.
51/G2 Gura Humorului, Rom.
91/F2 Gural (mts.), Braz.
62/B2 Gurbantünggut (des.), China
61/L2 Gurdāspur, India
94/B3 Gurguéia (riv.), Braz.
101/J6 Guri, Embalse de (res.), Ven.
45/L3 Gurk (riv.), Aus.
45/K3 Gurkthaler (mts.), Aus.
116/Q15 Gurnee, Il,US
51/J5 Gürsu, Turk.
93/J6 Gurupi, Braz.
93/J4 Gurupi (mts.), Braz.
94/A1 Gurupi (riv.), Braz.
70/B3 Guru Sikhar (mtn.), India
62/G2 Gurvandzagal, Mong.
55/J3 Gur'yev, Kaz.
55/J3 Gur'yev Obl., Kaz.
52/J5 Gus'-Khrustal'nyy, Rus.
48/A3 Guspini, It.
38/G2 Güstrow, Ger.
41/F5 Gütersloh, Ger.
109/H4 Guthrie, Ok,US
109/G4 Guthrie, Tx,US
37/E3 Gutulia Nat'l Park, Nor.
92/G3 Guyana
31/S10 Guyancourt, Fr.
113/H2 Guyandotte (riv.), WV,US
66/B2 Guyang, China
44/C4 Guyenne (reg.), Fr.
77/E1 Guy Fawkes Riv. Nat'l Park, Austl.
35/G1 Guyhirn, Eng,UK
109/G3 Guymon, Ok,US
62/F4 Guyuan, China
62/H3 Guyuan, China
101/N7 Guzmán (lake), Mex.
61/H3 Gwādar, Pak.
70/C2 Gwalior, India
87/E5 Gwanda, Zim.
35/F1 Gwash (riv.), Eng,UK
34/C2 Gwaunceste (mtn.), Wal,UK
39/J2 Gwda (riv.), Pol.
34/A6 Gweek, Eng,UK
34/D3 Gwent (co.), Wal,UK
33/E5 Gwersyllt, Wal,UK
87/E4 Gweru, Zim.
77/D1 Gwydir (riv.), Austl.
32/D5 Gwynedd (co.), Wal,UK
55/H4 Gyandzhe, Azer.
63/D5 Gyaring (lake), China
85/F5 Gyasikan, Gha.
56/H2 Gyda (pen.), Rus.
76/D4 Gympie, Austl.
71/G4 Gyobingauk, Burma
50/E2 Gyoma, Hun.
50/D2 Gyöngyös, Hun.
50/C2 Győr, Hun.
50/C2 Győr-Sopron (co.), Hun.
50/E2 Gyula, Hun.

H

42/D2 Haacht, Belg.
40/D4 Haaksbergen, Neth.
42/D2 Haaltert, Belg.
40/E6 Haan, Ger.
79/H6 Ha'apai Group (isls.), Tonga
37/H2 Haapavesi, Fin.
52/D4 Haapsalu, Est.
45/J2 Haar, Ger.
45/G2 Haardt (mts.), Ger.
40/B4 Haarlem, Neth.
75/Q11 Haast, NZ
61/J3 Hab (riv.), Pak.
43/E4 Habay, Belg.
60/D2 Habbānīyah, Iraq
71/F3 Habiganj, Bang.
65/L10 Habikino, Japan
63/N3 Haboro, Japan
41/F3 Hache (riv.), Ger.
63/N5 Hachijō (isl.), Japan
65/F3 Hachiōji, Japan
115/C3 Hacienda Heights, Ca,US
59/C2 Hacılar, Turk.
115/F5 Hackensack, NJ,US
115/F5 Hackettstown, NJ,US
31/N7 Hackney (bor.), Eng,UK
69/D1 Ha Coi, Viet.
45/H1 Hadamar, Ger.
65/F3 Hadano, Japan
86/D4 Hadarba, Ras (cape), Sudan
83/J4 Haddad (wadi), Chad
35/F3 Haddenham, Eng,UK
36/D3 Haddington, Sc,UK
115/E6 Haddonfield, NJ,US
115/E6 Haddon (township), NJ,US
61/G4 Ḩadd, Ra's al (pt.), Oman
85/H3 Hadejia (riv.), Nga.
41/F1 Hadelner (can.), Ger.
59/K5 Hadera, Isr.
38/E1 Haderslev, Den.
59/C3 Hadım, Turk.
81/S15 Hadjout, Alg.
50/E2 Hadjú-Bihar (co.), Hun.
102/F1 Hadley (bay), NW,Can
31/Q8 Hadlow, Eng,UK
33/F1 Hadrian's Wall (ruins), Eng,UK
37/E1 Hadselfjorden (fjord), Nor.
63/K4 Haeju, NKor.
104/S9 Haena (pt.), Hi,US
59/D2 Hafik, Turk.
61/K2 Hāfizābād, Pak.
37/N7 Hafnarfjördhur, Ice.
60/E3 Ḩafr al Bāţin, SAr.
60/E2 Haft Gel, Iran
81/H3 Hafun, Ras (pt.), Som.
114/F4 Hagemeister (isl.), Ak,US
41/E6 Hagen, Ger.
41/E4 Hagen am Teutoburger Wald, Ger.
38/F2 Hagenow, Ger.
109/F4 Hagerman, NM,US
110/E4 Hagerstown, Md,US
64/B3 Hagi, Japan
69/D1 Ha Giang, Viet.
34/D2 Hagley, Eng,UK
43/F5 Hagondange, Fr.
36/A4 Hags Head (pt.), Ire.
107/G2 Hague, Sk,Can
44/C2 Hague, Cap de la (cape), Fr.
43/G6 Haguenau, Fr.
40/B4 Hague, The ('s-Gravenhage) (cap.), Neth.
78/D2 Hahashima (isl.), Jap.
41/H6 Hahle (riv.), Ger.
43/G3 Hahnenbach (riv.), Ger.
66/D3 Hai (riv.), China
65/L10 Haibara, Japan
63/J3 Haicheng, China
69/D1 Hai Duong, Viet.
59/K5 Haifa (dist.), Isr.
59/K5 Haifa (Hefa), Isr.
43/H2 Haiger, Ger.
69/D1 Hai Hau, Viet.
67/B3 Haikou, China
63/H2 Hailar, China
63/J2 Hailar (riv.), China
110/E2 Haileybury, On,Can
35/G5 Hailsham, Eng,UK
71/J4 Hainan (prov.), China
67/B3 Hainan (str.), China
42/B2 Hainaut (prov.), Belg.
45/H1 Hainburg, Ger.
113/H4 Haines City, Fl,US
114/L3 Haines Junction, Yk,Can
41/H6 Hainich (mts.), Ger.
66/L9 Haining, China
69/D1 Haiphong (Hai Phong), Viet.
101/G4 Haiti
69/E2 Hai Van (pass), Viet.
71/K3 Haixia (str.), China
66/D4 Haizhou (bay), China
39/L5 Hajdú-Bihar (co.), Hun.
50/E2 Hajdúboszormény, Hun.
50/E2 Hajdúdorog, Hun.
50/E2 Hajdúhadház, Hun.
50/E2 Hajdúnánás, Hun.
50/E2 Hajdúszoboszló, Hun.
65/F1 Hajiki-zaki (pt.), Japan
39/M2 Hajnówka, Pol.
71/F2 Hājo, India
79/L5 Hakahau, Fr.Pol.
64/D3 Hakken-san (mtn.), Japan
63/N3 Hakodate, Japan
65/H7 Hakone, Japan
65/H8 Hakone-Fuji-Izu Nat'l Park, Japan
65/E2 Hakui, Japan
65/M10 Hakusan, Japan
65/E2 Haku-san (mtn.), Japan
65/E2 Hakusan Nat'l Park, Japan
61/J3 Hāla, Pak.
59/D3 Ḩalab (Aleppo), Syria
60/E1 Ḩalabjah, Iraq
86/D4 Ḩalā'ib, Sudan
37/D4 Halden, Nor.
38/F2 Haldensleben, Ger.
111/Q10 Haldimand, On,Can
62/G2 Haldzan, Mong.
87/G2 Hale, Tanz.
33/F5 Hale, Eng,UK
104/T10 Haleakala Nat'l Park, Hi,US
43/D2 Halen, Belg.
116/P14 Hales Corners, Wi,US
34/D2 Halesowen, Eng,UK
35/H2 Halesworth, Eng,UK
113/G3 Haleyville, Al,US
84/E5 Half Assini, Gha.
67/C6 Half Moon (shoal)
116/K12 Half Moon Bay, Ca,US
59/K6 Ḩalḩūl, WBnk.
110/E2 Haliburton (hills), On,Can
76/B2 Halifax (bay), Austl.
111/J2 Halifax (cap.), NS,Can
33/G4 Halifax, Eng,UK
61/G3 Halīl (riv.), Iran
114/H1 Halkett (cape), Ak,US
103/K2 Hall (pen.), NW,Can
78/E4 Hall (isls.), Micr.
114/D3 Hall (isl.), Ak,US
37/E4 Halland (co.), Swe.
63/K5 Halla-san (mtn.), SKor.
42/D2 Halle, Belg.
41/F4 Halle, Ger.
37/E4 Hällefors, Swe.
45/K3 Hallein, Aus.
42/A4 Hallencourt, Fr.
38/F3 Halle-Neustadt, Ger.
98/M Hallett (cape), Ant.
112/D4 Hallettsville, Tx,US
107/J3 Hallock, Mn,US
38/B4 Hallu (riv.), Fr.
42/B3 Hallue (riv.), Fr.
42/C2 Halluin, Fr.
64/A3 Hallyŏ Haesang Nat'l Park, SKor.
73/G3 Halmahera (isl.), Indo.
73/G4 Halmahera (sea), Indo.
37/E4 Halmstad, Swe.
81/X17 Ḩalq al Wādī, Tun.
37/E4 Hälsingborg, Swe.
35/G3 Halstead, Eng,UK
40/B5 Halsteren, Neth.
62/C4 Haltang (riv.), China
33/H4 Haltemprice, Eng,UK
41/E5 Haltern, Ger.
111/Q8 Halton Hills, On,Can
33/F2 Haltwhistle, Eng,UK
41/E6 Halver, Ger.
41/E3 Halverder Aa (riv.), Ger.
42/C4 Ham, Fr.
64/C3 Hamada, Japan
60/E2 Hamadān, Iran
59/L4 Ḩamāh, Syria
65/M10 Hamajima, Japan
65/E3 Hamakita, Japan
65/E3 Hamamatsu, Japan
37/D3 Hamar, Nor.
86/C3 Ḩamāţah, Jabal (mtn.), Egypt
70/D6 Hambantota, SrL.
35/E5 Hamble, Eng,UK
33/G3 Hambleton (hills), Eng,UK
41/G3 Hambühren, Ger.
41/G1 Hamburg, Ger.
41/H1 Hamburg (state), Ger.
112/F3 Hamburg, Ar,US
110/E3 Hamburg, NY,US
37/G3 Häme (prov.), Fin.
37/G3 Hämeenkyrö, Fin.
37/H3 Hämeenlinna, Fin.
74/A5 Hamelin Pool (bay), Austl.
41/G4 Hameln, Ger.
74/B4 Hamersley (range), Austl.
35/H3 Hamford Water (inlet), Eng,UK
63/K3 Hamgyŏng (mts.), NKor.
63/K4 Hamhŭng, NKor.
62/C3 Hami, China
103/L3 Hamilton (inlet), Nf,Can
111/Q9 Hamilton, On,Can
75/S10 Hamilton, NZ
36/C3 Hamilton, Sc,UK
113/G3 Hamilton, Al,US
116/L12 Hamilton (mt.), Ca,US
106/E4 Hamilton, Mt,US
110/C4 Hamilton, Oh,US
112/D4 Hamilton, Tx,US
70/D2 Hamīrpur, India
81/V17 Hamma-Bouziane, Alg.
81/X17 Hammāmāt (gulf), Tun.
81/Q16 Hamman, Oued el (riv.), Alg.
42/D1 Hamme, Belg.
41/F2 Hamme (riv.), Ger.
37/G1 Hammerfest, Nor.
31/N7 Hammersmith & Fulham (bor.), Eng,UK
40/D5 Hamminkeln, Ger.
116/R16 Hammond, In,US
113/F4 Hammond, La,US
43/E1 Hamont-Achel, Belg.
35/E4 Hampshire (co.), Eng,UK
35/E4 Hampshire Downs (hills), Eng,UK
31/N7 Hampstead, Eng,UK
110/E4 Hampton, Va,US
31/M7 Hampton Court, Eng,UK
77/G6 Hampton Park, Austl.
82/H1 Ḩamrā (upland), Libya
116/F7 Hamtramck, Mi,US
65/H7 Hamura, Japan
66/C5 Han (riv.), China
67/C3 Han (riv.), China
63/K4 Han (riv.), SKor.
63/N4 Hanamaki, Japan
104/U11 Hanamalo (pt.), Hi,US
63/M5 Hanamatsu, Japan
87/G1 Hanang (peak), Tanz.
110/B2 Hancock, Mi,US
65/M10 Handa, Japan
66/C3 Handan, China
35/E1 Handsworth, Eng,UK
108/C3 Hanford, Ca,US
62/D2 Hangayn (mts.), Mong.
34/C5 Hangingstone (hill), Eng,UK
88/L11 Hangklip (cape), SAfr.
68/B5 Hangu, Pak.
66/L9 Hangzhou, China
62/C2 Hanhöhiy (mts.), Mong.
59/E2 Hani, Turk.
107/J4 Hankinson, ND,US
107/G3 Hanley, Sk,Can
106/F3 Hanna, Ab,Can
106/G5 Hanna, Wy,US
65/L10 Hannan, Japan
109/K3 Hannibal, Mo,US
65/H7 Hannō, Japan
41/G4 Hannover, Ger.
43/E2 Hannut, Belg.
37/E5 Hanöbukten (bay), Swe.
69/D1 Hanoi (Ha Noi) (cap.), Viet.
110/D2 Hanover, On,Can
97/J7 Hanover (isl.), Chile
111/F3 Hanover, NH,US
116/P16 Hanover Park, Il,US
70/C2 Hānsi, India
68/D3 Hantengri Feng (peak), China
103/J2 Hantzsch (riv.), NW,Can
70/B2 Hanumāngarh, India
62/E2 Hanuy (riv.), Mong.
62/F5 Hanzhong, China
79/L6 Hao (atoll), FrPol.
37/H2 Haparanda, Swe.
103/K3 Happy Valley-Goose Bay, Nf,Can
62/D4 Har (lake), China
62/C2 Har (lake), Mong.
62/F2 Haraa (riv.), Mong.
65/G2 Haramachi, Japan
61/K2 Harappa (ruins), Pak.
87/F4 Harare (cap.), Zim.
62/F2 Har-Ayrag, Mong.
84/C5 Harbel, Libr.
63/K2 Harbin, China
111/L2 Harbour Breton, Nf,Can
35/E2 Harbury, Eng,UK
70/C3 Hardā, India
37/C3 Hardangervidda Nat'l Park, Nor.
88/B2 Hardap (dam), Namb.
41/H3 Hardau (riv.), Ger.
41/G5 Hardegsen, Ger.
40/D3 Hardenberg, Neth.
40/C4 Harderwijk, Neth.
106/G4 Hardin, Mt,US
61/L3 Hardwār, India
97/K8 Hardy (pen.), Chile
111/L1 Hare (bay), Nf,Can
42/C2 Harelbeke, Belg.
41/E3 Haren, Ger.
40/D2 Haren, Neth.
83/P6 Hārer, Eth.
59/N8 Har Eval (Jabal 'Aybāl) (mtn.), WBnk.
83/P6 Hargeysa, Som.
51/G2 Harghita (co.), Rom.
51/G2 Harghita (peak), Rom.
72/B4 Hari (riv.), Indo.
70/C5 Harihar, India
64/D3 Harima (sound), Japan
40/B5 Haringvliet (chan.), Neth.
61/H2 Harī rūd (riv.), Afg.
110/D4 Harlan, Ky,US
32/D6 Harlech, Wal,UK
35/H2 Harleston, Eng,UK
40/C2 Harlingen, Neth.
112/D5 Harlingen, Tx,US
35/F3 Harlington, Eng,UK
31/P6 Harlow, Eng,UK
106/F4 Harlowton, Mt,US
40/B4 Harmelen, Neth.
42/B3 Harnes, Fr.
106/D5 Harney (lake), Or,US
106/D5 Harney (val.), Or,US
107/H5 Harney (peak), SD,US
37/F3 Härnösand, Swe.
101/M8 Haro (cape), Mex.
46/D1 Haro, Sp.
35/F3 Harpenden, Eng,UK
114/L3 Harper (mtn.), Yk,Can
84/D5 Harper, Libr.
114/K3 Harper (mtn.), Ak,US
112/D2 Harper, Ks,US
116/G7 Harper Woods, Mi,US
110/E1 Harricana (riv.), Qu,Can
113/G3 Harriman, Tn,US
74/F6 Harris (lake), Austl.
110/B4 Harrisburg, Il,US
109/G2 Harrisburg, Ne,US
38/E1 Harrislee, Ger.
88/E3 Harrismith, SAfr.
106/C3 Harrison (lake), BC,Can
103/L3 Harrison (cape), Nf,Can
114/H1 Harrison (bay), Ak,US
112/E2 Harrison, Ar,US
109/G2 Harrison, Ne,US
115/G5 Harrison, NY,US
110/E4 Harrisonburg, Va,US
110/C4 Harrodsburg, Ky,US
33/G4 Harrogate, Eng,UK
31/M7 Harrow (bor.), Eng,UK
109/J3 Harry S Truman (res.), Mo,US
41/G2 Harsefeld, Ger.
41/F5 Harsewinkel, Ger.
37/F1 Harstad, Nor.
102/C2 Hart (riv.), Yk,Can
108/C2 Hart (lake), Or,US
88/C3 Hartbeesrivier (dry riv.), SAfr.
37/C3 Hårteigen (peak), Nor.
40/B5 Hartelkanaal (can.), Neth.
110/C3 Hartford City, In,US
109/H2 Hartington, Ne,US
34/B5 Hartland, Eng,UK
34/B4 Hartland (pt.), Eng,UK
34/D2 Hartlebury, Eng,UK
33/G2 Hartlepool, Eng,UK
31/P7 Hartley, Eng,UK
107/H3 Hartney, Mb,Can
88/D3 Harts (riv.), SAfr.
115/G4 Hartsdale, NY,US
113/G3 Hartselle, Al,US
35/E1 Hartshill, Eng,UK
116/B3 Hartstene (isl.), Wa,US
113/H3 Hartwell, Ga,US
113/H3 Hartwell (lake), Ga, SC,US
77/C4 Hartz Mtn. Nat'l Park, Austl.
43/G6 Hartzviller, Fr.
61/K3 Hārūnābād, Pak.
73/E3 Harun, Bukit (peak), Indo.
68/F2 Har Us (lake), Mong.
62/D2 Har-Us (riv.), Mong.
61/H2 Hārūt (riv.), Afg.
116/Q16 Harvey, Il,US
107/J4 Harvey, ND,US
35/H3 Harwich, Eng,UK
33/G5 Harworth, Eng,UK
70/C2 Haryana (state), India
41/H5 Harz (mts.), Ger.
41/E3 Hase (riv.), Ger.
41/E3 Haselünne, Ger.
65/M9 Hashima, Japan
64/D3 Hashimoto, Japan
82/D2 Hasi el Farsía (well), WSah.
61/K3 Hāsilpur, Pak.
112/D3 Haskell, Tx,US
35/F4 Haslemere, Eng,UK
33/F4 Haslingden, Eng,UK
33/F5 Haslington, Eng,UK
70/C5 Hassan, India
103/S7 Hassel (sound), NW,Can
43/E2 Hasselt, Belg.
40/D3 Hasselt, Neth.
45/H1 Hassfurt, Ger.
81/S16 Hassi Bahbah, Alg.
82/G1 Hassi Messaoud, Alg.
37/E4 Hässleholm, Swe.
75/S10 Hastings, NZ
35/G5 Hastings, Eng,UK
110/C3 Hastings, Mi,US
107/K4 Hastings, Mn,US
109/H2 Hastings, Ne,US
115/G4 Hastings-on-Hudson, NY,US
65/H7 Hasuda, Japan
81/W18 Ḩaţab (riv.), Tun.
65/M9 Hatashō, Japan
115/E5 Hatboro, Pa,US
108/F4 Hatch, NM,US
69/B5 Hat Chao Mai Nat'l Park, Thai.
97/J7 Hatcher (peak), Arg.
50/F3 Haţeg, Rom.
31/N6 Hatfield, Eng,UK
77/E1 Hat Head Nat'l Park, Austl.
33/G5 Hathersage, Eng,UK
70/C2 Hāthras, India
60/C4 Ḩāţibah, Ra's (pt.), SAr.
69/D4 Ha Tien, Viet.
69/D2 Ha Tinh, Viet.
69/B5 Hat Nai Yang Nat'l Park, Thai.
65/H7 Hatogaya, Japan
101/H4 Hato Mayor, DRep.
65/H7 Hatoyama, Japan
70/C3 Hatta, India
77/B2 Hattah-Kulkyne Nat'l Park, Austl.
40/D4 Hattem, Neth.
47/F2 Hatten, Ger.
113/K3 Hatteras (cape), NC,US
113/F4 Hattiesburg, Ms,US
41/E6 Hattingen, Ger.
33/G6 Hatton, Eng,UK
50/D2 Hatvan, Hun.
69/C5 Hat Yai, Thai.
69/E3 Hau Bon, Viet.
42/B2 Haubourdin, Fr.
83/Q6 Haud (reg.), Eth., Som.
37/C4 Haugesund, Nor.
69/D4 Hau Giang (riv.), Viet.
37/H2 Haukipudas, Fin.
115/G5 Hauppauge, NY,US
75/S10 Hauraki (gulf), NZ
47/E1 Hauskoa (mtn.), Fr.
82/D1 Haut Atlas (mts.), Mor.
44/D2 Haute-Normandie (reg.), Fr.
111/G1 Hauterive, Qu,Can
43/E3 Hautes Fagnes (uplands), Belg.
42/C3 Hautmont, Fr.
31/S10 Hauts-de-Seine (dept.), Fr.
100/E3 Havana (La Habana) (cap.), Cuba
79/V13 Havannah (chan.), NCal.
35/F5 Havant, Eng,UK
108/D4 Havasu (lake), Az, Ca,US
39/G2 Havel (riv.), Ger.
38/G2 Havelland (reg.), Ger.
113/J3 Havelock, NC,US
75/S10 Havelock North, NZ
35/G3 Havengore (isl.), Eng,UK
34/B3 Haverfordwest, Wal,UK
35/G2 Haverhill, Eng,UK
111/G3 Haverhill, Ma,US
31/P7 Havering (bor.), Eng,UK
39/K4 Havířov, Czh.
41/E5 Havixbeck, Ger.
39/H4 Havlíčkuv Brod, Czh.
106/F3 Havre, Mt,US
111/J1 Havre-Saint-Pierre, Qu,Can
51/H5 Havsa, Turk.
104/S10 Hawaii (state), US
104/U11 Hawaii (isl.), Hi,US
79/H2 Hawaiian (isls.), Hi,US
104/U11 Hawaii Volcanoes Nat'l Park, Hi,US
60/E3 Ḩawallī, Kuw.
33/E5 Hawarden, Wal,UK
107/J5 Hawarden, Ia,US
75/R10 Hawera, NZ
33/F3 Hawes, Eng,UK
33/F2 Haweswater (res.), Eng,UK
36/D3 Hawick, Sc,UK
77/E2 Hawke (cape), Austl.
75/S10 Hawke (bay), NZ
76/G8 Hawkesbury (riv.), Austl.
106/A2 Hawkesbury (isl.), BC,Can
110/F2 Hawkesbury, On,Can
60/E2 Hawr al Ḩammār (lake), Iraq
59/H6 Ḩawsh 'Īsá, Egypt
115/B3 Hawthorne, Ca,US
108/C3 Hawthorne, Nv,US
33/G3 Haxby, Eng,UK
76/C3 Hay (pt.), Austl.
102/E3 Hay (riv.), Ab, NW,Can
65/H7 Hayama, Japan
43/F5 Hayange, Fr.
33/F5 Haydock, Eng,UK
33/F2 Haydon Bridge, Eng,UK
102/G3 Hayes (riv.), Mb,Can
102/G2 Hayes (riv.), NW,Can
103/T7 Hayes (pen.), Grld.
31/M7 Hayes, Eng,UK
114/J3 Hayes (mtn.), Ak,US
34/A6 Hayle, Eng,UK
34/A6 Hayle (riv.), Eng,UK
35/F5 Hayling (isl.), Eng,UK
112/E3 Haynesville, La,US
34/C2 Hay on Wye, Wal,UK
51/H5 Hayrabolu, Turk.

109/H3 **Hays**, Ks,US
109/H3 **Haysville**, Ks,US
116/K11 **Hayward**, Ca,US
110/B2 **Hayward**, Wi,US
35/F5 **Haywards Heath**, Eng,UK
61/G3 **Hazār** (mtn.), Iran
110/D4 **Hazard**, Ky,US
70/E3 **Hazāribag**, India
42/B2 **Hazebrouck**, Fr.
33/F5 **Hazel Grove**, Eng,UK
116/F7 **Hazel Park**, Mi,US
103/R7 **Hazen** (str.), NW,Can
114/E3 **Hazen** (bay), Ak,US
40/B4 **Hazerswoude-Dorp**, Neth.
113/F4 **Hazlehurst**, Ms,US
35/F3 **Hazlemere**, Eng,UK
115/F5 **Hazlet**, NJ,US
106/B2 **Hazleton** (mts.), BC,Can
110/F3 **Hazleton**, Pa,US
65/N10 **Hazu**, Japan
35/G1 **Heacham**, Eng,UK
35/G4 **Headcorn**, Eng,UK
33/G4 **Headingley**, Eng,UK
108/B3 **Healdsburg**, Ca,US
77/G5 **Healesville**, Austl.
33/G6 **Heanor**, Eng,UK
29/R8 **Heard** (isl.), Austl.
112/D4 **Hearne**, Tx,US
98/V **Hearst** (isl.), Ant.
110/D1 **Hearst**, On,Can
107/H4 **Heart** (riv.), ND,US
111/J1 **Heath** (pt.), Qu,Can
76/G9 **Heathcote Nat'l Park**, Austl.
35/G5 **Heathfield**, Eng,UK
112/D5 **Hebbronville**, Tx,US
33/F4 **Hebden Bridge**, Eng,UK
66/G6 **Hebei** (prov.), China
112/E3 **Heber Springs**, Ar,US
66/C4 **Hebi**, China
30/C3 **Hebrides** (isls.), Sc,UK
36/A2 **Hebrides, Outer** (isls.), Sc,UK
109/H2 **Hebron**, Ne,US
59/K6 **Hebron** (Al Khalīl), WBnk.
114/M5 **Hecate** (str.), BC,Can
71/J3 **Hechi**, China
43/E1 **Hechtel**, Belg.
33/H6 **Heckington**, Eng,UK
107/J4 **Hecla**, SD,US
103/R7 **Hecla and Griper** (bay), NW,Can
106/D3 **Hector** (peak), Ab,Can
37/E3 **Hedemora**, Swe.
37/D3 **Hedmark** (co.), Nor.
33/H4 **Hedon**, Eng,UK
41/E4 **Heek**, Ger.
40/B3 **Heemskerk**, Neth.
40/B4 **Heemstede**, Neth.
40/D4 **Heerde**, Neth.
40/C3 **Heerenveen**, Neth.
40/B3 **Heerhugowaard**, Neth.
43/E2 **Heerlen**, Neth.
43/E2 **Heers**, Belg.
40/C5 **Heesch**, Neth.
40/C6 **Heeze**, Neth.
59/K5 **Ḥefa** (Haifa), Isr.
66/D5 **Hefei**, China
63/L2 **Hegang**, China
45/H3 **Hegau** (reg.), Ger.
65/L10 **Heguri**, Japan
62/D4 **Hei** (riv.), China
66/B3 **Heicha Shan** (mtn.), China
38/E1 **Heide**, Ger.
77/G5 **Heidelberg**, Austl.
45/H2 **Heidelberg**, Ger.
89/E2 **Heidelberg**, SAfr.
113/F4 **Heidelberg**, Ms,US
40/D5 **Heiden**, Ger.
63/K1 **Heihe**, China
38/F1 **Heikendorf**, Ger.
88/D2 **Heilbron**, SAfr.
45/H2 **Heilbronn**, Ger.
38/F1 **Heiligenhafen**, Ger.
40/D6 **Heiligenhaus**, Ger.
41/H6 **Heiligenstadt**, Ger.
63/L2 **Heilong (Amur)** (riv.), China
40/B3 **Heiloo**, Neth.
37/N7 **Heimaey** (isl.), Ice.
40/D4 **Heino**, Neth.
37/H3 **Heinola**, Fin.
40/D6 **Heinsberg**, Ger.
66/C3 **Heituo Shan** (mtn.), China
65/M9 **Heiwa**, Japan
66/D3 **Hejian**, China
59/D2 **Hekimhan**, Turk.
65/M10 **Hekinan**, Japan
37/N7 **Hekla** (vol.), Ice.
62/F4 **Helan** (mts.), China
40/D6 **Helden**, Neth.
113/F3 **Helena**, Ar,US
106/E4 **Helena** (cap.), Mt,US
38/D1 **Helgoland** (isl.), Ger.
38/D1 **Helgoländer Bucht** (bay), Ger.
60/F3 **Helleh** (riv.), Iran
40/D4 **Hellendoorn**, Neth.
43/F3 **Hellenthal**, Ger.
40/B5 **Hellevoetsluis**, Neth.
46/E3 **Hellín**, Sp.
106/D4 **Hells Canyon Nat'l Rec. Area**, Id, Or,US
61/H2 **Helmand** (riv.), Afg.
38/F3 **Helme** (riv.), Ger.
114/K2 **Helmet** (mtn.), Ak,US
40/C6 **Helmond**, Neth.
33/G3 **Helmsley**, Eng,UK
38/F2 **Helmstedt**, Ger.
108/E3 **Helper**, Ut,US
33/F5 **Helsby**, Eng,UK
37/E4 **Helsingør**, Den.
37/H3 **Helsinki** (Helsingfors) (cap.), Fin.
34/A6 **Helston**, Eng,UK
37/G3 **Helvetinjärven Nat'l Park**, Fin.
42/C2 **Hem**, Fr.
42/B2 **Hem** (riv.), Fr.
31/M6 **Hemel Hempstead**, Eng,UK
41/E6 **Hemer**, Ger.
115/D3 **Hemet**, Ca,US
41/G4 **Hemmingen**, Ger.
41/G1 **Hemmoor**, Ger.
112/E4 **Hemphill**, Tx,US
115/G5 **Hempstead**, NY,US
35/H1 **Hemsby**, Eng,UK
33/G4 **Hemsworth**, Eng,UK
66/B4 **Henan** (prov.), China
46/D2 **Henares** (riv.), Sp.
44/C5 **Hendaye**, Fr.
51/K5 **Hendek**, Turk.
96/E3 **Henderson**, Arg.
79/N7 **Henderson** (isl.), Pitc.
110/C4 **Henderson**, Ky,US
113/J2 **Henderson**, NC,US
108/D3 **Henderson**, Nv,US
113/F3 **Henderson**, Tn,US
112/E3 **Henderson**, Tx,US
113/H3 **Hendersonville**, NC,US
113/G2 **Hendersonville**, Tn,US
31/N7 **Hendon**, Eng,UK
40/B5 **Hendrik-Ido-Ambacht**, Neth.
88/D3 **Hendrik Verwoerdam** (res.), SAfr.
35/F5 **Henfield**, Eng,UK
66/L8 **Heng** (isl.), China
71/G2 **Hengduan** (mts.), China
40/D4 **Hengelo**, Neth.
66/C3 **Heng Shan** (mtn.), China
66/C3 **Hengshui**, China
67/B2 **Hengyang**, China
42/B3 **Hénin-Beaumont**, Fr.
35/E2 **Henley-in-Arden**, Eng,UK
35/F3 **Henley-on-Thames**, Eng,UK
44/B3 **Hennebont**, Fr.
43/G2 **Hennef**, Ger.
43/E2 **Henri-Chapelle**, Belg.
112/D3 **Henrietta**, Tx,US
103/H3 **Henrietta Maria** (cape), On,Can
114/M5 **Henry** (cape), BC,Can
108/E3 **Henry** (mts.), Ut,US
109/J4 **Henryetta**, Ok,US
42/C3 **Hensies**, Belg.
62/F2 **Hentiyn** (mts.), Mong.
71/G4 **Henzada**, Burma
37/N6 **Heradhsvötn** (riv.), Ice.
61/H2 **Herāt**, Afg.
47/G1 **Hérault** (riv.), Fr.
76/B2 **Herbert** (riv.), Austl.
106/G3 **Herbert**, Sk,Can
76/B2 **Herbert Riv. Falls Nat'l Park**, Austl.
31/S10 **Herblay**, Fr.
50/D4 **Hercegnovi**, Yugo.
116/K10 **Hercules**, Ca,US
41/E6 **Herdecke**, Ger.
43/G2 **Herdorf**, Ger.
100/E6 **Heredia**, CR
34/D2 **Hereford**, Eng,UK
112/C3 **Hereford**, Tx,US
34/D2 **Hereford & Worcester** (co.), Eng,UK
79/L6 **Hereheretue** (isl.), FrPol.
51/J5 **Hereke**, Turk.
46/C3 **Herencia**, Sp.
43/D1 **Herentals**, Belg.
41/F4 **Herford**, Ger.
109/H3 **Herington**, Ks,US
45/H3 **Herisau**, Swi.
43/E2 **Herk** (riv.), Belg.
43/E2 **Herk-de-Stad**, Belg.
62/G2 **Herlen** (riv.), Mong.
113/F2 **Hermann**, Mo,US
41/H3 **Hermannsburg**, Ger.
42/B5 **Hermes**, Fr.
106/D4 **Hermiston**, Or,US
59/K5 **Hermon** (mtn.), Leb., Syria
115/B3 **Hermosa Beach**, Ca,US
101/M8 **Hermosillo**, Mex.
96/E2 **Hernando**, Arg.
113/F3 **Hernando**, Ms,US
46/E1 **Hernani**, Sp.
42/D2 **Herne**, Belg.
41/E5 **Herne**, Ger.
35/H4 **Herne Bay**, Eng,UK
37/D4 **Herning**, Den.
59/N9 **Herodian** (ruins), WBnk.
59/N9 **Herodion Nat'l Park**, WBnk.
101/M7 **Heroica Caborca**, Mex.
101/M7 **Heroica Nogales**, Mex.
100/D4 **Herrero** (pt.), Mex.
44/D5 **Hers** (riv.), Fr.
41/E6 **Herscheid**, Ger.
114/L2 **Herschel**, Yk,Can
43/D1 **Herselt**, Belg.
43/E2 **Herstal**, Belg.
35/G5 **Herstmonceux**, Eng,UK
41/E5 **Herten**, Ger.
35/F3 **Hertford**, Eng,UK
31/N6 **Hertfordshire** (co.), Eng,UK
43/E2 **Herve**, Belg.
76/D4 **Hervey Bay**, Austl.
41/H5 **Herzberg am Harz**, Ger.
41/F5 **Herzebrock-Clarholz**, Ger.
42/C2 **Herzele**, Belg.
59/M8 **Herzliyya**, Isr.
45/J2 **Herzogenaurach**, Ger.
50/B1 **Herzogenburg**, Aus.
43/F2 **Herzogenrath**, Ger.
43/D3 **Hesbaye** (plat.), Belg.
71/J3 **Heshan**, China
43/F4 **Hesperange**, Lux.
115/C2 **Hesperia**, Ca,US
114/M3 **Hess** (riv.), Yk,Can
41/G6 **Hesse** (state), Ger.
41/F5 **Hessel** (riv.), Ger.
41/G6 **Hessisch Lichtenau**, Ger.
41/G4 **Hessisch Oldendorf**, Ger.
33/H4 **Hessle**, Eng,UK
33/E5 **Heswall**, Eng,UK
107/H4 **Hettinger**, ND,US
33/G2 **Hetton-le-Hole**, Eng,UK
41/E5 **Heubach** (riv.), Ger.
39/H5 **Heukuppe** (peak), Aus.
43/E1 **Heusden-Zolder**, Belg.
43/F5 **Heusweiler**, Ger.
44/D2 **Hève, Cap de la** (cape), Fr.
50/E2 **Heves**, Hun.
39/L5 **Heves** (co.), Hun.
115/G5 **Hewlett** (pt.), NY,US
33/F2 **Hexham**, Eng,UK
63/H3 **Hexigten Qi**, China
88/L10 **Hex River** (mts.), SAfr.
88/L10 **Hex River** (pass), SAfr.
33/F3 **Heysham**, Eng,UK
40/C6 **Heythuysen**, Neth.
33/F4 **Heywood**, Eng,UK
66/C4 **Heze**, China
113/H5 **Hialeah**, Fl,US
109/J3 **Hiawatha**, Ks,US
107/K4 **Hibbing**, Mn,US
77/C4 **Hibbs** (pt.), Austl.
114/M4 **Hickman** (mtn.), BC,Can
110/B4 **Hickman**, Ky,US
113/H3 **Hickory**, NC,US
115/G5 **Hicksville**, NY,US
65/E3 **Hida** (riv.), Japan
65/H7 **Hidaka**, Japan
64/D4 **Hidaka** (riv.), Japan
100/B3 **Hidalgo** (state), Mex.
101/N8 **Hidalgo del Parral**, Mex.
41/F4 **Hiddenhausen**, Ger.
47/W17 **Hierro** (isl.), Canl.
41/E2 **Hieve** (lake), Ger.
65/H7 **Higashikurume**, Japan
65/H7 **Higashimurayama**, Japan
65/G1 **Higashine**, Japan
65/L10 **Higashi-Ōsaka**, Japan
65/K10 **Higashiura**, Japan
65/H7 **Higashiyamato**, Japan
106/C5 **High** (des.), Or,US
35/F2 **Higham Ferrers**, Eng,UK
34/D4 **Highbridge**, Eng,UK
115/F5 **High Bridge**, NJ,US
112/E4 **High Island**, Tx,US
115/C2 **Highland**, Ca,US
116/R18 **Highland**, In,US
116/Q15 **Highland Park**, Il,US
116/F7 **Highland Park**, Mi,US
115/F5 **Highland Park**, NJ,US
34/D2 **Highley**, Eng,UK
107/J4 **Highmore**, SD,US
113/H3 **High Point**, NC,US
106/D2 **High Prairie**, Ab,Can
107/H2 **Highrock** (lake), Mb,Can
33/F3 **High Street** (mtn.), Eng,UK
33/E4 **Hightown**, Eng,UK
115/F5 **Hightstown**, NJ,US
34/B5 **High Willhays** (hill), Eng,UK
35/E3 **Highworth**, Eng,UK
35/F3 **High Wycombe**, Eng,UK
101/H4 **Higüey**, DRep.
59/H6 **Hihyā**, Egypt
37/J3 **Hiidenportin Nat'l Park**, Fin.
52/D4 **Hiiumaa** (isl.), Est.
60/C3 **Hijāz, Jabal al** (mts.), SAr.
64/B4 **Hiji**, Japan
96/Q9 **Hijuelas de Conchali**, Chile
65/L9 **Hikami**, Japan
64/E3 **Hikone**, Japan
79/L6 **Hikueru** (atoll), FrPol.
75/S10 **Hikurangi** (peak), NZ
43/H2 **Hilchenbach**, Ger.
45/J1 **Hildburghausen**, Ger.
40/D6 **Hilden**, Ger.
41/G4 **Hildesheim**, Ger.
98/L **Hillary** (coast), Ant.
109/H3 **Hill City**, Ks,US
115/F4 **Hillcrest**, NY,US
41/F4 **Hille**, Ger.
40/B4 **Hillegom**, Neth.
37/E5 **Hillerød**, Den.
32/B2 **Hillhall**, NI,UK
31/M7 **Hillingdon** (bor.), Eng,UK
36/D2 **Hill of Fearn**, Sc,UK
107/J4 **Hillsboro**, ND,US
108/F4 **Hillsboro**, NM,US
110/D4 **Hillsboro**, Oh,US
106/C4 **Hillsboro**, Or,US
112/D3 **Hillsboro**, Tx,US
76/C3 **Hillsborough** (chan.), Austl.
32/B3 **Hillsborough**, NI,UK
116/K11 **Hillsborough**, Ca,US
115/F5 **Hillsborough**, NJ,US
110/C3 **Hillsdale**, Mi,US
115/F5 **Hillside**, NJ,US
32/B3 **Hilltown**, NI,UK
104/U11 **Hilo**, Hi,US
67/D5 **Hilongos**, Phil.
33/E3 **Hilpsford** (pt.), Eng,UK
113/H3 **Hilton Head Island**, SC,US
40/C6 **Hilvarenbeek**, Neth.
40/C4 **Hilversum**, Neth.
68/C5 **Himachal Pradesh** (state), India
70/D2 **Himalaya, Great** (range), Asia
67/D5 **Himamaylan**, Phil.
64/D3 **Himeji**, Japan
65/E2 **Himi**, Japan
83/N5 **Himora**, Eth.
59/L4 **Ḥimṣ**, Syria
114/J3 **Hinchinbrook** (chan.), Ak,US
76/B2 **Hinchinbrook I. Nat'l Park**, Austl.
35/E1 **Hinckley**, Eng,UK
33/H2 **Hinderwell**, Eng,UK
33/F4 **Hindley**, Eng,UK
77/B2 **Hindmarsh** (lake), Austl.
61/J1 **Hindu Kush** (mts.), Afg., Pak.
70/C5 **Hindupur**, India
113/H4 **Hinesville**, Ga,US
70/C3 **Hinganghāt**, India
61/J3 **Hingol** (riv.), Pak.
70/C4 **Hingoli**, India
61/J3 **Hingorja**, Pak.
59/E2 **Hınıs**, Turk.
65/H7 **Hino**, Japan
65/M9 **Hino** (riv.), Japan
65/H7 **Hinode**, Japan
46/C3 **Hinojosa del Duque**, Sp.
64/C3 **Hino-misaki** (cape), Japan
116/Q16 **Hinsdale**, Il,US
33/F6 **Hinstock**, Eng,UK
41/E2 **Hinte**, Ger.
106/D2 **Hinton**, Ab,Can
110/D4 **Hinton**, WV,US
40/B3 **Hippolytushoef**, Neth.
33/G3 **Hipswell**, Eng,UK
65/L9 **Hira** (mts.), Japan
64/A4 **Hirado**, Japan
64/D3 **Hirakata**, Japan
70/D3 **Hirakud** (res.), India
64/C3 **Hirata**, Japan
65/H7 **Hiratsuka**, Japan
51/H2 **Hîrlău**, Rom.
63/N3 **Hirosaki**, Japan
64/C3 **Hiroshima**, Japan
64/C3 **Hiroshima** (pref.), Japan
45/J2 **Hirschau**, Ger.
42/D4 **Hirson**, Fr.
51/H3 **Hîrşova**, Rom.
37/D4 **Hirtshals**, Den.
34/C3 **Hirwaun**, Wal,UK
64/E3 **Hisai**, Japan
70/C2 **Hisār**, India
62/E2 **Hishig-Öndör**, Mong.
101/G4 **Hispaniola** (isl.), DRep., Haiti
65/G2 **Hitachi**, Japan
65/G2 **Hitachi-ōta**, Japan
35/F3 **Hitchin**, Eng,UK
64/B4 **Hitoyoshi**, Japan
37/C3 **Hitra** (isl.), Nor.
79/M5 **Hiva Oa** (isl.), FrPol.
52/B2 **Hjartfjellet** (peak), Nor.
69/B1 **Hka** (riv.), Burma
71/G2 **Hkakabo** (peak), Burma
39/J4 **Hlohovec**, Slvk.
76/G8 **Hmas-Nirimba**, Austl.
71/G4 **Hmawbi**, Burma
85/F5 **Ho**, Gha.
69/D1 **Hoa Bin**, Viet.
69/E4 **Hoa Da**, Viet.
69/C1 **Hoang Lien** (mts.), Viet.
103/K2 **Hoare** (bay), NW,Can
65/G2 **Hobara**, Japan
77/C4 **Hobart**, Austl.
109/H4 **Hobart**, Ok,US
98/Q **Hobbs** (coast), Ant.
109/G4 **Hobbs**, NM,US
42/D1 **Hoboken**, Belg.
115/F5 **Hoboken**, NJ,US
83/Q6 **Hobyo**, Som.
50/A2 **Hochalmspitze** (peak), Aus.
69/D4 **Ho Chi Minh City** (Saigon), Viet.
45/K3 **Hochkönig** (peak), Aus.
45/L3 **Hochschwab** (peak), Aus.
43/G3 **Hochsimmer** (peak), Ger.
35/G3 **Hockley**, Eng,UK
33/F4 **Hodder** (riv.), Eng,UK
31/N6 **Hoddesdon**, Eng,UK
106/G3 **Hodgeville**, Sk,Can
84/C2 **Hodh** (reg.), Mrta.
59/M8 **Hod HaSharon**, Isr.
84/D2 **Hodh ech Chargui** (reg.), Mrta.
84/C2 **Hodh el Gharbi** (reg.), Mrta.
50/E2 **Hódmezővásárhely**, Hun.
81/T16 **Hodna, Chott el** (salt lake), Alg.
33/F6 **Hodnet**, Eng,UK
39/J4 **Hodonín**, Czh.
43/E2 **Hoegnel** (riv.), Belg.
40/B5 **Hoekse Waard** (polder), Neth.
43/G6 **Hoenheim**, Fr.
43/E2 **Hoensbroek**, Neth.
43/E2 **Hoeselt**, Belg.
40/C4 **Hoevelaken**, Neth.
40/B5 **Hoeven**, Neth.
45/J1 **Hof**, Ger.
116/P15 **Hoffman Estates**, Il,US
41/G6 **Hofgeismar**, Ger.
66/B3 **Hofong Qagan** (salt lake), China
37/P6 **Hofsá** (riv.), Ice.
37/N7 **Hofsjökull** (glac.), Ice.
64/B3 **Hōfu**, Japan
40/C4 **Hoge Veluwe Nat'l Park**, Neth.
41/G6 **Hohegrass** (peak), Ger.
45/H3 **Hohenems**, Aus.
41/H4 **Hohenhameln**, Ger.
45/H2 **Hohenloher Ebene** (plain), Ger.
45/K3 **Hoher Dachstein** (peak), Aus.
45/K3 **Hohe Tauern** (mts.), Aus.
45/K3 **Hohe Tauern Nat'l Park**, Aus.
66/B2 **Hohhot**, China
45/G2 **Hohneck** (mtn.), Fr.
43/G3 **Höhr-Grenzhausen**, Ger.
68/F4 **Hoh Sai** (lake), China
68/F4 **Hoh Xil** (lake), China
68/E4 **Hoh Xil** (mts.), China
69/E3 **Hoi An**, Viet.
112/D2 **Hoisington**, Ks,US
69/D1 **Hoi Xuan**, Viet.
64/C4 **Hōjō**, Japan
75/R11 **Hokitika**, NZ
63/N3 **Hokkaidō** (isl.), Japan
65/G2 **Hokota**, Japan
65/K10 **Hokudan**, Japan
65/M9 **Hokusei**, Japan
33/J6 **Holbeach**, Eng,UK
35/H3 **Holbrook**, Eng,UK
108/E4 **Holbrook**, Az,US
109/H4 **Holdenville**, Ok,US
33/H4 **Holderness** (pen.), Eng,UK
109/H2 **Holdrege**, Ne,US
101/F3 **Holguín**, Cuba
114/G3 **Holitna** (riv.), Ak,US
110/C3 **Holland**, Mi,US
113/F3 **Hollandale**, Ms,US
40/B4 **Hollandse IJssel** (riv.), Neth.
35/H2 **Hollesley**, Eng,UK
109/H4 **Hollis**, Ok,US
108/B3 **Hollister**, Ca,US
43/E2 **Hollogne-aux-Pierres**, Belg.
37/H3 **Hollola**, Fin.
113/F3 **Holly Springs**, Ms,US
113/H5 **Hollywood**, Fl,US
37/F3 **Holm**, Swe.
102/E1 **Holman**, NW,Can
115/F5 **Holmdel**, NJ,US
76/C2 **Holmes** (reefs), Austl.
106/F4 **Holmes** (peak), Wy,US
33/F5 **Holmes Chapel**, Eng,UK
31/N8 **Holmesdale** (val.), Eng,UK
33/H4 **Holme upon Spalding Moor**, Eng,UK
33/G4 **Holmfirth**, Eng,UK
98/C **Holm-Lützow** (bay), Ant.
37/F3 **Holmsjön** (lake), Swe.
59/K5 **Ḥolon**, Isr.
37/D4 **Holstebro**, Den.
113/H2 **Holston** (riv.), Tn,US
34/B5 **Holsworthy**, Eng,UK
35/H1 **Holt**, Eng,UK
40/D4 **Holten**, Neth.
109/J3 **Holton**, Ks,US
115/G5 **Holtsville**, NY,US
32/D5 **Holy** (isl.), Wal,UK
32/D5 **Holyhead**, Wal,UK
32/D5 **Holyhead** (mtn.), Wal,UK
36/E3 **Holy (Lindisfarne)** (isl.), Eng,UK
109/G2 **Holyoke**, Co,US
111/F3 **Holyoke**, Ma,US
33/E5 **Holywell**, Wal,UK
32/C2 **Holywood**, NI,UK
38/F5 **Holzkirchen**, Ger.
41/G5 **Holzminden**, Ger.
41/E6 **Holzwickede**, Ger.
88/B3 **Hom** (dry riv.), Namb.
40/D6 **Homberg**, Ger.
41/G6 **Homberg**, Ger.
85/E3 **Hombori Tondo** (peak), Mali
43/F5 **Hombourg-Haut**, Fr.
43/G5 **Homburg**, Ger.
103/K2 **Home** (bay), NW,Can
43/E5 **Homécourt**, Fr.
112/E3 **Homer**, La,US
113/H5 **Homestead**, Fl,US
113/G3 **Homewood**, Al,US
116/Q16 **Homewood**, Il,US
113/F4 **Homochitto** (riv.), Ms,US
70/B5 **Honāvar**, India
69/D4 **Hon Chong**, Viet.
34/C3 **Honddu** (riv.), Wal,UK
64/B4 **Hondo**, Japan
109/F4 **Hondo** (dry riv.), NM,US
112/D4 **Hondo**, Tx,US
40/D3 **Hondsrug** (reg.), Neth.
100/D4 **Honduras**
100/D4 **Honduras** (gulf), NAm.
108/B2 **Honey** (lake), Ca,US
35/E2 **Honeybourne**, Eng,UK
66/C5 **Hong** (lake), China
66/C4 **Hong** (riv.), China
71/J2 **Hongdu** (riv.), China
69/D1 **Hong Gai**, Viet.
66/C5 **Honghu**, China
71/J2 **Hongjiang**, China
67/B3 **Hong Kong** (dpcy.), UK
66/B3 **Hongliu** (riv.), China
69/C1 **Hong (Red)** (riv.), Viet.
71/J3 **Hongshui** (riv.), China
66/C3 **Hongtao Shan** (mtn.), China
111/H1 **Honguedo** (passg.), Qu,Can
66/D4 **Hongze** (lake), China
78/E5 **Honiara** (cap.), Sol.
34/C5 **Honiton**, Eng,UK
104/T10 **Honolulu** (cap.), Hi,US
69/D4 **Hon Quan**, Viet.
63/M5 **Honshu** (isl.), Japan
74/B6 **Hood** (pt.), Austl.
116/J10 **Hood** (mt.), Ca,US
106/C4 **Hood** (mt.), Or,US
106/C4 **Hood Canal** (inlet), Wa,US
40/B4 **Hoofddorp**, Neth.
40/C6 **Hoogeloon**, Neth.
40/B6 **Hoogerheide**, Neth.
40/D3 **Hoogeveen**, Neth.
40/D3 **Hoogeveensche Vaart** (can.), Neth.
40/D2 **Hoogezand**, Neth.
70/E3 **Hooghly-Chinsura**, India
42/C2 **Hooglede**, Belg.
40/B6 **Hoogstraten**, Belg.
76/C3 **Hook** (isl.), Austl.
35/F4 **Hook**, Eng,UK
36/B4 **Hook Head** (pt.), Ire.
110/C3 **Hoopeston**, Il,US
40/C3 **Hoorn**, Neth.
40/C3 **Hoornse Hop** (bay), Neth.
108/D3 **Hoover** (dam), Az,US
59/E2 **Hopa**, Turk.
115/F5 **Hopatcong**, NJ,US
115/F5 **Hopatcong** (lake), NJ,US
74/C6 **Hope** (lake), Austl.
106/C3 **Hope**, BC,Can
33/E5 **Hope**, Wal,UK
112/E3 **Hope**, Ar,US
103/K2 **Hopes Advance** (cape), Qu,Can
34/C6 **Hope's Nose** (pt.), Eng,UK
34/D2 **Hope under Dinmore**, Eng,UK
115/F5 **Hopewell**, NJ,US
110/E4 **Hopewell**, Va,US
74/D4 **Hopkins** (lake), Austl.
77/B3 **Hopkins** (riv.), Austl.
110/C4 **Hopkinsville**, Ky,US
41/F6 **Hoppecke** (riv.), Ger.
41/E4 **Hopsten**, Ger.
106/C4 **Hoquiam**, Wa,US
114/J2 **Horace** (mtn.), Ak,US
65/L9 **Hōrai-san** (peak), Japan
59/E2 **Horasan**, Turk.
59/K5 **Ḥorbat Qesari** (ruins), Isr.
33/G4 **Horbury**, Eng,UK
37/C3 **Hordaland** (co.), Nor.
33/G2 **Horden**, Eng,UK
51/G3 **Horezu**, Rom.
62/F3 **Hörh** (peak), Mong.
29/S6 **Horiara** (cap.), Sol.
31/N8 **Horley**, Eng,UK
45/L2 **Horn**, Aus.
37/M6 **Horn** (pt.), Ice.
39/L4 **Hornád** (riv.), Slvk.
37/E2 **Hornavan** (lake), Swe.
41/F5 **Horn-Bad Meinberg**, Ger.
111/Q8 **Hornby**, On,Can
33/H5 **Horncastle**, Eng,UK
31/P7 **Hornchurch**, Eng,UK
110/E3 **Hornell**, NY,US
110/C1 **Hornepayne**, On,Can
97/L8 **Horn (Hornos)** (cape), Chile
97/L8 **Hornos Nat'l Park, Cabo de**, Chile
42/A4 **Hornoy-le-Bourg**, Fr.
76/H8 **Hornsby**, Austl.
33/H4 **Hornsea**, Eng,UK
38/E1 **Hornum Odde** (cape), Ger.
63/N3 **Horoshiri-dake** (mtn.), Japan
34/B6 **Horrabridge**, Eng,UK
109/F2 **Horse** (cr.), Ne, Wy,US
110/C4 **Horse Cave**, Ky,US
106/C2 **Horsefly** (lake), BC,Can
37/D5 **Horsens**, Den.
35/H3 **Horsey** (isl.), Eng,UK
33/G4 **Horsforth**, Eng,UK
77/B3 **Horsham**, Austl.
35/F4 **Horsham**, Eng,UK
115/E5 **Horsham**, Pa,US
40/D6 **Horst**, Neth.
41/E4 **Hörstel**, Ger.
41/E4 **Horstmar**, Ger.
47/S12 **Horta**, Azor.,Port.
47/N9 **Hortaleza**, Sp.
50/E2 **Hortobágyi Nat'l Park**, Hun.
114/N2 **Horton** (riv.), NW,Can
31/P7 **Horton Kirby**, Eng,UK
59/K6 **Ḥorvot 'Avedat** (ruins), Isr.
59/K6 **Ḥorvot Meẓada** (Masada) (ruins), Isr.
33/F4 **Horwich**, Eng,UK
110/D2 **Horwood** (lake), On,Can
70/C3 **Hoshangābād**, India
70/C4 **Hospet**, India
97/K8 **Hoste** (isl.), Chile
65/E2 **Hotaka**, Japan
65/E2 **Hotaka-dake** (mtn.), Japan
68/D4 **Hotan** (riv.), China
107/H5 **Hot Springs**, SD,US
112/E3 **Hot Springs Nat'l Park**, Ar,US
102/E2 **Hottah** (lake), NW,Can
88/A2 **Hottentot** (bay), Namb.
88/A2 **Hottentots** (pt.), Namb.
42/B3 **Houdain**, Fr.
84/D4 **Houet** (prov.), Burk.
110/B2 **Houghton**, Mi,US
110/C2 **Houghton Lake**, Mi,US
33/G2 **Houghton-le-Spring**, Eng,UK
31/S10 **Houilles**, Fr.
111/H2 **Houlton**, Me,US
66/B4 **Houma**, China
113/F4 **Houma**, La,US
31/M7 **Hounslow** (bor.), Eng,UK
42/B2 **Houplines**, Fr.
42/A3 **Hourdel, Pointe du** (pt.), Fr.
108/D3 **House** (range), Ut,US
106/B2 **Houston**, BC,Can
109/K3 **Houston**, Mo,US
113/F3 **Houston**, Ms,US
112/E4 **Houston**, Tx,US
40/C4 **Houten**, Neth.
42/B2 **Houthulst**, Belg.
74/A5 **Houtman Abrolhos** (isls.), Austl.
40/C3 **Houtribdijk** (dam), Neth.
35/F5 **Hove**, Eng,UK
41/F5 **Hövelhof**, Ger.
108/E3 **Hovenweep Nat'l Mon.**, Co,US
35/H1 **Hoveton**, Eng,UK
37/E3 **Hovfjället** (peak), Swe.
33/H3 **Hovingham**, Eng,UK
62/E1 **Hövsgöl** (lake), Mong.
114/H2 **Howard** (hill), Ak,US
114/G2 **Howard** (pass), Ak,US
33/H4 **Howden**, Eng,UK
77/D3 **Howe** (cape), Austl.
110/D3 **Howell**, Mi,US
115/F5 **Howell**, NJ,US
89/E3 **Howick**, SAfr.
79/H4 **Howland** (isl.), PacUS
70/E3 **Howrah**, India
38/E3 **Höxter**, Ger.
39/H3 **Hoyerswerda**, Ger.
33/E5 **Hoylake**, Eng,UK
33/G5 **Hoyland Nether**, Eng,UK
47/N8 **Hoyo-de-Manzanares**, Sp.
43/E3 **Hoyoux** (riv.), Belg.
62/E2 **Hoyt Tamir** (riv.), Mong.
65/M9 **Hozumi**, Japan
39/H3 **Hradec Králové**, Czh.
50/D4 **Hrasnica**, Bosn.
50/B2 **Hrastnik**, Slov.
37/M6 **Hrolleifsborg** (peak), Ice.
39/K4 **Hron** (riv.), Slvk.
39/J3 **Hronov**, Czh.
39/M3 **Hrubieszów**, Pol.
39/J3 **Hrubý Jeseník** (mts.), Czh.
37/P6 **Hrútafjöll** (peak), Ice.
62/G5 **Hua** (peak), China
92/C6 **Huacho**, Peru
69/B3 **Hua Hin**, Thai.
79/K6 **Huahine** (isl.), FrPol.
66/C4 **Huai** (riv.), China
66/D4 **Huai'an**, China
62/H5 **Huaibei**, China
67/A2 **Huaihua**, China
66/C2 **Huailai**, China
66/D4 **Huainan**, China
66/C3 **Huairen**, China
66/D4 **Huaiyin**, China
100/B4 **Huajuapan de León**, Mex.
96/C2 **Hualañé**, Chile
67/D3 **Hualien**, Tai.
92/C5 **Huallaga** (riv.), Peru
92/C5 **Huamachuco**, Peru
87/C3 **Huambo**, Ang.
66/C5 **Huan** (riv.), China
92/C6 **Huancavelica**, Peru
92/C6 **Huancayo**, Peru
92/E8 **Huanchaca** (peak), Bol.
69/C2 **Huang** (riv.), Laos, Thai.
66/C4 **Huangchuan**, China
67/C2 **Huanggang** (peak), China
66/C2 **Huangqi** (lake), China
66/D5 **Huangshan**, China
66/C5 **Huangshi**, China
66/C5 **Huangtang** (lake), China
66/B4 **Huangtu** (plat.), China
63/H4 **Huang (Yellow)** (riv.), China
92/C5 **Huánuco**, Peru
92/E7 **Huanuni**, Bol.
92/C6 **Huaral**, Peru
92/C5 **Huaráz**, Peru
92/C6 **Huarmey**, Peru
92/C5 **Huascarán** (peak), Peru
92/C5 **Huascarán Nat'l Park**, Peru
66/B4 **Hua Shan** (peak), China
101/N8 **Huatabampo**, Mex.
92/E6 **Huatunas** (lake), Bol.
67/A1 **Huaying**, China
114/L3 **Hubbard** (mtn.), Ak,US, Yk,Can
109/H4 **Hubbard Creek** (res.), Tx,US
66/C5 **Hubei** (prov.), China
66/B4 **Hubei Kou** (pass), China
70/C4 **Hubli-Dhārwār**, India
40/D6 **Hückelhoven**, Ger.
41/E6 **Hückeswagen**, Ger.
33/G5 **Hucknall Torkard**, Eng,UK
42/A2 **Hucqueliers**, Fr.
33/G4 **Huddersfield**, Eng,UK
52/C4 **Huddinge**, Swe.
41/F2 **Hude**, Ger.
37/F3 **Hudiksvall**, Swe.
98/L **Hudson** (cape), Ant.
103/H2 **Hudson** (bay), Can.
103/J2 **Hudson** (str.), NW, Qu,Can
111/M7 **Hudson**, Qu,Can
110/F3 **Hudson** (riv.), NJ, NY,US
110/F3 **Hudson**, NY,US
107/H2 **Hudson Bay**, Sk,Can
102/D3 **Hudson's Hope**, BC,Can
69/D2 **Hue**, Viet.
50/F2 **Huedin**, Rom.
100/C4 **Huehuetenango**, Guat.
100/B3 **Huejutla**, Mex.
46/B4 **Huelva**, Sp.
46/B3 **Huelva** (riv.), Sp.
96/B4 **Huequi** (vol.), Chile
46/E4 **Huercal-Overa**, Sp.
109/F3 **Huerfano** (riv.), Co,US
47/E1 **Huesca**, Sp.
46/D4 **Huéscar**, Sp.
96/F3 **Huesos** (riv.), Arg.
100/A4 **Huetamo de Nuñez**, Mex.
70/E3 **Hugli** (riv.), India
109/G3 **Hugo**, Co,US
109/J4 **Hugo**, Ok,US
109/G3 **Hugoton**, Ks,US
62/H2 **Hui** (riv.), China
88/B2 **Huib-Hock** (plat.), Namb.
87/B4 **Huila** (plat.), Ang.
96/D2 **Huinca Renancó**, Arg.
66/E5 **Hui Shan** (mtn.), China
44/D2 **Huisne** (riv.), Fr.
40/C5 **Huissen**, Neth.
52/D3 **Huittinen**, Fin.
100/C4 **Huixtla**, Mex.
40/C4 **Huizen**, Neth.
67/B3 **Huizhou**, China
63/J5 **Hŭksan** (arch.), SKor.
62/K2 **Hulan** (riv.), China
62/F2 **Huld**, Mong.
107/G4 **Hulett**, Wy,US
110/F2 **Hull**, Qu,Can
33/H4 **Hull**, Eng,UK
33/H4 **Hull** (riv.), Eng,UK
41/F4 **Hüllhorst**, Ger.
79/H5 **Hull (Orona)** (atoll), Kiri.
40/B6 **Hulst**, Neth.
66/B3 **Hulu** (riv.), China
62/H2 **Hulun** (lake), China
63/K1 **Huma** (riv.), China
92/F5 **Humaitá**, Braz.
101/N8 **Humaya** (riv.), Mex.
87/B4 **Humbe**, Ang.
111/K2 **Humber** (riv.), Nf,Can
111/R8 **Humber** (bay), On,Can
111/Q8 **Humber** (riv.), On,Can
33/H4 **Humber** (riv.), Eng,UK
33/H4 **Humberside** (co.), Eng,UK
33/H4 **Humberston**, Eng,UK
112/E4 **Humble**, Tx,US
107/G2 **Humboldt**, Sk,Can
78/F7 **Humboldt** (peak), NCal.
108/C2 **Humboldt** (range), Nv,US
108/D2 **Humboldt** (riv.), Nv,US
113/F3 **Humboldt**, Tn,US
77/C2 **Hume** (lake), Austl.
39/L4 **Humenné**, Slvk.
114/K2 **Humphrey** (pt.), Ak,US
108/E4 **Humphreys** (peak), Az,US
33/F1 **Humshaugh**, Eng,UK
63/J3 **Hun** (riv.), China
63/K3 **Hun** (riv.), China
37/N6 **Húnaflói** (bay), Ice.
71/K2 **Hunan** (prov.), China
63/L3 **Hunchun**, China
50/F3 **Hunedoara**, Rom.
50/F2 **Hunedoara** (co.), Rom.
38/E3 **Hünfeld**, Ger.
50/D2 **Hungary**
45/H1 **Hungen**, Ger.
35/E4 **Hungerford**, Eng,UK
62/C2 **Hüngüy** (riv.), Mong.
69/D1 **Hung Yen**, Viet.
63/K3 **Hunjiang**, China
33/H3 **Hunmanby**, Eng,UK
43/G1 **Hunspatch**, Fr.
43/G4 **Hunsrück** (mts.), Ger.
35/G1 **Hunstanton**, Eng,UK
41/F2 **Hunte** (riv.), Ger.
77/C4 **Hunter** (isl.), Austl.
77/D2 **Hunter** (riv.), Austl.

106/A3 Hunter (isl.), BC,Can
114/H3 Hunter (mtn.), Ak,US
110/C4 Huntingburg, In,US
35/F2 Huntingdon, Eng,UK
33/G4 Huntington, Eng,UK
110/C3 Huntington, In,US
115/G5 Huntington, NY,US
110/D4 Huntington, WV,US
115/C3 Huntington Beach, Ca,US
115/B3 Huntington Park, Ca,US
116/F7 Huntington Woods, Mi,US
75/S10 Huntly, NZ
36/D2 Huntly, Sc,UK
114/M4 Hunts Inlet, BC,Can
110/E2 Huntsville, On,Can
113/G3 Huntsville, Al,US
112/E4 Huntsville, Tx,US
40/D5 Hünxe, Ger.
63/H2 Huolin Gol, China
69/D2 Huong Hoa, Viet.
69/D2 Huong Khe, Viet.
69/D2 Huong Son, Viet.
71/J4 Huong Thuy, Viet.
66/B3 Huo Shan (mtn.), China
83/R5 Hurdiyo, Som.
31/S11 Hurepoix (reg.), Fr.
108/E4 Hurley, NM,US
110/D2 Huron (lake), Can., US
116/F7 Huron (riv.), Mi,US
107/J4 Huron, SD,US
110/D4 Hurricane, WV,US
35/F5 Hurstpierpoint, Eng,UK
42/D4 Hurtaut (riv.), Fr.
43/F2 Hürth, Ger.
33/G3 Hurworth, Eng,UK
70/D3 Husainābād, India
35/E2 Husbands Bosworth, Eng,UK
51/J2 Huşi, Rom.
38/E1 Husum, Ger.
109/H3 Hutchinson, Ks,US
107/K4 Hutchinson, Mn,US
33/J5 Huttoft, Eng,UK
76/C4 Hutton (peak), Austl.
31/Q7 Hutton, Eng,UK
33/H4 Hutton Cranswick, Eng,UK
33/G3 Hutton Rudby, Eng,UK
111/Q8 Huttonville, On,Can
66/C3 Hutuo (riv.), China
43/E2 Huy, Belg.
33/F5 Huyton-with-Roby, Eng,UK
66/E5 Huzhou, China
37/P7 Hvannadalshnúkur (peak), Ice.
50/C4 Hvar (isl.), Cro.
37/N7 Hvítá (riv.), Ice.
87/E4 Hwange, Zim.
87/E4 Hwange (Wankie) Nat'l Park, Zim.
96/B5 Hyades (peak), Chile
62/C2 Hyargas, Mong.
62/C2 Hyargas (lake), Mong.
115/K8 Hyattsville, Md,US
33/F5 Hyde, Eng,UK
31/N7 Hyde Park, Eng,UK
70/C4 Hyderābād, India
61/J3 Hyderābād, Pak.
45/G5 Hyères, Fr.
45/G5 Hyères (isls.), Fr.
102/D2 Hyland (riv.), Yk,Can
64/D3 Hyōgo (pref.), Japan
64/D3 Hyō-no-sen (mtn.), Japan
108/E2 Hyrum, Ut,US
35/E5 Hythe, Eng,UK
35/H4 Hythe, Eng,UK
64/B4 Hyūga, Japan
37/H3 Hyvinkää, Fin.

I

94/B4 Iaçu, Braz.
50/A2 Iāf di Montasio (peak), It.
51/H3 Ialomiţa (riv.), Rom.
95/D1 Iapu, Braz.
51/H2 Iaşi, Rom.
51/H2 Iaşi (co.), Rom.
67/C4 Iba, Phil.
85/F5 Ibadan, Nga.
92/C3 Ibagué, Col.
95/B2 Ibaiti, Braz.
67/D5 Ibajay, Phil.
108/D2 Ibapah, Ut,US
50/E4 Ibar (riv.), Yugo.
64/C3 Ibara, Japan
65/L10 Ibaraki, Japan
65/F2 Ibaraki (pref.), Japan
92/C3 Ibarra, Ecu.
91/E2 Ibarreta, Arg.
83/L6 Ibba (riv.), Sudan
41/E4 Ibbenbüren, Ger.
85/F2 Ibdekhene (wadi), Mali
91/E2 Ibera, Esteros de (marshes), Arg.
46/D2 Ibérico, Sistema (range), Sp.
111/P7 Iberville, Qu,Can
64/E3 Ibi (riv.), Japan
47/E3 Ibi, Sp.
95/C1 Ibiá, Braz.
94/B2 Ibiapaba (mts.), Braz.
94/C4 Ibicaraí, Braz.
94/C3 Ibimirim, Braz.
95/B2 Ibitinga, Braz.
95/F8 Ibiúna, Braz.
47/F3 Ibiza, Sp.
47/F3 Ibiza (isl.), Sp.
64/D3 Ibo (riv.), Japan
94/B4 Ibotirama, Braz.
82/H8 Iboundji (peak), Gabon
39/L4 Ibrány, Hun.
86/B2 Ibshawāy, Egypt
35/E1 Ibstock, Eng,UK
73/G3 Ibu (mtn.), Indo.
65/M9 Ibuki, Japan
65/M9 Ibuki-yama (peak), Japan
92/C6 Ica, Peru
37/N7 Iceland
70/B4 Ichalkaranji, India
70/D4 Ichchāpuram, India
65/J7 Ichihara, Japan
65/L9 Ichijima, Japan
65/H7 Ichikawa, Japan
64/E3 Ichinomiya, Japan
63/N4 Ichinoseki, Japan
65/M10 Ichishi, Japan
42/C1 Ichtegem, Belg.
94/C2 Icó, Braz.
114/K4 Icy (bay), Ak,US
114/F1 Icy (cape), Ak,US
114/L4 Icy (str.), Ak,US
109/J4 Idabel, Ok,US
106/E5 Idaho (state), US
106/E5 Idaho Falls, Id,US
70/B3 Idar, India
43/G4 Idarkopf (peak), Ger.
43/G4 Idar-Oberstein, Ger.
65/L10 Ide, Japan
62/D2 Ider (riv.), Mong.
86/C3 Idfū, Egypt
49/J5 Idhi (peak), Gre.
59/H6 Idkū, Egypt
33/H5 Idle (riv.), Eng,UK
59/D3 Idlib, Syria
50/B3 Idrija, Slov.
81/M13 Idriss I (res.), Mor.
42/B2 Ieper, Belg.
49/J5 Ierápetra, Gre.
87/G2 Ifakara, Tanz.
78/D4 Ifalik (isl.), Micr.
89/H8 Ifanadiana, Madg.
85/G5 Ife, Nga.
65/M10 Iga, Japan
65/M10 Iga (riv.), Japan
95/C2 Igarapava, Braz.
93/J4 Igarapé-Miri, Braz.
94/D2 Igarassu, Braz.
56/J3 Igarka, Rus.
70/B4 Igatpuri, India
59/F2 Iğdır, Turk.
31/P8 Ightham, Eng,UK
114/H2 Igikpak (mtn.), Ak,US
48/A3 Iglesias, It.
110/B1 Ignace, On,Can
51/J5 İğneada (cape), Turk.
31/S10 Igny, Fr.
53/M4 Igra, Rus.
95/B3 Iguaçu (riv.), Braz.
91/F2 Iguaçu Nat'l Park, Braz.
94/B4 Iguaí, Braz.
100/B4 Iguala, Mex.
47/F2 Igualada, Sp.
91/E2 Iguapa (riv.), Braz.
95/C3 Iguape, Braz.
95/C3 Iguape (riv.), Braz.
94/C2 Iguatu, Braz.
91/F2 Iguazu Nat'l Park, Arg.
82/D2 Iguidi, 'Erg (des.), Afr.
89/H8 Ihosy, Madg.
89/G8 Ihotry (lake), Madg.
56/C3 Ii (riv.), Fin.
65/E3 Iida, Japan
65/F2 Iide-san (mtn.), Japan
52/E2 Iijoki (riv.), Fin.
65/M10 Iinan, Japan
37/H3 Iisalmi, Fin.
65/M10 Iitaka, Japan
52/E3 Iitti, Fin.
65/F2 Iiyama, Japan
64/B4 Iizuka, Japan
82/C3 Ijill (peak), Mrta.
40/C4 IJmeer (bay), Neth.
40/B4 IJmuiden, Neth.
84/B2 Ijnaoun (well), Mrta.
37/H2 Ijoki (riv.), Fin.
40/C4 IJssel (riv.), Neth.
40/C3 IJsselmeer (lake), Neth.
40/C3 IJsselmuiden, Neth.
40/C4 IJsselstein, Neth.
91/F2 Ijuí, Braz.
64/B5 Ijūin, Japan
42/B2 Ijzer (riv.), Belg.
53/M5 Ik (riv.), Rus.
89/H7 Ikahavo (plat.), Madg.
49/J4 Ikaría (isl.), Gre.
87/D1 Ikela, Zaire
65/M10 Ikenokoya-yama (peak), Japan
51/F4 Ikhtiman, Bul.
64/A4 Iki (chan.), Japan
64/A4 Iki (isl.), Japan
65/L10 Ikoma, Japan
89/H7 Ikopa (riv.), Madg.
67/D4 Ilagan, Phil.
60/E2 Īlām, Iran
70/E2 Ilam, Nepal
67/D3 Ilan, Tai.
39/K2 Iława, Pol.
83/M4 'Ilay, Sudan
34/D4 Ilchester, Eng,UK
106/G2 Ile-à-la-Crosse, Sk,Can
107/G2 Ile-à-la-Crosse (lake), Sk,Can
87/D1 Ilebo, Zaire
44/E2 Ile-de-France (reg.), Fr.
55/K2 Ilek (riv.), Kaz., Rus.
111/N7 Ile-Perrot, Qu,Can
84/E5 Iles Ehotilés Nat'l Park, IvC.
85/G5 Ilesha, Nga.
31/P7 Ilford, Eng,UK
76/B3 Ilfracombe, Austl.
34/B4 Ilfracombe, Eng,UK
54/E4 Ilgaz, Turk.
59/B2 Ilgın, Turk.
95/H8 Ilhabela, Braz.
95/J8 Ilha Grande (bay), Braz.
95/B1 Ilha Solteira (res.), Braz.
46/A2 Ílhavo, Port.
94/C4 Ilhéus, Braz.
68/C3 Ili (riv.), China, Kaz.
114/G4 Iliamna (lake), Ak,US
114/H3 Iliamna (vol.), Ak,US
67/D6 Iligan, Phil.
59/E3 Ilisu (res.), Turk.
51/H6 Ilium (Troy) (ruins), Turk.
33/G6 Ilkeston, Eng,UK
33/G4 Ilkley, Eng,UK
45/H3 Ill (riv.), Aus.
45/G2 Ill (riv.), Fr.
96/C1 Illapel, Chile
85/G3 Illéla, Niger
45/J3 Iller (riv.), Ger.
46/D2 Illescas, Sp.
92/E7 Illimani (peak), Bol.
43/G5 Illingen, Ger.
110/B4 Illinois (state), US
110/B3 Illinois (riv.), Il,US
34/A6 Illogan, Eng,UK
46/D4 Illora, Sp.
45/G3 Illzach, Fr.
45/J2 Ilm (riv.), Ger.
37/G3 Ilmajoki, Fin.
41/G5 Ilme (riv.), Ger.
52/F4 Il'men' (lake), Rus.
38/F3 Ilmenau, Ger.
41/H2 Ilmenau (riv.), Ger.
34/D5 Ilminster, Eng,UK
92/D7 Ilo, Peru
67/D5 Iloilo, Phil.
85/G4 Ilorin, Nga.
55/H2 Ilovlya (riv.), Rus.
41/H4 Ilse (riv.), Ger.
41/H4 Ilsede, Ger.
41/H5 Ilsenburg, Ger.
51/H5 Ilyas (pt.), Turk.
53/N3 Ilych (riv.), Rus.
45/K2 Ilz (riv.), Ger.
64/C3 Imabari, Japan
65/F2 Imaichi, Japan
89/H8 Imaloto (riv.), Madg.
59/C3 Imamoğlu, Turk.
52/F2 Imandra (lake), Rus.
64/A4 Imari, Japan
37/J3 Imatra, Fin.
64/E3 Imazu, Japan
65/J7 Imba, Japan
95/B4 Imbituba, Braz.
83/P6 Imī, Eth.
55/J5 Imishli, Azer.
49/L7 Imittós (mtn.), Gre.
108/C2 Imlay, Nv,US
41/G6 Immenhausen, Ger.
45/J3 Immenstadt im Allgäu, Ger.
33/H4 Immingham, Eng,UK
113/H5 Immokalee, Fl,US
114/J2 Imnavait (mtn.), Ak,US
85/G5 Imo (state), Nga.
45/J4 Imola, It.
94/A2 Imperatriz, Braz.
45/H5 Imperia, It.
107/G3 Imperial, Sk,Can
109/G2 Imperial, Ne,US
82/J7 Impfondo, Congo
71/F3 Imphāl, India
51/J5 İmralı (isl.), Turk.
59/D2 İmranlı, Turk.
45/J3 Imst, Aus.
65/E3 Ina, Japan
65/L10 Ina (riv.), Japan
39/H2 Ina (riv.), Pol.
65/M9 Inabe, Japan
65/L10 Inagawa, Japan
65/H7 Inagi, Japan
82/G2 I-n-Amenas, Alg.
65/K10 Inami, Japan
81/M13 Inaouene (riv.), Mor.
37/H1 Inari (lake), Fin.
51/G2 Inău (peak), Rom.
65/G2 Inawashiro (lake), Japan
65/M9 Inazawa, Japan
47/G3 Inca, Sp.
85/F2 I-n-Chaouâg (wadi), Mali
36/C3 Inchinnan, Sc,UK
84/B2 Inchiri (reg.), Mrta.
63/K4 Inch'ŏn, SKor.
82/E3 I-n-Dagouber (well), Mali
95/C1 Indaiá (riv.), Braz.
95/C2 Indaiatuba, Braz.
67/D6 Indanan, Phil.
43/F2 Inde (riv.), Ger.
43/F2 Inden, Ger.
100/D4 Independence, Belz.
108/C3 Independence, Ca,US
109/J3 Independence, Ks,US
109/J3 Independence, Mo,US
108/C2 Independence (mts.), Nv,US
115/E6 Independence Nat'l Hist. Park, Pa,US
94/B2 Independência, Braz.
55/J2 Inder (lake), Kaz.
58/G7 India
29/N6 Indian (ocean)
110/C3 Indiana (state), US
110/E3 Indiana, Pa,US
116/R16 Indiana Dunes Nat'l Lakesh., In,US
110/C4 Indianapolis (cap.), In,US
107/H3 Indian Head, Sk,Can
113/F3 Indianola, Ms,US
113/H5 Indiantown, Fl,US
95/B1 Indiaporã, Braz.
57/Q3 Indigirka (riv.), Rus.
50/E3 Indija, Yugo.
108/C4 Indio, Ca,US
69/C1 Indochina (reg.), Asia
73/E4 Indonesia
76/E6 Indooroopilly, Austl.
70/C3 Indore, India
72/B4 Indragiri (riv.), Indo.
72/C5 Indramayu (cape), Indo.
70/D4 Indrāvati (riv.), India
44/D3 Indre (riv.), Fr.
44/D3 Indrois (riv.), Fr.
58/F7 Indus (riv.), Asia
61/J4 Indus, Mouths of the, Pak.
59/C2 İnebolu, Turk.
85/E1 I-n-Echaï (well), Mali
59/B2 İnegöl, Turk.
50/E2 Ineu, Rom.
82/D1 Inezgane, Mor.
88/C4 Infanta (cape), SAfr.
100/A4 Infiernillo (res.), Mex.
46/C1 Infiesto, Sp.
94/D2 Ingá, Braz.
92/C4 Ingapirca, Ecu.
31/Q7 Ingatestone, Eng,UK
42/C2 Ingelmunster, Belg.
76/G8 Ingleburn, Austl.
32/G2 Ingleton, Eng,UK
111/Q8 Inglewood, On,Can
115/B3 Inglewood, Ca,US
116/C2 Inglewood-Finn Hill, Wa,US
113/H4 Inglis, Fl,US
62/G1 Ingoda (riv.), Rus.
33/J5 Ingoldmells, Eng,UK
45/J2 Ingolstadt, Ger.
31/Q7 Ingrave, Eng,UK
98/E Ingrid Christianson (coast), Ant.
85/G2 I-n-Guezzâm, Alg.
54/E3 Ingulets (riv.), Ukr.
55/G4 Inguri (riv.), Geo.
94/C3 Inhambupe, Braz.
93/J7 Inhumas, Braz.
32/A1 Inishowen (pen.), Ire.
32/B1 Inishowen Head (pt.), Ire.
116/F7 Inkster, Mi,US
64/C3 Inland (sea), Japan
71/G3 Inle (lake), Burma
85/E2 I-n-Milach (well), Mali
45/K2 Inn (riv.), Eur.
62/G3 Inner Mongolia (reg.), China
41/H4 Innerste (riv.), Ger.
45/K3 Innichen (San Candido), It.
76/B2 Innisfail, Austl.
106/E2 Innisfail, Ab,Can
114/G3 Innoko (riv.), Ak,US
45/J3 Innsbruck, Aus.
34/B5 Inny (riv.), Eng,UK
64/C4 Ino, Japan
87/C1 Inongo, Zaire
39/K4 Inovec (peak), Slvk.
39/K2 Inowrocław, Pol.
85/E1 I-n-Sâkâne, Erg (des.), Mali
82/F2 I-n-Salah, Alg.
36/D2 Insch, Sc,UK
71/G4 Insein, Burma
106/A2 Inside (passg.), BC,Can
53/P2 Inta, Rus.
85/F2 I-n-Tassik (well), Mali
106/B2 Interior (plat.), BC,Can
107/K3 International Falls, Mn,US
69/B2 Inthanon (peak), Thai.
51/H3 Intorsura Buzăului, Rom.
65/G3 Inubō-zaki (pt.), Japan
103/J3 Inukjuak, Qu,Can
97/K8 Inútil (bay), Chile
65/E3 Inuyama, Japan
36/C2 Inveraray, Sc,UK
75/Q12 Invercargill, NZ
77/D1 Inverell, Austl.
36/C2 Invergarry, Sc,UK
36/D2 Inverkeilor, Sc,UK
107/H3 Invermay, Sk,Can
111/J2 Inverness, NS,Can
36/C2 Inverness, Sc,UK
113/G3 Inverness, Al,US
113/H4 Inverness, Fl,US
36/D2 Inverurie, Sc,UK
67/B6 Investigator (shoal)
74/F7 Investigator (str.), Austl.
87/F4 Inyangani (peak), Zim.
114/D2 Inymney, Gora (mtn.), Rus.
108/C3 Inyo (mts.), Ca,US
55/H1 Inza, Rus.
65/J7 Inzai, Japan
49/G3 Ioánnina, Gre.
109/J3 Iola, Ks,US
61/H1 Iolotan', Trkm.
87/B4 Iona Nat'l Park, Ang.
110/C3 Ionia, Mi,US
49/F3 Ionian (sea), Eur.
49/F3 Ionian (isls.), Gre.
49/J4 Íos (isl.), Gre.
84/A2 Iouîk (cape), Mrta.
107/K5 Iowa (state), US
107/L5 Iowa (riv.), Ia,US
107/L5 Iowa City, Ia,US
107/K5 Iowa Falls, Ia,US
95/B1 Ipameri, Braz.
96/B5 Ipan (isl.), Chile
95/D1 Ipanema, Braz.
95/D1 Ipatinga, Braz.
39/K4 Ipel' (Ipoly) (riv.), Hun., Slvk.
92/C3 Ipiales, Col.
94/C4 Ipiaú, Braz.
94/C4 Ipirá, Braz.
72/B3 Ipoh, Malay.
39/K4 Ipoly (Ipel') (riv.), Hun., Slvk.
93/H7 Iporá, Braz.
49/K2 Ipsala, Turk.
76/E7 Ipswich, Austl.
35/H2 Ipswich, Eng,UK
107/J4 Ipswich, SD,US
94/B2 Ipu, Braz.
95/B2 Ipuã, Braz.
94/B2 Ipueiras, Braz.
92/D8 Iquique, Chile
92/D4 Iquitos, Peru
65/M10 Irago (chan.), Japan
65/E3 Irago-misaki (cape), Japan
49/J4 Iráklia (isl.), Gre.
49/J5 Iráklion, Gre.
60/F2 Iran
72/D3 Iran (mts.), Indo., Malay.
61/H3 Irānshahr, Iran
100/A3 Irapuato, Mex.
60/D2 Iraq
95/B3 Irati, Braz.
73/H4 Irau (mtn.), Indo.
59/K5 Irbid, Jor.
59/L5 Irbid (gov.), Jor.
59/F3 Irbīl, Iraq
94/B3 Irecê, Braz.
36/A4 Ireland
36/B3 Ireland, Northern, UK
32/B5 Ireland's Eye (isl.), Ire.
53/N5 Iremel', Gora (peak), Rus.
34/C2 Irfon (riv.), Wal,UK
85/G2 Irhazer Oua-n-Agadez (wadi), Niger
63/K4 Iri, SKor.
73/H4 Irian Jaya (reg.), Indo.
84/D2 Irîgui (reg.), Mali, Mrta.
55/L2 Iriklinskiy (res.), Rus.
87/G2 Iringa, Tanz.
67/D3 Iriomote (isl.), Japan
93/H4 Iriri (riv.), Braz.
32/C4 Irish (sea), Ire., UK
62/E1 Irkut (riv.), Rus.
62/E1 Irkutsk, Rus.
33/F5 Irlam, Eng,UK
34/D1 Iron Bridge, Eng,UK
50/F3 Iron Gate (gorge), Eur.
110/B2 Iron Mountain, Mi,US
110/B2 Iron River, Mi,US
110/D4 Ironton, Oh,US
110/B2 Ironwood, Mi,US
110/D1 Iroquois Falls, On,Can
65/F3 Irō-zaki (pt.), Japan
54/E1 Irput' (riv.), Bela., Rus.
71/G4 Irrawaddy (riv.), Burma
43/F4 Irrel, Ger.
43/F3 Irsen (riv.), Ger.
33/E3 Irt (riv.), Eng,UK
33/F1 Irthing (riv.), Eng,UK
35/F2 Irthlingborough, Eng,UK
56/G4 Irtysh (riv.), Kaz., Rus.
65/H7 Iruma, Japan
83/L7 Irumu, Zaire
46/E1 Irún, Sp.
36/C3 Irvine, Sc,UK
115/C3 Irvine, Ca,US
112/D3 Irving, Tx,US
115/F5 Irvington, NJ,US
76/C3 Isaac (riv.), Austl.
67/D6 Isabela, Phil.
103/K2 Isabella (bay), NW,Can
103/R7 Isachsen (cape), NW,Can
37/M6 Ísafjardhardjúp (fjord), Ice.
64/B4 Isahaya, Japan
89/H8 Isalo Nat'l Park, Madg.
89/H8 Isalo Ruiniform, Massif (plat.), Madg.
38/G4 Isar (riv.), Aus., Ger.
45/J3 Isarco (Eisack) (riv.), It.
48/C2 Ischia, It.
41/H3 Ise (riv.), Ger.
65/E3 Ise, Japan
65/M10 Ise (bay), Japan
35/F2 Ise (riv.), Eng,UK
65/F3 Isehara, Japan
115/F5 Iselin, NJ,US
45/K2 Isen (riv.), Ger.
45/J4 Iseo (lake), It.
44/F4 Isère (riv.), Fr.
41/E6 Iserlohn, Ger.
48/D2 Isernia, It.
65/F2 Isesaki, Japan
65/E3 Ise-Shima Nat'l Park, Japan
53/Q4 Iset' (riv.), Rus.
85/F5 Iseyin, Nga.
65/L10 Ishi (riv.), Japan
65/F2 Ishibashi, Japan
65/M9 Ishibe, Japan
78/B2 Ishigaki, Japan
67/D3 Ishigaki (isl.), Japan
65/F2 Ishige, Japan
65/G2 Ishikawa, Japan
65/E1 Ishikawa (pref.), Japan
65/N10 Ishiki, Japan
56/H4 Ishim (riv.), Kaz., Rus.
53/R4 Ishim, Rus.
55/L1 Ishimbay, Rus.
65/G1 Ishinomaki, Japan
65/G2 Ishioka, Japan
64/C4 Ishizuchi-san (mtn.), Japan
110/C2 Ishpeming, Mi,US
92/E7 Isiboro Securé Nat'l Park, Bol.
97/G1 Isidoro, Uru.
56/H4 Isil'kul', Rus.
83/L7 Isiro, Zaire
86/C4 Is, Jabal (peak), Sudan
59/D3 İskenderun, Turk.
59/C2 İskilip, Turk.
49/H1 Iskŭr (res.), Bul.
49/H1 Iskŭr (riv.), Bul.
36/D2 Isla (riv.), Sc,UK
46/B4 Isla Cristina, Sp.
96/Q9 Isla de Maipo, Chile
76/C4 Isla Gorge Nat'l Park, Austl.
101/N9 Isla Isabella Nat'l Park, Mex.
61/K2 Islāmābād (cap.), Pak.
96/B5 Isla Magdalena Nat'l Park, Chile
70/E2 Islāmpur, India
100/D3 Isla Mujeres, Mex.
107/K2 Island Lake, Mb,Can
111/K1 Islands (bay), Nf,Can
44/D4 Isle (riv.), Fr.
35/G2 Isleham, Eng,UK
32/D3 Isle of Man, UK
32/D2 Isle of Whithorn, Sc,UK
110/B2 Isle Royale Nat'l Park, Mi,US
31/N7 Islington (bor.), Eng,UK
115/G5 Islip, NY,US
53/X9 Ismailovo Park, Rus.
86/C2 Ismailia (Al Ismā'īlīyah), Egypt
86/C3 Isnā, Egypt
45/J3 Isny, Ger.
65/M10 Isobe, Japan
37/H3 Isojärven Nat'l Park, Fin.
87/F3 Isoka, Zam.
48/C2 Isola del Liri, It.
48/E3 Isola di Capo Rizzuto, It.
59/B3 Isparta, Turk.
44/C5 Ispéguy, Col d' (pass), Fr.
51/H4 Isperikh, Bul.
59/E2 Ispir, Turk.
59/J5 Israel
116/C2 Issaquah, Wa,US
40/D5 Issel (riv.), Ger.
40/D5 Isselburg, Ger.
84/D5 Issia, IvC.
44/E4 Issoire, Fr.
44/E3 Issoudun, Fr.
40/D5 Issum, Ger.
68/C3 Issyk-Kul' (lake), Kyr.
42/B6 Issy-les-Moulineaux, Fr.
50/E1 Istállós-kő (peak), Hun.
51/J5 İstanbul, Turk.
51/J5 İstanbul (prov.), Turk.
51/H5 Istranca (mts.), Turk.
44/F5 Istres, Fr.
50/A3 Istria (pen.), Cro.
73/F2 Isulan, Phil.
94/C3 Itabaiana, Braz.
94/D2 Itabaiana, Braz.
94/C3 Itabaianinha, Braz.
95/D2 Itabapoana (riv.), Braz.
94/B4 Itaberaba, Braz.
95/D1 Itabira, Braz.
95/D2 Itabirito, Braz.
95/L7 Itaboraí, Braz.
94/C4 Itabuna, Braz.
93/H5 Itacaiunas (riv.), Braz.
94/A4 Itacarambi, Braz.
92/G4 Itacoatiara, Braz.
92/D5 Itacuaí (riv.), Braz.
95/K7 Itaguaí, Braz.
92/C2 Itagüí, Col.
95/B2 Itaí, Braz.
95/B3 Itaiópolis, Braz.
91/F1 Itaipu (res.), Braz., Par.
93/G4 Itaituba, Braz.
95/B3 Itajaí, Braz.
95/B3 Itajai (riv.), Braz.
95/H7 Itajubá, Braz.
94/C4 Itajuípe, Braz.
65/G3 Itako, Japan
30/E4 Italy
94/C5 Itamaraju, Braz.
95/D1 Itamarandiba, Braz.
95/D1 Itambacuri, Braz.
94/B4 Itambé, Braz.
95/D1 Itambé (peak), Braz.
65/L10 Itami, Japan
71/F2 Itanagar, India
95/G9 Itanhaém, Braz.
95/C2 Itanhandu, Braz.
94/B5 Itanhém, Braz.
95/D1 Itanhém (riv.), Braz.
95/D1 Itanhomi, Braz.
94/B5 Itaobim, Braz.
95/D2 Itaocara, Braz.
94/C1 Itapagé, Braz.
94/C4 Itaparica (isl.), Braz.
95/C2 Itapecerica, Braz.
94/A1 Itapecuru-Mirim, Braz.
95/D2 Itapemirim, Braz.
95/D2 Itaperuna, Braz.
94/B4 Itapetinga, Braz.
95/B2 Itapetininga, Braz.
95/B2 Itapeva, Braz.
95/G8 Itapevi, Braz.
94/C3 Itapicuru (riv.), Braz.
94/A1 Itapicuru (riv.), Braz.
94/C1 Itapipoca, Braz.
95/G7 Itapira, Braz.
94/C4 Itapitanga, Braz.
95/B2 Itaporanga, Braz.
95/G8 Itaquaquecetuba, Braz.
94/B4 Itarantim, Braz.
95/B3 Itararé, Braz.
70/C3 Itārsi, India
94/B4 Itaruçu, Braz.
95/C2 Itatiaia Nat'l Park, Braz.
95/G8 Itatiba, Braz.
95/C2 Itatinga (res.), Braz.
94/B3 Itaueira (riv.), Braz.
95/C2 Itaúna, Braz.
63/N3 Itayanagi, Japan
67/D3 Itbayat (isl.), Phil.
35/E4 Itchen (riv.), Eng,UK
83/K7 Itembiri (riv.), Zaire
92/F6 Iténez (riv.), Bol.
87/E4 Itezhi-Tezhi (dam), Zam.
110/E3 Ithaca, NY,US
49/G3 Ithaca (Itháki) (isl.), Gre.
41/G5 Ith Hils (ridge), Ger.
34/C2 Ithon (riv.), Wal,UK
87/F2 Itigi, Tanz.
65/F3 Itō, Japan
65/E2 Itoigawa, Japan
44/D2 Iton (riv.), Fr.
94/B4 Itororó, Braz.
65/H7 Itsukaichi, Japan
41/F6 Itter (riv.), Ger.
48/A2 Ittiri, It.
95/C2 Itu, Braz.
94/C4 Ituberá, Braz.
92/D5 Ituí (riv.), Braz.
95/B1 Ituiutaba, Braz.
95/B1 Itumbiara, Braz.
95/B1 Itumbiara (res.), Braz.
107/H3 Ituna, Sk,Can
95/B3 Ituporanga, Braz.
95/B1 Iturama, Braz.
95/J6 Itutinga (res.), Braz.
95/C2 Ituverava, Braz.
92/E5 Ituxi (riv.), Braz.
59/H6 Ityāy al Bārūd, Egypt
38/E2 Itzehoe, Ger.
114/C2 Iul'tin, Gora (mtn.), Rus.
95/D2 Iuna, Braz.
95/B3 Ivaí (riv.), Braz.
95/B3 Ivaiporã, Braz.
37/H1 Ivalojoki (riv.), Fin.
45/M2 Ivančice, Czh.
50/D4 Ivangrad, Yugo.
110/D1 Ivanhoe (riv.), On,Can
50/E4 Ivanjica, Yugo.
54/C2 Ivano-Frankovsk, Ukr.
54/C2 Ivano-Frankovsk Obl., Ukr.
52/J4 Ivanovo, Rus.
53/J4 Ivanovo Obl., Rus.
49/J2 Ivaylovgrad (res.), Bul.
53/P3 Ivdel, Rus.
31/M7 Iver, Eng,UK
31/M7 Iver Heath, Eng,UK
82/H7 Ivindo (riv.), Gabon
89/H8 Ivohibe, Madg.
89/J7 Ivondro (riv.), Madg.
84/D5 Ivory Coast (Côte d'Ivoire)
45/G4 Ivrea, It.
42/B6 Ivry-sur-Seine, Fr.
34/C6 Ivybridge, Eng,UK
62/F1 Iwai, Japan
65/G2 Iwaki, Japan
64/C3 Iwakuni, Japan
65/M9 Iwakura, Japan
64/D3 Iwami, Japan
63/N3 Iwamizawa, Japan
65/G1 Iwanuma, Japan
65/E3 Iwata, Japan
63/N4 Iwate-san (mtn.), Japan
65/H7 Iwatsuki, Japan
85/G5 Iwo, Nga.
78/D2 Iwo Jima (isl.), Japan
38/C3 Ixelles, Belg.
100/B4 Ixtaltepec, Mex.
101/P9 Ixtlán del Río, Mex.
35/G2 Ixworth, Eng,UK
62/D1 Iya (riv.), Rus.
64/C4 Iyo, Japan
64/C4 Iyo (sea), Japan
100/D4 Izabal (lake), Guat.
55/H4 Izberbash, Rus.
42/C2 Izegem, Belg.
114/F4 Izembek Nat'l Wild. Ref., Ak,US
53/M4 Izhevsk, Rus.
53/M2 Izhma (riv.), Rus.
114/E5 Izigan (cape), Ak,US
61/G4 Izkī, Oman
51/J3 Izmail, Ukr.
59/A2 İzmir, Turk.
51/J5 İzmit, Turk.
51/J5 İzmit (gulf), Turk.
46/C4 Iznájar, Sp.
51/J5 İznik, Turk.
51/H5 İznik (lake), Turk.
59/L5 Izra', Syria
50/D2 Izsák, Hun.
63/M5 Izu (isls.), Japan
65/F3 Izu (pen.), Japan
100/B4 Izúcar de Matamoros, Mex.
65/H8 Izu-Fuji-Hakone Nat'l Park, Japan
64/A3 Izuhara, Japan
64/D3 Izumi, Japan
65/L10 Izumi-ōtsu, Japan
64/D3 Izumi-Sano, Japan
64/C3 Izumo, Japan
54/F2 Izyum, Ukr.

J

86/B5 Jabal Abyad (plat.), Sudan
59/K4 Jabal Lubnān (gov.), Leb.
46/D3 Jabalón (riv.), Sp.
70/C3 Jabalpur, India
59/K6 Jabālyah, Gaza
42/C1 Jabbeke, Belg.
86/C4 Jabjabah, Wādī (dry riv.), Egypt, Sudan
59/K4 Jablah, Syria
49/G2 Jablanica (mts.), Alb.
39/H3 Jablonec nad Nisou, Czh.
94/D3 Jaboatão, Braz.
95/B2 Jaboticabal, Braz.
50/E3 Jabuka, Yugo.
72/B4 Jabung (cape), Indo.
47/E1 Jaca, Sp.
94/B3 Jacaré (riv.), Braz.
95/C2 Jacareí, Braz.
83/Q5 Jaceel (riv.), Som.
111/G2 Jackman, Me,US
108/D2 Jackpot, Nv,US
112/D3 Jacksboro, Tx,US
113/G4 Jackson, Al,US
108/B3 Jackson, Ca,US
110/C3 Jackson, Mi,US
107/K5 Jackson, Mn,US
109/K3 Jackson, Mo,US
113/F3 Jackson (cap.), Ms,US
106/D5 Jackson (mts.), Nv,US
110/D4 Jackson, Oh,US
113/F3 Jackson, Tn,US
106/F5 Jackson, Wy,US
106/F4 Jackson (lake), Wy,US
113/G3 Jacksonville, Al,US
112/E3 Jacksonville, Ar,US
113/H4 Jacksonville, Fl,US
110/B4 Jacksonville, Il,US
113/J3 Jacksonville, NC,US
112/E4 Jacksonville, Tx,US
113/H4 Jacksonville Beach, Fl,US
101/G4 Jacmel, Haiti
61/J3 Jacobābād, Pak.
94/B3 Jacobina, Braz.
111/H1 Jacques-Cartier (mtn.), Qu,Can
111/G2 Jacques-Cartier (riv.), Qu,Can
91/F2 Jacuí (riv.), Braz.
94/C3 Jacuipe (riv.), Braz.
95/C3 Jacupiranga, Braz.
61/H3 Jaddi (pt.), Pak.
38/E2 Jade (bay), Ger.
41/F2 Jade (riv.), Ger.
41/F2 Jadebusen (bay), Ger.
46/D4 Jaén, Sp.
77/A3 Jaffa (cape), Austl.
70/D6 Jaffna, SrL.
70/D4 Jagdalpur, India
70/D2 Jagdīspur, India
67/D6 Jagna, Phil.
68/C5 Jagraon, India
45/J2 Jagst (riv.), Ger.
70/C4 Jagtiāl, India
94/C4 Jaguaquara, Braz.
97/G2 Jaguarão, Braz.
97/G2 Jaguarão (riv.), Braz.
95/G7 Jaguari (riv.), Braz.
95/B3 Jaguariaíva, Braz.
94/C2 Jaguaribe, Braz.
94/C2 Jaguaribe (riv.), Braz.
95/G7 Jaguariúna, Braz.
94/C2 Jaguaruana, Braz.
77/D3 Jagungal (peak), Austl.
60/F3 Jahrom, Iran
73/G3 Jailolo, Indo.
70/C2 Jaipur, India
70/B2 Jaisalmer, India
50/C3 Jajce, Bosn.
70/E3 Jājpur, India
72/C5 Jakarta (cap.), Indo.
37/G3 Jakobstad, Fin.
109/G4 Jal, NM,US
61/K2 Jalālābād, Afg.
37/G3 Jalasjärvi, Fin.
95/B2 Jales, Braz.
70/C3 Jālgaon, India
82/H6 Jalingo, Nga.
101/P9 Jalisco (state), Mex.
48/A4 Jālitah, Jazī rat (isl.), Tun.
70/C4 Jālna, India
46/E2 Jalon (riv.), Sp.
70/B2 Jālor, India
70/E2 Jalpaiguri, India
83/K2 Jālū, Libya
78/F4 Jaluit (atoll), Mrsh.
60/E2 Jalūlā', Iraq
83/P7 Jamaame, Som.
85/H4 Jamaare (riv.), Nga.
101/F4 Jamaica
101/F4 Jamaica (chan.), NAm.
70/E3 Jamālpur, Bang.
70/E2 Jamālpur, India
93/G5 Jamanxim (riv.), Braz.
92/F5 Jamari (riv.), Braz.
72/B4 Jambi, Indo.
72/A2 Jambuair (cape), Indo.
105/K1 James (lake), On,Can
103/H3 James (bay), On, Qu,Can
96/B5 James (pt.), Chile
107/J4 James (riv.), ND, SD,US
110/E4 James (riv.), Va,US
115/F5 Jamesburg, NJ,US
102/G1 James Ross (str.), NW,Can
107/J4 Jamestown, ND,US
110/E3 Jamestown, NY,US
113/G2 Jamestown, Tn,US
100/B4 Jamiltepec, Mex.
68/B5 Jammu, India
68/C5 Jammu and Kashmīr (state), India
70/B3 Jāmnagar, India
61/K3 Jāmpur, Pak.
37/H3 Jämsä, Fin.
70/E3 Jamshedpur, India
37/E3 Jämtland (co.), Swe.
70/E3 Jamūī, India
107/H2 Jan (lake), Sk,Can

52/E3 **Janakkala,** Fin.
94/B4 **Janaúba,** Braz.
93/J3 **Janaucu** (isl.), Braz.
95/B2 **Jandaia do Sul,** Braz.
46/C4 **Jándula** (riv.), Sp.
110/B3 **Janesville,** Wi,US
70/C4 **Jangaon,** India
70/E3 **Jangipur,** India
39/K2 **Janikowo,** Pol.
59/K5 **Janīn,** WBnk.
50/D3 **Janja,** Bosn.
30/D1 **Jan Mayen** (isl.), Nor.
50/D2 **Jánoshalma,** Hun.
39/M3 **Janów Lubelski,** Pol.
94/A4 **Januária,** Braz.
86/C2 **Janūb Sīnā'** (gov.), Egypt
70/C3 **Jaora,** India
63/M4 **Japan**
63/L4 **Japan** (sea), Asia
65/E3 **Japanese Alps** (range), Japan
65/E2 **Japanese Alps Nat'l Park,** Japan
92/E4 **Japurá** (riv.), Braz.
59/D3 **Jarābulus,** Syria
46/C2 **Jaraíz de la Vera,** Sp.
59/K5 **Jarash,** Jor.
82/H1 **Jarbah** (isl.), Tun.
94/C2 **Jardim do Seridó,** Braz.
91/E2 **Jardín América,** Arg.
95/C2 **Jardinópolis,** Braz.
93/H3 **Jari** (riv.), Braz.
70/E3 **Jaridih,** India
82/H1 **Jarjīs,** Tun.
43/E5 **Jarny,** Fr.
39/J3 **Jarocin,** Pol.
39/H3 **Jaroměř,** Czh.
39/M3 **Jarosław,** Pol.
33/G2 **Jarrow,** Eng,UK
69/C2 **Jars** (plain), Laos
43/F6 **Jarville-la-Malgrange,** Fr.
79/J5 **Jarvis** (isl.), PacUS
39/L4 **Jasło,** Pol.
106/D2 **Jasper,** Ab,Can
113/G3 **Jasper,** Al,US
113/H4 **Jasper,** Fl,US
113/G3 **Jasper,** Ga,US
110/C4 **Jasper,** In,US
112/E4 **Jasper,** Tx,US
106/D2 **Jasper Nat'l Park,** Ab, BC,Can
70/C2 **Jaspur,** India
39/J2 **Jastrowie,** Pol.
39/K4 **Jastrzębie Zdroj,** Pol.
50/E2 **Jászapáti,** Hun.
50/D2 **Jászárokszállás,** Hun.
50/D2 **Jászberény,** Hun.
50/E2 **Jászladány,** Hun.
50/E2 **Jász-Nagykun-Szolnok** (co.), Hun.
95/B1 **Jataí,** Braz.
92/G4 **Jatapu** (riv.), Braz.
47/E3 **Játiva,** Sp.
95/B2 **Jaú,** Braz.
92/F4 **Jaú** (riv.), Braz.
92/F3 **Jauaperi** (riv.), Braz.
93/H4 **Jauaru** (mts.), Braz.
92/F3 **Jaua Sarisarinama Nat'l Park,** Ven.
92/C6 **Jauja,** Peru
45/G3 **Jaunpass** (pass), Swi.
72/C5 **Java** (isl.), Indo.
72/D5 **Java** (sea), Indo.
92/D5 **Javari** (riv.), Braz.
47/F3 **Jávea,** Sp.
97/J6 **Javier** (isl.), Chile
50/D1 **Javorie** (peak), Slvk.
83/Q7 **Jawhar** (Giohar), Som.
39/J3 **Jawor,** Pol.
73/J4 **Jaya** (peak), Indo.
73/K4 **Jayapura,** Indo.
112/C3 **Jayton,** Tx,US
35/H3 **Jaywick,** Eng,UK
60/D5 **Jazā'ir Farasān** (isls.), SAr.
39/L3 **Jędrzejów,** Pol.
38/F2 **Jeetze** (riv.), Ger.
106/C4 **Jefferson** (peak), Or,US
112/E3 **Jefferson,** Tx,US
109/J3 **Jefferson City** (cap.), Mo,US
110/C4 **Jeffersonville,** In,US
106/G5 **Jeffrey City,** Wy,US
96/B5 **Jeinemeni** (peak), Chile
52/E4 **Jēkabpils,** Lat.
39/J3 **Jelcz-Laskowice,** Pol.
39/H3 **Jelenia Góra,** Pol.
39/H3 **Jelenia Góra** (prov.), Pol.
70/E2 **Jelep** (pass), China
52/D4 **Jelgava,** Lat.
42/C3 **Jemappes,** Belg.
72/D5 **Jember,** Indo.
108/F4 **Jemez Pueblo,** NM,US
73/E4 **Jempang** (riv.), Indo.
86/C3 **Jemsa,** Egypt
38/F3 **Jena,** Ger.
112/E4 **Jena,** La,US
73/E5 **Jeneponto,** Indo.
112/E4 **Jennings,** La,US
102/F2 **Jenny Lind** (isl.), NW,Can
103/H2 **Jens Muck** (isl.), NW,Can
94/B4 **Jequié,** Braz.
94/B5 **Jequitinhonha,** Braz.
94/C5 **Jequitinhonha** (riv.), Braz.
81/N13 **Jerada,** Mor.
101/G4 **Jérémie,** Haiti
101/P9 **Jerez de García Salinas,** Mex.
46/B4 **Jerez de la Frontera,** Sp.
46/B3 **Jerez de los Caballeros,** Sp.
115/G5 **Jericho,** NY,US
59/K6 **Jericho** (Arīḩā), WBnk.
106/E5 **Jerome,** Id,US
115/F5 **Jersey City,** NJ,US
110/B4 **Jerseyville,** Il,US
59/M9 **Jerusalem** (dist.), Isr.
59/N9 **Jerusalem Walls Nat'l Park,** Isr.
59/K6 **Jerusalem** (Yerushalayim) (cap.), Isr.
106/C3 **Jervis** (inlet), BC,Can
50/B2 **Jesenice,** Slov.
45/K5 **Jesi,** It.
70/E3 **Jessore,** Bang.
113/H4 **Jesup,** Ga,US
111/N6 **Jésus** (isl.), Qu,Can
91/D3 **Jesús María,** Arg.
101/F3 **Jesús Menéndez,** Cuba
84/A4 **Jeta** (isl.), GBis.
109/H3 **Jetmore,** Ks,US
70/B3 **Jetpur,** India
42/D3 **Jeumont,** Fr.
41/E1 **Jever,** Ger.
107/G5 **Jewel Cave Nat'l Mon.,** SD,US
70/D4 **Jeypore,** India
49/F1 **Jezerce** (peak), Alb.
39/K2 **Jeziorák** (lake), Pol.
70/E3 **Jhā Jhā,** India
70/C3 **Jhālawār,** India
61/K2 **Jhang Sadar,** Pak.
70/C2 **Jhānsi,** India
70/D3 **Jhārsuguda,** India
61/K2 **Jhelum** (riv.), India, Pak.
61/K2 **Jhelum,** Pak.
70/E3 **Jiaganj,** India
62/F5 **Jialing** (riv.), China
66/C4 **Jialu** (riv.), China
63/L2 **Jiamusi,** China
67/B2 **Ji'an,** China
67/B3 **Jian** (riv.), China
69/E1 **Jiang** (riv.), China
67/B3 **Jiangmen,** China
66/D4 **Jiangsu** (prov.), China
66/D5 **Jiangxi** (prov.), China
66/E5 **Jiangyin,** China
67/C2 **Jianyang,** China
67/D2 **Jiaojiang,** China
63/J3 **Jiaolai** (riv.), China
66/C4 **Jiaozuo,** China
68/C4 **Jiashi,** China
66/E5 **Jiaxing,** China
62/D4 **Jiayuguan,** China
51/F2 **Jibou,** Rom.
61/G4 **Jibsh, Ra's** (pt.), Oman
39/H3 **Jičín,** Czh.
39/H4 **Jihlava,** Czh.
45/L2 **Jihočeský** (reg.), Czh.
39/J4 **Jihomoravský** (reg.), Czh.
81/U17 **Jijel,** Alg.
81/U17 **Jijel** (gov.), Alg.
51/H2 **Jijia** (riv.), Rom.
83/P6 **Jijiga,** Eth.
47/E3 **Jijona,** Sp.
86/A4 **Jilf al Kabīr, Ḩadabat al** (upland), Egypt
95/B2 **Jilhá** (res.), Braz.
39/J4 **Jilhava** (riv.), Czh.
68/E2 **Jili** (lake), China
63/K3 **Jilin,** China
63/J1 **Jiliu** (riv.), China
47/E2 **Jiloca** (riv.), Sp.
83/N6 **Jīma,** Eth.
50/E3 **Jimbolia,** Rom.
46/C4 **Jimena de la Frontera,** Sp.
62/B3 **Jimsar,** China
67/C2 **Jin** (riv.), China
71/K2 **Jin** (riv.), China
66/D3 **Jinan,** China
70/C2 **Jīnd,** India
39/H4 **Jindřichuv Hradec,** Czh.
66/B4 **Jing** (riv.), China
67/C2 **Jingdezhen,** China
67/B2 **Jinggangshan,** China
66/D3 **Jinghai,** China
66/C5 **Jingmen,** China
67/C2 **Jinhua,** China
66/C2 **Jining,** China
66/D4 **Jining,** China
83/M7 **Jinja,** Ugan.
100/D5 **Jinotega,** Nic.
100/D5 **Jinotepe,** Nic.
66/B4 **Jinqian** (riv.), China
66/E5 **Jinshan,** China
71/K2 **Jinshi,** China
67/D5 **Jintotolo** (chan.), Phil.
70/C4 **Jintūr,** India
66/E2 **Jinxi,** China
67/C2 **Jinxi,** China
66/E2 **Jinzhou,** China
92/F6 **Ji-Paraná,** Braz.
92/F5 **Jiparaná** (riv.), Braz.
92/B4 **Jipijapa,** Ecu.
86/B3 **Jirgā,** Egypt
67/A2 **Jishou,** China
59/D3 **Jisr ash Shughūr,** Syria
51/F4 **Jiu** (riv.), Rom.
67/C2 **Jiujiang,** China
67/A2 **Jiuwan** (mts.), China
66/D5 **Jixi,** China
66/C4 **Ji Xian,** China
66/D2 **Ji Xian,** China
86/B2 **Jīzah, Pyramids of** (Giza) (ruins), Egypt
66/C3 **Jize,** China
45/L1 **Jizera** (riv.), Czh.
64/C3 **Jizō-zaki** (pt.), Japan
60/F5 **Jiz', Wādī al** (dry riv.), Yem.
95/B3 **Joaçaba,** Braz.
94/B5 **Joaíma,** Braz.
94/D2 **João Câmara,** Braz.
94/A2 **João Lisboa,** Braz.
95/D1 **João Monlevade,** Braz.
94/D2 **João Pessoa,** Braz.
95/C1 **João Pinheiro,** Braz.
91/D2 **Joaquín V. González,** Arg.
101/F3 **Jobabo,** Cuba
46/D4 **Jódar,** Sp.
70/B2 **Jodhpur,** India
43/D2 **Jodoigne,** Belg.
37/J3 **Joensuu,** Fin.
65/F2 **Jōetsu,** Japan
43/F5 **Joeuf,** Fr.
88/E2 **Johannesburg,** SAfr.
108/C4 **Johannesburg,** Ca,US
106/D4 **John Day,** Or,US
106/C4 **John Day** (riv.), Or,US
106/C4 **John Day Fossil Beds Nat'l Mon.,** Or,US
112/C2 **John Martin** (res.), Co,US
113/H2 **Johnson City,** Tn,US
112/D4 **Johnson City,** Tx,US
109/G3 **Johnson** (Johnson City), Ks,US
114/M3 **Johnsons Crossing,** Yk,Can
74/C6 **Johnston** (lake), Austl.
79/J3 **Johnston** (atoll), PacUS
34/B3 **Johnston,** Wal,UK
110/E3 **Johnstown,** Pa,US
72/B3 **Johor Baharu,** Malay.
44/E3 **Joigny,** Fr.
95/B3 **Joinville,** Braz.
98/W **Joinville** (isl.), Ant.
83/M6 **Jokau,** Sudan
37/F2 **Jokkmokk,** Swe.
37/P6 **Jökulsárgljúfur Nat'l Park,** Ice.
116/P16 **Joliet,** Il,US
110/F2 **Joliette,** Qu,Can
112/D4 **Jollyville,** Tx,US
67/D6 **Jolo,** Phil.
67/D6 **Jolo** (isl.), Phil.
72/D5 **Jombang,** Indo.
45/H3 **Jona,** Swi.
39/N1 **Jonava,** Lith.
103/S7 **Jones** (sound), NW,Can
113/F3 **Jonesboro,** Ar,US
112/E3 **Jonesboro,** La,US
32/B3 **Jonesborough,** NI,UK
37/E4 **Jönköping,** Swe.
37/E4 **Jönköping** (co.), Swe.
111/G1 **Jonquière,** Qu,Can
109/J3 **Joplin,** Mo,US
60/C2 **Jordan**
111/R9 **Jordan,** On,Can
59/K6 **Jordan** (riv.), Jor., WBnk.
106/G4 **Jordan,** Mt,US
108/E2 **Jordan** (riv.), Ut,US
111/R9 **Jordan Station,** On,Can
106/D5 **Jordan Valley,** Or,US
97/J7 **Jorge** (cape), Chile
71/F2 **Jorhāt,** India
41/G1 **Jork,** Ger.
112/B3 **Jornada del Muerto** (val.), NM,US
85/H4 **Jos** (plat.), Nga.
67/E6 **Jose Abad Santos,** Phil.
95/B2 **José Bonifacio,** Braz.
94/B2 **José de Freitas,** Braz.
74/D2 **Joseph Bonaparte** (gulf), Austl.
65/F2 **Joshin-Etsu Kogen Nat'l Park,** Japan
108/D4 **Joshua Tree Nat'l Mon.,** Ca,US
37/C3 **Jotunheimen Nat'l Park,** Nor.
44/C2 **Jouanne** (riv.), Fr.
42/C6 **Jouarre,** Fr.
44/D3 **Joué-lès-Tours,** Fr.
76/B2 **Jourama Falls Nat'l Park,** Austl.
112/D4 **Jourdanton,** Tx,US
40/C3 **Joure,** Neth.
37/J3 **Joutseno,** Fin.
31/S10 **Jouy-en-Josas,** Fr.
31/S9 **Jouy-le-Moutier,** Fr.
60/G1 **Joveyn** (riv.), Iran
71/F2 **Jowai,** India
114/M3 **Joy** (mtn.), Yk,Can
65/L10 **Jōyō,** Japan
84/A2 **Jreïda,** Mrta.
66/B5 **Ju** (riv.), China
101/P9 **Juan Aldama,** Mex.
106/B3 **Juan de Fuca** (str.), Can., US
89/G7 **Juan de Nova** (isl.), Reun.
90/A6 **Juan Fernández** (isls.), Chile
101/J5 **Juangriego,** Ven.
92/C5 **Juanjuí,** Peru
97/T12 **Juan L. Lacaze,** Uru.
96/F3 **Juárez,** Arg.
95/J8 **Juatinga** (pt.), Braz.
94/B3 **Juazeiro,** Braz.
94/C2 **Juazeiro do Norte,** Braz.
83/M7 **Juba,** Sudan
83/P7 **Jubba** (riv.), Eth., Som.
47/Y17 **Juby** (cape), Mor.
48/D3 **Júcar** (riv.), Sp.
40/D6 **Jüchen,** Ger.
94/B5 **Jucurucu** (riv.), Braz.
59/N9 **Judaea** (reg.), WBnk.
45/L3 **Judenburg,** Aus.
106/F4 **Judith** (riv.), Mt,US
86/B3 **Juhaynah,** Egypt
100/D5 **Juigalpa,** Nic.
31/U9 **Juilly,** Fr.
44/E2 **Juine** (riv.), Fr.
67/D3 **Juishui,** Tai.
40/D1 **Juist** (isl.), Ger.
95/K6 **Juiz de Fora,** Braz.
109/G2 **Julesburg,** Co,US
92/D7 **Juliaca,** Peru
45/K3 **Julian Alps** (mts.), It., Slov.
43/F2 **Jülich,** Ger.
101/F3 **Julio A. Mella,** Cuba
61/L2 **Jullundur,** India
66/C3 **Juma** (riv.), China
46/E3 **Jumilla,** Sp.
81/W17 **Jūmīn** (riv.), Tun.
70/D2 **Jumla,** Nepal
41/E2 **Jümme** (riv.), Ger.
70/B3 **Jūnāgadh,** India
96/C2 **Juncal** (peak), Arg., Chile
112/D4 **Junction,** Tx,US
108/D3 **Junction,** Ut,US
109/H3 **Junction City,** Ks,US
106/C4 **Junction City,** Or,US
95/G8 **Jundiaí,** Braz.
66/H6 **Jundu** (mts.), China
81/W17 **Jundūbah,** Tun.
81/W17 **Jundūbah** (gov.), Tun.
114/M4 **Juneau** (cap.), Ak,US
45/G3 **Jungfrau** (peak), Swi.
97/C6 **Junín,** Peru
42/D5 **Juniville,** Fr.
66/C3 **Junji Guan** (pass), China
113/H5 **Juno Beach,** Fl,US
95/B2 **Junqueirópolis,** Braz.
95/E1 **Juparaná** (lake), Braz.
111/J1 **Jupiter** (riv.), Qu,Can
113/H5 **Jupiter,** Fl,US
116/A2 **Jupiter** (mtn.), Wa,US
95/C3 **Juquiá,** Braz.
95/F8 **Juquitiba,** Braz.
83/L6 **Jur** (riv.), Sudan
44/F3 **Jura** (mts.), Fr.
44/C5 **Jurançon,** Fr.
42/C2 **Jurbise,** Belg.
32/D3 **Jurby Head** (pt.), IM,UK
52/D4 **Jūrmala,** Lat.
92/E4 **Juruá** (riv.), Braz.
92/G6 **Juruena** (riv.), Braz.
93/G4 **Juruti,** Braz.
65/M9 **Jushiyama,** Japan
96/D2 **Justo Daract,** Arg.
92/E4 **Jutaí** (riv.), Braz.
100/D5 **Jutiapa,** Guat.
100/D5 **Juticalpa,** Hon.
37/D4 **Jutland** (pen.), Den.
37/H3 **Juva,** Fin.
100/E3 **Juventud** (Pinos) (isl.), Cuba
31/T10 **Juvisy-sur-Orge,** Fr.
66/D4 **Juye,** China
66/C5 **Juzhang** (riv.), China
50/E4 **Južna Morava** (riv.), Yugo.
37/H3 **Jyväskylä,** Fin.

K

68/C4 **K2** (Godwin Austen) (mtn.), China, Pak.
82/F5 **Ka** (riv.), Nga.
88/C3 **Kaap** (plat.), SAfr.
52/D3 **Kaarina,** Fin.
40/D6 **Kaarst,** Ger.
50/E2 **Kaba,** Hun.
73/F5 **Kabaena** (isl.), Indo.
100/D3 **Kabah** (ruins), Mex.
83/L8 **Kabale,** Ugan.
83/M7 **Kabalega Nat'l Park,** Ugan.
87/E2 **Kabalo,** Zaire
87/E2 **Kabamba** (lake), Zaire
73/F2 **Kabankalan,** Phil.
55/G4 **Kabardin-Balkar Aut. Rep.,** Rus.
110/C1 **Kabinakagami** (lake), On,Can
87/D2 **Kabinda,** Zaire
81/V17 **Kabīr** (riv.), Alg.
48/A5 **Kabīyah** (lag.), Tun.
87/D3 **Kabompo** (riv.), Zam.
87/E2 **Kabongo,** Zaire
61/J2 **Kabul** (riv.), Afg.
61/J2 **Kābul** (Kābol) (cap.), Afg.
73/G3 **Kaburuang** (isl.), Indo.
87/E3 **Kabwe,** Zam.
50/E4 **Kačanik,** Yugo.
114/H4 **Kachemak** (bay), Ak,US
71/G2 **Kachin** (state), Burma
70/C6 **Kadaianallur,** India
69/B3 **Kadan** (isl.), Burma
45/K1 **Kadaň,** Czh.
78/G6 **Kadavu** (isl.), Fiji
82/J7 **Kadéï** (riv.), CAfr., Congo
51/H5 **Kadıköy,** Turk.
59/C2 **Kadınhanı,** Turk.
85/E3 **Kadiogo** (prov.), Burk.
70/C5 **Kadiri,** India
59/D3 **Kadirli,** Turk.
107/H5 **Kadoka,** SD,US
65/L10 **Kadoma,** Japan
87/E4 **Kadoma,** Zim.
85/G4 **Kaduna,** Nga.
85/G4 **Kaduna** (riv.), Nga.
85/G4 **Kaduna** (state), Nga.
83/L5 **Kāduqlī,** Sudan
84/B2 **Kaédi,** Mrta.
82/H5 **Kaélé,** Camr.
69/C2 **Kaeng Khlo,** Thai.
69/B3 **Kaeng Krachan Nat'l Park,** Thai.
63/K4 **Kaesŏng,** NKor.
55/H5 **Kafan,** Arm.
61/J2 **Kafar Jar Ghar** (mts.), Afg.
88/D4 **Kaffraria** (reg.), SAfr.
84/B3 **Kaffrine,** Sen.
83/K6 **Kafia Kingi,** Sudan
49/J3 **Kafirévs, Akra** (cape), Gre.
59/H6 **Kafr ad Dawwār,** Egypt
59/H6 **Kafr ash Shaykh,** Egypt
59/H6 **Kafr ash Shaykh** (gov.), Egypt
59/H6 **Kafr az Zayyāt,** Egypt
59/N8 **Kafr Qari',** Isr.
59/M8 **Kafr Qāsim,** Isr.
87/E4 **Kafue,** Zam.
87/E4 **Kafue** (riv.), Zam.
87/E4 **Kafue Nat'l Park,** Zam.
64/E2 **Kaga,** Japan
82/J6 **Kaga Bandoro,** CAfr.
56/G6 **Kagan,** Uzb.
64/D3 **Kagawa** (pref.), Japan
51/J5 **Kağıthane,** Turk.
59/E2 **Kağızman,** Turk.
64/B5 **Kagoshima,** Japan
64/B5 **Kagoshima** (bay), Japan
64/B5 **Kagoshima** (pref.), Japan
51/J3 **Kagul,** Mol.
104/W12 **Kahana,** Hi,US
72/D4 **Kahayan** (riv.), Indo.
87/C2 **Kahemba,** Zaire
62/D1 **Kahmsara** (riv.), Rus.
109/K2 **Kahoka,** Mo,US
104/T10 **Kahoolawe** (isl.), Hi,US
37/G1 **Kahperusvaara** (peak), Fin.
59/D3 **Kahramanmaraş,** Turk.
61/K3 **Kahror Pakka,** Pak.
59/D3 **Kâhta,** Turk.
104/T10 **Kahuku** (pt.), Hi,US
104/T10 **Kahului,** Hi,US
87/E1 **Kahuzi-Biega Nat'l Park,** Zaire
73/H5 **Kai** (isls.), Indo.
75/R11 **Kaiapoi,** NZ
108/D3 **Kaibab** (plat.), Az,US
65/L9 **Kaibara,** Japan
73/H5 **Kai Besar** (isl.), Indo.
68/C3 **Kaidu** (riv.), China
62/G5 **Kaifeng,** China
64/D4 **Kaifu,** Japan
73/H5 **Kai Kecil** (isl.), Indo.
75/R10 **Kaikohe,** NZ
75/R11 **Kaikoura,** NZ
71/J2 **Kaili,** China
104/U11 **Kailua,** Hi,US
88/B2 **Kainab** (dry riv.), Namb.
50/B2 **Kainach** (riv.), Aus.
64/D3 **Kainan,** Japan
85/G4 **Kainji** (lake), Nga.
75/R10 **Kaipara** (har.), NZ
65/H7 **Kaisei,** Japan
43/G5 **Kaiserslautern,** Ger.
75/R10 **Kaitaia,** NZ
68/C6 **Kaithal,** India
104/T10 **Kaiwi** (chan.), Hi,US
66/F2 **Kaiyuan,** China
71/H3 **Kaiyuan,** China
65/M9 **Kaizu,** Japan
65/M10 **Kaizuka,** Japan
30/F2 **Kajaani,** Fin.
64/A3 **Kaji-san** (mtn.), SKor.
83/M5 **Kākā,** Sudan
37/G3 **Kakaanpää,** Fin.
83/M7 **Kakamega,** Kenya
65/E3 **Kakamigahara,** Japan
50/D3 **Kakanj,** Bosn.
114/M4 **Kaketsa** (mtn.), BC,Can
54/E3 **Kakhovka,** Ukr.
54/E3 **Kakhovka** (res.), Ukr.
70/D4 **Kākināda,** India
65/L9 **Kako** (riv.), Japan
84/B4 **Kakrima** (riv.), Gui.
65/G2 **Kakuda,** Japan
83/M7 **Kakuma,** Kenya
83/M8 **Kakuto,** Ugan.
81/X18 **Kalaa-Kebira,** Tun.
99/N2 **Kalaallit Nunaat** (Greenland) (dpcy.), Den.
87/D3 **Kalabo,** Zam.
55/G2 **Kalach,** Rus.
56/H4 **Kalachinsk,** Rus.
55/G2 **Kalach-na-Donu,** Rus.
71/F3 **Kaladan** (riv.), Burma
104/U11 **Ka Lae** (cape), Hi,US
87/D5 **Kalahari** (des.), Afr.
88/C2 **Kalahari-Gemsbok Nat'l Park,** SAfr.
49/L7 **Kalamáki,** Gre.
82/H5 **Kalamaloué Nat'l Park,** Camr.
49/H2 **Kalamariá,** Gre.
49/H4 **Kalamáta,** Gre.
110/C3 **Kalamazoo,** Mi,US
69/C2 **Kalasin,** Thai.
61/J3 **Kalāt,** Pak.
81/X18 **Kalbīyah** (lake), Tun.
37/N7 **Kaldakvísl** (riv.), Ice.
41/H5 **Kalefeld,** Ger.
87/E2 **Kalemie,** Zaire
39/K3 **Kalety,** Pol.
74/C6 **Kalgoorlie-Boulder,** Austl.
51/J4 **Kaliakra, Nos** (pt.), Bul.
72/C5 **Kalianda,** Indo.
67/D5 **Kalibo,** Phil.
87/E1 **Kalima,** Zaire
72/D4 **Kalimantan** (reg.), Indo.
59/A3 **Kálimnos,** Gre.
39/L1 **Kaliningrad,** Rus.
52/H5 **Kaliningrad,** Rus.
39/K1 **Kaliningrad** (lag.), Rus.
52/D5 **Kaliningrad Obl.,** Rus.
55/H2 **Kalininsk,** Rus.
54/D1 **Kalinkovichi,** Bela.
83/M8 **Kalisizo,** Ugan.
106/E3 **Kalispell,** Mt,US
39/K3 **Kalisz,** Pol.
39/J3 **Kalisz** (prov.), Pol.
37/G2 **Kalix,** Swe.
37/G2 **Kalixälv** (riv.), Swe.
70/E2 **Kāliyāganj,** India
110/C2 **Kalkaska,** Mi,US
49/L7 **Kallithea,** Gre.
37/E3 **Kallsjön** (lake), Swe.
37/F4 **Kalmar,** Swe.
37/E4 **Kalmar** (co.), Swe.
40/B6 **Kalmthout,** Belg.
55/H3 **Kalmyk Aut. Rep.,** Rus.
50/D2 **Kalocsa,** Hun.
104/T10 **Kalohi** (chan.), Hi,US
70/B3 **Kālol,** India
87/E4 **Kalomo,** Zam.
70/C2 **Kālpi,** India
38/E2 **Kaltenkirchen,** Ger.
45/F4 **Kaltern** (Caldaro), It.
70/D6 **Kalu** (riv.), SrL.
52/H5 **Kaluga,** Rus.
52/G5 **Kaluga Obl.,** Rus.
38/F1 **Kalundborg,** Den.
54/C2 **Kalush,** Ukr.
70/C6 **Kalutara,** SrL.
70/B4 **Kalyān,** India
53/M4 **Kama** (res.), Rus.
53/M3 **Kama** (riv.), Rus.
87/E1 **Kama,** Zaire
65/J7 **Kamagaya,** Japan
63/N4 **Kamaishi,** Japan
104/T10 **Kamakou** (peak), Hi,US
65/H7 **Kamakura,** Japan
68/B5 **Kamālia,** Pak.
59/C2 **Kaman,** Turk.
84/E2 **Kamango** (lake), Mali
70/C4 **Kāmāreddi,** India
70/E3 **Kāmārhāti,** India
70/A2 **Kambar,** Pak.
87/E3 **Kambove,** Zaire
73/F4 **Kambuno** (peak), Indo.
57/R4 **Kamchatka** (pen.), Rus.
57/R4 **Kamchatka Obl.,** Rus.
51/H4 **Kamchiya** (riv.), Bul.
41/E5 **Kamen,** Ger.
54/C2 **Kamenets-Podol'skiy,** Ukr.
50/A3 **Kamenjak, Rt** (cape), Cro.
55/H1 **Kamenka,** Rus.
68/D1 **Kamen'-na-Obi,** Rus.
54/G2 **Kamensk-Shakhtinskiy,** Rus.
53/P4 **Kamensk-Ural'skiy,** Rus.
64/D3 **Kameoka,** Japan
65/M10 **Kameyama,** Japan
106/D4 **Kamiah,** Id,US
39/H2 **Kamień Pomorski,** Pol.
65/H7 **Kamifukuoka,** Japan
63/N3 **Kamiisco,** Japan
65/M9 **Kamiishizu,** Japan
104/U11 **Kamilo** (pt.), Hi,US
87/E2 **Kamina,** Zaire
65/G1 **Kaminoyama,** Japan
114/H4 **Kamishak** (bay), Ak,US
64/B5 **Kamiyaku,** Japan
106/C3 **Kamloops,** BC,Can
69/C4 **Kamlot,** Camb.
65/L10 **Kammaki,** Japan
50/B2 **Kamnik,** Slov.
65/J7 **Kamo** (riv.), Japan
65/G3 **Kamogawa,** Japan
64/D3 **Kamojima,** Japan
45/L2 **Kamp** (riv.), Aus.
83/M7 **Kampala** (cap.), Ugan.
72/B3 **Kampar** (riv.), Indo.
72/B3 **Kampar,** Malay.
40/C3 **Kampen,** Neth.
69/B2 **Kamphaeng Phet,** Thai.
39/L2 **Kampinoski Nat'l Park,** Pol.
40/D6 **Kamp-Lintfort,** Ger.
69/D4 **Kampong Cham,** Camb.
69/D3 **Kampong Chhnang,** Camb.
69/D3 **Kampong Khleang,** Camb.
69/C4 **Kampong Saom,** Camb.
69/C4 **Kampong Saom** (bay), Camb.
69/D4 **Kampong Spoe,** Camb.
69/D3 **Kampong Thum,** Camb.
69/D4 **Kampong Trabek,** Camb.
69/D4 **Kampot,** Camb.
73/H4 **Kamrau** (bay), Indo.
107/H3 **Kamsack,** Sk,Can
107/H1 **Kamuchawie** (lake), Sk,Can
100/E6 **Kámuk** (mt.), CR
55/H2 **Kamyshin,** Rus.
103/J3 **Kanaaupscow** (riv.), Qu,Can
108/D3 **Kanab** (riv.), Az, Ut,US
108/D3 **Kanab,** Ut,US
114/C6 **Kanaga** (isl.), Ak,US
114/C6 **Kanaga** (vol.), Ak,US
65/F3 **Kanagawa** (pref.), Japan
103/K3 **Kanairiktok** (riv.), Nf,Can
65/L10 **Kanan,** Japan
87/D2 **Kananga,** Zaire
53/K5 **Kanash,** Rus.
110/D4 **Kanawha** (riv.), WV,US
65/E2 **Kanazawa,** Japan
69/B3 **Kanchanaburi,** Thai.
70/C5 **Kānchīpuram,** India
52/G2 **Kandalaksha,** Rus.
52/G2 **Kandalaksha** (gulf), Rus.
79/Y18 **Kandavu** (passg.), Fiji
61/J3 **Kandhkot,** Pak.
70/E3 **Kāndi,** India
73/F3 **Kandi** (cape), Indo.
51/K5 **Kandıra,** Turk.
70/C4 **Kandukūr,** India
70/D6 **Kandy,** SrL.
103/T7 **Kane Basin** (sound), NW,Can
82/H5 **Kanem** (reg.), Chad
104/W13 **Kaneohe,** Hi,US
104/W13 **Kaneohe** (bay), Hi,US
87/D5 **Kang,** Bots.
59/D2 **Kangal,** Turk.
72/B2 **Kangar,** Malay.
74/F7 **Kangaroo** (isl.), Austl.
60/E2 **Kangāvar,** Iran
73/E5 **Kangean** (isls.), Indo.
103/K3 **Kangiqsualujjuaq,** Qu,Can
103/J2 **Kangiqsujuaq,** Qu,Can
103/J2 **Kangirsuk,** Qu,Can
64/A2 **Kangnŭng,** SKor.
68/D5 **Kangrinboqê Feng** (peak), China
71/F2 **Kangto** (peak), China
70/C3 **Kanhān** (riv.), India
65/N9 **Kani,** Japan
65/M9 **Kanie,** Japan
53/K2 **Kanin** (pen.), Rus.
30/H2 **Kanin Nos** (pt.), Rus.
50/E2 **Kanjiža,** Yugo.
110/C3 **Kankakee,** Il,US
110/C3 **Kankakee** (riv.), Il, In,US
84/C4 **Kankan,** Gui.
84/C4 **Kankan** (comm.), Gui.
70/D3 **Kānker,** India
64/C3 **Kanmuri-yama** (mtn.), Japan
113/H3 **Kannapolis,** NC,US
70/C2 **Kannauj,** India
65/H7 **Kannon-zaki** (pt.), Japan
85/H4 **Kano,** Nga.
85/H3 **Kano** (state), Nga.
64/C3 **Kan'onji,** Japan
64/B5 **Kanoya,** Japan
70/D2 **Kānpur,** India
109/H3 **Kansas** (state), US
109/H3 **Kansas** (riv.), Ks,US
109/J3 **Kansas City,** Ks, Mo,US
56/K4 **Kansk,** Rus.
70/D3 **Kantābānji,** India
65/F2 **Kantō** (prov.), Japan
92/G3 **Kanuku** (mts.), Guy.
65/F2 **Kanuma,** Japan
114/H2 **Kanuti Nat'l Wild. Ref.,** Ak,US
88/D2 **Kanye,** Bots.
69/D3 **Kaoh Nhek,** Camb.
67/D3 **Kaohsiung,** Tai.
87/B4 **Kaokoveld** (reg.), Namb.
84/A3 **Kaolack,** Sen.
84/B3 **Kaolack** (reg.), Sen.
87/D3 **Kaoma,** Zam.
104/S9 **Kapaa,** Hi,US
67/E6 **Kapalong,** Phil.
87/D2 **Kapanga,** Zaire
50/E4 **Kapaonik** (upland), Yugo.
68/C3 **Kapchagay,** Kaz.
68/C3 **Kapchagay** (res.), Kaz.
40/B6 **Kapellen,** Belg.
45/L3 **Kapfenberg,** Aus.
51/H5 **Kapidaği** (pen.), Turk.
78/E4 **Kapingamarangi** (isl.), Micr.
87/E3 **Kapiri Mposhi,** Zam.
103/H3 **Kapiskau** (riv.), On,Can
83/M7 **Kapoeta,** Sudan
50/C2 **Kapos** (riv.), Hun.
50/C2 **Kaposvár,** Hun.
39/M1 **Kapsukas,** Lith.
72/C4 **Kapuas** (riv.), Indo.
72/D3 **Kapuas Hulu** (mts.), Indo., Malay.
110/D1 **Kapuskasing,** On,Can
110/D1 **Kapuskasing** (riv.), On,Can
50/C2 **Kapuvár,** Hun.
55/H5 **Kapydzhik, Gora** (peak), Azer.
53/Q1 **Kara** (riv.), Rus.
56/G2 **Kara** (sea), Rus.
55/K4 **Kara-Bogaz-Gol** (gulf), Trkm.
73/H4 **Karabra** (riv.), Indo.
59/C2 **Karabük,** Turk.
59/D3 **Karaca** (peak), Turk.
59/B2 **Karacabey,** Turk.
55/G4 **Karachay-Cherkass Aut. Obl.,** Rus.
54/E1 **Karachev,** Rus.
61/J4 **Karāchi,** Pak.
70/B4 **Karād,** India
68/B2 **Karaganda,** Kaz.
58/R4 **Karaginskiy** (isl.), Rus.
68/E1 **Karagoš** (peak), Rus.
70/C5 **Kāraikkudi,** India
60/F1 **Karaj,** Iran
55/L3 **Karakalpak Aut. Rep.,** Uzb.
68/C4 **Karakax** (riv.), China
59/D2 **Karakaya** (res.), Turk.
73/G3 **Karakelong** (isl.), Indo.
62/E3 **Karakhoto** (ruins), China
59/E2 **Karakoçan,** Turk.
68/C4 **Karakoram** (range), Asia
68/C4 **Karakoram** (pass), China, India
84/C3 **Karakoro** (riv.), Mali, Mrta.
62/E2 **Karakorum** (ruins), Mong.
59/E2 **Karaköse,** Turk.
68/B4 **Karakul'** (lake), Taj.
55/L5 **Karakumy** (des.), Trkm.
55/K4 **Karakyon, Gora** (peak), Trkm.
61/H1 **Karakyr** (peak), Trkm.
73/E4 **Karam** (riv.), Indo.
59/C3 **Karaman,** Turk.
68/D2 **Karamay,** China
75/R11 **Karamea,** NZ
75/R11 **Karamea** (bight), NZ
68/D4 **Karamiran** (riv.), China
68/E4 **Karamiran Shankou** (pass), China
51/J5 **Karamürsel,** Turk.
71/G4 **Karan** (state), Burma
73/E5 **Karangasem,** Indo.
57/S4 **Karanginskiy** (bay), Rus.
57/S4 **Karanginskiy** (isl.), Rus.
70/C3 **Kāranja,** India
69/B2 **Karan** (Kayin) (state), Burma
59/C3 **Karapınar,** Turk.
64/A3 **Kara-saki** (pt.), Japan
65/M10 **Karasu,** Japan
51/K5 **Karasu,** Turk.
68/C1 **Karasuk,** Rus.
68/C2 **Karatal** (riv.), Kaz.
68/B3 **Karatau,** Kaz.
68/A3 **Karatau** (mts.), Kaz.
64/A4 **Karatsu,** Japan
49/G3 **Karáva** (peak), Gre.
68/B2 **Karazhal,** Kaz.
86/C5 **Karbaka,** Sudan
60/D2 **Karbalā',** Iraq
50/E2 **Karcag,** Hun.
49/G3 **Kardhítsa,** Gre.
56/D3 **Karelian Aut. Rep.,** Rus.
87/F2 **Karema,** Tanz.
62/H1 **Karenga** (riv.), Rus.
87/E4 **Kariba** (lake), Zam., Zim.
87/E4 **Kariba,** Zim.
72/C4 **Karimata** (isl.), Indo.
72/C4 **Karimata** (str.), Indo.
70/C4 **Karīmnagar,** India
87/E1 **Karisimbi** (vol.), Rwa.
65/M10 **Kariya,** Japan
83/Q6 **Karkaar** (mts.), Som.
70/B5 **Kārkāl,** India
78/D5 **Karkar** (isl.), PNG
54/E3 **Karkinitsk** (gulf), Ukr.
68/B4 **Karla Marksa, Pik** (peak), Taj.
50/B3 **Karlovac,** Slov.
51/G4 **Karlovo,** Bul.
45/K1 **Karlovy Vary** (Karlsbad), Czh.
37/E4 **Karlshamn,** Swe.
37/E4 **Karlskoga,** Swe.
37/E4 **Karlskrona,** Swe.
45/H2 **Karlsruhe,** Ger.
37/E4 **Karlstad,** Swe.
86/B5 **Karmah,** Sudan
70/C4 **Karmāla,** India
59/K5 **Karmel, Har** (Mount Carmel) (mtn.), Isr.
70/C2 **Karnāl,** India
70/C4 **Karnataka** (state), India
112/D4 **Karnes City,** Tx,US
51/H4 **Karnobat,** Bul.
50/A2 **Kärnten** (prov.), Aus.
87/F2 **Karonga,** Malw.
88/C4 **Karoo Nat'l Park,** SAfr.
61/K2 **Karor,** Pak.
73/E5 **Karoso** (cape), Indo.
59/A3 **Kárpathos** (isl.), Gre.
74/B4 **Karratha,** Austl.
88/M11 **Kars** (riv.), SAfr.
59/E2 **Kars,** Turk.
56/G6 **Karshi,** Uzb.
55/M1 **Kartaly,** Rus.
51/L3 **Kartinitsk** (gulf), Ukr.
39/K1 **Kartuzy,** Pol.
60/E2 **Kārūn** (riv.), Iran
39/K4 **Karviná,** Czh.
70/B5 **Karwar,** India
107/L2 **Kasabonika** (lake), On,Can
70/E3 **Kāsai** (riv.), India
64/D3 **Kasai,** Japan
87/C1 **Kasai** (riv.), Zaire
65/G2 **Kasama,** Japan
87/F3 **Kasama,** Zam.
65/M9 **Kasamatsu,** Japan
87/E4 **Kasane,** Bots.
64/C3 **Kasaoka,** Japan
70/C5 **Kāsaragod,** India
86/D5 **Kasar, Ras** (cape), Sudan
65/M10 **Kasartori-yama** (peak), Japan
102/F2 **Kasba** (lake), NW,Can
64/B5 **Kaseda,** Japan
70/C2 **Kāsganj,** India
61/H1 **Kashaf** (riv.), Iran
60/F2 **Kāshān,** Iran

Kashi – Kohun

68/C4 **Kashi,** China
65/L10 **Kashiba,** Japan
64/D3 **Kashihara,** Japan
64/B4 **Kashima,** Japan
65/G3 **Kashima,** Japan
52/H4 **Kashin,** Rus.
65/H7 **Kashiwa,** Japan
65/L10 **Kashiwara,** Japan
65/F2 **Kashiwazaki,** Japan
61/G1 **Kāshmar,** Iran
70/A2 **Kashmor,** Pak.
52/J5 **Kasimov,** Rus.
73/G4 **Kasiruta** (isl.), Indo.
73/H4 **Kasiui** (isl.), Indo.
110/B4 **Kaskaskia** (riv.), Il,US
106/D3 **Kaslo,** BC,Can
87/E1 **Kasongo,** Zaire
87/C2 **Kasongo-Lunda,** Zaire
55/H4 **Kaspiysk,** Rus.
83/N4 **Kassala,** Sudan
49/H3 **Kassándra** (pen.), Gre.
41/G6 **Kassel,** Ger.
107/K4 **Kasson,** Mn,US
59/C2 **Kastamonu,** Turk.
43/D1 **Kasterlee,** Belg.
49/G2 **Kastoría,** Gre.
49/G3 **Kastrakíou** (lake), Gre.
65/E3 **Kasugai,** Japan
65/F3 **Kasukabe,** Japan
87/F1 **Kasulu,** Tanz.
65/G2 **Kasumiga** (lake), Japan
87/F3 **Kasungu,** Malw.
61/K2 **Kasūr,** Pak.
87/E4 **Kataba,** Zam.
111/G2 **Katahdin** (mtn.), Me,US
87/E2 **Katanga** (reg.), Zaire
65/L10 **Katano,** Japan
87/F2 **Katavi Nat'l Park,** Tanz.
71/F6 **Katchall** (isl.), India
87/D2 **Katea,** Zaire
87/E2 **Katea,** Zaire
49/H2 **Kateríni,** Gre.
114/M4 **Kates Needle** (mtn.), Ak,US
87/F3 **Katete,** Zam.
71/G3 **Katha,** Burma
70/C2 **Kāthgodām,** India
61/K4 **Kathiawar** (pen.), India
70/E2 **Kāthmāndu** (cap.), Nepal
61/L2 **Kathua,** India
84/C3 **Kati,** Mali
84/D4 **Katiola,** IvC.
41/H5 **Katlenburg-Lindau,** Ger.
114/H4 **Katmai** (vol.), Ak,US
114/G4 **Katmai Nat'l Park & Prsv.,** Ak,US
39/K3 **Katowice,** Pol.
39/K3 **Katowice** (prov.), Pol.
83/M2 **Kātrīnā, Jabal** (Mt. Catherine) (peak), Egypt
36/C2 **Katrine, Loch** (lake), Sc,UK
85/G3 **Katsina,** Nga.
85/G3 **Katsina** (state), Nga.
85/H5 **Katsina Ala** (riv.), Camr., Nga.
65/L9 **Katsura** (riv.), Japan
64/D3 **Katsuragi,** Japan
65/L10 **Katsuragi-san** (peak), Japan
65/G2 **Katsuta,** Japan
65/G3 **Katsuura,** Japan
110/E1 **Kattawagami** (riv.), On,Can
87/F3 **Katumbi,** Malw.
68/E1 **Katun'** (riv.), Rus.
68/E1 **Katun'chuya** (riv.), Rus.
40/B4 **Katwijk aan Zee,** Neth.
45/H2 **Katzenbuckel** (peak), Ger.
104/S10 **Kauai** (chan.), Hi,US
104/S9 **Kauai** (isl.), Hi,US
45/J3 **Kaufbeuren,** Ger.
112/D3 **Kaufman,** Tx,US
41/G6 **Kaufungen,** Ger.
37/G3 **Kauhajoki,** Fin.
37/G3 **Kauhanevan-Pohjankankaan Nat'l Park,** Fin.
37/G3 **Kauhava,** Fin.
104/U10 **Kauhola** (pt.), Hi,US
104/U10 **Kauiki Head** (pt.), Hi,US
87/C5 **Kaukaveld** (mts.), Namb.
79/L6 **Kaukura** (atoll), FrPol.
104/R9 **Kaulakahi** (chan.), Hi,US
39/M1 **Kaunas,** Lith.
39/N1 **Kaunas** (res.), Lith.
69/B4 **Kau-ye** (isl.), Burma
50/F5 **Kavadarci,** Macd.
49/F2 **Kavajë,** Alb.
49/J2 **Kavála,** Gre.
63/M3 **Kavalerovo,** Rus.
70/C5 **Kāvali,** India
78/C4 **Kavangel** (isls.), Palau
70/B5 **Kavaratti,** India
51/J4 **Kavarna,** Bul.
78/E5 **Kavieng,** PNG
112/D2 **Kaw** (lake), Ok,US
86/B5 **Kawa** (ruins), Sudan
65/L10 **Kawachi-Nagano,** Japan
65/M10 **Kawage,** Japan
65/F3 **Kawagoe,** Japan
65/M9 **Kawagoe,** Japan
65/F3 **Kawaguchi,** Japan
104/R10 **Kawaihoa** (pt.), Hi,US
104/S9 **Kawaikini** (peak), Hi,US
65/H7 **Kawajima,** Japan
65/G2 **Kawamata,** Japan
87/E2 **Kawambwa,** Zam.
65/L10 **Kawanishi,** Japan
70/D3 **Kawardha,** India
110/E2 **Kawartha** (lakes), On,Can
65/F3 **Kawasaki,** Japan
65/M9 **Kawashima,** Japan
104/V12 **Kawela Bay** (Kawela), Hi,US
75/S10 **Kawerau,** NZ
86/C3 **Kawm Umbū,** Egypt
68/D3 **Kax** (riv.), China
68/C3 **Kaxgar** (riv.), China
114/L2 **Kay** (pt.), Yk,Can
85/E4 **Kaya,** Burk.
82/J6 **Kayagangiri** (peak), CAfr.
69/B2 **Kayah** (state), Burma
73/E3 **Kayan** (riv.), Indo.
84/B3 **Kayanga** (riv.), Sen.
106/G5 **Kaycee,** Wy,US
108/E3 **Kayenta,** Az,US
84/C3 **Kayes,** Mali
84/C3 **Kayes** (reg.), Mali
69/B2 **Kayin** (Karan) (state), Burma
43/F5 **Kayl,** Lux.
73/G3 **Kayoa** (isl.), Indo.
59/C2 **Kayseri,** Turk.
72/B4 **Kayuagung,** Indo.
68/B2 **Kazakh** (uplands), Kaz.
56/G5 **Kazakhstan**
102/F2 **Kazan** (riv.), NW,Can
53/L5 **Kazan',** Rus.
51/G4 **Kazanlŭk,** Bul.
54/D2 **Kazatin,** Ukr.
55/H4 **Kazbek** (peak), Geo.
60/F3 **Kāzerūn,** Iran
39/L3 **Kazimierza Wielka,** Pol.
50/E1 **Kazincbarcika,** Hun.
63/N3 **Kazuno,** Japan
49/J4 **Kéa** (isl.), Gre.
32/B3 **Keady,** NI,UK
115/F5 **Keansburg,** NJ,US
109/H2 **Kearney,** Ne,US
32/C3 **Kearny** (pt.), NI,UK
115/F5 **Kearny,** NJ,US
104/U11 **Keawekaheka** (pt.), Hi,US
59/D2 **Keban** (res.), Turk.
37/F2 **Kebnekaise** (peak), Swe.
83/P6 **K'ebri Dehar,** Eth.
72/C5 **Kebumen,** Indo.
50/D2 **Kecel,** Hun.
50/D2 **Kecskemét,** Hun.
39/M1 **Kédainiai,** Lith.
43/F5 **Kédange-sur Canner,** Fr.
72/D5 **Kediri,** Indo.
84/B3 **Kédougou,** Sen.
39/K3 **Kędzierzyn-Koźle,** Pol.
116/F6 **Keego Harbor,** Mi,US
102/D2 **Keele** (riv.), NW,Can
102/C2 **Keele** (peak), Yk,Can
67/D2 **Keelung,** Tai.
111/F3 **Keene,** NH,US
76/A1 **Keer-weer** (cape), Austl.
88/B2 **Keetmanshoop,** Namb.
49/G3 **Kefallinía** (isl.), Gre.
59/M8 **Kefar Sava,** Isr.
37/M7 **Keflavík,** Ice.
71/J5 **Ke Ga** (cape), Viet.
70/D6 **Kegalla,** SrL.
33/G6 **Kegworth,** Eng,UK
43/G6 **Kehl,** Ger.
33/G4 **Keighley,** Eng,UK
65/L9 **Keihoku,** Japan
77/F5 **Keilor,** Austl.
83/J6 **Kéita** (riv.), Chad
36/D2 **Keith,** Sc,UK
111/H2 **Kejimkujik Nat'l Park,** NS,Can
50/D2 **Kékes** (peak), Hun.
73/G4 **Kelang** (isl.), Indo.
72/B3 **Kelang,** Malay.
85/H3 **Kélé-Kélé,** Niger
45/J2 **Kelheim,** Ger.
59/D2 **Kelkit,** Turk.
59/D2 **Kelkit** (riv.), Turk.
102/D2 **Keller** (lake), NW,Can
115/C2 **Keller** (peak), Ca,US
102/D1 **Kellett** (cape), NW,Can
106/D4 **Kellogg,** Id,US
32/B2 **Kells,** NI,UK
112/D4 **Kelly A.F.B.,** Tx,US
82/J6 **Kélo,** Chad
106/D3 **Kelowna,** BC,Can
33/F5 **Kelsall,** Eng,UK
34/A6 **Kelsey Head** (pt.), UK
36/D3 **Kelso,** Sc,UK
106/C4 **Kelso,** Wa,US
72/B3 **Keluang,** Malay.
35/G3 **Kelvedon,** Eng,UK
107/H2 **Kelvington,** Sk,Can
52/G2 **Kem',** Rus.
52/G2 **Kem'** (riv.), Rus.
34/D3 **Kemble,** Eng,UK
72/D3 **Kemena** (riv.), Malay.
56/J4 **Kemerovo,** Rus.
37/H2 **Kemi,** Fin.
37/H2 **Kemijärvi,** Fin.
37/H2 **Kemijoki** (riv.), Fin.
42/B2 **Kemmel,** Belg.
106/F5 **Kemmerer,** Wy,US
98/W **Kemp** (pen.), Ant.
109/H4 **Kemp** (lake), Tx,US
37/H2 **Kempele,** Fin.
40/D6 **Kempen,** Ger.
40/C6 **Kempenland** (reg.), Belg.
40/B6 **Kempisch** (can.), Belg.
77/E1 **Kempsey,** Austl.
35/F2 **Kempston,** Eng,UK
110/F2 **Kempt** (lake), Qu,Can
45/J3 **Kempten,** Ger.
88/E2 **Kempton Park,** SAfr.
73/E3 **Kemul** (peak), Indo.
114/H3 **Kenai,** Ak,US
114/J3 **Kenai Fjords Nat'l Park,** Ak,US
81/V18 **Kenchela** (gov.), Alg.
33/F3 **Kendal,** Eng,UK
113/H5 **Kendall,** Fl,US
110/C3 **Kendallville,** In,US
73/F4 **Kendari,** Indo.
40/D5 **Kendel** (riv.), Neth., Ger.
70/E3 **Kendrāpāra,** India
84/D4 **Kénédougou** (prov.), Burk.
84/C5 **Kenema,** SLeo.
71/J4 **Keng Deng,** Laos
87/C1 **Kenge,** Zaire
69/B1 **Kēng Tung,** Burma
84/C3 **Kenié-Baoulé Rsv.,** Mali
35/E2 **Kenilworth,** Eng,UK
81/L13 **Kenitra,** Mor.
32/D1 **Ken, Loch** (lake), Sc,UK
107/H3 **Kenmare,** ND,US
111/S10 **Kenmore,** NY,US
116/C2 **Kenmore,** Wa,US
75/K4 **Kenn** (reef), Austl.
111/G2 **Kennebec** (riv.), Me,US
111/G3 **Kennebunk,** Me,US
103/T6 **Kennedy** (chan.), NW,Can
114/H4 **Kennedy** (str.), Ak,US
40/B4 **Kennemerduinen Nat'l Park,** Neth.
113/F4 **Kenner,** La,US
34/D4 **Kennet** (can.), Eng,UK
35/E4 **Kennet** (riv.), Eng,UK
110/B4 **Kennett,** Mo,US
106/D4 **Kennewick,** Wa,US
110/C1 **Kenogami** (riv.), On,Can
114/L3 **Keno Hill,** Yk,Can
110/A1 **Kenora,** On,Can
116/Q14 **Kenosha,** Wi,US
31/N7 **Kensington & Chelsea** (bor.), Eng,UK
102/F2 **Kent** (pen.), NW,Can
31/P8 **Kent** (co.), Eng,UK
33/F3 **Kent** (riv.), Eng,UK
110/D3 **Kent,** Oh,US
116/C3 **Kent,** Wa,US
68/A3 **Kentau,** Kaz.
77/C3 **Kent Group** (isls.), Austl.
110/D3 **Kenton,** Oh,US
110/C4 **Kentucky** (state), US
110/C4 **Kentucky** (riv.), Ky,US
113/F2 **Kentucky** (lake), Ky, Tn,US
35/G4 **Kent, Vale of** (val.), Eng,UK
111/H2 **Kentville,** NS,Can
32/D1 **Ken, Water of** (riv.), Sc,UK
80/F4 **Kenya**
83/M8 **Kenya** (mtn.), Kenya
65/H7 **Ken-zaki** (pt.), Japan
107/L5 **Keokuk,** Ia,US
70/E3 **Keonjhar,** India
39/J3 **Kępno,** Pol.
70/C5 **Kerala** (state), India
85/F4 **Kéran Nat'l Park,** Togo
49/H4 **Keratéa,** Gre.
54/F3 **Kerch'** (str.), Rus., Ukr.
54/F3 **Kerch',** Ukr.
106/D3 **Keremeos,** BC,Can
83/N4 **Keren,** Erit.
52/G2 **Keret'** (lake), Rus.
29/N8 **Kerguélen** (isl.), FrAnt.
75/R9 **Kerikeri** (cape), NZ
72/B4 **Kerinci** (peak), Indo.
68/D4 **Keriya** (riv.), China
68/D4 **Keriya Shankou** (pass), China
40/C5 **Kerkdriel,** Neth.
40/D6 **Kerken,** Ger.
56/G6 **Kerki,** Trkm.
49/H2 **Kerkínis** (lake), Gre.
49/F3 **Kérkira** (Corfu), Gre.
43/F2 **Kerkrade,** Neth.
40/C5 **Kerkwijk,** Neth.
78/G7 **Kermadec** (isls.), NZ
61/G2 **Kermān,** Iran
112/C4 **Kermit,** Tx,US
108/C4 **Kern** (riv.), Ca,US
49/J4 **Kéros** (isl.), Gre.
113/J2 **Kerr** (res.), NC, Va,US
109/J4 **Kerr** (lake), Ok,US
106/F3 **Kerrobert,** Sk,Can
112/D4 **Kerrville,** Tx,US
34/C2 **Kerry,** Wal,UK
81/N13 **Kert** (riv.), Mor.
62/G2 **Kerulen** (riv.), China, Mong.
110/D1 **Kesagami** (riv.), On,Can
51/H5 **Keşan,** Turk.
63/N4 **Kesen'numa,** Japan
35/H2 **Kesgrave,** Eng,UK
70/B3 **Keshod,** India
59/C2 **Keskin,** Turk.
37/H3 **Keski-Suomi** (prov.), Fin.
35/H2 **Kessingland,** Eng,UK
40/C5 **Kesteren,** Neth.
33/E2 **Keswick,** Eng,UK
50/C2 **Keszthely,** Hun.
56/J4 **Ket'** (riv.), Rus.
85/F5 **Keta,** Gha.
56/K2 **Keta** (riv.), Rus.
114/M4 **Ketchikan,** Ak,US
106/E5 **Ketchum,** Id,US
85/E5 **Kete Krachi,** Gha.
40/C3 **Ketelmeer** (lake), Neth.
39/L1 **Kętrzyn,** Pol.
35/F2 **Kettering,** Eng,UK
110/C4 **Kettering,** Oh,US
106/D3 **Kettle** (riv.), Can., US
33/F3 **Kettlewell,** Eng,UK
40/B4 **Keukenhof,** Neth.
37/H3 **Keuruu,** Fin.
40/D5 **Kevelaer,** Ger.
101/G3 **Kew,** Trks.
110/B2 **Keweenaw** (bay), Mi,US
110/B2 **Keweenaw** (pen.), Mi,US
31/N7 **Kew Gardens,** Eng,UK
113/H5 **Key Largo,** Fl,US
34/D4 **Keynsham,** Eng,UK
115/F5 **Keyport,** NJ,US
110/E4 **Keyser,** WV,US
112/D2 **Keystone** (lake), Ok,US
113/H5 **Key West,** Fl,US
33/G6 **Keyworth,** Eng,UK
39/L4 **Kežmarok,** Slvk.
83/Q5 **Khaanziir** (cape), Som.
63/M2 **Khabarovsk,** Rus.
55/J4 **Khachmas,** Azer.
60/E3 **Khafjī, Ra's al,** SAr.
70/D2 **Khairābād,** India
61/J3 **Khairpur,** Pak.
49/H3 **Khalándrion,** Gre.
49/H2 **Khalkhidhikhi** (pen.), Gre.
49/H3 **Khalkís,** Gre.
62/E1 **Khamar-Daban** (mts.), Rus.
70/D3 **Khamaria,** India
61/J4 **Khambaliya,** India
70/C3 **Khāmgaon,** India
60/D5 **Khamīs Mushayţ,** SAr.
70/D4 **Khammam,** India
61/J1 **Khānābād,** Afg.
60/E2 **Khānaqīn,** Iraq
70/C3 **Khandwa,** India
82/F1 **Khanem** (well), Alg.
61/K2 **Khānewāl,** Pak.
49/J5 **Khaniá,** Gre.
63/L3 **Khanka** (lake), Rus.
62/E1 **Khankh,** Mong.
68/C5 **Khanna,** India
61/K3 **Khānpur,** Pak.
56/G3 **Khanty-Mansiysk,** Rus.
56/G3 **Khanty-Mansiysk Aut. Okr.,** Rus.
59/K6 **Khān Yūnus,** Gaza
69/C3 **Khao Chamao-Khao Wong Nat'l Park,** Thai.
69/C3 **Khao Khitchakut Nat'l Park,** Thai.
69/B3 **Khao Laem** (res.), Thai.
69/B3 **Khao Sam Roi Yot Nat'l Park,** Thai.
69/C3 **Khao Yai Nat'l Park,** Thai.
70/E3 **Kharagpur,** India
68/B5 **Kharak,** Pak.
61/J3 **Khārān,** Pak.
70/C3 **Khargon,** India
86/B3 **Khārijah, Al Wāḩāt al** (oasis), Egypt
86/C3 **Kharīt, Wādī al** (dry riv.), Egypt
54/F2 **Khar'kov,** Ukr.
54/F2 **Khar'kov Obl.,** Ukr.
51/G5 **Kharmanli,** Bul.
52/J4 **Kharovsk,** Rus.
81/M13 **Kharrour** (riv.), Mor.
83/M4 **Khartoum** (Kharţūm) (cap.), Sudan
83/M4 **Khartoum North,** Sudan
55/H4 **Khasavyurt,** Rus.
61/H2 **Khāsh** (riv.), Afg.
61/H3 **Khāsh,** Iran
55/G4 **Khashuri,** Geo.
51/G5 **Khaskovo,** Bul.
51/G5 **Khaskovo** (reg.), Bul.
57/L2 **Khatanga** (gulf), Rus.
57/L2 **Khatanga** (riv.), Rus.
86/C2 **Khatmia** (pass), Egypt
61/G3 **Khaymah, Ra's al,** UAE
83/M4 **Khazzān Jabal Al Awliyā** (dam), Sudan
81/S15 **Khemis el Khechna,** Alg.
81/S15 **Khemis Miliana,** Alg.
81/V18 **Khenchela,** Alg.
82/D1 **Khenifra,** Mor.
60/F2 **Khersān** (riv.), Iran
54/E3 **Kherson,** Ukr.
54/E3 **Kherson Obl.,** Ukr.
62/G1 **Khilok,** Rus.
62/F1 **Khilok** (riv.), Rus.
49/K3 **Khíos,** Gre.
49/J3 **Khíos** (isl.), Gre.
51/G4 **Khisarya,** Bul.
56/G5 **Khiva,** Uzb.
54/C2 **Khmel'nitskiy,** Ukr.
61/J2 **Khojak** (pass), Pak.
69/C3 **Khok Samrong,** Thai.
61/J1 **Kholm,** Afg.
63/N2 **Kholmsk,** Rus.
60/F2 **Khomeynīshahr,** Iran
69/C2 **Khon Kaen,** Thai.
55/G2 **Khopër** (riv.), Rus.
63/M2 **Khor** (riv.), Rus.
68/B4 **Khorog,** Taj.
60/E2 **Khorramābād,** Iran
60/E2 **Khorramshahr,** Iran
69/C2 **Kho Sawai** (plat.), Thai.
114/G3 **Khotol** (mtn.), Ak,US
82/D1 **Khouribga,** Mor.
71/F3 **Khowai,** India
61/J2 **Khowst,** Afg.
49/J2 **Khrisoúpolis,** Gre.
55/L2 **Khromtau,** Kaz.
49/J5 **Khrysi** (isl.), Gre.
69/C2 **Khuan Ubon Ratana** (res.), Thai.
68/A3 **Khudzhand,** Taj.
70/E3 **Khulna,** Bang.
61/L1 **Khūnjerāb** (pass), Pak.
70/C3 **Khurai,** India
70/E3 **Khurda,** India
70/C2 **Khurja,** India
54/B2 **Khust,** Ukr.
61/J3 **Khuzdār,** Pak.
63/L3 **Khvalynka,** Rus.
60/F2 **Khvonsār,** Iran
59/F2 **Khvoy,** Iran
68/B5 **Khyber** (pass), Afg., Pak.
77/D2 **Kiama,** Austl.
112/E3 **Kiamichi** (mts.), Ok,US
33/G2 **Kibblesworth,** Eng,UK
37/J1 **Kibergneset** (pt.), Nor.
87/F1 **Kibondo,** Tanz.
50/E5 **Kičevo,** Macd.
73/F2 **Kidapawan,** Phil.
34/D2 **Kidderminster,** Eng,UK
83/M7 **Kidepo Valley Nat'l Park,** Ugan.
33/F5 **Kidsgrove,** Eng,UK
34/B3 **Kidwelly,** Wal,UK
38/F1 **Kiel** (bay), Den., Ger.
38/F1 **Kiel,** Ger.
39/L3 **Kielce,** Pol.
39/L3 **Kielce** (prov.), Pol.
33/F1 **Kielder,** Eng,UK
33/F1 **Kielder** (res.), Eng,UK
69/D1 **Kien An,** Viet.
69/D4 **Kien Duc,** Viet.
69/D4 **Kien Thanh,** Viet.
41/E6 **Kierspe,** Ger.
54/D2 **Kiev** (Kiyev) (cap.), Ukr.
54/D2 **Kiev Obl.,** Ukr.
84/C2 **Kiffa,** Mrta.
49/L6 **Kifisiá,** Gre.
60/D2 **Kifrī,** Iraq
87/F1 **Kigali** (cap.), Rwa.
87/E1 **Kigoma,** Tanz.
104/T10 **Kihei,** Hi,US
64/D4 **Kii** (chan.), Japan
64/D4 **Kii** (mts.), Japan
68/D3 **Kiines** (riv.), China
104/R9 **Kikepa** (pt.), Hi,US
114/H2 **Kikiktat** (mtn.), Ak,US
50/E3 **Kikinda,** Yugo.
87/C2 **Kikwit,** Zaire
36/C3 **Kilbirnie,** Sc,UK
111/Q9 **Kilbride,** On,Can
32/B5 **Kildare** (co.), Ire.
52/G1 **Kil'den** (isl.), Rus.
112/E3 **Kilgore,** Tx,US
33/H3 **Kilham,** Eng,UK
103/R7 **Kilian** (isl.), NW,Can
51/K5 **Kilimli,** Turk.
87/G2 **Kilindoni,** Tanz.
59/D3 **Kilis,** Turk.
54/D3 **Kiliya,** Ukr.
32/B3 **Kilkeel,** NI,UK
36/B4 **Kilkenny,** Ire.
32/A6 **Kilkenny** (co.), Ire.
49/H2 **Kilkís,** Gre.
106/F2 **Killam,** Ab,Can
33/G5 **Killamarsh,** Eng,UK
76/H8 **Killara,** Austl.
107/J3 **Killarney,** Mb,Can
36/A4 **Killarney,** Ire.
107/H4 **Killdeer,** ND,US
36/C2 **Killearn,** Sc,UK
112/D4 **Killeen,** Tx,US
36/C2 **Killin,** Sc,UK
32/C3 **Killinchy,** NI,UK
103/K2 **Killinek** (isl.), NW,Can
49/H4 **Killíni** (peak), Gre.
32/C3 **Killough,** NI,UK
32/A2 **Killyclogher,** NI,UK
32/C3 **Killyleagh,** NI,UK
32/B5 **Kilmacanoge,** Ire.
36/C3 **Kilmarnock,** Sc,UK
34/B5 **Kilmar Tor** (hill), Eng,UK
32/B6 **Kilmichael** (pt.), Ire.
32/B1 **Kilraghts,** NI,UK
32/B2 **Kilrea,** NI,UK
87/G2 **Kilwa Masoko,** Tanz.
32/C2 **Kilwaughter,** NI,UK
36/C3 **Kilwinning,** Sc,UK
107/H5 **Kimball,** Ne,US
107/J5 **Kimball,** SD,US
78/E5 **Kimbe,** PNG
76/B2 **Kimberley** (cape), Austl.
74/D3 **Kimberley** (plat.), Austl.
106/E3 **Kimberley,** BC,Can
88/D3 **Kimberley,** SAfr.
63/K3 **Kimch'aek,** NKor.
64/A2 **Kimch'ŏn,** SKor.
64/A3 **Kimhae,** SKor.
65/F3 **Kimitsu,** Japan
63/K4 **Kimje,** SKor.
49/J4 **Kímolos** (isl.), Gre.
54/F1 **Kimovsk,** Rus.
87/D2 **Kimpanga,** Zaire
52/H4 **Kimry,** Rus.
73/E2 **Kinabalu, Gunung** (peak), Malay.
73/E2 **Kinabatangan** (riv.), Malay.
106/D2 **Kinbasket** (lake), BC,Can
106/G3 **Kincaid,** Sk,Can
110/D2 **Kincardine,** On,Can
77/B2 **Kinchega Nat'l Park,** Austl.
87/D2 **Kindambi,** Zaire
45/L3 **Kindberg,** Aus.
33/G5 **Kinder Scout** (mtn.), Eng,UK
84/B4 **Kindia,** Gui.
84/B4 **Kindia** (comm.), Gui.
87/E1 **Kindu,** Zaire
55/J1 **Kinel',** Rus.
52/J4 **Kineshma,** Rus.
35/E2 **Kineton,** Eng,UK
77/C3 **King** (isl.), Austl.
74/B6 **King** (lake), Austl.
76/B4 **King** (peak), Austl.
74/C3 **King** (sound), Austl.
106/B2 **King** (isl.), BC,Can
114/N4 **King** (mtn.), BC,Can
114/K3 **King** (peak), Yk,Can
76/C4 **Kingaroy,** Austl.
103/R7 **King Christian** (isl.), NW,Can
99/P3 **King Christian IX Land** (reg.), Grld.
99/Q2 **King Christian X Land** (reg.), Grld.
111/Q8 **King City,** On,Can
108/B3 **King City,** Ca,US
109/H4 **Kingfisher,** Ok,US
99/N3 **King Frederik VI Coast** (reg.), Grld.
99/Q2 **King Frederik VIII Land** (reg.), Grld.
79/L6 **King George** (isl.), FrPol.
110/E4 **King George,** Va,US
77/C3 **Kinglake Nat'l Park,** Austl.
74/D3 **King Leopold** (ranges), Austl.
79/J4 **Kingman** (reef), PacUS
108/D4 **Kingman,** Az,US
109/H3 **Kingman,** Ks,US
115/E5 **King of Prussia,** Pa,US
108/C3 **Kings** (riv.), Ca,US
108/E2 **Kings** (peak), Ut,US
34/C6 **Kingsbridge,** Eng,UK
108/C3 **Kings Canyon Nat'l Park,** Ca,US
35/E4 **Kingsclere,** Eng,UK
35/F1 **King's Cliffe,** Eng,UK
34/D2 **Kingsland,** Eng,UK
31/M6 **Kings Langley,** Eng,UK
35/G1 **King's Lynn,** Eng,UK
113/H2 **Kingsport,** Tn,US
35/E2 **Kings Sutton,** Eng,UK
34/C5 **Kingsteignton,** Eng,UK
77/C4 **Kingston,** Austl.
110/E2 **Kingston,** On,Can
101/F4 **Kingston** (cap.), Jam.
78/F7 **Kingston,** Norfl.
110/F3 **Kingston,** NY,US
77/A3 **Kingston South East,** Austl.
31/N7 **Kingston upon Thames** (bor.), Eng,UK
101/J5 **Kingstown** (cap.), StV.
113/J3 **Kingstree,** SC,US
86/C3 **Kings, Valley of the,** Egypt
112/D5 **Kingsville,** Tx,US
34/D2 **Kingswinford,** Eng,UK
34/D4 **Kingswood,** Eng,UK
34/C2 **Kington,** Eng,UK
102/G2 **King William** (isl.), NW,Can
88/D4 **King William's Town,** SAfr.
114/L4 **Kinkaid** (mtn.), Ak,US
87/B1 **Kinkala,** Congo
64/D3 **Kinki** (prov.), Japan
84/B4 **Kinkon, Chutes de** (falls), Gui.
32/E5 **Kinmel,** Wal,UK
37/E4 **Kinna,** Swe.
36/E2 **Kinnairds Head** (pt.), Sc,UK
64/D3 **Kino** (riv.), Japan
43/E1 **Kinrooi,** Belg.
36/D2 **Kinross,** Sc,UK
111/R8 **Kinsale,** On,Can
87/C1 **Kinshasa** (cap.), Zaire
109/H3 **Kinsley,** Ks,US
113/J3 **Kinston,** NC,US
85/E4 **Kintampo,** Gha.
36/D2 **Kintore,** Sc,UK
32/C1 **Kintyre, Mull of** (pt.), Sc,UK
65/F2 **Kinu** (riv.), Japan
83/M7 **Kinyeti** (peak), Sudan
49/G4 **Kiparissía** (gulf), Gre.
110/E2 **Kipawa** (lake), Qu,Can
87/F2 **Kipili,** Tanz.
107/H3 **Kipling,** Sk,Can
32/B5 **Kippure** (mtn.), Ire.
87/E3 **Kipushi,** Zaire
65/N10 **Kira,** Japan
49/H3 **Kira Panayía** (isl.), Gre.
41/F6 **Kirchhundem,** Ger.
41/F4 **Kirchlengern,** Ger.
41/G3 **Kirchlinteln,** Ger.
32/C3 **Kircubbin,** NI,UK
32/D2 **Kircudbright** (bay), Sc,UK
57/L4 **Kirensk,** Rus.
68/B3 **Kirgizskiy** (mts.), Kyr.
56/F5 **Kirgiz Steppe** (grsld.), Kaz., Rus.
78/H5 **Kiribati**
59/D3 **Kırıkhan,** Turk.
59/C2 **Kırıkkale,** Turk.
62/C3 **Kirikkuduk,** China
52/G4 **Kirishi,** Rus.
64/B5 **Kirishima-Yaku Nat'l Park,** Japan
64/B5 **Kirishima-yama** (mtn.), Japan
79/K4 **Kiritimati** (Christmas) (atoll), Kiri.
33/G4 **Kirkburton,** Eng,UK
33/F5 **Kirkby,** Eng,UK
33/G5 **Kirkby in Ashfield,** Eng,UK
33/F3 **Kirkby Lonsdale,** Eng,UK
33/H3 **Kirkbymoorside,** Eng,UK
33/F3 **Kirkby Stephen,** Eng,UK
36/D2 **Kirkcaldy,** Sc,UK
32/C2 **Kirkcolm,** Sc,UK
32/D2 **Kirkcowan,** Sc,UK
32/D2 **Kirkcudbright,** Sc,UK
70/B4 **Kirkee,** India
37/J1 **Kirkenes,** Nor.
33/F4 **Kirkham,** Eng,UK
32/D2 **Kirkinner,** Sc,UK
111/N7 **Kirkland,** Qu,Can
116/C2 **Kirkland,** Wa,US
110/D1 **Kirkland Lake,** On,Can
51/H5 **Kırklareli,** Turk.
51/H5 **Kırklareli** (prov.), Turk.
32/D3 **Kirkmichael,** IM,UK
51/L2 **Kirkovgrad Obl.,** Ukr.
98/M **Kirkpatrick** (mtn.), Ant.
109/J2 **Kirksville,** Mo,US
36/D2 **Kirkton of Glenisla,** Sc,UK
59/F3 **Kirkūk,** Iraq
43/G4 **Kirn,** Ger.
54/E1 **Kirov,** Rus.
55/H4 **Kirovakan,** Arm.
53/L4 **Kirovo-Chepetsk,** Rus.
54/E2 **Kirovograd,** Ukr.
54/D2 **Kirovograd Obl.,** Ukr.
36/D2 **Kirriemuir,** Sc,UK
55/G1 **Kirsanov,** Rus.
59/C2 **Kırşehir,** Turk.
33/H6 **Kirton,** Eng,UK
33/H5 **Kirton in Lindsey,** Eng,UK
37/G2 **Kiruna,** Swe.
65/F2 **Kiryū,** Japan
83/L7 **Kisangani,** Zaire
65/F3 **Kisarazu,** Japan
39/K5 **Kisbér,** Hun.
56/J4 **Kiselevsk,** Rus.
70/E2 **Kishanganj,** India
70/B2 **Kishangarh,** India
51/J2 **Kishinëv** (cap.), Mol.
64/D3 **Kishiwada,** Japan
70/F3 **Kishorganj,** Bang.
61/L2 **Kishtwar,** India
116/N15 **Kishwaukee** (riv.), Il,US
83/M8 **Kisii,** Kenya
114/B6 **Kiska** (isl.), Ak,US
114/B5 **Kiska** (vol.), Ak,US
106/C2 **Kiskatinaw** (riv.), BC,Can
107/J2 **Kiskitto** (lake), Mb,Can
50/D2 **Kiskőrös,** Hun.
50/D2 **Kiskunfélegyháza,** Hun.
50/D2 **Kiskunhalas,** Hun.
50/D2 **Kiskunmajsa,** Hun.
50/D2 **Kiskunsági Nat'l Park,** Hun.
55/G4 **Kislovodsk,** Rus.
83/P8 **Kismaayo** (Chisimayu), Som.
65/E3 **Kiso** (riv.), Japan
65/M9 **Kisogawa,** Japan
113/H4 **Kissimmee,** Fl,US
113/H4 **Kissimmee** (lake), Fl,US
107/H2 **Kississing** (lake), Mb,Can
50/E2 **Kisújszállás,** Hun.
83/M8 **Kisumu,** Kenya
50/F1 **Kisvárda,** Hun.
65/G2 **Kita** (inlet), Japan
84/C3 **Kita,** Mali
65/M9 **Kitagata,** Japan
65/G2 **Kita-Ibaraki,** Japan
65/F2 **Kitakata,** Japan
64/B4 **Kitakyūshū,** Japan
83/N7 **Kitale,** Kenya
63/N3 **Kitami,** Japan
63/N2 **Kitami** (mts.), Japan
65/H6 **Kitamoto,** Japan
110/D3 **Kitchener,** On,Can
37/J3 **Kitee,** Fin.
49/H4 **Kíthira** (isl.), Gre.
49/J4 **Kíthnos** (isl.), Gre.
106/A2 **Kitimat,** BC,Can
106/A2 **Kitimat Arm** (inlet), BC,Can
116/B2 **Kitsap Lake-Erlands Point,** Wa,US
115/E4 **Kittatinny** (mts.), NJ, Pa,US
111/G3 **Kittery,** Me,US
87/E3 **Kitwe,** Zam.
45/K3 **Kitzbühel,** Aus.
45/J2 **Kitzingen,** Ger.
37/H3 **Kiuruvesi,** Fin.
37/H2 **Kivalo** (mts.), Fin.
52/E4 **Kiviõli,** Est.
87/E1 **Kivu** (lake), Rwa., Zaire
54/D2 **Kiyev** (res.), Ukr.
54/D2 **Kiyev** (Kiev) (cap.), Ukr.
65/H7 **Kiyose,** Japan
65/M9 **Kiyosu,** Japan
87/C2 **Kizamba,** Zaire
53/N4 **Kizel,** Rus.
68/B4 **Kizil** (riv.), China
59/C2 **Kızılcahamam,** Turk.
59/C2 **Kizilirmak** (riv.), Turk.
59/E3 **Kızıltepe,** Turk.
55/H4 **Kizlyar,** Rus.
65/L10 **Kizu,** Japan
64/E3 **Kizu** (riv.), Japan
55/L5 **Kizyl-Arvat,** Trkm.
52/C1 **Kjerkestinden** (peak), Nor.
37/E2 **Kjølen** (Kölen) (mts.), Nor., Swe.
50/D3 **Kladanj,** Bosn.
45/L1 **Kladno,** Czh.
50/F3 **Kladovo,** Yugo.
45/L3 **Klagenfurt,** Aus.
52/D5 **Klaipėda,** Lith.
106/C5 **Klamath** (mts.), Ca, Or,US
106/C5 **Klamath** (riv.), Ca, Or,US
106/C5 **Klamath Falls,** Or,US
56/B3 **Klar** (riv.), Swe.
37/E3 **Klarälven** (riv.), Swe.
40/E3 **Klazienaveen,** Neth.
43/G5 **Kleinblittersdorf,** Ger.
111/Q8 **Kleinburg,** On,Can
39/G3 **Kleine Elster** (riv.), Ger.
43/E2 **Kleine Gete** (riv.), Belg.
40/B6 **Kleine Nete** (riv.), Belg.
88/Q12 **Kleinolifants** (riv.), SAfr.
37/C3 **Kleppestø,** Nor.
88/D2 **Klerksdorp,** SAfr.
40/D5 **Kleve,** Ger.
54/E1 **Klintsy,** Rus.
88/E2 **Klip** (riv.), SAfr.
50/C3 **Ključ,** Bosn.
39/K2 **Kłodawa,** Pol.
39/J3 **Kłodzko,** Pol.
41/F3 **Klosterbach** (riv.), Ger.
45/M2 **Klosterneuburg,** Aus.
45/L3 **Klosterwappen** (peak), Aus.
38/F2 **Klötze,** Ger.
114/L3 **Kluane,** Yk,Can
114/K3 **Kluane Nat'l Park,** Yk,Can
39/K3 **Kluczbork,** Pol.
114/L3 **Klukshu,** Yk,Can
40/B5 **Klundert,** Neth.
41/E3 **Klüstenkanal** (can.), Ger.
52/J4 **Klyaz'ma** (riv.), Rus.
57/S4 **Klyuchevskaya** (peak), Rus.
33/G3 **Knaresborough,** Eng,UK
35/F3 **Knebworth,** Eng,UK
107/K2 **Knee** (lake), Mb,Can
51/G4 **Knezha,** Bul.
106/B3 **Knight** (inlet), BC,Can
34/C2 **Knighton,** Wal,UK
50/C3 **Knin,** Cro.
45/L3 **Knittelfeld,** Aus.
50/F4 **Knjaževac,** Yugo.
74/B6 **Knob** (cape), Austl.
73/F1 **Knob** (peak), Phil.
32/B2 **Knockcloghrim,** NI,UK
32/B1 **Knocklayd** (mtn.), NI,UK
42/C1 **Knokke-Heist,** Belg.
88/A2 **Knoll** (pt.), Namb.
49/J5 **Knosós** (Knossos) (ruins), Gre.
33/F4 **Knott End,** Eng,UK
33/G4 **Knottingley,** Eng,UK
98/G **Knox** (coast), Ant.
77/G5 **Knox,** Austl.
114/M4 **Knox** (cape), BC,Can
113/H3 **Knoxville,** Tn,US
33/F5 **Knutsford,** Eng,UK
88/C4 **Knysna,** SAfr.
63/M2 **Ko** (peak), Rus.
64/B5 **Kobayashi,** Japan
64/D3 **Kōbe,** Japan
38/G1 **København** (Copenhagen) (cap.), Den.
73/G4 **Kobipato** (peak), Indo.
43/G3 **Koblenz,** Ger.
39/N2 **Kobrin,** Bela.
114/G2 **Kobuk** (riv.), Ak,US
114/G2 **Kobuk Valley Nat'l Park,** Ak,US
65/F3 **Kobushi-ga-take** (mtn.), Japan
51/J5 **Kocaeli** (prov.), Turk.
50/F5 **Kočani,** Macd.
50/B3 **Kočevje,** Slov.
103/J2 **Koch** (isl.), NW,Can
45/H2 **Kocher** (riv.), Ger.
64/C4 **Kōchi,** Japan
64/C4 **Kōchi** (pref.), Japan
114/H4 **Kodiak,** Ak,US
114/H4 **Kodiak** (isl.), Ak,US
114/H4 **Kodiak Nat'l Wild. Ref.,** Ak,US
70/B3 **Kodinār,** India
83/M6 **Kodok,** Sudan
51/H2 **Kodry** (hills), Mol.
42/B1 **Koekelare,** Belg.
70/D3 **Koel** (riv.), India
43/F5 **Koenigsmacker,** Fr.
108/D4 **Kofa** (mts.), Az,US
73/G4 **Kofiau** (isl.), Indo.
85/E5 **Koforidua,** Gha.
65/F3 **Kōfu,** Japan
65/F2 **Koga,** Japan
65/H7 **Koganei,** Japan
38/G1 **Køge,** Den.
38/G1 **Køge Bugt** (bay), Den.
84/B4 **Kogon** (riv.), Gui.
61/K2 **Kohāt,** Pak.
71/F2 **Kohīma,** India
52/E4 **Kohtla-Järve,** Est.
63/K5 **Kohŭng,** SKor.
100/D4 **Kohunlich** (ruins), Mex.

88/A2 **Koichab** (dry riv.), Namb.
114/K3 **Koidern**, Yk,Can
64/A3 **Kŏje** (isl.), SKor.
39/L4 **Kojšovská Hoľa** (peak), Slvk.
69/B1 **Kok** (riv.), Burma
65/M10 **Kōka**, Japan
65/J7 **Kokai** (riv.), Japan
68/B3 **Kokand**, Uzb.
68/A1 **Kokchetav**, Kaz.
37/G3 **Kokkola**, Fin.
84/C3 **Kokofata**, Mali
104/W13 **Koko Head** (crater), Hi,US
83/L7 **Kokola**, Zaire
110/C3 **Kokomo**, In,US
70/F2 **Kokrajhar**, India
68/C3 **Kokshaal-Tau** (mts.), Kyr.
42/B1 **Koksijde**, Belg.
103/K3 **Koksoak** (riv.), Qu,Can
88/E3 **Kokstad**, SAfr.
64/B5 **Kokubu**, Japan
52/H1 **Kola** (pen.), Rus.
52/G1 **Kola** (riv.), Rus.
73/F4 **Kolaka**, Indo.
70/C5 **Kolār**, India
50/D4 **Kolašin**, Yugo.
38/G5 **Kolbermoor**, Ger.
39/L3 **Kolbuszowa**, Pol.
84/B3 **Kolda**, Sen.
84/B3 **Kolda** (reg.), Sen.
38/E1 **Kolding**, Den.
37/E2 **Kölen (Kjølen)** (mts.), Nor., Swe.
78/C5 **Kolepom** (isl.), Indo.
52/F4 **Kolgompya** (cape), Rus.
53/K1 **Kolguyev** (isl.), Rus.
70/B4 **Kolhāpur**, India
84/B3 **Koliba** (riv.), Gui.
39/H3 **Kolín**, Czh.
52/D4 **Kolkasrags** (pt.), Lat.
40/D2 **Kollum**, Neth.
40/D7 **Köln** (Cologne), Ger.
39/L2 **Kolno**, Pol.
54/A1 **Koło**, Pol.
87/G1 **Kolo**, Tanz.
39/H1 **Kołobrzeg**, Pol.
84/C3 **Kolokani**, Mali
54/F1 **Kolomna**, Rus.
54/C2 **Kolomyya**, Ukr.
70/C6 **Kolonnawa**, SrL.
84/D3 **Kolossa** (riv.), Mali
56/J4 **Kolpashevo**, Rus.
52/F4 **Kolpino**, Rus.
50/E3 **Kolubara** (riv.), Yugo
39/K3 **Koluszki**, Pol.
68/A1 **Koluton** (riv.), Kaz.
53/N2 **Kolva** (riv.), Rus.
87/E3 **Kolwezi**, Zaire
57/R2 **Kolyma** (lowland), Rus.
57/R3 **Kolyma** (range), Rus.
57/R3 **Kolyma** (riv.), Rus.
50/F4 **Kom** (peak), Bul.
65/H7 **Koma** (riv.), Japan
50/E2 **Komádi**, Hun.
85/H4 **Komadugu Gana** (riv.), Nga.
85/H3 **Komadugu Yobé** (riv.), Nga.
65/H7 **Komae**, Japan
65/E3 **Komagane**, Japan
65/M9 **Komaki**, Japan
57/S4 **Komandorskiye** (isls.), Rus.
39/K5 **Komárno**, Slvk.
50/D2 **Komárom**, Hun.
50/D2 **Komárom-Esztergom** (co.), Hun.
64/E2 **Komatsu**, Japan
64/D4 **Komatsushima**, Japan
53/L2 **Komi Aut. Rep.**, Rus.
53/M3 **Komi-Permyak Aut. Okr.**, Rus.
50/D2 **Komló**, Hun.
54/F2 **Kommunarsk**, Ukr.
68/B4 **Kommunizma** (Communism) (peak), Taj.
73/E5 **Komodo Isl. Nat'l Park**, Indo.
84/E5 **Komoé** (riv.), IvC.
64/E3 **Komono**, Japan
49/J2 **Komotiní**, Gre.
88/D3 **Kompasberg** (peak), SAfr.
51/J2 **Komrat**, Mol.
57/L1 **Komsomolets** (isl.), Rus.
53/P2 **Komsomol'skiy**, Rus.
63/M1 **Komsomol'sk-na-Amure**, Rus.
49/K3 **Kömür** (pt.), Turk.
68/A2 **Kon** (riv.), Kaz.
52/H4 **Konakovo**, Rus.
65/M10 **Kōnan**, Japan
65/M9 **Kōnan**, Japan
77/D2 **Konangra-Boyd Nat'l Park**, Austl.
73/F4 **Konaweha** (riv.), Indo.
62/G1 **Konda** (riv.), Rus.
52/G3 **Kondopoga**, Rus.
61/J1 **Kondūz**, Afg.
69/C4 **Kong** (isl.), Camb.
69/D3 **Kong** (riv.), Laos
63/K4 **Kongju**, SKor.
87/E2 **Kongolo**, Zaire
65/L10 **Kongō-zan** (peak), Japan
37/D4 **Kongsberg**, Nor.
37/E3 **Kongsvinger**, Nor.
68/C4 **Kongur Shan** (peak), China
87/G2 **Kongwa**, Tanz.
39/K3 **Koniecpol**, Pol.
41/H4 **Königslutter am Elm**, Ger.
43/G2 **Königswinter**, Ger.
39/G2 **Königs Wusterhausen**, Ger.
39/K2 **Konin**, Pol.
39/K2 **Konin** (prov.), Pol.
45/G3 **Köniz**, Swi.
50/C4 **Konjic**, Bosn.
88/B2 **Konkiep** (dry riv.), Namb.
84/B4 **Konkouré** (riv.), Gui.
54/E2 **Konotop**, Ukr.
68/E3 **Konqi** (riv.), China
39/L3 **Końskie**, Pol.
39/L2 **Konstancin-Jeziorna**, Pol.
54/F2 **Konstantinovka**, Ukr.
39/K3 **Konstantynów Łódzki**, Pol.
45/H3 **Konstanz**, Ger.
42/D1 **Kontich**, Belg.
37/J3 **Kontiolahti**, Fin.
69/E3 **Kon Tum**, Viet.
59/C3 **Konya**, Turk.
43/F4 **Konz**, Ger.
106/E3 **Koocanusa** (lake), Can., US
106/D3 **Kootenai** (riv.), Id, Mt,US
106/D3 **Kootenay** (lake), BC,Can
106/D3 **Kootenay Nat'l Park**, BC,Can
70/B4 **Kopargaon**, India
37/N7 **Kópavogur**, Ice.
84/D5 **Kope** (peak), IvC.
39/G2 **Köpenick**, Ger.
53/P5 **Kopeysk**, Rus.
54/G4 **Kop Gecidi** (pass), Turk.
83/K7 **Kopia**, Zaire
52/C4 **Köping**, Swe.
73/F5 **Kopondei** (cape), Indo.
37/E3 **Kopparberg** (co.), Swe.
63/M2 **Koppi** (riv.), Rus.
50/C2 **Koprivnica**, Cro.
60/F2 **Kor** (riv.), Iran
65/M9 **Kōra**, Japan
49/G2 **Korab** (peak), Alb.
45/L4 **Korana** (riv.), Bosn., Cro.
70/D4 **Koraput**, India
70/D3 **Korba**, India
41/F6 **Korbach**, Ger.
49/G2 **Korçë**, Alb.
50/C4 **Korčula** (isl.), Cro.
50/C4 **Korčulanski** (chan.), Cro.
60/F1 **Kord Kūy**, Iran
63/J4 **Korea** (bay), China, NKor.
64/A4 **Korea** (str.), Japan, SKor.
63/K3 **Korea, North**
63/K4 **Korea, South**
54/F3 **Korenovsk**, Rus.
84/D4 **Korhogo**, IvC.
49/H4 **Kórinthos** (Corinth), Gre.
50/C2 **Kőris-hegy** (peak), Hun.
65/G2 **Kōriyama**, Japan
82/J3 **Korizo, Passe de** (pass), Chad
57/R3 **Korkodon** (riv.), Rus.
59/B3 **Korkuteli**, Turk.
68/E3 **Korla**, China
59/J4 **Kormakiti** (cape), Cyp.
50/B4 **Kornat** (isl.), Cro.
79/Z18 **Koro** (isl.), Fiji
78/G6 **Koro** (sea), Fiji
51/K5 **Köroğlu** (peak), Turk.
87/G2 **Korogwe**, Tanz.
67/E6 **Koronadal**, Phil.
49/H2 **Korónia** (lake), Gre.
39/J2 **Koronowo**, Pol.
49/L7 **Koropí**, Gre.
78/C4 **Koror** (cap.), Palau
50/E2 **Körös** (riv.), Hun.
54/D2 **Korosten'**, Ukr.
54/D2 **Korostyshev**, Ukr.
53/P1 **Korotaikha** (riv.), Rus.
82/J4 **Koro Toro**, Chad
114/D5 **Korovin** (vol.), Ak,US
63/N2 **Korsakov**, Rus.
40/D6 **Korschenbroich**, Ger.
38/F1 **Korsør**, Den.
42/C1 **Kortemark**, Belg.
43/E2 **Kortenaken**, Belg.
42/D2 **Kortenberg**, Belg.
43/E2 **Kortessem**, Belg.
42/C2 **Kortrijk**, Belg.
85/H5 **Korup Nat'l Park**, Camr.
58/R3 **Koryak** (range), Rus.
57/S3 **Koryak Aut. Okr.**, Rus.
53/K3 **Koryazhma**, Rus.
65/L10 **Koryō**, Japan
59/A3 **Kós** (isl.), Gre.
65/E3 **Kosai**, Japan
64/A3 **Ko-saki** (pt.), Japan
69/C3 **Ko Samut Nat'l Park**, Thai.
39/J2 **Kościan**, Pol.
39/J1 **Kościerzyna**, Pol.
77/D3 **Kosciusko** (mt.), Austl.
113/F3 **Kosciusko**, Ms,US
77/D3 **Kosciusko Nat'l Park**, Austl.
65/M10 **Kosei**, Japan
86/B4 **Kosha**, Sudan
65/F3 **Koshigaya**, Japan
61/H2 **Koshk**, Afg.
70/E2 **Kosi** (riv.), India
39/L4 **Košice**, Slvk.
68/C2 **Kosoba, Gora** (peak), Kaz.
50/E4 **Kosovo** (aut. reg.), Yugo.
50/E4 **Kosovo Polje**, Yugo.
50/E4 **Kosovska Mitrovica**, Yugo.
78/F4 **Kosrae** (isl.), Micr.
84/D3 **Kossi** (prov.), Burk.
84/D5 **Kossou** (lake), IvC.
51/F4 **Kostinbrod**, Bul.
54/C2 **Kostopol'**, Ukr.
52/J4 **Kostroma**, Rus.
52/J4 **Kostroma** (riv.), Rus.
52/J4 **Kostroma Obl.**, Rus.
39/H2 **Kostrzyn**, Pol.
39/J2 **Kostrzyn**, Pol.
53/N4 **Kos'va** (riv.), Rus.
53/N2 **Kos'yu** (riv.), Rus.
39/J1 **Koszalin**, Pol.
39/H2 **Koszalin** (prov.), Pol.
70/C2 **Kota**, India
65/N10 **Kōta**, Japan
72/B5 **Kotaagung**, Indo.
72/B2 **Kota Baharu**, Malay.
73/E4 **Kotabaru**, Indo.
72/C4 **Kotabumi**, Indo.
61/K2 **Kot Addu**, Pak.
51/H4 **Kotel**, Bul.
53/L4 **Kotel'nich**, Rus.
55/G3 **Kotel'nikovo**, Rus.
57/P2 **Kotel'nyy** (isl.), Rus.
38/F3 **Köthen**, Ger.
37/H3 **Kotka**, Fin.
52/E3 **Kotka**, Fin.
61/K2 **Kot Kapūra**, India
53/K3 **Kotlas**, Rus.
65/M9 **Kotō**, Japan
50/D4 **Kotor**, Yugo.
55/H2 **Kotovo**, Rus.
55/G1 **Kotovsk**, Rus.
61/J3 **Kotri**, Pak.
70/D4 **Kottagūdem**, India
70/C6 **Kottayam**, India
70/C6 **Kotte**, SrL.
83/K6 **Kotto** (riv.), CAfr.
57/L3 **Kotuy** (riv.), Rus.
114/E2 **Kotzebue** (sound), Ak,US
111/H2 **Kouchibouguac Nat'l Park**, NB,Can
85/E3 **Koudougou**, Burk.
49/J5 **Koufonísion** (isl.), Gre.
114/E2 **Kougarok** (mtn.), Ak,US
67/D3 **Kouhu**, Tai.
103/J2 **Koukdjuak** (riv.), NW,Can
87/B1 **Koula-Moutou**, Gabon
84/D3 **Koulikoro**, Mali
84/B3 **Koulountou** (riv.), Gui., Sen.
84/D3 **Koumbi Saleh** (ruins), Mrta.
82/J6 **Koumra**, Chad
68/C2 **Kounradskiy**, Kaz.
112/E4 **Kountze**, Tx,US
85/H5 **Koupé** (peak), Camr.
85/E3 **Koupela**, Burk.
85/E3 **Kouritenga** (prov.), Burk.
93/H2 **Kourou**, FrG.
82/J4 **Koussi** (peak), Chad
84/D3 **Koutiala**, Mali
37/H3 **Kouvola**, Fin.
50/E3 **Kovačica**, Yugo.
52/F2 **Kovdozero** (lake), Rus.
54/C2 **Kovel'**, Ukr.
70/C6 **Kovilpatti**, India
52/J4 **Kovrov**, Rus.
70/C5 **Kovūr**, India
55/G1 **Kovylkino**, Rus.
61/J1 **Kowkcheh** (riv.), Afg.
61/H2 **Kowl-e Namaksār** (lake), Afg., Iran
67/B3 **Kowloon**, HK
64/B5 **Kōyama**, Japan
51/G4 **Koynare**, Bul.
114/H2 **Koyukuk** (riv.), Ak,US
65/N10 **Kozakai**, Japan
59/C3 **Kozan**, Turk.
49/G2 **Kozáni**, Gre.
50/C3 **Kozara Nat'l Park**, Bosn.
70/C5 **Kozhikode**, India
52/H3 **Kozhozero** (lake), Rus.
53/M2 **Kozhva** (riv.), Rus.
39/L3 **Kozienice**, Pol.
51/F4 **Kozloduy**, Bul.
59/E2 **Kozluk**, Turk.
39/J3 **Koźmin**, Pol.
51/F4 **Koznitsa** (peak), Bul.
39/H3 **Kożuchów**, Pol.
85/F5 **Kpalimé**, Togo
85/F5 **Kpandu**, Gha.
69/B4 **Kra** (isth.), Burma, Thai.
88/D3 **Kraai** (riv.), SAfr.
88/L10 **Kraaifontein**, SAfr.
69/B4 **Krabi**, Thai.
69/D3 **Kracheh**, Camb.
37/D4 **Kragerø**, Nor.
50/E3 **Kragujevac**, Yugo.
45/H2 **Kraichgau** (reg.), Ger.
72/C5 **Krakatoa** (vol.), Indo.
69/D3 **Krakor**, Camb.
39/K3 **Kraków**, Pol.
39/K3 **Kraków** (prov.), Pol.
69/C3 **Kralanh**, Camb.
101/H5 **Kralendijk**, NAnt.
50/E4 **Kraljevo**, Yugo.
45/L1 **Kralupy nad Vltavou**, Czh.
54/F2 **Kramatorsk**, Ukr.
37/F3 **Kramfors**, Swe.
40/B5 **Krammer** (chan.), Neth.
40/D5 **Kranenburg**, Ger.
50/B2 **Kranj**, Slov.
39/J3 **Krapkowice**, Pol.
39/M3 **Kraśnik**, Pol.
39/M3 **Kraśnik Fabryczny**, Pol.
55/H2 **Krasnoarmeysk**, Rus.
54/F3 **Krasnodar**, Rus.
54/F3 **Krasnodar** (kray), Rus.
54/F1 **Krasnogorsk**, Rus.
54/E2 **Krasnograd**, Ukr.
63/H1 **Krasnokamensk**, Rus.
53/M4 **Krasnokamsk**, Rus.
55/H2 **Krasnoslobodsk**, Rus.
56/G4 **Krasnotur'insk**, Rus.
53/P4 **Krasnoural'sk**, Rus.
55/K5 **Krasnovodsk**, Trkm.
56/K4 **Krasnoyarsk**, Rus.
39/M3 **Krasnystaw**, Pol.
55/H2 **Krasnyy Kut**, Rus.
54/F2 **Krasnyy Luch**, Ukr.
54/G3 **Krasnyy Sulin**, Rus.
69/C4 **Kravanh** (mts.), Camb.
72/C5 **Krawang**, Indo.
40/D6 **Krefeld**, Ger.
41/G5 **Kreiensen**, Ger.
49/G3 **Kremastón** (lake), Gre.
54/E2 **Kremenchug**, Ukr.
54/E2 **Kremenchug** (res.), Ukr.
108/F2 **Kremmling**, Co,US
45/L2 **Krems an der Donau**, Aus.
57/T3 **Kresta** (gulf), Rus.
37/G5 **Kretinga**, Lith.
43/F2 **Kreuzau**, Ger.
43/G2 **Kreuztal**, Ger.
82/G7 **Kribi**, Camr.
54/D1 **Krichev**, Bela.
63/N2 **Kril'on, Mys** (cape), Rus.
40/B5 **Krimpen aan de IJssel**, Neth.
70/D4 **Krishna** (riv.), India
70/C5 **Krishnagiri**, India
37/C4 **Kristiansand**, Nor.
37/E4 **Kristianstad**, Swe.
39/H1 **Kristianstad** (co.), Swe.
37/C3 **Kristiansund**, Nor.
37/E4 **Kristinehamn**, Swe.
50/F4 **Kriva Palanka**, Macd.
54/E3 **Krivoy Rog**, Ukr.
50/B3 **Krk**, Cro.
50/C3 **Krka** (riv.), Cro.
39/J3 **Krnov**, Czh.
89/E2 **Krokodil** (riv.), SAfr.
88/D2 **Krokodilrivier** (riv.), SAfr.
54/E2 **Krolovets**, Ukr.
39/J4 **Kroměříž**, Czh.
45/J1 **Kronach**, Ger.
69/C4 **Krong Kaoh Kong**, Camb.
69/D4 **Krong Keb**, Camb.
37/E4 **Kronoberg** (co.), Swe.
52/F4 **Kronshtadt**, Rus.
76/C4 **Kroombit Tops Nat'l Park**, Austl.
88/D2 **Kroonstad**, SAfr.
55/G3 **Kropotkin**, Rus.
39/L4 **Krosno**, Pol.
39/L4 **Krosno** (prov.), Pol.
39/H2 **Krosno Odrzańskie**, Pol.
39/J3 **Krotoszyn**, Pol.
50/B3 **Krško**, Slov.
41/G1 **Kruckau** (riv.), Ger.
87/F5 **Kruger Nat'l Park**, SAfr.
88/P13 **Krugersdorp**, SAfr.
53/N5 **Kruglitsa, Gora** (peak), Rus.
114/A5 **Krugloi** (pt.), Ak,US
40/B6 **Kruibeke**, Belg.
50/D5 **Krujë**, Alb.
51/G5 **Krumovgrad**, Bul.
69/C3 **Krung Thep** (Bangkok) (cap.), Thai.
39/K4 **Krupina**, Slvk.
114/F2 **Krusenstern** (cape), Ak,US
50/E4 **Kruševac**, Yugo.
45/K1 **Krušné Hory** (Erzgebirge) (mts.), Czh., Ger.
39/K2 **Kruszwica**, Pol.
114/L4 **Kruzof** (isl.), Ak,US
54/F3 **Krymsk**, Rus.
39/L4 **Krynica**, Pol.
39/M3 **Krzna** (riv.), Pol.
39/J2 **Krzyż**, Pol.
81/M13 **Ksar el Kebir**, Mor.
66/D4 **Kuai** (riv.), China
72/D3 **Kuala Belait**, Bru.
72/B3 **Kuala Dungun**, Malay.
72/B3 **Kuala Lipis**, Malay.
72/B3 **Kuala Lumpur** (cap.), Malay.
72/B3 **Kuala Pilah**, Malay.
72/B2 **Kuala Terengganu**, Malay.
72/B3 **Kuantan**, Malay.
55/J4 **Kuba**, Azer.
54/F3 **Kuban'** (riv.), Rus.
52/H4 **Kubenskoye** (lake), Rus.
64/C4 **Kubokawa**, Japan
51/H4 **Kubrat**, Bul.
72/D3 **Kuching**, Malay.
49/F2 **Kuçovë**, Alb.
64/B4 **Kudamatsu**, Japan
72/D5 **Kudus**, Indo.
53/M4 **Kudymkar**, Rus.
83/K3 **Kufrah** (oasis), Libya
59/K5 **Kufrinjah**, Jor.
45/K3 **Kufstein**, Aus.
37/J2 **Kuhmo**, Fin.
40/D3 **Kuinder of Tjonger** (riv.), Neth.
89/E1 **Kuishan** (mtn.), China
87/C3 **Kuito**, Ang.
114/M4 **Kuiu** (isl.), Ak,US
85/E5 **Kujani Game Rsv.**, Gha.
39/K2 **Kujawy** (reg.), Pol.
63/N3 **Kuji**, Japan
64/B4 **Kujū-san** (mtn.), Japan
49/G1 **Kukës**, Alb.
65/F2 **Kuki**, Japan
65/J7 **Kukizaki**, Japan
61/G3 **Kūl** (riv.), Iran
50/D3 **Kula**, Yugo.
72/B3 **Kulai**, Malay.
55/J3 **Kulaly** (isl.), Kaz.
55/K4 **Kulandag** (mts.), Trkm.
55/G4 **Kulashi**, Geo.
52/D4 **Kuldīga**, Lat.
52/J5 **Kulebaki**, Rus.
69/D3 **Kulen**, Camb.
77/B2 **Kulkyne-Hattah Nat'l Park**, Austl.
61/L2 **Kullu**, India
45/J1 **Kulmbach**, Ger.
53/J2 **Kuloy** (riv.), Rus.
55/K3 **Kul'sary**, Kaz.
59/C2 **Kulu**, Turk.
56/H4 **Kulunda**, Rus.
68/C1 **Kulunda** (lake), Rus.
68/D1 **Kulunda** (riv.), Rus.
68/C1 **Kulunda Steppe** (grsld.), Kaz., Rus.
61/J1 **Kulyab**, Taj.
55/H3 **Kuma** (riv.), Rus.
65/F2 **Kumagaya**, Japan
64/B4 **Kumamoto**, Japan
64/B4 **Kumamoto** (pref.), Japan
64/E4 **Kumano**, Japan
64/D4 **Kumano** (riv.), Japan
50/E4 **Kumanovo**, Macd.
85/E5 **Kumasi**, Gha.
65/L10 **Kumatori**, Japan
55/G4 **Kumayri**, Arm.
85/H5 **Kumba**, Camr.
85/H5 **Kumbo**, Camr.
55/K5 **Kum-Dag**, Trkm.
67/E2 **Kumé** (isl.), Japan
55/K1 **Kumertau**, Rus.
64/A2 **Kumi**, SKor.
65/L10 **Kumiyama**, Japan
37/E4 **Kumla**, Swe.
59/B3 **Kumluca**, Turk.
30/F2 **Kumo** (riv.), Fin.
71/G2 **Kumon** (range), Burma
70/B5 **Kumta**, India
104/U11 **Kumukahi** (cape), Hi,US
63/P3 **Kunashiri** (isl.), Rus.
70/C2 **Kūnch**, India
87/E3 **Kundelungu Nat'l Park**, Zaire
61/K2 **Kundiān**, Pak.
70/B3 **Kundla**, India
37/E4 **Kungsbacka**, Swe.
83/J7 **Kungu**, Zaire
53/N4 **Kungur**, Rus.
50/E2 **Kunhegyes**, Hun.
64/B4 **Kunimi-dake** (mtn.), Japan
72/C5 **Kuningan**, Indo.
65/H7 **Kunitachi**, Japan
68/C4 **Kunjirap Daban** (pass), China
68/C4 **Kunlun** (mts.), China
50/E2 **Kunmadaras**, Hun.
71/H2 **Kunming**, China
63/K4 **Kunsan**, SKor.
66/E5 **Kunshan**, China
50/E2 **Kunszentmárton**, Hun.
66/E3 **Kunyu Shan** (mtn.), China
37/H3 **Kuopio**, Fin.
37/H3 **Kuopio** (prov.), Fin.
50/B3 **Kupa** (riv.), Cro., Slov.
73/F6 **Kupang**, Indo.
56/H4 **Kupino**, Rus.
114/M4 **Kupreanof** (isl.), Ak,US
54/F2 **Kupyansk**, Ukr.
63/L1 **Kur** (riv.), Rus.
55/J5 **Kura** (riv.), Azer., Geo.
65/L9 **Kurama-yama** (peak), Japan
64/C3 **Kurashiki**, Japan
86/B5 **Kuraymah**, Sudan
64/C3 **Kurayoshi**, Japan
60/D1 **Kurdistan** (reg.), Asia
51/G5 **Kŭrdzhali**, Bul.
49/J2 **Kŭrdzhali** (res.), Bul.
64/C3 **Kure**, Japan
59/C2 **Küre** (mts.), Turk.
78/H2 **Kure** (isl.), Hi,US
52/D4 **Kuressaare**, Est.
56/K3 **Kureyka** (riv.), Rus.
53/Q5 **Kurgan**, Rus.
53/Q5 **Kurgan Obl.**, Rus.
61/J1 **Kurgan-Tyube**, Taj.
78/G4 **Kuria** (isl.), Kiri.
60/G5 **Kuria Muria** (isls.), Oman
57/Q5 **Kuril** (isls.), Rus.
76/H8 **Ku-Ring-Gai Nat'l Park**, Austl.
83/M5 **Kurmuk**, Sudan
70/C4 **Kurnool**, India
65/K9 **Kurodashō**, Japan
65/G2 **Kuroiso**, Japan
65/M10 **Kuroso-yama** (peak), Japan
61/K2 **Kurram** (riv.), Pak.
52/D5 **Kuršėnai**, Lith.
70/E2 **Kurseong**, India
54/F2 **Kursk**, Rus.
39/L1 **Kurskaya** (spit), Lith., Rus.
39/L1 **Kurskiy** (lag.), Rus.
54/E2 **Kursk Obl.**, Rus.
50/E4 **Kuršumlija**, Yugo.
59/E3 **Kurtalan**, Turk.
41/E6 **Kürten**, Ger.
86/B5 **Kūrtī**, Sudan
83/L6 **Kuru** (riv.), Sudan
55/G4 **Kuruçay** (riv.), Turk.
68/E3 **Kuruktag** (mts.), China
64/B4 **Kurume**, Japan
70/D6 **Kurunegala**, SrL.
86/B4 **Kurur, Jabal** (peak), Sudan
76/E6 **Kurwongbah** (lake), Austl.
59/A3 **Kuşadası**, Turk.
83/M7 **Kusania** (lake), Ugan.
69/C2 **Ku Sathan** (peak), Thai.
65/L9 **Kusatsu**, Japan
65/M9 **Kusatsu**, Japan
65/M10 **Kushida** (riv.), Japan
64/B5 **Kushikino**, Japan
64/B5 **Kushima**, Japan
64/D4 **Kushimoto**, Japan
63/N3 **Kushiro**, Japan
53/Q5 **Kushmurun** (lake), Kaz.
62/F4 **Kushui** (riv.), China
55/J2 **Kushum** (riv.), Kaz.
114/F4 **Kuskokwim** (bay), Ak,US
114/G3 **Kuskokwim** (mts.), Ak,US
114/F3 **Kuskokwim** (riv.), Ak,US
55/M1 **Kustanay**, Kaz.
55/M2 **Kustanay Obl.**, Kaz.
83/M5 **Kūstī**, Sudan
65/M10 **Kusu**, Japan
69/C4 **Kut** (isl.), Thai.
59/B2 **Kütahya**, Turk.
55/G4 **Kutaisi**, Geo.
70/A3 **Kutch** (gulf), India
70/A3 **Kutch** (reg.), India
61/J4 **Kutch, Rann of** (swamp), India, Pak.
39/H4 **Kutná Hora**, Czh.
39/K2 **Kutno**, Pol.
87/C1 **Kutu**, Zaire
83/K5 **Kutum**, Sudan
102/E1 **Kuujjua** (riv.), NW,Can
103/K3 **Kuujjuaq** (Fort-Chimo), Qu,Can
103/J3 **Kuujjuarapik**, Qu,Can
37/J2 **Kuusamo**, Fin.
37/H3 **Kuusankoski**, Fin.
37/H4 **Kuutse Mägi** (mt.), Est.
55/L2 **Kuvandyk**, Rus.
60/E3 **Kuwait**
60/E3 **Kuwait** (Al Kuwait) (cap.), Kuw.
70/D2 **Kuwānā** (riv.), India
64/E3 **Kuwana**, Japan
53/L5 **Kuybyshev** (res.), Rus.
66/B3 **Kuye** (riv.), China
59/F3 **Kūysanjaq**, Iraq
52/F2 **Kuyto** (lake), Rus.
68/E3 **Kuytun**, China
68/D2 **Kuytun** (riv.), China
100/E5 **Kuyu Tingni**, Nic.
114/E2 **Kuzitrin** (riv.), Ak,US
55/H1 **Kuznetsk**, Rus.
37/F1 **Kvaløy** (isl.), Nor.
50/B3 **Kvarner** (chan.), Cro.
50/B3 **Kvarnerić** (chan.), Cro.
37/E2 **Kvigtinden** (peak), Nor.
37/C4 **Kvinnherad**, Nor.
87/C1 **Kwa** (riv.), Zaire
69/B3 **Kwai, River** (bridge), Thai.
78/F4 **Kwajelein** (atoll), Mrsh.
88/Q12 **Kwandebele** (homeland), SAfr.
63/K4 **Kwangju**, SKor.
87/C1 **Kwango** (riv.), Zaire
85/G4 **Kwara** (state), Nga.
110/D1 **Kwataboahegan** (riv.), On,Can
87/E4 **Kwekwe**, Zim.
39/K2 **Kwidzyn**, Pol.
83/N5 **Kwīha**, Eth.
80/D5 **Kwilu** (riv.), Zaire
82/J6 **Kyabé**, Chad
69/B2 **Kyaikkami**, Burma
69/B2 **Kyaikto**, Burma
62/F1 **Kyakhta**, Rus.
71/G4 **Kyangin**, Burma
69/D2 **Ky Anh**, Viet.
69/B1 **Kyaukme**, Burma
71/F4 **Kyaukpyu**, Burma
69/B1 **Kyaukse**, Burma
39/J4 **Kyjov**, Czh.
106/F3 **Kyle**, Sk,Can
43/F3 **Kyll** (riv.), Ger.
43/F3 **Kyllburg**, Ger.
35/F2 **Kym** (riv.), Eng,UK
37/H3 **Kymi** (prov.), Fin.
70/C3 **Kymore**, India
83/M7 **Kyoga** (lake), Ugan.
64/D3 **Kyōga-misaki** (cape), Japan
65/F3 **Kyonan**, Japan
64/A3 **Kyŏngju**, SKor.
64/A3 **Kyŏngju Nat'l Park**, SKor.
64/A2 **Kyŏngsang-bukto** (prov.), SKor.
64/A3 **Kyŏngsang-namdo** (prov.), SKor.
64/D3 **Kyōto**, Japan
64/D3 **Kyōto** (pref.), Japan
59/J4 **Kyrenia** (dist.), Cyp.
68/B3 **Kyrgyzstan**
38/G2 **Kyritz**, Ger.
71/H4 **Ky Son**, Viet.
64/B5 **Kyūshū** (isl.), Japan
64/B4 **Kyūshū** (mts.), Japan
64/B4 **Kyūshū** (prov.), Japan
50/F4 **Kyustendil**, Bul.
68/F1 **Kyzyl**, Rus.
56/G5 **Kyzylkum** (des.), Kaz.,Uzb.
56/G5 **Kzyl-Orda**, Kaz.

L

38/G2 **Laage**, Ger.
45/K3 **Laakirchen**, Aus.
46/B4 **La Algaba**, Sp.
100/E6 **La Amistad Int'l Park**
96/B3 **La Araucanía** (reg.), Chile
42/C1 **Laarne**, Belg.
101/N7 **La Ascensión**, Mex.
101/J5 **La Asunción**, Ven.
41/G4 **Laatzen**, Ger.
82/C2 **Laayoune**, WSah.
111/G1 **La Baie**, Qu,Can
46/A1 **La Baña**, Sp.
91/D2 **La Banda**, Arg.
46/C1 **La Bañeza**, Sp.
67/D6 **Labason**, Phil.
42/B2 **La Bassée**, Fr.
44/B3 **La Baule-Escoublac**, Fr.
48/B1 **Labbro** (peak), It.
82/H1 **Labdah** (Leptis Magna) (ruins), Libya
84/B4 **Labé**, Gui.
84/B4 **Labé** (comm.), Gui.
39/H3 **Labe** (Elbe) (riv.), Czh.
113/H5 **La Belle**, Fl,US
50/B3 **Labin**, Cro.
55/G3 **Labinsk**, Rus.
47/G2 **La Bisbal**, Sp.
100/D3 **Labná** (ruins), Mex.
39/L4 **Laborec** (riv.), Slvk.
96/E2 **Laboulaye**, Arg.
103/K3 **Labrador** (reg.), Nf,Can
99/M4 **Labrador** (sea), Can., Grld.
103/K3 **Labrador City**, Nf,Can
92/F5 **Lábrea**, Braz.
73/E2 **Labuk** (bay), Malay.
73/E2 **Labuk** (riv.), Malay.
71/F4 **Labutta**, Burma
49/F2 **Laç**, Alb.
96/C2 **La Calera**, Chile
111/N6 **Lac-Alouette**, Qu,Can
96/C2 **La Campana Nat'l Park**, Chile
115/B2 **La Cañada-Flintridge**, Ca,US
96/E2 **La Carlota**, Arg.
46/C4 **La Carlota**, Sp.
46/D3 **La Carolina**, Sp.
70/B5 **Laccadive** (sea), India
107/J3 **Lac du Bonnet**, Mb,Can
100/D4 **La Ceiba**, Hon.
31/S10 **La Celle-Saint-Cloud**, Fr.
77/A3 **Lacepede** (bay), Austl.
116/B3 **Lacey**, Wa,US
52/H3 **Lacha** (lake), Rus.
42/A5 **Lachapelle-aux-Pots**, Fr.
44/F2 **La Chapelle-Saint-Luc**, Fr.
44/C3 **La Chapelle-sur-Erdre**, Fr.
111/N6 **Lachenaie**, Qu,Can
111/N7 **Lachine**, Qu,Can
77/C2 **Lachlan** (riv.), Austl.
101/F6 **La Chorrera**, Pan.
41/H3 **Lachte** (riv.), Ger.
109/F4 **La Cienega**, NM,US
46/A1 **La Ciñiza**, Sp.
44/F5 **La Ciotat**, Fr.
101/N9 **La Ciudad Nat'l Park**, Mex.
111/S10 **Lackawanna**, NY,US
106/F2 **Lac La Biche**, Ab,Can
111/G2 **Lac-Mégantic**, Qu,Can
34/D4 **Lacock**, Eng,UK
106/E2 **Lacombe**, Ab,Can
100/E6 **La Concepción**, Pan.
101/G5 **La Concepcíon**, Ven.
111/G3 **Laconia**, NH,US
46/A1 **La Coruña**, Sp.
31/T10 **La Courneuve**, Fr.
44/D4 **La Couronne**, Fr.
107/L5 **La Crescent**, Mn,US
115/B2 **La Crescenta-Montrose**, Ca,US
110/B3 **La Crosse**, Wi,US
96/Q9 **La Cruz**, Chile
100/D5 **La Cruz**, CR
101/N9 **La Cruz**, Mex.
69/D1 **Lac Son**, Viet.
72/C1 **Lac Thien**, Viet.
61/L2 **Ladakh** (mts.), Pak., India
77/B3 **Laddon** (riv.), Austl.
39/J3 **Lądek-Zdrój**, Pol.
48/C2 **Ladispoli**, It.
52/F3 **Ladoga** (lake), Rus.
92/D2 **La Dorada**, Col.
97/J8 **Ladrillero** (mtn.), Chile
88/D3 **Ladybrand**, SAfr.
89/E3 **Ladysmith**, SAfr.
110/B2 **Ladysmith**, Wi,US
78/F4 **Lae** (atoll), Mrsh.
78/D5 **Lae**, PNG
100/D5 **La Esperanza**, Hon.
101/J6 **La Esperanza**, Ven.
46/B1 **La Estaca de Bares, Punta de** (cape), Sp.
46/A1 **La Estrada**, Sp.
91/D3 **La Falda**, Arg.
116/K11 **Lafayette**, Ca,US
113/G3 **La Fayette**, Ga,US
110/C3 **Lafayette**, In,US
112/E4 **Lafayette**, La,US
44/D2 **La Ferté-Bernard**, Fr.
44/C2 **La Ferté-Macé**, Fr.
42/C6 **La Ferté-sous-Jouarre**, Fr.
110/E1 **Laflamme** (riv.), Qu,Can
44/C3 **La Flèche**, Fr.
45/L3 **Lafnitz** (riv.), Aus.
111/M6 **Lafontaine**, Qu,Can
45/G4 **La Font Sancte, Pic de** (peak), Fr.
101/G6 **La Fría**, Ven.
71/F6 **Lāfūl**, India
32/B3 **Lagan** (riv.), NI,UK
31/S10 **La Garenne-Colombes**, Fr.
112/B2 **La Garita** (mts.), Co,US
47/L6 **La Garriga**, Sp.
94/C3 **Lagarto**, Braz.
67/D4 **Lagawe**, Phil.
82/H6 **Lagdo** (riv.), Camr.
41/F5 **Lage**, Ger.
95/B3 **Lages**, Braz.
40/C4 **Lage Vaart** (can.), Neth.
82/F1 **Laghouat**, Alg.
31/U9 **Lagny-le-Sec**, Fr.
31/U10 **Lagny-sur-Marne**, Fr.
95/C2 **Lagoa da Prata**, Braz.
95/C1 **Lagoa Formosa**, Braz.
95/B4 **Lagoa Vermelha**, Braz.
94/A2 **Lago da Pedra**, Braz.
96/C4 **Lago Puelo Nat'l Park**, Arg.
85/F5 **Lagos**, Nga.
85/F5 **Lagos** (state), Nga.
46/A4 **Lagos**, Port.
100/A3 **Lagos de Moreno**, Mex.
99/K4 **La Grande** (riv.), Can.
106/D4 **La Grande**, Or,US
45/G4 **La Grande Ruine** (mtn.), Fr.
113/G3 **La Grange**, Ga,US
110/C4 **La Grange**, Ky,US
112/D4 **La Grange**, Tx,US
92/F2 **La Gran Sabana** (plain), Ven.
46/A2 **La Guardia**, Sp.
96/D3 **La Guerra** (peak), Arg.
95/B4 **Laguna**, Braz.
116/M10 **Laguna** (cr.), Ca,US
96/C3 **Laguna Blanca Nat'l Park**, Arg.
46/C2 **Laguna de Duero**, Sp.
96/C3 **Laguna del Laja Nat'l Park**, Chile
115/C3 **Laguna Hills**, Ca,US
97/J6 **Laguna San Rafael Nat'l Park**, Chile
100/C4 **Lagunas de Montebello Nat'l Park**, Mex.
101/G6 **Lagunillas**, Ven.
115/C3 **La Habra**, Ca,US
72/B4 **Lahat**, Indo.
111/H2 **La Have** (riv.), NS,Can
91/B2 **La Higuera**, Chile
60/F1 **Lāhījān**, Iran
38/E3 **Lahn** (riv.), Ger.
43/G3 **Lahnstein**, Ger.
37/E4 **Laholm**, Swe.
61/K2 **Lahore**, Pak.
45/G2 **Lahr**, Ger.
37/H3 **Lahti**, Fin.
82/J6 **Laï**, Chad
69/C1 **Lai Chau**, Viet.
67/A2 **Laifeng Tujiazu Zizhixian**, China
44/D2 **L'Aigle**, Fr.
37/G3 **Laihia**, Fin.
37/G2 **Lainioälven** (riv.), Swe.
37/G3 **Laitila**, Fin.
45/J3 **Laives** (Leifers), It.
66/D3 **Laiwu**, China
66/D3 **Laizhou** (bay), China
96/C3 **Laja** (lake), Chile
95/B4 **Lajeado**, Braz.
94/C3 **Lajedo**, Braz.
47/S12 **Lajes do Pico**, Azor.,Port.
95/D2 **Lajinha**, Braz.
50/D2 **Lajosmizse**, Hun.
109/G3 **La Junta**, Co,US
107/J5 **Lake Andes**, SD,US
115/C2 **Lake Arrowhead**, Ca,US
112/E4 **Lake Charles**, La,US
108/F3 **Lake City**, Co,US
113/H4 **Lake City**, Fl,US
107/K4 **Lake City**, Mn,US
114/H3 **Lake Clark Nat'l Park & Prsv.**, Ak,US
33/E2 **Lake District Nat'l Park**, Eng,UK
115/C3 **Lake Elsinore**, Ca,US
76/B1 **Lakefield Nat'l Park**, Austl.
116/Q15 **Lake Forest**, Il,US
112/E3 **Lake Fork** (res.), Tx,US
108/D4 **Lake Havasu City**, Az,US
115/F5 **Lakehurst**, NJ,US
112/E4 **Lake Jackson**, Tx,US
113/H4 **Lakeland**, Fl,US
106/D3 **Lake Louise**, Ab,Can
87/F3 **Lake Malawi Nat'l Park**, Malw.
83/M8 **Lake Mburo Nat'l Park**, Ugan.
108/D4 **Lake Mead Nat'l Rec. Area**, Az, Nv,US
49/G2 **Lake Mikri Prespa Nat'l Park**, Gre.
115/F4 **Lake Mohawk**, NJ,US
35/G2 **Lakenheath**, Eng,UK
109/J3 **Lake of the Ozarks** (lake), Mo,US

107/K3 **Lake of the Woods** (lake), Can., US
116/F6 **Lake Orion**, Mi,US
108/B3 **Lakeport**, Ca,US
112/F3 **Lake Providence**, La,US
115/G5 **Lake Ronkonkoma**, NY,US
77/C4 **Lake Saint Clair-Cradle Mountain Nat'l Park**, Austl.
37/H1 **Lakesfjorden** (fjord), Nor.
115/K7 **Lake Shore**, Md,US
110/E4 **Lakeside**, Va,US
116/R16 **Lake Station**, In,US
106/C5 **Lakeview**, Or,US
116/F6 **Lakeville** (lake), Mi,US
113/H5 **Lake Wales**, Fl,US
115/B3 **Lakewood**, Ca,US
109/F3 **Lakewood**, Co,US
116/P15 **Lakewood**, Il,US
115/F5 **Lakewood**, NJ,US
106/C3 **Lakewood**, Wa,US
113/H5 **Lake Worth**, Fl,US
116/P15 **Lake Zurich**, Il,US
70/D2 **Lakhīmpur**, India
37/N7 **Laki** (vol.), Ice.
61/K2 **Lakki**, Pak.
49/H4 **Lakonía** (gulf), Gre.
70/B5 **Lakshadweep** (isls.), India
70/B6 **Lakshadweep** (terr.), India
47/X16 **La Laguna**, Canl.
61/K2 **Lāla Mūsa**, Pak.
89/H8 **Lalana** (riv.), Madg.
72/B4 **Lalang** (riv.), Indo.
70/E3 **Lālgola**, India
83/N5 **Lalībela**, Eth.
92/B4 **La Libertad**, Ecu.
100/C4 **La Libertad**, Guat.
101/M8 **La Libertad**, Mex.
96/C2 **La Ligua**, Chile
63/K3 **Lalin** (riv.), China
46/A1 **Lalín**, Sp.
46/C4 **La Línea de la Concepción**, Sp.
70/C3 **Lalitpur**, India
47/L6 **La Llagosta**, Sp.
106/F1 **La Loche**, Sk,Can
42/D3 **La Louvière**, Belg.
46/C4 **La Luisiana**, Sp.
46/B4 **La Luz, Costa de** (coast), Sp.
32/D1 **Lamachan** (mtn.), Sc,UK
48/A2 **La Maddalena**, It.
42/C2 **La Madeleine**, Fr.
85/F4 **Lama-Kara**, Togo
111/G2 **La Malbaie**, Qu,Can
100/D4 **Lamanai** (ruins), Belz.
72/D4 **Lamandau** (riv.), Indo.
109/G3 **Lamar**, Co,US
102/E2 **La Martre** (lake), NW,Can
44/B2 **Lamballe**, Fr.
91/E2 **Lambaré**, Par.
87/B1 **Lambaréné**, Gabon
95/H6 **Lambari**, Braz.
32/B5 **Lambay** (isl.), Ire.
92/C5 **Lambayeque**, Peru
32/B3 **Lambeg**, NI,UK
84/C3 **Lambé Koba** (riv.), Mali
98/E **Lambert** (glac.), Ant.
110/D3 **Lambertville**, Mi,US
115/F5 **Lambertville**, NJ,US
31/N7 **Lambeth** (bor.), Eng,UK
35/E3 **Lambourn**, Eng,UK
46/B2 **Lamego**, Port.
111/H2 **Lamèque** (isl.), NB,Can
92/C6 **La Merced**, Peru
44/F3 **La Mère Boitier, Signal de** (mtn.), Fr.
112/C3 **Lamesa**, Tx,US
49/H3 **Lamía**, Gre.
76/D5 **Lamington Nat'l Park**, Austl.
115/B3 **La Mirada**, Ca,US
101/M8 **La Misa**, Mex.
67/D6 **Lamitan**, Phil.
110/B3 **La Moine** (riv.), Il,US
45/J4 **Lamone** (riv.), It.
108/C4 **Lamont**, Ca,US
92/D5 **La Montaña** (reg.), Peru
47/K7 **La Morella** (peak), Sp.
101/P8 **La Morita**, Mex.
31/T9 **Lamorlaye**, Fr.
78/D4 **Lamotrek** (isl.), Micr.
107/J4 **La Moure**, ND,US
96/Q9 **Lampa**, Chile
69/B2 **Lampang**, Thai.
69/C2 **Lam Pao** (res.), Thai.
112/D4 **Lampasas**, Tx,US
112/D4 **Lampasas** (riv.), Tx,US
48/C5 **Lampedusa** (isl.), It.
45/H2 **Lampertheim**, Ger.
34/B2 **Lampeter**, Wal,UK
34/B3 **Lamphey**, Wal,UK
69/B2 **Lamphun**, Thai.
107/H3 **Lampman**, Sk,Can
87/H1 **Lamu**, Kenya
104/T10 **Lanai** (isl.), Hi,US
104/T10 **Lanaihale** (peak), Hi,US
43/E2 **Lanaken**, Belg.
47/F3 **La Nao, Cabo de** (cape), Sp.
36/D3 **Lanark**, Sc,UK
69/B4 **Lanbi** (isl.), Burma
62/D5 **Lancang** (riv.), China
33/F4 **Lancashire** (co.), Eng,UK
33/F4 **Lancashire** (plain), Eng,UK
103/H1 **Lancaster** (sound), NW,Can
33/F3 **Lancaster**, Eng,UK
108/C4 **Lancaster**, Ca,US
111/S10 **Lancaster**, NY,US
110/D4 **Lancaster**, Oh,US
113/H3 **Lancaster**, SC,US
110/B3 **Lancaster**, Wi,US
33/G2 **Lanchester**, Eng,UK
48/D1 **Lanciano**, It.
39/M3 **Łańcut**, Pol.
45/K2 **Landau an der Isar**, Ger.
45/H2 **Landau in der Pfalz**, Ger.
45/J3 **Landeck**, Aus.
43/E2 **Landen**, Belg.
106/F5 **Lander**, Wy,US
44/A2 **Landerneau**, Fr.
44/C4 **Landes** (reg.), Fr.
44/B3 **Landes de Lanvaux** (reg.), Fr.
106/F2 **Landis**, Sk,Can
44/A2 **Landivisiau**, Fr.
41/G1 **Land Kehdingen** (reg.), Ger.
76/B3 **Landsborough** (cr.), Austl.
34/A6 **Land's End** (pt.), Eng,UK
45/K2 **Landshut**, Ger.
40/B4 **Landsmeer**, Neth.
43/G5 **Landstuhl**, Ger.
33/F2 **Lanercost**, Eng,UK
44/B3 **Lanester**, Fr.
113/G3 **Lanett**, Al,US
107/J3 **Langdon**, ND,US
88/C3 **Langeberg** (mts.), SAfr.
88/L10 **Langeberg** (mts.), SAfr.
38/F1 **Langeland** (isl.), Den.
41/H5 **Langelsheim**, Ger.
41/F1 **Langen**, Ger.
41/E6 **Langenberg**, Ger.
107/H3 **Langenburg**, Sk,Can
40/D6 **Langenfeld**, Ger.
41/G4 **Langenhagen**, Ger.
39/H4 **Langenlois**, Aus.
45/G3 **Langenthal**, Swi.
41/E1 **Langeoog** (isl.), Ger.
66/D3 **Langfang**, China
106/G2 **Langham**, Sk,Can
35/F1 **Langham**, Eng,UK
33/F1 **Langholm**, Sc,UK
115/F5 **Langhorne**, Pa,US
37/N7 **Langjökull** (glac.), Ice.
72/A2 **Langkawi** (isl.), Malay.
69/B4 **Lang Kha Tuk** (peak), Thai.
31/M7 **Langley**, Eng,UK
35/G5 **Langney** (pt.), UK
37/E1 **Langøya** (isl.), Nor.
68/C5 **Langqên** (riv.), China
44/F3 **Langres**, Fr.
44/F3 **Langres** (plat.), Fr.
72/A3 **Langsa**, Indo.
69/D1 **Lang Son**, Viet.
111/R8 **Langstaff**, On,Can
112/C4 **Langtry**, Tx,US
47/G1 **Languedoc** (hist. reg.), Fr.
44/E5 **Languedoc-Roussillon** (reg.), Fr.
41/G3 **Langwedel**, Ger.
66/C3 **Langya Shan** (mtn.), China
115/K8 **Lanham-Seabrook**, Md,US
107/G3 **Lanigan**, Sk,Can
96/C3 **Lanín** (vol.), Chile
96/C3 **Lanín Nat'l Park**, Arg.
44/D5 **Lannemezan**, Fr.
44/D5 **Lannemezan** (plat.), Fr.
34/A6 **Lanner**, Eng,UK
44/B2 **Lannion**, Fr.
44/B2 **Lannion** (bay), Fr.
31/S11 **La Norville**, Fr.
69/B2 **Lan Sang Nat'l Park**, Thai.
115/E5 **Lansdale**, Pa,US
115/E6 **Lansdowne**, Pa,US
115/K7 **Lansdowne-Baltimore Highlands**, Md,US
110/B2 **L'Anse**, Mi,US
114/M3 **Lansing**, Yk,Can
116/Q16 **Lansing**, Il,US
110/C3 **Lansing** (cap.), Mi,US
69/B5 **Lanta** (isl.), Thai.
97/S12 **Lanús**, Arg.
48/A3 **Lanusei**, It.
67/C2 **Lanxi**, China
47/Y16 **Lanzarote** (isl.), Canl.
62/E4 **Lanzhou**, China
67/D4 **Laoag**, Phil.
67/E5 **Laoang**, Phil.
69/C1 **Lao Cai**, Viet.
63/H3 **Laoha** (riv.), China
66/B4 **Laohekou**, China
32/A6 **Laois (Leix)** (co.), Ire.
66/B4 **Laojun Shan** (mtn.), China
42/C4 **Laon**, Fr.
101/H5 **La Orchila** (isl.), Ven.
92/C6 **La Oroya**, Peru
69/C2 **Laos**
66/E3 **Lao Shan** (peak), China
66/E3 **Laotie Shan** (mtn.), China
66/F2 **Laotuding Shan** (peak), China
81/M13 **Laou** (riv.), Mor.
95/B3 **Lapa**, Braz.
85/G4 **Lapai**, Nga.
47/X16 **La Palma** (isl.), Canl.
96/D3 **La Pampa** (prov.), Arg.
92/E7 **La Paz** (cap.), Bol.
100/D5 **La Paz**, Hon.
101/M9 **La Paz**, Mex.
101/M9 **La Paz** (bay), Mex.
97/F2 **La Paz**, Uru.
110/F2 **La Pêche**, Qu,Can
52/F3 **Lapeenranta**, Fin.
116/F5 **Lapeer**, Mi,US
100/E6 **La Peña**, Pan.
101/P8 **La Perla**, Mex.
100/A3 **La Piedad Cavadas**, Mex.
37/H3 **Lapinlahti**, Fin.
37/F1 **Lapland** (reg.), Eur.
97/F2 **La Plata**, Arg.
92/C3 **La Plata**, Col.
112/B2 **La Plata** (peak), Co,US
110/E4 **La Plata**, Md,US
42/D3 **La Plate Taille, Barrage de** (dam), Belg.
111/G2 **La Pocatière**, Qu,Can
46/C1 **La Pola de Gordón**, Sp.
110/C3 **La Porte**, In,US
63/N1 **Lapotina** (mtn.), Rus.
50/E3 **Lapovo**, Yugo.
101/M8 **La Poza Grande**, Mex.
37/J3 **Lappeenranta**, Fin.
45/K2 **Lappersdorf**, Ger.
37/H2 **Lappi** (prov.), Fin.
111/N7 **La Prairie**, Qu,Can
112/D4 **La Pryor**, Tx,US
57/N2 **Laptev** (sea), Rus.
37/G3 **Lapua**, Fin.
47/G3 **La Puebla**, Sp.
46/C4 **La Puebla de Cazalla**, Sp.
46/B4 **La Puebla del Río**, Sp.
46/C3 **La Puebla de Montalbán**, Sp.
115/C2 **La Puente**, Ca,US
92/B4 **La Puntilla** (pt.), Ecu.
101/M8 **La Purísima**, Mex.
39/M2 **Łapy**, Pol.
86/B4 **Laqiyat al Arba'īn**, Sudan
92/E8 **La Quiaca**, Arg.
48/C1 **L'Aquila**, It.
61/F3 **Lār**, Iran
46/A1 **Laracha**, Sp.
81/L13 **Larache**, Mor.
46/C4 **La Rambla**, Sp.
109/F2 **Laramie** (riv.), Co, Wy,US
107/G5 **Laramie**, Wy,US
106/G5 **Laramie** (mts.), Wy,US
107/G5 **Laramie** (peak), Wy,US
95/A3 **Laranjeiras do Sul**, Braz.
73/H5 **Larat** (isl.), Indo.
81/S15 **Larba**, Alg.
44/B2 **L'Arcouest, Pointe de** (pt.), Fr.
106/A2 **Laredo** (sound), BC,Can
46/D1 **Laredo**, Sp.
112/D5 **Laredo**, Tx,US
40/C4 **Laren**, Neth.
113/H5 **Largo**, Fl,US
115/K8 **Largo**, Md,US
36/C3 **Largs**, Sc,UK
46/E1 **La Rhune** (mtn.), Fr.
73/F4 **Lariang** (riv.), Indo.
46/C4 **La Rinconada**, Sp.
91/C2 **La Rioja**, Arg.
46/D1 **La Rioja** (aut. comm.), Sp.
49/H3 **Lárisa**, Gre.
35/G2 **Lark** (riv.), Eng,UK
61/J3 **Lārkāna**, Pak.
35/E4 **Larkhill**, Eng,UK
116/J11 **Larkspur**, Ca,US
44/B3 **Larmor-Plage**, Fr.
59/J4 **Larnaca**, Cyp.
32/C2 **Larne**, NI,UK
32/C2 **Larne** (dist.), NI,UK
109/H3 **Larned**, Ks,US
32/C2 **Larne Lough** (inlet), NI,UK
106/F1 **La Roche** (lake), Sk,Can
44/C3 **La Rochelle**, Fr.
45/G3 **La Roche-sur-Foron**, Fr.
44/C3 **La Roche-sur-Yon**, Fr.
46/D3 **La Roda**, Sp.
101/H4 **La Romana**, DRep.
107/G2 **La Ronge**, Sk,Can
107/G2 **La Ronge** (lake), Sk,Can
113/F4 **Larose**, La,US
102/G1 **Larsen** (sound), NW,Can
98/V **Larsen Ice Shelf**, Ant.
38/A3 **L'Artois, Collines de** (hills), Fr.
46/B1 **La Rúa**, Sp.
111/N7 **La Salle**, Qu,Can
110/B3 **La Salle**, Il,US
109/G3 **Las Animas**, Co,US
110/E1 **La Sarre**, Qu,Can
45/G5 **La Sauvette** (mtn.), Fr.
101/H5 **Las Aves** (isls.), Ven.
91/D2 **Las Breñas**, Arg.
46/C4 **Las Cabezas de San Juan**, Sp.
96/C2 **Las Cabras**, Chile
100/D5 **Las Cañas**, CR
97/G2 **Lascano**, Uru.
100/C4 **Las Choapas**, Mex.
111/L1 **La Scie**, Nf,Can
108/F4 **Las Cruces**, NM,US
91/B2 **La Serena**, Chile
47/F1 **La Seu d'Urgell**, Sp.
44/F5 **La Seyne-sur-Mer**, Fr.
96/F3 **Las Flores**, Arg.
71/G3 **Lashio**, Burma
61/H2 **Lashkar Gāh**, Afg.
48/E3 **La Sila** (mts.), It.
97/J8 **La Silueta** (peak), Chile
96/C3 **Las Lajas** (peak), Arg.
91/D1 **Las Lomitas**, Arg.
101/G4 **Las Matas de Farfán**, DRep.
101/H6 **Las Mercedes**, Ven.
42/D2 **Lasne-Chapelle-Saint-Lambert**, Belg.
101/N8 **Las Nieves**, Mex.
46/D3 **La Solana**, Sp.
73/F4 **Lasolo** (riv.), Indo.
42/B4 **La Somme, Canal de** (can.), Fr.
96/C2 **Las Palmas de Cocalán Nat'l Park**, Chile
47/X16 **Las Palmas de Gran Canaria** (cap.), Canl.
46/D3 **Las Pedroñeras**, Sp.
45/H4 **La Spezia**, It.
97/F2 **Las Piedras**, Uru.
96/E2 **Las Rosas**, Arg.
47/N9 **Las Rozas**, Sp.
108/B2 **Lassen Volcanic Nat'l Park**, Ca,US
98/V **Lassiter** (coast), Ant.
101/E6 **Las Tablas**, Pan.
46/D3 **Las Tablas de Daimiel Nat'l Park**, Sp.
91/D2 **Las Termas**, Arg.
107/G3 **Last Mountain** (lake), Sk,Can
50/C4 **Lastovo** (isl.), Cro.
50/C4 **Lastovski** (chan.), Cro.
101/N8 **Las Varas**, Mex.
101/N9 **Las Varas**, Mex.
96/E1 **Las Varillas**, Arg.
109/F4 **Las Vegas**, NM,US
108/D3 **Las Vegas**, Nv,US
111/K1 **La Tabatière**, Qu,Can
92/C4 **Latacunga**, Ecu.
98/U **Latady** (isl.), Ant.
59/K4 **Latakia** (Al Lādhiqīyah), Syria
85/F4 **L'Atakora** (prov.), Ben.
48/E2 **Laterza**, It.
44/C4 **La Teste-de-Buch**, Fr.
44/C3 **Lathan** (riv.), Fr.
116/M11 **Lathrop**, Ca,US
31/M7 **Latimer**, Eng,UK
48/C2 **Latina**, It.
39/L4 **Latorica** (riv.), Slvk.
101/H5 **La Tortuga** (isl.), Ven.
74/B3 **Latouche Treville** (cape), Austl.
77/C3 **Latrobe** (peak), Austl.
77/C3 **Latrobe** (riv.), Austl.
44/E5 **Lattes**, Fr.
111/F2 **La Tuque**, Qu,Can
70/C4 **Lātūr**, India
52/E4 **Latvia**
92/E7 **Lauca Nat'l Park**, Chile
45/G3 **Lauch** (riv.), Fr.
36/D3 **Lauder**, Sc,UK
116/N14 **Lauderdale** (lakes), Wi,US
41/H2 **Lauenburg**, Ger.
45/J2 **Lauf**, Ger.
34/B3 **Laugharne**, Wal,UK
112/C4 **Laughlin A.F.B.**, Tx,US
78/H6 **Lau Group** (isls.), Fiji
37/G3 **Lauhanvuoren Nat'l Park**, Fin.
37/H3 **Laukaa**, Fin.
77/C4 **Launceston**, Austl.
34/B5 **Launceston**, Eng,UK
96/B4 **La Unión**, Chile
100/D5 **La Unión**, ESal.
47/E4 **La Unión**, Sp.
115/K7 **Laurel**, Md,US
113/F4 **Laurel**, Ms,US
106/F4 **Laurel**, Mt,US
32/B3 **Laurelvale**, NI,UK
36/D2 **Laurencekirk**, Sc,UK
113/H3 **Laurens**, SC,US
110/C1 **Laurentian** (plat.), Can.
32/D2 **Laurieston**, Sc,UK
113/J3 **Laurinburg**, NC,US
110/B2 **Laurium**, Mi,US
45/G3 **Lausanne**, Swi.
73/E4 **Laut** (isl.), Indo.
96/B3 **Lautaro**, Chile
43/G5 **Lauter** (riv.), Fr., Ger.
45/H2 **Lauter** (riv.), Ger.
38/E3 **Lauterbach**, Ger.
78/G6 **Lautoka**, Fiji
40/D2 **Lauwers** (chan.), Neth.
40/D2 **Lauwersmeer** (lake), Neth.
108/B2 **Lava Beds Nat'l Mon.**, Ca,US
111/N6 **Laval**, Qu,Can
44/C2 **Laval**, Fr.
97/G2 **Lavalleja** (dept.), Uru.
45/L3 **Lavant** (riv.), Aus.
96/B3 **Lavapié** (pt.), Chile
44/D5 **Lavelanet**, Fr.
48/D2 **Lavello**, It.
115/C2 **La Verne**, Ca,US
31/R10 **La Verrière**, Fr.
92/E1 **La Victoria**, Ven.
95/C2 **Lavras**, Braz.
94/C2 **Lavras da Mangabeira**, Braz.
49/J4 **Lávrion**, Gre.
61/K1 **Lawarai** (pass), Pak.
72/D3 **Lawit** (mtn.), Indo.
115/B3 **Lawndale**, Ca,US
109/J3 **Lawrence**, Ks,US
111/G3 **Lawrence**, Ma,US
110/C4 **Lawrenceburg**, In,US
113/G2 **Lawrenceburg**, Ky,US
113/G3 **Lawrenceburg**, Tn,US
32/B3 **Lawrencetown**, NI,UK
113/H3 **Lawrenceville**, Ga,US
115/F5 **Lawrenceville**, NJ,US
109/H4 **Lawton**, Ok,US
72/D5 **Lawu** (peak), Indo.
60/C3 **Lawz, Jabal al** (mtn.), SAr.
32/D3 **Laxey**, IM,UK
43/F6 **Laxou**, Fr.
44/C3 **Lay** (riv.), Fr.
53/N2 **Laya** (riv.), Rus.
73/E4 **Layar** (cape), Indo.
79/H2 **Laycan** (isl.), Hi,US
60/E4 **Laylá**, SAr.
44/C3 **Layon** (riv.), Fr.
108/E2 **Layton**, Ut,US
50/D3 **Lazarevac**, Yugo.
100/A4 **Lazaro Cardenas**, Mex.
48/C1 **Lazio** (reg.), It.
33/F2 **Lazonby**, Eng,UK
35/F3 **Lea** (riv.), Eng,UK
69/C3 **Leach**, Camb.
35/E3 **Leach** (riv.), Eng,UK
107/H4 **Lead**, SD,US
33/H5 **Leadenham**, Eng,UK
106/F3 **Leader**, Sk,Can
34/D2 **Leadon** (riv.), Eng,UK
112/B2 **Leadville**, Co,US
113/F4 **Leaf** (riv.), Ms,US
77/B2 **Leaghur** (lake), Austl.
109/J5 **League City**, Tx,US
112/D4 **Leakey**, Tx,US
35/E2 **Leam** (riv.), Eng,UK
116/G7 **Leamington**, On,Can
35/F4 **Leatherhead**, Eng,UK
42/D3 **L'Eau d'Heure** (riv.), Belg.
109/J3 **Leavenworth**, Ks,US
106/C4 **Leavenworth**, Wa,US
43/F5 **Lebach**, Ger.
50/E4 **Lebane**, Yugo.
59/K5 **Lebanon**
59/K5 **Lebanon** (mts.), Leb.
110/C3 **Lebanon**, In,US
110/C4 **Lebanon**, Ky,US
109/J3 **Lebanon**, Mo,US
111/F3 **Lebanon**, NH,US
106/C4 **Lebanon**, Or,US
113/G2 **Lebanon**, Tn,US
110/D4 **Lebanon**, Va,US
42/D2 **Lebbeke**, Belg.
54/E2 **Lebedin**, Ukr.
110/E1 **Lebel-sur-Quévillon**, Qu,Can
81/M13 **Lebene** (riv.), Mor.
44/D3 **Le Blanc**, Fr.
31/T10 **Le Blanc-Mesnil**, Fr.
39/J1 **Lębork**, Pol.
88/Q12 **Lebowa** (homeland), SAfr.
46/B4 **Lebrija**, Sp.
91/B4 **Lebu**, Chile
46/A2 **Leça da Palmeira**, Port.
45/G5 **Le Cannet**, Fr.
42/C3 **Le Cateau**, Fr.
49/F2 **Lecce**, It.
45/H4 **Lecco**, It.
45/J2 **Lech** (riv.), Aus., Ger.
67/B2 **Lechang**, China
31/S10 **Le Chesnay**, Fr.
35/E3 **Lechlade**, Eng,UK
38/E1 **Leck**, Ger.
45/J5 **Le Cornate** (peak), It.
44/F3 **Le Creusot**, Fr.
39/M3 **Łęczna**, Pol.
41/E2 **Leda** (riv.), Ger.
72/B3 **Ledang** (peak), Malay.
34/D2 **Ledbury**, Eng,UK
42/C2 **Lede**, Belg.
42/C2 **Ledegem**, Belg.
106/E2 **Leduc**, Ab,Can
107/K4 **Leech** (lake), Mn,US
33/G4 **Leeds**, Eng,UK
33/G4 **Leeds and Liverpool** (can.), Eng,UK
40/D2 **Leek**, Neth.
33/F5 **Leek**, Eng,UK
31/N7 **Lee (Lea)** (riv.), Eng,UK
41/E2 **Leer**, Ger.
40/C5 **Leerdam**, Neth.
40/C4 **Leersum**, Neth.
113/H4 **Leesburg**, Fl,US
110/E4 **Leesburg**, Va,US
112/E4 **Leesville**, La,US
77/C2 **Leeton**, Austl.
88/L10 **Leeu** (riv.), SAfr.
40/C2 **Leeuwarden**, Neth.
74/B6 **Leeuwin** (cape), Austl.
108/C3 **Lee Vining**, Ca,US
101/J4 **Leeward** (isls.), NAm.
44/B2 **Leff** (riv.), Fr.
85/H5 **Lefo** (peak), Camr.
74/C6 **Lefroy** (lake), Austl.
46/D2 **Leganés**, Sp.
46/D1 **Legazpia**, Sp.
77/C4 **Legges Tor** (peak), Austl.
39/L2 **Legionowo**, Pol.
45/J4 **Legnago**, It.
45/H4 **Legnano**, It.
39/J3 **Legnica**, Pol.
39/H3 **Legnica** (prov.), Pol.
68/C5 **Leh**, India
44/D2 **Le Havre**, Fr.
115/E5 **Lehigh** (riv.), Pa,US
113/H5 **Lehigh Acres**, Fl,US
41/G4 **Lehrte**, Ger.
67/B2 **Lei** (riv.), China
61/K2 **Leiah**, Pak.
45/L3 **Leibnitz**, Aus.
35/E1 **Leicester**, Eng,UK
35/E1 **Leicestershire** (co.), Eng,UK
76/B3 **Leichhardt** (mts.), Austl.
74/F3 **Leichhardt** (riv.), Austl.
40/E6 **Leichlingen**, Ger.
40/B4 **Leiden**, Neth.
40/B4 **Leiderdorp**, Neth.
40/B4 **Leidschendam**, Neth.
40/A7 **Leie** (riv.), Belg.
45/J3 **Leifers** (Laives), It.
31/N8 **Leigh**, Eng,UK
31/P8 **Leigh**, Eng,UK
35/F3 **Leighton Buzzard**, Eng,UK
41/G5 **Leine** (riv.), Ger.
41/H6 **Leinefelde**, Ger.
36/B4 **Leinster** (mtn.), Ire.
36/B4 **Leinster** (prov.), Ire.
34/D2 **Leintwardine**, Eng,UK
38/G3 **Leipzig**, Ger.
42/C2 **Leir** (riv.), Belg.
46/A3 **Leiria**, Port.
46/A3 **Leiria** (dist.), Port.
35/H2 **Leiston cum Sizewell**, Eng,UK
110/C4 **Leitchfield**, Ky,US
35/F4 **Leith** (hill), Eng,UK
50/C2 **Leitha** (riv.), Aus.
32/A6 **Leix (Laois)** (co.), Ire.
32/B5 **Leixlip**, Ire.
67/B2 **Leiyang**, China
66/B4 **Leiyuanzhen**, China
67/A3 **Leizhou** (pen.), China
40/B5 **Lek** (riv.), Neth.
40/B5 **Lekkerkerk**, Neth.
85/G5 **Lekki** (lag.), Nga.
37/E3 **Leksands-Noret**, Swe.
52/F3 **Leksozero** (lake), Rus.
73/G3 **Lelai** (cape), Indo.
113/F3 **Leland**, Ms,US
78/F4 **Lelu**, Micro.
45/G5 **Le Luc**, Fr.
40/C3 **Lelystad**, Neth.
97/L8 **Le Maire** (str.), Arg.
45/G3 **Léman** (Geneva) (lake), Fr., Swi.
44/D3 **Le Mans**, Fr.
107/J5 **Le Mars**, Ia,US
43/G5 **Lembach**, Fr.
72/A3 **Lembu** (peak), Indo.
95/C2 **Leme**, Braz.
31/T11 **Le Mée-sur-Seine**, Fr.
37/H1 **Lemenjoen Nat'l Park**, Fin.
31/S10 **Le Mesnil-le-Roi**, Fr.
31/R10 **Le Mesnil-Saint-Denis**, Fr.
41/F4 **Lemgo**, Ger.
40/C3 **Lemmer**, Neth.
101/M7 **Lemmon** (peak), Az,US
107/H4 **Lemmon**, SD,US
44/E4 **Le Moure de la Gardille** (mtn.), Fr.
48/E2 **Le Murge** (upland), It.
53/P2 **Lemva** (riv.), Rus.
41/F2 **Lemwerder**, Ger.
37/D3 **Lena**, Nor.
57/N3 **Lena** (riv.), Rus.
94/B1 **Lençóis Maranhenses Nat'l Park**, Braz.
95/B2 **Lençóis Paulista**, Braz.
45/J4 **Lendinara**, It.
41/H4 **Lengede**, Ger.
41/E4 **Lengerich**, Ger.
67/B2 **Lengshuijiang**, China
67/B2 **Lengshuitan**, China
91/B3 **Lengua de Vaca** (pt.), Chile
68/B4 **Lenina, Pik** (peak), Kyr.
52/F4 **Leningrad** (Saint Petersburg), Rus.
53/V7 **Leningrad** (Saint Petersburg) (inset), Rus.
98/L **Leningradskaya**, Ant.
68/D1 **Leninogorsk**, Kaz.
53/M5 **Leninogorsk**, Rus.
56/J4 **Leninsk-Kuznetskiy**, Rus.
50/E2 **Leninváros**, Hun.
31/H5 **Lenkoran'**, Azer.
41/E6 **Lenne** (riv.), Ger.
41/F6 **Lennestadt**, Ger.
97/L8 **Lennox** (isl.), Chile
113/H3 **Lenoir**, NC,US
113/G3 **Lenoir City**, Tn,US
42/B3 **Lens**, Fr.
57/M3 **Lensk**, Rus.
37/F1 **Lenvik**, Nor.
85/E4 **Léo**, Burk.
45/L3 **Leoben**, Aus.
42/B2 **Leoberghe**, Fr.
107/J4 **Leola**, SD,US
34/D2 **Leominster**, Eng,UK
44/C4 **Leon** (lag.), Fr.
100/A3 **León**, Mex.
100/D5 **León**, Nic.
46/C1 **León**, Sp.
112/D3 **Leon** (riv.), Tx,US
116/F6 **Leonard**, Mi,US
45/L2 **Leonding**, Aus.
96/E2 **Leones**, Arg.
48/D4 **Leonforte**, It.
98/F **Leopold and Astrid** (coast), Ant.
95/L6 **Leopoldina**, Braz.
42/C1 **Leopoldkanaal** (can.), Belg.
43/E1 **Leopoldsburg**, Belg.
41/F4 **Leopoldshöhe**, Ger.
109/G3 **Leoti**, Ks,US
106/G2 **Leoville**, Sk,Can
44/D4 **Le Passage**, Fr.
46/B4 **Lepe**, Sp.
31/S10 **Le Pecq**, Fr.
50/F3 **Lepenski Vir**, Yugo.
31/U9 **Le Plessis-Belleville**, Fr.
31/T10 **Le Plessis-Trévise**, Fr.
45/H3 **Lepontine Alps** (mts.), It., Swi.
89/R15 **Le Port**, Reun.
42/A2 **Le Portel**, Fr.
37/H3 **Leppävirta**, Fin.
68/C2 **Lepsy** (riv.), Kaz.
44/E4 **Le Puy**, Fr.
67/D5 **Legaspi**, Phil.
84/D4 **Léraba** (riv.), Burk., IvC.
31/T10 **Le Raincy**, Fr.
48/C4 **Lercara Friddi**, It.
45/H4 **Lerici**, It.
47/F2 **Lérida** (Lleida), Sp.
88/D3 **Le Rouxdam, P. K.** (res.), SAfr.
42/A5 **Les Andelys**, Fr.
101/G4 **Les Cayes**, Haiti
111/M7 **Les Cèdres**, Qu,Can
31/R10 **Les Clayes-sous-Bois**, Fr.
71/H2 **Leshan**, China
44/C3 **Les Herbiers**, Fr.
31/T10 **Lésigny**, Fr.
50/E4 **Leskovac**, Yugo.
36/D2 **Leslie**, Sc,UK
31/T10 **Les Lilas**, Fr.
31/S10 **Les Molières**, Fr.
42/A6 **Les Mureaux**, Fr.
44/A2 **Lesneven**, Fr.
89/D3 **Lesotho**
63/L2 **Lesozavodsk**, Rus.
47/G1 **L'Espinouse, Sommet de** (peak), Fr.
44/C3 **Les Sables-d'Olonne**, Fr.
43/E4 **Lesse** (riv.), Belg.
37/E4 **Lessebo**, Swe.
101/H4 **Lesser Antilles** (arch.), NAm.
55/G4 **Lesser Kavkaz** (mts.), Eur.
106/D2 **Lesser Slave** (lake), Ab,Can
73/E5 **Lesser Sunda** (isls.), Indo.
42/C2 **Lessines**, Belg.
43/E5 **L'Est, Canal de** (can.), Fr.
45/G3 **Le Suchet** (peak), Swi.
42/B6 **Les Ulis**, Fr.
72/D3 **Lesung** (peak), Indo.
49/J3 **Lésvos** (isl.), Gre.
32/C2 **Leswalt**, Sc,UK
39/J3 **Leszno**, Pol.
39/J3 **Leszno** (prov.), Pol.
89/R15 **Le Tampon**, Reun.
31/S10 **L'Étang-la-Ville**, Fr.
35/F3 **Letchworth**, Eng,UK
106/E3 **Lethbridge**, Ab,Can
41/F2 **Lethe** (riv.), Ger.
73/G5 **Leti** (isls.), Indo.
92/E4 **Leticia**, Col.
87/E5 **Letlhakane**, Bots.
87/D5 **Letlhakeng**, Bots.
71/G4 **Letpadan**, Burma
42/A3 **Le Tréport**, Fr.
69/B4 **Letsôk-Aw** (isl.), Burma
40/C4 **Leusden-Zuid**, Neth.
72/A3 **Leuser** (peak), Indo.
45/J3 **Leutkirch im Allgäu**, Ger.
43/D2 **Leuven** (Louvain), Belg.
42/C2 **Leuze-en-Hainaut**, Belg.
49/H3 **Levádhia**, Gre.
31/S10 **Levallois-Perret**, Fr.
37/D3 **Levanger**, Nor.
96/B5 **Level** (isl.), Chile
112/C3 **Levelland**, Tx,US
89/F2 **Leven** (pt.), SAfr.
33/H4 **Leven**, Eng,UK
33/F3 **Leven** (riv.), Eng,UK
33/G3 **Leven** (riv.), Eng,UK
36/D2 **Leven**, Sc,UK
74/C3 **Leveque** (cape), Austl.
40/D6 **Leverkusen**, Ger.
31/S10 **Le Vésinet**, Fr.
39/K4 **Levice**, Slvk.
75/S11 **Levin**, NZ
111/G2 **Lévis**, Qu,Can
31/R10 **Lévis-Saint-Nom**, Fr.
115/G5 **Levittown**, NY,US
115/F5 **Levittown**, Pa,US
49/G3 **Levkás**, Gre.
49/G3 **Levkás** (isl.), Gre.
39/L4 **Levoča**, Slvk.
51/G4 **Levski**, Bul.
35/G5 **Lewes**, Eng,UK
111/K1 **Lewis** (hills), Nf,Can
75/R11 **Lewis** (pass), NZ
106/E3 **Lewis** (range), Mt,US
106/C4 **Lewis** (riv.), Wa,US
107/J5 **Lewis & Clark** (lake), Ne, SD,US
113/G3 **Lewisburg**, Tn,US
110/D4 **Lewisburg**, WV,US
31/N7 **Lewisham** (bor.), Eng,UK
111/L1 **Lewisporte**, Nf,Can
113/G3 **Lewis Smith** (lake), Al,US
106/D4 **Lewiston**, Id,US
111/G2 **Lewiston**, Me,US
111/R9 **Lewiston**, NY,US
106/F4 **Lewistown**, Mt,US
110/E3 **Lewistown**, Pa,US
73/F5 **Lewotobi** (peak), Indo.
110/C4 **Lexington**, Ky,US
113/H3 **Lexington**, NC,US
109/H2 **Lexington**, Ne,US
113/H3 **Lexington**, SC,US
113/F3 **Lexington**, Tn,US
110/E4 **Lexington**, Va,US
110/E4 **Lexington Park**, Md,US
33/G3 **Leyburn**, Eng,UK
33/F4 **Leyland**, Eng,UK
67/D5 **Leyte** (isl.), Phil.
31/N7 **Leyton**, Eng,UK
44/F4 **Lez** (riv.), Fr.
39/M3 **Leżajsk**, Pol.
49/F2 **Lezhë**, Alb.
44/E5 **Lézignan-Corbières**, Fr.
54/E2 **L'gov**, Rus.
70/F2 **Lhasa**, China
70/E2 **Lhazê**, China
47/G2 **L'Hospitalet**, Sp.
71/G2 **Lhünzê**, China
66/B5 **Li** (riv.), China
66/C4 **Li** (riv.), China
71/K2 **Li** (riv.), China
67/B3 **Lian** (riv.), China
42/B5 **Liancourt**, Fr.
64/B2 **Liancourt** (rocks), Japan, SKor.
66/C2 **Liangcheng**, China
72/D3 **Liangpran** (peak), Indo.
66/D4 **Liang Shan** (mtn.), China
66/C5 **Liangzi** (lake), China
66/D4 **Lianyungang**, China
63/J3 **Liao** (riv.), China
66/C3 **Liaocheng**, China
66/E2 **Liaodong** (gulf), China
63/J3 **Liaoyang**, China
66/F2 **Liaoyuan**, China
61/K3 **Liāquatpur**, Pak.
102/D2 **Liard** (riv.), Can.
106/E3 **Libby**, Mt,US
83/J7 **Libenge**, Zaire
109/G3 **Liberal**, Ks,US
42/C3 **Libercourt**, Fr.
93/H6 **Liberdade** (riv.), Braz.
39/H3 **Liberec**, Czh.
84/C5 **Liberia**
100/D5 **Liberia**, CR
100/D4 **Libertad**, Belz.
97/F2 **Libertad**, Uru.
91/D1 **Libertador General San Martín**, Arg.
113/G2 **Liberty**, Ky,US
115/K7 **Liberty** (res.), Md,US
112/E1 **Liberty**, Mo,US
113/F4 **Liberty**, Ms,US
112/E4 **Liberty**, Tx,US
116/Q15 **Libertyville**, Il,US
73/G4 **Libobo** (cape), Indo.
45/K1 **Liboc** (riv.), Czh.
67/D5 **Libon**, Phil.
82/G7 **Libreville** (cap.), Gabon
83/J2 **Libya**
83/K2 **Libyan** (des.), Afr.
83/K1 **Libyan** (plat.), Libya
96/C2 **Licantén**, Chile
48/C4 **Licata**, It.
59/E2 **Lice**, Turk.
45/H1 **Lich**, Ger.
35/E1 **Lichfield**, Eng,UK
45/J1 **Lichtenfels**, Ger.
40/D5 **Lichtenvoorde**, Neth.
42/C1 **Lichtervelde**, Belg.
66/B5 **Lichuan**, China
110/C4 **Licking** (riv.), Ky,US
48/D2 **Licosa** (cape), It.
52/E5 **Lida**, Bela.
33/F1 **Liddell Water** (riv.), Sc,UK
103/R7 **Liddon** (gulf), NW,Can
35/F2 **Lidlington**, Eng,UK
45/K4 **Lido**, It.
48/C2 **Lido di Ostia**, It.
39/K2 **Lidzbark**, Pol.
39/L1 **Lidzbark Warmiński**, Pol.
88/E2 **Liebenbergsvlei** (riv.), SAfr.
45/H3 **Liechtenstein**
42/D2 **Liedekerke**, Belg.
43/E2 **Liège**, Belg.
43/E3 **Liège** (prov.), Belg.
37/J3 **Lieksa**, Fin.
40/C5 **Lienden**, Neth.
41/E4 **Lienen**, Ger.
45/K3 **Lienz**, Aus.
52/D4 **Liepāja**, Lat.
42/D1 **Lier**, Belg.
44/E1 **Lies** (riv.), Belg.
43/F3 **Lieser** (riv.), Ger.
37/G3 **Liesjärven Nat'l Park**, Fin.
45/G3 **Liestal**, Swi.
37/G3 **Lieto**, Fin.
42/B3 **Liévin**, Fr.
110/F2 **Lièvre** (riv.), Qu,Can
45/L3 **Liezen**, Aus.
32/B5 **Liffey** (riv.), Ire.
79/V12 **Lifou** (isl.), NCal.
34/B5 **Lifton**, Eng,UK
73/F1 **Ligao**, Phil.
45/H4 **Ligure, Appenino** (mts.), It.
45/H4 **Liguria** (reg.), It.
45/H5 **Ligurian** (sea), Eur.
75/J3 **Lihou** (reef), Austl.
71/H2 **Lijiang** (Lijiang Naxizu Zizhixian), China
87/E3 **Likasi**, Zaire
106/C2 **Likely**, BC,Can
87/F3 **Likoma** (isl.), Malw.
82/J8 **Likouala** (riv.), Congo
48/A1 **L'Ile-Rousse**, Fr.
31/T10 **L'Ile-Saint-Denis**, Fr.
41/F2 **Lilienthal**, Ger.
71/K2 **Liling**, China
43/D1 **Lille**, Belg.
42/C2 **Lille**, Fr.

37/D3 **Lillehammer,** Nor.
42/B2 **Lillers,** Fr.
37/D4 **Lillestrøm,** Nor.
106/C3 **Lillooet,** BC,Can
106/C3 **Lillooet** (riv.), BC,Can
87/F3 **Lilongwe** (cap.), Malw.
77/G5 **Lilydale,** Austl.
50/D4 **Lim** (riv.), Yugo.
92/C6 **Lima** (cap.), Peru
46/A2 **Lima** (riv.), Port.
107/L4 **Lima** (peak), Mn,US
110/C3 **Lima,** Oh,US
96/Q9 **Limache,** Chile
95/K6 **Lima Duarte,** Braz.
39/L4 **Limanowa,** Pol.
59/J4 **Limassol,** Cyp.
32/B1 **Limavady,** NI,UK
32/A2 **Limavady** (dist.), NI,UK
96/C4 **Limay** (riv.), Arg.
42/A6 **Limay,** Fr.
48/A2 **Limbara** (peak), It.
70/B3 **Limbdi,** India
43/E2 **Limburg** (prov.), Belg.
43/E1 **Limburg** (prov.), Neth.
45/H1 **Limburg an der Lahn,** Ger.
111/Q8 **Limehouse,** On,Can
31/T10 **Limeil-Brévannes,** Fr.
95/C2 **Limeira,** Braz.
36/A4 **Limerick,** Ire.
46/B2 **Limia** (riv.), Sp.
74/F2 **Limmen** (bight), Austl.
49/J3 **Límnos** (isl.), Gre.
94/D2 **Limoeiro,** Braz.
94/C2 **Limoeiro do Norte,** Braz.
44/D4 **Limoges,** Fr.
44/D4 **Limogne** (plat.), Fr.
100/E5 **Limón,** CR
109/G3 **Limon,** Co,US
31/S11 **Limours,** Fr.
44/D4 **Limousin** (mts.), Fr.
44/D4 **Limousin** (reg.), Fr.
44/E5 **Limoux,** Fr.
87/F5 **Limpopo** (riv.), Afr.
31/P8 **Limpsfield,** Eng,UK
69/E2 **Limu** (mtn.), China
67/C5 **Linapacan** (isl.), Phil.
96/C2 **Linares,** Chile
100/B3 **Linares,** Mex.
46/D3 **Linares,** Sp.
67/C2 **Linchuan,** China
96/E2 **Lincoln,** Arg.
111/R9 **Lincoln,** On,Can
99/L1 **Lincoln** (sea), Can., Grld.
33/H5 **Lincoln,** Eng,UK
110/B3 **Lincoln,** Il,US
111/G2 **Lincoln,** Me,US
109/H2 **Lincoln** (cap.), Ne,US
106/B4 **Lincoln Beach,** Or,US
106/B4 **Lincoln City,** Or,US
33/H5 **Lincoln Heath** (woodl.), Eng,UK
116/F7 **Lincoln Park,** Mi,US
115/F5 **Lincoln Park,** NJ,US
33/H5 **Lincolnshire** (co.), Eng,UK
33/H5 **Lincolnshire Wolds** (hills), Eng,UK
113/H3 **Lincolnton,** NC,US
115/F5 **Lincroft,** NJ,US
48/A2 **L'Incudine, Mont** (mtn.), Fr.
40/D3 **Linde** (riv.), Neth.
76/C3 **Lindeman** (isl.), Austl.
92/G2 **Linden,** Guy.
113/G3 **Linden,** Al,US
115/F5 **Linden,** NJ,US
45/H3 **Lindenberg im Allgäu,** Ger.
116/P15 **Lindenhurst,** Il,US
115/G5 **Lindenhurst,** NY,US
115/F6 **Lindenwold,** NJ,US
52/B4 **Lindesberg,** Swe.
87/G3 **Lindi,** Tanz.
36/E3 **Lindisfarne** (Holy) (isl.), Eng,UK
41/E6 **Lindlar,** Ger.
77/D3 **Lind Nat'l Park,** Austl.
110/E2 **Lindsay,** On,Can
108/C3 **Lindsay,** Ca,US
112/D2 **Lindsborg,** Ks,US
79/K4 **Line** (isls.), Kiri.
66/B3 **Linfen,** China
66/C4 **Lingchuan,** China
67/B2 **Lingchuan,** China
40/C5 **Linge** (riv.), Neth.
41/E3 **Lingen,** Ger.
31/N8 **Lingfield,** Eng,UK
72/B3 **Lingga** (isls.), Indo.
43/G6 **Lingolsheim,** Fr.
84/B3 **Linguère,** Sen.
66/D3 **Ling Xian,** China
67/B2 **Ling Xian,** China
66/E5 **Lingyang Shan** (mtn.), China
66/L8 **Lingyen Shan** (mtn.), China
66/E5 **Lingyin Si,** China
67/D2 **Linhai,** China
95/D1 **Linhares,** Braz.
37/E4 **Linköping,** Swe.
66/C3 **Linliu Shan** (mtn.), China
37/J3 **Linnansaaren Nat'l Park,** Fin.
34/A3 **Linney Head** (pt.), Wal,UK
36/C2 **Linnhe, Loch** (inlet), Sc,UK
43/F2 **Linnich,** Ger.
48/C5 **Linosa** (isl.), It.
66/C3 **Linqing,** China
95/B2 **Lins,** Braz.
89/H9 **Linta** (riv.), Madg.
35/G2 **Linton,** Eng,UK
110/C4 **Linton,** In,US
107/H4 **Linton,** ND,US
33/H5 **Linwood,** Eng,UK
66/B4 **Linyi,** China
66/D3 **Linyi,** China
66/D4 **Linyi,** China
45/L2 **Linz,** Aus.
44/E5 **Lions** (gulf), Fr.
48/D3 **Lipari** (isls.), It.
37/J3 **Liperi,** Fin.
54/F1 **Lipetsk,** Rus.
54/F1 **Lipetsk Obl.,** Rus.
92/E8 **Lípez** (range), Bol.
92/E8 **Lípez** (riv.), Bol.
35/F4 **Liphook,** Eng,UK
50/E4 **Lipljan,** Yugo.
39/K2 **Lipno,** Pol.
50/E2 **Lipova,** Rom.
40/E5 **Lippe** (riv.), Ger.
41/F5 **Lippetal,** Ger.
41/F5 **Lippstadt,** Ger.
39/K4 **Liptovský Mikuláš,** Slvk.
77/C3 **Liptrap** (cape), Austl.
68/D5 **Lipu La** (pass), India
68/D5 **Lipu Lehk Shankou** (pass), China
83/M7 **Lira,** Ugan.
87/C1 **Liranga,** Congo
48/C2 **Liri** (riv.), It.
47/E3 **Liria,** Sp.
83/K7 **Lisala,** Zaire
46/A3 **Lisboa** (dist.), Port.
111/G2 **Lisbon,** Me,US
107/J4 **Lisbon,** ND,US
46/A3 **Lisbon** (Lisboa) (cap.), Port.
47/P10 **Lisbon** (Lisboa) (inset) (cap.), Port.
32/B2 **Lisburn,** NI,UK
32/B3 **Lisburn** (dist.), NI,UK
114/E2 **Lisburne** (cape), Ak,US
66/B4 **Li Shan** (mtn.), China
71/H2 **Lishe** (riv.), China
67/C2 **Lishui,** China
79/H2 **Lisianski** (isl.), Hi,US
54/F2 **Lisichansk,** Ukr.
44/D2 **Lisieux,** Fr.
34/B6 **Liskeard,** Eng,UK
116/P16 **Lisle,** Il,US
42/B5 **L'Isle-Adam,** Fr.
44/F5 **L'Isle-sur-!a-Sorgue,** Fr.
77/E1 **Lismore,** Austl.
32/B3 **Lisnacree,** NI,UK
35/F4 **Liss,** Eng,UK
40/B4 **Lisse,** Neth.
31/T11 **Lisses,** Fr.
41/E6 **Lister** (riv.), Ger.
110/D3 **Listowel,** On,Can
71/H2 **Litang** (riv.), China
59/K5 **Līţanī** (riv.), Leb.
110/B4 **Litchfield,** Il,US
107/K4 **Litchfield,** Mn,US
40/C5 **Lith,** Neth.
33/F5 **Litherland,** Eng,UK
77/D2 **Lithgow,** Austl.
52/D5 **Lithuania**
52/E5 **Litovskiy Nat'l Park,** Lith.
76/D4 **Littabella Nat'l Park,** Austl.
113/H4 **Little** (riv.), Ga,US
109/J4 **Little** (riv.), La,US
113/J3 **Little** (riv.), NC,US
109/J4 **Little** (riv.), Ok,US
112/D4 **Little** (riv.), Tx,US
110/D1 **Little Abitibi** (riv.), On,Can
39/J5 **Little Alföld** (plain), Hun.
71/F5 **Little Andaman** (isl.), India
106/F4 **Little Belt** (mts.), Mt,US
31/N6 **Little Berkhamstead,** Eng,UK
106/G4 **Little Bighorn Nat'l Mon.,** Mt,US
109/H2 **Little Blue** (riv.), Ks, Ne,US
33/F4 **Littleborough,** Eng,UK
101/E4 **Little Cayman** (isl.), Cay.
31/M7 **Little Chalfont,** Eng,UK
108/E4 **Little Colorado** (riv.), Az,US
110/D2 **Little Current,** On,Can
110/C1 **Little Current** (riv.), On,Can
34/C5 **Little Dart** (riv.), Eng,UK
77/B3 **Little Desert Nat'l Park,** Austl.
114/E2 **Little Diomede** (isl.), Ak,US
107/K4 **Little Falls,** Mn,US
112/C3 **Littlefield,** Tx,US
107/K4 **Little Fork** (riv.), Mn,US
35/F5 **Littlehampton,** Eng,UK
101/G3 **Little Inagua** (isl.), Bahm.
88/C4 **Little Karoo** (reg.), SAfr.
111/K2 **Little Miquelon** (isl.), StP.
109/J4 **Little Missouri** (riv.), Ar,US
107/H4 **Little Missouri** (riv.), ND, SD,US
71/F6 **Little Nicobar** (isl.), India
35/G2 **Little Ouse** (riv.), Eng,UK
35/G2 **Littleport,** Eng,UK
109/J4 **Little Red** (riv.), Ar,US
112/E3 **Little Rock** (cap.), Ar,US
114/L3 **Little Salmon,** Yk,Can
84/B4 **Little Scarcies** (riv.), Gui., SLeo.
107/K5 **Little Sioux** (riv.), Ia,US
114/B5 **Little Sitkin** (isl.), Ak,US
106/D2 **Little Smoky** (riv.), Ab,Can
108/E2 **Little Snake** (riv.), Co, Wy,US
35/G4 **Little Stour** (riv.), Eng,UK
35/F2 **Little Stukeley,** Eng,UK
111/G2 **Littleton,** NH,US
110/B4 **Little Wabash** (riv.), Il,US
109/G2 **Little White** (riv.), SD,US
106/E5 **Little Wood** (riv.), Id,US
59/F3 **Little Zab** (riv.), Iraq
63/J3 **Liu** (riv.), China
63/K3 **Liu** (riv.), China
67/A3 **Liu** (riv.), China
87/D3 **Liuwa Pan Nat'l Park,** Zam.
71/J3 **Liuzhou,** China
113/H4 **Live Oak,** Fl,US
43/F6 **Liverdun,** Fr.
116/L11 **Livermore,** Ca,US
112/B4 **Livermore** (peak), Tx,US
76/G8 **Liverpool,** Austl.
111/H2 **Liverpool,** NS,Can
114/M2 **Liverpool** (bay), NW,Can
103/J1 **Liverpool** (cape), NW,Can
33/F5 **Liverpool,** Eng,UK
33/E5 **Liverpool** (bay), Eng,UK
33/H2 **Liverton,** Eng,UK
106/F4 **Livingston,** Mt,US
115/F5 **Livingston,** NJ,US
112/E4 **Livingston,** Tx,US
109/J5 **Livingston** (lake), Tx,US
106/E3 **Livingstone** (range), Ab,Can
87/E4 **Livingstone,** Zam.
87/B1 **Livingstone, Chutes de** (Livingstone) (falls), Congo
50/C4 **Livno,** Bosn.
54/F1 **Livny,** Rus.
37/H2 **Livojoki** (riv.), Fin.
116/F7 **Livonia,** Mi,US
45/J5 **Livorno,** It.
94/B4 **Livramento do Brumado,** Braz.
44/F4 **Livron-sur-Drôme,** Fr.
42/B6 **Livry-Gargan,** Fr.
87/G2 **Liwale,** Tanz.
34/A7 **Lizard,** Eng,UK
34/A7 **Lizard** (pt.), Eng,UK
34/A6 **Lizard, The** (pen.), Eng,UK
50/B2 **Ljubljana** (cap.), Slov.
50/C4 **Ljubuški,** Cro.
37/F3 **Ljungan** (riv.), Swe.
37/E4 **Ljungby,** Swe.
52/C3 **Ljusdal,** Swe.
37/E3 **Ljusnan** (riv.), Swe.
96/C2 **Llaillay,** Chile
96/C3 **Llaima** (vol.), Chile
92/E7 **Llallagua,** Bol.
34/B2 **Llanarth,** Wal,UK
32/D5 **Llanberis,** Wal,UK
32/D5 **Llanberis, Pass of** (pass), Wal,UK
96/C2 **Llancañelo** (lake), Arg.
34/C3 **Llandeilo,** Wal,UK
34/D3 **Llandogo,** Wal,UK
34/C3 **Llandovery,** Wal,UK
32/E6 **Llandrillo,** Wal,UK
34/C2 **Llandrindod Wells,** Wal,UK
32/E5 **Llandudno,** Wal,UK
34/C3 **Llandybie,** Wal,UK
34/B2 **Llandyssul,** Wal,UK
34/B3 **Llanelli,** Wal,UK
34/C1 **Llanelltyd,** Wal,UK
32/D6 **Llanenddwyn,** Wal,UK
32/D5 **Llanerchymedd,** Wal,UK
46/C1 **Llanes,** Sp.
34/C1 **Llanfair Caereinion,** Wal,UK
32/E5 **Llanfairfechan,** Wal,UK
32/D5 **Llanfair-Pwllgwyngyll,** Wal,UK
34/C1 **Llanfyllin,** Wal,UK
34/C2 **Llangammarch Wells,** Wal,UK
34/C3 **Llangattock,** Wal,UK
33/E6 **Llangollen,** Wal,UK
34/C2 **Llangurig,** Wal,UK
34/C2 **Llanidloes,** Wal,UK
32/D5 **Llanllyfni,** Wal,UK
34/B3 **Llannon,** Wal,UK
112/D4 **Llano,** Tx,US
109/H5 **Llano** (riv.), Tx,US
108/G4 **Llano Estacado** (plain), NM, Tx,US
34/B2 **Llanon,** Wal,UK
92/D3 **Llanos** (plain), Col., Ven.
96/B4 **Llanquihue** (lake), Chile
33/E5 **Llanrhaeadr,** Wal,UK
34/B2 **Llanrhystyd,** Wal,UK
34/A3 **Llanrian,** Wal,UK
32/E5 **Llanrwst,** Wal,UK
34/C3 **Llanthony,** Wal,UK
34/C3 **Llantrisant,** Wal,UK
34/C4 **Llantwit Major,** Wal,UK
32/E6 **Llanuwchllyn,** Wal,UK
34/C1 **Llanwnog,** Wal,UK
34/C2 **Llanwrtyd Wells,** Wal,UK
33/E5 **Llay,** Wal,UK
34/C2 **Lledrod,** Wal,UK
47/F2 **Lleida** (Lérida), Sp.
100/B3 **Llera,** Mex.
32/D6 **Lleyn** (pen.), Wal,UK
47/F1 **Llobregat** (riv.), Sp.
46/D1 **Llodio,** Sp.
47/G2 **Lloret de Mar,** Sp.
100/E6 **Llorona** (pt.), CR
115/G5 **Lloyd** (pt.), NY,US
106/F2 **Lloydminster,** Ab, Sk,Can
111/K1 **Lloyds** (riv.), Nf,Can
47/G3 **Lluchmayor,** Sp.
91/C1 **Llullaillaco** (vol.), Chile
34/C3 **Llynfi** (riv.), Wal,UK
69/D1 **Lo** (riv.), Viet.
91/C1 **Loa** (riv.), Chile
108/E3 **Loa,** Ut,US
45/H4 **Loano,** It.
47/N8 **Loaoya** (can.), Sp.
88/D2 **Lobatse,** Bots.
96/F3 **Lobería,** Arg.
87/B3 **Lobito,** Ang.
84/D5 **Lobo** (riv.), IvC.
96/F2 **Lobos,** Arg.
92/B5 **Lobos de Tierra** (isl.), Peru
96/B2 **Lobos, Punta de** (pt.), Chile
45/H3 **Locarno,** Swi.
32/D2 **Lochans,** Sc,UK
32/E1 **Locharbriggs,** Sc,UK
40/D4 **Lochem,** Neth.
36/C2 **Lochgilphead,** Sc,UK
32/E1 **Lochmaben,** Sc,UK
42/C1 **Lochristi,** Belg.
36/C2 **Lochy, Loch** (lake), Sc,UK
33/E1 **Lockerbie,** Sc,UK
112/D4 **Lockhart,** Tx,US
110/E3 **Lock Haven,** Pa,US
77/C3 **Lockington,** Austl.
116/P16 **Lockport,** Il,US
111/S9 **Lockport,** NY,US
69/D4 **Loc Ninh,** Viet.
48/E3 **Locri,** It.
109/J3 **Locust** (cr.), Ia, Mo,US
59/M9 **Lod,** Isr.
75/G7 **Loddon** (riv.), Austl.
35/H1 **Loddon,** Eng,UK
35/E4 **Loddon** (riv.), Eng,UK
44/E5 **Lodève,** Fr.
52/G3 **Lodeynoye Pole,** Rus.
106/F3 **Lodge** (cr.), Mt,US
109/G2 **Lodgepole** (cr.), Ne, Wy,US
45/H4 **Lodi,** It.
116/M10 **Lodi,** Ca,US
115/F5 **Lodi,** NJ,US
87/D1 **Lodja,** Zaire
83/N7 **Lodwar,** Kenya
39/K3 **Ł ódź,** Pol.
39/K3 **Ł ódź** (prov.), Pol.
47/N9 **Loeches,** Sp.
69/C2 **Loei,** Thai.
40/C4 **Loenen,** Neth.
84/C5 **Lofa** (co.), Libr.
84/C5 **Lofa** (riv.), Libr.
37/D2 **Lofoten** (isls.), Nor.
33/H2 **Loftus,** Eng,UK
77/C4 **Lofty** (range), Austl.
76/F7 **Logan,** Austl.
114/K3 **Logan** (mtn.), Yk,Can
109/G4 **Logan,** NM,US
110/D4 **Logan,** Oh,US
108/E2 **Logan,** Ut,US
110/D4 **Logan,** WV,US
32/D2 **Logan, Mull of** (pt.), Sc,UK
110/C3 **Logansport,** In,US
82/J6 **Logone** (riv.), Camr., Chad
46/D1 **Logroño,** Sp.
41/G6 **Lohfelden,** Ger.
52/E3 **Lohja,** Fin.
43/G2 **Lohmar,** Ger.
38/E2 **Lohne,** Ger.
41/F3 **Löhne,** Ger.
45/H2 **Lohr,** Ger.
71/G3 **Loi Lun** (range), Burma, China
44/E2 **Loing** (riv.), Fr.
44/C3 **Loir** (riv.), Fr.
44/C3 **Loire** (riv.), Fr.
43/E5 **Loisin** (riv.), Fr.
83/N8 **Loita** (hills), Kenya
92/C4 **Loja,** Ecu.
46/C4 **Loja,** Sp.
42/D1 **Lokeren,** Belg.
87/D1 **Lokolia,** Zaire
83/K8 **Lokolo** (riv.), Zaire
83/J8 **Lokoro** (riv.), Zaire
103/K2 **Loks** (isl.), NW,Can
83/L6 **Lol** (riv.), Sudan
38/F1 **Lolland** (isl.), Den.
106/E4 **Lolo** (peak), Mt,US
87/E1 **Lolo,** Zaire
78/G5 **Lolua,** Tuv.
51/F4 **Lom,** Bul.
84/C4 **Loma** (mts.), Gui., SLeo.
100/B4 **Loma Bonita,** Mex.
115/C2 **Loma Linda,** Ca,US
84/C4 **Loma Mansa** (peak), SLeo.
83/K8 **Lomami** (riv.), Zaire
97/S12 **Lomas de Zamora,** Arg.
116/P16 **Lombard,** Il,US
93/H3 **Lombarda** (mts.), Braz.
45/J4 **Lombardy** (reg.), It.
73/F5 **Lomblen** (isl.), Indo.
73/E5 **Lombok** (isl.), Indo.
85/F5 **Lomé** (cap.), Togo
87/D1 **Lomela,** Zaire
83/K8 **Lomela** (riv.), Zaire
115/B3 **Lomita,** Ca,US
44/E1 **Lomme,** Fr.
43/E1 **Lommel,** Belg.
36/C2 **Lomond, Loch** (lake), Sc,UK
73/E5 **Lompobatang** (peak), Indo.
108/B4 **Lompoc,** Ca,US
69/C2 **Lom Sak,** Thai.
39/M2 **Ł omża,** Pol.
39/M2 **Ł omża** (prov.), Pol.
70/B4 **Lonāvale,** India
96/B3 **Loncoche,** Chile
42/D2 **Londerzeel,** Belg.
42/A4 **Londinières,** Fr.
110/D3 **London,** On,Can
35/F3 **London** (cap.), Eng,UK
110/C4 **London,** Ky,US
31/N6 **London Colney,** Eng,UK
74/D2 **Londonderry** (cape), Austl.
97/J8 **Londonderry** (isl.), Chile
32/A2 **Londonderry,** NI,UK
32/A2 **Londonderry** (dist.), NI,UK
31/N7 **London** (inset) (cap.), Eng,UK
95/B2 **Londrina,** Braz.
109/H4 **Lone Grove,** Ok,US
76/E7 **Lone Pine Sanct.,** Austl.
76/C4 **Lonesome Nat'l Park,** Austl.
101/F3 **Long** (isl.), Bahm.
107/J2 **Long** (pt.), Mb,Can
110/C1 **Long** (lake), On,Can
67/A3 **Long** (riv.), China
57/T2 **Long** (str.), Rus.
34/C1 **Long** (mtn.), Wal,UK
111/F3 **Long** (isl.), NY,US
94/B1 **Longá** (riv.), Braz.
96/C2 **Longaví,** Chile
111/R10 **Long Beach,** On,Can
115/B3 **Long Beach,** Ca,US
115/F6 **Long Beach** (isl.), NJ,US
115/G5 **Long Beach,** NY,US
33/G1 **Longbenton,** Eng,UK
113/H5 **Longboat Key,** Fl,US
115/G5 **Long Branch,** NJ,US
35/E2 **Long Buckby,** Eng,UK
69/D1 **Long Chau,** Viet.
67/C3 **Longchuan,** China
71/G3 **Longchuan,** China
35/F3 **Long Crendon,** Eng,UK
31/N7 **Long Ditton,** Eng,UK
33/G6 **Long Eaton,** Eng,UK
43/E5 **Longeau** (riv.), Fr.
111/G2 **Longfellow** (mts.), Me,US
31/P7 **Longfield,** Eng,UK
36/B4 **Longford,** Ire.
67/B2 **Longhui,** China
115/G5 **Long Island** (sound), Ct,NY,US
31/S10 **Longjumeau,** Fr.
110/C1 **Longlac,** On,Can
34/D4 **Longleat House,** Eng,UK
66/B4 **Longmen Shan** (mtn.), China
66/C4 **Longmen Shiyao** (caves), China
109/F2 **Longmont,** Co,US
34/D1 **Long Mynd, The** (hill), Eng,UK
33/G5 **Longnor,** Eng,UK
69/D4 **Long Phu,** Viet.
31/S11 **Longpont-sur-Orge,** Fr.
111/K2 **Long Range** (mts.), Nf,Can
33/F4 **Longridge,** Eng,UK
62/E4 **Longshou** (mts.), China
33/J6 **Long Sutton,** Eng,UK
33/F2 **Longtown,** Eng,UK
42/B2 **Longuenesse,** Fr.
111/N6 **Longueuil,** Qu,Can
43/E5 **Longuyon,** Fr.
44/F3 **Longvic,** Fr.
112/E3 **Longview,** Tx,US
106/C4 **Longview,** Wa,US
43/E4 **Longwy,** Fr.
69/D4 **Long Xuyen,** Viet.
67/C2 **Longyan,** China
41/E3 **Löningen,** Ger.
44/C5 **Lons,** Fr.
44/F3 **Lons-le-Saunier,** Fr.
34/B6 **Looe,** Eng,UK
34/B6 **Looe** (isl.), Eng,UK
76/B1 **Lookout** (pt.), Austl.
113/J3 **Lookout** (cape), NC,US
87/G1 **Loolmalasin** (peak), Tanz.
106/F2 **Loon Lake,** Sk,Can
40/C5 **Loon op Zand,** Neth.
36/G7 **Loop Head** (pt.), Ire.
42/C2 **Loos,** Fr.
68/F3 **Lop** (lake), China
57/R4 **Lopatka, Mys** (cape), Rus.
69/C3 **Lop Buri,** Thai.
82/G8 **Lopez** (cape), Gabon
40/B5 **Lopik,** Neth.
83/K7 **Lopori** (riv.), Zaire
37/G1 **Lopphavet** (bay), Nor.
61/J3 **Lora** (riv.), Pak.
46/C4 **Lora del Río,** Sp.
61/J3 **Lora, Hāmūn-i-** (lake), Pak.
110/D3 **Lorain,** Oh,US
61/J2 **Loralai,** Pak.
47/E4 **Lorca,** Sp.
75/K6 **Lord Howe** (isl.), Austl.
108/E4 **Lordsburg,** NM,US
43/G3 **Lorelei** (cliff), Ger.
95/H7 **Lorena,** Braz.
73/J5 **Lorentz** (riv.), Indo.
40/C2 **Lorentzsluizen** (dam), Neth.
107/J3 **Lorette,** Mb,Can
83/N7 **Lorian** (swamp), Kenya
101/F6 **Lorica,** Col.
44/B3 **Lorient,** Fr.
81/N13 **L'Oriental** (reg.), Mor.
102/G2 **Lorillard** (riv.), NW,Can
50/D2 **Lorinci,** Hun.
111/Q8 **Lorne Park,** On,Can
45/G3 **Lörrach,** Ger.
43/F6 **Lorrain** (plat.), Fr.
111/N6 **Lorraine,** Qu,Can
45/G2 **Lorraine** (reg.), Fr.
33/E2 **Lorton,** Eng,UK
115/J8 **Lorton,** Va,US
115/B3 **Los Alamitos ,** Ca,US
108/B4 **Los Alamos,** Ca,US
109/F4 **Los Alamos,** NM,US
96/C4 **Los Alerces Nat'l Park,** Arg.
116/K12 **Los Altos,** Ca,US
96/C2 **Los Andes,** Chile
96/B3 **Los Ángeles,** Chile
115/B2 **Los Angeles,** Ca,US
115/B2 **Los Angeles** (riv.), Ca,US
108/B3 **Los Banos,** Ca,US
46/C4 **Los Barrios,** Sp.
90/B7 **Los Chonos** (arch.), Chile
46/C1 **Los Corrales de Buelna,** Sp.
97/J7 **Los Glaciares Nat'l Park,** Arg.
43/F4 **Losheim,** Ger.
101/N8 **Los Herreras,** Mex.
39/M2 **Ł osice,** Pol.
50/B3 **Lošinj** (isl.), Cro.
96/B3 **Los Lagos,** Chile
96/B4 **Los Lagos** (reg.), Chile
108/F4 **Los Lunas,** NM,US
101/N8 **Los Mochis,** Mex.
96/B4 **Los Muermos,** Chile
92/C2 **Los Orquideas Nat'l Park,** Col.
46/C4 **Los Palacios y Villafranca,** Sp.
97/J8 **Los Pingüinos Nat'l Park,** Chile
100/A4 **Los Reyes,** Mex.
101/H5 **Los Roques** (isls.), Ven.
46/B3 **Los Santos de Maimona,** Sp.
96/B3 **Los Sauces,** Chile
40/E4 **Losser,** Neth.
101/H5 **Los Teques,** Ven.
108/D1 **Lost River** (range), Id,US
34/B6 **Lostwithiel,** Eng,UK
96/C1 **Los Vilos,** Chile
46/D3 **Los Yébenes,** Sp.
44/D4 **Lot** (riv.), Fr.
96/B3 **Lota,** Chile
61/G1 **Lotfābād,** Trkm.
41/E4 **Lotte,** Ger.
66/B5 **Lou** (riv.), China
69/C2 **Louangphrabang,** Laos
87/B1 **Loubomo,** Congo
44/B2 **Loudéac,** Fr.
67/B2 **Loudi,** China
44/D3 **Loudun,** Fr.
44/F3 **Loue** (riv.), Fr.
84/A3 **Louga,** Sen.
84/B3 **Louga** (reg.), Sen.
33/G6 **Loughborough,** Eng,UK
32/B3 **Loughbrickland,** NI,UK
103/R7 **Lougheed** (isl.), NW,Can
32/B3 **Loughgall,** NI,UK
31/P7 **Loughton,** Eng,UK
110/E4 **Louisa,** Va,US
78/E6 **Louisiade** (arch.), PNG
112/E4 **Louisiana** (state), US
110/C4 **Louisville,** Ky,US
113/F3 **Louisville,** Ms,US
103/J3 **Louis XIV** (pt.), Qu,Can
81/M13 **Loukkos** (riv.), Mor.
46/A4 **Loulé,** Port.
45/K1 **Louny,** Czh.
109/H2 **Loup** (riv.), Ne,US
32/B2 **Loup, The,** NI,UK
31/U10 **L'Ourcq** (can.), Fr.
44/C5 **Lourdes,** Fr.
47/P10 **Loures,** Port.
46/A3 **Louriçal,** Port.
46/A3 **Lourinhã,** Port.
46/A2 **Lousã,** Port.
47/P10 **Lousa,** Port.
32/B4 **Louth** (co.), Ire.
33/H5 **Louth,** Eng,UK
49/H4 **Loutrákion,** Gre.
43/D2 **Louvain** (Leuven), Belg.
95/G8 **Louveira,** Braz.
42/A5 **Louviers,** Fr.
31/T9 **Louvres,** Fr.
42/C3 **Louvroil,** Fr.
42/B2 **Lovaart** (can.), Belg.
52/F4 **Lovat'** (riv.), Bela., Rus.
50/D4 **Lovćen Nat'l Park,** Yugo.
51/G4 **Lovech,** Bul.
51/G4 **Lovech** (reg.), Bul.
109/F2 **Loveland,** Co,US
106/F4 **Lovell,** Wy,US
108/C2 **Lovelock,** Nv,US
45/J4 **Lovere,** It.
109/F4 **Loving,** NM,US
109/G4 **Lovington,** NM,US
52/G2 **Lovozero** (lake), Rus.
103/H2 **Low** (cape), NW,Can
83/L8 **Lowa** (riv.), Zaire
33/H6 **Lowdham,** Eng,UK
111/G3 **Lowell,** Ma,US
88/B2 **Löwen** (dry riv.), Namb.
106/D3 **Lower Arrow** (lake), BC,Can
45/L2 **Lower Austria** (prov.), Aus.
35/E2 **Lower Brailes,** Eng,UK
77/B3 **Lower Glenelg Nat'l Park,** Austl.
77/C4 **Lower Gordon-Franklin Wild Rivers Nat'l Park,** Austl.
35/E3 **Lower Heyford,** Eng,UK
75/R11 **Lower Hutt,** NZ
31/P6 **Lower Nazeing,** Eng,UK
107/K4 **Lower Red** (lake), Mn,US
38/E2 **Lower Saxony** (state), Ger.
56/K3 **Lower Tunguska** (riv.), Rus.
87/E4 **Lower Zambezi Nat'l Park,** Zam.
35/H2 **Lowestoft,** Eng,UK
87/E1 **Lowi** (riv.), Zaire
39/K2 **Ł owicz,** Pol.
32/E1 **Lowther** (hills), Sc,UK
111/Q9 **Lowville,** On,Can
41/F2 **Loxstedt,** Ger.
79/V12 **Loyalty** (isls.), NCal.
50/D3 **Loznica,** Yugo.
54/F2 **Lozovaya,** Ukr.
50/E3 **Lozovik,** Yugo.
66/C5 **Lu** (riv.), China
87/D2 **Luachimo,** Ang.
87/E1 **Lualaba** (riv.), Zaire
66/J6 **Luam** (riv.), China
104/T10 **Lua Makika** (crater), Hi,US
66/D5 **Lu'an,** China
66/D2 **Luan** (riv.), China
46/C1 **Luanco,** Sp.
87/B2 **Luanda** (cap.), Ang.
69/C5 **Luang** (lag.), Thai.
69/B4 **Luang** (peak), Thai.
69/C2 **Luang Prabang** (range), Laos
87/F3 **Luangwa** (riv.), Moz., Zam.
87/E3 **Luanshya,** Zam.
66/D3 **Luan Xian,** China
87/D3 **Luao,** Ang.
46/B1 **Luarca,** Sp.
87/D3 **Luashi,** Zaire
82/G7 **Luba,** EqG.
100/D4 **Lubaantun** (ruins), Belz.
39/M3 **Lubaczów,** Pol.
39/H3 **Lubań,** Pol.
87/B3 **Lubango,** Ang.
39/M3 **Lubartów,** Pol.
39/K2 **Lubawa,** Pol.
41/F4 **Lübbecke,** Ger.
43/D2 **Lubbeek,** Belg.
112/C3 **Lubbock,** Tx,US
38/F2 **Lübeck,** Ger.
87/D1 **Lubefu,** Zaire
39/M3 **Lubelska** (upland), Pol.
83/L8 **Lubero,** Zaire
39/J3 **Lubin,** Pol.
39/M3 **Lublin,** Pol.
39/M3 **Lublin** (prov.), Pol.
39/K3 **Lubliniec,** Pol.
54/E2 **Lubny,** Ukr.
39/J2 **Luboń,** Pol.
39/H3 **Lubsko,** Pol.
87/E2 **Lubudi,** Zaire
72/B4 **Lubuklinggau,** Indo.
72/B3 **Lubuksikaping,** Indo.
87/E3 **Lubumbashi,** Zaire
87/E2 **Lubunda,** Zaire
87/C2 **Lucala,** Ang.
32/B5 **Lucan,** Ire.
69/D1 **Luc An Chau,** Viet.
114/K3 **Lucania** (mtn.), Yk,Can
87/D2 **Lucapa,** Ang.
45/J5 **Lucca,** It.
32/D2 **Luce** (bay), Sc,UK
113/F4 **Lucedale,** Ms,US
95/B2 **Lucélia,** Braz.
67/D5 **Lucena,** Phil.
46/C4 **Lucena,** Sp.
39/K4 **Lučenec,** Slvk.
45/H3 **Lucerne** (Luzern), Swi.
45/H3 **Lucerne** (Vierwaldstättersee) (lake), Swi.
38/F2 **Lüchow,** Ger.
39/G2 **Luckenwalde,** Ger.
70/D2 **Lucknow,** India
106/G3 **Lucky Lake,** Sk,Can
101/F3 **Lucrecia** (cape), Cuba
87/D3 **Lucusse,** Ang.
51/H4 **Luda Kamchiya** (riv.), Bul.
41/E6 **Lüdenscheid,** Ger.
88/A2 **Lüderitz,** Namb.
35/E4 **Ludgershall,** Eng,UK
61/L2 **Ludhiāna,** India
41/E5 **Ludinghausen,** Ger.
110/C3 **Ludington,** Mi,US
34/D2 **Ludlow,** Eng,UK
51/H4 **Ludogorie** (reg.), Bul.
51/G2 **Luduş,** Rom.
37/E3 **Ludvika,** Swe.
45/H2 **Ludwigsburg,** Ger.
39/G2 **Ludwigsfelde,** Ger.
38/F2 **Ludwigslust,** Ger.
87/D2 **Luebo,** Zaire
112/E4 **Lufkin,** Tx,US
52/F4 **Luga,** Rus.
45/H3 **Lugano,** Swi.
54/F2 **Lugansk,** Ukr.
54/F2 **Lugansk Obl.,** Ukr.
41/G5 **Lügde,** Ger.
87/G3 **Lugenda** (riv.), Moz.
34/D2 **Lugg** (riv.), Eng,UK
32/B6 **Lugnaquillia** (mtn.), Ire.
46/B1 **Lugo,** Sp.
50/E3 **Lugoj,** Rom.
41/H2 **Lühe** (riv.), Ger.
87/D4 **Luiana,** Ang.
45/H4 **Luino,** It.
98/X **Luitpold** (coast), Ant.
50/D3 **Lukavac,** Bosn.
87/C1 **Lukenie** (riv.), Zaire
51/G4 **Lukovit,** Bul.
39/M3 **Ł uków,** Pol.
78/E4 **Lukunor** (atoll), Micr.
37/G2 **Luleå,** Swe.
37/G2 **Luleälv** (riv.), Swe.
51/H5 **Lüleburgaz,** Turk.
66/B4 **Luling Guan** (pass), China
80/E4 **Lulonga** (riv.), Zaire
78/G5 **Lulua,** Tuv.
87/D2 **Lulua** (riv.), Zaire
87/D3 **Lumai,** Ang.
68/D5 **Lumajamgdong** (lake), China
113/J3 **Lumberton,** NC,US
112/E4 **Lumberton,** Tx,US
87/H4 **Lumbo,** Moz.
106/D3 **Lumby,** BC,Can
71/F2 **Lumding,** India
43/E2 **Lummen,** Belg.
69/D3 **Lumphat,** Camb.
107/G3 **Lumsden,** Sk,Can
75/Q12 **Lumsden,** NZ
87/D3 **Lunache,** Ang.
39/G1 **Lund,** Swe.
108/D3 **Lund,** Nv,US
87/F5 **Lundi** (riv.), Zim.
34/B4 **Lundy** (isl.), Eng,UK
41/F2 **Lune** (riv.), Ger.
33/F3 **Lune** (riv.), Eng,UK
41/H2 **Lüneburg,** Ger.
41/G2 **Lüneburger Heide** (reg.), Ger.
44/F5 **Lunel,** Fr.
41/E5 **Lünen,** Ger.
111/H2 **Lunenburg,** NS,Can
87/E3 **Lunga** (riv.), Zam.
71/F3 **Lunglei,** India
87/D3 **Lungue-Bungo** (riv.), Ang.
70/B3 **Luni** (riv.), India
66/B3 **Luo** (riv.), China
66/B4 **Luo** (riv.), China
66/C4 **Luohe,** China
66/D4 **Luoma** (lake), China
69/C1 **Luong** (mts.), Viet.
66/C4 **Luoyang,** China
87/B1 **Luozi,** Zaire
87/E4 **Lupane,** Zim.
71/H2 **Lupanshui,** China
51/F3 **Lupeni,** Rom.
71/H2 **Luquan,** China
61/J2 **Lūrah** (riv.), Afg.
110/E4 **Luray,** Va,US
32/B3 **Lurgan,** NI,UK
87/H3 **Lúrio,** Moz.
87/G3 **Lúrio** (riv.), Moz.
87/E4 **Lusaka** (cap.), Zam.
87/E1 **Lusamba,** Zaire
87/D1 **Lusambo,** Zaire
66/D3 **Lu Shan** (mtn.), China
66/C5 **Lu Shan** (peak), China
49/F2 **Lushnje,** Alb.
107/G5 **Lusk,** Wy,US
83/J7 **Lutanga** (riv.), Zaire
115/K7 **Lutherville,** Md,US
40/D1 **Lütjehorn** (isl.), Ger.
35/F3 **Luton,** Eng,UK
54/C2 **Lutsk,** Ukr.
41/F5 **Lutter** (riv.), Ger.
98/C **Lützow-Holm** (bay), Ant.
83/P7 **Luuq,** Som.
107/J5 **Luverne,** Mn,US
43/E4 **Luxembourg**
43/E4 **Luxembourg** (prov.), Belg.
43/F4 **Luxembourg** (cap.), Lux.
43/F4 **Luxembourg** (dist.), Lux.
71/J2 **Lu Xian,** China
86/C3 **Luxor** (Al Uqşur), Egypt
44/C5 **Luy** (riv.), Fr.
66/B3 **Luya Shan** (mtn.), China
95/C1 **Luz,** Braz.
53/L3 **Luza** (riv.), Rus.
45/H3 **Luzern** (Lucerne), Swi.
71/J2 **Luzhou,** China
94/A5 **Luziânia,** Braz.
94/B1 **Luzilândia,** Braz.
67/D4 **Luzon** (isl.), Phil.
54/C2 **L'viv,** Ukr.
54/B2 **L'viv Obl.,** Ukr.
69/C1 **Lwi** (riv.), Burma
53/P3 **Lyapin** (riv.), Rus.
51/G4 **Lyaskovets,** Bul.
37/F2 **Lycksele,** Swe.
35/G5 **Lydd,** Eng,UK
98/Y **Lyddan** (isl.), Ant.
89/E2 **Lydenburg,** SAfr.
34/D3 **Lydney,** Eng,UK
106/F5 **Lyman,** Wy,US
34/C5 **Lyme** (bay), Eng,UK
34/D5 **Lyme Regis,** Eng,UK
35/E5 **Lymington,** Eng,UK
33/F5 **Lymm,** Eng,UK

Łyna – Marin

39/L1 Łyna (riv.), Pol.
32/D5 Lynas (pt.), Wal,UK
115/G5 Lynbrook, NY,US
110/E4 Lynchburg, Va,US
113/H3 Lynches (riv.), SC,US
76/A2 Lynd (riv.), Austl.
35/E5 Lyndhurst, Eng,UK
115/F5 Lyndhurst, NJ,US
33/F1 Lyne (riv.), Eng,UK
37/G1 Lyngen (fjord), Nor.
111/G3 Lynn, Ma,US
113/G4 Lynn Haven, Fl,US
116/C2 Lynnwood, Wa,US
34/C4 Lynton, Eng,UK
115/B3 Lynwood, Ca,US
102/F2 Lynx (lake), NW,Can
44/F4 Lyon, Fr.
109/H3 Lyons, Ks,US
34/C4 Lype (hill), Eng,UK
78/E5 Lyra (reef), PNG
42/B2 Lys (riv.), Fr.
39/K4 Lysá (peak), Czh.
52/E5 Lysaya, Gora (hill), Bela.
39/L3 Łysica (peak), Pol.
42/C2 Lys-lez-Lannoy, Fr.
53/N4 Lys'va, Rus.
34/D5 Lytchett Matravers, Eng,UK
33/E4 Lytham Saint Anne's, Eng,UK
53/X9 Lytkarino, Rus.
106/C3 Lytton, BC,Can
54/F1 Lyubertsy, Rus.
51/H5 Lyubimets, Bul.
54/E2 Lyubotin, Ukr.
54/E1 Lyudinovo, Rus.
34/C3 Lywd (riv.), Wal,UK

M

69/C1 Ma (riv.), Laos, Viet.
59/K5 Ma'alot, Isr.
52/F2 Maanselkä (mts.), Fin.
66/D5 Ma'anshan, China
40/C6 Maarheeze, Neth.
40/C4 Maarssen, Neth.
38/D3 Maas (riv.), Eur.
40/C6 Maasbracht, Neth.
40/D6 Maasbree, Neth.
43/E1 Maaseik, Belg.
67/D5 Maasin, Phil.
43/E2 Maasmechelen, Belg.
40/B5 Maassluis, Neth.
43/E2 Maastricht, Neth.
59/N7 Ma'ayan Harod Nat'l Park, Isr.
67/D4 Mabalacat, Phil.
87/F5 Mabalane, Moz.
33/J5 Mablethorpe, Eng,UK
87/F5 Mabote, Moz.
96/B5 Macá (peak), Chile
95/D2 Macaé, Braz.
94/D2 Macaíba, Braz.
93/H3 Macapá, Braz.
92/C4 Macará, Ecu.
94/B4 Macarani, Braz.
94/C2 Macau, Braz.
67/B3 Macau (cap.), Macau
67/B3 Macau (dpcy.), Port.
78/H7 Macauley (isl.), NZ
92/D3 Macaya (riv.), Col.
101/G4 Macaya (pk.), Haiti
113/H4 Macclenny, Fl,US
33/F5 Macclesfield, Eng,UK
33/F5 Macclesfield (can.), Eng,UK
88/D3 Macdhui (peak), SAfr.
74/D4 MacDonald (lake), Austl.
74/E4 Macdonnell (ranges), Austl.
36/D2 Macduff, Sc,UK
49/G2 Macedonia
49/G2 Macedonia (reg.), Gre., Macd.
94/D3 Maceió, Braz.
94/C2 Maceió (pt.), Braz.
48/C1 Macerata, It.
98/E Macey (peak), Ant.
88/D3 Machache (peak), Les.
95/H6 Machado, Braz.
83/N8 Machakos, Kenya
92/C4 Machala, Ecu.
92/B4 Machalilla Nat'l Park, Ecu.
87/F5 Machanga, Moz.
32/D2 Machars, The (pen.), Sc,UK
74/G5 Machattie (lake), Austl.
87/F5 Machaze, Moz.
87/E5 Machemma (ruins), SAfr.
34/C3 Machen, Wal,UK
66/C5 Macheng, China
111/H2 Machias, Me,US
46/D1 Machichaco (cape), Sp.
47/V15 Machico, Madr.,Port.
65/H7 Machida, Japan
70/D4 Machilipatnam, India
101/G5 Machiques, Ven.
92/D6 Machu Picchu (ruins), Peru
92/F6 Machupo (riv.), Bol.
34/C1 Machynlleth, Wal,UK
51/J3 Măcin, Rom.
84/D3 Macina (reg.), Mali
77/D1 Macintyre (riv.), Austl.
108/E3 Mack, Co,US
76/C3 Mackay, Austl.
74/D4 Mackay (lake), Austl.
98/E MacKenzie (bay), Ant.
76/C3 Mackenzie (riv.), Austl.
106/C2 Mackenzie, BC,Can
114/N2 Mackenzie (riv.), NW,Can
103/C2 Mackenzie (bay), NW, Yk,Can
102/C2 Mackenzie (mts.), NW, Yk,Can
103/R7 Mackenzie King (isl.), NW,Can
110/C2 Mackinac Island, Mi,US
113/F1 Mackinaw (riv.), Il,US
110/C2 Mackinaw City, Mi,US
106/F2 Macklin, Sk,Can
76/F7 Macleay (isl.), Austl.
114/L3 Macmillan (riv.), Yk,Can
48/A2 Macomer, It.
44/F3 Mâcon, Fr.
109/K4 Macon (bayou), Ar, La,US
113/H3 Macon, Ga,US
109/J3 Macon, Mo,US
32/B1 Macosquin, NI,UK
77/C4 Macquarie (har.), Austl.
29/S8 Macquarie (isl.), Austl.
77/C1 Macquarie (riv.), Austl.
98/D Mac-Robertson Land (reg.), Ant.
92/F5 Macuim (riv.), Braz.
74/F5 Macumba (riv.), Austl.
106/C5 Mad (riv.), Ca,US
59/K6 Ma'dabā, Jor.
89/H8 Madagascar
82/H3 Madama, Niger
51/G5 Madan, Bul.
70/C5 Madanapalle, India
78/D5 Madang, PNG
82/H1 Madanīyīn, Tun.
85/G3 Madaoua, Niger
70/F3 Mādārīpur, Bang.
110/E2 Madawaska (riv.), On,Can
111/G2 Madawaska, Me,US
92/F5 Madeira (riv.), Braz.
47/V15 Madeira (isl.), Madr., Port.
47/U14 Madeira (aut. reg.), Port.
107/L4 Madelin (isl.), Wi,US
101/N8 Madera, Mex.
100/D5 Madera (vol.), Nic.
70/E2 Madhipura, India
70/C3 Madhya Pradesh (state), India
92/E6 Madidi (riv.), Bol.
109/H4 Madill, Ok,US
87/B1 Madingo-Kayes, Congo
113/G3 Madison, Al,US
113/H4 Madison, Fl,US
110/C4 Madison, In,US
113/F3 Madison, Ms,US
106/F4 Madison (riv.), Mt,US
109/H2 Madison, Ne,US
115/F5 Madison, NJ,US
107/J4 Madison, SD,US
110/B3 Madison (cap.), Wi,US
110/D4 Madison, WV,US
116/F6 Madison Heights, Mi,US
110/C4 Madisonville, Ky,US
112/E4 Madisonville, Tx,US
72/D5 Madiun, Indo.
62/D5 Madoi, China
45/G2 Madon (riv.), Fr.
48/C4 Madonie Nebrodi (mts.), It.
61/G5 Madrakah, Ra's al (pt.), Oman
70/D5 Madras, India
106/C4 Madras, Or,US
100/B2 Madre (lag.), Mex.
112/D5 Madre (lag.), Tx,US
90/C4 Madre de Dios (riv.), Bol., Peru
97/J7 Madre de Dios (isl.), Chile
44/E5 Madrès (mtn.), Fr.
46/C2 Madrid (aut. comm.), Sp.
46/D2 Madrid (cap.), Sp.
46/D3 Madridejos, Sp.
47/N9 Madrid (inset) (cap.), Sp.
70/D4 Madugula, India
70/C6 Madurai, India
65/F2 Maebashi, Japan
69/C2 Mae Charim, Thai.
69/B2 Mae Ping Nat'l Park, Thai.
34/C3 Maesteg, Wal,UK
69/B2 Mae Tho (peak), Thai.
78/F6 Maewo (isl.), Van.
69/B2 Mae Ya (mtn.), Thai.
87/H2 Mafia (isl.), Tanz.
88/D2 Mafikeng, SAfr.
84/C4 Mafou (riv.), Gui.
95/B3 Mafra, Braz.
46/A3 Mafra, Port.
57/R4 Magadan, Rus.
83/N8 Magadi, Kenya
88/P12 Magalies Berg (range), SAfr.
97/K8 Magallanes (Magellan) (str.), Arg., Chile
97/K8 Magallanes y Antártica Chilena (reg.), Chile
101/G6 Magangué, Col.
67/D6 Maganoy, Phil.
85/H3 Magaria, Niger
67/D4 Magat (riv.), Phil.
109/J4 Magazine (peak), Ar,US
63/K1 Magdagachi, Rus.
111/J2 Magdalen (isls.), Qu,Can
97/T12 Magdalena, Arg.
92/D3 Magdalena (riv.), Col.
101/M7 Magdalena de Kino, Mex.
73/E3 Magdalena, Gunung (peak), Malay.
38/F2 Magdeburg, Ger.
38/F2 Magdeburger Börde (plain), Ger.
75/J3 Magdelaine (cays), Austl.
95/K7 Magé, Braz.
113/F4 Magee, Ms,US
32/C2 Magee, Island (pen.), NI,UK
72/C5 Magelang, Indo.
97/K8 Magellan (Magallanes) (str.), Arg., Chile
74/B6 Magenta (lake), Austl.
37/H1 Magerøya (isl.), Nor.
45/H4 Maggiore (lake), It., Swi.
86/B2 Maghāghah, Egypt
32/B2 Maghera, NI,UK
32/B2 Magherafelt, NI,UK
32/B2 Magherafelt (dist.), NI,UK
81/W18 Maghīla (peak), Tun.
81/P13 Maghnia, Alg.
33/F4 Maghull, Eng,UK
32/B1 Magilligan, NI,UK
32/B1 Magilligan (pt.), NI,UK
50/D3 Maglaj, Bosn.
50/D4 Maglić (peak), Yugo.
49/F2 Maglie, It.
110/D2 Magnetawan (riv.), On,Can
76/B2 Magnetic (passg.), Austl.
76/B2 Magnetic I. Nat'l Park, Austl.
53/N5 Magnitogorsk, Rus.
112/E3 Magnolia, Ar,US
31/S10 Magny-les-Hameaux, Fr.
111/F2 Magog, Qu,Can
83/N6 Mago Nat'l Park, Eth.
34/D3 Magor, Wal,UK
111/H1 Magpie (riv.), Qu,Can
83/L7 Maguerite (peak), Zaire
71/F3 Magwe, Burma
71/F4 Magwe (div.), Burma
60/E1 Mahābād, Iran
70/B4 Mahād, India
79/X15 Mahaena, FrPol.
92/G2 Mahaica, Guy.
89/H6 Mahajamba (bay), Madg.
89/H7 Mahajamba (riv.), Madg.
89/H6 Mahajanga (prov.), Madg.
89/H7 Mahajilo (riv.), Madg.
73/E3 Mahakam (riv.), Indo.
87/E5 Mahalapye, Bots.
60/F2 Mahallāt, Iran
61/G2 Māhān, Iran
70/D3 Mahānadī (riv.), India
84/D4 Mahandiabani (riv.), IvC.
70/C2 Mahārajpur, India
70/B4 Mahārāshtra (state), India
70/D3 Mahāsamund, India
69/C2 Maha Sarakham, Thai.
89/H7 Mahavavy (riv.), Madg.
70/C4 Mahbubnagar, India
61/L2 Mahe, India
81/H5 Mahé (isl.), Sey.
89/S15 Mahébourg, Mrts.
75/S10 Mahia (pen.), NZ
71/G3 Mahlaing, Burma
81/V18 Mahmel (peak), Alg.
70/C2 Mahoba, India
47/H3 Mahón, Sp.
70/B3 Mahuva, India
115/F4 Mahwah, NJ,US
76/E6 Maiala Nat'l Park, Austl.
78/G4 Maiana (atoll), Kiri.
79/W15 Maiao (isl.), FrPol.
92/D1 Maicao, Col.
93/H3 Maicuru (riv.), Braz.
35/F3 Maidenhead, Eng,UK
34/D5 Maiden Newton, Eng,UK
32/D1 Maidens, Sc,UK
116/G7 Maidstone, On,Can
106/F2 Maidstone, Sk,Can
35/G4 Maidstone, Eng,UK
82/H5 Maiduguri, Nga.
42/B4 Maignelay-Montigny, Fr.
36/A4 Maigue (riv.), Ire.
70/D3 Maihar, India
64/E3 Maihara, Japan
83/L8 Maiko Nat'l Park, Zaire
104/V13 Maili, Hi,US
61/K3 Mailsi, Pak.
45/H2 Main (riv.), Ger.
32/B2 Main (riv.), NI,UK
74/G6 Main Barrier (range), Austl.
31/U11 Maincy, Fr.
87/C1 Mai-Ndombe (lake), Zaire
111/G3 Maine (gulf), Can., US
44/C2 Maine (hills), Fr.
36/A4 Maine (riv.), Ire.
111/G2 Maine (state), US
76/C5 Main Range Nat'l Park, Austl.
45/H2 Mainz, Ger.
80/K10 Maio (isl.), CpV.
96/C2 Maipo (vol.), Arg., Chile
96/Q9 Maipo (riv.), Chile
96/F3 Maipú, Arg.
96/C2 Maipú, Chile
45/G4 Maira (riv.), It.
94/B3 Mairi, Braz.
95/G8 Mairiporã, Braz.
101/G3 Maisí (cape), Cuba
31/T10 Maisons-Alfort, Fr.
31/S10 Maisons-Laffitte, Fr.
110/D3 Maitland (riv.), On,Can
43/F5 Maizières-lès-Metz, Fr.
64/D3 Maizuru, Japan
47/N9 Majadahonda, Sp.
49/G2 Maja e Zezë (peak), Alb.
81/W17 Majardah (mts.), Alg., Tun.
81/W17 Majardah (riv.), Tun.
50/E3 Majdanpek, Yugo.
82/J2 Majdūl, Libya
73/E4 Majene, Indo.
83/N6 Majī, Eth.
66/D3 Majia (riv.), China
47/G3 Majorca (Mallorca) (isl.), Sp.
78/G4 Majuro (atoll), Mrsh.
87/B1 Makabana, Congo
104/V13 Makaha, Hi,US
104/V13 Makakilo City, Hi,US
63/N2 Makarov, Rus.
50/C4 Makarska, Cro.
72/E4 Makassar (str.), Indo.
79/L6 Makatea (isl.), FrPol.
89/H8 Makay (massif), Madg.
79/L6 Makemo (atoll), FrPol.
84/B4 Makeni, SLeo.
54/F2 Makeyevka, Ukr.
87/D5 Makgadikgadi (salt pans), Bots.
55/H4 Makhachkala, Rus.
73/G3 Makian (isl.), Indo.
78/G4 Makin (atoll), Kiri.
68/B1 Makinsk, Kaz.
60/C4 Makkah (Mecca), SAr.
50/E2 Makó, Hun.
82/H7 Makokou, Gabon
39/L2 Maków Mazowiecki, Pol.
61/H3 Makran (reg.), Iran, Pak.
61/K3 Makrāna, India
59/F2 Mākū, Iran
87/F2 Makumbako, Tanz.
64/B5 Makurazaki, Japan
114/E5 Makushin (vol.), Ak,US
92/C6 Mala, Peru
70/B5 Malabar (coast), India
82/G7 Malabo (cap.), EqG.
95/D1 Malacacheta, Braz.
69/B5 Malacca (str.), Malay., Indo.
39/J4 Malacky, Slvk.
106/E5 Malad City, Id,US
46/C4 Málaga, Sp.
46/D3 Malagón, Sp.
32/B5 Malahide, Ire.
78/F5 Malaita (isl.), Sol.
83/M6 Malakāl, Sudan
70/D4 Malakangiri, India
101/G5 Malambo, Col.
72/D5 Malang, Indo.
87/C2 Malange, Ang.
96/C2 Malargüe, Arg.
110/E1 Malartic, Qu,Can
73/E5 Malasoro (pt.), Indo.
59/D2 Malatya, Turk.
87/F3 Malawi
69/B5 Malay (pen.), Malay.
52/G4 Malaya Vishera, Rus.
67/E6 Malaybalay, Phil.
60/E2 Malāyer, Iran
72/C2 Malaysia
53/L2 Malazemel'skaya (tundra), Rus.
59/E2 Malazgirt, Turk.
111/G2 Malbaie (riv.), Qu,Can
85/G3 Malbaza-Usine, Niger
39/K1 Malbork, Pol.
44/D5 Malcaras, Pic de (peak), Fr.
38/G2 Malchin, Ger.
62/C2 Malchin, Mong.
42/C1 Maldegem, Belg.
79/K5 Malden (isl.), Kiri.
110/B4 Malden, Mo,US
58/G9 Maldives
35/G3 Maldon, Eng,UK
97/G2 Maldonado, Uru.
97/G2 Maldonado (dept.), Uru.
58/G9 Male (cap.), Mald.
49/H4 Maléa, Akra (cape), Gre.
70/B3 Mālegaon, India
78/F6 Malekula (isl.), Van.
44/D4 Malemort-sur-Corrèze, Fr.
38/F1 Malente, Ger.
61/L2 Māler Kotla, India
55/H4 Malgobek, Rus.
47/G2 Malgrat de Mar, Sp.
83/L4 Malha Wells, Sudan
106/D5 Malheur (lake), Or,US
106/D5 Malheur (riv.), Or,US
89/S14 Malheureux (cape), Mrts.
84/E2 Mali
69/B3 Mali (isl.), Burma
62/F4 Malian (riv.), China
115/B2 Malibu, Ca,US
83/L4 Malik (wadi), Sudan
54/D2 Malin, Ukr.
73/E3 Malinau, Indo.
87/H1 Malindi, Kenya
42/D1 Malines (Mechelen), Belg.
66/C3 Maling Guan (pass), China
89/H8 Malio (riv.), Madg.
69/D1 Malipo, China
61/J4 Malīr Cantonment, Pak.
67/E6 Malita, Phil.
83/P7 Malka Mari Nat'l Park, Kenya
51/H5 Malkara, Turk.
85/H3 Malkammaduri, Nga.
81/W17 Mallāq, Wādī (riv.), Tun.
86/B3 Mallawī, Egypt
77/B2 Mallee Cliffs Nat'l Park, Austl.
96/Q10 Malloa, Chile
47/G3 Mallorca (Majorca) (isl.), Sp.
36/A4 Mallow, Ire.
37/G2 Malmberget, Swe.
43/F3 Malmédy, Belg.
88/B4 Malmesbury, SAfr.
34/D3 Malmesbury, Eng,UK
38/G1 Malmö, Swe.
39/G1 Malmöhus (co.), Swe.
53/L4 Malmyzh, Rus.
93/H5 Maloca, Braz.
78/G4 Maloelap (atoll), Mrsh.
110/F2 Malone, NY,US
39/L3 Małopolska (upland), Pol.
37/C3 Måløy, Nor.
33/F5 Malpas, Eng,UK
92/B3 Malpelo (isl.), Col.
46/A1 Malpica, Sp.
48/D5 Malta
48/D5 Malta (isl.), Malta
106/G3 Malta, Mt,US
33/G2 Maltby, Eng,UK
33/G5 Maltby, Eng,UK
111/Q8 Malton, On,Can
33/H3 Malton, Eng,UK
87/C1 Maluku, Zaire
37/E3 Malung, Swe.
70/B4 Malvan, India
47/P10 Malveira, Port.
77/G5 Malvern, Austl.
112/E3 Malvern, Ar,US
34/D2 Malvern (Great Malvern), Eng,UK
97/M8 Malvinas, Islas (Falkland Islands) (dpcy.), UK
55/J2 Malyy Uzen' (riv.), Kaz.
62/D1 Malyy Yenisey (riv.), Rus.
43/F6 Malzéville, Fr.
94/D2 Mamanguape, Braz.
115/G5 Mamaroneck, NY,US
87/E4 Mamba, Zam.
67/D6 Mambajao, Phil.
83/L7 Mambasa, Zaire
73/J4 Mamberamo (riv.), Indo.
82/J6 Mambéré (riv.), CAfr.
59/D3 Mambij, Syria
67/D5 Mamburao, Phil.
43/F4 Mamer, Lux.
44/D2 Mamers, Fr.
42/B2 Mametz, Fr.
85/H5 Mamfé, Camr.
110/C4 Mammoth Cave Nat'l Park, Ky,US
113/F2 Mammoth Spring, Ar,US
92/E6 Mamoré (riv.), Bol.
85/E5 Mampong, Gha.
39/L1 Mamry (lake), Pol.
73/E4 Mamuju, Indo.
87/D5 Mamuno, Bots.
93/G4 Mamuri (riv.), Braz.
66/C5 Man (riv.), China
84/D5 Man, IvC.
92/F4 Manacapuru, Braz.
34/A6 Manacle (pt.), UK
47/G3 Manacor, Sp.
73/F3 Manado, Indo.
100/D5 Managua (cap.), Nic.
100/D5 Managua (lake), Nic.
89/J8 Manakara, Madg.
115/F5 Manalapan, NJ,US
60/F3 Manama (Al Manāmah) (cap.), Bahr.
89/H7 Manambaho (riv.), Madg.
89/H7 Manambolo (riv.), Madg.
89/J7 Mananara, Madg.
89/H8 Mananara (riv.), Madg.
89/J8 Mananjary, Madg.
89/H8 Mananjary (riv.), Madg.
68/D2 Manas (lake), China
68/E3 Manas (riv.), China
70/D2 Manāslu (mtn.), Nepal
115/F5 Manasquan, NJ,US
115/F5 Manasquan (riv.), NJ,US
109/F3 Manassa, Co,US
110/E4 Manassas, Va,US
49/G1 Manastir Dečani, Yugo.
49/G1 Manastir Gračanica, Yugo.
49/G1 Manastir Sopoćani, Yugo.
65/H7 Manatsuru, Japan
92/F4 Manaus, Braz.
59/B3 Manavgat, Turk.
107/H2 Manawan (lake), Sk,Can
65/H7 Manazuru-misaki (cape), Japan
32/D3 Man, Calf of (isl.), IM,UK
46/D4 Mancha Real, Sp.
70/C4 Mancherāl, India
76/E6 Manchester (lake), Austl.
33/F5 Manchester, Eng,UK
110/D4 Manchester, Ky,US
111/G3 Manchester, NH,US
113/G3 Manchester, Tn,US
63/J3 Manchuria (reg.), China
60/F3 Mand (riv.), Iran
87/F3 Manda, Tanz.
95/B2 Mandaguari, Braz.
37/C4 Mandal, Nor.
73/K4 Mandala (peak), Indo.
69/B1 Mandalay, Burma
69/A1 Mandalay (div.), Burma
57/L5 Mandalgovĭ, Mong.
60/E2 Mandalī, Iraq
107/H4 Mandan, ND,US
83/J6 Manda Nat'l Park, Chad
66/D4 Mandang Shan (mtn.), China
73/F5 Mandasavu (peak), Indo.
67/D5 Mandaue, Phil.
81/G3 Mandeb, BAb el (str.), Afr., Asia
45/H4 Mandello del Lario, It.
43/F3 Manderscheid, Ger.
101/F4 Mandeville, Jam.
61/L2 Māndi, India
87/F4 Mandié, Moz.
73/G4 Mandiola (isl.), Indo.
70/D3 Mandla, India
38/E1 Mandø (isl.), Den.
49/K6 Mándra, Gre.
89/H9 Mandrare (riv.), Madg.
89/J6 Mandritsara, Madg.
70/C3 Mandsaur, India
74/B6 Mandurah, Austl.
49/E2 Manduria, It.
70/A3 Māndvi, India
70/C5 Mandya, India
70/D2 Mane (pass), Nepal
35/G2 Manea, Eng,UK
70/D3 Manendragarh, India
85/H5 Manéngouba, Massif du (peak), Camr.
45/J4 Manerbio, It.
60/B3 Manfalūt, Egypt
48/D2 Manfredonia, It.
48/E2 Manfredonia (gulf), It.
66/B4 Mang (riv.), China
94/B4 Manga, Braz.
94/A3 Mangabeiras (hills), Braz.
87/C1 Mangai, Zaire
79/K7 Mangaia (isl.), CookIs.
71/F2 Mangaldai, India
67/D4 Mangaldan, Phil.
51/J4 Mangalia, Rom.
70/B5 Mangalore, India
79/M7 Mangareva (isl.), FrPol.
55/K4 Mangistau Obl., Kaz.
73/E3 Mangkalihat (cape), Indo.
61/K2 Mangla, Pak.
92/C3 Manglares (pt.), Col.
85/F4 Mango, Togo
87/G3 Mangoche, Malw.
89/H8 Mangoky (riv.), Madg.
73/G4 Mangole (isl.), Indo.
89/J7 Mangoro (riv.), Madg.
34/D4 Mangotsfield, Eng,UK
70/B3 Māngrol, India
97/G2 Mangueira (lake), Braz.
109/H4 Mangum, Ok,US
55/J3 Mangyshlak (pen.), Kaz.
55/K4 Mangyshlak (plat.), Kaz.
109/H3 Manhattan, Ks,US
106/F4 Manhattan, Mt,US
115/B3 Manhattan Beach, Ca,US
95/D2 Manhuaçu, Braz.
95/D2 Manhumirim, Braz.
49/H4 Máni (pen.), Gre.
89/H7 Mania (riv.), Madg.
87/F4 Manica, Moz.
92/F5 Manicoré, Braz.
92/F5 Manicoré (riv.), Braz.
107/J3 Manicouagan, Mb,Can
111/G1 Manicouagan (res.), Qu,Can
111/G1 Manicouagan (riv.), Qu,Can
111/H1 Manicouagan, Petit Lac (lake), Qu,Can
76/C3 Manifold (cape), Austl.
79/L6 Manihi (isl.), FrPol.
79/J6 Manihiki (atoll), CookIs.
67/D5 Manila (cap.), Phil.
108/E2 Manila, Ut,US
89/J7 Maningory (riv.), Madg.
73/G4 Manipa (str.), Indo.
71/F3 Manipur (state), India
59/A2 Manisa, Turk.
32/D3 Man, Isle of (isl.), UK
110/C2 Manistee, Mi,US
110/C2 Manistee (riv.), Mi,US
102/G3 Manitoba (prov.), Can.
107/J3 Manitoba (lake), Mb,Can
111/H1 Manitou (riv.), Qu,Can
110/D2 Manitoulin (isl.), On,Can
112/B2 Manitou Springs, Co,US
110/C1 Manitouwadge, On,Can
110/C2 Manitowoc, Wi,US
110/F2 Maniwaki, Qu,Can
92/C2 Manizales, Col.
70/C4 Manjlegaon, India
61/L5 Mānjra (riv.), India
107/K4 Mankato, Mn,US
84/D4 Mankono, IvC.
62/F3 Manlay, Mong.
46/D2 Manlleu, Sp.
76/H8 Manly, Austl.
70/B3 Manmād, India
69/B4 Man Mia (peak), Thai.
70/C6 Mannar (gulf), India, SrL.
70/C6 Mannar, SrL.
70/C5 Mannārgudi, India
88/C4 Mannetjiesberg (peak), SAfr.
45/H2 Mannheim, Ger.
103/Q7 Manning (cape), NW,Can
113/H3 Manning, SC,US
35/H3 Manningtree, Eng,UK
84/C5 Mano (riv.), Libr., SLeo.
87/E2 Manono, Zaire
115/H5 Manorville, NY,US
44/F5 Manosque, Fr.
111/G1 Manouane (lake), Qu,Can
111/G1 Manouane (riv.), Qu,Can
79/H5 Manra (Sydney) (atoll), Kiri.
47/F2 Manresa, Sp.
87/E3 Mansa, Zam.
84/B3 Mansa Konko, Gam.
73/F1 Mansalay, Phil.
103/H2 Mansel (isl.), NW,Can
33/G5 Mansfield, Eng,UK
112/E3 Mansfield, La,US
110/D3 Mansfield, Oh,US
33/G5 Mansfield Woodhouse, Eng,UK
92/B4 Manta, Ecu.
73/E2 Mantalingaian (mt.), Phil.
92/C6 Mantaro (riv.), Peru
108/B3 Manteca, Ca,US
70/D1 Mantena, Braz.
42/A6 Mantes-la-Jolie, Fr.
42/A6 Mantes-la-Ville, Fr.
70/C4 Manthani, India
108/E3 Manti, Ut,US
115/G5 Manticock (pt.), NY,US
95/C2 Mantiquiera (range), Braz.
66/C3 Mantou Shan (mtn.), China
45/J4 Mantova, It.
100/E3 Mantua, Cuba
53/K4 Manturovo, Rus.
37/H3 Mäntyharju, Fin.
92/E6 Manú (riv.), Peru
79/J6 Manua (isls.), ASam.
79/K6 Manuae (atoll), CookIs.
104/W13 Manuawili, Hi,US
93/J6 Manuel Alves (riv.), Braz.
72/C5 Manuk (riv.), Indo.
75/R10 Manukau, NZ
92/D6 Manú Nat'l Park, Peru
92/E6 Manuripe (riv.), Bol.
78/D5 Manus (isl.), PNG
115/F5 Manville, NJ,US
112/E4 Many, La,US
55/G3 Manych (riv.), Rus.
55/G3 Manych-Gudilo (lake), Rus.
108/E3 Many Farms, Az,US
87/F2 Manyoni, Tanz.
46/D3 Manzanares, Sp.
47/N8 Manzanares (riv.), Sp.
101/P10 Manzanillo, Mex.
112/B3 Manzano (mts.), NM,US
63/H2 Manzhouli, China
86/C2 Manzilah, Buḩayrat al (lake), Egypt
81/W17 Manzil bū Ruqaybah, Tun.
81/X17 Manzil Tamīn, Tun.
89/E2 Manzini, Swaz.
101/G4 Mao, DRep.
73/J4 Maoke (mts.), Indo.
67/B3 Maoming, China
68/D5 Mapam (lake), China
100/C4 Mapastepec, Mex.
101/P8 Mapimí, Bolsón de (val.), Mex.
111/Q8 Maple, On,Can
107/K5 Maple (riv.), Ia,US
107/J4 Maple (riv.), ND,US
106/F3 Maple Creek, Sk,Can
115/F6 Maple Shade, NJ,US
115/F5 Maplewood, NJ,US
74/G2 Mapoon Mission Sta., Austl.
92/G4 Mapuera (riv.), Braz.
70/B4 Mapusa, India
89/F2 Maputo (cap.), Moz.
86/D5 Maqdam, Ras (cape), Sudan
61/J2 Maqor, Afg.
68/D5 Maquan (riv.), China
87/C2 Maquela do Zombo, Ang.
109/K2 Maquoketa (riv.), Ia,US
95/B3 Mar (range), Braz.
93/J5 Marabá, Braz.
93/J3 Maracá (isl.), Braz.
101/G5 Maracaibo, Ven.
101/G6 Maracaibo (lake), Ven.
93/H7 Maracaju (mts.), Braz.
94/B4 Maracás, Braz.
94/B4 Maracás (hills), Braz.
101/H5 Maracay, Ven.
46/D4 Maracena, Sp.
85/G3 Maradi, Niger
85/G3 Maradi (dept.), Niger
60/E1 Marāgheh, Iran
92/E3 Marahuaca (peak), Ven.
109/J3 Marais des Cygnes (riv.), Ks, Mo,US
93/J4 Marajó, Braz.
93/J4 Marajó (bay), Braz.
90/D3 Marajó (isl.), Braz.
67/E6 Maramag, Phil.
95/K8 Marambaia (isl.), Braz.
113/F2 Maramec (riv.), Mo,US
51/F2 Maramureş (co.), Rom.
108/E4 Marana, Az,US
94/C1 Maranguape, Braz.
94/A4 Maranhão (riv.), Braz.
94/A2 Maranhão (state), Braz.
76/C4 Maranoa (riv.), Austl.
92/C4 Marañón (riv.), Peru
84/D5 Maraoue Nat'l Park, IvC.
72/B4 Marapi (peak), Indo.
72/C4 Maras (peak), Indo.
51/H3 Mărăşeşti, Rom.
110/C1 Marathon, On,Can
113/H5 Marathon, Fl,US
112/C4 Marathon, Tx,US
95/A4 Marau, Braz.
67/D6 Marawi, Phil.
86/B5 Marawī, Sudan
34/A6 Marazion, Eng,UK
46/C4 Marbella, Sp.
106/F5 Marbleton, Wy,US
38/E3 Marburg, Ger.
50/C2 Marcali, Hun.
87/B4 Marca, Ponta da (pt.), Ang.
35/G1 March, Eng,UK
44/D3 Marche (mts.), Fr.
45/K5 Marche (reg.), It.
43/E3 Marche-en-Famenne, Belg.
46/C4 Marchena, Sp.
91/D3 Mar Chiquita (lake), Arg.
42/A2 Marck, Fr.
113/H5 Marco, Fl,US
92/C7 Marcona, Peru
106/E3 Marconi (peak), BC,Can
96/E2 Marcos Juárez, Arg.
42/C2 Marcq-en-Baroeul, Fr.
114/J3 Marcus Baker (mtn.), Ak,US
110/F2 Marcy (peak), NY,US
61/K2 Mardān, Pak.
97/F3 Mar del Plata, Arg.
35/G4 Marden, Eng,UK
59/E3 Mardin, Turk.
79/V12 Maré (isl.), NCal.
76/B2 Mareeba, Austl.
36/C2 Maree, Loch (lake), Sc,UK
33/H5 Mareham le Fen, Eng,UK
35/G5 Maresfield, Eng,UK
112/B4 Marfa, Tx,US
34/C3 Margam, Wal,UK
54/E3 Marganets, Ukr.
70/B4 Margao, India
101/J5 Margarita (isl.), Ven.
35/H4 Margate, Eng,UK
44/E4 Margeride (mts.), Fr.
83/L7 Margherita (peak), Ugan.
50/F2 Marghita, Rom.
68/B3 Margilan, Uzb.
68/E5 Margog Caka (lake), China
67/D6 Margosatubig, Phil.
43/E2 Margraten, Neth.
98/V Margurite (bay), Ant.
77/D4 Maria (peak), Austl.
79/K7 Maria (isl.), FrPol.
77/D4 Maria Island Nat'l Park, Austl.
113/F3 Marianna, Ar,US
113/G4 Marianna, Fl,US
100/E3 Mariano, Cuba
45/K2 Mariánské Lázně (Marienbad), Czh.
106/F3 Marias (riv.), Mt,US
50/B2 Maribor, Slov.
95/L7 Maricá, Braz.
92/E4 Marié (riv.), Braz.
98/S Marie Byrd Land (reg.), Ant.
101/J4 Marie-Galante (isl.), Guad.
37/F3 Mariehamn, Fin.
45/K2 Marienbad (Mariánské Lázně), Czh.
41/E6 Marienheide, Ger.
37/E4 Mariestad, Swe.
113/G3 Marietta, Ga,US
110/D4 Marietta, Oh,US
44/F5 Marignane, Fr.
95/B2 Marília, Braz.
46/A1 Marin, Sp.
115/B3 Marina del Rey, Ca,US

31/R9 Marines, Fr.
110/C2 Marinette, Wi,US
95/B2 Maringá, Braz.
46/A3 Marinha Grande, Port.
75/J3 Marion (reef), Austl.
113/G3 Marion, Al,US
110/B4 Marion, Il,US
110/C3 Marion, In,US
110/B4 Marion, Ky,US
110/C2 Marion, Mi,US
110/D3 Marion, Oh,US
113/H3 Marion (lake), SC,US
110/D4 Marion, Va,US
108/C3 Mariposa, Ca,US
51/H5 Maritsa (riv.), Bul., Turk.
54/F3 Mariupol', Ukr.
53/K4 Mariy Aut. Rep., Rus.
59/K5 Marj 'Uyūn, Leb.
40/B6 Mark (riv.), Belg.
62/B2 Markakol (lake), Kaz.
83/P7 Marka (Merca), Som.
37/E4 Markaryd, Swe.
40/C4 Marken (isl.), Neth.
40/C4 Markerwaard (polder), Neth.
35/E1 Market Bosworth, Eng,UK
35/F1 Market Deeping, Eng,UK
33/F6 Market Drayton, Eng,UK
35/F2 Market Harborough, Eng,UK
32/B3 Markethill, NI,UK
33/H5 Market Rasen, Eng,UK
33/H4 Market Weighton, Eng,UK
103/J2 Markham (bay), NW,Can
111/R8 Markham, On,Can
39/L2 Marki, Pol.
108/C3 Markleeville, Ca,US
49/L7 Markópoulon, Gre.
55/H2 Marks, Rus.
112/E4 Marksville, La,US
45/K2 Marktredwitz, Ger.
109/J3 Mark Twain (lake), Mo,US
41/E5 Marl, Ger.
115/F5 Marlboro, NJ,US
35/E4 Marlborough, Eng,UK
42/B3 Marles-les-Mines, Fr.
35/F3 Marlow, Eng,UK
115/F6 Marlton, NJ,US
42/C3 Marly, Fr.
31/T9 Marly-la-Ville, Fr.
31/S10 Marly-le-Roi, Fr.
43/F5 Marly-sur-Seille, Fr.
44/D4 Marmande, Fr.
51/H5 Marmara (isl.), Turk.
51/J5 Marmara (sea), Turk.
59/B3 Marmaris, Turk.
92/F5 Marmelos (riv.), Braz.
74/C5 Marmion (lake), Austl.
110/A1 Marmion (lake), On,Can
45/J3 Marmolada (peak), It.
46/C3 Marmolejo, Sp.
42/C6 Marne (dept.), Fr.
44/E2 Marne (riv.), Fr.
43/D6 Marne au Rhin, Canal de la (can.), Fr.
34/D5 Marnhull, Eng,UK
82/J6 Maro, Chad
79/H2 Maro (reef), Hi,US
89/J6 Maroantsetra, Madg.
79/L6 Marokau (atoll), FrPol.
81/G7 Marolambo, Madg.
31/S11 Marolles-en-Hurepoix, Fr.
89/J6 Maromokotro (peak), Madg.
87/F4 Marondera, Zim.
93/H3 Maroni (riv.), FrG., Sur.
76/D4 Maroochydore-Mooloolaba, Austl.
82/H5 Maroua, Camr.
89/H7 Marovoay, Madg.
43/G5 Marpingen, Ger.
33/F5 Marple, Eng,UK
62/D5 Marqên Gangri (peak), China
78/D8 Marquarie (riv.), Austl.
79/M5 Marquesas (isls.), FrPol.
110/C2 Marquette, Mi,US
83/K5 Marrah (mts.), Sudan
82/D1 Marrakech, Mor.
83/N7 Marsabit, Kenya
48/C4 Marsala, It.
83/L1 Marsá Matrūh, Egypt
31/U10 Marsange (riv.), Fr.
41/F6 Marsberg, Ger.
48/C1 Marsciano, It.
33/G4 Marsden, Eng,UK
40/B3 Marsdiep (chan.), Neth.
44/F5 Marseille, Fr.
112/E4 Marsh (isl.), La,US
106/F2 Marshall, Sk,Can
107/K4 Marshall, Mn,US
109/J3 Marshall, Mo,US
112/E3 Marshall, Tx,US
78/G3 Marshall Islands
107/K5 Marshalltown, Ia,US
109/J3 Marshfield, Mo,US
110/B2 Marshfield, Wi,US
35/E3 Marsh Gibbon, Eng,UK
33/G2 Marske-by-the-Sea, Eng,UK
69/B2 Martaban (gulf), Burma
106/G2 Martensville, Sk,Can
111/G3 Martha's Vineyard (isl.), Ma,US
45/G3 Martigny, Swi.
44/F5 Martigues, Fr.
98/S Martin (pen.), Ant.
39/K4 Martin, Slvk.
113/G3 Martin (lake), Al,US
107/H5 Martin, SD,US
113/F2 Martin, Tn,US
48/E2 Martina Franca, It.
116/K10 Martinez, Ca,US
113/H3 Martinez, Ga,US
100/B3 Martínez de la Torre, Mex.
101/J4 Martinique (passage), Dom., Mart.
101/J5 Martinique (isl.), Fr.
95/B2 Martinópolis, Braz.
110/E4 Martinsburg, WV,US
110/C4 Martinsville, In,US
110/E4 Martinsville, Va,US
28/H7 Martin Vaz (isls.), Braz.
34/D2 Martley, Eng,UK
34/D5 Martock, Eng,UK
47/F2 Martorell, Sp.
46/D4 Martos, Sp.
110/F1 Martre (riv.), Qu,Can
107/J5 Marty, SD,US
64/C3 Marugame, Japan
65/F2 Maruko, Japan
40/D2 Marum, Neth.
64/E2 Maruoka, Japan
79/M7 Marutea (atoll), FrPol.
65/H7 Maruyama, Japan
60/F3 Marv Dasht, Iran
76/D4 Mary (riv.), Austl.
61/H1 Mary, Trkm.
76/D4 Maryborough, Austl.
77/B3 Maryborough, Austl.
113/G4 Mary Esther, Fl,US
107/H3 Maryfield, Sk,Can
84/C5 Maryland (co.), Libr.
110/E4 Maryland (state), US
115/K7 Maryland City, Md,US
32/E2 Maryport, Eng,UK
111/L2 Marystown, Nf,Can
109/H3 Marysville, Ks,US
116/H6 Marysville, Mi,US
116/C1 Marysville, Wa,US
109/J2 Maryville, Mo,US
113/H3 Maryville, Tn,US
48/D2 Marzano (peak), It.
82/H2 Marzūq, Libya
82/H3 Marzūq, Şaḩrā (des.), Libya
59/K6 Masada (Horvot Mezada) (ruins), Isr.
87/G1 Masai Steppe (grsld.), Tanz.
83/M8 Masaka, Ugan.
81/X18 Masākin, Tun.
47/E3 Masamagrell, Sp.
73/F4 Masamba, Indo.
64/A3 Masan, SKor.
87/G3 Masasi, Tanz.
100/D5 Masaya, Nic.
67/D5 Masbate, Phil.
67/D5 Masbate (isl.), Phil.
81/R16 Mascara, Alg.
89/S15 Mascarene (isls.), Mrts., Reun.
101/P9 Mascota, Mex.
111/N6 Mascouche, Qu,Can
88/D3 Maseru (cap.), Les.
58/E6 Mashad, Iran
33/G3 Masham, Eng,UK
61/G1 Mashhad, Iran
61/H3 Māshkel, Hāmūn-i- (lake), Pak.
61/H3 Māshkīd (riv.), Iran
55/L1 Masim (peak), Rus.
61/G5 Masira (gulf), Oman
61/G4 Maşīrah (isl.), Oman
60/E2 Masjed-e Soleymān, Iran
36/A4 Mask, Lough (lake), Ire.
89/J6 Masoala (cape), Madg.
89/J6 Masoala (pen.), Madg.
110/C3 Mason, Mi,US
112/D4 Mason, Tx,US
116/A3 Mason (lake), Wa,US
107/K5 Mason City, Ia,US
47/X17 Maspalomas, Canl.,Sp.
47/K6 Masquefa, Sp.
45/J4 Massa, It.
111/G3 Massachusetts (state), US
111/G3 Massachusetts (bay), Ma,US
48/E2 Massafra, It.
94/B1 Massapê, Braz.
115/G5 Massapequa, NY,US
110/F2 Massena, NY,US
103/S7 Massey (sound), NW,Can
87/D3 Massibi, Ang.
44/E4 Massif Central (plat.), Fr.
110/D3 Massillon, Oh,US
98/G Masson (isl.), Ant.
31/S10 Massy, Fr.
75/S11 Masterton, NZ
40/B5 Mastgat (chan.), Neth.
115/H5 Mastic, NY,US
61/J3 Mastung, Pak.
64/B3 Masuda, Japan
72/B4 Masurai (peak), Indo.
87/F5 Masvingo, Zim.
59/L4 Maşyāf, Syria
49/F2 Mat (riv.), Alb.
87/B2 Matadi, Zaire
112/C3 Matador, Tx,US
100/D5 Matagalpa, Nic.
110/E1 Matagami (lake), Qu,Can
112/D4 Matagorda (bay), Tx,US
112/D4 Matagorda (isl.), Tx,US
101/G3 Mayaguana (isl.), Bahm.
70/D6 Matale, SrL.
84/B3 Matam, Sen.
100/A2 Matamoros, Mex.
100/B2 Matamoros, Mex.
83/K3 Ma'ṭan as Sarra (well), Libya
111/H1 Matane, Qu,Can
111/H1 Matane (riv.), Qu,Can
100/E3 Matanzas, Cuba
95/B2 Matão, Braz.
111/H1 Matapedia (riv.), Qu,Can
96/C2 Mataquito (riv.), Chile
60/C6 Matara (ruins), Egypt
70/D6 Matara, SrL.
73/E5 Mataram, Indo.
47/G2 Mataró, Sp.
79/L7 Mataura, FrPol.
78/H6 Mata Utu (cap.), Wall.
115/F5 Matawan, NJ,US
100/A3 Matehuala, Mex.
48/E2 Matera, It.
101/F3 Maternillos (pt.), Cuba
50/F2 Mátészalka, Hun.
115/C3 Mathews (lake), Ca,US
112/D4 Mathis, Tx,US
70/C2 Mathurā, India
67/E6 Mati, Phil.
95/K6 Matias Barbosa, Braz.
100/B4 Matías Romero, Mex.
81/W17 Mātir, Tun.
33/G5 Matlock, Eng,UK
92/G7 Mato Grosso, Braz.
93/G6 Mato Grosso (plat.), Braz.
95/A1 Mato Grosso do Sul (state), Braz.
87/E5 Matopos, Zim.
46/A2 Matosinhos, Port.
94/B4 Mato Verde, Braz.
61/G4 Maṭraḩ, Oman
94/D3 Matriz de Camaragibe, Braz.
88/B4 Matroosberg (peak), SAfr.
86/A2 Maṭrūḩ, Egypt
86/B2 Maṭrūḩ (gov.), Egypt
89/H8 Matsiatra (riv.), Madg.
65/L10 Matsubara, Japan
65/H7 Matsubushi, Japan
65/H7 Matsuda, Japan
65/H7 Matsudo, Japan
64/C3 Matsue, Japan
63/N3 Matsumae, Japan
65/E2 Matsumoto, Japan
64/E3 Matsusaka, Japan
65/G1 Matsushima, Japan
64/E2 Matsutō, Japan
64/C4 Matsuyama, Japan
110/D1 Mattagami (riv.), On,Can
110/E2 Mattawa, On,Can
45/G4 Matterhorn (pk.), It., Swi.
116/Q16 Matteson, Il,US
114/H2 Matthews (mtn.), Ak,US
101/G3 Matthew Town, Bahm.
64/E2 Mattō, Japan
32/B4 Mattock (riv.), Ire.
110/B4 Mattoon, Il,US
101/J6 Maturín, Ven.
87/E4 Matusadona Nat'l Park, Zim.
73/F2 Matutum (mt.), Phil.
92/G3 Maú (riv.), Braz., Guy.
95/C2 Mauá, Braz.
42/C3 Maubeuge, Fr.
71/G4 Ma-ubin, Burma
36/D2 Maud, Sc,UK
70/D2 Maudaha, India
92/G4 Maués, Braz.
92/G4 Maués Açu (riv.), Braz.
78/D3 Maug (isls.), NMar.
32/D3 Maughold, IM,UK
32/D3 Maughold Head (pt.), IM,UK
44/F5 Mauguio, Fr.
104/T10 Maui (isl.), Hi,US
79/K7 Mauke (isl.), Cookls.
42/A6 Mauldre (riv.), Fr.
96/B2 Maule (reg.), Chile
96/C1 Maule (riv.), Chile
44/C3 Mauléon, Fr.
96/B4 Maullín, Chile
110/C3 Maumee (riv.), In, Oh,US
87/D4 Maun, Bots.
104/U11 Mauna Kea (vol.), Hi,US
104/U11 Mauna Loa (vol.), Hi,US
79/K6 Maupiti (isl.), FrPol.
70/C2 Mau Rānīpur, India
31/S10 Maurecourt, Fr.
42/A6 Maurepas, Fr.
74/E5 Maurice (lake), Austl.
111/F2 Mauricie Nat'l Park, Qu,Can
84/B2 Mauritania
94/C2 Mauriti, Braz.
81/H6 Mauritius
110/B3 Mauston, Wi,US
50/E5 Mavrovo Nat'l Park, Macd.
69/B4 Maw Daung (pass), Thai.
98/D Mawson (coast), Ant.
98/E Mawson (sta.), Ant.
100/D3 Maxcanú, Mex.
43/F6 Maxéville, Fr.
110/F4 May (cape), NJ,US
72/C4 Maya (isl.), Indo.
57/P4 Maya (riv.), Rus.
101/H4 Mayagüez, PR
61/K1 Mayakovskogo (peak), Taj.
101/F3 Mayarí, Cuba
65/L10 Maya-san (peak), Japan
32/D1 Maybole, Sc,UK
83/N5 Maych'ew, Eth.
43/G3 Mayen, Ger.
44/C2 Mayenne, Fr.
44/C3 Mayenne (riv.), Fr.
106/E2 Mayerthorpe, Ab,Can
110/B4 Mayfield, Ky,US
54/G3 Maykop, Rus.
35/G3 Mayland, Eng,UK
71/G3 Maymyo, Burma
96/C5 Mayo (riv.), Arg.
114/L3 Mayo, Yk,Can
101/N8 Mayo (riv.), Mex.
46/D1 Mayor (cape), Sp.
89/H6 Mayotte (terr.), Fr.
101/F4 May Pen, Jam.
110/D4 Maysville, Ky,US
107/J4 Mayville, ND,US
116/Q16 Maywood, Il,US
87/E4 Mazabuka, Zam.
44/E5 Mazamet, Fr.
48/C4 Mazara (val.), It.
48/C4 Mazara del Vallo, It.
61/J1 Mazār-e Sharīf, Afg.
46/A1 Mazaricos, Sp.
46/E4 Mazarrón, Sp.
92/G2 Mazaruni (riv.), Guy.
100/C5 Mazatenango, Guat.
101/N9 Mazatlán, Mex.
52/D4 Mažeikiai, Lith.
76/B3 Mazeppa Nat'l Park, Austl.
32/B3 Mazetown, NI,UK
42/B3 Mazingarbe, Fr.
87/C2 Mazingu, Zaire
62/D3 Mazong (peak), China
39/L2 Mazury (reg.), Pol.
86/C2 Ma'ān, Jor.
89/E2 Mbabane (cap.), Swaz.
82/H6 Mbabo (peak), Camr.
82/J7 Mbaïki, CAfr.
83/H6 Mbakaou (lake), Camr.
87/F2 Mbala, Zam.
82/H7 Mbalam, Camr.
83/M7 Mbale, Ugan.
82/H7 Mbalmayo, Camr.
85/H5 Mbam (riv.), Camr.
85/H5 Mbam, Massif du (peak), Camr.
83/J7 Mbandaka, Zaire
83/M8 Mbarara, Ugan.
83/J7 Mbata, CAfr.
79/Y18 Mbengga (isl.), Fiji
87/F2 Mbeya, Tanz.
87/F2 Mbeya (range), Tanz.
87/B1 M'Bigou, Gabon
82/G7 Mbini, EqG.
82/H7 Mbini (riv.), EqG.
83/L6 Mbomou (riv.), CAfr.
84/B3 Mboune, Vallée du (wadi), Sen.
84/A3 M'Bour, Sen.
87/D2 Mbuji-Mayi, Zaire
109/J4 McAlester, Ok,US
112/D5 McAllen, Tx,US
106/C2 McBride, BC,Can
106/D4 McCall, Id,US
112/C4 McCamey, Tx,US
116/C3 McChord A.F.B., Wa,US
116/M9 McClellan A.F.B., Ca,US
107/H4 McClusky, ND,US
113/F4 McComb, Ms,US
109/G2 McConaughy (lake), Ne,US
109/G2 McCook, Ne,US
113/H3 McCormick, SC,US
107/J3 McCreary, Mb,Can
108/C2 McDermitt, Nv,US
29/N8 McDonald (isls.), Austl.
114/F3 McDonald (mtn.), Ak,US
114/L2 McDougall (pass), NW, Yk,Can
112/F3 McGehee, Ar,US
113/F3 McGehee, Ar,US
106/C2 McGregor (riv.), BC,Can
116/G7 McGregor, On,Can
116/P15 McHenry, Il,US
79/H5 McKean (atoll), Kiri.
103/K2 McKeand (riv.), NW,Can
110/E3 McKeesport, Pa,US
113/F2 McKenzie, Tn,US
114/H3 McKinley (mtn.), Ak,US
114/J3 McKinley Park, Ak,US
106/B5 McKinleyville, Ca,US
112/D3 McKinney, Tx,US
107/H4 McLaughlin, SD,US
115/J8 McLean, Va,US
106/D2 McLennan, Ab,Can
74/A4 McLeod (lake), Austl.
106/D2 McLeod (riv.), Ab,Can
102/E2 McLeod (bay), NW,Can
106/C2 McLeod Lake, BC,Can
102/F1 M'Clintock (chan.), NW,Can
103/Q7 M'Clure (str.), NW,Can
106/C4 McMinnville, Or,US
113/G3 McMinnville, Tn,US
98/M McMurdo, Ant.
116/B3 McNeil (isl.), Wa,US
87/F3 Mcocha, Malw.
109/H3 McPherson, Ks,US
62/E5 Mê (riv.), China
108/D3 Mead (lake), Az, Nv,US
114/G2 Meade (riv.), Ak,US
106/F2 Meadow Lake, Sk,Can
111/Q8 Meadowvale, On,Can
108/D3 Meadow Valley (riv.), Nv,US
113/F4 Meadville, Ms,US
110/D3 Meadville, Pa,US
94/A1 Mearim (riv.), Braz.
35/E1 Measham, Eng,UK
114/F2 Meat (mtn.), Ak,US
32/B4 Meath (co.), Ire.
107/G2 Meath Park, Sk,Can
31/U10 Meaux, Fr.
60/C4 Mecca (Makkah), SAr.
42/D1 Mechelen (Malines), Belg.
38/F1 Mecklenburger Bucht (bay), Ger.
38/F2 Mecklenburg-Western Pomerania (state), Ger.
87/G3 Mecuia (peak), Moz.
70/C4 Medak, India
72/A3 Medan, Indo.
97/L7 Medanosa (pt.), Arg.
35/F1 Medbourne, Eng,UK
81/S15 Médéa, Alg.
41/F6 Medebach, Ger.
94/B5 Medeiros Neto, Braz.
92/C2 Medellín, Col.
40/C3 Medemblik, Neth.
33/G5 Meden (riv.), Eng,UK
115/H5 Medford, NY,US
106/C5 Medford, Or,US
110/B2 Medford, Wi,US
51/J3 Medgidia, Rom.
51/G2 Mediaş, Rom.
106/D4 Medical Lake, Wa,US
108/F2 Medicine Bow (range), Co, Wy,US
107/G5 Medicine Bow, Wy,US
106/F3 Medicine Hat, Ab,Can
94/B5 Medina, Braz.
35/E5 Medina (riv.), Eng,UK
107/J4 Medina, ND,US
110/D3 Medina, Oh,US
109/H5 Medina, Tx,US
60/C4 Medina (Al Madīnah), SAr.
46/C2 Medina del Campo, Sp.
46/C4 Medina-Sidonia, Sp.
29/K4 Mediterranean (sea)
106/F2 Medley, Ab,Can
55/L2 Mednogorsk, Rus.
55/H2 Medveditsa, Gora (riv.), Rus.
57/S2 Medvezh'i (isls.), Rus.
52/G3 Medvezh'yegorsk, Rus.
31/P8 Medway (riv.), Eng,UK
108/F2 Meeker, Co,US
41/G3 Meerbach (riv.), Ger.
40/D6 Meerbusch, Ger.
43/E1 Meerhout, Belg.
43/E2 Meerssen, Neth.
70/C2 Meerut, India
35/E1 Meese (riv.), Eng,UK
106/F4 Meeteetse, Wy,US
83/N7 Mēga, Eth.
83/P6 Megalo, Eth.
111/G2 Megantic (peak), Qu,Can
49/H3 Megara, Gre.
71/F2 Meghalaya (state), India
59/N7 Megiddo (ruins), Isr.
110/E1 Mégiscane (lake), Qu,Can
110/E1 Mégiscane (riv.), Qu,Can
59/B3 Megista (isl.), Gre.
43/E2 Mehaigne (riv.), Belg.
81/R16 Mehdia, Alg.
41/G1 Mehe (riv.), Ger.
70/C3 Mehkar, India
61/F3 Mehrān (riv.), Iran
60/F2 Mehriz, Iran
70/B3 Mehsāna, India
67/C2 Mei (riv.), China
67/C3 Mei (riv.), China
95/B1 Meia Ponte (riv.), Braz.
82/H6 Meiganga, Camr.
103/R6 Meighen (isl.), NW,Can
63/K3 Meihekou, China
69/A1 Meiktila, Burma
41/H4 Meine, Ger.
41/E6 Meinerzhagen, Ger.
45/J1 Meiningen, Ger.
66/C5 Meishan (res.), China
39/G3 Meissen, Ger.
41/G6 Meissner (peak), Ger.
65/M10 Meiwa, Japan
67/C3 Meizhou, China
82/H7 Mekambo, Gabon
83/N5 Mek'elē, Eth.
81/M14 Meknès, Mor.
58/K8 Mekong (riv.), Asia
73/F4 Mekongga (peak), Indo.
69/D4 Mekong, Mouths of the, Viet.
72/B3 Melaka, Malay.
78/E5 Melanesia (reg.)
70/C6 Melappālaiyam, India
72/D4 Melawi (riv.), Indo.
35/G2 Melbourn, Eng,UK
77/C3 Melbourne, Austl.
102/F2 Melbourne (isl.), NW,Can
33/G6 Melbourne, Eng,UK
113/H4 Melbourne, Fl,US
77/F5 Melbourne (inset), Austl.
96/B5 Melchor (isl.), Chile
100/D4 Melchor de Mencos, Mex.
100/A2 Melchor Múzquiz, Mex.
34/D5 Melcombe Regis, Eng,UK
38/E1 Meldorf, Ger.
50/E3 Melenci, Yugo.
52/J5 Melenki, Rus.
55/K1 Meleuz, Rus.
103/J3 Mélèzes (riv.), Qu,Can
82/J5 Melfi, Chad
48/D2 Melfi, It.
107/G2 Melfort, Sk,Can
37/D3 Melhus, Nor.
81/N13 Melilla, Sp.
96/B5 Melimoyu (peak), Chile
96/D9 Melipilla, Chile
49/F3 Melissano, It.
107/H3 Melita, Mb,Can
48/D4 Melito di Porto Salvo, It.
54/E3 Melitopol', Ukr.
45/L2 Melk, Aus.
83/P7 Melka Meri, Eth.
34/D4 Melksham, Eng,UK
42/C2 Melle, Belg.
41/F4 Melle, Ger.
81/W17 Mellègue (riv.), Alg.
37/E4 Mellerud, Swe.
46/B1 Mellid, Sp.
33/F3 Melling, Eng,UK
75/K3 Mellish (reef), Austl.
97/J7 Mellizo Sur (peak), Chile
45/J1 Mellrichstadt, Ger.
41/F1 Mellum (isl.), Ger.
45/L1 Mělník, Czh.
97/G2 Melo, Uru.
116/Q16 Melrose Park, Il,US
41/G6 Melsungen, Ger.
33/G4 Meltham, Eng,UK
77/C3 Melton, Austl.
33/H6 Melton Mowbray, Eng,UK
31/T11 Melun, Fr.
74/F2 Melville (bay), Austl.
76/B1 Melville (cape), Austl.
74/E2 Melville (isl.), Austl.
103/L3 Melville (lake), Nf,Can
103/R7 Melville (isl.), NW,Can
103/H2 Melville (pen.), NW,Can
107/H3 Melville, Sk,Can
73/E2 Melville (cape), Phil.
115/G5 Melville, NY,US
116/F7 Melvindale, Mi,US
50/D2 Mélykút, Hun.
68/D5 Mêmar (lake), China
40/D1 Memmert (isl.), Ger.
45/J3 Memmingen, Ger.
69/D4 Memot, Camb.
86/B2 Memphis (ruins), Egypt
116/G6 Memphis, Mi,US
109/J2 Memphis, Mo,US
113/F3 Memphis, Tn,US
112/C3 Memphis, Tx,US
112/E3 Mena, Ar,US
32/D5 Menai (str.), Wal,UK
32/D5 Menai Bridge, Wal,UK
40/C2 Menaldum, Neth.
89/H9 Menarandra (riv.), Madg.
112/D4 Menard, Tx,US
110/B2 Menasha, Wi,US
89/H7 Menavava (riv.), Madg.
72/D4 Mendawai (riv.), Indo.
44/E4 Mende, Fr.
41/E6 Menden, Ger.
114/E4 Mendenhall (cape), Ak,US
59/B3 Menderes, Büyük (riv.), Turk.
95/K7 Mendes, Braz.
83/N6 Mendī, Eth.
43/G3 Mendig, Ger.
34/D4 Mendip (hills), Eng,UK
108/B3 Mendocino, Ca,US
104/B3 Mendocino (cape), Ca,US
96/C2 Mendoza, Arg.
96/C2 Mendoza (prov.), Arg.
89/H9 Mendrare (riv.), Madg.
50/F3 Menedinţi (co.), Rom.
101/G6 Mene Grande, Ven.
59/A2 Menemen, Turk.
42/C2 Menen, Belg.
83/N8 Menengai Crater, Kenya
62/H2 Menengiyn (plain), Mong.
48/C4 Menfi, It.
72/C4 Menggala, Indo.
46/D4 Mengibar, Sp.
66/D4 Menglianggu (mtn.), China
97/B2 Menindee (lake), Austl.
96/B5 Menlolat (peak), Chile
116/K12 Menlo Park, Ca,US
31/T11 Mennecy, Fr.
110/C2 Menominee, Mi,US
110/B3 Menomonee Falls, Wi,US
110/B2 Menomonie, Wi,US
47/H3 Menorca (Minorca) (isl.), Sp.
72/A4 Mentawai (isls.), Indo.
72/A4 Mentawai (str.), Indo.
115/C2 Mentone, Ca,US
112/C4 Mentone, Tx,US
110/D3 Mentor, Oh,US
31/R9 Menucourt, Fr.
73/E3 Menyapa (peak), Indo.
81/W17 Menzel Bourguiba, Tun.
114/M3 Menzie (mtn.), Yk,Can
35/E5 Meon (riv.), Eng,UK
31/Q7 Meopham, Eng,UK
101/N8 Meoquí, Mex.
73/H4 Meos Waar (isl.), Indo.
87/B2 Mepala, Ang.
55/G4 Mepistskaro (peak), Geo.
40/D3 Meppel, Neth.
41/E3 Meppen, Ger.
47/E2 Mequinenzo (res.), Sp.
109/K3 Meramec (riv.), Mo,US
45/J3 Merano, It.
72/D4 Meratus (mts.), Indo.
78/D5 Merauke, Indo.
83/P7 Merca, Som.
45/G4 Mercantour Nat'l Park, Fr.
108/B3 Merced, Ca,US
108/C3 Merced (riv.), Ca,US
96/C1 Mercedario (peak), Arg.
96/D2 Mercedes, Arg.
96/F2 Mercedes, Arg.
97/F2 Mercedes, Uru.
116/C2 Mercer Island, Wa,US
115/F5 Mercerville-Hamilton Square, NJ,US
42/D2 Merchtem, Belg.
111/N7 Mercier, Qu,Can
106/D2 Mercoal, Ab,Can
108/D3 Mercury, Nv,US
103/K2 Mercy (cape), Yk,Can
44/E5 Merdellou (mtn.), Fr.
34/D4 Mere, Eng,UK
97/M8 Meredith (cape), Falk.
112/C3 Meredith (lake), Tx,US
54/F2 Merefa, Ukr.
42/C2 Merelbeke, Belg.
69/D3 Mereuch, Camb.
31/Q8 Mereworth, Eng,UK
63/J2 Mergel (riv.), China
69/B3 Mergui, Burma
69/B4 Mergui (arch.), Burma
42/B3 Méricourt, Fr.
100/D3 Mérida, Mex.
46/B3 Mérida, Sp.
101/G6 Mérida, Ven.
92/D2 Mérida, Ven.
113/F3 Meridian, Ms,US
112/D4 Meridian, Tx,US
116/C2 Meridian-East Hill, Wa,US
44/C4 Mérignac, Fr.
42/D1 Merksem, Belg.
40/B6 Merksplas, Belg.
83/M4 Meroe (ruins), Sudan
59/K5 Meron, Har (mtn.), Isr.
77/F5 Merri (cr.), Austl.
115/G5 Merrick, NY,US
110/B2 Merrill, Wi,US
111/G3 Merrimack, NH,US
34/D5 Merriott, Eng,UK
106/C3 Merritt, BC,Can
113/H4 Merritt Island, Fl,US
33/F5 Mersey (riv.), Eng,UK
33/F5 Merseyside (co.), Eng,UK
59/C3 Mersin, Turk.
72/B3 Mersing, Malay.
31/N8 Merstham, Eng,UK
43/F5 Merten, Fr.
34/C3 Merthyr Tydfil, Wal,UK
31/N7 Merton (bor.), Eng,UK
98/K Mertz (glac.), Ant.
112/C4 Mertzon, Tx,US
42/B5 Méru, Fr.
83/N7 Meru, Kenya
42/B2 Merville, Fr.
40/C5 Merwedekanaal (can.), Neth.
31/S9 Méry-sur-Oise, Fr.
43/F2 Merzenich, Ger.
59/C2 Merzifon, Turk.
43/F5 Merzig, Ger.
97/K7 Mesa (peak), Arg.
114/G3 Mesa (mtn.), Ak,US
108/E4 Mesa, Az,US
107/K4 Mesabi (range), Mn,US
101/M8 Mesa del Seri, Mex.
49/E2 Mesagne, It.
49/J5 Mesarás (gulf), Gre.
108/E3 Mesa Verde Nat'l Park, Co,US
112/C3 Mescalero (ridge), NM,US
41/F6 Meschede, Ger.
45/H4 Mesco, Punta di (pt.), It.
110/F1 Mesgouez (lake), Qu,Can
49/G3 Mesolóngion, Gre.
96/F2 Mesopotamia (reg.), Arg.
60/D2 Mesopotamia (reg.), Iraq
48/E3 Mesoraca, It.
112/D3 Mesquite, Tx,US
82/E1 Mesrouh (peak), Mor.
82/F1 Messaad, Alg.
97/J7 Messier (chan.), Chile
48/D3 Messina, It.
48/D4 Messina (str.), It.
87/F5 Messina, SAfr.
49/H4 Messíni, Gre.
49/H4 Messini (gulf), Gre.
31/U10 Messy, Fr.
51/F5 Mesta (riv.), Bul.
45/K4 Mestre, It.
84/C5 Mesurado (cape), Libr.
111/G1 Métabetchouan, Qu,Can
111/G1 Métabetchouane (riv.), Qu,Can
103/K2 Meta Incognita (pen.), NW,Can
113/F4 Metairie, La,US
91/D2 Metán, Arg.
48/E2 Metapontum (ruins), It.
49/G3 Metéora, Gre.
33/H5 Metheringham, Eng,UK
49/G4 Methóni, Gre.
50/C4 Metković, Cro.
110/B4 Metropolis, Il,US
43/D3 Mettet, Belg.
41/E4 Mettingen, Ger.
43/F5 Mettlach, Ger.
40/D6 Mettmann, Ger.
83/N6 Metu, Eth.
115/F5 Metuchen, NJ,US
43/F5 Metz, Fr.
31/S10 Meudon, Fr.
42/C2 Meulebeke, Belg.
43/E6 Meurthe-et-Moselle (dept.), Fr.
43/E3 Meuse (riv.), Belg., Fr.
42/E6 Meuse (dept.), Fr.
43/E5 Meuse, Cotes de (uplands), Fr.
59/N9 Mevasseret Ziyyon, Isr.
33/G5 Mexborough, Eng,UK
112/D4 Mexia, Tx,US
93/J3 Mexiana, Braz.
101/L7 Mexicali, Mex.
100/A3 Mexico
100/B4 México (state), Mex.
109/J5 Mexico (gulf), NAm
109/K3 Mexico, Mo,US
100/B4 Mexico City (cap.), Mex.
60/F2 Meybod, Iran
88/Q13 Meyerton, SAfr.
61/H1 Meymaneh, Afg.
59/K6 Meẕada, Ḩorvot (Masada) (ruins), Isr.
51/F4 Mezdra, Bul.
52/J2 Mezen' (bay), Rus.
53/K2 Mezen' (riv.), Rus.
56/J4 Mezhdurechensk, Rus.
56/E2 Mezhdusharskiy (isl.), Rus.
50/E2 Mezőberény, Hun.
50/E2 Mezőkovácsháza, Hun.
50/E2 Mezőkövesd, Hun.
50/E2 Mezőtúr, Hun.
70/C3 Mhow, India
66/D3 Mi (riv.), China
100/B4 Miahuatlán, Mex.
46/C3 Miajadas, Sp.
108/E4 Miami, Az,US
113/H5 Miami, Fl,US
109/J3 Miami, Ok,US
113/H5 Miami Beach, Fl,US
66/B4 Mianchi, China
60/E1 Mīāndoāb, Iran
60/E1 Mīāneh, Iran
115/G4 Mianus (riv.), Ct,US
61/K2 Miānwāli, Pak.
62/E5 Mianyang, China
67/B2 Miao'er (peak), China
63/E6 Miaodao (isls.), China
66/H6 Miaofeng Shan (mtn.), China
53/P5 Miass, Rus.
53/Q5 Miass (riv.), Rus.
39/J2 Miastko, Pol.
86/C5 Miberika, Sudan
106/D2 Mica Creek, BC,Can
39/L4 Michalovce, Slvk.
114/K2 Michelson (mtn.), Ak,US
110/C3 Michigan (lake), Can., US
110/C2 Michigan (state), US
110/C3 Michigan City, In,US
110/C2 Michipicoten (isl.), On,Can
100/A4 Michoacán (state), Mex.
55/G1 Michurinsk, Rus.
33/F2 Mickle Fell (mtn.), Eng,UK
33/F2 Mickleton, Eng,UK
100/E5 Mico (riv.), Nic.
101/J5 Micoud, StL.
78/E3 Micronesia (reg.)
78/D4 Micronesia, Fed. States of
85/G2 Midal (well), Niger
107/H3 Midale, Sk,Can
40/A6 Middelburg, Neth.
88/D3 Middelburg, SAfr.
89/E2 Middelburg, SAfr.
38/E1 Middelfart, Den.
40/B5 Middelharnis, Neth.
42/B1 Middelkerke, Belg.
108/C2 Middle Alkali (lake), Ca,US
71/F5 Middle Andaman (isl.), India
111/F2 Middlebury, Vt,US
112/C4 Middle Concho (riv.), Tx,US
33/G3 Middleham, Eng,UK

109/G2 Middle Loup (riv.), Ne,US
109/J2 Middle Raccoon (riv.), Ia,US
115/K7 Middle River, Md,US
110/D4 Middlesboro, Ky,US
33/G2 Middlesbrough, Eng,UK
35/F4 Middlesex (reg.), Eng,UK
115/F5 Middlesex, NJ,US
106/C4 Middle Sister (peak), Or,US
33/F4 Middleton, Eng,UK
35/E2 Middleton Cheney, Eng,UK
33/F2 Middleton-in-Teesdale, Eng,UK
32/B3 Middletown, NI,UK
115/F5 Middletown, NJ,US
33/F5 Middlewich, Eng,UK
34/C3 Mid Glamorgan (co.), Wal,UK
35/F5 Midhurst, Eng,UK
44/D5 Midi (can.), Fr.
44/D4 Midi-Pyrénées (reg.), Fr.
110/E2 Midland, On,Can
110/C3 Midland, Mi,US
112/C4 Midland, Tx,US
116/Q16 Midlothian, Il,US
74/G6 Midona (lake), Austl.
44/C5 Midou (riv.), Fr.
67/D6 Midsayap, Phil.
34/D4 Midsomer Norton, Eng,UK
78/H2 Midway (isls.), PacUS
77/C4 Midway Point-Sorell, Austl.
109/H4 Midwest City, Ok,US
60/C3 Midyan (reg.), SAr.
59/E3 Midyat, Turk.
54/B4 Midzhur (peak), Bul.
50/F4 Midžor (peak), Yugo.
64/B4 Mie, Japan
64/E3 Mie (pref.), Japan
39/H2 Międzychód, Pol.
39/M3 Międzyrzec Podlaski, Pol.
39/H2 Międzyrzecz, Pol.
39/L3 Mielec, Pol.
82/J7 Miéle I, Congo
51/G2 Miercurea Ciuc, Rom.
46/C1 Mieres, Sp.
45/J3 Miesbach, Ger.
83/P6 Mī'ēso, Eth.
44/E3 Migennes, Fr.
100/A3 Miguel Auza, Mex.
94/B3 Miguel Calmon, Braz.
95/B2 Miguelópolis, Braz.
95/K7 Miguel Pereira, Braz.
46/D3 Miguelturra, Sp.
64/D3 Mihama, Japan
64/C3 Mihara, Japan
65/G2 Miharu, Japan
61/J3 Mihrābpur, Pak.
47/E2 Mijares (riv.), Sp.
46/C4 Mijas, Sp.
40/B4 Mijdrecht, Neth.
65/N10 Mikawa (bay), Japan
65/N9 Mikawa-Mino (mts.), Japan
55/G4 Mikha Tskhakaya, Geo.
51/F4 Mikhaylovgrad, Bul.
50/F4 Mikhaylovgrad (reg.), Bul.
55/G2 Mikhaylovka, Rus.
65/K10 Miki, Japan
37/H3 Mikkeli, Fin.
37/H3 Mikkeli (prov.), Fin.
49/J4 Míkonos (isl.), Gre.
49/G2 Mikri Prespa (lake), Gre.
65/M10 Mikuma, Japan
87/G2 Mikumi, Tanz.
87/G2 Mikumi Nat'l Park, Tanz.
64/E2 Mikuni, Japan
65/F2 Mikuni-tōge (pass), Japan
81/V17 Mila, Alg.
81/U17 Mila (gov.), Alg.
94/C2 Milagres, Braz.
92/C4 Milagro, Ecu.
45/H4 Milan (Milano), It.
59/A3 Milas, Turk.
48/D3 Milazzo, It.
34/D5 Milborne Port, Eng,UK
35/G2 Mildenhall, Eng,UK
77/B2 Mildura, Austl.
112/C4 Miles, Tx,US
107/G4 Miles City, Mt,US
45/K1 Milešovka (peak), Czh.
107/G3 Milestone, Sk,Can
48/D2 Miletto (peak), It.
35/F4 Milford, Eng,UK
32/B3 Milford, NI,UK
112/D2 Milford (lake), Ks,US
108/D3 Milford, Ut,US
34/A3 Milford Haven, Wal,UK
35/E5 Milford on Sea, Eng,UK
78/G4 Mili (atoll), Mrsh.
81/S15 Miliana, Alg.
39/J3 Milicz, Pol.
104/V13 Mililani Town, Hi,US
106/F3 Milk (riv.), Can., US
35/E4 Milk (hill), Eng,UK
106/E3 Milk River, Ab,Can
98/G Mill (isl.), Ant.
103/J2 Mill (isl.), NW,Can
44/E4 Millau, Fr.
116/K11 Millbrae, Ca,US
34/B6 Millbrook, Eng,UK
113/H3 Milledgeville, Ga,US
111/N6 Mille Iles (riv.), Qu,Can
110/B1 Mille Lacs (lake), On,Can
107/K4 Mille Lacs (lake), Mn,US
107/J4 Miller, SD,US
55/G2 Millerovo, Rus.
32/C1 Milleur (pt.), Sc,UK
44/D4 Millevaches (plat.), Fr.
111/Q9 Millgrove, On,Can
111/R8 Milliken, On,Can
111/G2 Millinocket, Me,US
32/C2 Millisle, NI,UK
33/E3 Millom, Eng,UK
107/G5 Mills, Wy,US
115/F5 Millstone (riv.), NJ,US
33/F3 Millthrop, Eng,UK
116/J11 Mill Valley, Ca,US
112/E3 Millwood (lake), Ar,US
78/E5 Milne (bay), PNG
33/F4 Milnrow, Eng,UK
84/C4 Milo (riv.), Gui.
111/G2 Milo, Me,US
49/J4 Milos (isl.), Gre.
116/L12 Milpitas, Ca,US
45/H1 Milseburg (peak), Ger.
111/Q8 Milton, On,Can
75/Q12 Milton, NZ
33/F2 Milton, Eng,UK
35/G4 Milton, Eng,UK
113/G4 Milton, Fl,US
111/G3 Milton, NH,US
106/D4 Milton-Freewater, Or,US
111/Q8 Milton Heights, On,Can
35/F2 Milton Keynes, Eng,UK
36/H7 Miltown Malbay, Ire.
67/B2 Miluo, China
34/C4 Milverton, Eng,UK
116/Q13 Milwaukee, Wi,US
64/B4 Mimi (riv.), Japan
44/C4 Mimizan, Fr.
67/C2 Min (riv.), China
71/H2 Min (riv.), China
81/R16 Mina (riv.), Alg.
108/C3 Mina, Nv,US
73/F3 Minahasa (pen.), Indo.
65/M10 Minakuchi, Japan
64/B4 Minamata, Japan
65/F3 Minami-Alps Nat'l Park, Japan
65/M10 Minamichita, Japan
78/D2 Minamiiō (isl.), Japan
78/E2 Minami-Tori-Shima (isl.), Japan
97/G2 Minas, Uru.
100/E3 Minas de Matahambre, Cuba
46/B4 Minas de Ríotinto, Sp.
95/H6 Minas Gerais (state), Braz.
94/B5 Minas Novas, Braz.
71/F3 Minbu, Burma
96/C1 Mincha, Chile
34/D3 Minchinhampton, Eng,UK
96/B4 Minchinmávida (vol.), Chile
67/D6 Mindanao (isl.), Phil.
67/D6 Mindanao (sea), Phil.
45/J2 Mindel (riv.), Ger.
80/J10 Mindelo, CpV.
41/F4 Minden, Ger.
112/E3 Minden, La,US
109/H2 Minden, Ne,US
67/D5 Mindoro (isl.), Phil.
67/D5 Mindoro (str.), Phil.
34/C4 Minehead, Eng,UK
93/H7 Mineiros, Braz.
115/G5 Mineola, NY,US
55/G3 Mineral'nye Vody, Rus.
112/D3 Mineral Wells, Tx,US
45/H5 Minerbio (pt.), Fr.
66/C3 Ming (riv.), China
111/J1 Mingan (riv.), Qu,Can
61/K2 Mingāora, Pak.
55/H4 Mingechaur, Azer.
55/H4 Mingechaur (res.), Azer.
69/A1 Mingun (ruins), Burma
46/B1 Minho (riv.), Sp.
74/C5 Minigwal (lake), Austl.
107/L3 Miniss (lake), On,Can
107/H2 Minitonas, Mb,Can
107/K4 Minneapolis, Mn,US
107/J3 Minnedosa, Mb,Can
107/K4 Minnesota (state), US
107/K4 Minnesota (riv.), Mn,US
32/D2 Minnigaff, Sc,UK
110/B1 Minnis (lake), On,Can
110/A1 Minnitaki (lake), On,Can
65/E3 Mino, Japan
65/F3 Minobu, Japan
65/N9 Mino-Mikawa (mts.), Japan
65/L10 Mino'o, Japan
65/L10 Mino'o (riv.), Japan
47/G3 Minorca (Menorca) (isl.), Sp.
107/H3 Minot, ND,US
67/C2 Minqing, China
41/F1 Minsener Oog (isl.), Ger.
54/C1 Minsk (cap.), Bela.
39/L2 Mińsk Mazowiecki, Pol.
54/C1 Minsk Obl., Bela.
35/G4 Minster, Eng,UK
68/B4 Mintaka (pass), China
111/H2 Minto, NB,Can
102/E1 Minto (inlet), NW,Can
114/L3 Minto, Yk,Can
48/C2 Minturno, It.
86/B2 Minūf, Egypt
56/K4 Minusinsk, Rus.
111/K2 Miquelon, StP.
92/C3 Mira (riv.), Col., Ecu.
46/A2 Mira, Port.
46/A4 Mira (riv.), Port.
111/M6 Mirabel, Qu,Can
95/D2 Miracema, Braz.
93/J5 Miracema do Norte, Braz.
96/C4 Mirador (pass), Chile
70/B4 Miraj, India
115/C2 Mira-Loma, Ca,US
49/J5 Mirambéllou (gulf), Gre.
115/A2 Mira Monte, Ca,US
93/G8 Miranda (riv.), Braz.
46/D1 Miranda de Ebro, Sp.
45/J4 Mirandola, It.
95/B2 Mirandópolis, Braz.
95/B2 Mirante do Paranapanema, Braz.
95/B2 Mirassol, Braz.
100/D5 Miravalles (vol.), CR
46/B1 Miravalles (mtn.), Sp.
45/G2 Mirecourt, Fr.
33/G4 Mirfield, Eng,UK
54/E2 Mirgorod, Ukr.
97/G2 Mirim (lake), Braz., Uru.
61/H3 Mirjāveh, Iran
98/G Mirnyy, Ant.
57/M3 Mirnyy, Rus.
107/H2 Mirond (lake), Sk,Can
49/H4 Mirtóön (sea), Gre.
64/A3 Miryang, SKor.
70/D2 Mirzāpur, India
83/M7 Misa, Zaire
86/A4 Misāha, Bi'r (well), Egypt
64/D3 Misaki, Japan
110/C3 Mishawaka, In,US
114/F2 Misheguk (mtn.), Ak,US
65/F3 Mishima, Japan
48/C3 Misilmeri, It.
101/L7 Misión del Rosario, Mex.
91/F2 Misiones (mts.), Arg.
101/L8 Misión San Fernando, Mex.
50/E1 Miskolc, Hun.
65/M10 Misono, Japan
73/H4 Misool (isl.), Indo.
107/L4 Misquah (hills), Mn,US
82/J1 Mişrātah, Libya
83/L1 Mişrātah (pt.), Libya
94/C2 Missão Velha, Braz.
110/D1 Missinaibi (lake), On,Can
110/D1 Missinaibi (riv.), On,Can
112/D5 Mission, Tx,US
108/C4 Mission Viejo, Ca,US
107/M2 Missisa (lake), On,Can
110/E1 Missisicabi (riv.), On,Can
111/Q8 Mississauga, On,Can
105/J6 Mississippi (delta), US
105/H5 Mississippi (riv.), US
113/F3 Mississippi (state), US
78/C5 Missol (isl.), Indo.
106/E4 Missoula, Mt,US
105/G3 Missouri (riv.), US
109/J3 Missouri (state), US
112/E4 Missouri City, Tx,US
107/H3 Missouri, Coteau du (upland), Can., US
76/B3 Mistake (cr.), Austl.
111/L2 Mistaken (pt.), Can.
111/F1 Mistassibi (riv.), Qu,Can
110/F1 Mistassini, Qu,Can
110/F1 Mistassini (lake), Qu,Can
111/F1 Mistassini (riv.), Qu,Can
39/J4 Mistelbach an der Zaya, Aus.
35/H3 Mistley, Eng,UK
49/H4 Mistrás (ruins), Gre.
48/D4 Mistretta, It.
114/M4 Misty Fjords Nat'l Mon., Ak,US
65/M10 Misugi, Japan
101/N9 Mita (pt.), Mex.
65/H7 Mitaka, Japan
34/D3 Mitcheldean, Eng,UK
76/A1 Mitchell (riv.), Austl.
113/H3 Mitchell (mtn.), NC,US
109/G2 Mitchell, Ne,US
107/J5 Mitchell, SD,US
76/A1 Mitchell & Alice Rivers Nat'l Park, Austl.
59/H6 Mīt Ghamr, Egypt
70/B2 Mithankot, Pak.
61/J4 Mithi, Pak.
79/K6 Mitiaro (isl.), CookIs.
49/K3 Mitilíni, Gre.
86/C2 Mitla (pass), Egypt
100/B4 Mitla (ruins), Mex.
65/G2 Mito, Japan
82/G7 Mitra (peak), EqG.
97/L8 Mitre (pen.), Arg.
31/T10 Mitry-Mory, Fr.
89/H7 Mitsinjo, Madg.
89/J6 Mitsio, Nosy (isl.), Madg.
83/N4 Mits'iwa, Erit.
65/F2 Mitsukaidō, Japan
65/F2 Mitsuke, Japan
41/F4 Mittelland (can.), Ger.
41/E3 Mittelradde (riv.), Ger.
38/G3 Mittweida, Ger.
87/E2 Mitumba (mts.), Zaire
87/E2 Mitwaba, Zaire
65/H7 Miura, Japan
65/H7 Miura (pen.), Japan
100/C5 Mixco Viejo (ruins), Guat.
65/M10 Miya (riv.), Japan
65/G1 Miyagi (pref.), Japan
63/N4 Miyako, Japan
67/E3 Miyako (isl.), Japan
64/B5 Miyakonojō, Japan
64/B5 Miyanojō, Japan
65/H6 Miyashiro, Japan
64/B4 Miyazaki (pref.), Japan
64/D3 Miyazu, Japan
66/D2 Miyun, China
66/D2 Miyun (res.), China
32/B6 Mizen Head (pt.), Ire.
51/H3 Mizil, Rom.
71/F3 Mizoram (state), India
65/E3 Mizunami, Japan
37/E4 Mjölby, Swe.
37/D3 Mjøsa (lake), Nor.
82/D1 Mkorn (peak), Mor.
89/F2 Mkuze (riv.), SAfr.
45/L1 Mladá Boleslav, Czh.
50/E3 Mladenovac, Yugo.
39/L2 Mł'awa, Pol.
50/C4 Mljet (isl.), Cro.
50/C4 Mljet Nat'l Park, Cro.
37/E2 Mo, Nor.
73/G5 Moa (isl.), Indo.
84/C5 Moa (riv.), Libr., SLeo.
108/E3 Moab, Ut,US
78/H6 Moala Group (isls.), Fiji
46/A1 Moaña, Sp.
87/B1 Moanda, Gabon
60/F2 Mobārakeh, Iran
109/J3 Moberly, Mo,US
106/C2 Moberly Lake, BC,Can
113/F4 Mobile, Al,US
107/H4 Mobridge, SD,US
93/J4 Mocajuba, Braz.
87/B4 Moçâmedes, Ang.
69/D4 Moc Hoa, Viet.
88/D2 Mochudi, Bots.
92/C3 Mocoa, Col.
95/G6 Mococa, Braz.
70/B3 Modāsa, India
34/C6 Modbury, Eng,UK
88/D3 Modderrivier (riv.), SAfr.
45/J4 Modena, It.
45/G2 Moder (riv.), Fr., Ger.
108/B3 Modesto, Ca,US
48/D4 Modica, It.
82/H4 Modjigo (reg.), Niger
39/J4 Mödling, Aus.
50/D3 Modriča, Bosn.
69/E3 Mo Duc, Viet.
48/E2 Modugno, It.
77/C3 Moe, Austl.
88/A2 Moeb (bay), Namb.
44/B3 Moëlan-sur-Mer, Fr.
33/E5 Moel Fammau (mtn.), Wal,UK
33/E6 Moel Fferna (mtn.), Wal,UK
34/C1 Moelfre (mtn.), UK
34/C2 Moel Hywel (mtn.), Wal,UK
33/E6 Moel Sych (mtn.), Wal,UK
34/C2 Moel y Llyn (mtn.), UK
78/E4 Moen, Micr.
108/E3 Moenkopi (dry riv.), Az,US
79/K7 Moerai, FrPol.
40/D6 Moers, Ger.
42/C1 Moervaart (can.), Belg.
32/E1 Moffat, Sc,UK
61/L2 Moga, India
83/Q7 Mogadishu (cap.), Som.
65/G2 Mogami (riv.), Japan
47/L6 Mogent (riv.), Sp.
95/G8 Mogi das Cruzes, Braz.
95/G7 Mogi-Guaçu, Braz.
54/D1 Mogilëv, Bela.
54/D1 Mogilëv Obl., Bela.
54/C2 Mogilev-Podol'skiy, Ukr.
39/J2 Mogilno, Pol.
95/F7 Mogi-Mirim, Braz.
63/H1 Mogocha, Rus.
71/G3 Mogok, Burma
97/F3 Mogotes (pt.), Arg.
46/B4 Moguer, Sp.
50/D3 Mohács, Hun.
107/H3 Mohall, ND,US
81/R16 Mohammadia, Alg.
81/L14 Mohammedia, Mor.
110/F3 Mohawk (riv.), NY,US
89/G6 Mohéli (isl.), Com.
87/D4 Mohembo, Bots.
114/E3 Mohican (cape), Ak,US
41/F6 Möhne (riv.), Ger.
41/F6 Möhnestausee (res.), Ger.
51/H2 Moineşti, Rom.
68/A3 Moinkum (des.), Kaz.
85/E5 Moinsi (hills), Gha.
110/E2 Moira (riv.), On,Can
44/F4 Moirans, Fr.
103/K3 Moisie (riv.), Qu,Can
44/D4 Moissac, Fr.
47/Q10 Moita, Port.
108/C4 Mojave (des.), Ca,US
95/G7 Moji-Guaçu (riv.), Braz.
107/L3 Mojikit (lake), On,Can
92/E6 Mojos (plain), Bol.
93/J4 Moju (riv.), Braz.
65/F2 Mōka, Japan
104/W13 Mokapu (pt.), Hi,US
108/B3 Mokelumne (riv.), Ca,US
116/Q16 Mokena, Il,US
78/F4 Mokil (atoll), Micr.
69/B3 Mokochu (peak), Thai.
71/F2 Mokokchūng, India
82/H5 Mokolo, Camr.
63/K5 Mokp'o, SKor.
50/E3 Mokrin, Yugo.
55/G1 Moksha (riv.), Rus.
43/E1 Mol, Belg.
50/E3 Mol, Yugo.
48/E2 Mola di Bari, It.
50/B3 Molat (isl.), Cro.
46/E3 Molatón (mtn.), Sp.
33/E5 Mold, Wal,UK
51/H2 Moldavia (reg.), Rom.
51/G2 Moldavian Carpathians (range), Rom.
37/C3 Molde, Nor.
54/C3 Moldova
51/H2 Moldova (riv.), Rom.
50/E3 Moldova Nouă, Rom.
51/G3 Moldoveanu (peak), Rom.
31/M7 Mole (riv.), Eng,UK
88/D2 Molepolole, Bots.
48/E2 Molfetta, It.
66/F2 Molihong Shan (peak), China
96/C2 Molina, Chile
46/E3 Molina de Segura, Sp.
110/B3 Moline, Il,US
48/D2 Molise (reg.), It.
45/K3 Möll (riv.), Aus.
37/D5 Møllebjerg (peak), Den.
92/D7 Mollendo, Peru
47/F2 Mollerussa, Sp.
96/C2 Molles (pt.), Chile
47/L6 Mollet del Vallès, Sp.
47/L7 Mollins de Rei, Sp.
38/F2 Mölln, Ger.
52/E5 Molodechno, Bela.
98/D Molodezhnaya, Ant.
52/H4 Mologa (riv.), Rus.
104/T10 Molokai (isl.), Hi,US
53/L4 Moloma (riv.), Rus.
88/C2 Molopo (Moloporivier) (dry riv.), Bots., SAfr.
82/J7 Moloundou, Camr.
107/J2 Molson (lake), Mb,Can
73/H5 Molu (isl.), Indo.
73/G4 Molucca (sea), Indo.
73/G3 Moluccas (isls.), Indo.
94/C2 Mombaça, Braz.
87/G1 Mombasa, Kenya
63/N3 Mombetsu, Japan
51/G5 Momchilgrad, Bul.
73/H4 Momfafa (cape), Indo.
101/G6 Mompós, Col.
71/F3 Mon (riv.), Burma
69/B3 Mon (state), Burma
38/G1 Møn (isl.), Den.
101/H4 Mona (passage), DRep., PR
45/G5 Monaco
45/G5 Monaco (cap.), Mona.
32/B3 Monaghan, Ire.
32/A3 Monaghan (co.), Ire.
101/E6 Monagrillo (ruins), Pan.
112/C4 Monahans, Tx,US
106/D3 Monashee (mts.), BC,Can
76/H8 Mona Vale, Austl.
47/E3 Moncada, Sp.
45/G4 Moncalieri, It.
67/E6 Moncayo, Phil.
46/D2 Moncayo (range), Sp.
52/G2 Monchegorsk, Rus.
40/D6 Mönchengladbach, Ger.
46/A4 Monchique, Port.
46/A4 Monchique (range), Port.
113/H3 Moncks Corner, SC,US
100/A2 Monclova, Mex.
111/H2 Moncton, NB,Can
46/A2 Mondego (cape), Port.
46/A2 Mondego (riv.), Port.
46/B1 Mondoñedo, Sp.
43/F5 Mondorf-les-Bains, Lux.
45/G4 Mondovì, It.
46/D1 Mondragón, Sp.
48/C2 Mondragone, It.
46/B1 Monesterio, Sp.
109/J3 Monett, Mo,US
32/C2 Money Head (pt.), Sc,UK
32/B2 Moneymore, NI,UK
32/C2 Moneyreagh, NI,UK
45/K4 Monfalcone, It.
45/H4 Monferrato (reg.), It.
46/B1 Monforte, Sp.
95/G9 Mongaguá, Braz.
69/D1 Mong Cai, Viet.
74/B5 Mongers (lake), Austl.
70/E2 Monghyr, India
83/J5 Mongo, Chad
84/C4 Mongo (riv.), Gui., SLeo.
62/D2 Mongolia
83/K5 Mongororo, Chad
87/B1 Mongoungou, Gabon
87/D4 Mongu, Zam.
68/F2 Mönh Hayrhan Uul (peak), Mong.
62/E1 Mönh Sarĭdag (peak), Mong.
32/E1 Moniaive, Sc,UK
47/K6 Monistrol de Montserrat, Sp.
108/C3 Monitor (range), Nv,US
39/M2 Mońki, Pol.
87/D1 Monkoto, Zaire
34/D3 Monmouth, Eng,UK
110/B3 Monmouth, Il,US
106/C4 Monmouth, Or,US
115/G5 Monmouth Beach, NJ,US
34/D2 Monnow (riv.), UK
40/C4 Monnickendam, Neth.
85/F5 Mono (prov.), Ben.
85/F5 Mono (riv.), Ben., Togo
108/C3 Mono (lake), Ca,US
48/E2 Monopoli, It.
50/D2 Monor, Hun.
111/Q8 Mono Road, On,Can
47/E3 Monóvar, Sp.
48/C3 Monreale, It.
113/H3 Monroe, Ga,US
112/E3 Monroe, La,US
110/D3 Monroe, Mi,US
113/H3 Monroe, NC,US
108/D3 Monroe, Ut,US
110/B3 Monroe, Wi,US
113/G4 Monroeville, Al,US
84/C5 Monrovia (cap.), Libr.
115/C2 Monrovia, Ca,US
42/C3 Mons, Belg.
43/F2 Monschau, Ger.
45/J4 Monselice, It.
115/F4 Monsey, NY,US
40/B4 Monster, Neth.
37/F4 Mönsteras, Swe.
89/J6 Montagne d'Ambre Nat'l Park, Madg.
31/U9 Montagny-Sainte-Félicité, Fr.
111/J2 Montague, PE,Can
114/L3 Montague, Yk,Can
114/J4 Montague (isl.), Ak,US
114/J4 Montague (str.), Ak,US
112/D3 Montague, Tx,US
48/E2 Montalbano Jonico, It.
106/F4 Montana (state), US
95/D1 Montanha, Braz.
44/E3 Montargis, Fr.
42/B5 Montataire, Fr.
44/D4 Montauban, Fr.
87/E6 Mont aux Sources (peak), Les.
44/F3 Montbard, Fr.
45/G3 Montbéliard, Fr.
47/L7 Montcada i Reixac, Sp.
44/F3 Montceau-les-Mines, Fr.
115/C2 Montclair, Ca,US
44/C5 Mont-de-Marsan, Fr.
42/B4 Montdidier, Fr.
100/B4 Monte Albán (ruins), Mex.
93/H4 Monte Alegre, Braz.
94/D2 Monte Alegre, Braz.
95/B1 Monte Alegre de Minas, Braz.
94/A3 Monte Alegre do Piauí, Braz.
95/B2 Monte Alto, Braz.
94/B4 Monte Azul, Braz.
74/A4 Montebello (isls.), Austl.
115/B2 Montebello, Ca,US
91/F2 Montecarlo, Arg.
95/C1 Monte Carmelo, Braz.
101/G6 Monte Carmelo, Ven.
91/E3 Monte Caseros, Arg.
101/G4 Monte Cristo, DRep.
48/B1 Montecristo (isl.), It.
46/C4 Montefrío, Sp.
101/F4 Montego Bay, Jam.
94/C2 Monteiro, Braz.
47/P10 Montelavar, Port.
44/F4 Montélimar, Fr.
46/C4 Montellano, Sp.
108/D2 Montello, Nv,US
96/D5 Montemayor (plat.), Arg.
100/B2 Montemorelos, Mex.
46/A3 Montemor-o-Novo, Port.
46/A2 Montemuro (mtn.), Port.
95/B4 Montenegro, Braz.
50/D4 Montenegro (rep.), Yugo.
48/D2 Montenero di Bisaccia, It.
38/B5 Montenoison, Butte de (mtn.), Fr.
94/C5 Monte Pascoal Nat'l Park, Braz.
44/E2 Montereau-faut-Yonne, Fr.
108/B3 Monterey, Ca,US
108/B3 Monterey (bay), Ca,US
115/B2 Monterey Park, Ca,US
101/F6 Montería, Col.
92/F7 Montero, Bol.
91/C2 Monteros, Arg.
48/C1 Monterotondo, It.
100/A2 Monterrey, Mex.
97/K7 Montes (pt.), Arg.
48/D2 Monte Sant'Angelo, It.
48/E2 Montescaglioso, It.
94/B5 Montes Claros, Braz.
48/D1 Montesilvano Marina, It.
31/S10 Montesson, Fr.
44/F4 Monteux, Fr.
97/F2 Montevideo (cap.), Uru.
97/T12 Montevideo (dept.), Uru.
107/K4 Montevideo, Mn,US
31/U10 Montévrain, Fr.
43/E5 Montfaucon, Fr.
31/T10 Montfermeil, Fr.
40/B4 Montfoort, Neth.
31/T10 Montgeron, Fr.
34/C1 Montgomery, Wal,UK
113/G3 Montgomery (cap.), Al,US
110/D4 Montgomery, WV,US
115/J7 Montgomery Village, Md,US
115/E5 Montgomeryville, Pa,US
44/E5 Montgrand (mtn.), Fr.
45/G3 Monthey, Swi.
31/U9 Monthyon, Fr.
112/F3 Monticello, Ar,US
116/K9 Monticello (dam), Ca,US
113/H4 Monticello, Fl,US
110/C3 Monticello, In,US
110/C4 Monticello, Ky,US
109/K2 Monticello, Mo,US
108/E3 Monticello, Ut,US
110/E4 Monticello, Va,US
42/B3 Montigny-en-Gohelle, Fr.
31/S10 Montigny-le-Bretonneux, Fr.
31/S10 Montigny-lès-Cormeilles, Fr.
43/F5 Montigny-lès-Metz, Fr.
42/D3 Montigny-le-Tilleul, Belg.
46/A3 Montijo, Port.
46/B3 Montijo, Sp.
46/C4 Montilla, Sp.
44/D2 Montivilliers, Fr.
111/G1 Mont-Joli, Qu,Can
110/F2 Mont-Laurier, Qu,Can
31/S11 Montlhéry, Fr.
44/E3 Montluçon, Fr.
111/G2 Montmagny, Qu,Can
31/S10 Montmorency, Fr.
44/D3 Montmorillon, Fr.
46/C3 Montoro, Sp.
84/D5 Mont Peko Nat'l Park, IvC.
106/F5 Montpelier, Id,US
111/F2 Montpelier (cap.), Vt,US
44/E5 Montpellier, Fr.
110/C2 Montreal (riv.), On,Can
111/N7 Montréal, Qu,Can
107/G2 Montreal (lake), Sk,Can
42/A3 Montreuil, Fr.
45/G3 Montreux, Swi.
36/D2 Montrose, Sc,UK
108/F3 Montrose, Co,US
31/S10 Montrouge, Fr.
111/N6 Mont-Royal, Qu,Can
31/U10 Montry, Fr.
111/P6 Mont-Saint-Hilaire, Qu,Can
43/E4 Mont-Saint-Martin, Fr.
110/F2 Mont-Saint-Michel, Qu,Can
44/C2 Mont-Saint-Michel, Fr.
44/C2 Mont-Saint-Michel (bay), Fr.
84/D4 Mont Sangbé Nat'l Park, IvC.
47/L6 Montseny Nat'l Park, Sp.
84/C5 Montserrado (co.), Libr.
47/F2 Montserrat (mtn.), Sp.
101/J4 Montserrat (isl.), UK
31/S9 Montsoult, Fr.
115/F5 Montville, NJ,US
109/G4 Monument Draw (cr.), NM, Tx,US
71/G3 Monywa, Burma
45/H4 Monza, It.
87/E4 Monze, Zam.
47/F2 Monzón, Sp.
88/P13 Mool (riv.), SAfr.
76/D4 Mooloolaba-Maroochydore, Austl.
77/G5 Moorabbin, Austl.
107/G4 Moorcroft, Wy,US
74/B5 Moore (lake), Austl.
111/R8 Moore (pt.), On,Can
109/H4 Moore, Ok,US
79/K6 Moorea (isl.), FrPol.
113/H5 Moore Haven, Fl,US
115/F6 Moorestown, NJ,US
113/H3 Mooresville, NC,US
107/J4 Moorhead, Mn,US
42/C2 Moorslede, Belg.
45/J2 Moosburg, Ger.
110/D1 Moose (riv.), On,Can
107/H3 Moose (mtn.), Sk,Can
110/D1 Moose Factory, On,Can
111/G2 Moosehead (lake), Me,US
114/H3 Mooseheart (mtn.), Ak,US
107/G3 Moose Jaw, Sk,Can
107/H3 Moosomin, Sk,Can
110/D1 Moosonee, On,Can
84/D3 Mopti, Mali
84/E3 Mopti (reg.), Mali
92/D7 Moquegua, Peru
50/D2 Mór, Hun.
82/H5 Mora, Camr.
46/D3 Mora, Sp.
37/E3 Mora, Swe.
109/F4 Mora, NM,US
109/F4 Mora (riv.), NM,US
49/F1 Morača (riv.), Yugo.
70/C2 Morādābād, India
94/C2 Morada Nova, Braz.
95/C1 Morada Nova de Mina, Braz.
96/C2 Morado Nat'l Park, Chile
89/H7 Morafenobe, Madg.
39/K2 Morąg, Pol.
116/K11 Moraga, Ca,US
31/R10 Morainvilliers, Fr.
96/B5 Moraleda (chan.), Chile
46/B2 Moraleja, Sp.
100/D4 Morales, Guat.
108/E2 Moran, Wy,US
76/C3 Moranbah, Austl.
79/M7 Morane (isl.), FrPol.
31/T10 Morangis, Fr.
46/E3 Moratalla, Sp.
39/J4 Morava (riv.), Czh.
49/G1 Morava (riv.), Yugo.
39/J4 Moravia (reg.), Czh.
39/J4 Moravská Třebová, Czh.
39/H4 Moravské Budějovice, Czh.
43/G4 Morbach, Ger.
42/B2 Morbecque, Fr.
45/H3 Morbegno, It.
37/F4 Mörbylånga, Swe.
107/J3 Morden, Mb,Can
35/G4 Morden, Eng,UK
77/G6 Mordialloc, Austl.
55/G1 Mordvian Aut. Rep., Rus.
107/H4 Moreau (riv.), SD,US
36/D3 Morebattle, Sc,UK
33/F3 Morecambe, Eng,UK
33/E3 Morecambe (bay), Eng,UK
77/D1 Moree, Austl.
110/D4 Morehead, Ky,US
113/J3 Morehead City, NC,US
100/A4 Morelia, Mex.
100/B4 Morelos (state), Mex.
70/C2 Morena, India
46/C3 Morena (range), Sp.
51/G3 Moreni, Rom.
115/C3 Moreno Valley, Ca,US
37/C3 Møre og Romsdal (co.), Nor.
115/B2 Morepack, Ca,US
102/C3 Moresby (isl.), BC,Can
76/F6 Moreton (bay), Austl.
76/D4 Moreton (cape), Austl.
31/P6 Moreton, Eng,UK
34/C5 Moretonhampstead, Eng,UK
76/D4 Moreton I. Nat'l Park, Austl.
35/E3 Moreton in Marsh, Eng,UK
53/N2 Moreyu (riv.), Rus.
44/G3 Morez, Fr.
113/F4 Morgan City, La,US
110/C4 Morganfield, Ky,US
48/D4 Morgantina (ruins), It.
113/H3 Morganton, NC,US
110/C4 Morgantown, Ky,US
110/E4 Morgantown, WV,US
44/E3 Morge (riv.), Fr.
45/G3 Morges, Swi.
61/H1 Morghāb (riv.), Afg.
96/B3 Morguilla (pt.), Chile
62/C3 Mori, China
45/J4 Mori, It.
109/F4 Moriarty, NM,US
106/B2 Morice (lake), BC,Can
65/L10 Moriguchi, Japan
41/G5 Moringen, Ger.
106/E2 Morinville, Ab,Can
63/N4 Morioka, Japan
65/H7 Moriya, Japan
64/D3 Moriyama, Japan
44/B2 Morlaix, Fr.
42/D3 Morlanwelz, Belg.
33/G4 Morley, Eng,UK
70/B4 Mormugao, India
76/F6 Morningside, Austl.
74/F3 Mornington (isl.), Austl.
97/J7 Mornington (isl.), Chile
61/J3 Moro, Pak.
67/D6 Moro (gulf), Phil.
82/C1 Morocco
87/G2 Morogoro, Tanz.
77/C3 Moroka-Wonnangatta Nat'l Park, Austl.
89/G8 Morombe, Madg.
96/F2 Morón, Arg.
101/F3 Morón, Cuba
92/C4 Morona (riv.), Ecu., Peru
89/H8 Morondara (riv.), Madg.
89/H8 Morondava, Madg.
46/C4 Morón de la Frontera, Sp.
89/G5 Moroni (cap.), Com.
73/G3 Morotai (isl.), Indo.
73/G3 Morotai (str.), Indo.
83/M7 Moroto, Ugan.
65/H7 Moroyama, Japan
55/G2 Morozovsk, Rus.
33/G1 Morpeth, Eng,UK
59/J4 Morphou, Cyp.
59/J4 Morphou (bay), Cyp.
40/C3 Morra (lake), Neth.
109/G2 Morrill, Ne,US
95/B1 Morrinhos, Braz.
107/J3 Morris, Mb,Can
110/B3 Morris, Il,US

107/K4 **Morris,** Mn,US
99/P1 **Morris Jesup** (cape), Grld.
115/F5 **Morris Plains,** NJ,US
34/C3 **Morriston,** Wal,UK
115/F5 **Morristown,** NJ,US
113/H2 **Morristown,** Tn,US
115/F5 **Morrisville,** Pa,US
108/B4 **Morro Bay,** Ca,US
87/C3 **Morro de Môco** (peak), Ang.
95/B3 **Morro do Capão Doce** (hill), Braz.
94/B3 **Morro do Chapéu,** Braz.
31/T11 **Morsang-sur-Orge,** Fr.
43/G2 **Morsbach,** Ger.
55/G1 **Morshansk,** Rus.
55/J3 **Morskoy** (isl.), Kaz.
34/B4 **Morte** (pt.), UK
93/H6 **Mortes** (riv.), Braz.
35/E4 **Mortimer,** Eng,UK
34/D2 **Mortimers Cross,** Eng,UK
110/B3 **Morton,** Il,US
116/Q15 **Morton Grove,** Il,US
77/D2 **Morton Nat'l Park,** Austl.
42/D1 **Mortsel,** Belg.
44/E3 **Morvan** (plat.), Fr.
70/B3 **Morvi,** India
77/C3 **Morwell,** Austl.
46/A1 **Mos,** Sp.
45/H2 **Mosbach,** Ger.
47/P10 **Moscavide,** Port.
52/G5 **Moscow** (upland), Rus.
106/D4 **Moscow,** Id,US
52/H5 **Moscow** (Moskva) (cap.), Rus.
53/X9 **Moscow** (Moskva) (inset) (cap.), Rus.
52/H5 **Moscow Obl.,** Rus.
98/H **Moscow Univ. Ice Shelf,** Ant.
43/F4 **Mosel** (riv.), Ger.
42/F5 **Moselle** (dept.), Fr.
43/F5 **Moselle** (riv.), Fr.
106/D4 **Moses Lake,** Wa,US
75/R12 **Mosgiel,** NZ
88/C2 **Moshaweng** (dry riv.), SAfr.
87/G1 **Moshi,** Tanz.
39/J2 **Mosina,** Pol.
37/E2 **Mosjøen,** Nor.
52/G5 **Moskva** (riv.), Rus.
53/X9 **Moskva** (Moscow) (inset) (cap.), Rus.
50/C2 **Mosonmagyaróvár,** Hun.
109/G4 **Mosquero,** NM,US
100/E6 **Mosquitos** (gulf), Pan.
100/E5 **Mosquitos, Costa de** (coast), Nic.
37/D4 **Moss,** Nor.
84/E4 **Mossi Highlands** (upland), Burk.
45/H2 **Mössingen,** Ger.
33/F4 **Mossley,** Eng,UK
32/C2 **Mossley,** NI,UK
94/C2 **Mossoró,** Braz.
113/F4 **Moss Point,** Ms,US
32/B1 **Moss-side,** NI,UK
45/K1 **Most,** Czh.
81/R16 **Mostaganem,** Alg.
50/C4 **Mostar,** Bosn.
46/D2 **Móstoles,** Sp.
33/E5 **Mostyn,** Wal,UK
59/E3 **Mosul** (Al Mawçil), Iraq
100/D4 **Motagua** (riv.), Guat.
37/E4 **Motala,** Swe.
66/E2 **Motian Ling** (mtn.), China
70/D2 **Motīhāri,** India
65/G2 **Motomiya,** Japan
37/K1 **Motovskiy** (gulf), Rus.
46/D4 **Motril,** Sp.
107/H4 **Mott,** ND,US
75/R11 **Motueka,** NZ
100/D3 **Motul,** Mex.
56/K4 **Motygino,** Rus.
84/B2 **Mougris** (well), Mrta.
84/E3 **Mouhoun** (prov.), Burk.
87/B1 **Mouila,** Gabon
82/H4 **Moul** (well), Niger
77/C2 **Moulamein** (riv.), Austl.
33/F5 **Mouldsworth,** Eng,UK
44/E3 **Moulins,** Fr.
69/B2 **Moulmein,** Burma
81/N13 **Moulouya** (riv.), Mor.
35/G2 **Moulton,** Eng,UK
113/H4 **Moultrie,** Ga,US
113/H3 **Moultrie** (lake), SC,US
109/J3 **Mound City,** Ks,US
82/J6 **Moundou,** Chad
110/D4 **Moundsville,** WV,US
69/C3 **Moung Roessei,** Camb.
69/D3 **Mounlapamok,** Laos
76/B3 **Mount Aberdeen Nat'l Park,** Austl.
70/B3 **Mount Abu,** India
102/D2 **Mountain** (riv.), NW,Can
34/C3 **Mountain Ash,** Wal,UK
113/G3 **Mountain Brook,** Al,US
109/J3 **Mountain Grove,** Mo,US
112/E2 **Mountain Home,** Ar,US
106/E5 **Mountain Home,** Id,US
112/E3 **Mountain View,** Ar,US
116/K12 **Mountain View,** Ca,US
88/D4 **Mountain Zebra Nat'l Park,** SAfr.
113/H2 **Mount Airy,** NC,US
74/B6 **Mount Barker,** Austl.
77/A2 **Mount Barker,** Austl.
76/C5 **Mount Barney Nat'l Park,** Austl.
77/C3 **Mount Buffalo Nat'l Park,** Austl.
110/C4 **Mount Carmel,** Il,US
83/M2 **Mount Catherine** (peak), Egypt
116/G6 **Mount Clemens,** Mi,US
76/E6 **Mount Coot'tha,** Austl.
87/F4 **Mount Darwin,** Zim.
77/B3 **Mount Eccles Nat'l Park,** Austl.
76/B2 **Mount Elliot Nat'l Park,** Austl.
77/B3 **Mount Emu** (cr.), Austl.
77/C4 **Mount Field Nat'l Park,** Austl.
77/B3 **Mount Gambier,** Austl.
78/D5 **Mount Hagen,** PNG
115/F6 **Mount Holly,** NJ,US
111/Q9 **Mount Hope,** On,Can
77/D3 **Mount Imlay Nat'l Park,** Austl.
74/F4 **Mount Isa,** Austl.
77/D1 **Mount Kaputar Nat'l Park,** Austl.
115/G4 **Mount Kisco,** NY,US
116/C2 **Mountlake Terrace,** Wa,US
115/F6 **Mount Laurel,** NJ,US
74/F6 **Mount Lofty** (ranges), Austl.
75/S10 **Mount Maunganui,** NZ
76/D4 **Mount Mistake Nat'l Park,** Austl.
110/D3 **Mount Morris,** Mi,US
76/E6 **Mount Nebo,** Austl.
31/Q7 **Mountnessing,** Eng,UK
113/J3 **Mount Olive,** NC,US
49/H3 **Mount Parnes Nat'l Park,** Gre.
111/L2 **Mount Pearl,** Nf,Can
107/L5 **Mount Pleasant,** Ia,US
110/C3 **Mount Pleasant,** Mi,US
112/E3 **Mount Pleasant,** Tx,US
108/E3 **Mount Pleasant,** Ut,US
116/Q15 **Mount Prospect,** Il,US
115/K8 **Mount Rainier,** Md,US
106/C4 **Mount Rainier Nat'l Park,** Wa,US
106/D3 **Mount Revelstoke Nat'l Park,** BC,Can
77/B3 **Mount Richmond Nat'l Park,** Austl.
109/G2 **Mount Rushmore Nat'l Mem.,** SD,US
34/A6 **Mount's** (bay), Eng,UK
76/B2 **Mount Spec Nat'l Park,** Austl.
110/D4 **Mount Sterling,** Ky,US
110/B4 **Mount Vernon,** Il,US
110/C4 **Mount Vernon,** In,US
115/G5 **Mount Vernon,** NY,US
110/D3 **Mount Vernon,** Oh,US
115/J8 **Mount Vernon,** Va,US
106/C3 **Mount Vernon,** Wa,US
76/C4 **Mount Walsh Nat'l Park,** Austl.
77/E1 **Mount Warning Nat'l Park,** Austl.
77/D4 **Mount William Nat'l Park,** Austl.
46/B3 **Moura,** Port.
44/C5 **Mourenx,** Fr.
32/B3 **Mourne** (dist.), NI,UK
32/B3 **Mourne** (mts.), NI,UK
42/C2 **Mouscron,** Belg.
82/J5 **Moussoro,** Chad
31/T9 **Moussy-le-Neuf,** Fr.
42/C2 **Mouvaux,** Fr.
94/C3 **Moxotó** (riv.), Braz.
32/B3 **Moy,** NI,UK
83/N7 **Moyalē,** Eth.
82/D1 **Moyen Atlas** (mts.), Mor.
43/F5 **Moyeuvre-Grande,** Fr.
32/B2 **Moygashel,** NI,UK
32/B1 **Moyle** (dist.), NI,UK
73/E5 **Moyo** (isl.), Indo.
68/C4 **Moyu,** China
87/G4 **Mozambique**
87/G5 **Mozambique** (chan.), Afr.
52/H5 **Mozhaysk,** Rus.
53/M4 **Mozhga,** Rus.
54/D1 **Mozyr',** Bela.
87/F2 **Mpanda,** Tanz.
87/C4 **Mpangu,** Namb.
87/F3 **Mpika,** Zam.
87/F2 **Mporokoso,** Zam.
85/E5 **Mpraeso,** Gha.
39/L2 **Mrągowo,** Pol.
50/C3 **Mrkonjić Grad,** Bosn.
81/T16 **M'Sila,** Alg.
81/T16 **M'Sila** (riv.), Alg.
81/N13 **Msoun** (riv.), Mor.
52/G4 **Msta** (riv.), Rus.
39/L4 **Mszana Dolna,** Pol.
54/F1 **Mtsensk,** Rus.
87/H3 **Mtwara,** Tanz.
87/G4 **Mualama,** Moz.
69/D2 **Muang Gnommarat,** Laos
69/C2 **Muang Kenthao,** Laos
69/D3 **Muang Khong,** Laos
69/D3 **Muang Khongxedon,** Laos
69/D3 **Muang Lakhonpheng,** Laos
69/D1 **Muang Soy,** Laos
69/C2 **Muang Thathom,** Laos
69/D2 **Muang Xamteu,** Laos
69/D2 **Muang Xepon,** Laos
72/B3 **Muar,** Malay.
72/B4 **Muarabungo,** Indo.
61/J4 **Muāri** (pt.), Pak.
82/H5 **Mubi,** Nga.
92/F3 **Mucajaí** (riv.), Braz.
43/G2 **Much,** Ger.
87/F3 **Muchinga** (mts.), Zam.
34/D1 **Much Wenlock,** Eng,UK
32/B2 **Muckamore Abbey,** NI,UK
87/H3 **Mucojo,** Moz.
59/C2 **Mucur,** Turk.
95/D1 **Mucuri** (riv.), Braz.
87/D3 **Mucussueje,** Ang.
63/K3 **Mudanjiang,** China
51/J5 **Mudanya,** Turk.
63/K2 **Muddan** (riv.), China
37/F2 **Muddas Nat'l Park,** Swe.
108/E3 **Muddy** (riv.), Ut,US
109/H4 **Muddy Boggy** (cr.), Ok,US
43/G2 **Mudersbach,** Ger.
77/D2 **Mudgee,** Austl.
106/G1 **Mudjatik** (riv.), Sk,Can
116/D3 **Mud Mountain** (lake), Wa,US
69/B2 **Mudon,** Burma
97/J8 **Muela** (peak), Chile
59/N8 **Mufjir, Nahr** (dry riv.), WBnk.
87/E3 **Mufulira,** Zam.
46/A1 **Mugardos,** Sp.
45/K4 **Muggia,** It.
46/A1 **Mugia,** Sp.
59/B3 **Muğla,** Turk.
55/L2 **Mugodzharskoye** (mts.), Kaz.
87/F2 **Mugombazi,** Tanz.
86/D4 **Muḩammad Qawl,** Sudan
86/C3 **Muḩammad, Ra's** (pt.), Egypt
87/E3 **Muhila** (mts.), Zaire
45/K2 **Mühlviertel** (reg.), Aus.
37/H2 **Muhos,** Fin.
60/C2 **Mūḩ, Sabkhat al** (lake), Syria
52/D4 **Muhu** (isl.), Est.
40/C4 **Muiden,** Neth.
36/C3 **Muirkirk,** Sc,UK
36/C2 **Muir of Ord,** Sc,UK
116/J11 **Muir Woods Nat'l Mon.,** Ca,US
63/K4 **Muju,** SKor.
54/B2 **Mukachevo,** Ukr.
86/D4 **Mukawwar** (isl.), Sudan
107/M2 **Muketei** (riv.), On,Can
59/L5 **Mukhayyam al Yarmūk,** Syria
116/C2 **Mukilteo,** Wa,US
65/L10 **Mukō,** Japan
78/D2 **Mukoshima** (isls.), Japan
69/B4 **Mu Ko Similan Nat'l Park,** Thai.
69/B4 **Mu Ko Surin Nat'l Park,** Thai.
61/K2 **Muktsar,** India
46/E3 **Mula,** Sp.
87/G4 **Mulanje,** Malw.
114/G4 **Mulchatna** (riv.), Ak,US
96/B3 **Mulchén,** Chile
38/G3 **Mulde** (riv.), Ger.
98/D **Mule** (pt.), Ant.
46/D4 **Mulhacén, Cerro de** (mtn.), Sp.
38/F3 **Mülhausen,** Ger.
40/D6 **Mülheim an der Ruhr,** Ger.
45/G3 **Mulhouse,** Fr.
66/D3 **Muling** (pass), China
63/L2 **Muling** (riv.), China
79/R9 **Mulinu'u** (cape), WSam.
61/L2 **Mulkila** (mtn.), India
32/B5 **Mullaghcleevaun** (mtn.), Ire.
32/B2 **Mullaghmore** (mtn.), NI,UK
109/G2 **Mullen,** Ne,US
72/D4 **Muller** (mts.), Indo.
45/G3 **Müllheim,** Ger.
36/B4 **Mullingar,** Ire.
113/J3 **Mullins,** SC,US
34/A6 **Mullion,** Eng,UK
87/C4 **Mulondo,** Ang.
61/K2 **Multān,** Pak.
106/C3 **Multnomah** (falls), Or,US
72/D3 **Mulu, Gunung** (peak), Malay.
86/B5 **Mulwad,** Sudan
87/C3 **Mumbué,** Ang.
87/E3 **Mumbwa,** Zam.
69/B5 **Mum Nauk** (pt.), Thai.
69/C3 **Mun** (riv.), Thai.
73/F4 **Muna** (isl.), Indo.
37/H4 **Munamägi** (hill), Est.
45/J2 **München** (Munich), Ger.
110/C3 **Muncie,** In,US
116/P15 **Mundelein,** Il,US
85/H5 **Mundemba,** Camr.
38/E3 **Munden,** Ger.
41/G6 **Münden,** Ger.
35/H1 **Mundesley,** Eng,UK
35/G2 **Mundford,** Eng,UK
70/C3 **Mungaolī,** India
77/B2 **Mungo Nat'l Park,** Austl.
68/F1 **Mungun-Tayga, Gora** (peak), Rus.
45/J2 **Munich** (München), Ger.
110/C2 **Munising,** Mi,US
57/L4 **Munku-Sardyk** (peak), Rus.
62/D1 **Munku-Sasan** (peak), Rus.
97/J8 **Muñoz Gamero** (pen.), Chile
41/E5 **Münster,** Ger.
41/H3 **Munster,** Ger.
36/A4 **Munster** (prov.), Ire.
116/Q16 **Munster,** In,US
41/E4 **Münsterland** (reg.), Ger.
51/F2 **Muntele Mare** (peak), Rom.
72/C4 **Muntok,** Indo.
69/D1 **Muong Khuong,** Viet.
37/G1 **Muonioälv** (riv.), Swe.
37/G1 **Muoniojoki** (riv.), Fin.
87/C4 **Mupa Nat'l Park,** Moz.
83/Q7 **Muqdisho** (Mogadishu) (cap.), Som.
45/L3 **Mur** (riv.), Aus.
50/C2 **Mura** (riv.), Slvk.
59/E2 **Muradiye,** Turk.
65/F1 **Murakami,** Japan
97/J7 **Murallón** (peak), Chile
83/N8 **Murang'a,** Kenya
59/E2 **Murat** (riv.), Turk.
54/D5 **Murat Daği** (peak), Turk.
74/B5 **Murchison** (riv.), Austl.
75/R11 **Murchison,** NZ
47/E4 **Murcia,** Sp.
46/E4 **Murcia** (aut. comm.), Sp.
111/H1 **Murdochville,** Qu,Can
76/B1 **Murdock** (pt.), Austl.
51/G2 **Mureş** (co.), Rom.
51/G2 **Mureş** (riv.), Rom.
44/D5 **Muret,** Fr.
112/E3 **Murfreesboro,** Ar,US
113/G3 **Murfreesboro,** Tn,US
61/H1 **Murgab** (riv.), Trkm.
72/D5 **Muria** (peak), Indo.
95/D2 **Muriaé,** Braz.
61/G3 **Mūrīān, Hāmūn-e Jaz** (lake), Iran
94/D3 **Murici,** Braz.
38/G2 **Müritz See** (lake), Ger.
83/N6 **Murle,** Eth.
52/G1 **Murmansk,** Rus.
52/G2 **Murmansk Obl.,** Rus.
65/M10 **Muro,** Japan
47/G3 **Muro,** Sp.
52/J5 **Murom,** Rus.
63/N3 **Muroran,** Japan
46/A1 **Muros,** Sp.
64/D4 **Muroto,** Japan
64/D4 **Muroto-zaki** (pt.), Japan
39/J2 **Murowana Goślina,** Pol.
113/G3 **Murphy,** NC,US
110/B4 **Murphysboro,** Il,US
77/D2 **Murramarang Nat'l Park,** Austl.
77/A2 **Murray** (riv.), Austl.
78/D5 **Murray** (lake), PNG
110/B4 **Murray,** Ky,US
113/H3 **Murray** (lake), SC,US
77/A2 **Murray Bridge,** Austl.
77/C2 **Murrumbidgee** (riv.), Austl.
50/C2 **Murska Sobota,** Slov.
33/G2 **Murton,** Eng,UK
75/S10 **Murupara,** NZ
79/M7 **Mururoa** (isl.), FrPol.
70/D3 **Murwāra,** India
77/E1 **Murwillumbah,** Austl.
39/H5 **Mürz** (riv.), Aus.
45/L3 **Mürzzuschlag,** Aus.
59/E2 **Muş,** Turk.
51/F4 **Musala** (peak), Bul.
61/G3 **Musandam** (pen.), Oman
65/H7 **Musashino,** Japan
61/G4 **Muscat** (Musqaţ) (cap.), Oman
115/E5 **Musconetcong** (riv.), NJ,US
115/C2 **Muscoy,** Ca,US
87/E5 **Musekwapoort** (pass), SAfr.
74/E5 **Musgrave** (ranges), Austl.
111/L1 **Musgrave Harbour,** Nf,Can
70/E3 **Mushābani,** India
59/N9 **Mushāsh, Wādī** (dry riv.), WBnk.
87/C1 **Mushie,** Zaire
72/B4 **Musi** (riv.), Indo.
116/P14 **Muskego,** Wi,US
110/C3 **Muskegon,** Mi,US
110/C3 **Muskegon** (riv.), Mi,US
110/D4 **Muskingum** (riv.), Oh,US
109/J4 **Muskogee,** Ok,US
110/E2 **Muskoka** (lake), On,Can
87/F1 **Musoma,** Tanz.
61/G4 **Musqaţ** (Muscat) (cap.), Oman
111/J1 **Musquaro** (riv.), Qu,Can
78/D5 **Mussau** (isl.), PNG
106/F4 **Musselshell** (riv.), Mt,US
48/C4 **Mussomeli,** It.
59/B2 **Mustafakemalpaşa,** Turk.
70/D2 **Mustāng,** Nepal
109/H4 **Mustang,** Ok,US
45/K2 **Můstek** (peak), Czh.
96/C5 **Musters** (lake), Arg.
63/K3 **Musu-dan** (pt.), NKor.
100/D5 **Musún** (mt.), Nic.
77/D2 **Muswellbrook,** Austl.
86/B3 **Mūt,** Egypt
59/C3 **Mut,** Turk.
94/C4 **Mutá, Ponta do** (pt.), Braz.
87/F4 **Mutare,** Zim.
73/F5 **Mutis** (peak), Indo.
89/H6 **Mutsamudu,** Com.
63/N3 **Mutsu,** Japan
95/D1 **Mutum,** Braz.
55/L4 **Muynak,** Uzb.
61/K2 **Muzaffargarh,** Pak.
70/C2 **Muzaffarnagar,** India
70/E2 **Muzaffarpur,** India
95/G6 **Muzambinho,** Braz.
68/D3 **Muzat** (riv.), China
68/D4 **Muztag** (peak), China
68/E4 **Muztag** (peak), China
68/C4 **Muztagata** (peak), China
87/C2 **Mwadi-Kalumbu,** Zaire
87/F1 **Mwanza,** Tanz.
36/H7 **Mweelrea** (mtn.), Ire.
87/D1 **Mweka,** Zaire
87/D2 **Mwene-Ditu,** Zaire
87/E2 **Mweru** (lake), Zaire, Zam.
77/E2 **Myall Lakes Nat'l Park,** Austl.
71/G4 **Myanaung,** Burma
62/C2 **Myangad,** Mong.
71/G2 **Myanmar** (Burma)
71/F4 **Myaungmya,** Burma
71/G3 **Myingyan,** Burma
71/G2 **Myitkyina,** Burma
39/J4 **Myjava,** Slvk.
34/C2 **Mynydd Eppynt** (mts.), Wal,UK
34/B2 **Mynydd Pencarreg** (mtn.), Wal,UK
71/F3 **Myohaung,** Burma
65/F2 **Myōkō-san** (mtn.), Japan
113/J3 **Myrtle Beach,** SC,US
106/C5 **Myrtle Creek,** Or,US
37/D4 **Mysen,** Nor.
39/K4 **Myślenice,** Pol.
39/H2 **Myślibórz,** Pol.
69/E3 **My Son** (ruins), Viet.
70/C5 **Mysore,** India
39/K3 **Myszków,** Pol.
69/D4 **My Tho,** Viet.
52/H5 **Mytishchi,** Rus.
45/K2 **Mže** (riv.), Czh.
87/F3 **Mzuzu,** Malw.

N

69/C1 **Na** (riv.), Viet.
45/J2 **Naab** (riv.), Ger.
40/B5 **Naaldwijk,** Neth.
40/C4 **Naarden,** Neth.
32/B5 **Naas,** Ire.
88/B3 **Nababeep,** SAfr.
70/E3 **Nabadwīp,** India
64/E3 **Nabari,** Japan
65/M10 **Nabari** (riv.), Japan
74/C5 **Nabberu** (lake), Austl.
53/M5 **Naberezhnye Chelny,** Rus.
60/D5 **Nabī Shu'ayb, Jabal an** (mtn.), Yem.
111/J1 **Nabisipi** (riv.), Qu,Can
67/D5 **Nabua,** Phil.
81/X17 **Nābul,** Tun.
81/X17 **Nābul** (gov.), Tun.
59/K5 **Nābulus,** WBnk.
64/D4 **Nachi-Katsuura,** Japan
39/J3 **Náchod,** Czh.
41/E6 **Nachrodt-Wiblingwerde,** Ger.
96/B3 **Nacimiento,** Chile
112/E4 **Nacogdoches,** Tx,US
34/D4 **Nadder** (riv.), Eng,UK
78/G6 **Nadi,** Fiji
70/B3 **Nadiād,** India
50/E2 **Nădlac,** Rom.
81/N13 **Nador,** Mor.
33/H3 **Nafferton,** Eng,UK
61/J3 **Nag,** Pak.
67/D5 **Naga,** Phil.
64/C4 **Nagahama,** Japan
64/E3 **Nagahama,** Japan
65/G1 **Nagai,** Japan
71/F2 **Nāgāland** (state), India
65/F2 **Nagano,** Japan
65/E3 **Nagano** (pref.), Japan
65/F2 **Nagaoka,** Japan
64/D3 **Nagaokakyō,** Japan
65/J7 **Nagara,** Japan
65/E3 **Nagara** (riv.), Japan
65/H7 **Nagareyama,** Japan
70/B4 **Nagar Haveli, Dadrak** (terr.), India
70/C4 **Nāgārjuna Sāgar** (res.), India
100/D5 **Nagarote,** Nic.
114/M5 **Nagas** (pt.), BC,Can
64/A4 **Nagasaki,** Japan
64/A4 **Nagasaki** (pref.), Japan
65/M9 **Nagashima,** Japan
64/B3 **Nagato,** Japan
70/B2 **Nāgaur,** India
70/C3 **Nāgda,** India
70/C6 **Nāgercoil,** India
68/F2 **Nagoonnuur,** Mong.
55/H5 **Nagorno-Karabakh Aut. Obl.,** Azer.
65/E3 **Nagoya,** Japan
70/C3 **Nāgpur,** India
62/C5 **Nagqu** (riv.), China
50/C2 **Nagyatád,** Hun.
50/E1 **Nagyhalász,** Hun.
50/E2 **Nagykálló,** Hun.
50/C2 **Nagykanizsa,** Hun.
50/D2 **Nagykáta,** Hun.
50/D2 **Nagykőrös,** Hun.
50/E1 **Nagy-Milic** (peak), Hun.
67/E2 **Naha,** Japan
102/D2 **Nahanni Nat'l Park,** NW,Can
59/K5 **Nahariyya,** Isr.
78/D2 **Nahashima** (isls.), Japan
60/E2 **Nahāvand,** Iran
43/G4 **Nahe** (riv.), Ger.
85/E4 **Nahouri** (prov.), Burk.
96/B3 **Nahuelbuta Nat'l Park,** Chile
96/C4 **Nahuel Huapí Nat'l Park,** Arg.
101/N8 **Naica,** Mex.
62/C4 **Naij Gol** (riv.), China
64/C3 **Naikai-Seto Nat'l Park,** Japan
34/D4 **Nailsea,** Eng,UK
34/D3 **Nailsworth,** Eng,UK
70/D3 **Nainpur,** India
36/D2 **Nairn,** Sc,UK
36/D2 **Nairn** (riv.), Sc,UK
83/N8 **Nairobi** (cap.), Kenya
83/N8 **Nairobi Nat'l Park,** Kenya
60/F2 **Najafābād,** Iran
60/D3 **Najd** (des.), SAr.
46/D1 **Nájera,** Sp.
70/C2 **Najībābād,** India
65/K9 **Naka,** Japan
64/D4 **Naka** (riv.), Japan
65/G2 **Naka** (riv.), Japan
65/H7 **Nakai,** Japan
65/F1 **Nakajō,** Japan
104/T10 **Nakalele** (pt.), Hi,US
65/G2 **Nakaminato,** Japan
64/C4 **Nakamura,** Japan
65/F2 **Nakano,** Japan
64/C3 **Nakano** (lake), Japan
64/B5 **Nakatane,** Japan
65/E3 **Nakatsugawa,** Japan
83/N4 **Nak'fa,** Erit.
55/H5 **Nakhichevan',** Azer.
55/H5 **Nakhichevan Aut. Rep.,** Azer.
63/L3 **Nakhodka,** Rus.
69/C3 **Nakhon Nayok,** Thai.
69/C3 **Nakhon Pathom,** Thai.
69/D2 **Nakhon Phanom,** Thai.
69/C3 **Nakhon Ratchasima,** Thai.
69/C3 **Nakhon Sawan,** Thai.
69/B4 **Nakhon Si Thammarat,** Thai.
37/G3 **Nakkila,** Fin.
39/J2 **Nakľo nad Notecią,** Pol.
38/F1 **Nakskov,** Den.
64/A3 **Naktong** (riv.), SKor.
83/N8 **Nakuru,** Kenya
106/D3 **Nakusp,** BC,Can
61/J3 **Nāl** (riv.), Pak.
62/F2 **Nalayh,** Mong.
43/F5 **Nalbach,** Ger.
71/F2 **Nalbāri,** India
77/D3 **Nalbaugh Nat'l Park,** Austl.
55/G4 **Nal'chik,** Rus.
69/C2 **Nale,** Laos
70/C4 **Nalgonda,** India
51/K5 **Nallıhan,** Turk.
46/B1 **Nalón** (riv.), Sp.
82/H1 **Nālūt,** Libya
60/F2 **Namak** (lake), Iran
61/G2 **Namakzār-e Shadād** (salt dep.), Iran
68/B3 **Namangan,** Uzb.
88/B3 **Namaqualand** (reg.), SAfr.
73/J4 **Namaripi** (cape), Indo.
43/G4 **Namborn,** Ger.
76/D4 **Nambour,** Austl.
69/D4 **Nam Can,** Viet.
69/C1 **Nam Cum,** Viet.
69/D1 **Nam Dinh,** Viet.
110/B2 **Namekagon** (riv.), Wi,US
85/E3 **Namemtenga** (prov.), Burk.
65/E2 **Namerikawa,** Japan
87/B5 **Namib** (des.), Namb.
87/C5 **Namibia**
88/A2 **Namib-Naukluft Park,** Namb.
65/G2 **Namie,** Japan
70/D2 **Namja** (pass), Nepal
71/G2 **Namjagbarwa** (peak), China
69/C2 **Nam Nao Nat'l Park,** Thai.
69/B4 **Namnoi** (peak), Burma
77/D1 **Namoi** (riv.), Austl.
78/E4 **Namonuito** (atoll), Micr.
78/F4 **Namorik** (atoll), Mrsh.
106/D5 **Nampa,** Id,US
63/K4 **Namp'o,** NKor.
87/G4 **Nampula,** Moz.
68/D6 **Namsê Shankou** (pass), China
37/D2 **Namsos,** Nor.
69/B2 **Nam Tok Mae Surin Nat'l Park,** Thai.
78/F4 **Namu** (atoll), Mrsh.
69/C2 **Nam Un** (res.), Thai.
43/D3 **Namur,** Belg.
43/D3 **Namur** (prov.), Belg.
39/J3 **Namysłów,** Pol.
66/B4 **Nan** (riv.), China
69/C2 **Nan,** Thai.
69/C2 **Nan** (riv.), Thai.
106/C3 **Nanaimo,** BC,Can
104/V13 **Nanakuli,** Hi,US
65/E2 **Nanao,** Japan
92/D4 **Nanay** (riv.), Peru
96/C2 **Nancagua,** Chile
67/C2 **Nanchang,** China
67/C2 **Nancheng,** China
43/F6 **Nancy,** Fr.
70/C4 **Nānded,** India
71/G3 **Nanding** (riv.), China
67/A4 **Nandu** (riv.), China
70/B3 **Nandurbār,** India
31/T11 **Nandy,** Fr.
70/C4 **Nandyāl,** India
61/K1 **Nanga Parbat** (mtn.), Pak.
72/D4 **Nangapinoh,** Indo.
66/C3 **Nangong,** China
73/F1 **Nangtud** (mt.), Phil.
66/D4 **Nanjing,** China
64/C4 **Nankoku,** Japan
71/J3 **Nanliu** (riv.), China
63/K3 **Nanlou** (peak), China
71/J3 **Nanning,** China
65/M9 **Nannō,** Japan
32/B4 **Nanny** (riv.), Ire.
70/D2 **Nānpāra,** India
67/C2 **Nanping,** China
65/M10 **Nansei,** Japan
103/S6 **Nansen** (sound), NW,Can
87/F1 **Nansio,** Tanz.
65/F2 **Nantai-san** (mtn.), Japan
31/S10 **Nanterre,** Fr.
44/C3 **Nantes,** Fr.
31/U9 **Nanteuil-le-Haudouin,** Fr.
110/D3 **Nanticoke,** On,Can
106/E3 **Nanton,** Ab,Can
66/E4 **Nantong,** China
111/G3 **Nantucket** (isl.), MA,US
33/F5 **Nantwich,** Eng,UK
34/C3 **Nantyglo,** Wal,UK
115/F4 **Nanuet,** NY,US
79/Z18 **Nanuku** (chan.), Fiji
78/G5 **Nanumanga** (atoll), Tuv.
78/G5 **Nanumea** (isl.), Tuv.
95/D1 **Nanuque,** Braz.
66/C4 **Nanwon** (res.), China
66/B4 **Nanwutai** (mtn.), China
66/D4 **Nanyang,** China
66/D4 **Nanyang** (lake), China
83/N7 **Nanyuki,** Kenya
103/J3 **Naococane** (lake), Qu,Can
70/A3 **Naokot,** Pak.
63/L2 **Naoli** (riv.), China
84/D5 **Naoua** (falls), IvC.
116/K10 **Napa,** Ca,US
116/K10 **Napa** (riv.), Ca,US
110/E2 **Napanee,** On,Can
86/B5 **Napata** (ruins), Sudan
116/P16 **Naperville,** Il,US
75/S10 **Napier,** NZ
88/L11 **Napier,** SAfr.
113/H5 **Naples,** Fl,US
48/D2 **Naples** (Napoli), It.
48/D2 **Napoli** (gulf), It.
76/A4 **Nappa Merrie,** Austl.
35/E2 **Napton on the Hill,** Eng,UK
79/L6 **Napuka** (isl.), FrPol.
64/D3 **Nara,** Japan
64/D3 **Nara** (pref.), Japan
84/D3 **Nara,** Mali
61/J4 **Nāra** (riv.), Pak.
68/D5 **Nara Logna** (pass), Nepal
70/D4 **Narasannapeta,** India
65/J7 **Narashino,** Japan
69/C5 **Narathiwat,** Thai.
70/F3 **Nārāyanganj,** Bang.
70/C4 **Nārāyanpet,** India
34/B3 **Narberth,** Wal,UK
44/E5 **Narbonne,** Fr.
46/B1 **Narcea** (riv.), Sp.
49/F2 **Nardò,** It.
34/B6 **Nare** (pt.), UK
103/T7 **Nares** (str.), NW,Can
39/L2 **Narew** (riv.), Pol.
101/F6 **Narganá,** Pan.
89/H6 **Narinda** (bay), Madg.
97/K8 **Nariz** (peak), Chile
70/D2 **Narkatiāganj,** India
70/C3 **Narmada** (riv.), India
59/E2 **Narman,** Turk.
48/C1 **Narni,** It.
31/K2 **Narodnaya** (peak), Rus.
46/A1 **Narón,** Sp.
61/K2 **Nārowāl,** Pak.
37/G3 **Närpes,** Fin.
67/C6 **Narra,** Phil.
77/D1 **Narrabri,** Austl.
70/C3 **Narsimhapur,** India
70/C3 **Narsingarh,** India
64/D3 **Naruto,** Japan
52/F4 **Narva,** Est.
52/E4 **Narva** (riv.), Est., Rus.
67/D4 **Narvacan,** Phil.
37/F1 **Narvik,** Nor.
53/M2 **Nar'yan-Mar,** Rus.
68/C3 **Naryn,** Kyr.
68/B3 **Naryn** (riv.), Kyr.
51/G2 **Năsăud,** Rom.
35/F3 **Nash,** Eng,UK
34/C4 **Nash** (pt.), Wal,UK
111/G3 **Nashua,** NH,US
112/E3 **Nashville,** Ar,US
113/G2 **Nashville** (cap.), Tn,US
50/D3 **Našice,** Cro.
39/L2 **Nasielsk,** Pol.
70/B4 **Nāsik,** India
83/M6 **Nāşir,** Sudan
70/B2 **Nasīrābād,** India
61/J3 **Nasīrābād,** Pak.
73/F1 **Naso** (pt.), Phil.
79/Z17 **Nasorolevu** (peak), Fiji
114/N4 **Nass** (riv.), BC,Can
101/F2 **Nassau** (cap.), Bahm.
97/L8 **Nassau** (bay), Chile
79/J6 **Nassau** (isl.), CookIs.
86/C4 **Nasser** (res.), Egypt
37/E4 **Nässjö,** Swe.
103/J3 **Nastapoka** (isls.), NW,Can
38/F1 **Næstved,** Den.
65/F2 **Nasu-dake** (mtn.), Japan
69/B2 **Nat** (peak), Burma
87/E5 **Nata,** Bots.
110/C1 **Natagani** (riv.), On,Can
94/D2 **Natal,** Braz.
89/E3 **Natal** (prov.), SAfr.
111/J1 **Natashquan** (riv.), Qu,Can
113/F4 **Natchez,** Ms,US
112/E4 **Natchitoches,** La,US
45/G3 **Naters,** Swi.
79/Z17 **Natewa** (bay), Fiji
70/B3 **Nāthdwāra,** India
106/B2 **Nation** (riv.), BC,Can
108/C4 **National City,** Ca,US
71/G4 **Nattaung** (peak), Burma
72/C3 **Natuna** (isls.), Indo.
108/E3 **Natural Bridges Nat'l Mon.,** Ut,US
74/A6 **Naturaliste** (cape), Austl.
77/D4 **Naturaliste** (cape), Austl.
74/A5 **Naturaliste** (chan.), Austl.
100/B4 **Naucalpan,** Mex.
88/E3 **Naudesnek** (pass), SAfr.
67/D5 **Naujan,** Phil.
52/D4 **Naujoji-Akmenė,** Lith.
88/A2 **Naukluft-Namib Game Rsv.,** Namb.
78/F5 **Nauru**
47/N8 **Navacarrada** (pass), Sp.
108/E3 **Navajo Nat'l Mon.,** Az,US
47/M9 **Navalcarnero,** Sp.
46/C3 **Navalmoral de la Mata,** Sp.
32/B4 **Navan,** Ire.
57/T3 **Navarin** (cape), Rus.
97/L8 **Navarino** (isl.), Chile
46/D1 **Navarre** (aut. comm.), Sp.
96/F2 **Navarro,** Arg.
34/A6 **Navax** (pt.), UK
46/B1 **Navia,** Sp.
46/B1 **Navia** (riv.), Sp.
96/C2 **Navidad,** Chile
93/H8 **Naviraí,** Braz.
51/J3 **Năvodari,** Rom.
56/G5 **Navoi,** Uzb.
101/N8 **Navojoa,** Mex.
101/N9 **Navolato,** Mex.
49/G3 **Návpaktos,** Gre.
49/H4 **Návplion,** Gre.
70/B3 **Navsāri,** India
103/H1 **Navy Board** (inlet), NW,Can
70/E3 **Nawābganj,** Bang.
70/D2 **Nawābganj,** India
61/J3 **Nawābshāh,** Pak.
61/G5 **Nawş, Ra's** (pt.), Oman
49/J4 **Náxos** (isl.), Gre.
101/P9 **Nayarit** (state), Mex.
35/G3 **Nayland,** Eng,UK
62/B2 **Nayramadlïn** (peak), Mong.
68/B4 **Nayzatash, Pereval** (pass), Taj.
46/A3 **Nazaré,** Port.
42/C2 **Nazareth,** Belg.
59/K5 **Nazareth** (Naẕerat), Isr.
101/P8 **Nazas** (riv.), Mex.
92/D6 **Nazca,** Peru
92/C6 **Nazca Lines** (ruins), Peru
78/B2 **Naze,** Japan
35/H3 **Naze, The** (pt.), Eng,UK
59/B3 **Nazilli,** Turk.
83/N6 **Nazrēt,** Eth.
56/H4 **Nazyvayevsk,** Rus.
87/E2 **Nchelenge,** Zam.
87/F3 **Ncheu,** Malw.
87/B2 **Ndalatando,** Ang.
83/K6 **Ndele,** CAfr.
78/F6 **Ndende** (isl.), Sol.
82/J5 **N'Djamena** (cap.), Chad
82/H8 **N'Djolé,** Gabon
87/E3 **Ndola,** Zam.
85/H5 **Ndop,** Camr.
84/B2 **Ndrhamcha, Sebkha de** (dry lake), Mrta.
44/C4 **Né** (riv.), Fr.
49/J5 **Néa Alikarnassós,** Gre.

32/B2 **Neagh, Lough** (lake), NI,UK
49/H3 **Néa Ionía**, Gre.
74/E4 **Neale** (lake), Austl.
51/H2 **Neamţ** (co.), Rom.
114/A6 **Near** (isls.), Ak,US
34/C3 **Neath**, Wal,UK
34/C3 **Neath** (riv.), Wal,UK
32/D3 **Neb** (riv.), IM,UK
55/K5 **Nebit-Dag**, Trkm.
76/E6 **Nebo** (mtn.), Austl.
109/G2 **Nebraska** (state), US
109/J2 **Nebraska City**, Ne,US
48/C4 **Nebrodi, Madonie** (mts.), It.
106/B2 **Nechako** (riv.), BC,Can
112/E4 **Neches** (riv.), Tx,US
83/N6 **Nechisar Nat'l Park**, Eth.
45/H2 **Neckar** (riv.), Ger.
79/J2 **Necker** (isl.), Hi,US
96/F3 **Necochea**, Arg.
48/C1 **Necropoli** (ruins), It.
46/A1 **Neda**, Sp.
40/C6 **Nederweert**, Neth.
40/D4 **Neede**, Neth.
35/H2 **Needham Market**, Eng,UK
35/F2 **Needingworth**, Eng,UK
108/D4 **Needles**, Ca,US
35/E5 **Needles, The** (seastacks), UK
110/B2 **Neenah**, Wi,US
107/J3 **Neepawa**, Mb,Can
43/E1 **Neerpelt**, Belg.
41/H2 **Neetze** (riv.), Ger.
43/F2 **Neffelbach** (riv.), Ger.
53/M4 **Neftekamsk**, Rus.
58/C7 **Nefud** (des.), SAr.
32/D6 **Nefyn**, Wal,UK
110/C2 **Negaunee**, Mi,US
83/N6 **Negēlē**, Eth.
86/D2 **Negev** (phys. reg.), Isr.
51/G3 **Negoiu** (peak), Rom.
70/C6 **Negombo**, SrL.
50/F3 **Negotin**, Yugo.
50/F5 **Negotino**, Maced.
94/A3 **Negra** (mts.), Braz.
92/B5 **Negra** (pt.), Peru
71/F4 **Negrais** (cape), Burma
46/A1 **Negreira**, Sp.
51/H2 **Negreşti**, Rom.
96/C3 **Negro** (peak), Arg.
96/D3 **Negro** (riv.), Arg.
92/F7 **Negro** (riv.), Bol.
93/G7 **Negro** (riv.), Braz.
92/F4 **Negro** (riv.), Braz., Ven.
97/F2 **Negro** (riv.), Uru., Braz.
67/D6 **Negros** (isl.), Phil.
101/G4 **Neiba**, DRep.
89/R15 **Neiges, Piton des** (peak), Reun.
66/C4 **Neihuang**, China
66/B2 **Nei Monggol** (aut. reg.), China
62/G3 **Nei Monggol** (plat.), China
92/C3 **Neiva**, Col.
102/G3 **Nejanilini** (lake), Mb,Can
83/N6 **Nejo**, Eth.
83/N6 **Nek'emtē**, Eth.
52/G4 **Nelidovo**, Rus.
109/H2 **Neligh**, Ne,US
70/C5 **Nellore**, India
77/B3 **Nelson** (cape), Austl.
106/D3 **Nelson**, BC,Can
102/G3 **Nelson** (riv.), Mb,Can
97/J7 **Nelson** (str.), Chile
75/R11 **Nelson**, NZ
33/F4 **Nelson**, Eng,UK
34/C3 **Nelson**, Wal,UK
114/F3 **Nelson** (isl.), Ak,US
77/E2 **Nelson Bay**, Austl.
89/E2 **Nelspruit**, SAfr.
84/D2 **Néma**, Mrta.
84/D2 **Néma, Dhar** (hills), Mrta.
45/H4 **Nembro**, It.
51/H2 **Nemira** (peak), Rom.
63/J2 **Nemor** (riv.), China
44/E2 **Nemours**, Fr.
63/P3 **Nemuro**, Japan
63/J2 **Nen** (riv.), China
35/G1 **Nene** (riv.), Eng,UK
53/M2 **Nenets Aut. Okr.**, Rus.
109/J3 **Neosho** (riv.), Ks, Mo,US
109/J3 **Neosho**, Mo,US
58/H7 **Nepal**
70/D2 **Nepālganj**, Nepal
70/C3 **Nepanagar**, India
76/G8 **Nepean** (riv.), Austl.
110/F2 **Nepean**, Can.
108/E3 **Nephi**, Ut,US
36/A3 **Nephin** (mtn.), Ire.
111/H2 **Nepisiguit** (riv.), NB,Can
62/H1 **Nercha** (riv.), Rus.
52/J4 **Nerekhta**, Rus.
50/D4 **Neretva** (riv.), Bosn., Cro.
52/E5 **Neris** (riv.), Lith.
46/D4 **Nerja**, Sp.
46/B4 **Nerva**, Sp.
54/C4 **Nesebūr**, Bul.
31/S9 **Nesles-la-Vallée**, Fr.
109/H3 **Ness City**, Ks,US
41/H6 **Nesse** (riv.), Ger.
114/M4 **Nesselrode** (mtn.), Ak,US
36/C2 **Ness, Loch** (lake), Sc,UK
33/E5 **Neston**, Eng,UK
49/J2 **Néstos** (riv.), Gre.
59/M9 **Nes Ziyyona**, Isr.
59/K5 **Netanya**, Isr.
115/F5 **Netcong**, NJ,US
41/G5 **Nethe** (riv.), Ger.
34/D3 **Netherend**, Eng,UK
40/B5 **Netherlands**
101/H5 **Netherlands Antilles** (isls.), Neth.
35/E5 **Netley**, Eng,UK
48/E3 **Neto** (riv.), It.
43/H2 **Netphen**, Ger.
40/D6 **Nette** (riv.), Ger.
41/H5 **Nette** (riv.), Ger.
43/G3 **Nettebach** (riv.), Ger.
43/F3 **Nettersheim**, Ger.
40/D6 **Nettetal**, Ger.
103/J2 **Nettilling** (lake), NW,Can
33/H5 **Nettleham**, Eng,UK
48/C2 **Nettuno**, It.
39/G2 **Neubrandenburg**, Ger.
45/G3 **Neuchâtel**, Swi.
45/G3 **Neuchâtel** (lake), Swi.
39/G2 **Neuenhagen**, Ger.
40/D4 **Neuenhaus**, Ger.
41/E4 **Neuenkirchen**, Ger.
41/F3 **Neuenkirchen**, Ger.
41/E6 **Neuenrade**, Ger.
43/E4 **Neufchâteau**, Belg.
44/F2 **Neufchâteau**, Fr.
42/B5 **Neuilly-en-Thelle**, Fr.
42/C5 **Neuilly-Saint-Front**, Fr.
31/T10 **Neuilly-sur-Marne**, Fr.
31/S10 **Neuilly-sur-Seine**, Fr.
45/J2 **Neumarkt in der Oberpfalz**, Ger.
38/E1 **Neumünster**, Ger.
50/C2 **Neunkirchen**, Aus.
43/G5 **Neunkirchen**, Ger.
43/H2 **Neunkirchen**, Ger.
43/G2 **Neunkirchen-Seelscheid**, Ger.
96/C3 **Neuquén**, Arg.
96/C3 **Neuquén** (prov.), Arg.
96/C3 **Neuquén** (riv.), Arg.
38/G2 **Neuruppin**, Ger.
113/J3 **Neuse** (riv.), NC,US
40/D6 **Neuss**, Ger.
41/G4 **Neustadt am Rübenberge**, Ger.
45/J2 **Neustadt an der Donau**, Ger.
45/H2 **Neustadt an der Weinstrasse**, Ger.
45/J1 **Neustadt bei Coburg**, Ger.
38/F1 **Neustadt in Holstein**, Ger.
38/G2 **Neustrelitz**, Ger.
45/J2 **Neu-Ulm**, Ger.
44/G2 **Neuves-Maisons**, Fr.
41/F1 **Neuwerk** (isl.), Ger.
43/G3 **Neuwied**, Ger.
55/V7 **Neva** (riv.), Rus.
46/D4 **Nevada** (mts.), Sp.
108/C3 **Nevada** (state), US
109/J3 **Nevada**, Mo,US
96/C4 **Nevado Cónico** (peak), Chile
91/C1 **Nevado de Chañi** (peak), Arg.
101/P10 **Nevado de Colima Nat'l Park**, Mex.
91/C2 **Nevado del Candado** (peak), Arg.
92/C3 **Nevado del Huila** (peak), Col.
96/C2 **Nevado, Sierra del** (mts.), Arg.
52/F4 **Nevel'**, Rus.
42/C1 **Nevele**, Belg.
63/N2 **Nevel'sk**, Rus.
44/E3 **Nevers**, Fr.
50/D4 **Nevesinje**, Bosn.
55/G3 **Nevinnomyssk**, Rus.
101/J4 **Nevis** (isl.), StK.
59/C2 **Nevşehir**, Turk.
92/G3 **New** (riv.), Guy.
35/E5 **New** (for.), Eng,UK
110/D4 **New** (riv.), WV,US
32/E2 **New Abbey**, Sc,UK
110/C4 **New Albany**, In,US
113/F3 **New Albany**, Ms,US
35/E4 **New Alresford**, Eng,UK
93/G2 **New Amsterdam**, Guy.
33/H5 **New Ancholme** (riv.), Eng,UK
116/K11 **Newark**, Ca,US
115/F5 **Newark**, NJ,US
110/D3 **Newark**, Oh,US
33/H5 **Newark-on-Trent**, Eng,UK
116/G6 **New Baltimore**, Mi,US
111/G3 **New Bedford**, Ma,US
116/P14 **New Berlin**, Wi,US
113/J3 **New Bern**, NC,US
110/C2 **Newberry**, Mi,US
113/H3 **Newberry**, SC,US
33/G1 **Newbiggin-by-the-Sea**, Eng,UK
112/D4 **New Braunfels**, Tx,US
34/C2 **Newbridge on Wye**, Wal,UK
78/D5 **New Britain** (isl.), PNG
111/F3 **New Britain**, Ct,US
111/H2 **New Brunswick** (prov.), Can.
115/F5 **New Brunswick**, NJ,US
32/A2 **New Buildings**, NI,UK
33/G2 **Newburn**, Eng,UK
35/E4 **Newbury**, Eng,UK
33/F3 **Newby Bridge**, Eng,UK
78/F6 **New Caledonia** (terr.), Fr.
79/U12 **New Caledonia** (isl.), NCal.
115/G4 **New Canaan**, Ct,US
77/D2 **Newcastle**, Austl.
111/H2 **Newcastle**, NB,Can
111/S8 **Newcastle**, On,Can
89/E2 **Newcastle**, SAfr.
32/C3 **Newcastle**, NI,UK
110/C4 **New Castle**, In,US
110/D3 **New Castle**, Pa,US
107/G5 **Newcastle**, Wy,US
34/B2 **Newcastle Emlyn**, Wal,UK
33/F1 **Newcastleton**, Sc,UK
33/F5 **Newcastle-under-Lyme**, Eng,UK
33/G2 **Newcastle upon Tyne**, Eng,UK
115/G4 **New City**, NY,US
36/C3 **New Cumnock**, Sc,UK
70/C2 **New Delhi** (cap.), India
106/D3 **New Denver**, BC,Can
31/N8 **Newdigate**, Eng,UK
115/F5 **New Egypt**, NJ,US
77/E1 **New England Nat'l Park**, Austl.
114/F4 **Newenham** (cape), Ak,US
34/D3 **Newent**, Eng,UK
111/S9 **Newfane**, NY,US
103/K3 **Newfoundland** (prov.), Can.
111/L1 **Newfoundland** (isl.), Nf,Can
32/D1 **New Galloway**, Sc,UK
78/E5 **New Georgia** (isls.), Sol.
78/E5 **New Georgia** (sound), Sol.
111/J2 **New Glasgow**, NS,Can
111/N6 **New Glasgow**, Qu,Can
78/C5 **New Guinea** (isl.), Indo., PNG
31/P7 **Newham** (bor.), Eng,UK
111/G3 **New Hampshire** (state), US
78/D5 **New Hanover** (isl.), PNG
35/F5 **Newhaven**, Eng,UK
110/F3 **New Haven**, Ct,US
116/G6 **New Haven**, Mi,US
78/F6 **New Hebrides** (isls.), Van.
115/F5 **New Hope**, Pa,US
112/F4 **New Iberia**, La,US
35/G5 **Newick**, Eng,UK
78/E5 **New Ireland** (isl.), PNG
110/F3 **New Jersey** (state), US
110/E3 **New Kensington**, Pa,US
112/D2 **Newkirk**, Ok,US
116/Q16 **New Lenox**, Il,US
110/E2 **New Liskeard**, On,Can
111/F3 **New London**, Ct,US
110/B2 **New London**, Wi,US
34/A6 **Newlyn**, Eng,UK
109/K3 **New Madrid**, Mo,US
76/F6 **Newmarket**, Austl.
110/E2 **Newmarket**, On,Can
35/G2 **Newmarket**, Eng,UK
110/D4 **New Martinsville**, WV,US
106/D4 **New Meadows**, Id,US
108/F4 **New Mexico** (state), US
33/F5 **New Mills**, Eng,UK
113/G3 **Newnan**, Ga,US
34/D3 **Newnham**, Eng,UK
77/C4 **New Norfolk**, Austl.
113/F4 **New Orleans**, La,US
110/D3 **New Philadelphia**, Oh,US
75/R10 **New Plymouth**, NZ
33/F6 **Newport**, Eng,UK
35/E5 **Newport**, Eng,UK
34/B2 **Newport**, Wal,UK
34/D3 **Newport**, Wal,UK
113/F3 **Newport**, Ar,US
110/C4 **Newport**, Ky,US
106/B4 **Newport**, Or,US
111/G3 **Newport**, RI,US
110/D5 **Newport**, Tn,US
111/F2 **Newport**, Vt,US
106/D3 **Newport**, Wa,US
115/C3 **Newport Beach**, Ca,US
110/E4 **Newport News**, Va,US
35/F2 **Newport Pagnell**, Eng,UK
113/H4 **New Port Richey**, Fl,US
101/F3 **New Providence** (isl.), Bahm.
34/A6 **Newquay**, Eng,UK
34/B2 **New Quay**, Wal,UK
34/C2 **New Radnor**, Wal,UK
111/H1 **New Richmond**, Qu,Can
115/G5 **New Rochelle**, NY,US
107/J4 **New Rockford**, ND,US
35/G5 **New Romney**, Eng,UK
33/G5 **New Rossington**, Eng,UK
32/B3 **Newry**, NI,UK
32/B3 **Newry** (can.), NI,UK
98/Z **New Schwabenland** (reg.), Ant.
57/P2 **New Siberian** (isls.), Rus.
113/H4 **New Smyrna Beach**, Fl,US
77/C2 **New South Wales** (state), Austl.
34/D2 **Newton**, Eng,UK
33/E1 **Newton**, Sc,UK
109/H3 **Newton**, Ks,US
111/G3 **Newton**, Ma,US
115/F4 **Newton**, NJ,US
112/E4 **Newton**, Tx,US
34/C5 **Newton Abbot**, Eng,UK
33/G2 **Newton Aycliffe**, Eng,UK
34/B6 **Newton Ferrers**, Eng,UK
33/F5 **Newton-le-Willows**, Eng,UK
36/C2 **Newtonmore**, Sc,UK
33/G1 **Newton on the Moor**, Eng,UK
32/D2 **Newton Stewart**, Sc,UK
77/B3 **Newtown**, Austl.
34/C1 **Newtown**, Wal,UK
107/H4 **New Town**, ND,US
115/F5 **Newtown**, Pa,US
32/C2 **Newtownabbey**, NI,UK
32/C2 **Newtownards**, NI,UK
36/B3 **Newtownbutler**, NI,UK
32/B3 **Newtownhamilton**, NI,UK
36/D3 **Newtown Saint Boswells**, Sc,UK
32/A2 **Newtownstewart**, NI,UK
34/C3 **New Tredegar**, Wal,UK
107/K4 **New Ulm**, Mn,US
111/J2 **New Waterford**, NS,Can
106/C3 **New Westminster**, BC,Can
110/F3 **New York** (state), US
115/G5 **New York**, NY,US
75/Q10 **New Zealand**
98/L **New Zealand** (peak), Ant.
65/L10 **Neyagawa**, Japan
34/B3 **Neyland**, Wal,UK
61/F3 **Neyrīz**, Iran
61/G1 **Neyshābūr**, Iran
53/P4 **Neyva** (riv.), Rus.
70/C5 **Neyveli**, India
70/C6 **Neyyāttinkara**, India
54/D2 **Nezhin**, Ukr.
106/D4 **Nezperce**, Id,US
72/C3 **Ngabang**, Indo.
73/H5 **Ngabordamlu** (cape), Indo.
87/F4 **Ngabu**, Malw.
82/H5 **Ngala**, Nga.
68/D5 **Ngangla Ringco** (lake), China
68/E5 **Ngangzê** (lake), China
82/H6 **Ngaoundéré**, Camr.
77/B2 **Ngarkat Consv. Park**, Austl.
78/E4 **Ngatik** (isl.), Micr.
79/Z18 **Ngau** (isl.), Fiji
75/S10 **Ngauruhoe** (vol.), NZ
69/D2 **Nghia Dan**, Viet.
69/D1 **Nghia Lo**, Viet.
87/C4 **Ngiva**, Ang.
87/C1 **Ngo**, Congo
69/E4 **Ngoan Muc** (pass), Viet.
71/J4 **Ngoc Linh** (peak), Viet.
87/D4 **Ngonye** (falls), Zam.
63/D5 **Ngoring** (lake), China
82/H8 **Ngounié** (riv.), Gabon
82/H5 **Nguigmi**, Niger
78/C4 **Ngulu** (atoll), Micr.
69/C2 **Ngum** (riv.), Laos
69/D1 **Nguyen Binh**, Viet.
89/E2 **Ngwenya** (peak), Swaz.
92/G4 **Nhamundá** (riv.), Braz.
69/E3 **Nha Trang**, Viet.
84/E3 **Niafounké**, Mali
111/R9 **Niagara** (riv.), Can., US
111/R9 **Niagara Falls**, On,Can
111/R9 **Niagara Falls**, NY,US
85/F3 **Niamey** (cap.), Niger
85/F3 **Niamey** (dept.), Niger
84/C4 **Niandan** (riv.), Gui.
83/L7 **Niangara**, Zaire
84/E3 **Niangay** (lake), Mali
66/C3 **Niangzi Guan** (pass), China
72/A3 **Nias** (isl.), Indo.
100/D5 **Nicaragua**
100/E5 **Nicaragua** (lake), Nic.
48/E3 **Nicastro-Sambiase**, It.
45/G5 **Nice**, Fr.
113/G4 **Niceville**, Fl,US
64/B5 **Nichinan**, Japan
74/B4 **Nickol** (bay), Austl.
71/F6 **Nicobar** (isls.), India
111/F2 **Nicolet**, Qu,Can
59/J4 **Nicosia** (cap.), Cyp.
48/D4 **Nicosia**, It.
100/D5 **Nicoya**, CR
100/D5 **Nicoya** (gulf), CR
100/D6 **Nicoya** (pen.), CR
33/G4 **Nidd** (riv.), Eng,UK
45/H1 **Nidda**, Ger.
43/F2 **Nideggen**, Ger.
43/G6 **Niderviller**, Fr.
39/L2 **Nidzica**, Pol.
38/E1 **Niebüll**, Ger.
45/G2 **Nied** (riv.), Fr.
43/F5 **Nied** (riv.), Ger.
45/K3 **Niedere Tauern** (mts.), Aus.
39/G3 **Niederlausitz** (reg.), Ger.
43/H4 **Nieder-Olm**, Ger.
41/E1 **Niedersächsisches Wattenmeer Nat'l Park**, Ger.
50/B1 **Niederösterreich** (prov.), Aus.
43/F2 **Niederzier**, Ger.
39/L2 **Niegocin** (lake), Pol.
41/G5 **Nieheim**, Ger.
39/J3 **Niemodlin**, Pol.
41/G3 **Nienburg**, Ger.
84/D5 **Niénokoué** (peak), IvC.
42/B2 **Nieppe**, Fr.
84/B3 **Niéri Ko** (riv.), Sen.
40/D5 **Niers** (riv.), Ger.
69/D4 **Niet Ban Tinh Xa**, Viet.
40/D5 **Nieuw-Bergen**, Neth.
40/C4 **Nieuwegein**, Neth.
40/B5 **Nieuwerkerk aan de IJssel**, Neth.
40/B4 **Nieuwkoop**, Neth.
40/D3 **Nieuwleusen**, Neth.
40/C4 **Nieuw-Loosdrecht**, Neth.
93/G2 **Nieuw-Nickerie**, Sur.
42/B1 **Nieuwpoort**, Belg.
40/D3 **Nieuw-Schoonebeek**, Neth.
59/C3 **Niğde**, Turk.
88/E2 **Nigel**, SAfr.
85/G2 **Niger**
85/G5 **Niger** (riv.), Afr.
85/G4 **Niger** (state), Nga.
85/G4 **Nigeria**
85/G5 **Niger, Mouths of the** (delta), Nga.
110/D1 **Nighthawk** (lake), On,Can
46/A1 **Nigrán**, Sp.
49/H2 **Nigríta**, Gre.
79/J2 **Nihoa** (isl.), Hi,US
65/G2 **Nihonmatsu**, Japan
65/F3 **Nii** (isl.), Japan
65/F2 **Niigata**, Japan
65/F2 **Niigata** (pref.), Japan
64/C4 **Niihama**, Japan
104/R10 **Niihau** (isl.), Hi,US
64/C3 **Niimi**, Japan
65/F2 **Niitsu**, Japan
65/H7 **Niiza**, Japan
46/D4 **Níjar**, Sp.
40/C4 **Nijkerk**, Neth.
42/D1 **Nijlen**, Belg.
40/C5 **Nijmegen**, Neth.
52/F1 **Nikel'**, Rus.
65/F2 **Nikkō**, Japan
65/F2 **Nikkō Nat'l Park**, Japan
54/E3 **Nikolayev**, Ukr.
54/D3 **Nikolayev Obl.**, Ukr.
57/Q4 **Nikolayevsk-na-Amure**, Rus.
55/H1 **Nikol'sk**, Rus.
54/E3 **Nikopol'**, Ukr.
59/D2 **Niksar**, Turk.
50/D4 **Nikšić**, Yugo.
79/H5 **Nikumaroro** (Gardner) (atoll), Kiri.
79/S5 **Nikunau** (isl.), Kiri.
83/M2 **Nile** (riv.), Afr.
59/H6 **Nile** (delta), Egypt
116/Q15 **Niles**, Il,US
110/C3 **Niles**, Mi,US
110/D3 **Niles**, Oh,US
95/K7 **Nilópolis**, Braz.
37/J3 **Nilsiä**, Fin.
70/B3 **Nīmach**, India
63/L1 **Niman** (riv.), Rus.
84/C5 **Nimba** (peak), IvC.
84/C5 **Nimba** (co.), Libr.
44/F5 **Nîmes**, Fr.
98/L **Nimrod** (glac.), Ant.
43/F4 **Nimsbach** (riv.), Ger.
83/M7 **Nimule Nat'l Park**, Sudan
60/D1 **Nineveh** (ruins), Iraq
96/D4 **Ninfas** (pt.), Arg.
67/D2 **Ningbo**, China
66/C4 **Ningling**, China
66/B3 **Ningxia Huizu Zizhiqu** (aut. reg.), China
69/D1 **Ninh Binh**, Viet.
69/E3 **Ninh Hoa**, Viet.
78/D5 **Ninigo** (isl.), PNG
98/K **Ninnis** (glac.), Ant.
65/H7 **Ninomiya**, Japan
42/D2 **Ninove**, Belg.
109/G2 **Niobrara** (riv.), Ne,US
84/B3 **Niokolo-Koba Nat'l Park**, Sen.
84/D3 **Niono**, Mali
84/B3 **Nioro-du-Rip**, Sen.
84/C3 **Nioro du Sahel**, Mali
44/C3 **Niort**, Fr.
107/H2 **Nipawin**, Sk,Can
110/B1 **Nipigon**, On,Can
110/B1 **Nipigon** (lake), On,Can
110/E2 **Nipissing** (lake), On,Can
96/C3 **Niquén**, Chile
65/F3 **Nirasaki**, Japan
76/H8 **Nirimba-Hmas**, Austl.
70/C4 **Nirmal**, India
50/E4 **Niš**, Yugo.
46/B3 **Nisa**, Port.
49/H1 **Nišava** (riv.), Yugo.
48/D4 **Niscemi**, It.
64/B4 **Nishiharu**, Japan
64/C3 **Nishiki** (riv.), Japan
65/L10 **Nishinomiya**, Japan
64/B5 **Nishino'omote**, Japan
65/E3 **Nishio**, Japan
64/D3 **Nishiwaki**, Japan
39/M3 **Nisko**, Pol.
116/B3 **Nisqually Reach** (str.), Wa,US
78/E5 **Nissan** (isl.), PNG
65/N9 **Nisshin**, Japan
107/K4 **Nisswa**, Mn,US
95/K7 **Niterói**, Braz.
32/E1 **Nith** (riv.), Sc,UK
32/E1 **Nithsdale** (val.), Sc,UK
68/C5 **Niti** (pass), India
39/K4 **Nitra**, Slvk.
39/K4 **Nitra** (riv.), Slvk.
53/P4 **Nitsa** (riv.), Rus.
79/H6 **Niuafo'ou** (isl.), Tonga
79/H6 **Niuatoputapu Group** (isls.), Tonga
79/J7 **Niue** (terr.), NZ
78/G6 **Niulakita** (isl.), Tuv.
71/H2 **Niulan** (riv.), China
72/C3 **Niut** (peak), Indo.
78/G5 **Niutau** (isl.), Tuv.
42/D2 **Nivelles**, Belg.
44/E3 **Nivernais** (hills), Fr.
107/J3 **Niverville**, Mb,Can
108/C3 **Nixon**, Nv,US
68/D4 **Niya** (riv.), China
64/C4 **Niyodo** (riv.), Japan
70/C4 **Nizāmābād**, India
53/K4 **Nizhegorod Obl.**, Rus.
53/M4 **Nizhnekama** (res.), Rus.
53/L5 **Nizhnekamsk**, Rus.
57/K4 **Nizhneudinsk**, Rus.
56/H3 **Nizhnevartovsk**, Rus.
55/G1 **Nizhniy Lomov**, Rus.
53/K4 **Nizhniy Novgorod** (Gor'kiy), Rus.
53/N4 **Nizhniy Tagil**, Rus.
59/D3 **Nizip**, Turk.
39/K4 **Nízke Tatry Nat'l Park**, Slvk.
87/F2 **Njombe**, Tanz.
85/H5 **Nkambe**, Camr.
87/B1 **Nkayi**, Congo
87/F3 **Nkhata Bay**, Malw.
85/H5 **Nkogam, Massif du** (peak), Camr.
85/H5 **N'Kongsamba**, Camr.
71/G2 **Nmai** (riv.), Burma
42/B5 **Noailles**, Fr.
70/F3 **Noākhāli**, Bang.
70/E3 **Noāmundi**, India
114/F2 **Noatak** (riv.), Ak,US
114/F2 **Noatak Nat'l Prsv.**, Ak,US
64/B4 **Nobeoka**, Japan
109/H4 **Noble**, Ok,US
110/C3 **Noblesville**, In,US
111/Q8 **Nobleton**, On,Can
63/N3 **Noboribetsu**, Japan
50/C5 **Noci**, It.
65/H7 **Noda**, Japan
81/P13 **Noé** (cape), Alg.
42/B3 **Noeux-les-Mines**, Fr.
108/E5 **Nogales**, Az,US
64/B4 **Nogata**, Japan
44/D2 **Nogent-le-Rotrou**, Fr.
31/T10 **Nogent-sur-Marne**, Fr.
42/B5 **Nogent-sur-Oise**, Fr.
52/H5 **Noginsk**, Rus.
76/B4 **Nogoa** (riv.), Austl.
62/C2 **Nogoonuur**, Mong.
96/F2 **Nogoyá**, Arg.
39/K5 **Nógrád** (co.), Hun.
47/F1 **Noguera Pallarosa** (riv.), Sp.
64/A2 **Nogwak-san** (mtn.), SKor.
70/B2 **Nohar**, India
43/G4 **Nohfelden**, Ger.
110/E2 **Noire** (riv.), Qu,Can
44/B2 **Noires** (mts.), Fr.
44/B3 **Noirmoutier** (isl.), Fr.
42/B6 **Noisiel**, Fr.
31/T10 **Noisy-le-Grand**, Fr.
31/S10 **Noisy-le-Roi**, Fr.
42/B6 **Noisy-le-Sec**, Fr.
65/F3 **Nojima-zaki** (pt.), Japan
37/G3 **Nokia**, Fin.
73/F4 **Nokilalaki** (peak), Indo.
61/H3 **Nok Kundi**, Pak.
82/J7 **Nola**, CAfr.
77/D2 **Nomadgi Nat'l Park**, Austl.
114/F3 **Nome** (cape), Ak,US
64/B5 **Nomo-misaki** (cape), Japan
64/A4 **Nomo-zaki** (pt.), Japan
62/D2 **Nōmrōg**, Mong.
102/F2 **Nonacho** (lake), NW,Can
45/G4 **None**, It.
42/B5 **Nonette** (riv.), Fr.
67/F1 **Nong'an**, China
69/D2 **Nong Han** (res.), Thai.
69/C2 **Nong Het**, Laos
69/C2 **Nong Khai**, Thai.
69/C2 **Nong Pet**, Laos
43/F4 **Nonnweiler**, Ger.
78/G5 **Nonouti** (atoll), Kiri.
66/E5 **Nonri** (isl.), China
63/K4 **Nonsan**, SKor.
40/A5 **Noordbeveland** (isl.), Neth.
40/B3 **Noorderhaaks** (isl.), Neth.
40/B3 **Noordhollandsch** (can.), Neth.
40/C3 **Noordostpolder** (polder), Neth.
40/B4 **Noordwijk aan Zee**, Neth.
40/B4 **Noordwijkerhout**, Neth.
40/B4 **Noordzeekanaal** (can.), Neth.
76/D4 **Noosa-Tewantin**, Austl.
106/B3 **Nootka** (isl.), BC,Can
106/B3 **Nootka** (sound), BC,Can
100/B4 **Nopala**, Mex.
63/L1 **Nora** (riv.), Rus.
52/B4 **Nora**, Swe.
73/F2 **Norala**, Phil.
115/C3 **Norco**, Ca,US
111/M6 **Nord** (riv.), Qu,Can
42/C3 **Nord** (dept.), Fr.
42/B3 **Nord, Canal du** (can.), Fr.
41/E1 **Norden**, Ger.
41/F2 **Nordenham**, Ger.
56/K2 **Nordenskjöld** (arch.), Rus.
41/E1 **Norderney**, Ger.
41/E1 **Norderney** (isl.), Ger.
41/G1 **Norderstedt**, Ger.
38/F3 **Nordhausen**, Ger.
41/F1 **Nordholz**, Ger.
41/E4 **Nordhorn**, Ger.
37/H1 **Nordkapp** (North) (cape), Nor.
37/H1 **Nordkinn** (pt.), Nor.
41/E5 **Nordkirchen**, Ger.
37/E2 **Nordland** (co.), Nor.
37/F3 **Nordmaling**, Swe.
38/E1 **Nord-Ostsee** (can.), Ger.
85/H5 **Nord-Ouest** (prov.), Camr.
81/M13 **Nord Ouest** (reg.), Mor.
44/D1 **Nord-Pas-de-Calais** (reg.), Fr.
41/E3 **Nord-Radde** (riv.), Ger.
41/E3 **Nord-Sud** (can.), Ger.
37/E2 **Nord-Trøndelag** (co.), Nor.
41/E4 **Nordwalde**, Ger.
36/B4 **Nore** (riv.), Ire.
44/E5 **Nore, Pic de** (peak), Fr.
75/M5 **Norfolk** (isl.), Austl.
77/C4 **Norfolk** (peak), Austl.
35/G1 **Norfolk** (co.), Eng,UK
109/H2 **Norfolk**, Ne,US
110/E4 **Norfolk**, Va,US
35/H1 **Norfolk Broads** (swamp), Eng,UK
109/J3 **Norfork** (lake), Ar, Mo,US
40/D2 **Norg**, Neth.
65/E2 **Norikura-dake** (mtn.), Japan
56/J3 **Noril'sk**, Rus.
110/B3 **Normal**, Il,US
76/A2 **Norman** (riv.), Austl.
109/H4 **Norman**, Ok,US
78/E6 **Normanby** (isl.), PNG
116/C3 **Normandy Park**, Wa,US
33/G4 **Normanton**, Eng,UK
88/B3 **Norotshama** (peak), Namb.
107/H3 **Norquay**, Sk,Can
37/F2 **Norrbotten** (co.), Swe.
46/B1 **Norrea** (riv.), Sp.
42/B2 **Norrent-Fontes**, Fr.
116/Q16 **Norridge**, Il,US
113/H2 **Norris** (lake), Tn,US
115/E5 **Norristown**, Pa,US
37/F4 **Norrköping**, Swe.
37/F2 **Norrland** (reg.), Swe.
37/F4 **Norrtälje**, Swe.
96/E4 **Norte** (pt.), Arg.
97/F3 **Norte** (pt.), Arg.
92/G6 **Norte** (mts.), Braz.
93/J3 **Norte, Cabo do** (cape), Braz.
97/J6 **Norte, Campo de Hielo** (glacier), Chile
93/G6 **Nortelândia**, Braz.
41/G5 **Nörten-Hardenberg**, Ger.
77/C3 **North** (pt.), Austl.
77/C4 **North** (pt.), Austl.
110/D2 **North** (chan.), On,Can
111/J2 **North** (cape), PE,Can
30/D3 **North** (sea), Eur.
75/R9 **North** (cape), NZ
75/R10 **North** (isl.), NZ
32/C1 **North** (chan.), UK
114/D5 **North** (cape), Ak,US
114/F3 **North** (peak), Ak,US
50/D4 **North Albanian Alps** (mts.), Alb., Yugo.
33/G3 **Northallerton**, Eng,UK
74/B6 **Northam**, Austl.
34/B4 **Northam**, Eng,UK
99/* **North America**
35/F2 **Northampton**, Eng,UK
35/E2 **Northampton** (uplands), Eng,UK
110/F3 **Northampton**, Ma,US
115/E5 **Northampton**, Pa,US
35/F2 **Northamptonshire** (co.), Eng,UK
71/F5 **North Andaman** (isl.), India
103/K3 **North Aulatsivik** (isl.), Nf,Can
31/N6 **Northaw**, Eng,UK
36/C2 **North Ballachulish**, Sc,UK
32/D3 **North Barrule** (mtn.), IM,UK
106/F2 **North Battleford**, Sk,Can
110/E2 **North Bay**, On,Can
106/B5 **North Bend**, Or,US
115/F5 **North Bergen**, NJ,US
36/D2 **North Berwick**, Sc,UK
40/C5 **North Brabant** (prov.), Neth.
116/Q15 **Northbrook**, Il,US
115/F5 **North Brunswick**, NJ,US
109/H3 **North Canadian** (riv.), Ok,US
107/L2 **North Caribou** (lake), On,Can
113/H3 **North Carolina** (state), US
106/C3 **North Cascades Nat'l Park**, Wa,US
113/J3 **North Charleston**, SC,US
116/Q15 **North Chicago**, Il,US
33/H5 **North Collingham**, Eng,UK
106/C3 **North Cowichan**, BC,Can
107/H4 **North Dakota** (state), US
34/D5 **North Dorset Downs** (uplands), Eng,UK
32/C2 **North Down** (dist.), NI,UK
35/F4 **North Downs** (hills), Eng,UK
76/C3 **North East** (pt.), Austl.
101/G3 **Northeast** (pt.), Bahm.
114/E3 **Northeast** (cape), Ak,US
56/C2 **Northeast Land** (isl.), Sval.
41/G5 **Northeim**, Ger.
35/G1 **North Elmham**, Eng,UK
74/E3 **Northern** (terr.), Austl.
85/E4 **Northern** (reg.), Gha.
59/K5 **Northern** (dist.), Isr.
84/B4 **Northern** (prov.), SLeo.
86/B4 **Northern** (reg.), Sudan
68/B4 **Northern Areas** (terr.), Pak.
79/J6 **Northern Cook** (isls.), CookIs.
30/H2 **Northern Dvina** (riv.), Rus.
36/B3 **Northern Ireland**, UK
110/B1 **Northern Light** (lake), On,Can, Mn,US
78/D3 **Northern Marianas**, US
56/G3 **Northern Sos'va** (riv.), Rus.
49/J3 **Northern Sporades** (isls.), Gre.
53/N3 **Northern Ural** (mts.), Rus.
53/K4 **Northern Uval** (hills), Rus.
56/E4 **Northern Wals** (upland), Rus.
114/K2 **Northern Yukon Nat'l Park**, Yk,Can
107/K4 **Northfield**, Mn,US
31/P7 **Northfleet**, Eng,UK
35/H4 **North Foreland** (pt.), Eng,UK
113/H5 **North Fort Myers**, Fl,US
110/D1 **North French** (riv.), On,Can
38/E1 **North Frisian** (isls.), Den., Ger.
111/F2 **North Hero**, Vt,US
116/M9 **North Highlands**, Ca,US
116/C3 **North Hill-Edgewood**, Wa,US
40/B3 **North Holland** (prov.), Neth.
33/H5 **North Hykeham**, Eng,UK
53/Q5 **North Kazakhstan Obl.**, Rus.
63/K3 **North Korea**
71/F2 **North Lakhimpur**, India
108/D3 **North Las Vegas**, Nv,US
112/E3 **North Little Rock**, Ar,US
87/F3 **North Luangwa Nat'l Park**, Zam.
103/R7 **North Magnetic Pole**, NAm
107/J2 **North Moose** (lake), Mb,Can
113/J3 **North Myrtle Beach**, SC,US
37/H1 **North** (Nordkapp) (cape), Nor.
55/G4 **North Ossetian Aut. Rep.**, Rus.
111/R9 **North Pelham**, On,Can
34/C4 **North Petherton**, Eng,UK
76/E6 **North Pine** (riv.), Austl.
115/F5 **North Plainfield**, NJ,US
109/G2 **North Platte** (riv.), US
109/G2 **North Platte**, Ne,US
113/G3 **Northport**, Al,US
115/G5 **Northport** (Old Northport), NY,US
115/J7 **North Potomac**, Md,US
38/E3 **North Rhine-Westphalia** (state), Ger.
108/D3 **North Rim**, Az,US
106/F2 **North Saskatchewan** (riv.), Ab, Sk,Can
33/G2 **North Shields**, Eng,UK
56/K2 **North Siberian** (plain), Rus.
33/J5 **North Somercotes**, Eng,UK

76/D4 **North Stradbroke** (isl.), Austl.
75/R10 **North Taranaki** (bight), NZ
115/G4 **North Tarrytown**, NY,US
33/H5 **North Thoresby**, Eng,UK
35/E4 **North Tidworth**, Eng,UK
111/S9 **North Tonawanda**, NY,US
33/F1 **North Tyne** (riv.), Eng,UK
111/J2 **Northumberland** (str.), Can.
33/F1 **Northumberland** (co.), Eng,UK
33/F1 **Northumberland Nat'l Park**, Eng,UK
108/B2 **North Umpqua** (riv.), Or,US
102/D4 **North Vancouver**, BC,Can
116/F7 **Northville**, Mi,US
35/H1 **North Walsham**, Eng,UK
31/P6 **North Weald Bassett**, Eng,UK
74/A4 **North West** (cape), Austl.
68/B4 **Northwest Frontier** (prov.), Pak.
111/L1 **North West Gander** (riv.), Nf,Can
36/C2 **North West Highlands** (mts.), Sc,UK
102/E2 **Northwest Territories** (terr.), Can.
33/H5 **North Wheatley**, Eng,UK
33/F5 **Northwich**, Eng,UK
33/G5 **North Wingfield**, Eng,UK
107/J4 **Northwood**, ND,US
111/R8 **North York**, On,Can
33/H3 **North York Moors Nat'l Park**, Eng,UK
33/G3 **North Yorkshire** (co.), Eng,UK
114/F3 **Norton** (bay), Ak,US
114/E3 **Norton** (sound), Ak,US
109/H3 **Norton**, Ks,US
110/D4 **Norton**, Va,US
33/F6 **Norton Bridge**, Eng,UK
110/C3 **Norton Shores**, Mi,US
38/E1 **Nortorf**, Ger.
111/Q8 **Norval**, On,Can
98/Z **Norvegia** (cape), Ant.
43/F2 **Nörvenich**, Ger.
115/B3 **Norwalk**, Ca,US
115/G4 **Norwalk**, Ct,US
110/D3 **Norwalk**, Oh,US
37/B3 **Norway**
107/J2 **Norway House**, Mb,Can
103/S7 **Norwegian** (bay), NW,Can
30/C2 **Norwegian** (sea), Eur.
35/H1 **Norwich**, Eng,UK
110/F3 **Norwich**, NY,US
65/L10 **Nose**, Japan
61/K1 **Noshaq** (mtn.), Pak.
63/N3 **Noshiro**, Japan
51/H4 **Nos Maslen Nos** (pt.), Bul.
72/E2 **Nosong** (cape), Malay.
88/C2 **Nosop** (dry riv.), Bots.
54/D2 **Nosovka**, Ukr.
61/G3 **Noşratābād**, Iran
94/C3 **Nossa Senhora da Glória**, Braz.
94/C3 **Nossa Senhora das Dores**, Braz.
97/J7 **Notch** (cape), Chile
39/J2 **Notec** (riv.), Pol.
48/D4 **Noto**, It.
48/D4 **Noto** (gulf), It.
65/E2 **Noto** (pen.), Japan
48/D4 **Noto Antica** (ruins), It.
65/M9 **Notogawa**, Japan
111/L1 **Notre Dame** (bay), Nf,Can
111/G1 **Notre Dame** (mts.), Qu,Can
111/N7 **Notre-Dame-de-l'Ile-Perrot**, Qu,Can
110/E1 **Nottaway** (riv.), Qu,Can
103/H2 **Nottingham** (isl.), NW,Can
33/G6 **Nottingham**, Eng,UK
33/H5 **Nottinghamshire** (co.), Eng,UK
41/E5 **Nottuln**, Ger.
82/B3 **Nouadhibou**, Mrta.
84/B2 **Nouakchott** (cap.), Mrta.
79/V13 **Nouméa** (cap.), NCal.
88/D3 **Noupoort**, SAfr.
42/A3 **Nouvion**, Fr.
43/D4 **Nouzonville**, Fr.
93/H8 **Nova Andradina**, Braz.
51/F3 **Novaci**, Rom.
94/D2 **Nova Cruz**, Braz.
39/K4 **Nová Dubnica**, Slvk.
95/L7 **Nova Friburgo**, Braz.
50/C3 **Nova Gradiška**, Cro.
95/K7 **Nova Iguaçu**, Braz.
94/C2 **Nova Olinda**, Braz.
92/G4 **Nova Olinda do Norte**, Braz.
50/E3 **Nova Pazova**, Yugo.
95/B4 **Nova Prata**, Braz.
45/H4 **Novara**, It.
94/B2 **Nova Russas**, Braz.
111/J2 **Nova Scotia** (prov.), Can.
94/C3 **Nova Soure**, Braz.
116/J10 **Novato**, Ca,US
50/D4 **Nova Varoš**, Yugo.
95/D1 **Nova Venécia**, Braz.
93/H6 **Nova Xavantina**, Braz.
54/E3 **Novaya Kakhovka**, Ukr.
57/R2 **Novaya Sibir'** (isl.), Rus.
56/E2 **Novaya Zemlya** (isl.), Rus.
51/H4 **Nova Zagora**, Bul.
47/E3 **Novelda**, Sp.
39/J4 **Nové Mesto nad Váhom**, Slvk.
39/K5 **Nové Zámky**, Slvk.
52/F4 **Novgorod**, Rus.
52/G4 **Novgorod Obl.**, Rus.
116/F7 **Novi**, Mi,US
50/E3 **Novi Bečej**, Yugo.
51/F4 **Novi Iskŭr**, Bul.
45/H4 **Novi Ligure**, It.
51/H4 **Novi Pazar**, Bul.
50/E4 **Novi Pazar**, Yugo.
50/D3 **Novi Sad**, Yugo.
95/K6 **Novo** (riv.), Braz.
55/G2 **Novoanninskiy**, Rus.
92/F5 **Novo Aripuanã**, Braz.
53/K4 **Novocheboksarsk**, Rus.
54/G3 **Novocherkassk**, Rus.
54/C2 **Novograd-Volynskiy**, Ukr.
52/E5 **Novogrudok**, Bela.
95/B4 **Novo Hamburgo**, Braz.
95/B2 **Novo Horizonte**, Braz.
56/G5 **Novokazalinsk**, Kaz.
55/J1 **Novokuybyshevsk**, Rus.
56/J4 **Novokuznetsk**, Rus.
98/A **Novolazarevskaya**, Ant.
50/B3 **Novo Mesto**, Slov.
50/E3 **Novo Miloševo**, Yugo.
54/F1 **Novomoskovsk**, Rus.
54/E3 **Novomoskovsk**, Ukr.
94/B2 **Novo Oriente**, Braz.
52/F5 **Novopolotsk**, Bela.
54/F3 **Novorossiysk**, Rus.
54/F3 **Novoshakhtinsk**, Rus.
56/J4 **Novosibirsk**, Rus.
55/L2 **Novotroitsk**, Rus.
54/D2 **Novoukrainka**, Ukr.
54/C2 **Novovolynsk**, Ukr.
53/L4 **Novovyatsk**, Rus.
54/D1 **Novozybkov**, Rus.
50/C3 **Novska**, Cro.
39/K4 **Nový Jičín**, Czh.
55/K4 **Novyy Uzen'**, Kaz.
39/L3 **Nowa Dęba**, Pol.
39/J3 **Nowa Ruda**, Pol.
39/M3 **Nowa Sarzyna**, Pol.
39/H3 **Nowa Sól**, Pol.
109/J3 **Nowata**, Ok,US
39/K2 **Nowe**, Pol.
39/K2 **Nowe Miasto Lubawskie**, Pol.
70/C2 **Nowgong**, India
71/F2 **Nowgong**, India
114/H3 **Nowitna** (riv.), Ak,US
114/H3 **Nowitna Nat'l Wild. Ref.**, Ak,US
39/H2 **Nowogard**, Pol.
108/F1 **Nowood** (riv.), Wy,US
61/K2 **Nowshera**, Pak.
39/K1 **Nowy Dwór Gdański**, Pol.
39/L4 **Nowy Sącz**, Pol.
39/L4 **Nowy Sącz** (prov.), Pol.
39/L4 **Nowy Targ**, Pol.
39/J2 **Nowy Tomyśl**, Pol.
46/A1 **Noya**, Sp.
42/B5 **Noye** (riv.), Fr.
42/C4 **Noyon**, Fr.
87/G4 **Nsanje**, Malw.
85/E5 **Nsawam**, Gha.
62/D5 **Nu** (riv.), China
83/M5 **Nūbah** (mts.), Sudan
86/C4 **Nubian** (des.), Sudan
108/E3 **Nucla**, Co,US
112/D4 **Nueces** (riv.), Tx,US
102/G2 **Nueltin** (lake), NW,Can
40/C6 **Nuenen**, Neth.
66/E2 **Nü'er** (riv.), China
100/C5 **Nueva Concepción**, Guat.
100/E3 **Nueva Gerona**, Cuba
97/F2 **Nueva Helvecia**, Uru.
96/B3 **Nueva Imperial**, Chile
92/C3 **Nueva Loja**, Ecu.
97/S11 **Nueva Palmira**, Uru.
100/A2 **Nueva Rosita**, Mex.
101/F3 **Nuevitas**, Cuba
96/D4 **Nuevo** (gulf), Arg.
101/N7 **Nuevo Casas Grandes**, Mex.
101/N9 **Nuevo Ideal**, Mex.
100/B2 **Nuevo Laredo**, Mex.
100/A2 **Nuevo León** (state), Mex.
97/S11 **Nuevo Palmira**, Uru.
78/E5 **Nuguria** (isls.), PNG
79/J2 **Nuhau** (isl.), Hi,US
41/F6 **Nuhne** (riv.), Ger.
78/G5 **Nui** (atoll), Tuv.
65/N10 **Nukata**, Japan
114/F4 **Nuklunek** (mtn.), Ak,US
79/H7 **Nuku'alofa** (cap.), Tonga
78/G5 **Nukufetau** (atoll), Tuv.
79/L5 **Nuku Hiva** (isl.), FrPol.
78/H5 **Nukulaelae** (isl.), Tuv.
78/F5 **Nukumanu** (atoll), PNG
79/H5 **Nukunonu** (atoll), Tok.
78/E4 **Nukuoro** (isl.), Micr.
56/F5 **Nukus**, Uzb.
79/M6 **Nukutavake** (isl.), FrPol.
47/E3 **Nules**, Sp.
74/D6 **Nullarbor** (plain), Austl.
82/H6 **Numan**, Nga.
40/B5 **Numansdorp**, Neth.
65/F2 **Numata**, Japan
65/F3 **Numazu**, Japan
43/G2 **Nümbrecht**, Ger.
73/H4 **Numfoor** (isl.), Indo.
77/G5 **Nunawading**, Austl.
35/E1 **Nuneaton**, Eng,UK
77/D3 **Nungatta Nat'l Park**, Austl.
114/E4 **Nunivak** (isl.), Ak,US
40/C4 **Nunspeet**, Neth.
33/G2 **Nunthorpe**, Eng,UK
63/J1 **Nuomin** (riv.), China
84/C5 **Nuon** (riv.), IvC., Libr.
48/A2 **Nuoro**, It.
68/B2 **Nura** (riv.), Kaz.
43/F3 **Nürburgring**, Ger.
59/D3 **Nurhak**, Turk.
86/B5 **Nuri** (ruins), Sudan
45/J2 **Nürnberg**, Ger.
77/C1 **Nurri** (peak), Austl.
45/H2 **Nürtingen**, Ger.
59/L4 **Nuşarī'yah, Jabal an** (mts.), Syria
59/E3 **Nusaybin**, Turk.
114/G4 **Nushagak** (riv.), Ak,US
61/J3 **Nushki**, Pak.
43/E2 **Nuth**, Neth.
115/F5 **Nutley**, NJ,US
99/M3 **Nuuk** (Godthåb), Grld.
79/X15 **Nuupere** (pt.), FrPol.
86/C2 **Nuwaybi'**, Egypt
88/L10 **Nuy** (riv.), SAfr.
87/E4 **Nxai Pan Nat'l Park**, Bots.
115/G4 **Nyack**, NY,US
87/F2 **Nyahua**, Tanz.
68/F5 **Nyainqêntanglha Feng** (peak), China
83/K5 **Nyala**, Sudan
83/L6 **Nyamlell**, Sudan
52/J3 **Nyandoma**, Rus.
87/E1 **Nyanza-Lac**, Buru.
87/F3 **Nyasa** (Malawi) (lake), Afr.
38/F1 **Nyborg**, Den.
37/E4 **Nybro**, Swe.
39/L5 **Nyíradony**, Hun.
50/F2 **Nyírbátor**, Hun.
50/E2 **Nyíregyháza**, Hun.
83/N7 **Nyiru** (peak), Kenya
38/F1 **Nykøbing**, Den.
37/F4 **Nyköping**, Swe.
88/E2 **Nylstroom**, SAfr.
37/F4 **Nynäshamn**, Swe.
45/G3 **Nyon**, Swi.
45/K2 **Nýřany**, Czh.
39/J3 **Nysa**, Pol.
106/D5 **Nyssa**, Or,US
63/M4 **Nyūdo-zaki** (pt.), Japan
52/F2 **Nyuk** (lake), Rus.
87/E2 **Nyunzu**, Zaire
65/E2 **Nyūzen**, Japan
84/C5 **Nzérékoré**, Gui.
84/C4 **Nzérékoré** (comm.), Gui.
84/D5 **Nzi** (riv.), IvC.

O

35/E1 **Oadby**, Eng,UK
107/H4 **Oahe** (lake), ND, SD,US
104/V13 **Oahu** (isl.), Hi,US
107/J3 **Oakbank**, Mb,Can
116/Q14 **Oak Creek**, Wi,US
107/J4 **Oakes**, ND,US
116/Q16 **Oak Forest**, Il,US
35/F1 **Oakham**, Eng,UK
110/D4 **Oak Hill**, WV,US
108/C3 **Oakhurst**, Ca,US
116/K11 **Oakland**, Ca,US
115/F4 **Oakland**, NJ,US
116/A3 **Oakland** (bay), Wa,US
116/Q16 **Oak Lawn**, Il,US
35/E3 **Oakley**, Eng,UK
35/F2 **Oakley**, Eng,UK
116/L11 **Oakley**, Ca,US
109/G3 **Oakley**, Ks,US
74/C4 **Oakover** (riv.), Austl.
116/Q16 **Oak Park**, Il,US
116/F7 **Oak Park**, Mi,US
106/C5 **Oakridge**, Or,US
110/C4 **Oak Ridge**, Tn,US
111/R8 **Oak Ridges**, On,Can
34/D3 **Oaksey**, Eng,UK
115/A2 **Oak View**, Ca,US
111/Q9 **Oakville**, On,Can
75/R12 **Oamaru**, NZ
100/B4 **Oaxaca**, Mex.
100/B4 **Oaxaca** (state), Mex.
56/H3 **Ob'** (gulf), Rus.
56/G3 **Ob'** (riv.), Rus.
78/F6 **Oba** (isl.), Van.
110/D2 **Obabika** (lake), On,Can
64/D3 **Obama**, Japan
85/H5 **Oban** (hills), Camr., Nga.
75/Q12 **Oban**, NZ
110/D1 **Obasatika** (riv.), On,Can
65/M10 **Obata**, Japan
91/E2 **Oberá**, Arg.
40/D6 **Oberhausen**, Ger.
39/H3 **Oberlausitz** (reg.), Ger.
109/G3 **Oberlin**, Ks,US
45/H2 **Oberndorf am Neckar**, Ger.
41/G4 **Obernkirchen**, Ger.
43/G4 **Oberthal**, Ger.
45/L3 **Oberwölz**, Aus.
73/G4 **Obi** (isls.), Indo.
73/G4 **Obi** (str.), Indo.
93/G4 **Óbidos**, Braz.
63/N3 **Obihiro**, Japan
50/E4 **Obilić**, Yugo.
65/J7 **Obitsu** (riv.), Japan
69/B2 **Ob Luang Gorge**, Thai.
63/L2 **Obluch'ye**, Rus.
52/H5 **Obninsk**, Rus.
83/P5 **Obock**, Djib.
39/J2 **Oborniki**, Pol.
39/J3 **Oborniki Śląskie**, Pol.
39/J2 **Obra** (riv.), Pol.
50/E3 **Obrenovac**, Yugo.
65/M10 **Ōbu**, Japan
85/E5 **Obuasi**, Gha.
113/H4 **Ocala**, Fl,US
44/C5 **Occabe, Sommet d'** (peak), Fr.
92/E7 **Occidental, Cordillera** (range), SAm.
114/L4 **Ocean** (cape), Ak,US
115/G5 **Ocean Beach**, NY,US
110/F4 **Ocean City**, Md,US
106/B2 **Ocean Falls**, BC,Can
115/F5 **Ocean Grove**, NJ,US
78/* **Oceania**
108/C4 **Oceanside**, Ca,US
115/G5 **Oceanside**, NY,US
69/D4 **Oc-Eo** (ruins), Viet.
55/G4 **Ochamchira**, Geo.
63/P3 **Ochiishi-misaki** (cape), Japan
101/F4 **Ocho Rios**, Jam.
41/E4 **Ochtrup**, Ger.
41/F2 **Ochtum** (riv.), Ger.
35/E3 **Ock** (riv.), Eng,UK
52/C3 **Ockelbo**, Swe.
113/H4 **Ocmulgee** (riv.), Ga,US
51/F2 **Ocna Mureş**, Rom.
113/H3 **Oconee** (lake), Ga,US
113/H3 **Oconee** (riv.), Ga,US
100/D5 **Ocotal**, Nic.
100/A3 **Ocotlán**, Mex.
100/B4 **Ocotlán**, Mex.
44/C2 **Octeville**, Fr.
57/L1 **October Revolution** (isl.), Rus.
85/E5 **Oda**, Gha.
64/C3 **Oda**, Japan
65/M10 **Ōdai**, Japan
64/E3 **Ōdaigahara-san** (mtn.), Japan
86/D4 **Oda, Jabal** (peak), Sudan
63/N3 **Ōdate**, Japan
65/F3 **Odawara**, Japan
37/C3 **Odda**, Nor.
83/P7 **Oddur**, Som.
41/F6 **Odeborn** (riv.), Ger.
46/A4 **Odemira**, Port.
59/A2 **Ödemiş**, Turk.
88/D2 **Odendaalsrus**, SAfr.
38/F1 **Odense**, Den.
41/E6 **Odenthal**, Ger.
115/K7 **Odenton**, Md,US
39/H2 **Oderhaff** (lag.), Ger., Pol.
39/H2 **Oder** (Odra) (riv.), Ger., Pol.
45/K4 **Oderzo**, It.
54/D3 **Odessa**, Ukr.
112/C4 **Odessa**, Tx,US
106/D4 **Odessa**, Wa,US
51/J2 **Odessa Obl.**, Ukr.
44/B2 **Odet** (riv.), Fr.
84/D4 **Odienné**, IvC.
52/H5 **Odintsovo**, Rus.
67/D5 **Odiongan**, Phil.
47/P10 **Odivelas**, Port.
51/H3 **Odobeşti**, Rom.
44/C2 **Odon** (riv.), Fr.
69/D4 **Odongk**, Camb.
40/D3 **Odoorn**, Neth.
51/G2 **Odorheiu Secuiesc**, Rom.
39/H2 **Odra** (Oder) (riv.), Ger., Pol.
50/D3 **Odžaci**, Yugo.
82/J7 **Odzala Nat'l Park**, Congo
65/L9 **Ōe**, Japan
40/B4 **Oegstgeest**, Neth.
94/B2 **Oeiras**, Braz.
41/F5 **Oelde**, Ger.
45/K1 **Oelsnitz**, Ger.
79/M7 **Oeno** (atoll), Pitc.,UK
41/E5 **Oer-Erkenschwick**, Ger.
43/E4 **Oesling** (mts.), Lux.
40/B6 **Oesterdam** (dam), Neth.
45/H2 **Oestrich-Winkel**, Ger.
49/H3 **Oeta Nat'l Park**, Gre.
59/E2 **Of**, Turk.
48/D2 **Ofanto** (riv.), It.
59/K6 **Ofaqim**, Isr.
32/A5 **Offaly** (co.), Ire.
45/H1 **Offenbach**, Ger.
45/G2 **Offenburg**, Ger.
45/G3 **Oftringen**, Swi.
63/M4 **Oga**, Japan
83/P6 **Ogadēn** (reg.), Eth.
64/E3 **Ōgaki**, Japan
109/G2 **Ogallala**, Ne,US
78/D2 **Ogasawara**, Japan
85/G4 **Ogbomosho**, Nga.
108/E2 **Ogden**, Ut,US
110/F2 **Ogdensburg**, NY,US
113/H3 **Ogeechee** (riv.), Ga,US
110/D2 **Ogidaki** (mtn.), On,Can
114/L3 **Ogilvie** (mts.), Yk,Can
102/C2 **Ogilvie** (riv.), Yk,Can
45/J4 **Oglio** (riv.), It.
34/C4 **Ogmore by Sea**, Wal,UK
44/F3 **Ognon** (riv.), Fr.
73/F3 **Ogoamas** (peak), Indo.
107/M3 **Ogoki** (lake), On,Can
107/L3 **Ogoki** (res.), On,Can
107/M3 **Ogoki** (riv.), On,Can
82/G8 **Ogooué** (riv.), Gabon
65/H7 **Ogose**, Japan
51/F4 **Ogosta** (riv.), Bul.
52/E4 **Ogre**, Lat.
65/M9 **Oguchi**, Japan
50/B3 **Ogulin**, Cro.
85/F5 **Ogun** (riv.), Nga.
85/F5 **Ogun** (state), Nga.
55/K5 **Ogurchinskiy** (isl.), Trkm.
82/G2 **Ohanet**, Alg.
76/G8 **O'Hares** (cr.), Austl.
41/E2 **Ohe** (riv.), Ger.
97/J7 **O'Higgins** (lake), Chile
110/B4 **Ohio** (riv.), US
110/D3 **Ohio** (state), US
33/F1 **Oh Me Edge** (hill), Eng,UK
113/H3 **Ohoopee** (riv.), Ga,US
45/K1 **Ohře** (riv.), Czh.
38/F2 **Ohre** (riv.), Ger.
50/E5 **Ohrid** (lake), Alb., Macd.
50/E5 **Ohrid**, Macd.
71/G2 **Oi** (riv.), China
65/H7 **Ōi**, Japan
65/F3 **Ōi** (riv.), Japan
93/H3 **Oiapoque** (riv.), Braz.
47/P10 **Oieras**, Port.
42/B3 **Oignies**, Fr.
110/E3 **Oil City**, Pa,US
40/C5 **Oirschot**, Neth.
42/B5 **Oise** (dept.), Fr.
42/B5 **Oise** (riv.), Fr.
42/C5 **Oise à l'Aisne, Canal de** (can.), Fr.
42/A4 **Oisemont**, Fr.
65/H7 **Ōiso**, Japan
40/C5 **Oisterwijk**, Neth.
42/C3 **Oisy-le-Verger**, Fr.
64/B4 **Ōita**, Japan
64/B4 **Ōita** (pref.), Japan
64/B4 **Ōita** (riv.), Japan
115/A2 **Ojai**, Ca,US
39/K3 **Ojcowski Nat'l Park**, Pol.
65/L10 **Ōji**, Japan
101/P8 **Ojinaga**, Mex.
65/F2 **Ojiya**, Japan
100/A3 **Ojocaliente**, Mex.
91/C2 **Ojos del Salado** (peak), Arg., Chile
101/L7 **Ojos Negros**, Mex.
53/J4 **Oka** (riv.), Rus.
103/K3 **Okak** (isl.), Nf,Can
106/C3 **Okanagan** (lake), BC,Can
106/D3 **Okanagan Falls**, BC,Can
87/B1 **Okanda Nat'l Park**, Gabon
106/D3 **Okanogan**, Wa,US
106/D3 **Okanogan** (riv.), Wa,US
61/K2 **Okāra**, Pak.
87/C4 **Okaukuejo**, Namb.
87/D4 **Okavango Delta** (reg.), Bots.
64/B4 **Ōkawa**, Japan
65/F2 **Okaya**, Japan
64/C3 **Okayama**, Japan
64/C3 **Okayama** (pref.), Japan
65/E3 **Okazaki**, Japan
113/H5 **Okeechobee**, Fl,US
113/H5 **Okeechobee** (lake), Fl,US
65/H7 **Okegawa**, Japan
34/C5 **Okehampton**, Eng,UK
34/B5 **Okement** (riv.), Eng,UK
41/H4 **Oker** (riv.), Ger.
57/Q4 **Okha**, Rus.
49/J3 **Ókhi** (peak), Gre.
57/Q4 **Okhotsk** (sea), Japan, Rus.
64/C2 **Oki** (isls.), Japan
64/C2 **Oki-Daisen Nat'l Park**, Japan
67/E2 **Okinawa** (isls.), Japan
78/C2 **Okino-Tori-Shima** (Parece Vela) (isl.), Japan
71/G4 **Okkan**, Burma
109/H4 **Oklahoma** (state), US
109/H4 **Oklahoma City** (cap.), Ok,US
113/H4 **Oklawaha** (riv.), Fl,US
109/J4 **Okmulgee**, Ok,US
107/K5 **Okoboji** (lakes), Ia,US
113/F3 **Okolona**, Ms,US
106/E3 **Okotoks**, Ab,Can
80/E6 **Okovango** (riv.), Afr.
86/C4 **Oko, Wādī** (dry riv.), Sudan
37/E2 **Oksskolten** (peak), Nor.
55/J1 **Oktyabr'sk**, Rus.
53/M5 **Oktyabr'skiy**, Rus.
52/G4 **Okulovka**, Rus.
63/M3 **Okushiri** (isl.), Japan
65/H7 **Okutama**, Japan
87/D5 **Okwa** (riv.), Bots.
108/C3 **Olancha**, Ca,US
100/D4 **Olanchito**, Hon.
37/F4 **Öland** (isl.), Swe.
37/F4 **Ölands södra udde** (pt.), Swe.
45/G4 **Olan, Pic d'** (peak), Fr.
48/D2 **Olanto** (riv.), It.
108/F3 **Olathe**, Co,US
109/J3 **Olathe**, Ks,US
96/E3 **Olavarría**, Arg.
39/J3 **Oława**, Pol.
41/F5 **Olbach** (riv.), Ger.
48/A2 **Olbia**, It.
45/J2 **Olching**, Ger.
111/S9 **Olcott**, NY,US
116/D3 **Old Baldy** (mtn.), Wa,US
115/F5 **Old Bridge**, NJ,US
114/L2 **Old Crow**, Yk,Can
40/C4 **Oldebroek**, Neth.
41/F2 **Oldenburg**, Ger.
40/D4 **Oldenzaal**, Neth.
33/F4 **Oldham**, Eng,UK
106/E3 **Oldman** (riv.), Ab,Can
32/E3 **Old Man of Coolston, The** (mtn.), Eng,UK
35/F2 **Old Nene** (riv.), Eng,UK
115/G5 **Old Northport** (Northport), NY,US
41/F1 **Oldoog** (isl.), Ger.
111/G2 **Old Town**, Me,US
31/M7 **Old Windsor**, Eng,UK
107/G3 **Old Wives** (lake), Sk,Can
110/E3 **Olean**, NY,US
39/M1 **Olecko**, Pol.
46/A1 **Oleiros**, Sp.
57/N4 **Olekma** (riv.), Rus.
116/B2 **Olele** (pt.), Wa,US
52/G1 **Olenegorsk**, Rus.
57/N2 **Olenëk** (bay), Rus.
57/N2 **Olenëk** (riv.), Rus.
68/B1 **Olenty** (riv.), Kaz.
44/C4 **Oléron** (isl.), Fr.
47/K6 **Olesa de Montserrat**, Sp.
39/J3 **Oleśnica**, Pol.
39/K3 **Olesno**, Pol.
41/E5 **Olfen**, Ger.
62/B2 **Ölgiy**, Mong.
46/B4 **Olhão**, Port.
94/C3 **Olho d'Água dos Flores**, Braz.
45/L4 **Olib** (isl.), Cro.
48/A2 **Oliena**, It.
88/B2 **Olifants** (dry riv.), Namb.
88/B3 **Olifants** (riv.), SAfr.
88/E2 **Olifantsrivier** (riv.), SAfr.
78/D4 **Olimarao** (atoll), Micr.
49/H2 **Olimbos** (Mount Olympus) (peak), Gre.
95/B2 **Olímpia**, Braz.
94/D3 **Olinda**, Braz.
94/C3 **Olindina**, Braz.
96/E2 **Oliva**, Arg.
47/E3 **Oliva**, Sp.
46/B3 **Oliva de la Frontera**, Sp.
46/A3 **Olivais**, Port.
95/C2 **Oliveira**, Braz.
46/B3 **Olivenza**, Sp.
106/D3 **Oliver**, BC,Can
44/D3 **Olivet**, Fr.
92/E8 **Ollagüe** (vol.), Bol.
31/S11 **Ollainville**, Fr.
47/E3 **Olleria**, Sp.
70/C5 **Ollūr**, India
96/Q9 **Olmué**, Chile
35/F2 **Olney**, Eng,UK
110/B4 **Olney**, Il,US
115/J7 **Olney**, Md,US
111/J1 **Olomane** (riv.), Qu,Can
39/J4 **Olomouc**, Czh.
67/D5 **Olongapo**, Phil.
44/C3 **Olonne-sur-Mer**, Fr.
44/C5 **Oloron-Sainte-Marie**, Fr.
47/G1 **Olot**, Sp.
57/S3 **Oloy** (range), Rus.
41/E6 **Olpe**, Ger.
41/F6 **Olsberg**, Ger.
40/D4 **Olst**, Neth.
39/L2 **Olsztyn**, Pol.
39/L2 **Olsztyn** (prov.), Pol.
39/L2 **Olsztynek**, Pol.
51/G3 **Olt** (co.), Rom.
51/G4 **Olt** (riv.), Rom.
96/C4 **Olte** (mts.), Arg.
45/G3 **Olten**, Swi.
51/H3 **Olteniţa**, Rom.
51/F3 **Olteţ** (riv.), Rom.
59/E2 **Oltu**, Turk.
59/E2 **Oltu** (riv.), Turk.
67/D3 **Oluanpi**, Tai.
46/C4 **Olvera**, Sp.
116/B3 **Olympia** (cap.), Wa,US
49/G4 **Olympia** (Olimbía) (ruins), Gre.
106/B4 **Olympic** (mts.), Wa,US
106/B4 **Olympic Nat'l Park**, Wa,US
59/J4 **Olympus** (mtn.), Cyp.
106/C4 **Olympus** (peak), Wa,US
49/H2 **Olympus, Mount** (Ólimbos) (peak), Gre.
49/H2 **Olympus Nat'l Park**, Gre.
57/S3 **Olyutorskiy** (bay), Rus.
53/K2 **Oma** (riv.), Rus.
65/E2 **Ōmachi**, Japan
65/F3 **Omae-zaki** (pt.), Japan
32/A2 **Omagh**, NI,UK
32/A2 **Omagh** (dist.), NI,UK
109/J2 **Omaha**, Ne,US
106/D3 **Omak**, Wa,US
61/G4 **Oman**
61/G4 **Oman** (gulf), Asia
87/C4 **Omatako** (riv.), Namb.
73/F5 **Ombai** (str.), Indo.
34/D2 **Ombersley**, Eng,UK
87/B4 **Ombombo**, Namb.
87/A1 **Omboué**, Gabon
48/B1 **Ombrone** (riv.), It.
83/M4 **Omdurman** (Umm Durmān), Sudan
65/H7 **Ōme**, Japan
45/H4 **Omegna**, It.
100/B4 **Ometepec**, Mex.
65/M9 **Ōmihachiman**, Japan
48/E1 **Omiš**, Cro.
65/G2 **Ōmiya**, Japan
114/M4 **Ommaney** (cape), Ak,US
40/D3 **Ommen**, Neth.
62/F2 **Ömnödelger**, Mong.
62/C2 **Ömnögovi**, Mong.
48/A2 **Omodeo** (lake), It.
58/Q3 **Omolon** (riv.), Rus.
83/N6 **Omo Nat'l Park**, Eth.
83/N6 **Omo Wenz** (riv.), Eth.
56/H4 **Omsk**, Rus.
51/G3 **Omul** (peak), Rom.
51/H4 **Omurtag**, Bul.
64/B4 **Ōmuta**, Japan
53/M4 **Omutninsk**, Rus.
65/G1 **Onagawa**, Japan
109/J5 **Onalaska**, Tx,US
46/D1 **Oñate**, Sp.
110/C2 **Onaway**, Mi,US
96/E1 **Oncativo**, Arg.
32/D3 **Onchan**, IM,UK
87/B4 **Oncocúa**, Ang.
47/E3 **Onda**, Sp.
87/C4 **Ondangua**, Namb.
39/L4 **Ondava** (riv.), Slvk.
87/C4 **Ondjiva**, Ang.
85/G5 **Ondo** (state), Nga.
62/G2 **Öndörhaan**, Mong.
62/C2 **Öndorhangay**, Mong.
52/H3 **Onega**, Rus.
52/H2 **Onega** (bay), Rus.
52/G3 **Onega** (lake), Rus.
52/H2 **Onega** (pen.), Rus.
52/H3 **Onega** (riv.), Rus.
106/C3 **One Hundred Mile House**, BC,Can
110/F3 **Oneida**, NY,US
109/H2 **O'Neill**, Ne,US
110/F3 **Oneonta**, NY,US
62/E2 **Ongiyn** (riv.), Mong.
70/D4 **Ongole**, India
107/H4 **Onida**, SD,US
47/E3 **Onil**, Sp.
89/G8 **Onilahy** (riv.), Madg.
85/G5 **Onitsha**, Nga.
89/H7 **Onive** (riv.), Madg.
42/C3 **Onnaing**, Fr.
34/D2 **Onny** (riv.), Eng,UK
64/D3 **Ono**, Japan
64/E3 **Ōno**, Japan
64/B4 **Onoda**, Japan
64/C3 **Onomichi**, Japan
62/G1 **Onon** (riv.), Mong., Rus.
78/G5 **Onotoa** (atoll), Kiri.
65/E3 **Ontake-san** (mtn.), Japan
102/H3 **Ontario** (prov.), Can.
110/E3 **Ontario** (lake), Can., US
115/C2 **Ontario**, Ca,US
106/D4 **Ontario**, Or,US
47/E3 **Onteniente**, Sp.
110/B2 **Ontonagon**, Mi,US
78/F5 **Ontong Java** (isl.), Sol.
112/E2 **Oologan** (lake), Ok,US
40/A6 **Oostburg**, Neth.
40/C4 **Oostelijk Flevoland** (polder), Neth.
42/B1 **Oostende**, Belg.
40/B5 **Oosterhout**, Neth.
40/A5 **Oosterschelde** (chan.), Neth.
42/C2 **Oosterzele**, Belg.
42/C1 **Oostkamp**, Belg.
40/C4 **Oostvaardersplassen** (lake), Neth.
40/B4 **Oostzaan**, Neth.
70/C5 **Ootacamund**, India
107/B2 **Ootsa** (lake), BC,Can
87/D1 **Opala**, Zaire
39/J2 **Opalenica**, Pol.
50/B3 **Opatija**, Cro.
39/L3 **Opatów**, Pol.
39/J4 **Opava**, Czh.
113/G3 **Opelika**, Al,US
112/E4 **Opelousas**, La,US
110/E2 **Opeongo** (lake), On,Can
43/E1 **Opglabbeek**, Belg.
40/C5 **Oploo**, Neth.
40/B3 **Opmeer**, Neth.
39/L3 **Opoczno**, Pol.
39/J3 **Opole**, Pol.
39/J3 **Opole** (prov.), Pol.
39/L3 **Opole Lubelskie**, Pol.
113/G4 **Opp**, Al,US
37/D3 **Oppdal**, Nor.
37/D3 **Oppland** (co.), Nor.
106/D4 **Opportunity**, Wa,US
42/D2 **Opwijk**, Belg.
50/E2 **Oradea**, Rom.
50/E4 **Orahovac**, Yugo.
70/C2 **Orai**, India
81/Q16 **Oran**, Alg.
88/B3 **Orange** (riv.), Afr.
77/D2 **Orange**, Austl.
44/F4 **Orange**, Fr.
93/H3 **Orange** (mts.), Sur.
115/C3 **Orange**, Ca,US
115/F5 **Orange**, NJ,US
112/E4 **Orange**, Tx,US
110/E4 **Orange**, Va,US
113/H3 **Orangeburg**, SC,US
88/D3 **Orange Free State** (prov.), SAfr.
113/H4 **Orange Park**, Fl,US
110/D3 **Orangeville**, On,Can
100/D4 **Orange Walk**, Belz.
84/A4 **Orango** (isl.), GBis.
39/G2 **Oranienburg**, Ger.
40/D3 **Oranjekanaal** (can.), Neth.
101/G5 **Oranjestad** (cap.), Aru.
81/Q16 **Oran, Sebkha d'** (lake), Alg.
87/E5 **Orapa**, Bots.
59/M8 **Or 'Aqiva**, Isr.
67/E5 **Oras**, Phil.
51/F3 **Orăştie**, Rom.
50/E3 **Oraviţa**, Rom.
44/E5 **Orb** (riv.), Fr.
46/C1 **Órbigo** (riv.), Sp.
112/B2 **Orchard City**, Co,US
106/E4 **Orchard Homes**, Mt,US
116/F6 **Orchard Lake Village**, Mi,US
67/D3 **Orchid** (isl.), Tai.
45/G4 **Orco** (riv.), It.
44/F3 **Or, Côte d'** (uplands), Fr.
109/H2 **Ord**, Ne,US
46/A1 **Ordenes**, Sp.
47/F1 **Ordesa y Monte Perdido Nat'l Park**, Sp.
66/B3 **Ordos** (des.), China
59/D2 **Ordu**, Turk.
109/G3 **Ordway**, Co,US
37/E4 **Örebro**, Swe.
37/E4 **Örebro** (co.), Swe.
106/C4 **Oregon** (state), US
108/B2 **Oregon Caves Nat'l Mon.**, Or,US
106/C4 **Oregon City**, Or,US
54/F1 **Orël**, Rus.
54/E2 **Orel'** (riv.), Ukr.
54/E1 **Orel Obl.**, Rus.
108/E2 **Orem**, Ut,US
55/K2 **Orenburg**, Rus.
55/K1 **Orenburg Obl.**, Rus.
46/B1 **Orense**, Sp.
49/K2 **Orestiás**, Gre.
35/H2 **Orford**, Eng,UK
35/H2 **Orford Ness** (pt.), UK
108/D4 **Organ Pipe Cactus Nat'l Mon.**, Az,US
95/L7 **Órgãos** (mts.), Braz.
31/S11 **Orge** (riv.), Fr.
31/R10 **Orgeval**, Fr.
51/J2 **Orgeyev**, Mol.
54/D5 **Orhaneli**, Turk.
51/J5 **Orhangazi**, Turk.
62/F2 **Orhon** (riv.), Mong.
44/C5 **Orhy, Pic d'** (peak), Fr.
91/C6 **Oriental** (val.), Arg.
92/D6 **Oriental, Cordillera** (range), SAm.
47/E3 **Orihuela**, Sp.
110/E2 **Orillia**, On,Can
116/K11 **Orinda**, Ca,US
92/F2 **Orinoco** (riv.), Col., Ven.
101/J6 **Orinoco** (delta), Ven.
116/F6 **Orion** (lake), Mi,US
70/D3 **Orissa** (state), India
48/A3 **Oristano**, It.
48/A3 **Oristano** (gulf), It.
37/H3 **Orivesi**, Fin.
93/G4 **Oriximiná**, Braz.
100/B4 **Orizaba**, Mex.
50/D4 **Orjen** (peak), Yugo.
41/F6 **Orke** (riv.), Ger.
30/C3 **Orkney** (isls.), Sc,UK
112/C4 **Orla**, Tx,US
95/C2 **Orlândia**, Braz.
113/H4 **Orlando**, Fl,US
48/D3 **Orlando, Capo d'** (cape), It.
116/Q16 **Orland Park**, Il,US
44/D2 **Orléanais** (hist. reg.), Fr.
44/D3 **Orléans**, Fr.
108/B2 **Orleans**, Ca,US
39/K4 **Orlová**, Czh.
31/T10 **Orly**, Fr.
67/D5 **Ormoc**, Phil.
113/H4 **Ormond Beach**, Fl,US
33/F4 **Ormskirk**, Eng,UK
44/F2 **Ornain** (riv.), Fr.
43/F5 **Orne** (riv.), Fr.
37/E2 **Ørnes**, Nor.
39/L1 **Orneta**, Pol.
37/F3 **Örnsköldsvik**, Swe.
101/N8 **Oro** (riv.), Mex.
45/J3 **Orobie, Alpi** (range), It.
84/D4 **Orodara**, Burk.
47/E1 **Oroel** (peak), Sp.
106/D4 **Orofino**, Id,US
79/L6 **Orohena** (peak), FrPol.
78/E4 **Oroluk** (atoll), Micr.
111/H2 **Oromocto**, NB,Can
48/A1 **Oro, Monte d'** (mtn.), Fr.
79/H5 **Orona** (Hull) (atoll), Kiri.
111/G2 **Orono**, Me,US
59/L4 **Orontes** (riv.), Asia
63/J1 **Oroqen Zizhiqi**, China
73/F2 **Oroquieta**, Phil.
94/C2 **Orós**, Braz.
94/C2 **Orós** (res.), Braz.
48/A2 **Orosei** (gulf), It.
50/E2 **Orosháza**, Hun.
50/D2 **Oroszlány**, Hun.
108/C2 **Orovada**, Nv,US
108/E4 **Oro Valley**, Az,US
108/B3 **Oroville**, Ca,US
106/D3 **Oroville**, Wa,US
31/P7 **Orpington**, Eng,UK
33/F4 **Orrell**, Eng,UK
31/T9 **Orry-la-Ville**, Fr.
37/E3 **Orsa**, Swe.
31/S10 **Orsay**, Fr.

Orset – Pearl

31/Q7 **Orsett**, Eng,UK
52/F5 **Orsha**, Bela.
55/L2 **Orsk**, Rus.
50/F3 **Orşova**, Rom.
37/C3 **Ørsta**, Nor.
45/H4 **Orta** (lake), It.
59/C2 **Orta**, Turk.
59/B3 **Ortaca**, Turk.
48/D2 **Orta Nova**, It.
46/B1 **Ortegal** (cape), Sp.
44/C5 **Orthez**, Fr.
46/B1 **Ortigueira**, Sp.
45/J3 **Ortles** (mts.), It., Swi.
92/E6 **Ortón** (riv.), Bol.
63/H2 **Orton** (riv.), China
48/D1 **Ortona**, It.
116/F6 **Ortonville**, Mi,US
107/J4 **Ortonville**, Mn,US
41/H3 **Örtze** (riv.), Ger.
59/F3 **Orūmīyeh**, Iran
92/E7 **Oruro**, Bol.
48/C1 **Orvieto**, It.
98/V **Orville** (coast), Ant.
35/H2 **Orwell** (riv.), Eng,UK
62/H2 **Orxon** (riv.), China
51/F4 **Oryakhovo**, Bul.
59/M8 **Or Yehuda**, Isr.
53/M4 **Osa**, Rus.
109/J3 **Osage** (riv.), Mo,US
109/J3 **Osage Beach**, Mo,US
64/D3 **Ōsaka**, Japan
65/L10 **Ōsaka** (bay), Japan
64/D3 **Ōsaka** (pref.), Japan
64/L10 **Ōsaka** (inset), Japan
63/K4 **Osan**, SKor.
95/G8 **Osasco**, Braz.
114/E3 **Osborn** (mtn.), Ak,US
109/H3 **Osborne**, Ks,US
113/F3 **Osceola**, Ar,US
38/F2 **Oschersleben**, Ger.
112/B3 **Oscura** (mts.), NM,US
68/B3 **Osh**, Kyr.
87/C4 **Oshakati**, Namb.
111/S8 **Oshawa**, On,Can
63/M3 **Oshima** (pen.), Japan
87/C4 **Oshivelo**, Namb.
107/H5 **Oshkosh**, Ne,US
110/B2 **Oshkosh**, Wi,US
59/F3 **Oshnovīyeh**, Iran
85/G5 **Oshogbo**, Nga.
87/C1 **Oshwe**, Zaire
50/D3 **Osijek**, Cro.
45/K5 **Osimo**, It.
54/D1 **Osipovichi**, Bela.
107/K5 **Oskaloosa**, Ia,US
37/F4 **Oskarshamn**, Swe.
54/F2 **Oskol** (riv.), Rus., Ukr.
37/D4 **Oslo** (cap.), Nor.
70/C4 **Osmānābād**, India
59/C2 **Osmancık**, Turk.
51/K5 **Osmaneli**, Turk.
59/D3 **Osmaniye**, Turk.
41/F4 **Osnabrück**, Ger.
31/S9 **Osny**, Fr.
95/B4 **Osório**, Braz.
96/B4 **Osorno**, Chile
106/D3 **Osoyoos**, BC,Can
76/B1 **Osprey** (reef), Austl.
40/C5 **Oss**, Neth.
77/C4 **Ossa** (peak), Austl.
49/H3 **Ossa** (mtn.), Gre.
46/B3 **Ossa** (range), Port.
85/G5 **Osse** (riv.), Nga.
33/G4 **Ossett**, Eng,UK
115/G4 **Ossining**, NY,US
52/G4 **Ostashkov**, Rus.
41/E4 **Ostbevern**, Ger.
41/G1 **Oste** (riv.), Ger.
42/B1 **Ostend** (Oostende), Belg.
38/F2 **Osterburg**, Ger.
41/F4 **Ostercappeln**, Ger.
40/D1 **Osterems** (chan.), Neth.
37/E4 **Östergötland** (co.), Swe.
45/K2 **Osterhofen**, Ger.
41/F2 **Osterholz-Scharmbeck**, Ger.
41/H5 **Osterode**, Ger.
38/F3 **Osterode am Harz**, Ger.
37/E3 **Östersund**, Swe.
37/D4 **Østfold** (co.), Nor.
41/E2 **Ostfriesland** (reg.), Ger.
37/F3 **Östhammar**, Swe.
48/C2 **Ostia Antica** (ruins), It.
45/J4 **Ostiglia**, It.
39/K4 **Ostrava**, Czh.
41/E2 **Ostrhauderfehn**, Ger.
42/C3 **Ostricourt**, Fr.
50/D4 **Oštri Rt** (cape), Yugo.
39/K2 **Ostróda**, Pol.
54/F2 **Ostrogozhsk**, Rus.
39/L2 **Ostrołęka**, Pol.
39/L2 **Ostrołęka** (prov.), Pol.
45/K1 **Ostrov**, Czh.
52/F4 **Ostrov**, Rus.
39/L3 **Ostrowiec Świętokrzyski**, Pol.
39/L2 **Ostrów Mazowiecka**, Pol.
39/J3 **Ostrów Wielkopolski**, Pol.
39/J3 **Ostrzeszów**, Pol.
41/H1 **Oststeinbek**, Ger.
48/E2 **Ostuni**, It.
49/G2 **Osum** (riv.), Alb.
51/G4 **Osŭm** (riv.), Bul.
64/B5 **Ōsumi** (isls.), Japan
64/B5 **Ōsumi** (pen.), Japan
64/B5 **Ōsumi** (str.), Japan
46/C4 **Osuna**, Sp.
95/B2 **Osvaldo Cruz**, Braz.
33/G3 **Oswaldkirk**, Eng,UK
33/F4 **Oswaldtwistle**, Eng,UK
110/E3 **Oswego**, NY,US
33/E6 **Oswestry**, Eng,UK
39/K3 **Oświęcim** (Auschwitz), Pol.
64/F2 **Ōta**, Japan
64/C3 **Ōta** (riv.), Japan
64/C3 **Ōtake**, Japan
65/G2 **Ōtakine-yama** (mtn.), Japan
45/K2 **Otava** (riv.), Czh.
65/G2 **Ōtawara**, Japan
50/F3 **Oţelu Roşu**, Rom.
79/L6 **Otepa**, FrPol.
101/N8 **Oteros** (riv.), Mex.
62/D2 **Otgon**, Mong.
62/D2 **Otgon Tenger** (peak), Mong.
106/D4 **Othello**, Wa,US
31/U9 **Othis**, Fr.
49/F3 **Othonoí** (isl.), Gre.
85/F4 **Oti** (riv.), Gui.
75/R11 **Otira**, NZ
87/C5 **Otjikango**, Namb.
87/C5 **Otjinene**, Namb.
87/C5 **Otjiwarongo**, Namb.
87/B4 **Otjokavare**, Namb.
33/G4 **Otley**, Eng,UK
66/A3 **Otog Qi**, China
107/L3 **Otoskwin** (riv.), On,Can
65/N10 **Otowa**, Japan
37/C4 **Otra** (riv.), Nor.
55/J1 **Otradnyy**, Rus.
49/F2 **Otranto** (str.), Alb., It.
39/J4 **Otrokovice**, Czh.
64/D3 **Ōtsu**, Japan
37/D3 **Otta**, Nor.
110/F2 **Ottawa** (cap.), Can.
103/H3 **Ottawa** (isls.), NW,Can
110/E2 **Ottawa** (riv.), On, Qu,Can
110/B3 **Ottawa**, Il,US
109/J3 **Ottawa**, Ks,US
110/C3 **Ottawa**, Oh,US
34/C5 **Otter** (riv.), Eng,UK
33/F1 **Otterburn**, Eng,UK
41/F1 **Otterndorf**, Ger.
41/G2 **Ottersberg**, Ger.
31/M7 **Ottershaw**, Eng,UK
34/C5 **Ottery Saint Mary**, Eng,UK
42/D2 **Ottignies-Louvain-La-Neuve**, Belg.
45/J2 **Ottobrunn**, Ger.
107/K5 **Ottumwa**, Ia,US
43/G5 **Ottweiler**, Ger.
77/B3 **Otway** (cape), Austl.
97/J8 **Otway** (bay), Chile
97/K8 **Otway** (sound), Chile
77/B3 **Otway Nat'l Park**, Austl.
39/L2 **Otwock**, Pol.
69/C1 **Ou** (riv.), Laos
112/E3 **Ouachita** (riv.), Ar, La,US
109/J4 **Ouachita** (mts.), Ar, Ok,US
82/C3 **Ouadane**, Mrta.
83/J5 **Ouaddaï** (reg.), Chad
85/E3 **Ouagadougou** (cap.), Burk.
83/K6 **Ouaka** (riv.), CAfr.
84/D2 **Oualâta, Dhar** (hills), Mrta.
44/E3 **Ouanne** (riv.), Fr.
82/C3 **Ouarane** (reg.), Mrta.
82/G1 **Ouargla**, Alg.
82/D1 **Ouarzazate**, Mor.
111/F1 **Ouasiemsca** (riv.), Qu,Can
81/S16 **Ouassel, Nahr** (riv.), Alg.
83/J6 **Oubangui** (riv.), CAfr.
85/E3 **Oubritenga** (prov.), Burk.
65/L10 **Ōuda**, Japan
85/E3 **Oudalan** (prov.), Burk.
40/B5 **Oud-Beijerland**, Neth.
40/A5 **Ouddorp**, Neth.
40/D5 **Oude IJssel** (riv.), Neth.
42/C2 **Oudenaarde**, Belg.
40/B5 **Oudenbosch**, Neth.
42/B1 **Oudenburg**, Belg.
40/E2 **Oude Pekela**, Neth.
44/C3 **Oudon** (riv.), Fr.
88/C4 **Oudtshoorn**, SAfr.
40/B6 **Oud-Turnhout**, Belg.
84/E2 **Oued el Hadjar** (well), Mali
81/R16 **Oued Rhiou**, Alg.
82/D1 **Oued Zem**, Mor.
85/F5 **Ouémé** (prov.), Ben.
85/F4 **Ouémé** (riv.), Ben.
79/V13 **Ouen** (isl.), NCal.
81/W18 **Ouenza**, Alg.
81/M13 **Ouerrha** (riv.), Mor.
44/A2 **Ouessant** (isl.), Fr.
82/J7 **Ouesso**, Congo
85/H5 **Ouest** (prov.), Camr.
101/G4 **Ouest** (pt.), Haiti
81/M13 **Ouezzane**, Mor.
83/J6 **Ouham** (riv.), CAfr., Chad
42/C5 **Ouichy-le-Château**, Fr.
81/P13 **Oujda**, Mor.
37/J2 **Oulangan Nat'l Park**, Fin.
77/A2 **Oulnina** (peak), Austl.
37/H2 **Oulu**, Fin.
37/H2 **Oulu** (prov.), Fin.
37/H2 **Oulujärvi** (lake), Fin.
81/V18 **Oum El Bouaghi**, Alg.
82/D1 **Oum er Rhia** (riv.), Mor.
83/J5 **Oum Hadjer**, Chad
52/E2 **Ounasjoki** (riv.), Fin.
35/F2 **Oundle**, Eng,UK
83/K4 **OuniangaKebir**, Chad
43/E2 **Oupeye**, Belg.
43/F4 **Our** (riv.), Eur.
44/F3 **Ource** (riv.), Fr.
42/C5 **Ourcq** (riv.), Fr.
37/H1 **Øvre Anarjokka Nat'l Park**, Nor.
37/F1 **Øvre Dividal Nat'l Park**, Nor.
83/J3 **Ouri**, Chad
94/B2 **Ouricuri**, Braz.
95/B2 **Ourinhos**, Braz.
85/H3 **Ourofané**, Niger
95/G7 **Ouro Fino**, Braz.
95/D2 **Ouro Preto**, Braz.
43/E3 **Ourthe** (riv.), Belg.
33/H4 **Ouse** (riv.), Eng,UK
35/G5 **Ouse** (riv.), Eng,UK
44/B3 **Oust** (riv.), Fr.
47/Q11 **Outão**, Port.
110/E2 **Outaouais** (riv.), Qu,Can
111/G1 **Outardes** (riv.), Qu,Can
111/G1 **Outardes Quatre** (res.), Qu,Can
84/D2 **Outeïd Arkas** (well), Mali
36/A2 **Outer Hebrides** (isls.), Sc,UK
46/A1 **Outes**, Sp.
106/G3 **Outlook**, Sk,Can
42/A2 **Outreau**, Fr.
111/N6 **Outremont**, Qu,Can
79/V12 **Ouvéa** (atoll), NCal.
45/H4 **Ovada**, It.
79/Y18 **Ovalau** (isl.), Fiji
91/B3 **Ovalle**, Chile
46/A2 **Ovar**, Port.
43/G2 **Overath**, Ger.
40/B5 **Overflakkee** (isl.), Neth.
42/D2 **Overijse**, Belg.
40/D3 **Overijssel** (prov.), Neth.
40/D4 **Overijssels** (can.), Neth.
109/J3 **Overland Park**, Ks,US
115/K7 **Overlea**, Md,US
96/C5 **Overo** (peak), Arg.
43/E1 **Overpelt**, Belg.
35/E1 **Overseal**, Eng,UK
35/H1 **Overstrand**, Eng,UK
35/E4 **Overton**, Eng,UK
33/F6 **Overton**, Wal,UK
108/D3 **Overton**, Nv,US
37/G2 **Övertorneå**, Swe.
46/C1 **Oviedo**, Sp.
37/J1 **Øvre Pasvik Nat'l Park**, Nor.
87/C1 **Owando**, Congo
65/N9 **Owariasahi**, Japan
64/E3 **Owase**, Japan
109/J3 **Owasso**, Ok,US
107/K4 **Owatonna**, Mn,US
110/E3 **Owego**, NY,US
67/B6 **Owen** (shoal)
75/R11 **Owen** (peak), NZ
32/A2 **Owenkillew** (riv.), NI,UK
108/C3 **Owens** (riv.), Ca,US
110/C4 **Owensboro**, Ky,US
110/D2 **Owen Sound**, On,Can
108/C2 **Owhyee** (mts.), Id,US
115/K7 **Owings Mills**, Md,US
106/F4 **Owl Creek** (mts.), Wy,US
110/C3 **Owosso**, Mi,US
106/D5 **Owyhee** (riv.), Id, Or,US
108/C2 **Owyhee**, Nv,US
108/C2 **Owyhee** (lake), Or,US
60/E1 **Owzan** (riv.), Iran
107/H3 **Oxbow**, Sk,Can
107/K2 **Oxford** (lake), Mb,Can
35/E3 **Oxford**, Eng,UK
35/E3 **Oxford** (can.), Eng,UK
116/F6 **Oxford**, Mi,US
113/F3 **Oxford**, Ms,US
110/C4 **Oxford**, Oh,US
35/E3 **Oxfordshire** (co.), Eng,UK
31/M7 **Oxhey**, Eng,UK
76/E7 **Oxley** (cr.), Austl.
115/A2 **Oxnard**, Ca,US
115/K8 **Oxon Hill-Glassmanor**, Md,US
31/M8 **Oxshott**, Eng,UK
31/N8 **Oxted**, Eng,UK
65/E2 **Oyabe**, Japan
65/F2 **Oyama**, Japan
65/M10 **Ōyamada**, Japan
65/L10 **Ōyamazaki**, Japan
93/H3 **Oyapock** (riv.), FrG.
82/H7 **Oyem**, Gabon
106/F3 **Oyen**, Ab,Can
85/F5 **Oyo**, Nga.
85/F4 **Oyo** (state), Nga.
65/L10 **Ōyodo**, Japan
64/B5 **Ōyodo** (riv.), Japan
115/G5 **Oyster Bay**, NY,US
41/G2 **Oyten**, Ger.
67/D6 **Ozamiz**, Phil.
44/D2 **Ozanne** (riv.), Fr.
109/J3 **Ozark** (plat.), US
113/G4 **Ozark**, Al,US
112/E3 **Ozark**, Ar,US
112/E3 **Ozark** (mts.), Ar, Mo,US
109/J3 **Ozarks, Lake of the** (lake), Mo,US
50/E1 **Ózd**, Hun.
57/S4 **Ozernoy** (cape), Rus.
106/B3 **Ozette** (lake), Wa,US
107/L3 **Ozhiski** (lake), On,Can
48/A2 **Ozieri**, It.
39/K3 **Ozimek**, Pol.
31/U10 **Ozoir-la-Ferrière**, Fr.
112/C4 **Ozona**, Tx,US
39/K3 **Ozorków**, Pol.
31/U11 **Ozouer-le-Voulgis**, Fr.
64/C4 **Ōzu**, Japan

P

45/J2 **Paar** (riv.), Ger.
88/B4 **Paarl**, SAfr.
39/K3 **Pabianice**, Pol.
70/E3 **Pābna**, Bang.
92/F6 **Pacaás Novos** (mts.), Braz.
92/F6 **Pacaás Novos Nat'l Park**, Braz.
93/H4 **Pacajá** (riv.), Braz.
94/C2 **Pacajus**, Braz.
92/C5 **Pacasmayo**, Peru
48/C4 **Paceco**, It.
92/C6 **Pachacamac** (ruins), Peru
48/D4 **Pachino**, It.
70/C3 **Pachmarhī**, India
28/B4 **Pacific** (ocean)
106/B3 **Pacific** (ranges), BC,Can
116/K11 **Pacifica**, Ca,US
115/B2 **Pacifico** (mtn.), Ca,US
102/D4 **Pacific Rim Nat'l Park**, BC,Can
72/D5 **Pacinan** (cape), Indo.
72/D5 **Pacitan**, Indo.
47/P10 **Paço de Arcos**, Port.
72/B4 **Padang**, Indo.
72/B4 **Padangpanjang**, Indo.
72/A3 **Padangsidempuan**, Indo.
31/N7 **Paddington**, Eng,UK
35/G4 **Paddock Wood**, Eng,UK
41/F5 **Paderborn**, Ger.
61/J3 **Pad Idan**, Pak.
33/F4 **Padiham**, Eng,UK
50/E3 **Padina**, Yugo.
37/E2 **Padjelanta Nat'l Park**, Swe.
45/J4 **Padova** (Padua), It.
87/B2 **Padrão, Ponta do** (pt.), Ang.
112/D5 **Padre Island Nat'l Seashore**, Tx,US
46/A1 **Padrón**, Sp.
88/D4 **Padrone** (cape), SAfr.
34/B5 **Padstow**, Eng,UK
45/J4 **Padua** (Padova), It.
110/B4 **Paducah**, Ky,US
112/C3 **Paducah**, Tx,US
64/A2 **Paektŏk-san** (mtn.), SKor.
63/K3 **Paektu-San** (mtn.), NKor.
63/J4 **Paengnyŏng** (isl.), SKor.
50/B3 **Pag** (isl.), Cro.
67/D6 **Pagadian**, Phil.
72/B4 **Pagai Selatan** (isl.), Indo.
72/A4 **Pagai Utara** (isl.), Indo.
78/D3 **Pagan** (isl.), NMar.
108/E3 **Page**, Az,US
79/H6 **Pago Pago** (cap.), ASam.
108/F3 **Pagosa Springs**, Co,US
110/C1 **Pagwachuan** (riv.), On,Can
72/B3 **Pahang** (riv.), Malay.
108/D3 **Pahrump**, Nv,US
108/C3 **Pahute Mesa** (upland), Nv,US
66/C5 **Pai** (lake), China
49/L7 **Paiania**, Gre.
34/C6 **Paignton**, Eng,UK
37/H3 **Päijänne** (lake), Fin.
69/C3 **Pailin**, Camb.
104/T10 **Pailolo** (chan.), Hi,US
52/D3 **Paimio**, Fin.
96/C2 **Paine**, Chile
97/J7 **Paine** (peak), Chile
110/D3 **Painesville**, Oh,US
34/C2 **Painscastle**, Wal,UK
107/J2 **Paint** (lake), Mb,Can
108/E4 **Painted** (des.), Az,US
112/D4 **Paint Rock**, Tx,US
110/D4 **Paintsville**, Ky,US
36/C3 **Paisley**, Sc,UK
70/C4 **Paithan**, India
37/G2 **Pajala**, Swe.
39/K3 **Pajęczno**, Pol.
94/C3 **Pajeú** (riv.), Braz.
101/E6 **Pajonal Abajo**, Pan.
72/B3 **Pakanbaru**, Indo.
77/G6 **Pakenham**, Austl.
97/J7 **Pakenham** (cape), Chile
49/J5 **Pákhnes** (peak), Gre.
53/X9 **Pakhra** (riv.), Rus.
61/H3 **Pakistan**
50/B3 **Paklenica Nat'l Park**, Cro.
71/G3 **Pakokku**, Burma
106/F3 **Pakowki** (lake), Ab,Can
61/K2 **Pākpattan**, Pak.
71/H6 **Pak Phanang**, Thai.
50/C3 **Pakrac**, Cro.
50/D2 **Paks**, Hun.
69/D3 **Pakxe**, Laos
82/H6 **Pala**, Chad
47/N9 **Palacio Real**, Sp.
47/G2 **Palafrugell**, Sp.
48/D4 **Palagonia**, It.
48/E1 **Palagruža** (isls.), Cro.
49/K6 **Palaiokastritsa**, Gre.
31/S10 **Palaiseau**, Fr.
70/D4 **Pālakolla**, India
47/G2 **Palamós**, Sp.
72/D4 **Palangkaraya**, Indo.
70/B3 **Pālanpur**, India
104/T10 **Palaoa** (pt.), Hi,US
87/E5 **Palapye**, Bots.
70/C5 **Palar** (riv.), India
46/B1 **Palas de Rey**, Sp.
116/P15 **Palatine**, Il,US
113/H4 **Palatka**, Fl,US
78/C4 **Palau** (terr.), US
67/C6 **Palawan** (isl.), Phil.
67/C5 **Palawan** (passage), Phil.
70/C6 **Pālayankottai**, India
48/D4 **Palazzolo Acreide**, It.
82/G8 **Palé**, EqG.
73/F3 **Paleleh**, Indo.
72/B4 **Palembang**, Indo.
96/B4 **Palena** (riv.), Chile
46/C1 **Palencia**, Sp.
111/Q9 **Palermo**, On,Can
48/C3 **Palermo**, It.
112/E4 **Palestine**, Tx,US
112/E3 **Palestine** (lake), Tx,US
61/K5 **Pālghar**, India
64/A2 **P'algong-san** (mtn.), SKor.
95/B3 **Palhoça**, Braz.
70/B2 **Pāli**, India
97/K8 **Pali Aike Nat'l Park**, Chile
50/D2 **Palić**, Yugo.
104/V13 **Palikea** (peak), Hi,US
49/H3 **Palioúrion, Akra** (cape), Gre.
115/F5 **Palisades Park**, NJ,US
70/B3 **Pālitāna**, India
50/C3 **Paljenik** (peak), Bosn.
70/C6 **Palk** (str.), India, SrL.
45/J3 **Palla Blanca** (Weisskugel) (mt.), Aus., It.
37/H1 **Pallas-Ounastunturin Nat'l Park**, Fin.
37/H1 **Pallastunturi** (peak), Fin.
75/S11 **Palliser** (cape), NZ
75/H3 **Palm** (isls.), Austl.
94/A4 **Palma** (riv.), Braz.
47/G3 **Palma**, Sp.
46/C4 **Palma del Río**, Sp.
48/C4 **Palma di Montechiaro**, It.
94/D3 **Palmares**, Braz.
95/B3 **Palmas**, Braz.
84/D5 **Palmas** (cape), Libr.
101/F3 **Palma Soriano**, Cuba
113/H4 **Palm Bay**, Fl,US
76/H8 **Palm Beach**, Austl.
115/B1 **Palmdale**, Ca,US
95/B3 **Palmeira**, Braz.
94/C3 **Palmeira dos Índios**, Braz.
94/A3 **Palmeiras** (riv.), Braz.
87/B2 **Palmeirinhas, Ponta das** (pt.), Ang.
47/Q10 **Palmela**, Port.
98/V **Palmer** (arch.), Ant.
98/V **Palmer Land** (reg.), Ant.
76/C3 **Palmerston** (cape), Austl.
79/J6 **Palmerston** (atoll), CookIs.
75/R12 **Palmerston**, NZ
76/B2 **Palmerston Nat'l Park**, Austl.
75/S11 **Palmerston North**, NZ
113/H5 **Palmetto**, Fl,US
113/H4 **Palm Harbor**, Fl,US
48/D3 **Palmi**, It.
96/C2 **Palmilla**, Chile
92/C3 **Palmira**, Col.
108/C4 **Palm Springs**, Ca,US
79/J4 **Palmyra** (isl.), PacUS
60/C2 **Palmyra** (ruins), Syria
70/E3 **Palmyras** (pt.), India
32/E2 **Palnackie**, Sc,UK
70/C5 **Palni**, India
67/D5 **Palo**, Phil.
116/K12 **Palo Alto**, Ca,US
101/M8 **Palo Bola**, Mex.
109/G3 **Palo Duro** (cr.), Ok, Tx,US
45/J4 **Palon** (peak), It.
112/D3 **Palo Pinto**, Tx,US
47/E4 **Palos, Cabo de** (cape), Sp.
116/Q16 **Palos Hills**, Il,US
115/B3 **Palos Verdes Estates**, Ca,US
100/D5 **Palo Verde Nat'l Park**, Mex.
70/D2 **Pālpa**, Nepal
91/C1 **Palpalá**, Arg.
73/G4 **Palpetu** (cape), Indo.
59/D2 **Palu**, Turk.
67/D5 **Paluan**, Phil.
72/C3 **Pamangkat**, Indo.
44/D5 **Pamiers**, Fr.
68/B4 **Pamir** (riv.), Afg., Taj.
68/B4 **Pamir** (reg.), China, Taj.
113/J3 **Pamlico** (riv.), NC,US
113/J3 **Pamlico** (sound), NC,US
112/C3 **Pampa**, Tx,US
96/E2 **Pampa Humida** (plain), Arg.
96/E3 **Pampas** (plain), Arg.
96/D3 **Pampa Seca** (plain), Arg.
92/D2 **Pamplona**, Col.
46/E1 **Pamplona**, Sp.
51/K5 **Pamukova**, Turk.
67/E6 **Panabo**, Phil.
108/D3 **Panaca**, Nv,US
70/C6 **Panadura**, SrL.
51/G4 **Panagyurishte**, Bul.
72/B5 **Panaitan** (isl.), Indo.
70/B4 **Pānāji**, India
101/E6 **Panama**
101/E6 **Panama** (can.), Pan.
101/F6 **Panamá** (cap.), Pan.
101/F6 **Panama** (gulf), Pan.
101/F6 **Panama** (isth.), Pan.
113/G4 **Panama City**, Fl,US
108/C3 **Panamint** (range), Ca,US
45/J4 **Panaro** (riv.), It.
67/D5 **Panay** (isl.), Phil.
108/C3 **Pancake** (range), Nv,US
50/E3 **Pančevo**, Yugo.
50/E4 **Pančicev vrh** (peak), Yugo.
51/H3 **Panciu**, Rom.
87/E4 **Pandamatenga**, Bots.
91/B2 **Pan de Azúcar Nat'l Park**, Chile
70/C4 **Pandharpur**, India
97/G2 **Pando**, Uru.
71/F2 **Pandu**, India
52/E5 **Panevėžys**, Lith.
68/D3 **Panfilov**, Kaz.
69/B1 **Pang** (riv.), Burma
79/H7 **Pangai**, Tonga
49/J2 **Pangaíon** (peak), Gre.
87/G1 **Pangani** (riv.), Tanz.
35/E4 **Pangbourne**, Eng,UK
72/A3 **Pangkalanberandan**, Indo.
73/F4 **Pangkalaseang** (cape), Indo.
72/C4 **Pangkalpinang**, Indo.
108/D3 **Panguitch**, Ut,US
73/F2 **Pangutaran**, Phil.
67/D6 **Pangutaran** (isl.), Phil.
112/C3 **Panhandle**, Tx,US
73/J4 **Paniai** (lake), Indo.
104/R10 **Paniau** (peak), Hi,US
78/F7 **Panié** (peak), NCal.
70/C2 **Pānīpat**, India
61/K1 **Panj** (Pyandzh) (riv.), Afg., Taj.
70/D3 **Panna**, India
76/F7 **Pannikin** (isl.), Austl.
95/B2 **Panorama**, Braz.
33/E6 **Pant**, Eng,UK
35/G3 **Pant** (riv.), Eng,UK
93/G7 **Pantanal Matogrossense Nat'l Park**, Braz.
48/B4 **Pantelleria** (isl.), It.
31/T10 **Pantin**, Fr.
46/B1 **Pantón**, Sp.
100/B3 **Pánuco**, Mex.
100/B3 **Pánuco** (riv.), Mex.
71/H2 **Panzhihua**, China
94/C3 **Pão de Açúcar**, Braz.
48/E3 **Paola**, It.
109/J3 **Paola**, Ks,US
108/F3 **Paonia**, Co,US
82/J6 **Paoua**, CAfr.
69/C3 **Paoy Pet**, Camb.
50/C2 **Pápa**, Hun.
100/D5 **Papagayo** (gulf), CR
100/B3 **Papantla de Olarte**, Mex.
79/X15 **Papara**, FrPol.
79/X15 **Papeete** (cap.), FrPol.
41/E2 **Papenburg**, Ger.
40/B5 **Papendrecht**, Neth.
79/X15 **Papenoo**, FrPol.
79/X15 **Papetoai**, FrPol.
59/J4 **Paphos**, Cyp.
109/H2 **Papillion**, Ne,US
49/G2 **Papingut, Maj'e** (peak), Alb.
73/H4 **Papisoi** (cape), Indo.
78/D5 **Papua** (gulf), PNG
78/D5 **Papua New Guinea**
95/C1 **Pará** (riv.), Braz.
94/A1 **Pará** (state), Braz.
95/K7 **Paracambi**, Braz.
94/A5 **Paracatu**, Braz.
94/A5 **Paracatu** (riv.), Braz.
67/B4 **Paracel** (isls.)
58/N7 **Parace Vela** (Okino-Tori-Shima) (isl.), Japan
50/E4 **Paraćin**, Yugo.
47/N8 **Paracuellos**, Sp.
94/C1 **Paracuru**, Braz.
95/C1 **Pará de Minas**, Braz.
70/E3 **Paradip**, India
106/F2 **Paradise Hill**, Sk,Can
94/A1 **Paragominas**, Braz.
113/F2 **Paragould**, Ar,US
92/F6 **Paraguá** (riv.), Bol.
92/F2 **Paragua** (riv.), Ven.
95/H6 **Paraguaçu**, Braz.
94/B4 **Paraguaçu** (riv.), Braz.
95/B2 **Paraguaçu Paulista**, Braz.
93/G6 **Paraguai** (riv.), Braz.
101/G5 **Paraguaná** (pen.), Ven.
91/E2 **Paraguarí**, Par.
90/D5 **Paraguay**
94/C2 **Paraíba** (state), Braz.
95/D2 **Paraíba do Sul** (riv.), Braz.
94/A2 **Paraibano**, Braz.
95/H8 **Paraibuna** (riv.), Braz.
94/A3 **Paraim** (riv.), Braz.
93/J6 **Paraíso do Norte de Goiás**, Braz.
95/G7 **Paraisópolis**, Braz.
85/F4 **Parakou**, Ben.
93/G2 **Paramaribo** (cap.), Sur.
94/B2 **Parambu**, Braz.
92/C2 **Paramillo Nat'l Park**, Col.
94/B4 **Paramirim** (riv.), Braz.
115/B3 **Paramount**, Ca,US
115/F5 **Paramus**, NJ,US
57/R4 **Paramushir** (isl.), Rus.
95/B3 **Paraná** (state), Braz.
90/D5 **Paraná** (riv.), SAm.
95/B3 **Paranaguá**, Braz.
95/B1 **Paranaíba**, Braz.
95/B1 **Paranaíba** (riv.), Braz.
95/B2 **Paranapanema** (riv.), Braz.
95/B3 **Paranapiacaba** (range), Braz.
90/D4 **Paranatinga** (riv.), Braz.
93/H8 **Paranavai**, Braz.
73/F2 **Parang**, Phil.
95/C1 **Paraopeba**, Braz.
93/J8 **Parapanema** (riv.), Braz.
75/S11 **Paraparaumu**, NZ
92/F7 **Parapetí** (riv.), Bol.
95/J8 **Parati**, Braz.
95/H8 **Paratinga** (riv.), Braz.
31/T10 **Paray-Vieille-Poste**, Fr.
70/C4 **Parbhani**, India
38/F2 **Parchim**, Ger.
39/M3 **Parczew**, Pol.
59/M8 **Pardes Hanna-Karkur**, Isr.
70/B3 **Pārdi**, India
95/G6 **Pardo** (riv.), Braz.
39/H3 **Pardubice**, Czh.
72/D5 **Pare**, Indo.
92/F6 **Parecis** (mts.), Braz.
47/P10 **Parede**, Port.
96/C2 **Paredones**, Chile
110/E1 **Parent** (lake), Qu,Can
73/E4 **Parepare**, Indo.
47/L6 **Parets del Vallès**, Sp.
49/G3 **Párga**, Gre.
101/J5 **Paria** (gulf), Trin., Ven.
108/E3 **Paria** (riv.), Az, Ut,US
101/J5 **Paria** (pen.), Ven.
101/J6 **Pariaguán**, Ven.
72/B4 **Pariaman**, Indo.
92/E7 **Parinacota** (peak), Bol.
93/G4 **Parintins**, Braz.
42/B6 **Paris** (cap.), Fr.
112/E3 **Paris**, Ar,US
110/B4 **Paris**, Tn,US
112/E3 **Paris**, Tx,US
31/T10 **Paris** (inset) (cap.), Fr.
108/F2 **Park** (range), Co,US
108/D4 **Parker**, Az,US
109/F3 **Parker**, Co,US
110/D4 **Parkersburg**, WV,US
77/D2 **Parkes**, Austl.
35/H3 **Parkeston**, Eng,UK
110/B2 **Park Falls**, Wi,US
32/B2 **Parkgate**, NI,UK
34/A5 **Park Head** (pt.), UK
35/E5 **Parkhurst**, Eng,UK
116/C3 **Parkland**, Wa,US
107/K4 **Park Rapids**, Mn,US
116/Q15 **Park Ridge**, Il,US
115/F4 **Park Ridge**, NJ,US
107/J3 **Park River**, ND,US
115/K7 **Parkville**, Md,US
116/L9 **Parkway-Sacramento**, Ca,US
46/D2 **Parla**, Sp.
70/D4 **Parlakhemundi**, India
70/C4 **Parli**, India
45/J4 **Parma**, It.
110/D3 **Parma**, Oh,US
31/S9 **Parmain**, Fr.
94/B1 **Parnaíba**, Braz.
94/B1 **Parnaíba** (riv.), Braz.
49/H3 **Parnassos Nat'l Park**, Gre.
49/H3 **Párnis** (peak), Gre.
49/H4 **Párnon** (mts.), Gre.
52/E4 **Pärnu**, Est.
75/G5 **Paroo** (riv.), Austl.
49/J4 **Páros** (isl.), Gre.
88/B4 **Parow**, SAfr.
108/D3 **Parowan**, Ut,US
96/C3 **Parral**, Chile
76/H8 **Parramatta**, Austl.
100/A2 **Parras de la Fuente**, Mex.
34/D4 **Parrett** (riv.), Eng,UK
100/E6 **Parrita**, CR
103/H2 **Parry** (bay), NW,Can
102/F1 **Parry** (chan.), NW,Can
103/R7 **Parry** (isls.), NW,Can
110/D2 **Parry Sound**, On,Can
45/J3 **Parseierspitze** (peak), Aus.
107/H4 **Parshall**, ND,US
115/F5 **Parsippany**, NJ,US
106/C2 **Parsnip** (riv.), BC,Can
109/J3 **Parsons**, Ks,US
52/C2 **Pårtefjället** (peak), Swe.
44/C3 **Parthenay**, Fr.
48/C3 **Partinico**, It.
63/L3 **Partizansk**, Rus.
110/D1 **Partridge** (riv.), On,Can
70/C4 **Partūr**, India
93/H4 **Paru** (riv.), Braz.
70/D4 **Pārvathīpuram**, India
33/G5 **Parwich**, Eng,UK
88/D2 **Parys**, SAfr.
111/K1 **Pasadena**, Nf,Can
115/B2 **Pasadena**, Ca,US
115/K7 **Pasadena**, Md,US
112/E4 **Pasadena**, Tx,US
92/C4 **Pasaje**, Ecu.
69/C3 **Pa Sak** (riv.), Thai.
72/B3 **Pasaman** (peak), Indo.
113/F4 **Pascagoula**, Ms,US
51/H2 **Paşcani**, Rom.
106/D4 **Pasco**, Wa,US
97/J7 **Pascua** (riv.), Chile
42/A3 **Pas-de-Calais** (dept.), Fr.
42/B3 **Pas-en-Artois**, Fr.
67/D5 **Pasig**, Phil.
71/G2 **Pāsighāt**, India
59/E2 **Pasinler**, Turk.
39/K1 **Pasłęk**, Pol.
39/L2 **Pasłęka** (riv.), Pol.
50/B4 **Pašman** (isl.), Cro.
61/H3 **Pasni**, Pak.
91/E2 **Paso de Los Libres**, Arg.
96/C2 **Paso del Planchón** (peak), Chile
108/B4 **Paso Robles** (El Paso de Robles), Ca,US
114/M3 **Pass** (peak), Yk,Can
115/F5 **Passaic**, NJ,US
115/F5 **Passaic** (riv.), NJ,US
95/J7 **Passa Quatro**, Braz.
45/K2 **Passau**, Ger.
42/C2 **Passendale**, Belg.
48/D4 **Passero** (pt.), It.
91/F2 **Passo Fundo**, Braz.
95/A3 **Passo Fundo** (res.), Braz.
85/E3 **Passoré** (prov.), Burk.
95/C2 **Passos**, Braz.
45/G4 **Passy**, Fr.
92/C4 **Pastaza** (riv.), Ecu., Peru
92/C3 **Pasto**, Col.
114/F3 **Pastol** (bay), Ak,US
72/D5 **Pasuruan**, Indo.
50/D2 **Pásztó**, Hun.
96/D4 **Patagonia** (reg.), Arg.
72/B4 **Patah** (peak), Indo.
70/B3 **Pātan**, India
115/K7 **Patapsco** (riv.), Md,US
115/G5 **Patchogue**, NY,US
34/D3 **Patchway**, Eng,UK
33/G3 **Pateley Bridge**, Eng,UK
47/E3 **Paterna**, Sp.
115/F5 **Paterson**, NJ,US
61/L2 **Pathānkot**, India
106/G5 **Pathfinder** (res.), Wy,US
72/D5 **Pati**, Indo.
92/C3 **Patía** (riv.), Col.
61/L2 **Patiāla**, India
73/F2 **Patikul**, Phil.
70/E2 **Patna**, India
32/D1 **Patna**, Sc,UK
73/F1 **Patnongon**, Phil.
59/E2 **Patnos**, Turk.
95/A3 **Pato Branco**, Braz.
113/G2 **Patoka** (riv.), In,US
49/F2 **Patos**, Alb.
94/C2 **Patos**, Braz.
95/B4 **Patos** (lake), Braz.
95/C1 **Patos de Minas**, Braz.
49/G3 **Pátrai**, Gre.
49/G3 **Patrai** (gulf), Gre.
97/J7 **Patricio Lynch** (isl.), Chile
33/H4 **Patrington**, Eng,UK
95/C1 **Patrocínio**, Braz.
69/C5 **Pattani**, Thai.
69/C3 **Pattaya**, Thai.
41/G4 **Pattensen**, Ger.
48/D3 **Patti**, It.
34/D1 **Pattingham**, Eng,UK
70/C5 **Pattukkottai**, India
114/N4 **Pattullo** (mtn.), BC,Can
94/C2 **Patu**, Braz.
100/E4 **Patuca** (pt.), Hon.
100/D5 **Patuca** (riv.), Hon.
115/K8 **Patuxent** (riv.), Md,US
44/C5 **Pau**, Fr.
94/C4 **Pau Brasil**, Braz.
94/C2 **Pau dos Ferros**, Braz.
92/E5 **Pauini** (riv.), Braz.
95/F7 **Paulínia**, Braz.
94/C3 **Paulo Afonso**, Braz.
94/C3 **Paulo Afonso Nat'l Park**, Braz.
115/E6 **Paulsboro**, NJ,US
109/H4 **Pauls Valley**, Ok,US
34/D4 **Paulton**, Eng,UK
71/G4 **Paungde**, Burma
68/C5 **Pauri**, India
45/H4 **Pavia**, It.
51/G4 **Pavlikeni**, Bul.
68/C1 **Pavlodar**, Kaz.
114/F4 **Pavlof** (vol.), Ak,US
54/E2 **Pavlograd**, Ukr.
52/J5 **Pavlovo**, Rus.
45/J4 **Pavullo nel Frignano**, It.
72/D4 **Pawan** (riv.), Indo.
109/H3 **Pawhuska**, Ok,US
69/B2 **Pawn** (riv.), Burma
109/H3 **Pawnee** (riv.), Ks,US
110/C3 **Paw Paw**, Mi,US
111/G3 **Pawtucket**, RI,US
49/F3 **Paxoí** (isl.), Gre.
49/G3 **Paxoí** (Yáios), Gre.
72/B4 **Payakumbuh**, Indo.
96/C3 **Payén, Altiplanicie del** (plat.), Arg.
106/D4 **Payette**, Id,US
106/D5 **Payette** (riv.), Id,US
53/P1 **Pay-Khoy** (mts.), Rus.
103/J3 **Payne** (lake), Qu,Can
97/F2 **Paysandú**, Uru.
97/F1 **Paysandú** (dept.), Uru.
31/T9 **Pays de France** (plain), Fr.
44/C3 **Pays de la Loire** (reg.), Fr.
108/E4 **Payson**, Az,US
108/E2 **Payson**, Ut,US
96/C3 **Payún** (peak), Arg.
59/D3 **Pazarcık**, Turk.
51/G4 **Pazardzhik**, Bul.
54/D5 **Pazaryeri**, Turk.
95/A2 **Peabiru**, Braz.
102/E3 **Peace** (riv.), Ab, BC,Can
113/H5 **Peace** (riv.), Fl,US
106/D1 **Peace River**, Ab,Can
106/D3 **Peachland**, BC,Can
113/G3 **Peachtree City**, Ga,US
33/G5 **Peak District Nat'l Park**, Eng,UK
104/W13 **Pearl** (har.), Hi,US
113/F4 **Pearl** (riv.), La, Ms,US
113/F3 **Pearl**, Ms,US

115/B1 Pearland, Ca,US
79/H2 Pearl and Hermes (reef), Hi,US
104/W13 Pearl City, Hi,US
67/B3 Pearl River (inlet), China
115/F4 Pearl River, NY,US
112/D4 Pearsall, Tx,US
103/R7 Peary (chan.), NW,Can
109/H4 Pease (riv.), Tx,US
35/E2 Pebworth, Eng,UK
50/E4 Peć, Yugo.
53/N2 Pechora, Rus.
53/M1 Pechora (bay), Rus.
53/M2 Pechora (riv.), Rus.
109/G5 Pecos (riv.), NM, Tx,US
112/C4 Pecos, Tx,US
109/F4 Pecos Nat'l Mon., NM,US
42/C3 Pecquencourt, Fr.
50/D2 Pécs, Hun.
101/E6 Pedasí, Pan.
77/C4 Pedder (lake), Austl.
101/G4 Pedernales, DRep.
95/B2 Pederneiras, Braz.
115/C3 Pedley, Ca,US
94/B5 Pedra Azul, Braz.
95/G7 Pedreira, Braz.
94/B2 Pedreiras, Braz.
70/D6 Pedro (pt.), SrL.
101/F4 Pedro Cays (isls.), Jam.
92/E3 Pedro II, Braz.
91/E1 Pedro Juan Caballero, Par.
95/C1 Pedro Leopoldo, Braz.
95/A4 Pedro Osório, Braz.
94/B2 Pedro Segundo, Braz.
36/D3 Peebles, Sc,UK
76/F6 Peel (isl.), Austl.
102/G1 Peel (sound), NW,Can
114/L2 Peel (riv.), Yk,Can
32/D3 Peel, IM,UK
33/F1 Peel Fell (mtn.), Eng,UK
43/E1 Peer, Belg.
75/R11 Pegasus (bay), NZ
45/J2 Pegnitz, Ger.
45/J2 Pegnitz (riv.), Ger.
47/E3 Pego, Sp.
33/G1 Pegswood, Eng,UK
69/B2 Pegu, Burma
69/B2 Pegu (mts.), Burma
69/B2 Pegu (riv.), Burma
69/B2 Pegu (Bago) (div.), Burma
35/H4 Pegwell (bay), Eng,UK
96/E2 Pehuajó, Arg.
96/C2 Pehuenche (pass), Chile
66/B3 Peijiachuankou, China
41/H4 Peine, Ger.
37/H4 Peipus (lake), Est., Rus.
95/K6 Peixe (riv.), Braz.
95/C2 Peixoto (res.), Braz.
72/C5 Pekalongan, Indo.
72/B3 Pekan Nanas, Malay.
110/B3 Pekin, Il,US
96/C5 Pelada (plain), Arg.
48/C5 Pelagie (isls.), It.
50/F3 Peleaga, Vîrful (peak), Rom.
111/D3 Pelee (isl.), On,Can
110/D3 Pelee (pt.), On,Can
101/J5 Pelée (mt.), Mart.
111/R9 Pelham, On,Can
113/G3 Pelham, Al,US
39/H4 Pelhřimov, Czh.
106/E2 Pelican (mts.), Ab,Can
107/H2 Pelican (lake), Sk,Can
107/H2 Pelican Narrows, Sk,Can
84/A4 Pelindã, Ponta de (pt.), GBis.
50/E5 Pelister Nat'l Park, Macd.
50/C4 Pelješac (pen.), Cro.
114/M3 Pelly (riv.), Yk,Can
102/H2 Pelly Bay, NW,Can
114/L3 Pelly Crossing, Yk,Can
49/G3 Peloponnisos (reg.), Gre.
48/D3 Peloritani (mts.), It.
95/A4 Pelotas, Braz.
95/B3 Pelotas (riv.), Braz.
39/K2 Pelplin, Pol.
73/F5 Pemali (cape), Indo.
72/A3 Pematangsiantar, Indo.
81/G5 Pemba (isl.), Tanz.
106/C3 Pemberton, BC,Can
106/E2 Pembina (riv.), Ab,Can
107/J3 Pembina (riv.), Can., US
107/J3 Pembina, ND,US
110/E2 Pembroke, On,Can
34/B3 Pembroke, Wal,UK
31/P8 Pembury, Eng,UK
96/B3 Pemuco, Chile
46/A2 Penafiel, Port.
96/Q9 Peñaflor, Chile
46/D2 Peñalara (mtn.), Sp.
94/A1 Penalva, Braz.
95/B2 Penápolis, Braz.
46/C2 Peñaranda de Bracamonte, Sp.
47/E2 Peñarroya (mtn.), Sp.
46/C3 Peñarroya-Pueblonuevo, Sp.
34/C4 Penarth, Wal,UK
97/L8 Peñas (cape), Arg.
97/J6 Penas (gulf), Chile
46/C1 Peñas (cape), Sp.
96/B3 Penco, Chile
49/L6 Pendelikón (mtn.), Gre.
94/C2 Pendências, Braz.
85/F4 Pendjari (riv.), Ben., Burk.
85/F4 Pendjari Nat'l Park, Ben.
33/F4 Pendle (hill), Eng,UK
106/D4 Pendleton, Or,US
106/D4 Pend Oreille (lake), Id,US
106/D3 Pend Oreille (riv.), Id, Wa,US
46/A2 Peneda-Gerês Nat'l Park, Port.
94/C3 Penedo, Braz.
34/C1 Penegoes, Wal,UK
110/E2 Penetanguishene, On,Can
70/C4 Penganga (riv.), India
31/N7 Penge, Eng,UK
67/C3 Penghu (Pescadores) (isls.), Tai.
95/B3 Penha, Braz.
106/E2 Penhold, Ab,Can
46/C4 Penibético, Sistema (range), Sp.
46/A3 Peniche, Port.
94/A3 Penitente (mts.), Braz.
34/D1 Penkridge, Eng,UK
32/E5 Penmaenmawr, Wal,UK
44/A3 Penmarch, Fr.
44/A3 Penmarc'h, Pointe de (pt.), Fr.
48/D1 Penna, Punta della (cape), It.
50/C5 Penne (pt.), It.
70/C5 Penner (riv.), India
110/E3 Penn Hills, Pa,US
45/G4 Pennine Alps (mts.), It., Swi.
33/F2 Pennine Chain (range), Eng,UK
115/F5 Pennington, NJ,US
115/E6 Pennsauken, NJ,US
110/E3 Pennsylvania (state), US
103/S7 Penny (str.), NW,Can
110/E3 Penn Yan, NY,US
110/G2 Penobscot (riv.), Me,US
101/E6 Penonomé, Pan.
32/E1 Penpont, Sc,UK
32/D5 Penrhyn Mawr (pt.), Wal,UK
79/K5 Penrhyn (Tongareva) (atoll), Cookls.
76/G8 Penrith, Austl.
33/F2 Penrith, Eng,UK
34/A6 Penryn, Eng,UK
98/X Pensacola (mts.), Ant.
113/G4 Pensacola, Fl,US
107/G3 Pense, Sk,Can
31/P8 Penshurst, Eng,UK
34/B5 Pensilva, Eng,UK
115/J8 Pentagon, Va,US
78/F6 Pentecost (isl.), Van.
94/C1 Pentecoste, Braz.
51/H3 Penteleu (peak), Rom.
106/D3 Penticton, BC,Can
34/B5 Pentire (pt.), UK
36/D3 Pentland (hills), Sc,UK
34/C3 Pentyrch, Wal,UK
96/C2 Peñuelas Nat'l Park, Chile
34/A6 Penwith (pen.), Eng,UK
33/E6 Pen-y-Cae, Wal,UK
33/F3 Pen-y-Ghent (mtn.), Eng,UK
32/E5 Pen-y-Gogarth (pt.), Wal,UK
34/C2 Pen y Gurnos (mtn.), Wal,UK
55/H1 Penza, Rus.
34/A6 Penzance, Eng,UK
55/G1 Penza Obl., Rus.
45/J3 Penzberg, Ger.
57/S3 Penzhina (bay), Rus.
57/S3 Penzhina (riv.), Rus.
110/B3 Peoria, Il,US
43/E2 Pepinster, Belg.
115/F5 Pequannock, NJ,US
75/G2 Pera (head), Austl.
72/B4 Perabumulih, Indo.
47/M9 Perales (riv.), Sp.
111/H1 Percé, Qu,Can
44/D2 Perche (hills), Fr.
39/J4 Perchtoldsdorf, Aus.
74/C4 Percival (lakes), Austl.
76/C3 Percy (isls.), Austl.
94/A3 Perdida (riv.), Braz.
47/F1 Perdido (mtn.), Sp.
92/C3 Pereira, Col.
95/B2 Pereira Barreto, Braz.
96/E2 Pergamino, Arg.
45/K5 Pergola, It.
111/G1 Péribonca (riv.), Qu,Can
44/D4 Périgueux, Fr.
101/G6 Perija, Sierra de (range), Col., Ven.
60/D6 Perim (isl.), Yem.
49/J3 Peristéra (isl.), Gre.
49/L6 Peristéri, Gre.
97/K6 Perito Moreno Nat'l Park, Arg.
70/C5 Periyakulam, India
115/E5 Perkasie, Pa,US
43/F5 Perl, Ger.
100/E5 Perlas (lag.), Nic.
100/E5 Perlas (pt.), Nic.
38/F2 Perleberg, Ger.
53/N4 Perm', Rus.
53/M4 Perm' Obl., Rus.
94/C3 Pernambuco (state), Braz.
44/F4 Pernes-les-Fontaines, Fr.
50/F4 Pernik, Bul.
52/D3 Perniö, Fin.
42/B4 Péronne, Fr.
53/X9 Perovo, Rus.
44/E5 Perpignan, Fr.
115/C3 Perris, Ca,US
44/B2 Perros-Guirec, Fr.
111/N7 Perrot (isl.), Qu,Can
102/F2 Perry (riv.), NW,Can
113/H4 Perry, Fl,US
113/H3 Perry, Ga,US
109/H3 Perry, Ok,US
115/K7 Perry Hall, Md,US
112/C2 Perryton, Tx,US
109/K3 Perryville, Mo,US
31/S9 Persan, Fr.
60/F3 Persepolis (ruins), Iran
34/D2 Pershore, Eng,UK
60/E3 Persian (gulf), Asia
59/D2 Pertek, Turk.
110/E2 Perth, On,Can
36/D2 Perth, Sc,UK
115/F5 Perth Amboy, NJ,US
44/F5 Pertuis, Fr.
44/C3 Pertuis Breton (inlet), Fr.
48/A2 Pertusato (cape), Fr.
92/C5 Peru
110/B3 Peru, Il,US
110/C3 Peru, In,US
50/D4 Perućačko (lake), Bosn.
48/C1 Perugia, It.
95/G9 Peruíbe, Braz.
42/C2 Péruwelz, Belg.
59/E3 Pervari, Turk.
53/J5 Pervomaysk, Rus.
54/D2 Pervomaysk, Ukr.
53/N4 Pervoural'sk, Rus.
72/B4 Pesagi (peak), Indo.
45/K5 Pesaro, It.
67/C3 Pescadores (Penghu) (isls.), Tai.
48/D1 Pescara, It.
55/J4 Peschanyy, Mys (cape), Kaz.
53/L2 Pesha (riv.), Rus.
61/K2 Peshāwar, Pak.
51/G4 Peshtera, Bul.
110/B2 Peshtigo (riv.), Wi,US
94/C3 Pesqueira, Braz.
44/C4 Pessac, Fr.
44/D5 Pessons, Pic dels (peak), And.
50/D2 Pest (co.), Hun.
52/G4 Pestovo, Rus.
59/K5 Petah Tiqwa, Isr.
113/F4 Petal, Ms,US
49/J4 Petalión (gulf), Gre.
116/J10 Petaluma, Ca,US
43/E4 Pétange, Lux.
100/B4 Petapa, Mex.
101/H5 Petare, Ven.
87/F3 Petauke, Zam.
110/E2 Petawawa (riv.), On,Can
110/E2 Petawawa, On,Can
107/L4 Petenwell (lake), Wi,US
110/E2 Peterborough, On,Can
35/F1 Peterborough, Eng,UK
36/E2 Peterhead, Sc,UK
98/T Peter I (isl.), Ant.
28/E9 Peter I (isl.), Nor.
33/G2 Peterlee, Eng,UK
96/C2 Peteroa (vol.), Arg.
106/F1 Peter Pond (lake), Sk,Can
110/E4 Petersburg, Va,US
35/F5 Petersfield, Eng,UK
41/F4 Petershagen, Ger.
48/E3 Petilia Policastro, It.
111/H2 Petitcodiac, NB,Can
101/G4 Petite Riviere de l'Artibonite, Haiti
43/F5 Petite-Rosselle, Fr.
42/C6 Petit Morin (riv.), Fr.
37/J3 Petkeljärven Nat'l Park, Fin.
70/B3 Petlād, India
100/D3 Peto, Mex.
96/C2 Petorca, Chile
110/C2 Petoskey, Mi,US
57/M2 Petra (isls.), Rus.
86/C2 Petra (Baṭrā) (ruins), Jor.
47/E3 Petrel, Sp.
48/C2 Petrella (peak), It.
51/F5 Petrich, Bul.
108/E4 Petrified Forest Nat'l Park, Az,US
51/F3 Petrila, Rom.
52/F4 Petrodvorets, Rus.
51/F4 Petrokhanski Prokhod (pass), Bul.
94/C3 Petrolândia, Braz.
94/B3 Petrolina, Braz.
56/G4 Petropavlovsk, Kaz.
57/R4 Petropavlovsk-Kamchatskiy, Rus.
95/K7 Petrópolis, Braz.
51/F3 Petroşani, Rom.
50/D3 Petrovaradin, Yugo.
55/H1 Petrovsk, Rus.
62/F1 Petrovsk-Zabaykal'skiy, Rus.
52/G3 Petrozavodsk, Rus.
33/F2 Petterill (riv.), Eng,UK
35/F5 Petworth, Eng,UK
50/A2 Petzeck (peak), Aus.
114/G4 Peulik (mtn.), Ak,US
96/C2 Peumo, Chile
35/G5 Pevensey, Eng,UK
116/P13 Pewaukee (lake), Wi,US
35/E4 Pewsey, Eng,UK
53/K2 Peza (riv.), Rus.
44/E5 Pézenas, Fr.
43/G5 Pfälzer Wald (for.), Ger.
41/G6 Pfieffe (riv.), Ger.
45/H2 Pforzheim, Ger.
45/H2 Pfungstadt, Ger.
69/C1 Phak (riv.), Laos
70/B2 Phalodi, India
69/C3 Phanat Nikhom, Thai.
69/B4 Phangan (isl.), Thai.
69/C3 Phang Hoei (range), Thai.
69/C3 Phanom Dongrak (mts.), Camb., Thai.
69/E4 Phan Rang, Viet.
69/E4 Phan Thiet, Viet.
112/D5 Pharr, Tx,US
69/C5 Phatthalung, Thai.
69/C2 Phaya Fo (peak), Thai.
69/B2 Phayao, Thai.
113/G3 Phenix City, Al,US
88/C2 Phepane (dry riv.), SAfr.
69/B3 Phet Buri, Thai.
69/C2 Phetchabun, Thai.
69/C2 Phichit, Thai.
113/F3 Philadelphia, Ms,US
115/E6 Philadelphia, Pa,US
60/B4 Philae (ruins), Egypt
107/H4 Philip, SD,US
42/D3 Philippeville, Belg.
110/D4 Philippi, WV,US
78/B3 Philippine (sea), Asia
67/D5 Philippines
101/J4 Philipsburg, NAnt.
106/E4 Philipsburg, Mt,US
40/B5 Philipsdam (dam), Neth.
109/H3 Phillipsburg, Ks,US
115/E5 Phillipsburg, NJ,US
69/C3 Phimai (ruins), Thai.
69/C2 Phitsanulok, Thai.
69/D4 Phnom Penh (Phnum Penh) (cap.), Camb.
69/D3 Phnum Tbeng Meanchey, Camb.
69/C5 Pho (pt.), Thai.
79/H5 Phoenix (isls.), Kiri.
108/D4 Phoenix (cap.), Az,US
113/H2 Phoenix (peak), NC,US
79/H5 Phoenix (Rawaki) (atoll), Kiri.
115/E5 Phoenixville, Pa,US
69/C1 Phongsali, Laos
69/C2 Phou Bia (peak), Laos
69/D2 Phou Huatt (peak), Viet.
69/C1 Phou Loi (peak), Laos
69/D2 Phou Xai Lai Leng (peak), Laos
69/C2 Phrae, Thai.
69/C3 Phra Nakhon Si Ayutthaya, Thai.
69/B4 Phra Thong (isl.), Thai.
69/C4 Phsar Ream, Camb.
69/D2 Phuc Loi, Viet.
71/J3 Phuc Yen, Viet.
69/C2 Phu Hin Rong Kla Nat'l Park, Thai.
69/E4 Phu Hoi, Viet.
69/B5 Phuket, Thai.
69/B5 Phuket (isl.), Thai.
69/C2 Phu Kradung Nat'l Park, Thai.
70/D3 Phulabāni, India
69/D2 Phu Loc, Viet.
69/D1 Phu Luong, Viet.
69/D1 Phu Luong (peak), Viet.
69/D1 Phu Ly, Viet.
69/D4 Phumi Banam, Camb.
69/C4 Phumi Choan, Camb.
69/D3 Phumi Kampong Trabek, Camb.
69/D4 Phumi Krek, Camb.
69/D3 Phumi Labang Siek, Camb.
69/D3 Phumi Prek Preah, Camb.
69/C3 Phumi Samraong, Camb.
69/C3 Phumi Toek Sok, Camb.
69/E3 Phu My, Viet.
69/E3 Phu Nhon, Viet.
69/D2 Phu Phan Nat'l Park, Thai.
69/C4 Phu Quoc (isl.), Viet.
69/D4 Phu Rieng Sron, Viet.
69/C2 Phu Rua Nat'l Park, Thai.
69/D1 Phu Tho, Viet.
69/D2 Phu Vang, Viet.
66/D4 Pi (riv.), China
94/C3 Piaçabuçu, Braz.
45/H4 Piacenza, It.
94/C2 Piancó, Braz.
48/A1 Pianosa (isl.), It.
39/L2 Piaseczno, Pol.
51/H2 Piatra Neamţ, Rom.
94/B3 Piauí (riv.), Braz.
94/B2 Piauí (state), Braz.
45/K3 Piave (riv.), It.
101/N9 Piaxtla (riv.), Mex.
47/G2 Piazza Armerina, It.
83/M6 Pibor Post, Sudan
110/C1 Pic (riv.), On,Can
101/P8 Picacho del Centinela (peak), Mex.
42/B4 Picardy (Picardie) (reg.), Fr.
113/F4 Picayune, Ms,US
48/E2 Piccolo (lag.), It.
96/C2 Pichidegua, Chile
96/C2 Pichilemu, Chile
111/R8 Pickering, On,Can
33/H3 Pickering, Eng,UK
33/H3 Pickering, Vale of (val.), Eng,UK
107/L3 Pickle Lake, On,Can
47/S12 Pico (isl.), Azor.,Port.
92/F3 Pico da Neblina Nat'l Park, Braz.
100/A4 Pico de Tancitaro Nat'l Park, Mex.
115/B3 Pico Rivera, Ca,US
94/B2 Picos, Braz.
96/D5 Pico Truncado, Arg.
42/B4 Picquigny, Fr.
110/E3 Picton, On,Can
111/J2 Pictou, NS,Can
34/D5 Piddle (riv.), Eng,UK
70/D6 Pidurutagala (peak), SrL.
45/G4 Piedmont (reg.), It.
116/K11 Piedmont, Ca,US
97/F2 Piedras (pt.), Arg.
92/D6 Piedras (riv.), Peru
39/K3 Piekary Śląskie, Pol.
88/B4 Piekenierskloof (pass), SAfr.
37/H3 Pieksämäki, Fin.
37/J3 Pielinen (lake), Fin.
39/L4 Pieniński Nat'l Park, Pol.
47/K6 Piera, Sp.
109/H2 Pierce, Ne,US
106/F2 Pierceland, Sk,Can
107/H4 Pierre (cap.), SD,US
31/T10 Pierrefitte-sur-Seine, Fr.
111/N7 Pierrefonds, Qu,Can
42/C5 Pierrefonds, Fr.
44/F4 Pierrelatte, Fr.
31/S9 Pierrelaye, Fr.
89/E3 Pietermaritzburg, SAfr.
87/E5 Pietersburg, SAfr.
89/E2 Piet Retief, SAfr.
51/G2 Pietrosul (peak), Rom.
106/E2 Pigeon (lake), Ab,Can
107/L3 Pigeon (riv.), Can., US
110/B4 Piggott, Ar,US
100/E3 Pigs (bay), Cuba
96/E3 Pigüé, Arg.
100/C4 Pijijiapan, Mex.
40/B4 Pijnacker, Neth.
78/D4 Pikelot (isl.), Micr.
109/F3 Pikes (peak), Co,US
115/K7 Pikesville, Md,US
110/D4 Pikeville, Ky,US
67/D6 Pikit, Phil.
39/J2 Piła, Pol.
39/J2 Piła (prov.), Pol.
88/P12 Pilanesberg (range), SAfr.
91/E2 Pilar, Par.
73/F1 Pilar, Phil.
92/F8 Pilaya (riv.), Bol.
116/D1 Pilchuck (riv.), Wa,US
90/C5 Pilcomayo (riv.), SAm.
31/P7 Pilgrims Hatch, Eng,UK
67/D5 Pili, Phil.
54/B2 Pilica (riv.), Pol.
49/H3 Pílion (peak), Gre.
50/D2 Pilis, Hun.
50/D2 Pilis (peak), Hun.
39/K5 Pilisvörösvár, Hun.
70/C2 Pilkhua, India
77/C4 Pillar (cape), Austl.
33/E2 Pillar (mtn.), Eng,UK
116/K12 Pillar (pt.), Ca,US
94/A5 Pilões (mts.), Braz.
113/G2 Pilot (peak), Tn,US
45/K2 Pilsen (Plzeň), Czh.
108/E4 Pima, Az,US
70/B4 Pimpri-Chinchwad, India
101/M7 Pinacote (mt.), Mex.
97/J7 Pináculo (peak), Arg.
67/D5 Pinamalayan, Phil.
72/A2 Pinang (isl.), Malay.
59/D2 Pınarbaşı, Turk.
100/E3 Pinar del Río, Cuba
51/H5 Pınarhisar, Turk.
92/C4 Piñas, Ecu.
67/D4 Pinatubo (mt.), Phil.
107/K3 Pinawa, Mb,Can
33/H6 Pinchbeck, Eng,UK
106/E3 Pincher Creek, Ab,Can
110/D3 Pinconning, Mi,US
50/E2 Pîncota, Rom.
111/N7 Pincourt, Qu,Can
39/L3 Pińczów, Pol.
95/H7 Pindamonhangaba, Braz.
94/A2 Pindaré (riv.), Braz.
94/A1 Pindaré-Mirim, Braz.
61/K2 Pindi Gheb, Pak.
49/G3 Pindos Nat'l Park, Gre.
49/G2 Píndus (mts.), Gre.
70/B3 Pindwāra, India
113/F4 Pine (hills), Ms,US
107/G4 Pine (hills), Mt,US
115/F6 Pine Barrens (reg.), NJ,US
112/E3 Pine Bluff, Ar,US
107/G5 Pine Bluffs, Wy,US
47/G2 Pineda de Mar, Sp.
106/F5 Pinedale, Wy,US
107/J3 Pine Falls, Mb,Can
52/J2 Pinega (riv.), Rus.
115/F6 Pine Hill, NJ,US
107/L2 Pineimuta (riv.), On,Can
98/T Pine Island (bay), Ant.
110/A2 Pine Island, Mn,US
88/L10 Pinelands, SAfr.
107/H5 Pine Ridge, SD,US
45/G4 Pinerolo, It.
89/E3 Pinetown, SAfr.
69/B2 Ping (riv.), Thai.
66/C4 Pingdingshan, China
66/D3 Pingdu, China
78/F4 Pingelap (atoll), Micr.
66/C5 Pingjing Guan (pass), China
66/D2 Pingquan, China
66/C3 Pingshan, China
67/D3 Pingtung, Tai.
66/C3 Pingxiang, China
67/B2 Pingxiang, China
69/D1 Pingxiang, China
66/C3 Pingxing Guan (pass), China
63/J4 Pingyang, China
95/G7 Pinhal, Braz.
47/Q10 Pinhal Novo, Port.
95/B3 Pinhão, Braz.
94/A1 Pinheiro, Braz.
95/D1 Pinheiros, Braz.
49/G3 Piniós (riv.), Gre.
49/G4 Piniós (riv.), Gre.
40/C2 Pinkegat (chan.), Neth.
108/B3 Pinnacles Nat'l Mon., Ca,US
41/G1 Pinnau (riv.), Ger.
41/G1 Pinneberg, Ger.
96/C3 Pino Hachado (pass), Arg.
116/K10 Pinole, Ca,US
108/C4 Pinos (peak), Ca,US
100/E3 Pinos (Juventud) (isl.), Cuba
46/D4 Pinos-Puente, Sp.
100/B4 Pinotepa Nacional, Mex.
73/E4 Pinrang, Indo.
78/F7 Pins, Ile des (isl.), NCal.
54/C1 Pinsk, Bela.
96/C3 Pinto, Chile
47/N9 Pinto, Sp.
108/D3 Pioche, Nv,US
94/B2 Pio IX, Braz.
48/B1 Piombino, It.
56/J2 Pioner (isl.), Rus.
39/L3 Pionki, Pol.
92/F4 Piorini (riv.), Braz.
39/K3 Piotrków (prov.), Pol.
39/K3 Piotrków Trybunalski, Pol.
94/A1 Pio XII, Braz.
70/B2 Pīpār, India
108/D3 Pipe Spring Nat'l Mon., Az,US
107/H3 Pipestone (cr.), Mb, Sk,Can
107/L2 Pipestone (riv.), On,Can
107/J4 Pipestone, Mn,US
107/J4 Pipestone Nat'l Mon., Mn,US
61/K2 Piplān, Pak.
111/G1 Pipmuacan (res.), Qu,Can
110/C3 Piqua, Oh,US
95/H7 Piquete, Braz.
95/A3 Piquiri (riv.), Braz.
95/B1 Piracanjuba, Braz.
95/C2 Piracicaba, Braz.
94/B1 Piracuruca, Braz.
95/K7 Piraí, Braz.
95/B3 Piraí do Sul, Braz.
49/H4 Piraiévs, Gre.
95/B2 Piraju, Braz.
95/B2 Pirajuí, Braz.
97/J7 Pirámide (peak), Chile
91/E2 Pirané, Arg.
95/D2 Piranga (riv.), Braz.
94/C2 Piranhas (riv.), Braz.
94/C2 Piranji (riv.), Braz.
95/C1 Pirapora, Braz.
95/B2 Pirapòzinho, Braz.
95/C2 Pirássununga, Braz.
96/C1 Pircas (peak), Arg.
95/B1 Pires do Rio, Braz.
51/F5 Pirin (mtn.), Bul.
51/F5 Pirin (mts.), Bul.
51/F5 Pirin Nat'l Park, Bul.
94/B2 Piripiri, Braz.
94/B3 Piritaba, Braz.
43/G5 Pirmasens, Ger.
39/G3 Pirna, Ger.
50/F4 Pirot, Yugo.
54/E2 Piryatin, Ukr.
45/J5 Pisa, It.
73/E2 Pisau, Tanjong (cape), Malay.
92/D2 Pisba Nat'l Park, Col.
115/F5 Piscataway, NJ,US
92/C6 Pisco, Peru
92/C6 Pisco (riv.), Peru
45/L2 Písek, Czh.
61/J2 Pishīn, Pak.
91/C2 Pissis (peak), Arg.
42/B4 Pissy, Fr.
116/P15 Pistakee (lake), Il,US
48/E2 Pisticci, It.
45/J5 Pistoia, It.
46/C1 Pisuerga (riv.), Sp.
39/L2 Pisz, Pol.
108/B2 Pit (riv.), Ca,US
92/C3 Pitalito, Col.
95/B3 Pitanga, Braz.
79/N7 Pitcairn Islands (terr.), UK
37/G2 Piteå, Swe.
37/F2 Piteälv (riv.), Swe.
51/G3 Piteşti, Rom.
44/E2 Pithiviers, Fr.
36/D2 Pitlochry, Sc,UK
115/E6 Pitman, NJ,US
36/D2 Pitmedden, Sc,UK
96/B3 Pitrufquén, Chile
76/H8 Pitt (lake), Austl.
36/D2 Pittenweem, Sc,UK
116/L10 Pittsburg, Ca,US
109/J3 Pittsburg, Ks,US
112/E3 Pittsburg, Tx,US
110/E3 Pittsburgh, Pa,US
111/F3 Pittsfield, Ma,US
111/G2 Pittsfield, Me,US
95/C2 Piũí, Braz.
92/B5 Piura, Peru
70/D2 Piuthān, Nepal
49/F1 Piva (riv.), Yugo.
101/G5 Pivijay, Col.
50/D4 Pivsko (lake), Yugo.
53/K4 Pizhma (riv.), Rus.
48/E3 Pizzo, It.
48/C1 Pizzuto (peak), It.
88/D3 P. K. Le Rouxdam (res.), SAfr.
111/L2 Placentia (bay), Nf,Can
115/C3 Placentia, Ca,US
67/D5 Placer, Phil.
31/T9 Plailly, Fr.
69/C3 Plai Mat (riv.), Thai.
115/F5 Plainfield, NJ,US
112/C3 Plains, Tx,US
115/F5 Plainsboro, NJ,US
110/A2 Plainview, Mn,US
115/G5 Plainview, NY,US
112/C3 Plainview, Tx,US
109/H3 Plainville, Ks,US
31/R10 Plaisir, Fr.
73/E5 Plampang, Indo.
94/A4 Planaltina, Braz.
95/D1 Planalto do Brasil (plat.), Braz.
101/F6 Planeta Rica, Col.
112/D3 Plano, Tx,US
113/H5 Plantation, Fl,US
113/H4 Plant City, Fl,US
113/F4 Plaquemine, La,US
46/B2 Plasencia, Sp.
48/C4 Platani (riv.), It.
97/F2 Plata, Río de la (estuary), Arg.
85/H4 Plateau (state), Nga.
101/G6 Plato, Col.
109/J2 Platte (riv.), Mo,US
109/H2 Platte (riv.), Ne,US
107/J5 Platte, SD,US
110/B3 Platteville, Wi,US
45/K2 Plattling, Ger.
110/F2 Plattsburgh, NY,US
45/K1 Plauen, Ger.
50/D4 Plav, Yugo.
100/D4 Playa de los Muertos (ruins), Hon.
92/B4 Playas, Ecu.
108/E5 Playas (lake), NM,US
69/E3 Play Cu (Pleiku), Viet.
107/J2 Playgreen (lake), Mb,Can
116/K11 Pleasant Hill, Ca,US
116/L11 Pleasanton, Ca,US
112/D4 Pleasanton, Tx,US
116/Q14 Pleasant Prairie, Wi,US
115/F5 Pleasantville, NY,US
69/E3 Pleiku (Play Cu), Viet.
38/G3 Pleisse (riv.), Ger.
77/G5 Plenty (riv.), Austl.
75/S10 Plenty (bay), NZ
107/G3 Plentywood, Mt,US
44/B2 Plérin, Fr.
39/J3 Pleszew, Pol.
111/G1 Plétipi (lake), Qu,Can
41/E6 Plettenberg, Ger.
51/G4 Pleven, Bul.
50/B3 Plitvice Lakes Nat'l Park, Cro.
45/L4 Plitvička Jezera Nat'l Park, Cro.
50/D4 Pljevlja, Yugo.
50/B4 Ploča, Rt (pt.), Yugo.
39/K2 Płock, Pol.
39/K2 Płock (prov.), Pol.
50/C4 Pločno (peak), Bosn.
44/B3 Ploemeur, Fr.
51/H3 Ploieşti, Rom.
38/F1 Plön, Ger.
106/G2 Plonge (lake), Sk,Can
39/L2 Płońsk, Pol.
39/H3 Ploučnice (riv.), Czh.
44/B2 Ploufragan, Fr.
44/A2 Plougastel-Daoulas, Fr.
51/G4 Plovdiv, Bul.
51/G5 Plovdiv (reg.), Bul.
110/B2 Plover, Wi,US
32/A2 Plumbridge, NI,UK
52/D5 Plungė, Lith.
101/J4 Plymouth (cap.), Monts.
34/B6 Plymouth, Eng,UK
34/B6 Plymouth (sound), Eng,UK
110/C3 Plymouth, In,US
111/G3 Plymouth, NH,US
110/C3 Plymouth, Wi,US
34/C2 Plynlimon (mtn.), UK
45/K2 Plzeň (Pilsen), Czh.
39/J2 Pniewy, Pol.
85/E4 Pô, Burk.
45/J4 Po (riv.), It.
45/J4 Po (val.), It.
95/G8 Poá, Braz.
68/D3 Pobedy, Pik (peak), Kyr.
39/J2 Pobiedziska, Pol.
113/F2 Pocahontas, Ar,US
94/A2 Poção de Pedra, Braz.
106/E5 Pocatello, Id,US
54/E1 Pochep, Rus.
45/K2 Pöcking, Ger.
78/E6 Pocklington (reef), PNG
33/H4 Pocklington, Eng,UK
94/B4 Poções, Braz.
95/H6 Poço Fundo, Braz.
109/J4 Pocola, Ok,US
93/G7 Poconé, Braz.
115/E4 Pocono (lake), Pa,US
95/G6 Poços de Caldas, Braz.
39/K3 Poddębice, Pol.
39/M3 Podlasie (reg.), Pol.
52/H5 Podol'sk, Rus.
84/B2 Podor, Sen.
52/G3 Podporozh'ye, Rus.
50/C3 Podravska Slatina, Cro.
50/E4 Podujevo, Yugo.
45/J5 Poggibonsi, It.
49/G2 Pogradec, Alb.
114/F5 Pogromni (vol.), Ak,US
64/A2 P'ohang, SKor.
111/G2 Pohénégamook, Qu,Can
37/G3 Pohjanmaa (reg.), Fin.
78/E4 Pohnpei (isl.), Micr.
115/E5 Pohopoco Mtn. (ridge), Pa,US
98/H Poinsett (cape), Ant.
102/E2 Point (lake), NW,Can
113/F4 Point au Fer (isl.), La,US
101/J4 Pointe-à-Pitre, Guad.
111/N7 Pointe-Claire, Qu,Can
111/F2 Pointe-du-Lac, Qu,Can
87/B1 Pointe-Noire, Congo
47/G4 Pointe Pescade, Cap de la (cape), Alg.
101/J5 Point Fortin, Trin.
77/E1 Point Lookout (peak), Austl.
110/D3 Point Pelee Nat'l Park, On,Can
115/F5 Point Pleasant, NJ,US
110/C4 Point Pleasant, Oh,US
110/D4 Point Pleasant, WV,US
31/S10 Poissy, Fr.
44/D3 Poitiers, Fr.
44/C3 Poitou (hist. reg.), Fr.
44/C3 Poitou-Charentes (reg.), Fr.
37/J3 Pojois-Karjala (prov.), Fin.
94/C4 Pojuca, Braz.
70/B2 Pokaran, India
70/D2 Pokhara, Nepal
55/K1 Pokhvistnevo, Rus.
69/E4 Po Klong Garai Cham Towers, Viet.
83/L7 Poko, Zaire
45/L1 Polabská Nížina (reg.), Czh.
46/C1 Pola de Laviana, Sp.
46/C1 Pola de Lena, Sp.
46/C1 Pola de Siero, Sp.
54/A2 Pol'ana (peak), Slvk.
39/K2 Poland
39/L3 Pol'aniec, Pol.
53/P2 Polar Urals (mts.), Rus.
59/C2 Polatlı, Turk.
39/J2 Pol'czyn-Zdrój, Pol.
61/J1 Pol-e-Khomri, Afg.
35/E1 Polesworth, Eng,UK
50/E2 Polgár, Hun.
49/J4 Poliaigos (isl.), Gre.
48/D3 Policastro (gulf), It.
39/H2 Police, Pol.
48/E2 Policoro, It.
49/H2 Políkhni, Gre.
67/D4 Polillo (isl.), Phil.
48/E3 Polistena, It.
39/J3 Polkowice, Pol.
47/G3 Pollensa, Sp.
67/E6 Polomolok, Phil.
97/G2 Polonia (cape), Uru.
70/D6 Polonnaruwa, SrL.
54/C2 Polonnoye, Ukr.
52/F5 Polotsk, Bela.
34/B6 Polperro, Eng,UK
51/G4 Polski Trŭmbesh, Bul.
106/E4 Polson, Mt,US
54/E2 Poltava, Ukr.
54/E2 Poltava Obl., Ukr.
52/F3 Polvijärvi, Fin.
52/G1 Polyarnyy, Rus.
79/J3 Polynesia (reg.)
95/D2 Pomba (riv.), Braz.
94/C2 Pombal, Braz.
46/A3 Pombal, Port.
39/H2 Pomerania (reg.), Pol.
39/H1 Pomeranian (bay), Ger., Pol.
95/B3 Pomerode, Braz.
32/B2 Pomeroy, NI,UK
106/D4 Pomeroy, Wa,US
78/E5 Pomio, PNG
115/C2 Pomona, Ca,US
51/H4 Pomorie, Bul.
113/H5 Pompano Beach, Fl,US
48/D2 Pompei (ruins), It.
95/C1 Pompeu, Braz.
115/F4 Pompton Lakes, NJ,US
85/E4 Pô Nat'l Park, Burk.
109/H3 Ponca City, Ok,US
101/H4 Ponce, PR
110/E1 Poncheville (lake), Qu,Can
103/J1 Pond (inlet), NW,Can
70/B5 Pondicherry (terr.), India
70/C5 Pondicherry (terr.), India
70/D4 Pondicherry (terr.), India
46/B1 Ponferrada, Sp.
89/E2 Pongolo (riv.), SAfr.
84/E4 Poni (prov.), Burk.
39/M3 Poniatowa, Pol.
106/E2 Ponoka, Ab,Can
52/H2 Ponoy (riv.), Rus.
42/D3 Pont-à-Celles, Belg.
94/C5 Ponta da Baleia (pt.), Braz.
47/S12 Ponta da Pico (mtn.), Azor.,Port.
47/T13 Ponta Delgada, Azor.,Port.

47/U15 **Ponta do Sol,** Madr.,Port.
95/B3 **Ponta Grossa,** Braz.
95/B1 **Pontalina,** Braz.
43/F6 **Pont-à-Mousson,** Fr.
93/G8 **Ponta Porã,** Braz.
34/C3 **Pontardawe,** Wal,UK
34/B3 **Pontardulais,** Wal,UK
45/G3 **Pontarlier,** Fr.
31/T10 **Pontault-Combault,** Fr.
110/E1 **Pontax** (riv.), Qu,Can
113/F4 **Pontchartrain** (lake), La,US
44/B3 **Pontchâteau,** Fr.
44/E4 **Pont-du-Château,** Fr.
48/C2 **Pontecorvo,** It.
46/A3 **Ponte de Sor,** Port.
33/G4 **Pontefract,** Eng,UK
33/G1 **Ponteland,** Eng,UK
95/D2 **Ponte Nova,** Braz.
34/C2 **Ponterwyd,** Wal,UK
34/D1 **Pontesbury,** Eng,UK
92/G7 **Pontes e Lacerda,** Braz.
46/A1 **Pontevedra,** Sp.
110/B3 **Pontiac,** Il,US
116/F6 **Pontiac,** Mi,US
72/C4 **Pontianak,** Indo.
44/B2 **Pontivy,** Fr.
31/S9 **Pontoise,** Fr.
113/F3 **Pontotoc,** Ms,US
34/C2 **Pontrhydfendigaid,** Wal,UK
34/D3 **Pontrilas,** Eng,UK
42/B5 **Pont-Sainte Maxence,** Fr.
44/F4 **Pont-Saint-Esprit,** Fr.
34/B3 **Pontyates,** Wal,UK
34/C3 **Pontyclun,** Wal,UK
34/C3 **Pont y Cymmer,** Wal,UK
34/C3 **Pontypool,** Wal,UK
34/C3 **Pontypridd,** Wal,UK
48/C2 **Ponziane** (isls.), It.
34/E5 **Poole,** Eng,UK
35/E5 **Poole** (bay), Eng,UK
70/B4 **Poona,** India
92/E7 **Poopó** (lake), Bol.
92/C3 **Popayán,** Col.
42/B2 **Poperinge,** Belg.
77/B2 **Popilta** (lake), Austl.
77/B2 **Popio** (lake), Austl.
107/K2 **Poplar** (riv.), Mb, On,Can
107/G3 **Poplar,** Mt,US
107/G3 **Poplar** (riv.), Mt,US
109/K3 **Poplar Bluff,** Mo,US
113/F4 **Poplarville,** Ms,US
82/J6 **Popokabaka,** Zaire
78/D5 **Popondetta,** PNG
51/H4 **Popovo,** Bul.
39/L4 **Poprad,** Slvk.
39/L4 **Poprad** (riv.), Slvk.
93/J6 **Porangatu,** Braz.
70/A3 **Porbandar,** India
46/C4 **Porcuna,** Sp.
114/K2 **Porcupine** (riv.), Yk,Can, Ak,US
76/B3 **Porcupine Gorge Nat'l Park,** Austl.
107/H2 **Porcupine Plain,** Sk,Can
45/K4 **Pordenone,** It.
37/G3 **Pori,** Fin.
75/R11 **Porirua,** NZ
52/E4 **Porkhov,** Rus.
101/J5 **Porlamar,** Ven.
34/C4 **Porlock,** Eng,UK
63/N2 **Poronaysk,** Rus.
98/J **Porpoise** (bay), Ant.
46/A1 **Porriño,** Sp.
37/H1 **Porsangen** (fjord), Nor.
37/D4 **Porsgrunn,** Nor.
59/B2 **Porsuk** (riv.), Turk.
92/F7 **Portachuelo,** Bol.
32/B3 **Portadown,** NI,UK
32/C3 **Portaferry,** NI,UK
110/C3 **Portage,** Mi,US
110/B3 **Portage,** Wi,US
107/J3 **Portage la Prairie,** Mb,Can
106/B3 **Port Alberni,** BC,Can
46/B3 **Portalegre,** Port.
46/B3 **Portalegre** (dist.), Port.
109/G4 **Portales,** NM,US
88/D4 **Port Alfred,** SAfr.
106/B3 **Port Alice,** BC,Can
106/C3 **Port Angeles,** Wa,US
101/F4 **Port Antonio,** Jam.
36/C2 **Port Appin,** Sc,UK
112/E4 **Port Arthur,** Tx,US
111/K1 **Port au Choix,** Nf,Can
74/F6 **Port Augusta,** Austl.
101/G4 **Port-au-Prince** (cap.), Haiti
32/C3 **Portavogie,** NI,UK
41/F4 **Porta Westfalica,** Ger.
71/F5 **Port Blair,** India
112/E4 **Port Bolivar,** Tx,US
84/E5 **Port-Bouët,** IvC.
103/K2 **Port Burwell,** Qu,Can
111/H1 **Port-Cartier,** Qu,Can
113/H5 **Port Charlotte,** Fl,US
115/G5 **Port Chester,** NY,US
110/D3 **Port Clinton,** Oh,US
111/R10 **Port Colborne,** On,Can
111/Q8 **Port Credit,** On,Can
111/S8 **Port Darlington,** On,Can
77/C4 **Port Davey** (har.), Austl.
101/G4 **Port-de-Paix,** Haiti
72/B3 **Port Dickson,** Malay.
114/M4 **Port Edward,** BC,Can
94/B4 **Porteirinha,** Braz.
93/H4 **Portel,** Braz.
110/D2 **Port Elgin,** Can.
88/D4 **Port Elizabeth,** SAfr.
32/D3 **Port Erin,** IM,UK
88/L10 **Porterville,** SAfr.
108/C3 **Porterville,** Ca,US
44/F4 **Portes-lès-Valence,** Fr.
82/B3 **Port-Étienne,** Mrta.
44/D5 **Portet-sur-Garonne,** Fr.
34/B3 **Port Eynon,** Wal,UK
34/B3 **Port Eynon** (pt.), Wal,UK
87/A1 **Port-Gentil,** Gabon
36/C3 **Port Glasgow,** Sc,UK
32/B2 **Portglenone,** NI,UK
34/C3 **Porth,** Wal,UK
85/G5 **Port Harcourt,** Nga.
106/B3 **Port Hardy,** BC,Can
111/J2 **Port Hawkesbury,** NS,Can
34/C4 **Porthcawl,** Wal,UK
74/B4 **Port Hedland,** Austl.
34/A6 **Porthleven,** Eng,UK
32/D6 **Porthmadog,** Wal,UK
115/A2 **Port Hueneme,** Ca,US
116/H6 **Port Huron,** Mi,US
46/A4 **Portimão,** Port.
34/B5 **Port Isaac,** Eng,UK
34/D4 **Portishead,** Eng,UK
115/G5 **Port Jefferson,** NY,US
77/C4 **Portland** (cape), Austl.
101/F4 **Portland** (pt.), Jam.
34/D6 **Portland** (pt.), Eng,UK
114/N4 **Portland** (inlet), BC,Can, Ak,US
110/C3 **Portland,** In,US
111/G3 **Portland,** Me,US
106/C4 **Portland,** Or,US
113/G2 **Portland,** Tn,US
34/D5 **Portland, Isle of** (pen.), Eng,UK
112/D4 **Port Lavaca,** Tx,US
74/F6 **Port Lincoln,** Austl.
89/S15 **Port Louis** (cap.), Mrts.
77/E1 **Port Macquarie,** Austl.
32/B5 **Portmarnock,** Ire.
106/B3 **Port McNeill,** BC,Can
111/H1 **Port-Menier,** Qu,Can
78/D5 **Port Moresby** (cap.), PNG
111/G1 **Portneuf** (riv.), Qu,Can
48/A1 **Porto** (gulf), Fr.
46/A2 **Porto,** Port.
46/A2 **Porto** (dist.), Port.
95/B4 **Pôrto Alegre,** Braz.
87/B3 **Porto Amboim,** Ang.
94/D3 **Pôrto Calvo,** Braz.
45/K5 **Portocivitanova,** It.
94/C3 **Pôrto da Fôlha,** Braz.
48/C4 **Porto Empedocle,** It.
48/B1 **Portoferraio,** It.
95/C2 **Pôrto Ferreira,** Braz.
94/A2 **Pôrto Franco,** Braz.
101/J5 **Port-of-Spain** (cap.), Trin.
45/K4 **Portogruaro,** It.
45/J4 **Portomaggiore,** It.
93/J6 **Pôrto Nacional,** Braz.
85/F5 **Porto-Novo** (cap.), Ben.
113/H4 **Port Orange,** Fl,US
48/C1 **Porto San Giorgio,** It.
48/B1 **Porto Santo Stefano,** It.
94/C5 **Porto Seguro,** Braz.
48/A2 **Porto Torres,** It.
95/B3 **Porto União,** Braz.
92/F5 **Porto Velho,** Braz.
92/B4 **Portoviejo,** Ecu.
32/C2 **Portpatrick,** Sc,UK
77/C3 **Port Phillip** (bay), Austl.
74/F6 **Port Pirie,** Austl.
32/B1 **Portrush,** NI,UK
86/C2 **Port Said** (Būr Sa'īd), Egypt
113/G4 **Port Saint Joe,** Fl,US
44/F5 **Port-Saint-Louis-du-Rhône,** Fr.
113/H5 **Port Saint Lucie,** Fl,US
32/D3 **Port Saint Mary,** IM,UK
35/E5 **Portsea** (isl.), Eng,UK
114/M4 **Port Simpson,** BC,Can
35/F5 **Portslade by Sea,** Eng,UK
35/E5 **Portsmouth,** Eng,UK
111/G3 **Portsmouth,** NH,US
110/D4 **Portsmouth,** Oh,US
110/E4 **Portsmouth,** Va,US
77/E2 **Port Stephens** (bay), Austl.
32/B1 **Portstewart,** NI,UK
86/D5 **Port Sudan** (Būr Sūdān), Sudan
34/C3 **Port Talbot,** Wal,UK
106/C3 **Port Townsend,** Wa,US
46/A3 **Portugal**
46/D1 **Portugalete,** Sp.
101/H6 **Portuguesa** (riv.), Ven.
115/G5 **Port Washington,** NY,US
110/C3 **Port Washington,** Wi,US
32/D2 **Port William,** Sc,UK
91/E2 **Posadas,** Arg.
46/C4 **Posadas,** Sp.
50/C3 **Posavina** (val.), Bosn., Cro.
73/F4 **Poso** (lake), Indo.
63/K5 **Posŏng,** SKor.
94/A4 **Posse,** Braz.
116/C2 **Possession** (sound), Wa,US
112/C3 **Post,** Tx,US
52/E5 **Postavy,** Bela.
82/F3 **Poste Maurice Cortier** (ruins), Alg.
82/F3 **Poste Weygand** (ruins), Alg.
106/D4 **Post Falls,** Id,US
88/C3 **Postmasburg,** SAfr.
50/B3 **Postojna,** Slov.
88/D2 **Potchefstroom,** SAfr.
109/J4 **Poteau,** Ok,US
48/D2 **Potenza,** It.
48/C1 **Potenza** (riv.), It.
106/D4 **Potholes** (res.), Wa,US
94/B2 **Poti** (riv.), Braz.
55/G4 **Poti,** Geo.
45/J5 **Poti, Alpe di** (peak), It.
115/J7 **Potomac,** Md,US
110/E4 **Potomac** (riv.), Md, Va,US
92/E7 **Potosí,** Bol.
109/K3 **Potosi,** Mo,US
91/C2 **Potrerillos,** Chile
38/G2 **Potsdam,** Ger.
110/F2 **Potsdam,** NY,US
31/N6 **Potters Bar,** Eng,UK
35/F2 **Potterspury,** Eng,UK
35/F2 **Potton,** Eng,UK
70/D6 **Pottuvil,** SrL.
110/F3 **Poughkeepsie,** NY,US
32/B5 **Poulaphouca** (res.), Ire.
33/G5 **Poulter** (riv.), Eng,UK
33/F4 **Poulton-le-Fylde,** Eng,UK
45/G4 **Pourri** (mtn.), Fr.
95/H7 **Pouso Alegre,** Braz.
69/C3 **Pouthisat,** Camb.
69/C3 **Pouthisat** (riv.), Camb.
39/K4 **Považská Bystrica,** Slvk.
46/A2 **Póvoa de Varzim,** Port.
55/G2 **Povorino,** Rus.
63/L3 **Povorotnyy, Mys** (cape), Rus.
103/J2 **Povungnituk** (riv.), Qu,Can
107/G4 **Powder** (riv.), Mt, Wy,US
108/E3 **Powell** (lake), Az, Ut,US
106/F4 **Powell,** Wy,US
106/B3 **Powell River,** BC,Can
111/R9 **Power** (res.), NY,US
34/C1 **Powys, Vale** (val.), Wal,UK
93/H7 **Poxoréo,** Braz.
67/C2 **Poyang** (lake), China
33/F5 **Poynton,** Eng,UK
46/A1 **Poyo,** Sp.
50/E3 **Požarevac,** Yugo.
100/B3 **Poza Rica,** Mex.
50/E4 **Požega,** Yugo.
39/J2 **Poznań,** Pol.
39/J2 **Poznań** (prov.), Pol.
46/D4 **Pozo Alcón,** Sp.
46/C3 **Pozoblanco,** Sp.
47/N9 **Pozuelo de Alarcón,** Sp.
48/D4 **Pozzallo,** It.
48/C1 **Pozzoni** (peak), It.
39/K2 **Prabuty,** Pol.
69/B4 **Pracham Hiang** (pt.), Thai.
45/L2 **Prachatice,** Czh.
69/C3 **Prachin Buri,** Thai.
69/C3 **Prachin Buri** (riv.), Thai.
69/B4 **Prachuap Khiri Khan,** Thai.
39/J3 **Praděd** (peak), Czh.
94/C5 **Prado,** Braz.
115/C3 **Prado** (dam), Ca,US
45/L1 **Prague (Praha)** (cap.), Czh.
45/L1 **Praha** (reg.), Czh.
51/G3 **Prahova** (co.), Rom.
80/K11 **Praia** (cap.), CpV.
47/S12 **Praia de Victória,** Azor.,Port.
95/G9 **Praia Grande,** Braz.
110/B3 **Prairie du Chien,** Wi,US
111/N6 **Prairies** (riv.), Qu,Can
107/J4 **Prairies, Coteau des** (upland), US
112/E4 **Prairie View,** Tx,US
69/B3 **Pran Buri** (res.), Thai.
70/D4 **Prānhita** (riv.), India
72/A3 **Prapat,** Indo.
69/D3 **Prasat Preah Vihear,** Camb.
39/K3 **Praszka,** Pol.
95/B1 **Prata,** Braz.
45/J5 **Prato,** It.
48/C1 **Pratola Peligna,** It.
97/J7 **Pratt** (isl.), Chile
109/H3 **Pratt,** Ks,US
113/G3 **Prattville,** Al,US
46/B1 **Pravia,** Sp.
34/C6 **Prawle** (pt.), Eng,UK
73/E5 **Praya,** Indo.
51/G3 **Predeal,** Rom.
107/H3 **Preeceville,** Sk,Can
33/F6 **Prees,** Eng,UK
33/F4 **Preesall,** Eng,UK
38/F1 **Preetz,** Ger.
39/L1 **Pregolya** (riv.), Rus.
110/E1 **Preissac** (lake), On,Can
69/D4 **Prek Pouthi,** Camb.
47/L7 **Premià de Mar,** Sp.
39/G2 **Prenzlau,** Ger.
39/J4 **Přerov,** Czh.
45/J3 **Presanella** (peak), It.
33/F5 **Prescot,** Eng,UK
110/F2 **Prescott,** On,Can
108/D4 **Prescott,** Az,US
50/E4 **Preševo,** Yugo.
91/D2 **Presidencia Roque Sáenz Peña,** Arg.
94/A2 **Presidente Dutra,** Braz.
95/A2 **Presidente Epitácio,** Braz.
95/B2 **Presidente Prudente,** Braz.
96/B5 **Presidente Ríos** (lake), Chile
95/B2 **Presidente Venceslau,** Braz.
112/B4 **Presidio,** Tx,US
51/H4 **Preslav,** Bul.
31/U10 **Presles-en-Brie,** Fr.
39/L4 **Prešov,** Slvk.
49/G2 **Prespa** (lake), Eur.
111/G2 **Presque Isle,** Me,US
33/E5 **Prestatyn,** Wal,UK
85/E5 **Prestea,** Gha.
34/D2 **Presteigne,** Wal,UK
45/K2 **Přeštice,** Czh.
77/G5 **Preston,** Austl.
33/F4 **Preston,** Eng,UK
34/D5 **Preston,** Eng,UK
106/F5 **Preston,** Id,US
110/D4 **Prestonsburg,** Ky,US
33/F4 **Prestwich,** Eng,UK
36/C3 **Prestwick,** Sc,UK
35/F3 **Prestwood,** Eng,UK
94/A3 **Prêto** (riv.), Braz.
94/A5 **Prêto** (riv.), Braz.
88/E2 **Pretoria** (cap.), SAfr.
41/F4 **Preussisch Oldendorf,** Ger.
49/G3 **Préveza,** Gre.
114/D4 **Pribilof** (isls.), Ak,US
50/D4 **Priboj,** Yugo.
45/L2 **Příbram,** Czh.
108/E3 **Price,** Ut,US
108/E3 **Price** (riv.), Ut,US
113/F4 **Prichard,** Al,US
46/C4 **Priego de Córdoba,** Sp.
88/C3 **Prieska,** SAfr.
106/D3 **Priest** (lake), Id,US
106/D3 **Priest River,** Id,US
46/C1 **Prieta** (mtn.), Sp.
39/K4 **Prievidza,** Slvk.
38/F2 **Prignitz** (reg.), Ger.
50/C3 **Prijedor,** Bosn.
50/D4 **Prijepolje,** Yugo.
55/H3 **Prikaspian** (plain), Kaz., Rus.
55/H3 **Prikumsk,** Rus.
50/E5 **Prilep,** Macd.
54/E2 **Priluki,** Ukr.
48/C2 **Prima Porta,** It.
97/J7 **Primero** (cape), Chile
35/E1 **Primethorpe,** Eng,UK
57/P5 **Primorsk Kray,** Rus.
54/F3 **Primorsko-Akhtarsk,** Rus.
106/F2 **Primrose** (lake), Ab, Sk,Can
43/F5 **Prims** (riv.), Ger.
102/E1 **Prince Albert** (pen.), NW,Can
102/E1 **Prince Albert** (sound), NW,Can
107/G2 **Prince Albert,** Sk,Can
107/G2 **Prince Albert Nat'l Park,** Sk,Can
102/D1 **Prince Alfred** (cape), NW,Can
103/J2 **Prince Charles** (isl.), NW,Can
29/L8 **Prince Edward** (isls.), SAfr.
111/J2 **Prince Edward Island** (prov.), Can.
111/J2 **Prince Edward Island Nat'l Park,** PE,Can
106/C2 **Prince George,** BC,Can
103/R7 **Prince Gustav Adolf** (sea), NW,Can
98/C **Prince Harold** (coast), Ant.
102/G1 **Prince Leopold** (isl.), NW,Can
40/C2 **Princenhof** (lake), Neth.
74/G2 **Prince of Wales** (isl.), Austl.
102/G1 **Prince of Wales** (isl.), NW,Can
102/E1 **Prince of Wales** (str.), NW,Can
114/M4 **Prince of Wales** (isl.), Ak,US
98/C **Prince Olav** (coast), Ant.
103/R7 **Prince Patrick** (isl.), NW,Can
102/G1 **Prince Regent** (inlet), NW,Can
114/M4 **Prince Rupert,** BC,Can
35/F3 **Princes Risborough,** Eng,UK
98/A **Princess Astrid** (coast), Ant.
76/A1 **Princess Charlotte** (bay), Austl.
103/S6 **Princess Margaret** (range), NW,Can
98/Z **Princess Martha** (coast), Ant.
98/B **Princess Ragnhild** (coast), Ant.
106/A2 **Princess Royal** (isl.), BC,Can
101/J5 **Princes Town,** Trin.
106/C3 **Princeton,** BC,Can
110/B3 **Princeton,** Il,US
110/C4 **Princeton,** In,US
110/C4 **Princeton,** Ky,US
107/K4 **Princeton,** Mn,US
115/F5 **Princeton,** NJ,US
110/D4 **Princeton,** WV,US
114/J3 **Prince William** (sound), Ak,US
82/G7 **Príncipe** (isl.), SaoT.
114/K3 **Prindle** (vol.), Ak,US
106/C4 **Prineville,** Or,US
40/B5 **Prinsenbeek,** Neth.
40/C2 **Prinses Margriet** (can.), Neth.
100/E5 **Prinzapolka,** Nic.
48/D4 **Priolo di Gargallo,** It.
46/A1 **Prior** (cape), Sp.
52/F3 **Priozersk,** Rus.
54/C2 **Pripet** (marshes), Bela., Ukr.
50/E4 **Priština,** Yugo.
38/G2 **Pritzwalk,** Ger.
44/F4 **Privas,** Fr.
55/H2 **Privolzhskiy,** Rus.
55/K1 **Priyutovo,** Rus.
50/E4 **Prizren,** Yugo.
50/C3 **Prnjavor,** Bosn.
72/D5 **Probolinggo,** Indo.
112/D3 **Proctor** (lake), Tx,US
70/C5 **Proddatūr,** India
43/D3 **Profondeville,** Belg.
100/E6 **Progreso,** Pan.
97/T12 **Progreso,** Uru.
63/K2 **Progress,** Rus.
55/H4 **Prokhladnyy,** Rus.
68/E1 **Prokop'yevsk,** Rus.
50/E4 **Prokuplje,** Yugo.
71/G4 **Prome,** Burma
95/B2 **Promissão,** Braz.
95/B2 **Promissão** (res.), Braz.
94/C3 **Propriá,** Braz.
39/J2 **Prosna** (riv.), Pol.
114/L3 **Prospector** (mtn.), Yk,Can
67/E6 **Prosperidad,** Phil.
39/J4 **Prostějov,** Czh.
39/L3 **Prószowice,** Pol.
51/H4 **Provadiya,** Bul.
45/G5 **Provence** (mts.), Fr.
44/F5 **Provence** (reg.), Fr.
45/G4 **Provence-Alpes-Côte d'Azur** (reg.), Fr.
92/F6 **Providência** (mts.), Braz.
100/E5 **Providencia** (isl.), Col.
44/E2 **Provins,** Fr.
108/E2 **Provo,** Ut,US
47/T13 **Provoação,** Azor.,Port.
106/F2 **Provost,** Ab,Can
50/C4 **Prozor,** Bosn.
95/B3 **Prudentópolis,** Braz.
33/G2 **Prudhoe,** Eng,UK
114/J1 **Prudhoe** (bay), Ak,US
39/J3 **Prudnik,** Pol.
43/F3 **Prüm** (riv.), Ger.
39/K1 **Pruszcz Gdański,** Pol.
39/L2 **Pruszków,** Pol.
51/J2 **Prut** (riv.), Eur.
98/F **Prydz** (bay), Ant.
112/E2 **Pryor** (cr.), Ok,US
39/L2 **Przasnysz,** Pol.
39/H3 **Przemków,** Pol.
39/M4 **Przemyśl,** Pol.
39/M4 **Przemyśl** (prov.), Pol.
39/M3 **Przeworsk,** Pol.
68/C3 **Przheval'sk,** Kyr.
52/C5 **Przylądek Rozewie** (cape), Pol.
39/L3 **Przysucha,** Pol.
49/J3 **Psará** (isl.), Gre.
52/F4 **Pskov** (lake), Est., Rus.
52/F4 **Pskov,** Rus.
52/F4 **Pskov Obl.,** Rus.
39/K4 **Pszczyna,** Pol.
49/G2 **Ptolemaís,** Gre.
50/B2 **Ptuj,** Slov.
69/C2 **Pua,** Thai.
92/D5 **Pucallpa,** Peru
116/G7 **Puce,** On,Can
66/B4 **Pucheng,** China
96/Q9 **Puchuncaví,** Chile
51/G3 **Pucioasa,** Rom.
39/K1 **Puck,** Pol.
35/G3 **Puckeridge,** Eng,UK
96/C3 **Pucón,** Chile
37/H2 **Pudasjärvi,** Fin.
34/D5 **Puddletown,** Eng,UK
33/G4 **Pudsey,** Eng,UK
71/H2 **Pudu** (riv.), China
70/C5 **Pudukkottai,** India
100/B4 **Puebla,** Mex.
100/B4 **Puebla** (state), Mex.
46/A1 **Puebla del Caramiñal,** Sp.
109/F3 **Pueblo,** Co,US
100/C5 **Pueblo Nuevo Tiquisate,** Guat.
96/C2 **Puente Alto,** Chile
46/A1 **Puenteareas,** Sp.
46/A1 **Puente Caldelas,** Sp.
46/A1 **Puente-Ceso,** Sp.
96/C2 **Puente del Inca,** Arg.
46/A1 **Puentedeume,** Sp.
46/C4 **Puente-Genil,** Sp.
46/B1 **Puentes de García Rodríguez,** Sp.
104/R10 **Pueo** (pt.), Hi,US
108/E4 **Puerco** (riv.), Az, NM,US
108/F4 **Puerco** (riv.), NM,US
96/B5 **Puerto Aisén,** Chile
92/C3 **Puerto Asís,** Col.
92/E2 **Puerto Ayacucho,** Ven.
100/D4 **Puerto Barrios,** Guat.
101/H5 **Puerto Cabello,** Ven.
100/E5 **Puerto Cabezas,** Nic.
101/H5 **Puerto Cumarebo,** Ven.
47/X16 **Puerto de la Cruz,** Canl.
46/A1 **Puerto del Son,** Sp.
100/B4 **Puerto Escondido,** Mex.
91/F2 **Puerto Iguazú,** Arg.
101/J5 **Puerto La Cruz,** Ven.
100/E4 **Puerto Lempira,** Hon.
46/C3 **Puertollano,** Sp.
46/E4 **Puerto Lumbreras,** Sp.
96/D4 **Puerto Madryn,** Arg.
92/E6 **Puerto Maldonado,** Peru
96/B4 **Puerto Montt,** Chile
100/D3 **Puerto Morelos,** Mex.
97/J7 **Puerto Natales,** Chile
101/F6 **Puerto Obaldía,** Pan.
101/G4 **Puerto Plata,** DRep.
67/C6 **Puerto Princesa,** Phil.
96/B4 **Puerto Quellón,** Chile
46/B4 **Puerto Real,** Sp.
101/H4 **Puerto Rico** (commonwealth), US
100/C5 **Puerto San José,** Guat.
92/G7 **Puerto Suárez,** Bol.
101/N9 **Puerto Vallarta,** Mex.
96/B4 **Puerto Varas,** Chile
96/C5 **Pueyrredón** (lake), Arg.
32/D5 **Puffin** (isl.), Wal,UK
55/J1 **Pugachev,** Rus.
116/C2 **Puget** (sound), Wa,US
48/E2 **Puglia** (reg.), It.
44/E5 **Puigmal** (mtn.), Fr.
47/G1 **Puigsacalm** (mtn.), Sp.
72/C5 **Pujut** (cape), Indo.
79/J6 **Pukapuka** (isl.), Cookls.
79/M6 **Puka Puka** (atoll), FrPol.
79/M6 **Pukarua** (isl.), FrPol.
110/C1 **Pukaskwa Nat'l Park,** On,Can
73/F1 **Pulanduta** (pt.), Phil.
78/D4 **Pulap** (atoll), Micr.
113/G3 **Pulaski,** Tn,US
110/D4 **Pulaski,** Va,US
39/L3 **Puławy,** Pol.
35/F5 **Pulborough,** Eng,UK
64/A3 **Pulguk-sa,** SKor.
40/D7 **Pulheim,** Ger.
73/G3 **Pulisan** (cape), Indo.
106/D4 **Pullman,** Wa,US
45/G3 **Pully,** Swi.
39/G3 **Pulsnitz** (riv.), Ger.
39/L2 **Pułtusk,** Pol.
78/D4 **Puluwat** (atoll), Micr.
34/C2 **Pumpsaint,** Wal,UK
71/F2 **Pumu** (pass), China
79/X15 **Punaauia,** FrPol.
92/E7 **Punata,** Bol.
61/K2 **Pūnch,** India
72/B3 **Punggai** (cape), Malay.
87/E1 **Punia,** Zaire
68/C5 **Punjab** (state), India
61/K2 **Punjab** (plains), Pak.
61/K3 **Punjab** (prov.), Pak.
92/D7 **Puno,** Peru
100/D4 **Punta Allen,** Mex.
97/K8 **Punta Arenas,** Chile
101/G5 **Punta Cardón,** Ven.
101/J6 **Punta de Mata,** Ven.
100/D4 **Punta Gorda,** Belz.
100/E5 **Punta Gorda** (bay), Nic.
113/H5 **Punta Gorda,** Fl,US
101/M7 **Punta Peñasco,** Mex.
100/E6 **Puntarenas,** CR
46/B4 **Punta Umbría,** Sp.
104/S10 **Puolo** (pt.), Hi,US
92/D6 **Puquio,** Peru
56/H3 **Pur** (riv.), Rus.
92/C3 **Puracé Nat'l Park,** Col.
34/D5 **Purbeck, Isle of** (pen.), Eng,UK
109/H4 **Purcell,** Ok,US
96/B3 **Purén,** Chile
109/G3 **Purgatoire** (riv.), Co,US
70/D3 **Purī,** India
52/E4 **Purikari** (pt.), Est.
31/N8 **Purley,** Eng,UK
40/B3 **Purmerend,** Neth.
70/C4 **Pūrna,** India
70/C3 **Pūrna** (riv.), India
91/B5 **Purranque,** Chile
35/E3 **Purton,** Eng,UK
92/F4 **Purús** (riv.), Braz.
51/G4 **Purvomay,** Bul.
72/C5 **Purwokerto,** Indo.
70/C4 **Pusad,** India
64/A3 **Pusan,** SKor.
72/A2 **Pusat Gayo** (mts.), Indo.
52/F4 **Pushkin,** Rus.
50/E2 **Püspökladány,** Hun.
96/C2 **Putaendo,** Chile
72/D4 **Puting** (cape), Indo.
100/B4 **Putla,** Mex.
96/B4 **Putumayo** (riv.), Col.
56/K3 **Putorana** (mts.), Rus.
96/C4 **Putrachoique** (peak), Arg.
70/C6 **Puttalam,** SrL.
42/D1 **Putte,** Belg.
40/C4 **Putten,** Neth.
40/B5 **Putten** (isl.), Neth.
43/F5 **Püttlingen,** Ger.
84/C5 **Putu** (range), Libr.
92/D4 **Putumayo** (riv.), SAm.
72/D3 **Putussibau,** Indo.
104/T10 **Puu Kukui** (peak), Hi,US
42/D1 **Puurs,** Belg.
66/B3 **Pu Xian,** China
116/C3 **Puyallup,** Wa,US
116/C3 **Puyallup** (riv.), Wa,US
66/C4 **Puyang,** China
44/E4 **Puy de Barbier** (peak), Fr.
44/E4 **Puy de Sancy** (peak), Fr.
96/B4 **Puyehué** (vol.), Chile
96/B4 **Puyehué Nat'l Park,** Chile
44/D5 **Puymorens, Col de** (pass), Fr.
47/E3 **Puzal,** Sp.
87/E2 **Pweto,** Zaire
32/D6 **Pwllheli,** Wal,UK
61/K1 **Pyandzh** (Panj) (riv.), Afg., Taj.
52/F2 **Pyaozero** (lake), Rus.
71/G4 **Pyapon,** Burma
56/J2 **Pyasina** (riv.), Rus.
55/G3 **Pyatigorsk,** Rus.
44/F4 **Pyfara** (mtn.), Fr.
37/H3 **Pyhä-Häkin Nat'l Park,** Fin.
37/H3 **Pyhäjärvi,** Fin.
37/H2 **Pyhätunturi** (peak), Fin.
69/B2 **Pyinmana,** Burma
34/C3 **Pyle,** Wal,UK
63/K4 **Pyŏngt'aek,** SKor.
63/K4 **P'yŏngyang** (cap.), NKor.
114/M4 **Pyramid** (mtn.), BC,Can
115/B1 **Pyramid** (lake), Ca,US
108/C3 **Pyramid** (lake), Nv,US
47/E1 **Pyrenees** (range), Eur.
44/C5 **Pyrénées Occidentales Nat'l Park,** Fr.
39/H2 **Pyrzyce,** Pol.
53/Q4 **Pyshma** (riv.), Rus.
69/B2 **Pyu,** Burma

Q

59/L6 **Qā'al Jafr** (salt pan), Jor.
59/K5 **Qabātiyah,** WBnk.
82/H1 **Qābis,** Tun.
60/F1 **Qā'emshahr,** Iran
49/G1 **Qafa e Malit** (pass), Alb.
82/G1 **Qafşah,** Tun.
63/J2 **Qagan** (lake), China
66/C2 **Qahar Youyi Qianqi,** China
62/C4 **Qaidam** (basin), China
59/M8 **Qalansuwa,** Isr.
59/F3 **Qal'at Dizah,** Iraq
59/H6 **Qallīn,** Egypt
59/K5 **Qalqīlyah,** WBnk.
60/F5 **Qamar, Ghubbat al** (bay), Yem.
59/N8 **Qanah, Wādī** (dry riv.), WBnk.
61/J2 **Qandahār,** Afg.
59/E3 **Qarah Qōsh,** Iraq
81/W17 **Qar'at al Ashkal** (lake), Tun.
83/Q6 **Qardho,** Som.
60/E2 **Qareh Chāy** (riv.), Iran
68/F4 **Qarqan** (riv.), China
49/G2 **Qarrit, Qaf'e** (pass), Alb.
48/B4 **Qarţājannah** (ruins), Tun.
86/B2 **Qārūn, Birkat** (lake), Egypt
60/E2 **Qaşr-e-Shīrīn,** Iran
86/A3 **Qaşr Farāfirah,** Egypt
59/L5 **Qaţanā,** Syria
60/F3 **Qatar**
86/A2 **Qattara** (depr.), Egypt
59/L4 **Qaţţīnah** (lake), Syria
70/A2 **Qāzi Ahmad,** Pak.
60/F1 **Qazvīn,** Iran
49/F2 **Qendrevica** (peak), Alb.
61/G3 **Qeshm** (isl.), Iran
60/E1 **Qezel** (riv.), Iran
71/J2 **Qi** (riv.), China
66/D4 **Qian** (can.), China
66/D5 **Qian** (riv.), China
66/D5 **Qianqiu Guan** (pass), China
66/E2 **Qian Shan** (peak), China
66/B5 **Qifeng Guan** (pass), China
62/D4 **Qilian** (mts.), China
62/D4 **Qilian** (peak), China
59/N9 **Qilt, Wādī** (dry riv.), WBnk.
68/F4 **Qimantag** (mts.), China
66/B4 **Qin** (mts.), China
66/C4 **Qin** (riv.), China
86/C3 **Qinā,** Egypt
86/C3 **Qinā** (gov.), Egypt
67/B1 **Qing** (riv.), China
66/E3 **Qingdao,** China
62/D4 **Qinghai** (lake), China
62/D4 **Qinghai** (mts.), China
67/C2 **Qingjiang,** China
67/A2 **Qingshui** (riv.), China
63/H4 **Qingzhou,** China
66/D3 **Qinhuangdao,** China
66/C3 **Qinyuan,** China
67/B4 **Qiongshan,** China
63/J2 **Qiqihar,** China
59/K5 **Qiryat Ata,** Isr.
59/K5 **Qiryat Bialik,** Isr.
59/K6 **Qiryat Gat,** Isr.
59/M9 **Qiryat Mal'akhi,** Isr.
59/K5 **Qiryat Shemona,** Isr.
59/K5 **Qiryat Yam,** Isr.
63/L2 **Qitaihe,** China
66/C4 **Qi Xian,** China
63/L2 **Qixing** (riv.), China
60/F2 **Qom,** Iran
60/F2 **Qom** (riv.), Iran
70/E2 **Qomolangma** (Everest) (peak), China
61/J1 **Qondūz** (riv.), Afg.
67/C2 **Qu** (riv.), China
111/F3 **Quabbin** (res.), Ma,US
35/F3 **Quainton,** Eng,UK
41/E3 **Quakenbrück,** Ger.
115/E5 **Quakertown,** Pa,US
62/H5 **Quan** (riv.), China
112/D3 **Quanah,** Tx,US
66/B4 **Quanbao Shan** (mtn.), China
69/E3 **Quang Ngai,** Viet.
69/D2 **Quang Trach,** Viet.
69/D2 **Quang Tri,** Viet.
34/C4 **Quantocks** (hills), Eng,UK
67/B2 **Quanzhou,** China
107/G3 **Qu'Appelle** (riv.), Mb, Sk,Can
107/H3 **Qu'Appelle,** Sk,Can
107/G3 **Qu'Appelle** (dam), Sk,Can
103/K2 **Quaqtaq,** Qu,Can
42/C3 **Quaregnon,** Belg.
72/E4 **Quarles** (mts.), Indo.
45/J5 **Quarrata,** It.
48/A3 **Quartu Sant'Elena,** It.
115/B1 **Quartz Hill,** Ca,US
81/W17 **Quballāt,** Tun.
61/G1 **Qūchān,** Iran
77/D2 **Queanbeyan,** Austl.
103/J3 **Québec** (prov.), Can.
111/G2 **Québec** (cap.), Qu,Can
95/J7 **Quebra-Cangalha** (mts.), Braz.
96/B4 **Quedal** (pt.), Chile
34/D3 **Quedgeley,** Eng,UK
102/C3 **Queen Charlotte** (isls.), BC,Can
102/C3 **Queen Charlotte** (sound), BC,Can
106/B3 **Queen Charlotte** (str.), BC,Can
112/E3 **Queen City,** Tx,US
103/R7 **Queen Elizabeth** (isls.), NW,Can
98/G **Queen Mary** (coast), Ant.
98/P **Queen Maud** (mts.), Ant.
102/F2 **Queen Maud** (gulf), NW,Can
98/Z **Queen Maud Land** (reg.), Ant.
74/D2 **Queens** (chan.), Austl.
103/S7 **Queens** (chan.), NW,Can
32/E1 **Queensberry** (mtn.), Sc,UK
33/G4 **Queensbury,** Eng,UK
33/E5 **Queensferry,** Wal,UK
76/B3 **Queensland** (state), Austl.
111/R9 **Queenston,** On,Can
75/Q12 **Queenstown,** NZ
88/D3 **Queenstown,** SAfr.
96/B4 **Queilén,** Chile
93/H4 **Queimada,** Braz.
94/C3 **Queimadas,** Braz.
87/G4 **Quelimane,** Moz.
46/A3 **Queluz,** Port.
35/E3 **Quenington,** Eng,UK
96/F3 **Quequén,** Arg.
96/F3 **Quequén Grande** (riv.), Arg.
100/A3 **Querétaro,** Mex.
100/A3 **Querétaro** (state), Mex.
100/E5 **Quesada,** CR
46/D4 **Quesada,** Sp.
66/C4 **Queshan,** China
106/C2 **Quesnel,** BC,Can
106/C2 **Quesnel** (lake), BC,Can
69/E3 **Que Son,** Viet.
109/F3 **Questa,** NM,US
61/J2 **Quetta,** Pak.
96/B5 **Queulat Nat'l Park,** Chile
92/C4 **Quevedo,** Ecu.
100/C5 **Quezaltenango,** Guat.
67/E6 **Quezon,** Phil.
67/D5 **Quezon City,** Phil.
66/D4 **Qufu,** China
87/B3 **Quibala,** Ang.
92/C2 **Quibdó,** Col.
44/B3 **Quiberon** (bay), Fr.
87/B2 **Quiçama Nat'l Park,** Ang.
41/G1 **Quickborn,** Ger.
43/G5 **Quierschied,** Ger.
108/D4 **Quijotoa,** Az,US
96/B4 **Quilán** (cape), Chile
96/Q9 **Quilicura,** Chile
107/G2 **Quill** (lakes), Sk,Can
92/D6 **Quillabamba,** Peru
92/E7 **Quillacollo,** Bol.
96/B4 **Quillagua** (pt.), Chile
96/C3 **Quilleco,** Chile
96/C2 **Quillota,** Chile
70/C6 **Quilon,** India
96/C2 **Quilpué,** Chile
44/A3 **Quimper,** Fr.
113/G4 **Quincy,** Fl,US
110/B4 **Quincy,** Il,US
111/G3 **Quincy,** Ma,US
106/D4 **Quincy,** Wa,US
31/T10 **Quincy-sous-Sénart,** Fr.
69/E3 **Qui Nhon,** Viet.
108/C2 **Quinn** (riv.), Nv,US
46/D3 **Quintanar de la Orden,** Sp.
100/D4 **Quintana Roo** (state), Mex.
96/Q9 **Quintero,** Chile
96/D2 **Quinto** (riv.), Arg.
94/C3 **Quipapá,** Braz.
101/N8 **Quiriego,** Mex.
96/B3 **Quirihue,** Chile
87/H3 **Quirimba** (arch.), Moz.

95/B1 **Quirinópolis,** Braz.
101/J6 **Quiriquire,** Ven.
111/H2 **Quispamsis,** NB,Can
91/D2 **Quitilipi,** Arg.
113/H4 **Quitman,** Ga,US
113/F3 **Quitman,** Ms,US
112/E3 **Quitman,** Tx,US
92/C4 **Quito** (cap.), Ecu.
94/C2 **Quixadá,** Braz.
94/C2 **Quixeramobim,** Braz.
71/H2 **Qujing,** China
62/C4 **Qumar** (riv.), China
102/G2 **Quoich** (riv.), NW,Can
32/C3 **Quoile** (riv.), NI,UK
88/B4 **Quoin** (pt.), SAfr.
59/L4 **Qurnat as Sawdā'** (mtn.), Leb.
86/C3 **Qūş,** Egypt
62/F4 **Quwu** (mts.), China
69/C1 **Quynh Nhai,** Viet.
66/C3 **Quzhou,** China
67/C2 **Quzhou,** China
50/D5 **Qyteti Stalin,** Alb.

R

45/L3 **Raab** (riv.), Aus.
37/H2 **Raahe,** Fin.
40/D4 **Raalte,** Neth.
40/B5 **Raamsdonk,** Neth.
59/M8 **Ra'ananna,** Isr.
103/S7 **Raanes** (pen.), NW,Can
83/P8 **Raas Jumbo,** Som.
50/B3 **Rab** (isl.), Cro.
50/C2 **Rába** (riv.), Hun.
48/D5 **Rabat,** Malta
81/L13 **Rabat** (cap.), Mor.
78/E5 **Rabaul,** PNG
45/K4 **Rabbi** (riv.), It.
39/K4 **Rabka,** Pol.
70/C4 **Rabkavi,** India
111/S8 **Raby** (pt.), On,Can
45/G4 **Racconigi,** It.
113/F4 **Raccoon** (pt.), La,US
103/L4 **Race** (cape), Nf,Can
69/D4 **Rach Gia,** Viet.
69/D4 **Rach Gia** (bay), Viet.
39/K3 **Racibórz,** Pol.
116/Q14 **Racine,** Wi,US
50/D2 **Ráckeve,** Hun.
51/G2 **Rădăuţi,** Rom.
45/K2 **Radbuza** (riv.), Czh.
33/F4 **Radcliffe,** Eng,UK
33/G6 **Radcliffe on Trent,** Eng,UK
50/A2 **Radenthein,** Aus.
41/E6 **Radevormwald,** Ger.
110/D4 **Radford,** Va,US
70/B3 **Rādhanpur,** India
106/G2 **Radisson,** Sk,Can
31/N6 **Radlett,** Eng,UK
51/G4 **Radnevo,** Bul.
39/L3 **Radom,** Pol.
39/L3 **Radom** (prov.), Pol.
50/F4 **Radomir,** Bul.
39/K3 **Radomsko,** Pol.
50/F5 **Radoviš,** Macd.
34/D4 **Radstock,** Eng,UK
52/D5 **Radviliškis,** Lith.
34/C3 **Radyr,** Wal,UK
39/K2 **Radziejów,** Pol.
39/L2 **Radzymin,** Pol.
39/M3 **Radzyń Podlaski,** Pol.
103/H3 **Rae** (isth.), NW,Can
102/E2 **Rae** (riv.), NW,Can
70/D2 **Rāe Bareli,** India
113/J3 **Raeford,** NC,US
43/F2 **Raeren,** Belg.
40/D5 **Raesfeld,** Ger.
74/C5 **Raeside** (lake), Austl.
91/D3 **Rafaela,** Arg.
59/K6 **Rafaḩ,** Gaza
61/G2 **Rafsanjān,** Iran
106/E5 **Raft** (riv.), Id, Ut,US
83/L6 **Raga,** Sudan
97/J8 **Ragged** (pt.), Chile
32/A1 **Raghtin More** (mtn.), Ire.
34/D3 **Raglan,** Wal,UK
37/E2 **Rago Nat'l Park,** Nor.
31/P8 **Ragstone** (range), Eng,UK
48/D4 **Ragusa,** It.
41/F4 **Rahden,** Ger.
61/K3 **Rahīmyār Khān,** Pak.
115/F5 **Rahway,** NJ,US
79/K6 **Raiatea** (isl.), FrPol.
70/C4 **Raichūr,** India
70/D3 **Raigarh,** India
108/E3 **Rainbow Bridge Nat'l Mon.,** Ut,US
33/F4 **Rainford,** Eng,UK
31/P7 **Rainham,** Eng,UK
106/C4 **Rainier** (mt.), Wa,US
113/G3 **Rainsville,** Al,US
33/G5 **Rainworth,** Eng,UK
107/K3 **Rainy** (lake), Can., US
107/K3 **Rainy** (riv.), Can., US
110/A1 **Rainy River,** On,Can
70/D3 **Raipur,** India
38/F1 **Raisdorf,** Ger.
116/E8 **Raisin** (riv.), Mi,US
37/G3 **Raisio,** Fin.
42/C3 **Raismes,** Fr.
79/L7 **Raivavae** (isl.), FrPol.
72/A3 **Raja** (pt.), Indo.
70/D4 **Rājahmundry,** India
70/C5 **Rājampet,** India
72/D3 **Rajang** (riv.), Malay.
61/K3 **Rājanpur,** Pak.
70/C6 **Rājapālaiyam,** India
70/B4 **Rājāpur,** India
70/B2 **Rājasthān** (state), India
61/L3 **Rajgarh,** India
70/C3 **Rājgarh,** India
70/B3 **Rājkot,** India
70/D3 **Rāj-Nāndagaon,** India
61/L2 **Rājpura,** India
70/E3 **Rājshāhi,** Bang.
70/B3 **Rājula,** India
79/J5 **Rakahanga** (atoll), CookIs.
61/K1 **Rakaposhi** (mtn.), Pak.
71/F4 **Rakhine** (state), Burma
61/H3 **Rakhshān** (riv.), Pak.
87/D5 **Rakops,** Bots.
51/G4 **Rakovski,** Bul.
52/E4 **Rakvere,** Est.
113/J3 **Raleigh** (cap.), NC,US
78/F4 **Ralik Chain** (arch.), Mrsh.
106/F3 **Ralston,** Ab,Can
94/A4 **Ramalho** (mts.), Braz.
59/K6 **Rām Allāh,** WBnk.
70/B4 **Ramas** (cape), India
59/K5 **Ramat Gan,** Isr.
59/M8 **Ramat HaSharon,** Isr.
79/Z17 **Rambi** (isl.), Fiji
42/A6 **Rambouillet,** Fr.
34/B6 **Rame** (pt.), UK
70/E2 **Rāmechhāp,** Nepal
70/C6 **Rāmeshwaram,** India
60/E2 **Rāmhormoz,** Iran
59/K6 **Ramla,** Isr.
86/C2 **Ramm, Jabal** (mt.), Jor.
32/A4 **Ramor, Lough** (lake), Ire.
71/F4 **Ramree** (isl.), Burma
60/F1 **Ramsar** (Sakht Sar), Iran
33/F4 **Ramsbottom,** Eng,UK
35/E4 **Ramsbury,** Eng,UK
110/D2 **Ramsey** (lake), On,Can
35/F2 **Ramsey,** Eng,UK
32/D3 **Ramsey,** IM,UK
34/A3 **Ramsey** (isl.), Wal,UK
35/H4 **Ramsgate,** Eng,UK
43/G5 **Ramstein-Miesenbach,** Ger.
78/D5 **Ramu** (riv.), PNG
70/E3 **Rānāghāt,** India
96/C2 **Rancagua,** Chile
44/B2 **Rance** (riv.), Fr.
95/B2 **Rancharia,** Braz.
106/G4 **Ranchester,** Wy,US
70/E3 **Rānchī,** India
116/M9 **Rancho Cordova,** Ca,US
115/C2 **Rancho Cucamonga** (Cucamonga), Ca,US
115/B3 **Rancho Palos Verdes,** Ca,US
96/B4 **Ranco** (lake), Chile
83/P5 **Randa,** Djib.
115/K7 **Randallstown,** Md,US
32/B2 **Randalstown,** NI,UK
48/D4 **Randazzo,** It.
88/P13 **Randburg,** SAfr.
37/D4 **Randers,** Den.
115/F5 **Randolph,** NJ,US
39/H2 **Randow** (riv.), Ger.
76/H8 **Randwick,** Austl.
69/C2 **Rang** (peak), Thai.
71/F3 **Rāngāmāti,** Bang.
73/E4 **Rangasa** (cape), Indo.
108/E2 **Rangely,** Co,US
112/D3 **Ranger,** Tx,US
75/R11 **Rangiora,** NZ
79/L6 **Rangiroa** (atoll), FrPol.
69/B2 **Rangoon** (div.), Burma
69/B2 **Rangoon** (Yangon) (cap.), Burma
70/E2 **Rangpur,** Bang.
70/C5 **Rānībennur,** India
112/C4 **Rankin,** Tx,US
69/B4 **Ranong,** Thai.
43/G3 **Ransbach-Baumbach,** Ger.
111/S9 **Ransomville,** NY,US
42/D1 **Ranst,** Belg.
73/F4 **Rantekombola** (peak), Indo.
110/B3 **Rantoul,** Il,US
69/D2 **Rao Co** (peak), Laos
45/G2 **Raon-L'Étape,** Fr.
78/H7 **Raoul** (isl.), NZ
66/C3 **Raoyang,** China
79/L7 **Rapa** (isl.), FrPol.
96/Q10 **Rapel** (lake), Chile
96/B5 **Raper** (cape), Chile
107/H4 **Rapid City,** SD,US
110/E4 **Rappahannock** (riv.), Va,US
70/D2 **Rapti** (riv.), India
115/F5 **Raritan** (bay), NJ,US
115/F5 **Raritan** (riv.), NJ,US
79/L6 **Raroia** (atoll), FrPol.
79/J7 **Rarotonga** (isl.), CookIs.
96/E4 **Rasa** (pt.), Arg.
59/E3 **Ra's al 'Ayn,** Syria
83/J7 **Ra's al Unūf,** Libya
81/Q16 **Râs el Ma,** Alg.
81/T16 **Râs el Oued,** Alg.
86/C2 **Ras Gharib,** Egypt
32/B2 **Rasharkin,** NI,UK
59/K5 **Rāshayyā,** Leb.
59/H6 **Rashīd** (Rosetta), Egypt
60/E1 **Rasht,** Iran
50/E4 **Raška,** Yugo.
102/G2 **Rasmussen** (basin), NW,Can
47/P10 **Raso** (cape), Port.
74/C5 **Rason** (lake), Austl.
55/G1 **Rasskazovo,** Rus.
45/H2 **Rastatt,** Ger.
41/F2 **Rastede,** Ger.
114/B6 **Rat** (isls.), Ak,US
72/B5 **Rata** (cape), Indo.
70/B2 **Ratangarh,** India
69/B3 **Rat Buri,** Thai.
70/C2 **Rāth,** India
107/K5 **Rathbun** (lake), Ia,US
38/G2 **Rathenow,** Ger.
32/B3 **Rathfriland,** NI,UK
32/B1 **Rathlin** (isl.), NI,UK
32/B1 **Rathlin** (sound), NI,UK
78/F4 **Ratik Chain** (arch.), Mrsh.
40/D6 **Ratingen,** Ger.
70/C3 **Ratlām,** India
70/B4 **Ratnāgiri,** India
70/D6 **Ratnapura,** SrL.
109/F3 **Raton,** NM,US
37/E3 **Rättvik,** Swe.
38/F2 **Ratzeburg,** Ger.
72/B3 **Raub,** Malay.
96/F3 **Rauch,** Arg.
37/D3 **Raufoss,** Nor.
95/D2 **Raul Soares,** Braz.
35/F2 **Raunds,** Eng,UK
75/S10 **Raupehu** (vol.), NZ
70/D3 **Raurkela,** India
48/C4 **Ravanusa,** It.
40/C6 **Ravels,** Belg.
33/E3 **Ravenglass,** Eng,UK
45/K4 **Ravenna,** It.
45/H3 **Ravensburg,** Ger.
33/G5 **Ravenshead,** Eng,UK
110/D4 **Ravenswood,** WV,US
61/K2 **Rāvi** (riv.), India, Pak.
50/B2 **Ravne na Koroškem,** Slov.
79/H5 **Rawaki** (Phoenix) (atoll), Kiri.
61/K2 **Rāwalpindi,** Pak.
39/L3 **Rawa Mazowiecka,** Pol.
39/J3 **Rawicz,** Pol.
106/G5 **Rawlins,** Wy,US
33/G5 **Rawmarsh,** Eng,UK
96/D4 **Rawson,** Arg.
33/F4 **Rawtenstall,** Eng,UK
111/K2 **Ray** (cape), Nf,Can
72/D4 **Raya** (peak), Indo.
70/C5 **Rāyadrug,** India
70/D4 **Rāyagada,** India
63/K2 **Raychikhinsk,** Rus.
35/G3 **Rayleigh,** Eng,UK
106/E3 **Raymond,** Ab,Can
112/D5 **Raymondville,** Tx,US
107/G3 **Raymore,** Sk,Can
69/C3 **Rayong,** Thai.
55/H4 **Razdan,** Arm.
51/J3 **Razelm** (lake), Rom.
51/H4 **Razgrad,** Bul.
49/K1 **Razgrad** (reg.), Bul.
51/F5 **Razlog,** Bul.
44/A2 **Raz, Pointe du** (pt.), Fr.
44/C3 **Ré** (isl.), Fr.
34/D2 **Rea** (riv.), Eng,UK
35/F4 **Reading,** Eng,UK
69/C3 **Reang Kesei,** Camb.
79/M6 **Reao** (atoll), FrPol.
74/C6 **Rebecca** (lake), Austl.
63/N2 **Rebun** (isl.), Japan
45/K5 **Recanati,** It.
74/C6 **Recherche** (arch.), Austl.
43/F6 **Réchicourt-le-Château,** Fr.
54/D1 **Rechitsa,** Bela.
94/D3 **Recife,** Braz.
88/D4 **Recife** (cape), SAfr.
41/E4 **Recke,** Ger.
41/E5 **Recklinghausen,** Ger.
38/G2 **Recknitz** (riv.), Ger.
69/B2 **Reclining Buddha** (Shwethalyaung) (ruins), Burma
91/E2 **Reconquista,** Arg.
60/C4 **Red** (sea), Afr., Asia
71/H3 **Red** (riv.), China, Viet.
32/B1 **Red** (bay), NI,UK
109/J5 **Red** (riv.), US
112/D2 **Red** (hills), Ks,US
39/K1 **Reda,** Pol.
115/F5 **Red Bank,** NJ,US
108/B2 **Red Bluff,** Ca,US
109/G4 **Red Bluff** (lake), NM, Tx,US
35/F3 **Redbourn,** Eng,UK
31/P7 **Redbridge** (bor.), Eng,UK
33/G2 **Redcar,** Eng,UK
106/F3 **Redcliff,** Ab,Can
76/F6 **Redcliffe,** Austl.
109/H2 **Red Cloud,** Ne,US
106/E2 **Red Deer,** Ab,Can
106/F3 **Red Deer** (riv.), Ab,Can
107/H2 **Red Deer** (lake), Mb,Can
107/H2 **Red Deer** (riv.), Mb, Sk,Can
108/B2 **Redding,** Ca,US
35/E2 **Redditch,** Eng,UK
33/F1 **Rede** (riv.), Eng,UK
107/J4 **Redfield,** SD,US
116/F7 **Redford,** Mi,US
31/N8 **Redhill,** Eng,UK
104/T10 **Red Hill** (peak), Hi,US
111/K1 **Red Indian** (lake), Nf,Can
43/G6 **Réding,** Fr.
107/K3 **Red Lake,** On,Can
107/K3 **Red Lake** (riv.), Mn,US
115/J7 **Redland,** Md,US
76/F7 **Redland Bay,** Austl.
115/C2 **Redlands,** Ca,US
106/F4 **Red Lodge,** Mt,US
106/C4 **Redmond,** Or,US
116/C2 **Redmond,** Wa,US
44/B3 **Redon,** Fr.
46/A1 **Redondela,** Sp.
46/B3 **Redondo,** Port.
115/B3 **Redondo Beach,** Ca,US
114/H3 **Redoubt** (vol.), Ak,US
107/J3 **Red River of the North** (riv.), Can., US
107/K5 **Red Rock** (lake), Ia,US
34/A6 **Redruth,** Eng,UK
86/D4 **Red Sea** (hills), Sudan
102/D2 **Redstone** (riv.), NW,Can
107/K2 **Red Sucker** (lake), Mb,Can
107/H3 **Redvers,** Sk,Can
85/E4 **Red Volta** (riv.), Burk., Gui.
106/E2 **Redwater,** Ab,Can
108/B2 **Redway,** Ca,US
109/G2 **Red Willow** (cr.), Ne,US
110/A2 **Red Wing,** Mn,US
116/K12 **Redwood City,** Ca,US
107/K4 **Redwood Falls,** Mn,US
108/A2 **Redwood Nat'l Park,** Ca,US
110/C3 **Reed City,** Mi,US
35/H1 **Reedham,** Eng,UK
108/C3 **Reedley,** Ca,US
110/B3 **Reedsburg,** Wi,US
106/B5 **Reedsport,** Or,US
77/B3 **Reedy** (cr.), Austl.
78/F6 **Reef** (isls.), Sol.
75/R11 **Reefton,** NZ
36/A4 **Ree, Lough** (lake), Ire.
35/H1 **Reepham,** Eng,UK
40/D5 **Rees,** Ger.
108/C3 **Reese** (riv.), Nv,US
40/D3 **Reest** (riv.), Neth.
33/G3 **Reeth,** Eng,UK
40/B4 **Reeuwijk,** Neth.
112/D4 **Refugio,** Tx,US
39/H2 **Rega** (riv.), Pol.
95/E1 **Regência, Pontal de** (pt.), Braz.
94/B2 **Regeneração,** Braz.
45/K2 **Regensburg,** Ger.
45/K2 **Regenstauf,** Ger.
76/H8 **Regents Park,** Austl.
82/F2 **Reggane,** Alg.
40/D4 **Regge** (riv.), Neth.
48/D3 **Reggio di Calabria,** It.
45/J4 **Reggio nell'Emilia,** It.
51/G2 **Reghin,** Rom.
107/G3 **Regina** (cap.), Sk,Can
108/F3 **Regina,** NM,US
107/G3 **Regina Beach,** Sk,Can
95/C3 **Registro,** Braz.
45/J2 **Regnitz** (riv.), Ger.
46/B3 **Reguengosde Monsaraz,** Port.
41/G4 **Rehburg-Loccum,** Ger.
43/F5 **Rehlingen-Siersburg,** Ger.
87/C5 **Rehoboth,** Namb.
59/M9 **Reẖovot,** Isr.
43/G2 **Reichshof,** Ger.
106/F3 **Reid** (lake), Sk,Can
113/J2 **Reidsville,** NC,US
31/N8 **Reigate,** Eng,UK
42/D5 **Reims,** Fr.
97/J7 **Reina Adelaida** (arch.), Chile
41/H1 **Reinbek,** Ger.
107/J2 **Reindeer** (isl.), Mb,Can
107/H1 **Reindeer** (lake), Mb, Sk,Can
107/H1 **Reindeer** (riv.), Sk,Can
46/C1 **Reinosa,** Sp.
37/G1 **Reisduoddarhal'di** (peak), Nor.
40/D2 **Reitdiep** (riv.), Neth.
106/F5 **Reliance,** Wy,US
81/R16 **Relizane,** Alg.
41/G1 **Rellingen,** Ger.
43/G2 **Remagen,** Ger.
94/B3 **Remanso,** Braz.
31/S11 **Remarde** (riv.), Fr.
72/D5 **Rembang,** Indo.
81/Q16 **Remchi,** Alg.
93/H3 **Rémire,** FrG.
45/H2 **Rems** (riv.), Ger.
41/E6 **Remscheid,** Ger.
66/B5 **Ren** (riv.), China
96/C2 **Renca,** Chile
113/F2 **Rend** (lake), Il,US
38/E1 **Rendsburg,** Ger.
45/G3 **Renens,** Swi.
110/E2 **Renfrew,** On,Can
72/B4 **Rengat,** Indo.
96/C2 **Rengo,** Chile
54/D3 **Reni,** Ukr.
40/C5 **Renkum,** Neth.
78/F6 **Rennell** (isl.), Sol.
44/C2 **Rennes,** Fr.
45/J4 **Reno** (riv.), It.
108/C3 **Reno,** Nv,US
88/C3 **Renoster** (riv.), SAfr.
88/D2 **Renoster** (riv.), SAfr.
66/D3 **Renqiu,** China
110/C3 **Rensselaer,** In,US
46/E1 **Rentería,** Sp.
116/C3 **Renton,** Wa,US
111/P6 **Repentigny,** Qu,Can
33/G6 **Repton,** Eng,UK
106/D3 **Republic,** Wa,US
109/H2 **Republican** (riv.), Ks, Ne,US
76/C3 **Repulse** (bay), Austl.
92/D4 **Requena,** Peru
47/E3 **Requena,** Sp.
96/C2 **Requiñoa,** Chile
96/B5 **Rescue** (pt.), Chile
50/E5 **Resen,** Macd.
95/J7 **Resende,** Braz.
108/E4 **Reserve,** NM,US
91/E2 **Resistencia,** Arg.
50/E3 **Reşiţa,** Rom.
102/G1 **Resolute,** NW,Can
103/K2 **Resolution** (isl.), NW,Can
34/C3 **Resolven,** Wal,UK
95/D1 **Resplendor,** Braz.
42/B4 **Ressons-sur-Matz,** Fr.
111/H2 **Restigouche** (riv.), NB,Can
107/H3 **Reston,** Mb,Can
115/J8 **Reston,** Va,US
116/C2 **Restoration** (pt.), Wa,US
100/C5 **Retalhuleu,** Guat.
42/D4 **Rethel,** Fr.
49/J5 **Réthimnon,** Gre.
43/E1 **Retie,** Belg.
50/F3 **Retrezap Nat'l Park,** Rom.
89/R15 **Réunion** (dpcy.), Fr.
47/F2 **Reus,** Sp.
40/C6 **Reusel,** Neth.
38/G2 **Reuterstadt Stavenhagen,** Ger.
45/H2 **Reutlingen,** Ger.
52/H5 **Reutov,** Rus.
44/D5 **Revel,** Fr.
106/D3 **Revelstoke,** BC,Can
76/H8 **Revesby,** Austl.
42/D4 **Revin,** Fr.
68/B4 **Revolyutsii, Pik** (peak), Taj.
37/G1 **Revsbotn** (fjord), Nor.
70/D3 **Rewa,** India
70/C2 **Rewāri,** India
114/J3 **Rex** (mtn.), Ak,US
106/F5 **Rexburg,** Id,US
42/B2 **Rexpoëde,** Fr.
101/F6 **Rey** (isl.), Pan.
35/H2 **Reydon,** Eng,UK
108/B3 **Reyes** (pt.), Ca,US
59/D3 **Reyhanlı,** Turk.
30/A2 **Reykjanestá** (cape), Ice.
37/N7 **Reykjavík** (cap.), Ice.
100/B2 **Reynosa,** Mex.
44/C3 **Rezé,** Fr.
52/E4 **Rēzekne,** Lat.
45/H3 **Rhaetian Alps** (mts.), It., Swi.
34/C2 **Rhayader,** Wal,UK
41/F5 **Rheda-Wiedenbrück,** Ger.
40/D5 **Rheden,** Neth.
35/F2 **Rhee** (Cam) (riv.), Eng,UK
43/F2 **Rheinbach,** Ger.
40/D5 **Rheinberg,** Ger.
41/E4 **Rheine,** Ger.
82/E2 **Rhemiles** (well), Alg.
40/C5 **Rhenen,** Neth.
38/D3 **Rhine** (riv.), Eur.
41/E5 **Rhine-Herne** (can.), Ger.
110/B2 **Rhinelander,** Wi,US
43/F3 **Rhineland-Palatinate** (state), Ger.
81/R16 **Rhiou** (riv.), Alg.
43/D3 **Rhisnes,** Belg.
34/C1 **Rhiw** (riv.), Wal,UK
111/G3 **Rhode Island** (state), US
59/B3 **Rhodes** (isl.), Gre.
59/B3 **Rhodes** (Ródhos), Gre.
51/F4 **Rhodope** (mts.), Bul.
34/C3 **Rhondda,** Wal,UK
44/F4 **Rhône** (riv.), Fr., Swi.
44/F4 **Rhône-Alpes** (reg.), Fr.
42/C3 **Rhonelle** (riv.), Fr.
33/E6 **Rhosllanerchrugog,** Wal,UK
34/B3 **Rhossili,** Wal,UK
32/E5 **Rhuddlan,** Wal,UK
41/H5 **Rhume** (riv.), Ger.
81/V17 **Rhumel** (riv.), Alg.
34/C2 **Rhyddhywel** (mtn.), Wal,UK
34/B2 **Rhydowen,** Wal,UK
32/E5 **Rhyl,** Wal,UK
34/C3 **Rhymney,** Wal,UK
94/C3 **Riachão do Jacuípe,** Braz.
94/B4 **Riacho de Santana,** Braz.
115/C2 **Rialto,** Ca,US
46/A1 **Rianjo,** Sp.
72/B3 **Riau** (isls.), Indo.
46/A1 **Ribadavia,** Sp.
46/B1 **Ribadeo,** Sp.
46/C1 **Ribadesella,** Sp.
89/H8 **Riban'i Manamby** (mts.), Madg.
33/F4 **Ribble** (riv.), Eng,UK
38/E1 **Ribe,** Den.
38/E1 **Ribe** (co.), Den.
95/B3 **Ribeira** (riv.), Braz.
94/C3 **Ribeira do Pombal,** Braz.
47/T13 **Ribeira Grande,** Azor.
80/J9 **Ribeira Grande,** CpV.
94/D3 **Ribeirão,** Braz.
95/B2 **Ribeirão do Pinha,** Braz.
95/C2 **Ribeirão Preto,** Braz.
42/C4 **Ribemont,** Fr.
48/C4 **Ribera,** It.
92/E6 **Riberalta,** Bol.
38/G1 **Ribnitz-Damgarten,** Ger.
110/E2 **Rice** (lake), On,Can
110/B2 **Rice Lake,** Wi,US
102/C2 **Richards** (isl.), NW,Can
111/G2 **Richardson** (lakes), Me,US
40/C2 **Richel** (isl.), Neth.
108/D3 **Richfield,** Ut,US
32/B3 **Richhill,** NI,UK
106/D4 **Richland,** Wa,US
113/H3 **Richland Balsam** (peak), NC,US
110/B3 **Richland Center,** Wi,US
112/D4 **Richland Creek** (res.), Tx,US
77/D2 **Richmond,** Austl.
111/F2 **Richmond,** Qu,Can
33/G3 **Richmond,** Eng,UK
116/K11 **Richmond,** Ca,US
110/C4 **Richmond,** In,US
110/C4 **Richmond,** Ky,US
112/E4 **Richmond,** Tx,US
110/E4 **Richmond** (cap.), Va,US
116/C2 **Richmond Beach-Innis Arden,** Wa,US
111/R8 **Richmond Hill,** On,Can
76/G8 **Richmond-Raaf,** Austl.
31/N7 **Richmond upon Thames** (bor.), Eng,UK
31/M7 **Rickmansworth,** Eng,UK
40/B5 **Ridderkerk,** Neth.
110/E2 **Rideau** (lake), On,Can
108/C4 **Ridgecrest,** Ca,US
115/F5 **Ridgewood,** NJ,US
33/G2 **Riding Mill,** Eng,UK
107/H3 **Riding Mtn. Nat'l Park,** Mb,Can
45/K2 **Ried im Innkreis,** Aus.
43/F5 **Riegelsberg,** Ger.
43/E2 **Riemst,** Belg.
39/G3 **Riesa,** Ger.
97/J8 **Riesco** (isl.), Chile
88/D3 **Riet** (riv.), SAfr.
41/F5 **Rietberg,** Ger.
48/C1 **Rieti,** It.
33/G3 **Rievaulx,** Eng,UK
106/C4 **Riffe** (lake), Wa,US
108/F3 **Rifle,** Co,US
37/N6 **Rifsnes** (pt.), Ice.
52/E4 **Riga** (Rīga) (cap.), Lat.
106/F5 **Rigby,** Id,US
61/H2 **Rīgestan** (reg.), Afg.
106/D4 **Riggins,** Id,US
70/D3 **Rihand Sāgar** (res.), India
37/H3 **Riihimäki,** Fin.
98/C **Riiser-Larsen** (pen.), Ant.
37/J2 **Riisitunturin Nat'l Park,** Fin.
50/B3 **Rijeka,** Cro.
40/B4 **Rijnsburg,** Neth.
40/D4 **Rijssen,** Neth.
40/B4 **Rijswijk,** Neth.
79/M7 **Rikitea,** FrPol.
51/F4 **Rila** (mts.), Bul.
49/H1 **Rilski Manastir,** Bul.
79/K7 **Rimatara** (isl.), FrPol.
39/L4 **Rimavská Sobota,** Slvk.
60/D3 **Rīma, Wādi** (dry riv.), SAr.
106/E2 **Rimbey,** Ab,Can
83/J5 **Rimé** (wadi), Chad
45/K4 **Rimini,** It.
51/H3 **Rîmnicu Sărat,** Rom.
51/G3 **Rîmnicu Vîlcea,** Rom.
111/G1 **Rimouski,** Qu,Can
62/D1 **Rinchinlhümbe,** Mong.
46/C4 **Rincón de la Victoria,** Sp.
100/D5 **Rincon de la Vieja Nat'l Park,** CR
101/P9 **Rincón de Romos,** Mex.
32/C3 **Ringboy** (pt.), NI,UK
37/D4 **Ringkøbing,** Den.
35/G5 **Ringmer,** Eng,UK
115/F5 **Ringoes,** NJ,US
32/B1 **Ringsend,** NI,UK
38/F1 **Ringsted,** Den.
40/B4 **Ringvaart** (can.), Neth.
37/F1 **Ringvassøy** (isl.), Nor.
77/G5 **Ringwood,** Austl.
35/E5 **Ringwood,** Eng,UK
115/F4 **Ringwood,** NJ,US
49/J4 **Rínia** (isl.), Gre.
32/C2 **Rinns, The** (pen.), Sc,UK
41/G4 **Rinteln,** Ger.
92/C5 **Río Abiseo Nat'l Park,** Peru
92/C4 **Riobamba,** Ecu.
95/L7 **Rio Bonito,** Braz.
92/E5 **Rio Branco,** Braz.
97/G2 **Río Branco,** Uru.
95/B3 **Rio Branco do Sul,** Braz.
110/C4 **Río Bravo del Norte** (Río Grande) (riv.), Mex., US
96/B4 **Río Bueno,** Chile
95/D2 **Rio Casca,** Braz.
97/T12 **Riochuelo,** Uru.
96/C2 **Río Clarillo Nat'l Park,** Chile
95/J7 **Rio Claro,** Braz.
96/D3 **Río Colorado,** Arg.
96/D2 **Río Cuarto,** Arg.
94/B4 **Rio de Contas,** Braz.
95/K7 **Rio de Janeiro,** Braz.
95/K7 **Rio de Janeiro** (state), Braz.
106/B5 **Rio Dell,** Ca,US
95/B3 **Rio do Sul,** Braz.
47/Q10 **Rio Frio,** Port.
97/K7 **Río Gallegos,** Arg.
97/L8 **Río Grande,** Arg.
95/A5 **Rio Grande,** Braz.
112/C4 **Rio Grande** (riv.), Mex., US
112/D5 **Rio Grande City,** Tx,US
95/G8 **Rio Grande da Serra,** Braz.
100/E5 **Río Grande de Matagalpa** (riv.), Nic.
94/C2 **Rio Grande do Norte** (state), Braz.
94/B2 **Rio Grande do Piauí,** Braz.
95/A4 **Rio Grande do Sul** (state), Braz.
101/G5 **Riohacha,** Col.
101/E6 **Río Hato,** Pan.
92/C5 **Rioja,** Peru
92/F4 **Rio Jaú Nat'l Park,** Braz.
94/D3 **Rio Largo,** Braz.
44/E4 **Riom,** Fr.
46/A3 **Rio Maior,** Port.
106/D3 **Riondel,** BC,Can
96/C4 **Río Negro** (prov.), Arg.
97/F2 **Río Negro** (dept.), Uru.
97/F2 **Río Negro** (res.), Uru.
48/D2 **Rionero in Vulture,** It.
95/C1 **Rio Paranaíba,** Braz.
95/A4 **Rio Pardo,** Braz.
91/E2 **Río Pilcomayo Nat'l Park,** Arg.
94/A5 **Rio Prêto** (mts.), Braz.
108/F4 **Rio Rancho,** NM,US
94/C3 **Rio Real,** Braz.
44/F3 **Riorges,** Fr.
96/E1 **Río Segundo,** Arg.
96/B5 **Río Simpson Nat'l Park,** Chile
96/D2 **Río Tercero,** Arg.
94/D2 **Rio Tinto,** Braz.
95/B1 **Rio Verde,** Braz.
100/B3 **Ríoverde,** Mex.
93/H7 **Rio Verde de Mato Grosso,** Braz.
50/E3 **Ripanj,** Yugo.
31/M8 **Ripley,** Eng,UK
113/F3 **Ripley,** Ms,US
113/F3 **Ripley,** Tn,US
47/G1 **Ripoll,** Sp.
47/L6 **Ripoll** (riv.), Sp.
47/L6 **Ripollet,** Sp.
33/G3 **Ripon,** Eng,UK
107/L5 **Ripon,** Wi,US
48/D4 **Riposto,** It.
33/G4 **Ripponden,** Eng,UK
34/C3 **Risca,** Wal,UK
63/N2 **Rishiri** (isl.), Japan
59/K6 **Rishon LeẔiyyon,** Isr.
44/D2 **Risle** (riv.), Fr.
50/B3 **Risnjak** (peak), Cro.
50/B3 **Risnjak Nat'l Park,** Cro.
51/G3 **Rîşnov,** Rom.
112/E3 **Rison,** Ar,US
37/D4 **Risør,** Nor.
31/T11 **Ris-Orangis,** Fr.
92/D2 **Ritacuba** (peak), Col.
78/C2 **Ritaiō** (isl.), Japan
41/F2 **Ritterhude,** Ger.
65/L9 **Rittō,** Japan
106/D4 **Ritzville,** Wa,US
45/J4 **Riva,** It.
96/E2 **Rivadavia,** Arg.
45/G4 **Rivarolo Canavese,** It.
100/D5 **Rivas,** Nic.
44/F4 **Rive-de-Gier,** Fr.
96/B5 **Rivera** (isl.), Chile
91/E3 **Rivera,** Uru.
97/G1 **Rivera** (dept.), Uru.
75/H7 **Riverina** (reg.), Austl.
116/F7 **River Rouge,** Mi,US
106/B3 **Rivers** (inlet), BC,Can
107/H3 **Rivers,** Mb,Can
85/G5 **Rivers** (state), Nga.
88/C4 **Riversdale,** SAfr.
115/C3 **Riverside,** Ca,US
76/G8 **Riverstone,** Austl.
107/J3 **Riverton,** Mb,Can
75/Q12 **Riverton,** NZ
106/F5 **Riverton,** Wy,US
111/H2 **Riverview,** NB,Can
116/F7 **Riverview,** Mi,US
113/H5 **Riviera Beach,** Fl,US
115/K7 **Riviera Beach,** Md,US
111/G2 **Rivière-du-Loup,** Qu,Can
88/L11 **Riviersonde-rendreeks** (mts.), SAfr.
45/G4 **Rivoli,** It.
42/D2 **Rixensart,** Belg.
60/E4 **Riyadh** (Ar Riyāḑ) (cap.), SAr.
59/E2 **Rize,** Turk.
66/D4 **Rizhao,** China
48/E3 **Rizzuto** (cape), It.
37/D4 **Rjukan,** Nor.
84/B2 **Rkîz** (lake), Mrta.
37/D3 **Roa,** Nor.
35/F2 **Roade,** Eng,UK
36/D2 **Roadside,** Sc,UK
101/J4 **Road Town** (cap.), BVI
108/E3 **Roan** (plat.), Co,US
33/F1 **Roan Fell** (hill), Sc,UK
113/H2 **Roan High** (peak), NC,US
44/F3 **Roanne,** Fr.
113/G3 **Roanoke,** Al,US
113/J2 **Roanoke** (riv.), NC, Va,US
110/E4 **Roanoke,** Va,US
113/J2 **Roanoke Rapids,** NC,US
100/D4 **Roatán** (isl.), Hon.
77/C4 **Robbins** (isl.), Austl.
77/B1 **Robe** (peak), Austl.
36/A4 **Robe** (riv.), Ire.
43/E6 **Robert-Espagne,** Fr.
112/C4 **Robert Lee,** Tx,US
114/E4 **Roberts** (mtn.), Ak,US
35/G5 **Robertsbridge,** Eng,UK
37/G2 **Robertsfors,** Swe.
70/D3 **Robertsganj,** India
88/B4 **Robertson,** SAfr.
111/F1 **Roberval,** Qu,Can
33/H3 **Robin Hood's Bay,** Eng,UK
74/B5 **Robinson** (ranges), Austl.
110/C4 **Robinson,** Il,US
116/C3 **Robinson** (pt.), Wa,US
90/B6 **Robinson Crusoe** (isl.), Chile
76/C4 **Robinson Gorge Nat'l Park,** Austl.
107/H3 **Roblin,** Mb,Can
92/G7 **Roboré,** Bol.
106/D2 **Robson** (peak), BC,Can
112/D5 **Robstown,** Tx,US
112/C3 **Roby,** Tx,US
46/A3 **Roca, Cabo da** (cape), Port.
100/B4 **Roca Partida** (pt.), Mex.
93/M4 **Rocas,** Braz.
45/G4 **Rocciamelone** (peak), It.
44/E5 **Roc de France** (mtn.), Fr.
97/G2 **Rocha,** Uru.
97/G2 **Rocha** (dept.), Uru.
33/F4 **Rochdale,** Eng,UK
34/B6 **Roche,** Eng,UK
44/C4 **Rochefort,** Fr.
35/G4 **Rochester,** Eng,UK
110/C3 **Rochester,** In,US
116/F6 **Rochester,** Mi,US
107/K4 **Rochester,** Mn,US
111/G3 **Rochester,** NH,US
110/E3 **Rochester,** NY,US
116/F6 **Rochester Hills,** Mi,US
35/G3 **Rochford,** Eng,UK
110/B3 **Rock** (riv.), Il, Wi,US
106/C4 **Rock** (cr.), Or,US
30/B3 **Rockall** (isl.), UK
114/L3 **Rock Creek,** Yk,Can
76/H8 **Rockdale,** Austl.
98/R **Rockefeller** (plat.), Ant.
110/B3 **Rockford,** Il,US
111/G2 **Rock Forest,** Qu,Can
107/G3 **Rockglen,** Sk,Can
76/C3 **Rockhampton,** Austl.
113/H3 **Rock Hill,** SC,US
74/B6 **Rockingham,** Austl.
113/J3 **Rockingham,** NC,US
110/B3 **Rock Island,** Il,US
110/F2 **Rockland,** On,Can
111/G2 **Rockland,** Me,US
77/B3 **Rocklands** (res.), Austl.
113/H4 **Rockledge,** Fl,US
112/D4 **Rockport,** Tx,US
112/C4 **Rocksprings,** Tx,US
106/F5 **Rock Springs,** Wy,US
115/J7 **Rockville,** Md,US
115/G5 **Rockville Center,** NY,US
112/D3 **Rockwall,** Tx,US
113/G3 **Rockwood,** Tn,US
99/E4 **Rocky** (mts.), NAm
110/D4 **Rocky** (peak), Ky,US
77/C4 **Rocky Cape Nat'l Park,** Austl.
111/K1 **Rocky Harbour,** Nf,Can
110/D2 **Rocky Island** (lake), On,Can
113/J3 **Rocky Mount,** NC,US
110/E4 **Rocky Mount,** Va,US
106/E2 **Rocky Mountain House,** Ab,Can
109/F2 **Rocky Mountain Nat'l Park,** Co,US
115/H5 **Rocky Point,** NY,US
43/G5 **Rodalben,** Ger.
111/K1 **Roddickton,** Nf,Can
34/D1 **Roden** (riv.), Eng,UK
116/K10 **Rodeo,** Ca,US
44/E4 **Rodez,** Fr.
59/B3 **Ródhos** (Rhodes), Gre.
45/K2 **Roding,** Ger.
31/P7 **Roding** (riv.), Eng,UK
41/F4 **Rödinghausen,** Ger.
49/F2 **Rodonit, Kep i** (cape), Alb.
29/N6 **Rodrigues** (isl.), Mrts.
32/B2 **Roe** (riv.), NI,UK
74/C3 **Roebuck** (bay), Austl.
40/D6 **Roer** (riv.), Neth.
40/C6 **Roermond,** Neth.
42/C2 **Roeselare,** Belg.
116/D2 **Roesiger** (lake), Wa,US
103/H2 **Roes Welcome** (sound), NW,Can
54/D1 **Rogachev,** Bela.
37/C4 **Rogaland** (co.), Nor.
50/D4 **Rogatica,** Bosn.
112/E2 **Rogers,** Ar,US
110/D4 **Rogers** (peak), Va,US
110/D2 **Rogers City,** Mi,US
113/H2 **Rogersville,** Tn,US
44/F2 **Rognon** (riv.), Fr.
39/J2 **Rogoźno,** Pol.
108/B2 **Rogue** (riv.), Or,US
83/L6 **Rohl** (riv.), Sudan
61/J3 **Rohri,** Pak.
69/C2 **Roi Et,** Thai.
42/C4 **Roisel,** Fr.
31/T10 **Roissy,** Fr.
31/T9 **Roissy-en-France,** Fr.
96/E2 **Rojas,** Arg.
100/B3 **Rojo** (cape), Mex.
101/H4 **Rojo** (cape), PR
72/B3 **Rokan** (riv.), Indo.
76/A1 **Rokeby-Croll Creek Nat'l Park,** Austl.
84/C4 **Rokel** (riv.), SLeo.
65/L10 **Rokkō-san** (peak), Japan
95/B2 **Rolândia,** Braz.
40/D3 **Rolde,** Neth.

Rolla – Saint

106/C2 **Rolla**, BC,Can
109/K3 **Rolla**, Mo,US
107/J3 **Rolla**, ND,US
116/P15 **Rolling Meadows**, Il,US
76/C4 **Roma**, Austl.
44/E4 **Romagnat**, Fr.
43/E5 **Romagne-sous-Montfaucon**, Fr.
113/J3 **Romain** (cape), SC,US
103/K3 **Romaine** (riv.), Qu,Can
51/H2 **Roman**, Rom.
73/G5 **Romang** (isl.), Indo.
73/G5 **Romang** (str.), Indo.
51/F3 **Romania**
44/F4 **Romans-sur-Isère**, Fr.
114/E3 **Romanzof** (cape), Ak,US
48/C2 **Roma** (Rome) (cap.), It.
43/F5 **Rombas**, Fr.
67/D5 **Romblon**, Phil.
113/G3 **Rome**, Ga,US
110/F3 **Rome**, NY,US
116/P16 **Romeoville**, Il,US
48/C2 **Rome** (Roma) (cap.), It.
31/P7 **Romford**, Eng,UK
44/E2 **Romilly-sur-Seine**, Fr.
40/D6 **Rommerskirchen**, Ger.
35/G4 **Romney Marsh** (reg.), Eng,UK
54/E2 **Romny**, Ukr.
38/E1 **Rømø** (isl.), Den.
44/D3 **Romorantin-Lanthenay**, Fr.
35/E5 **Romsey**, Eng,UK
116/F7 **Romulus**, Mi,US
69/D2 **Ron**, Viet.
106/E4 **Ronan**, Mt,US
93/H6 **Roncador** (mts.), Braz.
101/F5 **Roncador Cay** (isl.), Col.
48/C1 **Ronciglione**, It.
42/C2 **Roncq**, Fr.
46/C4 **Ronda**, Sp.
37/D3 **Rondane Nat'l Park**, Nor.
93/H7 **Rondonópolis**, Braz.
71/J2 **Rong** (riv.), China
107/G2 **Ronge** (lake), Sk,Can
78/F3 **Rongelap** (atoll), Mrsh.
78/F3 **Rongerik** (atoll), Mrsh.
79/X15 **Roniu** (peak), FrPol.
115/G5 **Ronkonkoma**, NY,US
39/H1 **Rønne**, Den.
37/E4 **Ronneby**, Swe.
98/U **Ronne Entrance** (inlet), Ant.
41/G4 **Ronnenberg**, Ger.
42/C2 **Ronse**, Belg.
93/H6 **Ronuro** (riv.), Braz.
88/P13 **Roodeport-Maraisburg**, SAfr.
88/B2 **Rooiberg** (peak), Namb.
70/C2 **Roorkee**, India
40/B5 **Roosendaal**, Neth.
98/N **Roosevelt** (isl.), Ant.
92/F6 **Roosevelt** (riv.), Braz.
102/D3 **Roosevelt** (mtn.), BC,Can
108/E2 **Roosevelt**, Ut,US
114/L4 **Root** (mtn.), Ak,US
116/Q14 **Root** (riv.), Wi,US
46/D4 **Roquetas de Mar**, Sp.
92/F2 **Roraima** (peak), Guy.
107/J3 **Rorketon**, Mb,Can
81/W17 **Rosa** (cape), Alg.
96/E2 **Rosario**, Arg.
94/A1 **Rosário**, Braz.
101/N9 **Rosario**, Mex.
97/F2 **Rosario**, Uru.
91/D2 **Rosario de la Frontera**, Arg.
97/S11 **Rosario del Tala**, Arg.
91/F3 **Rosário do Sul**, Braz.
101/M8 **Rosarito**, Mex.
47/G1 **Rosas** (gulf), Sp.
92/C3 **Rosa Zárate**, Ecu.
41/G6 **Rosdorf**, Ger.
79/J6 **Rose** (isl.), ASam.
114/M4 **Rose** (pt.), BC,Can
107/J3 **Roseau** (riv.), Can., US
101/J4 **Roseau** (cap.), Dom.
107/K3 **Roseau**, Mn,US
89/S15 **Rose Belle**, Mrts.
106/C5 **Roseburg**, Or,US
115/K7 **Rosedale**, Md,US
113/F3 **Rosedale**, Ms,US
36/D2 **Rosehearty**, Sc,UK
116/P16 **Roselle**, Il,US
115/N5 **Roselle**, NJ,US
111/N6 **Rosemère**, Qu,Can
112/E4 **Rosenberg**, Tx,US
38/G5 **Rosenheim**, Ger.
47/G1 **Roses**, Sp.
48/D1 **Roseto degli Abruzzi**, It.
106/G3 **Rosetown**, Sk,Can
59/H6 **Rosetta** (Rashīd), Egypt
116/M9 **Roseville**, Ca,US
116/G6 **Roseville**, Mi,US
59/M8 **Rosh Ha'Ayin**, Isr.
59/K5 **Rosh HaNiqra** (pt.), Isr.
51/G3 **Roşiori de Vede**, Rom.
38/G1 **Roskilde**, Den.
38/F1 **Roskilde** (co.), Den.
54/E1 **Roslavl'**, Rus.
40/C5 **Rosmalen**, Neth.
31/T10 **Rosny-sous-Bois**, Fr.
48/D4 **Rosolini**, It.
44/B3 **Rosporden**, Fr.
43/G2 **Rösrath**, Ger.
98/M **Ross** (isl.), Ant.
98/P **Ross** (sea), Ant.
107/J2 **Ross** (isl.), Mb,Can
45/K3 **Rossa** (peak), It.
33/E4 **Rossall** (pt.), Eng,UK
48/E3 **Rossano**, It.
78/E6 **Rossel** (isl.), PNG
98/N **Ross Ice Shelf**, Ant.
111/H2 **Rossignol** (lake), NS,Can
36/H6 **Rosskeeragh** (pt.), Ire.
106/D3 **Rossland**, BC,Can
32/A3 **Rosslea**, NI,UK
84/B2 **Rosso**, Mrta.
34/D3 **Ross on Wye**, Eng,UK
54/F2 **Rossosh'**, Rus.
114/M3 **Ross River**, Yk,Can
107/G2 **Rosthern**, Sk,Can
38/G1 **Rostock**, Ger.
54/F3 **Rostov**, Rus.
55/G2 **Rostov Obl.**, Rus.
32/B3 **Rostrevor**, NI,UK
113/G3 **Roswell**, Ga,US
109/F4 **Roswell**, NM,US
45/H2 **Rot** (riv.), Ger.
78/D3 **Rota** (isl.), NMar.
46/B4 **Rota**, Sp.
41/G2 **Rotenburg**, Ger.
41/G7 **Rotenburg an der Fulda**, Ger.
43/F2 **Rötgen**, Ger.
38/E3 **Rothaargebirge** (mts.), Ger.
33/G1 **Rothbury**, Eng,UK
33/G5 **Rother** (riv.), Eng,UK
35/F5 **Rother** (riv.), Eng,UK
33/G5 **Rotherham**, Eng,UK
36/D2 **Rothes**, Sc,UK
43/E2 **Rotheux-Rimière**, Belg.
35/F2 **Rothwell**, Eng,UK
73/F6 **Roti** (isl.), Indo.
75/S10 **Rotorua**, NZ
43/D2 **Rotselaar**, Belg.
45/K2 **Rott** (riv.), Ger.
43/F6 **Rotte** (riv.), Fr.
40/B5 **Rotterdam**, Neth.
40/D2 **Rottumeroog** (isl.), Neth.
40/D2 **Rottumerplaat** (isl.), Neth.
45/H2 **Rottweil**, Ger.
78/G6 **Rotuma** (isl.), Fiji
42/C2 **Roubaix**, Fr.
44/F4 **Roubion** (riv.), Fr.
44/D2 **Rouen**, Fr.
110/F2 **Rouge** (riv.), Qu,Can
116/F6 **Rouge** (riv.), Mi,US
113/G2 **Rough** (riv.), Ky,US
76/C4 **Round Hill** (pt.), Austl.
32/B1 **Round Knowe** (mtn.), NI,UK
116/P15 **Round Lake**, Il,US
116/P15 **Round Lake Beach**, Il,US
108/C3 **Round Mountain**, Nv,US
112/D4 **Round Rock**, Tx,US
106/F4 **Roundup**, Mt,US
34/E4 **Roundway** (hill), Eng,UK
76/G8 **Rouse Hill**, Austl.
43/E5 **Rouvres-en-Woëvre**, Fr.
110/E1 **Rouyn-Noranda**, Qu,Can
37/H2 **Rovaniemi**, Fin.
69/D3 **Rovieng Tbong**, Camb.
45/J4 **Rovigo**, It.
54/C2 **Rovno**, Ukr.
54/C2 **Rovno Obl.**, Ukr.
74/B3 **Rowley** (shoals), Austl.
103/J2 **Rowley** (isl.), NW,Can
84/B4 **Roxa** (isl.), GBis.
67/C5 **Roxas**, Phil.
67/D4 **Roxas**, Phil.
73/F1 **Roxas City**, Indo.
113/J2 **Roxboro**, NC,US
101/J5 **Roxborough**, Trin.
84/A3 **Roxo** (cape), Sen.
109/F4 **Roy**, NM,US
108/D2 **Roy**, Ut,US
45/G4 **Roya** (riv.), Fr.
36/B4 **Royal** (can.), Ire.
102/H4 **Royale** (isl.), Mi,US
35/E2 **Royal Leamington Spa**, Eng,UK
35/G4 **Royal Military** (can.), Eng,UK
88/E3 **Royal Natal Nat'l Park**, SAfr.
76/H9 **Royal Nat'l Park**, Austl.
116/F6 **Royal Oak**, Mi,US
35/G4 **Royal Tunbridge Wells**, Eng,UK
44/C4 **Royan**, Fr.
35/F2 **Royston**, Eng,UK
33/F4 **Royton**, Eng,UK
50/E4 **Rožaje**, Yugo.
39/L4 **Rožňava**, Slvk.
42/D4 **Rozoy-sur-Serre**, Fr.
39/M3 **Roztoczański Nat'l Park**, Pol.
112/E3 **R.S. Kerr** (lake), Ok,US
55/G1 **Rtishchevo**, Rus.
33/E6 **Ruabon**, Wal,UK
87/B4 **Ruacana** (falls), Ang.
87/B4 **Ruacana**, Namb.
87/F2 **Ruaha Nat'l Park**, Tanz.
60/E5 **Rub' al Khali** (des.), SAr.
31/U11 **Rubelles**, Fr.
54/F2 **Rubezhnoye**, Ukr.
47/G2 **Rubi**, Sp.
115/C3 **Rubidoux**, Ca,US
94/B5 **Rubim**, Braz.
68/D1 **Rubtsovsk**, Rus.
108/D2 **Ruby** (mts.), Nv,US
108/D2 **Ruby Valley**, Nv,US
40/B5 **Rucphen**, Neth.
39/K2 **Ruda Woda** (lake), Pol.
33/G6 **Ruddington**, Eng,UK
39/G2 **Rüdersdorf**, Ger.
39/M3 **Rudnik**, Pol.
55/M1 **Rudnyy**, Kaz.
56/F1 **Rudolf** (isl.), Rus.
38/F3 **Rudolstadt**, Ger.
60/F1 **Rūdsar**, Iran
33/H3 **Rudston**, Eng,UK
32/B1 **Rue** (pt.), NI,UK
31/S10 **Rueil-Malmaison**, Fr.
44/D4 **Ruelle-sur-Touvre**, Fr.
50/F4 **Ruen** (Rujen) (peak), Bul., Mac.
83/M5 **Rufā'ah**, Sudan
49/F3 **Ruffano**, It.
87/G2 **Rufiji** (riv.), Tanz.
96/E2 **Rufino**, Arg.
35/E2 **Rugby**, Eng,UK
107/J3 **Rugby**, ND,US
34/E1 **Rugeley**, Eng,UK
39/G1 **Rügen** (isl.), Ger.
40/D6 **Ruhr** (riv.), Ger.
41/D6 **Ruhrgebiet** (reg.), Ger.
109/F4 **Ruidoso**, NM,US
40/D3 **Ruinen**, Neth.
31/M7 **Ruislip**, Eng,UK
101/N9 **Ruiz**, Mex.
50/F4 **Rujen** (Ruen) (peak), Bul., Macd.
83/J8 **Ruki** (riv.), Zaire
87/F2 **Rukwa** (lake), Tanz.
50/D3 **Ruma**, Yugo.
83/L6 **Rumbek**, Sudan
101/G3 **Rum Cay** (isl.), Bahm.
111/G2 **Rumford**, Me,US
39/K1 **Rumia**, Pol.
34/C4 **Rumney**, Wal,UK
63/N3 **Rumoi**, Japan
87/F3 **Rumphi**, Malw.
115/F5 **Rumson**, NJ,US
42/D1 **Rumst**, Belg.
32/B1 **Runabay Head** (pt.), NI,UK
33/F5 **Runcorn**, Eng,UK
83/L7 **Rungu**, Zaire
87/F2 **Rungwa**, Tanz.
87/F2 **Rungwe** (peak), Tanz.
115/F6 **Runnemede**, NJ,US
115/C2 **Running Springs**, Ca,US
62/D3 **Ruo** (riv.), China
68/E4 **Ruoqiang**, China
72/B3 **Rupat** (isl.), Indo.
51/G2 **Rupea**, Rom.
42/D1 **Rupel** (riv.), Belg.
110/E1 **Rupert** (riv.), Qu,Can
106/E5 **Rupert**, Id,US
103/J3 **Rupert House** (Waskaganish), Qu,Can
43/G2 **Ruppichteroth**, Ger.
43/F1 **Rur** (riv.), Ger.
79/K7 **Rurutu** (isl.), FrPol.
87/F4 **Rusape**, Zim.
35/E4 **Rushall**, Eng,UK
107/K4 **Rush City**, Mn,US
35/F2 **Rushden**, Eng,UK
110/C4 **Rushville**, In,US
109/G2 **Rushville**, Ne,US
112/E4 **Rusk**, Tx,US
33/H5 **Ruskington**, Eng,UK
94/C2 **Russas**, Braz.
76/F7 **Russell** (isl.), Austl.
107/H3 **Russell**, Mb,Can
107/H1 **Russell** (lake), Mb,Can
102/F1 **Russell** (isl.), NW,Can
113/H3 **Russell** (lake), Ga, SC,US
109/H3 **Russell**, Ks,US
113/G3 **Russellville**, Al,US
112/E3 **Russellville**, Ar,US
110/C4 **Russellville**, Ky,US
56/* **Russia**
108/B3 **Russian** (riv.), Ca,US
55/H4 **Rustavi**, Geo.
88/D2 **Rustenburg**, SAfr.
112/E3 **Ruston**, La,US
46/C4 **Rute**, Sp.
73/F5 **Ruteng**, Indo.
87/F5 **Rutenga**, Zim.
108/D3 **Ruth**, Nv,US
41/F6 **Rüthen**, Ger.
33/E5 **Ruthin**, Wal,UK
111/F3 **Rutland**, Vt,US
35/F1 **Rutland Water** (res.), Eng,UK
68/C5 **Rutog**, China
87/E1 **Rutshuru**, Zaire
40/D4 **Ruurlo**, Neth.
48/E2 **Ruvo di Puglia**, It.
59/F3 **Ruwandūz**, Iraq
94/B4 **Ruy Barbosa**, Braz.
55/H1 **Ruzayevka**, Rus.
39/K4 **Ružomberok**, Slvk.
87/E1 **Rwanda**
77/D2 **Ryan** (mt.), Austl.
32/C2 **Ryan, Loch** (inlet), Sc,UK
54/F1 **Ryazan'**, Rus.
52/J5 **Ryazan' Obl.**, Rus.
54/G1 **Ryazhsk**, Rus.
52/G1 **Rybachiy** (pen.), Rus.
68/C3 **Rybach'ye**, Kyr.
52/H4 **Rybinsk**, Rus.
52/H4 **Rybinsk** (res.), Rus.
39/K3 **Rybnik**, Pol.
51/J2 **Rybnitsa**, Mol.
106/D2 **Rycroft**, Ab,Can
76/H8 **Ryde**, Austl.
35/E5 **Ryde**, Eng,UK
35/G5 **Rye**, Eng,UK
35/G5 **Rye** (bay), Eng,UK
33/H3 **Rye** (riv.), Eng,UK
108/C2 **Rye Patch** (res.), Nv,US
39/L3 **Ryki**, Pol.
55/J2 **Ryn-Peski** (des.), Kaz.
65/F1 **Ryōtsu**, Japan
65/M9 **Ryōzen-yama** (peak), Japan
39/K2 **Rypin**, Pol.
54/B2 **Rysy** (peak), Slvk.
33/G2 **Ryton**, Eng,UK
35/E2 **Ryton on Dunsmore**, Eng,UK
39/H1 **Rytterknægten** (peak), Den.
65/G3 **Ryūgasaki**, Japan
65/M9 **Ryūō**, Japan
39/M3 **Rzeszów**, Pol.
39/L3 **Rzeszów** (prov.), Pol.
52/G4 **Rzhev**, Rus.

S

41/G4 **Saale** (riv.), Ger.
38/F3 **Saalfeld**, Ger.
45/K3 **Saalfelden am Steinernen Meer**, Aus.
106/C3 **Saanich**, BC,Can
43/F5 **Saar** (riv.), Ger.
43/F5 **Saarbrücken**, Ger.
52/D4 **Saaremaa** (isl.), Est.
43/F5 **Saarland** (state), Ger.
43/F5 **Saarlouis**, Ger.
69/D3 **Sab** (riv.), Camb.
101/J4 **Saba** (isl.), NAnt.
50/D3 **Šabac**, Yugo.
47/G2 **Sabadell**, Sp.
64/E3 **Sabae**, Japan
73/E2 **Sabah** (state), Malay.
72/A2 **Sabang**, Indo.
101/F6 **Sabanita**, Pan.
83/M6 **Sabat** (riv.), Eth., Sudan
61/H2 **Şāberī, Hāmūn-e** (lake), Afg.
82/H2 **Sabhā**, Libya
86/B3 **Sabie**, Egypt
89/F2 **Sabie** (Sabierivier) (riv.), Moz., SAfr.
47/E1 **Sabiñánigo**, Sp.
100/A2 **Sabinas**, Mex.
100/A2 **Sabinas** (riv.), Mex.
100/A2 **Sabinas Hidalgo**, Mex.
112/E4 **Sabine** (lake), La, Tx,US
112/E4 **Sabine** (riv.), La, Tx,US
109/J5 **Sabine Pass** (waterway), La, Tx,US
48/C1 **Sabini** (mts.), It.
95/D1 **Sabinópolis**, Braz.
60/F4 **Sabkhat Maţţī** (salt marsh), UAE
73/F1 **Sablayan**, Phil.
111/J3 **Sable** (isl.), Can.
111/H3 **Sable** (cape), NS,Can
113/H5 **Sable** (cape), Fl,US
44/C3 **Sablé-sur-Sarthe**, Fr.
46/B2 **Sabor** (riv.), Port.
73/H4 **Sabra** (cape), Indo.
98/J **Sabrina** (coast), Ant.
61/G1 **Sabzevār**, Iran
106/D4 **Sacajawea** (peak), Or,US
108/E4 **Sacaton**, Az,US
46/A3 **Sacavém**, Port.
48/C2 **Sacco** (riv.), It.
51/G3 **Săcele**, Rom.
107/L2 **Sachigo** (lake), On,Can
107/L2 **Sachigo** (riv.), On,Can
111/H2 **Sackville**, NB,Can
31/S10 **Saclay**, Fr.
111/G3 **Saco**, Me,US
95/C1 **Sacramento**, Braz.
116/M9 **Sacramento** (cap.), Ca,US
108/B2 **Sacramento** (riv.), Ca,US
109/F4 **Sacramento** (mts.), NM,US
46/D4 **Sacratif** (cape), Sp.
104/W12 **Sacred** (falls), Hi,US
33/G2 **Sacriston**, Eng,UK
48/E2 **Sacro** (peak), It.
46/A1 **Sada**, Sp.
106/C2 **Saddle** (hills), Ab, BC,Can
33/G4 **Saddleworth**, Eng,UK
69/D4 **Sa Dec**, Viet.
61/K3 **Sādiqābād**, Pak.
71/G2 **Sadiya**, India
65/F2 **Sado** (isl.), Japan
46/A3 **Sado** (riv.), Port.
64/B4 **Sadowara**, Japan
70/B2 **Sādri**, India
82/H1 **Safāqis**, Tun.
81/X18 **Safāqis** (gov.), Tun.
60/E3 **Saffānīyah, Ra's as** (pt.), SAr.
37/E4 **Säffle**, Swe.
108/E4 **Safford**, Az,US
35/G2 **Saffron Walden**, Eng,UK
82/D1 **Safi**, Mor.
61/H2 **Safīd** (mts.), Afg.
61/J1 **Safīd** (riv.), Afg.
61/K1 **Safīd Khers** (mts.), Afg., Taj.
59/L4 **Şāfītā**, Syria
52/G5 **Safonovo**, Rus.
59/C2 **Safranbolu**, Turk.
70/E2 **Saga**, China
64/B4 **Saga**, Japan
64/A4 **Saga** (pref.), Japan
65/G1 **Sagae**, Japan
71/G3 **Sagaing**, Burma
71/F3 **Sagaing** (div.), Burma
65/H7 **Sagami** (bay), Japan
65/H7 **Sagami** (riv.), Japan
65/F3 **Sagami** (sea), Japan
65/F3 **Sagamihara**, Japan
65/H7 **Sagamiko**, Japan
70/C3 **Sāgar**, India
114/J2 **Sagavanirktok** (riv.), Ak,US
73/F1 **Sagay**, Phil.
110/D3 **Saginaw**, Mi,US
110/D3 **Saginaw** (bay), Mi,US
103/K3 **Saglek** (bay), Nf,Can
48/A1 **Sagone** (gulf), Fr.
46/A4 **Sagres**, Port.
68/E2 **Sagsay** (riv.), Mong.
101/F3 **Sagua de Tánamo**, Cuba
108/E4 **Saguaro Nat'l Mon.**, Az,US
111/G1 **Saguenay** (riv.), Qu,Can
82/C2 **Saguia el Hamra** (wadi), Mor., WSah.
47/E3 **Sagunto**, Sp.
31/R9 **Sagy**, Fr.
70/E2 **Sa'gya**, China
55/K2 **Sagyz** (riv.), Kaz.
59/L6 **Saḩāb**, Jor.
86/B5 **Sahaba**, Sudan
101/F6 **Sahagún**, Col.
60/E1 **Sahand** (mtn.), Iran
82/G3 **Sahara** (des.), Afr.
61/L3 **Sahāranpur**, India
70/E2 **Saharsa**, India
70/E2 **Sāhibganj**, India
61/K2 **Sāhīwāl**, Pak.
82/H2 **Şaḩrā' Awbārī** (des.), Libya
83/K2 **Sahra' Rabyānah** (des.), Libya
100/A3 **Sahuayo**, Mex.
70/D2 **Sai** (riv.), India
65/E2 **Sai** (riv.), Japan
81/R16 **Saïda**, Alg.
70/D2 **Saidpur**, India
64/C2 **Saigō**, Japan
69/D4 **Saigon** (Ho Chi Minh City), Viet.
64/C4 **Saijō**, Japan
64/A4 **Saikai Nat'l Park**, Japan
64/B4 **Saiki**, Japan
70/C4 **Sailu**, India
37/J3 **Saimaa** (lake), Fin.
42/C4 **Sains-Richaumont**, Fr.
36/D3 **Saint Abb's Head** (pt.), Sc,UK
44/E5 **Saint-Affrique**, Fr.
34/A6 **Saint Agnes**, Eng,UK
111/L2 **Saint Alban's**, Nf,Can
31/N6 **Saint Albans**, Eng,UK
31/M6 **Saint Albans** (val.), Eng,UK
111/F2 **Saint Albans**, Vt,US
110/D4 **Saint Albans**, WV,US
106/E2 **Saint Albert**, Ab,Can
34/D5 **Saint Aldhelm's Head** (pt.), Eng,UK
42/C3 **Saint-Amand-les-Eaux**, Fr.
44/E3 **Saint-Amand-Montrond**, Fr.
111/G1 **Saint-Ambroise**, Qu,Can
89/R15 **Saint-André**, Reun.
44/F2 **Saint-André-les-Vergers**, Fr.
36/D2 **Saint Andrews**, Sc,UK
84/B5 **Saint Ann** (cape), SLeo.
101/F4 **Saint Ann's Bay**, Jam.
44/B2 **Saint Anne**, Chl,UK
111/Q9 **Saint Anns**, On,Can
34/A3 **Saint Ann's** (pt.), UK
111/L1 **Saint Anthony**, Nf,Can
106/F5 **Saint Anthony**, Id,US
111/N6 **Saint-Antoine**, Qu,Can
42/D6 **Saint-Armand-sur-Fion**, Fr.
31/R11 **Saint-Arnoult-en-Yvelines**, Fr.
32/E5 **Saint Asaph**, Wal,UK
34/C4 **Saint Athan**, Wal,UK
44/B2 **Saint Aubin**, Chl,UK
111/N6 **Saint-Augustin**, Qu,Can
113/H4 **Saint Augustine**, Fl,US
34/B6 **Saint Austell**, Eng,UK
44/B3 **Saint-Avé**, Fr.
43/F5 **Saint-Avold**, Fr.
44/D5 **Saint-Barthélemy, Pic de** (peak), Fr.
32/E3 **Saint Bees**, Eng,UK
32/E2 **Saint Bees Head** (pt.), Eng,UK
111/M6 **Saint-Benoît**, Qu,Can
89/R15 **Saint-Benoît**, Reun.
111/P7 **Saint-Blaise**, Qu,Can
88/C4 **Saint Blaize** (cape), SAfr.
34/D3 **Saint Briavels**, Eng,UK
31/T10 **Saint-Brice-sous-Forêt**, Fr.
34/A3 **Saint Brides** (bay), Wal,UK
44/B2 **Saint-Brieuc**, Fr.
44/B2 **Saint-Brieuc** (bay), Fr.
111/P6 **Saint-Bruno-de-Montarville**, Qu,Can
111/M6 **Saint-Canut**, Qu,Can
111/R9 **Saint Catharines**, On,Can
101/J5 **Saint Catherine** (mt.), Gren.
35/E5 **Saint Catherine's** (pt.), Eng,UK
44/F4 **Saint-Chamond**, Fr.
116/P16 **Saint Charles**, Il,US
110/E4 **Saint Charles**, Md,US
109/K3 **Saint Charles**, Mo,US
31/S11 **Saint-Chéron**, Fr.
116/G7 **Saint Clair** (lake), On,Can, Mi,US
116/H6 **Saint Clair** (riv.), On,Can, Mi,US
116/G6 **Saint Clair Shores**, Mi,US
44/F3 **Saint-Claude**, Fr.
34/B3 **Saint Clears**, Wal,UK
31/S10 **Saint-Cloud**, Fr.
107/K4 **Saint Cloud**, Mn,US
34/B6 **Saint Columb Major**, Eng,UK
111/N7 **Saint-Constant**, Qu,Can
107/K4 **Saint Croix** (riv.), Mn, Wi,US
101/H4 **Saint Croix** (isl.), USVI
114/M3 **Saint Cyr** (mtn.), Yk,Can
31/S10 **Saint-Cyr-l'École**, Fr.
31/S11 **Saint-Cyr-sous-Dourdan**, Fr.
34/A3 **Saint David's**, Wal,UK
34/A3 **Saint David's Head** (pt.), Wal,UK
31/T10 **Saint-Denis**, Fr.
89/R15 **Saint-Denis** (cap.), Reun.
45/G2 **Saint-Dié**, Fr.
44/F2 **Saint-Dizier**, Fr.
44/E3 **Saint-Doulchard**, Fr.
110/F2 **Sainte-Agathe-des-Monts**, Qu,Can
111/H1 **Sainte-Anne-des-Monts**, Qu,Can
111/N6 **Sainte-Anne-des-Plaines**, Qu,Can
111/G2 **Sainte-Foy**, Qu,Can
109/K3 **Sainte Genevieve**, Mo,US
31/T11 **Sainte-Geneviève-des-Bois**, Fr.
111/P6 **Sainte-Julie-de-Verchères**, Qu,Can
111/J2 **Saint Eleanors**, PE,Can
114/K3 **Saint Elias** (mts.), Can., US
114/K4 **Saint Elias** (cape), Ak,US
114/K3 **Saint Elias** (mt.), Ak,US
114/K3 **Saint Elias-Wrangell Nat'l Park and Prsv.**, Ak,US
111/H1 **Sainte-Marguerite** (riv.), Qu,Can
111/G2 **Sainte-Marie**, Qu,Can
89/J7 **Sainte Marie, Nosy** (isl.), Madg.
45/G5 **Sainte-Maxime**, Fr.
42/C5 **Sainte-Erme-Outre-et-Ramecourt**, Fr.
107/J3 **Sainte Rose du Lac**, Mb,Can
44/C4 **Saintes**, Fr.
111/M6 **Sainte-Scholastique**, Qu,Can
44/F5 **Saint-Estève**, Fr.
111/N6 **Sainte-Thérèse**, Qu,Can
44/F4 **Saint-Étienne**, Fr.
44/D2 **Saint-Étienne-du-Rouvray**, Fr.
111/N6 **Saint-Eustache**, Qu,Can
31/T11 **Saint-Fargeau-Ponthierry**, Fr.
111/F1 **Saint-Félicien**, Qu,Can
32/C3 **Saintfield**, NI,UK
44/E2 **Saint-Florentin**, Fr.
44/E3 **Saint-Florent-sur-Cher**, Fr.
83/K6 **Saint-Floris Nat'l Park**, CAfr.
44/E4 **Saint-Flour**, Fr.
88/D4 **Saint Francis** (cape), SAfr.
109/K4 **Saint Francis** (riv.), Ar, Mo,US
109/G3 **Saint Francis**, Ks,US
116/Q14 **Saint Francis**, Wi,US
113/F4 **Saint Francisville**, La,US
113/F2 **Saint Francois** (mts.), Mo,US
44/D5 **Saint-Gaudens**, Fr.
111/H2 **Saint George**, Nb,Can
111/K1 **Saint George** (cape), Nf,Can
114/E4 **Saint George** (isl.), Ak,US
108/A2 **Saint George** (pt.), Ca,US
113/H3 **Saint George**, SC,US
108/D3 **Saint George**, Ut,US
111/K1 **Saint George's**, Nf,Can
111/J2 **Saint Georges** (bay), NS,Can
111/G2 **Saint-Georges**, Qu,Can
101/J5 **Saint George's** (cap.), Gren.
32/C6 **Saint George's** (chan.), Ire., UK
31/S10 **Saint-Germain-en-Laye**, Fr.
31/T11 **Saint-Germain-lès-Corbeil**, Fr.
31/U10 **Saint-Germain-sur-Morin**, Fr.
42/A5 **Saint-Germer-de-Fly**, Fr.
42/C3 **Saint-Ghislain**, Belg.
44/F5 **Saint-Gilles**, Fr.
44/C3 **Saint-Gilles-Croix-de-Vie**, Fr.
44/D5 **Saint-Girons**, Fr.
34/B3 **Saint Govan's Head** (pt.), Wal,UK
31/S10 **Saint-Gratien**, Fr.
76/F6 **Saint Helena** (isl.), Austl.
88/B4 **Saint Helena** (bay), SAfr.
80/B6 **Saint Helena** (isl.), UK
116/J9 **Saint Helena** (mtn.), Ca,US
77/D4 **Saint Helens** (pt.), Austl.
33/F5 **Saint Helens**, Eng,UK
106/C4 **Saint Helens**, Or,US
106/C4 **Saint Helens, Mount** (vol.), Wa,US
44/B2 **Saint Helier**, Chl,UK
44/C3 **Saint-Herblain**, Fr.
111/M6 **Saint-Hermas**, Qu,Can
70/E3 **Sainthia**, India
111/G1 **Saint-Honoré**, Qu,Can
111/P7 **Saint-Hubert**, Qu,Can
111/F2 **Saint-Hyacinthe**, Qu,Can
110/C1 **Saint Ignace** (isl.), On,Can
110/C2 **Saint Ignace**, Mi,US
76/H8 **Saint Ives**, Austl.
34/A6 **Saint Ives**, Eng,UK
35/F2 **Saint Ives**, Eng,UK
111/P7 **Saint-Jacques-le-Mineur**, Qu,Can
102/C3 **Saint James** (cape), BC,Can
107/K5 **Saint James**, Mn,US
115/G5 **Saint James**, NY,US
111/G1 **Saint-Jean** (lake), Qu,Can
111/H1 **Saint-Jean** (riv.), Qu,Can
44/C4 **Saint-Jean-d'Angély**, Fr.
44/D3 **Saint-Jean-de-la-Ruelle**, Fr.
44/C5 **Saint-Jean-de-Luz**, Fr.
111/G2 **Saint-Jean-Port-Joli**, Qu,Can
111/F2 **Saint-Jean-sur-Richelieu**, Qu,Can
111/N6 **Saint-Jérôme**, Qu,Can
106/D4 **Saint Joe** (riv.), Id,US
111/H2 **Saint John**, NB,Can
111/H2 **Saint John** (riv.), Can., US
44/B2 **Saint John**, Chl,UK
101/J4 **Saint John's** (cap.), Anti.
32/C3 **Saint John's** (pt.), IM,UK
108/E4 **Saint Johns**, Az,US
105/K6 **Saint Johns** (riv.), Fl,US
111/F2 **Saint Johnsbury**, Vt,US
110/B1 **Saint Joseph** (lake), On,Can
89/R15 **Saint-Joseph**, Reun.
110/C2 **Saint Joseph** (isl.), Mi,US
110/C3 **Saint Joseph** (riv.), Mi,US
109/J3 **Saint Joseph**, Mo,US
44/E5 **Saint-Juéry**, Fr.
44/D4 **Saint-Junien**, Fr.
34/A6 **Saint Just**, Eng,UK
34/A6 **Saint Just in Roseland**, Eng,UK
77/F5 **Saint Kilda**, Austl.
36/A2 **Saint Kilda** (isl.), Sc,UK
101/J4 **Saint Kitts and Nevis**
111/P6 **Saint-Lambert**, Qu,Can
107/J3 **Saint Laurent**, Mb,Can
111/N6 **Saint-Laurent**, Qu,Can
42/B3 **Saint-Laurent-Blangy**, Fr.
93/H2 **Saint-Laurent du Maroni**, FrG.
111/J1 **Saint Lawrence** (gulf), Can.
111/L2 **Saint Lawrence**, Nf,Can
111/G1 **Saint Lawrence** (riv.), Can, US
114/D3 **Saint Lawrence** (isl.), Ak,US
110/E2 **Saint Lawrence Islands Nat'l Park**, Can.
111/M7 **Saint-Lazare**, Qu,Can
77/G5 **Saint Leonard** (mtn.), Austl.
111/N6 **Saint-Léonard**, Qu,Can
89/R15 **Saint-Leu**, Reun.
31/S9 **Saint-Leu-la-Forêt**, Fr.
44/C2 **Saint-Lô**, Fr.
111/N7 **Saint Louis** (lake), Qu,Can
107/G2 **Saint Louis**, Sk,Can
89/R15 **Saint-Louis**, Reun.
84/A2 **Saint-Louis**, Sen.
84/B3 **Saint-Louis** (reg.), Sen.
106/A2 **Saint Louis** (riv.), Mn,US
109/K3 **Saint Louis**, Mo,US
111/H2 **Saint-Louis-de-Kent**, NB,Can
101/G4 **Saint-Louis du Nord**, Haiti
111/P7 **Saint-Luc**, Qu,Can
101/J5 **Saint Lucia**
89/F3 **Saint Lucia, Lake** (lag.), SAfr.
44/C3 **Saint-Maixent-l'École**, Fr.
107/J3 **Saint Malo**, Mb,Can
44/B2 **Saint-Malo**, Fr.
44/B2 **Saint-Malo** (gulf), Fr.
31/T10 **Saint-Mandé**, Fr.
44/F5 **Saint-Mandrier-sur-Mer**, Fr.
31/U9 **Saint-Mard**, Fr.
35/H4 **Saint Margaret's at Cliffe**, Eng,UK
106/D4 **Saint Maries**, Id,US
107/J3 **Saint Martin** (lake), Mb,Can
101/J4 **Saint-Martin** (isl.), Fr.
42/A2 **Saint-Martin-Boulogne**, Fr.
42/C6 **Saint-Martin-d'Ablois**, Fr.
44/F4 **Saint-Martin-d'Hères**, Fr.
31/T9 **Saint-Martin-du-Tertre**, Fr.
84/A3 **Saint Mary** (cape), Gam.
76/G8 **Saint Marys**, Austl.
110/D3 **Saint Mary's**, Nf,Can
111/J2 **Saint Marys** (riv.), NS,Can
114/F3 **Saint Marys**, Ak,US
113/H4 **Saint Marys**, Ga,US
110/E3 **Saint Marys**, Pa,US
111/N7 **Saint-Mathieu**, Qu,Can
114/D3 **Saint Matthew** (isl.), Ak,US
113/H3 **Saint Matthews**, SC,US
78/E5 **Saint Matthias** (isls.), PNG
31/T10 **Saint-Maur-des-Fossés**, Fr.
110/F1 **Saint-Maurice** (riv.), Qu,Can
34/A6 **Saint Mawes**, Eng,UK
43/F6 **Saint-Max**, Fr.
34/C3 **Saint Mellons**, Wal,UK
42/D6 **Saint-Memmie**, Fr.
31/S11 **Saint-Michel-sur-Orge**, Fr.
44/B3 **Saint-Nazaire**, Fr.
35/F2 **Saint Neots**, Eng,UK
43/E2 **Saint-Nicolas**, Belg.
31/S10 **Saint-Nom-la-Bretèche**, Fr.
42/B2 **Saint-Omer**, Fr.
42/A4 **Saint-Omer-en-Chaussée**, Fr.
31/S9 **Saint-Ouen-l'Aumône**, Fr.
111/G2 **Saint-Pamphile**, Qu,Can
111/G2 **Saint-Pascal**, Qu,Can
31/U9 **Saint-Pathus**, Fr.
28/H5 **Saint Paul** (isls.), Braz.
106/F2 **Saint Paul**, Ab,Can
29/N7 **Saint Paul** (isl.), FrAnt.
85/F5 **Saint Paul** (cape), Gha.
84/C5 **Saint Paul** (riv.), Gui., Libr.
89/R15 **Saint-Paul**, Reun.
114/E4 **Saint Paul** (isl.), Ak,US
109/J3 **Saint Paul**, Ks,US
107/K4 **Saint Paul** (cap.), Mn,US
44/C5 **Saint-Paul-lès-Dax**, Fr.
76/B1 **Saint Pauls** (peak), Austl.
44/F4 **Saint-Paul-Trois-Châteaux**, Fr.
107/K4 **Saint Peter**, Mn,US
93/M3 **Saint Peter and Saint Paul** (rocks), Braz.
44/B2 **Saint Peter Port**, Chl,UK
35/H4 **Saint Peter's**, Eng,UK
53/V7 **Saint Petersburg** (inset), Rus.
113/H5 **Saint Petersburg**, Fl,US
52/F4 **Saint Petersburg** (Leningrad), Rus.
52/G3 **Saint Petersburg Obl.**, Rus.
111/P7 **Saint-Philippe-de-La Prairie**, Qu,Can
101/J5 **Saint-Pierre**, Mart.
89/R15 **Saint-Pierre**, Reun.
111/K2 **Saint Pierre & Miquelon** (dpcy.), Fr
44/D3 **Saint-Pierre-des-Corps**, Fr.
44/C5 **Saint-Pierre-du-Mont**, Fr.
31/T11 **Saint-Pierre-du-Perray**, Fr.
107/J3 **Saint Pierre-Jolys**, Mb,Can
44/B2 **Saint-Pol-de-Léon**, Fr.
42/B1 **Saint-Pol-sur-Mer**, Fr.
44/E5 **Saint-Pons** (mtn.), Fr.
31/S9 **Saint-Prix**, Fr.
42/C4 **Saint-Quentin**, Fr.
45/G5 **Saint-Raphaël**, Fr.
44/F5 **Saint-Rémy-de-Provence**, Fr.
31/S10 **Saint-Rémy-lès-Chevreuse**, Fr.
42/A3 **Saint-Riquier**, Fr.
44/B2 **Saint Sampson's**, Chl,UK
42/C3 **Saint-Saulve**, Fr.
113/H4 **Saint Simons Island**, Ga,US

31/U9 Saint-Soupplets, Fr.
111/H2 Saint Stephen, NB,Can
34/B6 Saint Stephen in Brannel, Eng,UK
110/D3 Saint Thomas, On,Can
101/H4 Saint Thomas (isl.), USVI
111/N7 Saint-Urbain-Premier, Qu,Can
44/F3 Saint-Vallier, Fr.
42/B2 Saint-Venant, Fr.
74/F6 Saint Vincent (gulf), Austl.
77/C4 Saint Vincent (pt.), Austl.
101/J5 Saint Vincent & the Grenadines
43/F3 Saint Vith, Belg.
31/T11 Saint-Vrain, Fr.
106/F2 Saint Walburg, Sk,Can
31/T9 Saint-Witz, Fr.
70/D2 Sāipal (mtn.), Nepal
78/D3 Saipan (isl.), NMar.
65/F2 Saitama (pref.), Japan
64/B4 Saito, Japan
69/B3 Sai Yok Nat'l Park, Thai.
92/E7 Sajama Nat'l Park, Bol.
50/E1 Sajószentpéter, Hun.
88/C3 Sak (riv.), SAfr.
65/H7 Sakado, Japan
65/J7 Sakae, Japan
65/M9 Sakahogi, Japan
65/F2 Sakai, Japan
64/C3 Sakaide, Japan
64/C3 Sakaiminato, Japan
107/H3 Sakakawea (lake), ND,US
103/J3 Sakami (lake), Qu,Can
51/K5 Sakarya (prov.), Turk.
59/B2 Sakarya (riv.), Turk.
63/M4 Sakata, Japan
64/C4 Sakawa, Japan
57/Q4 Sakhalin (gulf), Rus.
57/Q4 Sakhalin (isl.), Rus.
60/F1 Sakht Sar (Ramsar), Iran
54/E3 Saki, Ukr.
67/D3 Sakishima (isls.), Japan
55/L1 Sakmara (riv.), Rus.
69/D2 Sakon Nakhon, Thai.
61/J3 Sakrand, Pak.
65/F2 Saku, Japan
65/J7 Sakura, Japan
65/L10 Sakurai, Japan
80/K10 Sal (isl.), CpV.
55/G3 Sal (riv.), Rus.
39/J4 Šal'a, Slvk.
37/F4 Sala, Swe.
48/D2 Sala Consilina, It.
91/E2 Saladas, Arg.
96/F2 Saladillo, Arg.
96/D3 Salado (riv.), Arg.
96/F2 Salado (riv.), Arg.
100/B2 Salado (riv.), Mex.
90/C5 Salado del Norte (riv.), Arg.
85/E4 Salaga, Gha.
73/G4 Salahatu (mtn.), Indo.
50/F2 Sălaj (co.), Rom.
82/J5 Salal, Chad
86/D4 Şalālah, Sudan
96/D5 Salamanca (plain), Arg.
96/C1 Salamanca, Chile
100/A3 Salamanca, Mex.
46/C2 Salamanca, Sp.
110/E3 Salamanca, NY,US
83/J6 Salamat (riv.), Chad
49/H3 Salamís, Gre.
49/L7 Salamís (isl.), Gre.
59/L4 Salamīyah, Syria
69/C1 Sala Mok, Laos
46/B1 Salas, Sp.
55/K1 Salavat, Rus.
78/B5 Salayar (isl.), Indo.
28/D7 Sala y Gomez (isls.), Chile
44/E3 Salbris, Fr.
34/C6 Salcombe, Eng,UK
77/C3 Sale, Austl.
81/L13 Salé, Mor.
33/F5 Sale, Eng,UK
73/G3 Salebabu (isl.), Indo.
56/G3 Salekhard, Rus.
70/C5 Salem, India
110/C4 Salem, In,US
109/K3 Salem, Mo,US
111/G3 Salem, NH,US
106/C4 Salem (cap.), Or,US
110/D4 Salem, Va,US
48/C4 Salemi, It.
48/F2 Salentina (pen.), It.
48/D2 Salerno, It.
48/D2 Salerno (gulf), It.
35/G3 Sales (pt.), UK
33/F5 Salford, Eng,UK
50/D1 Salgótarján, Hun.
94/C3 Salgueiro, Braz.
109/F3 Salida, Co,US
59/B2 Salihli, Turk.
87/F3 Salima, Malw.
86/B4 Salīmah (oasis), Sudan
46/B1 Salime (res.), Sp.
101/G3 Salina (pt.), Bahm.
48/D3 Salina (isl.), It.
109/H3 Salina, Ks,US
108/E3 Salina, Ut,US
100/B4 Salina Cruz, Mex.
94/B5 Salinas, Braz.
100/A3 Salinas, Mex.
108/B3 Salinas, Ca,US
108/B3 Salinas (riv.), Ca,US
47/G3 Salinas, Cabo de (cape), Sp.
109/F4 Salinas Nat'l Mon., NM,US
48/D2 Saline (marsh), It.
109/J4 Saline (riv.), Ar,US
109/G3 Saline (riv.), Ks,US
93/J4 Salinópolis, Braz.
103/J2 Salisbury (isl.), NW,Can
35/E4 Salisbury, Eng,UK
34/D4 Salisbury (plain), Eng,UK
110/F4 Salisbury, Md,US
113/H3 Salisbury, NC,US
94/B3 Salitre (riv.), Braz.
37/J2 Salla, Fin.
45/G4 Sallanches, Fr.
40/D4 Salland (reg.), Neth.
84/B4 Sallatouk (pt.), Gui.
42/B3 Sallaumines, Fr.
47/F2 Sallent, Sp.
109/J4 Sallisaw, Ok,US
86/D5 Sallūm, Sudan
70/D2 Sallyāna, Nepal
32/B5 Sally Gap (pass), Ire.
43/F3 Salm (riv.), Ger.
59/F2 Salmās, Iran
106/D4 Salmon (riv.), Id,US
106/D3 Salmon Arm, BC,Can
108/D2 Salmon Falls (riv.), Id, Nv,US
106/E4 Salmon River (mts.), Id,US
37/G3 Salo, Fin.
44/F3 Salon (riv.), Fr.
44/F5 Salon-de-Provence, Fr.
83/K8 Salonga Nat'l Park, Zaire
49/H3 Salonika (Thermaic) (gulf), Gre.
49/H2 Salonika (Thessaloníki), Gre.
50/E2 Salonta, Rom.
46/B3 Salor (riv.), Sp.
84/B3 Saloum, Vallée du (wadi), Sen.
55/G3 Sal'sk, Rus.
48/C4 Salso (riv.), It.
88/C3 Salt (riv.), SAfr.
108/E4 Salt (riv.), Az,US
91/C1 Salta, Arg.
34/B6 Saltash, Eng,UK
33/H2 Saltburn, Eng,UK
36/B4 Saltee (isls.), Ire.
37/E2 Saltfjorden (fjord), Nor.
34/D4 Saltford, Eng,UK
113/H4 Saltilla (riv.), Ga,US
100/A2 Saltillo, Mex.
108/E2 Salt Lake City (cap.), Ut,US
96/E2 Salto, Arg.
95/C2 Salto, Braz.
48/C1 Salto (riv.), It.
91/E3 Salto, Uru.
97/F1 Salto (dept.), Uru.
91/E3 Salto Grande (res.), Arg., Uru.
108/C4 Salton Sea (lake), Ca,US
95/A3 Salto Santiago (res.), Braz.
113/H3 Saluda (riv.), SC,US
67/D6 Salug, Phil.
70/D4 Sālūr, India
93/H2 Salut (isls.), FrG.
45/G4 Saluzzo, It.
97/J7 Salvación (bay), Chile
94/C4 Salvador, Braz.
46/A3 Salvaterra de Magos, Port.
46/A1 Salvatierra de Miño, Sp.
58/J8 Salween (riv.), Asia
55/J5 Sal'yany, Azer.
110/D4 Salyersville, Ky,US
39/H5 Salza (riv.), Aus.
41/E4 Salzbergen, Ger.
45/K3 Salzburg, Aus.
45/K3 Salzburg (prov.), Aus.
41/H4 Salzgitter, Ger.
41/G4 Salzhemmendorf, Ger.
41/F5 Salzkotten, Ger.
38/F2 Salzwedel, Ger.
46/C1 Sama, Sp.
72/C4 Samak (cape), Indo.
73/F2 Samales (isls.), Phil.
70/D4 Sāmalkot, India
86/B2 Samālūt, Egypt
101/H4 Samaná (cape), DRep.
59/C3 Samandağı, Turk.
59/H6 Samannūd, Egypt
67/E5 Samar (isl.), Phil.
55/J1 Samara, Rus.
55/K1 Samara (riv.), Rus.
55/J1 Samara Obl., Rus.
63/M2 Samarga (riv.), Rus.
59/N8 Samaria (reg.), WBnk.
59/N8 Samaria Nat'l Park, WBnk.
49/H5 Samarias Gorge Nat'l Park, Gre.
73/E4 Samarinda, Indo.
56/G6 Samarkand, Uzb.
60/D2 Sāmarrā', Iraq
61/K3 Samasata, Pak.
70/D3 Sambalpur, India
87/C2 Samba Lucala, Ang.
89/H7 Sambao (riv.), Madg.
72/D4 Sambar (cape), Indo.
72/C3 Sambas, Indo.
89/J6 Sambava, Madg.
54/B2 Sambor, Ukr.
97/F2 Samborombón (bay), Arg.
69/D3 Sambor Prei Kuk (ruins), Camb.
42/C3 Sambre (riv.), Belg.,Fr.
42/C4 Sambre à l'Oise, Canal de (can.), Fr.
64/A2 Samch'ŏk, SKor.
87/G1 Same, Tanz.
69/C4 Samit (cape), Camb.
69/C3 Samkos (peak), Camb.
116/C2 Sammamish (lake), Wa,US
64/A3 Samnangjin, SKor.
50/B3 Samobor, Cro.
51/F4 Samokov, Bul.
47/Q10 Samora Correia, Port.
59/A3 Sámos, Gre.
49/J2 Samothráki (isl.), Gre.
96/D2 Sampacho, Arg.
72/D4 Sampit, Indo.
72/D4 Sampit (riv.), Indo.
112/E4 Sam Rayburn (res.), Tx,US
69/C1 Sam Sao (mts.), Laos, Viet.
76/E6 Samson (mtn.), Austl.
69/D2 Sam Son, Viet.
76/E6 Samsonvale (lake), Austl.
59/D2 Samsun, Turk.
69/B4 Samui (isl.), Thai.
65/H7 Samukawa, Japan
55/J4 Samur (riv.), Azer., Rus.
69/C3 Samut Prakan, Thai.
69/C3 Samut Sakhon, Thai.
69/C3 Samut Songkhram, Thai.
69/D3 San (riv.), Camb.
63/H5 San (riv.), China
84/D3 San, Mali
39/M3 San (riv.), Pol.
50/C3 Sana (riv.), Bosn.
46/A1 San Adrián, Cabo de (cape), Sp.
80/D4 Sanaga (riv.), Afr.
67/E6 San Agustin (cape), Phil.
47/N8 San Agustin de Guadalix, Sp.
114/F5 Sanak (isl.), Ak,US
73/G4 Sanama (isl.), Indo.
90/B5 San Ambrosio (isl.), Chile
60/E1 Sanandaj, Iran
116/K11 San Andreas (lake), Ca,US
100/E5 San Andrés, Col.
100/E5 San Andrés (isl.), Col.
108/F4 San Andres (mts.), NM,US
97/S12 San Andrés de Giles, Arg.
46/C1 San Andrés del Rabanedo, Sp.
100/B4 San Andrés Tuxtla, Mex.
112/C4 San Angelo, Tx,US
116/J11 San Anselmo, Ca,US
97/F3 San Antonio (cape), Arg.
96/C2 San Antonio, Chile
101/M9 San Antonio, Mex.
115/C2 San Antonio (mt.), Ca,US
108/F4 San Antonio, NM,US
112/D4 San Antonio, Tx,US
112/D4 San Antonio (riv.), Tx,US
47/F3 San Antonio Abad, Sp.
96/F2 San Antonio de Areco, Arg.
101/J5 San Antonio del Golfo, Ven.
96/D4 San Antonio Oeste, Arg.
112/E4 San Augustine, Tx,US
70/C3 Sānāwad, India
48/D2 San Bartolomeo in Galdo, It.
48/C1 San Benedetto del Tronto, It.
115/C2 San Bernardino, Ca,US
115/C2 San Bernardino (mts.), Ca,US
96/C2 San Bernardo, Chile
101/F6 San Bernardo (pt.), Col.
101/N8 San Blas, Mex.
113/G4 San Blas (cape), Fl,US
112/E3 San Bois (mts.), Ok,US
45/J4 San Bonifacio, It.
92/E6 San Borja, Bol.
111/S9 Sanborn, NY,US
116/K11 San Bruno, Ca,US
100/A2 San Buenaventura, Mex.
115/A2 San Buenaventura (Ventura), Ca,US
96/C3 San Carlos, Chile
100/A2 San Carlos, Mex.
100/E5 San Carlos, Nic.
67/D4 San Carlos, Phil.
97/G2 San Carlos, Uru.
108/E4 San Carlos (lake), Az,US
116/K11 San Carlos, Ca,US
101/H6 San Carlos, Ven.
96/C4 San Carlos de Bariloche, Arg.
101/G6 San Carlos del Zulia, Ven.
49/F2 San Cataldo, It.
96/C2 San Clemente, Chile
46/D3 San Clemente, Sp.
108/C4 San Clemente (isl.), Ca,US
91/D3 San Cristóbal, Arg.
100/E3 San Cristóbal, Cuba
100/D5 San Cristobal (vol.), Nic.
78/F6 San Cristobal (isl.), Sol.
92/D2 San Cristóbal, Ven.
100/C4 San Cristóbal de las Casas, Mex.
101/F3 Sancti Spíritus, Cuba
106/F2 Sand (riv.), Ab,Can
88/D3 Sand (riv.), SAfr.
109/G2 Sand (hills), Ne,US
64/D3 Sanda, Japan
32/C1 Sanda (isl.), Sc,UK
69/D3 Sandan, Camb.
51/F5 Sandanski, Bul.
33/F5 Sandbach, Eng,UK
41/F2 Sande, Ger.
37/D4 Sandefjord, Nor.
98/Q Sanders (coast), Ant.
112/C4 Sanderson, Tx,US
113/H3 Sandersville, Ga,US
76/F6 Sandgate, Austl.
32/D2 Sandhead, Sc,UK
111/Q8 Sandhill, On,Can
35/F4 Sandhurst, Eng,UK
97/L8 San Diego (cape), Arg.
108/C4 San Diego, Ca,US
112/D5 San Diego, Tx,US
59/B2 Sandıklı, Turk.
115/C2 San Dimas, Ca,US
48/D4 San Dimitri, Ras (pt.), Malta
100/E3 Sandino, Cuba
73/E3 Sandkan, Malay.
37/C4 Sandnes, Nor.
37/E2 Sandnessjøen, Nor.
87/D2 Sandoa, Zaire
39/L3 Sandomierz, Pol.
45/K4 San Donà di Piave, It.
84/B3 Sandougou (riv.), Gam., Sen.
35/E5 Sandown, Eng,UK
106/D3 Sandpoint, Id,US
77/F5 Sandringham, Austl.
35/G1 Sandringham, Eng,UK
110/D3 Sandusky, Mi,US
110/D3 Sandusky, Oh,US
37/D4 Sandvika, Nor.
37/F3 Sandviken, Swe.
76/B2 Sandwich (cape), Austl.
35/H4 Sandwich, Eng,UK
76/D4 Sandy (cape), Austl.
107/K2 Sandy (lake), On,Can
35/F2 Sandy, Eng,UK
108/E2 Sandy, Ut,US
107/H2 Sandy Bay, Sk,Can
115/F5 Sandy Hook (bay), NJ,US
113/G3 Sandy Springs, Ga,US
43/E4 Sanem, Lux.
48/C2 San Felice Circeo, It.
96/C2 San Felipe, Chile
101/M7 San Felipe, Mex.
92/E1 San Felipe, Ven.
90/A5 San Félix (isl.), Chile
97/S12 San Fernando, Arg.
96/C2 San Fernando, Chile
100/B3 San Fernando, Mex.
67/D4 San Fernando, Phil.
46/B4 San Fernando, Sp.
115/B2 San Fernando, Ca,US
101/H6 San Fernando de Apure, Ven.
47/N9 San Fernando-de-Henares, Sp.
37/E3 Sånfjällets Nat'l Park, Swe.
114/K3 Sanford (mtn.), Ak,US
113/H4 Sanford, Fl,US
111/G3 Sanford, Me,US
113/J3 Sanford, NC,US
91/D3 San Francisco, Arg.
101/M7 San Francisco, Mex.
67/E6 San Francisco, Phil.
108/E4 San Francisco (riv.), Az, NM,US
116/K11 San Francisco, Ca,US
116/K11 San Francisco (bay), Ca,US
101/G5 San Francisco, Ven.
100/D5 San Francisco de la Paz, Hon.
101/N8 San Francisco del Oro, Mex.
101/G4 San Francisco de Macorís, DRep.
96/C2 San Francisco de Mostazal, Chile
70/B4 Sangamner, India
110/B3 Sangamon (riv.), Il,US
61/H2 Sangān (mtn.), Afg.
92/C4 Sangay Nat'l Park, Ecu.
46/A1 Sangenjo, Sp.
66/C2 Sanggan (riv.), China
72/D3 Sanggau, Indo.
82/J7 Sangha (riv.), CAfr., Congo
61/J3 Sanghar, Pak.
73/F3 Sangihe (isls.), Indo.
92/D2 San Gil, Col.
48/E2 San Giorgio Ionico, It.
48/C4 San Giovanni Gemini, It.
48/E3 San Giovanni in Fiore, It.
45/J4 San Giovanni in Persiceto, It.
62/D2 Sangiyn Dalay (lake), Mong.
64/A2 Sangju, SKor.
73/E3 Sangkulirang, Indo.
70/B4 Sāngli, India
82/H7 Sangmélima, Camr.
65/L10 Sangō, Japan
108/C4 San Gorgonio (peak), Ca,US
109/F3 Sangre de Cristo (mts.), Co, NM,US
101/J5 Sangre Grande, Trin.
48/D2 Sangro (riv.), It.
92/G6 Sangue (riv.), Braz.
85/E4 Sanguie (prov.), Burk.
101/M8 San Hipólito (pt.), Mex.
88/E3 Sani (pass), SAfr.
100/D4 San Ignacio, Belz.
92/E6 San Ignacio, Bol.
92/F7 San Ignacio, Bol.
96/B3 San Ignacio, Chile
101/M8 San Ignacio, Mex.
101/N9 San Ignacio, Mex.
64/D3 San'in Kaigin Nat'l Park, Japan
101/F6 San Jacinto, Col.
115/C3 San Jacinto (riv.), Ca,US
96/C2 San Javier, Chile
47/E4 San Javier, Sp.
65/F2 Sanjō, Japan
92/F6 San Joaquín, Bol.
108/B3 San Joaquin (val.), Ca,US
96/E1 San Jorge, Arg.
96/D5 San Jorge (cape), Arg.
96/D5 San Jorge (gulf), Arg.
101/M7 San Jorge (bay), Mex.
47/F2 San Jorge (gulf), Sp.
96/D4 San José (gulf), Arg.
100/D4 San Jose, Belz.
100/E6 San José (cap.), CR
101/M8 San José (isl.), Mex.
67/D4 San Jose, Phil.
47/F3 San José, Sp.
97/F2 San José (dept.), Uru.
97/T11 San José (riv.), Uru.
116/L12 San Jose, Ca,US
101/G5 San José, Ven.
101/J6 San José de Amacuro, Ven.
67/D5 San Jose de Buenavista, Phil.
92/F7 San José de Chiquitos, Bol.
101/M8 San José de Gracia, Mex.
101/J6 San José de Guanipa, Ven.
101/H6 San José de Guaribe, Ven.
91/C3 San José de Jáchal, Arg.
101/N9 San José del Cabo, Mex.
96/Q9 San José de Maipo, Chile
97/F2 San José de Mayo, Uru.
101/M8 San José de Pimas, Mex.
96/C1 San Juan, Arg.
97/M8 San Juan (cape), Arg.
96/C1 San Juan (prov.), Arg.
91/C3 San Juan (riv.), Arg.
100/E5 San Juan (riv.), CR, Nic.
101/G4 San Juan, DRep.
101/H4 San Juan (cap.), PR
108/F3 San Juan (mts.), Co,US
108/E3 San Juan (riv.), Co, Ut,US
112/A2 San Juan (basin), NM,US
91/E2 San Juan Bautista, Par.
47/E3 San Juan de Alicante, Sp.
46/B4 San Juan de Aznalfarache, Sp.
101/P10 San Juan de Lima (pt.), Mex.
100/E5 San Juan del Norte, Nic.
101/P9 San Juan de los Lagos, Mex.
101/H6 San Juan de los Morros, Ven.
97/K7 San Julián, Gran Bajo de (val.), Arg.
91/D3 San Justo, Arg.
84/C4 Sankanbiriwa (peak), SLeo.
84/C4 Sankoroni (riv.), Gui., Mali
45/L3 Sankt Andrä, Aus.
43/G2 Sankt Augustin, Ger.
45/H3 Sankt Gallen, Swi.
43/G5 Sankt Ingbert, Ger.
45/K3 Sankt Johann im Pongau, Aus.
45/K3 Sankt Johann in Tirol, Aus.
45/L2 Sankt Pölten, Aus.
45/L3 Sankt Veit an der Glan, Aus.
43/G5 Sankt Wendel, Ger.
101/M9 San Lázaro (cape), Mex.
116/K11 San Leandro, Ca,US
92/E6 San Lorenzo, Bol.
97/J6 San Lorenzo (peak), Chile
92/C3 San Lorenzo, Ecu.
92/B4 San Lorenzo (cape), Ecu.
48/A3 San Lorenzo (cape), It.
101/N8 San Lorenzo, Mex.
116/K11 San Lorenzo, Ca,US
46/C2 San Lorenzo de El Escorial, Sp.
46/B4 Sanlúcar de Barrameda, Sp.
101/N9 San Lucas, Mex.
101/N9 San Lucas (cape), Mex.
96/D2 San Luis, Arg.
96/D2 San Luis (mts.), Arg.
96/D2 San Luis (prov.), Arg.
101/F3 San Luis, Cuba
100/D4 San Luis, Guat.
112/B2 San Luis (val.), Co,US
108/B4 San Luis Obispo, Ca,US
100/A3 San Luis Potosí, Mex.
100/A3 San Luis Potosí (state), Mex.
101/M7 San Luis Río Colorado, Mex.
108/E4 San Manuel, Az,US
101/F6 San Marcos, Col.
100/B4 San Marcos, Mex.
112/D4 San Marcos, Tx,US
67/D4 San Mariano, Phil.
45/K5 San Marino
45/K5 San Marino (cap.), SMar.
96/C2 San Martín, Arg.
97/J7 San Martín (lake), Arg.
92/F6 San Martín (riv.), Bol.
96/C4 San Martín de los Andes, Arg.
85/E3 Sanmatenga (prov.), Burk.
116/K11 San Mateo, Ca,US
112/B3 San Mateo (mts.), NM,US
96/D4 San Matías (gulf), Arg.
92/G7 San Matías, Bol.
66/B4 Sanmenxia, China
92/F6 San Miguel (riv.), Bol.
100/D5 San Miguel, ESal.
100/A3 San Miguel de Allende, Mex.
96/F2 San Miguel del Monte, Arg.
91/C2 San Miguel de Tucumán, Arg.
67/C2 Sanming, China
65/L9 Sannan, Japan
83/M5 Sannār, Sudan
48/D2 Sannicandro Garganico, It.
108/C4 San Nicolas (isl.), Ca,US
96/E2 San Nicolás de los Arroyos, Arg.
100/A2 San Nicolás de los Garzas, Mex.
57/P2 Sannikova (str.), Rus.
31/S10 Sannois, Fr.
65/F2 Sano, Japan
39/M4 Sanok, Pol.
96/B4 San Pablo, Chile
67/D5 San Pablo, Phil.
116/K11 San Pablo, Ca,US
116/K10 San Pablo (bay), Ca,US
96/F2 San Pedro, Arg.
100/D4 San Pedro, Belz.
96/C2 San Pedro, Chile
91/C1 San Pedro (vol.), Chile
84/D5 San Pédro, IvC.
91/E1 San Pedro, Par.
46/B3 San Pedro (range), Sp.
108/E4 San Pedro (riv.), Az,US
115/B3 San Pedro (bay), Ca,US
100/C4 San Pedro Carchá, Guat.
100/A2 San Pedro de las Colinas, Mex.
92/C5 San Pedro de Lloc, Peru
47/E4 San Pedro del Pinatar, Sp.
101/H4 San Pedro de Macorís, DRep.
100/B4 San Pedro Pochutla, Mex.
100/D4 San Pedro Sula, Hon.
48/A3 San Pietro (isl.), It.
32/E1 Sanquhar, Sc,UK
92/C3 Sanquianga Nat'l Park, Col.
101/L7 San Quintín, Mex.
101/L7 San Quintín (cape), Mex.
96/C2 San Rafael, Arg.
116/J11 San Rafael, Ca,US
108/E3 San Rafael (riv.), Ut,US
101/G5 San Rafael, Ven.
97/G2 San Ramón, Uru.
116/L11 San Ramon, Ca,US
91/D1 San Ramón de la Nueva Orán, Arg.
45/G5 San Remo, It.
46/C4 San Roque, Sp.
96/B3 San Rosendo, Chile
112/D4 San Saba, Tx,US
109/H5 San Saba (riv.), Tx,US
100/D5 San Salvador (cap.), ESal.
97/S11 San Salvador (riv.), Uru.
91/C1 San Salvador de Jujuy, Arg.
101/G3 San Salvador (Watling) (isl.), Bahm.
48/D1 San Salvo, It.
46/E1 San Sebastián, Sp.
46/D2 San Sebastián de los Reyes, Sp.
45/J4 San Sebastiano, It.
48/D2 San Severo, It.
62/F2 Sant, Mong.
100/D5 Santa Ana, ESal.
101/M7 Santa Ana, Mex.
115/C3 Santa Ana, Ca,US
115/C3 Santa Ana (mts.), Ca,US
101/H5 Santa Ana, Ven.
95/D1 Santa Bárbara, Braz.
96/B3 Santa Bárbara, Chile
100/D5 Santa Bárbara, Hon.
101/N8 Santa Bárbara, Mex.
115/A2 Santa Barbara, Ca,US
115/A2 Santa Barbara (chan.), Ca,US
92/E3 Santa Bárbara, Ven.
95/C2 Santa Bárbara d'Oeste, Braz.
67/D6 Santa Catalina, Phil.
108/C4 Santa Catalina (gulf), Ca,US
108/C4 Santa Catalina (isl.), Ca,US
95/B3 Santa Catarina (isl.), Braz.
95/B3 Santa Catarina (state), Braz.
95/B3 Santa Cecília, Braz.
101/F3 Santa Clara, Cuba
46/A4 Santa Clara (res.), Port.
116/L12 Santa Clara, Ca,US
115/B2 Santa Clara (riv.), Ca,US
101/J6 Santa Clara, Ven.
115/B2 Santa Clarita, Ca,US
47/G2 Santa Coloma de Farners, Sp.
47/L7 Santa Coloma de Gramanet, Sp.
46/A1 Santa Comba, Sp.
97/K7 Santa Cruz (prov.), Arg.
97/K7 Santa Cruz (riv.), Arg.
92/F7 Santa Cruz, Bol.
94/C2 Santa Cruz, Braz.
96/C2 Santa Cruz, Chile
100/D5 Santa Cruz, CR
67/D5 Santa Cruz, Phil.
67/E6 Santa Cruz, Phil.
78/F6 Santa Cruz (isls.), Sol.
108/B3 Santa Cruz, Ca,US
115/A2 Santa Cruz (isl.), Ca,US
47/S12 Santa Cruz da Graciosa, Azor.,Port.
47/R12 Santa Cruz das Flores, Azor.,Port.
94/C4 Santa Cruz da Vitória, Braz.
100/C4 Santa Cruz del Quiché, Guat.
101/F3 Santa Cruz del Sur, Cuba
47/X16 Santa Cruz de Tenerife, Canl.
94/C2 Santa Cruz do Capibaribe, Braz.
95/B2 Santa Cruz do Rio Pardo, Braz.
91/F2 Santa Cruz do Sul, Braz.
47/L7 Sant Adrià de Besòs, Sp.
96/D5 Santa Elena (peak), Arg.
100/D5 Santa Elena (cape), CR
46/A1 Santa Eugenia de Ribeira, Sp.
47/F3 Santa Eulalia del Río, Sp.
96/E1 Santa Fé, Arg.
96/E2 Santa Fé (prov.), Arg.
46/D4 Santa Fé, Sp.
113/H4 Santa Fe (riv.), Fl,US
109/F4 Santa Fe (cap.), NM,US
95/B2 Santa Fe do Sul, Braz.
48/D3 Sant'Agata di Militello, It.
95/B1 Santa Helena de Goiás, Braz.
94/A1 Santa Inês, Braz.
94/C4 Santa Inês, Braz.
97/J8 Santa Inés (isl.), Chile
95/G8 Santa Isabel, Braz.
100/E5 Santa Isabel, Col.
78/E5 Santa Isabel (isl.), Sol.
82/G7 Santa Isabel, Pico de (peak), EqG.
97/F2 Santa Lucía, Uru.
97/G2 Santa Lucía (riv.), Uru.
94/C3 Santa Luz, Braz.
94/A1 Santa Luzia, Braz.
94/C2 Santa Luzia, Braz.
95/D1 Santa Luzia, Braz.
80/J10 Santa Luzia (isl.), CpV.
96/E2 Santa Magdalena, Arg.
101/M8 Santa Magdalena (isl.), Mex.
101/M9 Santa Margarita (isl.), Mex.
91/F2 Santa Maria, Braz.
94/A4 Santa Maria (hills), Braz.
96/C2 Santa María, Chile
96/B3 Santa María (isl.), Chile
47/T13 Santa Maria (isl.), Azor.,Port.
108/B4 Santa Maria, Ca,US
46/B4 Santa María, Cabo de (cape), Port.
48/D2 Santa Maria Capua Vetere, It.
94/C3 Santa Maria da Boa Vista, Braz.
94/A4 Santa Maria da Vitória, Braz.
49/F3 Santa Maria di Leuca (cape), It.
95/D1 Santa Maria do Suaçi, Braz.
101/G5 Santa Marta, Col.
95/B4 Santa Marta Grande, Cabo de (cape), Braz.
115/B2 Santa Monica, Ca,US
115/B3 Santa Monica (bay), Ca,US
115/B2 Santa Monica Mts. Nat'l Rec. Area, Ca,US
94/A4 Santana, Braz.
94/B1 Santana (isl.), Braz.
47/P11 Santana, Port.
47/V15 Santana, Madr.,Port.
94/B1 Santana do Acaraú, Braz.
94/C3 Santana do Ipanema, Braz.
91/E3 Santana do Livramento, Braz.
92/C3 Santander, Col.
46/D1 Santander, Sp.
48/A3 Sant'Antioco, It.
115/A2 Santa Paula, Ca,US
47/E3 Santa Pola, Sp.
47/E3 Santa Pola, Cabo de (cape), Sp.
94/B2 Santa Quitéria, Braz.
93/H4 Santarém, Braz.
46/A3 Santarém, Port.
46/A3 Santarém (dist.), Port.
94/A2 Santa Rita, Braz.
94/D2 Santa Rita, Braz.
94/A3 Santa Rita de Cássia, Braz.
95/H7 Santa Rita do Sapucaí, Braz.
96/D3 Santa Rosa, Arg.
96/D4 Santa Rosa (val.), Arg.
91/F2 Santa Rosa, Braz.
92/C4 Santa Rosa, Ecu.
108/B3 Santa Rosa, Ca,US
108/B4 Santa Rosa (isl.), Ca,US
109/F4 Santa Rosa, NM,US
108/C2 Santa Rosa (range), Nv,US
96/D2 Santa Rosa de Calamuchita, Arg.
100/D5 Santa Rosa de Copán, Hon.
95/C2 Santa Rosa de Viterbo, Braz.
101/M8 Santa Rosalía, Mex.
101/H6 Santa Rosalía, Ven.
100/D5 Santa Rosa Nat'l Park, CR
115/B2 Santa Susana (mts.), Ca,US
93/J6 Santa Teresa (riv.), Braz.
97/G2 Santa Teresa Nat'l Park, Uru.
93/H6 Santa Teresinha, Braz.
97/F3 Santa Teresita, Arg.
95/B1 Santa Vitória, Braz.
97/G2 Santa Vitória do Palmar, Braz.
47/L7 Sant Boi de Llobregat, Sp.
47/F2 Sant Carles de la Ràpita, Sp.
47/G2 Sant Celoni, Sp.
47/G2 Sant Cugat del Vallès, Sp.
113/H3 Santee (dam), SC,US
113/J3 Santee (riv.), SC,US
101/P10 San Telmo (pt.), Mex.
45/J4 Santerno (riv.), It.
48/D3 Sant'Eufemia (gulf), It.
47/G2 Sant Feliu de Guíxols, Sp.
47/G2 Sant Feliu de Llobregat, Sp.
47/F1 Sant Gervàs (peak), Sp.
91/F2 Santiago, Braz.
96/C2 Santiago (cap.), Chile
97/J7 Santiago (cape), Chile
101/G4 Santiago, DRep.
112/B5 Santiago (riv.), Mex.
100/E6 Santiago, Pan.
100/E6 Santiago (mt.), Pan.
67/D4 Santiago, Phil.
115/C3 Santiago (peak), Ca,US
112/C4 Santiago (mts.), Tx,US
46/A1 Santiago de Compostela, Sp.
101/F4 Santiago de Cuba, Cuba
91/D2 Santiago del Estero, Arg.
96/Q9 Santiago (inset) (cap.), Chile
101/N9 Santiago Ixcuintla, Mex.
100/B4 Santiago Jamiltepec, Mex.
101/N8 Santiago Papasquiaro, Mex.
96/Q9 Santiago, Región Metropolitana de (reg.), Chile
45/H3 Säntis (peak), Swi.
47/K6 Sant Jeroni (mtn.), Sp.
47/K6 Sant Llorenc del Munt Nat'l Park, Sp.
65/K9 Santō, Japan
94/C4 Santo Amaro, Braz.
95/G8 Santo Amaro (isl.), Braz.
94/C3 Santo Amaro das Brotas, Braz.
95/B2 Santo Anastácio, Braz.

95/G8 Santo André, Braz.
91/F2 Santo Ângelo, Braz.
80/J9 Santo Antão (isl.), CpV.
82/G7 Santo António, SaoT.
94/C4 Santo Antônio de Jesus, Braz.
95/D2 Santo Antônio de Pádua, Braz.
101/H4 Santo Domingo (cap.), DRep.
92/C4 Santo Domingo de los Colorados, Ecu.
94/C4 Santo Estêvão, Braz.
47/E3 Santomera, Sp.
46/D1 Santoña, Sp.
94/B4 Santo Onofre (riv.), Braz.
49/J4 Santorini (Thíra), Gre.
95/G8 Santos, Braz.
95/K6 Santos Dumont, Braz.
101/L7 Santo Tomás, Mex.
101/N8 Santo Tomás, Mex.
96/E1 Santo Tomé, Arg.
47/K7 Sant Pere de Ribes, Sp.
47/K7 Sant Sadurní d'Anoia, Sp.
46/D1 Santurce-Antiguo, Sp.
47/K6 Sant Vincenç de Castellet, Sp.
47/L7 Sant Vincenç dels Hort, Sp.
96/B6 San Valentín (peak), Chile
96/C2 San Vicente, Chile
100/D5 San Vicente, ESal.
101/L7 San Vicente, Mex.
46/B3 San Vicente de Alcántara, Sp.
92/C6 San Vicente de Cañete, Peru
47/E3 San Vicente del Raspeig, Sp.
48/B1 San Vincenzo, It.
48/C3 San Vito (cape), It.
69/E2 Sanya, China
71/J4 Sanya, China
94/B2 São Benedito, Braz.
94/A1 São Bento, Braz.
94/C3 São Bento do Una, Braz.
95/G8 São Bernardo do Campo, Braz.
91/E2 São Borja, Braz.
94/C3 São Cristóvão, Braz.
95/B1 São Domingos (riv.), Braz.
94/A2 São Domingos do Maranhão, Braz.
95/D2 São Fidélis, Braz.
94/A4 São Francisco, Braz.
91/G2 São Francisco (isl.), Braz.
94/B3 São Francisco (mts.), Braz.
93/L5 São Francisco (riv.), Braz.
95/B3 São Francisco do Sul, Braz.
95/B4 São Fransisco de Paula, Braz.
91/F3 São Gabriel, Braz.
95/D1 São Gabriel da Palha, Braz.
95/K7 São Gonçalo, Braz.
95/H6 São Gonçalo do Sapucaí, Braz.
95/C1 São Gotardo, Braz.
95/C2 São Joachim da Barra, Braz.
93/K4 São João, Braz.
92/F5 São João (mts.), Braz.
95/D2 São João da Barra, Braz.
95/G6 São João da Boa Vista, Braz.
46/A2 São João da Madeira, Port.
47/P10 São João das Lampas, Port.
95/C2 São João del Rei, Braz.
95/K7 São João de Meriti, Braz.
94/B3 São João do Piauí, Braz.
94/B2 São João dos Patos, Braz.
95/K6 São João Nepomuceno, Braz.
95/B4 São Joaquim, Braz.
95/B4 São Joaquim Nat'l Park, Braz.
47/S12 São Jorge (isl.), Azor.,Port.
95/B3 São José, Braz.
94/D2 São José de Mipibu, Braz.
94/A1 São José de Ribamar, Braz.
94/C2 São José do Belmonte, Braz.
94/D2 São José do Campestre, Braz.
94/C2 São José do Egito, Braz.
95/A5 São José do Norte, Braz.
95/G6 São José do Rio Pardo, Braz.
95/B2 São José do Rio Preto, Braz.
95/H8 São José dos Campos, Braz.
95/B3 São José dos Pinhais, Braz.
95/B4 São Leopoldo, Braz.
95/H7 São Lourenço, Braz.
93/G7 São Lourenço (riv.), Braz.
95/B4 São Lourenço do Sul, Braz.
87/C3 São Lucas, Ang.
94/A1 São Luís, Braz.
94/D3 São Luís do Quitunde, Braz.
95/B2 São Manoel, Braz.
94/A1 São Marcos (bay), Braz.
94/A5 São Marcos (riv.), Braz.
95/E1 São Mateus, Braz.
94/A2 São Mateus do Maranhão, Braz.
95/B3 São Mateus do Sul, Braz.
94/C2 São Miguel, Braz.
47/T13 São Miguel (isl.), Azor.,Port.
95/C2 São Miguel Arcanjo, Braz.
94/C3 São Miguel dos Campos, Braz.
94/B2 São Miguel do Tapuio, Braz.
44/F3 Saône (riv.), Fr.
80/J10 São Nicolau (isl.), CpV.
95/G8 São Paulo, Braz.
95/H8 São Paulo (state), Braz.
92/E4 São Paulo de Olivença, Braz.
94/D2 São Paulo do Potengi, Braz.
95/D2 São Pedro da Aldeia, Braz.
94/B2 São Pedro do Piauí, Braz.
94/C2 São Rafael, Braz.
94/A2 São Raimundo das Mangabeiras, Braz.
94/B3 São Raimundo Nonato, Braz.
65/M9 Saori, Japan
94/A5 São Romão, Braz.
90/F3 São Roque (cape), Braz.
47/S12 São Roque do Pico, Azor.,Port.
95/H8 São Sebastião, Braz.
87/G5 São Sebastião (pt.), Moz.
95/C2 São Sebastião do Paraíso, Braz.
95/B1 São Simão (res.), Braz.
46/A4 São Teotónio, Port.
95/C2 São Tiago, Braz.
80/K10 São Tiago (isl.), CpV.
90/E5 São Tomé (cape), Braz.
82/G7 São Tomé (cap.), SaoT.
82/F7 São Tomé and Príncipe
82/E1 Saouru (dry riv.), Alg.
95/G8 São Vicente, Braz.
80/J10 São Vicente (isl.), CpV.
46/A4 São Vicente, Cabo de (cape), Port.
51/K5 Sapanca, Turk.
49/H1 Sapareva Banya, Bul.
94/D2 Sapé, Braz.
113/H4 Sapelo (isl.), Ga,US
49/G4 Sapiéndza (isl.), Gre.
40/D2 Sappemeer, Neth.
63/N3 Sapporo, Japan
48/D2 Sapri, It.
95/H7 Sapucaí (riv.), Braz.
60/E1 Saqqez, Iran
50/E4 Šar (mts.), Yugo.
60/E1 Sarāb, Iran
69/C3 Sara Buri, Thai.
47/E2 Saragossa (Zaragoza), Sp.
50/D4 Sarajevo (cap.), Bosn.
113/F4 Saraland, Al,US
72/D4 Saran (peak), Indo.
68/B2 Saran', Kaz.
110/F2 Saranac Lake, NY,US
49/L6 Sarandapótamos (riv.), Gre.
49/G3 Sarandë, Alb.
97/G2 Sarandí Del Yi, Uru.
70/C3 Sārangpur, India
55/H1 Saransk, Rus.
53/M4 Sarapul, Rus.
113/H5 Sarasota, Fl,US
116/K12 Saratoga, Ca,US
106/G5 Saratoga, Wy,US
110/F3 Saratoga Springs, NY,US
55/H2 Saratov, Rus.
55/J1 Saratov (res.), Rus.
55/H2 Saratov Obl., Rus.
72/D3 Sarawak (state), Malay.
59/B3 Saraykōy, Turk.
59/C2 Sarayōnü, Turk.
50/D2 Sárbogárd, Hun.
31/T10 Sarcelles, Fr.
70/B2 Sardārshahar, India
48/A2 Sardegna (reg.), It.
45/G5 Sardinaux, Cap de (cape), Fr.
48/A2 Sardinia (isl.), It.
109/K4 Sardis (lake), Ms,US
109/J4 Sardis (lake), Ok,US
37/F2 Sareks Nat'l Park, Swe.
37/F2 Sarektjåkko (peak), Swe.
73/E4 Sarempaka (peak), Indo.
61/K2 Sargodha, Pak.
83/J6 Sarh, Chad
60/F1 Sārī, Iran
73/J4 Saribi (cape), Indo.
78/D3 Sarigan (isl.), NMar.
59/E2 Sarıkamış, Turk.
59/C2 Sarıkaya, Turk.
45/G3 Sarine (riv.), Swi.
83/K2 Sarīr Kalanshiyū (des.), Libya
83/J3 Sarīr Tibasti (des.), Libya
112/D5 Sarita, Tx,US
50/E2 Sarkad, Hun.
55/L4 Sarkamyshskoye (lake), Trkm., Uzb.
56/H5 Sarkand, Kaz.
59/B2 Şarkîkaraağaç, Turk.
59/D2 Şarkışla, Turk.
51/H5 Şarköy, Turk.
44/D4 Sarlat-La-Canéda, Fr.
97/K8 Sarmiento (peak), Chile
45/H3 Sarnen, Swi.
116/H6 Sarnia, On,Can
54/C2 Sarny, Ukr.
49/H4 Saronic (gulf), Gre.
49/L7 Saronikós (gulf), Gre.
51/H5 Saros (gulf), Turk.
50/E1 Sárospatak, Hun.
43/F6 Sarre (riv.), Fr.
43/G6 Sarrebourg, Fr.
43/G5 Sarreguemines, Fr.
46/B1 Sarria, Sp.
41/G4 Sarstedt, Ger.
57/P3 Sartang (riv.), Rus.
44/C3 Sarthe (riv.), Fr.
31/S10 Sartrouville, Fr.
50/D2 Sárvíz (riv.), Hun.
68/C2 Sary Ishikotrau (des.), Kaz.
68/B2 Saryshagan, Kaz.
68/A2 Sarysu (riv.), Kaz.
45/H4 Sarzana, It.
107/K3 Saskatchewan (lake), Mb,Can
70/D3 Sasarām, India
65/L9 Sasayama, Japan
65/L9 Sasayama (riv.), Japan
64/A4 Sasebo, Japan
102/F3 Saskatchewan (prov.), Can.
106/F3 Saskatchewan (riv.), Can.
106/G2 Saskatoon, Sk,Can
100/D5 Saslaya (mt.), Nic.
55/G1 Sasovo, Rus.
84/D5 Sassandra, IvC.
84/D5 Sassandra (riv.), IvC.
48/A2 Sassari, It.
41/F5 Sassenberg, Ger.
40/B4 Sassenheim, Neth.
39/G1 Sassnitz, Ger.
45/J4 Sassuolo, It.
40/A6 Sas Van Gent, Neth.
68/D2 Sasykkol (lake), Kaz.
64/B5 Sata-misaki (cape), Japan
70/B4 Sātāra, India
78/E4 Satawan (atoll), Micr.
92/D6 Satipo, Peru
33/G2 Satley, Eng,UK
70/D3 Satna, India
50/E1 Sátoraljaújhely, Hun.
68/A2 Satpayev, Kaz.
70/C3 Satpura (range), India
50/F2 Satu Mare, Rom.
50/F2 Satu Mare (co.), Rom.
69/C5 Satun, Thai.
79/R9 Satupaitea, WSam.
96/E3 Sauce Grande (riv.), Arg.
60/D4 Saudi Arabia
43/F4 Sauer (riv.), Ger., Lux.
43/G1 Sauerland (reg.), Ger.
92/G6 Saúeruiná (riv.), Braz.
107/K4 Sauk (riv.), Mn,US
107/K4 Sauk Centre, Mn,US
107/K4 Sauk Rapids, Mn,US
44/D3 Sauldre (riv.), Fr.
110/C2 Sault Sainte Marie, On,Can
110/C2 Sault Sainte Marie, Mi,US
43/E6 Saulx (riv.), Fr.
76/D3 Saumarez (reefs), Austl.
44/C3 Saumur, Fr.
34/B3 Saundersfoot, Wal,UK
87/D2 Saurimo, Ang.
116/K11 Sausalito, Ca,US
31/S9 Sausseron (riv.), Fr.
50/C3 Sava (riv.), Eur.
48/E2 Sava, It.
79/H6 Savai'i (isl.), WSam.
111/G1 Savane (riv.), Qu,Can
113/H3 Savannah, Ga,US
113/H3 Savannah (riv.), Ga, SC,US
113/F3 Savannah, Tn,US
71/H4 Savannakhet, Laos
69/D2 Savannakhet, Laos
101/F4 Savanna-la-Mar, Jam.
110/B1 Savant (lake), On,Can
70/B4 Sāvantvādi, India
87/C4 Savate, Ang.
87/F5 Save (riv.), Moz., Zim.
60/F1 Sāveh, Iran
51/H2 Săveni, Rom.
43/G6 Saverne, Fr.
45/G4 Savigliano, It.
45/K4 Savignano sul Rubicone, It.
31/T11 Savigny-le-Temple, Fr.
31/T10 Savigny-sur-Orge, Fr.
45/K5 Savio (riv.), It.
106/C3 Savona, BC,Can
45/H4 Savona, It.
37/J3 Savonlinna, Fin.
37/E4 Sävsjö, Swe.
73/F5 Savu (sea), Indo.
72/B4 Sawahlunto, Indo.
86/D5 Sawākin, Sudan
69/B2 Sawankhalok, Thai.
65/G3 Sawara, Japan
65/F2 Sawasaki-bana (pt.), Japan
108/F3 Sawatch (range), Co,US
35/G3 Sawbridgeworth, Eng,UK
82/J2 Sawdā (mts.), Libya
60/D5 Sawdā', Jabal (mtn.), SAr.
83/L5 Sawdirī, Sudan
73/H4 Saweba (cape), Indo.
32/A2 Sawel (mtn.), NI,UK
86/B3 Sawhāj, Egypt
86/B3 Sawhāj (gov.), Egypt
71/F6 Sāwi, India
60/G5 Sawqirah, Ghubbat (bay), Oman
35/G2 Sawston, Eng,UK
77/E1 Sawtell, Austl.
106/E4 Sawtooth (range), Id,US
73/F6 Sawu (isls.), Indo.
47/E3 Sax, Sp.
33/H5 Saxilby, Eng,UK
35/H2 Saxmundham, Eng,UK
39/G3 Saxony (state), Ger.
38/F3 Saxony-Anhalt (state), Ger.
65/F3 Sayama, Japan
100/D3 Sayil (ruins), Mex.
43/G2 Saynbach (riv.), Ger.
68/D3 Sayram (lake), China
115/F5 Sayreville, NJ,US
115/G5 Sayville, NY,US
49/F2 Sazan (isl.), Alb.
45/L2 Sázava (riv.), Czh.
33/E3 Scafell Pikes (mtn.), Eng,UK
33/H3 Scalby, Eng,UK
48/D3 Scalea, It.
45/J5 Scandicci, It.
67/C4 Scarborough (shoal)
111/R8 Scarborough, On,Can
33/H3 Scarborough, Eng,UK
42/B3 Scarpe (riv.), Fr.
115/G4 Scarsdale, NY,US
32/E1 Scar Water (riv.), Sc,UK
31/S10 Sceaux, Fr.
42/D2 Schaerbeek, Belg.
45/H3 Schaffhausen, Swi.
40/B3 Schagen, Neth.
40/C5 Schaijk, Neth.
41/E6 Schalksmühle, Ger.
77/C3 Schanck (cape), Austl.
41/F1 Scharhorn (isl.), Ger.
116/P15 Schaumburg, Il,US
40/D2 Scheemda, Neth.
41/G2 Scheessel, Ger.
42/C2 Schelde (Scheldt) (riv.), Belg.
108/D3 Schell Creek (range), Nv,US
41/H4 Schellerten, Ger.
110/F3 Schenectady, NY,US
41/G1 Schenefeld, Ger.
116/R16 Schererville, In,US
40/D5 Schermbeck, Ger.
40/C3 Scherpenzeel, Neth.
40/B5 Schiedam, Neth.
41/G5 Schieder-Schwalenberg, Ger.
40/D2 Schiermonnikoog (isl.), Neth.
43/G5 Schiffweiler, Ger.
40/C5 Schijndel, Neth.
42/D1 Schilde, Belg.
40/D2 Schildmeer (lake), Neth.
41/F1 Schillighörn (cape), Ger.
43/G6 Schiltigheim, Fr.
43/E2 Schinnen, Neth.
40/D4 Schipbeek (riv.), Neth.
49/G2 Schkumbin (riv.), Alb.
45/J3 Schlanders (Silandro), It.
41/F5 Schlangen, Ger.
43/F2 Schleiden, Ger.
38/E1 Schleswig, Ger.
41/H1 Schleswig-Holstein (state), Ger.
38/E1 Schleswig-Holsteinisches Wattenmeer Nat'l Park, Ger.
41/F5 Schloss Holte-Stukenbrock, Ger.
45/H1 Schlüchtern, Ger.
38/F3 Schmalkalden, Ger.
41/F6 Schmallenberg, Ger.
43/F5 Schmelz, Ger.
43/F3 Schneifel (upland), Ger.
41/G2 Schneverdingen, Ger.
104/V12 Schofield Barracks, Hi,US
97/L7 Scholl, Cerro (mtn.), Arg.
38/F2 Schönebeck, Ger.
38/F2 Schöningen, Ger.
40/D3 Schoonebeek, Neth.
40/B5 Schoonhoven, Neth.
40/B3 Schoorl, Neth.
41/E1 Schortens, Ger.
42/D1 Schoten, Belg.
77/D4 Schouten (isl.), Austl.
78/C5 Schouten (isls.), Indo.
40/A5 Schouwen (isl.), Neth.
44/D5 Schrader (peak), Fr.
82/H3 Şchrā Marzūq (des.), Libya
45/H2 Schramberg, Ger.
110/C1 Schreiber, On,Can
88/B2 Schroffenstein (peak), Namb.
112/D4 Schulenburg, Tx,US
41/H4 Schunter (riv.), Ger.
41/E4 Schüttorf, Ger.
115/E5 Schuylkill (riv.), Pa,US
45/J2 Schwabach, Ger.
45/H2 Schwäbische Alb (range), Ger.
45/H2 Schwäbisch Hall, Ger.
43/F5 Schwalbach, Ger.
41/G6 Schwalm (riv.), Ger.
40/D6 Schwalmtal, Ger.
45/K2 Schwandorf im Bayern, Ger.
72/D4 Schwaner (mts.), Indo.
41/F2 Schwanewede, Ger.
39/G3 Schwartz Elster (riv.), Ger.
88/B2 Schwartzerberg (peak), Namb.
41/H2 Schwarzenbek, Ger.
43/F3 Schwarzer Mann (peak), Ger.
45/J3 Schwaz, Aus.
39/J4 Schwechat, Aus.
39/H2 Schwedt, Ger.
45/J1 Schweinfurt, Ger.
41/E6 Schwelm, Ger.
38/F2 Schwerin, Ger.
38/F2 Schweriner (lake), Ger.
41/E6 Schwerte, Ger.
41/G1 Schwinge (riv.), Ger.
41/G5 Schwülme (riv.), Ger.
45/H3 Schwyz, Swi.
48/C4 Sciacca, It.
48/D4 Scicli, It.
110/D4 Scioto (riv.), Oh,US
107/G3 Scobey, Mt,US
35/G1 Scolt (pt.), UK
48/D4 Scordia, It.
33/G3 Scotch Corner, Eng,UK
115/F5 Scotch Plains, NJ,US
98/W Scotia (sea), Ant.
36/C2 Scotland, UK
98/M Scott, Ant.
98/L Scott (coast), Ant.
74/C2 Scott (reef), Austl.
102/D3 Scott (cape), BC,Can
103/R7 Scott (cape), NW,Can
102/F2 Scott (lake), NW,Can
109/G3 Scott City, Ks,US
109/G2 Scottsbluff, Ne,US
109/F2 Scotts Bluff Nat'l Mon., Ne,US
113/G3 Scottsboro, Al,US
110/C4 Scottsburg, In,US
108/E4 Scottsdale, Az,US
77/C4 Scotts Peak (dam), Austl.
110/C4 Scottsville, Ky,US
110/C3 Scottville, Mi,US
33/H4 Scunthorpe, Eng,UK
50/D4 Scutari (lake), Alb., Yugo.
105/K5 Sea (isls.), Ga,US
35/G5 Seaford, UK
32/C3 Seaforde, NI,UK
33/G2 Seaham, Eng,UK
103/H2 Seahorse (pt.), NW,Can
102/G3 Seal (riv.), Mb,Can
96/B5 Seal (pt.), Chile
88/C4 Seal (cape), SAfr.
31/P8 Seal, Eng,UK
115/B3 Seal Beach, Ca,US
33/H3 Seamer, Eng,UK
108/D4 Searchlight, Nv,US
112/F3 Searcy, Ar,US
32/E3 Seascale, Eng,UK
106/C4 Seaside, Or,US
116/C3 SeaTac, Wa,US
34/C5 Seaton, Eng,UK
34/B6 Seaton (riv.), Eng,UK
33/G2 Seaton Carew, Eng,UK
33/G1 Seaton Valley, Eng,UK
116/C2 Seattle, Wa,US
81/T15 Sebaou (riv.), Alg.
113/H5 Sebastian, Fl,US
101/M8 Sebastián Vizcaíno (bay), Mex.
77/B3 Sebastopol, Austl.
72/D4 Sebayan (peak), Indo.
81/Q16 Sebdou, Alg.
51/F3 Sebeş, Rom.
59/D2 Şebinkarahisar, Turk.
50/F2 Sebiş, Rom.
39/H3 Sebnitz, Ger.
73/F2 Seboto (pt.), Phil.
81/M13 Sebou (riv.), Mor.
113/H5 Sebring, Fl,US
73/E4 Sebuku (isl.), Indo.
45/J4 Secchia (riv.), It.
92/B5 Sechura, Peru
92/B5 Sechura (bay), Peru
92/B5 Sechura (des.), Peru
42/C2 Seclin, Fr.
97/L7 Seco (riv.), Arg.
70/C4 Secunderābād, India
92/E7 Securé (riv.), Bol.
109/J3 Sedalia, Mo,US
43/D4 Sedan, Fr.
69/B3 Sedaung (mtn.), Burma
33/F3 Sedbergh, Eng,UK
86/B4 Seddenga Temple (ruins), Sudan
59/K6 Sederot, Isr.
33/G2 Sedgefield, Eng,UK
114/L2 Sedgwick (mtn.), Yk,Can
84/B3 Sédhiou, Sen.
45/L1 Sedlo (peak), Czh.
108/E4 Sedona, Az,US
81/V17 Sedrata, Alg.
39/L3 Sędziszów, Pol.
44/C2 Sée (riv.), Fr.
88/D3 Seekooi (riv.), SAfr.
41/H5 Seesen, Ger.
41/G2 Seeve (riv.), Ger.
81/M14 Sefrou, Mor.
72/B3 Segamat, Malay.
51/F3 Segarcea, Rom.
48/C4 Segesta (ruins), It.
52/G3 Segezha, Rus.
47/E3 Segorbe, Sp.
84/D3 Ségou, Mali
84/D3 Ségou (reg.), Mali
46/C2 Segovia, Sp.
52/G3 Segozero (lake), Rus.
44/C3 Segré, Fr.
47/F2 Segre (riv.), Sp.
114/D5 Seguam (isl.), Ak,US
82/H3 Séguédine, Niger
84/D5 Séguéla, IvC.
112/D4 Seguin, Tx,US
46/D3 Segura (riv.), Sp.
87/D5 Sehithwa, Bots.
70/C3 Sehore, India
61/J3 Sehwān, Pak.
65/L10 Seika, Japan
109/H3 Seiling, Ok,US
43/F6 Seille (riv.), Fr.
37/G3 Seinäjoki, Fin.
107/L3 Seine (riv.), On,Can
44/C2 Seine (bay), Fr.
44/D2 Seine (riv.), Fr.
31/U10 Seine-et-Marne (dept.), Fr.
31/T10 Seine-Saint-Denis (dept.), Fr.
37/G3 Seitsemisen Nat'l Park, Fin.
65/M10 Seiwa, Japan
65/E3 Seki, Japan
65/M9 Sekigahara, Japan
65/H6 Sekiyado, Japan
85/E5 Sekondi, Gha.
106/C4 Selah, Wa,US
48/A3 Selargius, It.
73/H5 Selaru (isl.), Indo.
72/D4 Selatan (cape), Indo.
114/F2 Selawik (lake), Ak,US
73/F5 Selayar (isl.), Indo.
45/K1 Selb, Ger.
33/G4 Selby, Eng,UK
107/H4 Selby, SD,US
115/G5 Selden, NY,US
48/D2 Sele (riv.), It.
87/E5 Selebi-Phikwe, Bots.
63/L1 Selemdzha (riv.), Rus.
62/F1 Selenga (riv.), Rus.
62/E2 Selenge, Mong.
62/E2 Selenge (riv.), Mong.
45/G2 Sélestat, Fr.
68/B1 Selety (riv.), Kaz.
68/B1 Seletyteniz (lake), Kaz.
52/G4 Seliger (lake), Rus.
108/D4 Seligman, Az,US
48/C4 Selinunte (ruins), It.
106/D3 Selkirk (mts.), BC,Can
107/J3 Selkirk, Mb,Can
36/D3 Selkirk, Sc,UK
108/E5 Sells, Az,US
34/E2 Selly Oak, Eng,UK
41/E5 Selm, Ger.
113/G3 Selma, Al,US
113/F3 Selmer, Tn,US
114/M3 Selous (mtn.), Yk,Can
35/F5 Selsey, Eng,UK
35/F5 Selsey Bill (pt.), Eng,UK
44/C2 Sélune (riv.), Fr.
92/E5 Selvas (for.), Braz.
45/H2 Selz (riv.), Ger.
82/C2 Semara, WSah.
72/D5 Semarang, Indo.
59/F3 Şemdinli, Turk.
53/K4 Semenov, Rus.
72/D5 Semeru (peak), Indo.
114/G4 Semidi (isls.), Ak,US
54/F2 Semiluki, Rus.
106/G5 Seminoe (res.), Wy,US
113/G4 Seminole (lake), Ga,US
112/C3 Seminole, Tx,US
68/D1 Semipalatinsk, Kaz.
114/B5 Semisopochnoi (isl.), Ak,US
72/D4 Semitau, Indo.
60/F1 Semnān, Iran
44/C3 Semnon (riv.), Fr.
43/E4 Semois (riv.), Belg.
43/D4 Semoy (riv.), Fr.
52/B2 Semskefjellet (peak), Nor.
69/D3 Sen (riv.), Camb.
69/C3 Sena, Thai.
94/C2 Senador Pompeu, Braz.
67/C6 Senaja, Malay.
87/D4 Senanga, Zam.
113/F3 Senatobia, Ms,US
35/E2 Sence (riv.), Eng,UK
64/B5 Sendai, Japan
65/G1 Sendai (bay), Japan
64/B5 Sendai (riv.), Japan
64/D3 Sendai (riv.), Japan
41/E5 Senden, Ger.
41/E5 Sendenhorst, Ger.
39/J4 Senec, Slvk.
42/D2 Seneffe, Belg.
84/B3 Senegal
84/B2 Sénégal (riv.), Afr.
88/D3 Senekal, SAfr.
39/H3 Senftenberg, Ger.
68/D5 Sêngê (riv.), China
96/C5 Senguerr (riv.), Arg.
94/B3 Senhor do Bonfim, Braz.
39/J4 Senica, Slvk.
45/K5 Senigallia, It.
59/B2 Senirkent, Turk.
48/E2 Senise, It.
50/B3 Senj, Cro.
37/F1 Senja (isl.), Nor.
42/B5 Senlis, Fr.
65/L10 Sennan, Japan
83/M5 Sennar (dam), Sudan
42/D2 Senne (riv.), Belg.
110/E1 Senneterre, Qu,Can
34/C3 Sennybridge, Wal,UK
85/F3 Séno (prov.), Burk.
44/E2 Sens, Fr.
50/E3 Senta, Yugo.
87/E2 Sentery, Zaire
106/C2 Sentinel (peak), BC,Can
78/E4 Senyavin (isls.), Micr.
70/C3 Seoni, India
70/C3 Seonī Mālwā, India
63/K4 Seoul (Sŏul) (cap.), SKor.
95/K8 Sepetiba (bay), Braz.
78/D5 Sepik (riv.), PNG
39/J2 Sępólno Krajeńskie, Pol.
51/G4 Septemvri, Bul.
111/H1 Sept-Îles, Qu,Can
116/A1 Sequim (bay), Wa,US
108/C3 Sequoia Nat'l Park, Ca,US
43/E2 Seraing, Belg.
72/C5 Serang, Indo.
72/C3 Serasan (str.), Indo., Malay.
50/E4 Serbia (rep.), Yugo.
55/H1 Serdobsk, Rus.
114/D2 Serdtse-Kamen, Mys (pt.), Rus.
59/C2 Şereflikoçhisar, Turk.
44/F3 Serein (riv.), Fr.
72/B3 Seremban, Malay.
87/F1 Serengeti (plain), Tanz.
87/F1 Serengeti Nat'l Park, Tanz.
87/F3 Serenje, Zam.
53/K5 Sergach, Rus.
56/J2 Sergeya Kirova (isls.), Rus.
94/C3 Sergipe (state), Braz.
52/H4 Sergiyev Posad, Rus.
72/D3 Seria, Bru.
45/H4 Seriate, It.
49/J4 Sérifos (isl.), Gre.
59/B3 Serik, Turk.
93/H5 Seringa (mts.), Braz.
59/B3 Serinhisar, Turk.
73/G5 Sermata (isl.), Indo.
56/G4 Serov, Rus.
87/E5 Serowe, Bots.
46/B4 Serpa, Port.
48/A3 Serpeddi (peak), It.
74/D5 Serpentine (lakes), Austl.
84/C3 Serpent, Vallée du (wadi), Mali
52/H5 Serpukhov, Rus.
95/D2 Serra, Braz.
95/J8 Serra da Bocaina Nat'l Park, Braz.
95/C2 Serra da Canastra Nat'l Park, Braz.
94/B3 Serra de Capivara Nat'l Park, Braz.
95/D1 Serra do Cipo Nat'l Park, Braz.
95/K7 Serra dos Órgãos Nat'l Park, Braz.
49/H2 Sérrai, Gre.
48/E3 Serralta di San Vito (peak), It.
48/A3 Serramanna, It.
101/F5 Serrana (bank), Col.
92/E3 Serranía de la Neblina Nat'l Park, Ven.
101/F4 Serranilla (bank), Col.
81/W17 Serrat (cape), Tun.
94/C2 Serra Talhada, Braz.
42/C4 Serre (riv.), Fr.
94/C3 Serrinha, Braz.
46/A3 Sertã, Port.
94/C3 Sertânia, Braz.
95/C2 Sertãozinho, Braz.
62/C4 Serteng (mts.), China
72/D4 Seruyan (riv.), Indo.
86/B4 Sesebi (ruins), Sudan
45/H4 Sesia (riv.), It.
46/A3 Sesimbra, Port.
46/D1 Sestao, Sp.
45/J5 Sesto Fiorentino, It.
45/H4 Sesto San Giovanni, It.
48/A3 Sestu, It.
50/C3 Sesvete, Cro.
44/E5 Sète, Fr.
94/B2 Sete Cidades Nat'l Park, Braz.
95/C1 Sete Lagoas, Braz.
61/J3 Sethārja, Pak.
81/U17 Sétif, Alg.
65/E3 Seto, Japan
64/C3 Seto-Naikai Nat'l Park, Japan
45/G4 Settimo Torinese, It.
107/J2 Setting (lake), Mb,Can
33/F3 Settle, Eng,UK
65/L10 Settsu, Japan
46/A3 Setúbal, Port.
47/Q11 Setúbal (bay), Port.
46/A3 Setúbal (dist.), Port.
44/C4 Seudre (riv.), Fr.
44/C4 Seugne (riv.), Fr.
110/A1 Seul (lake), On,Can
55/H4 Sevan (lake), Arm.
54/E3 Sevastopol', Ukr.
36/G7 Seven Hogs, The (isls.), Ire.
31/P8 Sevenoaks, Eng,UK
107/L2 Severn (riv.), On,Can
34/D3 Severn (riv.), Eng,UK
115/K7 Severn, Md,US
115/K7 Severna Park, Md,US
53/P3 Severnaya Sos'va (riv.), Rus.
58/K2 Severnaya Zemlya (arch.), Rus.
34/C4 Severn, Mouth of the (estuary), Eng,UK
53/Q2 Severnyy, Rus.
39/G3 Severočeský (reg.), Czh.
54/F2 Severodonetsk, Ukr.
52/H2 Severodvinsk, Rus.
57/R4 Severo-Kuril'sk, Rus.
39/J4 Severomoravský (reg.), Czh.
52/G1 Severomorsk, Rus.
53/N3 Severoural'sk, Rus.
108/D3 Sevier (des.), Ut,US
108/D3 Sevier (riv.), Ut,US
113/H3 Sevierville, Tn,US
46/C4 Seville, Sp.
51/G4 Sevlievo, Bul.
31/T10 Sevran, Fr.
31/S10 Sèvres, Fr.
84/C5 Sewa (riv.), SLeo.
114/E2 Seward (pen.), Ak,US
109/H2 Seward, Ne,US
114/M5 Sewell Inlet, BC,Can
106/D2 Sexsmith, Ab,Can
81/V17 Seybouse (riv.), Alg.
81/H5 Seychelles
59/B3 Seydişehir, Turk.
59/C2 Seyhan (riv.), Turk.
77/C3 Seymour, Austl.
112/D3 Seymour, Tx,US
42/C6 Sézanne, Fr.
46/A3 Sezimbra, Port.
48/C2 Sezze, It.
51/G3 Sfintu Gheorghe, Rom.
81/Q16 Sfizef, Alg.
40/C4 's-Graveland, Neth.
40/B5 's-Gravendeel, Neth.
40/B4 's-Gravenhage (The Hague) (cap.), Neth.
36/C2 Sgurr Mór (mtn.), Sc,UK
66/C4 Sha (riv.), China
66/B4 Shaanxi (prov.), China
83/P7 Shabeelle, Webi (riv.), Som.
87/E1 Shabunda, Zaire
98/M Shackleton (coast), Ant.
98/G Shackleton Ice Shelf, Ant.
53/P4 Shadrinsk, Rus.
112/B4 Shafter, Tx,US
34/D4 Shaftesbury, Eng,UK
68/C2 Shagan (riv.), Kaz.
61/J3 Shāhdādkot, Pak.
61/J3 Shāhdādpur, Pak.
70/D3 Shahdol, India
83/K1 Shaḩḩāt, Libya
70/C2 Shāhjahānpur, India
61/K3 Shahpura, India
70/A2 Shāhpur Chākar, Pak.
86/C3 Shā'ib al Banāt, Jabal (mtn.), Egypt
70/C3 Shājāpur, India
61/L2 Shakargarh, Pak.
87/D4 Shakawe, Bots.
56/H5 Shakhtinsk, Kaz.
54/G3 Shakhty, Rus.
52/K4 Shakhun'ya, Rus.
55/H4 Shalbuzdag, Gora (peak), Rus.
34/C5 Shaldon, Eng,UK
87/F2 Shama (riv.), Tanz.
59/J6 Shamal Sīnā' (gov.), Egypt
107/M2 Shamattawa (riv.), On,Can
70/C3 Shāmgarh, India
70/C2 Shāmli, India
60/D3 Shammar, Jabal (mts.), SAr.
114/L3 Shamrock (mtn.), Yk,Can
112/C3 Shamrock, Tx,US
69/B1 Shan (plat.), Burma
69/B1 Shan (state), Burma
81/W18 Sha'nabī, Jabal ash (peak), Tun.
83/M4 Shandī, Sudan
66/D3 Shandong (pen.), China
66/C5 Shangcheng, China
66/E5 Shanghai, China
66/L8 Shanghai (inset), China
66/C4 Shangqiu, China
67/C2 Shangrao, China
35/E5 Shanklin, Eng,UK
36/A4 Shannon (riv.), Ire.
57/P4 Shantar (isls.), Rus.
67/C3 Shantou, China
67/B3 Shaoguan, China
67/D2 Shaoxing, China
67/B2 Shaoyang, China
33/F2 Shap, Eng,UK
98/L Shapeless (peak), Ant.
53/M2 Shapkina (riv.), Rus.
59/F3 Shaqlāwah, Iraq
61/G5 Sharbatāt, Ra's ash (pt.), Oman
74/A5 Shark (bay), Austl.
86/C3 Sharm ash Shaykh, Egypt
35/F2 Sharnbrook, Eng,UK
110/D3 Sharon, Pa,US
107/K2 Sharpe (lake), Mb,Can
107/J4 Sharpe (lake), SD,US
53/K4 Shar'ya, Rus.

83/N6 **Shashemenē**, Eth.
66/C5 **Shashi**, China
108/B2 **Shasta** (dam), Ca,US
108/B2 **Shasta** (peak), Ca,US
54/B2 **Shatskiy Nat'l Park**, Ukr.
82/G1 **Shaṭṭ al Jarīd** (dry lake), Tun.
109/H3 **Shattuck**, Ok,US
106/F3 **Shaunavon**, Sk,Can
35/E4 **Shaw**, Eng,UK
110/B2 **Shawano**, Wi,US
111/M6 **Shawbridge**, Qu,Can
34/D1 **Shawbury**, Eng,UK
111/F2 **Shawinigan**, Qu,Can
109/H4 **Shawnee**, Ok,US
59/E3 **Shaykhān**, Iraq
54/C1 **Shchara** (riv.), Bela.
54/F1 **Shchekino**, Rus.
53/X9 **Shchelkovo**, Rus.
54/F2 **Shchigry**, Rus.
68/B1 **Shchuchinsk**, Kaz.
83/P6 **Shebelē Wenz** (riv.), Eth.
61/J1 **Sheberghān**, Afg.
110/C3 **Sheboygan**, Wi,US
111/H2 **Shediac**, NB,Can
32/A4 **Sheelin, Lough** (lake), Ire.
114/F2 **Sheep** (mtn.), Ak,US
40/D5 **'s-Heerenberg**, Neth.
33/G5 **Sheffield**, Eng,UK
113/G3 **Sheffield**, Al,US
35/F2 **Shefford**, Eng,UK
83/P6 **Shēh Husēn**, Eth.
97/K7 **Shehuen** (riv.), Arg.
110/C1 **Shekak** (riv.), On,Can
61/K2 **Shekhūpura**, Pak.
55/H4 **Sheki**, Azer.
57/T2 **Shelagskiy** (cape), Rus.
111/H3 **Shelburne**, NS,Can
113/F3 **Shelby**, Ms,US
106/F3 **Shelby**, Mt,US
113/H3 **Shelby**, NC,US
113/F2 **Shelbyville** (lake), Il,US
110/C4 **Shelbyville**, In,US
113/G3 **Shelbyville**, Tn,US
57/R3 **Shelekhov** (gulf), Rus.
114/H4 **Shelikof** (str.), Ak,US
107/G2 **Shellbrook**, Sk,Can
110/B2 **Shell Lake**, Wi,US
107/K5 **Shell Rock** (riv.), Ia,US
116/A3 **Shelton**, Wa,US
55/J4 **Shemakha**, Azer.
114/A5 **Shemya** (isl.), Ak,US
107/K5 **Shenandoah**, Ia,US
110/E4 **Shenandoah Nat'l Park**, Va,US
84/B5 **Shenge** (pt.), SLeo.
68/E3 **Shengli Daban** (pass), China
66/B5 **Shennongjia**, China
35/E1 **Shenstone**, Eng,UK
63/J3 **Shenyang**, China
71/K3 **Shenzhen**, China
70/B2 **Sheoganj**, India
70/C2 **Sheopur**, India
54/C2 **Shepetovka**, Ukr.
112/E4 **Shepherd**, Tx,US
78/F6 **Shepherd** (isls.), Van.
35/G4 **Sheppey** (isl.), Eng,UK
35/E1 **Shepshed**, Eng,UK
34/D4 **Shepton Mallet**, Eng,UK
103/H1 **Sherard** (cape), NW,Can
34/D5 **Sherborne**, Eng,UK
84/B5 **Sherbro** (isl.), SLeo.
111/G2 **Sherbrooke**, Qu,Can
33/G2 **Sherburn**, Eng,UK
85/H4 **Shere** (hill), Nga.
70/D3 **Sherghāti**, India
112/E3 **Sheridan**, Ar,US
106/G4 **Sheridan**, Wy,US
35/H1 **Sheringham**, Eng,UK
112/D3 **Sherman**, Tx,US
40/C5 **'s-Hertogenbosch**, Neth.
106/E2 **Sherwood Park**, Ab,Can
30/C2 **Shetland** (isls.), Sc,UK
55/J4 **Shevchenko**, Kaz.
66/D4 **Sheyang** (riv.), China
107/J4 **Sheyenne** (riv.), ND,US
66/C4 **Shi** (riv.), China
116/E6 **Shiawassee** (riv.), Mi,US
65/F2 **Shibata**, Japan
86/B2 **Shibīn al Kaum**, Egypt
107/L2 **Shibogama** (lake), On,Can
64/B5 **Shibushi** (bay), Japan
68/B1 **Shiderty** (riv.), Kaz.
64/D3 **Shido**, Japan
34/D1 **Shifnal**, Eng,UK
55/L9 **Shiga**, Japan
64/E3 **Shiga** (pref.), Japan
65/M10 **Shigaraki**, Japan
66/C3 **Shigu Shan** (mtn.), China
68/E3 **Shihezi**, China
49/F2 **Shijak**, Alb.
66/C3 **Shijiazhuang**, China
61/J3 **Shikārpur**, Pak.
65/M9 **Shikatsu**, Japan
65/H7 **Shiki**, Japan
64/C4 **Shikoku** (isl.), Japan
64/C4 **Shikoku** (mts.), Japan
63/P3 **Shikotan** (isl.), Rus.
33/G2 **Shildon**, Eng,UK
62/H1 **Shilka**, Rus.
63/H1 **Shilka** (riv.), Rus.
61/L2 **Shilla** (mtn.), India
59/N8 **Shillo, Naḥal** (dry riv.), WBnk.
71/F2 **Shillong**, India
62/D2 **Shilüüstey**, Mong.
65/M10 **Shima** (pen.), Japan
64/B4 **Shimabara**, Japan
64/D3 **Shimamoto**, Japan
64/C3 **Shimane** (pref.), Japan
63/K1 **Shimanovsk**, Rus.
65/M9 **Shimasahi**, Japan
83/Q5 **Shimber Berris** (peak), Som.
71/H2 **Shimian**, China
65/F3 **Shimizu**, Japan
65/F3 **Shimoda**, Japan
65/F2 **Shimodate**, Japan
70/C5 **Shimoga**, India
65/L10 **Shimoichi**, Japan
64/A5 **Shimo-koshiki** (isl.), Japan
64/B4 **Shimonoseki**, Japan
65/F2 **Shinano** (riv.), Japan
61/H2 **Shindand**, Afg.
64/D4 **Shingū**, Japan
64/C3 **Shinji** (lake), Japan
63/N4 **Shinjō**, Japan
65/M9 **Shinkawa**, Japan
65/E2 **Shinminato**, Japan
65/M9 **Shinsei**, Japan
87/F1 **Shinyanga**, Tanz.
65/G1 **Shiogama**, Japan
64/D4 **Shio-no-misaki** (cape), Japan
31/P8 **Shipbourne**, Eng,UK
33/G4 **Shipley**, Eng,UK
111/H2 **Shippegan**, NB,Can
65/M9 **Shippo**, Japan
108/E3 **Shiprock**, NM,US
35/E2 **Shipston on Stour**, Eng,UK
68/C5 **Shipuqi Shankou** (pass), China
60/F2 **Shīr** (mtn.), Iran
65/H8 **Shirahama**, Japan
64/E3 **Shirakawa-tōge** (pass), Japan
65/F3 **Shirane-san** (mtn.), Japan
65/H6 **Shiraoka**, Japan
60/F3 **Shīrāz**, Iran
59/H6 **Shirbīn**, Egypt
33/G1 **Shiremoor**, Eng,UK
66/C5 **Shirjiu** (lake), China
65/J7 **Shiroi**, Japan
65/G2 **Shiroishi**, Japan
65/F2 **Shirone**, Japan
65/H7 **Shiroyama**, Japan
61/G1 **Shīrvān**, Iran
66/D2 **Shi San Ling**, China
114/F5 **Shishaldin** (vol.), Ak,US
62/D1 **Shishhid** (riv.), Mong.
66/C5 **Shishou**, China
65/J7 **Shisui**, Japan
70/C2 **Shivpurī**, India
66/B4 **Shiyan**, China
62/F4 **Shizuishan**, China
63/N3 **Shizunai**, Japan
65/F3 **Shizuoka**, Japan
65/F3 **Shizuoka** (pref.), Japan
49/F1 **Shkodër**, Alb.
49/G2 **Shkumbin** (riv.), Alb.
114/C2 **Shmidta, Mys** (pt.), Rus.
77/D2 **Shoalhaven** (riv.), Austl.
107/H3 **Shoal Lake**, Mb,Can
76/C3 **Shoalwater** (bay), Austl.
64/C3 **Shōbara**, Japan
64/D3 **Shōdō** (isl.), Japan
35/G3 **Shoeburyness**, Eng,UK
70/C4 **Sholāpur**, India
59/N8 **Shomron** (ruins), WBnk.
65/M9 **Shonai** (riv.), Japan
65/J7 **Shōnan**, Japan
70/C4 **Shorāpur**, India
35/F5 **Shoreham by Sea**, Eng,UK
116/P16 **Shorewood**, Il,US
116/Q13 **Shorewood**, Wi,US
61/K2 **Shorkot**, Pak.
76/F6 **Shorncliffe**, Austl.
113/G3 **Short** (peak), Tn,US
78/E5 **Shortland** (isl.), Sol.
35/E5 **Shorwell**, Eng,UK
108/C3 **Shoshone** (mts.), Nv,US
106/F4 **Shoshone** (riv.), Wy,US
106/F5 **Shoshoni**, Wy,US
54/E2 **Shostka**, Ukr.
35/H3 **Shotley**, Eng,UK
33/G2 **Shotton**, Eng,UK
65/H7 **Shōwa**, Japan
108/E4 **Show Low**, Az,US
54/D2 **Shpola**, Ukr.
112/E3 **Shreveport**, La,US
34/D1 **Shrewsbury**, Eng,UK
34/D1 **Shropshire** (co.), Eng,UK
33/F6 **Shropshire Union** (can.), Eng,UK
66/D4 **Shu** (riv.), China
66/D5 **Shu** (riv.), China
63/K3 **Shuangyang**, China
63/L2 **Shuangyashan**, China
59/H6 **Shubrā Khīt**, Egypt
59/K6 **Shu'fāṭ**, WBnk.
66/D5 **Shuiyang** (riv.), China
61/K3 **Shujāābād**, Pak.
62/D4 **Shule** (riv.), China
114/G4 **Shumagin** (isls.), Ak,US
51/H4 **Shumen**, Bul.
53/K5 **Shumerlya**, Rus.
68/B2 **Shunak, Gora** (peak), Kaz.
66/C3 **Shuo Xian**, China
61/G2 **Shūr** (riv.), Iran
87/F4 **Shurugwi**, Zim.
68/F1 **Shushenskoye**, Rus.
60/E2 **Shūshtar**, Iran
106/D3 **Shuswap** (lake), BC,Can
83/N5 **Shuwak**, Sudan
52/J4 **Shuya**, Rus.
69/A1 **Shwebo**, Burma
69/B2 **Shwemawdaw Pagoda** (ruins), Burma
68/C5 **Shyok** (riv.), India
61/H2 **Siāh** (mts.), Afg.
72/B3 **Siak** (riv.), Indo.
61/K2 **Siālkot**, Pak.
67/E6 **Siargao** (isl.), Phil.
67/D6 **Siasi**, Phil.
73/F2 **Siaton** (pt.), Phil.
73/G3 **Siau** (isl.), Indo.
52/D5 **Šiauliai**, Lith.
67/D5 **Sibalom**, Phil.
55/L1 **Sibay**, Rus.
50/B4 **Šibenik**, Cro.
56/K3 **Siberia** (reg.), Rus.
61/J3 **Sibi**, Pak.
83/N7 **Sibiloi Nat'l Park**, Kenya
87/B1 **Sibiti**, Congo
51/G3 **Sibiu**, Rom.
51/G2 **Sibiu** (co.), Rom.
35/G3 **Sible Hedingham**, Eng,UK
72/A3 **Sibolga**, Indo.
71/F2 **Sibsāgar**, India
73/F2 **Sibuco**, Phil.
73/F2 **Sibuko**, Phil.
73/F1 **Sibuyan** (isl.), Phil.
67/D5 **Sibuyan** (sea), Phil.
106/D3 **Sicamous**, BC,Can
71/H2 **Sichuan** (prov.), China
48/C4 **Sicilia** (reg.), It.
48/C3 **Sicily** (isl.), It.
48/B4 **Sicily** (str.), It., Tun.
100/D4 **Sico** (riv.), Hon.
92/D6 **Sicuani**, Peru
50/D3 **Šid**, Yugo.
31/P7 **Sidcup**, Eng,UK
70/C4 **Siddipet**, India
48/E3 **Siderno Marina**, It.
95/B4 **Siderópolis**, Braz.
115/C1 **Sidewinder** (mtn.), Ca,US
49/F3 **Sidhári**, Gre.
70/D3 **Sidhi**, India
49/H2 **Sidhirókastron**, Gre.
70/B3 **Sidhpur**, India
81/S16 **Sidi Aïssa**, Alg.
86/A2 **Sīdī Barrānī**, Egypt
81/Q16 **Sidi Bel-Abbes**, Alg.
81/W18 **Sīdī Bū Zayd** (gov.), Tun.
82/C2 **Sidi Ifni**, Mor.
81/M13 **Sidi Kacem**, Mor.
59/H6 **Sīdī Sālim**, Egypt
98/R **Sidley** (mtn.), Ant.
76/A1 **Sidmouth** (cape), Austl.
34/C5 **Sidmouth**, Eng,UK
106/C3 **Sidney**, BC,Can
107/G4 **Sidney**, Mt,US
109/G2 **Sidney**, Ne,US
110/C3 **Sidney**, Oh,US
113/G3 **Sidney Lanier** (lake), Ga,US
59/K5 **Sidon** (Ṣaydā), Leb.
82/J1 **Sidra** (gulf), Libya
41/F3 **Siede** (riv.), Ger.
39/M2 **Siedlce**, Pol.
39/L2 **Siedlce** (prov.), Pol.
43/G2 **Sieg** (riv.), Ger.
43/G2 **Siegburg**, Ger.
43/H2 **Siegen**, Ger.
39/M2 **Siemianówka** (lake), Pol.
39/M2 **Siemiatycze**, Pol.
69/D3 **Siempang**, Camb.
69/C3 **Siemreab**, Camb.
45/J5 **Siena**, It.
44/C2 **Sienne** (riv.), Fr.
39/K3 **Sieradz**, Pol.
39/K3 **Sieradz** (prov.), Pol.
43/F5 **Sierk-les-Bains**, Fr.
39/K2 **Sierpc**, Pol.
112/B4 **Sierra Blanca**, Tx,US
92/D3 **Sierra de la Macarena Nat'l Park**, Col.
100/A2 **Sierra del Carmen Nat'l Park**, Mex.
101/M7 **Sierra de San Pedro Mártir**, Mex.
96/D4 **Sierra Grande**, Arg.
84/B4 **Sierra Leone**
84/B4 **Sierra Leone** (cape), SLeo.
115/B2 **Sierra Madre**, Ca,US
100/B4 **Sierra Madre del Sur** (mts.), Mex.
101/N8 **Sierra Madre Occidental** (range), Mex.
100/B3 **Sierra Madre Oriental** (mts.), Mex.
100/A2 **Sierra Mojada**, Mex.
108/B3 **Sierra Nevada** (range), Ca,US
101/G5 **Sierra Nevada de Santa Marta**, Col.
101/G6 **Sierra Nevada Nat'l Park**, Ven.
108/E5 **Sierra Vista**, Az,US
45/G3 **Sierre**, Swi.
47/M8 **Siete** (peak), Sp.
96/C2 **Siete Tazas Nat'l Park**, Chile
49/J4 **Sífnos** (isl.), Gre.
81/Q16 **Sig**, Alg.
51/F2 **Sighetu Marmaţiei**, Rom.
51/G2 **Sighişoara**, Rom.
33/F1 **Sighty Crag** (hill), Eng,UK
81/T15 **Sigli** (cape), Alg.
72/A2 **Sigli**, Indo.
45/H2 **Sigmaringen**, Ger.
52/C4 **Sigtuna**, Swe.
70/D3 **Sihorā**, India
37/H3 **Siilinjärvi**, Fin.
59/E3 **Siirt**, Turk.
102/D3 **Sikanni Chief** (riv.), BC,Can
70/C2 **Sīkar**, India
84/D4 **Sikasso**, Mali
84/D4 **Sikasso** (reg.), Mali
109/K3 **Sikeston**, Mo,US
63/M2 **Sikhote-Alin'** (mts.), Rus.
49/J4 **Síkinos** (isl.), Gre.
70/E2 **Sikkim** (state), India
50/D3 **Siklós**, Hun.
46/B1 **Sil** (riv.), Sp.
100/A3 **Silao**, Mex.
67/D5 **Silay**, Phil.
71/F3 **Silchar**, India
51/J5 **Şile**, Turk.
35/E1 **Sileby**, Eng,UK
39/H3 **Silesia** (reg.), Pol.
82/F3 **Silet**, Alg.
59/C3 **Silifke**, Turk.
70/E2 **Silīguri**, India
68/E5 **Siling** (lake), China
79/H6 **Silisili** (peak), WSam.
51/H3 **Silistra**, Bul.
51/J5 **Silivri**, Turk.
37/D4 **Silkeborg**, Den.
33/G2 **Silksworth**, Eng,UK
47/E3 **Silla**, Sp.
52/E4 **Sillamäe**, Est.
46/A1 **Silleda**, Sp.
33/E2 **Silloth**, Eng,UK
112/E2 **Siloam Springs**, Ar,US
60/D1 **Silopi**, Turk.
112/E4 **Silsbee**, Tx,US
33/G4 **Silsden**, Eng,UK
82/J4 **Siltou** (well), Chad
39/L1 **Šilutė**, Lith.
59/E2 **Silvan**, Turk.
70/B3 **Silvassa**, India
106/D5 **Silver** (cr.), Or,US
108/B2 **Silver** (lake), Or,US
107/L4 **Silver Bay**, Mn,US
108/E4 **Silver City**, NM,US
114/L3 **Silver Creek**, Yk,Can
33/F3 **Silverdale**, Eng,UK
116/B2 **Silverdale**, Wa,US
116/C2 **Silver Lake-Fircrest**, Wa,US
115/J8 **Silver Spring**, Md,US
35/E2 **Silverstone**, Eng,UK
34/C5 **Silverton**, Eng,UK
108/F3 **Silverton**, Co,US
106/C4 **Silverton**, Or,US
112/C3 **Silverton**, Tx,US
46/A4 **Silves**, Port.
48/D1 **Silvi**, It.
108/C2 **Silvies** (riv.), Or,US
81/W17 **Silyānah** (gov.), Tun.
72/D3 **Simanggang**, Malay.
94/C3 **Simão Dias**, Braz.
110/E2 **Simard** (lake), Qu,Can
59/B2 **Simav**, Turk.
55/J1 **Simbirsk**, Rus.
55/H1 **Simbirsk Obl.**, Rus.
110/D3 **Simcoe**, On,Can
110/E2 **Simcoe** (lake), On,Can
83/N5 **Simēn** (mts.), Eth.
50/F3 **Simeria**, Rom.
72/A3 **Simeulue** (isl.), Indo.
54/E3 **Simferopol'**, Ukr.
66/E5 **Siming** (mtn.), China
51/F5 **Simitli**, Bul.
115/B2 **Simi Valley**, Ca,US
61/L2 **Simla**, India
50/F2 **Şimleu Silvaniei**, Rom.
45/G3 **Simme** (riv.), Swi.
43/F2 **Simmerath**, Ger.
43/G4 **Simmerbach** (riv.), Ger.
94/C4 **Simões Filho**, Braz.
100/C4 **Simojovel**, Mex.
106/D2 **Simonette** (riv.), Ab,Can
88/B4 **Simonstown**, SAfr.
40/D1 **Simonszand** (isl.), Neth.
72/A3 **Simpang-kiri** (riv.), Indo.
43/E2 **Simpelveld**, Neth.
74/F4 **Simpson** (des.), Austl.
102/H2 **Simpson** (pen.), NW,Can
102/G2 **Simpson** (riv.), NW,Can
39/H1 **Simrishamn**, Swe.
73/E3 **Simunul**, Phil.
83/Q6 **Sinadhago**, Som.
60/B3 **Sinafir** (isl.), SAr.
86/C2 **Sinai** (pen.), Egypt
101/N8 **Sinaloa** (state), Mex.
101/F6 **Sincelejo**, Col.
113/H3 **Sinclair** (lake), Ga,US
106/G5 **Sinclair**, Wy,US
94/B4 **Sincorá** (mts.), Braz.
70/C2 **Sind** (riv.), India
61/J3 **Sind** (prov.), Pak.
67/D6 **Sindañgan**, Phil.
72/C5 **Sindangbarang**, Indo.
45/H2 **Sindelfingen**, Ger.
46/A4 **Sines**, Port.
46/A4 **Sines, Cabo de** (cape), Port.
84/D5 **Sinfra**, IvC.
72/B3 **Singapore**
72/B3 **Singapore** (cap.), Sing.
69/C3 **Sing Buri**, Thai.
45/H3 **Singen**, Ger.
51/G2 **Singeorz-Băi**, Rom.
87/F1 **Singida**, Tanz.
49/H2 **Singitic** (gulf), Gre.
73/F4 **Singkang**, Indo.
72/C3 **Singkawang**, Indo.
72/B4 **Singkep** (isl.), Indo.
77/D2 **Singleton**, Austl.
48/A2 **Siniscola**, It.
83/M5 **Sinjah**, Sudan
59/E3 **Sinjār**, Iraq
86/D5 **Sinkāt**, Sudan
42/C3 **Sin-le-Noble**, Fr.
70/B4 **Sinnar**, India
48/E2 **Sinni** (riv.), It.
50/E2 **Sînnicolau Mare**, Rom.
86/B2 **Sinnūris**, Egypt
84/C5 **Sino** (co.), Libr.
51/J3 **Sinoe** (lake), Rom.
93/G6 **Sinop**, Braz.
59/C1 **Sinop**, Turk.
72/D3 **Sintang**, Indo.
42/D2 **Sint-Genesius-Rode**, Belg.
42/D1 **Sint-Gillis-Waas**, Belg.
42/D1 **Sint-Katelijne-Waver**, Belg.
42/C1 **Sint-Laureins**, Belg.
101/J4 **Sint Maarten** (isl.), NAnt.
40/C5 **Sint-Michielsgestel**, Neth.
42/D1 **Sint-Niklaas**, Belg.
40/C5 **Sint-Oedenrode**, Neth.
112/D4 **Sinton**, Tx,US
42/D2 **Sint-Pieters-Leeuw**, Belg.
46/A3 **Sintra**, Port.
47/P10 **Sintra** (mts.), Port.
43/E2 **Sint-Truiden**, Belg.
101/F6 **Sinú** (riv.), Col.
63/J3 **Sinŭiju**, NKor.
43/G2 **Sinzig**, Ger.
50/D2 **Sió** (riv.), Hun.
73/F2 **Siocon**, Phil.
50/D2 **Siófok**, Hun.
87/D4 **Sioma Ngwezi Nat'l Park**, Zam.
45/G3 **Sion**, Swi.
44/E4 **Sioule** (riv.), Fr.
107/J5 **Sioux City**, Ia,US
107/J5 **Sioux Falls**, SD,US
110/B1 **Sioux Lookout**, On,Can
48/E1 **Šipan** (isl.), Cro.
66/F2 **Siping**, China
107/J2 **Sipiwesk** (lake), Mb,Can
98/Q **Siple** (coast), Ant.
98/R **Siple** (isl.), Ant.
113/G3 **Sipsey** (riv.), Al,US
72/A4 **Sipura** (isl.), Indo.
95/B2 **Siqueira Campos**, Braz.
100/E5 **Siquia** (riv.), Nic.
37/C4 **Sira** (riv.), Nor.
48/D4 **Siracusa** (Syracuse), It.
70/E3 **Sirājganj**, Bang.
106/C2 **Sir Alexander** (peak), BC,Can
59/D2 **Şiran**, Turk.
74/F3 **Sir Edward Pellew Group** (isls.), Austl.
51/H2 **Siret**, Rom.
51/H3 **Siret** (riv.), Rom.
72/D3 **Sirik** (cape), Malay.
69/C2 **Sirikit** (res.), Thai.
94/D3 **Sirinhaém**, Braz.
71/H4 **Sirit** (res.), Thai.
114/B5 **Sirius** (pt.), Ak,US
102/D2 **Sir James MacBrien** (peak), NW,Can
61/G3 **Sīrjān**, Iran
77/D4 **Sir John** (cape), Austl.
59/E3 **Şırnak**, Turk.
70/B3 **Sirohi**, India
70/C3 **Sironj**, India
49/J4 **Síros** (isl.), Gre.
70/C2 **Sirsa**, India
70/B5 **Sirsi**, India
50/C3 **Sisak**, Cro.
69/D3 **Sisaket**, Thai.
71/H4 **Si Sa Ket**, Thai.
69/B2 **Si Satchanalai** (ruins), Thai.
107/H2 **Sisipuk** (lake), Mb, Sk,Can
69/C3 **Sisophon**, Camb.
107/J4 **Sisseton**, SD,US
85/E4 **Sissili** (prov.), Burk.
113/H2 **Sissonville**, WV,US
71/F3 **Sitākunda**, Bang.
47/F2 **Sitges**, Sp.
49/H2 **Sithoniá** (pen.), Gre.
49/K5 **Sitía**, Gre.
114/M2 **Sitidgi** (lake), NW,Can
114/L4 **Sitka**, Ak,US
39/K4 **Sitno** (peak), Slvk.
69/B2 **Sittang** (riv.), Burma
40/C7 **Sittard**, Neth.
35/G4 **Sittingbourne**, Eng,UK
71/F3 **Sittwe** (Akyab), Burma
50/D3 **Sivac**, Yugo.
70/C6 **Sivakāsi**, India
59/D2 **Sivas**, Turk.
59/D3 **Siverek**, Turk.
59/B2 **Sivrihisar**, Turk.
42/D3 **Sivry-Rance**, Belg.
83/L2 **Sīwah**, Egypt
70/D2 **Siwān**, India
32/A2 **Sixmilecross**, NI,UK
114/K3 **Sixtymile**, Yk,Can
62/G3 **Siziwang**, China
37/D5 **Sjælland** (isl.), Den.
50/E4 **Sjenica**, Yugo.
37/M6 **Sjónfridh** (peak), Ice.
37/P7 **Skaftafell Nat'l Park**, Ice.
37/D4 **Skagen**, Den.
37/D4 **Skagens** (cape), Den.
37/D4 **Skagerrak** (str.), Eur.
37/P6 **Skálfandafljót** (riv.), Ice.
39/J4 **Skalica**, Slvk.
45/K2 **Skalice** (riv.), Czh.
49/J3 **Skantzoura** (isl.), Gre.
37/E4 **Skaraborg** (co.), Swe.
39/L3 **Skarżysko-Kamienna**, Pol.
39/K4 **Skawina**, Pol.
102/D3 **Skeena** (range), BC,Can
106/A2 **Skeena** (riv.), BC,Can
33/J5 **Skegness**, Eng,UK
37/G2 **Skellefteå**, Swe.
37/F2 **Skellefteälv** (riv.), Swe.
33/G4 **Skelmanthorpe**, Eng,UK
33/F4 **Skelmersdale**, Eng,UK
33/H2 **Skelton**, Eng,UK
33/G2 **Skerne** (riv.), Eng,UK
32/B4 **Skerries**, Ire.
49/G4 **Skhiza** (isl.), Gre.
109/H3 **Skiatook**, Ok,US
33/E2 **Skiddaw** (mtn.), Eng,UK
37/D4 **Skien**, Nor.
39/L3 **Skierniewice**, Pol.
39/K3 **Skierniewice** (prov.), Pol.
81/V17 **Skikda**, Alg.
49/G4 **Skinári, Ákra** (cape), Gre.
33/H4 **Skipsea**, Eng,UK
33/F4 **Skipton**, Eng,UK
33/F3 **Skirfare** (riv.), Eng,UK
49/J3 **Skíros** (isl.), Gre.
37/D4 **Skjeberg**, Nor.
52/B2 **Skjelåtinden** (peak), Nor.
37/D5 **Skjern**, Den.
34/A3 **Skokholm** (isl.), Wal,UK
116/Q15 **Skokie**, Il,US
34/A3 **Skomer** (isl.), Wal,UK
69/D3 **Skon**, Camb.
49/H3 **Skópelos** (isl.), Gre.
54/F1 **Skopin**, Rus.
50/E5 **Skopje** (cap.), Macd.
37/E4 **Skövde**, Swe.
63/J1 **Skovorodino**, Rus.
111/G2 **Skowhegan**, Me,US
114/L3 **Skukum** (mtn.), Yk,Can
109/K2 **Skunk** (riv.), Ia,US
39/H2 **Skwierzyna**, Pol.
116/D2 **Skykomish** (riv.), Wa,US
97/J8 **Skyway** (sound), Chile
37/D5 **Slagelse**, Den.
33/F4 **Slaidburn**, Eng,UK
39/L4 **Slaná** (riv.), Slvk.
36/B4 **Slaney** (riv.), Ire.
52/F4 **Slantsy**, Rus.
51/G3 **Slatina**, Rom.
99/F3 **Slave** (riv.), Can.
85/F5 **Slave Coast** (reg.), Afr.
106/E2 **Slave Lake**, Ab,Can
68/C1 **Slavgorod**, Rus.
50/C3 **Slavonia** (reg.), Cro.
50/C3 **Slavonska Požega**, Cro.
50/D3 **Slavonski Brod**, Cro.
54/C2 **Slavuta**, Ukr.
54/F2 **Slavyansk**, Ukr.
54/F3 **Slavyansk-na-Kubani**, Rus.
39/J1 **Sławno**, Pol.
107/K5 **Slayton**, Mn,US
33/H6 **Sleaford**, Eng,UK
40/D3 **Sleen**, Neth.
103/H3 **Sleeper** (isls.), NW,Can
107/K4 **Sleepy Eye**, Mn,US
32/A4 **Sliabh na Cailliighe** (mtn.), Ire.
113/F4 **Slidell**, La,US
40/B5 **Sliedrecht**, Neth.
48/D5 **Sliema**, Malta
32/A3 **Slieve Beagh** (mtn.), NI,UK
32/C3 **Slieve Binnian** (mtn.), NI,UK
32/C3 **Slieve Croob** (mtn.), NI,UK
32/C3 **Slieve Donard** (mtn.), NI,UK
32/B3 **Slieve Gullion** (mtn.), NI,UK
32/A1 **Slieve Snaght** (mtn.), Ire.
36/A3 **Sligo**, Ire.
36/A3 **Sligo** (bay), Ire.
51/H4 **Sliven**, Bul.
50/F4 **Slivnitsa**, Bul.
111/S10 **Sloan**, NY,US
53/L4 **Slobodskoy**, Rus.
51/H3 **Slobozia**, Rom.
40/D2 **Slochteren**, Neth.
54/C1 **Slonim**, Bela.
40/C3 **Slotermeer** (lake), Neth.
31/M7 **Slough**, Eng,UK
39/K4 **Slovakia**
50/B3 **Slovenia**
50/B2 **Slovenska Bistrica**, Slov.
39/L4 **Slovenské Rudohorie** (mts.), Slvk.
39/J1 **Słowiński Nat'l Park**, Pol.
39/H2 **Słubice**, Pol.
54/C2 **Sluch'** (riv.), Ukr.
39/J2 **Słupca**, Pol.
39/J1 **Słupia** (riv.), Pol.
39/J1 **Słupsk**, Pol.
39/J1 **Słupsk** (prov.), Pol.
54/C1 **Slutsk**, Bela.
62/E1 **Slyudyanka**, Rus.
31/N8 **Smallfield**, Eng,UK
103/K3 **Smallwood** (res.), Nf,Can
107/G2 **Smeaton**, Sk,Can
50/E3 **Smederevo**, Yugo.
50/E3 **Smederevska Palanka**, Yugo.
37/E3 **Smedjebacken**, Swe.
54/D2 **Smela**, Ukr.
81/V17 **Smendou** (riv.), Alg.
40/D3 **Smilde**, Neth.
98/V **Smith** (pen.), Ant.
106/B3 **Smith** (inlet), BC,Can
103/J2 **Smith** (isl.), NW,Can
106/F4 **Smith** (riv.), Mt,US
106/B2 **Smithers**, BC,Can
113/J3 **Smithfield**, NC,US
108/E2 **Smithfield**, Ut,US
110/E4 **Smith Mtn.** (lake), Va,US
110/E2 **Smiths Falls**, On,Can
115/G5 **Smithtown**, NY,US
111/Q9 **Smithville**, On,Can
109/J4 **Smithville**, Ok,US
77/E1 **Smoky** (cape), Austl.
106/D2 **Smoky** (riv.), Ab,Can
109/H3 **Smoky** (hills), Ks,US
109/G3 **Smoky Hill** (riv.), Ks,US
106/E2 **Smoky Lake**, Ab,Can
37/C3 **Smøla** (isl.), Nor.
52/G5 **Smolensk**, Rus.
52/F5 **Smolensk Obl.**, Rus.
49/G2 **Smólikas** (peak), Gre.
51/G5 **Smolyan**, Bul.
98/U **Smyley** (isl.), Ant.
113/G3 **Smyrna**, Ga,US
32/D3 **Snaefell** (mtn.), IM,UK
114/M2 **Snake** (riv.), Yk,Can
106/D4 **Snake** (riv.), US
109/G2 **Snake** (riv.), Ne,US
75/Q12 **Snares** (isls.), NZ
40/C2 **Sneek**, Neth.
40/C2 **Sneekermeer** (lake), Neth.
88/D3 **Sneeuberg** (mts.), SAfr.
88/B4 **Sneeuberg** (peak), SAfr.
111/Q8 **Snelgrove**, On,Can
35/G1 **Snettisham**, Eng,UK
39/H3 **Sněžka** (peak), Czh.
50/B3 **Snežnik** (peak), Yugo.
39/L2 **Śniardwy** (lake), Pol.
35/G4 **Snodland**, Eng,UK
37/D3 **Snøhetta** (peak), Nor.
116/C2 **Snohomish**, Wa,US
116/C2 **Snohomish** (riv.), Wa,US
116/D2 **Snoqualmie** (riv.), Wa,US
37/E2 **Snøtind** (peak), Nor.
32/D5 **Snowdon** (mtn.), Wal,UK
32/D5 **Snowdonia Nat'l Park**, Wal,UK
108/E4 **Snowflake**, Az,US
107/H2 **Snow Lake**, Mb,Can
114/K2 **Snowy** (peak), Ak,US
77/D3 **Snowy River Nat'l Park**, Austl.
112/C3 **Snyder**, Tx,US
89/H7 **Soalala**, Madg.
89/J7 **Soanierana-Ivongo**, Madg.
33/G6 **Soar** (riv.), Eng,UK
45/L2 **Soběslav**, Czh.
73/K4 **Sobger** (riv.), Indo.
61/J3 **Sobhādero**, Pak.
94/B3 **Sobradinho** (res.), Braz.
94/B1 **Sobral**, Braz.
65/M9 **Sobue**, Japan
39/L2 **Sochaczew**, Pol.
54/F4 **Sochi**, Rus.
79/K6 **Society** (isls.), FrPol.
95/G7 **Socorro**, Braz.
108/F4 **Socorro**, NM,US
112/B4 **Socorro**, Tx,US
58/E8 **Socotra** (isl.), Yem.
69/D4 **Soc Trang**, Viet.
46/D3 **Socuéllamos**, Sp.
37/H2 **Sodankylä**, Fin.
106/F5 **Soda Springs**, Id,US
65/H7 **Sodegaura**, Japan
37/F3 **Söderhamn**, Swe.
37/F4 **Södertälje**, Swe.
83/N6 **Sodo**, Eth.
41/F5 **Soest**, Ger.
40/C4 **Soest**, Neth.
41/E3 **Soeste** (riv.), Ger.
89/J6 **Sofia** (riv.), Madg.
51/F4 **Sofia** (Sofiya) (cap.), Bul.
50/F4 **Sofiya** (reg.), Bul.
92/D2 **Sogamoso**, Col.
37/B3 **Sognafjorden** (fjord), Nor.
37/C3 **Sogn og Fjordane** (co.), Nor.
82/J4 **Sogollé** (well), Chad
63/K5 **Sŏgwip'o**, SKor.
35/G2 **Soham**, Eng,UK
42/D2 **Soignies**, Belg.
31/U11 **Soignolles-en-Brie**, Fr.
42/C5 **Soissons**, Fr.
31/T11 **Soisy-sur-Seine**, Fr.
64/C3 **Sōja**, Japan
70/B2 **Sojat**, India
55/J1 **Sok** (riv.), Rus.
69/C3 **Sok** (pt.), Thai.
65/H7 **Sōka**, Japan
63/K4 **Sokch'o**, SKor.
59/A3 **Söke**, Turk.
62/F1 **Sokhor** (peak), Rus.
50/E4 **Sokobanja**, Yugo.
85/F4 **Sokodé**, Togo
52/J4 **Sokol**, Rus.
39/M2 **Sokółka**, Pol.
45/K1 **Sokolov**, Czh.
39/M2 **Sokołów Podlaski**, Pol.
85/G4 **Sokoto** (plains), Nga.
85/G4 **Sokoto** (riv.), Nga.
85/G3 **Sokoto** (state), Nga.
37/C4 **Sola**, Nor.
67/D4 **Solana**, Phil.
94/D2 **Solânea**, Braz.
92/C2 **Solano** (pt.), Col.
46/C4 **Sol, Costa del** (coast), Sp.
47/P10 **Sol, Costa do** (reg.), Port.
109/J2 **Soldier** (riv.), Ia,US
101/G5 **Soledad**, Col.
115/B2 **Soledad** (canyon), Ca,US
101/J6 **Soledad**, Ven.
100/A3 **Soledad Diez Guiterrez**, Mex.
95/A4 **Soledade**, Braz.
35/E5 **Solent** (chan.), Eng,UK
43/E4 **Soleuvre** (mtn.), Lux.
59/E2 **Solhan**, Turk.
54/C1 **Soligorsk**, Bela.
35/E2 **Solihull**, Eng,UK
53/N4 **Solikamsk**, Rus.
55/K2 **Sol'-Iletsk**, Rus.
41/E6 **Solingen**, Ger.
37/F3 **Sollefteå**, Swe.
47/G3 **Sóller**, Sp.
41/G5 **Solling** (mts.), Ger.
37/D3 **Søln** (peak), Nor.
44/F3 **Solnan** (riv.), Fr.
72/D5 **Solo** (riv.), Indo.
72/B4 **Solok**, Indo.
100/C5 **Sololá**, Guat.
78/E5 **Solomon** (sea), PNG, Sol.
112/D2 **Solomon** (riv.), Ks,US
78/E6 **Solomon Islands**
55/L4 **Solonchak Goklenkui** (salt marsh), Trkm.
45/G3 **Solothurn**, Swi.
52/G2 **Solovetskiy** (isls.), Rus.
47/F2 **Solsona**, Sp.
50/D2 **Solt**, Hun.
50/B4 **Šolta** (isl.), Cro.
41/G3 **Soltau**, Ger.
50/D2 **Soltvadkert**, Hun.
50/E5 **Solunska** (peak), Macd.
34/A3 **Solva** (riv.), Wal,UK
108/B4 **Solvang**, Ca,US
37/E4 **Sölvesborg**, Swe.
32/E2 **Solway Firth** (inlet), Eng, Sc,UK
87/E3 **Solwezi**, Zam.
65/G2 **Sōma**, Japan
59/A2 **Soma**, Turk.
42/C3 **Somain**, Fr.
81/G4 **Somalia**
111/F1 **Somaqua** (riv.), Qu,Can
50/D3 **Sombor**, Cro.
101/P9 **Sombrerete**, Mex.
95/B4 **Sombrio**, Braz.
33/G5 **Somercotes**, Eng,UK
40/C6 **Someren**, Neth.
37/G3 **Somero**, Fin.
106/E3 **Somers**, Mt,US
102/G1 **Somerset** (isl.), NW,Can
34/D4 **Somerset** (co.), Eng,UK
110/C4 **Somerset**, Ky,US
115/F5 **Somerset**, NJ,US
111/S9 **Somerset**, NY,US
77/C4 **Somerset-Burnie**, Austl.
88/D4 **Somerset East**, SAfr.
88/B4 **Somerset West**, SAfr.
35/F2 **Somersham**, Eng,UK
111/G3 **Somersworth**, NH,US
34/D4 **Somerton**, Eng,UK
108/D4 **Somerton**, Az,US
115/F5 **Somerville**, NJ,US
109/H5 **Somerville** (lake), Tx,US
51/F2 **Someş** (riv.), Rom.
51/G2 **Someşul Mare** (riv.), Rom.
81/T15 **Sommam** (riv.), Alg.
44/D1 **Somme** (bay), Fr.
42/B4 **Somme** (dept.), Fr.
42/A3 **Somme** (riv.), Fr.
42/D6 **Somme** (riv.), Fr.
42/D5 **Somme-Soude** (riv.), Fr.
50/C2 **Somogy** (co.), Hun.
100/D5 **Somoto**, Nic.
35/F5 **Somptin**, Eng,UK
37/D5 **Sønderborg**, Den.
88/L11 **Sonderend** (riv.), SAfr.
38/E1 **Sønderjylland** (co.), Den.
45/H3 **Sondrio**, It.
70/C2 **Sonepat**, India
70/D3 **Sonepur**, India
69/E3 **Song Cau**, Viet.
69/D4 **Song Dinh**, Viet.
87/G3 **Songea**, Tanz.
66/F1 **Songhua** (riv.), China
68/B3 **Song-Kel'** (lake), Kyr.
69/C5 **Songkhla**, Thai.
69/C2 **Songkhram** (riv.), Thai.
63/J2 **Songling**, China
69/C1 **Song Ma**, Viet.
87/F4 **Songo**, Moz.
66/C4 **Song Shan** (peak), China
63/K4 **Songt'an**, SKor.
66/C5 **Songzi Guan** (pass), China
69/E3 **Son Ha**, Viet.
62/G3 **Sonid Youqi**, China

62/G3 Sonid Zuoqi, China
69/C1 Son La, Viet.
61/J3 Sonmiāni (bay), Pak.
45/J1 Sonneberg, Ger.
35/F4 Sonning, Eng,UK
38/G5 Sonntagshorn (peak), Ger.
93/J5 Sono (riv.), Braz.
94/A5 Sono (riv.), Braz.
64/D3 Sonobe, Japan
116/K10 Sonoma, Ca,US
116/J10 Sonoma (mts.), Ca,US
101/M8 Sonora (riv.), Mex.
101/M8 Sonora (state), Mex.
108/B3 Sonora, Ca,US
112/C4 Sonora, Tx,US
101/M7 Sonoyta (riv.), Mex.
60/E2 Sonqor, Iran
40/D5 Sonsbeck, Ger.
46/D3 Sonseca, Sp.
100/D5 Sonsonate, ESal.
78/C4 Sonsorol (isls.), Palau
50/D3 Sonta, Yugo.
69/D1 Son Tay, Viet.
41/G6 Sontra, Ger.
73/G3 Sopi (cape), Indo.
69/C1 Sopka, Laos
61/K2 Sopore, India
51/G4 Sopot, Bul.
39/K1 Sopot, Pol.
50/C2 Sopron, Hun.
34/D3 Sôr (riv.), Wal,UK
48/C2 Sora, It.
63/K4 Sŏrak-san (mtn.), SKor.
111/F2 Sorel, Qu,Can
59/M9 Soreq, Nabel (dry riv.), Isr.
45/H4 Soresina, It.
44/F5 Sorgues, Fr.
59/C2 Sorgun, Turk.
46/D2 Soria, Sp.
97/F2 Soriano (dept.), Uru.
72/A3 Sorikmerapi (peak), Indo.
55/K3 Sor Karatuley (salt pan), Kaz.
55/K3 Sor Kaydak (salt marsh), Kaz.
55/K3 Sor Mertvyy Kultuk (salt marsh), Kaz.
42/D4 Sormonne (riv.), Fr.
38/F1 Sorø, Den.
95/C2 Sorocaba, Braz.
55/K1 Sorochinsk, Rus.
51/J1 Soroki, Mol.
78/D4 Sorol (atoll), Micr.
73/H4 Sorong, Indo.
83/M7 Soroti, Ugan.
37/G1 Sørøya (isl.), Nor.
37/G1 Sørøysundet (chan.), Nor.
41/E6 Sorpestausee (res.), Ger.
46/A3 Sorraia (riv.), Port.
48/D2 Sorrento, It.
87/B5 Sorris-Sorris, Namb.
48/A2 Sorso, It.
67/D5 Sorsogon, Phil.
52/F3 Sortavala, Rus.
52/D4 Sõrve (pt.), Est.
41/H5 Söse (riv.), Ger.
54/F1 Sosna (riv.), Rus.
96/C2 Sosneado (peak), Arg.
53/M3 Sosnogorsk, Rus.
53/L4 Sosnovka, Rus.
39/K3 Sosnowiec, Pol.
101/G4 Sosúa, DRep.
42/D6 Soude (riv.), Fr.
101/J4 Soufrière (mt.), Guad.
101/J5 Soufrière (mt.), StV.
81/V17 Souk Ahras, Alg.
43/G1 Soultz-sous-Forets, Fr.
85/E3 Soum (prov.), Burk.
43/E2 Soumagne, Belg.
88/E3 Sources, Mont aux (peak), Les.
93/J4 Soure, Braz.
46/A2 Soure, Port.
81/S15 Sour El Ghozlane, Alg.
107/H3 Souris, Mb,Can
111/J2 Souris, PE,Can
107/H3 Souris (riv.), Can., US
84/E3 Sourou (prov.), Burk.
82/D2 Sous (wadi), Mor.
94/C2 Sousa, Braz.
46/B3 Sousel, Port.
88/C3 Sout (riv.), SAfr.
76/G8 South (cr.), Austl.
111/H2 South (mts.), NS,Can
103/H2 South (bay), NW,Can
75/Q12 South (cape), NZ
75/Q11 South (isl.), NZ
87/D6 South Africa
31/M7 Southall, Eng,UK
35/E2 Southam, Eng,UK
90/* South America
103/H2 Southampton (cape), NW,Can
103/H2 Southampton (isl.), NW,Can
110/D2 Southampton, On,Can
35/E5 Southampton, Eng,UK
71/F5 South Andaman (isl.), India
113/J2 South Anna (riv.), Va,US
113/H3 South Augusta, Ga,US
103/K3 South Aulatsivik (isl.), Nf,Can
74/E5 South Australia (state), Austl.
113/F3 Southaven, Ms,US
32/D3 South Barrule (mtn.), IM,UK
110/C3 South Bend, In,US
31/P8 Southborough, Eng,UK
110/E4 South Boston, Va,US
35/F5 Southbourne, Eng,UK
34/C6 South Brent, Eng,UK
111/F2 South Burlington, Vt,US
113/H3 South Carolina (state), US
58/L8 South China (sea), Asia
107/H4 South Dakota (state), US
34/D5 South Dorset Downs (uplands), Eng,UK
35/F5 South Downs (hills), Eng,UK
29/S8 South East (cape), Austl.
77/C3 South East (pt.), Austl.
101/G3 Southeast (pt.), Bahm.
114/E3 Southeast (cape), Ak,US
116/P16 South Elgin, Il,US
33/G4 South Elmsall, Eng,UK
32/C1 Southend, Sc,UK
35/G3 Southend-on-Sea, Eng,UK
59/K6 Southern (dist.), Isr.
84/B5 Southern (prov.), SLeo.
75/Q11 Southern Alps (range), NZ
79/J6 Southern Cook (isls.), CookIs.
102/G3 Southern Indian (lake), Mb,Can
113/J3 Southern Pines, NC,US
32/D1 Southern Uplands (mts.), Sc,UK
35/G1 Southery, Eng,UK
77/C4 South Esk (riv.), Austl.
74/D3 Southesk Tablelands (plat.), Austl.
116/F7 Southfield, Mi,US
35/H4 South Foreland (pt.), Eng,UK
108/F3 South Fork, Co,US
113/F2 South Fulton, Tn,US
31/N7 Southgate, Eng,UK
115/B3 South Gate, Ca,US
116/F7 Southgate, Mi,US
98/X South Georgia (isl.), UK
34/C4 South Glamorgan (co.), Wal,UK
34/C6 South Hams (plain), Eng,UK
35/F5 South Hayling, Eng,UK
110/E4 South Hill, Va,US
40/B5 South Holland (prov.), Neth.
116/Q16 South Holland, Il,US
31/N8 South Holmwood, Eng,UK
33/G4 South Kirkby, Eng,UK
63/K4 South Korea
108/C3 South Lake Tahoe, Ca,US
87/F3 South Luangwa Nat'l Park, Zam.
98/K South Magnetic Pole, Ant.
116/Q14 South Milwaukee, Wi,US
35/G3 Southminster, Eng,UK
34/C4 South Molton, Eng,UK
107/J2 South Moose (lake), Mb,Can
114/M5 South Moresby Nat'l Park Rsv., BC,Can
33/G5 South Normanton, Eng,UK
31/P7 South Ockenden, Eng,UK
98/W South Orkney (isls.), UK
55/G4 South Ossetian Aut. Obl., Geo.
31/M7 South Oxhey, Eng,UK
34/D5 South Petherton, Eng,UK
76/E6 South Pine (riv.), Austl.
115/F5 South Plainfield, NJ,US
109/G2 South Platte (riv.), Co, Ne,US
98/A South Pole, Ant.
33/E4 Southport, Eng,UK
113/J3 Southport, NC,US
115/F5 South River, NJ,US
98/Y South Sandwich (isls.), UK
116/K11 South San Francisco, Ca,US
106/F3 South Saskatchewan (riv.), Ab, Sk,Can
98/W South Shetland (isls.), UK
33/G2 South Shields, Eng,UK
109/H2 South Sioux City, Ne,US
70/E3 South Suburban, India
75/R10 South Taranaki (bight), NZ
33/F2 South Tyne (riv.), Eng,UK
73/F2 South Ubian, Phil.
31/N7 Southwark (bor.), Eng,UK
33/H5 Southwell, Eng,UK
77/C4 South West (cape), Austl.
77/C4 South West Nat'l Park, Austl.
35/H2 Southwold, Eng,UK
35/G3 South Woodham Ferrers, Eng,UK
76/C4 Southwood Nat'l Park, Austl.
33/G5 South Yorkshire (co.), Eng,UK
51/G2 Sovata, Rom.
48/E3 Soverato Marina, It.
39/L1 Sovetsk, Rus.
52/D5 Sovetsk, Rus.
52/L4 Sovetsk, Rus.
63/N2 Sovetskaya Gavan', Rus.
33/G4 Sowerby Bridge, Eng,UK
88/D2 Soweto, SAfr.
52/J2 Soyana (riv.), Rus.
64/A2 Soyang (lake), SKor.
44/D4 Soyaux, Fr.
98/E Soyuz, Ant.
54/D1 Sozh (riv.), Eur.
43/E3 Spa, Belg.
98/U Spaatz (isl.), Ant.
46/C2 Spain
33/H6 Spalding, Eng,UK
116/C3 Spanaway, Wa,US
101/F4 Spanish Town, Jam.
108/C3 Sparks, Nv,US
113/H2 Sparta, NC,US
115/F4 Sparta, NJ,US
113/G3 Sparta, Tn,US
110/B3 Sparta, Wi,US
113/H3 Spartanburg, SC,US
49/H4 Sparta (Spárti), Gre.
81/M13 Spartel (cape), Mor.
48/A3 Spartivento (cape), It.
48/E4 Spartivento (cape), It.
106/E3 Sparwood, BC,Can
63/L3 Spassk-Dal'niy, Rus.
49/H5 Spátha, Ákra (cape), Gre.
36/C2 Spean (riv.), Sc,UK
36/C2 Spean Bridge, Sc,UK
107/H4 Spearfish, SD,US
33/F5 Speke, Eng,UK
74/F7 Spencer (cape), Austl.
74/F6 Spencer (gulf), Austl.
114/E2 Spencer (pt.), Ak,US
107/K5 Spencer, Ia,US
41/F4 Spenge, Ger.
33/G2 Spennymoor, Eng,UK
49/H3 Sperkhiós (riv.), Gre.
32/A2 Sperrin (mts.), NI,UK
36/D2 Spey (riv.), Sc,UK
45/H2 Speyer, Ger.
111/Q8 Speyside, On,Can
48/E3 Spezzano Albanese, It.
103/H2 Spicer (isl.), NW,Can
41/E1 Spiekeroog (isl.), Ger.
45/G3 Spiez, Swi.
40/B5 Spijkenisse, Neth.
114/K2 Spike (mtn.), Ak,US
50/A2 Spilimbergo, It.
33/J5 Spilsby, Eng,UK
48/A2 Spina, Bruncu (peak), It.
61/J2 Spin Būldak, Afg.
43/E5 Spincourt, Fr.
106/D2 Spirit River, Ab,Can
106/G2 Spiritwood, Sk,Can
39/L4 Spišská Nová Ves, Slvk.
35/E5 Spithead (chan.), Eng,UK
56/B2 Spitsbergen (isl.), Sval.
45/K3 Spittal an der Drau, Aus.
107/K2 Split (lake), Mb,Can
50/C4 Split, Cro.
45/H3 Splugenpass (Passo dello Spluge) (pass), It., Swi.
106/D4 Spokane (riv.), Id, Wa,US
106/D4 Spokane, Wa,US
48/C1 Spoleto, It.
110/B3 Spoon (riv.), Il,US
110/B2 Spooner, Wi,US
107/K3 Sprague, Mb,Can
40/C5 Sprang-Capelle, Neth.
67/B5 Spratly (isls.)
39/H2 Spree (riv.), Ger.
45/K4 Spresiano, It.
43/E3 Sprimont, Belg.
113/G4 Spring (cr.), Ga,US
112/D4 Spring, Tx,US
111/K1 Springdale, Nf,Can
112/E2 Springdale, Ar,US
41/G4 Springe, Ger.
109/F4 Springer, NM,US
108/E4 Springerville, Az,US
109/G3 Springfield, Co,US
110/B4 Springfield (cap.), Il,US
111/F3 Springfield, Ma,US
109/J3 Springfield, Mo,US
110/D4 Springfield, Oh,US
106/C4 Springfield, Or,US
113/G2 Springfield, Tn,US
115/J8 Springfield, Va,US
111/F3 Springfield, Vt,US
111/J2 Springhill, NS,Can
112/E3 Springhill, La,US
88/E2 Springs, SAfr.
107/H3 Springside, Sk,Can
77/G5 Springvale
107/K5 Spring Valley, Mn,US
115/F4 Spring Valley, NY,US
41/E6 Sprockhövel, Ger.
35/H1 Sprowston, Eng,UK
110/E4 Spruce (peak), WV,US
115/E5 Spruce Run (res.), NJ,US
40/B5 Spui (riv.), Neth.
33/J4 Spurn Head (pt.), Eng,UK
106/C3 Squamish, BC,Can
48/E3 Squillace (gulf), It.
49/F2 Squinzano, It.
50/D3 Srbobran, Yugo.
69/C4 Sre Ambel, Camb.
50/D3 Srebrenica, Bosn.
51/G4 Sredna (mts.), Bul.
51/G4 Srednogorie, Bul.
69/D3 Sre Khtum, Camb.
39/J2 Śrem, Pol.
50/E3 Sremčica, Yugo.
50/D3 Sremska Mitrovica, Yugo.
69/C3 Sreng (riv.), Camb.
69/D3 Sre Noy, Camb.
69/D3 Srepok (riv.), Camb.
63/H1 Sretensk, Rus.
61/K3 Sri Dungargarh, India
61/K3 Sri Gangānagar, India
70/D4 Srikākulam, India
70/D6 Sri Lanka
61/K2 Srīnagar, India
70/B4 Srīvardhan, India
39/J3 Środa Śląska, Pol.
39/J2 Środa Wielkopolska, Pol.
76/A2 Staaten River Nat'l Park, Austl.
37/H1 Stabbursdalen Nat'l Park, Nor.
40/B6 Stabroek, Belg.
41/G1 Stade, Ger.
42/C2 Staden, Belg.
40/D3 Stadskanaal, Neth.
41/G4 Stadthagen, Ger.
40/D5 Stadtlohn, Ger.
45/H3 Stäfa, Swi.
39/G1 Staffanstorp, Swe.
33/F6 Stafford, Eng,UK
34/D2 Stafford & Worcester (can.), Eng,UK
33/F5 Staffordshire (co.), Eng,UK
48/B4 Stagnone (isls.), It.
33/G2 Staindrop, Eng,UK
31/M7 Staines, Eng,UK
31/T10 Stains, Fr.
116/M12 Stakes (mtn.), Ca,US
54/F2 Stakhanov, Ukr.
34/D5 Stalbridge, Eng,UK
35/H1 Stalham, Eng,UK
103/S6 Stallworthy (cape), NW,Can
39/M3 Stalowa Wola, Pol.
33/F5 Stalybridge, Eng,UK
51/G4 Stamboliyski, Bul.
35/F1 Stamford, Eng,UK
115/G4 Stamford, Ct,US
33/H4 Stamford Bridge, Eng,UK
37/E1 Stamsund, Nor.
32/B4 Stamullin, Ire.
88/E2 Standerton, SAfr.
33/F4 Standish-with-Langtree, Eng,UK
35/G4 Stanford le Hope, Eng,UK
31/P6 Stanford Rivers, Eng,UK
37/D3 Stange, Nor.
89/E3 Stanger, SAfr.
33/F2 Stanhope, Eng,UK
115/F5 Stanhope, NJ,US
108/B3 Stanislaus (riv.), Ca,US
51/F4 Stanke Dimitrov, Bul.
77/C4 Stanley (peak), Austl.
111/H2 Stanley, NB,Can
70/C5 Stanley (res.), India
33/G2 Stanley, Eng,UK
107/H3 Stanley, ND,US
83/L8 Stanley (falls), Zaire
57/E4 Stanovo, Yugo.
57/N4 Stanovoy (range), Rus.
31/P8 Stansted, Eng,UK
35/G3 Stansted Mountfitchet, Eng,UK
35/G2 Stanton, Eng,UK
115/C3 Stanton, Ca,US
110/D4 Stanton, Ky,US
112/C3 Stanton, Tx,US
31/M7 Stanwell, Eng,UK
40/D3 Staphorst, Neth.
35/E4 Stapleford, Eng,UK
31/P7 Stapleford Abbotts, Eng,UK
35/G4 Staplehurst, Eng,UK
39/L3 Starachowice, Pol.
50/E3 Stara Pazova, Yugo.
50/F3 Stara Planina (mts.), Yugo.
52/F4 Staraya Russa, Rus.
51/G4 Stara Zagora, Bul.
79/K5 Starbuck (isl.), Kiri.
76/B1 Starcke Nat'l Park, Austl.
39/H2 Stargard Szczeciński, Pol.
113/H4 Starke, Fl,US
113/F3 Starkville, Ms,US
54/F3 Staroderevyan-kovskaya, Rus.
54/E1 Starodub, Rus.
39/K2 Starogard Gdański, Pol.
54/F3 Staroshcher-binovskaya, Rus.
34/C6 Start (bay), Eng,UK
34/C6 Start (pt.), Eng,UK
39/L3 Staszów, Pol.
110/E3 State College, Pa,US
115/F5 Staten (isl.), NY,US
113/H3 Statesboro, Ga,US
113/H3 Statesville, NC,US
38/E3 Staufenberg, Ger.
34/D3 Staunton, Eng,UK
110/E4 Staunton, Va,US
34/D2 Staunton on Wye, Eng,UK
37/C4 Stavanger, Nor.
33/F3 Staveley, Eng,UK
33/G5 Staveley, Eng,UK
55/G3 Stavropol', Rus.
55/G3 Stavropol' Kray, Rus.
77/B3 Stawell, Austl.
106/C4 Stayton, Or,US
108/F2 Steamboat Springs, Co,US
41/H3 Stederau (riv.), Ger.
77/F5 Steele (cr.), Austl.
107/J4 Steele, ND,US
89/E2 Steelpoortrivier (riv.), SAfr.
40/B5 Steenbergen, Neth.
108/C2 Steens (mtn.), Or,US
103/J1 Steensby (inlet), NW,Can
40/D3 Steenwijk, Neth.
74/A5 Steep (pt.), Austl.
107/G1 Steephill (lake), Sk,Can
34/C4 Steep Holm (isl.), Eng,UK
33/J5 Steeping (riv.), Eng,UK
114/J2 Steese Nat'l Rec. Area, Ak,US
102/F1 Stefansson (isl.), NW,Can
96/C5 Steffen (peak), Chile
45/G3 Steffisburg, Swi.
50/A2 Steiermark (prov.), Aus.
45/J2 Steigerwald (for.), Ger.
38/F4 Stein, Ger.
43/E2 Stein, Neth.
107/J3 Steinbach, Mb,Can
41/F5 Steinhagen, Ger.
41/G5 Steinheim, Ger.
41/G4 Steinhuder Meer (lake), Ger.
37/D2 Steinkjer, Nor.
42/D1 Stekene, Belg.
111/J2 Stellarton, NS,Can
41/H2 Stelle, Ger.
88/B4 Stellenbosch, SAfr.
45/H5 Stello (mtn.), Fr.
45/J3 Stelvio Nat'l Park, It.
38/F2 Stendal, Ger.
51/G4 Stenento Nat'l Park, Bul.
37/D4 Stenungsund, Swe.
55/H5 Stepanakert, Azer.
77/B1 Stephens Creek, Austl.
111/K1 Stephenville, Nf,Can
112/D3 Stephenville, Tx,US
109/G2 Sterling, Co,US
112/C4 Sterling City, Tx,US
116/F6 Sterling Heights, Mi,US
55/K1 Sterlitamak, Rus.
45/J3 Sterzing (Vipiteno), It.
106/E2 Stettler, Ab,Can
110/D3 Steubenville, Oh,US
35/F3 Stevenage, Eng,UK
107/J2 Stevenson (lake), Mb,Can
114/H4 Stevenson (str.), Ak,US
110/B2 Stevens Point, Wi,US
106/E4 Stevensville, Mt,US
40/C3 Stevinsluizen (dam), Neth.
74/E2 Stewart (cape), Austl.
114/L3 Stewart (riv.), Yk,Can
75/Q12 Stewart (isl.), NZ
114/L3 Stewart Crossing, Yk,Can
114/L3 Stewart River, Yk,Can
32/B2 Stewartstown, NI,UK
107/K5 Stewartville, Mn,US
35/F5 Steyning, Eng,UK
45/L2 Steyr, Aus.
45/L3 Steyr (riv.), Aus.
40/C2 Stiens, Neth.
109/J4 Stigler, Ok,US
114/M4 Stikine (riv.), BC,Can
107/K4 Stillwater, Mn,US
108/C3 Stillwater (range), Nv,US
109/H3 Stillwater, Ok,US
109/J4 Stilwell, Ok,US
32/D1 Stinchar (riv.), Sc,UK
112/C3 Stinnett, Tx,US
50/F5 Štip, Macd.
43/F5 Stiring-Wendel, Fr.
36/D2 Stirling, Sc,UK
111/L2 St. John's (cap.), Nf,Can
37/D3 Stjørdal, Nor.
35/E4 Stockbridge, Eng,UK
39/J4 Stockerau, Aus.
37/F4 Stockholm (cap.), Swe.
33/F5 Stockport, Eng,UK
33/F4 Stocks (res.), Eng,UK
33/G5 Stocksbridge, Eng,UK
116/M11 Stockton, Ca,US
109/J3 Stockton (lake), Mo,US
112/C4 Stockton (plat.), Tx,US
33/G2 Stockton-on-Tees, Eng,UK
69/D3 Stoeng Treng, Camb.
34/B6 Stoke (pt.), Eng,UK
33/F5 Stoke-on-Trent, Eng,UK
77/B4 Stokes (pt.), Austl.
50/C4 Stolac, Bosn.
43/F2 Stolberg, Ger.
57/P2 Stolbovoy (isl.), Rus.
88/K10 Stompneuspunt (pt.), SAfr.
33/F6 Stone, Eng,UK
36/D2 Stonehaven, Sc,UK
35/E4 Stonehenge (ruins), Eng,UK
34/D3 Stonehouse, Eng,UK
107/J3 Stonewall, Mb,Can
111/Q9 Stoney Creek, On,Can
107/J2 Stony (pt.), Mb,Can
115/G5 Stony Brook, NY,US
107/J3 Stony Mountain, Mb,Can
115/G4 Stony Point, NY,US
56/K3 Stony Tunguska (riv.), Rus.
110/D1 Stooping (riv.), On,Can
103/S7 Stor (isl.), NW,Can
41/G1 Stör (riv.), Ger.
37/F2 Stora Sjöfallets Nat'l Park, Swe.
37/F2 Storavan (lake), Swe.
38/F1 Store Bælt (chan.), Den.
37/D3 Støren, Nor.
77/C4 Storm (bay), Austl.
107/K5 Storm Lake, Ia,US
32/C2 Stormont, NI,UK
35/F5 Storrington, Eng,UK
37/F1 Storsteinsfjellet (peak), Nor.
38/F1 Storstrøm (co.), Den.
35/G3 Stort (riv.), Eng,UK
37/F2 Storuman, Swe.
106/G4 Story, Wy,US
97/J7 Stosch (isl.), Chile
35/F2 Stotfold, Eng,UK
107/H3 Stoughton, Sk,Can
34/D5 Stour (riv.), Eng,UK
35/E2 Stour (riv.), Eng,UK
35/H3 Stour (riv.), Eng,UK
35/H4 Stour (riv.), Eng,UK
34/D2 Stourbridge, Eng,UK
35/G4 Stour, Great (riv.), Eng,UK
34/D2 Stourport on Severn, Eng,UK
35/G2 Stowmarket, Eng,UK
35/E3 Stow on the Wold, Eng,UK
32/A2 Strabane (dist.), NI,UK
36/D2 Strachan, Sc,UK
36/C2 Strachur, Sc,UK
45/H4 Stradella, It.
40/D6 Straelen, Ger.
45/K2 Strakonice, Czh.
51/H4 Straldzha, Bul.
38/G1 Stralsund, Ger.
88/B4 Strand, SAfr.
32/C3 Strangford, NI,UK
32/C3 Strangford Lough (inlet), NI,UK
52/C4 Strängnäs, Swe.
32/B1 Stranocum, NI,UK
32/C2 Stranraer, Sc,UK
107/G3 Strasbourg, Sk,Can
45/G2 Strasbourg, Fr.
110/D3 Stratford, On,Can
75/R10 Stratford, NZ
115/E6 Stratford, NJ,US
35/E2 Stratford upon Avon, Eng,UK
36/C3 Strathaven, Sc,UK
32/D1 Strathclyde (reg.), Sc,UK
106/E3 Strathmore, Ab,Can
34/B5 Stratton, Eng,UK
45/K2 Straubing, Ger.
37/M6 Straumnes (pt.), Ice.
39/G2 Strausberg, Ger.
115/B2 Strawberry (peak), Ca,US
74/E6 Streaky (bay), Austl.
116/P15 Streamwood, Il,US
31/N7 Streatham, Eng,UK
35/E3 Streatley, Eng,UK
110/B3 Streator, Il,US
45/L2 Středočeská Žulová Vrchovina (mts.), Czh.
45/L2 Středočeský (reg.), Czh.
39/K4 Středoslovenský (reg.), Slvk.
34/D4 Street, Eng,UK
111/Q8 Streetsville, On,Can
51/F3 Strehaia, Rom.
52/H2 Strel'na (riv.), Rus.
33/F5 Stretford, Eng,UK
35/G2 Stretham, Eng,UK
40/B5 Strijen, Neth.
49/H2 Strimón (gulf), Gre.
49/H2 Strimónas (riv.), Gre.
97/K7 Strobel (lake), Arg.
49/G4 Strofádhes (isls.), Gre.
48/D3 Stromboli (isl.), It.
37/D4 Strømmen, Nor.
37/D4 Strömstad, Swe.
37/E3 Strömsund, Swe.
39/J3 Stronie Śląskie, Pol.
34/D3 Stroud, Eng,UK
50/E5 Struga, Macd.
88/C4 Struisbaai (bay), SAfr.
32/A2 Strule (riv.), NI,UK
49/H2 Struma (riv.), Bul., Gre.
34/A2 Strumble Head (pt.), UK
50/F5 Strumica, Macd.
37/C3 Stryn, Nor.
39/J3 Strzegom, Pol.
39/H2 Strzelce Krajeńskie, Pol.
76/A5 Strzelecki (cr.), Austl.
77/D4 Strzelecki (peak), Austl.
39/J3 Strzelin, Pol.
39/L4 Strzyżów, Pol.
106/B2 Stuart (lake), BC,Can
106/B2 Stuart (riv.), BC,Can
113/H5 Stuart, Fl,US
110/E4 Stuarts Draft, Va,US
39/G1 Stubbenkammer (pt.), Ger.
35/E5 Studland, Eng,UK
35/E2 Studley, Eng,UK
39/J4 Stupava, Slvk.
52/H5 Stupino, Rus.
107/J3 Sturgeon (bay), Mb,Can
110/B1 Sturgeon (lake), On,Can
110/C2 Sturgeon Bay, Wi,US
110/E2 Sturgeon Falls, On,Can
110/C3 Sturgis, Mi,US
107/H4 Sturgis, SD,US
34/D5 Sturminster Newton, Eng,UK
35/H4 Sturry, Eng,UK
76/A5 Sturt (des.), Austl.
77/B1 Sturt (peak), Austl.
77/B1 Sturt Nat'l Park, Austl.
88/D4 Stutterheim, SAfr.
45/H2 Stuttgart, Ger.
113/F3 Stuttgart, Ar,US
54/C2 Styr (riv.), Ukr.
45/L3 Styria (prov.), Aus.
95/D1 Suaçui Grande (riv.), Braz.
86/D5 Suakin (arch.), Sudan
67/D3 Suao, Tai.
72/C5 Subang, Indo.
48/C1 Subasio (peak), It.
81/W18 Subaytilah, Tun.
72/C3 Subi (isl.), Indo.
50/D2 Subotica, Yugo.
115/F5 Succasunna-Kenvil, NJ,US
51/H2 Suceava, Rom.
51/G2 Suceava (co.), Rom.
39/L3 Suchedniów, Pol.
36/A4 Suck (riv.), Ire.
92/E7 Sucre (cap.), Bol.
92/G5 Sucunduri (riv.), Braz.
95/B2 Sucuriú (riv.), Braz.
31/T10 Sucy-en-Brie, Fr.
52/H4 Suda (riv.), Rus.
83/L5 Sudan
82/H5 Sudan (phys. reg.), Afr.
110/D2 Sudbury, On,Can
35/G2 Sudbury, Eng,UK
41/H2 Sude (riv.), Ger.
39/H3 Sudeten (mts.), Czh., Pol.
40/D5 Südlohn, Ger.
85/H5 Sud-Ouest (prov.), Camr.
83/L6 Sue (riv.), Sudan
47/E3 Sueca, Sp.
51/G4 Sŭedinenie, Bul.
86/C2 Suez (can.), Egypt
86/C2 Suez (gulf), Egypt
86/C2 Suez (As Suways), Egypt
59/K5 Sūf, Jor.
115/F4 Suffern, NY,US
35/G2 Suffolk (co.), Eng,UK
110/E4 Suffolk, Va,US
109/K2 Sugar (riv.), Il, Wi,US
112/E4 Sugar Land, Tx,US
75/J6 Sugarloaf (pt.), Austl.
34/C3 Sugar Loaf (mtn.), Wal,UK
113/H2 Sugarloaf (peak), Ky,US
62/F1 Sühbaatar, Mong.
45/J1 Suhl, Ger.
59/B2 Şuhut, Turk.
67/B3 Sui (riv.), China
69/B4 Sui (pt.), Thai.
93/H6 Suia-Missu (riv.), Braz.
63/L2 Suibin, China
63/L3 Suifenhe, China
63/K2 Suihua, China
63/K2 Suileng, China
42/D5 Suippe (riv.), Fr.
36/B4 Suir (riv.), Ire.
116/K10 Suisun City, Ca,US
65/L10 Suita, Japan
115/K8 Suitland-Silver Hill, Md,US
62/G5 Suizhou, China
70/B2 Sūjāngarh, India
72/C5 Sukabumi, Indo.
72/C4 Sukadana, Indo.
72/C4 Sukadana (bay), Indo.
65/G2 Sukagawa, Japan
54/E1 Sukhinichi, Rus.
52/J4 Sukhona (riv.), Rus.
69/B2 Sukhothai, Thai.
55/G4 Sukhumi, Geo.
61/J3 Sukkur, Pak.
64/C4 Sukumo, Japan
73/G2 Sula (isls.), Indo.
53/L2 Sula (riv.), Rus.
61/J3 Sulaimān (range), Pak.
73/E4 Sulawesi (Celebes) (isl.), Indo.
86/B4 Sulb Temple (ruins), Sudan
32/D3 Sulby (riv.), IM,UK
39/H2 Sulechów, Pol.
39/H2 Sulęcin, Pol.
39/L2 Sulejówek, Pol.
41/F3 Sulingen, Ger.
62/D4 Sulin Gol (riv.), China
37/F2 Sulitjelma (peak), Nor.
92/B4 Sullana, Peru
106/F3 Sullivan (lake), Ab,Can
110/C4 Sullivan, In,US
110/E1 Sullivan Mines, Qu,Can
34/C4 Sully, Wal,UK
48/C1 Sulmona, It.
109/J4 Sulphur (riv.), Ar, Tx,US
112/E4 Sulphur, La,US
109/H4 Sulphur, Ok,US
112/E3 Sulphur Springs, Tx,US
73/E2 Sulu (sea), Malay., Phil.
67/D6 Sulu (arch.), Phil.
59/C2 Suluova, Turk.
83/K1 Sulūq, Libya
43/G2 Sülz (riv.), Ger.
43/G5 Sulzbach, Ger.
45/J2 Sulzbach-Rosenberg, Ger.
98/P Sulzberger (bay), Ant.
98/Q Sulzberger Ice Shelf, Ant.
50/E3 Šumadija (reg.), Yugo.
92/D3 Sumapaz Nat'l Park, Col.
72/B4 Sumatra (isl.), Indo.
72/E5 Sumba (isl.), Indo.
73/E5 Sumba (str.), Indo.
55/L5 Sumbar (riv.), Trkm.
72/E5 Sumbawa (isl.), Indo.
73/E5 Sumbawa Besar, Indo.
87/F2 Sumbawanga, Tanz.
87/B3 Sumbe, Ang.
62/F2 Sümber, Mong.
114/M4 Sumdum (mtn.), Ak,US
94/C2 Sumé, Braz.
50/C2 Sümeg, Hun.
72/D5 Sumenep, Indo.
55/J4 Sumgait, Azer.
33/G3 Summer Bridge, Eng,UK
106/D3 Summerland, BC,Can
111/J2 Summerside, PE,Can
110/D4 Summersville, WV,US
113/G3 Summerville, Ga,US
113/H3 Summerville, SC,US
115/F5 Summit, NJ,US
116/C3 Sumner, Wa,US
64/D3 Sumoto, Japan
39/J4 Šumperk, Czh.
113/H3 Sumter, SC,US
54/E2 Sumy, Ukr.
54/E2 Sumy Obl., Ukr.
106/E4 Sun (riv.), Mt,US
65/M9 Sunami, Japan
77/C3 Sunbury, Austl.
35/F4 Sunbury on Thames, Eng,UK
63/K5 Sunch'ŏn, SKor.
108/D4 Sun City, Az,US
115/C3 Sun City, Ca,US
111/G3 Suncook, NH,US
72/B5 Sunda (str.), Indo.
107/G4 Sundance, Wy,US
70/E3 Sundarbans (reg.), Bang., India
70/D3 Sundargarh, India
61/L2 Sundarnagar, India
88/D4 Sundays (riv.), SAfr.
33/G2 Sunderland, Eng,UK
41/F6 Sundern, Ger.
77/D1 Sundown Nat'l Park, Austl.
106/E3 Sundre, Ab,Can
37/F3 Sundsvall, Swe.
72/B4 Sungaipenuh, Indo.
72/B2 Sungai Petani, Malay.
59/C2 Sungurlu, Turk.
112/B4 Sunland Park, NM,US
37/D3 Sunndalsøra, Nor.
37/E4 Sunne, Swe.
35/F4 Sunninghill, Eng,UK
116/K12 Sunnyvale, Ca,US
65/H8 Su-no-saki (cape), Japan
110/B3 Sun Prairie, Wi,US
115/B3 Sunset Beach, Ca,US
77/B2 Sunset Country (reg.), Austl.
108/E4 Sunset Crater Nat'l Mon., Az,US
77/F5 Sunshine, Austl.
57/P3 Suntar-Khayata (mts.), Rus.
41/G4 Süntel (mts.), Ger.
85/E5 Sunyani, Gha.
87/F2 Sunzu (peak), Zam.
64/B4 Suo (sea), Japan
69/D1 Suoi Rut, Viet.
37/H3 Suomenselkä (reg.), Fin.
69/D4 Suong, Camb.
92/C6 Supe, Peru
110/C2 Superior (lake), Can., US
108/E4 Superior, Az,US
106/E4 Superior, Mt,US
110/A2 Superior, Wi,US
110/B2 Superior (upland), Wi,US
69/C3 Suphan Buri, Thai.
73/J4 Supiori (isl.), Indo.
60/E2 Sūq ash Shuyūkh, Iraq
59/L4 Şuqaylabīyah, Syria
66/D4 Suqian, China
97/F3 Sur (pt.), Arg.
43/E4 Sûr (riv.), Belg.
108/B3 Sur (pt.), Ca,US
55/H1 Sura (riv.), Rus.
72/D5 Surabaya, Indo.
70/D4 Surada, India
72/D5 Surakarta, Indo.
67/D6 Surallah, Phil.
39/K4 Šurany, Slvk.
70/B3 Surat, India
70/B2 Suratgarh, India
69/B4 Surat Thani, Thai.
43/G6 Surbourg, Fr.
97/J7 Sur, Campo de Hielo (glacier), Chile
50/E3 Surčin, Yugo.
50/F4 Surdulica, Yugo.
43/E4 Sûre (riv.), Belg., Lux.
70/B3 Surendranagar, India
44/C3 Surgères, Fr.
56/H3 Surgut, Rus.
70/E3 Sūri, India
47/F2 Súria, Sp.
67/E6 Surigao, Phil.

69/C3 Surin, Thai.
93/G3 Suriname
68/A4 Surkhob (riv.), Taj.
115/K8 Surrattsville (Clinton), Md,US
106/C3 Surrey, BC,Can
31/M8 Surrey (co.), Eng,UK
82/J1 Surt, Libya
37/D3 Sur-Trøndelag (co.), Nor.
59/K5 Şūr (Tyre), Leb.
94/D2 Surubim, Braz.
59/D3 Sürüç, Turk.
65/F3 Suruga (bay), Japan
31/T9 Survilliers, Fr.
81/X18 Sūsah, Tun.
81/X17 Sūsah (gov.), Tun.
64/C4 Susaki, Japan
60/E2 Sūsangerd, Iran
108/B2 Susanville, Ca,US
59/D2 Suşehri, Turk.
66/B4 Sushui (riv.), China
114/J3 Susitna (riv.), Ak,US
65/F3 Susono, Japan
110/E3 Susquehanna (riv.), US
111/H2 Sussex, NB,Can
35/F4 Sussex, Vale of (val.), Eng,UK
40/C6 Susteren, Neth.
57/Q3 Susuman, Rus.
76/H9 Sutherland, Austl.
50/D4 Sutjeska Nat'l Park, Bosn.
61/K2 Sutlej (riv.), India, Pak.
33/H6 Sutterton, Eng,UK
31/N7 Sutton (bor.), Eng,UK
33/J6 Sutton Bridge, Eng,UK
35/E1 Sutton Coldfield, Eng,UK
33/G5 Sutton in Ashfield, Eng,UK
33/J5 Sutton on Sea, Eng,UK
33/H5 Sutton on Trent, Eng,UK
88/D4 Suurberge (mts.), SAfr.
78/G6 Suva (cap.), Fiji
65/F2 Suwa, Japan
39/M1 Suwałki, Pol.
39/M2 Suwałki (prov.), Pol.
113/H4 Suwannee (riv.), Fl,US
79/J6 Suwarrow (atoll), Cookls.
59/K5 Şuwaylih, Jor.
66/D4 Suzhou, China
66/E5 Suzhou, China
65/E2 Suzu, Japan
64/E3 Suzuka, Japan
65/M10 Suzuka (range), Japan
65/E2 Suzu-misaki (cape), Japan
45/J4 Suzzara, It.
56/C2 Svalbard (arch.), Nor.
69/D4 Svay Rieng, Camb.
37/E4 Svealand (reg.), Swe.
38/F1 Svendborg, Den.
103/S7 Svendsen (pen.), NW,Can
37/E4 Svenljunga, Swe.
53/P4 Sverdlovsk (Yekaterinburg), Rus.
103/S7 Sverdrup (chan.), NW,Can
103/R7 Sverdrup (isls.), NW,Can
56/H2 Sverdrup (isl.), Rus.
54/D1 Svetlogorsk, Bela.
55/G3 Svetlograd, Rus.
50/E4 Svetozarevo, Yugo.
37/P7 Svíahnúkar (peak), Ice.
50/E3 Svilajnac, Yugo.
51/H5 Svilengrad, Bul.
51/G4 Svishtov, Bul.
39/J4 Svitavy, Czh.
63/K1 Svobodnyy, Rus.
51/F4 Svoge, Bul.
37/E1 Svolvær, Nor.
57/Q2 Svyatyy Nos (cape), Rus.
35/E1 Swadlincote, Eng,UK
35/G1 Swaffham, Eng,UK
76/D3 Swain (reefs), Austl.
113/H3 Swainsboro, Ga,US
79/H5 Swains Island (atoll), ASam.
87/C2 Swa-Kibula, Zaire
87/B5 Swakopmund, Namb.
33/G3 Swale (riv.), Eng,UK
35/H4 Swalecliffe, Eng,UK
35/G4 Swale, The (chan.), Eng,UK
40/D6 Swalmen, Neth.
106/D2 Swan (hills), Ab,Can
107/H2 Swan (riv.), Mb, Sk,Can
100/E4 Swan (isls.), Hon.
35/E5 Swanage, Eng,UK
77/B2 Swan Hill, Austl.
31/P7 Swanley, Eng,UK
35/G4 Swanley Hextable, Eng,UK
107/H2 Swan River, Mb,Can
31/P7 Swanscombe, Eng,UK
34/C3 Swansea, Wal,UK
34/C3 Swansea (bay), Wal,UK
115/E6 Swarthmore, Pa,US
88/D3 Swart Kei (riv.), SAfr.
39/J2 Swarzędz, Pol.
88/B2 Swarzrand (mts.), Namb.
32/B2 Swatragh, NI,UK
35/E5 Sway, Eng,UK
89/E2 Swaziland
37/E3 Sweden
106/C4 Sweet Home, Or,US
112/C3 Sweetwater, Tx,US
106/F5 Sweetwater (riv.), Wy,US
88/C4 Swellendam, SAfr.
39/J3 Świdnica, Pol.
39/M3 Świdnik, Pol.
39/H2 Świdwin, Pol.
39/J3 Świebodzice, Pol.
39/H2 Świebozin, Pol.
39/K2 Świecie, Pol.
106/G3 Swift Current, Sk,Can
35/E3 Swindon, Eng,UK
33/H6 Swineshead, Eng,UK
39/H2 Świnoujście, Pol.
33/G5 Swinton, Eng,UK
45/G3 Swiss (plat.), Swi.
43/F2 Swist Bach (riv.), Ger.
45/G3 Switzerland
32/B5 Swords, Ire.
52/G3 Syamozero (lake), Rus.
39/J3 Syców, Pol.
77/D2 Sydney, Austl.
111/J2 Sydney, NS,Can
76/H8 Sydney (inset), Austl.
79/H5 Sydney (Manra) (atoll), Kiri.
111/J2 Sydney Mines, NS,Can
41/F3 Syke, Ger.
53/L3 Syktyvkar, Rus.
113/G3 Sylacauga, Al,US
37/E3 Sylarna (peak), Swe.
71/F3 Sylhet, Bang.
38/E1 Sylt (isl.), Ger.
53/N4 Sylva (riv.), Rus.
110/D3 Sylvania, Oh,US
116/F6 Sylvan Lake, Mi,US
49/L6 Syntagma Square, Gre.
115/G5 Syosset, NY,US
98/C Syowa, Ant.
109/G3 Syracuse, Ks,US
110/E3 Syracuse, NY,US
48/D4 Syracuse (Siracusa), It.
56/G5 Syrdar'ya (riv.), Asia
60/C1 Syria
71/G4 Syriam, Burma
53/L3 Sysola (riv.), Rus.
35/E1 Syston, Eng,UK
55/J1 Syzran', Rus.
50/E1 Szabolcs-Szatmár-Bereg (co.), Hun.
39/J2 Szamotuły, Pol.
50/E2 Szarvas, Hun.
50/D2 Százhalombatta, Hun.
39/H2 Szczecin, Pol.
39/H2 Szczecin (prov.), Pol.
39/J2 Szczecinek, Pol.
39/L2 Szczytno, Pol.
50/E2 Szeged, Hun.
50/E2 Szeghalom, Hun.
50/E2 Szegvár, Hun.
50/D2 Székesfehérvár, Hun.
50/D2 Szekszárd, Hun.
50/D2 Szentendre, Hun.
50/E2 Szentes, Hun.
50/E1 Szerencs, Hun.
39/M1 Szeskie (peak), Pol.
50/C2 Szigetvár, Hun.
50/E2 Szolnok, Hun.
50/C2 Szombathely, Hun.
39/H3 Szprotawa, Pol.
39/K2 Sztum, Pol.
39/J2 Szubin, Pol.
39/L3 Szydłowiec, Pol.

T

67/D5 Tabaco, Phil.
61/G2 Tabas, Iran
100/C4 Tabasco (state), Mex.
94/A3 Tabatinga (mts.), Braz.
106/E3 Taber, Ab,Can
47/E3 Tabernes de Valldigna, Sp.
94/C2 Tabira, Braz.
78/G5 Tabiteuea (atoll), Kiri.
67/D5 Tablas (isl.), Phil.
88/B4 Table (bay), SAfr.
88/L10 Table (mtn.), SAfr.
109/J3 Table Rock (lake), Ar, Mo,US
46/B1 Taboada, Sp.
45/L2 Tábor, Czh.
87/F2 Tabora, Tanz.
84/D5 Tabou, IvC.
79/K4 Tabuaeran (Fanning) (atoll), Kiri.
67/D4 Tabuk, Phil.
60/C3 Tabūk, SAr.
94/C2 Tabuleiro do Norte, Braz.
78/F6 Tabwemasana (mtn.), Van.
101/F6 Tacarcuna (mt.), Pan.
68/D2 Tacheng, China
67/D3 Tachia (riv.), Tai.
64/A4 Tachibana (bay), Japan
65/F3 Tachikawa, Japan
67/D3 Tachoshui, Tai.
45/K2 Tachov, Czh.
67/E5 Tacloban, Phil.
92/D7 Tacna, Peru
116/C3 Tacoma, Wa,US
92/E7 Tacora (vol.), Chile
47/X16 Tacoronte, Canl.,Sp.
97/G1 Tacuarembó, Uru.
97/G2 Tacuarembó (dept.), Uru.
65/F2 Tadami (riv.), Japan
65/L10 Tadaoka, Japan
33/G4 Tadcaster, Eng,UK
82/F2 Tademaït (plat.), Alg.
70/D4 Tadepallegūdem, India
79/V12 Tadine, NCal.
35/E4 Tadley, Eng,UK
60/C2 Tadmur, Syria
65/M9 Tado, Japan
64/C3 Tadotsu, Japan
70/C5 Tādpatri, India
82/H2 Tadrart (mts.), Alg., Libya
31/N8 Tadworth, Eng,UK
63/K4 T'aebaek (mts.), NKor., SKor.
63/K4 Taech'ŏn, SKor.
63/K4 Taegang-got (pt.), NKor.
64/A3 Taegu, SKor.
63/K4 Taejŏn, SKor.
34/B3 Taf (riv.), Wal,UK
46/E1 Tafalla, Sp.
34/C3 Taff (riv.), Wal,UK
91/C2 Tafí Viejo, Arg.
60/F2 Taft, Iran
61/H3 Taftān (mtn.), Iran
65/M9 Taga, Japan
54/F3 Taganrog, Rus.
54/F3 Taganrog (gulf), Rus., Ukr.
84/C2 Tagant (reg.), Mrta.
61/G1 Tagarav (peak), Trkm.
64/B4 Tagawa, Japan
67/D6 Tagbilaran, Phil.
45/G5 Taggia, It.
82/E1 Taghit, Alg.
114/M3 Tagish, Yk,Can
45/K3 Tagliamento (riv.), It.
42/D5 Tagnon, Fr.
73/F2 Tagolo (pt.), Phil.
78/E6 Tagula (isl.), PNG
67/E6 Tagum, Phil.
53/P4 Tagun (riv.), Rus.
46/B3 Tagus (riv.), Port., Sp.
72/B3 Tahan (peak), Malay.
65/N10 Tahara, Japan
82/G3 Tahat (peak), Alg.
81/R16 Tahat, Oued et (riv.), Alg.
79/L6 Tahenea (atoll), FrPol.
79/L6 Tahiti (isl.), FrPol.
112/E3 Tahlequah, Ok,US
114/J3 Tahneta (pass), Ak,US
108/C3 Tahoe (lake), Ca, Nv,US
112/C3 Tahoka, Tx,US
85/G3 Tahoua, Niger
85/G3 Tahoua (dept.), Niger
106/B3 Tahsis, BC,Can
86/B3 Tahtā, Egypt
79/L6 Tahuata (isl.), FrPol.
73/G3 Tahulandang (isl.), Indo.
66/L8 Tai (lake), China
63/H4 Tai'an, China
79/X15 Taiarapu (pen.), FrPol.
66/C3 Taibai Shan (mtn.), China
67/D3 Taichung, Tai.
66/C3 Taihang (mts.), China
67/D3 Taihsi, Tai.
65/L10 Taima, Japan
36/C2 Tain, Sc,UK
67/D3 Tainan, Tai.
49/H4 Tainaron, Ákra (cape), Gre.
84/D5 Taï Nat'l Park, IvC.
94/B4 Taiobeiras, Braz.
79/L5 Taiohae, FrPol.
67/D2 Taipei (cap.), Tai.
63/J2 Taiping (peak), China
72/B3 Taiping, Malay.
64/C3 Taisha, Japan
65/L10 Taishi, Japan
67/C2 Taishun, China
96/B5 Taitao (pen.), Chile
67/D3 Taitung, Tai.
67/D3 Taiwan
67/C3 Taiwan (str.), China, Tai.
49/H4 Taíyetos (mts.), Gre.
66/C3 Taiyuan, China
66/D4 Taizhou, China
66/E2 Taizi (riv.), China
72/C4 Tajam (peak), Indo.
82/H3 Tajarhī, Libya
56/H6 Tajikistan
65/F2 Tajima, Japan
65/E3 Tajimi, Japan
65/L10 Tajiri, Japan
46/C3 Tajo (Tagus) (riv.), Sp.
60/F1 Tajrīsh, Iran
100/C4 Tajumulco (vol.), Guat.
46/D2 Tajuña (riv.), Sp.
69/B2 Tak, Thai.
65/G2 Takahagi, Japan
64/D3 Takahama, Japan
64/C3 Takahashi, Japan
64/C3 Takahashi (riv.), Japan
65/G2 Takahata, Japan
65/L10 Takaishi, Japan
64/D3 Takamatsu, Japan
65/M10 Takami-yama (peak), Japan
64/B4 Takanabe, Japan
65/E2 Takaoka, Japan
75/R10 Takapuna, NZ
65/L10 Takarazuka, Japan
79/L6 Takaroa (isl.), FrPol.
65/F2 Takasaki, Japan
65/M9 Takashima, Japan
65/L10 Takatori, Japan
64/D3 Takatsuki, Japan
65/E2 Takayama, Japan
64/E3 Takefu, Japan
64/C3 Takehara, Japan
60/E1 Tākestān, Iran
64/B4 Taketa, Japan
65/M10 Taketoyo, Japan
69/D4 Takev, Camb.
71/H4 Ta Khli, Thai.
83/R2 Takht-e Jamshīd (Persepolis) (ruins), Iran
65/M10 Taki, Japan
102/E2 Takijuq (lake), NW,Can
63/N3 Takikawa, Japan
65/K10 Takino, Japan
106/B2 Takla (lake), BC,Can
68/D4 Takla Makan (des.), China
85/E5 Takoradi, Gha.
59/H6 Talā, Egypt
33/E5 Talacre, Wal,UK
96/Q9 Talagante, Chile
70/B3 Talāja, India
85/G2 Talak (reg.), Niger
87/C2 Tala Mugongo, Ang.
72/B4 Talang (peak), Indo.
43/F5 Talange, Fr.
44/F3 Talant, Fr.
92/B4 Talara, Peru
68/B3 Talas (riv.), Kaz.
59/C2 Talas, Turk.
73/G3 Talaud (isls.), Indo.
46/C3 Talavera de la Reina, Sp.
70/D6 Talawakele, SrL.
83/M5 Talawdī, Sudan
46/C3 Talayuela, Sp.
74/D2 Talbot (cape), Austl.
96/C2 Talca, Chile
96/B3 Talcahuano, Chile
70/E3 Tālcher, India
68/C3 Taldy-Kurgan, Kaz.
44/C4 Talence, Fr.
56/H5 Talgar, Kaz.
34/C3 Talgarth, Wal,UK
73/F4 Taliabu (isl.), Indo.
83/M6 Tali Post, Sudan
73/E5 Taliwang, Indo.
59/H6 Talkhā, Egypt
113/G3 Talladega, Al,US
59/E3 Tall 'Afar, Iraq
113/G4 Tallahassee (cap.), Fl,US
113/F3 Tallahatchie (riv.), Ms,US
59/N9 Tall 'Āşūr (Ba'al Hazor) (mtn.), WBnk.
115/E6 Talleyville, De,US
52/E4 Tallinn (cap.), Est.
59/E3 Tall Kayf, Iraq
113/H3 Tallulah (falls), Ga,US
113/F3 Tallulah, La,US
83/N5 Talo (peak), Eth.
70/B3 Taloda, India
61/J1 Tāloqān, Afg.
91/B2 Taltal, Chile
102/E2 Taltson (riv.), NW,Can
69/C4 Talumphuk (pt.), Thai.
61/L2 Talwāra, India
65/H7 Tama, Japan
65/H7 Tama (riv.), Japan
65/M10 Tamaki, Japan
85/E4 Tamale, Gha.
78/G5 Tamana (atoll), Kiri.
80/C2 Tamanghasset, Alg.
34/B5 Tamar (riv.), Eng,UK
50/D2 Tamási, Hun.
100/B3 Tamazunchale, Mex.
65/L9 Tamba, Japan
65/L9 Tamba (hills), Japan
84/B3 Tambacounda, Sen.
84/B3 Tambacounda (reg.), Sen.
84/C3 Tambaoura, Falaise de (escarp.), Mali
72/C3 Tambelan (isls.), Indo.
73/E5 Tambora (peak), Indo.
77/C3 Tamboritha (peak), Austl.
55/G1 Tambov, Rus.
55/G1 Tambov Obl., Rus.
46/A1 Tambre (riv.), Sp.
83/L6 Tambura, Sudan
35/E1 Tame (riv.), Eng,UK
46/B2 Tâmega (riv.), Port.
85/H2 Tamgak (peak), Niger
84/B3 Tamgué, Massif du (reg.), Gui., Sen.
70/C5 Tamil Nadu (state), India
69/E3 Tam Ky, Viet.
69/D2 Tam Le, Viet.
113/H5 Tampa, Fl,US
37/G3 Tampere, Fin.
100/B3 Tampico, Mex.
72/A3 Tampulonanjing (peak), Indo.
100/B3 Tamuín, Mex.
100/B3 Tamulipas (state), Mex.
77/D1 Tamworth, Austl.
35/E1 Tamworth, Eng,UK
71/K3 Tan (riv.), China
83/N5 Tana (lake), Eth.
80/F5 Tana (riv.), Kenya
37/H1 Tana (riv.), Nor.
64/D4 Tanabe, Japan
95/B2 Tanabi, Braz.
37/J1 Tanafjorden (fjord), Nor.
114/C6 Tanaga (isl.), Ak,US
48/D2 Tanagro (riv.), It.
65/G2 Tanagura, Japan
69/C5 Tanah Merah, Malay.
74/E3 Tanami (des.), Austl.
69/D4 Tan An, Viet.
114/J3 Tanana (riv.), Ak,US
45/H4 Tanaro (riv.), It.
70/C2 Tānda, India
70/D2 Tandā, India
84/D3 Tanda (lake), Mali
83/M5 Tandaltī, Sudan
51/H3 Ţăndărei, Rom.
96/F3 Tandil, Arg.
61/J3 Tando Ādam, Pak.
61/J3 Tando Allāhyār, Pak.
61/J3 Tando Muhammad Khān, Pak.
77/B2 Tandou (lake), Austl.
32/B3 Tandragee, NI,UK
64/B5 Tanega (isl.), Japan
69/B2 Tanem (range), Burma, Thai.
82/E3 Tanezrouft (des.), Alg., Mali
66/C3 Tang (riv.), China
66/C4 Tang (riv.), China
87/G2 Tanga, Tanz.
89/H8 Tangainony, Madg.
87/F2 Tanganyika (lake), Afr.
93/G6 Tangará da Serra, Braz.
114/G1 Tangent (pt.), Ak,US
38/F2 Tangerhütte, Ger.
81/M13 Tanger (Tangier), Mor.
68/E5 Tanggula (mts.), China
68/F5 Tanggula Shankou (pass), China
81/M13 Tangier (Tanger), Mor.
116/B3 Tanglewilde-Thompson Place, Wa,US
68/E5 Tangra (lake), China
67/D6 Tangub, Phil.
73/H5 Tanimbar (isls.), Indo.
67/D6 Tanjay, Phil.
72/A3 Tanjungbalai, Indo.
72/C5 Tanjungkarang-Telukbetung, Indo.
72/C4 Tanjungpandan, Indo.
72/A3 Tanjungpura, Indo.
61/K2 Tānk, Pak.
78/F6 Tanna (isl.), Van.
65/L9 Tannan, Japan
68/F1 Tannu-Ola (mts.), Mong., Rus.
85/E5 Tano (riv.), Ghana, IvC.
59/H6 Ţanţā, Egypt
83/M1 Ţanţā, Egypt
82/C2 Tan-Tan, Mor.
100/B3 Tantoyuca, Mex.
70/D4 Tanuku, India
87/F2 Tanzania
65/H7 Tanzawa-yama (peak), Japan
67/B2 Tao (riv.), China
69/B4 Tao (isl.), Thai.
63/J2 Tao'er (riv.), China
48/D4 Taormina, It.
109/F3 Taos, NM,US
82/E3 Taoudenni, Mali
81/N13 Taourirt, Mor.
67/B2 Taoyuan, China
67/D3 Taoyuan, Tai.
52/E4 Tapa, Est.
100/C5 Tapachula, Mex.
93/G4 Tapajós (riv.), Braz.
93/G3 Tapanahoni (riv.), Sur.
92/E5 Tapauá (riv.), Braz.
67/D5 Tapaz, Phil.
95/B4 Tapejara, Braz.
95/B4 Tapes, Braz.
72/B3 Tapis (peak), Malay.
85/F3 Tapoa (prov.), Burk.
50/C2 Tapolca, Hun.
110/E4 Tappahannock, Va,US
115/G4 Tappan, NY,US
115/G4 Tappan Zee (reach), NY,US
116/C3 Tapps (lake), Wa,US
70/B3 Tāpti (riv.), India
86/B5 Taqab, Sudan
86/D5 Taqātu' Hayyā, Sudan
95/B4 Taquara, Braz.
95/B4 Taquari, Braz.
93/G7 Taquari (riv.), Braz.
95/B2 Taquaritinga, Braz.
95/B2 Taquarituba, Braz.
68/B3 Tar (riv.), Kyr.
50/D4 Tara (riv.), Bosn., Yugo.
56/H4 Tara, Rus.
85/H4 Taraba (riv.), Nga.
59/K4 Tarābulus (Tripoli), Leb.
82/H1 Ţarābulus (Tripoli) (cap.), Libya
32/B4 Tara, Hill of (hill), Ire.
73/E3 Tarakan, Indo.
46/D2 Tarancón, Sp.
87/G1 Tarangire Nat'l Park, Tanz.
48/E2 Taranto, It.
48/E3 Taranto (gulf), It.
92/C5 Tarapoto, Peru
44/F4 Tarare, Fr.
44/F5 Tarascon, Fr.
92/D5 Tarauacá, Braz.
79/M7 Taravai (isl.), FrPol.
78/G4 Tarawa (atoll), Kiri.
46/E2 Tarazona, Sp.
46/E3 Tarazona de la Mancha, Sp.
68/D2 Tarbagatay (mts.), Kaz.
61/K2 Tarbela (res.), Pak.
44/D5 Tarbes, Fr.
113/J3 Tarboro, NC,US
50/A2 Tarcento, It.
44/E3 Tardes (riv.), Fr.
44/D4 Tardoire (riv.), Fr.
63/M2 Tardoki-Jani (peak), Rus.
77/E1 Taree, Austl.
81/V18 Tarf (lake), Alg.
86/C2 Ţarfā', Wādī al (dry riv.), Egypt
86/B4 Tarfāwī, Bīr (well), Egypt
32/D2 Tarf Water (riv.), Sc,UK
82/H1 Tarhūnah, Libya
46/C4 Tarifa, Sp.
92/F8 Tarija, Bol.
73/J4 Tariku (riv.), Indo.
73/J4 Tariku-taritatu (plain), Indo.
62/B4 Tarim (basin), China
68/D3 Tarim (riv.), China
61/J2 Tarin (riv.), Afg.
73/J4 Taritatu (riv.), Indo.
54/E3 Tarkhankut, Mys (cape), Ukr.
85/E5 Tarkwa, Gha.
67/D4 Tarlac, Phil.
92/C6 Tarma, Peru
44/D5 Tarn (riv.), Fr.
62/E2 Tarna (riv.), Mong.
61/J2 Tarnak (riv.), Afg.
39/L3 Tarnobrzeg, Pol.
39/L3 Tarnobrzeg (prov.), Pol.
39/L3 Tarnów, Pol.
39/L3 Tarnów (prov.), Pol.
68/D5 Taro (lake), China
45/J4 Taro (riv.), It.
82/D1 Taroudannt, Mor.
113/H4 Tarpon Springs, Fl,US
33/F5 Tarporley, Eng,UK
48/B1 Tarquinia, It.
47/F2 Tarragona, Sp.
47/F2 Tàrrega, Sp.
115/G4 Tarrytown, NY,US
59/C3 Tarsus, Turk.
52/E4 Tartu, Est.
59/K4 Ţarţūs, Syria
59/K4 Ţarţūs (dist.), Syria
65/M9 Tarui, Japan
64/B5 Tarumizu, Japan
69/B5 Tarutao Nat'l Park, Thai.
62/D2 Tarvagatay (mts.), Mong.
33/F5 Tarvin, Eng,UK
69/D3 Ta Seng, Camb.
68/E2 Tashanta, Rus.
56/F5 Tashauz, Trkm.
55/L4 Tashauz Obl., Trkm.
68/A3 Tashkent (cap.), Uzb.
68/B3 Tash-Kumyr, Kyr.
72/C5 Tasikmalaya, Indo.
59/C3 Taşkent, Turk.
59/C2 Taşköprü, Turk.
75/* Tasman (sea)
77/C4 Tasman (pen.), Austl.
75/R11 Tasman (bay), NZ
77/C4 Tasman Head (cape), Austl.
77/C4 Tasmania (state), Austl.
50/F2 Tăşnad, Rom.
50/D2 Tata, Hun.
82/D2 Tata, Mor.
50/D2 Tatabánya, Hun.
110/D2 Tatachikapika (riv.), On,Can
79/M6 Tatakoto (isl.), FrPol.
62/D4 Tatalin (riv.), China
63/N2 Tatar (str.), Rus.
53/L5 Tatar Aut. Rep., Rus.
56/H4 Tatarsk, Rus.
82/H1 Tatāwīn, Tun.
65/F3 Tateyama, Japan
65/E2 Tate-yama (mtn.), Japan
102/E2 Tathlina (lake), NW,Can
84/B2 Tatilt (well), Mrta.
102/G3 Tatnam (cape), Mb,Can
85/H3 Tatokou, Niger
39/K4 Tatranský Nat'l Park, Slvk.
39/K4 Tatrzański Nat'l Park, Pol.
31/P8 Tatsfield, Eng,UK
65/E3 Tatsuno, Japan
33/H5 Tattershall, Eng,UK
59/E2 Tatvan, Turk.
94/B2 Tauá, Braz.
95/H8 Taubaté, Braz.
45/H2 Tauberbischofsheim, Ger.
45/K3 Tauern, Hohe (mts.), Aus.
45/K2 Taufkirchen, Ger.
109/K3 Taum Sauk (peak), Mo,US
71/G3 Taungdwingyi, Burma
69/B1 Taunggyi, Burma
61/K2 Taunsa, Pak.
111/S8 Taunton, On,Can
34/C4 Taunton, Eng,UK
111/G3 Taunton, Ma,US
45/H1 Taunusstein, Ger.
75/S10 Taupo, NZ
75/S10 Taupo (lake), NZ
39/M1 Tauragė, Lith.
75/S10 Tauranga, NZ
44/D3 Taurion (riv.), Fr.
59/C3 Taurus (mts.), Turk.
46/E2 Tauste, Sp.
44/C2 Taute (riv.), Fr.
79/X15 Tautira, FrPol.
78/E5 Tauu (isls.), PNG
108/E3 Tavaputs (plat.), Ut,US
113/H4 Tavares, Fl,US
59/B3 Tavas, Turk.
53/Q4 Tavda (riv.), Rus.
35/H1 Taverham, Eng,UK
31/S9 Taverny, Fr.
79/Z17 Taveuni (isl.), Fiji
46/B4 Tavira, Port.
34/B5 Tavistock, Eng,UK
69/B3 Tavoy, Burma
63/L3 Tavrichanka, Rus.
59/B2 Tavşanlı, Turk.
34/B5 Tavy (riv.), Eng,UK
34/B4 Taw (riv.), Eng,UK
65/L10 Tawaramoto, Japan
110/D2 Tawas City, Mi,US
73/E3 Tawau, Malay.
34/C3 Tawe (riv.), Wal,UK
67/C6 Tawi-tawi (isl.), Phil.
86/D5 Tawkar, Sudan
82/G1 Tawzar, Tun.
100/B4 Taxco, Mex.
61/K2 Taxila (ruins), Pak.
68/C4 Taxkorgan (Taxkorgan Tajik Zizhixian), China
36/D2 Tay (riv.), Sc,UK
36/C2 Tay, Loch (lake), Sc,UK
109/H2 Taylor, Ne,US
110/B4 Taylorville, Il,US
57/L2 Taymyr (isl.), Rus.
56/K2 Taymyr (pen.), Rus.
56/K2 Taymyr (riv.), Rus.
56/J2 Taymyr Aut. Okr., Rus.
69/D4 Tay Ninh, Viet.
56/K4 Tayshet, Rus.
67/C5 Taytay, Phil.
56/J3 Taz (riv.), Rus.
81/M13 Taza, Mor.
81/M13 Tazekka (peak), Mor.
113/H2 Tazewell, Tn,US
110/D4 Tazewell, Va,US
83/K2 Tāzirbū (oasis), Libya
100/D5 Tazumal (ruins), ESal.
55/H4 Tbilisi (cap.), Geo.
87/B1 Tchibanga, Gabon
82/H6 Tcholliré, Camr.
39/K1 Tczew, Pol.
92/E4 Tea (riv.), Braz.
33/H5 Tealby, Eng,UK
75/Q12 Te Anau, NZ
75/Q12 Te Anau (lake), NZ
115/F5 Teaneck, NJ,US
100/C4 Teapa, Mex.
75/S10 Te Araroa, NZ
75/S10 Te Aroha, NZ
75/S10 Te Awamutu, NZ
72/B4 Tebak (peak), Indo.
81/W18 Tébessa, Alg.
81/W18 Tebessa (mts.), Alg., Tun.
85/F2 Tebesselamane (well), Mali
91/E2 Tebicuary (riv.), Par.
72/A3 Tebingtinggi, Indo.
55/H4 Tebulos-mta (peak), Rus.
47/E5 Tech (riv.), Fr.
44/J3 Techirghiol, Rom.
96/C4 Tecka (riv.), Arg.
101/P10 Tecomán, Mex.
101/N9 Tecuala, Mex.
51/H3 Tecuci, Rom.
116/G7 Tecumseh, On,Can
110/D3 Tecumseh, Mi,US
109/H2 Tecumseh, Ne,US
61/H1 Tedzhen, Trkm.
56/G6 Tedzhen (riv.), Trkm.
33/G2 Tees (bay), Eng,UK
33/G2 Tees (riv.), Eng,UK
92/F4 Tefé, Braz.
92/E4 Tefé (riv.), Braz.
72/C5 Tegal, Indo.
40/D6 Tegelen, Neth.
82/H2 Tegheri (well), Libya
32/E6 Tegid, Llyn (lake), Wal,UK
85/H3 Tégouma (wadi), Niger
100/D5 Tegucigalpa (cap.), Hon.
102/G2 Tehek (lake), NW,Can
60/F1 Tehrān (cap.), Iran
68/C5 Tehri, India
101/L8 Tehuacán, Mex.
100/B4 Tehuantepec (gulf), Mex.
100/C4 Tehuantepec (isth.), Mex.
47/X16 Teide (peak), Canl.,Sp.
34/B2 Teifi (riv.), Wal,UK
83/L4 Teiga (plat.), Sudan
34/C5 Teignmouth, Eng,UK
46/B3 Tejo (Tagus) (riv.), Port.
109/H2 Tekamah, Ne,US
75/R9 Te Kao, NZ
100/D3 Tekax, Mex.
68/C3 Tekeli, Kaz.
68/C3 Tekes (riv.), China
60/C6 Tekezē Wenz (reg.), Eth.
83/N5 Tekezē Wenz (riv.), Eth., Sudan
68/D4 Tekiliktag (peak), China
51/H5 Tekirdağ, Turk.
70/D4 Tekkali, India
75/S10 Te Kuiti, NZ
70/D3 Tel (riv.), India
100/D4 Tela, Hon.
81/Q16 Télagh, Alg.
55/H4 Telavi, Geo.
59/K5 Tel Aviv (dist.), Isr.
59/K5 Tel Aviv-Yafo, Isr.
47/X17 Telde, Canl.
84/E2 Télé (lake), Mali
68/G2 Telem (lake), Mong.
95/B3 Telemaco Borba, Braz.
37/D4 Telemark (co.), Nor.
73/E3 Telen (riv.), Indo.
51/G4 Teleorman (co.), Rom.
82/G3 Telertheba (peak), Alg.
93/G5 Teles Pires (riv.), Braz.
34/D1 Telford, Eng,UK
45/J3 Telfs, Aus.
41/E5 Telgte, Ger.
84/B4 Télimélé, Gui.
59/N9 Tel Jericho Nat'l Park, WBnk.
106/B2 Telkwa, BC,Can
81/Q16 Tell Atlas (mts.), Alg.
110/C4 Tell City, In,US
70/C5 Tellicherry, India
108/F3 Telluride, Co,US
59/N7 Tel Megiddo Nat'l Park, Isr.
62/D2 Telmen (lake), Mong.
72/B3 Telok Anson, Malay.
68/E1 Telotskoye (lake), Rus.
52/D5 Telšiai, Lith.
39/G2 Teltow (reg.), Ger.
85/E5 Tema, Gha.
110/D2 Temagami (lake), On,Can
88/E2 Tembisa, SAfr.
101/J6 Temblador, Ven.
87/C2 Tembo, Zaire
34/D2 Teme (riv.), Eng,UK
50/D3 Temerin, Yugo.
72/B3 Temerloh, Malay.
68/B1 Temirtau, Kaz.
111/F1 Témiscamie (riv.), Qu,Can
110/E2 Témiscaming, Qu,Can
62/E1 Temnik (riv.), Rus.
79/M7 Temoe (isl.), FrPol.
108/E4 Tempe, Az,US
48/A2 Tempio Pausania, It.
112/D4 Temple, Tx,US
32/B2 Templepatrick, NI,UK
77/G5 Templestowe, Austl.
39/G2 Templin, Ger.
100/B3 Tempoal, Mex.
87/C3 Tempué, Ang.
54/F3 Temryuk, Rus.
42/D1 Temse, Belg.
96/B3 Temuco, Chile
75/R11 Temuka, NZ
82/D5 Tena Kourou (peak), Burk.
70/D4 Tenāli, India
69/B3 Tenasserim (range), Burma
69/B4 Tenasserim (Thanintharyi) (div.), Burma
40/D2 Ten Boer, Neth.
34/D2 Tenbury, Eng,UK
34/B3 Tenby, Wal,UK
83/P5 Tendaho, Eth.
65/G1 Tendō, Japan
82/G3 Ténéré du Tafassasset (des.), Niger
85/H2 Ténéré, 'Erg du (des.), Niger
47/X16 Tenerife (isl.), Canl.
81/R15 Ténès, Alg.
47/L6 Tenes (riv.), Sp.
69/B1 Teng (riv.), Burma
73/E4 Tenggarong, Indo.
62/E4 Tengger (des.), China
68/A1 Tengiz (lake), Kaz.
45/G4 Tenibres (peak), It.
91/D1 Teniente Enciso Nat'l Park, Par.
50/D3 Tenja, Cro.
85/E4 Tenkodogo, Burk.
113/F2 Tennessee (riv.), US
113/G3 Tennessee (state), US
96/C2 Teno, Chile
37/H1 Tenojoki (riv.), Fin.
100/C4 Tenosique, Mex.
65/L10 Tenri, Japan
65/E3 Tenryū (riv.), Japan
35/G4 Tenterden, Eng,UK
69/B2 Ten Thousand Buddhas, Cave of, Burma
73/F3 Tentolomatinan (peak), Indo.
46/A1 Teo, Sp.
100/A3 Teocaltiche, Mex.
95/A2 Teodoro Sampaio, Braz.
95/D1 Teófilo Otoni, Braz.
101/P9 Tepatitlán de Morelos, Mex.
101/P9 Tepic, Mex.
39/G3 Teplice, Czh.
101/M7 Tepoca (cape), Mex.
79/L6 Tepoto (isl.), FrPol.
101/P9 Tequila, Mex.
47/G1 Ter (riv.), Sp.
85/F3 Téra, Niger
46/B1 Tera (riv.), Sp.
40/B4 Ter Aar, Neth.
79/K4 Teraina (Washington) (atoll), Kiri.
48/C1 Teramo, It.
59/E2 Tercan, Turk.
47/S12 Terceira (isl.), Azor.,Port.
96/E2 Tercero (riv.), Arg.
51/K2 Terderovsk (bay), Ukr.
55/H4 Terek (riv.), Rus.
94/B2 Teresina, Braz.
95/L7 Teresópolis, Braz.
42/C4 Tergnier, Fr.
62/D4 Tergun Daba (mts.), China
40/B5 Terheijden, Neth.
52/G1 Teriberskiy, Mys (pt.), Rus.
40/C2 Terkaplesterpoelen (lake), Neth.
51/H5 Terkirdağ (prov.), Turk.
61/J1 Termez, Uzb.
48/C4 Termini Imerese, It.
100/C4 Términos (lag.), Mex.
108/B2 Termo, Ca,US
48/D1 Termoli, It.
34/D1 Tern (riv.), Eng,UK
73/G3 Ternate, Indo.
40/A6 Terneuzen, Neth.
48/C1 Terni, It.
44/F3 Ternin (riv.), Fr.
42/B3 Ternoise (riv.), Fr.
54/C2 Ternopol', Ukr.
54/C2 Ternopol' Obl., Ukr.

63/N2 Terpeniya (bay), Rus.
106/A2 Terrace, BC,Can
110/C1 Terrace Bay, On,Can
48/C2 Terracina, It.
111/Q8 Terra Cotta, On,Can
48/A3 Terralba, It.
94/B4 Terra Nova, Braz.
94/C3 Terra Nova, Braz.
111/L1 Terra Nova Nat'l Park, Nf,Can
47/G2 Terrassa, Sp.
44/D4 Terrasson-la-Villedieu, Fr.
111/N6 Terrebonne, Qu,Can
113/G2 Terre Haute, In,US
76/H8 Terrey Hills, Austl.
35/G1 Torrington Saint Clement, Eng,UK
107/G4 Terry, Mt,US
68/A1 Tersakkan (riv.), Kaz.
40/C2 Terschelling (isl.), Neth.
47/E2 Teruel, Sp.
69/B5 Terutao (isl.), Thai.
51/H4 Tervel, Bul.
45/K3 Terza Grande (peak), It.
62/C1 Tes, Mong.
62/D2 Tes, Mong.
44/D5 Tescou (riv.), Fr.
114/G1 Teshekpuk (lake), Ak,US
63/N3 Teshio-dake (mtn.), Japan
62/D2 Tesiyn (riv.), Mong.
62/C1 Tes-Khem (riv.), Rus.
50/C3 Teslić, Bosn.
102/C3 Teslin (lake), BC,Can
114/M3 Teslin, Yk,Can
102/C2 Teslin (riv.), Yk,Can
85/G3 Tessaoua, Niger
43/E1 Tessenderlo, Belg.
35/E4 Test (riv.), Eng,UK
47/G1 Têt (riv.), Fr.
34/D3 Tetbury, Eng,UK
45/G4 Tête de l'Estrop (peak), Fr.
51/G4 Teteven, Bul.
33/H5 Tetford, Eng,UK
79/L6 Tetiaroa (isl.), FrPol.
43/F5 Teting-sur-Nied, Fr.
114/K3 Tetlin Nat'l Wild. Ref., Ak,US
106/F4 Teton (riv.), Mt,US
81/M13 Tétouan, Mor.
50/E4 Tetovo, Macd.
47/N9 Tetuan, Sp.
91/D1 Teuco (riv.), Arg.
48/A3 Teulada (cape), It.
107/J3 Teulon, Mb,Can
41/F4 Teutoburger Wald (for.), Ger.
45/K5 Tevere (Tiber) (riv.), It.
59/K5 Teverya (Tiberias), Isr.
36/D3 Teviot (riv.), Sc,UK
76/D4 Tewantin-Noosa, Austl.
34/D3 Tewkesbury, Eng,UK
112/E3 Texarkana, Ar, Tx,US
112/C4 Texas (state), US
112/E4 Texas City, Tx,US
40/B2 Texel (isl.), Neth.
109/G3 Texoma, Ok,US
52/J4 Teykovo, Rus.
100/B4 Teziutlán, Mex.
71/F2 Tezpur, India
69/C1 Tha (riv.), Laos
102/G2 Tha-anne (riv.), NW,Can
88/E3 Thabana-Ntlenyana (peak), Les.
89/E2 Thabankulu (peak), SAfr.
88/D2 Thabazimbi, SAfr.
69/B3 Tha Chin (riv.), Thai.
69/B4 Thaen (pt.), Thai.
69/D1 Thai Binh, Viet.
69/C3 Thailand
69/C4 Thailand (gulf), Thai.
69/D1 Thai Nguyen, Viet.
61/K2 Thal, Pak.
68/B5 Thal (des.), Pak.
69/C5 Thaleban Nat'l Park, Thai.
60/E6 Thamar, Jabal (mtn.), Yem.
35/F3 Thame, Eng,UK
35/F3 Thame (riv.), Eng,UK
110/D3 Thames (riv.), On,Can
75/S10 Thames, NZ
35/G3 Thames (riv.), Eng,UK
70/B4 Thāna, India
35/H4 Thanet, Isle of (isl.), Eng,UK
71/J5 Thang Duc, Viet.
69/D2 Thanh Hoa, Viet.
71/J4 Thanh Lang Xa, Viet.
69/D4 Thanh Phu, Viet.
69/D4 Thanh Tri, Viet.
69/B4 Thanintharyi (Tenasserim) (div.), Burma
70/C5 Thanjavur, India
61/J3 Thar (des.), India, Pak.
70/B3 Tharād, India
71/G4 Tharrawaddy, Burma
49/J2 Thásos (isl.), Gre.
35/E4 Thatcham, Eng,UK
69/D1 That Khe, Viet.
69/B2 Thaton, Burma
71/H4 Tha Uthen, Thai.
35/G3 Thaxted, Eng,UK
39/H4 Thaya (riv.), Aus.
71/G4 Thayetmyo, Burma
71/G3 Thazi, Burma
35/E4 Theale, Eng,UK
86/C3 Thebes (ruins), Egypt
112/C3 The Caprock (cliffs), NM,US
106/C4 The Dalles, Or,US
77/B3 The Grampians (mts.), Austl.
40/B4 The Hague ('s-Gravenhage) (cap.), Neth.
77/C3 The Lakes Nat'l Park, Austl.
102/F2 Thelon (riv.), NW,Can
32/B2 The Loup, NI,UK
107/H3 Theodore, Sk,Can
108/E4 Theodore Roosevelt (lake), Az,US
107/G4 Theodore Roosevelt Nat'l Park, ND,US
107/H2 The Pas, Mb,Can
42/B5 Thérain (riv.), Fr.
49/H3 Thermaic (Salonika) (gulf), Gre.
49/H3 Thermopílai (Thermopylae) (pass), Gre.
106/F5 Thermopolis, Wy,US
31/U9 Thérouanne (riv.), Fr.
110/D2 Thessalon, On,Can
49/H2 Thessaloníki (Salonika), Gre.
49/H3 Thessaly (reg.), Gre.
35/G2 Thet (riv.), Eng,UK
35/G2 Thetford, Eng,UK
111/G2 Thetford Mines, Qu,Can
43/E2 Theux, Belg.
101/J4 The Valley (cap.), Angu.
31/T9 Thève (riv.), Fr.
35/G1 The Wash (bay), Eng,UK
35/G4 The Weald (reg.), Eng,UK
112/E4 The Woodlands, Tx,US
34/D1 The Wrekin (hill), Eng,UK
31/P7 Theydon Bois, Eng,UK
31/T10 Thiais, Fr.
49/G3 Thíamis (riv.), Gre.
113/F4 Thibodaux, La,US
107/J3 Thief River Falls, Mn,US
106/C5 Thielsen (peak), Or,US
69/D4 Thien Ngon, Viet.
44/E4 Thiers, Fr.
31/T9 Thiers-sur-Thève, Fr.
84/A3 Thiès, Sen.
84/A3 Thiès (reg.), Sen.
87/G1 Thika, Kenya
70/E2 Thimphu (cap.), Bhu.
37/N7 Thingvellir Nat'l Park, Ice.
43/F5 Thionville, Fr.
49/J4 Thíra (isl.), Gre.
33/E2 Thirlmere (lake), Eng,UK
33/G3 Thirsk, Eng,UK
37/D4 Thisted, Den.
37/P6 Thistilfjördhur (bay), Ice.
114/L3 Thistle (mtn.), Yk,Can
79/Z18 Thithia (isl.), Fiji
67/B5 Thitu (isl.)
49/H3 Thívai, Gre.
37/N7 Thjórsa (riv.), Ice.
102/G2 Thlewiaza (riv.), NW,Can
69/D4 Thoi Binh, Viet.
40/B5 Tholen, Neth.
40/B5 Tholen (isl.), Neth.
43/G5 Tholey, Ger.
113/G3 Thomaston, Ga,US
113/G4 Thomasville, Al,US
113/H4 Thomasville, Ga,US
113/H3 Thomasville, NC,US
75/G4 Thompson (riv.), Austl.
106/C3 Thompson (riv.), BC,Can
107/J2 Thompson, Mb,Can
109/J2 Thompson (riv.), Ia, Mo,US
106/E4 Thompson Falls, Mt,US
116/B3 Thompson Place-Tanglewilde, Wa,US
102/E1 Thomsen (riv.), NW,Can
76/A4 Thomson (riv.), Austl.
113/H3 Thomson, Ga,US
69/C3 Thon Buri, Thai.
71/J4 Thon Cam Lo, Viet.
69/B2 Thongwa, Burma
69/E4 Thon Lac Nghiep, Viet.
45/G3 Thonon-les-Bains, Fr.
69/E4 Thon Song Pha, Viet.
108/E4 Thoreau, NM,US
106/E2 Thorhild, Ab,Can
31/U10 Thorigny-sur-Marne, Fr.
33/G2 Thornaby-on-Tees, Eng,UK
34/D3 Thornbury, Eng,UK
33/H4 Thorne, Eng,UK
111/R8 Thornhill, On,Can
32/E1 Thornhill, Sc,UK
33/G2 Thornley, Eng,UK
33/G3 Thornthwaite, Eng,UK
33/E4 Thornton Cleveleys, Eng,UK
33/H3 Thornton Dale, Eng,UK
111/R9 Thorold, On,Can
31/M7 Thorpe, Eng,UK
35/H3 Thorpe le Soken, Eng,UK
33/G2 Thorpe Thewles, Eng,UK
44/C3 Thouars, Fr.
44/C3 Thouet (riv.), Fr.
115/B2 Thousand Oaks, Ca,US
54/C4 Thracian (sea), Gre., Turk.
106/F4 Three Forks, Mt,US
114/L4 Three Guardsmen (mtn.), BC,Can
106/E3 Three Hills, Ab,Can
77/C4 Three Hummock (isl.), Austl.
75/R9 Three Kings (isls.), NZ
69/B3 Three Pagodas (pass), Burma
85/E5 Three Points (cape), Gha.
110/C3 Three Rivers, Mi,US
112/D3 Throckmorton, Tx,US
74/C5 Throssell (lake), Austl.
34/B5 Thrushel (riv.), Eng,UK
34/D2 Thruxton, Eng,UK
69/D4 Thu Dau Mot, Viet.
69/D4 Thu Duc, Viet.
42/D3 Thuin, Belg.
44/E5 Thuir, Fr.
103/T7 Thule Air Base, Grld.
45/G3 Thun, Swi.
110/B1 Thunder Bay, On,Can
69/C2 Thung Salaeng Luang Nat'l Park, Thai.
45/H3 Thur (riv.), Swi.
45/H1 Thüringer Wald (for.), Ger.
38/F3 Thuringia (state), Ger.
35/E2 Thurlaston, Eng,UK
36/B4 Thurles, Ire.
98/T Thurston (isl.), Ant.
100/B4 Tiacolula, Mex.
92/E7 Tiahuanco (ruins), Bol.
114/M5 Tian (pt.), BC,Can
94/B1 Tianguá, Braz.
66/D3 Tianjin, China
66/D3 Tianjin (prov.), China
66/C5 Tianmen, China
66/K9 Tianmu (mts.), China
56/H5 Tian Shan (range), Asia
62/F5 Tianshui, China
66/C5 Tiantangzhai (mtn.), China
81/R16 Tiaret, Alg.
79/S9 Tiavea, WSam.
95/B2 Tibaji (riv.), Braz.
82/H6 Tibati, Camr.
33/F6 Tibberton, Eng,UK
84/C4 Tibé, Pic de (peak), Gui.
59/K5 Tiberias (Sea of Galilee) (lake), Isr., Syria
59/K5 Tiberias (Teverya), Isr.
45/K5 Tiber (Tevere) (riv.), It.
82/J3 Tibesti (mts.), Chad, Libya
68/D5 Tibet (Xizang) Aut. Reg., China
47/L7 Tibidabo (peak), Sp.
82/H1 Ţīb, Ra's aţ (Cape Bon) (cape), Tun.
33/G5 Tibshelf, Eng,UK
101/G4 Tiburon (cape), Haiti
101/M8 Tiburón (isl.), Mex.
116/K11 Tiburon, Ca,US
35/G4 Ticehurst, Eng,UK
116/P14 Tichigan (lake), Wi,US
84/C2 Tichît, Dhar (hills), Mrta.
82/C3 Tichla, WSah.
45/H4 Ticino (riv.), It.
33/G5 Tickhill, Eng,UK
110/F3 Ticonderoga, NY,US
100/D3 Ticul, Mex.
37/E4 Tidaholm, Swe.
33/G5 Tideswell, Eng,UK
82/F2 Tidikelt (plain), Alg.
84/C2 Tidjikdja, Mrta.
73/G3 Tidore (isl.), Indo.
84/A2 Tidra (isl.), Mrta.
47/X16 Tiede Nat'l Park
40/C5 Tiel, Neth.
63/J3 Tieling, China
47/N9 Tielmes, Sp.
42/C1 Tielt, Belg.
43/D2 Tielt-Winge, Belg.
84/D4 Tiemba (riv.), IvC.
68/E3 Tiemen Guan (pass), China
43/D2 Tienen, Belg.
58/H5 Tien Shan (range), China
69/D1 Tien Yen, Viet.
69/D2 Tien Yen, Viet.
82/J3 Tieroko (peak), Chad
37/F3 Tierp, Swe.
108/F3 Tierra Amarilla, NM,US
97/L8 Tierra del Fuego (isl.), Arg., Chile
97/L8 Tierra del Fuego, Antártida e Islas del Atlántico Sur (prov.), Arg.
97/K8 Tierra del Fuego Nat'l Park, Arg.
46/C2 Tiétar (riv.), Sp.
95/B2 Tietê (riv.), Braz.
82/C2 Tifariti, WSah.
110/D3 Tiffin, Oh,US
113/H4 Tifton, Ga,US
79/V12 Tiga (isl.), NCal.
82/H6 Tignère, Camr.
97/S12 Tigre, Arg.
92/C4 Tigre (riv.), Peru
101/J6 Tigre (riv.), Ven.
60/D1 Tigris (riv.), Iraq, Turk.
82/J4 Tigui (well), Chad
85/G2 Tiguidit, Falaise de (escarp.), Niger
100/B3 Tihuatlán, Mex.
37/J3 Tiilikkajärven Nat'l Park, Fin.
84/B1 Tijirît (reg.), Mrta.
101/L7 Tijuana, Mex.
95/K8 Tijuca Nat'l Park, Braz.
95/B3 Tijucas, Braz.
95/B1 Tijuco (riv.), Braz.
100/C4 Tikal Nat'l Park, Guat.
70/C3 Tīkamgarh, India
114/G3 Tikchik (lakes), Ak,US
79/L6 Tikehau (atoll), FrPol.
54/G3 Tikhoretsk, Rus.
52/G4 Tikhvin, Rus.
49/H2 Tikveš (lake), Macd.
40/C5 Tilburg, Neth.
31/Q7 Tilbury, Eng,UK
112/D4 Tilden, Tx,US
33/H5 Till (riv.), Eng,UK
106/C4 Tillamook, Or,US
44/F3 Tille (riv.), Fr.
37/D4 Tilst, Den.
36/D2 Tilt (riv.), Sc,UK
96/Q9 Tiltil, Chile
53/L2 Timan (ridge), Rus.
75/R11 Timaru, NZ
54/F3 Timashevsk, Rus.
94/D2 Timbaúba, Braz.
107/H4 Timber Lake, SD,US
95/B3 Timbó, Braz.
84/E2 Timbuktu (Tombouctou), Mali
73/H4 Timbuni (riv.), Indo.
49/G3 Timfristós (peak), Gre.
81/V18 Timgad (ruins), Alg.
82/F2 Timimoun, Alg.
84/A2 Timiris (cape), Mrta.
50/E3 Timiş (co.), Rom.
50/E3 Timiş (riv.), Rom.
50/E3 Timişoara, Rom.
85/G2 Ti-m-Mershoï (wadi), Niger
110/D1 Timmins, On,Can
110/B2 Timms (hill), Wi,US
94/B2 Timon, Braz.
115/K7 Timonium, Md,US
74/D2 Timor (sea)
73/G5 Timor (isl.), Indo.
95/D1 Timóteo, Braz.
57/N4 Timpton (riv.), Rus.
37/F3 Timrå, Swe.
113/G3 Tims Ford (lake), Tn,US
88/E3 Tina (riv.), SAfr.
67/E6 Tinaca (pt.), Phil.
70/C5 Tindivanam, India
82/D2 Tindouf, Alg.
46/B1 Tineo, Sp.
67/C2 Ting (riv.), China
76/F7 Tingalpa (res.), Austl.
77/D3 Tingaringy Nat'l Park, Austl.
82/H2 Tinghert (upland), Libya
84/C4 Tingi (mts.), Gui., SLeo.
114/F2 Tingmerkpuk (mtn.), Ak,US
92/C5 Tingo María, Peru
96/C2 Tinguirrica (vol.), Chile
93/L6 Tinharé, Braz.
94/C4 Tinharé (isl.), Braz.
69/D2 Tinh Gia, Viet.
78/D3 Tinian (isl.), NMar.
84/C4 Tinkisso (riv.), Gui.
116/Q16 Tinley Park, Il,US
91/C2 Tinogasta, Arg.
49/J4 Tínos (isl.), Gre.
42/C5 Tinqueux, Fr.
82/G2 Tinrhert (plat.), Alg.
82/D1 Tinrhir, Mor.
71/G2 Tinsukia, India
34/B5 Tintagel, Eng,UK
46/B4 Tinto (riv.), Sp.
115/F5 Tinton Falls, NJ,US
33/G5 Tintwistle, Eng,UK
82/F4 Ti-n-Zaouâten, Alg.
107/H3 Tioga, ND,US
72/B3 Tioman (isl.), Malay.
81/S15 Tipaza, Alg.
35/G3 Tiptree, Eng,UK
70/C5 Tiptūr, India
79/L6 Tiputa, FrPol.
94/A1 Tiracambu (mts.), Braz.
86/C2 Tiran (str.), Egypt
49/F2 Tiranë (cap.), Alb.
86/C3 Tiran, Jazīrat (isl.), Egypt
45/J3 Tirano, It.
51/J2 Tiraspol', Mol.
59/A2 Tire, Turk.
54/F4 Tirebolu, Turk.
85/F1 Tirest (well), Mali
53/G3 Tîrgovişte, Rom.
51/H3 Tîrgu Bujor, Rom.
51/F3 Tîrgu Cărbuneşti, Rom.
51/H2 Tîrgu Frumos, Rom.
51/F3 Tîrgu Jiu, Rom.
51/F2 Tîrgu Lăpuş, Rom.
51/G2 Tîrgu Mureş, Rom.
51/H2 Tîrgu Neamţ, Rom.
51/H2 Tîrgu Ocna, Rom.
51/H3 Tîrgu Secuiesc, Rom.
61/K1 Tirich Mīr (mtn.), Pak.
51/G2 Tîrnava Mare (riv.), Rom.
51/G2 Tîrnava Mică (riv.), Rom.
51/G2 Tîrnăveni, Rom.
49/H3 Tírnavos, Gre.
45/J3 Tirol (prov.), Aus.
34/C1 Tir Rhiwiog (mtn.), Wa,UK
45/K2 Tirschenreuth, Ger.
48/A2 Tirso (riv.), It.
70/C5 Tiruchchendūr, India
70/C5 Tiruchchirāppalli, India
70/C6 Tiruchendūr, India
70/C6 Tirunelveli, India
70/C5 Tirupati, India
70/C5 Tiruppattūr, India
70/C5 Tiruppūr, India
70/C5 Tirūr, India
70/C5 Tiruvannāmalai, India
54/B2 Tisa (riv.), Eur.
34/D4 Tisbury, Eng,UK
107/G2 Tisdale, Sk,Can
109/H4 Tishomingo, Ok,US
81/R16 Tissemsilt, Alg.
50/E2 Tisza (riv.), Hun.
50/E2 Tiszaföldvár, Hun.
50/E2 Tiszafüred, Hun.
50/E2 Tiszakécske, Hun.
50/E1 Tiszalök, Hun.
50/E2 Tiszavasvári, Hun.
50/E3 Titel, Yugo.
92/E7 Titicaca (lake), Bol., Peru
70/D3 Titlagarh, India
45/H3 Titlis (peak), Swi.
50/D4 Titograd, Yugo.
50/D4 Titovo Užice, Yugo.
50/E5 Titov Veles, Macd.
50/E5 Titov vrh (peak), Macd.
31/P8 Titsey, Eng,UK
51/G3 Titu, Rom.
113/H4 Titusville, Fl,US
84/A3 Tivaouane, Sen.
50/D4 Tivat, Yugo.
34/C5 Tiverton, Eng,UK
100/D3 Tizimín, Mex.
81/T15 Tizi Ouzou, Alg.
61/L1 Tiznap (riv.), China
82/D2 Tiznit, Mor.
40/C3 Tjeukemeer (lake), Neth.
101/P8 Tlahualilo de Zaragoza, Mex.
100/B4 Tlalnepantla, Mex.
100/B4 Tlapa, Mex.
100/B4 Tlaxcala, Mex.
100/B4 Tlaxcala (state), Mex.
81/Q16 Tlemcen, Alg.
82/J3 Tmassah, Libya
51/G2 Toaca (peak), Rom.
89/H8 Toamasina, Madg.
89/J7 Toamasina (prov.), Madg.
116/B2 Toandos (pen.), Wa,US
79/L6 Toau (atoll), FrPol.
106/B3 Toba (inlet), BC,Can
62/D5 Toba, China
72/A3 Toba (lake), Indo.
63/L5 Toba, Japan
101/J5 Tobago (isl.), Trin.
61/J2 Toba Kākar (range), Pak.
46/E3 Tobarra, Sp.
68/B5 Toba Tek Singh, Pak.
32/B2 Tobermore, NI,UK
94/C3 Tobias Barreto, Braz.
74/D4 Tobin (lake), Austl.
107/H2 Tobin (lake), Sk,Can
111/H2 Tobique (riv.), NB,Can
53/Q4 Tobol (riv.), Kaz., Rus.
56/G4 Tobol'sk, Rus.
83/K1 Tobruk, Libya
115/E4 Tobyhanna (lake), Pa,US
53/L2 Tobysh (riv.), Rus.
93/J5 Tocantinópolis, Braz.
94/A2 Tocantins (riv.), Braz.
94/A3 Tocantins (state), Braz.
113/H3 Toccoa, Ga,US
45/H3 Toce (riv.), It.
65/F2 Tochigi, Japan
65/F2 Tochigi (pref.), Japan
65/F2 Tochio, Japan
46/C4 Tocina, Sp.
91/B1 Tocopilla, Chile
101/F6 Tocumen, Pan.
101/H5 Tocuyito, Ven.
101/H5 Tocuyo (riv.), Ven.
65/H7 Toda, Japan
70/C2 Toda Bhīm, India
35/F3 Toddington, Eng,UK
48/C1 Todi, It.
33/F4 Todmorden, Eng,UK
94/C4 Todos os Santos (bay), Braz.
101/M9 Todos Santos, Mex.
93/G3 Toekomstig (res.), Sur.
106/E2 Tofield, Ab,Can
37/E3 Töfsingdalens Nat'l Park, Swe.
79/H6 Tofua (isl.), Tonga
84/C2 Togba (well), Mrta.
114/G4 Togiak Nat'l Wild. Ref., Ak,US
85/F4 Togo
65/N9 Tōgō, Japan
108/E4 Tohatchi, NM,US
79/X15 Tohivea (peak), FrPol.
65/F2 Tōhoku (prov.), Japan
65/F3 Toi, Japan
65/M9 Tōin, Japan
108/C3 Toiyabe (range), Nv,US
64/C3 Tojō, Japan
65/L10 Tōjō, Japan
65/E3 Tōkai, Japan
65/F2 Tōkamachi, Japan
86/D5 Tokar, Sudan
78/B1 Tokara (isls.), Japan
86/D5 Tokar Game Rsv., Sudan
59/D2 Tokat, Turk.
79/H5 Tokelau (terr.), NZ
65/N9 Toki, Japan
65/N9 Toki (riv.), Japan
65/H6 Tokigawa, Japan
65/M10 Tokoname, Japan
75/S10 Tokoroa, NZ
65/F3 Tokorozawa, Japan
62/B2 Toksun, China
68/B3 Toktogul (res.), Kyr.
64/D3 Tokushima, Japan
64/C4 Tokushima (pref.), Japan
65/H7 Tokyo (bay), Japan
65/F3 Tōkyō (cap.), Japan
65/H7 Tōkyō (inset) (cap.), Japan
81/G7 Tôlañaro, Madg.
51/H4 Tolbukhin, Bul.
91/F1 Toledo, Braz.
67/D5 Toledo, Phil.
46/C3 Toledo, Sp.
46/C3 Toledo (mts.), Sp.
110/D3 Toledo, Oh,US
112/E4 Toledo Bend (res.), La, Tx,US
48/C1 Tolentino, It.
96/C3 Tolhuaca Nat'l Park, Chile
68/D2 Toli, China
89/G8 Toliara, Madg.
89/H8 Toliara (prov.), Madg.
73/F3 Tolitoli, Indo.
32/B5 Tolka (riv.), Ire.
50/A2 Tolmezzo, It.
50/D2 Tolna, Hun.
50/D2 Tolna (co.), Hun.
73/F4 Tolo (gulf), Indo.
46/D1 Tolosa, Sp.
116/D2 Tolt (riv.), Wa,US
96/B3 Toltén, Chile
96/B3 Toltén (riv.), Chile
100/B4 Toluca, Mex.
55/J1 Tol'yatti, Rus.
56/J4 Tom' (riv.), Rus.
110/B3 Tomah, Wi,US
63/N3 Tomakomai, Japan
78/G6 Tomanivi (peak), Fiji
46/A3 Tomar, Port.
49/G3 Tómaros (peak), Gre.
39/M3 Tomaszów Lubelski, Pol.
39/L3 Tomaszów Mazowiecki, Pol.
36/D2 Tomatin, Sc,UK
92/G6 Tombador (mts.), Braz.
83/M6 Tombe, Sudan
113/F4 Tombigbee (riv.), Al, Ms,US
87/B2 Tomboco, Ang.
84/E2 Tombouctou (Timbuktu), Mali
108/E5 Tombstone, Az,US
87/B4 Tombua, Ang.
96/B3 Tomé, Chile
44/B2 Tomé (isl.), Fr.
39/G1 Tomelilla, Swe.
46/D3 Tomelloso, Sp.
73/F4 Tomini (gulf), Indo.
46/A2 Tomiño, Sp.
65/H7 Tomiura, Japan
57/N4 Tommot, Rus.
92/E2 Tomo (riv.), Col.
110/C4 Tompkinsville, Ky,US
56/J4 Tomsk, Rus.
115/F6 Toms River, NJ,US
114/K3 Tom White (mtn.), Ak,US
106/D3 Tonasket, Wa,US
111/S9 Tonawanda, NY,US
31/P8 Tonbridge, Eng,UK
65/L10 Tondabayashi, Japan
73/F3 Tondano, Indo.
37/D5 Tönder, Den.
83/K6 Tondou (mts.), CAfr.
65/J7 Tone, Japan
65/G3 Tone (riv.), Japan
34/C4 Tone (riv.), Eng,UK
60/F1 Tonekābon, Iran
62/F5 Tong (riv.), China
79/H7 Tonga
79/K5 Tongareva (Penrhyn) (atoll), CookIs.
79/H7 Tonga-tapu (isl.), Tonga
62/F4 Tongchuan, China
43/E2 Tongeren, Belg.
67/B2 Tonggu, China
63/K3 Tonghua, China
73/E5 Tongo (peak), Indo.
71/J2 Tongren, China
70/F2 Tongsa (riv.), Bhu.
62/D5 Tongtian (riv.), China
106/G4 Tongue (riv.), Mt, Wy,US
40/D6 Tönisvorst, Ger.
83/L6 Tonj, Sudan
70/C2 Tonk, India
109/H3 Tonkawa, Ok,US
69/D1 Tonkin (gulf), China, Viet.
84/D5 Tonkoui (peak), IvC.
69/C3 Tonle Sap (lake), Camb.
44/D4 Tonneins, Fr.
108/D4 Tonopah, Az,US
108/C3 Tonopah, Nv,US
64/D3 Tonoshō, Japan
88/D2 Tonota, Bots.
37/D4 Tønsberg, Nor.
108/E4 Tonto Nat'l Mon., Az,US
108/D2 Tooele, Ut,US
77/G6 Toomuc (cr.), Austl.
76/C4 Toowoomba, Austl.
115/B2 Topanga, Ca,US
109/J3 Topeka (cap.), Ks,US
106/B2 Topley, BC,Can
51/G2 Topliţa, Rom.
39/K4 Topoľčany, Slvk.
51/G3 Topoloveni, Rom.
51/H4 Topolovgrad, Bul.
52/F2 Topozero (lake), Rus.
106/C4 Toppenish, Wa,US
34/C5 Topsham, Eng,UK
83/M6 Tor, Eth.
65/M9 Torahime, Japan
92/D7 Torata, Peru
73/G3 Torawitan (cape), Indo.
59/A2 Torbalı, Turk.
61/G1 Torbat-e Ḩeydarīyeh, Iran
44/B1 Torbay, Eng,UK
114/H3 Torbert (mtn.), Ak,US
38/E1 Törder, Den.
47/L6 Tordera (riv.), Sp.
46/C2 Tordesillas, Sp.
47/G1 Torelló, Sp.
39/G2 Torgelow, Ger.
42/C1 Torhout, Belg.
65/J7 Toride, Japan
65/E3 Torii-tōge (pass), Japan
46/A1 Toriñana (cape), Sp.
45/G4 Torino (Turin), It.
78/D1 Tori-Shima (isl.), Japan
83/M7 Torit, Sudan
61/H1 Torkestān (mts.), Afg.
46/D2 Tormes (riv.), Sp.
33/H4 Torne (riv.), Eng,UK
41/G1 Tornesch, Ger.
50/D4 Tornik (peak), Yugo.
37/G2 Torniojoki (Torneälven) (riv.), Fin., Swe.
46/C2 Toro, Sp.
91/C2 Toro, Cerro del (peak), Arg.
50/E2 Törökszentmiklós, Hun.
49/H2 Toronaic (gulf), Gre.
111/R8 Toronto, On,Can
52/F4 Toropets, Rus.
83/M7 Tororo, Ugan.
47/N8 Torote (riv.), Sp.
34/B6 Torpoint, Eng,UK
34/C6 Torquay, Eng,UK
115/B3 Torrance, Ca,US
46/D4 Torre del Campo, Sp.
46/D4 Torredonjimeno, Sp.
46/D2 Torrejón de Ardoz, Sp.
46/C1 Torrelavega, Sp.
47/N8 Torrelodones, Sp.
76/B3 Torrens (cr.), Austl.
74/F6 Torrens (lake), Austl.
47/E3 Torrente, Sp.
101/P6 Torreón, Mex.
47/E4 Torre-Pacheco, Sp.
46/D3 Torreperogil, Sp.
74/G2 Torres (str.), Austl.
95/B4 Tôrres, Braz.
78/F6 Torres (isls.), Van.
97/J7 Torres del Paine Nat'l Park, Chile
46/A3 Torres Novas, Port.
46/A3 Torres Vedras, Port.
47/E4 Torrevieja, Sp.
32/B1 Torr Head (pt.), NI,UK
34/B5 Torridge (riv.), Eng,UK
46/C3 Torrijos, Sp.
107/G5 Torrington, Wy,US
46/D4 Torrox, Sp.
30/C2 Tórshavn, Den.
44/B2 Torteval, Chl,UK
101/J4 Tortola (isl.), BVI
48/A3 Tortolì, It.
45/H4 Tortona, It.
47/F2 Tortosa, Sp.
47/F2 Tortosa (cape), Sp.
68/C3 Torugart, Pereval (pass), Kyr.
39/K2 Toruń, Pol.
39/K2 Toruń (prov.), Pol.
36/A3 Tory (isl.), Ire.
39/L4 Torysa (riv.), Slvk.
52/G4 Torzhok, Rus.
64/C4 Tosa, Japan
64/C4 Tosa (bay), Japan
64/C4 Tosashimizu, Japan
87/B5 Toscanini, Namb.
45/J4 Tosco-Emiliano (range), It.
62/D4 Toson (lake), China
62/D2 Tosontsengel, Mong.
45/H3 Töss (riv.), Swi.
33/G1 Tosson (hill), Eng,UK
91/D2 Tostado, Arg.
41/G2 Tostedt, Ger.
64/B4 Tosu, Japan
59/C2 Tosya, Turk.
46/E4 Totana, Sp.
35/E5 Totland, Eng,UK
34/C6 Totnes, Eng,UK
100/A4 Totolapan, Mex.
96/E2 Totoras, Arg.
98/H Totten (glac.), Ant.
31/N7 Tottenham, Eng,UK
33/F4 Tottington, Eng,UK
35/E5 Totton, Eng,UK
64/D3 Tottori, Japan
64/C3 Tottori (pref.), Japan
82/D1 Toubkal, Jebel (peak), Mor.
67/D3 Toucheng, Tai.
107/G3 Touchwood (hills), Sk,Can
84/E3 Tougan, Burk.
82/G1 Touggourt, Alg.
81/S16 Touiel (riv.), Alg.
43/E6 Toul, Fr.
111/H1 Toulnustouc (riv.), Qu,Can
44/F5 Toulon, Fr.
44/D5 Toulouse, Fr.
82/H3 Toumo (well), Niger
84/D5 Toumodi, IvC.
67/D3 Tounan, Tai.
69/B2 Toungoo, Burma
84/D5 Toura (mts.), IvC.
42/C2 Tourcoing, Fr.
44/C5 Tourettes, Pic de (peak), Fr.
46/A1 Touriñan (cape), Sp.
44/C2 Tourlaville, Fr.
42/C2 Tournai, Belg.
31/U10 Tournan-en-Brie, Fr.
44/F3 Tournus, Fr.
44/D3 Tours, Fr.
47/E3 Tous (res.), Sp.
44/B2 Toussaines, Signal de (peak), Fr.
82/J3 Toussidé (peak), Chad
83/K6 Toussoro (peak), CAfr.
88/C4 Touws (riv.), SAfr.
101/G6 Tovar, Ven.
35/E2 Tove (riv.), Eng,UK
62/E2 Tövshrüüleh, Mong.
65/G2 Towada, Japan
35/F2 Towcester, Eng,UK
31/N7 Tower Hamlets (bor.), Eng,UK
33/G2 Tow Law, Eng,UK
107/H3 Towner, ND,US
106/F4 Townsend, Mt,US
116/A2 Townsend (mt.), Wa,US
76/C3 Townshend (cape), Austl.
76/B2 Townsville, Austl.
61/H1 Towraghondi, Afg.
115/K7 Towson, Md,US
73/F4 Towuti (lake), Indo.
68/C3 Toxkan (riv.), China, Kyr.
112/C4 Toyah, Tx,US
112/C4 Toyahvale, Tx,US
65/E2 Toyama, Japan
65/E2 Toyama (bay), Japan
65/E2 Toyama (pref.), Japan
65/N9 Toyoake, Japan
65/E3 Toyohashi, Japan
65/E3 Toyokawa, Japan
65/L10 Toyonaka, Japan
65/L10 Toyono, Japan
64/D3 Toyo'oka, Japan
65/M9 Toyosato, Japan
65/E2 Toyoshina, Japan
65/E3 Toyota, Japan
65/M9 Toyoyama, Japan
114/H2 Tozi (mtn.), Ak,US
69/E3 Tra Bong, Viet.
59/D2 Trabzon, Turk.
111/H2 Tracadie, NB,Can
69/D4 Tra Cu, Viet.
111/F2 Tracy, Qu,Can
116/M11 Tracy, Ca,US
46/B4 Trafalgar (cape), Sp.
47/P10 Trafaria, Port.
96/B3 Traiguén, Chile
106/D3 Trail, BC,Can
45/L3 Traisen (riv.), Aus.
39/J4 Traiskirchen, Aus.
36/A4 Tralee, Ire.
69/D1 Tra Linh, Viet.
95/B4 Tramandaí, Braz.
69/E3 Tra Mi, Viet.
109/G3 Tramperos (cr.), NM, Tx,US
37/E4 Tranås, Swe.
43/D4 Tranet (mtn.), Fr.
69/B5 Trang, Thai.
73/H5 Trangan (isl.), Indo.
48/E2 Trani, It.
98/W Transantarctic (mts.), Ant.
51/F1 Trans-Carpathian Obl., Ukr.
88/E3 Transkei (ind. homeland), SAfr.
50/F2 Transylvania (reg.), Rom.
50/F3 Transylvanian Alps (range), Rom.
69/D4 Tra On, Viet.
48/C3 Trapani, It.
69/D3 Trapeang Veng, Camb.
106/E4 Trapper (peak), Mt,US
31/S10 Trappes, Fr.
77/C3 Traralgon, Austl.
84/B2 Trarza (reg.), Mrta.
48/C1 Trasimeno (lake), It.
46/B2 Trás-os-Montes e Alto Douro (dist.), Port.
88/E2 Trasvaal (prov.), SAfr.
69/C3 Trat, Thai.
45/L2 Traun, Aus.
45/L2 Traun (riv.), Aus.
45/K3 Traunreut, Ger.
45/K3 Traunsee (lake), Aus.
45/K3 Traunstein, Ger.
38/F2 Trave (riv.), Ger.
77/B2 Travellers (lake), Austl.
114/G2 Traverse (peak), Ak,US
107/J4 Traverse (lake), SD,US
110/C2 Traverse City, Mi,US
69/D4 Tra Vinh, Viet.
112/D4 Travis (lake), Tx,US
50/C3 Travnik, Bosn.
34/C2 Trawsalt (mtn.), Wal,UK
32/E6 Trawsfynydd, Wal,UK
32/E6 Trawsfynydd, Llyn (lake), Wal,UK
50/B2 Trbovlje, Slov.
45/H4 Trebbia (riv.), It.
38/G1 Trebel (riv.), Ger.
39/H4 Třebíč, Czh.
50/D4 Trebinje, Bosn.
48/E3 Trebisacce, It.
45/L2 Třeboň, Czh.
46/B4 Trebujena, Sp.

34/C3 Tredegar, Wal,UK
34/C2 Trefeglwys, Wal,UK
32/E5 Trefnant, Wal,UK
34/C2 Tregaron, Wal,UK
97/G2 Treinta y Tres, Uru.
97/G2 Treinta y Tres (dept.), Uru.
45/G4 Tré-la-Tête (mtn.), Fr.
44/C3 Trélazé, Fr.
34/B3 Trelech, Wal,UK
96/D4 Trelew, Arg.
44/D4 Trélissac, Fr.
38/G1 Trelleborg, Swe.
32/D6 Tremadoc (bay), Wal,UK
31/T10 Tremblay-lès-Gonesse, Fr.
32/B4 Tremblestown (riv.), Ire.
106/B2 Trembleur (lake), BC,Can
43/D2 Tremelo, Belg.
48/D1 Tremiti (isls.), It.
108/D2 Tremonton, Ut,US
111/F1 Trenche (riv.), Qu,Can
39/K4 Trenčín, Slvk.
96/E2 Trenque Lauquen, Arg.
33/H5 Trent (riv.), Eng,UK
33/F6 Trent and Mersey (can.), Eng,UK
45/J3 Trentino-Alto Adige (reg.), It.
45/J3 Trento, It.
110/E2 Trenton, On,Can
113/H4 Trenton, Fl,US
113/G3 Trenton, Ga,US
116/F7 Trenton, Mi,US
109/J2 Trenton, Mo,US
115/F5 Trenton (cap.), NJ,US
113/F3 Trenton, Tn,US
34/C3 Treorchy, Wal,UK
49/F2 Trepuzzi, It.
97/T11 Tres Arboles, Uru.
96/E3 Tres Arroyos, Arg.
95/H6 Três Corações, Braz.
95/B2 Três Irmãos (res.), Braz.
91/D2 Tres Isletas, Arg.
95/B2 Três Lagoas, Braz.
95/C1 Três Marias, Braz.
95/C1 Três Marias (res.), Braz.
101/N9 Tres Marías (isls.), Mex.
96/B5 Tres Montes (cape), Chile
96/C4 Tres Picos (peak), Arg.
96/E3 Tres Picos (peak), Arg.
95/H6 Três Pontas, Braz.
96/D5 Tres Puntas (cape), Arg.
95/K7 Três Rios, Braz.
45/J2 Treuchtlingen, Ger.
38/G2 Treuenbrietzen, Ger.
45/H4 Treviglio, It.
45/K4 Treviso, It.
34/A5 Trevose Head (pt.), Eng,UK
115/J7 Triadelphia (res.), Md,US
76/B2 Tribulation (cape), Austl.
49/F3 Tricase, It.
70/C5 Trichūr, India
73/J4 Tricora (peak), Indo.
67/B5 Trident (shoal)
42/A5 Trie-Château, Fr.
31/S10 Triel-sur-Seine, Fr.
43/F4 Trier, Ger.
48/E2 Triggiano, It.
51/G4 Triglav (peak), Bul.
50/A2 Triglav (peak), Slov.
50/A2 Triglav Nat'l Park, Slov.
48/D2 Trigno (riv.), It.
46/B4 Trigueros, Sp.
49/G3 Tríkala, Gre.
49/G3 Trikhonís (lake), Gre.
45/G3 Trimbach, Swi.
33/G2 Trimdon, Eng,UK
70/D6 Trincomalee, SrL.
93/J7 Trindade, Braz.
39/K4 Třinec, Czh.
35/F3 Tring, Eng,UK
96/E3 Trinidad (isl.), Arg.
92/F6 Trinidad, Bol.
97/J7 Trinidad (gulf), Chile
97/T11 Trinidad, Uru.
109/F3 Trinidad, Co,US
101/J5 Trinidad and Tobago
93/N8 Trinidade, Braz.
111/L2 Trinity (bay), Nf,Can
114/H4 Trinity (isls.), Ak,US
108/B2 Trinity (riv.), Ca,US
108/C2 Trinity (range), Nv,US
112/E4 Trinity (riv.), Tx,US
86/D5 Trinkitat, Sudan
89/S15 Triolet, Mrts.
49/H4 Trípolis, Gre.
82/H1 Tripolitania (reg.), Libya
59/K4 Tripoli (Ţarābulus), Leb.
82/H1 Tripoli (Ţarābulus) (cap.), Libya
70/C6 Tripunittura, India
71/F3 Tripura (state), India
28/J7 Tristan da Cunha (isls.), StH.
84/B4 Tristao (isls.), Guin.
96/D4 Triste (peak), Arg.
69/D4 Tri Ton, Viet.
41/H1 Trittau, Ger.
70/C6 Trivandrum, India
39/J4 Trnava, Slvk.
78/E5 Trobriand (isls.), PNG
42/A5 Troesne (riv.), Fr.
45/L3 Trofaiach, Aus.
48/D2 Troia, It.
47/Q11 Tróia, Port.
43/G2 Troisdorf, Ger.
43/G6 Troisfontaines, Fr.
81/N13 Trois Fourches, Cap des (cape), Mor.
111/G1 Trois-Pistoles, Qu,Can
111/F2 Trois-Rivières, Qu,Can
53/P5 Troitsk, Rus.
37/E4 Trollhättan, Swe.
93/G4 Trombetas (riv.), Braz.
81/H6 Tromelin (isl.), Reu.
37/F1 Troms (co.), Nor.
37/F1 Tromsø, Nor.
96/C4 Tronador (peak), Arg., Chile
37/D3 Trondheim, Nor.
48/C1 Tronto (riv.), It.
59/J4 Troodos (mts.), Cyp.
32/D1 Trool, Loch (lake), Sc,UK
36/C3 Troon, Sc,UK
48/D3 Tropea, It.
108/D3 Tropic, Ut,US
32/B1 Trostan (mtn.), NI,UK
31/Q8 Trottiscliffe, Eng,UK
102/D2 Trout (lake), NW,Can
107/K3 Trout (lake), On,Can
33/F3 Troutbeck, Eng,UK
106/E1 Trout Lake, BC,Can
34/D4 Trowbridge, Eng,UK
113/G4 Troy, Al,US
116/F6 Troy, Mi,US
110/F3 Troy, NY,US
113/G1 Troy, Oh,US
51/G4 Troyan, Bul.
51/G4 Troyanski Prokhod (pass), Bul.
44/F2 Troyes, Fr.
49/K3 Troy (Ilium) (ruins), Turk.
50/E4 Trstenik, Yugo.
114/M3 Truitt (peak), Yk,Can
100/D4 Trujillo, Hon.
92/C5 Trujillo, Peru
46/C3 Trujillo, Sp.
101/G6 Trujillo, Ven.
78/E4 Truk (isls.), Micr.
115/G4 Trumbull, Ct,US
34/D2 Trumpet, Eng,UK
69/D1 Trung Khanh, Viet.
111/J2 Truro, NS,Can
34/A6 Truro, Eng,UK
108/F4 Truth Or Consequences, NM,US
39/H3 Trutnov, Czh.
44/E4 Truyère (riv.), Fr.
32/D6 Trwyn Cilan (pt.), Wal,UK
51/G4 Tryavna, Bul.
37/E3 Trysil, Nor.
39/J2 Trzcianka, Pol.
39/H1 Trzebiatów, Pol.
39/J3 Trzebnica, Pol.
39/J2 Trzemeszno, Pol.
50/B2 Tržič, Slov.
62/D3 Tsagaan Bogd (peak), Mong.
62/G2 Tsagaan-Ovoo, Mong.
62/E1 Tsagaan-Üür, Mong.
89/J6 Tsaratanana Massif (plat.), Madg.
88/B2 Tsarisberge (mts.), Namb.
68/F2 Tsast Uul (peak), Mong.
88/E3 Tsatsana (peak), Les.
87/D5 Tsau, Bots.
87/G1 Tsavo, Kenya
87/G1 Tsavo East Nat'l Park, Kenya
87/G1 Tsavo West Nat'l Park, Kenya
68/B1 Tselinograd, Kaz.
62/F2 Tsenhermandal, Mong.
62/D2 Tsetsen-Uul, Mong.
87/B1 Tshela, Zaire
87/B2 Tshibwika, Zaire
87/D2 Tshikapa, Zaire
83/K8 Tshuapa (riv.), Zaire
81/G6 Tsiafajavona (peak), Madg.
53/L2 Tsil'ma (riv.), Rus.
55/G2 Tsimlyansk (res.), Rus.
89/H9 Tsiombe, Madg.
89/H7 Tsiribihina (riv.), Madg.
89/H7 Tsiroanomandidy, Madg.
88/C4 Tsitsikamma Forest & Coastal Nat'l Park, SAfr.
55/G4 Tskhinvali, Geo.
52/G4 Tsna (riv.), Rus.
62/D2 Tsogt, Mong.
62/F3 Tsogt-Ovoo, Mong.
62/F3 Tsogttsetsiy, Mong.
62/F2 Tsöh (riv.), Mong.
88/D3 Tsomo (riv.), SAfr.
64/E3 Tsu, Japan
64/A3 Tsu (isls.), Japan
65/F2 Tsubame, Japan
64/E2 Tsubata, Japan
65/G2 Tsuchiura, Japan
65/M10 Tsuchiyama, Japan
63/M3 Tsugaru (str.), Japan
65/L10 Tsuge, Japan
65/H7 Tsukui, Japan
64/B4 Tsukumi, Japan
87/C4 Tsumeb, Namb.
65/K10 Tsuna, Japan
65/F3 Tsuru, Japan
64/E3 Tsuruga, Japan
65/H7 Tsurugashima, Japan
65/E2 Tsurugi, Japan
64/D4 Tsurugi-san (mtn.), Japan
65/M9 Tsushima, Japan
64/D3 Tsuyama, Japan
72/C5 Tua (cape), Indo.
46/B2 Tua (riv.), Port.
96/B4 Tuamapu (chan.), Chile
79/L6 Tuamotu (arch.), FrPol.
66/B4 Tuan (riv.), China
72/A3 Tuan (pt.), Indo.
69/C1 Tuan Giao, Viet.
72/A3 Tuangku (isl.), Indo.
69/D2 Tuan Thuong, Viet.
67/D4 Tuao, Phil.
54/F3 Tuapse, Rus.
108/E3 Tuba City, Az,US
72/D5 Tuban, Indo.
60/D6 Tuban (riv.), Yem.
95/B4 Tubarão, Braz.
40/D4 Tubbergen, Neth.
45/H2 Tübingen, Ger.
42/D2 Tubize, Belg.
84/C5 Tubmanburg, Libr.
78/H6 Tubou, Fiji
83/K1 Ţubruq (Tobruk), Libya
79/K7 Tubuaï (isls.), FrPol.
79/K7 Tubuaï (isl.), FrPol.
94/C3 Tucano, Braz.
39/J2 Tuchola, Pol.
108/E4 Tucson, Az,US
109/G4 Tucumcari, NM,US
101/H6 Tucupido, Ven.
101/J6 Tucupita, Ven.
93/J4 Tucuruí, Braz.
93/H4 Tucuruí (res.), Braz.
46/E1 Tudela, Sp.
31/P8 Tudeley, Eng,UK
44/E5 Tude, Rochers de la (mtn.), Fr.
88/E3 Tugela (falls), SAfr.
89/E3 Tugela (riv.), SAfr.
113/H2 Tug Fork (riv.), WV,US
67/D4 Tuguegarao, Phil.
73/F5 Tukangbesi (isls.), Indo.
52/D4 Tukums, Lat.
72/D4 Tukung (peak), Indo.
116/C3 Tukwila, Wa,US
100/B3 Tula, Mex.
54/F1 Tula, Rus.
68/F4 Tulagt Ar (riv.), China
100/B3 Tulancingo, Mex.
54/F1 Tula Obl., Rus.
108/C3 Tulare, Ca,US
109/F4 Tularosa, NM,US
109/F4 Tularosa (val.), NM,US
88/L10 Tulbagh, SAfr.
92/C3 Tulcán, Ecu.
51/J3 Tulcea, Rom.
51/J3 Tulcea (co.), Rom.
112/C3 Tulia, Tx,US
114/E5 Tulik (vol.), Ak,US
78/E5 Tulin (isls.), PNG
59/K5 Ţülkarm, WBnk.
113/G3 Tullahoma, Tn,US
36/B4 Tullamore, Ire.
44/D4 Tulle, Fr.
39/J4 Tulln, Aus.
52/G1 Tuloma (riv.), Rus.
109/J3 Tulsa, Ok,US
92/C3 Tuluá, Col.
57/L4 Tulun, Rus.
100/D5 Tuma (riv.), Nic.
108/E5 Tumacacori Nat'l Mon., Az,US
93/H3 Tumac-Humac (mts.), Braz.
92/C3 Tumaco, Col.
67/D4 Tumauini, Phil.
83/J8 Tumba (lake), Zaire
92/B4 Tumbes, Peru
69/C3 Tumbot (peak), Camb.
63/K3 Tumen, China
101/J6 Tumeremo, Ven.
70/C5 Tumkūr, India
36/C2 Tummel (riv.), Sc,UK
63/M1 Tumnin (riv.), Rus.
72/B2 Tumpat, Malay.
73/F4 Tumpu (peak), Indo.
77/D2 Tumut, Austl.
116/B3 Tumwater, Wa,US
59/D2 Tunceli, Turk.
87/F2 Tunduma, Tanz.
87/G3 Tunduru, Tanz.
68/C1 Tundyk (riv.), Kaz.
50/H4 Tundzha (riv.), Bul., Turk.
70/C4 Tungabhadra (res.), India
70/C4 Tungabhadra (riv.), India
77/C3 Tungamah, Austl.
56/K3 Tunguska, Lower (riv.), Rus.
56/K3 Tunguska, Stony (riv.), Rus.
81/X17 Tūnis (cap.), Tun.
48/B4 Tunis (gov.), Tun.
81/X17 Tunis (gulf), Tun.
82/G1 Tunisia
92/D2 Tunjá, Col.
94/A2 Tuntum, Braz.
103/K3 Tunungayualuk (isl.), Nf,Can
96/C2 Tunuyán, Arg.
96/C2 Tunuyán (riv.), Chile
108/B3 Tuolumne (riv.), Ca,US
69/D2 Tuong Duong, Viet.
71/J3 Tuoniang (riv.), China
68/F5 Tuotuo (riv.), China
95/B1 Tupã, Braz.
95/B1 Tupaciguara, Braz.
79/K6 Tupai (isl.), FrPol.
113/F3 Tupelo, Ms,US
95/B2 Tupi Paulista, Braz.
92/E8 Tupiza, Bol.
110/F2 Tupper Lake, NY,US
96/C2 Tupungato (peak), Arg., Chile
70/F2 Tura, India
53/Q4 Tura (riv.), Rus.
63/L1 Turana (mts.), Rus.
75/S10 Turangi, NZ
56/G5 Turan Lowland (plain), Uzb.
101/F5 Turbaco, Col.
61/H3 Turbat, Pak.
101/F6 Turbo, Col.
51/F2 Turda, Rom.
79/M7 Tureia (atoll), FrPol.
39/K2 Turek, Pol.
56/G4 Turgay Obl., Kaz.
110/E1 Turgeon (riv.), Qu,Can
51/H4 Tŭrgovishte, Bul.
59/A2 Turgutlu, Turk.
59/D2 Turhal, Turk.
47/E3 Turia (riv.), Sp.
94/A1 Turiaçu (riv.), Braz.
45/G4 Turin (Torino), It.
83/N7 Turkana (lake), Eth., Kenya
68/A3 Turkestan, Kaz.
50/E2 Túrkeve, Hun.
59/C2 Turkey
56/F6 Turkmenistan
101/G3 Turks and Caicos (isls.), UK
37/G3 Turku (Åbo), Fin.
37/G3 Turku Ja Pori (prov.), Fin.
108/B3 Turlock, Ca,US
101/H5 Turmero, Ven.
32/D1 Turnberry, Sc,UK
100/D4 Turneffe (isls.), Belz.
40/B6 Turnhout, Belg.
106/F1 Turnor Lake, Sk,Can
39/H3 Turnov, Czh.
51/G4 Turnu Măgurele, Rom.
62/B3 Turpan, China
68/E3 Turpan (depr.), China
100/F4 Turquino (pk.), Cuba
36/D2 Turriff, Sc,UK
84/B5 Turtle (isls.), SLeo.
106/F2 Turtleford, Sk,Can
33/F4 Turton, Eng,UK
68/C3 Turugart Shankou (pass), China
95/J6 Turvo (riv.), Braz.
113/G3 Tuscaloosa, Al,US
48/B1 Tuscano (arch.), It.
45/J5 Tuscany (reg.), It.
108/C2 Tuscarora, Nv,US
113/G3 Tuskegee, Al,US
115/C3 Tustin, Ca,US
39/K3 Tuszyn, Pol.
52/H4 Tutayev, Rus.
33/G6 Tutbury, Eng,UK
70/C6 Tuticorin, India
50/E4 Tutin, Yugo.
72/D3 Tutong, Bru.
51/H3 Tutrakan, Bul.
109/H3 Tuttle Creek (lake), Ks,US
79/H6 Tutuila (isl.), ASam.
114/F2 Tututalak (mtn.), Ak,US
62/F2 Tuul (riv.), Mong.
37/H3 Tuusula, Fin.
56/K4 Tuva Aut. Rep., Rus.
78/G5 Tuvalu
60/E4 Ţuwayq, Jabal (mts.), SAr.
33/H5 Tuxford, Eng,UK
101/N9 Tuxpan, Mex.
100/B4 Tuxtepec, Mex.
100/C4 Tuxtla Gutiérrez, Mex.
46/A1 Túy, Sp.
69/D2 Tuyen Hoa, Viet.
69/D1 Tuyen Quang, Viet.
69/E3 Tuy Hoa, Viet.
53/M5 Tuymazy, Rus.
60/E2 Tūysarkān, Iran
59/C2 Tuz (lake), Turk.
108/D4 Tuzigoot Nat'l Mon., Az,US
60/D2 Ţūz Khurmātū, Iraq
50/D3 Tuzla, Bosn.
52/G4 Tver', Rus.
52/G4 Tver' Obl., Rus.
52/G4 Tvertsa (riv.), Rus.
51/G4 Tvŭrditsa, Bul.
39/J3 Twardogóra, Pol.
36/D3 Tweed (riv.), UK
77/E1 Tweed Heads, Austl.
40/D4 Twente (can.), Neth.
40/D4 Twente (reg.), Neth.
111/Q9 Twenty Mile (riv.), On,Can
109/G5 Twin Buttes (res.), Tx,US
106/E5 Twin Falls, Id,US
41/G6 Twiste (riv.), Ger.
41/F3 Twistringen, Ger.
75/R11 Twizel, NZ
109/G3 Two Buttes (riv.), Co,US
77/D3 Twofold (bay), Austl.
107/L4 Two Harbors, Mn,US
106/F2 Two Hills, Ab,Can
110/C2 Two Rivers, Wi,US
35/E1 Twycross, Eng,UK
35/F4 Twyford, Eng,UK
34/C1 Twymyn (riv.), Wal,UK
32/D2 Twynholm, Sc,UK
39/K3 Tychy, Pol.
35/G1 Tydd Saint Giles, Eng,UK
110/E2 Tyendinaga, On,Can
113/H3 Tygart (riv.), SC,US
33/F4 Tyldesley, Eng,UK
112/E3 Tyler, Tx,US
63/N1 Tymovskoye, Rus.
45/L2 Týn, Czh.
109/H2 Tyndall, SD,US
36/C2 Tyndrum, Sc,UK
33/F2 Tyne (riv.), Eng,UK
33/G2 Tyne & Wear (co.), Eng,UK
33/G1 Tynemouth, Eng,UK
60/C2 Tyre, Leb.
59/K5 Tyre (Şūr), Leb.
63/L2 Tyrma (riv.), Rus.
55/G4 Tyrnyauz, Rus.
77/B2 Tyrrell (cr.), Austl.
77/B2 Tyrrell (lake), Austl.
48/B2 Tyrrhenian (sea), It.
115/J8 Tysons Corner, Va,US
55/J3 Tyub-Karagan (pt.), Kaz.
55/J3 Tyulen'i (isls.), Kaz.
55/H3 Tyuleniy (isl.), Rus.
53/Q4 Tyumen', Rus.
53/Q4 Tyumen' Obl., Rus.
68/C3 Tyup, Kyr.
34/B3 Tywi (riv.), Wal,UK
34/B1 Tywyn, Wal,UK
87/F5 Tzaneen, SAfr.

U

79/M5 Ua Huka (isl.), FrPol.
79/L5 Ua Pou (isl.), FrPol.
92/G4 Uatumã (riv.), Braz.
92/E3 Uaupés (riv.), Braz.
50/E3 Ub, Yugo.
95/D2 Ubá, Braz.
43/F2 Übach-Palenberg, Ger.
53/Q5 Ubagan (riv.), Kaz.
94/C4 Ubaitaba, Braz.
94/B1 Ubajara, Braz.
94/B1 Ubajará Nat'l Park, Braz.
83/J7 Ubangi (riv.), Zaire
94/C4 Ubatã, Braz.
95/H8 Ubatuba, Braz.
67/D5 Ubay, Phil.
45/G4 Ubaye (riv.), Fr.
40/C5 Ubbergen, Neth.
64/B4 Ube, Japan
46/D3 Ubeda, Sp.
92/G7 Uberaba (lake), Bol.
95/C1 Uberaba, Braz.
43/F5 Überherrn, Ger.
95/B1 Uberlândia, Braz.
73/J4 Ubia (peak), Indo.
69/D3 Ubon Ratchathani, Thai.
46/C4 Ubrique, Sp.
92/D5 Ucayali (riv.), Peru
38/C3 Uccle, Belg.
53/N5 Uchaly, Rus.
53/X8 Uchinskoye, Rus.
63/N3 Uchiura (bay), Japan
38/F2 Uchte (riv.), Ger.
57/P4 Uchur (riv.), Rus.
43/F5 Uckange, Fr.
39/G2 Uckermark (reg.), Ger.
35/G5 Uckfield, Eng,UK
106/B3 Ucluelet, BC,Can
62/F1 Uda (riv.), Rus.
70/B3 Udaipur, India
37/D4 Uddevalla, Swe.
37/F2 Uddjaure (lake), Swe.
40/C5 Uden, Neth.
40/C5 Udenhout, Neth.
70/C4 Udgīr, India
61/L2 Udhampur, India
45/K3 Udine, It.
70/B5 Udipi, India
53/L4 Udmurt Aut. Rep., Rus.
69/C2 Udon Thani, Thai.
39/H2 Ueckermünde, Ger.
65/F2 Ueda, Japan
83/K7 Uele (riv.), Zaire
41/H3 Uelzen, Ger.
65/F3 Uenohara, Japan
41/G1 Uetersen, Ger.
41/H4 Uetze, Ger.
53/N5 Ufa, Rus.
53/N5 Ufa (riv.), Rus.
35/E3 Uffington, Eng,UK
87/F1 Uganda
49/F3 Ugento, It.
45/G4 Ugine, Fr.
63/N2 Uglegorsk, Rus.
52/H4 Uglich, Rus.
45/L4 Ugljan (isl.), Cro.
54/E1 Ugra (riv.), Rus.
62/F2 Ugtaaltsaydam, Mong.
39/J4 Uherské Hradiště, Czh.
45/K2 Úhlava (riv.), Czh.
87/C2 Uíge, Ang.
55/K2 Uil (riv.), Kaz.
88/L11 Uilkraal (riv.), SAfr.
55/G4 Uilpata, Gora (peak), Rus.
108/E2 Uinta (mts.), Ut,US
94/C2 Uiraúna, Braz.
64/A2 Ŭisŏng, SKor.
88/D4 Uitenhage, SAfr.
40/B3 Uitgeest, Neth.
40/B4 Uithoorn, Neth.
78/F4 Ujae (atoll), Mrsh.
78/F4 Ujelang (atoll), Mrsh.
50/E2 Újfehértó, Hun.
65/L10 Uji, Japan
65/L10 Ujitawara, Japan
70/C3 Ujjain, India
72/E5 Ujung Pandang, Indo.
53/M3 Ukhta, Rus.
108/B3 Ukiah, Ca,US
52/E5 Ukmergė, Lith.
54/D2 Ukraine
62/F2 Ulaanbaatar (cap.), Mong.
62/C2 Ulaangom, Mong.
62/B2 Ulaanhus, Mong.
62/F1 Ulan-Burgasy (mts.), Rus.
63/J2 Ulanhot, China
62/F1 Ulan-Ude, Rus.
68/F5 Ulan Ul (lake), China
87/G2 Ulaya, Tanz.
64/A2 Ulchin, SKor.
50/D5 Ulcinj, Yugo.
62/G2 Uldz (riv.), Mong.
63/H2 Ulgain (riv.), China
70/B4 Ulhāsnagar, India
62/D2 Uliastay, Mong.
83/L8 Ulindi (riv.), Zaire
78/D3 Ulithi (atoll), Micr.
46/A1 Ulla (riv.), Sp.
77/D2 Ulladulla, Austl.
37/F1 Ullsfjorden (fjord), Nor.
33/F2 Ullswater (lake), Eng,UK
64/B2 Ullŭng (isl.), SKor.
45/H2 Ulm, Ger.
64/A3 Ulsan, SKor.
32/A3 Ulster (reg.), Ire.
100/D4 Ulúa (riv.), Hon.
60/D1 Uludoruk (peak), Turk.
59/C3 Ulukışla, Turk.
62/B2 Ulungur (lake), China
62/B2 Ulungur (riv.), China
74/E5 Uluru (Ayers Rock) (peak), Austl.
68/A2 Ulutau, Gora (peak), Kaz.
33/E3 Ulverston, Eng,UK
77/C4 Ulverstone, Austl.
52/F4 Ul'yanovka, Rus.
112/C2 Ulysses, Ks,US
100/D3 Umán, Mex.
54/D2 Uman', Ukr.
94/C2 Umarizal, Braz.
70/D4 Umarkot, India
61/L2 Umāsi La (pass), India
78/D5 Umboi (isl.), PNG
48/C1 Umbria (reg.), It.
45/K5 Umbro-Marchigiano, Appenino (range), It.
56/B3 Ume (riv.), Swe.
37/G3 Umeå, Swe.
37/F2 Umeälv (riv.), Swe.
89/E3 Umfolozi (riv.), SAfr.
89/E3 Umgeni (riv.), SAfr.
61/F4 Umm as Samīm (salt dep.), Oman
83/M4 Umm Durmān (Omdurman), Sudan
59/K5 Umm el Fahm, Isr.
86/C4 Umm Hibal, Bi'r (well), Egypt
83/M5 Umm Ruwābah, Sudan
114/E5 Umnak (isl.), Ak,US
106/C5 Umpqua (riv.), Or,US
88/E3 Umtata, SAfr.
91/F1 Umuarama, Braz.
88/E3 Umzimvubu (riv.), SAfr.
50/B3 Una (riv.), Bosn., Cro.
75/R11 Una (peak), NZ
94/A5 Unaí, Braz.
114/E5 Unalaska (isl.), Ak,US
60/C2 'Unāzah, Jabal (mtn.), SAr.
108/E3 Uncompahgre (plat.), Co,US
107/H4 Underwood, ND,US
79/Z17 Undu (pt.), Fiji
51/E1 Unecha, Rus.
114/F4 Unga (isl.), Ak,US
87/H1 Ungama (bay), Kenya
103/K3 Ungava (bay), Qu,Can
103/J2 Ungava (pen.), Qu,Can
54/C3 Ungeny, Mol.
94/B2 União, Braz.
95/B3 União da Vitória, Braz.
94/C3 União dos Palmares, Braz.
114/E4 Unimak (isl.), Ak,US
92/F4 Unini (riv.), Braz.
109/K3 Union, Mo,US
115/F5 Union, NJ,US
106/D4 Union, Or,US
113/H3 Union, SC,US
116/K11 Union City, Ca,US
115/F5 Union City, NJ,US
113/F2 Union City, Tn,US
100/E3 Unión de Reyes, Cuba
113/G3 Union Springs, Al,US
110/E4 Uniontown, Pa,US
111/R8 Unionville, On,Can
109/J2 Unionville, Mo,US
60/F4 United Arab Emirates
36/* United Kingdom
102/* United States
103/T6 United States (range), NW,Can
106/F2 Unity, Sk,Can
112/D4 Universal City, Tx,US
70/B3 Unjha, India
41/E5 Unna, Ger.
70/D2 Unnāo, India
38/F3 Unstruct (riv.), Ger.
59/D2 Ünye, Turk.
64/A4 Unzen-Amakusa Nat'l Park, Japan
64/B4 Unzen-dake (mtn.), Japan
53/K4 Unzha (riv.), Rus.
65/E2 Uozu, Japan
101/J6 Upata, Ven.
87/E2 Upemba Nat'l Park, Zaire
88/C3 Upington, SAfr.
70/B3 Upleta, India
31/P7 Upminster, Eng,UK
104/U10 Upolu (pt.), Hi,US
79/H6 Upolu (isl.), WSam.
108/C2 Upper (lake), Ca,US
113/H1 Upper Arlington, Oh,US
106/D3 Upper Arrow (lake), BC,Can
45/K2 Upper Austria (prov.), Aus.
115/E6 Upper Darby, Pa,US
35/G5 Upper Dicker, Eng,UK
85/E4 Upper East (reg.), Gha.
75/S11 Upper Hutt, NZ
109/J2 Upper Iowa (riv.), Ia,US
106/C5 Upper Klamath (lake), Or,US
32/B2 Upperlands, NI,UK
110/C2 Upper Peninsula (pen.), Mi,US
107/L5 Upper Peoria (lake), Il,US
107/K3 Upper Red (lake), Mn,US
35/E3 Upper Thames (val.), Eng,UK
85/E4 Upper West (reg.), Gha.
35/F1 Uppingham, Eng,UK
37/F4 Uppsala, Swe.
37/F3 Uppsala (co.), Swe.
114/D3 Upright (cape), Ak,US
76/B2 Upstart (bay), Austl.
107/G4 Upton, Wy,US
34/D2 Upton upon Severn, Eng,UK
60/E2 Ur (ruins), Iraq
65/H7 Uraga (chan.), Japan
94/A1 Uraim (riv.), Braz.
56/F3 Ural (mts.), Rus.
56/F5 Ural (riv.), Rus., Kaz.
55/J2 Ural'sk, Kaz.
55/J2 Ural'sk Obl., Kaz.
102/F3 Uranium City, Sk,Can
92/F3 Uraricoera (riv.), Braz.
65/F3 Urawa, Japan
56/G3 Uray, Rus.
65/H7 Urayasu, Japan
110/B3 Urbana, Il,US
110/D3 Urbana, Oh,US
33/G3 Ure (riv.), Eng,UK
100/E6 Ureña, CR
108/E5 Ures, Mex.
65/M10 Ureshino, Japan
59/D3 Urfa, Turk.
41/G6 Urft (riv.), Ger.
56/G5 Urgench, Uzb.
37/H1 Urho Kekkosen Nat'l Park, Fin.
92/F2 Urimáan, Ven.
101/N8 Urique (riv.), Mex.
40/C3 Urk, Neth.
59/A2 Urla, Turk.
51/H3 Urlaţi, Rom.
63/L2 Urmi (riv.), Rus.
60/D1 Urmia (lake), Iran
33/F5 Urmston, Eng,UK
50/E4 Uroševac, Yugo.
32/E1 Urr Water (riv.), Sc,UK
93/J6 Uruaçu, Braz.
100/A4 Uruapan, Mex.
92/D6 Urubamba (riv.), Peru
92/G4 Urubu (riv.), Braz.
94/C1 Uruburetama, Braz.
94/C4 Uruçuca, Braz.
94/A2 Uruçuí, Braz.
94/A3 Uruçuí (mts.), Braz.
94/A5 Uruçuí (riv.), Braz.
94/A3 Uruçuí Prêto (riv.), Braz.
91/E2 Uruguaiana, Braz.
91/E3 Uruguay
91/E2 Uruguay (riv.), SAm.
62/B3 Ürümqi, China
57/R5 Urup (isl.), Rus.
95/B4 Urussanga, Braz.
63/H1 Uryumkan (riv.), Rus.
55/G2 Uryupinsk, Rus.
51/H3 Urziceni, Rom.
31/R9 Us, Fr.
64/B4 Usa, Japan
53/N2 Usa (riv.), Rus.
59/B2 Uşak, Turk.
97/N7 Usborne (peak), Falk.
64/B4 Ushibuka, Japan
65/J7 Ushiku, Japan
68/C2 Ushtobe, Kaz.
97/K8 Ushuaia, Arg.
70/C6 Usilampatti, India
31/H3 Usinsk, Rus.
34/D3 Usk, Wal,UK
34/D3 Usk (riv.), Wal,UK
51/J5 Üsküdar, Turk.
41/G5 Uslar, Ger.
54/F1 Usman', Rus.
62/E1 Usol'ye-Sibirskoye, Rus.
67/D5 Uson, Phil.
96/C2 Uspallata (pass), Arg., Chile
44/E4 Ussel, Fr.
44/F3 Usses (riv.), Fr.
63/L2 Ussuri (Wusuli) (riv.), Rus., China
63/L3 Ussuriysk, Rus.
48/C3 Ustica (isl.), It.
51/F4 Ust'-Ilimsk, Rus.
39/H3 Ústí nad Labem, Czh.
39/J1 Ustka, Pol.
57/S4 Ust'-Kamchatsk, Rus.
68/D2 Ust'-Kamenogorsk, Kaz.
57/L4 Ust'-Kut, Rus.
62/E1 Ust'-Ordynskiy, Rus.
39/M4 Ustrzyki Dolne, Pol.
53/K3 Ust'ya (riv.), Rus.
55/K4 Ustyurt (plat.), Kaz., Uzb.
68/D3 Usu, China
64/B4 Usuki, Japan
100/D5 Usulután, ESal.
100/C4 Usumacinta (riv.), Mex.
108/E3 Utah (state), US
108/D2 Utah (lake), Ut,US
65/L10 Utano, Japan
109/G3 Ute (cr.), NM,US
52/E5 Utena, Lith.
69/C3 Uthai Thani, Thai.
110/F3 Utica, NY,US
46/E3 Utiel, Sp.
107/K2 Utik (lake), Mb,Can
106/E2 Utikuma (lake), Ab,Can
78/G3 Utirik (atoll), Mrsh.
78/G5 Utiroa, Kiri.
70/D2 Utraulā, India
40/C4 Utrecht, Neth.
40/C4 Utrecht (prov.), Neth.
46/C4 Utrera, Sp.
65/F2 Utsunomiya, Japan
69/C2 Uttaradit, Thai.
68/C5 Uttarkashi, India
70/C2 Uttar Pradesh (state), India
33/G6 Uttoxeter, Eng,UK
101/H4 Utuado, PR
78/F6 Utupua (isl.), Sol.
79/K6 Uturoa, FrPol.
62/G2 Uulbayan, Mong.
62/E1 Üür (riv.), Mong.
62/C1 Üüreg (lake), Mong.
62/C1 Uus (lake), Mong.
37/H3 Uusimaa (prov.), Fin.
92/E3 Uva (riv.), Col.
112/D4 Uvalde, Tx,US
53/K4 Uval, Northern (hills), Rus.
55/G2 Uvarovo, Rus.
68/F1 Uvs Nuur (lake), Mong.
64/C4 Uwajima, Japan
83/L6 Uwayl, Sudan
31/M7 Uxbridge, Eng,UK
66/B3 Uxin Qi, China
100/D3 Uxmal (ruins), Mex.
53/P5 Uy (riv.), Kaz., Rus.
62/E2 Uyanga, Mong.
62/C2 Üyench, Mong.
92/E8 Uyuni, Bol.
56/G5 Uzbekistan
54/B2 Uzhgorod, Ukr.
54/F1 Uzlovaya, Rus.
51/H5 Uzunköprü, Turk.

V

88/C3 Vaal (riv.), SAfr.
88/E2 Vaaldam (res.), SAfr.
43/F2 Vaals, Neth.
43/E2 Vaalsberg (hill), Neth.
37/G3 Vaasa (prov.), Fin.
37/G3 Vaasa (Vasa), Fin.
40/C4 Vaassen, Neth.
50/D2 Vác, Hun.
116/K10 Vaca (mts.), Ca,US
95/B4 Vacaria, Braz.
116/L10 Vacaville, Ca,US
103/J2 Vachon (riv.), Qu,Can
45/H3 Vaduz (cap.), Lcht.
52/J3 Vaga (riv.), Rus.
50/B3 Vaganski vrh (peak), Cro.
53/K4 Vagay (riv.), Rus.
37/E4 Vaggeryd, Swe.
39/J4 Vah (riv.), Slvk.
79/M6 Vahitahi (isl.), FrPol.
61/K5 Vaijāpur, India
109/F3 Vail, Co,US
42/C5 Vailly-sur-Aisnes, Fr.
31/T10 Vaires-sur-Marne, Fr.
78/G5 Vaitupu (isl.), Tuv.
59/D2 Vakfıkebir, Turk.
56/J3 Vakh (riv.), Rus.
61/K1 Vākhān (mts.), Afg.
61/J1 Vakhsh (riv.), Trkm.
40/C5 Valburg, Neth.
52/G4 Valdai (hills), Rus.
43/F6 Val-de-Bide, Fr.
46/C3 Valdecañas (res.), Sp.
31/T10 Val-de-Marne (dept.), Fr.
37/F4 Valdemarsvik, Swe.
47/M8 Valdemorillo, Sp.
46/D3 Valdepeñas, Sp.
46/C2 Valderaduey (riv.), Sp.
96/E4 Valdés (pen.), Arg.
96/B3 Valdivia, Chile
42/A5 Val-d'Oise (dept.), Fr.
110/E1 Val d'Or, Qu,Can
113/H4 Valdosta, Ga,US
46/A1 Valdoviño, Sp.
106/D5 Vale, Or,US
106/D2 Valemount, BC,Can
95/K7 Valença, Braz.
94/B2 Valença do Piauí, Braz.
47/E3 Valencia, Sp.
47/E3 Valencia (aut. comm.), Sp.
47/F3 Valencia (gulf), Sp.
101/H5 Valencia, Ven.
46/B3 Valencia de Alcántara, Sp.
42/C3 Valenciennes, Fr.
51/H3 Vălenii de Munte, Rom.
94/B2 Valentim (mts.), Braz.
109/G2 Valentine, Ne,US
112/B4 Valentine, Tx,US
31/T10 Valenton, Fr.
45/H4 Valenza, It.
101/G6 Valera, Ven.
52/E4 Valga, Est.
95/G7 Valhinos, Braz.
44/D5 Valier (mtn.), Fr.
48/A2 Valinco (gulf), Fr.
50/D3 Valjevo, Yugo.
43/E2 Valkenburg, Neth.
40/C6 Valkenswaard, Neth.
100/D3 Valladolid, Mex.
46/C2 Valladolid, Sp.
47/E3 Vall de Uxó, Sp.
47/N9 Vallecas, Sp.
45/G5 Vallecrosia, It.

45/G4 Valle d'Aosta (reg.), It.
101/L7 Valle de Guadalupe, Mex.
101/H6 Valle de la Pascua, Ven.
47/M8 Valle de los Caídos, Sp.
101/N8 Valle de Zaragoza, Mex.
101/G5 Valledupar, Col.
92/F7 Vallegrande, Bol.
47/X16 Vallehermoso, Canl.,Sp.
40/C4 Valleikanaal (can.), Neth.
116/K10 Vallejo, Ca,US
91/B2 Vallenar, Chile
43/G3 Vallendar, Ger.
101/L7 Valle San Telmo, Mex.
48/D5 Valletta (cap.), Malta
107/J4 Valley City, ND,US
115/G4 Valley Cottage, NY,US
110/D2 Valley East, On,Can
111/M7 Valleyfield, Qu,Can
115/E5 Valley Forge Nat'l Hist. Park, Pa,US
115/G5 Valley Stream, NY,US
106/D2 Valleyview, Ab,Can
96/E3 Vallimanca (riv.), Arg.
47/F2 Valls, Sp.
106/G3 Val Marie, Sk,Can
47/M8 Valmayor (res.), Sp.
41/F6 Valme (riv.), Ger.
52/E4 Valmiera, Lat.
31/S9 Valmondois, Fr.
49/F2 Valona (bay), Alb.
70/C5 Vālpārai, India
96/C2 Valparaíso, Chile
96/C2 Valparaíso (reg.), Chile
101/P9 Valparaíso, Mex.
113/G4 Valparaiso, Fl,US
110/C3 Valparaiso, In,US
50/D3 Valpovo, Cro.
44/F4 Valréas, Fr.
88/D2 Vals (riv.), SAfr.
70/B3 Valsād, India
88/B4 Valsbaai (bay), SAfr.
54/F2 Valuyki, Rus.
115/B2 Val Verde, Ca,US
46/B4 Valverde del Camino, Sp.
37/G3 Vammala, Fin.
59/E2 Van, Turk.
59/E2 Van (lake), Turk.
79/L7 Vanavaro (isl.), FrPol.
112/E3 Van Buren, Ar,US
111/H2 Van Buren, Me,US
109/K3 Van Buren, Mo,US
106/C3 Vancouver, BC,Can
106/B3 Vancouver (isl.), BC,Can
106/C4 Vancouver, Wa,US
114/L3 Vancouver (mtn.), Yk,Can, Ak,US
98/L Vanda, Ant.
110/B4 Vandalia, Il,US
109/K3 Vandalia, Mo,US
88/D2 Vanderbijl Park, SAfr.
106/D2 Vanderhoof, BC,Can
74/F3 Vanderlin (isl.), Austl.
74/E2 Van Diemen (cape), Austl.
74/E2 Van Diemen (gulf), Austl.
43/F6 Vandoeuvre-lès-Nancy, Fr.
37/E4 Vänern (lake), Swe.
37/E4 Vänersborg, Swe.
89/H8 Vangaindrano, Madg.
40/C2 Van Harinxmakanaal (can.), Neth.
69/D1 Van Hoa, Viet.
112/B4 Van Horn, Tx,US
103/R7 Vanier (isl.), NW,Can
78/F6 Vanikoro (isl.), Sol.
73/K4 Vanimo, PNG
63/N2 Vanino, Rus.
37/F3 Vännäs, Swe.
44/E2 Vanne (riv.), Fr.
44/B3 Vannes, Fr.
69/E3 Van Ninh, Viet.
45/G4 Vanoise Nat'l Park, Fr.
88/E3 Vanreenenpas (pass), SAfr.
73/J4 Van Rees (mts.), Indo.
103/H2 Vansittart (isl.), NW,Can
37/H3 Vantaa, Fin.
78/G6 Vanua Levu (isl.), Fiji
78/F6 Vanuatu
31/S10 Vanves, Fr.
110/C3 Van Wert, Oh,US
69/D1 Van Yen, Viet.
45/G5 Var (riv.), Fr.
60/F1 Varāmīn, Iran
70/D2 Vārānāsi, India
37/J1 Varangerfjorden (fjord), Nor.
37/J1 Varangerhalvøya (pen.), Nor.
48/D2 Varano (lake), It.
50/C2 Varaždin, Cro.
45/H4 Varazze, It.
37/E4 Varberg, Swe.
50/E5 Vardar (riv.), Macd.
38/E1 Varde, Den.
41/F2 Varel, Ger.
111/P6 Varennes, Qu,Can
42/A4 Varennes (riv.), Fr.
31/T10 Varennes-Jarcy, Fr.
44/E3 Varennes-Vauzelles, Fr.
50/D3 Vareš, Bosn.
45/H4 Varese, It.
94/C3 Vargem (riv.), Braz.
95/G6 Vargem do Sul, Braz.
94/B1 Vargem Grande, Braz.
95/H6 Varginha, Braz.
37/C4 Varhaug, Nor.
37/H3 Varkaus, Fin.
37/E3 Värmland (co.), Swe.
51/H4 Varna, Bul.
51/H4 Varna (reg.), Bul.
37/E4 Värnamo, Swe.
50/D2 Várpalota, Hun.
59/E2 Varto, Turk.
32/B5 Vartry (res.), Ire.
32/B5 Vartry (riv.), Ire.
94/C2 Várzea Alegre, Braz.
95/C1 Várzea da Palma, Braz.
93/G7 Várzea Grande, Braz.
52/H2 Varzuga (riv.), Rus.
50/C2 Vas (co.), Hun.
94/C3 Vasa Barris (riv.), Braz.
39/M4 Vásárosnamény, Hun.
37/G3 Vasa (Vaasa), Fin.
53/K2 Vashka (riv.), Rus.
116/C3 Vashon (isl.), Wa,US
54/D2 Vasil'kov, Ukr.
51/H2 Vaslui, Rom.
51/H2 Vaslui (co.), Rom.
110/D3 Vassar, Mi,US
49/G4 Vassés (Bassae) (ruins), Gre.
95/K7 Vassouras, Braz.
37/F4 Västerås, Swe.
37/F2 Västerbotten (co.), Swe.
37/F4 Västerhaninge, Swe.
37/F3 Västernorrland (co.), Swe.
37/F4 Västervik, Swe.
37/F3 Västmanland (co.), Swe.
52/C3 Vastmanland (co.), Swe.
48/D1 Vasto, It.
45/J2 Vaterstetten, Ger.
48/C2 Vatican City
37/P7 Vatnajökull (glac.), Ice.
51/G2 Vatra Dornei, Rom.
37/E2 Vättern (lake), Swe.
79/Y18 Vatukoula, Fiji
111/M7 Vaudreuil, Qu,Can
111/Q8 Vaughan, On,Can
109/F4 Vaughn, NM,US
44/F4 Vaulx-en-Velin, Fr.
44/F5 Vauvert, Fr.
42/D4 Vaux (riv.), Fr.
106/E3 Vauxhall, Ab,Can
31/R9 Vaux-sur-Seine, Fr.
42/B3 Vaux-Vraucourt, Fr.
79/H6 Vava'u Group (isls.), Tonga
70/D6 Vavuniya, SrL.
37/E4 Växjö, Swe.
31/J2 Vaygach (isl.), Rus.
95/C1 Vazante, Braz.
95/G8 Vázea Paulista, Braz.
52/G5 Vazuza (res.), Rus.
40/D4 Vecht (riv.), Neth.
41/F3 Vechta, Ger.
41/E4 Vechte (riv.), Ger.
50/D2 Vecsés, Hun.
51/G3 Vedea (riv.), Rom.
96/E2 Vedia, Arg.
40/D2 Veendam, Neth.
40/C4 Veenendaal, Neth.
40/A5 Veerse Meer (res.), Neth.
37/D2 Vega (isl.), Nor.
114/B6 Vega (pt.), Ak,US
37/D2 Vegafjorden (fjord), Nor.
40/C5 Veghel, Neth.
49/G2 Vegorítis (lake), Gre.
106/E2 Vègreville, Ab,Can
37/H3 Vehkalahti, Fin.
46/C4 Vejer de la Frontera, Sp.
38/E1 Vejle, Den.
38/E1 Vejle (co.), Den.
101/G5 Vela (cape), Col.
47/S12 Velas, Azor,Port.
40/E6 Velbert, Ger.
45/L3 Velden am Wörthersee, Aus.
40/C6 Veldhoven, Neth.
40/D5 Velen, Ger.
50/B2 Velenje, Slov.
46/C4 Vélez-Málaga, Sp.
46/D4 Vélez-Rubio, Sp.
95/C1 Velhas (Araguari) (riv.), Braz.
50/C3 Velika Gorica, Cro.
50/E3 Velika Plana, Yugo.
52/F4 Velikaya (riv.), Rus.
52/F4 Velikiye Luki, Rus.
52/K3 Velikiy Ustyug, Rus.
51/G4 Veliko Tŭrnovo, Bul.
51/G4 Velingrad, Bul.
31/S10 Vélizy-Villacoublay, Fr.
39/J4 Velké Meziříčí, Czh.
39/K4 Veľký Krtíš, Slvk.
48/C2 Velletri, It.
41/G6 Vellmar, Ger.
47/N8 Vellón (res.), Sp.
70/C5 Vellore, India
52/J3 Vel'sk, Rus.
40/C4 Veluwe (reg.), Neth.
40/C4 Veluwemeer (lake), Neth.
40/C4 Veluwezoom Nat'l Park, Neth.
107/H3 Velva, ND,US
96/E2 Venado Tuerto, Arg.
48/D2 Venafro, It.
95/A4 Venâncio Aires, Braz.
45/G4 Venaria, It.
45/G5 Vence, Fr.
95/B2 Venceslau Brás, Braz.
46/A3 Vendas Novas, Port.
44/D3 Vendôme, Fr.
47/F2 Vendrell, Sp.
45/J4 Veneto (reg.), It.
45/K4 Venezia (gulf), It.
45/K4 Venezia (Venice), It.
92/E2 Venezuela
101/G5 Venezuela (gulf), Col., Ven.
70/B4 Vengurla, India
114/G4 Veniaminof (vol.), Ak,US
113/H5 Venice, Fl,US
45/K4 Venice (Venezia), It.
44/F4 Vénissieux, Fr.
70/C5 Venkatagiri, India
40/D6 Venlo, Neth.
37/C4 Vennesla, Nor.
48/D2 Venosa, It.
40/C5 Venray, Neth.
52/D4 Venta (riv.), Lat., Lith.
46/C2 Venta de Baños, Sp.
79/L6 Vent, Iles du (isls.), FrPol.
79/K6 Vent, Iles sous le (isls.), FrPol.
35/E5 Ventnor, Eng,UK
52/D4 Ventspils, Lat.
115/A2 Ventura (San Buenaventura), Ca,US
48/B1 Venturina, It.
79/X15 Vénus (pt.), FrPol.
100/C4 Venustiano Carranza, Mex.
91/D2 Vera, Arg.
100/B4 Veracruz, Mex.
100/B3 Veracruz (state), Mex.
95/B4 Veranópolis, Braz.
70/B3 Verāval, India
45/H4 Verbania, It.
45/H4 Vercelli, It.
37/D3 Verdal, Nor.
95/B1 Verdão (riv.), Braz.
96/E3 Verde (bay), Arg.
95/H6 Verde (riv.), Braz.
101/N8 Verde (riv.), Mex.
91/E1 Verde (riv.), Par.
82/B5 Verde (cape), Sen.
108/E4 Verde (riv.), Az,US
46/B1 Verde, Costa (coast), Sp.
94/B4 Verde Grande (riv.), Braz.
41/G3 Verden, Ger.
109/J3 Verdigris (riv.), Ks, Ok,US
95/B1 Verdinho (riv.), Braz.
44/F5 Verdon (riv.), Fr.
111/N7 Verdun, Qu,Can
43/E5 Verdun-sur-Meuse, Fr.
88/D2 Vereeniging, SAfr.
53/M4 Vereshchagino, Rus.
39/M4 Veretskiy Pereval (pass), Ukr.
84/B4 Verga (cape), Gui.
46/D1 Vergara, Sp.
111/F2 Vergennes, Vt,US
49/H2 Vergína (ruins), Gre.
46/B2 Verin, Sp.
52/F1 Verkhnetulomskiy (res.), Rus.
57/N3 Verkhoyansk (range), Rus.
41/F5 Verl, Ger.
42/C4 Vermand, Fr.
94/A3 Vermelho (riv.), Braz.
106/F2 Vermilion, Ab,Can
106/F2 Vermilion (riv.), Ab,Can
109/K2 Vermilion (riv.), Il,US
107/K4 Vermillion (range), Mn,US
107/J5 Vermillion, SD,US
109/H2 Vermillion (riv.), SD,US
111/F2 Vermont (state), US
108/E2 Vernal, Ut,US
44/D2 Verneuil-sur-Avre, Fr.
31/R10 Verneuil-sur-Seine, Fr.
88/C3 Verneukpan (salt pan), SAfr.
106/D3 Vernon, BC,Can
42/A5 Vernon, Fr.
112/D3 Vernon, Tx,US
116/Q15 Vernon Hills, Il,US
31/R10 Vernouillet, Fr.
43/F5 Verny, Fr.
113/H5 Vero Beach, Fl,US
49/H2 Véroia, Gre.
45/J4 Verona, It.
31/S10 Verrières-le-Buisson, Fr.
31/S10 Versailles, Fr.
110/C4 Versailles, Ky,US
54/E2 Verskla (riv.), Rus., Ukr.
41/F4 Versmold, Ger.
46/E1 Vert (riv.), Fr.
45/J3 Vertana (peak), It.
31/T11 Vert-le-Grand, Fr.
31/T11 Vert-le-Petit, Fr.
44/C3 Vertou, Fr.
31/T11 Vert-Saint-Denis, Fr.
43/E2 Verviers, Belg.
35/E5 Verwood, Eng,UK
34/B6 Veryan (bay), Eng,UK
43/F2 Vesdre (riv.), Belg.
53/G5 Veselyy (res.), Rus.
42/D5 Vesle (riv.), Fr.
45/G3 Vesoul, Fr.
37/C4 Vest-Agder (co.), Nor.
37/E1 Vesterålen (isls.), Nor.
37/E2 Vestfjorden (fjord), Nor.
37/D4 Vestfold (co.), Nor.
38/F1 Vest-Sjælland (co.), Den.
87/G4 Vestvågøya (isl.), Nor.
50/E2 Veszprém, Hun.
50/C2 Veszprém (co.), Hun.
50/E2 Vésztő, Hun.
88/D3 Vet (riv.), SAfr.
37/E4 Vetlanda, Swe.
53/K4 Vetluga (riv.), Rus.
48/C1 Vetralla, It.
44/D3 Veude (riv.), Fr.
42/B1 Veurne, Belg.
45/G3 Vevey, Swi.
43/F2 Veybach (riv.), Ger.
44/D4 Vézère (riv.), Fr.
59/C2 Vezirköprü, Turk.
92/E7 Viacha, Bol.
94/A1 Viana, Braz.
46/B1 Viana del Bollo, Sp.
46/A2 Viana do Castelo, Port.
46/A2 Viana do Castelo (dist.), Port.
40/C5 Vianen, Neth.
69/C2 Viangchan (Vientiane) (cap.), Laos
46/C4 Viar (riv.), Sp.
45/J5 Viareggio, It.
31/T9 Viarmes, Fr.
44/E4 Viaur (riv.), Fr.
37/D4 Viborg, Den.
48/E3 Vibo Valentia, It.
47/G2 Vic, Sp.
46/D4 Vicar, Sp.
97/S12 Vicente López, Arg.
45/J4 Vicenza, It.
52/J4 Vichuga, Rus.
44/E3 Vichy, Fr.
113/F3 Vicksburg, Ms,US
48/C1 Vico (lake), It.
94/C3 Viçosa, Braz.
95/D2 Viçosa, Braz.
49/G3 Vicou Gorge Nat'l Park, Gre.
42/C5 Vic-sur-Aisne, Fr.
43/F6 Vic-sur-Seille, Fr.
80/F5 Victoria (lake), Afr.
96/E2 Victoria, Arg.
74/E3 Victoria (riv.), Austl.
77/C3 Victoria (state), Austl.
100/D4 Victoria (peak), Belz.
71/F3 Victoria (peak), Burma
106/C3 Victoria (cap.), BC,Can
102/E1 Victoria (isl.), NW,Can
102/F2 Victoria (str.), NW,Can
111/Q8 Victoria, On,Can
96/B3 Victoria, Chile
67/B3 Victoria (cap.), HK
73/E2 Victoria (peak), Phil.
51/G3 Victoria, Rom.
112/D4 Victoria, Tx,US
101/F3 Victoria de las Tunas, Cuba
98/L Victoria Land (reg.), Ant.
83/M7 Victoria Nile (riv.), Ugan.
111/G2 Victoriaville, Qu,Can
115/C1 Victorville, Ca,US
89/F3 Vidal (cape), SAfr.
113/H3 Vidalia, Ga,US
113/F4 Vidalia, La,US
95/B3 Videira, Braz.
51/G3 Videle, Rom.
50/F4 Vidin, Bul.
70/C3 Vidisha, India
112/E4 Vidor, Tx,US
44/E5 Vidourle (riv.), Fr.
44/C3 Vie (riv.), Fr.
96/E4 Viedma, Arg.
97/J7 Viedma (lake), Arg.
46/C1 Vieja (mtn.), Sp.
112/B4 Vieja (mts.), Tx,US
43/E3 Vielsalm, Belg.
41/H5 Vienenburg, Ger.
115/J8 Vienna, Va,US
110/D4 Vienna, WV,US
39/J4 Vienna (Wien) (cap.), Aus.
44/F4 Vienne, Fr.
44/D3 Vienne (riv.), Fr.
69/C2 Vientiane (Viangchan) (cap.), Laos
43/D6 Viere (riv.), Fr.
40/D5 Vierlingsbeek, Neth.
43/E4 Vierre (riv.), Fr.
40/D6 Viersen, Ger.
45/H3 Vierwaldstättersee (Lucerne) (lake), Swi.
44/E3 Vierzon, Fr.
48/E2 Vieste, It.
69/D2 Vietnam
69/D1 Viet Tri, Viet.
42/C3 Vieux-Condé, Fr.
101/J5 Vieux Fort, StL.
67/D5 Viga, Phil.
67/D4 Vigan, Phil.
45/H4 Vigevano, It.
93/J4 Vigia, Braz.
48/C2 Viglio (peak), It.
44/C5 Vignemale (mtn.), Fr.
31/T10 Vigneux-sur-Seine, Fr.
45/J4 Vignola, It.
46/A1 Vigo, Sp.
43/F5 Vigy, Fr.
61/K2 Vihāri, Pak.
37/H3 Viitasaari, Fin.
70/D4 Vijayawada, India
49/F2 Vijosë (riv.), Alb.
37/D4 Vikersund, Nor.
51/F5 Vikhren (peak), Bul.
106/F2 Viking, Ab,Can
78/F6 Vila (cap.), Van.
47/G2 Viladecans, Sp.
47/V14 Vila de Porto Santo, Madr.,Port.
87/G4 Vila de Sena, Moz.
46/A2 Vila do Conde, Port.
47/T13 Vila do Porto, Azor,Port.
47/K7 Vilafranca del Penedès, Sp.
46/A3 Vila Franca de Xira, Port.
47/T13 Vila Franca do Campo, Azor.,Port.
44/B3 Vilaine (riv.), Fr.
89/H7 Vilanandro (cape), Madg.
46/A2 Vila Nova de Gaia, Port.
47/F2 Vilanova i la Geltrù, Sp.
47/K7 Vilanova i la Geltru, Sp.
46/B2 Vila Real, Port.
46/B2 Vila Real (dist.), Port.
46/B4 Vila Real de Santo António, Port.
95/D2 Vila Velha Argolas, Braz.
51/F3 Vîlcea (co.), Rom.
37/F2 Vilhelmina, Swe.
92/F6 Vilhena, Braz.
52/E5 Viliya (riv.), Bela.
52/E4 Viljandi, Est.
57/K2 Vil'kitsogo (str.), Rus.
96/Q9 Villa Alemana, Chile
91/D2 Villa Ángela, Arg.
46/E1 Villaba, Sp.
46/B1 Villablino, Sp.
101/H6 Villa Bruzual, Ven.
96/E2 Villa Cañas, Arg.
46/D3 Villacañas, Sp.
91/D3 Villa Carlos Paz, Arg.
46/D3 Villacarrillo, Sp.
45/K3 Villach, Aus.
96/E2 Villa Constitución, Arg.
46/A1 Villa de Cruces, Sp.
46/C4 Villa del Río, Sp.
46/E3 Villa Dolores, Arg.
100/C4 Villa Flores, Mex.
46/B3 Villafranca de los Barros, Sp.
100/A2 Villa Frontera, Mex.
46/A1 Villagarcía, Sp.
112/E4 Village Mills, Tx,US
97/F3 Villa Gesell, Arg.
96/F1 Villaguay, Arg.
100/C4 Villahermosa, Mex.
101/N7 Villa Hidalgo, Mex.
47/E3 Villajoyosa, Sp.
46/B1 Villalba, Sp.
46/B2 Villalcampo (res.), Sp.
96/E2 Villa María, Arg.
46/C4 Villamartín, Sp.
92/F8 Villa Montes, Bol.
100/D4 Villanueva, Hon.
46/A1 Villanueva de Arosa, Sp.
46/C3 Villanueva de Córdoba, Sp.
46/D3 Villanueva del Arzobispo, Sp.
46/C3 Villanueva de la Serena, Sp.
46/D3 Villanueva de los Infantes, Sp.
115/C3 Villa Park, Ca,US
116/Q16 Villa Park, Il,US
96/D3 Villa Regina, Arg.
47/E3 Villarreal de los Infantes, Sp.
96/B3 Villarrica, Chile
96/B3 Villarrica (lake), Chile
91/E2 Villarrica, Par.
96/C3 Villarrica Nat'l Park, Chile
46/D3 Villarrobledo, Sp.
46/D3 Villarrubia de los Ojos, Sp.
96/F2 Villa San José, Arg.
92/F7 Villa Serrano, Bol.
91/C2 Villa Unión, Arg.
101/N9 Villa Unión, Mex.
92/D3 Villavicencio, Col.
46/C1 Villaviciosa, Sp.
47/N9 Villaviciosa de Odon, Sp.
92/E8 Villazón, Bol.
31/T10 Villecresnes, Fr.
31/S10 Ville-d'Avray, Fr.
44/E4 Villefranche-de-Rouergue, Fr.
44/F4 Villefranche-sur-Saône, Fr.
31/T10 Villejuif, Fr.
31/T10 Villemomble, Fr.
47/E3 Villena, Sp.
42/C2 Villeneuve-d'Ascq, Fr.
31/S10 Villeneuve-la-Garenne, Fr.
31/U10 Villeneuve-le-Comte, Fr.
31/T10 Villeneuve-le-Roi, Fr.
44/F5 Villeneuve-lès-Avignon, Fr.
42/B6 Villeneuve-Saint-Georges, Fr.
44/D4 Villeneuve-sur-Lot, Fr.
44/D5 Villeneuve-Tolosane, Fr.
31/R10 Villennes-sur-Seine, Fr.
31/T10 Villeparisis, Fr.
112/E4 Ville Platte, La,US
31/S10 Villepreux, Fr.
42/C5 Villers-Cotterêts, Fr.
43/F6 Villers-lès-Nancy, Fr.
42/C3 Villers-Outreaux, Fr.
43/E5 Villerupt, Fr.
31/T10 Villevaudé, Fr.
31/T9 Villiers-le-Bel, Fr.
31/T10 Villiers-sur-Marne, Fr.
45/H2 Villingen-Schwenningen, Ger.
70/C5 Villupuram, India
39/N1 Vilnius (cap.), Lith.
37/H3 Vilppula, Fin.
45/K2 Vils (riv.), Ger.
45/K2 Vilshofen, Ger.
42/D2 Vilvoorde, Belg.
57/M3 Vilyuy (range), Rus.
57/N3 Vilyuy (riv.), Rus.
46/B1 Vimianzo, Sp.
37/E4 Vimmerby, Swe.
42/B3 Vimy, Fr.
82/H6 Vina (riv.), Camr.
96/C2 Viña del Mar, Chile
45/G5 Vinaigre (mtn.), Fr.
47/F2 Vinaroz, Sp.
98/H Vincennes (bay), Ant.
31/T10 Vincennes, Fr.
110/C4 Vincennes, In,US
115/B2 Vincent, Ca,US
37/F2 Vindeln, Swe.
111/R9 Vineland, On,Can
69/D2 Vinh, Viet.
95/G8 Vinhedo, Braz.
69/D4 Vinh Long, Viet.
69/D4 Vinh Quoi, Viet.
69/E3 Vinh Thanh, Viet.
69/D1 Vinh Yen, Viet.
50/F5 Vinica, Macd.
109/J3 Vinita, Ok,US
50/F3 Vînju Mare, Rom.
50/D3 Vinkovci, Cro.
54/D2 Vinnitsa, Ukr.
54/D2 Vinnitsa Obl., Ukr.
54/B2 Vinogradov, Ukr.
28/E9 Vinson (peak), Ant.
31/R9 Viosne (riv.), Fr.
67/D5 Virac, Phil.
59/D3 Viranşehir, Turk.
70/B4 Virār, India
107/H3 Virden, Mb,Can
44/C2 Vire, Fr.
87/B4 Virei, Ang.
91/C7 Virgenes (cape), Arg.
111/R9 Virgil, On,Can
101/J4 Virgin (isls.), UK, US
108/D3 Virgin (riv.), US
110/E5 Virginia (state), US
107/K4 Virginia, Mn,US
110/F4 Virginia Beach, Va,US
108/C3 Virginia City, Nv,US
69/D3 Virochey, Camb.
31/S10 Viroflay, Fr.
42/D3 Viroin (riv.), Belg.
110/B3 Viroqua, Wi,US
50/C3 Virovitica, Cro.
43/E4 Virton, Belg.
70/C6 Virudunagar, India
31/T10 Viry-Châtillon, Fr.
48/D1 Vis (isl.), Cro.
70/D4 Visākhapatnam, India
108/C3 Visalia, Ca,US
67/D5 Visayan (sea), Phil.
41/F3 Visbek, Ger.
37/F4 Visby, Swe.
95/D2 Visconde do Rio Branco, Braz.
103/R7 Viscount Melville (sound), NW,Can
43/E2 Visé, Belg.
50/D4 Višegrad, Bosn.
46/B2 Viseu, Port.
46/B2 Viseu (dist.), Port.
51/G2 Vişeu de Sus, Rom.
53/N3 Vishera (riv.), Rus.
88/B4 Vishoek, SAfr.
70/B3 Visnagar, India
50/D3 Višnjevac, Cro.
50/D4 Visoko, Bosn.
41/G3 Visselhövede, Ger.
108/C4 Vista, Ca,US
49/J2 Vistonís (lake), Gre.
39/K2 Vistula (Wisła) (riv.), Pol.
51/G4 Vit (riv.), Bul.
107/J3 Vita, Mb,Can
45/J5 Vitalba (peak), It.
52/F5 Vitebsk, Bela.
52/E5 Vitebsk Obl., Bela.
48/C1 Viterbo, It.
69/D4 Vi Thanh, Viet.
78/G6 Viti Levu (isl.), Fiji
62/G1 Vitim (plat.), Rus.
62/G1 Vitim (riv.), Rus.
95/D2 Vitória, Braz.
46/D1 Vitoria, Sp.
94/B4 Vitória da Conquista, Braz.
94/D3 Vitória de Santo Antão, Braz.
94/A1 Vitória do Mearim, Braz.
94/A2 Vitorino Freire, Braz.
51/F4 Vitosha Nat'l Park, Bul.
44/C2 Vitré, Fr.
44/F5 Vitrolles, Fr.
42/D6 Vitry-le-François, Fr.
31/T10 Vitry-sur-Seine, Fr.
48/D4 Vittoria, It.
45/K4 Vittorio Veneto, It.
44/F4 Vivarais (mts.), Fr.
46/B1 Vivero, Sp.
51/H5 Vize, Turk.
53/K2 Vizhas (riv.), Rus.
70/D4 Vizianagaram, India
40/B5 Vlaardingen, Neth.
50/F2 Vlădeasa (peak), Rom.
55/H4 Vladikavkaz, Rus.
52/J4 Vladimir, Rus.
52/J5 Vladimir Obl., Rus.
54/C2 Vladimir-Volynskiy, Ukr.
63/L3 Vladivostok, Rus.
41/E2 Vlagtwedde, Neth.
51/G2 Vlăhiţa, Rom.
50/E4 Vlajna (peak), Yugo.
50/D3 Vlasenica, Bosn.
39/H4 Vlašim, Czh.
50/F4 Vlasotince, Yugo.
40/B2 Vlieland (isl.), Neth.
40/C2 Vliestroom (chan.), Neth.
40/C5 Vlijmen, Neth.
40/A6 Vlissingen, Neth.
49/F2 Vlorë, Alb.
41/F4 Vlotho, Ger.
45/L1 Vltava (riv.), Czh.
45/K2 Vöcklabruck, Aus.
52/H3 Vodlozero (lake), Rus.
40/D5 Voerde, Ger.
45/H1 Vogelsberg (mts.), Ger.
45/H4 Voghera, It.
50/D4 Vogošća, Bosn.
45/J1 Vogtland (reg.), Ger.
79/U12 Voh, NCal.
45/K2 Vohenstrauss, Ger.
89/H9 Vohimena (cape), Madg.
89/G7 Vohipeno, Madg.
87/G1 Voi, Kenya
44/F4 Voiron, Fr.
44/D2 Voise (riv.), Fr.
103/K3 Voisey (bay), Nf,Can
42/B5 Voisne (riv.), Fr.
50/D5 Vojosë (riv.), Alb.
50/D3 Vojvodina (aut. prov.), Yugo.
43/F5 Vöklingen, Ger.
78/C2 Volcano (isls.), Japan
37/C3 Volda, Nor.
40/C4 Volendam, Neth.
31/H4 Volga (riv.), Rus.
52/H3 Volga-Baltic Wtwy., Rus.
55/G3 Volgodonsk, Rus.
55/H2 Volgograd, Rus.
55/H2 Volgograd (res.), Rus.
55/G2 Volgograd Obl., Rus.
40/B5 Volkerakdam (dam), Neth.
45/L3 Völkermarkt, Aus.
52/G4 Volkhov, Rus.
52/F4 Volkhov (riv.), Rus.
38/D4 Völklingen, Ger.
41/G6 Volkmarsen, Ger.
39/N2 Volkovysk, Bela.
89/E2 Volksrust, SAfr.
43/G5 Volmunster, Fr.
52/H4 Vologda, Rus.
52/J3 Vologda Obl., Rus.
45/G2 Vologne (riv.), Fr.
49/H3 Vólos, Gre.
49/H3 Volos (gulf), Gre.
55/H1 Vol'sk, Rus.
85/E4 Volta (lake), Gha.
85/F5 Volta (reg.), Gha.
85/F5 Volta (riv.), Gha.
95/J7 Volta Redonda, Braz.
45/J5 Volterra, It.
48/D2 Volturno (riv.), It.
81/M13 Volubilis (ruins), Mor.
49/H2 Vólvi (lake), Gre.
53/L5 Volzhsk, Rus.
55/H2 Volzhskiy, Rus.
114/H3 Von Frank (mtn.), Ak,US
44/D3 Vonne (riv.), Fr.
40/B4 Voorburg, Neth.
40/B5 Voorne (isl.), Neth.
40/B4 Voorschoten, Neth.
40/D4 Voorst, Neth.
45/H3 Vorarlberg (prov.), Aus.
40/D4 Vorden, Neth.
45/H3 Vorderrhein (riv.), Swi.
44/F4 Voreppe, Fr.
53/Q2 Vorkuta, Rus.
55/G1 Vorona (riv.), Rus.
54/F2 Voronezh, Rus.
54/F1 Voronezh (riv.), Rus.
55/G2 Voronezh Obl., Rus.
52/G1 Voron'ya (riv.), Rus.
43/E1 Vorst, Belg.
52/E4 Võru, Est.
45/G3 Vosges (mts.), Fr.
52/H5 Voskresensk, Rus.
37/C3 Voss, Nor.
98/V Vostock (cape), Ant.
98/H Vostok, Ant.
79/K6 Vostok (isl.), Kiri.
53/M4 Votkinsk, Rus.
53/M4 Votkinsk (res.), Rus.
95/C2 Votorantim, Braz.
95/B2 Votuporanga, Braz.
46/B2 Vouga (riv.), Port.
49/H5 Voúxa, Ákra (cape), Gre.
107/K3 Voyageurs Nat'l Park, Mn,US
98/J Voyeykov Ice Shelf, Ant.
53/M3 Voy-Vozh, Rus.
52/H3 Vozhe (lake), Rus.
54/D3 Voznesensk, Ukr.
51/H3 Vrancea (co.), Rom.
58/S2 Vrangelya (isl.), Rus.
50/E4 Vranje, Yugo.
39/L4 Vranov nad Teplou, Slvk.
51/F4 Vratsa, Bul.
50/C3 Vrbas (riv.), Bosn.
50/D3 Vrbas, Yugo.
88/E2 Vrede, SAfr.
40/D4 Vreden, Ger.
88/B4 Vredenburg, SAfr.
45/L4 Vrhnika, Slov.
40/D2 Vries, Neth.
40/D4 Vriezenveen, Neth.
38/B5 Vrin (riv.), Fr.
70/C2 Vrindāban, India
50/E4 Vrnjačka Banja, Yugo.
50/E3 Vršac, Yugo.
88/D2 Vryburg, SAfr.
89/E2 Vryheid, SAfr.
39/K4 Vsetín, Czh.
114/E5 Vsevidof (mtn.), Ak,US
39/K4 Vtáčnik (peak), Slvk.
50/E4 Vučitrn, Yugo.
40/C5 Vught, Neth.
50/D3 Vukovar, Cro.
106/E3 Vulcan, Ab,Can
51/F3 Vulcan, Rom.
48/D3 Vulcano (isl.), It.
51/F4 Vŭlchedrŭm, Bul.
48/B1 Vulci (ruins), It.
69/D2 Vu Liet, Viet.
69/D4 Vung Tau, Viet.
78/G7 Vunisea, Fiji
52/E1 Vuotso, Fin.
51/F4 Vŭrshets, Bul.
70/B3 Vyāra, India
53/L4 Vyatka, Rus.
53/L4 Vyatka (riv.), Rus.
53/L4 Vyatka Obl., Rus.
53/L4 Vyatskiye Polyany, Rus.
63/L2 Vyazemskiy, Rus.
52/G5 Vyaz'ma, Rus.
52/F3 Vyborg, Rus.
53/K3 Vychegda (riv.), Rus.
39/H3 Východočeský (reg.), Czh.
39/L4 Východoslovenský (reg.), Slvk.
52/G3 Vygozero (lake), Rus.
39/M4 Vyhorlat (peak), Slvk.
52/J5 Vyksa, Rus.
53/L3 Vym' (riv.), Rus.
34/C1 Vyrnwy (riv.), Wal,UK
52/G4 Vyshniy Volochek, Rus.
39/J4 Vyškov, Czh.

W

85/E4 Wa, Gha.
40/C5 Waal (riv.), Neth.
40/C6 Waalre, Neth.
40/C5 Waalwijk, Neth.
42/C1 Waarschoot, Belg.
106/E2 Wabasca, Ab,Can
102/E3 Wabasca (riv.), Ab,Can
110/C4 Wabash (riv.), Il, In,US
110/C3 Wabash, In,US
41/G6 Wabern, Ger.
107/K3 Wabigoon (lake), On,Can
107/J2 Wabowden, Mb,Can
39/K2 Wąbrzeźno, Pol.
66/D4 Wabu (lake), China
65/L9 Wachi, Japan
42/C1 Wachtebeke, Belg.
40/D6 Wachtendonk, Ger.
112/D4 Waco, Tx,US
112/D2 Waconda (lake), Ks,US
107/K4 Waconia, Mn,US
77/D3 Wadbilliga Nat'l Park, Austl.
82/J2 Waddān, Libya
40/C2 Waddenzee (sound), Neth.
106/B3 Waddington (mtn.), BC,Can
33/F4 Waddington, Eng,UK
33/H5 Waddington, Eng,UK
40/B4 Waddinxveen, Neth.
76/D4 Waddy (pt.), Austl.
34/B5 Wadebridge, Eng,UK
107/H3 Wadena, Sk,Can
107/K4 Wadena, Mn,US
45/H3 Wädenswil, Swi.
43/F4 Wadern, Ger.
41/F5 Wadersloh, Ger.
43/F5 Wadgassen, Ger.
35/G4 Wadhurst, Eng,UK
59/K6 Wādī As Sīr, Jor.
86/B4 Wādī Ḩalfā', Sudan
83/M5 Wad Medanī, Sudan
39/K4 Wadowice, Pol.
63/J4 Wafangdian, China
83/M7 Wagagai (peak), Ugan.
41/F3 Wagenfeld-Hasslingen, Ger.
40/C5 Wageningen, Neth.
102/G2 Wager (bay), NW,Can
77/C2 Wagga Wagga, Austl.
39/J2 Wągrowiec, Pol.
61/K2 Wāh, Pak.
73/G4 Wahai, Indo.
86/B4 Wāḩat Salīmah (well), Sudan
104/V12 Wahiawa, Hi,US
109/H2 Wahoo, Ne,US
107/J4 Wahpeton, ND,US
108/D3 Wah Wah (range), Ut,US
70/B4 Wai, India
104/V13 Waianae, Hi,US
45/L3 Waidhofen an der Ybbs, Aus.
73/H3 Waigeo (isl.), Indo.
73/E5 Waikabubak, Indo.
75/R11 Waikari, NZ
104/T10 Wailuku, Hi,US
75/R11 Waimate, NZ
104/V12 Waimea (falls), Hi,US
111/R10 Wainfleet, On,Can
33/J5 Wainfleet All Saints, Eng,UK
70/C3 Waingangā (riv.), India
73/F5 Waingapu, Indo.
106/F2 Wainwright, Ab,Can
104/V13 Waipahu, Hi,US
104/U10 Waipio, Hi,US
75/S11 Waipukurau, NZ
75/S10 Wairoa, NZ
75/R10 Waitara, NZ
75/R10 Waitemata, NZ

79/Z17 Waiyevu, Fiji
65/E2 Wajima, Japan
83/P7 Wajir, Kenya
73/G4 Waka (cape), Indo.
64/D3 Wakasa, Japan
64/D3 Wakasa (bay), Japan
107/G2 Wakaw, Sk,Can
64/D3 Wakayama, Japan
64/D4 Wakayama (pref.), Japan
78/F3 Wake (isl.), PacUS
112/D2 Wakeeney, Ks,US
33/G4 Wakefield, Eng,UK
110/B2 Wakefield, Mi,US
71/G4 Wakema, Burma
64/D3 Waki, Japan
63/N2 Wakkanai, Japan
65/H7 Wakō, Japan
110/D1 Wakwayowkastic (riv.), On,Can
51/G3 Walachia (range), Rom.
51/G3 Walachia (reg.), Rom.
39/J3 Wał brzych, Pol.
39/J3 Wał brzych (prov.), Pol.
35/E4 Walbury (hill), Eng,UK
40/A5 Walcheren (isl.), Neth.
42/D3 Walcourt, Belg.
39/J2 Wał cz, Pol.
43/G2 Waldbröl, Ger.
41/G6 Waldeck, Ger.
109/F2 Walden, Co,US
106/G2 Waldheim, Sk,Can
45/G2 Waldkirch, Ger.
45/L2 Waldviertel (reg.), Aus.
73/F4 Walea (str.), Indo.
73/F4 Waleabahi (isl.), Indo.
103/H2 Wales (isl.), NW,Can
36/C4 Wales, UK
98/T Walgreen (coast), Ant.
107/J3 Walhalla, ND,US
113/H3 Walhalla, SC,US
87/E1 Walikale, Zaire
88/L11 Walker (bay), SAfr.
108/C3 Walker (lake), Nv,US
108/C3 Walker (riv.), Nv,US
110/D2 Walkerton, On,Can
106/E4 Wallace, Id,US
116/H6 Wallaceburg, On,Can
33/E5 Wallasey, Eng,UK
106/D4 Walla Walla, Wa,US
116/F6 Walled (lake), Mi,US
116/F6 Walled Lake, Mi,US
41/F4 Wallenhorst, Ger.
42/C3 Wallers, Fr.
35/E3 Wallingford, Eng,UK
79/H6 Wallis (isls.), Wall.
78/G6 Wallis & Futuna (terr.), Fr.
106/D4 Wallowa (mts.), Or,US
33/G2 Wallsend, Eng,UK
33/E3 Walney, Isle of (isl.), Eng,UK
115/C2 Walnut, Ca,US
108/E4 Walnut Canyon Nat'l Mon., Az,US
116/K11 Walnut Creek, Ca,US
113/F2 Walnut Ridge, Ar,US
114/F4 Walrus (isls.), Ak,US
34/E1 Walsall, Eng,UK
103/K2 Walsingham (cape), NW,Can
35/G1 Walsingham, Eng,UK
41/G3 Walsrode, Ger.
113/H3 Walterboro, SC,US
113/G4 Walter F. George (res.), Al, Ga,US
31/P6 Waltham Abbey, Eng,UK
31/N7 Waltham Forest (bor.), Eng,UK
35/G3 Waltham Holy Cross, Eng,UK
33/F4 Walton-le-Dale, Eng,UK
35/F4 Walton on Thames, Eng,UK
35/H3 Walton on the Naze, Eng,UK
41/E5 Waltrop, Ger.
87/B5 Walvisbaai, SAfr.
87/C3 Wama, Ang.
83/L7 Wamba, Zaire
40/C5 Wamel, Neth.
33/E2 Wampool (riv.), Eng,UK
106/G5 Wamsutter, Wy,US
66/D5 Wan (riv.), China
75/Q11 Wanaka, NZ
115/F4 Wanaque, NJ,US
115/F4 Wanaque (res.), NJ,US
63/L2 Wanda (mts.), China
71/G3 Wanding, China
31/N7 Wandsworth (bor.), Eng,UK
69/B2 Wang (riv.), Thai.
75/S10 Wanganui, NZ
77/C3 Wangaratta, Austl.
45/H3 Wangen, Ger.
41/E1 Wangerooge (isl.), Ger.
73/F6 Wanggamet (peak), Indo.
69/B4 Wang Hip (peak), Thai.
66/E5 Wangpan (bay), China
73/F4 Wani (peak), Indo.
65/M9 Wanouchi, Japan
68/D5 Wanquan (lake), China
33/G1 Wansbeck (riv.), Eng,UK
31/P7 Wanstead, Eng,UK
35/E3 Wantage, Eng,UK
62/F5 Wanxian, China
43/E2 Wanze, Belg.
110/C3 Wapakoneta, Oh,US
107/G2 Wapawekka (lake), Sk,Can
106/D2 Wapiti (riv.), Ab, BC,Can
73/J4 Wapoga (riv.), Indo.
109/K3 Wappapello (lake), Mo,US
107/K5 Wapsipinicon (riv.), Ia,US
65/H7 Warabi, Japan
70/C4 Warangal, India
35/F2 Warboys, Eng,UK
41/G6 Warburg, Ger.
74/F5 Warburton (cr.), Austl.
43/F3 Warche (riv.), Belg.
75/R11 Ward, NZ
35/G4 Warden (pt.), Eng,UK
41/F2 Wardenburg, Ger.
70/C3 Wardha, India
33/F3 Ward's Stone (mtn.), Eng,UK
35/F3 Ware, Eng,UK
42/C2 Waregem, Belg.
34/D5 Wareham, Eng,UK
43/E2 Waremme, Belg.
38/G2 Waren, Ger.
41/E5 Warendorf, Ger.
35/F3 Wargrave, Eng,UK
69/D3 Warin Chamrap, Thai.
32/B3 Waringstown, NI,UK
33/F1 Wark, Eng,UK
39/L3 Warka, Pol.
75/R10 Warkworth, NZ
34/D2 Warley, Eng,UK
31/N8 Warlingham, Eng,UK
107/G2 Warman, Sk,Can
88/E2 Warmbad, SAfr.
41/G6 Warmebach (riv.), Ger.
41/H5 Warme Bode (riv.), Ger.
39/K1 Warmia (reg.), Pol.
34/D4 Warminster, Eng,UK
115/E5 Warminster, Pa,US
108/B2 Warner (mts.), Ca,US
113/H3 Warner Robins, Ga,US
38/G2 Warnow (riv.), Ger.
40/D4 Warnsveld, Neth.
74/F5 Warrandirinna (lake), Austl.
77/G5 Warrandybe, Austl.
76/B4 Warrego (range), Austl.
75/H5 Warrego (riv.), Austl.
114/M2 Warren (pt.), NW,Can
112/E3 Warren, Ar,US
116/F6 Warren, Mi,US
107/J3 Warren, Mn,US
115/F5 Warren, NJ,US
110/D3 Warren, Oh,US
110/E3 Warren, Pa,US
32/B3 Warrenpoint, NI,UK
109/J3 Warrensburg, Mo,US
88/D3 Warrenton, SAfr.
110/E4 Warrenton, Va,US
116/P16 Warrenville, Il,US
33/F5 Warrington, Eng,UK
113/G4 Warrington, Fl,US
77/B3 Warrnambool, Austl.
107/K3 Warroad, Mn,US
77/D1 Warrumbungle Nat'l Park, Austl.
110/C3 Warsaw, In,US
109/J3 Warsaw, Mo,US
39/L3 Warszawa (prov.), Pol.
39/L2 Warszawa (Warsaw) (cap.), Pol.
39/H5 Warscheneck (peak), Aus.
33/G5 Warslow, Eng,UK
33/G5 Warsop, Eng,UK
41/F6 Warstein, Ger.
39/H2 Warta (riv.), Pol.
76/D5 Warwick, Austl.
35/E2 Warwick, Eng,UK
111/G3 Warwick, RI,US
35/E2 Warwickshire (co.), Eng,UK
108/E2 Wasatch (range), Ut,US
108/C4 Wasco, Ca,US
107/K4 Waseca, Mn,US
102/F1 Washburn (lake), NW,Can
33/G4 Washburn (riv.), Eng,UK
107/M3 Washi (lake), On,Can
33/H5 Washingborough, Eng,UK
33/G2 Washington, Eng,UK
106/C4 Washington (state), US
115/J8 Washington (cap.), DC,US
110/B3 Washington, Il,US
110/C4 Washington, In,US
113/J3 Washington, NC,US
111/G2 Washington (mtn.), NH,US
115/F5 Washington, NJ,US
110/D3 Washington, Pa,US
116/C2 Washington (lake), Wa,US
110/C2 Washington (isl.), Wi,US
110/D4 Washington Court House, Oh,US
79/K4 Washington (Teraina) (atoll), Kiri.
109/H4 Washita (riv.), Ok, Tx,US
35/G1 Wash, The (bay), Eng,UK
39/M2 Wasilków, Pol.
110/E1 Waskaganish (Rupert House), Qu,Can
114/G4 Waskey (mtn.), Ak,US
40/B4 Wassenaar, Neth.
40/D6 Wassenberg, Ger.
45/H1 Wasserkuppe (peak), Ger.
104/C4 Wassuk (range), Nv,US
33/E3 Wast Water (lake), Eng,UK
110/E1 Waswanipi (lake), Qu,Can
73/E4 Watampone, Indo.
65/M10 Watarai, Japan
65/F2 Watarase (riv.), Japan
65/G1 Watari, Japan
34/C4 Watchet, Eng,UK
35/E3 Watchfield, Eng,UK
35/G2 Waterbeach, Eng,UK
111/F3 Waterbury, Ct,US
111/Q9 Waterdown, On,Can
113/H3 Wateree (lake), SC,US
113/H3 Wateree (riv.), SC,US
36/B4 Waterford, Ire.
116/F6 Waterford, Mi,US
34/A6 Watergate (bay), Eng,UK
107/J2 Waterhen (lake), Mb,Can
106/F2 Waterhen (riv.), Sk,Can
42/D2 Waterloo, Belg.
110/D3 Waterloo, On,Can
109/J2 Waterloo, Ia,US
110/B4 Waterloo, Il,US
42/D2 Waterloo Battlesite, Belg.
35/E5 Waterlooville, Eng,UK
42/D2 Watermael-Boitsfort, Belg.
106/E3 Waterton Lakes Nat'l Park, Ab,Can
110/F3 Watertown, NY,US
107/J4 Watertown, SD,US
110/B3 Watertown, Wi,US
89/E2 Waterval-Bo, SAfr.
111/G2 Waterville, Me,US
106/C4 Waterville, Wa,US
31/M7 Watford, Eng,UK
107/H4 Watford City, ND,US
33/G5 Wath-upon-Dearne, Eng,UK
101/G3 Watling (San Salvador) (isl.), Bahm.
35/F3 Watlington, Eng,UK
69/B2 Wat Mahathat, Thai.
109/H4 Watonga, Ok,US
73/G3 Watowato (peak), Indo.
69/D3 Wat Phu, Laos
107/G3 Watrous, Sk,Can
83/L7 Watsa, Zaire
110/C3 Watseka, Il,US
102/D2 Watson Lake, Yk,Can
108/B3 Watsonville, Ca,US
45/J3 Wattens, Aus.
42/C2 Wattignies, Fr.
35/G1 Watton, Eng,UK
42/C2 Wattrelos, Fr.
69/C2 Wat Xieng Thong, Laos
113/H5 Wauchula, Fl,US
116/P15 Wauconda, Il,US
74/C4 Waukarlycarly (lake), Austl.
116/Q15 Waukegan, Il,US
116/P13 Waukesha, Wi,US
34/C3 Waun Fâch (mtn.), Wal,UK
34/C1 Waun Oer (mtn.), Wal,UK
110/B3 Waupun, Wi,US
109/H4 Waurika, Ok,US
110/B2 Wausau, Wi,US
110/C3 Wauseon, Oh,US
116/P13 Wauwatosa, Wi,US
35/H2 Waveney (riv.), Eng,UK
33/E2 Waver (riv.), Eng,UK
77/G5 Waverley, Austl.
113/G2 Waverly, Tn,US
42/D2 Wavre, Belg.
42/B2 Wavrin, Fr.
83/L6 Wāw, Sudan
110/C2 Wawa, On,Can
110/E1 Wawagosic (riv.), Qu,Can
112/D3 Waxahachie, Tx,US
43/F3 Waxweiler, Ger.
113/H4 Waycross, Ga,US
116/F7 Wayne, Mi,US
109/H2 Wayne, Ne,US
115/F5 Wayne, NJ,US
113/H3 Waynesboro, Ga,US
113/F4 Waynesboro, Ms,US
110/E4 Waynesboro, Pa,US
110/E4 Waynesboro, Va,US
109/J3 Waynesville, Mo,US
113/H3 Waynesville, NC,US
42/C3 Waziers, Fr.
65/L10 Wazuka, Japan
38/K2 Wda (riv.), Pol.
85/F3 W du Niger Nat'l Park, Afr.
72/A2 We (isl.), Indo.
35/G4 Weald, The (reg.), Eng,UK
33/G2 Wear (riv.), Eng,UK
33/F2 Wear Head, Eng,UK
109/H4 Weatherford, Ok,US
112/D3 Weatherford, Tx,US
33/F5 Weaver (riv.), Eng,UK
108/B2 Weaverville, Ca,US
107/J4 Webster, SD,US
107/K5 Webster City, Ia,US
83/M7 Webuye, Kenya
98/W Weddell (sea), Ant.
97/M7 Weddell (isl.), Falk.
77/C2 Weddin Mountains Nat'l Park, Austl.
41/G1 Wedel, Ger.
41/G3 Wedemark, Ger.
34/D4 Wedmore, Eng,UK
34/D1 Wednesbury, Eng,UK
34/D1 Wednesfield, Eng,UK
108/B2 Weed, Ca,US
35/E2 Weedon Bec, Eng,UK
113/H4 Weeki Wachee Springs, Fl,US
34/B5 Week Saint Mary, Eng,UK
40/D4 Weerselo, Neth.
40/C6 Weert, Neth.
40/C4 Weesp, Neth.
40/D6 Wegberg, Ger.
39/L1 Węgorzewo, Pol.
39/M2 Węgrów, Pol.
41/G6 Wehre (riv.), Ger.
63/H4 Wei (riv.), China
63/H3 Weichang, China
38/G3 Weida, Ger.
45/K2 Weiden, Ger.
66/D3 Weifang, China
63/J4 Weihai, China
45/H1 Weilburg, Ger.
43/F2 Weilerswist, Ger.
45/J3 Weilheim, Ger.
38/F3 Weimar, Ger.
45/H3 Weingarten, Ger.
39/J4 Weinviertel (reg.), Aus.
110/D3 Weirton, WV,US
106/D4 Weiser, Id,US
106/D4 Weiser (riv.), Id,US
66/D4 Weishan (lake), China
43/F4 Weiskirchen, Ger.
113/G3 Weiss (lake), Al,US
45/J2 Weissenburg im Bayern, Ger.
38/F3 Weissenfels, Ger.
43/G3 Weissenthurm, Ger.
43/F3 Weisser Stein (peak), Ger.
45/J3 Weisskugel (Palla Bianca) (mt.), Aus., It.
45/G3 Weissmies (peak), Swi.
39/H3 Weisswasser, Ger.
45/L3 Weiz, Aus.
71/J3 Weizhou (isl.), China
39/K1 Wejherowo, Pol.
110/D4 Welch, WV,US
83/N5 Weldiya, Eth.
35/F2 Weldon, Eng,UK
83/M6 Welel (peak), Eth.
35/E4 Welford, Eng,UK
31/N6 Welham Green, Eng,UK
70/D6 Weligama, SrL.
43/E2 Welkenraedt, Belg.
88/D3 Welkom, SAfr.
111/R10 Welland, On,Can
111/R10 Welland (can.), On,Can
35/F1 Welland (riv.), Eng,UK
111/R10 Wellandport, On,Can
43/E2 Wellen, Belg.
74/F3 Wellesley (isls.), Austl.
35/F2 Wellingborough, Eng,UK
77/C3 Wellington (inlet), Austl.
103/S7 Wellington (chan.), NW,Can
97/J7 Wellington (isl.), Chile
75/R11 Wellington (cap.), NZ
88/B4 Wellington, SAfr.
34/C5 Wellington, Eng,UK
34/D2 Wellington, Eng,UK
112/D2 Wellington, Ks,US
112/C3 Wellington, Tx,US
74/C5 Wells (lake), Austl.
106/C2 Wells, BC,Can
34/D4 Wells, Eng,UK
106/E5 Wells, Nv,US
35/G1 Wells-next-the-Sea, Eng,UK
110/D4 Wellston, Oh,US
45/L2 Wels, Aus.
34/C1 Welshpool, Wal,UK
41/E5 Welver, Ger.
35/F3 Welwyn, Eng,UK
35/F3 Welwyn Garden City, Eng,UK
33/F6 Wem, Eng,UK
87/F1 Wembere (riv.), Tanz.
106/D2 Wembley, Ab,Can
34/B6 Wembury, Eng,UK
103/J3 Wemindji, Qu,Can
42/D2 Wemmel, Belg.
106/C4 Wenatchee, Wa,US
67/B4 Wenchang, China
85/E5 Wenchi, Gha.
41/H4 Wendeburg, Ger.
43/G2 Wenden, Ger.
35/F3 Wendover, Eng,UK
108/D2 Wendover, Nv,US
34/A6 Wendron, Eng,UK
34/D2 Wenlock Edge (ridge), Eng,UK
41/F6 Wenne (riv.), Ger.
41/G4 Wennigsen, Ger.
33/F3 Wennington, Eng,UK
33/F3 Wensleydale (val.), Eng,UK
35/H1 Wensum (riv.), Eng,UK
33/G4 Went (riv.), Eng,UK
67/D2 Wenzhou, China
38/G3 Werdau, Ger.
83/Q6 Werdēr, Eth.
41/E6 Werdohl, Ger.
40/B5 Werkendam, Neth.
41/E5 Werl, Ger.
41/E3 Werlte, Ger.
41/E6 Wermelskirchen, Ger.
41/E5 Werne an der Lippe, Ger.
45/J2 Werneck, Ger.
41/H5 Wernigerode, Ger.
77/D2 Werong (peak), Austl.
41/G6 Werra (riv.), Ger.
41/F4 Werre (riv.), Ger.
77/E1 Werrikimbe Nat'l Park, Austl.
33/F5 Werrington, Eng,UK
41/E5 Werse (riv.), Ger.
45/H2 Wertheim, Ger.
41/F4 Werther, Ger.
40/C3 Wervershoof, Neth.
42/C2 Wervik, Belg.
40/D5 Wesel, Ger.
41/E5 Wesel-Datteln-Kanal (can.), Ger.
41/F2 Weser (riv.), Ger.
41/G4 Wesergebirge (ridge), Ger.
112/D5 Weslaco, Tx,US
88/D2 Wes-Rand, SAfr.
74/F2 Wessel (cape), Austl.
74/F2 Wessel (isls.), Austl.
34/D4 Wessex (reg.), Eng,UK
107/J4 Wessington Springs, SD,US
77/C4 West (pt.), Austl.
116/P13 West Allis, Wi,US
113/H3 West Augusta, Ga,US
115/G5 West Babylon, NY,US
59/K5 West Bank (occ. zone)
110/B3 West Bend, Wi,US
70/E3 West Bengal (state), India
35/G3 West Bergholt, Eng,UK
110/C2 West Branch, Mi,US
33/G6 West Bridgford, Eng,UK
35/E1 West Bromwich, Eng,UK
34/D4 Westbury, Eng,UK
115/G5 Westbury, NY,US
116/P16 West Chicago, Il,US
31/M8 West Clandon, Eng,UK
34/B3 West Cleddau (riv.), Wal,UK
113/H3 West Columbia, SC,US
33/G2 West Cornforth, Eng,UK
115/C2 West Covina, Ca,US
40/A6 Westdorpe, Neth.
30/F3 West Dvina (riv.), Eur.
112/B2 West Elk (mts.), Co,US
40/D3 Westerbork, Neth.
31/P8 Westerham, Eng,UK
41/E4 Westerkappeln, Ger.
38/E1 Westerland, Ger.
43/D1 Westerlo, Belg.
86/B3 Western (des.), Egypt
85/E5 Western (reg.), Gha.
84/B4 Western (area), SLeo.
74/C4 Western Australia (state), Austl.
64/A3 Western Channel (str.), Japan, SKor.
56/C4 Western Dvina (riv.), Lat., Rus.
70/B4 Western Ghats (mts.), India
82/B3 Western Sahara
79/H6 Western Samoa
62/C1 Western Sayan (mts.), Rus.
40/A6 Westerschelde (chan.), Neth.
41/E2 Westerstede, Ger.
110/D3 Westerville, Oh,US
40/C5 Westervoort, Neth.
43/G2 Westerwald (for.), Ger.
41/F4 Westfalica, Porta (pass), Ger.
97/M8 West Falkland (isl.), Falk.
107/J4 West Fargo, ND,US
78/D4 West Fayu (isl.), Micr.
115/F5 Westfield, NJ,US
42/B2 West Flanders (prov.), Belg.
110/B4 West Frankfort, Il,US
40/C2 West Frisian (isls.), Neth.
34/C3 West Glamorgan (co.), Wal,UK
35/F1 West Glen (riv.), Eng,UK
31/P7 West Ham, Eng,UK
115/G4 West Haverstraw, NY,US
113/F3 West Helena, Ar,US
36/D2 Westhill, Sc,UK
31/Q7 West Horndon, Eng,UK
31/M8 West Horsley, Eng,UK
33/F4 Westhoughton, Eng,UK
111/Q8 West Humber (riv.), On,Can
101/F4 West Indies (isls.), NAm.
75/J4 West Islet (isl.), Austl.
115/G5 West Islip, NY,US
108/E2 West Jordan, Ut,US
31/P8 West Kingsdown, Eng,UK
33/E5 West Kirby, Eng,UK
116/F7 Westland, Mi,US
106/E2 Westlock, Ab,Can
87/E3 West Lunga Nat'l Park, Zam.
32/A4 Westmeath (co.), Ire.
113/F3 West Memphis, Ar,US
35/G3 West Mersea, Eng,UK
35/E2 West Midlands (co.), Eng,UK
115/F4 West Milford, NJ,US
115/B3 Westminster, Ca,US
31/N7 Westminster Abbey, Eng,UK
31/N7 Westminster, City of (bor.), Eng,UK
116/Q16 Westmont, Il,US
115/E6 Westmont (Haddon), NJ,US
33/F3 Westmoreland (reg.), Eng,UK
111/N7 Westmount, Qu,Can
109/J3 Weston, Mo,US
110/D4 Weston, WV,US
88/P13 Westonaria, SAfr.
34/D4 Weston-super-Mare, Eng,UK
34/D4 Weston Zoyland, Eng,UK
115/F5 West Orange, NJ,US
113/H5 West Palm Beach, Fl,US
31/Q8 West Peckham, Eng,UK
113/G4 West Pensacola, Fl,US
109/K3 West Plains, Mo,US
113/G3 West Point (lake), Al, Ga,US
113/F3 West Point, Ms,US
109/H2 West Point, Ne,US
75/R11 Westport, NZ
115/G4 Westport, Ct,US
106/B2 West Road (riv.), BC,Can
116/L9 West Sacramento, Ca,US
111/S10 West Seneca, NY,US
56/H3 West Siberian (plain), Rus.
35/F4 West Sussex (co.), Eng,UK
31/P7 West Thurrock, Eng,UK
108/E2 West Valley City, Ut,US
106/C3 West Vancouver, BC,Can
110/D4 West Virginia (state), US
34/B4 Westward Ho!, Eng,UK
115/F5 Westwood, NJ,US
33/G4 West Yorkshire (co.), Eng,UK
112/B2 Wet (mts.), Co,US
73/G5 Wetar (isl.), Indo.
73/G5 Wetar (str.), Indo.
106/E2 Wetaskiwin, Ab,Can
87/G2 Wete, Tanz.
110/E1 Wetetnagami (riv.), Qu,Can
33/F2 Wetheral, Eng,UK
33/G4 Wetherby, Eng,UK
77/B2 Wetherell (lake), Austl.
41/E6 Wetter, Ger.
42/C1 Wetteren, Belg.
41/E4 Wettringen, Ger.
42/C2 Wevelgem, Belg.
78/D5 Wewak, PNG
109/H4 Wewoka, Ok,US
36/B4 Wexford, Ire.
32/B6 Wexford (co.), Ire.
31/M8 Wey (riv.), Eng,UK
35/H1 Weybourne, Eng,UK
31/M7 Weybridge, Eng,UK
107/H3 Weyburn, Sk,Can
34/D5 Weymouth, Eng,UK
34/D5 Weymouth (bay), Eng,UK
75/S10 Whakatane, NZ
33/G5 Whaley Bridge, Eng,UK
33/F4 Whalley, Eng,UK
75/R10 Whangarei, NZ
33/G3 Wharfe (riv.), Eng,UK
112/D4 Wharton, Tx,US
107/G5 Wheatland, Wy,US
35/E3 Wheatley, Eng,UK
116/P16 Wheaton, Il,US
34/D1 Wheaton Aston, Eng,UK
115/J7 Wheaton-Glenmont, Md,US
113/G3 Wheeler (lake), Al,US
109/F3 Wheeler (peak), NM,US
108/D3 Wheeler (peak), Nv,US
116/Q15 Wheeling, Il,US
110/D3 Wheeling, WV,US
33/F3 Whernside (mtn.), Eng,UK
33/G2 Whickham, Eng,UK
116/B1 Whidbey (isl.), Wa,US
108/B2 Whiskeytown-Shasta-Trinity Nat'l Rec. Area, Ca,US
33/G2 Whitburn, Eng,UK
111/S8 Whitby, On,Can
33/H3 Whitby, Eng,UK
33/F6 Whitchurch, Eng,UK
35/E4 Whitchurch, Eng,UK
35/F3 Whitchurch, Eng,UK
34/C4 Whitchurch, Wal,UK
98/D White (isl.), Ant.
74/D4 White (lake), Austl.
111/K1 White (bay), Nf,Can
110/C1 White (lake), On,Can
52/H2 White (sea), Rus.
114/L4 White (pass), Ak,US
113/F3 White (riv.), Ar,US
108/E2 White (riv.), Co, Ut,US
110/C4 White (riv.), In,US
109/J5 White (lake), La,US
109/K4 White (riv.), La, Mo,US
109/G2 White (riv.), Ne, SD,US
108/D3 White (riv.), Nv,US
112/C3 White (riv.), Tx,US
110/D4 White (peak), Va,US
111/K1 White Bear (riv.), Nf,Can
107/G3 White City, Sk,Can
106/E2 Whitecourt, Ab,Can
33/E1 White Esk (riv.), Sc,UK
107/K4 Whiteface (riv.), Mn,US
33/F4 Whitefield, Eng,UK
110/C2 Whitefish (bay), On,Can, Mi,US
106/E3 Whitefish, Mt,US
114/L2 Whitefish Station, Yk,Can
34/B3 Whiteford (pt.), Wal,UK
107/G2 White Fox, Sk,Can
106/E4 Whitehall, Mt,US
115/E5 Whitehall (Fullerton), Pa,US
32/E2 Whitehaven, Eng,UK
32/C2 Whitehead, NI,UK
114/L3 Whitehorse (cap.), Yk,Can
35/E3 Whitehorse (hill), Eng,UK
115/K7 White Marsh, Md,US
114/J2 White Mountains Nat'l Rec. Area, Ak,US
107/K3 Whitemouth (riv.), Mb,Can
83/M5 White Nile (riv.), Sudan
115/K7 White Oak, Md,US
110/A1 White Otter (lake), On,Can
115/G4 White Plains, NY,US
110/C1 White River, On,Can
108/E4 Whiteriver, Az,US
112/B3 White Rock, NM,US
108/F4 White Sands, NM,US
108/F4 White Sands Nat'l Mon., NM,US
97/K8 Whiteside (chan.), Chile
106/F4 White Sulphur Springs, Mt,US
110/D4 White Sulphur Springs, WV,US
113/J3 Whiteville, NC,US
85/E4 White Volta (riv.), Burk., Gha.
107/L3 Whitewater (lake), On,Can
107/H3 Whitewood, Sk,Can
32/D2 Whithorn, Sc,UK
34/B3 Whitland, Wal,UK
33/G1 Whitley Bay, Eng,UK
108/C3 Whitney (mtn.), Ca,US
109/H4 Whitney (lake), Tx,US
34/B6 Whitsand (bay), Eng,UK
35/H4 Whitstable, Eng,UK
76/C3 Whitsunday I. Nat'l Park, Austl.
115/B3 Whittier, Ca,US
35/F1 Whittlesey, Eng,UK
33/G5 Whitwell, Eng,UK
33/F4 Whitworth, Eng,UK
102/F2 Wholdaia (lake), NW,Can
74/F6 Whyalla, Austl.
69/B2 Wiang Ko Sai Nat'l Park, Thai.
110/D2 Wiarton, On,Can
42/C2 Wichelen, Belg.
109/H3 Wichita, Ks,US
109/H4 Wichita (mts.), Ok,US
109/H4 Wichita (riv.), Tx,US
112/D3 Wichita Falls, Tx,US
108/D4 Wickenburg, Az,US
35/G3 Wickford, Eng,UK
77/C3 Wickham (cape), Austl.
35/H2 Wickham Market, Eng,UK
32/B6 Wicklow (co.), Ire.
32/B5 Wicklow (mts.), Ire.
32/B5 Wicklow Gap (pass), Ire.
32/C6 Wicklow Head (pt.), Ire.
41/F4 Wickriede (riv.), Ger.
33/F5 Widnes, Eng,UK
43/G2 Wied (riv.), Ger.
41/G2 Wiedau (riv.), Ger.
41/F2 Wiefelstede, Ger.
41/F4 Wiehengebirge (ridge), Ger.
43/G2 Wiehl, Ger.
39/L4 Wieliczka, Pol.
42/C2 Wielsbeke, Belg.
39/K3 Wieluń, Pol.
39/J4 Wien (prov.), Aus.
39/J5 Wiener Neustadt, Aus.
39/J4 Wien (Vienna) (cap.), Aus.
45/L2 Wienwald (reg.), Aus.
39/M3 Wieprz (riv.), Pol.
40/D4 Wierden, Neth.
40/B3 Wieringermeerpolder (polder), Neth.
40/C3 Wieringerwerf, Neth.
39/K3 Wieruszów, Pol.
45/H1 Wiesbaden, Ger.
45/G3 Wiese (riv.), Ger.
56/H2 Wiese (isl.), Rus.
41/E2 Wiesmoor, Ger.
41/E3 Wietmarschen, Ger.
41/G3 Wietze, Ger.
41/G3 Wietze (riv.), Ger.
39/K1 Wiezyca (peak), Pol.
33/F4 Wigan, Eng,UK
113/F4 Wiggins, Ms,US
35/E5 Wight, Isle of (isl.), Eng,UK
35/E1 Wigston, Eng,UK
33/E2 Wigton, Eng,UK
32/D2 Wigtown, Sc,UK
32/D2 Wigtown (bay), Sc,UK
40/C5 Wijchen, Neth.
40/D4 Wijhe, Neth.
40/C5 Wijk bij Duurstede, Neth.
83/N5 Wik'ro, Eth.
109/H2 Wilber, Ne,US
33/H4 Wilberfoss, Eng,UK
106/D4 Wilbur, Wa,US
109/J4 Wilburton, Ok,US
56/G1 Wilczek (isl.), Rus.
88/E4 Wild Coast (reg.), SAfr.
41/F3 Wildeshausen, Ger.
111/Q8 Wildfield, On,Can
107/J4 Wild Rice (riv.), Mn,US
45/J3 Wildspitze (peak), Aus.
115/K8 Wild World, Md,US
88/E2 Wilge (riv.), SAfr.
98/F Wilhelm II (coast), Ant.
93/G3 Wilhelmina (mts.), Sur.
40/C5 Wilhelminakanaal (can.), Neth.
41/G2 Wilhelmsburg, Ger.
41/F1 Wilhelmshaven, Ger.
113/H2 Wilkesboro, NC,US
98/J Wilkes Land (reg.), Ant.
106/F2 Wilkie, Sk,Can
98/V Wilkins (sound), Ant.
114/N4 Will (mtn.), BC,Can
106/C4 Willamette (riv.), Or,US
77/C2 Willandra Nat'l Park, Austl.
106/B4 Willapa (bay), Wa,US
33/F5 Willaston, Eng,UK
108/E4 Willcox, Az,US
41/G5 Willebadessen, Ger.
42/D1 Willebroek, Belg.
101/H5 Willemstad (cap.), NAnt.
31/N7 Willesden, Eng,UK
77/B3 William (peak), Austl.
108/D4 Williams, Az,US
110/C4 Williamsburg, Ky,US
110/E4 Williamsburg, Va,US
106/C2 Williams Lake, BC,Can
110/D4 Williamson, WV,US
77/F5 Williamstown, Austl.
111/S10 Williamsville, NY,US
40/D6 Willich, Ger.
115/F5 Willingboro, NJ,US
33/G2 Willington, Eng,UK
33/G6 Willington, Eng,UK
112/E4 Willis, Tx,US
75/J3 Willis Islets (isls.), Austl.
106/C2 Williston (lake), BC,Can
113/H4 Williston, Fl,US
107/H3 Williston, ND,US
34/C4 Williton, Eng,UK
108/B3 Willits, Ca,US
107/K4 Willmar, Mn,US
106/C2 Willow (riv.), BC,Can
106/D4 Willow (cr.), Or,US
116/Q16 Willowbrook, Il,US
107/G3 Willow Bunch, Sk,Can
115/E5 Willow Grove, Pa,US
106/C2 Willow River, BC,Can
108/B3 Willows, Ca,US
74/D4 Wills (lake), Austl.
116/Q15 Wilmette, Il,US
31/P7 Wilmington, Eng,UK
115/E6 Wilmington, De,US
113/J3 Wilmington, NC,US
110/D4 Wilmington, Oh,US
113/H4 Wilmington Island, Ga,US
33/F5 Wilmslow, Eng,UK
43/H2 Wilnsdorf, Ger.
40/B6 Wilrijk, Belg.
41/G2 Wilseder Berg (peak), Ger.
103/H2 Wilson (cape), NW,Can
115/B2 Wilson (mt.), Ca,US
113/J3 Wilson, NC,US
111/S9 Wilson, NY,US
115/E5 Wilson, Pa,US
77/C3 Wilsons Promontory Nat'l Park, Austl.
35/E4 Wilton, Eng,UK
35/E4 Wiltshire (co.), Eng,UK
31/N7 Wimbledon, Eng,UK
34/E5 Wimborne Minster, Eng,UK
42/A2 Wimereux, Fr.
88/D3 Winburg, SAfr.
34/D4 Wincanton, Eng,UK
35/E3 Winchcombe, Eng,UK
35/G5 Winchelsea, Eng,UK
35/E4 Winchester, Eng,UK
110/C4 Winchester, Ky,US
113/G3 Winchester, Tn,US
110/E4 Winchester, Va,US
106/F5 Wind (riv.), Wy,US
107/G5 Wind Cave Nat'l Park, SD,US
113/H3 Winder, Ga,US
33/F3 Windermere, Eng,UK
33/F3 Windermere (lake), Eng,UK
87/C5 Windhoek (cap.), Namb.
107/K5 Windom, Mn,US

108/E4 Window Rock, Az,US
106/F5 Wind River (range), Wy,US
35/E3 Windrush (riv.), Eng,UK
76/G8 Windsor, Austl.
111/L1 Windsor, NF,Can
111/H2 Windsor, NS,Can
116/F7 Windsor, On,Can
111/G2 Windsor, Qu,Can
35/F4 Windsor, Eng,UK
101/K5 Windward (isls.), NAm.
101/G4 Windward (passage), NAm.
106/D3 Winfield, BC,Can
109/H3 Winfield, Ks,US
35/F3 Wing, Eng,UK
33/G2 Wingate, Eng,UK
42/C1 Wingene, Belg.
111/R10 Winger, On,Can
35/H4 Wingham, Eng,UK
74/C4 Winifred (lake), Austl.
107/M2 Winisk, On,Can
107/M2 Winisk (lake), On,Can
107/M2 Winisk (riv.), On,Can
107/J3 Winkler, Mb,Can
85/E5 Winneba, Gha.
110/B3 Winnebago (lake), Wi,US
108/C2 Winnemucca, Nv,US
107/J5 Winner, SD,US
116/Q15 Winnetka, Il,US
106/F4 Winnett, Mt,US
112/E4 Winnfield, La,US
107/J3 Winnipeg (cap.), Mb,Can
107/J2 Winnipeg (lake), Mb,Can
107/K3 Winnipeg (riv.), Mb, On,Can
107/J3 Winnipeg Beach, Mb,Can
107/J3 Winnipegosis, Mb,Can
107/H2 Winnipegosis (lake), Mb,Can
112/F3 Winnsboro, La,US
113/H3 Winnsboro, SC,US
111/Q9 Winona, On,Can
107/L4 Winona, Mn,US
40/E2 Winschoten, Neth.
34/D4 Winscombe, Eng,UK
33/F5 Winsford, Eng,UK
34/D4 Winsley, Eng,UK
35/F3 Winslow, Eng,UK
108/E4 Winslow, Az,US
113/H2 Winston-Salem, NC,US
40/D2 Winsum, Neth.
41/F6 Winterberg, Ger.
88/D4 Winterberge (mts.), SAfr.
34/D3 Winterbourne, Eng,UK
113/H4 Winter Haven, Fl,US
113/H4 Winter Park, Fl,US
40/D5 Winterswijk, Neth.
45/H3 Winterthur, Swi.
111/G2 Winthrop, Me,US
116/Q15 Winthrop Harbor, Il,US
38/F3 Wipper (riv.), Ger.
41/H2 Wipperau (riv.), Ger.
41/E6 Wipperfürth, Ger.
33/G5 Wirksworth, Eng,UK
33/E5 Wirral (pen.), Eng,UK
35/G1 Wisbech, Eng,UK
110/B2 Wisconsin (state), US
110/B2 Wisconsin Rapids, Wi,US
107/J4 Wishek, ND,US
39/K4 Wisła, Pol.
39/K1 Wiślany (lag.), Pol.
39/K2 Wisła (Vistula) (riv.), Pol.
39/L4 Wisłok (riv.), Pol.
39/L4 Wisłoka (riv.), Pol.
38/F2 Wismar, Ger.
43/G5 Wissembourg, Fr.
43/G2 Wissen, Ger.
35/G1 Wissey (riv.), Eng,UK
88/E2 Witbank, SAfr.
88/A2 Witberg (peak), Namb.
35/G3 Witham, Eng,UK
33/H5 Witham (riv.), Eng,UK
34/C5 Witheridge, Eng,UK
33/J4 Withernsea, Eng,UK
114/J3 Witherspoon (mtn.), Ak,US
113/H4 Withlacoochee (riv.), Fl, Ga,US
33/F4 Withnell, Eng,UK
88/D3 Wit Kei (riv.), SAfr.
39/J2 Witkowo, Pol.
35/E3 Witney, Eng,UK
39/H2 Witnica, Pol.
43/E2 Witten, Neth.
41/E6 Witten, Ger.
38/G3 Wittenberg, Ger.
38/F2 Wittenberge, Ger.
45/G3 Wittenheim, Fr.
35/F1 Wittering, Eng,UK
41/H3 Wittingen, Ger.
43/F4 Wittlich, Ger.
41/E1 Wittmund, Ger.
39/G1 Witton (pen.), Ger.
38/G2 Wittstock, Ger.
88/P12 Witwatersrand (reg.), SAfr.
41/G6 Witzenhausen, Ger.
34/C4 Wiveliscombe, Eng,UK
75/J5 Wivenhoe (lake), Austl.
35/G3 Wivenhoe, Eng,UK
116/E6 Wixom, Mi,US
39/L2 Wkra (riv.), Pol.
39/K1 Władysławowo, Pol.
39/K2 Włocławek, Pol.
39/K2 Włocławek (prov.), Pol.
39/K2 Włocławskie (lake), Pol.
39/M3 Włodawa, Pol.
39/K3 Włoszczowa, Pol.
34/C1 Wnion (riv.), Wal,UK
35/F2 Woburn Sands, Eng,UK
77/C3 Wodonga, Austl.
39/K4 Wodzisław Śląski, Pol.
40/B4 Woerden, Neth.
43/G6 Woerth, Fr.
40/C3 Wognum, Neth.
43/F5 Woippy, Fr.
73/H5 Wokam (isl.), Indo.
63/K2 Woken (riv.), China
31/M8 Woking, Eng,UK
35/F4 Wokingham, Eng,UK
111/S9 Wolcottsville, NY,US
31/N8 Woldingham, Eng,UK
78/D4 Woleai (atoll), Micr.
114/H2 Wolf (mtn.), Ak,US
109/G3 Wolf (cr.), Ok, Tx,US
110/B2 Wolf (riv.), Wi,US
114/F3 Wolf Creek (mtn.), Ak,US
106/E4 Wolf Creek, Mt,US
38/G3 Wolfen, Ger.
41/H4 Wolfenbüttel, Ger.
41/G6 Wolfhagen, Ger.
107/G3 Wolf Point, Mt,US
41/H4 Wolfsburg, Ger.
39/G1 Wolgast, Ger.
39/H2 Woliński Nat'l Park, Pol.
102/E2 Wollaston (pen.), NW,Can
102/F3 Wollaston (lake), Sk,Can
97/L8 Wollaston (isl.), Chile
35/F2 Wollaston, Eng,UK
77/D2 Wollemi Nat'l Park, Austl.
77/D2 Wollongong, Austl.
88/D2 Wolmaransstad, SAfr.
45/J3 Wolnzach, Ger.
82/C6 Wologizi (range), Libr.
39/L2 Wołomin, Pol.
39/J3 Wołów, Pol.
88/L10 Wolseley, SAfr.
33/G2 Wolsingham, Eng,UK
39/J2 Wolsztyn, Pol.
42/D2 Woluwé-Saint-Lambert, Belg.
40/D3 Wolvega, Neth.
34/D1 Wolverhampton, Eng,UK
35/F2 Wolverton, Eng,UK
110/D2 Woman (riv.), On,Can
34/D1 Wombourne, Eng,UK
33/G4 Wombwell, Eng,UK
116/P15 Wonder (lake), Il,US
77/C1 Wongalarroo (lake), Austl.
77/C3 Wonnangatta-Moroka Nat'l Park, Austl.
63/K4 Wŏnsan, NKor.
107/H2 Wood (lake), Sk,Can
106/G3 Wood (mtn.), Sk,Can
114/K3 Wood (mtn.), Yk,Can
111/Q8 Woodbridge, On,Can
35/H2 Woodbridge, Eng,UK
115/F5 Woodbridge, NJ,US
102/E2 Wood Buffalo Nat'l Park, Ab, Yk,Can
111/Q9 Woodburn, On,Can
32/C2 Woodburn, NI,UK
106/C4 Woodburn, Or,US
115/E6 Woodbury, NJ,US
116/Q16 Wood Dale, Il,US
76/D4 Woodgate Nat'l Park, Austl.
33/H5 Woodhall Spa, Eng,UK
116/F7 Woodhaven, Mi,US
116/L9 Woodland, Ca,US
109/F3 Woodland Park, Co,US
78/E5 Woodlark (isl.), PNG
115/K7 Woodlawn, Md,US
35/F4 Woodley, Eng,UK
115/G5 Woodmere, NY,US
116/P16 Woodridge, Il,US
74/E5 Woodroffe (peak), Austl.
33/F6 Woodseaves, Eng,UK
111/H2 Woodstock, NB,Can
35/E3 Woodstock, Eng,UK
116/P15 Woodstock, Il,US
110/E4 Woodstock, Va,US
113/F4 Woodville, Ms,US
112/E4 Woodville, Tx,US
109/H3 Woodward, Ok,US
34/D5 Wool, Eng,UK
34/D4 Woolavington, Eng,UK
33/G1 Woolsington, Eng,UK
31/P7 Woolwich, Eng,UK
109/H1 Woonsocket, SD,US
33/F6 Woore, Eng,UK
110/D3 Wooster, Oh,US
35/E3 Wootton Basset, Eng,UK
88/B4 Worcester, SAfr.
34/D2 Worcester, Eng,UK
111/G3 Worcester, Ma,US
34/D2 Worcester & Birmingham (can.), Eng,UK
45/K3 Wörgl, Aus.
32/E2 Workington, Eng,UK
33/G5 Worksop, Eng,UK
106/G4 Worland, Wy,US
28/* World
40/B4 Wormer, Neth.
31/N6 Wormley, Eng,UK
45/H2 Worms, Ger.
45/J2 Wörnitz (riv.), Ger.
41/F2 Worpswede, Ger.
33/G4 Worsbrough, Eng,UK
116/Q16 Worth, Il,US
35/F5 Worthing, Eng,UK
107/K5 Worthington, Mn,US
78/F3 Wotho (atoll), Mrsh.
78/G4 Wotje (atoll), Mrsh.
34/D3 Wotton under Edge, Eng,UK
40/C4 Woudenberg, Neth.
40/C5 Woudrichem, Neth.
40/B5 Wouw, Neth.
73/F4 Wowoni (isl.), Indo.
33/H5 Wragby, Eng,UK
57/T2 Wrangel (isl.), Rus.
114/A5 Wrangell (cape), Ak,US
114/K3 Wrangell (mts.), Ak,US
114/K3 Wrangell-Saint Elias Nat'l Park & Prsv., Ak,US
33/J5 Wrangle, Eng,UK
109/G2 Wray, Co,US
31/M7 Wraysbury, Eng,UK
33/H6 Wreake (riv.), Eng,UK
75/K4 Wreck (reef), Austl.
88/B3 Wreck (pt.), SAfr.
34/D1 Wrekin, The (hill), Eng,UK
33/F5 Wrenbury, Eng,UK
33/F5 Wrexham, Wal,UK
107/G5 Wright, Wy,US
115/F5 Wrightstown, NJ,US
115/C2 Wrightwood, Ca,US
35/G3 Writtle, Eng,UK
39/J3 Wrocław, Pol.
39/J3 Wrocław (prov.), Pol.
31/P8 Wrotham, Eng,UK
102/D1 Wrottesley (cape), NW,Can
34/D1 Wroxeter, Eng,UK
35/H1 Wroxham, Eng,UK
39/J2 Września, Pol.
39/J3 Wschowa, Pol.
71/K2 Wu (riv.), China
66/C3 Wu'an, China
66/C5 Wuchang (lake), China
67/C3 Wudalianchi, China
66/B4 Wudang Shan (mtn.), China
66/B3 Wuding (riv.), China
66/C5 Wuhan, China
66/D5 Wuhu, China
62/F3 Wujia (riv.), China
40/E6 Wülfrath, Ger.
67/B2 Wuling (mts.), China
85/H5 Wum, Camr.
41/F2 Wümme (riv.), Ger.
70/C3 Wūn, India
41/F5 Wünnenberg, Ger.
41/G4 Wunstorf, Ger.
108/E4 Wupatki Nat'l Mon., Az,US
41/E6 Wüpper (riv.), Ger.
41/E6 Wuppertal, Ger.
68/C4 Wuqia, China
43/F2 Würm (riv.), Ger.
85/G3 Wurno, Nga.
43/F2 Würselen, Ger.
45/H2 Würzburg, Ger.
63/H5 Wushan (lake), China
66/C5 Wusheng Guan (pass), China
68/C3 Wushi, China
41/G6 Wüstegarten (peak), Ger.
63/L2 Wusuli (Ussuri) (riv.), China, Rus.
66/C3 Wutai Shan (peak), China
84/C4 Wuteve (peak), Libr.
40/B6 Wuustwezel, Belg.
66/C5 Wuwei, China
66/E5 Wuxi, China
66/C5 Wuxue, China
67/C2 Wuyi (mts.), China
63/K2 Wuyur (riv.), China
69/E2 Wuzhi (mts.), China
66/D2 Wuzhi Shan (peak), China
71/K3 Wuzhou, China
116/F7 Wyandotte, Mi,US
77/D2 Wyangale (dam), Austl.
115/F4 Wyckoff, NJ,US
34/D3 Wye (riv.), UK
34/D4 Wylye (riv.), Eng,UK
33/G6 Wymeswold, Eng,UK
35/H1 Wymondham, Eng,UK
113/F3 Wynne, Ar,US
76/F6 Wynnum, Austl.
107/G3 Wynyard, Sk,Can
106/F5 Wyoming (state), US
110/C3 Wyoming, Mi,US
106/F5 Wyoming (peak), Wy,US
108/E2 Wyoming (range), Wy,US
77/B2 Wyperfeld Nat'l Park, Austl.
33/F4 Wyre (riv.), Eng,UK
39/L2 Wyszków, Pol.
110/D4 Wytheville, Va,US

X

69/D4 Xa Binh Long, Viet.
100/B4 Xadani, Mex.
68/E5 Xainza, China
70/E2 Xaitongmoin, China
89/F2 Xai-Xai, Moz.
69/D1 Xam Nua, Laos
69/D3 Xan (riv.), Viet.
40/D5 Xanten, Ger.
49/J2 Xánthi, Gre.
95/A3 Xanxerê, Braz.
83/Q7 Xarardheere, Som.
69/E4 Xa Song Luy, Viet.
87/C3 Xassengue, Ang.
69/D3 Xa Tho Thanh, Viet.
93/J6 Xavantes (mts.), Braz.
95/B2 Xavantes (res.), Braz.
69/D4 Xa Vo Dat, Viet.
68/D3 Xayar, China
100/D3 Xel-há (ruins), Mex.
110/D4 Xenia, Oh,US
69/D2 Xeno, Laos
66/E2 Xi (lake), China
63/E3 Xi (riv.), China
63/F5 Xi (riv.), China
63/H5 Xi (riv.), China
67/B3 Xi (riv.), China
71/H2 Xiaguan, China
67/C3 Xiamen, China
66/B4 Xi'an, China
67/B2 Xiang (riv.), China
66/C4 Xiangfan, China
69/C2 Xiang Khoang (plat.), Laos
67/B2 Xiangtan, China
67/B2 Xiangxiang, China
66/C5 Xianning, China
66/C5 Xiantao, China
62/F5 Xianyang, China
66/C3 Xiao (riv.), China
67/B2 Xiao (riv.), China
71/H2 Xiao (riv.), China
63/J1 Xiaobole (peak), China
66/C5 Xiaogan, China
63/K2 Xiao Hinggang (mts.), China
66/D3 Xiaoqing (riv.), China
66/L9 Xiaoshan, China
66/C3 Xiaowutai Shan (peak), China
71/F2 Xibaxa (riv.), China
66/C4 Xicheng Shan (mtn.), China
100/B3 Xicohténcatl, Mex.
100/B3 Xicotepec, Mex.
66/C4 Xifei (riv.), China
62/F4 Xifeng, China
63/J3 Xifeng, China
67/A2 Xifeng, China
70/E2 Xigazê, China
62/E5 Xihan (riv.), China
68/F4 Xijir Ulan (lake), China
66/E2 Xiliao (riv.), China
67/C2 Xin (riv.), China
66/D5 Xin'an (riv.), China
66/D5 Xin'anjiang (res.), China
67/B3 Xinfengjiang (res.), China
66/E2 Xingcheng, China
87/C2 Xinge, Ang.
66/D4 Xinghua, China
68/D3 Xingjiang Uygur Aut. Reg., China
63/L3 Xingkai (lake), China
66/C3 Xingtai, China
93/H4 Xingu (riv.), Braz.
66/C4 Xingyang, China
62/E4 Xining (Xining Shi), China
66/C3 Xinji, China
58/J5 Xinjiang (reg.), China
66/D4 Xintai, China
66/C4 Xinxiang, China
66/C4 Xinyang, China
67/B2 Xinyu, China
68/D3 Xinyuan, China
62/E5 Xiqing (mts.), China
94/B3 Xique-Xique, Braz.
67/B2 Xiu (riv.), China
70/E2 Xixabangma (peak), China
71/J3 Xiyang (riv.), China
66/E3 Xizhong (isl.), China
67/C2 Xu (riv.), China
66/C2 Xuanhua, China
66/C4 Xuchang, China
83/P7 Xuddur (Oddur), Som.
66/E5 Xuedou (peak), China
62/D4 Xugin Gol (riv.), China
66/D4 Xun (riv.), China
67/B3 Xun (riv.), China
63/K2 Xunke, China
66/D4 Xuyi, China
66/D4 Xuzhou, China

Y

62/E6 Ya'an, China
82/G7 Yabassi, Camr.
83/N7 Yabēlo, Eth.
100/E5 Yablis, Nic.
62/F1 Yablonovyy (ridge), Rus.
65/G2 Yabuki, Japan
67/A2 Yachi (riv.), China
65/J7 Yachiyo, Japan
95/A4 Yacuí (riv.), Braz.
92/F8 Yacuiba, Bol.
70/C4 Yādgīr, India
65/L9 Yagi, Japan
82/J5 Yagoua, Camr.
62/D4 Yagradagzê (peak), China
97/G2 Yaguarón (riv.), Uru.
65/N10 Yahagi (riv.), Japan
59/C2 Yahyalı, Turk.
65/F3 Yaita, Japan
65/F3 Yaizu, Japan
63/J2 Yakeshi, China
106/C4 Yakima, Wa,US
106/C4 Yakima (riv.), Wa,US
85/E3 Yako, Burk.
83/K7 Yakoma, Zaire
51/F4 Yakoruda, Bul.
64/B5 Yaku-Kirishima Nat'l Park, Japan
65/K9 Yakuno, Japan
114/K4 Yakutat (bay), Ak,US
57/N3 Yakut Aut. Rep., Rus.
57/N3 Yakutsk, Rus.
69/C5 Yala, Thai.
109/K4 Yalobusha (riv.), Ms,US
82/J6 Yaloké, CAfr.
71/H2 Yalong (riv.), China
54/E3 Yalta, Ukr.
63/J3 Yalu (riv.), China, NKor.
64/B4 Yamaga, Japan
65/G1 Yamagata, Japan
65/F1 Yamagata (pref.), Japan
64/B3 Yamaguchi (pref.), Japan
56/G2 Yamal (pen.), Rus.
56/G3 Yamal-Nenets Aut. Okr., Rus.
65/F3 Yamanashi (pref.), Japan
76/B2 Yamanie Falls Nat'l Park, Austl.
53/N5 Yamantau, Gora (peak), Rus.
65/N9 Yamaoka, Japan
65/L10 Yamashiro, Japan
65/L10 Yamato-Kōriyama, Japan
64/D3 Yamatotakada, Japan
65/M10 Yamazoe, Japan
83/L7 Yambio, Sudan
51/H4 Yambol, Bul.
69/B1 Yamethin, Burma
73/K4 Yamin (peak), Indo.
76/A4 Yamma Yamma (lake), Austl.
65/G1 Yamoto, Japan
84/D5 Yamoussoukro (cap.), IvC.
108/F2 Yampa (riv.), Co,US
70/C2 Yamuna (riv.), India
61/L2 Yamunānagar, India
71/E2 Yamzho Yumco (lake), China
66/B3 Yan (riv.), China
70/D6 Yan (riv.), SrL.
57/P3 Yana (riv.), Rus.
64/B4 Yanagawa, Japan
64/C4 Yanai, Japan
53/M4 Yanaul, Rus.
66/C4 Yancheng, China
66/E4 Yancheng, China
79/T12 Yandé (isl.), NCal.
71/G4 Yandoon, Burma
83/K7 Yangambi, Zaire
71/G2 Yangbi (riv.), China
66/L8 Yangcheng (lake), China
67/C2 Yangdang (mts.), China
66/C2 Yanggao, China
63/K4 Yanggu, SKor.
69/B2 Yangon (Rangoon) (cap.), Burma
66/C3 Yangquan, China
71/K3 Yangshan, China
71/K3 Yangshuo, China
66/D5 Yangtze (Chang) (riv.), China
83/P5 Yangudi Rassa Nat'l Park, Eth.
64/A1 Yangyang, SKor.
66/C2 Yangyuan, China
66/D4 Yangzhou, China
63/K3 Yanji, China
85/H4 Yankari Game Rsv., Nga.
107/J5 Yankton, SD,US
66/C3 Yanmen Guan (pass), China
66/E3 Yantai, China
66/C2 Yantong Shan (mtn.), China
77/G5 Yan Yean (res.), Austl.
64/D3 Yao, Japan
82/H7 Yaoundé (cap.), Camr.
78/C4 Yap (isls.), Micr.
92/E3 Yapacana Nat'l Park, Ven.
73/J4 Yapen (isl.), Indo.
73/J4 Yapen (str.), Indo.
115/H5 Yaphank, NY,US
101/M8 Yaqui, Mex.
101/N8 Yaqui (riv.), Mex.
35/E5 Yar (riv.), Eng,UK
101/F3 Yara, Cuba
73/J4 Yaramaniapuka (mtn.), Indo.
53/K4 Yaransk, Rus.
59/B3 Yardımcı (pt.), Turk.
35/H1 Yare (riv.), Eng,UK
65/E2 Yari-ga-take (mtn.), Japan
51/J5 Yarımca, Turk.
68/C4 Yarkant (riv.), China
111/H3 Yarmouth, NS,Can
52/H4 Yaroslavl', Rus.
52/H4 Yaroslavl' Obl., Rus.
77/G5 Yarra (riv.), Austl.
92/C2 Yarumal, Col.
78/G6 Yasawa Group (isls.), Fiji
54/C1 Yasel'da (riv.), Bela.
65/H7 Yashio, Japan
65/K10 Yashiro, Japan
55/L2 Yasnyy, Rus.
69/D3 Yasothon, Thai.
60/F4 Yas, Sir Bani (isl.), UAE
65/M9 Yasu, Japan
65/M10 Yasu (riv.), Japan
64/C3 Yasugi, Japan
92/C4 Yasuni Nat'l Park, Ecu.
65/G2 Yatabe, Japan
59/B3 Yatağan, Turk.
34/D3 Yate, Eng,UK
35/F4 Yateley, Eng,UK
85/E3 Yatenga (prov.), Burk.
109/J3 Yates Center, Ks,US
102/G2 Yathkyed (lake), NW,Can
65/M9 Yatomi, Japan
65/E2 Yatsuo, Japan
64/B4 Yatsushiro, Japan
59/K6 Yaṭṭah, WBnk.
34/D4 Yatton, Eng,UK
92/D5 Yavari (riv.), Peru
70/C3 Yavatmāl, India
56/H2 Yavay (pen.), Rus.
101/F6 Yaviza, Pan.
59/M9 Yavne, Isr.
65/J7 Yawahara, Japan
65/L10 Yawata, Japan
64/C4 Yawatahama, Japan
100/C4 Yaxchilán (ruins), Mex.
35/F2 Yaxley, Eng,UK
61/F2 Yazd, Iran
113/F3 Yazoo (riv.), Ms,US
113/F3 Yazoo City, Ms,US
45/L2 Ybbs (riv.), Aus.
69/B3 Ye, Burma
33/G4 Yeadon, Eng,UK
34/B6 Yealmpton, Eng,UK
69/C4 Yeay Sen (cape), Camb.
68/C4 Yecheng, China
47/E3 Yecla, Sp.
54/F1 Yefremov, Rus.
55/G3 Yegorlak (riv.), Rus.
59/M8 Yehud, Isr.
83/M7 Yei, Sudan
53/P4 Yekaterinburg Obl., Rus.
53/P4 Yekaterinburg (Sverdlovsk), Rus.
53/M5 Yelabuga, Rus.
55/G2 Yelan', Rus.
54/F1 Yelets, Rus.
57/Q4 Yelizavety (cape), Rus.
57/R4 Yelizovo, Rus.
81/R16 Yellel, Alg.
63/J4 Yellow (sea), Asia
113/G4 Yellow (riv.), Al, Fl,US
107/G3 Yellow Grass, Sk,Can
63/H4 Yellow (Huang) (riv.), China
102/E2 Yellowknife (cap.), NW,Can
102/E2 Yellowknife (riv.), NW,Can
107/G4 Yellowstone (riv.), Mt,US
106/F4 Yellowstone (lake), Wy,US
106/F4 Yellowstone Nat'l Park, Wy,US
112/E2 Yellville, Ar,US
34/B6 Yelverton, Eng,UK
62/D4 Yema (riv.), China
60/E5 Yemen
54/F2 Yenakiyevo, Ukr.
71/F3 Yenangyaung, Burma
69/D1 Yen Bai, Viet.
85/E4 Yendi, Gha.
68/C4 Yengisar, China
54/E4 Yenice (riv.), Turk.
59/C2 Yeniceoba, Turk.
51/J5 Yenişehir, Turk.
56/J3 Yenisey (riv.), Rus.
56/K4 Yeniseysk, Rus.
69/D1 Yen Minh, Viet.
74/C5 Yeo (lake), Austl.
34/D5 Yeo (riv.), Eng,UK
61/K4 Yeola, India
34/D5 Yeovil, Eng,UK
76/C3 Yeppoon, Austl.
49/H3 Yerakovoúni (peak), Gre.
42/A4 Yères (riv.), Fr.
55/H4 Yerevan (cap.), Arm.
108/C3 Yerington, Nv,US
59/C2 Yerköy, Turk.
58/C1 Yermak, Kaz.
56/H4 Yermentau, Kaz.
59/K6 Yeroḥam, Isr.
31/T10 Yerres, Fr.
31/U11 Yerres (riv.), Fr.
92/C6 Yerupaja (peak), Peru
59/K6 Yerushalayim (Jerusalem) (cap.), Isr.
71/G3 Yesagyo, Burma
68/A1 Yesil', Kaz.
59/D2 Yeşilirmak (riv.), Turk.
55/G3 Yessentuki, Rus.
34/D5 Yetminster, Eng,UK
44/B3 Yeu (isl.), Fr.
70/B3 Yevla, India
55/H4 Yevlakh, Azer.
54/E3 Yevpatoriya, Ukr.
54/G3 Yeya (riv.), Rus.
54/F3 Yeysk, Rus.
66/C4 Yi (riv.), China
97/G2 Yi (riv.), Uru.
49/H2 Yiannitsá, Gre.
49/J4 Yíaros (isl.), Gre.
66/B5 Yichang, China
67/B2 Yichun, China
67/C2 Yihuang, China
63/K2 Yilan, China
59/D2 Yıldızeli, Turk.
63/J1 Yilehuli (mts.), China
66/B4 Yima, China
63/J2 Yimin (riv.), China
62/F3 Yin (mts.), China
62/F4 Yinchuan, China
74/C6 Yindarlgooda (lake), Austl.
66/C4 Ying (riv.), China
66/C5 Yingcheng, China
63/J3 Yingkou, China
67/C2 Yingtan, China
68/D3 Yining, China
83/M6 Yirol, Sudan
66/F2 Yitong (riv.), China
66/C4 Yiyang, China
67/B2 Yiyang, China
66/D4 Yizheng, China
32/E6 Y Llethr (mtn.), Wal,UK
37/G3 Ylöjärvi, Fin.
112/D4 Yoakum, Tx,US
64/D3 Yodo (riv.), Japan
57/P4 Yoduma (riv.), Rus.
82/J4 Yogoum (well), Chad
72/D5 Yogyakarta, Indo.
106/D3 Yoho Nat'l Park, BC,Can
82/J7 Yokadouma, Camr.
64/E3 Yōkaichi, Japan
64/D3 Yokawa, Japan
64/E3 Yokkaichi, Japan
65/F3 Yokohama, Japan
65/H7 Yokohama (inset), Japan
65/F3 Yokosuka, Japan
82/H6 Yola, Nga.
69/C2 Yom (riv.), Thai.
87/B1 Yombi, Gabon
67/A3 Yon (riv.), China
44/C3 Yon (riv.), Fr.
65/G2 Yonago, Japan
65/G2 Yonezawa, Japan
67/C2 Yong'an, China
64/A3 Yŏngch'ŏn, SKor.
71/G3 Yongde, China
66/H7 Yongding (riv.), China
64/A2 Yŏngdŏk, SKor.
71/J3 Yongfu, China
64/A2 Yŏngju, SKor.
66/C3 Yongnian, China
64/A2 Yŏngwŏl, SKor.
67/B2 Yongzhou, China
115/G5 Yonkers, NY,US
44/E2 Yonne (riv.), Fr.
65/H7 Yono, Japan
68/C4 Yopurga, China
115/C3 Yorba Linda, Ca,US
74/G2 York (cape), Austl.
74/C2 York (sound), Austl.
111/R8 York, On,Can
111/H1 York (riv.), Qu,Can
33/G4 York, Eng,UK
113/F3 York, Al,US
109/H2 York, Ne,US
113/H3 York, SC,US
110/E4 York (riv.), Va,US
74/F6 Yorke (pen.), Austl.
107/J1 York Landing, Mb,Can
33/G4 York Minster, Eng,UK
33/F3 Yorkshire Dales Nat'l Park, Eng,UK
33/H3 Yorkshire Wolds (hills), Eng,UK
107/H3 Yorkton, Sk,Can
33/G3 York, Vale of (val.), Eng,UK
100/D4 Yoro, Hon.
65/M9 Yorō, Japan
65/J7 Yōrō (riv.), Japan
65/M10 Yoroi-zaki (pt.), Japan
62/F2 Yöröö, Mong.
33/F6 Yorton, Eng,UK
85/F4 Yorubaland (plat.), Nga.
108/C3 Yosemite Nat'l Park, Ca,US
64/C4 Yoshida, Japan
64/D3 Yoshii (riv.), Japan
65/H7 Yoshikawa, Japan
64/D3 Yoshino (riv.), Japan
65/L10 Yoshino, Japan
64/E3 Yoshino-Kumano Nat'l Park, Japan
53/L4 Yoshkar-Ola, Rus.
63/K5 Yŏsu, SKor.
63/N3 Yōtei-san (mtn.), Japan
65/J7 Yotsukaidō, Japan
67/A2 You (riv.), China
67/A3 You (riv.), China
77/D2 Young, Austl.
97/F2 Young, Uru.
111/R9 Youngstown, NY,US
110/D3 Youngstown, Oh,US
63/L2 Youyi, China
92/E2 Yovi (peak), Ven.
59/C2 Yozgat, Turk.
116/E7 Ypsilanti, Mi,US
32/D6 Yr Eifl (mtn.), Wal,UK
108/B2 Yreka, Ca,US
42/B2 Yser (riv.), Fr.
39/G1 Ystad, Swe.
34/C3 Ystalyfera, Wal,UK
34/C3 Ystradgynlais, Wal,UK
34/C3 Ystrad Mynach, Wal,UK
34/C2 Ystwyth (riv.), Wal,UK
36/D2 Ythan (riv.), Sc,UK
71/J3 Yu (riv.), China
67/D3 Yū (peak), Tai.
66/C5 Yuan (lake), China
67/B2 Yuan (riv.), China
71/H3 Yuan (riv.), China
66/C3 Yuanping, China
108/B3 Yuba City, Ca,US
63/N3 Yūbari, Japan
115/C2 Yucaipa, Ca,US
100/D4 Yucatan (pen.), Mex.
100/D3 Yucatan (state), Mex.
100/D3 Yucatan (chan.), NAm.
108/D4 Yucca, Az,US
66/C3 Yuci, China
66/D5 Yuexi, China
71/H2 Yuexi, China
67/B2 Yueyang, China
53/K3 Yug (riv.), Rus.
53/P1 Yugorskiy (pen.), Rus.
50/D3 Yugoslavia
66/L9 Yuhang, China
65/F2 Yūki, Japan
102/B2 Yukon (riv.), Can., US
114/K2 Yukon-Charley Rivers Nat'l Prsv., Ak,US
114/L3 Yukon Crossing, Yk,Can
102/C2 Yukon Territory (terr.), Can.
59/F3 Yüksekova, Turk.
60/D1 Yüksekova, Turk.
64/B4 Yukuhashi, Japan
74/E5 Yulara, Austl.
69/E2 Yulin, China
71/K3 Yulin, China
66/B3 Yulin (riv.), China
66/D5 Yuling Guan (pass), China
108/D4 Yuma, Az,US
109/G2 Yuma, Co,US
96/B3 Yumbel, Chile
87/E1 Yumbi, Zaire
92/C3 Yumbo, Col.
62/D4 Yumen, China
66/C5 Yun (riv.), China
59/B2 Yunak, Turk.
92/E7 Yungas (reg.), Bol.
96/B3 Yungay, Chile
71/H3 Yunnan (prov.), China
66/D4 Yuntai Shan (peak), China
66/D2 Yunwu Shan (peak), China
66/D4 Yunyan (riv.), China
66/C3 Yunzhong Shan (mtn.), China
71/J2 Yuping, China
66/H7 Yuqiao (res.), China
64/D3 Yura (riv.), Japan
56/J4 Yurga, Rus.
92/C5 Yurimaguas, Peru
68/C4 Yurungkax (riv.), China
53/N5 Yuryuzan' (riv.), Rus.
66/D3 Yutian, China
43/F5 Yutz, Fr.
66/C3 Yu Xian, China
66/C4 Yu Xian, China
67/D1 Yuyao, China
63/N2 Yuzhno-Sakhalinsk, Rus.
54/D2 Yuzhnyy Bug (riv.), Ukr.
31/R10 Yvelines (dept.), Fr.
45/G3 Yverdon, Swi.
31/S10 Yvette (riv.), Fr.
43/D3 Yvoir, Belg.
44/E3 Yzeure, Fr.

Z

81/N13 Za (riv.), Mor.
40/B4 Zaandam, Neth.
39/L2 Ząbki, Pol.
39/J3 Ząbkowice Śląskie, Pol.
61/H2 Zābol, Iran
44/K2 Zábřeh, Czh.
39/K3 Zabrze, Pol.
100/D5 Zacapa, Guat.
100/A4 Zacapú, Mex.
100/A3 Zacatecas, Mex.
101/P9 Zacatecas, Mex.
100/A3 Zacatecas (state), Mex.
100/D5 Zacatecoluca, ESal.
113/F4 Zachary, La,US
100/B3 Zacualtipán, Mex.
50/B3 Zadar, Cro.
69/B4 Zadetkyi (isl.), Burma
62/D5 Zadoi, China
46/B3 Zafra, Sp.
39/H3 Żagań, Pol.
81/X17 Zaghwān, Tun.
81/W17 Zaghwān (gov.), Tun.
50/B2 Zagorjeob Savi, Slov.
50/C3 Zagreb (cap.), Cro.
60/E1 Zagros (mts.), Iran
68/E5 Za'gya (riv.), China
61/H3 Zāhedān, Iran
70/C4 Zahirābād, India
59/K5 Zaḩlah, Leb.
60/D5 Zahrān, SAr.
80/E5 Zaire
80/E4 Zaire (Congo) (riv.), Zaire
50/F4 Zaječar, Yugo.
62/E1 Zakamensk, Rus.
59/E3 Zākhū, Iraq
49/G4 Zákinthos, Gre.
49/G4 Zákinthos (isl.), Gre.
39/K4 Zakopane, Pol.
83/J5 Zakouma Nat'l Park, Chad
49/J5 Zakro (ruins), Gre.
50/C2 Zala (co.), Hun.
50/C2 Zala (riv.), Hun.
50/C2 Zalaegerszeg, Hun.
46/C3 Zalamea de la Serena, Sp.
63/J2 Zalantun, China
50/C2 Zalaszentgrót, Hun.
50/F2 Zalău, Rom.
82/J2 Zaltan (well), Libya
40/C5 Zaltbommel, Neth.
65/H7 Zama, Japan
87/F4 Zambezi (riv.), Afr.
87/D3 Zambezi, Zam.
87/E3 Zambia
73/F2 Zamboanga, Phil.
39/M2 Zambrów, Pol.
47/P11 Zambujal de Cima, Port.
85/G3 Zamfora (riv.), Nga.
69/B3 Zami (riv.), Burma
92/C4 Zamora, Ecu.
92/C4 Zamora (riv.), Ecu.
100/A4 Zamora, Mex.
46/C2 Zamora, Sp.
39/M3 Zamość, Pol.
39/M3 Zamość (prov.), Pol.
46/D3 Záncara (riv.), Sp.
68/C5 Zanda, China
40/A5 Zandkreekdam (dam), Neth.
40/B4 Zandvoort, Neth.

113/H2 **Zanesville,** Oh,US
60/E1 **Zanjān,** Iran
87/G2 **Zanzibar,** Tanz.
87/G2 **Zanzibar** (isl.), Tanz.
65/G1 **Zaō-san** (mtn.), Japan
66/D4 **Zaozhuang,** China
63/N2 **Zapadno-Sakhalin** (mts.), Rus.
45/K2 **Západočeský** (reg.), Czh.
39/J4 **Západoslovenský** (reg.), Slvk.
96/C3 **Zapala,** Arg.
91/C1 **Zapaleri** (peak), Arg.
112/D5 **Zapata,** Tx,US
92/D2 **Zapatoca,** Col.
52/F1 **Zapolyarnyy,** Rus.
54/E3 **Zaporozh'ye,** Ukr.
54/E3 **Zaporozh'ye Obl.,** Ukr.
50/B3 **Zaprešić,** Cro.
59/D2 **Zara,** Turk.
92/D2 **Zaragoza,** Col.
47/E2 **Zaragoza** (Saragossa), Sp.
85/H4 **Zaranda** (hill), Nga.
96/F2 **Zárate,** Arg.
46/D1 **Zarauz,** Sp.
101/H6 **Zaraza,** Ven.
60/F2 **Zard** (mtn.), Iran
60/F3 **Zargān,** Iran
85/G4 **Zaria,** Nga.
61/H2 **Zarmast** (pass), Afg.
51/G3 **Zărneşti,** Rom.
39/J4 **Záruby** (peak), Slvk.
39/H3 **Żary,** Pol.
46/A1 **Zas,** Sp.
61/L2 **Zāskar** (range), India
45/K1 **Žatec,** Czh.
42/D2 **Zaventem,** Belg.
50/D3 **Zavidovići,** Bosn.
63/K1 **Zavitinsk,** Rus.
39/K3 **Zawadzkie,** Pol.
39/K3 **Zawiercie,** Pol.
62/D6 **Zaya** (riv.), China
68/D2 **Zaysan,** Kaz.
68/D2 **Zaysan** (lake), Kaz.
71/G2 **Zayü,** China
71/G2 **Zayü** (riv.), China
39/H2 **Zbąszyń,** Pol.
39/H4 **Žďár nad Sázavou,** Czh.
39/K3 **Zduńska Wola,** Pol.
96/C5 **Zeballos** (peak), Arg.
81/R16 **Zeddine** (riv.), Alg.
42/C1 **Zedelgem,** Belg.
40/A5 **Zeeland** (prov.), Neth.
110/C3 **Zeeland,** Mi,US
88/D2 **Zeerust,** SAfr.
40/C4 **Zeewolde,** Neth.
59/K5 **Zefat,** Isr.
39/L2 **Zegrzyńskie** (lake), Pol.
39/G2 **Zehdenick,** Ger.
74/E4 **Zeil** (peak), Austl.
40/C4 **Zeist,** Neth.
38/G3 **Zeitz,** Ger.
42/D1 **Zele,** Belg.
53/L5 **Zelenodol'sk,** Rus.
52/F3 **Zelenogorsk,** Rus.
55/G3 **Zelenokumsk,** Rus.
40/D4 **Zelhem,** Neth.
45/K3 **Zell am See,** Aus.
39/K3 **Zelów,** Pol.
50/B2 **Zeltweg,** Aus.
42/C1 **Zelzate,** Belg.
48/B4 **Zembra** (isls.), Tun.
81/R16 **Zemmora,** Alg.
100/B4 **Zempoaltepec** (mt.), Mex.
42/D2 **Zemst,** Belg.
108/B2 **Zenia,** Ca,US
50/C3 **Zenica,** Bosn.
116/C3 **Zenith,** Wa,US
45/J2 **Zenn** (riv.), Ger.
107/H2 **Zenon Park,** Sk,Can
64/C3 **Zentsūji,** Japan
50/D3 **Žepče,** Bosn.
81/S15 **Zeralda,** Alg.
81/L13 **Zerga** (lake), Mor.
54/G3 **Zernograd,** Rus.
102/F1 **Zeta** (lake), NW,Can
41/E2 **Zetel,** Ger.
41/G2 **Zeven,** Ger.
40/D5 **Zevenaar,** Neth.
40/B5 **Zevenbergen,** Neth.
63/K1 **Zeya,** Rus.
63/K1 **Zeya** (res.), Rus.
63/K1 **Zeya** (riv.), Rus.
63/K1 **Zeya-Bureya** (plain), Rus.
46/A3 **Zêzere** (riv.), Port.
59/K4 **Zghartā,** Leb.
39/K3 **Zgierz,** Pol.
39/H3 **Zgorzelec,** Pol.
63/K2 **Zhan** (riv.), China
66/B5 **Zhang** (riv.), China
66/C5 **Zhangdu** (lake), China
63/K3 **Zhangguangcai** (mts.), China
66/C2 **Zhanghei,** China
66/C2 **Zhangjiakou,** China
66/D3 **Zhangqiu,** China
66/D3 **Zhangwei** (riv.), China
62/E4 **Zhangye,** China
67/C3 **Zhangzhou,** China
67/B3 **Zhanjiang,** China
63/K2 **Zhaodong,** China
67/B3 **Zhaoqing,** China
71/H2 **Zhaotong,** China
66/C3 **Zhao Xian,** China
68/D5 **Zhari Namco** (lake), China
66/L9 **Zhejiang** (prov.), China
56/G2 **Zhelaniya** (cape), Rus.
54/E1 **Zheleznogorsk,** Rus.
57/L4 **Zheleznogorsk-Ilimskiy,** Rus.
66/C3 **Zhengding,** China
66/C4 **Zhengzhou,** China
66/D4 **Zhenjiang,** China
66/C4 **Zhentou** (riv.), China
66/B3 **Zhenwu Shan** (mtn.), China
71/H3 **Zhenyuan,** China
66/B5 **Zhicheng,** China
55/J1 **Zhigulevsk,** Rus.
55/J4 **Zhiloy** (isl.), Azer.
54/D2 **Zhitomir,** Ukr.
54/C2 **Zhitomir Obl.,** Ukr.
54/D1 **Zhlobin,** Bela.
54/D2 **Zhmerinka,** Ukr.
61/J2 **Zhob,** Pak.
61/J2 **Zhob** (riv.), Pak.
52/F5 **Zhodino,** Bela.
57/R2 **Zhokhov** (isl.), Rus.
66/B4 **Zhongnan Shan** (mtn.), China
71/K3 **Zhongshan,** China
66/C4 **Zhoukou,** China
66/E5 **Zhoushan** (isls.), China
54/E3 **Zhovtnevoye,** Ukr.
63/J4 **Zhuanghe,** China
66/D4 **Zhucheng,** China
71/K3 **Zhuhai,** China
54/E1 **Zhukovka,** Rus.
52/H5 **Zhukovskiy,** Rus.
66/C4 **Zhumadian,** China
66/C2 **Zhuolu,** China
66/G7 **Zhuo Xian,** China
67/B2 **Zhuzhou,** China
67/B2 **Zi** (riv.), China
66/D3 **Zibo,** China
39/J3 **Ziębice,** Pol.
39/H3 **Zielona Góra,** Pol.
39/H2 **Zielona Góra** (prov.), Pol.
41/G6 **Zierenberg,** Ger.
40/A5 **Zierikzee,** Neth.
59/H6 **Ziftá,** Egypt
71/H2 **Zigong,** China
84/A3 **Ziguinchor,** Sen.
84/A3 **Ziguinchor** (reg.), Sen.
66/B3 **Zijing Shan** (mtn.), China
59/C2 **Zile,** Turk.
39/K4 **Žilina,** Slvk.
45/J3 **Ziller** (riv.), Aus.
62/E1 **Zima,** Rus.
100/B4 **Zimatlán,** Mex.
87/F2 **Zimba,** Tanz.
87/E4 **Zimbabwe**
51/G4 **Zimnicea,** Rom.
87/F5 **Zinave Nat'l Park,** Moz.
85/H3 **Zinder,** Niger
85/H3 **Zinder** (dept.), Niger
116/Q15 **Zion,** Il,US
108/D3 **Zion Nat'l Park,** Ut,US
50/C2 **Zirc,** Hun.
50/B4 **Žirje** (isl.), Cro.
39/K5 **Žitava** (riv.), Slvk.
39/H3 **Zittau,** Ger.
50/D3 **Živinice,** Bosn.
66/B4 **Ziwu** (mtn.), China
67/B2 **Zixing,** China
66/D3 **Ziya** (riv.), China
51/F2 **Zlatna,** Rom.
51/G5 **Zlatograd,** Bul.
50/E4 **Zlatorsko** (lake), Yugo.
53/N5 **Zlatoust,** Rus.
39/J4 **Zlin,** Czh.
39/J2 **Złocieniec,** Pol.
39/H3 **Złotoryja,** Pol.
39/J2 **Złotów,** Pol.
39/J3 **Żmigród,** Pol.
54/E2 **Znamenka,** Ukr.
39/J2 **Żnin,** Pol.
39/J4 **Znojmo,** Czh.
43/D1 **Zoersel,** Belg.
40/B4 **Zoetermeer,** Neth.
45/G3 **Zofingen,** Swi.
49/L7 **Zográfos,** Gre.
60/F2 **Zohreh** (riv.), Iran
54/E2 **Zolotonosha,** Ukr.
87/G4 **Zomba,** Malw.
34/B6 **Zone** (pt.), UK
51/K5 **Zonguldak,** Turk.
51/K5 **Zonguldak** (prov.), Turk.
43/E2 **Zonhoven,** Belg.
42/B2 **Zonnebeke,** Belg.
41/H5 **Zorge** (riv.), Ger.
45/G2 **Zorn** (riv.), Fr.
42/C2 **Zottegem,** Belg.
85/F5 **Zou** (prov.), Ben.
82/J3 **Zouar,** Chad
82/C3 **Zouîrât,** Mrta.
85/E4 **Zoundwéogo** (prov.), Burk.
88/L10 **Zout** (riv.), SAfr.
50/E3 **Zrenjanin,** Yugo.
46/D4 **Zubia,** Sp.
45/H3 **Zug,** Swi.
82/C3 **Zug,** WSah.
55/G4 **Zugdidi,** Geo.
45/J3 **Zugspitze** (peak), Ger.
40/A6 **Zuidbeveland** (isl.), Neth.
40/C4 **Zuidelijk Flevoland** (polder), Neth.
40/D2 **Zuidhorn,** Neth.
40/D2 **Zuidlaardermeer** (lake), Neth.
40/D2 **Zuidlaren,** Neth.
40/C6 **Zuid-Willemsvaart** (can.), Belg.
40/D3 **Zuidwolde,** Neth.
46/D4 **Zújar,** Sp.
46/C3 **Zújar** (res.), Sp.
46/C3 **Zújar** (riv.), Sp.
43/F2 **Zülpich,** Ger.
42/C2 **Zulte,** Belg.
89/E2 **Zululand** (reg.), SAfr.
46/D1 **Zumárraga,** Sp.
100/B4 **Zumpango,** Mex.
40/B6 **Zundert,** Neth.
66/D2 **Zunhua,** China
108/E4 **Zuni** (dry riv.), Az, NM,US
108/E4 **Zuni,** NM,US
112/A3 **Zuni** (mts.), NM,US
71/J2 **Zunyi,** China
71/J3 **Zuo** (riv.), China
69/D1 **Zuo Jiang** (riv.), China
50/D3 **Županja,** Cro.
60/D6 **Zuqar, Jabal** (isl.), Yemen
45/H3 **Zürich,** Swi.
45/H3 **Zürichsee** (lake), Swi.
39/K2 **Żuromin,** Pol.
45/J2 **Zusam** (riv.), Ger.
65/H7 **Zushi,** Japan
94/A2 **Zutiua** (riv.), Braz.
40/D4 **Zutphen,** Neth.
82/H1 **Zuwārah,** Libya
53/L4 **Zuyevka,** Rus.
50/D4 **Zvijesda Nat'l Park,** Yugo.
39/K4 **Zvolen,** Slvk.
50/D3 **Zvorničko** (lake), Yugo.
50/D3 **Zvornik,** Bosn.
40/C3 **Zwarte Meer** (lake), Neth.
43/G5 **Zweibrücken,** Ger.
42/C2 **Zwevegem,** Belg.
38/G3 **Zwickau,** Ger.
40/B6 **Zwijndrecht,** Belg.
40/B5 **Zwijndrecht,** Neth.
41/F2 **Zwischenahn,** Ger.
41/F2 **Zwischenahner Meer** (lake), Ger.
39/L3 **Zwoleń,** Pol.
40/D4 **Zwolle,** Neth.
39/K2 **Żychlin,** Pol.
39/L2 **Żyrardów,** Pol.
62/A2 **Zyryanovsk,** Kaz.
55/J3 **Zyudev** (isl.), Rus.
39/K4 **Żywiec,** Pol.

Acknowledgements

In 1986, we saw an opportunity to create a radically new map-making system. Advances in technology put within our grasp a means of producing maps more efficiently and more accurately than ever before. At the heart of our plan was a computerized geographic database – one which would enable maps to be created and changed at whim.

This world atlas is one of the first products of our new system. Behind it hums another world, a bustling, close-knit family of talented and innovative cartographers, researchers, editors, artists, technicians and scholars. In the five years it has taken to create our new system, their world has seen almost as many upheavals as our own planet. For their constancy and faith in a project which sometimes seemed so daunting, for their patience and creativity to explore new technologies, and for the teamwork which enabled us to realize such an ambitious goal, we are deeply grateful.

We are especially grateful for the support of our many contributors, whose efforts made this volume better. In particular, we wish to thank Mitchell Feigenbaum, a brilliant scientist and dear friend, whose illumination of the world around him extends to the art – and science – of cartography. His genius is ever-present in this atlas, from his revolutionary map projection to his pioneering software, which was crucial to the success of our computer mapping system.

At last, a map-making system that moves as fast as the world is changing. As new technology continues to redefine what is possible, we will continue to push the envelope, to pioneer a better way. We are committed to maintaining the highest level of quality – in accuracy and timeliness, in design and printing, and in service to our clients and readers. It is our goal to ensure that you can always turn to Hammond for the very best in map and atlas design and geographic information.

C. Dean and Kathleen Hammond

Computerized Cartographic Advisory Board

Mitchell J. Feigenbaum, Ph.D
Chief Technical Consultant
Toyota Professor, The Rockefeller University
Wolf Prize in Physics, 1986
Member, The National Academy of Sciences

Judson G. Rosebush, Ph.D
Computer Graphics Animation
Producer, Director and Author

Gary Martin Andrew, Ph.D
Consultant in Operations Research,
Planning and Management

Warren E. Schmidt, B.A.
Former U.S. Geological Survey,
Chief of the Branch of Geographic
and Cartographic Research

Hammond Publications Advisory Board

United States and Canada
Daniel Jacobson
Professor of Geography and Education,
Adjunct Professor of Anthropology,
Michigan State University

Latin and Middle America
John P. Augelli
Professor and Chairman,
Department of Geography-Meteorology,
University of Kansas

Western and Southern Europe
Norman J. W. Thrower
Professor, Department of Geography,
University of California, Los Angeles

Northern and Central Europe
Vincent H. Malmstrom
Professor, Department of Geography,
Dartmouth College

South and Southeast Asia
P. P. Karan
Professor, Department of Geography,
University of Kentucky

East Asia
Christopher L. Salter
Professor and Chairman,
Department of Geography,
University of Missouri

Australia, New Zealand & the Pacific Area
Tom L. McKnight
Professor, Department of Geography,
University of California, Los Angeles

Population and Demography
Kingsley Davis
Distinguished Professor of Sociology,
University of Southern California
and Senior Research Fellow,
The Hoover Institution,
Stanford University

Biblical Archaeology
Roger S. Boraas
Professor of Religion,
Upsala College

Flags
Whitney Smith
Executive Director,
The Flag Research Center,
Winchester, Massachusetts

Library Consultant
Alice C. Hudson
Chief, Map Division,
The New York Public Library

Special Advisors

Design Consultant
Pentagram

Contributing Writer
Frederick A. Shamlian

Hammond Incorporated

Charles G. Lees, Jr., V.P.
Editor in Chief, Cartography

William L. Abel, V.P.
Graphic Services

Chingliang Liang
Director, Technical Services

Martin A. Bacheller
Editor-In-Chief, Emeritus

Joseph F. Kalina, Jr.
Managing Editor

Phil Giouvanos
Manager, Computer Cartography

Shou-Wen Chen
Cartographic Systems Manager

Ernst G. Hofmann
Nadya Sazanets
Topographic Specialists

Michael E. Agishtein, Ph.D
Advanced Systems Development

Lauren Kaligo
Manager, Information & Statistics